**THE GREAT
CONTEMPORARY
ISSUES**

LOYALTY AND SECURITY IN A DEMOCRATIC STATE

The New York Times
ARNO PRESS
NEW YORK / 1977

RICHARD H. ROVERE
Advisory Editor

GENE BROWN
Editor

Library of Congress Cataloging in Publication Data

Main entry under title:

Loyalty and security in a democratic state.

   (The Great contemporary issues)
   Articles from the New York times.
   Bibliography: p.
   Includes index.
   SUMMARY: A collection of newspaper articles discussing
emphasis placed on national loyalty and security in the United
States.

   1. Loyalty-security program, 1947- —Addresses,
essays, lectures. 2. Internal security—United States—
Addresses, essays, lectures. 3. United States—National
security—Addresses, essays, lectures. [1. Subversive
activities. 2. National security] I. Rovere,
Richard Halworth, 1915-　II. Brown, Gene.
III. New York times. IV. Series.
E743.5.L65　　　323.4'9'0973　　　75-54570
ISBN 0-405-09864-2

Manufactured in the United States of America

The editors express special thanks to The Associated Press, United Press
International, and Reuters for permission to include in this series of books
a number of dispatches originally distributed by those news services.

Book design by Stephanie Rhodes

Contents

Publisher's Note About the Series

It would take even an accomplished speed-reader, moving at full throttle, some three and a half solid hours a day to work his way through all the news The New York Times prints. The sad irony, of course, is that even such indefatigable devotion to life's carnival would scarcely assure a decent understanding of what it was really all about. For even the most dutiful reader might easily overlook an occasional long-range trend of importance, or perhaps some of the fragile, elusive relationships between events that sometimes turn out to be more significant than the events themselves.

This is why "The Great Contemporary Issues" was created—to help make sense out of some of the major forces and counterforces at large in today's world. The philosophical conviction behind the series is a simple one: that the past not only can illuminate the present but must. ("Continuity with the past," declared Oliver Wendell Holmes, "is a necessity, not a duty.") Each book in the series, therefore has as its subject some central issue of our time that needs to be viewed in the context of its antecedents if it is to be fully understood. By showing, through a substantial selection of contemporary accounts from The New York Times, the evolution of a subject and its significance, each book in the series offers a perspective that is available in no other way. For while most books on contemporary affairs specialize, for excellent reasons, in predigested facts and neatly drawn conclusions, the books in this series allow the reader to draw his own conclusions on the basis of the facts as they appeared at virtually the moment of their occurrence. This is not to argue that there is no place for events recollected in tranquility; it is simply to say that when fresh, raw truths are allowed to speak for themselves, some quite distinct values often emerge.

For this reason, most of the articles in "The Great Contemporary Issues" are reprinted in their entirety, even in those cases where portions are not central to a given book's theme. Editing has been done only rarely, and in all such cases it is clearly indicated. (Such an excision occasionally occurs, for example, in the case of a Presidential State of the Union Message, where only brief portions are germane to a particular volume, and in the case of some names, where for legal reasons or reasons of taste it is preferable not to republish specific identifications.) Similarly, typographical errors, where they occur, have been allowed to stand as originally printed.

"The Great Contemporary Issues" inevitably encompasses a substantial amount of history. In order to explore their subjects fully, some of the books go back a century or more. Yet their fundamental theme is not the past but the present. In this series the past is of significance insofar as it suggests how we got where we are today. These books, therefore, do not always treat a subject in a purely chronological way. Rather, their material is arranged to point up trends and interrelationships that the editors believe are more illuminating than a chronological listing would be.

"The Great Contemporary Issues" series will ultimately constitute an encyclopedic library of today's major issues. Long before editorial work on the first volume had even begun, some fifty specific titles had already been either scheduled for definite publication or listed as candidates. Since then, events have prompted the inclusion of a number of additional titles, and the editors are, moreover, alert not only for new issues as they emerge but also for issues whose development may call for the publication of sequel volumes. We will, of course, also welcome readers' suggestions for future topics.

Introduction

In the *Oxford English Dictionary*, that stately product of 19th century English scholarship, the primary definition of "loyalty" is given as the state of being "true to obligations of duty, love, etc; faithful to plighted troth." In the *American Heritage Dictionary*, compiled in the turbulence of the Cold War, it is given as "steadfast in allegiance to one's homeland, government, or sovereign." The British lexicographers, then, accept the usage of moral philosophers and poets (loyalty, Seneca wrote, is "the holiest good in the human heart"), while the Americans narrow the concept to an assertive nationalism and acceptance of constituted authority. The difference could — and perhaps should — be cited as one more piece of evidence that as a people we are peculiarly obsessed by a notion of loyalty as synonymous with a patriotism that is uncritical and unexamining, except by those who think that some of us lack it or have it in insufficient supply. That we have at times carried this concern to an irrational degree is hardly open to doubt. Our nation was barely a decade old when Congress passed the Alien and Sedition Acts, which made political dissent and opposition a criminal offense, and although these laws were on the books for only three years, the spirit that motivated them has been a continuing presence in our life and one on which many politicians have built careers, a notable case being that of Richard Nixon, who first became a national figure as an aggressive young member of the House Committee on Un-American Activities. In 1975, that committee, then in its thirty-seventh year as a scourge of the allegedly disloyal, was abolished, but the good deed had hardly been done when we learned that the Central Intelligence Agency was more deeply and in some ways more outrageously engaged in the same line of work.

It is not difficult to make a case that there is some-thing perverse in the American temperament that accounts for all this. It seems a very American activity to investigate un-American activity and to try to frame laws proscribing it. Not only Congress but many state legislatures have had committees similar to the one in the House of Representatives: in California some years ago, a witness was told by a committee member that his political associations were "un-Californian" as well as un-American. No other modern democracy has worried the question of loyalty as we have. "Loyalty oaths" are demanded not only of public servants in sensitive positions but of many licensed tradesmen and many professionals, among them football coaches and professors of veterinary medicine. By far the most successful demagogue in our history — Senator Joseph McCarthy — was a man who exploited not our sufferings or our hopes, which is what most demagogues do, but a widespread fear that there was a threat to our national security posed not by the military might of adversary powers but by American citizens thought to be "loyalty risks" or "security risks." Although he uncovered no trace of the danger he said existed, his efforts to do so had, until shortly before he was perceived as a threat himself, the support of the United States Senate and the approval of fifty percent of Americans. Surely it is possible to conclude that paranoia of the sort McCarthy made into a political force is a national affliction.

It is a conclusion, however, that I find myself unable to draw. I believe that the difference between us and, say, the British, is to be explained not as an aberration on our part but as a product, an understandable and almost inevitable one, of our social and political history. In most societies, authoritarian no less than democratic ones, loyalty is rooted in shared experience, ethnicity, and established or traditional religion.

The early settlers here were diverse in their national origins and, though overwhelmingly Christian, differed widely and at times fiercely, over what their faith demanded of them and of their fellows. Some had come to escape tyrannies, some to extend them. They had come not to establish a new nation but to secure enclaves — some religious, some commercial, some military. This was not their "homeland," and their "sovereigns," if they acknowledged any, were an ocean away and often at war with one another. For a century and a half, Americans were not nationals of any sort, or even a people striving for nationhood, but, like Europeans, Africans, or Asians, inhabitants of a particular land mass. In time, they had a "government," but it was by design one of divided and diffused powers. There were few symbols of spiritual authority, and none of temporal authority except the President, who could be replaced every four years and could be overruled by the legislative and judicial branches. In the American Revolution, which was as much a civil war — Americans against Americans, Whigs against Tories — as it was a war of independence, a tenuous kind of unity was achieved, but the Articles of Confederation, adopted in 1781, gave the states that had been colonies sovereignty in everything but military affairs. The Confederation was a defensive alliance, like the North Atlantic Treaty Organization, and not a very stable one. When the Articles were superseded by the Constitution, a nation remained to be built. Loyalty to regions, to states, to institutions, to classes was stronger than loyalty to the central government, and one of the bloodiest internecine struggles in history was fought to prevent the two principal regions, North and South, from becoming separate and rival powers.

We began, then, as a people of uncertain and divided loyalties, and many of the uncertainties and divisions persist to this day. We are a nation now — a powerful one by almost any measure — but we are a nation of nations, of hyphenates, of minorities, of many creeds and of many and varied ancestral memories. In developing our country and in defending it with arms, we have acquired much in the way of shared experience. But at the core of our being as a nation there is still very little that holds us together. When we describe ourselves as loyal Americans, what is it that we are loyal to? The country, the land we inhabit? Of course, but this is an aspect of our humanity. The Czars and the Bolsheviks both loved Russia and gave it their allegiance. Is it the kind of society we have built? An industrious and democratic one, governed, we are often told, by laws, not men? Splendid as they may be, such abstractions do not in themselves command loyalty. Often they do not even command respect. Some years ago, Chief Justice Earl Warren ventured the opinion that if the Bill of Rights were put to a popular referendum, it might be found to have the approval of less than half the people. Supporting evidence could be found in the opinion polls and in the success of the likes of Senator McCarthy. Loyalty of the kind that we so often demand of our countrymen requires symbols, personifications, and we have few. There is, of course, the flag, to which, at least in school and in patriotic gatherings, we give the Pledge of Allegiance. But the flag itself is vividly emblematic of our diversity, and the Pledge is a statement of ideals yet to be fulfilled.

And so it is, I think, that we, the most unideological of people, have witnessed the development of a strange ideological test by means of which those who wish to monitor our loyalty can carry on. The test is adherence to the doctrine of "Americanism." This "ism" embraces patriotism and goes beyond it, though precisely where it seems impossible to say. "There can be no fifty-fifty patriotism in this country," Theodore Roosevelt once admonished us. "There is room here only for 100 per cent Americanism, only for those who are American and nothing else." Roosevelt was an uncommonly intelligent man and far from being illiberal, but he was party to the creation and promulgation of a doctrine that is the foundation for those who find "un-American activities" a legitimate description of a category of behavior, or misbehavior. It has persisted, I think, because without it there would be nothing else to be loyal or disloyal to. And this is because ours is so essentially a free and open society. We have had our moments of collective intolerance, and many of our leaders are constantly on the prowl for evidence of disloyalty, but in fact we tolerate dissent as few societies do and indeed can be said to have institutionalized dissent. As this book vividly demonstrates, loyalty and disloyalty are relative terms — they mean different things to different people and their meaning changes with time and place. There is no better way to illustrate the persistent importance of loyalty and security in American life than through the pages of one of our leading newspapers.

RICHARD H. ROVERE

THE GREAT
CONTEMPORARY
ISSUES

LOYALTY AND SECURITY IN A DEMOCRATIC STATE

CHAPTER 1

The Alien Threat

A. Mitchell Palmer, Attorney General of the United States
during the "Red Scare" of the early '20's.

Courtesy Compix

PRESIDENT SHOT AT BUFFALO FAIR

Wounded in the Breast and Abdomen.

HE IS RESTING EASILY

One Bullet Extracted, Other Cannot Be Found.

Assassin Is Leon Czolgosz of Cleveland, Who Says He Is an Anarchist and Follower of Emma Goldman.

BUFFALO, Sept. 6.—President McKinley, while holding a reception in the Temple of Music at the Pan-American Exposition at 4 o'clock this afternoon, was shot and twice wounded by Leon Czolgosz, an Anarchist, who lives in Cleveland.

One bullet entered the President's breast, struck the breast bone, glanced and was later easily extracted. The other bullet entered the abdomen, penetrated the stomach, and has not been found, although the wounds have been closed.

The physicians in attendance upon the President at 10:40 o'clock tonight issued the following bulletin:

"The President is rallying satisfactorily and is resting comfortably. 10:15 P.M., temperature, 100.4 degrees; pulse, 124; respiration, 24.

"P. M. RIXEY,
"M. B. MANN,
"R. E. PARKE,
"H. MYNTER,
"EUGENE WANBIN.

Signed by George B. Cortelyou, Secretary to the President."

This condition was maintained until 1 o'clock A.M., when the physicians issued the following bulletin:

"The President is free from pain and resting well. Temperature, 100.2; pulse, 120; respiration, 24."

The assassin was immediately overpowered and taken to a police station on the Exposition grounds, but not before a number of the throng had tried to lynch him. Later he was taken to Police Headquarters.

The exact nature of the President's injuries is described in the following bulletin issued by Secretary Cortelyou for the physicians who were called:

"The President was shot about 4 o'clock. One bullet struck him on the upper portion of the breast bone, glancing and not penetrating; the second bullet penetrated the abdomen five inches below the left nipple and one and one-half inches to the left of the median line. The abdomen was opened through the line of the bullet wound. It was found that the bullet had penetrated the stomach.

"The opening in the front wall of the stomach was carefully closed with silk sutures; after which a search was made for a hole in the back wall of the stomach. This was found and also closed in the same way. The further course of the bullet could not be discovered, although careful search was made. The abdominal wound was closed without drainage. No injury to the intestines or other abdominal organs was discovered.

"The patient stood the operation well, pulse of good quality, rate of 130, and his condition at the conclusion of operation was gratifying. The result cannot be foretold. His condition at present justifies hope of recovery."

Leon Czolgosz, the assassin, has signed a confession, covering six pages of foolscap, in which he states that he is an Anarchist and that he became an enthusiastic member of that body through the influence of Emma Goldman, whose writings he had read and whose lectures he had listened to. He denies having any confederate, and says he decided on the act three days ago and bought the revolver with which the act was committed in Buffalo.

He has seven brothers and sisters in Cleveland, and the Cleveland Directory has the names of about that number living in Hosmer Street and Ackland Avenue, which adjoin. Some of them are butchers and others are in other trades.

Czolgosz is now detained at Police Headquarters, pending the result of the President's injuries. He does not appear in the least degree uneasy or penitent for his action. He says he was induced by his attention to Emma Goldman's lectures and writings to decide that the present form of government in this country was all wrong, and he thought the best way to end it was by the killing of the President. He shows no sign of insanity, but is very reticent about much of his career.

While acknowledging himself an Anarchist, he does not state to what branch of the organization he belongs.

September 7, 1901

SUPPRESSING THE ANARCHISTS.

There is no short way with the Anarchists, as we shall find out if we adopt any of the preventive remedies proposed in such a glib, off-hand, confident fashion during the past week. Let us not forget that the Russian Government has unexceled facilities for suppressing every kind of seditious opinion or practice. No constitutional guarantees there limit the power or restrain the hand of the Czar, yet neither the vigilance of the famous Third Section of the Police nor the ruthless transportation to Siberian prisons of men and women on mere suspicion has sufficed to arrest the propaganda of the Russian Anarchists and Nihilists nor even to protect the person of the Czar himself. It was only twenty years ago that Alexander II was slain by the bomb of an assassin, and since then attempts and plots against the life of the ruler have been often reported.

We are told that the meetings of the Anarchists must be broken up, that we must stop their harangues, and that they must be driven from the country. It is seriously proposed that the civilized Powers unite in an agreement to expel them. But unless we can drive them into the ocean or off the earth this cooperative denial of the right of domicile would be futile. An Anarchist who took the simple precaution to keep his mouth shut would easily escape detection and be free to continue his insane dreaming and his plotting. Suppression of Anarchist meetings and speeches would seem to be an indicated remedy, since it is plain that the right of free speech cannot be claimed for the enemies of the Government that grants it. But if we close the mouths of the Anarchists we simply drive them into their holes and hiding places, where the evil of which they are capable will be planned in secret and society will be quite unaware of its peril. A den of rattlesnakes is not broken up by the killing of the reptiles that emerge and approach the habitations of men.

Nevertheless, communities that are infested by Anarchists must take thought about the matter and devise protective measures. England and the United States have pursued the policy of letting them alone. They have freely sought refuge in these two countries when driven out by Continental Governments, which have complained of our Anglo-Saxon hospitality. The policy of letting them alone does not work well. That is a sufficient reason for adopting a different treatment. Exclusion is the safeguard that first suggests itself, and it is the best and most practicable in a land of liberty and law. It is not a perfect safeguard, nor is capital punishment a perfect safeguard against murder. But it would be absurd to reject a remedy because it would merely diminish, not cure, the evil. We have let known Anarchists come here. We ought to shut them out.

In fact, we ought to shut out a considerable part of the immigration that flows to our shores. A system of diligent inquiry into the antecedents of persons of the immigrant class, the requirement that their neighborhood standing should be certified to by some form of official declaration, and that a Consular certificate from a representative of the United States in the country of their origin should be exhibited to the authorities here prior to their landing would exclude a part at least of the multitude of the undesirable, whether Anarchists, criminals, or paupers who in one way or another now pass the insufficient defenses we have erected. The system would give a great deal of trouble. It is worth while to be at some trouble to keep out even an occasional Anarchist; and it is time that reasonable obstacles were interposed to check indiscriminate immigration. Our Consuls could in no way more profitably busy themselves.

As to what we may do with Anarchists already on American soil we shall be instructed by the proceedings in the case of EMMA GOLDMAN. Czolgosz says that he was prompted by the speeches of this woman to attempt the life of the Presi-

dent. The woman has been arrested. What can we do with her? There is no record of the meetings at which Czolgosz heard her speak, there is no report of the speeches to put before the jury. It would be easy to draw the indictment, but where are the proofs? She has "done time" already for her dangerous talk, but in that trial she was confronted with a report of her utterances. If it could be shown that Czolgosz had in fact been incited to his crime by this woman's speeches she would be convicted as an accomplice. But it is not at all probable that the speeches to which he may have listened would have caused her arrest even if policemen had been present.

That is one of the most serious aspects of the problem. Czolgosz's confession creates a presumption that in one case the words of an Anarchist speaker provoked an attempt to assassinate the President of the United States. Shall we continue to incur that frightful risk, or shall we pass laws forbidding the public or private preaching of these perilous doctrines and try to shut the mouths of all the Anarchists? We know very well that we cannot altogether stop their

talking, and we have hitherto believed that it was the best policy to let them reveal themselves in this way. Of course we are not going to dodge the problem because it is difficult, nor are we going to confess that we are powerless. But those who study the evil most soberly will be least inclined to prescribe remedies off-hand. Doubtless what the newspapers call nests of Anarchists should be broken up by the application of existing laws. It is not safe or reasonable to permit enemies of the human race to spread their doctrines and gain confidence in complete immunity from molestation. Public opinion, awakened and concentrated by the attack on the President, will demand and sanction repressive measures of some kind. But neither newspapers nor ministers of the Gospel nor statesmen should delude themselves with the belief that it is going to be easy to extirpate these reptiles. On the other hand, it would be absurd to defer the attempt to provide safeguards because some critic points out the fact that the remedies suggested are not perfect. All laws are open to the amendments suggested by experience.

September 12, 1901

THE EXCLUSION OF ANARCHISTS.

To the Editor of The New York Times:
Of all the remedies that have been suggested for the suppression of anarchy, I think the one proposed in this morning's TIMES is decidedly the best—that is, to exclude them from the country.

As you rightly say, "exclusion is the safeguard that first suggests itself, and it is the most practicable. In fact, we ought to shut out a considerable part of the immigration that flows to our shores."

But past experience leads me to doubt very much if any such effective legislation will be adopted in the near future. The foreign steamship ring has such a grip on Congress that it is sure to block any legislation that will cut down its enormous dividends.

By the time Congress meets in December all this excitement will have blown over. Mr. Henderson will be re-elected Speaker, Mr. Shattuck of Ohio will be reappointed Chairman of the Immigration Committee, and with these two worthies in power, the friends of immigration restriction may whistle in vain for any effective legislation. Doubtless some kind of a bill will be brought forward as a sop to public opinion, but the ring will take care that it does not materially reduce its list of steerage passengers. If the American people really desire the adoption of such legislation as you recommend they will have to display more interest in the matter than they have shown thus far.   W. H. ALLEN.
Brooklyn, Sept. 12, 1901.

September 16, 1901

AN ANTIDOTE TO ANARCHY.

To the Editor of The New York Times:
The admirable article appearing on the editorial page of yesterday's issue of your paper entitled "Suppression of Anarchy," together with the later grave rumors regarding President McKinley's condition, must have given many of your readers food for thought.

That we are reaping a harvest of our own sowing in having for years permitted almost unlimited immigration is unquestionable, and the means by which we can effectually suppress or wholly eradicate anarchy must interest every loyal American man or woman. That this will require years of concerted, well-directed effort must needs be also true.

Let the patriotic societies, with many of whose members ancestor worship has been the principal occupation, actively interest themselves in this question, greater even than the negro question which confronts us. Let the Daughters of the American Revolution, with its approximate membership of 40,000, forget, for a brief interval, whether the "National woman" or one who has proved her fitness for office be more eligible for the office of President General, and emulate the example of one of its chapters, that of Buffalo, N. Y., by having lectures given in different languages in the slums of the cities where anarchy reigns, and endeavor gradually to inculcate a spirit of reverence for government, the only ligament between man and his country, and for the greatest of all Governments, that of the United States of America.
GRACE M. H. WAKEMAN,
Regent, D. A. R.
Southport, Conn., Sept. 13, 1901.

September 16, 1901

BOGUS AMERICANISM.

To the Editor of The New York Times:
A densely ignorant immigrant who reaches these shores learns in an incredibly short period that this is the freest of free countries. He scarce knows a dozen words of pidgin-English, but he has already absorbed enough of the spirit of so-called "Americanism" to impudently assert it to our oldest citizen. Fresh from the hard slavery of an obscure province, these folk arrive at a most hospitable shore inflamed with the exaggerated tales of the auriferous nature of our paving blocks, of a country whose only nobility is that of wealth, and where socialism and anarchy are punishable only in the deed.

In a generation, these crude opinions, tempered by a little education and some prosperity, are molded into what ultimately becomes the spirit of a very vicious kind of "Americanism," a spirit which, whether right or wrong, is clamorous for the one against the multitude, a spirit which rages against the uniform of the State Guard obeying its lawfully chosen magistrate, a spirit which howls for the freedom in a land for whose liberty neither they nor their ancestors fired a shot. It is oft a mob which is full of patron saints, "vaterlands," stilettos and unpronounceable names, headed by a mercenary with a small head and big voice whose waving arms is the only proceeding understood by the crowd. He talks "America, the land of the free." This is indeed a bogus "Americanism," which breeds cocoon-like in the seclusion of alien countries to finally emerge in full flight to these United States.

This blessed soil may be the promised abiding place, overflowing with milk and money to which the slaves of lands of oppression turn their steps, but with our unrestrained immigration, it will take many years to efface the flaming red paint with which the Goddess of Liberty is at present so plentifully bedaubed.
IRVING E. DOOB.
New York, March 20, 1903.

March 22, 1903

SUPREME COURT BARS TURNER.

Upholds Constitutionality of the Immigration Law Under Which His Deportation Was Ordered.

WASHINGTON, May 16.—In an opinion written by Chief Justice Fuller, the United States Supreme Court to-day sustained the

action of the immigration authorities at the Port of New York in ordering the deportation of the Englishman Turner, alleged to be an Anarchist.

The Chief Justice said in his opinion that Turner did not himself deny that he was an Anarchist. The opinion upheld the law for the exclusion of Anarchists and affirmed the decision of the Circuit Court for the Southern District of New York, which refused a writ of habeas corpus to Turner.

Chief Justice Fuller in his opinion first reviewed the facts in the case, including the claim of Turner that he is a lecturer on sociological questions and an Anarchist in theory merely. He then referred to the fact that Turner's counsel attacked the immigration law as unconstitutional, on the ground that it is in contravention of the First, Fifth, and Sixth Amendments and also of Section 1 of the Constitution, and because "no power is delegated by the Constitution to the General Government over alien friends with reference to their admission into the United States or otherwise, or over the beliefs of citizens, denizens, sojourners, or aliens, or over the freedom of speech or of the press."

All of these contentions were negatived by the decision of the Chief Justice, who said, among other things:

"Whether rested on the accepted principle of international law that every sovereign nation has the power, as inherent in sovereignty and essential to self-preservation, to forbid the entrance of foreigners within its dominions, or to admit them only in such cases and on such conditions as it may see fit to prescribe, or on the power to regulate commerce with foreign nations, which includes the entrance of ships, the importation of goods, and the bringing of persons into the ports of the United States, the act before us is not open to constitutional objection. Nor is the manner in which Congress has exercised the right,

although when such a case arises the objection may be taken."

The Chief Justice also expresses the surprise of the court that exception should be taken to the law on the ground that it is obnoxious to the Constitutional provision prohibiting the abridgment of freedom of speech, the exercise of religious privileges, &c.

"It has," he said, "no reference to an establishment of religion nor does it prohibit the free exercise thereof nor abridge the freedom of speech or of the press, nor the right of the people to assemble and petition the Government for redress of grievances. It is of course true that if an alien is not permitted to enter this country, or, having entered contrary to law, is expelled, he is in fact cut off from worshipping or speaking or publishing or petitioning in the country, but that is merely because of his exclusion therefrom.

"He is not one of the people to whom these things are secured, and cannot become such by an attempt forbidden by law."

Discussing the plea that the law should

not be applicable to Turner because he was not an active Anarchist Chief Justice Fuller said:

"Even if Turner, even though he did not so state to the immigration board of inquiry, only regarded the absence of government as a political ideal, yet when he sought to attain it by advocating, not simply for the benefit of workingmen, who are justly entitled to repel the charge of desiring the destruction of law and order, but 'at any rate as an Anarchist' the 'universal strike' to which he referred, and by discourses on what he called 'the legal murder of 1887,' referring to the Spies case, and by addressing mass meetings on that subject in association with Most, we cannot say that the inference was unjustifiable, either that he contemplated the ultimate realization of his ideal by the use of force or that his speeches were incitements to that end."

Turner is now in Europe, having been released on bail.

May 17, 1904

USE OF DYNAMITE GROWING.

113 Explosions Reported in 6 Years in Labor Dispute

Dynamite has been used in fights on the "open shop" idea for the last six years and dynamite outrages in those years have been steadily on the increase. In all 113 destructive explosions have been reported in connection with labor disputes. At first the use of dynamite was limited to physical work—particularly steel—in course of construction. More recently whole shops have been dynamited.

In the iron and steel industry alone seventy-two cases of dynamiting of structures in course of erection have been reported by one association. In most of these cases there was exhibited a wanton disregard for both life and property, the explosions often causing more damage to the poorly constructed and crowded surroundings than to the construction work under attack.

Detective Burns said in a recent interview:

"In 1908 the dynamitings amounted to a reign of terror. We were given a record for that year of twenty big explosions on different works. They were in all parts of the United States. The thing got so bad that a war couldn't have been much worse. For 1909 and down to the time of the Peoria affair, in September, 1910, we made a list of thirty-five destructive explosions, three other unsuccessful attempts, and seven assaults on workmen."

Nor did the dynamiting stop after The Los Angeles Times was blown up. Since then many explosions have been reported. A list of dynamiting cases in 1910 and 1911 follows:

1910.

March 27—McClintic-Marshall Construction Company, Indiana Harbor, Ind. Two bombs, obviously fitted with time fuses, exploded in building. Erected for American Steel Foundries Company.
April 5—Pan-American Bridge Company, Newcastle, Ind. Entire plant dynamited. After explosion the plant was unionized.
April 19—Second dynamiting of hotel in Salt Lake City, erected by R.D. Jones, sub-contractor for the American Bridge Company.
April 19—Power house of Mount Vernon Car and Manufacturing Company, Mount Vernon, Ill., dynamited. Erected

by McClintic-Marshall Construction Company.
April 19—Chicago & Eastern Illinois bridge across Wabash River at Clinton, Ind., wrecked.
May 24—Structural material stored in Interborough Rapid Transit yards, 223rd Street and Broadway, blown up by dynamite bomb. Construction work by Pennsylvania Steel Company of New York City.
June 4—Machine shop of Davenport Locomotive Works, Davenport, Iowa, dynamited. McClintic-Marshall Construction Company, contractor.
June 4—Bridge for Peoria & Pekin Union Railway Company at Peoria, Ill., dynamited. McClintic-Marshall Construction Company, contractor.
June 5—Material for Denison-Harvard bridge dynamited at Cleveland. McClinton-Marshall Construction Company, contractor.
July 9—Two dynamite explosions partially wrecked Lehigh Valley Railroad viaduct at Greenville, N. J. Phoenix Bridge Company, contractor.
July 15—Trestle work for West Side Belt Railroad of Pittsburgh wrecked by dynamite. McClintic-Marshall Construction Company, contractor.
July 21—Power plant for Omaha & Council Bluffs Street Railway dynamited. Wisconsin Bridge and Iron Company, contractor.
Aug. 1—While unloading a rig on dock of Philadelphia and Reading Coal and Iron Company two dynamite explosions in half hour. Heyl & Patterson, Superior, Wis., contractors.
Aug. 23—Material in McClintic-Marshall Construction Company's yard in Kansas City dynamited.
Sept. 4—Three dynamite explosions at Lucas Bridge and Iron Company's plat at Peoria, Ill. Six adjacent buildings wrecked.
Sept. 4—Two carloads of steel girders belonging to McClintic-Marshall Construction Company in East Orange, Ill., dynamited. Material intended for use in building bridge for Peoria & Pekin Union Railway. (It was in connection with this case Detective Burns's war against the dynamiters began.)
Sept. 28—Dynamite explosion at Reading Railway Bridge at Nicetown, Penn. American Bridge Company, contractors.

Oct. 1—Los Angeles Times Building destroyed by dynamite. Twenty-one men killed.

Oct. 10—Derrick car at New Boston & Albany Bridge in Worcester, Mass., dynamited. Phoenix Bridge Company, contractors.
Oct. 10—Street bridge over Boston & Albany Railroad tracks in Worcester, Mass., dynamited. Boston Bridge Works, contractors.
Nov. 28—Derrick at West Philadelphia National Bank dynamited. Bergdoll & Rawling, contractors.
Dec. 25—Llewellyn Iron Works of Los Angeles, Cal., dynamited. Alleged perpetrators of Los Angeles Times outrage indicted also for this crime.
Dec. 30—Walter Vanstan's Furnace and Sheet Metal Works of Kansas City practically wrecked by dynamite.

1911.

Jan. 29—Car dump being built for Susquehanna Company blown up by two charges of dynamite in Erie, Penn. McCain Construction Company.
Feb. 24—Plant of Iriquois Iron Company of South Chicago damaged by two dynamite explosions. Surrounding property shattered.
March 8—Viaduct for McKinley Traction system at Springfield, Ill., wrecked by two dynamite explosions. McClintic-Marshall Construction Company.
March 16—Unloading bridge of Milwaukee Western Fuel Company, Milwaukee, Wis., wrecked by two explosions. Heyl & Patterson.
March 24—Omaha County Court House badly damaged by two charges of dynamite. Caldwell & Drake Iron Works.
March 24—Caldwell & Drake Iron Works plant, at Columbus, Ind., dynamited simultaneously with Omaha County Court House.
March 25—Ore conveyors of Pickands & Mather of North Kendall, Ohio totally destroyed by dynamite. Heyl & Patterson.
April 2—St. Peter's Street (South Bend, Ind.) viaduct dynamited. Attempt to wreck Grand Trunk bridge across St. Joseph River thwarted.
April 4—Springfield (Mass.) Municipal Building, in course of construction, damaged by two dynamite explosions. A. E. Stephens Company of New York.
Sept. 3—Westchester & Boston Railway viaduct at Mount Vernon, N. Y., wrecked by dynamite.

December 2, 1911

THE NEW SOCIALISM THAT THREATENS THE SOCIAL SYSTEM

By Charles Willis Thompson.

SPRUNG from the fertile brain of a Catholic priest—of all unlikely persons in the world—a perfectly practicable scheme of non-political Socialism has been gradually spreading itself over the United States for the last seven years. Nothing much is known of it in the East even now, when its successful management of the Lawrence strike has focused the attention of the country upon it. To most Eastern-

ers the I. W. W. is merely a name; but the West learned that it was something more when Gov. Steunenberg of Idaho was blown to pieces and when Moyer, Haywood and Pettibone were placed on trial and acquitted of the crime.

The I. W. W., the full name of which is the Industrial Workers of the World, is an association which ought not to be overlooked or slighted. It is the business of every American citizen to acquaint himself fully with what it aims at and what it stands for.

For the I. W. W. is the most serious menace the present system of society has ever been called upon to face.

Socialism—the political variety—may seem more threatening, because of its rapid growth in numbers; but wherever Socialists get into office they turn out to be not very different from other people. Their theories are modified by the conditions they confront, and political Socialism in operation is entirely different from theoretical Socialism. Anarchism makes a great deal of noise, but

Elizabeth Gurley Flynn, the New York Girl Who Went to Jail in Spokane for Writing I. W. W. Articles.

never gets anywhere. But the I. W. W. stands for a plan which means business and which actually could be put in operation, if it got enough of the working class to stand with it; and its aims and methods are revolutionary.

The plan of the I. W. W. is to abolish the wage system. Not through politics; the I. W. W. has no intention of running the Government through commercial and manufacturing industries.

State Socialism approaches the problem from the Governmental end. It proposes to acquire control of the Nation's industries by voting its followers into public office. The I. W. W., on the contrary, proposes to have the workers of the world acquire control of the Nation's industries by gradually increasing the share of the workers in the profits of the industries until a point is reached where the capitalist will be forced out.

It begins by demanding an increase of 15 per cent. in wages. If it gets the increase it waits for awhile and then asks for 15 per cent. more. So it will go on until it has forced the wage scale up to 100 per cent., by which time it will have driven the capitalists out of the field and, as the I. W. W. men put it, have "taken possession of the machinery of production."

The I. W. W. differs from all previous labor organizations. All of them recognize the present system of society and tacitly acknowledge the right of capitalists to exist. All they do is to try to secure advantageous terms for the workers. But the I. W. W. declares war on capital—war to the death. It intends to tear down the whole social structure and build it anew.

This is why such men as William D. Haywood are perfectly unmoved when they are charged with being revolutionists; why they preserve a tranquil countenance when horrified society cries out, "But you are incendiaries!" "We are," Haywood and his like reply; "that's what we have been trying to make you understand. Glad you see the point." Denunciation is wasted on such men; it might as well have been addressed by horrified French society to Danton and Robe-

spierre.

If the plan sounds impracticable, the I. W. W. will frankly reply, "So it is, to-day. But there is nothing impracticable about it if we get a majority of the Nation's workers into our organization. So it is merely a matter of education. If we can't educate the workers up to our standpoint, why, then we fail. If we can educate them nothing can stop our success, for the machinery of production is already in the hands of the workers. All they have to do is to recognize that fact and take possession of it."

Now, so thoroughly obsessed is the American citizen with the idea that everything must be accomplished through politics—through Government, through having some law passed on the subject—that it is next to impossible for him to get the I. W. W. viewpoint through his head. The State Socialist, who of all Americans is the one most thoroughly possessed with the political or governmental idea, will be the last to understand. The State Socialist works from the top down, when he is planning his Utopia; the I. W. W. intends to work from the bottom up.

"Whereas," says Article XIV. of the I. W. W.'s by-laws, "the primary object of the Industrial Workers of the World is to unite the workers on the industrial battlefield; and

"Whereas, Organization in any sense implies discipline through the subordination of parts to the whole and of the individual member to the body of which he is a part; therefore be it

"Resolved, That to the end of promoting industrial unity and of securing necessary discipline within the organization, the I. W. W. refuses all alliances, direct or indirect, with existing political parties or anti-political sects, and disclaims responsibility for any individual opinion or act which may be at variance with the purposes herein expressed."

The old-fashioned labor organizations are much more concerned about the growth of the I. W. W. than are even the employers, for such organizations as the American Federation of Labor recognize in this new society something deadly, something which will wipe them out of existence if it continues to grow. This explains what must have seemed incomprehensible to uninformed newspaper readers—the hostility of John Golden and other labor leaders to the Lawrence strike. Golden and his like were fighting the battle of the employers in Lawrence, not because they especially love the employing class, but because the Lawrence strike was an I. W. W. strike. It was declared, not for the old A. F. of L. motive, that of securing better terms for the workers, but as the first step toward wiping out the capitalist class. Hence Gompers, for instance, who clearly understood what the strike was for, was more bitterly hostile to it than even the employers, whose interests were directly affected, but who did not understand what the fight is for.

"Are you organized in Philadelphia?" I asked an I. W. W. man.

"It's not much of a stronghold for us," he said, "for this reason. When the bosses read that preamble to our constitution it scared the life out of them. 'These people are not looking for wages, they want to own the factory,' one of the bosses said, and with the assistance of the A. F. of L. they drove us out of town."

What is this terrible preamble? It is the work of the Catholic priest already referred to, the Rev. Thomas J. Hagerty, and it declares war on the capitalist society of to-day in the following significant words:

"The working class and the employing class have nothing in common. There can be no peace so long as hunger and

want are found among millions of working people, and the few who make up the employing class have all the good things of life.

"Between these two classes a struggle must go on until all the toilers come together on the political as well as on the industrial field, and take and hold that which they produce by their labor through an economic organization of the working class, without affiliation with any political party.

"The rapid gathering of wealth and the centring of the management of industries into fewer and fewer hands makes the trades unions unable to cope with the ever-growing power of the employing class, because the trades unions foster a state of things which allows one set of workers to be pitted against another set of workers in the same industry, thereby helping defeat one another in wage wars. The trades unions aid the employing class to mislead the workers into the belief that the working class have interests in common with their employers.

"These sad conditions can be changed and the interests of the working class upheld only by an organization formed in such a way that all its members in any one industry, or in all industries, if necessary, cease work whenever a strike or lockout is on in any department thereof, thus making an injury to one an injury to all."

This was the original preamble as drawn up by Hagerty. It was afterward amended by striking out the third paragraph and inserting the following:

"We find that the centring of the management of industries into fewer and fewer hands makes the trades unions unable to cope with the ever growing power of the employing class. The trades unions foster a state of affairs which allows one set of workers to be pitted against another set of workers in the same industry, thereby helping defeat one another in wage wars. Moreover, the trades unions aid the employing class to mislead the workers into the belief that the working class have interests in common with their employers.

"Instead of the conservative motto, 'a fair day's wages for a fair day's work,' we must inscribe on our banner the revolutionary watchword 'abolition of the wage system.'

"It is the historic mission of the working class to do away with capitalism. The army of production must be organized, not only for the everyday struggle with capitalists, but also to carry on production when capitalism shall have been overthrown. By organizing industrially we are forming the structure of the new society within the shell of the old.

"Knowing, therefore, that such an organization is absolutely necessary for our emancipation, we unite under the following constitution."

I asked an I. W. W. man to tell me just what the organization stood for and how it worked. He said:

"In the first place, we don't ask to be recognized by the boss; in fact, we refuse to be recognized by the boss. In this Lawrence strike, for instance, if the workers want to go back they can go as individuals, or they can go back in groups, but they can't make any agreement to go back on behalf of the I. W. W. We don't recognize the boss, and we will not be recognized by him.

"There are two main planks in our platform: First, we use the strike as our predecessors did; second, we use the master lock-out.

"Our use of the strike, though, is not for the half-way purposes for which the old labor organizations used it. We don't strike because of some inequity in payment. We strike because we intend to get hold in time of the tools of production. Each one of our strikes is a step in that direction.

"We don't strike because in a given case the men are getting a dollar or so less than they ought, or are working an hour or two longer than they ought. We strike because the workers are entitled to what they produce, and because we intend to get them what they produce. In one case we strike for a 15 per cent. increase in wages; when we get that we will strike for another 15 per cent., and so on until we get 100 per cent., and then the capitalist will have nothing at all of what we earn, unless, indeed, he wants to go to work. If he does, we will give him a wheel and a bench.

"And, of course, we are going to get all this. We are going to keep at it until the men who produce the wealth shall have the wealth. It is a perfectly simple proposition. We may not get the 15 per cent. the first time we ask it, but we will get it the second or third time, and the same will be true of the 30 per cent., and so on up to the 100 per cent.

"So much for the strike. Now, as to the master lock-out. That means just what it says. We lock out the master.

"What we do is to find out the possibilities of production, and then cut down the production. For instance, if we find, as we did in a case in Minnesota, that the average production is five cars, we cut down the product to four cars. The workmen won't load more than that."

"What is the advantage of that?" I asked.

"To give work to the unemployed," was the reply. "The boss can't make the men load more than four cars. He has got to get extra men if he wants a fifth loaded.

"The matter is absolutely in the control of the men. All that is needed is education. If the men once grasp the idea that the boss is absolutely in their power they can do as they please with him.

"Don't you see? We have the game in our hands. Take the eight hour day. Let the boss say that we have got to work more than eight. All we have to do is to quit after eight hours. If you want a vacation, take it. Stay away as long as you please. When you get ready to come back, tell the boss that you have struck and have been defeated, and are ready to go back to work. Then go back to work, and after eight hours quit again."

"This, then, is war?" I asked.

"War between the working class and the master class," he nodded. "There is no use blinking facts. Such a state of things exists. We have the power, only we have never known how to use it. The I. W. W. is teaching us how to use it. When we use it the capitalist will be powerless. He is in the minority; we have the strength."

"All you need is to get the tools of your production in your hands?"

A smile of impatience crossed his face. "You don't understand. We have the tools of production already in our hands. All we need to do is to take them up. That is what all the labor movements of the past have missed.

"Stay on the job. That's our motto. Don't quit. Strike, if you feel like it, but strike always ready to come back. Strike not for a momentary advantage, but for the sake of stepping forward toward your control of the produce you make."

"Then," said I, "in the case, for instance, of the Lawrence strike, you would have won even if you had lost?"

"Of course," he said.

"And how about politics?"

"Well, you've seen our constitution and by-laws. We don't care a continental

about politics; we don't aim to pass any laws. We can break up the capitalistic system without that by simply taking hold of the machinery of production. As for voting a lot of the workers are not even American citizens, and couldn't vote if they tried. But they have just as much right to the wealth they produce as you or I, and if the I. W. W. accomplishes what it aims at they will get it."

No wonder Gompers does not like the I. W. W.

This organization was born in the brains of some half dozen or so Western radicals and labor men about eight years ago. The brains and driving force were centred in the brilliant mind and striking personality of Hagerty. The lesser lights were Haywood, shortly to be on trial for his life: Charles O. Sherman, William E. Trautmann, editor of the Brauer Zeitung; Frank Bohn, at that time an organizer of the Socialist Labor Party; Ernest Mills, now Secretary of the Western Federation of Miners, and another Haggerty, this one spelling his name with two "g's." He is now studying law at Harvard. The Western Federation of Miners was the backbone of the movement.

These men and eighteen or twenty others met in Chicago in 1904 and discussed their project for two or three days. They drew up an address—Father Hagerty wrote it—and sent it to all the different labor organizations. On January 2, 1905, the first real conference began, and on June 27 a convention was held.

Most of the delegates were from the West, and from that day to this the real strength of the I. W. W. has been from that section. The further West you go the stronger you find it. Haywood, who presided, struck the keynote in his opening speech:

"We are here to confederate the workers of the country into a working class movement that shall have for its purpose the emancipation of the working class from the slave bondage of capitalism. The aims and object of this organization should be to put the working class in possession of the economic power, the means of life, in control of the machinery of production and distribution, without regard to capitalist masters.

"The American Federation of Labor, which presumes to be the labor movement of this country, is not a working class movement. You are going to be confronted with the so-called labor leader, the man who will tell you and other workers that the interests of the capitalist and the workingman are identical. I want to say that a man who makes that assertion is a worse foe to the working class than is D. M. Parry or August Belmont. There is no man who has an ounce of honesty in his make-up but recognizes the fact that there is a continuous struggle between the two classes, and this organization will be formed, based and founded on the class struggle, having in view no compromise and no surrender, and but one object and one purpose; and that is to bring the workers of this country into the possession of the full value of the product of their toil."

After such a speech it is a mere waste of energy to hold up your hands in horror and tell the I. W. W. that it is revolutionary. "That's what we've been telling you," it will reply. Nor would it do Mr. Gompers any good to say, "But you are antagonizing everything the labor unions of the last fifty years have stood for." "Glad you see the point," it will answer Gompers, with an unruffled front.

The I. W. W. had hardly got a fair start when Moyer, Haywood, Pettibone and Vincent St. John, who is now its Secretary, were arrested for the murder of Steunenberg. St. John was promptly

liberated; the other three were tried and acquitted.

"It ought to have been a good ad for us," said an I. W. W. man to me; "but it was the Western Federation of Miners that got all the advertising. The public didn't associate us with the trial at all. We had to stop our organization work to raise funds for the defense, and altogether that trial didn't do us much good."

After this excitement was over the I. W. W. went ahead with its work. It abolished the office of President, and Secretary St. John is the highest officer it has. "In a labor organization," one of them explained to me, "the office of President tends to autocracy. The President can't stay in his office; he must go on the road. The position Gompers holds is not at all like the Presidency of a corporation. We saw that to have a President would be to Gomperize the organization, so we figured that it was better simply to have a Secretary, have the board called together at frequent intervals, and let it elect its own Chairman for the time being."

The first attack of the I. W. W. on the East was when it organized the electrical workers in Schenectady, the city which recently elected a Socialist Mayor. They tried to organize in New York City, but could not get anywhere with it because of the hostility of the building trades, which are a sort of labor aristocracy. In Newark they organized the metal workers and some others, but they found New York in the hands of the A. F. of L.—or, as they put it, "organized on the other side."

"However," said one of them, "we didn't go out to fight other organizations. Our chief purpose was to organize the unorganized."

The first conflict was in Schenectady, and the first big victory was in the Northwestern lumber camps. There was another big fight in Goldfield, Nev., but the thing which first advertised the I. W. W. in the East was not a strike at all, but a fight over the question of free speech, and it happened in Spokane in 1909.

The I. W. W. had been organizing in Missoula, Mont., and it extended its activities to Spokane. The city authorities determined to prevent it, and whenever an I. W. W. orator undertook to make a speech he or she was promptly arrested. One of the most celebrated of these cases was that of Elizabeth Gurley Flynn, a New York girl and now a Normal College student, who was then about 18 years old. Miss Flynn has since become very well known as a labor agitator. Another girl arrested at the time was Agnes Fair. Altogether the authorities arrested about 400 persons, for no crime except that of trying to make speeches advising workers to join the I. W. W.

"Nearly all of them were American born, and many of them had a long American lineage," said Miss Flynn's mother in telling me about it. "The Chief of Police who arrested them was named Sullivan—a name which the I. W. W. seems to run up against wherever it goes; the Lawrence Chief is named Sullivan, too. Some of the cases were very curious. One speaker got up on the platform and started to read the Declaration of Independence. He was promptly arrested. Amusing, wasn't it? Another speaker got badly scared when he mounted the platform and saw the police in front of him. He couldn't say anything for a moment or two, and then he desperately began: 'Fellow-workers!' That was as far as he got; he was immediately arrested for delivering an incendiary harangue.

"They put the editor of The Industrial Worker in jail, and my daughter promptly took his place. She was arrested. There were three editors arrested, and finally the police invaded the office, broke the press, and smashed the types. At last, however, the authorities lost their courage; Sullivan parleyed with Fred Hazlewood, the organizer, and an agreement was reached by which Hazlewood was allowed the right of free speech for his organizers. Some of those arrested, however, died as a result of their jail experience."

There was another "free speech fight" in Aberdeen, S. D., and another in Fresno, Cal. The East paid little or no attention to these things, until the great strike at McKees Rocks, Penn., in 1909. The Pennsylvania State Constabulary—the I. W. W. calls them "the Cossacks"—were brought into service, and a state of actual war resulted, in which pitched battles were fought between the strikers and the constabulary. The first killing was that of a striker. The strike committee thereupon served notice upon the commander of the constabulary that for every life his men took a life would be demanded by the strikers.

The strikers kept their word and an equal number were killed on both sides. In one battle ten strikers were killed and fifty wounded, and for every life taken a life was exacted from the constabulary. The result of this civil war was a victory for the strikers.

The I. W. W. still finds its chief strength in the Far West. It has made no impression on the State of New York, but has got a good foothold in New England, as the Lawrence strike proves.

In Chicago it has a very fair organization. In Newcastle, Penn., it is strong enough to support a newspaper. It is strong in New Bedford and in Olneyville, which is really a part of Providence, the part where most of the mills are located.

It extends through a large part of Massachusetts. It flourishes in Paterson and West Hoboken and one or two other New Jersey towns. It controls Hammond, Ind.

Its Northwestern strength, whereof Missoula is the centre, extends across the border and takes in all of British Columbia. All of Butte is organized by it except for the aristocratic building trades, and Butte has a Socialist Mayor. What there is of labor in Nevada is entirely in the hands of the I. W. W.; it has organized Tonopah, Goldfield, and Reno. I. W. W. organizers are now at work in Alaska. The whole metalliferous field is organized under the direction of the Western Federation of Miners. The fruit valleys of California belong to the I. W. W.

"And," said one of them, "we were the first people to organize the Chinese and Japs out there. It went against all the labor traditions of California."

"Shades of Dennis Kearney!" interrupted Mrs. Flynn, who was listening.

"How about negroes?"

"It's hard to do anything with them," said the I. W. W. man, "because you can't induce a colored man to buy only union goods. They are not dependable.

However, in New Orleans, where the negro workingman really is a factor to be considered, there are negro unions as well as white unions, and white and black meet in the central board."

In Florida they have organized the cigarmakers, and for a while they were strong in Porto Rico, but the A. F. of L. got it away from them. They control St. Joseph, Mo., and even in Philadelphia, the coldest of all cities to them, they have about 1,000 members. It was really the A. F. of L. that killed their chances in Philadelphia, working hand in hand with the "bosses." They were strong enough in Brooklyn last Winter to conduct a strike of shoe workers there, and they won a victory. They also have a strong organization in Youngstown, Ohio.

Many of the I. W. W. strikes have been successful, but in view of the fact that the organization is only seven years old the members don't regard that as an important matter. When they have won victories they have won big and decisive ones. In 1906 they established the eight-hour day for hotel and restaurant workers in Goldfield. In the same year they conducted a strike of sheet steel workers at Youngstown, but lost it. This defeat was the work of the American Federation, which sent men to fill the places of the strikers. In 1907 they won a victory for the textile workers at Skowhegan, although John Golden tried to break the strike by furnishing strikebreakers.

In Portland, Ore., they conducted a sawmill strike which was apparently a failure, though in the end the workers got what they wanted in the way of increased wages. In Bridgeport, Conn., the A. F. of L. again "scabbed" and defeated a tube mill strike, and the I. W. W. lost a silk mill strike in Lancaster, Penn. All these fights were in 1906.

In 1907 they again conducted a successful strike in Goldfield. In 1909 came the successful strike at McKees Rocks. That was followed by the "free speech fight" in Spokane, and by another, less noted, in Fresno, Cal. The Brooklyn strike of 1911, which was successful, and the victorious strike in Lawrence fill the list of the I. W. W.'s conflicts.

In a pamphlet issued by the I. W. W. the following statement of its tactics is given:

"As a revolutionary organization the Industrial Workers of the World aim to use any and all tactics that will get the results sought with the least expenditure of time and energy. The tactics used are determined solely by the power of the organization to make good in their use. The question of 'right' and 'wrong' does not concern us.

"No terms made with an employer are final. All peace so long as the wage system lasts is but an armed truce. At any favorable opportunity the struggle for more control of industry is renewed.

"The Industrial Workers realize that the day of successful long strikes is past. Under all ordinary circumstances a strike that is not won in four to six weeks cannot be won by remaining out longer. In

trustified industry the employer can better afford to fight one strike that lasts six months than he can six strikes that take place in that period.

"The organization does not allow any part to enter into time contracts with the employers. It aims, where strikes are used, to paralyze all branches of the industry involved, when the employers can least afford a cessation of work—during the busy season and when there are rush orders to be filled.

"The Industrial Workers of the World maintain that nothing will be conceded by the employers except that which we have the power to take and hold by the strength of our organization. Therefore we seek no agreements with the employers.

"Failing to force concessions from the employers by the strike, work is resumed and 'sabotage' is used to force the employers to concede the demands of the workers.

"The great progress made in machine production results in an ever-increasing army of unemployed. To counteract this the Industrial Workers of the World aims to establish the shorter workday, and to slow up the working pace, thus compelling the employment of more and more workers.

"To facilitate the work of organization large initiation fees and dues are prohibited by the I. W. W.

"During strikes the works are closely picketed and every effort made to keep the employers from getting workers into the shops. All supplies are cut off from strike-bound shops. All shipments are refused or missent, delayed, and lost if possible. Strikebreakers are also isolated to the full extent of the power of the organization. Interference by the Government is resented by open violation of the Government's orders, going to jail en masse, causing expense to the taxpayers—which are but another name for the employing class.

"In short, the I. W. W. advocates the use of militant 'direct action' tactics to the full extent of our power to make good."

Whether we believe in its aims and methods or hold them in abhorrence, let us all get acquainted with the I. W. W. without loss of time. We are going to hear more and more of it as time goes on, and it is just as well to make its acquaintance now as later. It is Socialism, but not political Socialism; it has more of the air of meaning business than either the Socialist Party or any labor organization. It calls itself "industrial unionism," which may sound vague, but which means something very definite and not at all Gomperish. It is not afraid of using violence and has no fear of violence being used against it. Since Camille Desmoulins climbed on that table in the Palais Royal in 1789 and unloosed the French Revolution there has been no movement about which it behooved conservative citizens to be more thoughtful.

March 17, 1912

FORCED TO KISS THE FLAG.

100 Anarchists Are Then Driven from San Diego.

SAN DIEGO, Cal., April 4.—Nearly 100 Industrial Workers of the World, all of whom admitted that they were anarchists, knelt on the ground and kissed the folds of an American flag at dawn to-day near San Onofre, a small settlement a short distance this side of the Orange County boundary line.

The ceremony, which was most unwillingly performed, was witnessed by forty-five deputy constables and a large body of armed citizens of San Diego. The men who were thus forced to show respect to the National emblem composed the party that left Santa Ana on a freight train the night before and whose coming was awaited by the deputies and armed citizens who had gone out in automobiles to meet them and drive them back.

The Industrial Workers were stopped at San Onofre and detained there until this morning.

After the flag kissing the Industrial Workers were divided into squads of five and placed in command of details of deputies. Then the march to the line was started, and the procession moved to the tune of the "Star Spangled Banner," in which the Industrial Workers were compelled to make at least a show of joining. At the Orange County line the men who had come from Santa Ana were given a parting caution to keep out of San Diego County. They started north on the railroad track.

April 5, 1912

CHARGES LABOR PLOT TO WRECK SAN DIEGO

Federal Attorney Says Industrial Workers Had Dynamite Cached There.

FIRST STEP IN REVOLUTION

Grand Jury Starts Inquiry—Secret Service Men to Seek More Evidence of Conspiracy.

Special to The New York Times.

LOS ANGELES, Cal., May 20.—When the Federal Grand Jury convened this afternoon it began in earnest an investigation of the Industrial Workers of the World which will last for weeks and be Nation wide in scope. It is predicted by officials of the Government that it will disclose that San Diego was selected as the ground for the organization to start in their own words, "An evolution that would result in a revolution for the overthrow of the Government."

Assistant United States Attorney Dudley Robinson, who has charge of the investigation, which is being conducted on orders from Washington, stated to-night that a condition of affairs exists in San Diego of which the outside world knows nothing, practically, as all the evidence that has been collected by San Diego authorities, working in conjunction with Federal authorities, has been reserved for the Federal Grand Jury.

"The evidence which has been brought to my attention in an unofficial manner," said Mr. Robinson, "discloses a state of affairs that is almost beyond comprehension. I have learned that a plot was hatched in this city by the Industrial Workers of the World some time ago to march on San Diego, and when the full force was gathered there they were to blow up the water works, the electric light plant, and the street railway simultaneously, and then start a free-for-all looting and pillaging. Three caches of dynamite have been found by Secret Service men in San Diego. The dynamite was hidden away for the purpose of blowing up these institutions. The plot was found out by Government Secret Service men in Los Angeles and frustrated.

"It is the purpose of the Government to make a thorough investigation of the organization and of some of the acts of the ring leaders, or heads of the order, who, we have reason to believe, are now in hiding at or near San Diego and directing affairs."

The officials of the Department of Justice of the United States Government, acting under orders of President Taft, have concluded to take the investigation out of the hands of the city authorities of San Diego and those of the State. This is indicated in a resumption of activities at San Diego by United States Secret Service agents of Los Angeles.

The telegram from the Department of Justice instructing the special agents to go to San Diego declared: "Important developments are at hand."

Police Commissioner C. H. Delacour of San Diego received a threatening letter signed by F. Garney at the Natick House to-day threatening him with death if he did not at once cease his efforts to bring the organization's activities before the Federal Grand Jury. The letter closed: "Yours for revolution. F. Garney."

Attorney Fred H. Moore, in arguing his motion before Judge W. R. Guy in San Diego that citation for contempt of court be issued this morning for John M. Porter and fifteen others of the vigilantes, was unable to name any of the others, and the case has narrowed down to Porter, who is a prominent business man.

Upon a vigorous protest of Attorney Moore, who demanded that the citation be issued forthwith in regard to Porter, and that John Doe citations be issued for the others, Judge Guy changed the continuance until Wednesday and denied the John Doe proceedings.

May 21, 1912

U. S. SAILORS RAID SEATTLE SOCIALISTS

Wreck I. W. W. Hall, Burn Furniture—Stirred by Daniels' Speech on Red Flag.

SEATTLE, July 18.—A party of United States marines and sailors from the Pacific reserve fleet, most of the sailors wearing the name bands of the cruisers Colorado and California, started to-night to "clean up the town" as they expressed it, by attacking Socialists' headquarters and Industrial Workers of the World. They dragged the furniture from the big I. W. W. hall in the southern part of the city, and made a bonfire of it.

A provost guard of fifty men from the fleet hurried ashore in cutters to arrest all the seamen.

Mr. Daniels, Secretary of the Navy, was dining on board the cruiser West Virginia at the time of the disturbance.

About a dozen bluejackets, all young, were in the first wrecking party to get under way. They were aided by several members of the Washington Naval Militia and by a hundred young civilians, who made most of the noise. Waving United States flags the storming party swooped down on the cart newsstand of Millard Price, a Socialist orator, at the intersection of Fourth Avenue and Westlake Boulevard, the busiest night corner of the city. The cart was broken to splinters in a moment and the big stock of Socialist papers and magazines was torn, tossed into the street, and jumped upon.

The mob then proceeded to the Socialist headquarters, on Fifth Avenue, near Stewart Street, smashing the plate-glass front, after which they nailed American flags on the front of the building.

The sailors tore the signs from the front of the building and broke them to pieces, and then started to drag the furniture and books into the street, but the police stopped them.

The mob reformed in the northern part of the city after it had been dispersed, and went back to the Socialist headquarters on Fifth Avenue and Virginia. This time they sacked the place, destroying the furniture and a large quantity of Socialist literature.

There were demands that the Industrial workers be hunted down, and a young civilian tried to induce the party to go to the headquarters of the Moderate Socialists in an old church on Olive Street near Seventh.

Another self-appointed leader led the party toward the old Unitarian Church on Seventh Avenue near Union Street, which had just been vacated by the Moderates.

As the sailors were crossing Pike Street, at Sixth, they were overhauled by an automobile full of policemen headed by a Captain, who told them if did not disperse he would arrest every one of them. The sailors shouted back:—"Your Mayor won't do anything to protect the flag, so we are saving your city."

A young civilian who had been endeavoring to incite the sailors kept shouting to them to "go and get Mayor Cotterill."

The mob finally scattered and no arrests were made.

During the Administration of Mayor George Cotterill all street speakers have been allowed to speak as much as they chose, provided they did not block traffic or display the red flag. The Industrial Workers of the World have held meetings every night at three public squares. Mayor Cotterill has been assailed in some of the newspapers for permitting the I. W. W. to hold their meetings.

During the Golden Potlatch celebration hundreds of men from the fleet were on shore leave, and yesterday many soldiers from Fort Lawton and Fort Flagler were at liberty. In a fight at an I. W. W. meeting last night three soldiers were badly beaten.

In his speech at a banquet last night Secretary Daniels praised the attitude of the Mayor of Boston, who stopped a red flag parade.

"The red flag has no place in this country," he said, "and believers in it have no place in this country. A Mayor who does not enforce the law against the red flag is not fit to hold office, and people who believe in the red flag should be driven from the country."

His red flag remarks occupied only a minute and those who observed him closely said he had no intention of making them apply locally. However, word was passed about the street to-day that the Secretary had made a long address devoted to the two flags and had urged that all believers in the red flag be driven out of the country. It was also asserted that he had made a direct attack upon Mayor Cotterill who sat near him. The fact was that the Mayor accompanied the Secretary from the banquet to the Press Club reception.

It is not believed Mr. Daniels had any knowledge of the Seattle controversy over the red flag.

July 19, 1913

DANIELS CONDEMNS RIOTERS

Directs the Punishment of Sailors Who Destroyed Socialist Property.

Special to The New York Times.

WASHINGTON, Aug. 20.—Secretary Daniels has issued an order for the punishment of the enlisted men of the Colorado, the Charleston, the St. Louis, and other vessels of the Pacific reserve fleet stationed at Bremerton, Wash., who engaged in the riots at Seattle, on July 17, 18 and 19, against the Industrial Workers of the World and the Socialists. This action follows a thorough investigation by a special board appointed by Rear Admiral Alfred Reynolds, Commander in Chief of the fleet, and consisting of Commander Thomas Washington, Lieut. Commander Henry E. Jensen, Lieut. Commander Walter E. Whitehead and Lieut. Harvey W. McCormack.

The board had difficulty in securing witnesses, as most citizens of Seattle sympathized with the attacks upon the Industrial Workers of the World and the Socialist orators, and would not give information against any of the individuals who participated in the riots. None of the sailors who had shore liberty could be proved to have taken part in the disorders. It is expected that Admiral Reynolds will therefore impose a collective punishment which all who went ashore will be obliged to bear, the innocent with the guilty.

The report of the board says that the direct responsibility for the riot rests upon the Seattle police, who were in sympathy with the rioters and their purpose, and took no steps to prevent violence. The idea of destroying the Industrial Workers of the World property did not originate with the enlisted men, but with citizens of Seattle, and there were comparatively few of the bluejackets in the crowd; but by reason of their wearing uniforms they were plainly known to be taking part.

Secretary Daniels in his order, which is to be published to the men of the various vessels of the fleet, denounces the Industrial Workers of the World for criticising the men of the navy and provoking them to violence.

The conduct of the persons who denounced the soldiers, abused the army and navy, reflected upon the flag, and made assault upon soldiers in the American uniform, says the Secretary, "is most reprehensible and deserving of condemnation. But their violence of language, unprovoked assault upon soldiers and lawlessness do not justify retaliation in kind.

"It is hereby directed that the Commander in Chief of the Pacific reserve fleet send a copy of this letter to the commanding officers of the ships upon which the enlisted men and marines are serving, who engaged in the unlawful action in Seattle, with instructions to have this letter read, and it is further ordered that the men engaged in this

affair be punished for their conduct as the Admiral may adjudge is adequate for the offense."

SEATTLE, Aug. 20.—Rear Admiral Alfred Reynolds, in transmitting Secretary Daniels's letter, appends a direction to commanders of all the ships of the Pacific reserve fleet to read the Secretary's statement at muster, but it adds that inasmuch as it has been impossible to obtain proof of the participation of any specified man in the demonstration, it will be impracticable to attempt any punishment.

August 21, 1913

HAYWOOD OPENLY STIRS SEDITION

I. W. W. Leader Threatens Wilson with Great Strike if War Comes.

SAYS MINERS HAVE PLANNED

Warns of Industrial Struggle Which He Says President Will Start Automatically.

EXPECT WASHINGTON TO ACT

Sedition, Says Washington
Special to The New York Times.
WASHINGTON, April 19.—Attorney General McReynolds could not be seen to-night, but it was learned that he had had under consideration

such an emergency as that suggested in Haywood's speech in New York to-night, and his course of action has been fully decided upon.

At the Department of Justice the view was expressed that the threat to bring on a general strike to prevent the Government from going to war with Mexico was seditious, and the summary arrest of any man who attempted to execute such a threat would speedily follow proof of the act.

"That is the vilest blackmail," said a prominent official of the Department of Justice when the declaration of Haywood was called to his attention. This official explained that the labor organizations concerned, baffled by the refusal of the United States Supreme Court to afford relief to President Ryan of the Structural Steel Workers and other labor leaders who were convicted of complicity in dynamiting The Los Angeles Times office building, have agreed to demand the pardon of Ryan and the rest. The threat of a strike in the event of war with Mexico is declared to be a part of their campaign.

William D. Haywood, founder and chief organizer of the I. W. W. told an audience which more than half filled Carnegie Hall last night that the minute President Wilson and Congress declared war against Mexico they would automatically start the greatest general strike this country had ever known.

Supplementing Haywood's threat, Ernest Bohm later told the audience that all Socialists would favor a general strike against war with Mexico. "It would be a test," he said, "of the working people's power to conduct a general strike against the capitalist class."

Haywood, in the course of his speech, said that he prophesied the great strike upon authority of the United Mine Workers of America and the Western Federation of Miners.

"The mine workers of this country," he shouted to his inflamed hearers, "will simply fold their arms, and when they fold their arms there will be no war.

"Sherman said war was hell. Well, then, let the bankers go to war, and let the interest-takers and the dividend-takers go to war with them. If only those parasites were out of the country it would be a pretty decent place to live in. They live on graft, and if they stay here the best that I can promise them is that we will speedily bring them to the day when they will turn over the keys of the city to the marching men such as Frank Tannenbaum led against the churches."

Haywood said that the mine workers already had made up their minds about what they would do in case of war. He said they had already done all the voting necessary, and that the situation purposely was arranged so that President Wilson might automatically start the general strike himself.

April 20, 1914

A "DEEPLY POETICAL SOUL."

In view of all the other incentives to excitement in this hour, it is scarcely worth while to give way to wrath over the extraordinary exhibition of disloyalty to the Government, demagogism, and sheer impudence at Carnegie Hall on Sunday night. We may be sure that HAYWOOD and his followers will be powerless to influence the course of events in this country. It seems strange that while the newspapers which fitly represent the Haywood quality of mind have been clamoring for war, that mob leader should turn a grave national situation, out of which war might grow, into an occasion to proclaim his superiority to the Government at Washington and announce that the successful prosecution of a war would be prevented by a general labor strike. It has been truthfully said that HAYWOOD's language on Sunday was seditious, but it is not at all likely at present that any serious notice will be taken of it at Washington.

If the situation were graver than it is, if we were actually embarking on a perilous war, the provocation for checking the rabid utterances of these fellows, who earn their living by fomenting discontent, would be greater. But, obviously, the naval expedition to the eastern coast of Mexico is made not to begin a war against the Mexican people but to teach a much-needed lesson to an insolent dictator, whose right to the Presidency of Mexico is denied by the United States Government and a very large majority of the Mexican people as well. Therefore HAYWOOD's sedition will probably go unnoticed. The "deeply poetical soul," ascribed to him by one of his admirers, will not be disturbed by tyrannical law officers.

But the citizens of New York are getting very tired of HAYWOOD and all the I. W. W. crowd. They do not recognize in them fellow-Americans. The methods of these malcontents are entirely un-American. They are

feeble imitators of the German and French anarchists and the riotous element in Spain, to which one of their heroes, FERRER, belonged. There is no excuse for their existence here. They abuse all the privileges granted to them, preach murder, disloyalty, and theft by violence, and there is no doubt that a large majority of the residents of New York, including all who work honestly for a living and have managed to lay by a few dollars to meet emergencies, would heartily favor stringent measures for their suppression. Perhaps it is just as well, however, to take them for what they are worth and not make too much of them. If there is a war, you may be sure that HAYWOOD's followers will not oppose it, but will enlist, if the recruiting officers find them physically fit. Some of them may turn out to be good soldiers in the end.

April 21, 1914

HIBBEN FOR PREPAREDNESS.

Princeton Head Also Would Stamp Out "Hyphenated Loyalty."

Dr. John Grier Hibben, President of Princeton University, has written for the American Defense Society an article on "Preparedness Against War," in the course of which he says that, in the event of war, the young men of the universities and colleges will "be led to slaughter like cattle to the shambles." Likewise he pays his respects to the man of "hyphenated loyalty," whom he brands as a traitor, and in this country, he adds, there should be "no place and no quarter for traitors."

"In the event of a grave national peril," he says, "our university students would be the first to offer their services. They would give the enthusiasm of faith and the loyal devotion of patriots, but without knowledge, skill, or experience in the art of warfare. It is like a hideous nightmare to think that, under the possible circumstances of sudden surprise of an invading enemy, these young men would be led to slaughter like cattle to the shambles. In the second place, the American youth of today need above all things to be given an opportunity to forget themselves and their selfish interests and pursuits in some form of disinterested service in which the spirit of unselfishness and manly endeavor richly latent in their natures may find concrete expression.

"Whatever views I may hold concerning military preparedness, therefore, cannot be ascribed to any feeling of panic due to brooding over the unspeakable horrors of the present world tragedy, whose daily progress we follow with anxious and depressed spirits. The war, however, has served to confirm my opinion of the necessity of a more adequate military preparedness."

"Finally," concludes Dr. Hibben, "there must be a preparedness for all that the future holds in store for us by a demand throughout our country for an undivided loyalty on the part of the entire body of our citizens, and an unconditional and unreserved acknowledgment that America is their one and only fatherland. Public sentiment must run so strong and so high as to make it impossible for any one who has taken the oath of citizenship to divide his allegiance between the claims of this country and those of the country upon which he turned his back long years past in order to seek a home in this new land beyond the sea.

"Let us not shrink from calling things by their right names, and therefore let us brand as a traitor whoever lives in our midst, enjoying the protection and prosperity of our country, and yet dares to express by word or deed the spirit of hyphenated loyalty. There is welcome within our border for all sorts and conditions of men, but no place and no quarter for traitors."

January 22, 1916

IS MONEY OUR KING?

Plea for National Institutions to Make New Citizens Coming to Our Shores Patriotic.

By MARK EISNER,
Collector of Internal Revenue.

IN a recent article on preparedness in The Metropolitan Magazine, Henry Reuterdahl makes the following statement:

Our patriotism is waning and drifting away on the ebb tide of indifference, and as a nation, our manhood is on the decline; national conscience we have not. No longer can an American hold up his head abroad. Our place in the world is that of a moneybag. In Germany we are laughed at, despised as spineless weaklings; our money alone is feared. England thinks we are cowards and American life a commodity which can be paid for in cash. The French shrug their shoulders.

The foregoing is but an echo of an assertion that is frequently heard these days and deserves particular attention because if untrue, it should be sharply challenged, and if true, something should be done to restore the fires of American patriotism that established and preserved our union of States upon the principles of liberty, equality, and justice.

It is quite true that there are superficial indications which might lead to a hasty generalization, such as that of Mr. Reuterdahl. There are signs in this country of an apathetic national conscience, but whether they proceed from causes which are only slight and inconclusive, or whether they are fundamental and organic, remains to be seen.

Quite recently there was a private dinner given to a former President of this country, at which were assembled men representing a capital of $12,000,000,000, and common belief has it that the purpose of this dinner was to discuss the availability of this former President as a candidate for re-election to the same office.

Now it does not make a particle of difference whether that was the object of the dinner or not. It is sufficient that the people of the United States generally believe that such was its object. Yet where has there been any general protest against the availability of a candidate being considered only by an aggregation of capital? There were no prominent educators at that dinner. No ministers' names appeared among the guests. No prominent representative of the agricultural community seems to have been there. No representative of labor shared the hospitality of the host. Nor was any public man there present who, in a non-partisan, unselfish and patriotic way has won the confidence of the people as a mouthpiece of their innermost sentiments and aspirations. But nobody appears surprised or indignant.

So that we, the people, seem to accept complacently and without a murmur, the fact that an aggregation of capitalists might dictate the nomination of a candidate for the highest office in the land.

When the Mexican controversy raged at its fiercest, those who sided with the President and those who opposed his course, never by argument faced the real issue. Most of the President's defenders spoke of the frightful loss of American lives which would follow armed intervention.

Which was quite true. But that was not the issue. Those who bitterly opposed Mr. Wilson's views had their arguments provided for them by persons interested financially in Mexico who feared the loss of their investments if this government did not plunge into war to save them.

How many considered the real patriotic issue which regarded the recognition of a government as the welcoming of the recognized government into the sisterhood of nations, and the implication that that government was in every way fit to associate, so to speak, with the nation so recognizing it? How many were there patriotic enough sincerely to feel that the United States ought not to welcome a government to an equality with itself, which was founded upon foul crime? The answer to this question would give us a measure of the really patriotic Americans; those whose love for their country is not a matter of dollars or of physical comfort, but is engendered upon devotion to ideals.

The statement has been made that, however wise and devoted to his country a man may be, whatever he has done, and no matter how much he has done toward realizing its destiny, and regardless of the intensity of his consecration, the extent of his sacrifice in the achievement of patriotic ends and the promotion of the general happiness of his people, such a man would stand little chance of election to the Presidency over another whose sole claim was the provision of a full dinner pail.

Can all this be true? Have we become a nation of materialists—capitalists, shopkeepers, and workers—each man among us a cosmos in himself, looking neither to the right nor to the left, and without ideals and devoid of the love of country, regarding our fair land with no further appreciation than that with which a cow looks upon its pasture field?

To a certain extent, particularly in the large centres of population, patriotism plays no part in the daily life of many people. This is especially the case with certain of our wealthy class, whose interest is largely the accumulation and retention of money. Abroad, these good people make it known immediately that they are Americans, and by their loud boasting, which they think is patriotism, bring derision and scorn to the name American. But at home, none of them regards his native land as the living-place of a posterity which should have guaranteed to it the largest measure of freedom and opportunity.

The real love of country today finds itself in the heart of the recently naturalized citizen who has in good faith renounced his former allegiance in the children of immigrants, and in the small communities, East, West, North and South, where the drive and grind of a never-ceasing material conflict do not obliterate the memories of our nation's past history, nor cause its future to be regarded with the cynical eye of him whose present existence is a hopeless struggle or an idle Sybaritism. In the smaller communities, likewise, a comparative economic independence has preserved independence in thought and action, which is essential if the Republic is to survive.

Thus there is still a considerable part of our population, Mr. Reuterdahl to the contrary notwithstanding, that has not lost all patriotism. But what are we to do to preserve it and to reclaim those who are indifferent?

Perhaps our greatest fault is a lack of national institutions. We have no folk songs, for example, which everybody, old and young, knows. Our national holidays are indifferently celebrated and without any uniformity of manner. They are for the most part "a day off" rather than a day of commemoration, in which all should participate. Our patriotic airs are familiar, but the words unknown to most of us. Go anywhere in Europe and you will hear, on national holidays, the deep-chested voices of men singing the national anthems from beginning to end. Have you ever been to a banquet, attended perhaps by the President of the United States, where an attempt has been made to sing "The Star-Spangled Banner" or "America"? If you have nothing further need be said.

How many adults in the United States know by heart a single poem describing either a great American historical event, or a poetic masterpiece, from a purely literary point of view? Have we a single song, not rag-time, which is national, and which our children's children will sing? Hardly. But every Frenchman can sing " La Marseillaise " from start to finish, and Béranger is familiar to all. In Germany, especially, can it be said that every citizen knows the national airs as well as his own name, and in addition an astonishing number of folk songs and poems, which are sung and recited on all occasions, formal, informal, in public, and in the family circle.

Might it not be said that our difficulties with hyphenated Americans are partly due to the fact that we have not provided sufficient national customs, institutions, and associations to wean them away from those of their parent countries, and make them forget what they have left behind in the absorption of the spirit of what they find here? Those Germans, for example, who came over after 1848 chose this country for its political freedom, which was full compensation for everything they renounced in assuming American citizenship. They and their children today are not " hypenated," any more than Mayflower descendants. Those who emigrated to America within the last thirty years, however, did so for economic reasons largely, the element of political freedom hardly entering into their calculations. Not finding purely American customs, associations, and ideals of sufficient strength and individuality to dissever those links which

bound them to the land from which they came, we now find a number, much smaller than the volume of sound which emanates from them would indicate, who place their former allegiance above that of their later choice.

It is therefore these ties that bind which go far toward instilling patriotism in the people. The remedy lies in education. We have a glorious history, with events worthy of commemoration. We have natio. al airs and a national literature. But our education is superficial. It is woefully lacking in drill and concentration. Your English child knows the 2,000 years of English history in minute detail, while our average college graduate has but a nodding acquaintance with the few hundred years of American history. Our colleges, which should be centres of patriotism, of lofty national ethics, are in the main seats of cynical abstraction and negation, unless that peculiar athletic state of mind known as " college spirit " may be considered a " pis aller " for a broader altruism.

If the State educational departments are too weak to cause the instruction of history in a way that will inspire our youth; if our national anthems and poems cannot be taught, under present auspices, in such a way as to remain firmly imbedded in the memory of our people; if our national holidays cannot now be observed in a uniformly fitting manner, then it is time for us as a nation to intervene, and instead of a national commissioner of education,

who is nothing more than a statistician, let us have a powerful secretary of education in the Cabinet, who will be charged with the duty of once more stimulating a love of country, which shall be affirmative, not negative. What we need is a spirit of patriotism in times of peace, which is the only true patriotism. Any brute animal will defend its home, if attacked. Of jingoism and Chauvinism we have an excess; of the subordination of ambition, of party, of all save honor to the general good, we have too little. The catch phrase " America first " may mean much; the word "America" should mean vastly more.

We must apply ourselves to the task of unification; of uprooting selfishness, greed, and interested commercialism; of shaking the dust off our principles and national ideals, and setting them up high where all can see and ever keep uppermost. It can be done. Now is the time—before the anaemia which is developing in America becomes pernicious and incurable. To every American, including the hyphenated, the following passage from Washington's farewell address is earnestly commended: *Citizens, by birth or choice, of a common country, that country has a right to concentrate your affections. The name of American, which belongs to you in your national capacity, must always exalt the just pride of patriotism more than any appellation derived from local discriminations.*

January 23, 1916

URGES CONSIDERATION FOR 8,000,000 ALIENS

Defense Council Calls Upon Citizens to Avoid Showing Suspicion of Them.

WASHINGTON, Feb. 28.—The Council of National Defense today issued an appeal to the people of the United States to show every consideration in the present international situation to aliens resident in this country.

" The United States," says the statement, " for many generations has been

the shelter of the oppressed of the world and of those who would become one with the spirit of the republic. It is the crucible of the nations. Many of those who have come to us are now citizens. Many are not. It is with the latter that we are chiefly concerned.

" The presence here at this time of perhaps 8,000,000 aliens is deeply and soberly to be weighed, not only in our own interests, but in their own. For so long a space as they are lawful dwellers within this country they are entitled to the generous consideration of the people and Government of the United States.

" Emphasizing anew our national doctrines of tolerance and personal liberty, of holding all persons within the land to be loyal unless by their own acts they shall prove the contrary, we call upon all citizens, if untoward events should come upon us, to present to these aliens, many of whom tomorrow will be

Americans, the attitude of neither suspicion nor aggressiveness.

" We urge on all Americans to meet these millions of foreign-born with unchanged manner and with unprejudiced mind. Any other course is unworthy of our traditions and against public policy and the free flow of Governmental affairs."

The act creating the Council of National Defense charges the council in times of stress to promote good-will within the country's borders and to make every effort to conserve the national unity.

Eighteen executives of railroads will meet here tomorrow to approve plans for making the country's rail lines available for Government uses in the event of a national emergency.

March 1, 1917

MILLION SIGN PLEDGE OF LOYALTY TO U. S.

Thousands of letters have been received daily by the Mayor's Committee on National Defense since it began circulating the "loyalty pledge" now to be found in hotels, clubs, stores, telegraph offices, and many other public places through the city, but up to last night fewer than a dozen of the letter writers had declined to sign the pledge, according to the committee's officials at its headquarters, at 50 East Forty-second Street. It was pointed out, however, that the committee would not know of such refusals unless the persons refusing were to write about it, until all of the pledge blanks had been turned in, and that even then, of course, the absence of a name might not mean refusal, but might show only that the person in question had not happened to see one of the blanks.

The purpose of the plan, it was pointed out, was partly to show the vast difference in numbers between those who were loyal and the small body that attended a recent mass meeting of "protest" against any firm action by this country.

Many inquiries came to the committee's headquarters yesterday asking if certain individuals who were considered by the inquirers to be disloyal to the country, or at least more loyal to the interests of Germany than to those of America, had signed the pledge. It was impossible to answer most of these questions, as thousands of the blanks have not yet been returned, and in view of the fact that from 50,000 to 100,000 new names were being added to the lists daily at the present time. It was estimated yesterday that the total number of signers was already in excess of 1,000,000.

Many of yesterday's inquiries as to whether certain individuals had signed were prompted by the report that Justice Daniel F. Cohalan of the Supreme Court had refused to sign the pledge of loyalty. Justice Cohalan yesterday issued a statement regarding his own refusal, in which he said in part:

"If any man or set of men feels that their devotion and loyalty require from them a public declaration as to their loyalty I have no objection to their making it, but in common with many thoughtful men to whom I have talked during the last week I do not think such action helps America, whatever else it may do."

A number of clergymen yesterday notified the committee that they were earnestly in favor of the plan, and that they intended to post the blanks in their churches today, and in their sermons to urge their congregations to place themselves on record as being "for America first" by signing the pledges. There has been such a constant call for the blanks from all sources that the committee has found itself unable to provide them rapidly enough to meet the public demand. Up to yesterday it was said at headquarters that about 250,000 had been printed and circulated thus far. The smallest of these have room for ten names. Blanks were, however, sent to clergymen of every denomination in time for use today.

The Rev. Dr. William T. Manning of Trinity and the Rev. Christian F. Reisner of Grace M. E. Church are among those supporting the plan.

The Rev. Dr. John Haynes Holmes, pastor of the Church of the Messiah, who has attracted considerable attention as an ultra-pacifist during recent months and who two weeks ago ordered the American flag taken down from his church and placed inside the edifice, declined to answer last night when asked if he had signed the "loyalty pledge" and said that he thought this was "of no interest to the public," and that he did not want to comment upon it.

The "loyalty pledge" movement as inaugurated in this city promises to spread rapidly all over the country. Requests for samples of the blanks have been received by the Mayor's committee from numerous large cities already, and the movement has thus far been on foot for only six days.

The New York Telephone Company, according to the committee's announcement last night, applied for 10,000 blanks during the day, and its officials explained that these were to be placed in their offices in every large Eastern city to stimulate the movement along the entire Eastern seaboard.

Feeling that teachers in public schools, to whom the education of the children of the country is intrusted, should be called on to give a more comprehensive statement of their attitude than comprised in the "loyalty pledge" deemed suitable for popular purposes, Wadleigh High School teachers yesterday circulated among the entire teaching staff of the institution a declaration addressed to the Board of Education and the Mayor which said, in part:

"We declare our unqualified loyalty to America, the land of our birth, (or adoption,) our faith in the principles upon which our Government was founded, and our hope in their perpetuation; and we pledge ourselves to inculcate by every precept and example the American ideals of justice, liberty, and humanity."

The Chairman of the Committee on Resolutions, J. S. Gibson, announced last night that every member of the Faculty of the school had signed the declaration with one exception. This person was a native-born citizen, it was said, but his name was withheld. It was pointed out that there are about 21,000 public school teachers in this city alone, and those behind this movement considered their attitude on the subject involved a matter of considerable public importance and interest.

March 18, 1917

500,000 WILL JOIN IN HUNT FOR SPIES

Entire Force of Government's Civilian Employes Enlisted in the Search for Plotters.

WHOLE NATION IS COVERED

Army of Postmasters and Letter Carriers Expected to Obtain Valuable Information.

WASHINGTON, March 30.—Virtually the entire force of the Federal Government's civilian employes, approximately 500,000 men and women engaged in every branch of service, has been summoned to aid the Bureau of Investigation and the Secret Service in the detection of spies and the apprehension of persons engaged in plots, intrigues, or other activities against the interests of the United States.

In addition, the Government has sought the active co-operation of the police and detective forces of every town and city of consequence throughout the country. Hundreds of letters requesting such co-operation have been mailed broadcast by the Department of Justice, and replies pledging unstinted aid are coming back in great numbers by telegraph and mail.

The largest single force which the Government has enrolled in its nation-wide spy hunt, with the possible exception of the municipal police and detective forces, is the army of Postmasters, all of whom have been instructed to permit no information regarding suspected individuals and their activities to go unreported. Under the Postmasters are working the letter carriers in the cities and the rural free delivery carriers in the country, a force, all told, of about 300,000 men.

Instructions to the Federal employes call for the prompt reporting to designated authorities of all information, no matter how unimportant it appears, which might seem to furnish clues in ferreting out agents of foreign Governments. Under this head come letters passing through the mails, telegrams, and even conversation indicating activity against the Government.

Such information will be promptly forwarded to the proper investigating body at Washington, the name of the informant held secret, and an inquiry quietly begun wherever, in the opinion of officials intrusted with such work, investigation is warranted.

Although no request for co-operation has been addressed to the general public, officials welcome and hold in strictest confidence co-operation on the part of all private citizens looking to the prevention of activities harmful to the national interest. A number of private citizens, impelled by patriotic motives, already have furnished much valuable information of this character, it is said, and have aided materially in the work of the two bureaus heretofore engaged in enforcing the maintenance of American neutrality. Officials want to encourage citizens to communicate such information through United States attorneys or direct to the Department of Justice here.

The idea of enlisting virtually all Government employes in the work originated with the Department of Justice, and was approved promptly by the heads of the various Government departments. Instructions already have been sent to most of the employes concerned.

March 31, 1917

TOASTS KAISER, IS HANGED.

Man In Wyoming Then Is Cut Down and Driven from Town.

Special to The New York Times.

THERMOPOLIS, Wyo., April 2.—A stranger believed to be a German who shouted "Hoch der Kaiser!" as he stood drinking at a saloon bar here narrowly escaped lynching at the hands of Thermopolitans.

As the stranger lifted the glass to his lips, after shouting his toast, he was knocked down by a miner, a rope appeared as if by magic, and in a moment the dazed man was hanging from a beam.

Before life was extinct, however, the counsel of cooler heads prevailed and he was cut down by the City Marshal. He was revived with cold water, forced to kneel and kiss the American flag, and then was warned to get out of town. He did.

April 3, 1917

HIS PEACE DIATRIBE COSTLY.

Kerr, Rescued from Angry Crowd, Gets Six Months.

Stephen Kerr, a Russian, 21 years old, of 1,416 Steffins Avenue, the Bronx, was sentenced to the workhouse for six months by Magistrate Murphy in the Yorkville Police Court yesterday for calling Americans a "lot of skunks" at an anti-militarist meeting in Madison Square Park on Tuesday. He was rescued from an angry crowd by Patrolman Chaffers.

April 6, 1917

DINERS RESENT SLIGHT TO THE ANTHEM

Attack a Man and Two Women Who Refuse to Stand When It Is Played.

There was much excitement in the main dining room at Rector's last night following the playing of the "Star-Spangled Banner." Frederick S. Boyd, a former reporter on The New York Call, a Socialist newspaper, was dining with Miss Jessie Ashley and Miss May R. Towle, both lawyers and suffragists. The three alone of those in the room remained seated. There were quiet, then loud and vehement protests, but they kept their chairs. The angry diners surrounded Boyd and the two women and blows were struck back and forth, the women fighting valiantly to defend Boyd. He cried out that he was an Englishman and did not have to get up, but the crowd would listen to no explanations.

Boyd was being beaten severely when Albert Dasburg, a head waiter, succeeded in reaching his side. Other waiters closed in and the fray was stopped. The guests insisted upon the ejection of Boyd and his companions, and they were asked to leave. They refused to do so, and were escorted to the street, and turned over to a policeman, who took Boyd to the West Forty-seventh Street Station, charged with disorderly conduct.

Before Magistrate Corrigan in Night Court Boyd repeated that he did not have to rise at the playing of the national anthem, but the Court told him that while there was no legal obligation, it was neither prudent nor courteous not to do so in these tense times. Boyd was found guilty of disorderly conduct and was released on suspended sentence.

Charged with having used an improper epithet in regard to this country, Andrew Kacin of 528 Avenue C, Bayonne, N. J., was held in $1,000 bail yesterday for a hearing by Recorder William J. Cain. John Melynk of 92 Andrew Street, Bayonne, who made the complaint, said he heard the remark and struck Kacin.

"That's good. Any man who insults the flag ought to get two or three years in jail," said the Recorder.

TRENTON, N. J., April 6.—Philip Madino, a Mexican, was sentenced today to six months in the workhouse by a police justice for spitting on the American flag.

April 7, 1917

URGE GERMAN LOYALTY.

Local Language Papers Again Warn Compatriots to Keep Quiet.

The New-Yorker Staats-Zeitung and the New Yorker Herold continued to remind their readers yesterday of the necessity for calmness and silence during the period of the war and drew the attention of German citizens to the President's proclamation regarding the treatment of alien enemies. The Staats-Zeitung concluded an editorial on this subject as follows:

"These orders are to be taken so seriously, because, in our opinion, the treatment of the Germans in general will depend upon their observance. Stick it out! Hold out! Keep your mouth shut! And submit! This is now the first duty of the German citizens in this country."

After pointing out the different opinions regarding the effect the entry into the lists by the United States would have upon the duration of the war, the New Yorker Herold said:

"For practical reasons our readers will do well not to give too much credence to the idea that the war will end soon. Every one of us will do well to prepare for a long duration of the war and to figure out how to arrange our personal affairs so as to be able to withstand possible disturbances in our economic life."

April 8, 1917

ALL SPY ARRESTS NOW KEPT SECRET

Prisoners Go Direct to Ellis Island Without Any Proceedings in Court.

ARREST IN CUSTOMS HOUSE

Man Seeking Job on German Ships Gives Forged Letter—Suspects Taken in Mount Vernon.

The round-up of German spies and aliens who have aroused the suspicion of the Government was continued yesterday, and while the officials refused to give out any information in regard to their work, there was good reason to believe that a great many persons were arrested whose names were not made public. It is easy for the Secret Service agents to keep the facts in these cases from becoming known as it is no longer necessary to take war prisoners to court. It is thought that fully 50 per cent. of those who are arrested are taken at once to the detention quarters on Ellis Island.

Of the arrests made public yesterday, the most important was that of a man who said he was Walter H. S. Griffiths, a "mariner." He tried to get work on one of the seized German ships by submitting recommendations which in at least one instance were found to be forged. Another arrest was that of an employe in the Navy Yard in Brooklyn, who was charged with uttering threats against President Wilson. Arrests in the neighborhood of Mount Vernon were reported, one of those taken into custody being a young woman who is said to have been in the employ of a woman prominent in Mount Vernon. A German who gave the name of Hans Erfurt and who admitted that he was a native of Mainz, Germany, was taken into custody in Mount Vernon also.

Griffiths appeared at the office in the Custom House of Thomas B. Hasler, who is representing the Government in making contracts for the repair of the German ships seized last week. Griffiths applied for the place of deck officer on one of the ships, and presented letters to prove that he was qualified for the job. He said that he was formerly Captain of the steam yacht Condor, which is owned by New York business men, among them A. De Wilde, Vice President of the Republic Steamship Company, and Deputy Dock Commissioner John E. Eastmond.

One of the letters was written on the stationery of the Republic Steamship Company and was signed, "A. De Wilde." Secret Service men were asked to investigate the references, and Mr. De Wilde, whose office is within a block of the Custom House, was sent for.

When Mr. De Wilde arrived, the Secret Service agents found that the letter purporting to have been written by him was missing. It had been put with the other letters on Mr. Hasler's desk. Griffiths was searched, and the letter, which had been torn up, was found in one of his pockets. It was pieced together, and Mr. De Wilde immediately pronounced the signature a forgery. The Secret Service agents then took Griffiths in hand and subjected him to a long examination, after which they took him to the Criminal Courts Building and turned him over to District Attorney Swann, as there is no Federal statute covering the offense with which he is charged.

John C. Bolden, who is said to be the Secretary of a shipmasters' organization of this city, and who it is alleged signed the forged letter presented by Griffiths, was arraigned with Griffiths before Magistrate Ten Eyck in the Tombs Court late yesterday afternoon. The prisoners were held in $5,000 bail each for examination tomorrow morning.

The workman arrested at the navy yard was John Wehnau, who had been employed there as a machinist since 1906. Other navy yard workmen declared that he made three statements: "The President of the United States is an English dog. He is yellow. He is no good. He ought to be assassinated. To hell with the American flag. Germany should sink every ship that goes over."

Wehnau is 42 years old, and was born in Hamburg. He lives at 77 Nassau Street, Brooklyn, with his wife and daughter. He denied the charge against him, and said that he was the victim of a "frame up." He was sent to the Raymond Street Jail in default of $10,000 bail.

Secret Service agents are looking up the record of the German newspaperman who was arrested Tuesday night, and who said he was "Frank Miller." They ascertained yesterday that the man's right name was Warner Tissmer, and that he was until recently in the employ of Dr. Carl A. Fucher, a representative in this country of the Transocean News Service, a German organization. Tissmer is held on Ellis Island, and details as to why he is under arrest are withheld.

The Federal Grand Jury returned sealed indictments yesterday against persons who are believed to have been implicated in German plots hatched in this country against Great Britain. Fritz Kolb, who was convicted of having high explosives in his possession in Hoboken, was sentenced by Judge Mark A. Sullivan in Jersey City yesterday to not less than three years and four months nor more than five years in State Prison.

April 13, 1917

WILSON PURPOSES TO GUARD RIGHTS

Will Take Up "at Proper Time" Guarantees of Democracy, the President Says.

REFERS TO WAR LEGISLATION

Special to The New York Times.

WASHINGTON, May 5.—In a letter sent to Miss Lillian D. Wald of the Henry Street Settlement, New York City, and others, who had written to him regarding the threatened war-time invasion of the rights of democracy, including the rights of free speech and a free press, President Wilson announced today that "at the right time" he purposed discussing ways and means of safeguarding those rights during war. The President's letter read:—

"The letter signed by yourself and others under date of April 16 has, of course, chimed in with my own feelings and sentiments. I do not know what steps it will be practicable to take in the immediate future to safeguard the things which, I agree with you in thinking, ought in any circumstances be safeguarded, but you may be sure I have the matter in mind and will act, I hope, at the right time in the spirit of suggestion."

The letter to which this was a response was signed by Herbert Croly, editor of The New Republic; Mathew Hale, the Progressive leader in Massachusetts; Judge Ben B. Lindsey of Denver, Charles C. Burlingham of New York City, Charles J. Rhoades of the Federal Reserve Board, Philadelphia; Lillian D. Wald, Jane Addams, Amos R. E. Pinchot, Owen R. Lovejoy of the National Child Labor Committee, Paul U. Kellogg, Mrs. Glendower Evans of Boston, and others. It read, in part, as follows:

"What we ask of you, Mr. President, whose utterances at this time must command the earnest attention of the country, is to make an impressive statement that will reach not only the officials of the Federal Government scattered throughout the Union, but the officials of the several States and of the cities, towns, and villages of the country, reminding them of the peculiar obligation devolving upon all Americans to uphold in every way our constitutional rights and liberties. This will give assurance that in attempting to administer war-time laws the spirit of democracy will not be broken. Such a statement, sent throughout the country, would reinforce your declaration that this is a war for democracy and liberty."

The letter went on to cite drastic ordinances which had been introduced in many places, as well as some of the extreme bureaucratic utterances credited to various officials. These, the writers urged, should be checked in their too great zeal and reminded that safeguards had been thrown by the legislation about discussions of public affairs.

May 6, 1917

WILSON DEMANDS PRESS CENSORSHIP

Special to The New York Times.

WASHINGTON, May 22.—The first break of the war between the Administration and the Republicans was threatened today when the minority party in the House held a caucus and voted to oppose any press censorship provision in the General Espionage bill, now in conference between the two houses following its passage by House and Senate. Soon after this action was taken Chairman Webb of the House Judiciary Committee received a letter from President Wilson insisting on the retention of the censorship clause.

In the caucus Representative Medill McCormick of Illinois moved to oppose the Gard amendment to the Spy bill. This amendment, a compromise, was adopted by the House after it had rejected the original censorship provision. Representative Graham of Pennsylvania, a Republican leader, approved Mr. McCormick's motion.

The President's letter, made public by Mr. Webb some hours after the Republican caucus, follows:

My Dear Mr. Webb: I have been very much surprised to find several of the public prints stating that the Administration has abandoned the position which it so distinctly took, and still holds, that authority to exercise censorship over the press, to the extent that censorship is embodied in the recent action of the House of Representatives, is absolutely necessary to the public safety. It, of course, has not been abandoned, because the reasons still exist why such authority is necessary for the protection of the nation.

I have every confidence that the great majority of the newspapers of the country will observe a patriotic reticence about everything whose publication could be of injury, but in every country there are some persons in a position to do mischief in this field who cannot be relied upon and whose interests or desires will lead to actions on their part highly dangerous to the nation in the midst of war. I want to say again that it seems to me imperative that powers of this sort should be granted. Cordially and sincerely yours,

WOODROW WILSON.

The President's letter caused some surprise because many members of Congress and some Administration leaders had understood for several days that no further attempt was to be made at present to put through any such provision. Sentiment in the Senate is strong against censorship, and unless the conferees agree upon a very mild form, it probably will not be accepted there.

Representative Webb announced upon receipt of the President's letter that he would wage a determined fight in behalf of the censorship amendment, written into the bill in the House by a narrow margin, just before it was sent to conference.

An incident of the caucus was the promise by Republican Leader Mann that he would name a steering committee of Republicans to consider legislation. Representatives Gillett of Massachusetts, Lenroot of Wisconsin, Moore of Pennsylvania, and Longworth of Ohio are mentioned for positions on the committee.

May 23, 1917

OUR APATHY IN WAR DEPLORED BY BORAH

American People Not Yet Awake to Fact That This Is Our Own Fight Rather than "Modern Crusade" for Humanity—Senator Decries Undue Centralization of Power and Un-American Curb on Free Speech

WILLIAM E. BORAH, United States Senator from Idaho, remarked the other day in the course of a conversation in Washington that the American people had not yet waked up to the great fact of the war.

"Do you mean the people out West?" asked an Atlantic Coast man to whom he was talking.

"No, I don't mean the people out West. I mean all the American people, out West and down East, up North and in the South. As a whole people we have not waked up, and it is because the reasons why this country is in the war have not been presented to the masses of the population in sufficiently tangible and concrete form.

"For nearly three years the American people have been led to look upon this war as a European war—a war with which they had little to do either in thought or act. This was thoroughly and persistently drilled into the minds of our people. The mere declaration of war did not wholly, it seems, revolutionize the public mind in this respect. A great many of our people, even those whose interests in the war are keen and whose patriotism is undoubted, look upon this war as a European war and continue to treat it as such. So long as that condition continues we shall make progress slowly in the mobilization of our military and industrial forces for the conflict. And if it should continue indefinitely, we would not in any true sense mobilize our forces at all.

"Legislation alone cannot save us; food dictators cannot save us; bureaus cannot save us; only the aroused and sustained interest, the concentration and devotion of a hundred million people can save us. This cannot be had until the people as a whole come to believe and understand beyond peradventure that this is now our war and involves the immediate and vital interests, the institutions and welfare of our own country and the security of our own people. No people should be called upon or should be expected to make the supreme sacrifice which the people of this country are now called upon to make other than for their own institutions and for the future safety and liberty of their children. We may have our deep sympathy for other people engaged in this war and justly so, but when it comes to the proposition of committing our country to war with all the suffering and sacrifice which is to follow, it should not be done other than when the immediate and vital interests of our own people are involved.

"Can we not Americanize this war? We have just and abundant reasons for doing so. Since we entered the war and as the situation now exists it is in every

Senator Borah of Idaho, Who Says We Entered World War Primarily to Protect Our Own Rights.

sense an American war, and no nation has more at stake or will be called upon to make greater sacrifice in the end, in all probability, than our own. If any man doubts the interest we have in the war let him reflect upon the future in case the opposing powers are successful. One shudders to think of the humiliation, the degradation, and the sacrifice which we shall then experience.

"It seems to me, therefore, in all candor, that we may well suspend for a time this surfeit of talk about democracy as an abstract principle of government to be applied benignantly and indiscriminately to every people wherever or however situated, and spend more time, write more editorials, and express more views relative to the interests and welfare of this particular democracy of ours. Its whole future and its whole existence are wrapped up now in the success of this fight in which we are engaged, and it is a theme, as it occurs to me, upon which we may well concentrate our minds and our thought. We are still continually and persistently and exclusively discussing and writing about the war as if it were a European war and how it will affect European matters when it is over, and what adjustments shall there be made, as if all the great interests involved were European interests and as if we had entered it to perform a service to mankind, a kind of modern crusade. We entered it, I assume, at least that is my understanding, to protect our own rights, to defend and make secure the lives of our own people, and to maintain our own dignity and honor and prestige among the nations of the earth. Why not say so? It is not only the truth, but it is infinitely more important that it be said than that we undertake to carry on the war upon the strength of vague and ever-receding generalities.

"But whatever might have been the reasons for entering the war and whether they were sound or unsound, whether out of sympathy for other nations or for reasons not satisfactory to many of our people, these propositions are no longer debatable, it seems to me. We are in, and never did a nation assume a greater burden and have involved more nearly all it is and all it cherishes.

"I quite agree with those who say we should not criticize merely for the sake of criticism. Certainly we should not. But I wholly disagree and shall, I am sure, continue to disagree with the proposition that a sincere interchange of views is unwise or unpatriotic.

"Not only have we not placed sufficient stress upon our own immediate interests in the war, but it seems to me that we may well in the methods and means of carrying on this war have some regard for the fundamental principles of our own Government and the ideas and ideals of the American people. In our willingness to engraft upon our program of war certain foreign practices and propositions we have created a feeling of uneasiness in the minds of a great many good people and chilled the ardor of many whose cooperation and support we shall have great need of before the conflict is over.

"We have read or heard for years how in certain foreign countries like Russia prior to the revolution opinions were restrained and freedom of speech and of the press were inhibited under the severest penalties. But if there is anything which has been accepted by our people as theirs beyond dispute, fixed and settled beyond all controversy, it was and is the right of free speech and of a free press.

"Some one well said many years ago, during the fight for the liberty of speech and of the press, that the greatest of all liberties is the liberty of opinion, and so the American people have ever regarded it. It is about as indispensable to the American citizen as the air he breathes. This principle has come down to us as a blessed inheritance, never questioned or doubted. It is found guaranteed in the Constitution so plainly that the wayfaring man may read and understand. I think it was something of a shock to this country that as soon as the people were called upon to fight it was practically announced that all discussions, all expressions of opinion, should be under the surveillance of the Government. And now comes the startling, the almost hideous proposition that peace, that which we all hope for and all right-minded people pray for, shall be one subject upon which the American people shall not exchange views and concerning which there shall be no discussion. Not only are we to fight a foreign war on foreign soil, but if our troops are generaled by incompetents or receive insufficient arms or are fed on poisoned food, all lips shall be sealed and all opinions restrained. And if the people entertain views with reference to peace, wise or unwise, there shall be no discussion of that subject.

"Then followed, naturally, of course, the proposition that in time of war we have no Constitution, that everything rests in the discretion of the Executive and Congress. When the question was asked, how could people be denied the right to express their opinion when the Constitution is clear and unmistakable in its terms, the reply came, the only reply that could be made, that during the war the guarantees in this fundamental law relative to liberty of speech and of private rights were in some way or other suspended; that, like Mohammed's coffin, they floated about in the upper air just beyond the reach of the people and would descend again only at the nod of the Congress and of the Executive. The doctrine is advanced that every citizen, his property, his rights, his liberty, his life are after the declaration of war the playthings of Congress and the Executive.

"Speaking with entire personal respect for those who entertain such an opinion, the doctrine seems to me perfectly monstrous. Our Constitution was not only made for war as well as for peace, but it was made sufficiently efficient for the purposes of war. It was made by men entirely familiar with war and the duties and obligations and responsibilities of a people at war. The powers plainly granted are efficient and sufficient to carry on war and to call forth and utilize all the powers of a people. As made and according to its terms, the Constitution holds good at all periods and shields the citizen and binds those in power in peace and in war. The Executive is bound by its terms, Congress is bound by its terms, and the private citizen is protected by its terms in war as well as in peace. The opposite doctrine is a foreign doctrine, it is the creed of foreign courts, it is the faith of Czars and Emperors. It is not only unnecessary for carrying on the war, not only un-

American, but it is a doctrine fraught with evils the consequences of which no man can foresee or foretell. If democracy cannot carry on war without jeopardizing the rights and liberties of all its citizens, if the moment war is declared all the guarantees relative to private rights and private citizens are to be swallowed up in a military despotism, then we must admit there is more in this doctrine of Kultur than we have been willing heretofore to concede.

"But all this is not true. The Constitution is the property of the nation and not of those who temporarily enjoy office. It contains no provision which is in conflict with any other provision. It provides no method under which modifications or amendments or suspensions can be had save through and by the consent of the people.

"The people adopted it not only as a restraint for those in power, but as a restraint upon the people themselves—that in the hour of passion, excitement or war, in times when power would be claimed and coveted, there might be a compass to steer us through the storm and maintain through it all the rights and liberties and freedom of the people. To make the Constitution the plaything of the hour, the occasion of peace or war, is infinitely more menacing to the happiness and future welfare of our own people than foreign foes.

"One could easily contemplate, for in-

stance, a Congress being elected on a peace issue which nevertheless, within thirty days after the members had taken the oath of office, would declare war, and then, to silence all criticism, announce that the Constitution, under whose authority Congress sits and of which it is the creature, is suspended and all private rights, such as liberty of speech and of the press, of the right of trial by jury, are no longer to be enjoyed. Could the effrontery of usurpation go further? And yet this might happen. Where, then, are the people who made the Constitution? What rights have they left? They are relegated to bloodshed and revolution, where the people must always go when their form of government is disregarded or usurped by those in power.

"This is now our war—the great burden is here, other nations are nearing exhaustion—we are entering a period of sacrifice. It is a war with foreign powers. In such a war there can be no divided allegiance. Every citizen should realize his individual responsibility and put forth to his utmost his individual efforts. In return, the Government should deal with the American people as they are—deal with them in confidence, respect their teachings and their traditions and scrupulously regard their rights and their liberties. Out of such a course will come confidence and unity, and out of unity victory."

June 3, 1917

HOUSE DEFEATS CENSORSHIP LAW BY 184 TO 144

Spy Bill Goes Back to Conference, with Orders to Eliminate Press Gag.

PARTY LINES SHATTERED

Thirty-six Democrats Join Forces Opposing the Measure —10 Republicans Support It.

GRAHAM LEADS THE FIGHT

Gard, Ohio Democrat, Author of First Censorship Measure, Votes with Majority.

Special to The New York Times.

WASHINGTON, May 31.—The House voted decisively today against a newspaper censorship, rejecting by a vote of 184 to 144 the censorship section of the Administration's Espionage bill. The bill was sent back to the Conference Committee with instructions to eliminate Section 4. Chairman Webb of the Judiciary Committee, who led the Administration's unsuccessful fight for a censorship, probably will ask the conferees to meet tomorrow to carry out the mandate of the House.

Representative George S. Graham of Pennsylvania, a Republican, aided by the Republican floor leader, Representative Mann, conducted the opposition to the censorship section. Closing a debate of two hours, Mr. Graham is believed to have brought several wavering members into line by showing that the so-called compromise on censorship was more drastic than the original House proposal. He assailed it as a "pernicious section."

Representative Gard, Democrat, of Ohio, who was the author of the censorship provision originally adopted by the House, repudiated the section as modified in conference and voted against the conference agreement. Mr. Gard stressed the fact that his draft of the censorship section provided that the President should declare what was not to be published, whereas the conference agreement invested the President with authority to say what might be published. Absence of Presidential approval of a certain class of information, it was insisted, would automatically place such matter in the prohibited class.

The motion to recommit the conference report was made by Mr. Graham. Thirty-six Democrats voted to recommit and ten Republicans and one independent voted against. The "Tammany Democrats," who were rumored to be opposed to censorship, finally voted with the Administration. The Ohio delegation furnished the largest percentage of Democratic votes in opposition to the Administration's program. Only two New York Democrats voted against it—Maher and Smith.

Dyer Supports Censorship.

Representatives Graham, Mann, Campbell of Kansas, McKenzie and McCormick of Illinois, and Gard of Ohio made the principal speeches against the conference report. The Administration speakers included Mr. Webb and Mr. Carlin, ranking Democratic members of the Judiciary Committee, and Mr. Dyer of Missouri, a Republican member of the committee. Mr. Dyer said that, although the Republican caucus had decided to oppose the censorship section, he regarded it as his duty "to stand up and support my country rather than to take orders from any caucus or conference of a political party."

"I am in favor of this," he added.

"because it will enable the President to protect my fellow-Americans who have to traverse the seas and fight in France for their country."

Mr. Graham in reply contended that a situation might arise wherein better protection would be afforded to American soldiers by a frank discussion than by silence.

"How can you criticize when criticism is needed," he asked, "without being able to state the basis of your criticism? The very fact of the distribution and movement of troops may bring about improper conditions which cannot be discussed under this provision." Mr. Graham refuted the suggestion that any American newspaper would furnish information of value to the enemy, but insisted that healthy criticism should not be withheld when it became necessary.

"My objection to this clause," said Mr. Campbell of Kansas, "is that it indirectly assumes the newspapers of this country are unpatriotic. All the patriotism is not in the bosom of men temporarily in office. The newspapers have proved themselves to be patriotic. They will continue to do so. There have been no leaks to the enemy from our newspapers."

Mr. Graham has led two successful contests in the House against censorship. On his motion the House several weeks ago struck from the Espionage bill the committee censorship section. Afterward the matter was again presented by a parliamentary ruse, and the House voted for a substitute section, which went to conference. In conference this substitute was modified and materially broadened, according to the analysis made by Mr. Graham today.

As soon as the conference report was presented notice was given that there would be a motion to send it back to the Conference Committee. No other portion of the conference report except the censorship section was discussed. Loud applause on the Republican side greeted the announcement that the motion to recommit had prevailed.

Graham and Carlin Clash.

Mr. Graham engaged in a spirited colloquy with Mr. Carlin of Virginia. Mr. Carlin insisted that Mr. Graham "had changed his mind four or five times about censorship," and had voted in committee for the bill as reported by the Judiciary Committee. Mr.

Graham hotly retorted that he voted "present" when accused of presenting to the Conference Committee suggestions for a compromise censorship clause. Mr. Graham said he had made such suggestions for others and merely in the hope of harmony on some mild legislation. He had never agreed, he said, to support anything approaching the drastic provisions of the Conference Committee report.

"No man in this House," said Representative Graham, "will go further in upholding, without regard to politics or to any other consideration, the hands of the President of the United States in prosecuting this war. Having voted for his proclamation, having voted for the selective draft, I pledged myself to do all that may be done by a man or a member of Congress to promote the President's work in bringing this war to a successful issue. But I want to say to you, my friends, that this section is not calculated to help, influence, or bring about that result.

"This section is a pernicious section and does not accomplish what I think, perhaps, the members of the Conference Committee hoped to accomplish by its adoption. One gentleman said a moment ago, 'Why, I am told that other parts of this bill would enable you to punish anybody that published information that was useful to the enemy.' Then he said, 'If that is so, why not pass Section 4 also, for it can do no harm?'

"Therein lies the vice of his reasoning, and when he reflects he will understand that is so, and I am sure he will vote, for he is an honest man, to strike out this section. There are other sections of this bill, the first and the second, under which the obtaining of any matter connected with the national defense is made a crime, and in the second section there is provision that the publication of any information with reference to the national defense is made a crime for which the man who willfully and intentionally and with the purpose of aiding the enemy, which is to be found by the jury, publishes it shall be punished under the severe penalties that are prescribed in these sections.

"No man can sit down and sanely and fairly read these two sections without arriving at the conclusion that there is ample power for the punishment of any villainous newspaper that will attempt to publish anything for the benefit of the enemy; but I ask your attention to this distinction. A publication might be alleged to be one that gave information to the enemy, and yet be a subject that the papers of the country and the men of the country in the exercise of freedom of speech ought to discuss, and the question would be—is it more harmful than beneficial?

"It may be something that would give information to the enemy, but at the same time if left without exposure it might bring a calamity upon one's own country. Under such circumstances who is to muzzle the press or who is to leave it to the jury to say whether or not on the single issue that it is helpful to the enemy, for that is what is left to the jury to try? I say that the statement made by my colleague, Mr. Gard, is worthy of serious attention of the members of this House on both sides of the aisle. His amendment was infinitely superior to the one that this Conference Committee has brought forth.

"This is a mongrel production, it is neither one thing nor the other, and when you read it honestly and squarely you must say that the condition of the press, the condition not alone of the press, but of every individual member of the House, will be ten-fold worse under this conference report than it could possibly be under the amendment that the House adopted on the motion of Mr. Gard.

"Why do I say that? When you read the first paragraph of Section 4 you find the prohibition of giving information to the enemy that will be useful to the enemy upon certain enumerated topics, but the language that is used, description and so forth, is so broad that it will cover everything connected with these particular subjects and make the publisher amenable to punishment.

"The next paragraph provides that the President shall from time to time—no not 'shall' even, but 'may'—that the President may from time to time designate what may be published. Ergo, whatever he does not designate is forbidden. Then think of the muzzle in the concluding paragraph of the section which has been amended since it left the House, wherein it attempts to provide the constitutional right of criticism and free speech, but winds up with the sting in the end and says, 'Provided it is not something that is prohibited in this section.'

"Suppose the President made no proclamation of what might be published, then I ask what could a paper say? Then in an attempt to preserve the freedom of the press it provides that only those things may be criticised which are not within the prohibition of this section. The first paragraph of the section prohibits it all. The second paragraph says that the President may from time to time designate what may be published. All else remains prohibited. Then the concluding paragraph of the section provides that nothing in the section shall be construed to limit or restrict any discussion, comment, or criticism of the act or policies of the Government or its representatives or the publication of the same. When you passed the bill you stopped there. But the conferees have added: 'If such discussion, comment, or criticism does not disclose information herein prohibited.'

"That paragraph has all its strength taken out of it and no lawyer will dare argue otherwise. That eliminates the power to criticise—so far as this section goes—anything and everything that is prohibited, and when you start with the thought that the first portion of the section prohibits all publications with relation to the enumerated topics, and when you consider that the President by refraining from ever saying that anything connected with those subjects is food for publication, you leave the whole matter prohibited, and then the press muzzler comes on and no comment can be made upon it at all.

"This is not merely a question of free press, however important that may be, but it involves also the sacred and inalienable rights of American citizens to free speech. Aye, if one of you obtained from the Department of War some information of value touching the question of the defense, and you were to come to me and communicate what you had found, then unless the President had permitted that publication you would be guilty of a crime. Remember the word 'publication' does not mean to print in type in a newspaper, but 'publication' means to utter, and that may be a publication just as much as a paragraph in a newspaper article would be."

Gard Rejects Changed Section.

Representative Gard said:

"I cannot accept the language framed by the conferees in the new Section 4 of this conference report. The particular language which I object to is that the President is not called upon to make a declaration of reasonable rules for the publication of matters affecting the national defense which may be useful to the enemy, but that the absolute power is given to the President to withhold all information concerning the movement, description, or distribution of the armed forces of the United States in naval or military operations, or in respect to any of the works intended for the fortification or defense of any place, which information is useful to the enemy, unless he shall first issue a proclamation, and determine by that proclamation the character of such above-desired information which in his opinion is not useful to the enemy, and thereupon it shall be lawful to publish the same.

"I do not think the question of authority which the Constitution contains, authorizing the President to make reasonable rules and regulations for the carrying on of a war, can at this time be held to include every publication which a newspaper can make, for as I read this language, if it means anything at all, it means that before any publication can be made of anything pertaining to the movement of troops or our fortifications the approval of the President must first be had. I assume that this is a provision which no man would want, and I am sure the present Chief Executive of the United States would not desire to be burdened with this idea of, being compelled every time a publication is to be made, concerning the movement of troops, to issue a proclamation saying whether or not in his opinion it is of such a character as is not useful to the enemy. And that thereupon the newspapers may publish it.

Trusts the Newspapers.

"Then, standing to the full for the freedom of speech and the freedom of the press, I yet realize that there may be newspapers—fortunately very few in number I believe they are—that might seek to transgress rules of the Government for our national welfare, and in that light such regulations restricting them or prohibiting them in a sense should be agreed to and should be in the law. But certainly the time is not here, and I trust it will never be here, when it is necessary to see the President of the United States before a newspaper can print anything at all."

Representative McCormick of Illinois said the Administration through Representative Webb had asked Mr. Graham and him to suggest a compromise on the censorship, but after thinking it over they decided they could not support any amendment.

"The difficulty with which we are to deal," said Mr. McCormick, "is that of drawing a censorship section which will meet the exigency in the case, to find language that will protect, without endangering the men enlisted in the army and navy of the United States; because censorship, gentlemen, not merely prohibits publication, but it prohibits misrepresentation, conscious or unconscious."

Mr. McCormick referred to newspaper articles appearing earlier in the week to the effect that the American fleet was in splendid fighting trim.

"Now, I think I am not transgressing the bounds of discretion," he said, "when I say that the fleet is far less ready for action today than when it came from Guantanamo."

Representative Butler of Pennsylvania asked him to give his reasons, but he declined to go into details. However, he said:

"The sick bays are overflowing, the hospitals are crowded, making it necessary to bring men here. I am informed at one point men were herded into sheds. At another point they have no bedding except such as was supplied by private charity."

The Democrats voting to recommit were:

Ashbrooks, Ohio; Bell, Georgia; Borland, Missouri; Brand, Georgia; Brodbeck, Pennsylvania; Burnett, Alabama; Church, California; Claypool, Ohio; Connelly, Kansas; Crosser, Ohio; Dill, Washington; Dominick, South Carolina; Evans, Montana; Gallagher, Illinois; Gard, Ohio; Gordon, Ohio; Hamill, New Jersey; Hilliard, Colorado; Huddleston, Alabama; Humphreys, Mississippi; Keating, Colorado; Kelly, Pennsylvania; Larsen, Georgia; Maher, New York; Olney, Massachusetts; Overmyer, Iowa; Overstreet, Georgia; Rouse, Kentucky; Scully, New Jersey; Sherwood, Ohio; Sisson, Mississippi; Slayden, Texas; Charles B. Smith, New York; Thompson, Oklahoma; Vandyke, Minnesota; Vinson, Georgia; White, Ohio.

Republicans voting against motion to recommit:

Dyer, Missouri; Elston, California; Griest, Pennsylvania; James, Michigan; King, Illinois; Little, Kansas; Moores, Indiana; Morgan, Oklahoma; Parker, New Jersey; Volstead, Minnesota; Fuller, Massachusetts. Independent, voted against.

June 1, 1917

ESPIONAGE BILL IS SIGNED.

Numerous Prosecutions Expected Under Its Provisions.

WASHINGTON, June 15.—President Wilson today signed the Espionage bill, which was passed by both Houses of Congress without the censorship provision. A Public Information Committee statement on the new law says:

"Department of Justice officials regard the Espionage act as one of the most important pieces of legislation enacted since the declaration of the state of war, and numerous prosecutions are anticipated under its provisions.

"For the time being the export control chapter is regarded by the War Trade Committee as the most important portion of the new law. That section of the act will not only prove effective in prompting the successs of the war by preventing shipments to the enemy, but it will prove a safeguard against the development of another embarrassing situation in the relations with Mexico, since under it shipments of arms and ammunitions across the border can be absolutely controlled.

"Another feature of the law which was designed to prevent embarrassing situations from arising in the nation's foreign relation prevents any other than a duly accredited diplomatic or consular official from serving as an agent of a foreign Government in the United States, unless the individual so serving first gives notice of his position to the Secretary of State."

June 16, 1917

EMMA GOLDMAN AND A. BERKMAN BEHIND THE BARS

Anarchist Headquarters Raided and Leaders Held for Anti-Draft Conspiracy.

MANY DOCUMENTS SEIZED

Card Index of Reds in the United States Simplifies Secret Service Men's Work.

RIOTERS MENACE SOLDIERS

Some 200 Without Registration Cards Detained at Anti-Conscription Gatherings in This City.

Emma Goldman and Alexander Berkman, the two most notorious anarchists in the United States, who for weeks have been conducting a campaign against all the aspirations and activities of this Government, particularly against our part in the war and army conscription, in the course of which they have at times almost preached sedition, were arrested by Federal agents yesterday afternoon in the anarchist headquarters at 20 East 125th Street.

For several weeks Secret Service agents have kept close watch on Emma Goldman and Berkman, and it has been known for some days that their arrest would be made immediately the Government obtained evidence of an overt act on their part to interfere with the nation's war program. Yesterday that evidence was forthcoming when the Government came into possession of copies of the anarchist publications known as Mother Earth, which is owned by Emma Goldman, and The Blast, the editor and proprietor of which is Berkman.

Important as are the prisoners to the Government, they are perhaps not nearly so important as is the mass documents and other written matter which has come into the possession of the Department of Justice. A wagon load of anarchist records and propaganda material was seized, and included in the lot is what is believed to be a complete registry of anarchy's friends in the United States. A splendidly kept card index was found, which the Federal agents believe will greatly simplify their task of identifying persons mentioned in the various record books and papers. The subscription lists of Mother Earth and the Blast, which contain 10,000 names, were also seized.

It was 4 o'clock yesterday afternoon when United States Marshal Thomas D. McCarthy was instructed to arrest Berkman and Miss Goldman. The complaint was signed by Lieutenant George D. Barnitz of the New York Police Department. It charged that since May 1 last, and until yesterday, the two anarchists had been conspiring "to aid, counsel, and induce" various men of conscript age not to comply with the provisions of the selective draft law. The complaint further alleges that Berkman and Miss Goldman, in the June issues of the Blast and Mother Earth, published signed articles meant to effect the conspiracy into which they had entered.

Slacker Arrested Also.

The raiding party which left the Federal Building at 4:10 P. M. under command of Marshal McCarthy included Assistant United States District Attorney E. M. Stanton, Lieutenant Barnitz, Deputy Marshals Doran, Hearne, and Meade, and Detectives Murphy and Kiely of the Police Department. A few minutes before 5 o'clock the Government automobiles arrived at 20 East 125th Street. In the publication office of the anarchist papers Marshal McCarthy and his aids found Miss Goldman, a Miss Fitzgerald, Walker Merchant, Carl Nawlander, and a young man named Bales, who was subsequently arrested when it was discovered that although of draft age he had failed to register on June 5.

"I have a warrant for your arrest," Marshal McCarthy said to Emma Goldman.

"I am not surprised, yet I would like to know what the warrant is based on," the woman said.

Marshal McCarthy answered by producing a copy of Mother Earth containing an article on the so-called No-Conscription League signed "Emma Goldman."

"Did you write that?" asked the Marshal.

Miss Goldman replied that she had written the article, and in answer to another question said she stood for everything in Mother Earth, because, she added, she was the sole owner of the publication.

Lieutenant Barnitz asked her if she knew where Berkman was, and she told him that Berkman was upstairs in another room. A few minutes later the man who in 1892 tried to murder H. C. Frick and subsequently served fourteen years in the penitentiary for his crime, appeared. He was taken completely by surprise and did not appear nearly so brave or defiant as his woman companion.

The young man, Bales, was busy in a corner of the room wrapping copies of the Blast and Mother Earth and addressing them when the officers entered. Mr. Stanton walked over and touched him on the shoulder. Bales looked up.

"How are you?" Mr. Stanton demanded.

"Who, me?"

"Yes, you."

"I don't care to make any statement at this time," young Bales answered.

"Where is your registration card?"

"I have no registration card."

A moment later Bales was under arrest and in the custody of a detective.

Miss Fitzgerald, who gave her address as the Hotel Brevoort, seemed completely upset. "I can't understand it at all," she said to a reporter, "for they (Berkman and Goldman) are fine and beautiful characters, and are hundreds of years ahead of their time."

A big crowd gathered in front of the anarchist headquarters and the reserves from the East 126th Street Police Station were summoned to keep order.

Arrayed in Royal Purple.

Marshal McCarthy told the prisoners to get ready for a quick trip to the Federal Building. Miss Goldman asked if she could have time to put on a more presentable gown. Permission was given, and she disappeared upstairs, to return a few minutes later dressed in royal purple.

In the meantime the Marshals and the police were busy searching the room. All the papers of every kind were seized, including some of George Bernard Shaw's works. The Shaw books, however, were later ordered to be left on the shelves, together with other works not of an anarchistic character. The entire unmailed editions of Mother Earth and The Blast were seized.

The issue of The Blast on which the arrest of Berkman was based is, in the opinion of the Federal officials, one of the vilest things ever sent through the United States mails, for several hundred copies were mailed before the paper was brought to the attention of the authorities.

The outside cover to the issue shows an American carrying on his back a fat man in uniform, who is labelled "American militarism." Near by stands a Russian peasant. Russia asks the American who is carrying the man in uniform. "What's the idea! and the American answers, "Democracy," whereupon the Russian remarks, "Well, you know how I got mine."

The article for the writing of which Berkman was arrested is captioned "Registration."

It follows another article captioned "To the Youth of America," in which the men of the country are urged to refuse to go to war against Germany.

Berkman's Offending Article.

The article on registration, which is the one specifically referred to in the complaint, reads:

Registration is the first step of conscription.

The war shouters and their prostitute press, bent on snaring you into the army, tell you that registration has nothing to do with conscription.

They lie.

Without registration, conscription is impossible.

Conscription is the abdication of your rights as a citizen. Conscription is the cemetery where every vestige of your liberty is to be buried. Registration is the undertaker.

No man with red blood in his veins can be forced to fight against his will.

But you cannot successfully oppose conscription if you approve of, or submit to, registration.

Every beginning is hard. But if the Government can induce you to register it will have little difficulty in putting over conscription.

By registering you wilfully supply the Government with the information it needs to make conscription effective.

Registration means placing in the hands of the authorities the despotic power of the machinery of passports which made darkest Russia what it was before the revolution.

There are thousands, perhaps hundreds of thousands of young men in this country who have never voted and who have never paid taxes, and who, legally speaking, have no official existence. Their registration means nothing short of suicide in a majority of cases.

Failure to register is punishable by imprisonment. Refusal to be conscripted may be punishable by death.

To register is to acknowledge the right of the Government to conscript.

The consistent conscientious objector to human slaughter will neither register nor be conscripted.

ALEXANDER BERKMAN.

Miss Goldman's Proclamation.

The article in Mother Earth, which is mentioned in the Barnitz complaint, is quite long. That part which counsels defiance of the Selective Draft law reads:

The No-Conscription League has been formed for the purpose of encouraging conscientious objectors to affirm their liberty of conscience, and to translate their objection to human slaughter by refusing to participate in the killing of their fellowmen. The No-Conscription League is to be the voice of protest against war, and against the coercion of conscientious objectors to participate in the war. Our platform may be summarized as follows:

We oppose conscription because we are internationalists, anti-militarists, and opposed to all wars waged by capitalistic Governments.

We will fight for what we choose to fight for; we will never fight simply because we are ordered to fight.

We believe that the militarization of America is an evil that far outweighs in its anti-social and anti-libertarian effects any good that may come from America's participation in the war.

We will resist conscription by every means in our power, and we will sustain those who, for similar reasons, refuse to be conscripted.

The prisoners arrived at the Federal Building at 6:30. They were taken to the office of United States Marshal McCarthy, where they remained until Harry Weinberger, their lawyer, could be communicated with. It was 7 o'clock when Weinberger, who is a non-conscriptionist and often spoke at the same meetings with Miss Goldman, arrived.

Assistant United States District Attorneys John C. Knox and Harold A. Content informed the prisoners that United States Commissioners Hitchcock and Gilchrist had left for the day, and that, unless they insisted on being arraigned before a United States Judge, they would be arraigned before Commissioner Hitchcock at 10:30 o'clock this morning. Berkman and Miss Goldman had both denounced the Judges at a meeting held on the east side Thursday night, and they shook their heads in unison when Mr. Content offered them the chance of an immediate arraignment before a Judge.

Will Demand Heavy Bail.

"We will go to the Tombs and be arraigned before a Commissioner in the morning," Miss Goldman said, after a whispered conference with Berkman.

A few minutes later a patrol wagon arrived at the Federal Building, and the prisoners were taken to the Tombs and locked up. They will be brought to the Federal Building this morning and arraigned at 10:30 o'clock. The Government will demand high bail in each case, it being rumored that the amount will be put at not less than $25,000 for each prisoner.

The Grand Jury does not meet again until Monday. The Goldman-Berkman case will be presented to that body as soon as it convenes, and it is believed the Government will ask for an indictment charging conspiracy to obstruct the operation of the draft law. A conviction will carry a sentence of two years in the penetentiary and the Judge

may also, in his discretion, impose fines as high as $10,000. The indictment, if returned, may also contain several counts, which would make possible a sentence in each case of six to ten years in prison.

It was also pointed out yesterday that neither Berkman nor Emma Goldman is a citizen of the United States, and that if convicted they may both be deported after their prison terms are served. The laws of the United States provide that where an alien has twice been convicted of crime in this country he may be deported, no matter how many years he has been in this country. Berkman served fourteen years for the attempted assassination of H. C. Frick, and Miss

Goldman has served a term of one year on Blackwell's Island for inciting others to riot.

Miss Goldman gave her age yesterday as 48 years. She said she was born in Russia, but as a young girl migrated to Prussia. She came to the United States in 1886. Berkman refused his pedigree, and sneeringly answered when asked his age that he was 250 years old.

"Anarchist activities in this country are at an end," said a Federal official yesterday as the patrol wagon in which the prisoners were taken to the Tombs sped away from the Federal Building.

June 16, 1917

BOSTON 'PEACE' PARADE MOBBED

Soldiers and Sailors Break Up Socialist Demonstration and Rescue Flag.

TWO DIVISIONS ATTACKED

Socialist Headquarters Ransacked and Contents Burned —Many Arrests for Fighting.

BOSTON, July 1.—Riotous scenes attended a Socialist parade today which was announced as a peace demonstration. The ranks of the marchers were broken up by self-organized squads of uniformed soldiers and sailors, red flags and banners bearing socialistic mottoes were trampled on, and literature and furnishings in the Socialist headquarters in Park Square were thrown into the street and burned.

Police reserves stopped the rioting af-

ter it had been in progress an hour and a half. Many arrests were made.

The police took into custody some of the participants in hundreds of fist fights which were waged on the Common and in the line of the parade on Tremont Street, while agents of the Federal Department of Justice, under the direction of Assistant District Attorney Goldberg, arrested in the crowd a number of persons who were alleged to have made unpatriotic remarks in the heat of the conflict. None of the soldiers and sailors who figured in the disturbance was arrested.

The procession, which consisted of hundreds of men and women, many of whom carried babies, formed in Park Square, and, passing through Eliot Street, marched along Tremont Street, one division going to the baseball ground on the Common, where a meeting had been arranged, and another proceeding to Scollay Square. Most of the marchers carried small red flags with white centres, emblematic of the peace demonstration, and there were large banners bearing inscriptions, some of which read:

"Russia has a six-hour day. Why not America?"

"Liberty Loan a first mortgage on labor."

A large American flag was at the head of the procession.

Half a hundred men in the uniform of Naval Reservists, National Guardsmen, marines, and Canadian "Kilties," who had watched the formation of the parade, marched across the common in a double column and intercepted the procession at the corner of West and Tremont Streets, and again at the corner of Winter and Tremont Streets. In both instances the contact resulted in a street fight. Blows were exchanged, and flags were snatched from the hands of the marchers, while women in the line screamed in fright.

At Scollay Square there was a similar scene. The American flag at the head of the line was seized by the attacking party, and the band, which had been

playing "The Marseillaise," with some interruptions, was forced to play "The Star-Spangled Banner," while cheers were given for the flag.

The police had just succeeded in quieting this disturbance, when the reserves were called out to quell a near-riot at the meeting place on the Common. The first of the "peace speakers" had barely begun his remarks when the reserves arrived. They formed a circle in the crowd, with the police wagon as a centre, in front of the speakers' stand, but in spite of their presence there were scores of individual fights in the big gathering. To restore quiet Supt. Crowley, as Acting Police Commissioner, revoked the permit for the speaking and the meeting was called off.

Meanwhile the Socialist headquarters in Park Square had been ransacked, and its contents destroyed in a bonfire. The American flag taken from the paraders was placed over a statue of "Lincoln the Emancipator" near the scene of the bonfire.

The peace demonstration was organized at a conference of Socialist branches, labor unions, and workmen's benefit societies of the metropolitan district, acting under the name of the Workmen's Council, in imitation of the Council of Workmen and Soldiers of Russia. It was announced that the organization represented 10,000 working men, and that its program would include the peace terms of the Russian workmen—no forcible annexations, no punitive indemnities, and free development of all nations.

Among the speakers who were announced as on the program for the meeting, on the Common were James H. Maurer, President of the Pennsylvania Federation of Labor; J. Edward Morgan of San Francisco, representing the Mooney Defense Movement; James O'Neal, State Secretary of the Socialist Party, and Joseph Murphy of Lowell.

July 2, 1917

BUREAU TO DEFEND LOVERS OF PEACE

A National Organization Formed to Protect Our 'Conscientious Objectors.

HILLQUIT AS A VOLUNTEER

Will Serve Unpaid with Other Lawyers—Amos Pinchot and the Rev. John Haynes Holmes in It, Too.

The National Civil Liberties Bureau, which has for its purpose, among other things, the defense of men who refuse to fight on the ground that they are "conscientious objectors," has come into existence, and announces that it has obtained the services, without pay, of a large number of lawyers in all parts of the country, who will render legal aid to the organization. Among the lawyers named are several who are members of the so-called People's Council of America, which is agitating for a world peace.

"The Civil Liberties Bureau," the statement issued yesterday says, "is formed to meet the increased demand all over the country for an agency to protect the rights of free speech, free press, free assembly, and liberty of conscience. Its chief purpose will be to give legal aid and advice through attorneys and committees of citizens in all parts of the United States to persons whose rights are invaded under pressure of war. The work in behalf of 'conscientious objectors' recently undertaken by the American Union Against Militarism will become a part of this larger bureau."

The office of the American Union Against Militarism, in the name of which organization yesterday's announcement was made, is at 70 Fifth Avenue. That is also the address of the People's Council of America. L. Hollingsworth Wood is announced as the director of the bureau, other members being the Rev. Dr. John Haynes Holmes, Amos Pinchot, Roger H. Baldwin, and John Lovejoy Elliott. Among the lawyers who will render their services free to the bureau are Morris Hillquit, Job Harriman, D. J. Meserole, Gilbert E. Roe, Eustace Seligman, and Alfred Jaretski, Jr. Miss Crystal Eastman, who is prominent in the People's Council, said yesterday:

"It is high time that all honest liberals in this country, whether for or against war, realize that all that is real in American democracy is in danger today. Yesterday's outrage in Boston is the most extreme example of what we mean by the danger of militarism." The breaking up of the Socialist Peace Parade in Boston was what she referred to. Miss Eastman added that the bureau would not oppose the "competent prosecution" of the war, and added: "We are not obstructionists or troublemakers."

Describing the activities of the new bureau, Roger Baldwin, one of the directors, said: "It will be the object of the Civil Liberties Bureau to act as a clearing house for complaints of injustice. Correspondents and newspaper clippings from all over the country will keep us informed of each case as it arises. We have already the names of lawyers in Chicago, Cincinnati, St. Louis, Pittsburgh, Boston, Philadelphia, Seattle, San Francisco, and thirty other large cities who have agreed to give their services free in investigating and defending cases we turn over to them. In addition to acting directly in the people's interest as a national clearing house, we are rapidly establishing legal complaint bureaus, with attorneys in charge, in all the large cities, to whom local complaints can be made direct and from whom immediate legal aid can be obtained."

William E. Williams, publicity director of the People's Council of America, denied yesterday that his organization had gone on record as approving a German peace. As Mr. Williams explained it, the council's goal is:

"An early, general, and democratic peace, to be obtained through negotiation in harmony with the principles outlined by the President and by revolutionary Russia, and accepted substantially by the progressive and democratic forces of France, England, Italy, Germany, Austria, and other countries, namely, no forcible annexation of territory, no punitive indemnities, and free development of all nationalities." He declared that no member of the organization had authority to vary that platform.

July 3, 1917

ARIZONA SHERIFF SHIPS 1,100 I.W.W'S OUT IN CATTLE CARS

Harry C. Wheeler of Bisbee Summons 2,000 Deputies and Clears the Town of Agitators.

TWO KILLED IN ROUNDUP

Lawyer W. B. Cleary and Other Sympathizers Driven Away with the Trouble Makers.

GOVERNOR ASKS FOR TROOPS

Whole Far West Awake to Threats of I. W. W. Men and Moving to Suppress Them.

BISBEE, Ariz., July 12.—More than eleven hundred Industrial Workers of the World were deported from Bisbee today, aboard twenty-four cattle cars. Their announced destination was Columbus, N. M. The special train carrying them left Warren, four miles from Bisbee, at noon.

When the train arrived in Columbus tonight, according to a dispatch received here, F. B. King, Division Superintendent of the El Paso & Southwestern Railway, was in charge, and was arrested by the local authorities for bringing in the deportees. The Columbus authorities refused to permit the men to be detrained. The army officer in command at Columbus threw out a strong guard about the military establishment. The train is said to be moving westward again. The men may be detrained at Hermanas, a small settlement twenty miles west of Columbus.

The men were driven from the city by Deputy Sheriffs and about 2,000 armed men, members of an organization known as the Citizens' Protective League. Two men were killed during the work of deportation.

The victims were Orson P. McRae, a member of the Citizens' Protective League and shift boss at one of the Copper Queen mines, and James Brew, a former employe of the Denn mine. McRae was killed when Brew fired through the door of his room at the deputy. McRae, it was said, was unarmed. Brew fired several more shots and then stepped out of his room. Three of McRae's companions fired at him and he fell dead beside his victim.

A strike was called here by the metal workers branch of the I. W. W., about two weeks ago. Since then, according to officials, scores of strangers have

been in Bisbee. These men are alleged to have prevented miners from returning to work. Plans for the " roundup " of alleged undesirables were made at midnight by Harry C. Wheeler, Sheriff of Cochise County. Within two hours the Sheriff had sworn in 1,200 men as deputies and ordered them to report at various points at 4 o'clock this morning. When the bands of citizens assembled, those who were not already armed received rifles and revolvers with instructions to use them only in self-defense.

" Until the last I. W. W. is run out," was the watchword passed to the waiting men.

At 6:30 o'clock special newspaper editions contained a proclamation by Sheriff Wheeler, ordering women and children to keep off the streets during the day. It also instructed deputies to arrest " on charges of vagrancy, treason, and of being disturbers of the peace of Cochize County, all men who have congregated here from other parts and sections for the purpose of harassing and intimidating all men who desire to pursue their daily toil."

Posses Gather as if By Magic.

Simultaneously five bands of armed citizens appeared as if by magic. Some hurried from alleys, others came streaming from storerooms, and some sprang down from low roofs of business buildings. All marched in a businesslike manner to the centre of the town. Every strange man on the streets was challenged.

" Hold on, stranger, what's your business? " " What are you doing in Bisbee? " and " How long have you been here? " were some of the questions asked by the little groups as they surrounded each man. Every suspicious-looking individual was placed under arrest.

Fifty pickets at the entrance to the Copper Queen mines, in front of the Post Office, were arrested when twenty-five armed citizens rushed from the lobby of the Post Office and surrounded them. Four squads of citizens, coming from different parts of the city, reached the centre of the town at the same time. Each band was marching with several hundred prisoners. As each man was detained he was ordered to put up his hands, and deputies quickly searched him for weapons. As the prisoners marched along the streets hundreds of rifles were leveled at their heads from all sides.

After an hour's wait, captors and captured marched to the railroad station, where another squad on duty had taken charge of several hundred more men. At 8:30 o'clock the prisoners were lined up two abreast. Flanked by 2,000 heavily armed citizens, the captives were ordered to march down the railroad tracks toward Warren. At Lowell, a suburb, about 800 more I. W. W.'s were merged into the procession.

Herded in a Ball Park.

The baseball park at Warren was chosen for the place of assembling the men to be deported. Word of the " clean up " preceded the Sheriff and his men, and when the prisoners reached the park the hundreds of spectators on the scene began to jeer.

When the prisoners were inside the inclosure, half the armed bands formed a guard around the park, while the other half started a systematic search of the entire district for the men who were identified with the I. W. W., or who could not account for their presence in a satisfactory manner.

Armed men went through lodging houses and restaurants questioning every one. Those who did not answer satisfactorily were marched between lines of citizens to the park. For two hours leaders of the I. W. W. attempted to make themselves heard above the hoots and jeers of the crowds. When it seemed as if the park would hold no more, six additional squads of prisoners were packed in and the guards were increased.

A few minutes before noon a special train of cattle cars rolled up to the park. The prisoners were marched in single file from the inclosure up the runways and on to the cars. As each man entered the car, according to the authorities he was asked if he wanted to go to work or if he could give the name of a reliable citizen who would vouch for him. Those who expressed a desire for employment were held for further investigation.

Several prominent citizens of Bisbee and Lowell who openly declared they were in sympathy with the I. W. W. movement were forced into the cars with the vagrants. Among these was William B. Cleary, an attorney widely known through Arizona, who was taken into custody when the raid started. Cleary was alleged to have spoken openly in sympathy with the I. W. W. movement.

The train left Warren at noon. As it pulled out cheers and jeers came from the crowd. Some of the deported ones waved their hands and their caps and shouted: " Goodby, Bisbee."

Throughout the afternoon the citizens contined the work of questioning every one on the streets. Tonight hundreds of men are patrolling the streets. Every male citizen is armed, some with shotguns and others with a variety of pistols, revolvers and rifles.

The proclamation posted by Sheriff Wheeler is as follows:

I have formed a Sheriff's posse of 1,200 men in Bisbee and 1,000 men in Douglas, all loyal Americans, for the purpose of arresting on the charges of vagrancy, treason, and of being disturbers of the peace of Cochise County all those strange men who have congregated here from other parts and sections for the purpose of harassing and intimidating all men who desire to pursue their daily toil.

I am continually told of threats and insults heaped upon the workingmen of this district by so-called strikers, who are strange to these parts yet who presume to dictate the manner of life of the people of this district. Appeal to patriotism does not move them nor do appeals to reason. At a time when our country needs her every resource these strangers persist in keeping from her the precious metal production of this entire district.

Today I heard threats to the effect that homes would be destroyed because the heads of families insisted upon their rights as Americans to work for themselves, their families, and their country.

Other threats have and are daily being made. Men have been assaulted and brutally beaten, and only today I heard the Mayor of Bisbee threatened and his request ignored.

We cannot longer stand nor tolerate such conditions. This is no labor trouble. We are sure of that. But it is a direct attempt to embarrass the Government of the United States. I therefore call upon all loyal Americans to aid me in peaceably arresting these disturbers of national and local peace. Let no shot be fired throughout this day unless in necessary self-defense, and I hereby give warning that each and every leader of so-called strikers will be held personally responsible for any injury inflicted upon any of the deputies while in the performance of their duty as deputies of my office, for whose acts, I in turn, assume full responsibility as Sheriff of this county.

All arrested persons will be treated humanely and their cases examined with justice and care.

I hope no resistance will be made, for I desire no bloodshed. However, I am determined, if resistance is made, it shall be effectively overcome.

HARRY C. WHEELER.

July 13, 1917

TROOPS TO BE SENT TO QUELL THE I. W. W.

Special to The New York Times.

WASHINGTON, July 11.—Secretary Baker, acting on an appeal from Governor Lister of the State of Washington, who represented the conditions due to I. W. W. activity as very bad in that State, took steps tonight to send Federal troops to North Yakima, Wenatchee, Ellensburg, and Cle Elum. The Governor telegraphed Secretary Baker that it was feared that the I. W. W. would destroy crops and blow up irrigation reservoirs upon which this apple-growing country depends for water.

Secretary Baker telegraphed to General Liggett, commanding the Western Military Department, with headquarters at San Francisco, to get into communication with Governor Lister and furnish any assistance he desired.

The Secretary of War has been informed that in Northern Idaho, a large part of Montana, especially the Butte region; practically all of the States of Washington and Arizona, and scattered communities in Oregon and California, the I. W. W. is paralyzing industry and terrifying labor. Many lumber camps have been compelled to close. Some mines have suspended; more are threatened. And now the I. W. W. has invaded the agricultural districts, organizing farm laborers and employees of related industries and intimidating laborers who refuse to join their organization.

The I. W. W. organization is opposed to the war with Germany. It has made the question of wages the pretext for its present activities. Its program calls for the destruction of industries until capital surrenders.

KINGMAN, Ariz., July 11.—Forty-two Industrial Workers of the World, rounded up by Home Guards after they were brought here by armed guards who had failed in attempting to deport the men from Jerome into California at Needles, armed Californians driving the agitators back into Arizona, were released today by order of Governor Thomas E. Campbell. County authorities exacted pledges from the men that they would leave this district. Some said they would return to Jerome.

GLOBE, Ariz., July 11. — The mine owners and striking copper miners in the Globe-Miami district are apparently deadlocked, but United States troops, mounted deputies, and home guards are in control of the situation.

Governor Campbell was warned today that he would be held responsible for the safety of I. W. W. leaders who were deported from Jerome and Mohave County, in a telegram from the I. W. W. Executive Committee of the Globe-Miami district.

Governor Campbell's reply to what he characterized over the long-distance telephone tonight as an "impudent message" read:

"If I receive another expression of that kind I will treat it as an intimidation of my executive action and will hold those who send it responsible accordingly."

ELLENSBURG, Wash., July 11.—Federal troops stationed near here today arrested between fifty and sixty Industrial Workers of the World, charged with interfering with crop harvesting and logging, in violation of the Federal statutes.

The men will be brought to Ellensburg and placed in a stockade.

July 12, 1917

ENTIRE WEST ALERT TO SUPPRESS I. W. W.

"Red Card" Agitators, Seeking to Establish Reign of Terror, Mysteriously Provided with Funds.

SAN FRANCISCO, July 12.—Deportation, undertaken today at Bisbee, Ariz., of more than 1,000 Industrial Workers of the World centred attention upon an agitation which has risen in the West to considerable proportions after manifesting itself sporadically from coast to coast for years. From the Canadian border to Mexico civic, State, and military authorities were alert tonight to suppress all disorder.

Disturbances, fomented admittedly by the I. W. W. and spreading into various branches of industry, carry with them in virtually every instance a demand for higher wages. Officials in some States pronounced the movement one to reduce production of supplies necessary to the conduct of the war, but, while German influence and financial support was charged by some of them, no direct substantiation of this accusation could be had. Organizers of the I. W. W., especially in Arizona, were reported to be well financed from sources unknown even to those well versed in the workings of the body.

Military censorship, which repressed accounts of immediate occurrences in Arizona, still permitted a fairly extensive view of the general situation. Strikes were on tonight in the copper mines of Arizona and Montana. They were threatened in the mines of Colorado, Nevada, and Utah. There were lumber strikes in Idaho and Washington, with agitation in the lumber districts of Oregon. Threats had been made to destroy the wheat fields of the Northwest, and the State Council of Defense of Washington appointed a committee especially to deal with the I. W. W. lest harm come to the crops. Existing disturbances reached into Mexico.

Aim to Destroy Property.

Bodily resistance to constituted and unconstituted authority has not manifested itself to any great extent in the recent Western operations of the organization. Sixty I. W. W.'s were deported from Jerome, Ariz., and redeported from Needles, Cal., without physical violence. Threats attributed to them are generally against property. They say they base their demands and actions upon the theories of George Sorel, a Frenchman, and got from him the plan of property destruction as a lever to gain their end, which they define as "industrial democracy." This property destruction as advocated and practiced in the West of late has taken many forms. Lumber mills have had their costly saws splintered by spikes driven into logs. In the orchard districts fruit trees have died after copper nails had been hammered into them.

The organizers proclaim the movement to be world-wide. The red flag is the proposed universal banner, and each member of the organization carries a red card. Membership is sought in all branches of industry. Organizers say that 52,000 farm laborers belong, and that the plantation labor of the South is being organized. It is the theory of the I. W. W. that each branch of industry should help the other in gaining its ends, and Rodger Culver, an I. W. W. speaker, recently said at Miami, Ariz., "If necessary to enforce the miners' demands there will be no wheat crop in the North American Continent." Threats of wholesale destruction of wheat have not materialized.

First-hand reports from Western States indicated the situation to be about as follows:

Arizona, Bisbee—Between 4,500 and 5,000 men on strike sponsored entirely by Industrial Workers of the World.

Globe-Miami—About 7,000 men on strike. Troops or guard since July 5.

Clifton-Morenci District — Mine shut down by operators following strike vote by 3,000 men.

Jerome—About sixty I. W. W. members deported and town at peace.

The strikers in Arizona are not all connected with the I. W. W. movement.

Reaches Into Mexico.

Mexico—State of Sonora—Labor disturbances at Cananea, El Tigre, and Nacozari, following visits from I. W. W. organizers from Douglas and Bisbee, Ariz.

Texas—El Paso—Three I. W. W.'s arrested in connection with alleged plots to blow up railroad bridge. Efforts now on foot to organize Mexican smelter labor.

Oregon—Marshfield—Lumber strike, interfering with production for army cantonments and wooden ships, broken up. Eastern Oregon farmers actively organizing against I. W. W. propaganda, with threatened destruction of crops.

Washington—West of Cascade Mountains. Timber workers at Gray's Harbor demand higher wages and shorter hours.

Seattle—About 500 I. W. W. members in town, passing to and from lumber camps where, they say, they seek to stir up trouble.

East of Cascades—Strikes among loggers and sawmill men in Upper Yakima Valley have followed appearance of I. W. W. organizers. I. W. W. headquarters have been established in numerous small towns, followed by promulgation of proposed scales for fruit and grain harvesting in accord with the organization's expressed views of what is due the workers. Proposals for these scales have been followed by threats of property destruction, eliciting a declaration from the State Council of Defense that stern measures were awaiting any burning of grain or laying waste of orchards.

Northern Idaho—Lumber camps shut down. Governor declares State quiet, no troops needed. State Council of Defense disagreed. Western Department of the army has received orders to co-operate in suppression of disorder, upon call of Governor. Governor Moses Alexander is making a study of the purposes of the I. W. W., listening to street speaking and studying their publications.

Western Montana—Butte copper mines nearly at a standstill, following organization of new union, encouraged by the I. W. W.

Throughout the States the organizers shuttle back and forth. In Washington it is said hundreds of them ride the trains unmolested. Through Bisbee, Morenci, Jerome, and other Arizona towns, and through the lumber camps of the Northwest, they have been active, according to reliable reports.

GOVERNOR ASKS FOR TROOPS.

Arizona Executive Telegraphs to Fort Sam Houston for Soldiers.

PHOENIX, Ariz., July 12.—Governor Campbell this afternoon wired to General Parker at Fort Sam Houston informing him of the situation with regard to I. W. W. deportations at Bisbee and requesting that United States troops be sent there at once.

Attorney General Whitney said he had been advised that two men had been killed at Bisbee. One was Deputy Sheriff McRae and the other a striker. Details are lacking, but it is understood they killed each other.

Mr. Whitney has telegraphed the following to Sheriff H. C. Wheeler at Bisbee:

"Kindly wire this office immediately details leading up to deportation now taking place in Bisbee. State by what authority of law you are acting. State fully what violations, if any, took place prior to decision to deport strikers."

"The situation is such," Governor Campbell said today, "that it is almost impossible for the State to handle it. The State has no troops at its command, the National Guard being in the service of the United States. It would be impracticable for me at this time to declare martial law, as I have no troops to enforce it. The situation is one for the Federal Government to handle."

Further details of the roundup are that the 1,500 members of the Citizens' Protective League were sworn in as deputies by the Sheriff and made a house-to-house canvass. Every man found who refused to go to work was escorted, under guard, to a ball park, where they were herded together.

It was said Attorney W. B. Cleary, who sent a telegram protesting against the deportation to ex-Governor Hunt at Globe, was among those caught in the dragnet.

A telephone message from Bisbee this afternoon at 1:30 o'clock said a train made up of twenty-four cattle cars left there with 1,103 persons on it, bound for some point in New Mexico. Included in the number are three women, who were sent out on account of their sympathy for the I. W. W. and their outspoken expression of it.

At this time Bisbee is quiet. It is announced that all of the mines will resume operations tomorrow with about 50 per cent. of the force at work. Every miner in Bisbee has not only expressed his willingness to work, but is anxious to do so. Every known agitator and sympathizer with the I. W. W. has been deported.

Shops are reopening for business and the camp is assuming a normal air.

OUTRAGE, SAYS HAYWOOD.

I. W. W. Official Denies That Union Is Backed by German Money.

CHICAGO, July 12.—W. D. Haywood, Secretary-Treasurer of the I. W. W., said tonight that the Attorney General of the United States was investigating what he termed a "series of outbreaks against the I. W. W." and branded as absolutely false the rumors that German influence and German money were behind the copper mine strikes at Bisbee, Ariz.; Butte, Mont., and elsewhere in the West.

"The deportation of I. W. W. members from Bisbee today was an outrage," said Haywood, "and only one of a series. I want to deny emphatically that German money, German influence, or war-time motives are behind the Western copper mine strikes. And I want to say that the deportations will not affect the general situation. They cannot mine copper with machine guns or dig it with bayonets.

"Senator Thomas of Colorado recently made the absurd statement that German influences were behind our movement. It is not German influence, but simply an effort to get living wages and just working conditions for our miners that is behind the strikes."

July 13, 1917

MALONE AIDS FIGHT OF ANTI-DRAFT PRESS

Collector Advises Papers Barred from the Mails to Appeal to Wilson.

F. C. HOWE HELPS ALSO

Authority of a Postmaster to Decide on Suppression Is Questioned.

The voices of Dudley Field Malone, Collector of the Port; Dr. Frederic C. Howe, Commissioner of Immigration, and, by proxy, George Creel, the Government's unofficial censor, were added yesterday to a protest of Socialists, internationalists, pacifists, and others against the methods by which a dozen or more periodicals have been excluded recently from the United States mails. The occasion was a luncheon in Haan's Park Row Restaurant under the auspices of the Civil Liberties Committee of the Union Against Militarism.

Various announcements were made of steps to be taken in behalf of the barred periodicals, and motions were passed contemplating action.

A motion was passed authorizing the appointment of a committee to go to Washington to take the matter up with the Postmaster General and the President, and Amos Pinchot, who presided, invited every one present to become a member of the committee. He said the date of the committee's departure would depend upon the time when it could obtain audiences with the officials in Washington. Another motion was passed authorizing the appointment of a committee to co-operate with the Civil Liberties Committee in arranging a mass meeting of protest against the suppression of periodicals by the Post Office Department.

Dr. Howe said that the policy by which the Post Office Department had excluded some fifteen periodicals from the mails was not in harmony with the country's motives in the war, and Ann Herendeen, one of the editors of the issue of Four Lights, which was barred from the mails, said that the Woman's Peace Party, which publishes the magazine, had been in correspondence with Mr. Creel, who had said that he deplored the action of the Post Office Department. After the meeting Mrs. Margaret Lane, managing editor of the magazine, said that she had seen Mr. Creel in Washington and enlisted his support in attempting to persuade the Post Office Department to let Four Lights go through the mails. Mr. Creel had taken the matter up, she said, and had admitted later that he could do nothing.

Collector Malone was not scheduled to speak, but when called upon for a speech, said that he had come merely to see "what it was all about," and that he would not criticise a Government department. He condemned, however, a policy which permitted Postmasters to pass upon the merits of magazines submitted to the mails.

"I don't think there is a Postmaster in the country," said Mr. Malone, "competent to decide what magazine shall go through the mails, and I do not think that the suppression without sufficient reason of any periodical is a contribution to the country's welfare."

Mr. Malone advised those dissatisfied to meet and form their protest, and then to take it to the Postmaster General, and, if they did not obtain satisfaction, to the President himself. He predicted that such procedure would result in justice.

Max Eastman said that he had been surprised at "the imperial talent" shown by officials at Washington, and predicted that, as men had been put in jail for quoting the Declaration of Independence and the Bible, some one would be given a life sentence for quoting President Wilson in the wrong connection.

"You can't even collect your thoughts without being arrested for unlawful assemblage," he said.

Abraham Cahan, editor of the Jewish Daily Forward, said that on the east side the people were looking to citizens of Petrograd to form societies for the furtherance of freedom in America as persons in New York had organized for freedom in Russia before the revolution there.

Mr. Pinchot said that he had been informed that socialist papers printed in Russia had been kept out of this country by the authorities here.

Charles Erbin of The New York Call said that he had printed in his newspapers several of the articles for the publication of which other periodicals had been kept out of the mails, and he could not understand why he had not been suppressed. He announced that he would print this morning a cartoon ridiculing the Post Office Department.

Several of the speakers made it clear that they did not hold pacifist views and thought there ought to be some regulation of the mails, but they agreed that the present policy of the Post Office Department was wrong.

CREEL WILL NOT HELP.

Says He Found Four Lights Was Clearly Obnoxious.

Special to The New York Times.
WASHINGTON, July 13. — George Creel, Chairman of the Committee on Public Information, denied tonight having been enlisted in the fight against the Post Office Department to prevent the suppression of treasonable publications.

"It is true that Mrs. Lane wrote me," said Mr. Creel, "asking my assistance in behalf of Four Lights, which is an outgrowth of The Survey. I did go to see Mr. Lamar, Attorney General for the Post Office Department, in regard to the publication, and found that it was clearly obnoxious to the espionage law. I am as firmly the friend of a free press as any man, and would fight for a free press. But publications which are trying to break down the Government are clearly treasonable, and I believe in enforcing the law against them. I replied to Mrs. Lane, saying I could not for one moment undertake to defend a publication that was violating the law, and that she must not expect to receive any help from me in contesting the action of the Post Office Department."

COURT CITES POSTMASTER.

The Masses Seeks to Enjoin Him from Barring the Paper.

Judge Learned Hand of the Federal District Court, on the motion of Lawyer Gilbert E. Roe of 55 Liberty Street, yesterday granted an order directing Postmaster Thomas G. Patten to show cause before him on Monday at 2 o'clock why he should not be enjoined from barring from the mails the August issue of The Masses, a monthly magazine published by The Masses Publishing Company of 34 Union Square East.

The complaint states that on July 5 the company was by letter informed by Postmaster Patten that according to advice from the Solicitor of the Post Office Department the August issue of "The Masses is non-mailable under the act of June 15, 1917." The Masses Publishing Company, in the complaint, alleges it was not and never has been afforded an opportunity by Postmaster Patten or any other postal official in the matter of determining the magazine to be non-mailable.

July 14, 1917

I. W. W. STRIKE CHIEF LYNCHED AT BUTTE

Frank Little Taken from Home by Six Masked Men in Auto and Hanged to Bridge.

VIGILANTES' SIGN ON BODY

Agitator Called Our Troops "Scabs in Uniform" and Denounced American Government.

BUTTE, Mon., Aug. 1.—Frank Little, member of the Executive Board of the Industrial Workers of the World and leader in labor troubles in Arizona, was taken from a lodging house early today by masked men annd hanged to a railroad trestle on the outskirts of the city.

Little, in a recent speech here, referred to United States troops as "Uncle Sam's scabs in uniform." Since his arrival in Butte recently from Globe, Ariz., he has made speeches to strikers, in all of which he had attacked the Government and urged the men to shut down the mines of the Butte district. He was bitter in his denunciation of the Government.

When his body was cut down by Chief of Police Jerry Murphy at 8 o'clock this morning, a card was found pinned to the underclothing on his right thigh. It bore in red crayon letters the inscription:

> Others Take Notice.
> First and Last Warning.
> 3-7-77.   L D C S S W T.

Sign of the Vigilantes.

A circle was about the letter L. The letters were inscribed with a lead pencil. The figures "3-7-77" are the old sign of the Vigilantes in Montana. The custom of the Vigilantes was to send three warnings to a marked man, the third and last being written in red.

Six masked men in an automobile drove up to the front of Little's lodgings at 5 minutes after 3 o'clock. One stood upon the sidewalk in front of the rooming house. The others entered. Without speaking, the men quickly broke into the Room No. 30, on the ground floor. Light from an electric torch showed them the room was unoccupied. Mrs. Nora Byrne, owner of the place, who was awakened by the noise, occupied an adjoining room at the front of the building.

"Some mistake here," she heard a voice say. Then she heard the men move to the door of her room, which they pushed slightly open. Mrs. Byrne sprang to the door and held it. "Wait until I get my clothes on," she said.

Then she asked who they were and what they wanted. "We are officers and we want Frank Little," she was told.

Mrs. Byrne hastily dressed, again went to the door and opened it. The leader of the masked men poked a revolver into the opening.

"Where is Frank Little?" he asked.

"He is in room 32," she answered.

The men ran down the hall and tried the door to that room. One of them gave it a kick that broke the lock and they entered. Mrs. Byrne said she heard them coming from the room and saw them half lead, half carry Little across the sidewalk and push him into a motor car.

Wounded on the Head.

The body was found hanging on the north side of the railroad trestle. The ties on the trestle are about fourteen feet above the roadway. Little's feet were about five feet from the ground. On the back of his head was a wound. The Coroner could not determine whether the mark was a gunshot wound or an abrasion from a blow. An autopsy was ordered held late today.

Little wore only his underclothing when taken from his room. He is not known to have made any outcry or demanded any explanation.

Following the identification of the body, Butte members of the I. W. W. telegraphed appeals for aid. A message was sent to William D. Haywood, at Chicago, and others went to I. W. W. organization leaders in the Southwest and the Pacific coast. It was said that a message was received later from Haywood, saying the resources of the organzation would be employed to bring the lynchers of Little to justice.

Early in the day men gathered at Finn Hall, headquarters of the Metal Mine Workers' Union, and threats were made against "gunmen" said to be employed here. At Union Hall threats were made by individuals against local newspapers.

Little's record was under investigation by the Federal authorities, whose attention had been called to his activities. On the other hand, the report was current that he was in the employ of a detective agency, and one theory was that he was the victim of the radical element' of whom he appeared to be a member.

The agitator took a leading part in recent labor troubles in Arizona. He addressed a letter to Governor Campbell of Arizona, protesting against the deportation of I. W. W. members from Bisbee. This letter was written from Salt Lake. Governor Campbell replied, telling Little he resented his interference and his threats. Little was understood to have the confidence of William D. Haywood, Secretary of the I. W. W. national organization and was regarded here as one of Haywood's confidential agents. He had letters in his baggage from various I. W. W. organizers, including Haywood.

Slurred American Troops.

Little began to make speeches on the day of his arrival in Butte three weeks ago. On July 19, before a mass meeting of miners, he referred to the United States soldiers as "Uncle Sam's scabs in uniform." In the same speech he said: "If the mines are taken under Federal control we will make it so hot for the Government that it will not be able to send any troops to France."

Referring in another address to his interview recently with Governor Campbell of Arizona, Little said that he used these words:

"Governor, I don't give a d—— what your country is fighting for; I am fighting for the solidarity of labor."

Last Friday night, at Finn Hall, before the Metal Mine Workers' Union, Little said:

"A city ordinance is simply a piece of paper which can be torn up. The same can be said of the Constitution of the United States."

When Governor Sam Stewart was asked at Helena if he contemplated any action in relation to the lynching he would give no opinion. Attorney General Ford said he had communicated with County Attorney Jackson at Butte asking for a statement of the facts.

"They got Little. He was the first man marked to go. We had received warnings and were told that Joe Shannon was the second in line, Tom Campbell third, and another man fourth," said William Sullivan, attorney for the Metal Mine Workers' Union, this morning. "I can't tell you how we received the warnings, but we knew they were marking some of the men."

Shannon, one of Little's associates in Butte, is prominent in the new mine workers' union and is Chairman of its Strike Committee. He had a leading part in the labor troubles of three years ago when the Western Federation of Miners organization was broken up, its hall destroyed and Charles H. Moyer ordered to leave Butte.

Sullivan shrugged his shoulders when asked if he himself were not the fourth man referred to as marked.

"We used every precaution and even had the marked men change rooms every so often," added Sullivan. "I cannot give the names of other men who were supposed to be designated as victims."

Speaking of possible trouble growing out of the lynching, Sullivan said there would be no outbreaks in Butte, "although the temper of the men is much tried.

"We have taken steps to provide against trouble," he said. "The men will not cause riot or other disturbance. We are going to the bottom of this thing, but in a legal way."

"Have you any idea of the identity of the men who composed the hanging party?" Sullivan was asked.

"We have practically proved who five of them were, we are uncertain as to a sixth. We soon will know who they all were," he replied.

Unwise, Says Prosecutor.

"It is the most unwise thing that has happened in Butte," said United States District Attorney B. K. Wheeler, in discussing the lynching. "The men who perpetrated the affair should be brought to justice."

Mr. Wheeler said he wrote yesterday to the United States Attorney General in Washington, asking if prosecution could be brought against Little on the ground of his unpatriotic utterances.

County Attorney Joseph R. Jackson said: "It is a cold-blooded murder and every effort will be used to apprehend the men who did it. If they are caught they will be prosecuted to the full extent of the law."

August 2, 1917

Uncle Sam as Cub Reporter and News Critic

How the Government, Through Creel Committee, Is Learning Business of Writing for the Papers, With Censorship as Side Line

Uncle Sam himself has turned cub reporter. But even though he is new at the job of writing news, he has undertaken a star assignment—the news of the war—through George Creel and his Committee on Public Information.

The activities of that committee present a queer mixture of nth degree press-agenting, news gathering, and news censoring. It may put out a "good story" one minute and be forced to kill a better one the next. Its "handout" may be a commonplace recital of fact or a colorful account of "an attack in force" by German submarines on American transport ships. The result is confusing. So perhaps the public would like to know how Washington "covers the war."

Within the last few days there has been a change in the committee's policy. Hereafter it intends to disseminate fewer "canned stories." It will confine itself largely to straightout official announcements and news from the Government departments. The facts will be furnished the newspaper correspondents, and there will be less attempt to write their articles for them. J. W. McConaughy, appointed Director of Publicity, is striving for a greater degree of cooperation between the committee and the correspondents. The publicity division also has to overcome the prejudices of army and navy officers, who have never relished the creation of a committee to furnish war news to the public.

While the publicity division is supplying matter for publication, the division of vise, an equally important branch of the general committee, is charged with the duty of saying what may not be published. This division now comprises Mr. McConaughy, Edgar Sisson, William Churchill, and Kenneth Durant. It maintains a twenty-four hour watch. There has been added to the committee's branches a "feature section," under direction of L. Ames Brown, who will try to bring about the publication of articles on America's part in the war by noted authors.

The committee undertakes to assemble and distribute, in circular mimeograph form, the daily news developments of the Government departments most intimately associated with the conduct of the war. It feeds these mimeograph sheets to the press associations and newspaper bureaus, deposits a large batch of "handouts" on a desk at the National Press Club, and maintains a "press room" at its headquarters, and notifies the associations and principal newspaper representatives in advance when something important is impending. The committee publishes also the Official Bulletin, first cousin to the Congressional Record. There are 80,000 copies daily, and they go to every Postmaster in the United States, each member of Congress, all army and navy officials, and all officers of the Government, including Collectors of the Port, District Attorneys, and Marshals.

No doubt the Creel committee sincerely strives to "cover" all the Governmental news which the committee thinks should become public. However, the Washington newspaper correspondent, who deals for the public with the committee, has a deep-rooted antipathy toward "handout stuff." This material heretofore has been the product of the paid press agents; paid press agents are always active in Washington, and their free offerings pile up on the desk of the correspondent. Furthermore, the news writer prefers, as a rule, to get his own story. He would rather discuss a news event with a Cabinet officer or other official, of course, than to have the Secretary of that official supply a typewritten statement prepared in advance on an expected question.

The Committee on Public Information covers the departments through its numerous reporters, but makes no at-

George Creel, Whose Committee on Public Information Employs Many News-Gatherers, Movie Film Distributers, and Bulletin Dispensers.

tempt to report or censor the news of Congress. The Department of State has its own Publicity and Censorship Bureau, headed by Phil Patchin. The Official Bulletin runs each day a digest of the happenings in the Senate and House, but this appears as a summary for purposes of record only.

With its publicity organizations, the committee soon was enabled to turn out many thousand words of copy each day. Some of it was "press agent stuff" of a dignified sort, intended to arouse patriotism throughout the country and keep the public advised at the same time of the Government's activities in a fight for democracy. Other announcements were simple statements of fact; for instance, the correspondence between President Wilson and Chairman Lever of the House Committee on Agriculture, concerning the Food Control bill. To a considerable extent the committee has become the medium through which Presidential announcements are made, although Secretary Tumulty still sees the newspaper men. On the day the Wilson-Lever correspondence was released, the committee notified the Washington correspondents that it was making public a letter written by the President.

The Red Cross publicity campaign and the Liberty Loan campaign were handled independently of the committee. Each organization had its temporary

staff of "boosters." Herbert C. Hoover's food control organization also has a separate publicity medium. The Creel committee performs, in a general way, these functions:

Dissemination of news relating to the Washington end of the war. Showing of war activities by the use of moving pictures. Enlistment of "four-minute men"—speakers who go into the moving-picture houses and theatres and make four-minute speeches on the object of the war, its progress, and its patriotic aspects. Placing in foreign language newspapers of articles showing America's aims. Distribution of pamphlets—such as the "Red, White, and Blue Book"—relating to the war.

Under the supervision of Mr. Creel there is also maintained a Division of External Communication, which exercises a censorship over wireless and telegraph messages. Staff officers of the navy apply this censorship with respect to cable messages, and officers of the army keep a watch upon messages that do not go abroad. These officers are designated at intervals by the Secretaries of War and the Navy.

William M. Blair and Henry Atwater have enlisted about 3,000 "four-minute speakers." It is felt by the committee that the theatre, next to the newspapers, affords the chief medium through which the people may be acquainted with the country's war aims. The Division of Pictures, directed by Kendall Banning, not only supplies films to the movie houses throughout the United States, in which one of the "four-minute men" may appear simultaneously, but it distributes enlistment posters and placards

appealing for the support of the public. William A. Brady, theatrical manager, has contributed his services to this division.

Professor Guy Stanton Ford directs the Division of Education, which prepares pamphlets on the war, annotated textbooks of the President's messages, and State papers, and other official data for the enlightenment of the public.

The Division of Visé, with authority gradually increased since its formation, is virtually a censorship board directly influencing what is printed in the newspapers. Under the voluntary censorship accepted by the press, this division gives its "O. K." or disapproval when newspapers submit "tips" and stories and seek to publish them. Naturally, there are disagreements at times between the newspaper and the Division of Visé. A story which a correspondent may regard as entirely proper for publication may be held up by the Visé Board. A paper which obeys the injunction may be "scooped" by another paper which has not thought it necessary to submit the article to the censors.

Conflict arises at times between the committee and officials of the War and Navy Departments. There are various avenues of information in these departments, and men of various opinions regarding the propriety of publishing war stories. The Creel committee may have the full sanction of the Secretary of either department to obtain and promulgate information of a certain sort, but the official directly in possession of that information may have entirely different ideas. First, he may disapprove of the Creel committee and its functions; second, he may have the hidebound conviction that it's none of the public's business how the details of the war are being worked out. The task of the Creel committee has not been an easy one. It is understood that in some cases direct orders from the Secretary of War and the Secretary of the Navy have been necessary to "loosen up" the more reticent Admirals, Captains, Generals, and Majors.

"Newspaper men who inveigh against the Creel censorship," said a confidant of Creel, "are unappreciative of the troubles he has undergone. Creel has been a shouter for free speech all his life. He is a two-fisted fighter in whose brain there could lodge no thought of muzzling the press. He wants a democratic country to know about its war. He has gone to the mat several times with men who wanted to kill the news and has taken the blame when it did not belong to him. Probably he and the committee have made mistakes now and then, and more tact might have been used on occasions, but it is idle to criticise Creel as a censor who would hold back any legitimate item from the press."

The whole thing, of course, has been much in the nature of an experiment, and experience is now gradually bringing better conditions and more co-operation. The President is reported to be determined that the public shall have information concerning the war whenever that information does not disclose military secrets and afford aid to the enemy. For this reason it is believed that the Creel committee chosen by the President is in Washington to stay so long as the war lasts.

August 12, 1917

THE REPRESSION OF SEDITION.

"We condemn," said the American Bar Association in one of a series of patriotic resolutions which are an honor to its members, "all attempts, "in Congress and out of it, to hinder "and embarrass the Government of "the United States in carrying on the "war with vigor and effectiveness. "Under whatever cover of pacifism "or technicality such attempts are "made, we deem them to be pro- "German, and in effect giving aid "and comfort to the enemy."

The more or less disguised pro-Germans in Congress may be hard to reach, save by time and the gathering disgust of their constituents. The Department of Justice, after a long and wide investigation, has fallen, in many cities, upon the I. W. W., and in Chicago upon the headquarters of the Socialist Party.

From the beginning of the war the majority of the Socialist Party has been uninterruptedly pro-German. Since the American declaration of war it has officially and bitterly and multifariously opposed the war. It has been and is anti-American, pro-German. It is a nursery of sedition. It is an industrious propagandist of sedition.

The I. W. W., whose Chicago headquarters were likewise seized, is ostensibly engaged in bringing the wage system and "capitalism" to an end. It is a believer in and practicer of violence in word and action. Its present war on the wage system, its devotion to sabotage, take the form of burning crops, crippling machinery, shutting up mines, promoting strikes, obstructing the production of needed war supplies of lumber, minerals, and food. If malicious mischief is its purpose, the effect of its diversions is to hamper the prosecution of the war and to aid Germany. It has been insolent, destructive, and seditious; it has been, in effect, a domestic ally of Germany altogether too long. The Government has been patient. Now the Government has struck hard.

Various societies, German-language and other-language magazines and newspapers and pamphlets, the whole colportage of treason, are said to be under investigation. The "dark forces" of sedition, of aid and comfort to the Germans, have abused their impunity. They have forgotten or braved the will of the majority, the sentiment of the nation, the implacable patriotic resolve of the American people. Sedition must stop. The country must protect itself against its enemies at home. The Government has made a good beginning.

September 7, 1917

BLOW AT I. W. W., 168 ARE INDICTED; SCORES ARRESTED

Seditious Conspiracy, Nearest Crime to Treason, Charged in Chicago True Bills.

LEADERS SUDDENLY SEIZED

Women Lend and Drive Autos of Federal Officers in Round-up at Headquarters.

HAYWOOD HELD IN $25,000

Bail for Others Fixed at $10,000— Two to Twenty Years' Imprisonment Possible.

Special to The New York Times.

CHICAGO, Ill., Sept. 28.—The Government today throttled the anti-war machine of the Industrial Workers of the World by a series of nation-wide raids, which ended in the arrest of practically all the leaders of the organization, including William D. ("Big Bill") Haywood, general secretary-treasurer. Raids started the minute the Federal Grand Jury sitting in Chicago returned true bills before Judge Evan Evans charging 168 members of the organization with four crimes against the Government.

The defendants are charged with seditious conspiracy, a crime ranking next to treason. The sections of the espionage law of the United States Criminal Code under which the men were indicted are as follows:

Whoever, when the United States is at war, shall cause insubordination, disloyalty, mutiny, or refusal of duty in the military or naval forces of the United States, or shall willfully obstruct the recruiting or enlistment service of the United States, to the injury of the service or of the United States, shall be punished by a fine of not more than $100,000 or imprisonment for twenty years or both.

Heavy Penalties Provided.

Section 6 of the United States Criminal Code forbids conspiracy to overthrow the Government or to take any of the property of the United States, and violations of this code are punishable by a fine of $5,000 or imprisonment for six years or both.

Section 19 prohibits intimidation of citizens and carries a fine of $5,000 and imprisonment for ten years. Any person convicted of a violation of this code, according to the language of the section, "shall thereafter be ineligible to hold any office or place of honor, profit or trust created by the Constitution or laws of this country."

Section 37 deals with general conspiracy against the Government and fixes a punishment of a fine of $10,000 or imprisonment for two years or both.

Arrests quickly followed the return. Almost before the court proceedings had reached the stage of the discharge of the jury Deputy Marshals were on their way to the local I. W. W. headquarters at 1001 West Madison Street in ten automobiles, given and driven by women, and quickly returned to the Federal Building, bringing prisoners with them. Among the first prisoners to be taken in custody was Haywood, who was questioned Sept. 5, when the headquarters of the I. W. W. in various cities were raided by the Government.

When the officers swooped down on the I. W. W. headquarters Haywood swung round in his whirling chair and smiled at Special Agent Sweep, who led the party. He was informed of the action of the Grand Jury and locked his desk preparatory to accompanying the officers. Meantime city policemen had surrounded the building and seized every employe and hanger-on. The men who invaded the meeting hall upstairs came down with more than fifty men. More than twenty employes of the I. W. W. printing office were taken from their work.

In ten minutes, before a crowd had an opportunity to collect, the raiders were on their way back to the Federal building with nearly 100 prisoners. The leaders were quickly separated from the rank and file of the organization, and United States Marshal John J. Bradley read his warrants.

The others taken in the cleanup were all held by Hinton G. Clabaugh, Divisional Chief of the Department of Justice. Several "John Does" were named in the indictments, and it is probable two or three of the men will be told later in the week they are the ones meant.

Mr. Clabaugh's aids held an all night inquisition of the men taken, hoping to get a confession from some of the lesser lights. It was understood none of the leaders would be allowed to tell his story if he hoped to obtain immunity by talking. The evidence taken in the raids was declared to have furnished all the proof required to obtain convictions.

September 29, 1917

ALL GERMANS HERE UNDER NEW WATCH

President Wilson Proclaims a Sweeping Surveillance and Plan of Registration.

WATERFRONTS WAR ZONES

Troops to Guard Piers When Necessary—Enemy Aliens Required to Leave Washington.

Special to The New York Times.

WASHINGTON, Nov. 19.—President Wilson today issued a sweeping proclamation to govern the conduct of enemy aliens in the United States and protect shipping and other property from the outrages which have greatly crippled the energies of the nation at war. The proclamation, which will be followed by regulations to be framed by the Attorney General, provides for the most drastic action yet taken against enemies within this country.

Machinery is created which will prevent, by means of military guards, the approach of enemy aliens within prescribed areas of waterfronts and within three miles of navigable streams. Enemy aliens are to be sent out of the District of Columbia and the Panama Canal Zone and denied re-entrance.

All enemy aliens must be registered and cannot travel or change their occupations without obtaining Government consent. In this way the police eye of the nation will be constantly upon these persons, who must report from time to time to Federal and municipal officers. The salient features of the proclamation which are now confirmed were outlined in a Washington dispatch in The Times last Sunday.

By its provisions every unnaturalized German in the United States will be under constant supervision. It is understood that within the next few months a proclamation will be issued to include nationals of Austria-Hungary, Turkey, and Bulgaria. Subjects of these countries are not yet considered enemy aliens, but it was said today that Congress shortly after assembling will be asked to include them in that classification. This would be an act of war.

Text of the Proclamation.

BY THE PRESIDENT OF THE UNITED STATES OF AMERICA.
A PROCLAMATION.

Whereas, The Congress of the United States, in the exercise of the constitutional authority vested in them, have resolved, by joint resolution of the Senate and House of Representatives bearing date of April 6, 1917, "that the state of war between the United States and the Imperial German Government which has been thrust upon the United States is hereby formally declared";

Whereas, it is provided by Section Four Thousand and Sixty-Seven of the Revised Statutes, as follows:

Whenever there is declared a war between the United States and any foreign nation or Government, or any invasion or predatory incursion is perpetrated, attempted, or threatened against the territory of the United States by any foreign nation or Government, and the President makes public proclamation of the event, all natives, citizens, denizens, or subjects of the hostile nation or Government, being males of the age of fourteen years and upwards, who shall be within the United States, and not actually naturalized, shall be liable to be apprehended, restrained, secured, and removed as alien enemies. The President is authorized, in any such event, by his proclamation thereof, or other public act, to direct the conduct to be observed on the part of the United States toward the aliens who become so liable; the manner and degree of the restraint to which they shall be subject, and in what cases and upon what security their residence shall be permitted, and to provide for the removal of those who, not being permitted to reside within the United States, refuse or neglect to depart therefrom; and to establish any other regulations which are found necessary in the premises and for the public safety.

Whereas, by Sections Four Thousand and Sixty-Eight, Four Thousand and Sixty-Nine, and Four Thousand and Seventy, of the Revised Statutes, further provision is made relative to alien enemies; and

Whereas, by a proclamation dated April 6th, 1917, I declared and established certain regulations prescribing the conduct of alien enemies;

Now, Therefore, I, Woodrow Wilson, President of the United States of America, pursuant to the authority vested in me, hereby declare and establish the following regulations, additional and supplemental to those declared and established by said proclamation of April 6th, 1917, which additional and supplemental regulations I find necessary in the premises and for the public safety:

13. An alien enemy shall not approach or be found within one hundred yards of any canal; nor within one hundred yards of any wharf, pier, or dock used directly or by means of lighters by any vessel or vessels of over five hundred (500) tons gross engaged in foreign or domestic trade other than fishing; nor within one hundred yards of any warehouse, shed, elevator, railroad terminal, or other terminal, storage, or transfer facility adjacent to or operated in connection with any such wharf, pier, or dock; and wherever the distance between any two of such wharves, piers, or docks, measured along the shore line connecting them, is less than eight hundred and eighty yards, an alien enemy shall not approach or be found within one hundred yards of such shore line.

14. Whenever the Attorney General of the United States deems it to be necessary, for the public saftey and the protection of transportation, to exclude alien enemies from the vicinity of any warehouse, elevator, or railroad depot, yard, or terminal which is not located within any prohibited area designated by this proclamation or the proclamation of April 6th, 1917, then an alien enemy shall not approach or be found within such distance of any such warehouse, elevator, depot, yard, or terminal as may be specified by the Attorney General by regulation duly made and declared by him; and the Attorney General is hereby authorized to fix, by regulations to be made and declared from time to time, the area surrounding any such warehouse, elevator, depot, yard, or terminal from which he deems it necessary, for the public safety and the protection of transportation, to exclude alien enemies.

15. An alien enemy shall not, except on public ferries, be found on any ocean, bay, river, or other waters within three miles of the shore line of the United States or its territorial possessions; said shore line for the purpose of this proclamation being hereby defined as the line of seacoast and the shores of all waters of the United States and its territorial possessions connected with the high seas and navigable by oceangoing vessels; nor on any of the Great Lakes, their connecting waters or harbors, within the boundaries of the United States.

16. No alien enemy shall ascend into the air in any airplane, balloon, airship, or flying machine.

17. An alien enemy shall not enter or be found within the District of Columbia.

18. An alien enemy shall not enter or be found within the Panama Canal Zone.

19. All alien enemies are hereby required to register at such times and places and in such manner as may be fixed by the Attorney General of the United States and the Attorney General is hereby authorized and directed to provide, as speedily as may be practicable, for registration of all alien enemies and for the issuance of registration cards to alien enemies and to make and declare such rules and regulations as he may deem necessary for effecting such registration; and all alien enemies and all other persons are hereby requested to comply with such rules and regulations; and the Attorney General in carrying out such registration is hereby authorized to utilize such agents, agencies, officers, and departments of the United States and of the several States, Territories, dependencies, and municipalities thereof and of the District of Columbia as he may select for the purpose, and all such agents, agencies, officers, and departments are hereby granted full authority for all acts done by them in the execution of this regulation when acting by the direction of the Attorney General. After the date fixed by the Attorney General for such registration, an alien enemy shall not be found within the limits of the United States, its Territories or possessions, without having his registration card on his person.

20. An alien enemy shall not change his place of abode or occupation or otherwise travel or move from place to place without full compliance with any such regulation as the Attorney General of the United States may, from time to time, make and declare; and the Attorney General is hereby authorized to make and declare, from time to time, such regulations concerning the movements of alien enemies as he may deem necessary in the premises and for the public safety, and to provide in such regulations for monthly, weekly, or other periodical report by alien enemies to Federal, State, or local authorities; and all alien enemies shall report at the times and places and to the authorities specified in such regulations.

This proclamation and the regulations herein contained shall extend and apply to all land and water, continental or insular, in any way within the jurisdiction of the United States.

In Witness Whereof, I have hereunto set my hand and caused the seal of the United States to be affixed.

Done in the District of Columbia, this Sixteenth day of November, in the year of Our Lord One Thousand Nine Hundred and Seventeen, and of the Independence of the United States the One Hundred and Forty-second.

WOODROW WILSON.

By the President:

Frank L. Polk,

Acting Secretary of State.

(Seal.)

Bars Dr. Muck from Washington.

Dr. Carl Muck, director of the Boston Symphony Orchestra, is an unnaturalized German, and as such cannot enter the District of Columbia unless the President should exempt him from the provisions of the proclamation. The Boston Symphony Orchestra gave its opening concert in Washington ten days ago and has a number of others scheduled here. Seats have been sold for the series.

In his opening concert Dr. Muck played the "Star-Spangled Banner," after a protest had been raised, because it had not been included in the program. Dr. Muck had said that it had not been included because it was out of place. He offered his resignation after the uproar, but Colonel Higginson, the patron of the orchestra, has not accepted it.

November 20, 1917

CENSORS OUR FOREIGN MAIL

Board Now Co-operating with British and French Inspectors.

WASHINGTON, Dec. 24.—Censorship of foreign mails, authorized by the Trading With the Enemy law, now is in full force under a board on which the Postoffice, War and Navy Departments, the War Trade Board and the Committee on Public Information are represented.

Through branch offices at New York, the Panama Canal Zone, Porto Rico and such other places as may be necessary, the board plans to carry on the work with as little interference to legitimate correspondence as is possible. The work of organization was begun on Nov. 1 and at the request of the Government the news was not published at that time. The Government now has withdrawn its request for secrecy.

The board is in close co-operation with the British and French censorship. It will combine with censorship of foreign mails the present censorship of wireless and cables.

December 25, 1917

PLAN TO CO-ORDINATE WORK AGAINST SPIES

President Expected to Bring About More Effective Way of Fighting the Enemy Within.

CENTRAL BUREAU FAVORED

Would Avoid the Present Overlapping of Activity and Clashes Over Authority.

Special to The New York Times.

WASHINGTON, Feb. 19.—Plans for the establishment of a central bureau or clearing house for the co-ordination of the activities of the Secret Service and other Government agencies engaged in espionage and intelligence work are being discussed in Administration circles.

and steps to bring about definite action along such lines may soon be taken by President Wilson.

Friends of the President have suggested that this could be accomplished most effectively under the powers incorporated in the Overman bill now before Congress. On the other hand, it is expected that some measures may be adopted shortly regardless of the fate of that measure.

In a general way the effort would be toward a more comprehensive administratio nof the various agents in all branches of the Government engaged in fighting the enemy within. A number of the Secret Service and intelligence agencies have taken up that work regardless of their stated duties, and there has been, it is alleged, an overlapping of activity which has affected the results.

The plan now under discussion would not necessarily abolish or rescind the powers of any of the existing agencies, or in any material way alter their status. By the establishment of a clearing house, it is believed, however, much more effective service could be rendered.

The Secret Service now is under the sole jurisdiction of the Treasury Department. Its work was limited by Congressional action, to the detection of counterfeiters and the protection of the President. The latter duty has been extended to take in the investigation of practically all pro-German intrigue and the German spy system.

The Department of Justice's division of investigation also is engaged in running down German spies, while the work of detecting violators of the Espionage and Trading with the Enemy acts, also has come within the Department of Justice. John Lord O'Brian has been put in charge of that section in co-operation with the Division of Investigation.

The State Department has its own secret service system, the agents of which are known to but few officials. In addition to these intelligence branches there are the Post Office Inspectors, the Army and Navy Intelligence Services, and the agents of the War Trade Board and the Department of Agriculture.

There have been clashes of authority in more than one instance, and such a situation, it was reported, led to the resignation of William J. Flynn, as Chief of the Secret Service.

February 20, 1918

ROUNDUP OF I.W.W. FOR DEPORTATION

Secretary Wilson Orders That All Aliens Urging Sabotage Be Seized.

WASHINGTON, March 2.—A vigorous policy for the suppression of anarchists and all who advocate sabotage and other forms of lawlessness was announced today by Secretary Wilson in orders to immigration officials in the Northwest to proceed immediately to arrest aliens guilty of spreading such doctrines. Even though they do not commit any overt act, they will be detained and deported.

The Secretary's action was in answer to requests from employers and civic organizations of Seattle and other cities that the department undertake the wholesale internment of Industrial Workers of the World, who were blamed

for industrial unrest, particularly in the logging camps.

Mr. Wilson held that membership in the I. W. W. organization was not in itself cause for arrest or deportation, but that alien industrial workers or any other aliens who preached overthrow of the Government by force, assassination, or who were in any other manner subject to deportation under the immigration laws should be taken into custody at once.

The department stands ready to support the round-up of anarchistic agitators by supplying funds to obtain additional quarters if the Seattle situation proves inadequate for interning them.

Orders for the suppression of radical propaganda by aliens are regarded by officials as the final step in the Government's determination to put a stop to extremists who seek to interfere with the prosecution of the war from motives sincere or otherwise. Citizens of the United States who preach anarchy will be handled by the Department of Justice, which brought about the arrest of scores of industrial workers in the nation-wide raids last year.

Secretary Wilson's order was issued with a full personal knowledge of the situation in the Northwest. As Chairman of the President's Mediation Commission, he investigated the unrest in the lumber camps and sawmills last

Fall and succeeded in quieting the situation to a marked degree.

SPOKANE, Wash., March 2.—Fifty-five thousand men in the United States are members of the Lumber Workers' Industrial Union No. 500, Industrial Workers of the World, according to Fred Hegge, District Secretary-Treasurer of the union, with headquarters here. Eighty per cent. of the membership, he said, was in the Northwest lumber camps.

Hegge admitted that members of the Industrial Workers advocated sabotage, but he gave a different definition of the destruction of property. He said sabotage to the Industrial Workers meant slowing up work if their demands were not met. In hope that the Industrial Workers would some day control all property, they did not advocate its destruction, Hegge declared.

Hegge expects the order issued today by Secretary Wilson will cause the arrest of some members of his organization. He said that all men of his office force were citizens of the United States. Many men of the Lumber Workers' Industrial Union were migratory workers, he explained, and they did not remain long enough in any one place to take out citizenship papers.

March 3, 1918

JAIL FOR DISLOYAL WORDS.

Newark Austrian Who Made Remarks Gets Ten Days.

" Just remember we still have those lampposts Gerard told the Kaiser about, and if your kind is not careful we'll be forced to make use of them." With this admonition Police Judge J. Victor D'Alvia of Newark sentenced Harry Worbrt, an Austrian, to jail for ten days for saying " To hell with the United States." Worbrt was arrested after he was made to kiss the flag and carry it through several streets in Newark.

Employes of the Heller Brothers Steel Works, Newark, where Worbrt worked, wanted to throw him in a furnace, but the Superintendent saved him and made him kiss the flag.

March 10, 1918

PRO-GERMANS MOBBED IN MIDDLE WEST

Disturbances Start in Ohio and Are Renewed in Illinois—Woman Among Victims.

LIMA, Ohio, March 25.—Five business men of Delphos, a German settlement in western Allen County near here, accused of pro-Germanism, were hunted out by a volunteer vigilance committee of 400 men and 50 women of the town, taken into a brilliantly lighted downtown street and forced to publicly salute and kiss the American Flag tonight under pain of being hanged from nearby telephone poles.

Three others, also business men, made their escape from the mob. Leaders declared tonight, according to word received here, that the demonstration will be repeated tomorrow night until all suspected pro-Germans have been punished.

Barney Lindermann, wealthy shoe merchant, was the first taken. After a flag had been nailed to the door of his store, he held the mob at bay with a revolver from his apartment over the place. Police Chief Clark Thompson induced him to come to the street at the request of the committee. He was forced to kiss the flag and salute it twice. He was told that if the flag was removed from his store he would be thrown into a nearby canal and drowned. Lindermann, reports here say, had refused to buy Liberty Bonds.

Efforts to find Carl Jettinger, publisher of The Delphos Herald, were futile, but the committee nailed a flag to his door. They charged he had not printed matter for the Liberty Loan in his paper. He is President of the Buckeye Printers' Association.

Jacob Marb, grocer, escaped after being taken from his store. Henry Schwartzengraber, retired merchant, was dragged from the lobby of a hotel and made to kiss and salute the flag. Next door, John Kohler, a wealthy German farmer, was taken from a saloon and forced to go through the public demonstration.

The vigilance committee members, according to reports here tonight, has a list of a score of prominent men in the Delphos neighborhood who are charged with pro-Germanism. Federal agents have been furnished a copy, it is said.

BENTON, Ill., March 25.—Five hundred members of the "Loyalty League" of West Frankfort, near here, late today seized Mrs. Frances Bergen, a woman of Bohemian birth, from municipal officers, rode her on a rail through the main street of the town and compelled her to wave an American flag throughout the demonstration. At frequent intervals the procession paused, while Mrs. Bergen was compelled to shout praise for President Wilson.

The trouble followed a quarrel between the woman and Henry Baker, who charged her with disloyal utterances. Both were arrested and found guilty of assault. Baker's fine was paid by public subscription. Mrs. Bergen was still in custody when taken away from officers by members of the "Loyalty League." Later she was arraigned before a United States Commissioner, who ordered her held for the Grand Jury.

Half a dozen other demonstrations against alleged disloyal persons have occurred recently in the southeastern section of Illinois, near where West Frankfort is situated.

March 26, 1918

GERMAN IS LYNCHED BY AN ILLINOIS MOB

Had Made Speeches to Miners on Socialism and Uttered Disloyal Sentiments.

POLICE TRIED TO SAVE HIM

Mob tSormed City Hall to Get Him and Then Hanged Him After Wrapping Him In an American Flag.

Special to The New York Times
ST. LOUIS, Mo., April 4.—Robert P. Prager, a German born Socialist, was dragged from the basement of the Collinsville, Ill., City Hall, twelve miles from St. Louis, tonight by leaders of a mob of from three to four hundred men, marched barefooted to a point one-half mile outside of the Collinsville limits and lynched. He was accused of having made disloyal remarks to Maryville, Ill. miners.

His capture by the mob and lynching came after he had been hidden by the Collinsville police among a lot of tiling in the basement of the City Hall while Mayor Siegel made a speech to the mob from the steps of the City Hall, pleading with his hearers to give the prisoner the right of trial. The police previously had rushed the mob and captured Prager while he was being marched through the main street of the city with an American flag tied about him.

Twice before the mob wreaked its vengeance on the man it appeared that he would have escaped from it—once when he fled from Maryville to Collinsville, a distance of four miles, and again when the police, after hiding their prisoner, told the mob he had been spirited out of the city. But the mob leaders each time took up the search for their victim, and stayed with it until they found him.

The lynching took place on the old National Road, leading toward St. Louis. While police were rushing toward the scene in an automobile from East St. Louis, Prager, who was a baker and miner, 32 years old, was strung up to a tree. The lynching took place about 12:30 o'clock Friday morning. The body was found a few minutes later and the Coroner of Edwardsville, Madison County, notified.

The trouble started at Maryville. Prager was employed there in the Bruno Bakery. Recently he made application to join the Miners' Union, and sought work in the coal mines.

He said he had worked as a miner in Germany.

While his application for membership in the union was pending Prager is said to have harrangued some of the miners on socialism. In the course of his remarks he made statements they interpreted as disloyal and pro-German. When a recent wave of patriotism swept over many Illinois towns the miners and others at Maryville organized a committee to deal with Prager.

The committee was to have taken him in custody yesterday afternoon. Prager heard of it, and fled to Maryville.

The committee followed and searched for him. He was found in a house here in which he formerly resided, and dragged into the street. His shoes were stripped off, and members of the mob began pulling off his clothes when some one produced an American flag. It was wrapped about him and tied.

With the prisoner bareheaded and stumbling every few steps a parade was started up the main street of the city. It had proceeded several blocks when a policeman led a squad of other officers in a dash into the crowd. They captured the prisoner. He was hurried to the police station, members of the mob following. Later he was retaken by the mob.

April 5, 1918

ILLINOIS GETS AID IN CURBING SEDITION

Federal Agents to be Sent to State in Response to Governor Lowden's Appeal.

WASHINGTON, April 9.—Federal cooperation in suppressing disloyalty and disorder in Illinois was promised today by Attorney General Gregory in response to a request from Governor Lowden. Special agents of the Department of Justice will be assigned to advise with State officials and aid in the conduct of investigations.

In announcing the Attorney General's decision, department officials let it be known that he was prepared to lend similar assistance to other States desiring it. Without new legislation, officials say, they are almost powerless to deal with disloyal utterances, the suppression of which they think is essential to the prevention of disorders, but the Federal agents are expected to accomplish something in cooperation with State authorities.

Lieutenant Governor John G. Oglesby of Illinois had long conferences today with Mr. Gregory and John Lord O'Brian, special assistant to the Attorney General for war work. He told them Federal aid was imperative to check increasing instances of mob violence against disloyalists, particularly in the mining districts of Southern Illinois.

While the recent lynching of a German at Collinsville, Ill., probably hastened the decision of the Illinois officials to seek Federal support, it is understood that any part the Department of Justice agents may play in investigating this particular case will be only incidental to a general plan of cooperation.

The Attorney General's representatives will report to Governor Lowden at Springfield for preliminary conferences before undertaking their work. There a general program probably will be mapped out.

April 10, 1918

27

SEDITION BILL PASSED BY SENATE

No Record Vote Taken, Measure Having Been Perfected in Protracted Debate.

NOW GOES TO CONFERENCE

Early Agreement by the Two Houses Expected — Heavy Penalties Provided for Disloyalty.

WASHINGTON, April 10.—The Sedition bill, prohibiting, under penalties of twenty years' imprisonment and $10,000 fine, language or acts of disloyalty, or obstruction of the army draft and Liberty Loans, was passed today by the Senate without a record vote. The bill now goes to conference between House and Senate, and final enactment is expected soon.

Protracted and bitter debate marked consideration of the measure, the passage of which had been strongly urged by Administration officials, to permit the Government to deal with disloyal agitators and check the growing danger of mob violence.

Although modified to meet the objections of Senators who contended that the original draft would curb legitimate freedom of speech, the bill retains the broad inhibition of words or acts which "support or favor the cause of the German Empire or its allies * * * or oppose the cause of the United States." It also would punish willful and "disloyal, profane, scurrilous, contemptuous, or abusive" language about the American form of government, Constitution, military or naval forces, flag or uniform," and willful utterances designed to curtail production of essential war materials.

The Senate adopted an amendment by Senator Jones of New Mexico providing for dismissal of Federal executive employes making disloyal statements. This was a substitute for one introduced by Senator Penrose of Pennsylvania several days ago after attacks had been made on George Creel, Chairman of the Committee on Public Information, and other officials on account of their writings in the past.

Senator Overman of North Carolina accused the Pennsylvania Senator of ":having some official in mind" in introducing his amendment. Senator Penrose replied that he "had several men in mind." Senator Nelson of Minnesota said he understood the proposed amendment was to apply to cases like that of George Creel.

Senator Lodge, after he and other Senators had denounced alleged disloyal publications in the German-American press, withdrew his amendment prohibiting German language publication unless paralleled by English translation. Senator Nelson opposed the amendment, declaring it an "insult" to loyal Americans of German blood. Senator Borah of Idaho did not press an amendment he had offered to repeal the Postmaster General's press censorship authority conferred in the original Espionage act.

With an intimation that it might be stricken out in conference, an amendment by Senator France of Maryland providing that the bill shall not impair liberty to speak "what is true, with good motives, and for justifiable ends," was adopted.

April 11, 1918

President Signs Sedition Bill.
WASHINGTON, May 21.—President Wilson today signed the Sedition bill, giving the Government wide powers to punish disloyal acts and utterances.

May 22, 1918

TARRED AND FEATHERED BY KNIGHTS OF LIBERTY

New Organization in California to Stamp Out Disloyalty Finds Three Victims.

SAN JOSE, Cal., May 2.—H. Steinmoltz, an Oakland tailor, was hanged here early today until he became unconscious; then he was tied to a tree, and later was taken away in an automobile by an organization known as the Knights of Liberty.

George Koelzer, who was tarred and feathered last night by members of the organization, was held in jail today for his own protection. Over the telephone today one of the "Knights" said:

"This organization has eighty-two members in San José and vicinity, with branches in San Francisco, Oakland, Stockton, Santa Rosa, Palo Alto, and other places. We are going to stamp out disloyalty. We give a fair and impartial trial, and, if the evidence warrants, we turn the man over to the military or civil authorities."

Koelzer, a brewery worker, who was accused of pro-German activities, told the police that "Knights of Liberty," wearing black coats over their heads, took him from his room, carried him in an automobile five miles into the country last night, where they applied a coat of tar and feathers, and then brought him back to the city and chained him to a brass cannon in a city park, where he was found by the police.

RICHMOND, Cal., May 2.—Guido Poenisch was taken from his home here last night by fifty white-robed persons, rushed to the municipal wharf, where he was "tried" for disloyalty, and then tarred and feathered. He was "found" not to have bought a Liberty bond and to have made disloyal remarks. Poenisch promised he would buy $100 worth of Liberty bonds and would join the Red Cross before his captors released him. He came here about ten years ago from Germany.

May 3, 1918

ASKS AID IN SEDITION HUNT.

Gregory Wants Every Citizen to be a Volunteer Detective.

WASHINGTON, May 12.—Every citizen may act as a volunteer detective to assist Government officers in ferreting out persons suspected of disloyal actions or utterances, says a statement issued today by Attorney General Gregory. United States attorneys have been told to cooperate with newspapers in their districts so that public notice can be given of the nearest offices of attorneys or the bureau of investigation to which citizens may refer information that they think will be valuable in running down suspicious persons.

"The District Attorneys are instructed to make it clear," says the Attorney General's statement, "that complaints of even the most informal or confidential nature are always welcome, and that citizens should feel free to bring their information or suspicions to the attention of the nearest representative of the Department of Justice; or if that is not convenient, communicate with the department in Washington."

Hundreds of letters are already being received daily by the department here from persons who believe they have discovered evidence of disloyalty. Although only a small part of the information proves to be of value, the department considers the system of sufficient worth to warrant its extension.

May 13, 1918

FIGHTING SEDITION WITHOUT HYSTERIA

Special to The New York Times.
WASHINGTON, May 30.—Attorney General Gregory today made public a letter addressed to Judge S. H. Howard of the Superior Court of Georgia, setting forth the attitude of himself and of the Department of Justice toward disloyal acts and violation of the various war statutes enacted by Congress.

In brief the Attorney General's attitude is that every case of disloyalty or violation will be vigorously prosecuted, but persons, whether aliens or citizens, who are law-abiding and loyal should not be subject to unjust suspicion and discrimination by private citizens or others. In his letter to the Georgia Judge the Attorney General urges the co-operation of citizens everywhere in the work of the Department of Justice.

Mr. Gregory's letter follows:

Honorable S. H. Howard, Superior Court Chambers, Columbus, Ga.:

Sir: I have the honor to acknowledge the receipt of your letter under date of the 15th of this month, wherein you say in substance that you have some apprehension that there is danger that through the well-intentioned activities of State or municipal officers or of bodies of citizens in endeavoring to bring about the surveillance or the prosecution of persons suspected of acts of disloyalty, many loyal citizens will suffer loss of business and may suffer otherwise by reason of the fact that it may be reported that they are under suspicion by the Government.

The Department of Justice is actively engaged in the prevention and detection of disloyal acts and the prosecution of violations of the various war statutes. It welcomes any information giving definite facts of specific instances of such offenses, and appreciates deeply the interest of the citizens of the country and the aid which they render to the department.

Much of the information and many of the suspicions that are communicated to the department do not, of course, upon an investigation by the department, disclose facts justifying any action. Nevertheless, all such information is investigated and, wherever the facts warrant it, the proper action promptly follows. On the other hand, the department deprecates unjust and unfounded criticism or suspicion of citizens or aliens who are law-abiding and loyal, and certainly it should not come about that by unwarranted suspicion such persons should be caused loss of business, loss of employment or other loss.

The Federal statutes punishing seditious acts, malicious destruction of property and other war crimes and the alien enemy laws and regulations are being and will be rigidly and aggressively enforced and the penalties prescribed for their violation imposed without exception, but no possible good will come from any unnecessary hardships or discrimination inflicted by private citizens upon those alien enemies who remain law-abiding and loyal or from any such hardship or discriminations unjustly inflicted upon loyal citizens of the United States. All persons who remain law-abiding and loyal contribute to the resources of the country and, therefore, to the strength of the country during the war.

Perhaps all this is best typified by the language of the President's proclamations of war with Germany and of war with Austria-Hungary, wherein the President expressly stated as to the conduct of citizens toward alien enemies and the conduct of alien enemies themselves that so long as alien enemies " shall conduct themselves in accordance with the law, they shall be undisturbed in the peaceful pursuit of their lives and occupations and be accorded the consideration due to all peaceful and law-abiding persons, except so far as restrictions may be necessary for their own protection and for the safety of the United States; and toward such alien enemies as conduct themselves in accordance with law, all citizens of the United States are enjoined to preserve the peace and to treat them with all such friendliness as may be compatible with loyalty and allegiance to the United States."

I trust that the foregoing clearly sets before you my attitude and that of the Department of Justice in relation to the subject matter of your letter. To sum it up, it is, briefly, that any case of disloyalty or of violation of the war statutes or of the President's proclamations and regulations by aliens or citizens will be vigorously prosecuted, but persons, whether aliens or citizens, who are law-abiding and loyal, should not be subject to unjust suspicion and discrimination by private citizens and others. Respectfully,

T. W. GREGORY,
May 23, 1918.   Attorney General.

May 31, 1918

LETTERS SEIZED BY MILLIONS IN RAIDS

Alleged Seditious Matter Taken After Over 300 Search Warrants Are Issued Secretly.

ANTI-WAR BODIES ON LIST

Socialist and I. W. W. Officials Named in Chicago Inquiry—Mail Sent Out Here Held Up.

CHICAGO, Aug. 29.—Upward of 2,000,000 letters and other mailed documents of alleged seditious import have been seized recently. As a result more than 300 search warrants were issued secretly to Post Office inspectors, co-operating with United States District Attorney Charles F. Clyne, it became known today.

According to reports, practically every pro-German and anti-war organization has been made a target and the use of the mails denied them.

Among those named in the search warrants are:

The Socialist Party and affiliated organizations, their officials and publications.

The I. W. W., its defense fund organizations, propagandists and officials.

Among the out-of-town individuals and organizations mentioned in the warrants are:

State Socialist Party, Huntington, W. Va.

Room 831, 70 Fifth Avenue, New York City.

Room 831, in the building 70 Fifth Avenue, which is named in the Chicago dispatch, is the office of the New York Bureau of Legal Advice, of which Miss Fanny Witherspoon, who was recently named as the Socialist candidate for Congress in the Fifteenth District of this city, is said to be the head.

During the selection of the first draft army Miss Witherspoon addressed several communications to Governor Whitman in which she protested against the way the draft was being conducted by the then Draft Director, Roscoe W. Conkling, who is now a Colonel and a member of General Crowder's staff in Washington. The protests were not seriously considered by the Governor.

At 70 Fifth Avenue it was said last night that Miss Witherspoon had not been in her office for nearly a month. It was said she was on a vacation.

That the Government has been quietly at work for several months in an effort to put an end to the circulation of anti-war and pro-German propaganda was also indicated yesterday, when it was announced that L. Hollingsworth Wood, the Rev. John Haynes Holmes, Helen Phelps Stokes, James P. Warbasse, and other persons associated together under the name of the National Civil Liberties Bureau had brought an equity suit in the Federal District Court against Postmaster Thomas G. Patten, for the purpose of compelling the Postmaster to circulate through the mails certain pamphlets and documents which have been excluded by the Post Office authorities.

The office of the National Civil Liberties Bureau is also at 70 Fifth Avenue, in Room 710, almost directly underneath the office of the New York Bureau of Legal Advice. The complainants in the case assert that the pamphlets which are withheld from circulation by Postmaster Patten, who is acting under instruction from the Postmaster General, are properly mailable under the postal laws, and the Federal Courts are asked to direct the Postmaster to forward them to the persons to whom they are addressed. They also ask that the Postmaster and his assistants be enjoined from hereafter holding up papers mailed by the Civil Liberties Bureau and upon which postage has been paid.

The pamphlets which have been held up are entitled "Liberty in War Time," "The Knights of Liberty Mob," "The Facts About Conscientious Objectors in the United States," "The Case of the Christian Pacifists of Los Angeles," several dealing with the troubles of the I. W. W., and a dozen or more others.

Chief Charles F. De Woody of the Bureau of Investigation of the Department of Justice would not discuss these cases yesterday. Whether certain raids which are said to have been made in New York were conducted by the Department of Justice or agents of the Post Office Inspection Service, was not disclosed.

At the offices of the People's Council for Peace and Democracy at 138 West Thirteenth Street, Louis P. Lochner, who was in charge last night, said he knew nothing about the reported raids. The People's Council moved out of 70 Fifth Avenue several months ago.

August 30, 1918

GERMAN BECOMING DEAD TONGUE HERE

Schools All Over America Banishing Study of the Tongue from Courses —A Survey of Their Attitude

By JOHN WALKER HARRINGTON.

EMPTY benches confront teachers of the German language all over the United States. Instruction in the Teutonic tongue has fallen off in American schools by at least 50 per cent. and possibly 65, and by next September it will be near the vanishing point in the elementary classes.

Action hostile to teaching the speech of the enemy has been taken either by State or local authorities in thirty-six out of the forty-eight American Commonwealths. In Delaware, Florida, Idaho, New Mexico, and Wyoming this amounts to prohibition direct from the officials at the capitals. Iowa and North Dakota, through their State Boards of Education, recommend the dropping of German from all schools, while Oklahoma bans it from elementary classes and gives the local educators their choice regarding advanced grades.

In many of the large centres of population the municipal Boards of Education have either banished German or so cut down schedules that it seems only a question of a year or so before its influence will have disappeared. In twenty States of the Union communities have been vigorously exercising their option and have been steadily eliminating the language.

Before proceeding with the details of this survey it should be said that the facts were gathered from many sources. They come from investigations made by the National Education Association's Commission on the Present Emergency in Education, from a canvass made by the National Security League of this city, from the American Universities Association, and from independent inquiries made in other directions. The close of the school year last month was marked by much feeling against the continuance of German language teaching, and there was an additional reflex of that sentiment in the annual meeting of the National Education Association held a few

29

days ago in Pittsburgh. On that occasion many attacks were made on the cultural value of Teuton language and ideals, and a resolution was adopted urging that in future the pupils of American schools be taught only in English.

Much information as to the attitude of our educational authorities throughout the United States was gained from their correspondence with the New York City Board of Education, which was among the first to proceed against German instruction. Acting on the recommendation of Dr. William L. Ettinger, City Superintendent of Schools, it ordered that no classes in German should begin next September in the high schools. Pupils in those schools who are trying to make certain credits for entering college may continue their German study. Under these conditions the language will have disappeared from the high schools in two years. It will not be taught in the elementary grades.

"There is every reason to believe," says the argument presented by the Board of Superintendents, "that the high school pupils will themselves abolish the teaching of German by refusing to elect it. This is shown by the fact there are at present in twenty-four high schools only 12,954 pupils studying German, whereas 23,898 were in German classes in February, 1917. There are only 1,097 at present enrolled in first term German classes, when in February, 1917, there were 5,859 in these same classes.

"Nevertheless, a hands-off policy is not meeting this issue squarely. New York should lead the way in the abolishing of the teaching of German as a means, though a slight means, of winning the war by making a dent in Pan Germanism, by shaking possibly the morale of the German people, as they come to realize that the great city of New York is unwilling to endure any longer their language, and desires to break off more completely the possibility of intimate relations with them through that medium."

The falling off in the study of German in the high schools of the metropolis, which was 50 per cent. before the action of the board, has been taken up by the Spanish classes. A few days ago a conference of New York public school teachers of Spanish was held, at which there were 140 present.

In the State of New York an order has been issued by the Department of Education that all schools must teach in English, and an investigation is being made of all foreign language schools. In Syracuse the classes in German were one-third of their usual size at the close of the academic year.

New Jersey through its State Board of Education began last April to stimulate the introduction of Spanish as a substitute for German in her schools whenever possible. Calvin N. Kendall, the State Superintendent of Public Instruction, on June 1 of this year sent a letter to all local boards of education throughout the Commonwealth recommending that they exclude textbooks, magazines, or newspaper publications from the schools which would tend, directly or indirectly, to establish German propaganda.

The cutting of German out of the schools of such a large industrial city as Newark had a marked effect. East Orange claims the distinction of being the first city in the United States whose school board passed a resolution, as it did in May, 1917, eliding German from the course of study in her schools. Paterson forbade the singing of any German songs in her schoolhouses; Glassborough got rid of German in her high school and two days later substituted French. Vineland dispensed with German in all classes.

The State Board of Education of Connecticut adopted a resolution that all books used in its schools, except in the high schools, should be in the English language. It is also provided that the use of any book, leaflet, periodical, or newspaper printed in any foreign language be prohibited in any class on and after July 18, 1918, except by authorization of an agent of the board.

Massachusetts adopted a law providing that every public high school of not less than 150 pupils, offering a business course, should give instruction in commercial Spanish. Boston is reluctant to exile German from its classic portals. Beginning with next Autumn, Worcester will reduce the schools where German is taught from five to two in the preparatory division of the grammar department. In smaller cities German is being dropped because the students are no longer electing it.

New Hampshire a few weeks ago passed a law that no textbooks should be used in her schools which favored any political party or sect. The statute was a thinly disguised attack on the German propaganda. Vermont is making an investigation of German influences on her pupils, Maine has never had much of a Teutonic tide, and there are only twenty-nine of her schools which teach German. In Rhode Island no definite action has yet been taken regarding the instruction in the language, although a committee was appointed to examine the courses used in the schools of Providence for evidences of German propaganda.

Even in the Keystone State, famed as the home of the "Pennsylvania Dutch," the trend against the learning of German is marked. The State Superintendent of Public Instruction has only gone so far as to direct the elimination of unpatriotic literature, but German is being dropped in many schools by the direction of the local boards. The Common Council of Philadelphia demanded that the language be barred from the public schools. In Pittsburgh the German texts were not only taken from the students, but tons of the volumes were burned as though they were under the ban of heresy. Harrisburg, which is in the centre of a population largely German by descent, drove the study of the language from many public schools, and in its high schools discontinued the German electives, although students already registered were permitted to continue. Johnstown dispensed with German last May, as did also Lebanon. Erie took it from all grammar grades and voted to keep it out of high schools next Fall.

The speech of Kultur has fallen out of educational favor along the Atlantic seaboard. The State Board of Education of Delaware forbade instruction in German in all the schools under its control after the academic year just closed. Although Maryland has not acted, the authorities of Baltimore directed that no German should be taught in the elementary schools of the City of Monuments.

Education in the District of Columbia is supervised by Congress and there are movements on foot destined to remove German from all the schedules in the national capital. In the five white high schools of Washington the attendance in the German classes last year decreased 50 per cent., as compared with the same terms in 1917. In the Central High School there were eleven classes in German in the term recently closed and thirty-five in the same period last year.

Opposition to the teaching of German rears an almost solid front in the South. "German will be discontinued and French taught instead in the ensuing year in the schools," writes Frank Evans, Superintendent of the schools of Spartanburg, S. C.

"I doubt whether German is being taught anywhere in Mississippi," reports W. F. Bond, the Superintendent of Public Instruction in that Commonwealth. "Practically all the schools of the State make it elective, but both pupils and parents have eliminated it by declining to elect it."

As so very few pupils wished German, the New Orleans Parish School Board voted to discontinue German instruction with the close of the academic year.

Florida discarded all German books from the State-adopted texts. Texas has taken no action. There is a strong sentiment against German instruction in Georgia, and such cities as Athens have dropped it from their high schools.

The State Superintendent of Alabama is ridding the classrooms of that region German propaganda, and it is the intention of the State Board, he writes, to submit a bill to the Legislature providing for the teaching of patriotism in the public schools.

In Tennessee, German was excluded from the entire county school system. Chattanooga will not have it in her public schools next year, but will emphasize French and Spanish. Virginia has as yet taken no action, but in West Virginia there is a strong anti-Teutonic movement. In Wheeling the lessons in German have been banished from the elementary classes and in some of the advanced grades.

"Many of our high schools," to quote the State Superintendent of Public Instruction in Kentucky, "have cut out German entirely, and others have censored their textbooks.

German immigration, especially in the period from 1848 until just before the civil war, swept into the Middle States and those of the Northwest, and so across to the prairies toward the Southwest. Some of the settlers became sturdy American citizens, others kept alive the traditions of Germany, founded clubs, societies, and schools for the perpetuation of speech and song. Here were communities as Teutonic as Berlin. The German became a factor in politics, and in return for the German vote so called, he was able to obtain special schools for his language. In many of the Central and Western Commonwealths laws were passed providing that on the petition of a certain number of inhabitants of a district schools might be started which would give instruction in a foreign language. There were a few Polish and Scandinavian schools, but usually this provision in the laws resulted in the establishment of German centres. Where the instruction was not given outright in German, the Teutons insisted that there should be classes for imparting their language. Many teachers of the language of their Fatherland established themselves in the public school systems of the central part of the United States and formed powerful associations which were always ready to battle and to lobby for the perpetuation of their calling. Efforts were made a quarter of a century ago to break the German grip in these regions, but as long as there were parts of these Western cities under Pan Germanic spells the task was difficult.

One of the surprises of the year was the abolishing of German in the schools of Cincinnati, for in that Ohio city the Germans were so numerous that when one spoke of going "over the Rhine," as the canal was called, he meant that he was disappearing into a realm where all English was left behind. At one time pupils had to go to the City Hall to make excuses for not studying German.

Cleveland, where year after year the German party had foisted their language on the schools, not only put the German textbooks out of the schools, but provided cans in the principal streets, where pupils and the public might throw all the volumes they wished to have destroyed. At Columbus German was dropped from the entire system, including the elementary, intermediate, and high school grades.

"German," writes Horace Ellis, State Superintendent of Public Instruction of Indiana, "is being practically excluded from the schools next year."

Indianapolis has eliminated the study of the language from all her elementary classes.

Illinois permits probably wider latitude to the local school boards than any State in the Union, and for this reason it is difficult to learn the attitude of her educators. In Chicago there has been much discussion and many conferences. The high schools at Peoria have discontinued German, and at Dundee the board voted the language out of the schools and disposed of all the textbooks.

Michigan's Superintendent of Public Instruction says that many of the high schools will discontinue all German instruction next year.

"Our students of German have been reduced 64 per cent.," writes W. W. Warner, at the head of the public schools of Saginaw. Houghton, Marine City, Ypsilanti, and Adrian are among the Michigan cities which are barring the language.

Milwaukee, famed for its Germans, has risen against the language to such an extent that in the high schools those electing to study German were fifty less than they were a year ago, and many have chosen French and Spanish from the modern language lists. Wisconsin leaves much of her education to local option, but strong adjurations to patriotism and unity of spirit have been issued by the State board.

"In Nebraska," said Richard L. Metcalfe of the State Council for Defense, "there are eighteen districts where the public school has been driven out by German schools. In those German schools nothing but the German language is spoken or taught. Out of 879 teachers investigated 350 were Germans. In three counties where those German schools predominated the German national hymn was generally sung. In 100 of these schools the American national anthem, up to thirty days ago, had never been sung."

Disclosures such as those made by Mr. Metcalfe led to the movement for the repeal of the Mulkey law, passed by the Nebraska Legislature a few years ago at the request of the German-American Alliance, which required a district to provide instruction in a foreign language when twelve citizens petitioned for it.

The Deputy State Superintendent writes that the teaching of German has been generally discontinued in the Nebraska high schools.

On the recommendation of the State Department of Public Instruction all public schools in Iowa decided last April to discontinue the training in German. This includes the high schools as well. German was dropped also from nearly every high school in the State of Arkansas. The State Superintendent of Public Instruction in North Dakota, a Commonwealth in which there are many citizens of Teutonic descent, recommended that umlaut drills be omitted for those in the elementary and high schools as rapidly as possible after July 1, 1918. The sister State of South Dakota has as yet taken no definite action.

Despite the fact that Missouri has a strong Teuton element, the State Superintendent of Schools declares that only one high school in the State, outside of the cities, is maintaining a German course. The urban high schools are confining their instruction of this kind to such students as are preparing for technical work. The common schools of St. Louis abolished German.

R. H. Wilson, State Superintendent of Public Instruction of Oklahoma, says in an official circular to local boards: "So far as I have been able to learn there will not be a high school in the State teaching German when school opens next September. The language has been removed from the elementary classes, and next Fall the State Board of Education will require every teacher who draws public money to subscribe to an oath to uphold the Constitution of the United States and that of the Commonwealth of Oklahoma."

Idaho has prohibited German entirely in her schools up to the ninth grade, and the advisability of such instruction in the high schools was left to the communities. Only a few of these schools of the higher grade include it in their courses. The local authorities in Wyoming dropped the German classes, while the City of Laramie burned all its German textbooks. The State Superintendent of Nevada writes that the teaching of German has been largely discontinued in his jurisdiction. The University of Colorado abolished its German courses after adopting scathing resolutions on the subject. The schools of that State are following its lead. Montana and Utah, at this writing, are making an investigation of their school books in quest of Prussian propaganda.

All courses in German were discarded from the high schools of California by a resolution of the State Board of Education. Los Angeles abandoned German the first of January, with the exception of instruction to a few advanced pupils who had already studied it and needed it for credits. No German will be taught in her elementary schools, high schools, and junior colleges hereafter. By order of the State Board of Education the study of the German language was discontinued in New Mexico. Arizona has not yet reached a decision. In Spokane schools have dropped it.

How greatly the demand for German language teachers is declining is shown in the falling off in the registration of normal courses for them at the Summer school of Teachers College, Columbia University, which opened last Monday. The program provided for demonstration classes in the pedagogy of German both in primary and secondary schools. There were four of these, in charge of educators of high ability and ordinarily there would have been from fifty to sixty students in each division. As there were no applicants, the courses will not be given. For the special class on German phonetics, which is of high value to instructors in English and language students in general, there were only four applications, and it was decided not to organize it.

In higher educational circles strong pressure is being brought upon the colleges and universities to withdraw credits for German for entrance to the freshman classes. The College of the City of New York has already abolished the study of German in the high school and junior high school departments, and has so lessened the credits for German in the collegiate courses as to discourage the study of the language. Members of the Faculties of Yale and Harvard Universities recommended to the National Educational Association the substitution of Spanish and French for German as entrance subjects as well as for college studies.

Many leading college educators, however, are disposed to uphold the study of German for advanced students, as they think it will be of value to them in scientific and technical work. Some of them believe, as does Dr. Nicholas Murray Butler, President of Columbia, that access would be cut off to the idealism of Goethe and Schiller if this Teuton tongue were removed from the curricula of our higher institutions of learning. This is the view, in a measure, which is taken by Philander P. Claxton, the United States Commissioner of Education.

Dr. L. D. Coffman, Dean of Education of the University of Minnesota, in his recent address on "Competent Teachers for American Children," delivered before the association, quoted from the official quarterly of the League for Germanism in Foreign Lands the following significant passage:

"Work rendered in the interest of the German school is a noble service rendered to the German nation; for the most effective means for perpetuating Germanism in foreign countries is the school. Within its sacred walls the strange land is transformed for children and teachers and parents into a fatherland."

"Not until recently," to quote Dr. Coffman further, "were we aware that there were many un-American schools and many un-American teachers. Our ignorance of the situation was appalling and our stupidity colossal. Not until we entered the world conflict did we pause, take stock, and discover the sinister influence of German Kultur in the schools of the country. Now we find that there has been an organized program for the Germanizing of America."

July 14, 1918

WHAT HAS BEEN PROVED AT I. W. W. TRIAL

So prolonged has been the I. W. W. trial in Chicago, and so intricate the procedure, that the news of each day has formed only a disjointed story of the case.

This article, in which is presented a concise statement of what the trial has brought to light, was written by an observer, acting under official auspices, having access to all the records and sources of information.

THE Industrial Workers of the World have been a storm centre in various communities for a dozen years past. State and local authorities have warred against them in vain. Charged with crime and disturbance, they have continued their activities in the field of industry, leaving behind a trail of bitterness and dissension.

After the declaration of war the Government began an investigation of the activities of this organization. On Sept. 5, 1917, the Department of Justice made a nation-wide raid on all I. W. W. headquarters. This was followed, on Sept. 28, by an indictment by the Federal Grand Jury, charging 166 officers and members of the organization with conspiracy to interfere with certain activities essential to the successful prosecution of the war.

The trial began in Chicago on April 1, before Judge Kenesaw Mountain Landis, one of the most able judicial officers on the Federal bench. The selection of a jury occupied a month's time.

The Government is represented by a Special Assistant United States Attorney General, Frank K. Nebeker of Salt Lake, assisted by Claude R. Porter of Iowa. The defendants' case is in charge of George Vanderveer of Seattle and William Cleary of Bisbee, Ariz.

Of those named in the indictment, 101 are on trial, some were never apprehended, and the case against others was dismissed. With one or two exceptions, all of these men are prominent officers of the I. W. W. More than half of them are foreign born, and the majority of these unnaturalized.

As the trial has proceeded there have been revealed clearly for the first time many of the reasons why all previous efforts to cope with the I. W. W. were unsuccessful. The inside history of the organization has been presented in letters and documents which passed between the officers and members. The attitude of the officers toward the Government, local authorities, and the courts, the methods used in inciting labor disorders, the attitude toward syndicalism, sabotage, "direct action," and others matters leading to the very heart of the long series of disturbances are made clear. It is a story that has grown in interest as the trial progressed, for it has a vital bearing upon what the majority of us have learned to call our "American institutions."

No understanding of the I. W. W. is possible without a knowledge of their "Preamble" or statement of the fundamental ideas which are the basis for all the activities of the organization. In view of the recent references to the "American Bolsheviki," it is worthy of note that this "Preamble" is said by officers of the I. W. W. to have been translated without alteration and adopted by the present Soviet Government of Russia. This document, one of the first placed in evidence by the Government, reads:

> The working class and the employing class have nothing in common. There can be no peace so long as hunger and want are found among the millions of working people, and the few, who make up the employing class, have all the good things of life.
>
> Between these two classes a struggle must go on until the workers of the world organize as a class, take possession of the earth and the machinery of production, and abolish the wage system.
>
> We find that the centring of management of industries into fewer and fewer hands makes the trade unions unable to cope with the ever-growing power of the employing class. The trade unions foster a state of affairs which allows one set of workers to be pitted against another set of workers in the same industry, thereby helping defeat one another in wage wars. Moreover, the trade unions aid the employing class to mislead the workers into the belief that the workers have interests in common with their employers.
>
> These conditions can be changed and the interest of the working class upheld only by an organization formed in such a way that all its members in any one industry, or in all industries, if necessary, cease work whenever a strike or lockout is on in any department thereof, thus making an injury to one an injury to all.
>
> Instead of the conservative motto, "A fair day's wage for a fair day's work," we must inscribe on our banner the revolutionary watchword, "Abolition of the wage system."
>
> It is the historic mission of the working class to do away with capitalism. The army of production must be organized not only for the everyday struggle with capitalists, but to carry on production when capitalism shall have been overthrown. By organizing industrially we are forming the structure of the new society within the shell of the old.

Here is the primary cause of all the antagonism and the resulting social disturbances with which the members of this revolutionary society of the I. W. W. have been charged. In accepting its tenets the members are committed to a course which inevitably leads to bitter opposition to the established order of things. Accepted standards of ethics are discarded, because they are held to be the outgrowth of, and devised for, the protection of a so-called "capitalistic society." Freed from the standards which bind the majority of mankind, it is not surprising that the members of the organization are continually running foul of the law and public opinion, no matter in what quarter they operate.

In his opening argument for the Government Mr. Nebeker said:

"The I. W. W. is unqualifiedly committed to the doctrine of 'direct action,' as distinguished from political action, and on this revolutionary principle as its fundamental premise the present organization has been built up.

"The expression 'direct action' has a well-defined meaning. Based on the theory that the modern State, however progressive, will do nothing in the interest of the proletariat, it urges that all wage workers unite in one organization to accomplish directly what cannot be obtained indirectly by means of parliamentary representative government. The employment of direct action, therefore, not only presupposes the nonuse of political methods of every kind, but it calls for unyielding opposition to all political institutions and laws whenever and wherever such opposition can be made effective. Members of the organization, therefore, are not supposed to participate in primaries, conventions, or elections. They are taught to believe that all laws are made in the interest of employers and capitalists; that legislative, executive, and judicial branches of the Government are capitalistic institutions and should be destroyed."

The I. W. W. literature on sabotage is extensive. Numerous books on the subject have been written by members of the organization, and translations have been made of foreign pamphlets. These publications have been circulated by the tens of thousands in all parts of the country. During the present trial all of these books have been placed in evidence by the Government. They contain suggestions of destructive methods to be used by employers in every branch of industry.

A letter from William D. Haywood, the chief executive officer, written to a member of the I. W. W., says:

"I do not understand how you are going to ignore the term sabotage in your educational campaign if you use the I. W. W. literature. Every leaflet, every pamphlet, and the song book are full of references to the great weapon."

Unquestionably the teaching was as extensive as this letter suggests. These would-be rulers of the industrial world overlooked no class of employes. Regarding all employers, no matter how humble, as enemies against whom continuous warfare was to be carried on, they did not forget the housemaid. The following suggestions for sabotage in the home are from one of their pamphlets:

> No longer does the family eat in peace. Soup is served, the family chokes. The soup has been sabotaged by emptying the contents of the red pepper shaker into it. The new cook declared her innocence. Woe again; a steak is served—the family loses its teeth. Cook had been ordered to buy the best—the butcher's bill shows that it cost $2, and it is more like leather than steak.
>
> Then there is a motion-picture of the new housemaid sabotaging the best china. It is most uncanny the way the dishes slip out of that girl's hands.
>
> Maybe the I. W. W. housemaid decides that the family does too much entertaining. She sabotages at the next bridge party by serving sherbet that is decidedly salty, or spilling a whole pot of tea on the $150 exclusive model frock of the honor guest—an accident, of course. Picture father putting on his favorite soft shirt only to find that the new laundress sabotaged it by using plenty of starch.

According to the testimony introduced, the I. W. W. strike is totally different from the ordinary strike because of the purpose behind it. The mere raising of wages, improvement of working conditions, or shortening of hours is not the goal for which they are striving. To quote once again from their literature, the members of the I. W. W. "deny that employers have any right to exist as employers. The employer, being in their eyes not a part of the social body but a parasite on the social body, must be driven out of existence by all available means just as pathogenic microbes must be driven out of the patient's system, the choice of remedies being determined solely by the physician's care not to affect any of the patient's vital organs."

It is charged by the Government that the I. W. W. planned and called a "general strike" as a protest against conscription. Evidence has been presented to bear out the contention that the lumber workers' strike in the Northwest, which so seriously handicapped the Government's airplane and ship program, was a part of a general conspiracy. Evidence that officers of the I. W. W. were cognizant of the fact that the strike was holding up the important products needed for war work has been introduced.

To workers in the iron mining regions this circular was sent:

> Your attention is called to the fact that in this Land of Liberty, the home of the free, hundreds of our fellow-workers have been arrested and thrown into jails that the workers have built, for the reason that they did not register, because they know that the Constitution of the United States does not allow any force to be practiced on any man under the jurisdiction of the United States, and because they do not believe in wars and practicing for killing their fellow-men for the benefit of a few overfed parasites while they themselves are in urgent need of the necessities of life.
>
> You fellow-workers think this over a minute in your head and you will soon see that if we workers do not help ourselves the master class will not help us. We are here producing the iron of which the war machineries is built from. Thousands of tons of our sweat and blood is sunk into the bottom of the oceans and millions of our fellow-men are being killed and others are wanted for cannons' fodder.
>
> You workers must stop of furnishing the master the material of which the war structures are made of, and same time defend our innocent fellow-workers, who believe that they will not murder your brothers or your father, nor destroy your home.
>
> We appeal to you workers of the iron industry to prepare for a walk-out from your jobs, and demand that the imprisoned fellow-workers are immediately released. Thousands of men in the copper industries in the State of Montana are on strike already to defend our fellow-workers. Thousands more will in a few days be out in the lumber industry of the West.
>
> Prepare yourselves miners and all other workers to go out on strike on the moment's notice. Do not be slackers to defend your own class.

The defense has contended that the I. W. W. strikes in 1917 were not inspired by their opposition to the war and conscription, but solely to get additional concessions in the matter of shorter hours and higher wages, taking advantage of the urgent demands and higher prices for the product to force the employers to a settlement. But the I. W. W. newspaper Solidarity, during the period following the declaration of war until it was suppressed in September, was filled with lengthy tirades against the Government and conscription. These articles are in evidence at the trial.

"Since its inception our organization has opposed all national and imperialistic wars," said one outburst. "We have proved beyond the shadow of doubt that war is a question with which we never have and never intend to compromise."

The paper bitterly attacked Samuel Gompers and the American Federation of Labor for their patriotic stand. The I. W. W. at all times has opposed the so-called craft unions by every means in its power.

There has been extensive testimony relating to the organization of the I. W. W. and the methods used in recruiting its membership. The executive officer is William D. Haywood, who as Secretary-Treasurer wields extensive powers. It is charged by the Government he has been the presiding spirit of the organization since its inception and has been responsible for the drawing together of the extreme radicals who fill all of the higher offices.

Among the hundred of translations which have been read to the jury in the course of the present trial were many lengthy tirades against registration and the draft and charges that the participation of the United States in the war had been forced by the capitalists.

In the entire record of the organization covering cases of hundreds of members arrested on charges varying from murder to vagrancy, there is no evidence that any member was ever expelled from the I. W. W. for the commission of crime. On the other hand, there was never a time when defense funds were not being raised by special assessment stamps or direct contribution for the defense of members charged with some offense against the law.

The attitude of the organization, the officers and members, is at all times defiant of the courts. During the preent trial there appeared in The Industrial Worker a threatening article addressed to "the gentlemen of the prosecution." It read in part as follows:

The crisis has come. The long suspense of waiting is over. We are now on trial for our life. Every morning now our boys file into your court to listen to the droning mockery of your justice. In a few more weeks—perhaps in a few more days—the farce will be over and we shall hear the verdict. What will it be?

It is a bitter thought that the fate of our superb organization now lies in the hands of one Judge and twelve jurymen and a bitter and vindictive prosecutor in a courtroom in Chicago.

It is one of the ironical twists of the insane present, but it is true. And we of the I. W. W. have no illusions about that court. We have no faith in the wisdom of its verdict.

We do not expect justice. The memories of our past are fresh in our minds and those memories have taught us that you of the Government are always our enemies. • • •

And so as we stand at the bar in Chicago we think of these things. Their memories are seared into our brains. And if your court shall return a verdict of guilty against the I. W. W. we shall know what it means and we shall remember.

There are 200,000 of us scattered about the country. There will be 200,000 of us whether your verdict be innocent or guilty, for the I. W. W. never lay down. We ask you gentlemen of the prosecution to think carefully what you are doing before you send Haywood and our leaders away to your prisons.

It is the duty of the jury in the present trial to determine whether the defendants conspired to interfere with the production of munitions and supplies for the army and navy, and whether they knowingly conspired to prevent certain persons from the exercise of their constitutional rights and to use the mails to defraud the employers of labor in general. These questions can only be decided when the evidence has been fully presented on both sides. This task has already consumed more than three months, and the end is not in sight.

No matter what the verdict may be, the revelations as to the inner workings of the Industrial Workers of the World have made it clear that the organization of our American Bolsheviki is more than a fledgling. The black cat with outstretched claws, so universally used by the organization, is indeed a fitting symbol for a revolutionary society which has openly declared again and again during the present trial that its purpose is unceasing warfare to exterminate the wage system and seize the industries of the nation.

August 4, 1918

I. W. W. LEADERS GET 20-YEAR TERMS

Haywood and 14 of His Chief Aids Also Fined $20,000 for Anti-War Activities.

EIGHTY OTHERS SENTENCED

Receive Terms of from Ten Years to Ten Days — Judge Landis Pleased with Verdict.

CHICAGO, Aug. 30.—William D. Haywood, "uncrowned king" of the Industrial Workers of the World, and fourteen of his chief aids in the conspiracy to overturn the American war program, were sentenced to serve twenty years in the Federal Penitentiary at Leavenworth, Kan., by Federal Judge K. M. Landis here late today.

Ten-year sentences were imposed upon thirty-three of the organization's leaders, five-year sentences on thirty-three, one year and one day on twelve defendants, and ten-day sentences on two others. The cases against Benjamin Schraeger, the Chicago writer, and Pietro Nigra of Spring Valley, Ill., were continued.

All sentences on the four counts in the indictment will run concurrently. Fines ranging from $20,000 on Haywood and his chief aids down to $5,000 were imposed. Ninety days is granted in which to file a bill of exceptions, and a stay of seven days in which to petition for bail.

"It is the closing chapter in America's biggest criminal case," said Frank K. Nebeker, chief prosecutor.

"We are confident a new trial will be granted," said George F. Vanderver, chief counsel for the defense.

Ovation for Haywood Squelched.

There was silence in the courtroom as Haywood and his fourteen chief assistants were called before the bar. As "Big Bill" arose from his seat a group of women, who had been weeping, started a mild ovation, which was silenced quickly. George Andreytchine, the young Russian poet, whose stormy career since his exile from Russia for plotting a revolution, is an outstanding phase of the I. W. W., was next called. As he stepped forward he smiled and blew a kiss to his pretty bride, who waved her handkerchief.

Vincent St. John, who formerly held Haywood's office of general Secretary-Treasurer, was sentenced to serve ten years at Leavenworth; J. A. MacDonald, Seattle, publisher of a radical paper, was sentenced to serve ten years, while J. T. ("Third-Rail Red") Doran, a Western leader, and Harrison George of Pittsburgh, whose printed vision of President Wilson and his Cabinet in flight before an army of I. W. W.'s was an important factor in the trial, received sentences of five years each.

For more than an hour Judge Landis read excerpts from Haywood's correspondence relative to opposition to the war.

"In light of the evidence before it, the jury had no avenue of escape from a verdict of guilty," the court said.

"I don't mean," said Judge Landis at another point in his statement, "that the I. W. W. started out deliberately to aid Germany." He added that their acts were an aid to the enemy and were aimed directly at their own country.

Some of the defendants chuckled as sentence was pronounced, others paled and swayed uncertainly, while still others tried to make their way to wives and other relatives.

Benjamin Fletcher of Philadelphia, the only colored member on trial, grinned broadly when he was sentenced to serve ten years. He was being led away when he remarked:

"Judge Landis is using poor English today. His sentences are too long."

August 31, 1918

FREE SPEECH.

In imposing sentence on the I. W. W. convicts Judge Landis said:

When the country is at peace it is a legal right of free speech to oppose going to war and to oppose even preparation for war. But when once war is declared that right ceases.

That is the law, never more clearly and compactly stated than in these two sentences. Those who have been talking about free speech as if it gave the right to speak and write and work against their country when it is in a fight for its life may learn from Judge Landis's words just how far they are wrong, and, what will be of more interest to them, just how far they are in danger.

September 2, 1918

FIND DEBS GUILTY OF DISLOYAL ACTS

Socialist Convicted of Violating Espionage Act — Jury Out Six Hours.

SATISFIED WITH THE TRIAL

Rose Pastor Stokes Holds Defendant's Hand When the Verdict Is Announced.

Special to The New York Times.

CLEVELAND, Ohio, Sept. 12.—Eugene V. Debs, four times Socialist candidate for President of the United States, today was found guilty on three counts of violation of the Espionage act. The penalty on each count is twenty years' imprisonment and a fine of $10,000. In the event of an adverse decision on his counsel's motion for a new trial, Debs probably will be sentenced Saturday morning immediately after the motion has been disposed of.

Seymour Stedman, leading counsel for the defense, gave notice of appeal, the grounds of which will be " admission of incompetent evidence " and " failure of the indictment properly to charge the offense."

United States District Judge Westenhaver intimated today that if he overruled the motion for a new trial he might make it a condition of defendant's bail that he obey the law pending the appeal. While not announcing a definite decision on the question of conditional bail, the Judge said he was " inclined to think he ought to make the condition " in view of the defendant's actions and attitude since his indictment.

The jury retired to consider its verdict at 11:12 o'clock this morning and did not announce its decision until 5:05 this evening.

Found Guilty on Three Counts.

The counts on which Debs was found guilty are:

Attempting to incite insubordination, disloyalty, mutiny, and refusal of duty in the military and naval forces;

Obstructing and attempting to obstruct the recruiting and enlistment service;

Uttering language intended to incite, provoke, and encourage resistance to the United States and to promote the cause of the enemy.

The only count left to the discretion of the jury on which it found Debs " not guilty " was the tenth, charging " opposition to the cause of the United States." At the direction of the Judge, the jury returned " not guilty " verdicts to counts 6 and 8, charging defendant with " uttering language intended to bring the form of government, Constitution, military and naval forces, the flag, and the uniform into contempt, scorn, contumely, and disrepute," and with " urging, inciting, and advocating the curtailment of the production of war necessaries." The four remaining counts of the ten originally contained in the indictment had previously been nolled on advice of Federal officials.

Verdict Interrupts Story Telling.

The return of the jury, nearly six hours after its retirement, interrupted Debs when he was half way through telling one of several typical Lincoln stories with which he was entertaining counsel and some of his friends. When Foreman Cyrus Stoner and the other jurors filed back into court Mrs. Rose Pastor Stokes took a seat beside the veteran Socialist leader. With one hand locked between the hands of Mrs. Stokes, Debs, as calm and imperturbable as he had been throughout the trial, awaited the reading of the verdict.

" In God's good time it will all come right," the defendant said, and the salutations of his sympathizers were those of congratulation rather than sorrow.

Outside the courtroom a girl pushed a bunch of flowers into Debs' outstretched hands. Then she fell, half fainting, into his arms. Debs stooped down and kissed her.

" I haven't one word of complaint either against the verdict or the trial," the defendant asserted. " The evidence was truthful, it was fairly presented by the prosecution, the jury was patient and attentive, and the Judge's charge was masterly and scrupulously fair."

Mrs. Stokes Expects Many Converts.

" To find ' Gene ' Debs guilty of disloyalty to his country will mean the conversion to our cause of many of the millions in this country who either know or have heard him," Rose Pastor Stokes declared at the close of the trial. " The verdict will greatly help the movement and makes us tremendously hopeful and joyous."

Judge Westenhaver in his charge declared that the Socialist Party was not on trial, and that defendant was not being tried because he was a member of the Socialist Party. He also made it clear that Debs was not on trial and was not to be tried for any other offense except his Canton speech. He ruled that the Espionage act did not conflict with the Constitution of the United States.

" The act was passed to protect the public peace and the public safety in time of war. The constitutional guarantee of free speech and a free press does not forbid the enactment of a law to protect the public peace and safety," he declared. " In the last analysis, the question for us today is whether the evidence proves beyond reasonable doubt that defendant intended to do the things forbidden by the law. Disapproval of the war or advocacy of peace is not a crime unless the words uttered shall be wilfully intended by the person uttering them to have the effect and consequences forbidden by law."

September 13, 1918

WILSON LIFTED 'NATION' BAN

Reverses Exclusion Order, Based on Criticism of Gompers.

Special to The New York Times.

WASHINGTON, Sept. 19.—The sudden overruling of Assistant Attorney General Lamar of the Post Office Department, who excluded the New York Nation from the mails, was directly due to President Wilson.

The matter was taken up at the Cabinet meeting Tuesday, and the President is understood to have expressed his unconditional disapproval of the action, sanctioned by Postmaster General Burleson, and directed that the order against The Nation be rescinded.

The article in The Nation that caused Mr. Lamar to issue the order was an editorial criticizing the selection of Samuel Gompers as the representative of the United States to the labor organizations of England and France. The fact that Gompers had led laboring men of this country to support the war solidly, it was held by Mr. Burleson, entitled him to protection from criticism. Mr. Lamar took the position that if the objectionable editorial was cut out of The Nation the edition would be passed.

Among the periodicals that have come under the ban of the Post Office Department is The World Tomorrow, which represents the Fellowship of Reconciliation, of which Jane Addams is President. The World Tomorrow has been practically ordered to cease publication. Tomorrow the Post Office Department, by the President's direction, will issue an order permitting it to continue.

September 20, 1918

100 PER CENT. AMERICAN.

Object of Educational Campaigns in Two Western Cities.

Special to The New York Times.

WASHINGTON, Dec. 26.—Two cities of the United States have entered upon a campaign to make themselves 100 per cent. American—Flint, Mich., and Sheboygan, Wis. The Bureau of Naturalization, the Department of Labor announces, is co-operating to the fullest extent.

In Sheboygan the work is in charge of a citizens' committee composed of the leading men and women in each ward, and an industrial committee, with one representative in each factory. Classes in English and citizenship are held in the factories, and at night at churches and clubs. The campaign in Flint is being conducted along similar lines.

December 27, 1918

BERGER CONVICTED WITH FOUR OTHERS

Accused Socialist Leaders Had Expected "Hung Jury" in Sedition Trial.

ON BAIL PENDING APPEAL

Verdict, Based on Socialist Anti-War Screeds, Bars Berger from Congress.

Special to The New York Times.

CHICAGO, Jan. 8.—Victor L. Berger, Milwaukee politician-publisher, the only Socialist elected last Fall to the Sixty-sixth Congress, and four other national leaders of the Socialist Party, were found guilty by a jury in Federal Court this evening of sedition and disloyalty under the Espionage act. Berger's conviction bars him from Congress.

Those convicted with Berger for obstructing the nation's war program against Germany and with him now facing sentences of from one to twenty years in prison, or fines of from $1,000 to $10,000, or both, are:

Adolph Germer, National Secretary of the Socialist Party.

William F. Kruse, National Secretary of the Young People's Socialist Party—the "Yipsels."

J. Louis Engdahl, editor of The American Socialist.

Irwin St. John Tucker, Protestant Episcopal rector and former newspaper man.

The five defendants were released under $10,000 bonds each, pending hearing of a motion for a new trial on Jan. 23. Sentence was withheld by Judge Landis until that time.

Surprise to the Defendants.

The verdict, a sweeping victory for the Government, came as a surprise to the defendants. They had believed that the five weeks of radical "preaching" before the jury had "converted" at least one member of that body. None, save Berger, had counted upon an acquittal, but had believed a "hung jury" would result.

While out from 11 A. M. until 4:48 P. M., the jury took only three ballots. The first stood 10 to 2 for conviction, the second 11 to 1, and the third unanimous.

The courtroom was jammed with Socialists, I. W. W., and Bolsheviki when the jury reported its finding. They made no demonstration, seeming stunned.

Berger seemed more deeply moved at the result than the other defendants, tears streaming down his cheeks.

Judge Landis made no comment on the verdict, confining himself to thanking the twelve men for their long service in the jury box.

Berger said somewhat shakily, his emotion greatly accentuating his broad German accent:

"I am completely surprised. I am no more guilty of this crime than the Judge on the bench. I have lived in accordance with these principles for thirty-seven years, and now I must suffer for them."

Germer made no statement except that the verdict was "a shocking surprise." The others "had nothing to say."

Seymour Stedman, chief of counsel, who, with William Cunnea, Swan Johnson, and Henry Cochems, defended the accused men, was cryptic in his utterances. He is one of the principal leaders of the Socialist Party.

"Now that the controlling faction has shown the dragon's teeth, we will see how far they can go," he said, adding that if such a step became necessary the conviction would be taken to the Supreme Court of the United States for review.

What Convinced the Jurors.

What transpired in the jury room was related by A. L. Hendee, the foreman:

"We paid more attention to the documentary evidence than to the testimony," he said. "We were unanimous in declaring the 'proclamation and war program' of the Socialist Party, passed at St. Louis, to be a traitorous document. Such gruesome and scurrilous pamphlets as 'The Price We Pay' and 'Why We Should Fight,' as well as the strong anti-war editorials in Berger's newspaper, The Milwaukee Leader, and the printed propaganda urging opposition to the draft, convicted the defendants on their face.

"The fact that the armistice has been signed cut no figure in our deliberations. The documentary evidence showed that these men had deliberately, in wartime, set out to hinder the nation and help the enemy and had broken laws well known to them. We could see nothing innocent in their intent."

The trial, regarded by the Government as being even more important than the famous I. W. W. case, in which ninety-three leaders were sentenced to terms of from one to twenty years for similar offenses under the Conspiracy act, was regarded by the defense as the placing of the Socialist Party in the dock.

The defendants were tried under the Espionage act passed in June, 1917. They were indicted in February, 1918, following spectacular raids on Socialist headquarters and a denial of second-class mailing privileges to Berger's paper, as well as The American Socialist, the national party organ. The trial started on Dec. 9.

In twenty-five overt acts cited in the indictment the defendants were accused of willfully obstructing the recruiting and enlistment service of the nation while it was at war, through speeches, articles, pamphlets, cartoons, and other means of propaganda, and with causing insubordination, disloyalty, and refusal of duty in the military and naval forces.

The "pro-German" factor was continuously in the trial. While no evidence was offered showing use of German funds or aid from the Imperial Government, German influences were constantly brought out, particularly as regards the operations of the "Yipsels," young Socialists of draft age, who took a "conscientious objector" stand. The city organizer in Chicago was shown to have boasted of being "a German agent," and he is now interned. Berger was shown to have been born in Austria and Germer in Prussia, while Kruse, another defendant, is of immediate German extraction.

January 9, 1919

SUPREME COURT RULES AGAINST PACIFISTS

Holds Enlistment Section of Espionage Act No Interference with "Free Speech."

WASHINGTON, March 3.—While not passing directly upon the question of the constitutionality of the Espionage act, the Supreme Court in disposing of proceedings involving an interpretation of that statute today in effect held that the so-called enlistment section was not an interference with the right of free speech provided by the Constitution.

"When a nation is at war," the court held in an opinion rendered by Justice Holmes, "many things that might be said in time of peace are such a hindrance to its effort that their utterance will not be endured so long as men fight, and no court could regard them as protected by any constitutional right."

The opinion was rendered in sustaining convictions of Charles T. Schenk and Elizabeth Baer of Philadelphia, who were charged with attempting to interfere with army enlistments by sending through the mails to men of draft ages circulars discussing subjects relative to the war.

The court also, in effect, sustained the convictions of Kate Richards O'Hare in North Dakota, under the Espionage Act, by refusing to review her case, and also the conviction of Abraham L. Sugerman of Minneapolis.

Appeals from convictions under the Espionage Act of Eugene V. Debs and Jacob Frohwerk of Kansas City were argued in the court prior to the February recess, but were not disposed of by the court today.

March 4, 1919

HARDING FREES DEBS AND 23 OTHERS HELD FOR WAR VIOLATIONS

Socialist Leader's Sentence of Ten Years Is Commuted, Effective Christmas.

NO RESTORATION OF RIGHTS

None of "Political" Prisoners Regains Citizenship—Some Are to Be Deported.

FIVE EX-SOLDIERS PARDONED

Men Serving Life Sentences for Murder of British Officer Released by President.

Special to The New York Times.

WASHINGTON, Dec. 23.—Announcement was made at the White House late this afternoon that President Harding had commuted the sentences of twenty-four so-called political prisoners, including Eugene V. Debs, who were convicted under the Espionage act and other wartime laws and sentenced to from two to twenty years. Debs will be released from Atlanta Penitentiary on Christmas Day.

Five soldiers who were sentenced to life imprisonment by a general court-martial at Coblenz for the killing of a former British officer were pardoned by the President.

Commutation of sentences of the twenty-four prisoners means that the President is not disposed, even in the case of Debs, to issue out-and-out pardons with consequent restoration of rights of citizenship.

Attorney General Daugherty, who called Debs to Washington for a personal interview last March, recommended to the President that it would be a "gracious act of mercy" to release the Socialist leader.

According to the summary of the Debs case as given out at the White House, "there is no question of his guilt and that he actively and purposely obstructed the draft. In fact, he admitted it at the time of his trial, but sought to justify his action. He was by no means, however, as rabid and outspoken in his expressions as many others, and but for his prominence and the resulting far-reaching effect of his words, very probably might not have received the sentence he did. He is an old man, not strong physically. He is a man of much personal charm and impressive personality, which qualifications make him a dangerous man calculated to mislead the unthinking and affording excuse for those with criminal intent."

No Sabotage Advocates Freed.

"The list, in the main," said an Executive statement issued from the White House, "is made up of those who opposed the war in one way or another, and it is made up of less than a third of I. W. W. prisoners, and these have either expressed full penitence or are booked for deportation. The Department of Justice has given no recommendation in behalf of the advocates of sabotage or the destruction of government by force, and the President let it be known he would not consider such cases. In addition to the five soldiers on the list, many other cases are under consideration.

"No comment was made by the President on the case of Debs. The President and the Attorney General had given very extended consideration to the Debs petitions, and it is known that the fact that he had twice been the Presidential candidate of a million voters had its influence in reaching a decision favorable to his release.

"The President expressed the wish that it be stated that the grant of clemency in the cases acted upon does not question the justice of any action of the courts in enforcing the law in a time of national peril, but he feels the ends of justice have been fairly met in view of the changed conditions. The vast majority of so-called political prisoners still imprisoned are the I. W. W. group, are rarely American citizens and have no good claim to Executive clemency. A number of convicted citizens have never been imprisoned, owing to appeals under bond. There are also many thousands of indictments under war legislation still pending. These do not come under Executive consideration."

The five soldiers pardoned by the President's order are Carl J. Bryan, James A. O'Dell, Roy Youngblood, George Van Gilder and J. R. Richardson. While serving with the American forces in Germany, they were tried before a general court-martial on the charge of murdering George Lancefield, a former British officer, and were sentenced to life imprisonment.

December 24, 1921

COOLIDGE RELEASES ALL WAR OFFENDERS AS CHRISTMAS GIFT

President Commutes the Terms of 31 Convicted Under the Espionage Act in 1919.

BAKER COMMITTEE FOR IT

Gen. Harbord Is Said to Have Dissented From Majority Report Favoring Amnesty.

BORAH COMMENDS ACTION

Special to The New York Times.

WASHINGTON, Dec. 15.—President Coolidge today pardoned the last of the wartime offenders, thirty-one in number, convicted for acts against the Government. The action was taken upon the recommendation of a special report prepared by former Secretary of War Baker, Bishop Charles H. Brent and General J. G. Harbord.

All those released were convicted under the Espionage act for speaking against the Government during the war and in inciting sentiment against the Selective Draft act. Among those released were a number of I. W. W. men.

Nicholas S. Sogg, a Mexican, convicted of aiding an American to escape the draft, for whom a pardon was asked by the American Amnesty Committee, now serving a ten-year sentence in California, was not pardoned.

The White House announcement, which will allow the prisoners to return to their homes by Christmas, follows:

"It is announced today that the President and Attorney General Daugherty, after conferring together and considering the joint report prepared by Hon. Newton D. Baker, Bishop Charles H. Brent and General J. G. Harbord upon wartime prisoners, have decided to adopt and follow the majority recommendation of the committee, and accordingly the President today, in conformity with the recommendation of the Attorney General, has commuted the sentences of all the remaining wartime prisoners convicted at Chicago, Kansas City and Sacramento to the terms already served.

"Warrants of commutation are being prepared and as soon as signed by the President will be sent to the wardens with instructions to release the prisoners."

In order to make certain that all of these prisoners will be able to spend Christmas outside of the prisons, President Coolidge will notify by telegraph the wardens of the Federal prisons of his action. This course was decided upon lest the warrants arrive too late to permit Christmas at home for the men released.

The men freed by the President are:

Convicted at Sacramento in January, 1919, and sentenced to ten-year terms: Elmer Anderson, Chris A. Luber, Harry Brewer, Phil McLaughlin, Robert Connellan, George O'Connell, Roy P. Connor, John Potthast, Pete de Bernardi, Edward Quigley, Mortimer Downing, James Quinlan, Frank Elliott, Myron Sprague, John Graves, Caesar Tabib, Henry Hammer, Jacob Tori, William Hood, George F. Voetter, Harry Gray, Vincent Santilli.

Convicted at Kansas City in December, 1919: Wencil Francik, serving seven years, six months, and F. J. Gallagher, eight years.

Convicted at Chicago in 1919, fined $20,000 each and sentenced to five to twenty years: C. J. Bourg, Alexander Cournos, Harry Lloyd, Burt Lorton, Charles H. McKinnon, James Rowan, James P. Thompson.

President Harding offered Francik and those convicted at Chicago conditional pardon last year, but they refused to accept the conditions, among which was that they should not engage in similar acts again.

In most cases those pardoned by President Harding were granted commutations after their cases had been individually passed upon by eminent lawyers. The demand for the pardoning of all the political prisoners became so insistent that President Harding referred the matter to the committee, upon whose majority report President Coolidge acted today. It is understood in War Department circles that General Harbord was not numbered with the majority.

Senator Pepper and Senator Borah were very active in requesting the release of the prisoners. The former made a special study of each case and it was due to his influence that Bishop Brent was appointed on the committee.

Discussing the pardons, Senator Borah said:

"I am delighted that a President of the United States has discovered the First Amendment to the Constitution and has had the courage to announce the discovery. It is a vindication of the right of free speech and free press, of that spirit which moved the fathers to incorporate that sublime principle in the Constitution.

"These men were not in prison for violence to either person or property. They were there because they expressed their political views upon matters of government, of the activities of government. Intolerance, bigotry, prejudice kept them there for many years.

"The President has performed a distinct service to the most fundamental principle of free government. I am certainly glad that the Chief Executive has gone as far as lies within his power to destroy the precedent which might obtain by reason of these prosecutions for political opinions. It far transcends in importance the releasing of these men from prison. It involves a great and vital principle."

Taken in California Red Raids.

SACRAMENTO, Cal., Dec. 15.—Twenty alleged members of the Industrial Workers of the World, included in the amnesty order by President Coolidge were convicted in Sacramento in 1919 on charges of violating the Espionage act.

The "round-up" of alleged radicals began late in 1918, after the Governor's mansion had been dynamited. Police investigations were held to determine whether the dynamiting was the result of an I.W.W. plot and several members of the organization were arrested.

Last of 26 Kansas City I. W. W.'s.

KANSAS CITY, Dec. 15.—Wencil Francik and F. J. Gallagher, ordered released today under Presidential amnesty, were among twenty-six alleged I.W.W. convicted in the Federal Court here Dec. 18, 1919. They were found guilty under a joint indictment of conspiracy to obstruct the draft, dissemination of radical propaganda and interference with production and transportation of food and coal.

The other twenty-four, including four women, have been released from time to time by commutation of sentences or by completion of terms.

Chicago Men Were With Haywood.

CHICAGO, Dec. 15.—The Chicago wartime prisoners who will be released by the order of President Coolidge are those associated with William D. ("Big Bill") Haywood, General Secretary-Treasurer of the I.W.W., who were convicted of conspiracy to violate the Espionage act. Haywood himself fled to Russia, while an appeal was pending, and is still there.

The explosion of a bomb in a doorway of the Federal Building and the receipt of a bomb by Federal Judge (now Baseball Commissioner) K. M. Landis, and Frank K. Nebker, a special prosecutor in the case, were incidents during the trial.

In addition to prison sentences Judge Landis imposed fines of $20,000 to $35,000 on the defendants following their conviction.

Asks Pardons for Negro Soldiers.

BOSTON, Dec. 15.—The National Equal Rights League, a Negro organization, today issued a call to all Negroes in the country to send letters to President Coolidge asking for a Christmas pardon for Negro soldiers of the Twenty-fourth Infantry in prison at Fort Leavenworth, Kansas, for participation in the Houston, Texas riots in 1917.

December 16, 1923

THE RED SCARE

SENATE ORDERS REDS HERE INVESTIGATED

Directs Overman Committee to Turn the Light on American Bolshevism.

MASS OF EVIDENCE AT HAND

Walsh, Borah, and Others Attack Congressmen Who Attended a Soviet Meeting.

Special to The New York Times.

WASHINGTON, Feb. 4.—The sub-committee of the Senate Committee on Judiciary, which, under the chairmanship of Senator Overman of North Carolina, has been investigating German propaganda in this country, was instructed by unanimous vote of the Senate this afternoon immediately to begin an investigation of Bolshevism and all other forms of anti-American radicalism in the United States. The resolution was offered by Senator Walsh of Montana and covers every phase of the radical propaganda which is now being preached in various parts of the country.

Major E. Lowry Humes, who has handled the investigation of the German propaganda, will direct the investigation of Bolshevism. Major Humes said tonight that he hoped to be ready to call the first witnesses Thursday or Friday.

The Walsh resolution passed by the Senate reads as follows:

Resolved, That the authority of the Committee on the Judiciary conferred by Senate Resolution 307 be and hereby is extended so as to include the power and duty to inquire concerning any efforts being made to propagate in this country the principles of any party exercising or claiming to exercise any authority in Russia, whether such efforts originate in this country or are financed from abroad, and further to inquire into any effort to incite the overthrow of the Government of this country or all government by force, or by the destruction of life or property, or the general cessation of industry.

The action of the Senate was hastened as a result of several radical meetings recently held in this city and also by a speech delivered yesterday by Senator Thomas of Colorado, who said that there was a powerful organization at work in this country to overthrow the present American system of Government.

Senator Weeks of Massachusetts, in supporting the Walsh resolution, said he was confident that Bolshevism would have no force in this country once the evil was understood by the rank and file of Americans. Senator Borah of Idaho, in his remarks, referred to the meeting held in a theatre Sunday night at which Congressman Mason of Illinois was one of the speakers.

"I am informed that at the meeting held in a theatre Sunday," said Senator Borah, "among the things advocated was the overthrow of our form of Government and the substitution in its place of a form of government known as the Soviet Government. It is but fair to say that the statement has been made to me that so far as the advocacy of the overthrow of our Government was concerned no such doctrine was preached at that meeting; that it was a defense of the Soviet Government in Russia under conditions and surroundings which confront the people of that country. But if the propaganda which seems to have been fathered at that meeting be the beginning of a movement in this country we may well consider how we are to meet such a serious situation."

Senator Overman called Senator Borah's attention to a bill which is in Congress to repeal the Espionage law. Senator Overman said that other laws must be placed on the statute books to deal with Bolshevism if the Espionage act was repealed. Senator Borah said that he did not regard the Espionage act as effective.

"I am opposed to Bolshevism," he said, "whether it is in tatters and rags or whether it is clothed in broadcloth. It is wholly immaterial to me from what source the attack comes upon the American Republic. These men may be hammering and battering away with a pickaxe and dynamite at one pillar of the republic, while other men in more powerful places are battering and hammering away at other pillars of the republic.

"The Soviet Government has its enthusiasts throughout the land and throughout the world, but who in this hour is preaching Americanism and the great fundamental principles of Americanism in this country? They held a meeting at the Poli Theatre. The League to Enforce Peace will begin its campaign in Boston on the 6th day of February, and if they succeed they will ultimately land us precisely where the Bolshevists would land us, and that is under the control of internationalism. They would tear down the fundamental principles of this republic just as successfully in the end and just as efficiently as the men who met at the Poli Theatre."

Immediately following the passage of the resolution the committee which will direct the investigation went into executive session. The committee comprises Senators Overman, Nelson, King, Sterling, and Wolcott.

Tomorrow Major Humes will confer with Secretary Baker, and he is expected to request that the entire evidence in the possession of the Government regarding radical propaganda be turned over to the committee. A member of the committee said tonight he was certain Secretary Baker would give the information asked. The report referred to is said to be one of the most complete ever compiled by the War Department.

February 5, 1919

37

TROOPS ON GUARD IN SEATTLE STRIKE

Soldiers from Camp Lewis Hurried There Upon Call from Governor Lister.

ENTIRE CITY IS TIED UP

Street Cars Stopped, Schools Closed, and Newspapers Suspended.

SEATTLE, Feb. 6.—Federal troops from Camp Lewis are quartered tonight in Seattle and Tacoma to "stand ready for any emergency," as army officers said today, in connection with the general strike this morning of 45,000 union men, in sympathy with 25,000 shipyard workers who walked out on Jan. 21 to enforce demands for higher wages.

Major John L. Hayren commands the contingent of 800 soldiers in Seattle, and General Frank B. Watson has under him in Tacoma, thirty-six miles from here, two battalions and a machine-gun company. Equipment of the soldiers included 200 hand grenades. Authority for the use of troops was granted by Secretary of War Baker upon advices from Governor Ernest Lister.

Thirty-five thousand union men in the vicinity of Seattle quit work today, labor leaders said, but in Tacoma the response was not so general, and the principal unions involved there were the carmen, timber workers, barbers, and retail clerks.

Street cars stopped running in Seattle, schools closed, restaurants and theatres closed their doors. Newspapers suspended and other industries ceased operating. Twelve "soup kitchens" were established by culinary unions to feed strikers and others who depend upon restaurants for meals. Patrons of the kitchens were lined up and served in military mess fashion. Barber shops closed and elevators stopped running.

Only emergency telegraph business from Seattle was handled by the telegraph companies. The telephone system continued in service.

The city government is prepared for any emergency, Mayor Ole Hanson said, and ten thousand extra police will be sworn in if necessary.

"Any man who attempts to take over control of municipal government functions here will be shot on sight," Mayor Hanson declared when told of a statement by Senator Thomas in the Senate today.

"Strikers have not taken over government functions in Seattle," the Mayor said. "They will not be allowed to take over any government functions despite their published statements that they intend to operate the light plant and help police the city. The seat of city government is still at the City Hall."

Police Have Machine Gun.

Seattle police said they were ready for any emergency. A big truck carrying a machine gun, with sand bags built up around its edges, stands at the police station. Three former army Lieutenants have been assigned to the truck.

Motor cycle police were instructed to watch sharply for offenders who might possibly spread tacks on the streets to puncture automobile tires. For several days stories of enormous sales of tacks for this purpose have been circulated here.

A statement issued by the Strike Committee of the Central Labor Council, which is directing the strike, said the walkout was a success. All lines of industry in which union workmen were employed were crippled, the statement said.

Steamship operators and others were worried over the handling of fresh fish shipments, due from Alaska, and fruits and vegetables coming from California, because of the strike of the longshoremen who, defying their international officers, have virtually tied up coastwise and off-shore traffic.

Vessels coming here to discharge, it was said, would be diverted to other ports nearby. Two Japanese steamers, the Hozan Maru and Mandasan, were ordered to San Francisco to load cargo for the Orient.

February 7, 1919

Anarchists Tried Revolution in Seattle, but Never Got to First Base, Says Mayor Hanson

By OLE HANSON,
Mayor of Seattle.
By Telegraph to THE NEW YORK TIMES.

SEATTLE, Wash., Feb. 8.—Two years ago our city had 15,000 industrial workers; today we have 65,000. The American Federation of Labor two years ago controlled our labor organizations. The influx of workmen from all over the country and from Russia brought in a very large radical and I. W. W. element. Under stress of the war the American Federation of Labor unions allowed these anarchists to join their unions.

The I. W. W. element, noisy and active, talked the loudest and promised the most, and secured partial control of the Central Labor Council and active control of a great many unions in Seattle. The shipyard workmen were dissatisfied with the Macey award; the radicals and I. W. W. demanded a general strike. The Soviet Government of Russia, duplicated here, was their plan. The conservative leaders acted the part of cowards in most instances, and the sympathetic strike was called.

The Central Labor Council, which is composed of the heads of the different unions, is controlled by the radicals, and the working people of Seattle were made to believe that a general strike would increase the pay of the shipyard workers. Many members of the labor organizations believed they could take over the industries, Government, &c.

The sympathetic revolution was called in the exact manner as was the revolution in Petrograd. Labor tried to run everything. Janitors and engineers in schools were called out, everything was stopped, except a few things, which were exempted.

We refused to ask for exemptions from any one. The seat of Government is at the City Hall. We organized 1,000 extra police, armed with rifles and shot guns, and told them to shoot on sight any one causing disorder. We got ready for business. We had already had trouble in two instances heretofore and had completely whipped the Bolsheviki. They knew we meant business, and they started no trouble.

I issued a proclamation that all life and property would be protected; that all business should go on as usual, and this morning all our municipal street cars, light, power plants, water, &c., were running full blast.

This was an attempted revolution which they expected to spread all over the United States. It never got to first base, and it never will if the men in control of affairs will tell all traitors and anarchists that death will be their portion if they start anything. Law and order are supreme in our city.

The labor unions must now cleanse themselves of their anarchistic element or the labor unions must fall. They are on trial before the people of this country. I take the position that our duty as citizens stands ahead of the demand of any organization on the face of the earth. The union men, the business men, the churchmen, must first of all be citizens. Any man who owes a higher allegiance to any organization than he does to the Government should be sent to a Federal prison or deported.

Let the National Government stop pandering to and conciliating the men who talk against it. Let us clean up the United States of America. Let all men stand up and be counted. If the majority of the people of this country are disloyal and owe superior allegiance to some other country or some other cause, now is the time to find it out. We refuse to treat with these revolutionists. Unconditional surrender are our only terms.

Among the proofs that this is a revolution and not a strike are the following extracts from an editorial in The Labor Union Record of Feb. 4:

We are undertaking the most tremendous move ever made by labor in this country, a move which will lead no one knows where. We do not need hysteria, we need the iron march of labor. The Strike Committee is arranging for guards, and it is expected that the stopping of the cars will keep people at home.

The closing down of Seattle's industries as a mere shutdown will not affect these Eastern gentlemen much. They could let the whole Northwest go to pieces as far as money alone is concerned. But the closing down of the capitalistically controlled industries of Seattle, while the workers organize to feed the people, to care for the babies and the sick, to preserve order—this will move them, for this looks too much like the taking over of power by the workers.

Labor will not only shut down the industries, but labor will reopen, under the management of the appropriate trades, such activities as are needed to preserve public health and public peace.

If the strike continues labor may feel led to avoid public suffering by reopening more and more activities under its own management, and that is why we say that we are starting on a road that leads no one knows where.

February 9, 1919

ROUND UP TO OUST ALIEN AGITATORS

54 Due from West Today Are First of Groups to be Deported.

RIGOROUS NEW ACT APPLIED

Undesirables to be Sent to Gothenburg—Caminetti Tells of Vigorous Action.

Special to The New York Times.

WASHINGTON, Feb. 10.—The two carloads of foreign labor agitators now on the way from the West to New York are to be passed through the immigration clearing house at Ellis Island for deportation to Russia and other countries as soon as ship transportation can be provided for them.

Most of this particular group, it was said here today, were rounded up in Seattle and the immediate vicinity, and more than fifty of them are in the party. There are also some odds and ends of agitators from other parts of the country who are being sent to Ellis Island for deportation.

The orders for their deportation have been signed by Anthony Caminetti, Commissioner General of Immigration, who has had a number of anarchist cases under consideration for some time. He is acting both under the authority of Section 19 of the immigration law of Feb. 5, 1917, and under the special enactment against anarchists passed by Congress in response to Mr. Caminetti's appeal on Oct. 16, 1918, which vests him with authority to expel from the United States aliens who are members of the anarchistic and similar classes.

More Cases Are Pending.

The movement of these agitators to New York and their deportation will continue for the next five or six weeks. A number of cases are pending for final action, and as soon as the order has been signed in their cases the men involved will be sent to Ellis Island for safe keeping, pending their deportation. Most of those now being sent to New York from Seattle are Russians, but there are some from Scandinavian and Mediterranean countries and several from England.

Some of these cases have been accumulating for several years. While the Government has had clear cases in many instances, the men could not be deported because shipping was not available, or because they came from Austria, Bulgaria, or enemy regions to which they could not be sent during the war.

One of the subjects that gave the officials of the Immigration Bureau great concern during the period preceding the signing of the armistice in November involved the activity of alien anarchists and persons affiliated with organizations, which, while they may not be avowedly anarchistic, spread the propaganda of destruction of property and the upsetting of the general doctrine of Government.

" Much evidence was obtained by Government agents as to the pernicious activities of this class of persons," said Commissioner Caminetti today. " It was hoped that the provisions incorporated in the immigration act of Feb. 5, 1917, would be sufficient to reach and deal effectively with them. While many of them were found, on investigation, to be subject to arrest and deportation under the immigration law and a large number of warrants were issued and served, there appeared to be a lack of conformity between the provisions of Sections 3 and 19 of the immigration act, as a result of which some persons of the anarchistic class, while subject to exclusion upon their original arrival, might be able to frustrate deportation upon warrant procedure."

Finding that these two provisions of the law were not strong enough to enable the Government to deport certain of the most troublesome classes who had succeeded in gaining admission and who might be able to frustrate deportation by probable judicial interpretation of the law pursuant to habeas corpus proceedings, the Government, in October, enacted a special law for the deportation of anarchists.

" When this situation came to be realized," said Mr. Caminetti, " it was deemed advisable to defer action upon all but the clearest cases until Congress could enact amendatory legislation which would serve to eliminate the supposed weaknesses of the immigration statute of 1917, and the law of Oct. 16, 1918, was passed, providing for the exclusion or expulsion from the United States of members of anarchistic and similar classes.

" Under that law the Secretary of Labor has authority to issue warrants for the arrest and deportation, irrespective of the time of their entry into the United States, of aliens who are anarchists, who believe in or advocate the overthrow by force or violence of the Government of the United States or all forms of law, who disbelieve in or are opposed to all organized government, who advocate or teach assassination of public officials, or the unlawful destruction of property, or who are members of or affiliated with any organization that hold such beliefs.

" If after they have been deported any such persons try to re-enter the United States it will be considered a felony, and on conviction they may be imprisoned for not more than five years."

Commissioner Caminetti was careful to explain that the deportation of the present large group of agitators was not related to the labor or other present activities at Seattle, but that orders for the deportations had been signed before the Seattle situation had developed.

February 11, 1919

CALLS ALIEN REDS INVADING ENEMIES

Deportation Will Proceed Under 1917 Law, Secretary Wilson Announces.

WASHINGTON, Feb. 17.—Aliens who are found advocating the destruction of property or the overthrow of the Government by force will be deported under the provision of the Immigration act of Feb. 5, 1917. This announcement was made today by Secretary Wilson in a letter sharply rebuking Micrometer Lodge 460, International Association of Machinists, of Brooklyn, for protesting against the deportation of fifty-eight " alien radicals." The Secretary denied that the aliens were being deported without due process of law, and asserted that they had received fair trials.

Mr. Wilson reiterated his previously announced decision that no person would be arrested simply for joining the Industrial Workers of the World, and said:

" It is my intention, as Secretary of Labor, now that the unusual danger of sea travel is over, to carry out the clear provisions of the law; first, because it is my sworn duty to do so, and, second, because any foreigner who comes to this country and advocates the overthrow of our form of Government by force is an invading enemy, who is treated with great leniency when he is simply deported to the land from which he came.

" When our own citizens desire to change the form of Government they can do so peaceably in the manner provided by the Constitution. If we cannot make progress by the peaceable process of discussing and voting, we are not likely to make any progress by the riotous process of cussing and shouting. The man who cannot be depended upon to vote right cannot be depended upon to shoot right."

Mr. Wilson called the Union's attention to the fact that the passage of the Immigration act was strongly supported by the American Federation of Labor, " of which you are a part."

Discussing the deportations, the Secretary said:

" Those you refer to as radicals are being sent out of the country because they have been found advocating the overthrow of our Government by force. * * * They have had every possible opportunity, both at the places where they were originally arrested some time ago and at the department in Washington, to defend themselves against the charges made under the immigration law. All were freely granted the privilege of employing counsel. Some did so; others declined; but all, irrespective of whether or not they employed counsel, were treated fairly, as the department never acts or allows any of its officials to act as prosecutor, but simply as an agency to ascertain the truth. The right to resort to the courts was not denied any of the aliens. Some of them availed themselves of the opportunity. Most of them preferred to abide by the department's decision."

Another measure designed to check radical agitation was introduced today by Senator Jones of Washington. If enacted it would punish persons who urge resistance to law or changes in the form of Government with five years' imprisonment at hard labor or a fine of $5,000. Aliens convicted under the law would be deported after serving their sentences.

February 18, 1919

BOLSHEVISM IN THE SCHOOLS.

" Down with everybody who wears a collar or a clean shirt!" That is the pemmican of Bolshevism. It is not only meat for strong men, it is milk for babes. Our high school boys are to be fed on it. The teacher of English at the Commercial High School finds his pupils reading " The Bolsheviks and the Soviets," a pamphlet by that industrious propagandist of Bolshevism in the United States, Mr. ALBERT RHYS WILLIAMS, and " A Letter to the American Workingman," ascribed to the master sculptor of Russian ruin, NIKOLAI LENINE.

If our youth are to learn the science of destruction at school; if, instead of filling the too brief time of their education with study of free representative government, of the democratic polity under which they live, they are to be indoctrinated in theories of class intolerance and supremacy put into bloody practice before their eyes in Russia; if the intolerable horror and shame that have brought a mighty nation to despair are to be the model and example of our future citizens, we had better close the schools or turn them into penitentiaries for the assassins they will breed.

Tobacco drugs, alcohol—how assiduously have our ingenuous youth been guarded from these poor perils! Their stomachs, their minor morals are the source of anxious paternalistic care. We teach them to play and to work. But the deadliest poison in the world is not forbidden to them. At their rawest and most impressionable time they are free to feed upon the insanest root that ever took the reason prisoner.

The City, the State pay to bring about their ultimate subversion. Focuses of wild radicalism and the gospel of disorder some of our "public forums" and high schools have notoriously been, long before the perihelion of massacre under Trotzky and Lenin. There have been teachers disloyal or of doubtful loyalty. The

desk has been a soapbox. School children have "struck," obeying some sinister command. Among the school teachers, if not to the same extent as among the professors, here and there has found lodgment the notion, too common among the semi-educated who have not learned "a wise and modest ignorance," that dissent from the common, accepted, and vital beliefs of the majority is a proof of intellectual superiority. Are the preparatory seminaries of American citizenship to be the nurseries of its overthrow?

A teacher of an old eighteenth century foundation, the Phillips Andover Academy in Massachusetts, descends upon the industrial City of Lawrence, as a "Comrade of the

World," crying for a strike, and imagining in his vealy way, doubtless, that it is a clever and noble thing to associate himself with the forces of trouble.

The intelligenzia has been pretty thoroughly wiped out in Russia. Some, too many, representatives of it here seem to be doing their best to wipe itself and the rest of the population out here. Nobody in particular is fighting Bolshevism anywhere. Here it is fighting openly or insidiously and in many ways to establish itself and disestablish law and democracy and equality.

February 21, 1919

EXTREMISTS HERE PLAN A REVOLT TO SEIZE POWER

Papers Taken in Mail and Sent to Senate Committee Reveal Existence of Plot.

I. W. W. LEADS PROPAGANDA

Special to The New York Times.

WASHINGTON, March 10.—That the I. W. W. anarchists, Radical Socialists and other groups of extreme views are combining with the object of overthrowing the American Government through a "bloody revolution," and establishing a Bolshevist republic, was disclosed by a memorandum from Solicitor General Lamar of the Post Office Department, which was read into the records at the session this afternoon of the Senate Propaganda Committee, by Major Hume, counsel to the committee.

The memorandum prefaced something like a hundred excerpts from publications seized in the mails since the signing of the armistice, and it read:

"These excerpts will readily convey to you the forceful activities of these organizations and the methods they advocated to accomplish the object of their purposes.

"This propaganda is being conducted with such regularity that its magnitude can be measured only by the bold and outspoken statements contained in these publications and the efforts made therein to inaugurate a nation-wide reign of terror and overthrow of the Government.

"In classifying these papers they are submitted in their major or general class as follows: I. W. W., anarchists, Radical Socialists and Socialists. It will be seen from these excerpts, and it is indeed significant, that this is the first time in the history of the so-called radical movement in the United States that these radical elements have found a common cause (Bolshevism) in which they can all unite. The I. W. W., anarchists, Socialistic radical and otherwise, in fact all dissatisfied elements, particularly the foreign elements, are perfecting an amalgamation with one object, and one object only in view, namely, the overthrow of the Government of the United States by means of a bloody revolution and the establishment of a Bolshevist republic.

I. W. W. the Most Dangerous.

"The organization of the Industrial Workers of the World is perhaps most

actively engaged in spreading this propaganda and has at its command a large field force known as recruiting agents, subscription agents, lecturers, &c., who work unceasingly in the furtherance of 'the cause.' This organization also publishes at least five newspapers in the English language and nine in foreign languages.

"It is the announced intention of this organization to publish their literature in practically every foreign language spoken in the United States, to change their monthly magazines into weeklies, their weeklies into dailies.

"In a recent issue of one of these publications there appears a notice to the effect that beginning in March a publication in the Chinese language will be published in New York, in the interests of the Chinese I. W. W., who have recently been organized.

"It will be seen from the foregoing that this organization will be able by this method to reach every foreign element in the United States and by means of its propaganda to weld them into one big 'revolutionary' unit.

"It also appears that the Socialists have joined the Bolshevist movement and are using the party organization to further the cause, and this will be seen from the various excerpts from socialistic publications.

"The anarchistic class, already outside the pale of the law, are to be found among the stanchest supporters of Bolshevism and have eagerly seized this opportunity to join forces with other radicals and overthrow the Government."

Attached to the memorandum was the following list of English and foreign language publications said to be conducted and published by the I. W. W.:

The New Solidarity, English, weekly, Chicago; One Big Union, English, monthly, Chicago; Industrial Unionist, English, weekly, Seattle; California Defense Bulletin, English, weekly, San Francisco; The Rebel Worker, English, bi-monthly, New York; La Neuva Solidaridad, Spanish, weekly, Chicago; Golos Truzenta, Russian, weekly, Chicago; Li Nuovo Proletario, Italian, weekly, Chicago; Nya Varlden, Swedish, weekly, Chicago; Der Industrialer Arbeiter, Jewish, weekly, Chicago; Probuda, Bulgarian, weekly, Chicago; A. Fels Badulas, Hungarian, weekly, Chicago; Loukkataistelu, Finnish, monthly, New York.

This list comprises only the official papers of the I. W. W. and does not take into account the large number of free-lance papers published in the interests of the organization.

What Some of Them Say.

Following are some of the excerpts submitted:

The Nuovo Proletario of Chicago, on Dec. 28 under the heading, "This Is Your Task Workingmen: First, defend the Russian revolution wherever you can, as it is the first true revolution of the proletariat ever accomplished in the history of humanity."

A Fels Badulas of Chicago, on Feb. 1:

"Slaves of America, awake! Things will hereafter change, no matter whether the American Huns, the industrial Kaisers, their associates and hirelings, like it or not."

Industrial Defense Bulletin of Seattle, Nov. 29: "Big things are just ahead. Don't you think it is time for all rebels to get into line and equip our propaganda and throw our enthusiasm and knowledge into the problem of educat-

ing and organizing the workers for victory?"

"Otelma" writes thus in Il Diritto of New York, Jan. 25: "Let us tell them (these Kaisers of wealth) once for all that we are disposed to obtain our liberty at the price of their stinking carcasses. That we are determined to obtain our liberty appearing in the night in their sanctuaries, as livid spectres because of the centuries of starvation and chains, with a dagger between our teeth tight because of wrath, and with dynamite we will bring down the roof of their dwellings, where infamy, dishonor, and slavery are perpetuated."

In the same issue the paper speaks of "Americanism, which is all-obsequious and servile to law."

From the Socialist papers, which, theoretically, are less violent in their doctrines, the following excerpts are taken:

L'Avanti of New York, on Nov. 1: "Certainly America will not be the privileged country where the workingmen and bourgeoise class will live in peace and harmony. The harmony of classes is not possible in America. The laborers of America should possess their country."

A Muncas, New York, Feb. 1: "We all are enthusiastic over the work of our revolutionary comrades in Russia and Germany, so why should we ourselves not come to an agreement? Let us think of the outbreak of the storm in which we have to take our stand."

Novy Mir, New York, Jan. 30: "Lenine and all those who are behind him are fighting for the establishment of the Socialist society throughout the entire world, but as real statesmen they know that this cannot be accomplished without revolutionary methods. There is hope that soon also the American workingman will come to understand that simple truth."

El Ore, New York, Jan. 20, 1919: "The hour of deeds has arrived. The International Socialists must leave their reserved attitude and must step out upon the field of action, the opportunity for action is here. The Bolshevist Government may give an opportunity, and not the Berne 'Socialist' Conference. The Socialist Party and its members have only one duty, and this is to oppose most decidedly all movements which purpose to weaken the Bolshevist internationale."

New York Call, Dec. 1, 1918: "The soldiers coming back from Europe have the spirit of Bolshevism. Influenza was brought to America in ships, and the same ship will carry back the soldiers, who will carry a more dangerous disease to the capitalists of America."

Nobitnyk of New York, Feb. 10, 1919: "To break off all relations with the dying corpse and organize all American workers into one communist party which should include us and the comrades of the Socialists' radical party and the I. W. W. will be the first step forward."

Socialist Leaflet—"The war has ended! The war has begun! Workingmen of the world, unite! You have nothing to lose but your chains! You have the world to gain!"

Anarchistic Leaflet—"The senile fossils ruling the United States see red! Smelling their destruction, they have decided to check the storm by passing the deportation law affecting all foreign radicals. We American anarchists do not protest, for it is futile to waste any energy on feeble-minded creatures led by His Majesty Phonograph Wilson! Do not think that only foreigners are anarchists, we are a mighty number right here at home."

Colonel Raymond Robins, former head of the American Red Cross Mission to

Russia, reappeared before the committee today in order to reply to certain statements which Ambassador Francis, according to a Chicago newspaper, made on the witness stand last Saturday.

Colonel Robins made particular reference to a statement of Ambassador Francis regarding Colonel Robins's first visit to Lenine, following the overthrow of the Kerensky Government by the Bolsheviki. The Ambassador said that Colonel Robins had gone to Lenine in order to ascertain the principles of the new Government. According to the account of the testimony which Colonel Robins said he had read, it was made to appear that the Ambassador had testified that Colonel Robins approved of Bolshevism.

"The Ambassador was quoted," said Colonel Robins, "as stating that I approved of the principles of Bolshevism. Of course, that was a ridiculous statement, for I knew the principles of the Bolsheviki and had fought them, and was opposed to them, and am still utterly opposed to them. If the Ambassador made the statement quoted, it was a misstatement, without a scintilla of foundation in fact."

Colonel Robins then placed into the record a number of letters, cablegrams, and other documents, ten of them being, he said, documents which originated with the Ambassador. One of them, written in Russian, was in the handwriting of Lenine, and the others were commendatory letters or cables to Colonel Robins from Secretary of State Lansing and various officials of the Red Cross.

The Francis documents, some of which were copies of official cablegrams to the State Department, were introduced, Colonel Robins said, in order to prove that during the time he was in Russia under the Bolshevist rule he was the unofficial representative of the Ambassador to the Lenine-Trotzky Government. The witness was reminded by Senator King that the Ambassador had himself testified to that fact on Saturday and that, furthermore, Mr. Francis had said that his relations with Colonel Robins had always been pleasant.

Colonel Robins offered first a document, which he said was an exact copy of a document in his possession which was O. K.'d and initialed by David R. Francis, the notations on the document being in the Ambassador's handwriting. It was dated at the American Embassy in Petrograd, Jan. 2, 1918, and was headed, "Suggested Communication to the Commissary for Foreign Affairs." It read:

"At the hour the Russian people shall require assistance from the United States to repel the action of Germany and her allies you may be assured that I will recommend to the American Government that it render them all aid and assistance within its power. If upon the termination of the present armistice Russia fails to conclude a democratic peace through the fault of the Central Powers, and is compelled to continue the war, I shall urge upon my Government the fullest assistance to Russia possible, including the shipment of supplies and munitions for the Russian armies, the extension of credits, the giving of such advice and technical assistance as may be welcome to the Russian people in the service of the common purpose to obtain through the defeat of the German autocracy the effective guarantee of a lasting and democratic peace.

"I am not authorized to speak for my Government on the question of recognition, but that is a question which will of necessity be decided by actual future events. I may add, however, that if the Russian armies now under command of the people's commissaries commence and seriously conduct hostilities against the forces of Germany and her allies, I will recommend to my Government the formal recognition of the de facto Government of the people's commissaries."

"The circumstances of the prepara-

tion, O. K.-ing and initialing of this document," Colonel Robins stated, "were as follows:

"For some days I had been working under the verbal instructions of the Ambassador of the United States, in conferences with Lenine and Trotzky and other officers of the Soviet Government, seeking to prevent the signing of a German peace at Brest-Litovsk. To provide against the possibility of error in statement and subsequent refutation of my authorization to represent the Ambassador in the manner indicated by his verbal instructions, this document was prepared by me and submitted to him as a correct statement of his verbal instructions to me and was O. K.'d by him.

"Document, filed as 'Robins Document No. 2,' is an actual copy of an original in my possession, the notations on this document being in the handwriting of the American Ambassador, written therein in my presence in his private office in the American Embassy at Petrograd on the evening of the 2d of January, 1918.

"The document is as follows:

"(Note in lead pencil 'To Colonel Robins: This is substance of cable I shall send to department on being advised by you that peace negotiations are terminated and Soviet Government decided to prosecute war against Germany and Austria-Hungary.—D. R. F.')

"From sources which I regard as reliable I have received information to the effect that Bolshevist leaders fear complete failure of peace negotiations because of probable demands by Germany of impossible terms.

"Desire for peace is so fundamental and widespread that it is impossible to foretell the results of the abrupt termination of these negotiations, with only alternatives a disgraceful peace or continuance of war.

"Bolshevist leaders will welcome information as to what assistance may be expected from our Government if continuance of war is decided upon. Assurances of American support in such event may decidedly influence their decision.

"Under these circumstances and notwithstanding previous cables I have considered it my duty to instruct General Judson to informally communicate to the Bolshevist leaders the assurance that in case the present armistice is terminated and Russia continues the war against the Central Powers I will recommend to the American Government that it render all aid and assistance possible. I have also told Robins of Red Cross to continue his relations with Bolshevist Government, which are necessary for the present.

"Present situation is so uncertain and liable to sudden change that immediate action upon my own responsibility is necessary, otherwise the opportunity for all action may be lost.

"Nothing that I shall do will in any event give formal recognition to the Bolshevist Government until I have explicit instructions, but the necessity for informal intercourse in the present hour is so vital that I should be remiss if I failed to take the responsibility of action."

"This document," continued Colonel Robins, "was prepared by me and submitted to the Ambassador and O. K.'d by him, for the same reasons and purposes stated in the circumstances of Document 1."

Feared Intervention by Japan.

Other documents presented evidenced further the nature of Colonel Robins's confidential relationship as the unofficial representative of Mr. Francis in dealing with the Soviet Government. One of these had reference to reports of a projected Japanese invasion of Russia, and was cabled in cipher to the Secretary of State at Washington on

March 9, 1918, by the Ambassador. It read:

"Colonel Robins arrived at midnight. He returned from Petrograd after an important conference with Trotzky on the fifth. The result of that conference he wired to me in the code of the military mission, but as the mission had left for Petrograd, of which fact you were advised, with the code, I did not learn of the conference until the arrival of Robins an hour ago.

"Since R. left Petrograd, Moscow, and Petrograd Soviets have both instructed their delegates to the conference of March 12 to support the ratification of the peace terms. I fear that such action is the result of a threatened Japanese invasion of Siberia, which I have anticipated by sending Wright eastward. Trotzky told Robins that he had heard that such invasion was countenanced by the Allies and especially by America, and it would not only force the Government to advocate the ratification of the humiliating peace, but would so completely estrange all factions in Russia that further resistance to Germany would be absolutely impossible.

"Trotzky furthermore asserted that neither his Government nor the Russian people would object to the supervision by America of all shipments from Vladivostok in Russia and a virtual control of the operations of the Siberian Railway, but a Japanese invasion would result in non-resistance and eventually make Russia a German province. In my judgment a Japanese advance now would be exceedingly unwise and this midnight cable is sent for the purpose of asking that our influence may be exerted to prevent same."

"The deduction to be drawn from those documents," said Senator King, "is that the Ambassador was doing all that he could to prevent the ratification of the treaty of Brest-Litovsk?"

"Yes, and also to prevent Japanese intervention. We both did all we could at all times to prevent ratification of that treaty."

"My impression of the testimony of Ambassador Francis," said Senator King, "was that he recognized the value of your services and he stated that he had requested you to continue your relations with the Bolsheviki in order to assist him."

"Yes, there is no doubt but that was the Ambassador's view," added Senator Overman.

"I am glad to hear that," said Colonel Robins.

"As far as I can see there is no conflict between your testimony and that of the Ambassador," said Senator Nelson.

Again Colonel Robins said he was glad to hear it.

Colonel Robins, in a reference to the recall of Sir George Buchanan as British Ambassador to Russia, said that the recall followed a conference that Colonel William B. Thompson of New York had with Lloyd George in London.

"Colonel Thompson," said Colonel Robins, "left Russia at my urgent request. In London he conferred with Lloyd George and shortly thereafter Sir George Buchanan, the Ambassador, and General Knox, the British Military Attaché, were recalled and Bruce-Lockhart was sent to Russia as British High Commissioner. Mr. Bruce-Lockhart and myself were in entire accord in every respect regarding the situation in Russia."

Colonel Robins also said that the Committee on Public Information had offered to assist in financing a group of Bolsheviki, who were ordered into Austria for propaganda work. He said Edgar G. Sisson of the committee turned over 75,000 rubles to him for the Bolsheviki, but the latter declined to accept the money.

March 11, 1919

PALMER WARNS SOCIETIES.

Cannot Recognize Private Bodies Formed to Combat Sedition.

Special to The New York Times.

WASHINGTON, March 31.—The various private organizations formed during and since the war to detect offenders against the laws of the country and to aid in securing the prosecution of seditionists, agitators and others, will receive no sanction from the Department of Justice, so Attorney-General Palmer announced today in a statement which reads in part as follows:

"Espionage conducted by private individuals or organizations is entirely at variance with our theories of government, and its operation in any community constitutes a grave menace to that feeling of public confidence which is the chief force making for the maintenance of good order.

"Furthermore, on reflection it must be obvious to every one that for a Government agency to maintain any relationship whatever with private bodies engaged in this work would in the end result in impairing the confidence of the public in disinterestedness and impartiality of Government investigations.

"I fully realize the patriotic and high-minded motives with which these organizations have been formed, and which have animated them in making proffers of assistance to this Department, but I am constrained to say frankly that I fear the work of these private organizations may produce harmful results. I, therefore, feel compelled to instruct the various officials of this department not to enter into relationship with them."

April 1, 1919

TO PUNISH TERRORISM.

Michigan House Passes Bill Against Criminal Syndicalism.

LANSING, Mich., April 1.—The lower house of the State Legislature, in committee of the whole, early this morning approved passage of legislation which would make criminal syndicalism a felony, punishable by maximum fine of $5,000 and imprisonment of not more than ten years.

Criminal syndicalism is defined in the bill as advocacy of crime, sabotage, violence, or "other terrorism" to accomplish political or industrial ends.

April 2, 1919

FINDS BOLSHEVIKI IN FEDERAL POSTS

Senate Committee Discovers Propaganda Is Spread Among Employes of the Government.

MAKES PUBLIC A LETTER

Government Employe Still in Army Writes in Praise of "Pure Socialism" Now Enjoyed by Russians.

Special to The New York Times.

WASHINGTON, April 12.—Evidence of the spread of insidious Bolshevist propaganda among certain Government employes has come to the hands of the subcommittee of the Senate Judiciary Committee, which made an exhaustive inquiry into Bolshevism up to the end of the last Congress. From information in possession of the Committee, it appears that agents of Bolshevism are attempting to gain converts in various Governmental departments, and that some employes themselves are undertaking the work of spreading the propaganda.

What is regarded as a startling evidence of the effect of the Bolshevist propaganda was contained in an anonymous letter from a Government employe, still, he writes, wearing a soldier's uniform. This letter reached the sub-committee today. In it the writer accused the Senate Committee of having attempted to suppress free speech in its investigation. He asserted that "there are millions in this country" who feel that there is less liberty in America today than there is in Russia. Bolshevism, he said, was preferred by these millions to the "suppression" of free speech, which, he intimated, is being done through the espionage law.

Along with the letter the committee made known today that an employe in the Pension Bureau, within the last ten days, had been distributing Bolshevist propaganda to fellow employes. The employe, a clerk, circulated typewritten data, done upon Government bond stationery, and placed inside envelopes of the War Risk Bureau. Some of the employes to whom the propaganda was handed approved it, while others threw it aside, declining to read it.

The effort to win converts to Bolshevism among Government employes has been made known by the Senate Committee to Government officials. It is understood that the Government is making an investigation.

Here is the unsigned letter from the Government employe:

Dear Sir:—

I am going to hide behind a nom de plume and tell you what I would not essay to speak otherwise, because I wish to keep my personal liberty as long as I can.

First—Why don't you give the rights of free speech, free press and freedom of assembly back to the people of this country?

Second—Why do you apply the "scare-word" Bolshevism to the pure socialism of Russia?

Third—Do you have any reason to think that you can suppress the freedom of this country any more successfully than did the Czar and the Kaiser in their respective countries? Why can't any fair-minded person subscribe to the dictum of Albert Hays Williams—"Let everybody give his views of things generally; let him give them freely and without stint or fear, so that we may all see all the different sides of all questions and so form some plan of action that will be to the advantage of the majority"?

Fourth—Why don't you let Russia, the biggest nation on earth, decide its own destiny in accordance with Wilson's "point" to the effect that all nations shall be protected in their rights to determine their own destinies? Why are our "boys" being sent into the most democratic nation on earth today to crush democracy by shooting peasants, women, children and half-starved and half-frozen people?

Now, you might think I am some blear-eyed foreign fanatic. I am not. I am a native-born American and am wearing the uniform of the United States Army, although I am discharged. I am also a Government employe, and I could love the U. S. A. above all other States if she would only drop her autocratic and imperialistic practices that have sprung up during the war.

If you could only mingle with the "rabble" as I do you would learn that there are millions and millions in this country that say we have less liberty, freedom, and justice today than we did before this "war for democracy" was fought. All that these millions want is to be allowed to think and say whatever they honestly think, and decide for themselves what kind of Government they wish. So I say let us have all the "Bolshevist" propaganda and all other kinds we want and let us decide for ourselves which we wish to accept. Why should you arrogate to yourselves the right to decide whether we shall have this country run under socialists or not? You were placed in office to represent the will of the people, and not to form and mould that will.

In conclusion let me say that I know there are millions in this country who believe and feel just like I do on this matter, but your suppression is keeping them quiet. If you continue this suppression you will engender a spirit of hatred in the masses against the classes that will result in terrorism that will equal Russia.

You may call me a coward for not signing my name to this, but that is your privilege. I am just an everyday citizen, and I know too much to risk having my personal liberty taken away from me when it would not do any good for the toiling masses. But if the time ever comes when I can retaliate upon you for your suppressive methods, believe me, I will make the terrorism of Russia look like "baby play." If I were in power and told you that you could not say what you honestly thought unless it agreed with my ideas, would you be able to turn the other cheek if your positions should become reversed? You would be Christ-like if you could.

Give me liberty or give me death, that's what the world is crying for today. So you had better be warned in time that your suppressive methods will not succeed in the U. S. A. any more than they did in Russia and Germany.

Respectfully,
GOVERNMENT EMPLOYE.

In connection with the Bolshevist propaganda interest has been aroused here over the suspension this week by the Board of Education of Miss Alice Wood, a teacher in a public school, pending an investigation into a Bolshevist debate that occurred in her class room. Miss Wood denies having attempted to spread Bolshevist propaganda or having expressed sympathy for Bolshevism.

April 13, 1919

MIDNIGHT BOMBS FOR OFFICIALS IN 8 CITIES; BOMBERS DIE AT ATTORNEY GENERAL'S HOUSE

PALMER AND FAMILY SAFE

On Second Floor When Explosion Wrecked Lower Part of House.

TWO MEN BLOWN TO BITS

Parts of Bodies of Bombers or Passersby Projected Through Windows Across Street.

RED LITERATURE FOUND

Defiance of Authority and Acclaim of the Social Revolution Voiced.

Special to The New York Times.

WASHINGTON, Tuesday, June 3.— An attempt to blow up the residence of A. Mitchell Palmer, Attorney General of the United States and former Alien Property Custodian, was made at 11:15 o'clock last night when a bomb, which had been placed on the front doorstep exploded, blowing in the lower front of the house and also wrecking windows, or otherwise damaging, homes of other well-known persons living in the same part of the fashionable northwest section of the city.

Attorney General Palmer and his family were just retiring and being in the upper part of the house escaped injury. Apparently two men who may have been placing the bomb were blown to bits by the explosion, which seemingly was premature.

That the attempt was made by anarchists or Bolsheviki was evident from the fact that anarchist literature and leaflets were scattered around the street in front of the wrecked home of the Attorney General, at 2,132 R Street, N. W. The literature was in the form of leaflets.

All the front windows of the residence of Franklin D. Roosevelt, at No. 2,131, just across the street from the Palmer residence, were blown in, and Mr. Roosevelt, from whom some of the details were obtained by telephone by THE NEW YORK TIMES correspondent soon after midnight, said that he was standing on glass while talking over the telephone.

Palmer Family's Narrow Escape.

When communicated with also over the telephone Attorney General Palmer said:

"The explosion took place about 11:15 o'clock. I had been in the library on the first floor, and had just turned out the lights and gone upstairs with Mrs. Palmer to retire. I had reached the upper floor and undressed, but had not yet retired.

"I heard a crash downstairs as if something had been thrown against the front door. It was followed immediately by an explosion which blew in the front of the house. The door against which it was thrown leads into the library in which we had been sitting, and the part of the house blown in was in front of the library.

"The police and other agents who hurried to the residence to make an investigation found in the street in front of the house the limbs of a man who had been blow to pieces by the bomb. No papers were found and no evidence has yet been uncovered to indicate his identity, and it is not yet known whether the limbs were those of the person who threw the bomb or of a passerby. I hope sincerely that they were not portions of the body of some innocent person passing the house.

"No one inside the house was injured by the explosion. It cracked the upper part of the first story of the house, blew in the front of the lower floor, broke windows, and knocked pictures from the walls. The damage done was chiefly downstairs."

Fragments of Bodies Widely Scattered.

As has been mentioned, portions of the bodies of two men were found in various parts of the neighborhood. Mr. Roosevelt said that from the kind of socks worn by the men they appeared to be poorly dressed. While it is not known whether the fragments and dismembered parts formed the bodies of passersby or of the principals in the outrage, it appears to be the idea of the police that the bomb was prematurely exploded, and that it may have resulted in the death of those who placed it on the front doorstep of the Palmer house.

A fragment of one of the bodies was blown across R Street and was found on the doorstep of the Franklin D. Roosevelt residence. Another part of a body also blown across the street, went through a front window of the residence of Helmer H. Bryn, the Envoy Extraordinary and Minister Plenipotentiary from Norway to the United States, who lives at No. 2,137. This fragment fell near a cot on which a baby was sleeping.

Senator Claude A. Swanson, who lives at 2,136, two doors down the street from Assistant Secretary Roosevelt, found the front windows of his house blown in, and a fragment of one of the bodies was found in front of his house.

Representative Ira C. Copley of Illinois, who lives at 2,201 R Street, also had the front windows of his house smashed to smithereens. This showed the force of the explosion, for Mr. Copley lives in the block between Twenty-second Street and Sheridan Circle, while the Palmer house stands in the block lower down, between Twenty - first and Twenty - second Streets.

The residence of Edgar L. Hill, at 2,133 R Street, adjoining that of Mr. Roosevelt, was considerably damaged.

The home of James R. Ellerson, at 2,134, next to that of Attorney General Palmer's residence, was almost as badly damaged as that of Mr. Palmer.

The neighborhood, which was at once roped off by the police on their arrival, is in what is known as the West End of Washington, between Dupont and Sheridan Circles, where there are many fine mansions, in which live officials, army and navy officers, society folks, diplomats, and members of Congress.

Assistant Secretary Roosevelt, who was interviewed again later, said:

"The bomb or infernal machine— there was hardly enough left of it found so far to indicate its character —was in a dress suit case. Perhaps it was the intention to place it against the entrance of the door of the Attorney General's house, but it appears from the examination so far made of the scene, that the suit case had been placed on the third step of the front door steps.

"This was a heavy stone step. The force of the explosion blew it downward. It was the only one of the steps blown downward. The front door to the house was blown in and the façade is a wreck. The front sitting room, or library, was badly shattered.

"I had just placed my automobile in the garage and walked home when the explosion took place. It happened about three minutes after I had entered my house. I went over to the Attorney General's immediately after the explosion and was very much gratified to find that no one had been injured despite the terrific wreckage of the front of the house. Blackhand literature and dodgers were found among the wreckage of the neighborhood. These dodgers had been blown around the street."

Major Pullman, the Chief of Police, his Chief Inspector, Acting Captain Stall of the Tenth Police Precinct, and special agents of the Department of Justice were soon upon the scene and the reserves were ordered out throughout Washington for the protection of the homes of other officials.

As Attorney General Palmer was one of the members of the Cabinet to whom bombs found in the New York City Post Office on April 20 were addressed, and the attempt to blow up his house bore every evidence of having been the work of anarchists or Bolsheviki, it was suspected attempts would be made to place bombs in front of the homes of other officials.

The Anarchist Document.

About fifty of the anarchistic dodgers were found. They measured about six by ten inches in size, were printed in black ink on pink paper, and read as follows:

"PLAIN WORDS.

"The powers that be make no secret of their will to stop here in America the worldwide spread of revolution. The powers that be must reckon that they will have to accept the fight they have provoked.

"A time has come when the social question's solution can be delayed no longer; class war is on, and cannot cease but with a complete victory for the international proletariat.

" The challenge is an old one, O democratic ' lords of the autocratic republic. We have been dreaming of freedom, we have talked of liberty, we have aspired to a better world, and you jailed us, you clubbed us, you deported us, you murdered us whenever you could.

" Now that the great war, waged to replenish your purses and build a pedestal to your saints, is over, nothing better can you do to protect your stolen millions, and your usurped fame, than to direct all the power of the murderous institutions you created for your exclusive defense, against the working multitudes rising to a more human conception of life.

" The jails, the dungeons you reared to bury all protesting voices, are now replenished with languishing conscientious workers, and never satisfied, you increase their number every day.

" It is history of yesterday that your gunmen were shooting and murdering unarmed masses by the wholesale; it has been the history of every day in your régime; and now all prospects are even worse.

" Do you expect us to sit down and pray and cry? We accept your challenge, and mean to stick to our war duties. We know that all you do is for your defense as a class. We know also that the proletariat has the same

right to protect itself. Since their press has been suffocated, their mouths muzzled, we mean to speak for them the voice of dynamite, through the mouths of guns.

" Do not say we are acting cowardly because we keep in hiding; do not say it is abominable; it is war, class war, and you were the first to wage it under cover of the powerful institutions you call order, in the darkness of your laws, behind the guns of your bone-headed slaves.

" No liberty do you accept but yours; the working people also have a right to freedom and their rights. Our own rights we have set our minds to protect at any price.

" We are not many, perhaps more than you dream of, though, but are all determined to fight to the last, till not a man remains buried in your bastiles, till not a hostage of the working class is left to the tortures of your police system, and will never rest till your fall is complete, and the laboring masses have taken possession of all that rightly belongs to them.

" There will have to be bloodshed; we will not dodge; there will have to be murder; we will kill, because it is necessary; there will have to be destruction; we will destroy to rid the world of your tyrannical institutions.

" We are ready to do anything and

everything to suppress the capitalist class; just as you are doing anything and everything to suppress the proletarian revolution.

" Our mutual position is pretty clear. What has been done by us so far is only a warning that there are friends of popular liberties still living. Only now we are getting into the fight; and you will have a chance to see what liberty-loving people can do.

" Do not seek to believe that we are the Germans or the devil's paid agents: you know well we are class-conscious men, with strong determination and no vulgar liability. And never hope that your cops and your hounds will ever succeed in ridding the country of the anarchistic germ that pulses in our veins.

" We know how we stand with you and know how to take care of ourselves.

" Besides, you will never get all of us * * * and we multiply nowadays.

" Just wait and resign yourselves to your fate, since privilege and riches have turned your heads.

" Long live social revolution! Down with tyranny!

" THE ANARCHIST FIGHTERS."

June 3, 1919

SENATORS TELL WHAT BOLSHEVISM IN AMERICA MEANS

Overman Committee Not Only Reports on German and Radical Propaganda Here, But Investigates Effect of Doctrines If Made Effective—Makes Suggestions as to Legislation

THE Senate Judiciary Committee will submit this week its report on German propaganda and Bolshevism. The report has been compiled after an investigation extending over more than eight months and it is the first official United States Government report on Bolshevism.

That part which deals with German propaganda is a résumé of the various activities directed by Boy-Ed, von Papen, and other plotters. The report on Bolshevism deals with the subject from a new angle. After telling what Bolshevism is, it applies the system, theoretically, to the United States and points out what would happen if the American Government were replaced by one patterned after the " red terror " of Russia.

In compiling the report Major E. Lowry Humes, counsel for the committee, had at his disposal the diplomatic and other information on Russian conditions in the archives of the American and British Governments.

Study of Bolshevist " Law."

" In order to determine the possible connection and relation between the principles of government advocated by those claiming to exercise authority in Russia and the several activities now being carried on in the United States, it was deemed essential that a careful inquiry be made to determine the exact nature of the so-called principles of government now being applied in Russia," says the report.

" The record includes the Constitution and a compilation of many of the so-called laws in force in Russia from which the nature of the paper government can be determined, and the testimony of many eyewitnesses of the attempted application of this paper government discloses the character and nature of the actual government in practical operation. The investigation which

your committee has conducted convinces it that few of either the advocates or opponents, in this country, of the present Russian Socialist Federal Soviet Republic are familiar with the fundamenal principles upon which this Government is attempting to perpetuate itself. Consequently the agitation growing out of developments in Russia has largely degenerated into appeals to the prejudices and the animosities that are inherent in the selfish natures of most individuals and little or no appeal has been made to the intelligence of the people.

" It is therefore not surpring that the word ' Bolshevism ' has now become merely a generic term, and in America is nothing more than a slogan of the elements of unrest and discontent.

" By reason of their ignorance as to what Bolshevism as a code of political and social morals in Russia means, almost every dissatisfied element, from the radical anarchist to the theoretical idealist, has seiz d upon it as approaching something of a Utopian nature. It is interesting to note that every witness called before your committee as a champion of the cause of the principles of the Russian Socialist Federal Soviet Republic admitted that he or she had never read the Constitution of the Government of which he was the champion.

" The word Bolshevism has been so promiscuously applied to various political and social programs that we feel that it is of paramount importance that the delusions and misconceptions as to what it really is, as it exists today in Russia, should be, as far as possible, removed and that the people of the United States should be thoroughly informed as to just what this much-discussed institution really is, both in theory and in practice.

" Your committee is of the opinion that the best answer that can be given to the argument of the champions of this Russian institution is a true ex-

planation of its real nature and the actual principles upon which it is founded as well as the unavoidable consequences that would follow its adoption. The word Bolshevik is the name of the party that controls the Russian Socialist Federal Soviet Republic and that dictated its Constitution. We are, therefore, justified in using this name to identify the Constitution which it dictated and in accepting that Constitution and the laws that have been prescribed under it as the platform and program of Bolshevism."

Dictatorship of Small Minority.

Here follow facts descriptive of the Government established by Lenin and Trotzky. The report then continues:

" It is perhaps difficult to realize that it has been possible to perpetuate a dictatorship of such a small minority through the many months which have passed since it came into power. Without some understanding of the nature and character of the actual activities of the Bolsheviki the casual observer would be persuaded that the tyranny of this autocracy would in a short time bring down upon its head the wrath of the majority, who with reasonable effort would have no difficulty in overthrowing the usurpers. A study of the actual methods and practices of the dictatorship, however, clearly establishes the helplessness of the great mass of the Russian populace. The Bolsheviki have inaugurated a reign of terror unparalleled in the history of modern civilization, in many of its aspects rivaling even the inhuman savagery of the Turk and the terrors of the French Revolution. Under the evidence your committee has been compelled to impose the responsibility for this terrorism upon the Government itself rather than attribute it merely to the excesses of individuals and groups undisciplined and untrained in the personal liberty acquired by them with the overthrowing of the centralized autocratic Government of the old monarchistic régime.

" Terrorism and excesses in a State are either attributable to the encouragement of the State or the weakness and inability of the State to restrain the same. In Bolshevist Russia every instrument available for the exercise of force and power is in the possession of that Government, and those opposed to the Government or who fail to render it whole-hearted support are completely suppressed and absolutely powerless.

" All these facts negative the suggestion of the existence of a degree of weakness which makes the Government impotent to exercise the necessary restraint. On the contrary, every act of terrorism is justified by the affirmative pronouncement of the Bolshevist Government, either through its Constitution and laws or the authoritative utterances of its officials. The Government is founded upon class hatred, its avowed purpose is the extermination of all elements of society that are opposed to or are capable of opposing the Bolshevist Party. ' Merciless ' suppression and ' extermination ' of all classes except the present governing class are familiar slogans of the Bolsheviki, and confiscation is adopted as an essential instrument in the governmental formula.

Citizens Have No Rights.

" As a guarantee of its perpetuation in power its underlying policy is that ' the end justifies the means,' and in the application of this policy the Government denies the existence of any inalienable right in the Russian citizen and respects neither the right to life, liberty, or property. In its so-called declaration of rights the Government adopts a policy which it hopes will result in ' the destruction of the parasitic classes of society,' and as an aid to this end has decreed as an essential part of its fundamental law the principle of arming one class and disarming another, with a view of making the extermination and destruction more effective. In practice this Government has classified all of those people who fail to sympathize with and support the existing dictatorship as the bourgeoisie, and has proclaimed the doctrine that their refusal to bow to the edict of the dictatorship should be answered by ' violence toward the bourgeoisie.' A careful survey of the innumerable acts of violence and terrorism committed in Russia will fail to disclose scarcely a single offense that has not been participated in either by the Red Guard, by Commissars, or by others having an official and Governmental status."

Major Humes points out here that the Bolshevist dictators, with the aid of Lettish and Chinese mercenaries, German and Austrian prisoners, and criminals, secured, following the overthrow of the Kerensky Government, all arms and ammunition, foodstuffs, clothing and household goods, and precious metals in those parts of Russia that passed under the control of Lenin and Trotzky in November, 1917. He continues:

" The following of the Bolshevist Government being more numerous in the cities, and these, by reason of their concentration within more restricted territorial limits, being more readily led and dominated, it was prescribed by constitutional direction that representation from cities in the Government should be five times as great as the representation from the provincial districts. In other words, representation from cities is in the ratio of one to every 25,000 of the population, while from the rural districts and the territory of the peasants, who constitute a large percentage of the Russian population, representation is one to every 125,000 of the population. Even this discrimination did not adequately safeguard the domination of the Bolshevist minority. Disfranchisement of large groups of the population was necessary. By constitutional provision they denied the right to participate in the Government and disfranchised the following classes:

" (a) All persons employing others in connection with the conduct of their business.

" (b) All persons receiving interest, rents, dividends, or an income from financial or industrial enterprises.

" (c) All merchants, traders, and dealers.

" (d) All clergymen, priests, and employes of churches and religious bodies.

" (e) Certain persons connected with the Czar's Government, persons mentally afflicted and persons convicted of certain crimes against the Bolshevist Government.

" Even with these restrictions upon suffrage the Bolshevist Government has refused to undertake the election of a constituent assembly. The elections that are permitted are conducted under supervision of the Red Guard, and local bodies or Soviets that are not satisfactory to the dictatorship are removed and in some instances so-called commissars or officials of unquestioned loyalty to the Government are imported from the cities to govern the affairs of the political unit (the local Soviet) sought to be dominated according to the Bolshevist faith.

" Confiscation on a wholesale scale has been used as a means of undertaking to create and maintain tangible assets that could be used as the economic foundation upon which could be built the industrial and financial superstructure of the Bolshevist State. By constitutional edict and by a series of decrees issued by the dictatorship all land, forests, and natural resources of Russia have been confiscated by the Government in order that the Bolshevist Government may become the landlord of the entire population and exercise the control incident thereto. Where a man shall live and toil and till the soil is determined by the State, and the right to determine the nature and extent of each man's domicile, and the power to compel the migration of the peasant from the locality of his birth or adoption, even to the extent of separating families as the population of the various communities expands or contracts, is exercised by the Bolshevist Government through the laws which it has decreed for the control of the people.

How the Peasant Was Cheated.

" The alleged purpose of the seizure of land by the Government was that the right to the land might be transferred to the rank and file of the people of Russia in order that the individual Russian peasant might become the unrestrained and unrestricted architect of his own future economic development, but the methods adopted by the Bolsheviki have merely transferred the landlordship from the large landowners, and in many instances from the peasant groups themselves, to the Bolshevist Government, and the present control by that Government is not confined to the land itself, as was the control of the landowners under the old régime, but extends as well to the persons and even the tools, implements, and products of the peasants. The aged and infirm are deprived of all right to utilize and enjoy during their declining years the soil their efforts may have enriched, because their physical strength makes them powerless to perform all of the labor incident to its full cultivation. They thereupon become mere pensioners of the State. This system guarantees to the peasant only the present enjoyment of a given piece of land, and consequently only warrants him in so utilizing the beneficence of the State in according him the right to use the same as to insure the maximum present production to the exclusion of a scientific development that will inure to future advantage.

" In other words, an uncertain tenure is naturally accompanied by an exploitation rather than by a systematic development of the leasehold interest. Under this system, the peasant can never become the owner of the land he tills or of any other land. To aid

in the system and to establish a larger control of peasant activities by the Government the principle of confiscation has also been invoked in the case of all live stock and all agricultural implements, and as a consequence these essential instruments of land cultivation, these chattels necessary to the production of both meat and vegetable foodstuffs, have become without regard to the rights of former owners or the advantage to the individual of future ownership therein, the property of the Bolshevist Government, and the only right thereto that the peasant can in the future acquire is a use upon such terms and conditions as the Government may prescribe.

Industrial Stagnation.

" Confiscation, under the milder term of nationalization, has eliminated from all industrial establishments, such as factories, mills, and mines the business acumen and scientific methods necessary to successful operation and competitive methods. The absolute control of their operation and management is placed in the hands of the employes. This has been followed by the stagnation of the industrial life of the country, and even those nationalized industries which have been able to operate under Government control have operated at an enormous percentage of loss, the deficiencies being met from the unlimited issue of fiat paper money printed by the Government. The nationalization of the enterprises essential to the production and delivery of raw materials has so handicapped their production as to restrict the quantity of raw materials available for the maintenance of industrial enterprises, and the whole economic condition of Russia has made it impossible to secure relief from foreign sources. These industrial conditions can only continue so long as the Government can succeed in monopolizing the means of subsistence, maintain an adequate military force to enforce the decrees of the dictatorship, and force the recognition of worthless fiat paper money as the basis of its financial system.

" As the economic formula of the Bolsheviki prescribes the confiscation of the property rights of others, likewise it proclaims the doctrine of the repudiation of financial obligations and the debts of Russia have been renounced. Repudiation is also invoked to secure the Government against the incumbrances upon and liabilities of the property and assets of the enterprises, land and chattels seized by it under its confiscation program.

" The destruction of all effective military and naval power and the removal of the leadership of capable officers was essential to the establishment of a powerful dictatorship as well as to the complete abandonment of the eastern front during the war.

Revolutionary Tribunals.

" All of the established courts and judicial institutions have been abolished and in their place have been created revolutionary tribunals. Under the dictatorship these new judicial tribunals disregard all laws that ' contradict the revolutionary conception of right.' In actual operation these revolutionary tribunals have tried and condemned men in their absence. No right to bail is recognized and the penalty imposed depends largely upon the caprice of the court. The death penalty, the re-establishment of which under the Provisional Government was vociferously denounced by the Bolsheviki, has been invoked for all sorts of crimes and misdemeanors. In fact, the procedure in the courts is a mere travesty on justice and most summary in its nature.

" Every activity of the Bolshevist Government indicates clearly the antipathy of the Bolsheviki toward Christianity and the Christian religion. Its program is a direct challenge to that religion. The Christian church and Bolshevism cannot both survive the program that is being developed by the Russian dictatorship and which it is undertaking to extend throughout the world. Not only have they confiscated all church property, real and personal, but they have established the right of anti-religious propaganda as a constitutionally recognized institution. Church and school have been divorced even to the extent of suppressing the Sunday school and the teaching of all religious doctrines in public, either in schools or educational institutions of any kind, is expressly forbidden. Religion can only be taught or studied privately. All church and religious organizations are prohibited from owning property of any kind. All recognition of a Supreme Being in both governmental and judicial oaths is abolished. The clergy and all servants or employes of church bodies are expressly disfranchised and deprived of all right to hold public positions.

"Bolshevism accords to the family no such sacred place in society as modern civilization accords to it. Conflicting reports have been passing current during the last few months relative to the nationalization of women by the new Russian Government. Two or three local Soviets have apparently thus degraded the womanhood of their particular districts, but the central Government has refrained from adopting any such policy in the whole nation. They have, however, promulgated decrees relating to marriage and divorce which practically establishes a state of free love. Their effect has been to furnish a vehicle for the legalization of prostitution by permitting the annulment of the marriage bonds at the whim of the parties, recognizing their collusive purposes as a ground for the severance of the matrimonial state.

No Freedom of Speech.

"The freedom of the press and of speech, though heralded by the advocates of Bolshevism as necessary to the intelligent participation of the people in popular government, has been abrogated in Russia, and by the usual confiscatory method of the accepted formula all of the mechanical devices and materials necessary for the publication of periodicals and all places of meeting and public assemblage have been seized by the Bolshevist Government.

"The apparent purpose of the Bolshevist Government is to make the Russian citizen, and especially the women and children, the wards and dependants of that Government. Not satisfied with the degree of dependency incurred by the economic and industrial control assumed by its functionaries, it has destroyed the moral obligation of the father to provide, care for and adequately protect the child of his blood and the mother of that child against the misfortunes of orphanhood and widowhood. To accomplish this it has by decree expressly abolished and prohibited all right of inheritance, either by law or will. Upon death all of the decedent's estate is confiscated by the State, and all heirs who are physically incapable of working become pensioners of the State to the extent that the assets confiscated by the Government make such pensions possible.

Program of Bolshevism.

"The salient features which constitute the program of Bolshevism as it exists today in Russia and is presented to the rest of the world as a panacea for all ills may be summarized as follows:

(1.) The repudiation of democracy and the establishment of a dictatorship.
(2.) The confiscation of all land and the improvements thereon.
(3.) The confiscation of all forests and natural resources.
(4.) The confiscation of all live stock and all agricultural implements.
(5.) The confiscation of all banks and banking institutions and the establishment of a State monopoly of the banking business.
(6) The confiscation of all factories, mills, mines, and industrial institutions and the delivery of the control and operation thereof to the employes therein.
(7) The confiscation of all churches

and all church property, real and personal.
(8) The confiscation of all newspapers and periodicals and all mechanical facilities and machinery used in the publication thereof.
(9) The seizure and confiscation of all public meeting places and assembly halls.
(10) The confiscation of all transportation and communication systems.
(11) The confiscation of the entire estate of all decedents.
(12) The monopolizing by the State of all advertisements of every nature, whether newspapers, periodicals, handbills, or programs.
(13) The repudiation of all debts against the Government, and all obligations due the non-Bolshevist elements of the population.
(14) The establishment of universal compulsory military service regardless of religious scruples and conscientious objections.
(15) The establishment of universal compulsory labor.
(16) The abolition of the Sunday school and all other schools and institutions that teach religion.
(17) The absolute separation of churches and schools.
(18) The establishment, through marriage and divorce laws, of a method for the legalization of prostitution, when the same is engaged in by consent of the parties.
(19) The refusal to recognize the existence of God in its governmental and judicial proceedings.
(20) The conferring of the rights of citizenship on aliens without regard to length of residence or intelligence.
(21) The arming of all so-called "toilers," and the disarming of all persons that had succeeded in acquiring property.
(22) The discrimination in favor of residents of cities and against residents of the rural districts through giving residents of cities five times as much voting power as is accorded to residents of rural districts in such elections as are permitted.
(23) The disfranchisement of all persons employing any other person in connection with their business.
(24) The disfranchisement of all persons receiving rent, interest, or dividends.
(25) The disfranchisement of all merchants, traders, and commercial agents.
(26) The disfranchisement of all priests, clergymen, or employes of churches and religious bodies.
(27) The denial of the existence of any "inalienable rights in the individual citizen.
(28) The establishment of a judicial system exercising autocratic power, convicting persons and imposing penalties in their absence, and without opportunity to be heard, and even adopting the death penalty for numerous crimes and misdemeanors.
(29) The inauguration of a reign of fear, terrorism, and violence.

"This is the program that the revolutionary elements and the so-called 'Parlor Bolshevik' would have this country accept as a substitute for the Government of the United States, which recognizes that 'all men are created equal,' and that 'life, liberty, and the pursuit of happiness' are the inalienable rights of all its citizens. This is the formula they would have adopted to supersede the Government which was established by all the people of the United States 'in order to form a more perfect union, establish justice, insure domestic tranquillity,' and 'promote the general welfare.' The mere recital of the program is a sufficient denunciation of it, and of the individuals and groups which advocate and defend it.

Blow to Civilization.

"During modern times the effort of civilization has been directed to lifting mankind to the highest possible level of intelligence and social material wellbeing, in order to attain the highest degree of social equality between man and man. For the first time since the Dark Ages has an organized government undertaken to invoke a process of equalization by establishing as the basis of social equality the minimum rather than the maximum degree of existing educational, industrial, social, and moral efficiency, yet such is the policy of the Bolshevist Government. It recognizes that the psychology of even the most illiterate elements of the Russian people is such that it cannot perpetuate this doctrine in practice unless the same reactionary methods of equalization are simultaneously destroying the social fabric, the efficiency, the individual initiative, the ambition, and the material prosperity of the peoples of all other

nations, whose competition and accomplishments would necessarily result in odious and destructive comparisons. Not content therefore in fathering in Russia this retrograde method of establishing the equality of mankind on the basis of the lowest strata of society, it has undertaken to arouse in the United States and in all other countries resentment, rancor, and hatred against those elements of society which have, by reason of their aptitude, perseverance, industry, and thrift attained that superior degree of intelligence and prosperity that has made possible the accomplishments of twentieth century civilization. The effort of progressing civilization has always been the uplifting of man to a higher and higher plane of living and a loftier place in society.

"The activities of the Bolsheviki constitute a complete repudiation of modern civilization and the promulgation of the doctrine that the best attainment of the most backward member of society shall be the level at which mankind shall find its final and victorious goal. The pulling down of the progressive rather than the lifting up of the retrogressive is presented as the doctrine of their new kind of civilization. To carry this message to the uttermost parts of the earth they have appropriated enormous sums of money, and, incidentally, their process of equalization in Russia was promoted by the starvation which the funds thus expended might have been utilized to alleviate. Their messengers and their friends have afflicted this country, and their new civilization has been represented as Utopian in its nature. Many well-disposed persons have been deceived into the belief that they were promoting a social welfare movement in advocating it. They have even given their substance that it might be perpetuated and extended.

"Yet, while these people who have been popularly called 'parlor Bolsheviki' are contributing to these Bolshevist agents, these same agents are appealing to the hatred and the lowest instincts of the more ignorant elements of the population, reinforced by the criminally inclined, to whom the doctrine of confiscation furnishes a form of legalized robbery and a means of livelihood without physical or mental effort, to rise en masse and destroy our civilization and the so-called bourgeoisie with whom, of course, must be classed these same 'parlor Bolsheviki' who are assisting, by lending funds and respectability to the movement, in bringing the temple down upon their own heads.

Rallying Cry Here.

"It is significant, however, that in the United States only a portion of the so-called radical revolutionary groups and organizations accept in its entirety the doctrine of the Bolsheviki. They have, however, all seized upon Bolshevism as a rallying cry and are undertaking to unite all of these elements under that banner for the purpose of accomplishing the initial step in their common formula, to wit, the overthrow of existing governmental institutions and the complete demoralization of modern society. With this accomplished each group hopes that it can muster sufficient strength to maintain a supremacy in the new social order and invoke the policies of its particular creed. Most of these groups accept the common ground that forcible, as distinguished from political, action should be used as the instrument to secure the overthrow of the present Government, and in so doing defy and repudiate the democratic form of government which guarantees under our Constitution the rule of the majority. Like the Bolsheviki in Russia, these groups recognize in the destruction of life, property, and personal security the necessary preliminary to the establishment of a Government founded upon the violence of the minority. They realize that riot, disorder, and hunger breed hatred, blood lust, and desperation, and that without these mankind cannot be driven to the use of force to accomplish an end attainable by lawful and peaceable political methods under the existing Government.

"The radical revolutionary elements in this country and the Bolshevist Government of Russia have, therefore, found a common cause in support of which they can unite their forces. They are both fanning the flame of discontent and endeavoring to incite revolution. Numerous newspapers are openly advocating revolution. Literature and circular matter demanding a resort to violence are being widely circulated. Bombs and high explosives have been used in many parts of the country in an attempt to inaugurate a reign of terror and to accomplish the assassination of public officials. The demonstration of the consequences of this movement in Russia, no matter how graphic the description, is a distant, far-away picture to the average citizen of the United States. While entertaining and perhaps amusing him, much as the novel in modern fiction does, it fails to impress him as an actual existing institution, in a world growing smaller and smaller through the accomplishments in transportation and communication, that must be considered and met as an actuality. To understand and realize its real consequences it must be brought home to the citizen and applied to the life and institutions which he knows.

What It Would Mean.

"With a view, therefore, of concretely illustrating just what this new social order would accomplish if transplanted into the political, educational, industrial, and religious life of the United States, attention is invited to the following unavoidable consequences:

(1) The application of force and violence, the shedding of blood and the destruction of life and property, the common incidents of all revolutions, and all this to destroy a democratic form of government under which the majority can secure just the kind of government that it desires. The advocacy of revolutionary methods is an admission, therefore, that minority rather than majority rule is the goal sought to be attained.

(2) To make possible the control of the minority as the dictators of the majority, the disfranchisement of millions of substantial, patriotic citizens who would fall in the so-called bourgeois or capitalistic class. This would deprive of the right to participate in affairs of government—

(a) Millions of farmers, merchants, and manufacturers, both large and small, employing persons in the conduct of their business, and all professional and business men utilizing the services of a clerk, bookkeeper, or stenographer.

(b) All persons receiving interest on borrowed money or bonds, rent from real estate or personal property, and dividends from stock of any kind.

(c) All traders, merchants, and dealers, even though tney do not employ another person in the conduct of their business.

(d) All preachers, priests, janitors, and employes of all churches and religious bodies.

It is apparent with the millions of persons falling into these several classes, disfranchised and deprived of all right to participate in the affairs of government, accompanied with the immediate enfranchisement of all aliens who do not fall within these prohibited classes, and the opening of the doors of all prisons and penitentiaries, the domination of the criminal and most undesirable alien elements of the country would be a comparatively easy matter. To simplify the question of this control, however, the substantial rural portion of the population would be further suppressed and restricted, and under the revolutionary formula the voting power of the cities would be five times as great as that of the rural communities, the ratio of the representation in cities being 1 to every 25,000 of the population, while that of the rural districts would be only 1 to every 125,000 of the population. In the United States the rural population under the 1910 census was considerably in excess of the urban. We must also remember that the application of the formula would include the disarming of all disfranchised classes and the arming to the teeth of these criminal and alien elements.

(3) It would result in the confiscation by the Government thus constituted of the land of the United States including 6,361,502 farms, of which 62.1 per cent., or 3,948,722 farms, are owned in fee by the farmers who cultivate them and represent the labor and toil of a lifetime. On the farms of the United States there are improvements, machinery, and live stock to the value of $40,991,449,090, [census of 1910,] all of which would be confiscated with the land. The confiscation program would include the more than 275,000 manufacturing establishments, including the $22,790,980,000 of invested capital, much of which is owned by the small investor whose livelihood depends upon the success of the respective enterprises. The confiscation would also include 203,432 church edifices. Forests aggregating 555,000,000 acres would be seized by the Government and an annual product of $1,375,000,000 would come under the control of the dictatorship. Dwellings to the number of 17,805,845, of which 9,093,675 are owned in fee, with 5,984,248 entirely free from debt, would be confiscated and the owners dispossessed at the pleasure of the Government.

(4) Although clamoring loudly for a free and unrestricted press the revolutionary program would require the seizure and confiscation of the 22,896 newspapers and periodicals in the United States, together with all mechanical equipment necessary for their publication, and a control and ownership of the public press by the Government.

(5) Complete control of all banking institutions and their assets is an essential part of the revolutionary program, and the 31,492 banks in the United States would be taken over by the Government and the savings of millions, including 11,397,553 depositors drawing interest on accounts in savings banks, and consequently belonging to the so-called bourgeois or capitalistic class, jeopardied.

(6) One of the most appalling and far-reaching consequences of an application of Bolshevism in the United States would be found in the confiscation and liquidation of its life insurance companies. There is 20 per cent. more life insurance in force in this country than in all the rest of the world, and nine-tenths of it is mutual insurance. Almost 50,000,000 life insurance policies, representing nearly $30,000,000,000 of insurance, the substantial protection of the women and children of the nation, would be rendered valueless.

(7) The atheism that permeates the whole Russian dictatorship is clearly reflected in the activities of their revolutionary confrères in the United States, and in their publications they have denounced our religion and our God as "lies." This gives added significance to the revolutionary attitude toward the Christian Church and the Christian religion. The prohibition of religious schools and the teaching or studying of religion, except in private, would necessitate the abolition of 194,759 Sunday schools in the United States and a great number of seminaries, colleges, and universities; 19,935,890 Sunday school scholars would be deprived and prevented from enjoying the institution that has become an important part of their lives and is one of the great moral influences of the nation. Catholic schools, colleges, and seminaries to the number of 6,681 would be suppressed. Church property of the value of $1,676,600,582 would be confiscated and 41,926,854 (census of 1916) members of 227,487 church organizations would be subjected to the domination of an atheist dictatorship.

"Notwithstanding the fact that every champion and defender of Bolshevism that testified before your committee unequivocally admitted that the Bolshevist formula was not adaptable to the economic and social life of the United States, they and their co-evangelists persist in their appeals to the passion of the people in an attempt to provoke discontent and hatred. In co-operation with the revolutionary elements, destruction of existing social and governmental institutions by violent methods is being promoted. They must, therefore, be condemned as the mere champions of discontent and disorder, offering no practical and acceptable ideal, as they profess to have, with which to soften and appease the wrath that they are undertaking to arouse.

General Statement.

"The testimony taken before this committee having been printed, a further review thereof is deemed unnecessary. A careful consideration of this record discloses certain well-defined abuses prejudicial to the best interests of the nation and calculated to undermine and destroy our form of government. The nation having engaged in the greatest war in history with the purpose of saving the world for democracy, now emerges from that struggle confronted with the paramount duty of preserving democracy for the world.

"The disclosures before this committee concerned (a) the political activities of the liquor interests in their effort to control and dominate elections and public officials, (b) the propaganda of the agents, representatives, and sympathizers of a foreign Government, the form of which and whose purposes, industrial, commercial, and political, were incompatible with and antagonistic to the form, ideals, and purposes of the Government of the United States, and (c) Bolshevism as it exists in Russia and the activities of its champions in the country. No useful purpose is to be served by reviewing and recounting the reprehensible activities of either of the elements whose conduct has been the subject matter of this inquiry. A perusal of the testimony furnishes adequate evidence of it. This testimony embodies such an exposure of all of these elements as to justify fully the investigation.

"The activities brought to the attention of the committee are so startling, however, that we believe that the real advantage of the inquiry will be lost unless Congress profits from the knowledge thus obtained by undertaking by appropriate legislation to make impossible a repetition of these activities, either on the part of the offenders who have been under investigation, and the many whose activities are still continuing, or by others who at some future time may seek to undermine the Government or pervert the popular will by the adoption of similar methods against which the Federal statutes seem to provide no adequate safeguard.

"With this end in view, therefore, this committee invites attention to certain abuses which are clearly established by the record of its hearings and a summary of proposed legislation the immediate adoption of which it earnestly recommends.

I.

"That millions of dollars have been expended in elections, in connection with which Federal officers were voted for by special interests through organizations of their own creation and by methods of their own adoption. That secrecy has surrounded these expenditures and the activities thereby induced. That the publicity and accounting sought for all political expenditures by the Corrupt Practices acts of the Federal and the several State Governments has been largely defeated. That the Federal corrupt practices statutes are entirely inadequate to meet present-day political methods and are easily evaded without involving a violation of the statute. Any effective Corrupt Practices act must provide—

(1) For full publicity of all receipts and expenditures intended to influence in any way the result of an election.

(2) To bring under legal control and supervision every committee and organization participating in a political activity.

(3) To perpetuate and preserve for a reasonable time a complete record of the financial transactions of all individuals, candidates, committees, and organizations.

(4) To define clearly the purposes and activities for which money can be legally expended.

(5) To require publicity that will unequivocally fix responsibility for all paid and inspired advertising or publicity matter used and intended either openly or secretly to affect the result of an election.

II.

"Newspapers printed in both English and foreign languages have been subsidized directly and indirectly for the purpose of undertaking to influence the minds, thoughts, and actions of the people of the United States without disclosing in any way the commercial or political influence financially interested. It is of great importance that every facility should be afforded to all elements of society and to every commercial industrial, social, religious, and educational interest to present openly and frankly its views on every subject not aimed at the impairment of the sovereignty of the nation or in disparagement of our form of government as established by the Constitution. But as the right to present these various contentions should be preserved as inalienable, so the public to whom the appeal is made have an inalienable right to know and to be advised as to who is the spokesman of a given cause. Newspapers have become such an educational medium that the public should be afforded an ample opportunity to know just who their instructors are.

"The act of Congress of Aug. 24, 1912, undertook to accomplish this, but in the light of experience it is now clearly established that this act is inadequate. It permits of the adoption of many subterfuges by which its purpose is defeated though its spirit is violated without the commission of a legal breach of its prohibitions.

"It is the opinion of this committee that this act should be amended and made more effective in several important particulars.

III.

"The foreign-language press of the country as now conducted has the effect and in many instances is inspired with the purpose of discouraging the assimilation of the foreign elements with the American people and has been utilized by special interests for political and propaganda purposes. The financial condition of many of these newspapers has made them the easy and cheap victims of designing persons and interests whose financial advantage is best secured by retarding the Americanization of the alien and limiting him to the use of the foreign-language paper as his sole source of information. The foreign-language press exerts a greater influence upon its readers than an English newspaper does because of the limited educational facilities of the persons who can only read and talk in such foreign tongues; and consequently the subsidization and domination of this press are proportionately more vicious in their effects than similar practices would be in the case of English newspapers.

"The experience of the last few years has clearly demonstrated the necessity of Americanizing the residents of this country, and especially those who from time to time are assuming the responsibility of citizenship. The aliens now residing within our borders or hereafter immigrating to our shores must either be assimilated by the Americans or they will be held together in their several nativistic groups, each group adhering to its own language and customs, with the consequent adherence, either consciously or unconsciously, to the land of their nativity. While it must be recognized that during the time when they are merely the guests of this nation a knowledge of their native language is all that can be expected, the Government is justified in requiring that before their status is changed to one of citizenship and before they can be permitted to participate in the government of the United States there should be some evidence at least of a purpose on their part toward that assimilation which is essential to the unity of purpose and substantial adherence to our institutions necessary to the healthy development of the nation.

"Foreign-language newspapers are a danger to the country unless they are utilized to assist in the assimilation of the alien element and to aid in the process of Americanization which is essential to the healthy development of the population into a homogeneous whole. This much-sought-for Americanization would be impeded by either depriving the alien of the educational value of a newspaper in the only language he can read or by withholding from him proper aid and facility for learning the English language and failing to encourage him to acquire the educational advantages incident to the mastering of the language of his adopted country. With this in mind, therefore, this committee recommends legislation to control and regulate the printing of foreign-language publications in this country.

IV.

"For a number of years prior to our entry into the world war agents of the German Government persistently carried on a great propaganda in the United States, the purpose of which was to promote the interests of the German Government and to create a sentiment in this country in favor of that Government to the prejudice of this nation. Every activity which tended to weaken our Government or to arouse antagonisms that would demoralize the unity and morale of our population and every movement that was aimed at involving us in foreign disputes or domestic difficulties was encouraged and frequently financed by the agents and representatives of the German Government.

"Today the forces of anarchy and violence are utilizing the financial resources plundered by them from the European people they have succeeded in exploiting, to import into this country money, literature, and hired agents for the purpose of promulgating the doctrine of force, violence, assassination, confiscation, and revolution.

"As an effect of these activities there has appeared in this country a large group of persons who advocate the overthrow of all organized government, and especially the Government of the United States, who favor revolutionary movements, repudiate the Constitution of the United States, and refuse to respect our national emblem and our governmental institutions. There are found among the leaders of this group many aliens who unhesitatingly abuse the hospitality which this country has extended to them and who because of that leadership are able to retard the real Americanization of the more ignorant residents possessing similar racial characteristics. These persons encourage and maintain a solidarity of the people of the several foreign tongues which is used to create and incite a class hatred that is quickly absorbed by and incorporated into the revolutionary movement led by them. The alien element in this country is the most susceptible and is the first to adopt violence as an effective weapon for supremacy.

"More reprehensible than the alien element is that class of American citizens, whether native born or naturalized, who, having obligated themselves to support and defend the Constitution of the United States, lightly disregard their responsibilities and promulgate the doctrine that the form of Government established by the Constitution should be overthrown and that a Government responsive to a class rather than to all the people should be forcibly substituted therefor. It is a significant fact that almost without exception the persons in this country who are today advocating revolution and violence and all of the suffering, pain, and bloodshed incident to such a movement, have during the great struggle of the last two years undertaken to handicap, check, and obstruct in every way possible the military operations of this Government under the pretext that their consciences would not permit them to take the life of their fellow-men even in war. The destruction of life, property, and Government has no horrors to them when directed toward the overthrow of the Government of the United States, but the use of force in defense of our country they conscientiously object to.

"Prior to the enactment of the statute of June 15, 1917, as amended by the statute of May 16, 1918, our Government was without laws adequate even to protect its own sovereignty. It is indeed unfortunate that this legislation should have been called an espionage act. Much of the complaint and criticism directed at this act was aimed more at the word used to designate it than at the text of the statute. Many of the provisions of this act are applicable only during time of war, and consequently the restoration of peace will leave the Government of the United States more helpless, and because of the growth of the revolutionary movement as a result of the world war more powerless, than it found itself prior to our entrance into that struggle.

"It is therefore imperative that there be enacted before the re-establishment of peace an act adequately protecting our national sovereignty and our established institutions.

V.

"That the American people have been victimized and deceived by the activities of special interests and the subtle practices of designing individuals, some of them the agents and representatives of foreign Governments, through the use of organizations having dignified and respectable names, which completely disarm all suspicion of the ulterior purposes of those who inspired their organization. By the use of euphonious names given to supposedly patriotic, idealistic, and charitable organizations, patriotic and philanthropic citizens have been innocent victims of conniving representatives of foreign interests and Governments and have been exploited by corrupt and dishonest elements. The Government of the United States long ago undertook by appropriate legislation to protect society from the fraudulent use of the mails commercially. The public has a right to some protection from deception being practiced by these mushroom organizations that have become so common.

"No legitimate organization is ashamed of its paternity, its purposes, or its activities, and a proper registration of all voluntary associations or organizations appealing to the public through the mails for popular approval, financial support, and the propagation of its notions of government, sociology, benevolence, or what not is a reasonable requirement that can be utilized to provide some security to a much imposed upon public, and legislation is therefore recommended to this end.

VI.

"Never have the Federal statutes provided adequate security against an unlawful and promiscuous use of high explosives. During the period of American neutrality, the representatives of the German Government, as well as many criminally inclined residents of our own country, resorted to the use of explosives for the destruction of life, property, and transportation facilities, and except for the provision in the Interstate Commerce act, which prohibited the shipping or carrying of explosives in interstate commerce, the offenses could not be reached by the Federal Government, and when reached under this act the penalties were entirely incommensurate with the offense. The act of Congress of Oct. 6, 1917, entitled ' An act to prohibit the manufacture, distribution, storage, use, and possession in time of war of explosives, providing regulations for the safe manufacture, distribution, storage, use, and possession of the same, and for other purposes,' was enacted by Congress as a purely war statute, and becomes inoperative upon the restoration of peace. The efficacious effect of this legislation during the period of the war has not only justified its enactment as a war statute, but has impressed upon the people of the country the merit of its provision in times of peace as well as in times of war.

"All law-abiding persons recognize the necessity of controlling and regulating the manufacture, distribution, and possession of the instruments of death and destruction relied upon by the criminal and lawless elements of society. The obligation of the Federal Government to protect the lives and property of its citizens would not be fully performed were Congress to permit the act of Oct. 6, 1917, to die by limitation without enact-

ing in its place a peace-time measure.

"The committee wishes to again express its thanks to Major Humes, Captain Lester, and Mr. Benham for their untiring zeal and great ability in aiding the committee in securing the great mass of testimony which, in our opinion, will be most useful to the public.

"All of which is respectfully submitted.
"LEE S. OVERMAN, Chairman.
"WILLIAM H. KING.
"JOSIAH O. WOLCOTT.
"KNUTE NELSON.
"THOMAS STERLING."

June 15, 1919

SOCIALISTS ASSAIL 'LEFT WING' PARTY

Executive Committee Says That a Plot Exists to Wreck the Regular Organization.

SEES "REIGN OF TERROR"

Statement Gives Reason for Expulsion of Michigan Body from the Party Councils.

A plot to wreck the Socialist Party and to substitute an organization composed of foreign language revolutionary federations, committed to the overthrow of the Government by force and violence if necessary, is charged against the so-called "Left Wing" Socialists in a statement issued by the National Executive Committee of the Socialist Party organization which became public yesterday.

The legislative committee investigating seditious activities last Saturday raided the headquarters of the "Left Wing" Socialists in West Twenty-ninth Street, as well as the East Fourth Street headquarters of the Russian Branch of the I. W. W., another element entering into the left wing movement. In both raids much frankly revolutionary propa-

ganda literature was seized.

The statement gives the reason for the expulsion of the Michigan State organization of the Socialist Party from the party councils, together with the Hungarian, Lettish, Lithuanian, Polish, South Slavic, Russian and Ukrainian branches.

"This action," the statement says, "is due to a defiance of national conventions, national referendums, the national Constitution, and decisions of the National Executive Committee. Accompanying this defiance and aggravating the offense was an incredible series of acts hitherto unknown in the Socialist Party in this country. Evidence in our possession indicates an organized and systematic attempt of nation-wide scope to capture the party organization by fair means or foul. An opera bouffe reign of terror was inaugurated in many locals or branches. Their plans were made to vote the whole foreign language federations for a slate, using the foreign language newspapers in a disgusting campaign of slander against the party and its elected officials. The party and its officials were helpless against the cowardly tirade, as we could not know what was taking place."

The canceling of the charter of the Michigan State organization the statement declares due to action taken by the Socialist State Convention in Michigan proposing the expulsion of any member, local, or branch advocating legislative reforms or supporting any organization advocating such reforms. After the Michigan organization thus definitely had turned its back on a program providing for the achievement of Socialist aims through processes of peaceful evolution, the Secretary of the organization was called before the Executive Committee, but refused to answer any questions.

An "emergency" national convention of the Socialist Party has been summoned to meet in Chicago

on Aug. 30, for the purpose of passing upon the action of the National Executive Committee in purging the party of its unruly elements. Among Socialists of both wings there is a strong belief that the split is final and that the solidarity of the party this Fall and in the Presidential, Congressional, and State elections next year is out of the question.

A national convention of the Left Wing Socialists, which has been in progress in this city since Saturday, is regarded by the regulars as ample indication that the revolutionary element of the party has left the fold for good and is determined to set up housekeeping for itself. The Left Wing Convention, which is meeting behind closed doors at the Manhattan Lyceum in East Fourth Street, was summoned for the purpose of effecting permanent organization and drafting a Red Wing Constitution and set of bylaws.

The bitterness of the factional fight and the wide divergence of "regular" and "left wing" policies are reflected in quotations from Left Wing pronunciamentos cited in the statement of the National Executive Committee. It was in this State that the first clash occurred after the New York local had expelled some twenty English-speaking Assembly District organization and foreign language branches. The Socialist Party of Queens went out in a body and joined the Left Wing. After the charter had been revoked, the Lithuanian, Lettish, Ukrainian, Hungarian, and South Slavic Federations proclaimed jointly that they had endorsed the Left Wing program and declared that they could take no orders from either State, City, or National Executive Committees.

June 24, 1919

LEFT WING PUT OUT BY SOCIALIST PARTY

Radicals Refused Admittance to Chicago Convention— Threaten to Join Communist Party.

JOHN REED LEADING THEM

Berger Says They Are Anarchists and That Chicago Meeting Will Continue Without Them.

CHICAGO, Aug. 30.—Strife developed in the ranks of the Socialist Party which presaged a split before Adolph Germer, National Secretary, was able to call to order the opening session of the national convention here today. Delegates of the so-called Left Wing of the party were forcibly put out of the hall by policemen because Secretary Germer said they were trying to pack the convention by seating delegates who had no credentials.

A candidate for President will not be named at the convention. Resolutions to that effect were adopted after U. Louis Engdahl of Chicago had proposed Eugene V. Debs, now serving a prison sentence for violation of the espionage law, for the nomination. Seymour Stedman, Temporary Chairman, declared that the nomination would injure Debs's chances for a pardon.

Ejection of John Reed, unrecognized Bolshevist Ambassador to the United States, and eighty-three other members of the left wing of the party, by members of the police anarchist squad on guard duty at the convention, enlivened the credentials fight in the morning.

A fist fight between two delegates threatened for a time to become a free-for-all affair, but the police were able to stop it before more irate Left Wing delegates could take part.

Immediately after their expulsion from the convention hall left wing supporters, led by John Reed of New York, held a meeting to decide on a course of action. They said they would continue to hold caucuses until it was decided whether they would organize a new radical Socialist Party or join with the Communist Party, which is scheduled to hold a national convention here on Monday.

"We are Revolutionary Socialists, and we don't want to talk to any reporters or members of the capitalistic press," Reed declared before he closed the doors of the Left Wing caucus.

Although many delegates were not

clear as to the difference between the left and right wings of the party the principal trouble appeared to be that the left wing want practically a proletariat dictatorship and some even go so far as to suggest the abolition of political action. It was explained that the breach in the party has been widening for some time, and the trouble today was the result of this schism. Some said the left wing side wanted to adopt a program modeled after the Russian Socialists.

The Communist Party, it was explained, also has a left and right wing, and the revolting left wing delegation of the Socialists have so far been unable to decide which side of the Communists they favor.

In the meantime, the main convention of the Socialist Party, headed by Congressman-elect Victor Berger of Wisconsin, Seymour Stedman, and Adolph Germer, is going ahead with its business, which, according to announcements, will consume a week.

"We are the party," Mr. Berger persisted, "the others are just a lot of anarchists. I have been through this experience before."

Among the left wing delegates who were making the fight today were Rose Pastor Stokes, Kate Sadler, and I. E. Ferguson, temporary Secretary of the radicals.

"The left wing represents about 80 per cent. of the Socialist Party," said Mr. Ferguson, "but we seem to be left out of the party's deliberations."

Only delegates who had white cards were admitted to the floor of the convention today, and most of the left wing delegates were unable to obtain these cards because, it was said by the right wing faction, they had obtained their election by fraud. The card of admission up to this year has been red.

August 31, 1919

49

NEW PARTY RAISES BOLSHEVIST BANNER

Communists Proclaim Sympathy with Lenin Program and Seek "Conquest of State."

SOCIALIST NUMBERS CUT

Before the War They Claimed 117,-000, Now There Are Only 42,217—Transactions of the Convention.

CHICAGO, Sept. 3.—The new Communist Labor Party of America adopted a platform today after wrangling nearly all day over the phraseology. It declares the party in full harmony with the revolutionary working class parties of all countries and stands by the principles stated by the third international program adopted at Moscow, Russia. Other planks in the platform read:

"We fully recognize the crying need for an immediate change in the social system. The time for parleying and compromise has passed and now it is only a question whether the full power remains in the hands of the capitalist or the working class.

"The Communist Labor Party of America has as its ultimate aim the overthrow of the present system of production in which the working class is mercilessly exploited, and the creation of an industrial republic, wherein the machinery of production shall be socialized so as to guarantee to the workers the full social value of their toil.

"To this end we ask the workers to unite with the Communist Labor Party of America industrially and politically in the struggle for the conquest of the State and the powers of government in the establishment of a co-operative Commonwealth."

John Reed of New York presented the report of the Committee on Program and Labor, which was said to be the most radical declaration of principles ever issued by a political party in this country. The lengthy document is said to have been largely copied from the program of the Soviet Republic of Russia. Action on the report was deferred until tomorrow.

The Communist Labor Party delegates sang social revolutionary songs for an hour before getting down to business. One of the songs was "The Gene Debs Gang," of which the words of the refrain are:

Glorious, glorious; we'll make the Bolshevik
    victorious;
Hail to the plutes; they are making more
    of us.
While 'Gene lies in prison for us all.

Another song ran:

All who right and justice seek,
Burst your bonds, no longer weak;
Unite and join the Bolshevik.
    Rise, rise, rise.

The insistence of H. Tichenor of St. Louis finally prevailed in the selection of a name for the party.

"There are fifty-seven varieties of socialism, and perhaps more than that," he said, "but there is only one kind of Bolshevism, and the world is having a hard time to stomach that. Communism knows no race, nation, breed, or creed. We've got to get the word 'communism' in the name some place."

The meeting of communists was thrown into a commotion when detectives arrested Dennis E. Batt, reputed to be an organizer for the I. W. W., and took him from the hall. They had been searching for him for a week on a charge of making a seditious speech.

War and the withdrawal of radical insurgent members have reduced the total membership of the National Socialist Party in this country to 42,217, according to a report read at the convention of the organization today. Before the war the Socialist Party claimed a membership of 117,000.

A summary of the more important business transacted by the convention follows:

Urged political freedom for Ireland and India.

Criticised Congress for declining to seat Victor Berger, Socialist, of Milwaukee pending an investigation of his claims to the office.

Indorsed the plan for a general industrial strike on Oct. 8 to compel the release of Tom Mooney, Eugene V. Debs and other prisoners.

Indorsed the co-operative store plan to reduce the high cost of living.

Sent telegrams of fraternal greeting to Debs and other radical leaders imprisoned during the war.

The delegates applauded for several minutes when a report was read that Emma Goldman had been released from prison two weeks ago.

September 4, 1919

SEEK SOVIET RULE HERE.

Communists at Chicago Plan Mass Action to Gain Control.

Special to The New York Times.

CHICAGO, Sept. 6.—A program embodying direct mass action to gain control of the national political state in order to establish a government on "Soviet" principles, was enacted here today by the new Communist party of America, now in convention. The party plans to enter into labor disturbances for the express purpose of inculcating Bolshevist or revolutionary principles.

The major part of the program was identical in wording with that adopted by the Lenin-Trotzky government convention in Moscow last June, copies of which were brought here yesterday by courier direct from Petrograd. Louis C. Fraina, well-known Radical, was named international secretary of the organization. An entire roster of officers was elected.

The right wing and left wing Socialists, who have been holding separate conventions here, both adjourned this morning. No Presidential candidates were selected by either party.

September 7, 1919

50,000 ALIENS HERE SPREAD RADICALISM

Government Official Tells of Wide Agitation on Bolshevist Lines.

BACKED BY A RABID PRESS

Special to The New York Times.

WASHINGTON, Oct. 16.—Thousands of aliens are now in this country agitating for the confiscation of property and the overthrow of the American system of constitutional government. These agitators are supported by many of the 3,000 newspapers published in foreign languages, and these are circulated especially in the great centres of industry.

A Federal official informed THE TIMES correspondent today that he estimated that there were at least 50,000 aliens in the United States who were openly or secretly working for a Bolshevist form of government for this country. Many agitators do not claim allegiance to the I. W. W., but proclaim themselves Bolshevists and Radical Socialists.

A thorough investigation is being made of these red foreign papers. Among their contributors are hundreds of writers who are not citizens of the United States. In most instances these newspapers still circulate through the mails. The most radical of these papers are printed in the Russian, Hungarian, Lithuanian, and the Finnish languages.

The evidence of the activities of these foreigners is now in the possession of the Federal authorities, and there is reason for stating that a strict enforcement of the deportation laws against these alien trouble makers is among the possibilities of the near future.

A Russian paper, which prints a long article dealing with the activities of Russians who are spreading Communistic propaganda in this country, says that "the struggle for the lifting of the blockade against Russia is interwoven with our common struggle for the triumph and fulfillment of Communist Bolshevist ideals, for the triumph of the Proletarian Soviet Government idea of the dictatorship of the proletariat, not only in Russia but the world over."

Another Russian paper, also published in New York City, on Oct. 11 printed an article which shows how far these foreign agitators go in their efforts to stir discontent among their fellow countrymen in the United States.

"We know," the article reads, "that the American Cossacks (the New York police) not only searched and beat up the Russian demonstrators in Washington Square, but that they also sent over some of them to the other world. Among those who were killed were children. They tell us that a policeman's horse stepped on a child and that the child's entrails were crushed out. They tell us that the police Cossacks wrapped up bodies and threw them into ambulances. Let the parents of the lost children come. The editors will use all means to find the killed and lost. So don't be afraid to talk about these horrors which happened in noisy New York under the very windows of the rich."

Still another newspaper, printed in Russian, has circularized within the last two weeks among Russian-speaking people the following denunciation of the United States and its citizens:

"The American 'freedom-loving Government does not pay the least attention to the demands of the workers. Persons leading the lives of exiles are daily waiting the happy moment when they can go back to their native land. And, all of a sudden, President Wilson, according to the newspapers, asked the Congress to extend the law for another year in order to oppress the defenseless foreigners.

"Many of you are working and loading ammunition for Kolchak and Denikin to be used in crushing the Russian revolution. * * * Your duty and obligation is to refuse to do it if the Russian Soviet republic is to live. * * * Comrades, your duty is to join the revolutionary ranks of the American proletariat and to say, 'No, we will not kill our fathers, mothers, sisters, brothers, and their children.'"

A paper in the language of Little Russia, an out-and-out Bolshevist organ that enjoys a large circulation, says of the steel strike:

"This strike with its shootings of workers and the disposing of their meetings shows once again that the Government and its organs always have been and always will be the enemies of the workers, the enemies of the unfortunate, and the friend of the strong and rich. It is necessary for the workers to remember this simple truth, and while struggling against and destroying the trusts, also to destroy the organs which serve these trusts. The Government sending its agents to kill the strikers and to abuse them in every way is the most terrible enemy of the workers. Therefore, workers struggling against the trusts, must also struggle against the Government, which is in the service of these trusts."

One of the most violent of all the Bolshevist papers, published in the Ukrainian language, also issued in New York, said recently:

"A bourgeois is a lazy, dangerous, bloodthirsty creature who has not the slightest right to exist. His character is just the opposite of the worker's character. He is a nature greedy, egotistic, vulgar. He cannot live without the exploitation of the worker, and unless he can feed upon the worker's life. Victims and more victims are needed for the upkeep of his existence. The bourgeoisie,

in other words, is a class of parasites, whose existence is not justified either by biological, moral, or economical laws."

The I. W. W. is now publishing in New York a monthly magazine in the Finnish language. In its October issue the magazine prints many revolutionary and inflammatory articles.

"The workers of the whole world," it says, "should organize economically—join everywhere wherever they may work, the one big union. In this way only, fighting as one body, one for all and all for one, can we change the prevailing conditions so that the capitalist class will disappear entirely. The present bourgeois order will then be replaced by the republic of labor, where no work will be done for business purposes but for the benefit of mankind of the whole world."

A radical paper printed in the German language within the past week refers as follows to the soldiers in Gary and their commander, Major Gen. Leonard Wood:

"It is understood that the brave General did not come to Gary to defend the civil rights of the strikers, but that he undertook to carry out with an iron hand the autocratic rule of the steel trust and the Mayor of Gary. He issued a ukase that no striker should be permitted to don the uniform. He forbade meetings, and, of course, picketing. It is worth while remarking that General Wood came to Gary directly from Omaha, where he defended the poor white population against the hatred of the negroes, who, according to the General, made a conspiracy to make a pogrom on the whites. The pogrom, of cours, was made by the whites against the negroes, but the conspiracy was discovered by the General among the negroes."

Jugoslav Radicalism.

A radical Jugoslav publication, called The Munkas, a week ago mailed to Jugoslavs in various parts of the country copies of resolutions adopted at a meeting of radical Jugoslavs in Akron, Ohio, a short while ago. After stating that the revolutionary upheavals in various parts of the world "have shaken the foundations of capitalistic brigandage, thus hastening the hour of the liberation of the International proletariat," the resolutions assert that the time is rapidly approaching when all working men will be freed from "wage slavery" and that "the soil has become entirely ripe for the spread of revolutionary socialistic ideas, which is proved by the fact that our party literature, press, and organizers are everywhere received with great enthusiasm by the discontented proletarian masses.

"In this country (the United States) the industrial situation brings before us the capitalistic class, thoroughly intrenched in the industries, in the gates of which, like true servitors, we find the political powers of the State, which fact brings us to the conclusion that the realization of our aims is not even to be imagined so long as we fail to force the capitalist class from its strategic fortress, the industries."

Within the last ten days a Slavic paper with a large circulation in the steel, iron, and coal-mining districts said:

"All the steel forces have been placed against the unarmed steel slaves. That means that the State is in the hands of the capitalists; that they do not think of the wants of the workers, and that the ruling class in this country shivers when the slaves commence to move. All of us wage slaves learn from this steel strike, for the same thing awaits us as soon as we awake from our sleep, the same as our comrades did."

On Oct. 3, this same paper circulated another article lauding what it terms was the inauguration of a communist movement in this country, in which movement it claims the Lithuanians in America will have a prominent part.

"The Lithuanian workers," the article reads, "will have a real class understanding, a real organization of the proletariat, which will lead them to final release from under the yoke of the damned capitalist. The Lithuanian Federation will go together with the whole world's revolutionary organization and will follow in the path of the Communist International."

"The world war of capitalism," says this radical paper, "has brought forth the catastrophe of the capitalist system. * * * The working class will rule the whole world. The rule of the working class is a social revolution. It signifies the victory of class struggle. With the abolishment of classes, the new system will have one class—the working class—at the head of society. That class will be the master over production. Therefore, when the capitalists tremblingly predicted the approach of the new danger they really felt the coming of their end, because the social revolution brings with it the merciless destruction of capitalism.

"In the other countries (than Russia) —England, France, and America—the bourgeoisie endeavors, with more or less success, to decrease, check, or entirely disarm the class struggle. In this line America is the first, unlike other countries, to try to break the class struggle by old played-out means. * * * However, the mad and despicable effort will not succeed because America undertakes alone an impossible fight, a fight that will be more fatal than the world war, and, in spite of everything, will have only one end, and that is the collapse of the capitalist system. * * * The earthquake will come, and, with the occurring strikes, the revolution will come in this country; (the United States,) slowly but surely."

A recent issue of a Hungarian newspaper, published in New York, refers as follows to the deportation of alien agitators:

"When these lines shall reach the light of day our fellow workers will have been several days on their enforced journey. The statue, made ridiculous by the name of Liberty, points with forbidding hand after the brethren dragged from our ranks."

The above extracts are from official translations.

October 17, 1919

SAYS RICH RADICALS FINANCE 'RED' PRESS

Samuel A. Berger Declares New York Parlor Socialists Furnish Propaganda Funds.

NO NAMES ARE MENTIONED

The radical propaganda among foreigners in the industrial centers of this country, aiming at the overthrow of the American Government and a general seizure of property after the Bolshevist example, is carried on largely by well-to-do New Yorkers of the parlor radical type, whose contributions keep the "Red" press alive.

This is established, according to Deputy State Attorney General Samuel A. Berger, by his survey of the radical publications of this city, in connection with the investigation by the Lusk Committee into Bolshevist propaganda.

Between forty and fifty extreme radical publications which reach 3,000,000 readers, largely in the

great industrial centers, are published in this city. Only two of these are self-supporting, and the rest are kept going by the subsidies of dilettante "Reds" of this city, including a number of well-known men and women, according to Mr. Berger. He said that a list of contributors who kept the foreign-language revolutionary press from going out of existence had been furnished to the Federal Government.

"I examined the editors and publishers of all these papers," said Mr. Berger, "and have made a study of their books. With two exceptions, the editors or publishers have admitted to me that the income from their papers would not pay expenses and that they would be bankrupt except for gifts from wealthy people of this city.

"I have not the authority to make public the names of those who are subsidizing radical publications, but they are in general the same people who subsidized the pro-German propaganda and furnished the money for the pacifist and peace-at-any-price campaigns and contributed to the cause of the conscientious objectors. My inquiry shows that a very large portion of the circulation of these newspapers is in the very centers where, during the past few months, there has been the greatest amount of radical disturbance and radical labor agitation.

"The keynote is the overthrow of the present system of Government, the abolition of the wage sys-

tem, and the dictatorship of the proletariat.

"This propaganda is carried on almost solely among foreigners. It makes little appeal to Americans or to foreigners who have become familiar with American institutions. Those who furnish the money and those who direct the propaganda are, however, mostly Americans.

"The Left Wing of the Socialist Party presents its 'program' as follows:

a. The organization of workmen's councils; the recognition of and propaganda for these mass organizations of the working class as instruments in the immediate struggle and as instruments for the seizure of the power of the State and the basis of the new proletariat State of the organized producers and the dictatorship of the proletariat.

b. Workers' control of industry to be exercised by the industrial organizations, or Soviets, as against Government ownership or the State control of industry.

c. Repudiation of all national debts.

d. Expropriation of banks.

e. Socialization of foreign trade.

Mr. Berger was asked if the Federal Government had made full use of its power to deal with the press preaching revolution. He refused to answer the question.

October 17, 1919

51

SENATE ASKS PALMER FOR DATA ON RADICALS

Passes Resolution Requesting What Action Has Been Taken Against Advocates of Revolution.

Special to The New York Times.

WASHINGTON, Oct. 17.—The resolution introduced in the Senate last Tuesday, which calls upon Attorney General Palmer to advise and inform the Senate what action, if any, has been taken by the Department of Justice to proceed legally against domestic and alien radicals who are or have been advocating the overthrow of the United States Government, and also what legal steps have been taken for the deportation of alien agitators, was passed unanimously by the Senate today.

Senator Poindexter expressed the hope that Attorney General Palmer would respond with the information requested within a week. Senator Poindexter expects soon to make a speech in the Senate, in which he will review the activities of I. W. W. agitators, Bolsheviki, and other disturbers in this country.

In an interview Senator Poindexter said that he had been informed that all but eight of the sixty or more alien agitators who were ordered deported as a result of the effort to overthrow the Seattle municipal government last Spring, instead of being sent to Europe, received their liberty after reaching Ellis Island. One of these, Leon Green, whom he described as a "Russian anarchist and alien," now is active in agitation in the Chicago district, he said.

"No steps have been taken," added Senator Poindexter, "to deport this man. There can, if necessary, be introduced a cabinet full of documentary proof and an army of witnesses to prove the existence of a revolutionary movement in this country, and we will find that it is not confined to Gary, Indiana, nor to the State of Indiana, but that it extends throughout the United States. We will find that this movement is well

supplied with funds and that a large number at least of the many strikes that have occurred during recent months and that are now in progress are based upon revolutionary purpose.

"A member of Congress from Ohio, who deserves a great deal of credit for the courageous stand which he has taken upon this question, a member of a labor union himself, told me the other day that recently one of the aliens working in the steel industry in Youngstown, Oh o, who had gone out on strike told him that they were on strike because Congress was going to take over these industries and give them to the workers.

"That is the idea behind the longshoremen's strike in New York. Confessedly or secretly they hold up food supplies which are stored upon these ships, which they refuse to unload because they want to put the community into discomfort.

"The demands which the longshoremen in New York are making if put into effect would give them and the Longshoremen's Union absolute control of the employment of men, their discharge, the fixing of their wages, and the fixing of their hours in that industry."

October 18, 1919

RAIDS ON RADICALS HERE AND IN OTHER CITIES

200 CAUGHT IN NEW YORK

Federal Agents Act on Second Anniversary of Soviet Revolution.

MANY WILL BE DEPORTED

Russian People's House Raided and Tons of Literature Carried Away.

RED FLAG WAVED IN BRONX

Speaker at Bolshevist Celebration There Threatens a Revolution in America.

Choosing the second anniversary of the Bolshevist revolution in Russia as the psychological moment to strike, the Federal Government, aided by municipal police in New York and several other large cities, last night dealt the most serious and sweeping blow it has yet aimed at criminal anarchists.

Armed with warrants for dangerous agitators whom Federal agents have trailed for months, the raiders swarmed into the Russian People's House in New York and into similar gathering places of alleged "Reds" in Philadelphia, Newark, Detroit, Jackson, Mich.; Ansonia, Conn., and other cities, broke up meetings, seized tons of literature and herded the gangs of foreign men and women into various offices for exami-

nation, whence many of those who proved to be the most sought after of the radicals found their way into cells.

"Reds" to be Deported.

Though the Federal authorities were most reticent as to their plans and purposes, the fact that the warrants upon which they held twenty-seven in New York, thirty in Philadelphia, fifty in Detroit, thirty-six in Newark, and six in Jackson, were signed by United States Commissioner of Immigration Caminetti, led to the inference that it is the Government's purpose to deport as many of those taken as can be proved to be criminal anarchists.

From one of those co-operating with Chief Flynn of the Bureau of Investigation of the Department of Justice, who, with Sergeant Gegan of the police Bomb Squad, led the raid in this city, came the declaration that many at least of those held were persons of provable criminal records. Twenty-five men were locked in cells in Police Headquarters here without their identity or the charges against them being disclosed, while two women, Ethel Bernstein and Dora Lipkin, were locked in a police station where there is a matron.

The police last night prevented a meeting of the Communist Labor Party which was to have been held in Laurel Garden to celebrate the Bolshevist anniversary while the Communist mass meeting scheduled for today in Rutgers Square was abandoned by those who sponsored it, with the assertion that they had discovered a "Secret Service plot," to "plant" operatives and force disorder.

Several meetings held in New York were marked by inflammatory speeches, one speaker at a meeting in the Bronx predicting the overthrow of the United States Government.

200 in Custody Here.

The police who raided headquarters in New York, the Russian People's House at 133 East Fifteenth Street, took about 200 men and women found there to the Department of Justice Headquarters in the Park Row Building for examination. The raid was carried out, it was said, under orders from Washington, and in addition to the men and women the police carried away several tons of documents, all of it said to be anarchist literature.

Those taken in the raid were examined

last night by agents of the Department of Justice, and those who were able to prove citizenship were released. The examination was still under way at a late hour, and it was said that the ones who couldn't give a good account of themselves would be held at the Old Slip Police Station for further interrogation today.

Sergeant Gegan in Charge.

The police, who included besides plain clothes men from headquarters a number of Department of Justice agents, were under direction of Sergeant J. J. Gegan of the Bomb Squad, who has been co-operating with Government officials here in the effort to root out the anarchists known to be in New York.

Neither Sergeant Gegan nor any of his men would discuss the raid, all of them asserting that they were silent under orders of Chief William Flynn, recently appointed head of the Bureau of Investigation of the Department, with orders to leave no stone unturned to end all symptoms of anarchy in the United States.

The raid was executed swiftly. Automobiles filled with detectives, uniformed police, and Federal agents drove up quietly one by one and parked on side streets. When the building at 133 was completely surrounded the men in charge of each section of the raiding party ordered their men to the ground, and they went forward.

Those within had not the slightest idea of what was coming and the police had penetrated the Russian People's House from top to bottom before any alarm was given. On one of the floors a class was in progress. Several of those in this class said afterward they were merely studying English when the police arrived.

"Out into the hall everybody," was the terse order. "Line up there and don't make any noise."

At first there was evidence that the presence of the policemen would be questioned, some of the women being especially vociferous in their demands to know the meaning of the raid. The harsh command to "Shut up, there, you, if you know what's good for you," brought silence, and those in the building were hustled into waiting automobiles and driven away.

Police Club Men in Building.

A number of those in the building were badly beaten by the police during the raid, their heads wrapped in bandages testifying to the rough manner in which they had been handled.

It was nearly an hour before the last machine had whirled off to the Park Row Building, but in the meantime the raiders had gone systematically through the building in search of incriminating literature of any kind. Doors were taken off, desks were ripped open, and even the few carpets were torn up to find possible hiding places for documents.

The papers seized filled several huge trucks, and the police worked like longshoremen unloading their booty at the Park Row Building.

The questioning followed general lines of "are you a citizen? How long have you been in this country? What is your occupation?" and "What were you doing in that building tonight?"

Chief Flynn is very anxious to get hold of documents vital to the cause of anarchy in this country as well as men believed to be high in the councils of the Soviet Government in Russia. It is also known that the Chief considers New York the headquarters for all kinds and degrees of Reds in America.

Since the bomb outrages last June, which led to the appointment of Flynn to take charge of the work of ferreting out anarchy, the police have been watching and cataloguing every act and every utterance of radicals in this city, even the so-called "harmless parlor Bolsheviki." It is hoped that sooner or later one of these raids will yield clues to the perpetrators of the bomb outrages.

It is only three weeks now since this city was placarded all along Third Avenue with circulars calling on the Reds to "arm yourselves" against their "oppressors, the capitalists and the police," and to strike terror into the hearts of all foes of the workers. The circular called for a "bloody revolution" in this country as the sole means of righting matters.

The police have never been able to trace the authorship of the circular, nor have they found the faintest clue to the mind which planned the bomb plots. The raid last night, it was said, was one of the drives which Federal, State, and municipal authorities have been making to apprehend those who would attempt to overthrow the Government.

The names of those taken in the raid last night were not made public, nor could it be learned last night just how many were detained. The interrogation was impeded, it was stated, by the fact that an interpreter had to be employed in nearly every case. Practically all of those examined were of Russian birth.

Communist Meeting in Bronx.

Two thousand persons attended a meeting of the Communist Labor Party, held in the Hunts Point Palace, 163rd Street and Southern Boulevard, the Bronx, last night, to celebrate the second anniversary of the establishment of the Russian Soviet Government.

Despite the presence of Inspector Walsh and Captain Meade of the Simpson Street Station and many uniformed patrolmen and detectives, the speakers denounced Mayor Hylan and Governor Coolidge of Massachusetts as "traitors" to the laboring classes of the United States. The alleged powers were assailed for their intervention in Russia. The presence of stenographers from the

office of District Attorney Martin and the United States Department of Justice led some of the speakers to harangue in the Russian language.

Prior to the speeches several persons attired in red costumes unfurled a crimson banner across the stage, upon which was an inscription "Long Live the Third International."

Mrs. Ella Reeve Bloor was introduced as "an American revolutionist." She attacked the capitalistic class and denounced public officials, terming them traitors to the proletariat. The mention of Mayor Hylan's and Governor Coolidge's names was the cause of booing and hissing, which continued for three minutes.

L. C. A. K. Martens, who was caught in the raid last summer conducted by the State Constabulary at the suggestion of the Lusk Committee, held a long conversation with Miss Bloor, and then addressed the audience in Russian.

At the conclusion of several speeches in Yiddish, Benjamin Gitlow spoke upon the sacrifices of his comrades in European countries.

"No matter what the police or courts may think," added the speaker, "we will work until we abolish this Government, the last to survive."

The Brownsville section of the Communist Labor Party of America celebrated the second anniversary of the founding of Soviet Government in Russia in Independence Hall, Osborn Street and Pitkin Avenue, last night. There were about 600 present, and the audience included many policemen as well as agents of the Department of Justice. L. C. A. K. Martens, the so-called Soviet Ambassador, did not appear as was expected.

The principal speaker was Dr. Morris Zucker, a dentist, who is out pending appeal for a sentence for seditious utterances. Among other things, Zucker said that the day was soon coming when the proletariat would be able to meet the capitalists bayonet for bayonet, machine gun for machine gun.

James Larkin and Ella Reeve Bloor also spoke. The speakers criticized Mayor Hylan, whose name was hissed because he had issued a letter urging the people not to attend a so-called communist meeting in Rutgers Square tonight. Larkin said that the Mayor was Irish in name only. He said that while he was receiving de Valera the police were smashing the heads of Russian revolutionists.

RED RAIDS IN OTHER CITIES.
Radicals Taken in Newark, Philadelphia, and St. Louis.

One hundred and fifty men and women were taken in Newark last night in a series of raids in radical circles made by agents of the Department of Justice. So quietly were the raids conducted that the local police did not learn of them until the Federal authorities began to bring in their prisoners to the Government headquarters in the Lawyers' Building, 164 Market Street.

Four automobiles and a large motor truck were used by the agents in carrying the prisoners and quantities of literature and other evidence which were found in the places visited during the evening. Many of

those who were rounded up had weapons on their persons, according to the officials. Forty agents took part in the raids.

PHILADELPHIA, Penn., Nov. 7.—Thirty men and women were arrested in two raids here tonight. All were locked up in the Federal Building, and Todd Daniels, special agent of the Department of Justice, said he could not give out any information on account of orders from Washington.

The principal raid took place at Eighth and Poplar Streets, where twenty persons were taken from a radical meeting hall. The other was on a hall at Second and Christian Streets, where ten additional arrests were made.

ANSONIA, Conn., Nov. 7.—Alleged radicals were arrested in raids conducted here tonight by agents of the Department of Justice, assisted by local police. Up to midnight twenty-seven prisoners had been locked up at police headquarters.

WATERBURY, Conn., Nov. 7.—Six alleged radicals were arrested by local police officials here tonight. The men were taken into custody on charges of attempting to circulate Bolshevist propaganda and stir up unrest.

NEW HAVEN, Conn., Nov. 7.—Three men were arrested by Department of Justice agents here tonight in the round-up of alleged radicals.

NEW LONDON, Conn., Nov. 7.—Department of Justice men swooped down upon New London tonight and searched for evidence of radicals. No arrests were made, but a quantity of radical literature was seized in the rooms of a local club. Local police assisted. In ten saloons raided liquor was seized.

HARTFORD, Conn., Nov. 7.—Federal agents took two alleged radicals into custody in this city tonight. They were locked up at police headquarters.

DETROIT, Mich., Nov. 7.—Department of Justice agents here tonight, reinforced by officers from several other cities, took into custody fifty alleged radical agitators. Twenty men were arrested at a hall used for anarchistic meetings and the others were rounded up at their homes. All are being held for further investigation.

CHICAGO, Nov. 7.—A wagon load of prisoners was taken to the Federal building shortly before midnight. It was said the arrests were made in connection with the national raids on radicals.

ST. LOUIS, Nov. 7.—Two men suspected of radical tendencies were arrested here tonight by Department of Justice operatives. They gave their names as Joe Norvelle, a Russian, and Antone Jurkovich, a Croatian.

November 8, 1919

73 RED CENTRES RAIDED HERE BY LUSK COMMITTEE

Hundreds of Prisoners and Tons of Seditious Literature Taken to Headquarters.

Seventy-three radical headquarters in all five boroughs of this city were raided simultaneously last night for evidence of revolutionary propaganda by more than 700 policemen and va-

rious agents of the Federal and State Governments acting under the authority of search warrants issued by Chief Magistrate McAdoo to the Lusk Committee.

After lawyers for the committee had completed a canvass of some 500 prisoners at Police Headquarters at 1 o'clock this morning, they directed the police to hold about 100 men on charges of criminal anarchy and release the rest. Radical literature by the ton was confiscated by the police.

Among the places raided were editorial offices, meeting rooms, and printing shops, from which issued a large part of the revolutionary propaganda which has made its effect felt in Gary, Omaha, Seattle, and other centres of industrial disturbance, according to testimony before the Lusk Committee.

The places raided were all connected with the so-called "Communist Party," the group of radicals which has broken away from the Socialist Party and attempted to form a union of anarchists,

I. W. W., syndicalists, and all other violent groups of radicals. The addresses of the seventy-three places, many of which are the editorial rooms of radical publications, were furnished by Associate Counsel Archibald E. Stevenson and Charles F. Donnelly of the Lusk Committee, who appeared yesterday morning before Magistrate McAdoo and obtained search warrants for the raids. Members of the New York State Constabulary took part in the raids.

One of the first prisoners brought in by them was the famous "Jim" Larkin, the Irish labor agitator, who led the shipping strike in England in 1914. Larkin, who is regarded as one of the most dangerous of the agitators in this country, was arrested in McDougall Alley.

Simultaneous Raids in Five Boroughs.

The plans for the raids were kept secret with great care, and shortly after 9 o'clock the raids started in all five boroughs. The raiders included members of the anarchist, narcotic and Italian squads, plainclothes men, 700 men in uniform, agents of the Department of Justice, inspectors of the Immigration Service, and the State Constabulary. The police were directed by Inspector Faurot, and the entire movement was directed by State Senator Clayton R. Lusk, whose committee has been for months accumulating evidence on the radical propaganda in this State.

The Lusk Committee made public last night a list of the places raided, and the branches of the Communist Party described in the list include Lettish, Esthonian, Lithuanian, Ukrainian, Jewish, Russian, Hungarian, German, Spanish, and Italian.

Fifty radical publications in various foreign languages, which are printed in this city, are the backbone of the Red movement in this country, according to Deputy Attorney General Berger, and many of these were raided last night. One of the purposes of th raids was to gather evidence as to the future plans for causing outbreaks like those in Seattle and at Gary, which have been laid largely to inflammatory publications, printed in this city, with the aid, according to Mr. Berger, of wealthy parlor Bolsheviki of New York City.

After the raids started patrol wagons and Brooklyn, mainly breaking into the drove up to Police Headquarters and policemen began to stagger in under the weight of the Red literature which they were carrying. Prisoners were taken in droves, the dangerous Reds to be divided later from the innocent bystanders.

While most of the raids were downtown, the police were active in Harlem small printing shops, from which inflammatory proclamations and weekly propaganda papers have been issued.

Plans for Revolution Confessed.

Senator Lusk, Chairman of the legislative committee investigating seditious activities, issued a statement last night in which he said that it was shown by the confession of leaders of the new Communist Party before the committee that they were aiming at the overthrow of the United States Government by revolution.

"It is the plain statement of the intention of the members of this organization to overthrow our established Government by force and unlawful means," said Senator Lusk. "The seventy-one local Communist organizations in New York City consisted of bodies of men and women openly and notoriously organized for the sole purpose of destroying our Government. They profess to believe and contend that the time has come when the Government is not strong enough to protect itself.

"These organizations are a direct public challenge to the authorities of the State and nation. A passive attitude on the part of the Government toward the disloyal agitators organizing its citizens against it has resulted in a constant growth of the movement, as has been clearly shown by the investigation made by this committee. It seems to me that the time has come to put into force stern measures to do away with this agitation and punish these disloyal leaders in the movement. The city and State officials are engaged in an effort to enforce the laws of the State.

The committee considers that the result of this effort will be very helpful in preparing recommendations for action on the part of the Legislature, and regards it as a legitimate part of its work to do everything that it can to assist in this matter. It is perfectly willing to accept the onus of anything which may happen through its activity in an effort to protect our Government and citizens.

"It has been the policy of certain individuals and publications to furnish aid and assistance to the enemies of our country by criticising any efforts made by public officials to enforce the laws against sedition and protect our institutions.

"The time has come for the people of this country to take a definite stand on this question in order that we may know who our enemies are and deal with them as they deserve."

Russian Model Followed.

The Lusk Committee made public last night an account of the proceedings before Magistrate McAdoo, which said:

"Mr. Stevenson testified that on Nov. 1, 1919, Morris S. Nessim, who was held a prisoner at Police Headquarters charged with criminal anarchy, gave him certain information which supplemented information already in possession of the Lusk Committee. As a result of this information, there was obtained an accurate list of all the Communist headquarters in this city. It was further shown that Dr. Maxmillian Cohen, one of the Red leaders in this city and the editor of The Communist World, had stated to agents of the Lusk Committee that the purpose of the Communist Party and of all the persons associated and affiliated therewith and who subscribed to its doctrines was the overthrow of the organized Government of the United States and the State of New York and the substitution therefor of a 'Dictatorship of the Proletariat.'

"He also stated that it was the purpose of the Communist Party to expropriate all land and property without compensation to the present owners, and that they proposed to accomplish this overthrow by 'stimulated mass strikes,' and that they did not propose to bring about any changes by the use of the ballot. Dr. Maxmilian Cohen further stated that it was the purpose of the Communist organization, as well as of all persons who are members of it, to use as much force as was necessary to accomplish the purpose and overcome the resistance of the present organized Governments of the State of New York and of the United States, and that if in accomplishing such purpose there was any bloodshed, the onus would be upon you, meaning the legal representatives of the organized Government of the State of New York and of the United States.

"It was also shown that the purpose of this organization and its object are clearly set forth in its manifesto, program and constitution. The program of the party states, 'Its aim is to direct this struggle (the class struggle) to the conquest of political power, the overthrow of capitalism and the destruction of the bourgeoisie State.' To make clear its purpose the manifesto of this organization states: 'Communism does not propose to capture the bourgeoise Parliamentary State, but to conquer and destroy it. • • • It rejects the idea of class reconciliation and the parliamentary conquest of capitalism.'

"Under the head of 'The Progress of the Party,' in the official manifesto and program appears the following: '(b) Participation in parliamentary campaigns, which in the general struggle of the proletariat is of secondary importance, is for the purpose of revolutionary propaganda only.'"

Hundreds of prisoners were landed at Police Headquarters in patrol wagons and automobiles of all descriptions. They were herded into the gymnasium, trial room, and all corners of the building, while the men considered to be the more important catches were questioned, generally through interpreters. One of the prisoners was a white-bearded man of 70 years. Several were carrying cases with musical instruments, protesting that they were merely taking their cases in their clubrooms when they had been arrested. One woman prisoner was taken to Police Headquarters by a plainclothes man.

The largest crowd of prisoners captured was taken at one of the Ukrainian branches at 222 East Fifth Street. The prisoners from this place, which had been raided some time previously, numbered 150. Thirty-five men were taken in a raid in East Broadway, near Rutgers Square, where the Communists were to have made their demonstration yesterday.

Several of the places raided were found locked and uninhabited, but membership books, records, and printed literature were carried away. Social functions were in progress at some of the resorts raided. A package party and dance was interrupted by the raiders at the Communist branch headquarters, 1,709 Pitkin Avenue, Brownsville, and thirty-eight merrymaking youths were arrested. The girls were detained for a time and then released.

The questioning of prisoners at Police Headquarters was done by counsel for the Lusk Committee, Major Archibald E. Stevenson, Frederick W. Rich, and Deputy Attorney General Berger. Scores of men judged to be innocent were turned loose with little delay. Some of them said that they had been attending benefits and parties with wives and children at the Communist halls when they had been arrested.

When Jim Larkin was questioned, he said that he claimed the protection of his Government, the Irish Republic. He was detained nevertheless.

WILL DEPORT REDS AS ALIEN PLOTTERS

Palmer's Blow Friday Hit Leaders of Russian Society, Worse Than Bolsheviki.

Special to The New York Times.

WASHINGTON, Nov. 8.—The arrest of more than 200 Russian Bolsheviki in various cities of the country last night ended the first phase of a campaign which the Department of Justice is waging to rid the United States of alien radial agitators who are urging the overthrow by violence of the Government. Other arrests, which will involve alien agitators of other nationalities, will soon be made.

"This is the first big step," it was stated in Attorney General Palmer's office this morning, "to rid the country of these foreign trouble makers."

It was pointed out that all the persons arrested, with the exception of some in New York City, had been investigated and the record of their activities in this country gone over in the Department of Justice before orders were issued for their arrest. In cases involving aliens the department will ask for deportation warrants.

In every instance in which an arrest was ordered the instructions to William J. Flynn, Director of the Department of Justice Bureau, came from the Attorney General.

It is stated in the Department of Justice that the Government is determined to rid the country of these foreign disloyalists, and the campaign will continue until this undesirable element is eliminated.

Every person whose arrest was ordered last night is a member of the Union of Russian Workers, the organization which held a convention in Youngstown last Summer and voted in favor of a campaign of confiscation of private property and substitution of soviet control of industry in this country. This convention, at the instance of Jacob Margolis, the I. W. W. lawyer of Pittsburgh, voted an indorsement of the steel strike.

The activities of this organization in the United States was disclosed by the Department of Justice today.

"More than 200 Russian Reds," the statement reads, "one of them with all the materials for making a bomb in his possession, were taken into custody last night by agents of the Department of Justice in a raid that covered more than fifteen of the largest industrial centres of this country.

"Raiders captured a complete counterfeiting plant at Newark, N. J. This included plates, presses, and bank notes ready for circulation. Red flags, guns, revolvers, and thousands of pieces of literature were also taken by the Department of Justice agents.

"The Reds taken into custody were all leaders of the Union of Russian Workers. This organization has more than 7,000 members throughout the country, and has been engaged in active propaganda against the present form of Government for many months. It has many locals scattered throughout the country. Last night's raids included leaders of the organization in New York, Chicago, Pittsburgh, Philadelphia, Cleveland, Detroit, Buffalo, Akron and Youngstown, Ohio, Baltimore, Newark and Elizabeth, N. J.; Hartford, Waterbury, Ansonia, Bridgeport, New Haven and Seymour, Conn.

"Romen Mosichok, organizer of the Union at Trenton, N. J., had the material for making bombs in his room at 109 Pemberton Street.

"These articles included gunpowder, copper and brass wire, electric batteries, wax paper, &c. Mosichok, when taken into custody, admitted that he had been member of the organization since December, 1915.

"The counterfeiting plant at Newark was found to be an elaborate affair. It was found in the rooms of two active members of the union. A large supply of counterfeit banknotes was on hand. These men will have to face additional charges.

"Agents of the department and of the Bureau of Immigration have been collecting evidence in these cases for two months. All of the prisoners are aliens, and the evidence collected will be presented to the Commissioner of Immigration and their deportation asked for.

"The Union of Russian Workers was organized in New York in 1907 by eleven men, led by one William Szatow, at present the Chief of Police of Petrograd. The purpose was to amalgamate all of the Russian groups in the United States into one organization.

"With the aid of newspaper and other propaganda, the membership of the Union of Russian Workers began to grow until at the present time it consists of sixty locals, located in the principal cities of the country, with a membership of 7,000.

"The most important convention of the union was held in Detroit in 1914, with delegates from all of the principal cities in the United States and Canada present. The delegates to this convention adopted resolutions which have become a part of the constitution of the federation and which has not been substantially changed since that time. The dues books of the members of this organization contain the following preamble to the constitution of the organization which reveals the purposes of the Union of Russian Workers:

"'The present society is divided into two opposing classes—the downtrodden workers and peasants on the one side, producing by their work all the riches of the world; the rich people on the other side, who have grabbed all the riches into their hands.

"'Many a time the class of the oppressed stood up against the rich parasites and their faithful servant and protector—the Government—to conquer its full liberation from the yoke of capitalism and political power, but every time it suffered defeat, not being fully conscious of its own final goal and means, by which victory can be accomplished thus remaining only a weapon in the hands of its enemies.

The struggle between these two classes is being fought also at the present time and will end only when the toiling masses, organized as a class, will understand their true interests, and will make themselves masters of all the riches of this world by means of a violent social revolution.

"'Having accomplished such a change and having annihilated at the same time all the institutions of Government and State, the class of the disowned must establish the Society of Free Producers, aiming at satisfying the needs of every individual person who, on its side, is giving to the society its labor and its knowledge.

"'For the attainment of these aims we consider as of the primal importance the necessity of building up a wide revolutionary organization of toilers which, by conducting a direct struggle with all the institutions of capital and government, must train the working class to initiative and an independent action in all its acts, thus educating in it the consciousness of the absolute necessity of a general strike—of the social revolution.'

"The Union of Russian Workers believes more in mass action, including armed action in time of great national strife. Its principles do not favor the Bolshevist form of Government, but they are willing to accept any radical or group of men as an expedient for furthering their own particular needs. And while not supporting the Bolshevist move in this country openly, they are secretly supporting it in order that they may through it achieve their ends."

Francis P. Garvan, Assistant Attorney General, stated tonight that all the leaders of the union were now in custody. The number arrested who are to be held, he added, was 211, distributed as follows: Newark, N. J., 81; Baltimore, Md., 10; Akron, Ohio, 6; Monessen, Penn., 2; Bentleyville, Penn., 1; Universal, Penn., 1; Cleveland, 17; Buffalo, 14; Philadelphia, 9; Trenton, N. J., 1; Hartford, Conn., 83; New York City, 83; Chicago, 7; Detroit, 40.

It was said today that nine radicals had also been taken into custody in Washington. Mr. Garvan declined to say anything regarding this report.

A Federal official was asked if Ludwig C. A. K. Martens, who styles himself Bolshevist representative in this country, had been arrested. He replied that, as yet, Martens had not been arrested. He made the same reply regarding Santori Nuorteva, Marten's chief assistant in the "Bolshevist embassy" in New York City.

The locals of the union, it was pointed out, were organized to spread the doctrines of the union among Russian immigrants, and propaganda was conducted by means of literature, newspapers and lectures. Lecturers were sent out by the Executive Committee to all parts of the country. Funds of the organization were derived from dues, lectures and concerts and the sale of radical literature.

Among the literature captured in the raid were:

1. "The Future Society," by John Gray, issued by the Union of Newark, and dealing with anarchistic doctrines.

2. "Program of the Anarchist Communists," a book issued by the New York branch of the Union of Russian Workers in 1919, dealing with the overthrow of Government by force.

3. "God and the Government," by Michael Bakunin, issued by the New York branch of the union in 1919. Bakunin is a leading Russian anarchist.

4. "The History and Structure of the I. W. W.," by Vincent St. John, published by the I. W. W.

5. "Revolutionary Industrialism," by Grover Perry, published by the I. W. W.

Following the suppression of "Golos Truda" by the Post Office Department, the official organ of the organization became the Khlieb y Nolya (Bread and Freedom), which appeared first on Feb. 26, 1919. This is barred from the mail in Canada and the United States, due to its anarchistic teachings. It is issued from the headquarters of the union, 133 East Fifteenth Street, New York City. The sheet of eight pages has a wide circulation among members of the union. An extract from the issue of Aug. 28 shows the nature of the articles:

"Complete destruction of private control of natural resources and capital, complete destruction of power to rule and the institutions invested with powers to enforce rule of one man over another, those are the outstanding features of social revolution."

The union supports the Russian I. W. W. paper Golos Truzienko and the Soviet publication Robotshi i Krestyanian, (Workman and Peasant).

An article in the union's organ, entitled "Thoughts on Social Revolution," says:

"Only social revolution can free the worker and only the working class can 'put over' a social revolution. There are no legal means nor can there be any whereby true liberty could be obtained, for the laws are the products of those that favor and defend the existing order of things.

"By the words 'social revolution' we mean a complete destruction of the present order and not merely the transfer of Government power into the hands of social democrats—in other words, not with a view of intrusting the political minority with the power we came out to destroy, a dream cherished by the social Jacobins. You cannot call a set of reforms, whatever they are, a revolution; you cannot apply this term to a play at parliamentary combinations."

The issue of Sept. 17, under the title "In Passing," says:

"Murder is always murder, and the man who kills is always a murderer.
* * * Not only he who has fired the shot or wielded the knife which kills is a murderer, but in equal measure, and often even more, those who send men subservient to them, (as for instance, in suppressing popular rebellions and in war,) to kill, are murderers, making use of blind instruments.

"The only service of this man has been in the fact that, being a professional of his craft, he came to be by a simple chance at the head of the American armies which fought in Europe, and there, obedient to the commands of those who had sent him, he, with ability and with brains, led the work of murder of men by men, and for this they raise him to the skies and honor him in every way."

The issues of Sept. 25, under the heading of "Anarchist Syndicalism and Communism," contains the following:

"The contemporary professionalism (unionism) does not contain anything anarchistic, because it is partisan and utterly materialistic—anarchists joining professional unions are forced to renounce the social-political teachings of anarchism.

"France was among the first who showed the world how to get rid of priests and autocratic monarchs and to introduce, constitutionally, a democratic form of government.

"Anarchism is going still farther, saying that we are not only obliged to destroy the political mechanism as it may be, either monarchism, constitutionalism, republicanism, democracy or even socialism, but that it is our duty to destroy all these forms of government, as they are unworthy of human freedom."

The House Committee on Immigration may investigate the problem of deporting aliens during the coming recess. The inquiry, if authorized, will go into the activities of Frederic C. Howe, former Commissioner of Immigration in New York, who is charged with having been indifferent to the deportation of undesirables.

Representative Albert Johnson, Chairman of the committee, said today:

"The investigation will be a comprehensive attempt to find the defects in the present system, and as a result we hope to be able to recommend to Congress changes that will rid the country of these men whom the Department of Labor has not deported. Congress more than a year ago provided for the deportation of all aliens who advocated the overthrow of this Government by force, and, yet, few of these undesirables have been sent back to their native countries. Three thousand of these aliens are waiting, and we propose to determine the cause of the delay.

"Many of the radicals have been able to check the deportation warrants by writs of habeas corpus. The deportation machinery set up a special court for the work, largely in the Department of Labor, and it may be found advisable to transfer all the proceedings to the Department of Justice and have the deportation trials in the regular courts."

November 9, 1919

35 TAKEN IN RAID HELD FOR ANARCHY

Most of 1,000 Men Caught in Lusk Descent Are Set Free.

7,500 COMMUNISTS HERE

Membership in Party Held to be Crime—John Reed on Way to Russia.

Twenty-five tons of radical literature, among which were several hundredweight of appeals in English from Lenin to the American people and the rest disguised or open pleas for revolution in many languages, was seized in the raids on seventy-one radical headquarters on Saturday night, according to State Senator Clayton R. Lusk, head of the Legislative Committee, investigating Bolshevist and seditious activities.

The money for printing revolutionary circulars, pamphlets and papers by millions, for maintaining the seventy-one radical headquarters which were raided and for keeping hundreds of Red agitators at work in disturbed industrial centres is furnished mainly by large contributors abroad and in this country, Senator Lusk said.

The Communist Party, which was organized in Chicago on Sept. 1 of this year as a coalition of all radicals who believe in overthrowing the Government by violence, apparently has unlimited funds at its disposal, and one of the purposes of the raids of Saturday night was to trace in detail the sources of its income. Senator Lusk pointed to the fact that the communists, officially born only a little more than two months ago, were able to set up seventy-three meeting places and business offices in this city and vast machinery for agitation throughout the country as proof of the great amount of money at their disposal.

Planned to Organize Red Guards.

Senator Lusk said that leaders of the communists, who had been questioned by the committee, had not only admitted that they planned to organize "Red Guards," after the Bolshevist pattern, to overthrow this Government, but that they were working in co-operation with Russia. When he was asked if the committee's investigations showed that the money supplied from abroad came from Russia, he said:

"We have established that they have received very substantial contributions here and substantial sums of money from abroad, but I am not ready to go further into that. This movement, however, did not start in Russia. It started in Germany.

"It has been completely established that the Red Government in Russia was established by 500 radicals, who were shipped by Germany from Switzerland into Russia and who organized the Red Guard and caused a large part of the securities held in Russia to fall into the hands of Germany. It is safe to say that Germany will not be distressed by any Bolshevist moves here. As to the local contributors to this movement, I am not ready to say anything at this time."

Senator Lusk said that Maximilian Cohen, editor of The Communist World and co-leader with John Reed of this communist movement, had admitted that the Communist leaders believed the time was now ripe for the overthrow of the Government of the United States and that they were prepared to take practical steps to organize the "American Red Guard" for the purpose of taking over all Government offices.

"He said that this would not necessarily be done by violence," Senator Lusk said. "He told us that trouble would be avoided, if the officeholders of the nations quietly handed over the keys of their offices and abdicated without disturbance. On the other hand, he said that there would necessarily be slaughter if resistance were offered to the Red Guard."

John Reed Going to Russia.

Dr. Maximilian Cohen was not taken in last night's raids, and is not under arrest. Senator Lusk would not discuss his case. The principal organizer of the Communist Party at the Chicago meeting was John Reed. After telling about the unlimited finances of the Communists, Senator Lusk said that Reed was at present en route to Russia again. No news of his arrest had yet reached the authorities here, and Senator Lusk refused to say whether or not there was a warrant out for his arrest.

The local contributors to the Communist movement, according to Deputy Attorney General Samuel A. Berger, are mainly New York "parlor radicals" of inherited wealth anxious to gain fame and importance as guarantors of the American Red revolution. While he stated some time ago that a list of these contributors had been turned over to the Federal Government, the representative of the Lusk Committee refused to say yesterday what further steps were to be taken regarding the American financial backers of the movement.

The twenty-five tons of literature seized in the raids on Saturday night is at Police Headquarters and in the offices of Chief City Magistrate McAdoo. Weeks of work will be required before the value of this as evidence has been ascertained. The most interesting printed matter so far noted are the appeals of Lenin to American workmen to follow the Bolshevist example.

Although more than 1,000 men were carted to Police Headquarters and questioned on Saturday night and early Sunday morning, only thirty-five of them were held. These are charged with criminal anarchy because of the fact that they belonged to the Communist Party. In the cases of two men charged with this crime, Chief Magistrate McAdoo has ruled that membership in the Communist Party in itself is proof of guilt, because the members sign a statement that they have read the by-laws of the

organization, which pledge members to an attempt to overthrow the institutions of this country. Many of the 1,000 or so who have been turned loose, Senator Lusk said, would probably be re-arrested.

After Evidence, Not Prisoners.

"The raids were made to get evidence, not prisoners," he said. "We chose last night for the raids, when there were no meetings being held at any of these headquarters and when there were important radical meetings in progress at Madison Square Garden, at the Rand School and elsewhere.

"Those who were arrested were gathered in incidentally, because they happened to be on the premises. There was no stretch of authority in taking these 1,000 people. The Criminal Anarchy statute of this State is very broad, and makes those aiding and abetting such movements guilty with the others. Those found at the meeting places were necessarily proper subjects for arrest, and there was not the slightest abuse of power in the proceeding."

According to those who took part in the raids on Saturday night, those who were taken were not beaten or mistreated in any way, which was in contrast to the raid on the Russian People's House on Friday night.

"I didn't hear of any case where there was any resistance," Senator Lusk said, "and there was no reason for hurting anybody."

The records of the Communist Party in this city show a membership of 7,500, according to investigators for the committee, while hundreds are being added every day by the expensive campaign which is being waged for new members from all radical groups. Members of the I. W. W., anarchists, Left Wing Socialists, syndicalists, and other groups are invited to join the Communist Party without breaking with the other radical groups.

Lusk's Statement on Raids.

Senator Lusk gave out the following statement on the raids:

"Over twenty-five tons of literature intended to be used in the campaign now being waged for the overthrow of our Government was seized.

"Over 1,000 persons were examined for the purpose of obtaining records of these individuals found in the rooms of organizations engaged in promoting criminal anarchy.

"Thirty-five were held on the charge of criminal anarchy and other charges on their admission and evidence found on them. The records will be given further investigation.

"Not over 5 per cent. of those brought in were citizens. Many of them stated that they had been in this country ten years but were unable to speak our language. The efforts on the part of some of those present to destroy their cards in the communist organizations indicate that they appreciate the criminal nature of the order.

"At their headquarters at 5 Maspeth Avenue, Brooklyn, a foreigner was taken who had previously told an agent of the committee that he was in charge of the organization there. A search of the premises revealed two loaded revolvers and a quantity of ammunition, also a quantity of chemicals. He was held on a charge of violating the Sullivan law.

"While the obtaining and execution of these search warrants was all planned and the papers prepared before the Federal raid on Friday night, the Federal agents and the immigration authorities were notified and assisted the representatives of the committee in the examinations. There is full harmony and co-operation between all branches of the Federal, State and city authorities. It is also our purpose to give the city and Federal authorities the benefit of the data that we have collected in efforts made by them to enforce the law.

"We believe that the time has come for a thorough, vigorous campaign for the protection of our institutions. We are anxious to have our present laws tested in order that we may know what additional legislation is needed. All that our city and State officials need to destroy this menace to our Government is proper backing by the Legislature. That they will have."

Senator Lusk said that it was originally intended to hold the raids earlier in the week, but that it was feared that riots might occur on Saturday, the second anniversary of the birth of the Bolshevist régime, and that the Lusk Committee raids might be regarded as the cause.

One of those held on a charge of criminal anarchy was Benjamin Gitlow, a former Assemblyman from the Bronx. Another was "Big Jim" Larkin, the Irish agitator, who became famous as the leader of the Dublin strike in 1914. He was found carrying a seaman's passport which bore his photograph, but was made out in the name of I. Wexler. The man arrested at 5 Maspeth Avenue on the charge of violating the Sullivan law was Henry Pearl.

The New York Board of Trade and Transportation announced yesterday that it would start a campaign this week to mobilize the businessmen of New York in a determined effort to crush Bolshevism and radicalism and to free American industry from the disturbing influences which have held it back since the signing of the armistice a year ago.

November 10, 1919

REDS SHOOT DOWN MARCHING VETERANS; MOB LYNCHES ONE

Jail Stormed at Night After Four Ex-Soldiers Are Killed in Parade.

I. W. W. TAKEN AND HANGED

Mob Lynches One Assailant.

SEATTLE, Wash., Nov. 11.—About 8 o'clock tonight the mob surrounding the Centralia Jail succeeded in getting one of the I. W. W.'s arrested out of the jail and into an automobile, rushing him away before the guards could prevent it, telephone reports here said.

At 7:30 tonight the city's lights suddenly were cut off and a volley of

shots rained down Pearl Street. It was during this period that the prisoner was taken from jail and spirited away. He was rushed toward a nearby wood, and at last accounts the crowd had disappeared with him.

According to a report telephoned to The Associated Press tonight from The Centralia Chronicle, the mob took the alleged I. W. W. from jail, escorted him to a point just outside the city limits, and hanged him on a bridge on the old Chehalis military road.

"The man's body is now hanging on a rope under the bridge about ten feet from the water," the message said. "The I. W. W. whom the mob lynched was the one who shot Dale Hubbard during the fight in the river bed."

CENTRALIA, Wash., Nov. 11.—Four former soldiers, members of the American Legion, were killed, two other service men were probably fatally wounded, and several other soldiers were less seriously hurt when members of the Industrial Workers of the World fired on an Armistice Day parade today as it passed the I. W. W. Hall.

The marching veterans raided the hall, seized supposed snipers to the number of eight, according to one account, and sixteen, according to another, and escorted them to jail, protecting them

from a mob that tried to seize them.

Early tonight a meeting to discuss the situation was held at a local club, and soon afterward the city's electric lights failed. In the darkness one man was removed from the jail. Apparently he was placed in an automobile, waiting in readiness, and, flanked by six other cars filled with men, was hurried into a wood near the town.

Reports say that the prisoner was hanged to a bridge. There seems to be no doubt that he was lynched. It became known tonight that the victim was Britt Smith, Secretary of the I. W. W. local here.

Rumors of more violence to come were current late tonight. More than one citizen remarked: "There will not be any I. W. W.'s left in the jail by morning."

The victims of the sudden attack by the Reds, which has infuriated the town and surrounding country, were as follows:

Dead.

McELFRESH, ARTHUR E., Centralia.
CASAGRANDA, Ben, Centralia.
GRIMM, WARREN C., Centralia.
HUBBARD, DALE, Centralia.

Wounded.

WATT, JOHN EARL, Centralia, probably fatally.
FRISCUS, ——, Chehalis.
WATT, ——, Chehalis.

The shooting began when the parade drew abreast of the Industrial Workers of the World Hall, according to witnesses, the bullets going over the heads of the crowds watching the parade. Onlookers say the shots came from every direction and that snipers in the upper windows of the I. W. W. headquarters building fired into the line.

McElfresh was killed instantly. Grimm, who formerly was a Lieutenant, was leading a platoon in the parade and fell at the second burst of fire, fatally wounded. He was an attorney and once a football star at the University of Washington. The death of this athletic idol especially angered the populace.

Casagranda, who was a real estate agent, received a fatal wound in the first fire.

A rifle bullet strick him in the body. "They got me this time," he said, as he doubled up and fell in the street.

Hubbard received his wound in pursuing a supposed I. W. W. According to ex-service men, Hubbard's party caught the man they were chasing on the banks of the Skookumchuck River, a small stream which runs through the town, Hubbard and the man grappled, and the supposed I. W. W. fired into Hubbard's body.

George Stevens, another of the party, kicked the pistol from the I. W. W.'s hands. A rope was thrown about the man's neck, put over the crossarm of a telephone pole, and he was hoisted into the air. The police persuaded the crowd to let the man down, and he was taken to jail nearly dead. It was this man, according to reports, that was taken from jail tonight and hanged.

A. C. Rogers, Mayor of Centralia, A. C. Hughes, Chief of Police, and other citizens addressed the crowd in front of the jail tonight, asking the citizens not to attempt to lynch the prisoners.

Bullets Poured Out on Soldiers.

The whole city had turned out to celebrate the anniversary of the suspension of hostilities, and a large parade was formed, headed by the city's boys who had helped bring about the glad day a year ago, wearing the uniforms that sheltered them in the trenches of France and on the picket lines of the German border.

As the column swung around the corner of Tower Avenue and Second Avenue, the band struck up a patriotic march. Then bullets came into the ranks from an unseen enemy. Men fell to the pavement and tiny rivulets of blood showed the spectators what had taken place, the crack of the rifles of the assassins having been drowned by the blare of the band.

Tiny puffs of smoke from the roof of a near-by building indicated whence the bullets had come, and the nearness of the I. W. W. hall led to the quick decision that the victims had been slain from ambush by radicals who opposed the American system of government. The marching soldiers did not await the order to fall out, but rushed into the near-by structure and made their way to the roofs. The snipers had disappeared (but the service men esarched the highways and byways for all suspicious persons, and then sent parties out into the timbered country around the city.

The service men soon stripped the hall of all furniture and documents and arrested about a dozen men. These were marched to jail, while they were guarded by the former soldiers to prevent their escape and at the same time to protect them from lynching. A mob seeking the prisoners was fought back by the overseas men.

A quantity of arms and ammunition was seized when the I. W. W. headquarters was ransacked. The people broke down the building front and threw into the street and burned all of the organization's literature and property which could be found.

Meanwhile wives, daughters, and sweethearts of the paraders, after a momentary pause from the sudden terror of the situation, had rushed to the aid of the fallen.

Tonight a mob carrying ropes surrounded the Centralia Jail, but it was still guarded by former soldiers. Other former soldiers were doing picket duty tonight in all parts of the city and searching for other suspects.

Farmers from surrounding points and citizens of nearby towns, including Chehalis and Olympia, are pouring into Centralia tonight. Many of them are offering their services.

November 12, 1919

NORTHWEST ROUSED AGAINST REDS; I. W. W. RAIDED IN 4 CITIES, 127 JAILED; RADICALS PLOTTED CENTRALIA ATTACK

PRISONER MAKES CONFESSION

Says Revolutionists Had Four Centralians Marked For Death.

SEATTLE WARNING TO REDS

Mayor Tells Them to Keep That City "Out of Their Future Itineraries."

TACOMA AND ABERDEEN ACT

Much Incendiary Literature Is Seized with Fourscore of Radicals.

CENTRALIA, Wash., Nov. 12.—Cities of western Washington joined Centralia today in arresting members of the Industrial Workers of the World and raiding their headquarters following the firing on an Armistice Day parade here yesterday when four former American soldiers were killed and several were wounded.

The body of "Brick" Smith, the I. W. W. Secretary, who was lynched last night, was found in the Chehalis River, the rope by which he was hanged to the bridge having been subsequently cut.

Twenty-five men and one woman, reported to have radical beliefs, were placed in jail here and later four of the prisoners, including the woman, were removed to the Lewis County jail at Chehalis by National Guardsmen who patrolled Centralia today.

Late tonight former service men entered a poolroom here, lined about 100 persons against the wall and searched them. Sixteen who were said to have carried Industrial Workers of the World membership cards were arrested.

In Seattle, eleven men and "tons of literature," according to the police, were taken to police headquarters, and the Mayor, C. B. Fitzgerald, issued a statement warning all radicals to "leave Seattle off their future itineraries."

Tonight thirty-nine more were arrested in Seattle, the aim being to learn if any orders directing the Centralia shooting were sent from the Seattle local.

The Tacoma police arrested thirty-four alleged members of the Industrial Workers of the World and seized a quantity of radical literature. At Aberdeen, large quantities of literature and the records of the Aberdeen local of the organization were taken.

Prisoners Make Confessions.

Herman Allen, prosecuting attorney, announced that D. Lamb, 16 years old, who was arrested here as an I. W. W., confessed to belonging to the organization. The boy, according to Allen, said he had heard his father, James Lamb, who also was arrested, talking of a plot to start trouble yesterday. The father, Allen added, confessed last night that the radicals had four former service men marked for death because of their activities in a fight that has been waged for some time by Centralia citizens to rid the city of the I. W. W.

"The I. W. W. expected trouble here yesterday, and they were prepared for it," Allen is quoted as saying. "When the parade was almost over without trouble appearing, they decided to start it themselves."

Dr. David Livingston, who served in the war as a Captain, was one of the four marked men, according to Lamb's alleged confession. He is the Coroner here, and will hold an inquest tomorrow over the bodies of the four victims of yesterday's outrage.

All of yesterday's shooting did not come from the buildings in the vicinity of the I. W. W. hall, as first believed, it was learned today when Berdine Fry, a 17-year-old boy, told the police that during the parade he saw a man shooting toward town from a hill not far from the scene of the tragedy. The hill lies east of Centralia's main street. Fry led the police to the spot and they discovered a suitcase containing a box of "soft-nosed" cartridges, a field glass, a man's coat, and a book containing I. W. W. songs.

Centralia was quiet today, and Judge George Dysart said citizens had promised to let the law take its course.

"Last night I talked to them and promised that every I. W. W. arrested here would have a quick and just trial," said Judge Dysart. "The former service men promised to aid officials jail the men."

Clashes between the I. W. W. and Centralia citizens have occurred at intervals during the last two years. The first trouble occurred when a radical spoke against a Red Cross bazaar. At that time a crowd removed all furniture from I. W. W. hall and burned it in the street. Recently a "Protective League" was organized. Every I. W. W. was to be listed, it was planned, and ordered to leave. As a direct answer to the citizens' declaration of war came the attack yesterday.

"Brick" Smith, the I. W. W. Secretary who was lynched, was reported by officials to have a police record in Washington. During the war it was said he caused trouble in Washington lumber camps and a lumber company wrote to a patriotic organization that he was a menace and asked that he be arrested.

Smith was arrested at Cedar Falls, July, 1917, when he and other alleged I. W. W.'s defied a freight train crew at a time farmers complained of sabotage being practiced in the grain fields and fruit orchards.

Following the attack on the parade yesterday, Smith darted from the rear of the I. W. W. headquarters firing an automatic revolver as he ran. Dale Hubbard, recently returned from overseas, gathered a small band and started after the fugitive. Hubbard overtook him and in the struggle that followed Smith shot him four times. An attempt to lynch Smith was made before he was lodged in the jail.

"You fellows can't hang me," he said. "I was sent to do my duty and I did it."

The lynching party worked silently and in darkness while taking him from the jail. At 7:30 o'clock all the city's electric lights were cut off, and eight men easily overcame the one man on guard inside the building. Smith was placed in one of about six darkened automobiles in waiting and rushed to the bridge over the river. Here a rope was tied about his neck while the other end was attached to the structure. Then the doomed man was thrown off, and as his squirming body dangled a volley of shots was sent into it.

No name was mentioned in a verdict rendered by a Coroner's jury which tonight held an inquest over the body believed to be that of Brick Smith.

The jury's verdict said:

"We find that deceased came to his death by gunshot wounds and by strangulation caused by persons unknown."

For a few hours tonight the body lay on the floor of the bridge under which the man was lynched last night. Later it was moved to the county jail. It was expected the Coroner would dispose of it.

No witnesses were examined at the inquest. The jury returned its verdict immediately after it examined the body and Justice of the Peace Charles F. Hoss accepted the verdict without comment.

Of the first twenty-five prisoners arrested an examination tonight disclosed that fourteen were American citizens. Three are Swedes, one Swiss, one Montenegrin, one Bohemian, and one Finn. The nationality of the others could not be learned.

Two groups of former soldiers, most of them members of the American Legion, under leadership of Captain Lloyd Dysart, a Centralia war veteran, returned tonight from Mendota, a coal and logging town near nere, where they searched for Industrial Workers believed to have escaped after the shooting yesterday. They had in custody P. J. Nolan and another man whose name was not learned.

Captain Dysart said the party failed to find Bert Brand, an alleged I. W. W., who, according to A. L. Cornier, adjutant of the parade yesterday, fired the shot that killed Grimm. It was thought today that Brand fled to Mendota.

TO BE DEPORTED TO RUSSIA.

Palmer Plans to Rid Country of Union of Russian Workers.

WASHINGTON, Nov. 12. — Aliens rounded up by Department of Justice agents in the recent raids on headquarters of the Union of Russian Workers in a score of cities will be deported as soon as hearings have been held by the Department of Labor, according to Attorney General Palmer.

Mr. Palmer said today arrangements for their deportation to Russia had been made, but added that he could not disclose to what part of Russia they would be sent.

REDS PLAN VAST CAMPAIGN.

Department of Justice Powerless to Prevent It, Palmer Says.

SPOKANE, Wash., Nov. 12.—Industrial Workers of the World are preparing to launch from their headquarters here a propaganda campaign throughout the Northwest and perhaps through the entire West, in the near future, according to officials of the Department of Justice.

So far, they said, no orders to proceed against them had been received.

Resolutions opposing clemency to any

one convicted of the murder of the four ex-service men at Centralia, and calling upon State and national authorities for a national campaign of suppression against radical organizations, were passed at a meeting of the executive committee of the local American Legion post here today.

Commissioner Tilsley of the Department of Public Safety, in a statement today, blamed the Federal authorities for failure to deport agitators in this section. He said the police were ready to round them up and furnish evidence for such procedure whenever the Government was ready to act.

WASHINGTON, Nov. 12.—Attorney General Palmer said today no orders had been sent to Department of Justice agents to prevent an I. W. W. propaganda campaign in the Northwest because the Department could not act under present laws until some overt act had been committed.

PORTLAND MOVES VIGOROUSLY

Alien Agitators Arrested Tuesday Night to be Deported.

PORTLAND, Ore., Nov. 12.—Immediate proceedings toward deportation of all aliens among the men arrested last night in a raid by the police at I. W. W. headquarters here, will be taken, according to announcement made today by Barnett Goldstein, Acting United States Attorney.

Federal officials today began an investigation of the antecedents and activities of the fifty-three men taken into custody. Reports that speakers at a meeting of the "Council of Workmen" had denounced the American Legion and charged members of the organization with responsibility for the riots at Centralia, caused Mayor Baker, to order the raid.

As soon as reports of the Centralia trouble reached here the chief of police summoned all available patrolmen. Agents of the police sent to the meeting of the council reported that the speeches were of an incendiary character and the raid followed.

One of the prisoners, Joseph Laundy, is a candidate for the presidency of the Central Labor Council. Two other prisoners have been prominent in radical agitation here.

November 13, 1919

PUTTING DOWN THE REDS.

President BUTLER of Columbia is right in saying that the instant and most vital thing for Americans to do now, the thing on which all Americans should unite without regard to politics, is the smashing of the Bolsheviki and the I. W. W. All over the country we catch sight every day of the unrelenting activities of these enemies of the United States and of every free, orderly Government. The number of these destructionists in our own city is great. The number of their organs in English and in foreign tongues is great. Rich, " superior " men and women of New York, persons who suppose themselves to be " intellectuals " because they have lost the prime and common feeling of American patriotism, endow and support Bolshevist periodicals with a circulation of 3,000,000.

" Do you realize," asks President BUTLER, " that within a mile or two of this " room there could be counted fifty " meetings, each attended by from a " score to a hundred men and women, " where everything for which this country stands is being attacked?" The enemy is here and everywhere. In President BUTLER'S words, " we must repeat " the great demonstration of 1917 and " summon all the resources of America " not for war overseas, but for a war at " home." We must repress, deport, make impotent the irreconcilable radicals. To them no mercy should be shown. The country is full of violent aliens who should be made to leave it for its good. Meanwhile the great mass, not yet hopeless, of aliens in the United States must be taught to know what the American institutions are which so many blatant agitators, alien and native, are seeking to subvert. And this immense foreign population, neither speaking nor thinking American, must be taught to speak and think American.

November 16, 1919

RADICALISM AND SEDITION AMONG THE NEGROES, AS REFLECTED IN THEIR PUBLICATIONS.

From the Report of the Department of Justice.

AT this time there can no longer be any question of a well-concerted movement among a certain class of negro leaders of thought and action to constitute themselves a determined and persistent source of a radical opposition to the Government, and to the established rule of law and order.

Among the more salient points to be noted in the present attitude of the negro leaders are, first, the ill-governed reaction toward negro rioting; second, the threat of retaliatory measures in connection with lynching; third, the more openly expressed demand for social equality, in which demand the sex problem is not infrequently included; fourth, the identification of the negro with such radical organizations as the I. W. W. and an outspoken advocacy of the Bolsheviki or Soviet doctrines; fifth, the political stand assumed toward the present Federal Administration, the South in general, and incidentally, toward the Peace Treaty and the League of Nations.

Underlying these more salient viewpoints is the increasingly emphasized feeling of a race consciousness, in many of these publications always antagonistic to the white race, and openly, defiantly assertive of its own equality and even superiority. When it is borne in mind that this boast finds its most frequent expression in the pages of those journals whose editors are men of education, in at least one instance men holding degrees conferred by Harvard University, it may be seen that the boast is not to be dismissed lightly as the ignorant vaporing of untrained minds.

Neither is the influence of the negro press in general to be reckoned with lightly. The Negro World for Oct. 18, 1919, states that "there are a dozen negro papers with a circulation of over 20,000, and scores with smaller circulation. There are half a dozen magazines with a large circulation, and other magazines with a smaller circulation, and there are easily over fifty writers who can write interesting editorials and special articles, written in fine, pure English, with a background of scholarship behind them." Notwithstanding the clumsiness of expression

of this particular assertion, the claim is not an idle one. It may be added that in several instances the negro magazines are expensive in manufacture, being on coated paper throughout, well printed, and giving evidence of the possession of ample funds.

In all the discussions of the recent race riots there is reflected the note of pride that the negro has found himself, that he has "fought back," that never again will he tamely submit to violence or intimidation.

The sense of oppression finds increasingly bitter expression. Defiance and insolently race-centred condemnation of the white race is to be met with in every issue of the more radical publications, and this one in moderateness of denunciation carries its own threat. The negro is "seeing red," and it is the prime object of the leading publications to induce a like quality of vision upon the part of their readers. A few of them deny this, notwithstanding the evidence of their work. Others of them openly admit the fact. The number of restrained and conservative publications is relatively negligible, and even some of these, it will later be shown, have indulged in most intemperate utterances, though it would be unfair not to state that certain papers—I can think of no magazine—maintain an attitude of well-balanced sanity. • • •

I call attention first to The Negro World, a weekly publication. • • • In its issue of July 26, 1919, The Negro World bore an editorial closing with these words:

"It is true that all races look forward to the time when spears shall be beaten into agricultural implements, but until that time arrives it devolves upon all oppressed peoples to avail themselves of every weapon that may be effective in defeating the fell motives of their oppressors.

"In a world of wolves one should go armed, and one of the most powerful defensive weapons within the reach of negroes • • •."

The Messenger, the monthly magazine published in New York, is by long odds the most able and the most dangerous of all the negro publications. It is representative of the most educated thought among the negroes. We find on its editorial

board men bearing degrees from Harvard University, and among its regular special contributors those actually engaged upon other negro publications and prominent among the negro radical movement. The March, 1919, number was the first to be published after the return of the editors from military service. There was no April issue, and the May-June issue is one. Since then The Messenger has come out regularly and with an increasing crystallization of radical purpose.

A glance at the relatively harmless nature of the March issue with that succeeding in May-June will show how speedily The Messenger took the bit in its teeth. • • •

The Messenger for October is significant for one thing above all others. In it for the first time a negro publication comes out openly for sex equality. It is the habit of most of the negro publications to deny that they advocate social equality. The Messenger claims it, and, furthermore, with it, sex equality.

In an article on "The Social Experience of the Negro Soldier Abroad," the matter of social equality is again advanced:

"Indeed, the social experience of the American negro abroad will continue to produce, from the present time on, the most favorable and proper reaction. Remembering the pleasantness of French life, he will not rest until he has caused to be ushered into the United States a state of complete and uncompromising economic, political, and social equality. This program will call for the benefit of every enjoyment, privilege, and immunity which the white race does or will possess in America."

Just what is implied by the above statement, if any doubt may exist, a preceding paragraph of this article will make unquestionable:

"Briefly stated, the principal points of social contact which the negro soldiers had were the towns, the cafés and restaurants, the leave areas, and the great cities. In each one of those groups of places they enjoyed with the French the common, everyday experience of life. It is needless to say that the French took

the negro soldiers on terms of absolute social equality, just as they took Englishmen or Belgians on terms of absolute social equality. Of all the American soldiers, the good-natured negro, who learned the French language and manners so easily, was without a doubt the best-liked American. Hundreds of unsolicited testimonials, verbal and written, attest to this undeniable fact. Many are the reminiscences with which black men refer to their fair treatment in all parts of France. Once the fine nature and high character of the negro Americans became manifest, the French people opened their homes welcomely to them. They wined and dined them at every opportunity. They made invidious comparisons between the whites and the blacks, but always in favor of the blacks.

"When the riots between French and American soldiers and sailors occurred at Brest, the French made it emphatically clear that American negroes, 'camarades,' could walk the streets without molestation. To show how well the French people received American negroes, various estimates place the number of marriages of American negroes and French girls between 1,000 and 2,000. Though most of these marriages were among the bourgeoisie and proletariat, a surprisingly fair percentage was found among women of culture and refinement. It was quite the custom for negro officers to spend their leaves with French families to whom they had become endeared. Barring misunderstandings, due to differences in language, American negroes in France enjoyed the highest degree of social equality compatible with current conditions.

"While enjoying unrestricted social equality among the French population, negroes saw, among other things, negro Deputies in the French Chamber, French negro officers commanding French soldiers, white and colored; no color or caste discrimination whatsoever; in short, a country characterized by the fullest social, religious, and political equality for every class and race and nationality."

November 23, 1919

RADICALS' ACTIVITY GROWS, SAYS PALMER

Attorney General Reports Agitation Increasing—Asks Stronger Laws.

PUTS BLAME ON CONDITIONS

WASHINGTON, Dec. 8.—The Department of Justice is confronted with "increasingly dangerous radical activities," Attorney General Palmer said in his annual report submitted today to Congress. He did not go into details as to "Red" activities in general, but said that of the total of 365,295 index record cards,

71,000 Bertillon records, and 262,712 fingerprint records now in the department, some 60,000 represented data concerning "Reds" and their work.

He mentioned that the department had increased steadily its contributory sources of investigation, adding that this meant better facilities for running down persons whose lives bore marks of crime.

Mr. Palmer quotes from the letter written recently to the Committee on Immigration and Naturalization of the House, asking for more effective legislation to permit the deportation of dangerous aliens and punishment for incendiary utterances.

Radicalism and labor unrest in the United States are due more to social and economic conditions than to the efforts of individual agitators, according to Mr. Palmer.

"On Aug. 1, 1919," Mr. Palmer says, "a definite division of the bureau was formed to deal with radicalism. As mentioned elsewhere in this report, the work of the bureau has not resulted in a large

number of criminal prosecutions since the armistice by reason of the present state of permanent legislation on the subject. The Federal statutes are exceedingly limited in so far as they affect persons of American citizenship engaged in radical agitation. The efforts of this division have, therefore, been largely centered upon the activities of alien agitators, with the object of securing the deportation of such persons. To this end very close relations have been established with the office of the Commissioner General of Immigration. Already this policy has shown results, and it is believed that, in the near future, the country may be freed of the presence of a considerable number of undesirable aliens who have come as missionaries of unrest rather than as emigrants from oppression.

"At the same time it is clearly recognized that the present unrest and tendency toward radicalism arise from social and economic conditions that are of greater consequence than the individual agitator."

December 9, 1919

249 REDS SAIL, EXILED TO SOVIET RUSSIA; BERKMAN THREATENS TO COME BACK; SECOND SHIPLOAD MAY LEAVE THIS WEEK

BUFORD LEAVES AT DAWN

Heads Eastward With Cargo of Sedition Under Heavy Soldier Guard.

THREE WOMEN IN PARTY

Emma Goldman Shows Bravado —Glad to Go, She Says, Predicting Triumphant Return.

SOME HAPPY, OTHERS CURSE

Carry Great Quantity of Baggage and Quarter Million Dollars in Cash.

Under the guns of Fort Wadsworth the leaden-colored transport Buford loomed vaguely in the beginning of yesterday's dawn, her port holes blinking out one by one as light came on. Shortly after 6 o'clock, splashing and rasping in the silence of the empty bay, the anchors came up to the bow, the Buford's prow swung lazily eastward, a patch of foam slipped from under the stern and 249 persons who didn't like America left it.

Some indifferent, some happy, some cursing, some sullen and some crying, the company of radicals guilty, by confession, of seeking the overthrow of American ideals and institutions, passed out to sea while the city slept—went out without the slightest chance to pose as the martyrs they considered themselves to be. Two hundred of them started on their way forty-four days after they were arrested.

Scarcely an hour after the Buford departed for Soviet Russia, bound, it was believed her secret sailing orders read, for Cronstadt, an hour's ride from Petrograd, it was ascertained that yesterday's action was the beginning of an extremely rigorous policy against radicals. Another shipload is going out, perhaps this week, and a drive to cut down the Department of Justice's list of 60,000 radicals in the nation already has been started, with Assistant Attorney General Francis P. Garvan and Chief William J. Flynn of the Secret Service cooperating in direction.

The action that ended yesterday had its beginning when Mr. Garvan joined the staff of Attorney General A. Mitchell Palmer, it was said yesterday. He took office determined to stamp out the Red menace. The first results of this determination were the wholesale raids of the Department of Justice on Nov. 7—action aimed chiefly at the Union of Russian Workers, the constitution of which advocated the destruction by any means of all government. Two hundred who went out yesterday—and there were sixty-one New Yorkers among them—were the fruits of these raids.

Buford Picked for Voyage.

Quietly conducted investigations and arrests in the industrial centres in New England, in the Middle West, in Seattle, San Francisco, Butte, and at a few Southern points followed. The goal of the Federal agents was the capture of the leaders, the "intellectuals," of agitation, and on the Buford, in the opinion of Chief Flynn, went the brains of the ultra-radical movement.

Many trains, starting from widely scattered points, converged on Ellis Island. The prisoners they brought mounted from tens to hundreds, until Saturday night more than 300 were caged there. As the island filled, official Washington seemed to find itself in a dilemma. No one seemed to know where to get a ship to deport the undesirables.

Finally, Mr. Garvan went to the War Department, talked it over with Secretary Baker, and a liner was obtained for Emma Goldman, who failed to find the kind of liberty she sought after thirty-four years here; for Alexander Berkman, anarchist and attempted assassin, and for the lesser fry.

The ship chosen was the old Buford, not quite 5,000 tons, which has done a deal of tossing about in her twenty-eight years of seafaring. Captain George J. Hitchcock, who commanded her when she carried troops in the Spanish war and A. E. F. doughboys more recently, was told last Wednesday to get his 125 American-born officers and men busy revamping troop quarters for a cargo of Reds.

He was instructed to load stores and provisions enough to last 500 persons sixty days, and was told that he probably would be cruising for eighteen days, allowing for the usual bad weather at this time of year. He also was told to issue automatic revolvers to a detail of guards to be picked from his crew.

250 Soldiers as Guard.

Over at the Port of Embarkation Colonel John Hilton was directed to prepare to sail on the Buford in command of a full company of 250 soldiers from Governors Island, assigned to supplement the crew. In the Military Intelligence Section of the General Staff at Washington Colonel A. Ely was informed that he was detailed to accompany the deportees to their destination. Men from the Department of Justice and Immigration Service also were assigned to make the trip.

Saturday evening the Government's preparations were completed. The transport had steam up. Commissioner General Anthony Caminetti came from Washington and went to Ellis Island. Also from Washington to witness the deportations came members of the House committee that has been investigating immigration methods, including Representative Isaac Siegel of New York, Representative Albert Johnson of Washington, Representative J. E. Raker of California, and Representative William N. Vaile of Colorado. Representative Rowe of Brooklyn was with the party.

After all agencies were ready, the Reds on the island were told that the warnings of the previous three days had materialized—that they were going away, and soon. The news was broken after they had savagely attacked frankfurters and cabbage, rice pudding, apple sauce and coffee. As the anarchistic vehemence of Peter J. Bianki's condemnation of the coffee as "too cold," was lapsing into the echo stage, Acting Commissioner Bryon H. Uhl went into the community dining room and said they were going to make a trip.

They took it calmly, and without rising from their seats, took a vote and elected Berkman leader of the expedition. The one-time assailant of the late Henry C. Frick, clothed with this authority, demanded to know "when we're going."

"A couple of hours from now," replied Mr. Uhl. According to an official who was present, the countenance of Emma Goldman lost some of its color, but she checked herself and became as stolid as the two other women prisoners, Dora Lipkin and Ethel Bernstein, who sat with emotionless faces.

Sing the "Internationale."

For a spell, the Reds sat at the tables silent. Then Berkman stood up, studying the faces keenly through his abnormally large tortoise shell rimmed spectacles. It seemed that he sensed a breakdown of bravado, that a minute more and the "comrades" might display what the guards would call "the yellow."

"Comrades, let us sing!" he shouted, and launched himself into the "Internationale."

With scores of Department of Justice operatives, Immigration Service agents and Ellis Island attaches accelerating their movements, the deportees were told to produce their luggage and their bundles—they must have had a thousand bulky packages, containing everything from canned soup to nuts—and congregate in the big room in the south wing of the main immigration building.

Lugging their grips and old-fashioned, foreign-looking portmanteaus, their Old World tin trunks—small affairs in weird colors—extra overcoats and boxes of apples and oranges, the Reds trooped into the big, warm, bare, brilliantly lighted room. They put their belongings down in heaps and squatted down on them. Some sat with hands under chin, elbows on knees; some read books; others glanced through tattered copies of newspapers. Groups talked noisily in Russian. Here and there a man strummed the melancholy strains of Russian peasant songs upon a battered banjo, guitar, or mandolin.

The ensemble looked for all the world like a party of immigrants waiting in Grand Central Station for a train to take them somewhere in the new land of opportunity. The simile was fortified by tags they wore. There the comparison ended, for there was none of the materials from which Americanism is made in the sullen faces or the conversation.

Berkman Expects Warm Welcome.

Seated apart was Berkman, tying extra twine around a paper bag of oranges. Beads of perspiration dotted his broad, bald head. Even his straggling black mustache looked weary. He had his coat off and was wearing a khaki shirt and black tie, that looked like army issue. His trousers also were identical with the kind issued to Private Jones or Smith or Brown when he was convalescent in France from wounds.

Berkman was asked what he expected to find in Russia.

"I have an uncle there," he said. "His name is N. Starick. It means 'old man.' About thirty years ago he was sentenced to death by the Czar. He escaped from Siberia and got to Paris, where he lived for fifteen years. While there he became the intellectual head of the revolutionary movement throughout Europe. At the beginning of the Russian revolution he went home, and now is in charge of the railways in Russia and also is head of the Moscow Soviet.

"You can see from that that I am going among friends. I expect to go to Petrograd and carry out my ideas. I intend to co-operate with Lenin and Trotzky. As for my fellow prisoners, some of these fellows were merely poor miners. They know nothing about anarchy, but on my way over I am going to convert them. I am happy to go back to Soviet Russia."

Emma Goldman, who began an unremitting preachment against America, "capitalism," church and State thirty-four years ago, when she landed at the age of 15 from Kovno, Russia, by way of Rhenish Prussia, was found coming out of a nap.

"I do not consider it a punishment to be sent to Soviet Russia," she said in strident tones. "On the contrary, I consider it an honor to be the first political agitator deported from the United States. The Czar of Russia never resorted to such autocratic methods as the Government of the United States has in dealing with Russians. I can assure you that any other American who comes to Russia will receive a greater hospitality than we have here.

"Am Coming Back," Says Emma.

"Incidentally, I am coming back. I am not going to stop my work as long as life remains. The plan we have considered, which I am going to work on particularly, is the immediate organization in Soviet Russia of the Russian Friends of American Freedom. I insist that I am an American. This practice of deportation means the beginning of the end of the United

States Government."

Emma Goldman was dressed entirely in black. She was interrupted by the arrival of Arthur Katzes and Ethel Bernstein. Katzes, who is noticeable for width of chin, and Miss Bernstein for breadth of jaw, are summed up in Government records as follows:

Both of these are members of the Union of Russian Workers, and from their own admissions they are anarchists and believe in violence. On Sept. 29, 1919, both were arrested, charged with distributing seditious literature, and since that time, it is said, have been indicted on charges of criminal anarchy. Both Katzes and the Bernstein woman are aged 22 years. The man was born in Russia and has been in the United States about five years, arriving by way of Canada. He claims employment as a pressman. Ethel Bernstein claims to be a dressmaker. She arrived in the United States from Russia eight years ago. Neither has ever made any attempt to become a citizen of this country."

Bianki "Glad to Go."

Both, according to the Government record, said they were happy to get away from America, Katzes adding that "the Government is just taking the top of the movement."

Over in a corner was Peter J. Bianki, atheist, exponent of free love, formerly General Secretary of the Union of Russian Workers, a black-looking person, listed by the Federal authorities as "exceedingly dangerous."

"Damn the country. Glad to go," he said curtly, without looking up from an expensive-looking shoe he was studying. Then he yelled after the departing questioner: "What time do we go?"

That was the question that buzzed through the room ceaselessly as the deportees watched the big clock's hand travel into morning. As 2 o'clock approached the various agencies of deportation began to move. With the departure of cutters from the Battery bearing the Congressmen, Chief Flynn, and a number of agents things began to speed up.

Almost as soon as the cutters had reached the island, where four searchlights were playing on the building and all else was dark, the Buford had slipped from her South Brooklyn berth and plowed through the drifting ice to the point off Fort Wadsworth. Arrived there, the signal was flashed to the island and the deportees were marched out to the departmental boat Immigrant.

Between lanes of agents the Reds walked, without a word, except Berkman, who, at the head of the gangplank, turned and caught a glimpse of the broad figure of Chief Flynn in the half light.

Threatens Vengeance on Flynn.

"Oh, it's you, Mr. Flynn," he said, sarcastically. "Well, we're coming back some day, and when we do—" a curse— "we'll fix you."

In five minutes the Reds were aboard and soldiers with fixed bayonets were lining the rails. The Immigrant backed out, and swinging across the bay made for the anchorage of the Buford. She moved slowly, and it was 4:45 o'clock before the bulk of the transport loomed superior to the solid blackness—a row of lighted portholes staring out of the darkness.

Close to the transport went the load of Reds. The Immigrant was made fast, a lower deck port was swung open, and Berkman and Goldman and the rest of them filed aboard, while one of their number, said to have been Bianki, shouted a farewell, "Long live the revolution in America!"

Once aboard, the deportees were ordered to bed. They were assigned to bunks once used by soldiers bound for France. The three women were assigned to a first-class cabin; the records in the deportation proceedings were turned over to Colonel Hilton and Captain Hitchcock; the lower deck port doors clanged closed, and, as dawn came, the Buford headed toward the Narrows and Soviet Russia.

The transport was far at sea before Harry Weinberger, counsel for Berkman and Goldman; Isaac Schorr, counsel for others of the Reds; friends, relatives, and former asso-

ciates of the Buford's passengers were aware of what had happened. Then came the type-written statements.

Mrs. Stella Ballentine, niece of Emma Goldman, gave out at her home at 36 Grove Street the Berkman-Goldman valedictory. The statement condemned the deportations. Weinberger's statement criticized the deportations. Mr. Schorr's statement declared that he had not been told what was to take place, but added that he felt certain the Government would take his late clients to Soviet Russia and not to anti-Bolshevist territory.

One Gets Habeas Corpus Writ.

"There were 249 deportees aboard, and would have been 250 but one, Alexis Gregorious, obtained a writ of habeas corpus yesterday," said Congressman Siegel last night. "I was surprised at the excellence of the arrangement on the Buford. The linen, pillows, and other equipment for the comfort of the passengers were of the very best. I might say they are traveling de luxe."

Terming the departure as "an impressive sight," Mr. Siegel remarked on the amount of baggage the Reds took with them and the $250,000 in cash.

"Speaking for myself, and my colleagues agree with me," he added, "this deportation is a good thing. We believe it will convince those who are left behind, and who feel as those who have been deported feel, that the Government is still here."

Neither Mr. Caminetti, who left last night for Washington, nor the local officers of the Department of Justice would supply a complete list of the radicals deported.

December 22, 1919

CAMBRIDGE TEACHER IN SEIZED RED LIST

Mary Peabody, Radcliffe Graduate, Declares She Is Thoroughly Radical.

Special to The New York Times.

CAMBRIDGE, Mass., Dec. 21.—Miss Mary Peabody, who was graduated from Radcliffe College last June and who is among the prominent persons on the lists

seized in the raid on the alleged Red headquarters, declared today she was a "radical through and through, forever."

Miss Peabody has just been suspended temporarily as a teacher in the Cambridge public schools.

"I glory in the strength of my convictions and I have never denied them. I am a radical," Miss Peabody asserts.

Miss Peabody will be married on Christmas Day, at her home at 13 Hilliard Street, to J. Leslie Hotson, a junior at Harvard. He spent fourteen months with the Quaker reconstruction unit during the war. When he graduates he plans to go to Russia with his wife, as members of the "Friends Reconstruction Unit," it is stated.

Miss Peabody was a leading member of the Radical Club at Radcliffe, which

recently changed its name to the Liberal Club. Her sister, now a student there, is a member of that organization.

Mrs. Peabody, the mother of the two sisters, said:

"I taught my girls to advocate reform without violence. We believe in reconstruction without bloodshed, in free speech and free assemblage. Arrests of radicals are foolish and they are bound to augment trouble."

Miss Caroline Eliot and Miss Rosamond Eliot, granddaughters of President Emeritus Eliot of Harvard, are members of the Radcliffe Liberal Club.

Miss Peabody criticised District Attorney Gallagher for his statement that the girl students were "dilettantes, with no anchorage in the moral world," and denied his charge that he was unable to find any of their names in connection with the Red Cross or other war relief activities.

December 22, 1919

"RED" WORKS IN LIBRARIES.

For Reference Only—Not for Young or in Branches, Director Says.

In reply to a published statement regarding radical propaganda and the part played by libraries in its dissemination through anarchistic literature, E. H. Anderson, Director of The New York Public Library (Astor, Lenox and Tilden foundations), issued the following statement yesterday:

"According to Saturday morning's papers, a special agent of the Lusk Legislative Committee testified on Friday that Bakunin's works were in the Public Library at Fifth Avenue and Forty-second Street, notwithstanding

the fact that he had seen denials in the press.

"We never made any such denial. We did deny a young Russian's statement that he had received his education in anarchy by reading Bakunin in one of our branches. Bakunin is in none of our branches, and the boy was never registered as a reader under the name given in the newspapers. We have repeatedly stated in the public press that, in the large reference collection in the Central Library, at Fifth Avenue and Forty-second Street, we gather all the literature we can, representing all shades of political or economic opinion. We do not permit the use of revolutionary printed matter by the young in the Central Building, nor do we have any of it for use in our branches.

"Hundreds of letters go out from the Central Library every day over my name, to all parts of the world, asking for the publications of this, that or the other organization. We collect radical as well as conservative literature so that students of economics and politics may know what even the wildest radicals are thinking, saying and advocating. The Lusk Committee has some of this radical material subpoenaed from us at this moment; and I hope we are not boasting when we express the opinion that our collections have materially assisted in their investigations.

"It seems to be difficult to get people to understand that the New York Public Library is really two libraries under one management. The Circulation Department of this institution includes forty-two branches, besides the circulation branch on the ground floor of the central building. The books available in these branches are quite different from those in the Reference Department, where we have considerably over a million volumes and pamphlets on all sides of every conceivable subject. It is harmful and misleading to print 'scare-heads' to the effect that the Library has this, that or the other objectionable book. We have here in the Reference Department thousands and thousands of books of which we do not approve. Those on anarchism and allied subjects are here for the student

of modern political conditions and for the use of our courts and officers of the law. This literature is in almost daily use in the courts of New York.

"To attempt to draw a line as to what in the realm of political theory should be included in our big reference collection, and what excluded, would not only be impracticable but absurd. The big reference collection here is for the use of grown men and women, who must find their own protection against folly and false doctrine.

"We agree with John Milton, who said 'Though all the winds of doctrine were let loose to play upon the earth, so Truth be in the field, we do ingloriously, by licensing and prohibiting, to misdoubt her strength. Let her and Falsehood grapple; who ever knew Truth put to the worse in a free and open encounter?'"

December 29, 1919

PALMER PLEDGES WAR ON RADICALS

WASHINGTON, Dec. 31.—Asserting that sympathizers in the Bolshevist movement in this country "are composed chiefly of criminals, mistaken idealists, social bigots, and many unfortunate men and women suffering with varying forms of hyperaesthesia," Attorney General Palmer tonight, in a New Year's message to the nation, pledged the Department of Justice to an unflinching and aggressive warfare against all forms of radicalism which sought to overthrow the Government.

During the coming year, Mr. Palmer said, leaders of such movements and all others who sought to arouse sympathy for radical proposals would be proceeded against and he predicted that their efforts would be defeated.

Mr. Palmer summed up his attitude toward the radical elements in the following statement:

"It would be extremely helpful to the cause of good government, the maintenance of law and order, and the preservation of peace and happiness in our country if the people on this New Year's Day would resolve to study, understand, and appreciate the so-called 'Red' movement. They can counteract it most effectively by teaching its purpose through the press, the church, the schools, patriotic organizations, and labor unions, all of which are within the range of its insidious attacks.

The 'Red' movement does not mean an attitude of protest against alleged defects in our present political and economic organization of society. It does not represent the radicalism of progress. It represents a specific doctrine, namely, the introduction of dictatorship the world over by force and violence. It is not a movement of liberty-loving persons, but a distinctly criminal and dishonest movement. Lenin himself made the statement at the Third Soviet Conference, 'Among 100 so-called Bolsheviki there is 1 real Bolshevik, 39 criminals and 60 fools.' It advocates the destruction of all ownership in property, the destruction of all religion and belief in God.

It is a movement organized against democracy and in favor of the power of the few built up by force. Bolshevism, syndicalism, the Soviet Government, sabotage, &c., are only new names for old theories of violence and criminality.

Tells of Russian Conditions.

"More than two years ago the fanatical doctrinaires of communism in Russia took advantage of the situation that has developed in that suffering country. The war had brought the Russian people to a state of acute economic distress. The first revolution, the democratic and national revolution of March, 1917, had inevitably caused much more confusion of mind in the masses of the people, who had been allowed to go hungry and ignorant under the old regime of the Czars.

"After more than two years the Bolsheviki, who, under these conditions, seized the Government, property and power, are still promising the workmen and peasants of Russia 'peace, bread and land'; but have been unable to satisfy or help them except through the wasteful consumption of accumulated stocks. Even their so-called 'Soviet Constitution' has been suspended, and the country is ruled by self-appointed communist commissionaries. The 'dictatorship of the proletariat' has degenerated into a military dictatorship of a subsidized and corrupt portion of the proletariat.

"Though their adherents in this country are advocating and fomenting strikes, Lenin and Trotzky forbid strikes and trade unions are being broken up and completely subordinated to the will of the few demagogues in control. This Bolshevist experiment on the living body of the Russian people has not proven in any sense of the word an experiment in democracy. The Bolshevist leaders frankly repudiate democratic principles as we understand them. It has been a gamble which meant for Russia, and, indeed, for the whole of humanity, enormous losses in lives as well as in material resources. The Bolshevism have run up a colossal bill which the Russian workmen and peasants will have to pay.

"Having lived at the expense of the Russian people for two years, these speculators in human lives and other peoples' earnings are trying to move to new fields, to the east and

to the west, hoping to take advantage of the economic distress and confusion of mind in which humanity finds itself after the terrific strain of five years of war.

"Its sympathizers in this country are composed chiefly of criminals, mistaken idealists, social bigots, and many unfortunate men and women suffering with varying forms of hyperaesthesia. They are enemies of the Government, of the Church and of the home, and advocate principles which mean the abolition of all three of these safeguards of civilization.

What the Reds Would Do.

"Twenty million people in this country own Liberty bonds. These the Reds propose to take away. Nine million eight hundred and thirty thousand people in the United States own farms, and 3,838,000 more own homes, which they would forfeit. Eleven million odd people have savings accounts in savings banks, and 18,000,000 people have deposits in our national banks, at which they aim. There are hundreds of thousands of churches and religious institutions, all of which they would abolish. In other words, 110,000,000 hard-working and saving people, who own property, love liberty and worship God, are asked to abandon all the ideals of religion, liberty and government which are the outcome of the struggles of their fathers and their own development, and to place themselves, their homes, their families and their religious faith in the keeping, and their property under the domination, of a small group of Lenins and Trotzkys.

"This department, as far as existing law allows, intends during the forthcoming year to keep up an unflinching, persistent, aggressive warfare against any movement, no matter how cloaked or dissembled, having for its purpose either the promulgation of these ideas or the excitation of sympathy for those who spread them. The movement will not be permitted to go far enough in this country to disturb our peace and well-being, or create any widespread distrust of the people's Government. It will fall away before the light of popular knowledge and appreciation of its aims and purposes."

January 1, 1920

REDS RAIDED IN SCORES OF CITIES; 2,600 ARRESTS, 700 IN NEW YORK; DEPORTATION HEARINGS BEGIN TODAY

RAID FROM COAST TO COAST

Special to The New York Times.

WASHINGTON, Jan. 2.—A nationwide raid on members of the Communist Party and the Communist Labor Party was conducted tonight by agents of the Department of Justice. In thirty-three cities of the country, extending from the

Pacific to the Atlantic, and many neighboring towns, Secret Service operatives, armed with thousands of warrants, set out to make wholesale arrests. According to reports reaching here the total of arrests up to a late hour had reached nearly 2,600.

Excerpts made public from a manifesto of the Communist Party revealed that the organization contemplates the overthrow of the American system of government and its replacement by a

"workers industrial republic," or Soviet system. It was said tonight at the Department of Justice that the Communist Party and the Communist Labor Party—between which there is little difference—supported the Third International,—which was formed under the auspices of Lenin and Trotzky at Moscow, March 6, 1919.

Totals of the Arrests.

Up to midnight these unofficial reports of total arrests from the centers of Red activities had been received:

Raiders Ordered to Make Cleanup Thorough; Warned Against Violence or Taking Valuables

The following instructions as to the conduct of the raids were issued in identical form to all Department of Justice men engaged in the action throughout the country:

INSTRUCTIONS.

Our activities will be directed against the radical organizations known as the Communist Party of America and the Communist Labor Party of America, also known as Communists.

The strike will be made promptly and simultaneously at 8:30 P. M. in all districts. The meeting places of the Communists in your territory, and the names and addresses of the officers and heads that you are to arrest, are on the attached lists.

You will also arrest all active members where found.

Particular efforts should be made to apprehend all the officers, irrespective of where they may be, and, with respect to such officers, their residence should be searched and in every instance all literature, membership cards, records and correspondence are to be taken.

When a citizen is arrested as a Communist, he must be present with the officers searching his home at the time of the search.

Meeting rooms should be thoroughly searched.

Locate and obtain the charter. All records, if not found in the meeting rooms, will probably be found in the home of the Recording Secretary or Financial Secretary, but in every instance, if possible records should be found and taken.

All literature, books, papers, pictures on the walls of the meeting places, should be gathered together and tagged with tags which will be supplied you, with the name and address of the person by whom obtained and where obtained.

In searching meeting places, a thorough search should be made and the walls sounded.

It is an order of the Government that violence to those apprehended should be scrupulously avoided.

Immediately upon the apprehension of the alien, or citizen, search him thoroughly. If found in groups in a meeting room, they should be lined up against the wall and searched. Particular efforts should be made to obtain membership cards on the persons who are taken.

Make an absolute search of the individual. No valuables, such as jewelry and moneys, to be taken away from those arrested.

After a search has been made of the person arrested you will take all the evidence you have obtained from his person and place in an envelope, which will be furnished you, placing the name, address, contents of the envelope, by whom taken and where, on the outside of the envelope and deliver to me with the alien.

Everybody will remain on duty until relieved, without exception.

Flashlights, string, tags and envelopes should be carried, as per instructions.

In searching rooms of an alien pay particular attention to everything in the room and make a thorough search thereof.

You are also warned to take notice " that no violence is to be used."

You will communicate with me by telephone from your several districts, the number of the telephone herewith given.

Attached you will find a list of those to be apprehended in your district, and you will also apprehend all those found arrested with these names at the time of the arrest whom you find to be active members of the Communist Party.

You are also instructed to use reasonable care and good judgment.

Ansonia	12	Louisville	21
Baltimore	35	Manchester, N. H.	65
Berlin, N. H.	40	Meriden	3
Boston	37	Milwaukee	30
Buffalo and vicinity	135	Nashua, N. H.	161
		New York City	700
Bridgeport	15	Oakland, Cal.	18
Cambridge	1	Portland, Ore.	30
Cleveland	100	Philadelphia	200
Chelsea	24	Pittsburgh	21
Chicopee	16	St. Paul	1
Detroit	400	St. Louis	23
Denver	6	Springfield, Mass.	65
Erie, Pa.	2	Toledo	8
Grand Rapids	6	Youngstown	16
Holyoke	20	Wellesley, Mass.	2
Haverhill	21	Waterbury	7
Hartford	2	Worcester	65
Kansas City	12	Wilkesbarre and vicinity	70
Lawrence	19	Connecticut towns	11
Lowell	46	Rhode Island cities	30
Lynn	47		
Los Angeles	1		
Total			2,585

Simultaneously with the announcement of the country-wide raids, Attorney General Palmer gave out a copy of a letter he sent on Dec. 29 to Maclay Hoyn, State's Attorney of Illinois, who last night put 200 radicals in jail on his own authority and declared that he had been asked by the Department of Justice to hold off. Mr. Hoyn asserted that this was "pussyfoot politics" on the part of the Attorney General, and also said that the Reds had been warned of the forthcoming raids.

Mr. Palmer's letter shows that raids upon an extensive scale were contemplated at the time he wrote to Mr. Hoyn. For this reason the Attorney General requested the State's Attorney to postpone independent action for ten days.

This formal statement on the raids was issued by the Department of Justice:

" Agents of the Department of Justice took into custody tonight several hundred members of the Communist Party and the Communist Labor Party of this country, located in thirty-three cities, on the charge that these organizations advocate and teach the overthrow of the United States Government by force and violence. The only difference between the Communist Party and the Communist Labor Party is one of leadership. Both of these parties, since their organization early last September, have been endeavoring to bring about the establishment of a Soviet form of Government in this country, similar to that which now obtains in Russia."

Quotes Communist Manifesto.

The extract from the manifesto of the Communist Party as made public was as follows:

" The Communist Party of America is the party of the working class. The Communist Party of America proposes to end capitalism and organize a workers' industrial republic. The workers must control industry and dispose of the products of industry. The Communist Party is a party realizing the limitations of all existing workers' organizations, and proposes to develop the revolutionary movement necessary to free the workers from the oppression of capitalism. The Communist Party insists that the problems of the American worker are identical with the problems of the workers of the world.

" The Communist Party is the conscious expression of the class struggle of the workers against capitalism. Its aim is to direct this struggle to the conquest of political power, the overthrow of capitalism and the destruction of the bourgeois State.

" The Communist Party prepares itself for the revolution in the measure that it develops a program of immediate action, expressing the mass struggles of the proletariat. These struggles must be inspired with revolutionary spirit and purposes.

" The Communist Party is fundamentally a party of action. It brings to the workers a consciousness of their oppression, of the impossibility of improving their conditions under capitalism. The Communist Party directs the workers' struggle against capitalism, developing fuller forms and purposes in this struggle culminating in the mass action of the revolution.

" In close connection with the unskilled workers is the problem of the negro worker. The negro problem is a political and economic problem. The racial oppression of the negro is simply the expression of his economic bondage and oppression, each intensifying the other. This complicates the negro problem, but does not alter its proletarian character. The Communist Party will carry on agitation among the negro workers to unite them with all class conscious workers."

Asked Hoyne to Defer Raid.

The Attorney General's letter to Mr. Hoyne was as follows:

" Dec. 29, 1919.

" Hon. Maclay Hoyne, State's Attorney of Cook County, Criminal Court Building, Chicago, Ill.:

" My Dear Mr. Hoyne—I have just concluded a conference with Assistant Attorney General Francis P. Garvan and Special Assistant to the Attorney General John B. Creighton regarding anticipated action by your office in Cook County which you have discussed with both of them.

" Mr. Creighton informs me that the State authorities under your jurisdiction at Cook County are contemplating extensive arrests of certain members of certain radical organizations in Chicago, with a view of prosecuting the individuals under the Illinois State laws, and, further, that you desire to initiate these arrests at a meeting which it is said will probably take place on the 1st of January, or soon thereafter.

" As doubtless you have inferred from your conversation with Mr. Garvan and Mr. Creighton, the Department of Justice is contemplating a nation-wide campaign against certain groups of radicals which, if things go as we expect, will take place in the very near future.

" The object of our activities will be to secure, to submit to the Department of Labor, cases for the deportation of a very large number of some of our most dangerous anarchists and radical agitators. It would be extremely unfortunate for the country at large, and for the Administration, if the local authorities in a city of such great importance as Chicago should conduct a raid directed at the same class of individuals on a date prior to that set for national action, and thereby, through the publicity which such local raid in Chicago would involve, send to cover all over the United States large numbers of individuals whom we have great hopes of apprehending for deportation.

" I am, therefore, asking that you defer the making of such extensive arrests for a short period of time, let us say not to exceed ten days, until the department can complete its arrangements for its nation-wide activities.

" Were the matter purely local I perhaps would not feel that the United States Government should call upon you for this favor, but inasmuch as the situation is national in scope, with such a tremendous result at stake, I feel it not improper to ask this of you at this time.

" Please rest assured that the department stands ready to render you any assistance in its power, consistent with its other official duties, in the preparation and prosecution of such cases under your State law as you may see fit to bring against offenders in Cook County, and will attempt in every possible way not to interfere with your plans.

" Mr. Creighton will leave shortly for Chicago and will have a further conference with you, after which I feel sure you will be able to come to a mutually acceptable understanding that will be beneficial to your office as well as to mine in the handling of these matters. Respectfully,

" A. MITCHEL PALMER."

It was intimated at the Department of Justice that many of the Reds arrested tonight would be deported, although this decision would ultimately rest with the Bureau of Immigration of the Department of Labor. Other raids will follow the ones made tonight and are expected soon.

The campaign against the anarchists and radicals has been personally conducted by William J. Flynn, Chief of the Bureau of Investigation, and has been going on quietly for six months. Ever since anarchists sent the bombs through the mails last Spring Flynn has had hundreds of his operatives scattered throughout the country, in many instances living in the actual camps of the Reds, mixing with them by day and sleeping with them by night.

During the steel strike, coal strike and the threatened railway strikes secret agents moved constantly among the more radical of the agitators and collected a mass of evidence. For months an elaborate card index of the utterances, habits and whereabouts of these men has been made. From time to time the Department of Justice will, from now on, round up these disturbers and either send them to the courts or out of the country.

Oakland Raid Nets Fifteen.

OAKLAND, Cal., Jan. 2.—Fifteen persons, several of them women, were arrested tonight by Federal agents on charges of violations of the immigration laws. Warrants were out for about fifteen more.

January 3, 1920

REDS PLOTTED COUNTRY-WIDE STRIKE; ARRESTS EXCEED 5,000, 2,635 HELD; THREE TRANSPORTS READY FOR THEM

FOMENTED TWO BIG STRIKES

Communists Planned to Extend Steel and Coal Walkouts.

REVOLUTION AS NEXT STEP

Evidence Procured in Seizure of Literature Before and During the Raids.

CENTRED DRIVE ON LABOR

Agitators Had Slush Fund of Millions with Which to Bail Arrested Workers.

WASHINGTON, Jan. 3.—Radical leaders planned to develop the recent steel and coal strike into a general strike and ultimately into a revolution to overthrow the Government, according to information gathered by Federal agents in Friday night's wholesale roundup of members of the Communist and Communist Labor parties. A definite program to expand the two labor disturbances for the purpose of blotting out every semblance of organized Government was disclosed in evidence gathered in half a score of cities. These data, officials said, tended to prove that the nation-wide raids had blasted the most menacing revolutionary plot yet unearthed.

The late figures received by the Department of Justice showed that out of more than 5,000 arrests 2,635 aliens were held on evidence thought sufficient to cause their deportation.

Officials indicated that both groups of radicals were awaiting only an opportune moment to carry on among other classes of workers the same sort

Communist Labor Party Sought to End Capitalism and Organize Workers to Be the Ruling Class

WASHINGTON, Jan. 3.—Assistant Attorney General Garvan made public tonight the department's memorandum, submitted to the Bureau of Immigration, upon which was based the Government classification of the Communist Labor Party as coming under the Espionage act. This disclosed that both groups were pledged to fight any suggestion of military action by America against the Soviet Russians. Membership applications revealed that both groups were indirectly under the control of the Russian Communist Council.

Significant among other features of the Communist Labor Party's doctrine was the enunciation of the following principles:

"The Communist Labor Party proposes the organization of the workers as a class, the overthrow of capitalist rule and the conquest of political power by the workers. The workers, organized as a ruling class, shall, through their Government, make and enforce the laws; they shall own and control land, factories, mills, mines, transportation systems and financial institutions. All power to the workers!

"The Communist Labor Party of America declares itself in complete accordance with the principles of communism as laid down in the manifesto of the Third International formed at Moscow.

"We maintain that the class struggle is essentially a political struggle; that is, a struggle by the proletariat to conquer the capitalist State, whether its form be monarchical or Democratic-Republican, and to replace it by a governmental structure adequately adapted to the Communist transformation.

"The most important means of capturing State power for the workers is the action of the masses, proceeding from the places where the workers are gathered together—in the shops and factories. The use of the political machinery of the capitalistic State is only secondary. The working class must organize and train itself for the capture of State power."

of agitation employed among steel workers and coal miners. Among the foreign element of the Communist and Communist Labor parties information described as conclusive revealed that the payrolls had been "loaded" with agitators to be sent suddenly to every fertile field in support of a general strike campaign.

Stopped Return to Coal Mines.

During the last two weeks of the coal strike communist agitators were discovered to have penetrated practically every mining centre east of the Mississippi River. Evidence showed that in several instances where miners had voted to return to work, the communists had spread their propaganda of distrust of the Government to such an extent that few, if any, miners actually went back to their jobs.

Attempts to incite the mine workers to violence were most bold in West Virginia, officials said, serious trouble being narrowly averted there. But all soft coal regions were infested, and much of the data leading up to Friday's nation-wide raids was gathered by secret agents and coming in contact with the agitators themselves.

The raids also disclosed that a "slush fund" has been created by the two parties, much of which, said to amount to several millions, had been set aside for use in bailing out radicals in case of arrest for sedition and the teaching of violence.

Proof also was said to have been obtained that the agitators who went among the steel and mine workers, made funds for bail available in every section they frequented. Their plans for the organization of the workers in support of the communist cause were pictured as more complete than even a political campaign. It was evident, officials declared, that the movement was "ripe" and that the settlement of the coal strike had been a keen disappointment to the radical leaders.

To Hasten Deportation Hearings.

Deportation hearings in the cases of those against whom there is sufficient evidence will begin as soon as possible, Anthony Caminetti, Commissioner General of Immigration, stated tonight. Consideration has already been given to the question of a special ship to carry away those ordered deported, he added, but no decision could be reached until the number to be deported was known.

Owing to the number of cases to be heard, the speedy deportation of those found guilty is an impossibility, John W. Abercrombie, Solicitor of the Department of Labor, said tonight. About 3,000 aliens a year were deported normally, he said, and to arrange for the sailing of the Buford with 349 deportees all the other work of the Bureau of Immigration had to be suspended. The task of deporting over 2,000 aliens in one group would tax the bureau to the utmost.

Federal officials deplored weaknesses in the present laws governing the procedure preliminary to deportation. It was pointed out that in most cases persons arrested as were those taken in the raids could obtain temporary freedom on bail of $1,000. There was an apparent feeling that if bail was granted some of the most dangerous of the "Reds" gladly would forfeit that amount to avoid deportation. The department plans, however, to keep all under surveillance and rearrest any who attempt to lose themselves in the masses of the foreign-born population here.

One of the features of the raids was the effort to break up sources of propaganda. The Communist Party alone had twenty-five newspapers printed in several languages actively supporting its cause. The Communist Labor group was said to have gained its strength chiefly through literature, tons of which were seized.

Mr. Garvan said that, although his information was incomplete, it was reasonably certain that the whole editorial staffs of most of the Communist Party newspapers had been taken.

MILWAUKEE HEARINGS START.

Only Two of Sixty-two Radical Prisoners Examined Yesterday.

Special to The New York Times.

MILWAUKEE, Jan. 3.—Federal authorities moved today to bring about the deportation of sixty-two Milwaukee ringleaders of the Communist movement. These Reds were captured by Federal officials in raids.

Eugene Kessler, Immigration Inspector and representative of the United States Government, opened hearings late today at the Federal Building, but only two prisoners were examined. The other cases will be taken up on Monday. Each

man is being asked if he wishes to be represented by counsel.

A record of the hearings will be forwarded to Secretary Wilson of the Department of Labor, who will pass on the question of deportation. Attorneys appearing for the Reds will be permitted to file briefs, which will be forwarded to Secretary Wilson.

Many women, some in tears and others talking excitedly, crowded the Federal Building to see the men under arrest.

Evidence consisting of books, newspapers, and other literature preaching the doctrine of anarchy, red flags, photographs of Lenin and Trotzky, Liebknecht, and Ferrer, colored posters depicting the rise of the proletariat in Russia and a framed charter of the Communist Party in Milwaukee was taken in the raid.

It is reported that a confession has been made by Harry Loeb, whose real name is said to be Loobisch, and who is the ringleader of the Bolshevist movement in Milwaukee, according to other members of the party under arrest.

The prisoners are held incommunicado at the County Jail and Federal Building, but will be allowed to have attorneys when the deportation proceedings start.

Some lawyers are urging the removal of the Socialist Sheriff Busch from office. He said the Federal officers were "a bunch of nuts" for making the raids."

TO ATTACK AMERICAN REDS.

Pennsylvania Plans Prosecutions Under State Law.

Special to The New York Times.

PHILADELPHIA, Jan. 3.—The Government's campaign against the radicals who seek to overthrow the Government by force and violence got going at full speed today when it was announced that an attempt would be made to prosecute those radicals who are protected from deportation proceedings by virtue of their American citizenship, for violation of the Flynn act, a Pennsylvania law that strikes at the Reds.

It was revealed today that this city was one of the large centres in which the Communist Party flourished. In the last month, according to the Government men, the membership here leaped from 2,600 to a figure close to 3,000.

Proletarian dictatorship, overthrow of the Government by force, seizure of the industries and overthrow of all Governments of the world are a few of the aims of the Communist Party as revealed in literature confiscated here and made public today.

Proof of a direct connection between the national headquarters of the American Communist Party and the Russian Communist International in Moscow, of which Lenin and Trotzky are the heads, was also found.

Further raids are contemplated by the local Government authorities in the campaign against the Communists, as it is said that all of the radicals liable to deportation have not yet been arrested.

PLAN MORE OHIO RAIDS.

41 of the 90 Arrested Are Held as Revolutionaries.

CLEVELAND, Jan. 3.—That there are in Cleveland and in the northeast section

of Ohio still more alien radicals to be arrested by Federal authorities in further raids was indicated today by the Department of Justice officials at the close of an all-day examination of the ninety alien radicals taken in raids Friday night.

Forty-one of those examined are being held on charges of believing in the overthrow of the Government, and will be turned over to immigration officials of the Department of Labor for deportation.

Examination of the alien radicals today by Bliss Morton, Special Agent in charge of the Bureau of Investigation of the Department of Justice, indicated most of the radicals belonged to the Communist Party or the Communist Labor Party and that they had been in America only from one to two years prior to the outbreak of the war.

Only three or four of the suspected radicals were found to have taken out citizenship papers, and in these cases the men were immediately released and the prosecution turned over to County Prosecutor Stephen M. Young. Of the thirty-nine men and two women held for deportation proceedings, fifteen are Russians, fourteen Austrians, seven Hungarians, three Germans, one Rumanian and one Greek.

BILLY SUNDAY LAUDS RAIDS.

Evangelist Says He Would Place Reds Before a Firing Squad.

Special to The New York Times.

WASHINGTON, Jan. 3.—Billy Sunday, the evangelist, hurrying through Washington today en route to Norfolk, praised the work of the Department of Justice in its raids on radicals throughout the country.

"I would stand every one of the ornery, wild-eyed I. W. W.'s, anarchists, crazy Socialists, and other types of Reds up before a firing squad and save space on our ships," he said. "Take it from me, Big Chief Flynn will scour the country clean and he should have the support of the whole country."

EVIDENCE IN PITTSBURGH.

Literature Seized Supported Overthrow of Government.

PITTSBURGH, Pa., Jan. 3.—Overthrow of the United States Government by mass strength and "direct force" was advocated in literature of the Communist Party of America, seized by Federal officers in raids here last night, R. B. Spencer, chief of the Department of Justice offices in Pittsburgh, said today.

Mr. Spencer examined today the twenty-three alleged radicals taken into custody during the raids and supervised translation of the confiscated literature, which, he declared, showed that the Communist organization was one of the most radical in existence.

Two of the prisoners were released today. One produced citizenship papers and the other was given his freedom when he showed an honorable discharge from the United States Army.

January 4, 1920

REDS BY THE THOUSAND.

If some or any of us, impatient for the swift confusion of the Reds, have ever questioned the alacrity, resolute will, and fruitful, intelligent vigor of the Department of Justice in hunting down those enemies of the United States, the questioners and the doubters have now cause to approve and applaud. The agents of the department have planned with shrewdness and a large wisdom, and carried out with extraordinary success, the nabbing of nearly four thousand radicals, Communists and Communist Labor-

ites, differentiated by name alone, all working for the destruction of the Government of the United States, and the establishing in its place of the Soviet State that has brought so much happiness and prosperity to Russia.

These energumens of proletarian autocracy and the knocking in the head of the "bourgeoisie"—which Americans are—have been gathered from many towns and cities. All over the country these devisers of social and economic ruin were found; and this "raid" is only a beginning. It is to be followed by others. Without

notice and without interruption the department will pursue and seize the conspirators against our Government. Some 60,000 Bolshevists' names are recorded in the department. Its future activities should be far-reaching and beneficent.

It deserves praise for its work. These Communists are continuing here the pernicious labors of Lenin and Trotzky. Some of them are making mischief, or trying to make it, in certain American labor organizations. One of their principles and hopes is agitation among the negroes, regarded as victims of " economic bondage " and material for proletarian propaganda. These Communists are a pernicious gang. In many languages they are denouncing the blockade of Russia and doing the bidding of their brother Reds in Russia.

The more of these dangerous anarchists are arrested, the more of them are sent back to Europe, the better for the United States. Let us hope that the Department of Labor will have no compassion for such of them as deserve deportation and are not, as most of them are not, American citizens.

January 5, 1920

FINDS COMMUNIST MEMBERSHIP REASON FOR DEPORTATION

Decision by Secretary Wilson Affects More Than 3,000 Reds Now Under Arrest.

CONDEMNS WHOLE PARTY

Advocacy of Violence to Destroy Government Cited as Shown in Constitution.

MORE ARRESTS TO FOLLOW

Decision Is the Outcome of an Appeal by Englebrert Preis, a Chicago Communist.

Special to The New York Times.

WASHINGTON, Jan. 24.—Secretary of Labor William B. Wilson rendered a decision today that the Communist Party of America advocates the overthrow of the Government by force or violence, and that it is the duty of the Department of Justice, under the provisions of a law passed by Congress and approved Oct. 16, 1918, to arrest and deport aliens who are members of the organization.

The decision, based on an appeal taken in behalf of Englebrert Preis, a Communist held for deportation at Chicago, is sweeping in its scope and apparently ends the hope of more than 3,000 foreigners, arrested as Communists in the recent raids conducted by the Department of Justice, that they might be permitted to remain in the United States.

It also is understood that as a result of the decision the Department of Justice will continue to make arrests as rapidly as provision can be made for the deportation of the undesirable aliens.

The case of the Communists was argued before Secretary of Labor Wilson during the week by Isaac E. Ferguson of Chicago, a member and general counsel of the Communist Party of America, and by other attorneys. The contention was then made that the Communist Party was political in nature and did not advocate the overthrow of the Governmnent by means which brought its members under the jurisdiction of the law. It also was held that the fact that a foreigner [•] become a member of the party did not necessarily subject him to deportation.

Secretary Wilson swept aside all of the objections raised, and, while stating that it was not for him to say whether Congress acted wisely in adopting the law, held that the law unquestionably made those foreigners who had joined the Communist Party subject to deportation.

The Secretary rules that the Communist Party is a revolutionary party, " seeking to destroy the State in open combat." He points out that the law is specific in stating that a foreigner who is a member of such a party must be deported.

Text of the Decision.

The text of the decision is as follows:
OPINION OF SECRETARY WILSON WITH REGARD TO MEMBERSHIP IN COMMUNIST PARTY.

IN RE ENGLEBRERT PREIS.

" Age 31; native of Austria; entered the United States at Port Huron, Mich., on Nov. 13, 1915, having arrived in Quebec by steamship Scotian June 14, 1914. This is a case arising under the provision of the act of Oct. 16, 1918.

" It is alleged that the alien is a member of the Communist Party of America, which is affiliated with the Communist International. The alien admits membership in the Communist Party of America, and that it is affiliated with the Communist International. The sole question therefore is to be determined by the Secretary of Labor is: Is the Communist Party of America such an organization as is described in the Act of Oct. 16, 1918, membership in which makes an alien liable to deportation? The language of the act applicable to this particular case is as follows:

Section 1. Aliens who are members of or affiliated with any organization that entertains a belief in, teaches, or advocates the overthrow by force or violence of the Government of the United States * * *

Section 2. * * * shall upon the warrant of the Secretary of Labor, be taken into custody and deported in the manner provided in the Immigration act of Feb. 5, 1917.

" It will be observed that teaching or advocating the overthrow of the Government of the United States is not alone sufficient to bring any organization within the scope of the act. There must in addition be a belief in, teaching or advocacy, of force or violence to accomplish the purpose. Bearing that in mind we may proceed to an examination of the facts.

" The manifesto and program and constitution of the Communist Party of America, and the manifesto of the Communist International, are submitted in evidence and their authenticity admitted. The constitution of the communist party (see page 10 of the manifesto) requires that:

" ' Section 1—Applicants for membership shall sign an application card reading as follows:

" ' The undersigned, after having read the constitution and program of the communist party, declares his adherence to the principles and tactics of the party and the Communist International; agrees to submit to the discipline of the party as stated in the constitution, and pledges himself to engage actively in its work.'

" An examination of the documents submitted clearly demonstrates the fact that it is the purpose of the Communist Party to overthrow the Government of the United States. There are many statements that might be quoted showing that purpose. The two following are typical. On Page 9 of the manifesto and program the statement is made:

" ' Communism does not propose to " capture " the bourgeois parliamentary state, but to conquer and destroy it.'

" And again on the same page:

" ' The proletarian class struggle is essentially a political struggle. * * * The objective is the conquest by the proletariat of the power of the State.'

" Many other statements of similar purport are to be found in the same document. After having found that it is the purpose of the Communist Party to conquer and destroy the Government of the United States, the next point of inquiry is as to how the conquest is to take place.

Says Parliamentarism Is Secondary.

" It is apparent that the Communist Party does not seek to attain its objective through the parliamentary machinery of this Government, established by, and operated under, the Constitution. That is made sufficiently clear by the following excerpt from Page 15 of the manifesto referred to:

" ' (b) Participation in parliamentary campaign, which in the general struggle of the proletariat is of secondary importance, is for the purpose of revolutionary propaganda only.'

" And again from Pages 9 and 10 of the same document:

" ' In those countries where the conditions for a workers' revolution are not yet ripe, the same process will go on. The use of parliamentarism, however, is only of secondary importance.'

" And further on Page 10:

" ' The parliamentarism of the Communist Party performs a service in mobilizing the proletariat against capitalism, empashizing the political character of the class struggle.'

" The parliamentary processes established by our Government are to be discarded or used for propaganda purposes only, and other means adopted for overthrowing the Government of the United States. These means are stated at considerable length, and frequently reiterated, seemingly for purpose of emphasis. The conquest of the power of the State is to be accomplished by the mass power of the proletariat.

" Strikes are to be broadened and deepened, making them general and militant, and efforts made to develop their revolutionary implications. The strike is to be used not simply as a means to secure redress of economic wrongs, but as a means through which the Government may be conquered, and destroyed. A few excerpts from the Communist Party and Communist International manifestos will make these statements evident.

" Thus on page 10 of the manifesto and program of the Communist Party of America is the following:

" ' The conquest of the power of the State is accomplished by the mass power of the proletariat. Political mass strikes are a vital factor in developing this mass power, preparing the working classes for the conquest of capitalism. The power of the proletariat lies fundamentally in its control of the industrial process. The mobilization of this control against capitalism means the initial form of the revolutionary mass action that will conquer the power of the State.'

" And again on Page 11 of the same document:

" ' Mass action is industrial in its origin, but it acquires political character as it develops fuller form. Mass action, in the form of general political strikes and demonstrations, unites the energy and forces of the proletariat, brings proletarian mass pressure upon the bourgeois state. The more general and conscious mass action becomes, the more it antagonizes the bourgeois state, the more it becomes political mass action. Mass action is responsive to life itself, the form of aggressive proletarian struggle under imperialism. Out of this struggle develops revolutionary mass action, the means for the proletarian conquest of power.'

" And, further, on Page 12 of the same document:

" ' Strikes of protest develop into general political strikes and then into revolutionary mass action for the conquest of the powerful State. Mass action becomes political in purpose while extra-parliamentary in form; it is equally a process of revolution and the revolution itself in operation.'

" Then on page 16:

" ' The Communist Party shall participate in mass strikes, not only to achieve the immediate purposes of the strike, but to develop the revolutionary implications of the mass strike.'

" And then, making the purpose still

more clear, we have the following from page 30 of the manifesto of the Communist International, with which the Communist Party of America is affiliated and whose manifesto is accepted as part of the policy of the party:

" 'The revolutionary era compels the proletariat to make use of the means of battle which will concentrate its entire energies, namely, mass action, with its logical resultant, direct conflict with the governmental machinery in open combat. All other methods, such as revolutionary use of bourgeois parliamentarism, will be of only secondary significance.'

"From these quotations and numerous other statements in the manifesto, not here quoted, it is apparent that the Communist Party of America is not merely a political party seeking the control of affairs of state, but a revolutionary party seeking to conquer and destroy the State in open combat. And the only conclusion is that the Communist Party of America is an organisation that believes in, teaches, and advocates the overthrow by force or violence of the Government of the United States.

"It does not devolve upon the Secretary of Labor officially to determine whether Congress was wise in creating the law or the Communist Party wise in creating the facts. It is his duty to apply the law to the facts as he finds them. It is mandatory upon him to take into custody aliens who are members of this organisation and deport them in the manner provided for in the Immigration act of Feb. 5, 1917.

"Your memorandum of Jan. 17, 1920, recommending that the department issue its warrant for the deportation of Englebrert Preis, such deportation to be to Austria, at Government expenses, is hereby approved.

"W. B. WILSON, Secretary."

January 25, 1920

LA GUARDIA SEES REAL PERIL IN REACTIONARIES, NOT REDS

Danger, He Says, Not So Much in Bolshevism as in Those Who Use the Word to Discredit Aspirations of Honest Workers

RIDICULING the fear that the American Government is in danger of being overthrown by Bolsheviki—as one faction of the State Legislature says it is—F. H. LaGuardia, President of the Board of Aldermen, declared in an interview that, if danger there were of a revolution, it lay in the ranks of the reactionary groups. Mr. LaGuardia had made a similar statement at a luncheon of the Albany County Republican Committee when he had forcibly declared, after an Assemblyman had stated the five Assemblymen were guilty of treason, that " if the five Socialists are guilty of the charges made against them they should be indicted, convicted and shot. If not, they should be immediately reseated."

"People," he began, "are much too prone to speak loosely. They choose their terms carelessly. Nine times out of ten, when pinned to the wall, they have no conception of the true meaning of a word. Today Bolshevism happens to be the very last word of reproach. It is used by the sweatshop owner when he speaks of his men demanding a living wage; it is howled by the profiteer when he insists that he is as pure as the driven snow; it is ranted forth by rotten political leaders when they try to justify themselves in the eyes of their constituents. And not one of them knows what it means.

"As a mere word, it means majority. Politically speaking, it means the rule of the majority through a soviet system. We have nothing of this nature to fear in this country. In spite of speeches to the contrary. In spite of columns of space in the newspapers to the contrary. In spite of the most insidious reactionary propaganda to the contrary.

A Negligible Minority.

"The number of advocates of a soviet rule are so few as to be negligible. It is the nonworking, nonproducing exploiters and corrupt politicians who are really the dangerous elements in the community. It is they and not the people erroneously called Bolsheviki who want to see blood spilled. It is they who are egging on dissatisfaction of every sort, distemper of every sort, distrust of every sort which may finally lead to destruction of every sort. I repeat, if there is fear of revolution, we have our smug reactionaries to thank for it.

"Let us get down to facts. For years and years, ever since this country became a nation, we have been preaching to all its members, 'You must not advocate force and violence in gaining any reform. This is a land of law and order. The power of the ballot is supreme. Our constitutional rights are supreme. If you want a change in legislation we have laws which will legally give you this change provided enough people want it.'

'Very good,' say our citizens. And 'very wonderful,' says our alien populations, also citizens, albeit naturalized ones.

"What happens? Five representatives of certain political leanings are elected in due course of law and order to sit in the lawmaking chamber of the State. Nobody objects to their nomination; nobody objects to their election. The matter is allowed to proceed quietly, according to due process of law. What happens next in this period of enlightenment, in this country where the right to life, liberty and the pursuit of happiness is part of the constitutional right of every individual? When the men enter the Assembly to take their seats, we throw them out. We use force and violence, forgetting that once not long ago we said something about not advocating force and violence. We forget that we said anything about the law being sufficient to meet every situation, and that if these men were indeed guilty of the crime charged against them, the law was all on our side, and that we could indict, convict and punish them.

"The effect of action such as this is most unfortunate. Any thinking group of people will naturally resent it. 'If we advocate violence, we commit a crime,' they will argue. 'If we proceed peacefully, a crime is committed against us. There's something wrong somewhere.'

"There most assuredly is. The result of the matter is that this group takes to meeting secretly and clandestinely. Fortunately, the display of feeling following the expulsion of the men was sufficient to assure the people all over the country that as a nation we did not support Czaristic action of this sort.

"The trouble at the present lies in the fact that the average citizen believes that the inherent right of life, liberty and happiness includes something more than a bite to eat and a place to sleep in. It means a chance to play, a chance to educate himself and a chance to be happy. The day has passed when the man who is willing to work can be poverty-stricken. He does not demand that everything be given him, but he does demand that something be given him. He demands also that the class of individuals who have lived like leeches on the profits produced by the men their fathers have exploited and whom they are continuing to exploit—that this class must go or else the members of it roll up their sleeves and get busy. There is nothing revolutionary or vicious in that.

"People are forgetting that we fought a war for democracy. They are forgetting that the minds of a large mass of people were aroused by the thought that the world was at arms in order that justice might be done to all. They forget that the brains of men awoke to the fact they could do something to help win the war. 'What are you doing to help make the world safe for democracy?' asked the posters and every man-jack in the factories, in the mines, in the railroads, as well as on the battlefront, thrilled at the question. There was a personal appeal and a personal response. They all wanted to count for something as they all did count for something in keeping the hand of autocracy off the throat of decent living and clean justice.

The New Question.

"The war is over. And with it apparently is the promise of five years ago. The question now is not the open, free and inspiring one of 'What are you doing to make the world safe for democracy?' but the vile, ugly, suspicious, half-hopeful one of 'What are you doing to make the world run riot with Bolshevism?' A very useful word is Bolshevism. Easy to say, hard to define, but most potent as an epithet.

"With the ending of the war the eyes of some of the political, industrial, and commercial leaders of the country grew blind to the legends on their former flaming banners. They forgot that they had told the workingman that he had the power and the strength to make what he would of the country. They forgot that it was they who had wakened him to the force that was within him.

"But the worker did not forget. Long dormant, his awakening was all the more potent. He refused to go to sleep again. He refused to be lulled by tales of 'war work' and 'war expediency.' He wanted to taste the fruits of peace. He had stinted himself for four years in order that he might more fully live at the end of that period. He began making demands, he didn't know they were demands. He thought it was justice. These demands grew louder in proportion as the ears of the war profiteer grew deafer. Finally they reached a pitch where none could disregard them. And then war profiteers, politicians, reactionaries of every type raised their voices in unison with a cry that held the country in a sudden grip of fear. 'Bolshevists' they cried. And 'Bolshevists' was echoed down every narrow valley of fear and slander and ignorance.

Putting the Blame on the Alien.

"I wonder greatly what these people would have done if there had been no revolution in Russia, and if the word Bolshevist had not been added to our English vocabulary. Mark this, whether or not Russia had had a revolution, we could not have escaped this period of unrest and dissatisfaction. Just as long as our leaders had not played fair with an awakened people, we were fore-doomed to go through a period of adjustment and change.

"A good many of our reactionary friends may come out with the assertion that they have no cause for disagreement with the mass of American citizenship; that it is the foreigners who are creating all the trouble. That statement, too, is false. What's more, it is creating more harm than is now appreciated in the northern section of the State. It is creating an anti-racial feeling, which, if allowed to grow, may in time reach a point where sanity will go by the board. 'All foreigners that come from Russia are Bolshevists.' That statement is made with as much conviction as the old syllogism that all men are mortal.

"If it were changed to say that all foreigners that come from Russia have suffered there might be more truth in it. For 'hey have. Government to them, in truth, is something to be feared. All their lives most of them have been crushed under by a régime that would breed distrust and hatred of control in the heart of the most hopeful. These people came over in the search of freedom and happiness. Most of them found their way into the sweatshops of the cities, where their labor was exploited. Very often by their kind. Their wages were poor, their type of living low, their pleasures few. To their short vision things weren't much better here than they were in Russia.

"There was just one thing that they looked forward to with hope. That was the gaining of the ballot, a right denied them in the land from which they had come. With it, they felt they could do the things that would insure them happiness for all time. The question

is, did it? The question also is, can it? There are factors outside of the political, which go toward the make-up of a man's life. These factors can be reached by the ballot. I mean among other things the economic, social and education factors.

"The recent fiasco at Albany has shown these people one thing. And that is that the ballot in which they have placed such faith has failed them. Their faith in mankind they lost long ago. If then, they talk louder than any other group, it is because their disappointment in the one safe American institution is so much greater. But this, let us hope, is only temporary.

Duped by War Promises.

"Added to this, it must not be forgotten that they too are part of the great mass who feel that they have been duped by war promises which have not been kept. But to call them Bolsheviste because of expressions of their disappointment is wrong and vicious.

"America is more greatly awake today than it has ever been before. Not only the leaders are conversant with the political and economic situation of the country, but the people as a whole, as well. They insist that the words of Lincoln in his Gettysburg address shall have meaning today and carried out with the spirit and sincerity of Roosevelt. They want to make this a government 'of the people' in the highest sense of the term. Bloodshed will not do that. They do not want bloodshed. They know that the primary laws, the short term office, the expression of public opinion through their votes and through an honest press can give them all that they desire. And it can, provided the law functions honestly.

"Honesty in administration and honesty in management of private industry are the demand of the people at the present time. It is dishonesty to which they are frankly antagonistic. It is the sort of dishonesty that makes them pay for an insolvent railroad when they know perfectly well that the Directors of that railroad have made heavy profits. Take any example of an insolvent railroad and you will find that as the corporation went more greatly into debt the wealth of favored Directors rose in inverse proportion. It is things of this nature, today more fully understood than ever by an awakened people, that is causing the word 'Bolshevist' to grow so popular. And it is the small but powerful handful of unscrupulous reactionaries who are doing most to make it popular.

"My opinion is that this wave will soon pass. In another year we will have a new administration. That administration will have in its power the most wonderful opportunity for honest reconstruction of the country's political and economic life. If it makes full use of it, the future holds little promise of strife; if it does not, however, and the reactionary spirit is in control, then I dread to think of what may happen. Not because of Bolshevism, mark my words, but because of an honest and natural reaction to a policy of dishonesty.

"Meanwhile, all we can do is wait and see what will happen next. The most pitiable aspect of this situation lies in the fact that not we alone are waiting, but that all the freed nations of the world who have turned to us for help also are anxiously watching to see how justice is meted out to the freemen of America."

February 29, 1920

WILL DEPORT ONLY REAL COMMUNISTS

Acting Secretary Post Rules Name on Party Roll Does Not Prove Alien Undesirable.

CRITICISES MANY ARRESTS

Declares Men Held as Suspects Are Not Anarchists, but Workers of Good Character.

WASHINGTON, April 9.—Bona fide membership in the Communist Party and guilty knowledge of the precepts of that organization by alleged undesirable aliens will be made the basis of deportation, Acting Secretary Post ruled

today in canceling the warrant issued in the case of Thomas Truss of Baltimore.

Appearance of a suspect's name in the membership list will not be accepted as proof of his connection with the party, it was held. Withdrawal from membership prior to the date of the ban against the organization will be taken, however, as indicating clean intent, and "where the accused appears to be a person of good general character, fit for American citizenship except for the accusation in hand, and there is reasonable doubt of his membership, the warrant will be canceled."

Mr. Post reviewed the case of Truss at length as typical of the thousands he will be called upon to decide. He criticised severely the apparent failure of local police and agents of the Department of Justice to protect the rights of aliens arrested, declaring in the case of Truss that no warrant was produced, that the prisoner was not informed of the reason or authority for his summary imprisonment and that he did not receive the privilege of obtaining counsel.

Examination of the records, Mr. Post said, showed that, far from being an anarchist, as charged, Truss was "a respected member and active worker for the St. Paul Polish Presbyterian Church in Baltimore."

"It is found in a large proportion of cases I have examined that there is no better reason for deportation than is disclosed in the present case," Mr. Post said. "As a rule the hearings show the aliens arrested to be working men of good character, who have never been arrested before, who are not anarchists or revolutionists, nor politically nor otherwise dangerous in any sense.

"It is pitiful to consider the hardship to which they and their families have been subjected during the past three or four months by arbitrary arrests, long detention in default of bail beyond the means of hard-working wage-earners to give, for nothing more dangerous than affiliating with friends of their own race, country and language, and without the slightest indication of sinister motive, or any unlawful act within their knowledge or intention.

"To permit aliens to violate the hospitality of this country by conspiring against it is something which no American can contemplate with patience. Equally impatient, however, must any patriotic American be with drastic proceedings on flimsy proof to deport aliens who are not conspiring against our laws, and do not intend to. Although these are not criminal proceedings, being wholly administrative in their character, in the effect on the innocent individual who in this summary way is found to be guilty is as distressing to him and his family, to his friend and his neighbors, as the effect of convictions for crime by regular judicial process."

April 10, 1920

SCORES GOVERNMENT AS ABETTOR OF REDS

Federal Judge at Boston Says Federal Agents Operate Part of Communist Party.

HEARS CASES OF DEPORTEES

BOSTON, April 20.—A declaration that "it is clear that the Government operates some part of the Communist Party in this country" was made from the bench of the Federal District Court today by Judge George W. Anderson. The Judge added that his view was based on evidence developed at the proceedings before him on applications for writs of habeas corpus for five persons ordered deported as alien radicals.

Officials of the Bureau of Investigation of the Department of Justice who had previously testified at the hearings had referred to the activities of Government agents operating as members of Communist and Socialist groups.

The court's statement came during the cross-examination by Assistant United States Attorney Goldberg of Isaac Ferguson of Chicago, who was testifying as an authority on the Communist Party and its principles. Goldberg sought to introduce through the witness a translation of a pamphlet written by a German, Karl Radek, entitled "Development of Socialism from Science to Action." Samuel Katzeff, counsel for the petitioners, objected on the ground that the author had never been in this country, but the Federal attorney argued that translations of the pamphlet had been circulated widely by Communist leaders.

Counsel for the petitioners then made a statement which the United States attorney asserted was an insinuation that Federal agents had distributed the pamphlets. He criticised the remarks of Katzeff and the latter had started to reply when Judge Anderson said:

"You needn't go any further. The admission by Government employes here that under cover informants planned to stimulate meetings of the Communists in order to make easy the arrest of members lays a solid foundation for any inference of this kind.

"This spotters' evidence and pseudo-membership of persons make it perfectly easy to argue that persons in the employ of the Government might have issued literature intended to bring into condemnation people connected with the party. I don't know anything about it, but the evidence here is clear that the Government owns and operates some part of the Communist Party. That means something to any one who has had experience with spies in private industry."

April 21, 1920

ASSAIL LOUIS POST FOR RELEASING REDS

Committeemen Say Assistant Secretary of Labor Nullified Justice Department's Work.

COUNSEL DEFENDS OFFICIAL

He Exercised Humanity, While the "Justice Officers Used Worse Than Russian Methods."

WASHINGTON, April 30.—Administration of radical deportation cases by Louis F. Post, Assistant Secretary of Labor, was attacked and defended today before the House Rules Committee, which is investigating Mr. Post's official conduct.

Members of the Immigration Committee, headed by Chairman Johnson, declared they had evidence that Government efforts to break up "the most damnable conspiracy in the nation's history" were practically nullified through release by the Department of Labor, largely at the instance of Mr. Post, of most of the 5,000 Communists arrested in the nation-wide raids.

The course of the Department of Labor, including that of the Assistant Secretary, was defended by Jackson H. Ralston, counsel for Mr. Post, who declared that the only criticism that could be directed against his administration was that he had "exercised humanity" and had proceeded on the theory that only in most exceptional cases should a man be torn from his family and sent from the country.

Mr. Ralston attacked the Department of Justice, asserting that its agents had used methods in dealing with alleged radicals that were not countenanced even in Russia when the Czarist regime was at the height of its power.

Representative Siegel of New York, Republican member of the Immigration Committee, declared that the secrecy maintained by the Department of Labor in deportation proceedings was without precedent and without authority.

The arrest of 5,000 Communists was followed by an "awful mix-up between the two departments," resulting in the release of the big majority of those held, said Chairman Johnson. The Department of Justice did its part, he said, but one obstacle appeared in Assistant Secretary Post.

Johnson told the committee that George Andreychine, described as "a prince of the I. W. W.," was released by the Department of Labor after letters had been exchanged by radical leaders saying "that if we can keep Secretary Wilson out making speeches Post will release Andreychine."

Later, he said, Andreychine was arrested for renewed radical activities in the Michigan copper district, indicted, convicted in the Federal court at Chicago and sent to Leavenworth penitentiary.

Johnson said the immigration committee had evidence that Emma Goldman, radical leader, had sent a plea by telegram to Assistant Secretary Post in behalf of one arrested Communist. Mr. Post, Mr. Johnson declared, referred the plea to the office of the Secretary of Labor with the notation that "Miss Goldman's representations of fact be given full credence."

Johnson said he did not introduce a resolution looking to the impeachment of Post because "the Assistant Secretary had already been impeached by eight-tenths of the people of the United States."

A statement by Mr. Ralston that "we in America have sunk to the level of the police Government of Russia under the Czarist regime," brought challenges and requests for modification from a half dozen members of the committee.

The witness first declared that he would stand on his assertion, but later modified it to exclude "a large part of the American people and the members of the Rules Committee," but not to exclude the representatives of the Department of Justice, who, he added, "were even lower in some of their methods than the old Russian officials."

CHICAGO, April 30.—George Andreychine was one of ninety-seven I. W. W. leaders convicted here in August, 1918, of conspiracy to prevent enforcement of the draft law and to encourage drafted men to resist induction into the army.

He was fined $20,000 and sentenced to twenty years in the Leavenworth penitentiary. He was one of thirty-six of the convicted men who joined William D. Haywood, former secretary of the I. W. W., in appealing. They were released on bail and their appeals will be argued here May 17.

May 1, 1920

LAWYERS DENOUNCE RAIDS ON RADICALS

Popular Government League Bitterly Attacks Palmer's Treatment of Reds.

CALLS HIS METHODS BRUTAL

WASHINGTON, May 27.—Charges that the anti-radical raids made by the Department of Justice last Winter were conducted with cruelty comparable to that employed by the Russian secret police are made in a report given out today by the National Popular Government League. Twelve lawyers signed the report, which alleges lawlessness, cruelty and persecution on a wholesale scale by the Government agents.

The signers of the report are: Roscoe Pound, Dean of the Law School, Harvard; Tyrrell Williams, Dean of the Washington University Law School; Frank P. Walsh of New York City, David Wallerstein of Philadelphia, Jackson H. Ralston of Washington, ex-Judge Alfred Niles of Baltimore, professor in Maryland University Law School; Francis Fisher Kane, who recently resigned as District Attorney in Philadelphia; Felix Frankfurter, professor of law at Harvard; Swinburne Hale of New York, Ernst Freund, professor in the Law School of the University of Chicago; R. G. Brown of Memphis, Tenn., and Professor Zechariah Chafee, Jr., of Harvard Law School.

Attorney General Palmer and William J. Flynn, Chief of the Bureau of Investigation, are violently attacked. On the other hand, lawyers praise Louis F. Post, Assistant Secretary of Labor, for his "courageous re-establishment of American constitutional law in deportation proceedings."

Among the charges made in the report are the following:

Maintenance by the department of agents provocateurs throughout the country for the purpose of joining and becoming officers of radical organizations and inciting their members to criminal activities.

Wholesale arrest and imprisonment of men and women without warrants, or pretense of warrants, and illegal searches and seizures, in violation of the Constitution.

Forgery by agents of the department to make cases against innocent persons caught in illegal raids.

Criminal thefts of money, watches, jewelry and other personal property from victims of raids by agents of the department.

Cruel and unusual punishments visited upon prisoners taken into custody with and without warrants, in violation of the Constitution.

Use of Government funds in violation of law to spread newspaper propaganda favorable to campaign of repression and to purchase "boiler plate" distributed free to country newspapers to create popular opinion favorable to acts of the department.

Compulsion of prisoners to be witnesses against themselves in violation of the Constitution.

Brutal and indecent treatment of women taken in raids.

Filthy conditions of confinement and

refusal to let prisoners communicate with friends or lawyers.

Report Disclaims Radicalism.

"We make no argument in favor of any radical doctrine as such, whether Socialist, Communist or anarchist," the report says. "No one of us belongs to any of these schools of thought nor do we now raise any question as to the constitutional protection of free speech and a free press. We are concerned solely with bringing to the attention of the American people the utterly illegal acts which have been committed by those charged with the highest duty of enforcing the laws, acts which have caused widespread suffering and unrest, have struck at the foundation of American free institutions and have brought the name of our country into disrepute."

The office of the Attorney General, "under guise of a campaign for suppression of radical activities," the report says, "acting by its local agents throughout the country and giving express instructions from Washington, has committed continual illegal acts. Wholesale arrests, both of aliens and citizens, have been made without warrant or any process of law; men and women have been jailed and held incommunicado without access of friends or counsel; homes have been entered without search warrant and property seized and removed; other property has been wantonly destroyed; working men and working women suspected of radical views have been shamefully abused and maltreated; agents of the Department of Justice have been introduced into radical organizations for the purpose of informing upon their members or inciting them to activities; these agents have been instructed from Washington to arrange meetings upon certain dates, for the express object of facilitating wholesale raids and arrests.

"In support of these illegal acts and to create sentiment in its favor, the Department of Justice has also constituted itself a propaganda bureau and has sent to newspapers and magazines of the country quantities of material designed to excite public opinion against radicals, all at the expense of the Government and outside the scope of the Attorney General's duties.

"American institutions have not in fact been protected by the Attorney General's ruthless suppression. On the contrary, those institutions have been seriously undermined and revolutionary unrest vastly intensified. No organization of radicals acting through propaganda over the last six months could have created as much revolutionary sentiment in America as has been created by the acts of the Department of Justice itself."

Brutality Charged in Raid Here.

The treatment of radicals in the steel and coal strikes in Hartford, Buffalo, Detroit and New York City is declared to have been "shocking" and brutal. The raid on the Russian People's House, 133 East Fifteenth Street, New York, last November, is dealt with at some length.

It is understood that the Department of Justice has seen copies of the report and will probably make a reply tomorrow.

May 28, 1920

REDS CARD INDEXED, PALMER DISCLOSES

More Than 200,000 References Kept—Blames Aliens for 90% of Radical Agitation.

WASHINGTON, Dec. 10.—The campaign against the high cost of living, efforts to break up trusts and combinations in restraint of trade and the Government's fight on radicalism are reviewed by Attorney General Palmer in his annual report sent today to Congress.

In a discussion of the radicals problem, Mr. Palmer discloses that the Department of Justice has developed a card index system, containing more than 200,000 cards, giving detailed data on the activities of ultra-radicals and their organizations as well as a complete library of reference on the general radical movement.

Ninety per cent. of the communist and anarchistic agitation during the last year, the Attorney General says, is traceable to aliens. This agitation, he adds, is not confined to the so-called "economic evils," but has been directed also toward the stirring up of racial prejudice. One of the fertile fields, he says, is among the negroes, who "have been appealed to directly for support in the movement to overthrow the Government of the United States."

The foreign-language press has been "particularly noticeable for its strong ultra-radical leanings," the Attorney General says. He declares that the spread of radical doctrines has been "aided" in twenty-six or more foreign-language newspapers in the country.

The results of the raids last January on the Communist and Communist Labor Party meetings, Mr. Palmer says, caused a "marked temporary cessation" in radical activities. Meetings of the communist and anarchist groups were suspended, and this was followed by the declaration of the American delegate to the Third Internationale at Amsterdam that the January raids had destroyed the hopes of the Communists in America.

He recommends practically a general increase in the salaries of United States Attorneys and Marshals. In most cases the increase is $500 a year.

December 11, 1920

PALMER DEFENDS HIS WAR ON REDS

Attorney General Tells Senate Committee Real Emergency Existed Early Last Year.

TELLS OF MARTENS AGENT

Deported Envoy Named New York Lawyer to Act Under Instructions of Soviet.

Special to The New York Times.

WASHINGTON, Feb. 18.—Attorney General Palmer, testifying today before the Senate Committee on the Judiciary, submitted a complete report of the activities of the Department of Justice in handling the so-called "Red" problem in this country.

"It must be remembered," he said, "that the Communist Party in the United States had affiliated with the Third Internationale in Moscow and had accepted its platform and manifesto, and we find in that platform and manifesto the specific statement that they intend to overthrow the Government of the United States by force and violence and we also find in the manifesto of the Communist Party of America that they do not intend to resort to the ballot for their reforms, but they are to resort to mass action and the general strike with revolutionary implications.

"There have been references made to the effect that aliens, who were members of this organization, knew nothing of its purposes, but I refer the committee to the provision in the constitution of the Communist Party which provides that an applicant for membership shall sign an application card in which he declares himself as having read the constitution and program of the party, and his adherence to the principles and tactics of the party and of the Third Internationale, and further agrees to engage actively as an agitator in its work. This provision is found in the organic law of the Communist Party."

The Government, the Attorney General contended, had no alternative but to accept the governing rules of membership in an organization as the law of that organization. He pointed out that at all of the meetings of the Communist Party in this country agitators were present who expounded the theories of the Russian Bolshevist system.

Attorney Appointed by Martens.

The Attorney General made the statement that Ludwig C. A. K. Martens, deported Bolshevist "Ambassador," when he found that it would be impossible to extend his stay in this country, designated Charles Recht, a New York lawyer, as the representative of Soviet Russia in the United States. In proof of his statement Attorney General Palmer read a letter said to have been written by Martens to Recht just prior to the former's departure from this country for Russia.

Mr. Palmer explained that the letter had been obtained from a Russian newspaper. The instructions from Martens to Recht as read into the record by the Attorney General were as follows:

"In view of my sailing I wish to make some arrangements and leave certain instructions which you should carry out during my absence.

"First, you are hereby authorized to act as my personal representative and to act for me in all matters of importance.

"Second, you are authorized, if necessary, and if so instructed by the Commissary of Foreign Affairs in Moscow, to receive all legal papers and in every way act as an attorney representing the Russian Socialist Federated Soviet Republic.

"Third, you are authorized to take action in the cases of needy and worthy Russians, who may appeal to you for aid, in accordance with instructions which will be sent you."

Mr. Recht was a recent witness before the Judiciary Committee, on which occasion he charged that persons arrested in the nation-wide raid against communists and anarchists in January of last year were deprived of their legal rights by the Department of Justice and in many instances maltreated by agents of the department who carried out the instructions of the Attorney General or his subordinates. He was attorney for many of the Russians arrested in the raids, among his clients being Gregory Weinstein, an intimate friend of Trotzky, and one of Martens's private secretaries.

Defending the course of the department, the Attorney General continued:

"I cannot agree with the contention that the sole justification for a nation-wide arrest of such alien communists would be a military operation in incubation, but if such contention were sound I believe that it existed when the arrests were made on Jan. 2, 1920. This country had just passed through a steel strike and a coal strike of great magnitude, and in each of these strikes thousands of leaflets were distributed by the communist parties, urging the workers to rise up and seize not only the shops in which they worked, but also the Government, and stating to the workers that they must control the State power, the police and the army and that the only way to control was to rise in open combat against the constituted governing authority using not parliamentary means but open mass action.

"Certainly no one can contend with any seriousness that the Government must stand idly by and wait for the actual throwing of the bomb, or the actual use of arms in military operation before it can act to protect itself against such onslaughts, and yet that is what practically all of the witnesses who have appeared before this comittee have in essence contended. Professor Chaffee is on record as being opposed to all legislation against sedition and anarchy and not a single witness who has come before the committee has failed to express his personal views that deportation is the wrong policy, that it is but taking a firebrand from one house and throwing it into another.

"The emergency existed, and I consider that the action of the Department of Justice, in moving deliberately and with thoroughness, is fully warranted and justified. I do not maintain that some mistakes were not made, and that some delays were experienced, which under ordinary conditions would not have been excusable, but in a great movement for the overthrow of the Government of the United States, sponsored and adhered to, by thousands of alien agitators, directed and engineered by the guiding hands of Lenin and Trotzky, I believe that it was the duty of the Department of Justice, the branch of the Government to whom the American people look for the protection of its institutions and Government, to move with dispatch in such matters.

"I believe that the Department of Justice took every necessary precaution to guard the rights of the persons taken into custody. The charges of brutality, forgery of names and theft of money have frequently been made, but I challenge a single substantiation of any of these deliberate, malicious falsehoods.

"I would refer also to the vagueness of the statements read into the record of the hearings before the committee taken from the report of the Inter-Church World Movement upon the steel strike. It is but another example of the diligent effort exercised by certain individuals to endeavor to belittle the efforts of the Department of Justice. When one charge fails we find another produced, and the charges made in the steel report are but typical of the indefiniteness of the general charges made against the administration of the department."

The Attorney General asserted that he had been and was now ready to answer all specific accusations, but that he could not answer generalities. Mr. Palmer then gave his view of what he termed "the type of mind" that has appeared before the Judiciary Committee.

"It is," he said, "a type of mind that would be horrified at the murder of a citizen but is unmoved in the plotting of those who would assassinate a State. Professor Chaffee referred to the fact that we had tolerated Emma Goldman for thirty years, and I believe that it is a just inference to draw from his testimony that we could have tolerated her a little longer. He at least states that he does not know but that she might be doing more harm in Russia than she would have done in this country.

"Swinburne Hale, another of these twelve lawyers, has admitted in open court that he did not believe that a person who undertook to preach the overthrow of the Government by force and violence should be punished as a criminal. I could cite without number similar expressions of views of these twelve lawyers, but I believe it is of little or no avail. It is significant that all criticisms which have been directed against the enforcement of the deportation statutes as participated in by the Department of Justice, have emanated from persons who are opposed to any law or legislation against sedition or anarchy, who would let foreign agitators disseminate by pamphlet and by word, doctrines wholly foreign to our American life and poisonous to our institutions."

The Attorney General filed with the committee various documents procured by the Department of Justice which he contends prove conclusively his conclusion regarding the mission and methods of the Communist Party in this country.

February 19, 1921

ANTI-RED ACTIVITY FOUND ON THE WANE

Civil Liberties Union Says in Report There Were Only a Few Outbursts Last Year.

INCREASE IN MOB VIOLENCE

Interference with meetings by the police, and sometimes by State and Federal authorities, "constituted the largest number of violations of civil rights" during the past year, according to a report just issued by the American Civil Liberties Union. The year also saw a "serious extension" of mob violence, due chiefly to the growth of the Ku Klux Klan, the report states. Most of the victims of mob violence were white persons, the record of negro lynchings for 1923 being "the lowest in thirty years."

Pennsylvania led the country in the number of "lawless police interferences" with labor and radicals, the report declares. Texas and Oklahoma led in mob violence and California in prosecutions under the criminal syndicalist laws. The Federal Government was "sporadically" active against radicals, "depending chiefly on the personal attitude of the head of the department involved."

Though the "big national drives" were over, a chart for the year published in the report shows that "local anti-radical groups still expressed themselves vigorously as a result of the nation-wide propaganda designed to serve larger interests." But the year also saw "a healthy farmer-working class reaction against the forces of repression, with the result that the chart shows a decline in some forms of active interference with civil rights."

The report outlines the work of the Civil Liberties Union in the past year. The fear of radicalism persisted "almost undiminished" during the year, the report states, but organized anti-red agitation was confined to "a few outbursts" from Samuel Gompers, William J. Burns, Ellis Searles of the United Mine Workers, Ralph M. Easley of the National Civic Federation and R. M. Whitney of the American Defense Society.

General Charles G. Dawes, Republican candidate for Vice President, is among those named in the report as specially active against the reds.

June 23, 1924

CHAPTER 2

Un-Americans

Humphrey Bogart is questioned about Communist influence in Hollywood
by Martin Dies, first chairman of the House Un-American
Activities Committee.

Courtesy Compix

REPUBLICAN CITES 'RADICAL DANGERS'

A. H. Laidlaw, in Party Organ, Lists Senators, House Members and Periodicals.

SEES REVOLUTION AS AIM

La Follette, Wheeler and Others Are Linked With W. Z. Foster, Debs and the I. W. W.

Special to The New York Times.

WASHINGTON, April 20.—In a leading article by Albert H. Laidlaw in this week's issue of the National Republican, organ of the Republican National Committee, the writer cites what he calls the dangers confronting the nation through radical movements. Senators La Follette, Norris, Wheeler, Brookhart, Magnus Johnson, Ladd and Dill, and many members of the farm bloc are declared to be attempting by their policies to overthrow "the present constitutional or republican form of government." The article reads in part:

"The personnel of the anti-Republican leadership, which is a leadership of forces contemplating not the 'reform' but the overthrow of the present constitutional or republican form of the American Government, I revealed in my article last week. This survey showed:

"1. That the following organizations, among many others to be discussed in later articles, constitute the vertebrae of the anti-Republican or radical movement in the United States:

"Radical bloc in the United States Congress.

"People's Legislative Service.

"Conference for Progressive Political Action.

"Workers Party of America; Farmers Labor Party.

"Non-Partisan League.

"Committee of Forty-Eight.

"Plumb Plan League.

"Emergency Foreign Policy Conference.

"National Board of Farm Organizations. Farmers' National Council for the Prevention of War.

"Women's International League for Peace and Freedom.

"Committee for the Recognition of Russia.

"Joint Amnesty Committee.

"I. W. W. Defense Committee.

"League for Industrial Democracy, known as the Intercollegiate Socialist Society, before it assumed its masquerade.

"American Civil Liberties Union.

"2—That the following individuals, among many others of less note, are the vitalizing spirits and active leaders of these vari-colored but closely interlocking anti-Republican organizations:

"Robert M. La Follette, United States Senator from Wisconsin, 'Czar' of the Radical bloc in Congress and Chairman of the Executive Committee of the People's Legislative Service.

"Burton K. Wheeler, United States Senator from Montana, La Follette's spectacular leader on the Democratic side of the Senate.

"Smith W. Brookhart, United States Senator from Iowa.

"George Huddleston, representative in Congress from Alabama.

"Hendrick Shipstead, United States Senator from Minnesota.

"Magnus Johnson, United States Senator from Minnesota.

"Edwin F. Ladd, United States Senator from North Dakota.

"Lynn J. Frazier, United States Senator from North Dakota.

"C. C. Dill, United States Senator from Washington.

"George W. Norris, United States Senator from Nebraska.

"Basil M. Manly, Director of the People's Legislative Service.

"Max S. Hayes, editor of the radical Cleveland Citizen.

"William Z. Foster, National Chairman of the Workers' Party.

"Charles E. Ruthenberg, Executive Secretary and Treasurer of the Workers' Party.

"William F. (Big Bill) Dunne, D. C. Dorman, Upton Sinclair, Scott Nearing, Eugene V. Debs, Charles A. Lyman, Benjamin C. Marsh and Roger Baldwin.

"William H. Johnston, head of the International Association of Machinists, Secretary-Treasurer of the People's Legislative Service and Chairman of the Conference for Progressive Political Action.

"James P. Noonan, Vice President of the Plumb Plan League.

"J. A. H. Hopkins, head of the Committee of Forty-Eight.

"Mary Heaton Vorse, Mrs. Arthur C. Watkins, Amy Woods, Harriet Connor Brown, Lucy Branham, Inez H. Irwin, Mrs. Florence Kelly and Madeline Z. Doty.

"3. That the following radical newspapers and periodicals, among many others widely circulated and heavily financed, are engaged in promulgating the propaganda which is intended to crystallize the radical movement into a unified political power in the American Government:

"Labor, a weekly, published in Washington, D. C.

"The Daily Worker, published in Chicago.

"The Liberator, a monthly, published in Chicago.

"The Nation, a weekly, published in New York City.

"The New Republic, a weekly, published in New York City."

April 21, 1924

DAUGHERTY LINKS HIS FOES AND REDS

Declares Wheeler and Brookhart Influenced by Communist Forces of Russia.

COLUMBUS, April 23.—Harry M. Daugherty told an audience of friends and neighbors here tonight that he had given up his Cabinet post rather than "contribute to a treasonable cause."

Files of the Department of Justice, he said, contained "abundant proof of the plans, purposes and hellish designs of the Communist International."

"Bear in mind," he added, "that the files which I refused to deliver to the Wheeler investigating committee at the time my resignation was requested, were demanded by Brookhart and Wheeler, two United States Senators who spent last Summer in Russia with their Soviet friends—those same Soviet and Communist leaders who preach destruction of constitutional government, destruction even to human life.

"I preferred to permit my integrity to be questioned and my honor to hang in the balance, for the time being, rather than surrender the files in the keeping of the Department of Justice. I gladly gave up a post of honor rather than contribute to a treasonable cause."

Mr. Daugherty charged that "pilgrimages to Moscow by United States Senators" had been arranged for by the Communist authorities after their efforts to capture American labor organizations had failed.

"There (in Russia) no doubt new inspirations were advanced," he continued, "as to what steps should be taken to cripple the Government of the United States and crumble the columns that support it.

"It may fairly be inferred that one step in this direction was to capture, by deceit and design, as many members of the Senate of the United States as possible and to spread throughout Washington City and in the cloakrooms of Congress a poison gas as deadly as that which sapped and destroyed brave soldiers in the late war.

"Time will not permit me to give on this occasion the details of the various plans and efforts undertaken to influence the Senate as a body and individual members thereof. When the country is willing to hear and in condition to comprehend it, the whole story will be made known. For protection of innocent persons much of it must now be withheld."

Communist Movement Charged.

Mr. Daugherty said that Department of Justice records showed that a Communist movement began in the United States three years ago to destroy confidence "in our form of government."

"To this end," he continued, "confidence in men of both political parties had to be destroyed, when they could not be dominated by the directors of the movement. At any cost, by any conceivable method, cruel, criminal or murderous, the character of men in authority had of necessity to be assassinated."

The former Attorney General declared that official Government records, obtained from official Russian sources, "contribute indisputable proof" of the assertions he made. He referred then to what he described as "the connection between the Communists and those members of the United States Senate and other individuals, who seemingly embrace the ideals of this strange and dangerous doctrine, especially as it may be applicable to the 'investigative mania' at Washington.

"The Senate was swept off its feet," Mr. Daugherty continued. "Precedent was cast to the winds. The protection of individual and official rights has been ignored. Under Senatorial immunity falsehoods were reeled off by slanderous tongues of conscienceless Senators. Groundless charges were made against those who had stood for the enforcement of law and for orderly processes."

The former Attorney General then paid his respects to the Daugherty committee. He declared it was well known that a majority of this committee "would make an adverse report without charges and without evidence."

"I have been advised," he added, "that a resolution condemning the Attorney General was prepared even before the hearings before the investigating committee commenced."

Declaring that had there been any indication that the committee investigation of the Department of Justice would be conducted with fairness and along proper lines, Mr. Daugherty said it had been his intention to "make public the private business transactions of my life."

"I would not have consented to do this," he said, "except for the fact that while I held office I did not want any man to feel that there was anything in my private or official life that I was disposed to conceal from a curious public. I did not abandon my intention to declare my private business transactions even when the unfair methods of the majority of the Wheeler committee became plain.

"But now, having withstood the tempest until forced off my official feet, I deny the right of the committee to investigate my private life or scrutinize my personal business transactions, though I am willing and anxious that my official acts while Attorney General of the United States shall be investigated and scrutinized by the public.

"When banks are attacked, houses burglarized, graves opened, liars encouraged, individuals shadowed by spies and the Wheeler committee pursues an unlawful inquisition against a private American citizen, I propose to stand my ground and deny its authority over me and advise other private citizens to do the same."

Mr. Daugherty devoted a large part of his address to a defense of his administration as Attorney General, saying that on the day when "President Coolidge was forced, through misrepresentations, to request my resignation," the department was functioning more efficiently "than at any time in the history of the Government."

"Constant and unjustifiable criticism has been heaped upon the Department of Justice and upon the Attorney General by those who anticipated and deserved action against them in war fraud cases, anti-trust cases, prohibition cases, postal fraud cases and radical cases," he said. "But notwithstanding all this, the department was shock-proof and driving along with most successful results in all its various branches.

"President Coolidge well knew this, and so expressed himself frequently. Many of those who struck the hardest blows against the Government, the Department of Justice and the Attorney General, officially and personally, were deceived and misled into doing so, but they cannot be altogether excused, because the reports of the department were available and dependable, and showed conclusively the wonderful accomplishments of the department since its organization, and especially during the past three years.

"In justice to the clean and capable men and women to whom credit is due for the almost incomprehensible results accomplished by the Department of Justice, and because you are entitled to know the facts, you will permit me, I am sure, to give you in concrete form and as briefly as possible some idea of what the department has done in the past three years as compared with the three years just preceding.

"In making this comparison I assure you it is with no disposition to criticize my predecessor or his assistants.

"In the years 1918, 1919 and 1920, the period just preceding the present administration, there had been 100,913 criminal cases disposed of.

"In the years 1921, 1922 and 1923, covering the period of my administration of the Department of Justice, there were disposed of 168,606 such cases.

"There was collected by the Government in the years 1918, 1919 and 1920 in such cases the total sum of $14,297,548; whereas in the three years of 1921, 1922 and 1923 there were collected in cases of this class $32,556,467.

"The increase of civil business disposed of by the department during the comparative periods was even greater in proportion than the criminal business to which I have referred.

"The number of anti-trust cases tried and disposed of in the past three years was greater by 33 1-3 per cent. than the number disposed of in the three years just preceding.

"Fines collected by the Government in this class of cases within the past three years were more than twice as much as the total amount in the three years preceding.

"Until the present Administration was installed not a single person had ever been sent to prison for violation of the anti-trust laws. In the trial of cases arising out of the violation of the anti-trust laws, the Department of Justice urged the courts to impose sentences as well as heavier fines upon those convicted. The courts held that in order to stop such violations prison sentences should be imposed, and during the past three years many violators were given prison sentences. Some of them happened to be millionaires. They were not sent to prison because they were millionaires. That was just an incident. I will say, however, that a prison is an uncomfortable place for millionaire offenders to take the rest cure, and they have many ways of representing to the public that the Attorney General is not a fit or proper man for the job.

Suits Over War Transactions.

"During the war and thereafter there was much cry and criticism against men and concerns who had transacted business with the Government in war time. But not until 1921, when the Harding Administration was installed, was anything done to investigate war time transactions or to recover moneys fraudulently obtained from the Government.

It takes many months after a change of administration to reorganize the Department of Justice, to establish its definite policies and to select the men and instruct them in the practical work of carrying out such policies.

"The law business of the Department of Justice, as far as suits and claims are concerned, originates in and comes to the Department of Justice from the several other governmental departments. This is true in the case of claims and disputes growing out of war transactions and contracts. The war ended in 1918, yet up to the time the new Administration was installed in 1921, the Department of Justice had not instituted a single suit or made any collections in so-called war transactions. Congress had made no appropriation to pay the extra expense of the department in investigating claims of this character and instituting suits on such as were found necessary. In May, 1922, upon the request of the Attorney General, Congress appriated $500,000 for this purpose. Thereafter the work progressed as fast as it could be done thoroughly, and on Feb. 5, 1924, there were pending 117 suits involving $62,343,741. Nineteen claims were pending with receivers or trustees in bankruptcy involving $2,668,418. Ten claims had been reduced to judgments amounting to $4[illegible]308. Eighty-two claims were disposed of and collections of over six millions in cash paid into the Government Treasury. Three hundred claims, involving a total of $41,000,000 were under investigation. The Department of Justice, therefore, has had before it in excess of $100,000,000 of war claims in dispute. On the first of March, 1924 there were settlements in process of consummation amounting to $4,480,000, which will shortly make the total amount received to date about $9,000,000, with an expense to the Government of about $1,000,000, and all the work of organization and preliminary legal study and investigation completed.

"In addition, there were pending in the court of claims in December, 1923, 2,200 cases, involving $1,783,830,467.72, and of these, 1,514 cases arose out of the World War.

"About thirty days before I resigned as Attorney General of the United States, claims against the Government aggregating more than $350,000,000, and which were involved in twenty-eight cases arising out of claims by German ship owners whose vessels were seized during the war, were won in the court of claims by the Department of Justice, acting in behalf of the Government. The court dismissed all of the bills in these twenty-eight cases outright, which means that this enormous amount was saved to the Government.

"In the period of a year and a half ended December, 1923, 387 cases growing out of the World War were handled by the Department of Justice in the Court of Claims alone. In these cases the total amount claimed against the Government was $13,052,794. The total amount of judgments obtained against the Government was $3,061,476, of which amount the Government had already admitted a liability of $1,250,000.

"Cases of this class take no priority over other cases in the courts, and considering the congested condition of the court dockets throughout the country, no additional number of men could have tried any greater number of cases than were tried in the past three years.

"Looking back over the four years during which the national prohibition act has been in force, one is amazed at the volume of business which the Federal courts have handled during that period. More than 115,000 criminal cases arising under the prohibition act have already been terminated. Of this great number of cases, 80 per cent., or 92,411, have resulted in convictions and have brought to the Government in fines $15,726,593.

"The volume of litigation arising under the prohibition act has increased so rapidly and enforcement speeded up so effectively that a glance at the number of cases terminated and convictions obtained is very interesting and at the same time gives conclusive answer to the critics whose criticism is not in good faith.

Fiscal year ending June 30	Cases commenced	Cases terminated	Convictions	Cases pending
1920 (6 mos.)...	7,291	5,095	4,315	2,196
1921	29,114	21,962	17,962	10,365
1922	34,984	28,743	22,749	16,713
1923	49,021	42,730	34,067	23,052

"Under my Administration of the Department of Justice a policy was adopted, under Section 22 of the national prohibition act, to employ the use of the injunction to close up, as nuisances, thousands of breweries and saloons throughout the country. I may also explain that two years ago I directed all United States Attorneys to make every effort to secure jail sentences, where possible, and to urge upon the courts that more severe sentences be imposed upon those violating the liquor laws.

"In 1922, for several months, industrial chaos prevailed in this country. Two strikes of greater proportion than ever before engaged in in this or any other country were waged simultaneously. The railroad strike alone cost the railroad companies and the striking shop crafts hundreds of millions of dollars. Had the violence and lawlessness growing out of the strikes been allowed to continue, the Government itself would have been imperiled. As Attorney General it was my plain duty to take cognizance of the lawlessness, the interference with interstate commerce and the transportation of the mails incident to the strike, and a Federal statute required that the Attorney General apply to a court of competent jurisdiction to prevent such lawlessness and the interference with interstate commerce and the transportation of the mails. This I did in compliance with the law and in accordance with precedents established by my predecessors in office. Any man occupying the office of Attorney General of the United States who failed to do just what was done in the situation existing would be, and should be, impeached. On full and final hearing, the action of the Attorney General in applying for an injunction under the circumstances was sustained by the courts. The injunction ended the strike in thirty-six hours, and as a consequence of the injunction the industrial life of America will never again be paralyzed by a general transportation strike. It settled the law on the subject in this country and determined once and for all the principle that the general public has the paramount interest in all industrial controversies and the right to protection by law from loss, violence, suffering and hardship incident to such controversies. While the radical element condemned the Attorney General who secured the injunction, and undertook but ignominiously failed to impeach him before the Congress of the United States for doing his duty, labor generally and the public as a whole will one day applaud that service.

"The principle of the injunction is not one-sided, but applies equally to capital and labor. During my Administration as Attorney General the injunction was successfully invoked in behalf of labor to sustain the United States Labor Board against the attack made by the Pennsylvania Railroad Company, and the case terminated favorably to labor in an opinion of the Supreme Court on Feb. 19, 1923. Again, in the case of the United States vs. San Francisco Builders Exchange, Federal Judge Dooling issued an injunction within the past year forbidding discrimination by dealers in building material against contractors employing union labor. This case had been tried in the California State courts and a jury refused to convict. Upon practically the same evidence the Federal Court found in favor of union labor and forbade any combination in restraint of interstate commerce which illegally interfered with the rights of laboring men to unite for their own protection. The case has been appealed to the Supreme Court of the United States and when decided will be a leading case upon this important subject.

"I have given you but a few of the most important activities of the Department of Justice in the three years ending about April 1, 1924. This I do in answer to the misrepresentations made on the floor of the United States Senate, under the protection of senatorial immunity, by those, who, for their own purposes, charged that the Department of Justice was not successfully functioning. Radical and irresponsible Senators indulged in such misrepresentations for no other purpose than to inflame the public mind and to influence the Senate to make an investigation of the Department of Justice and the Attorney General. I did not resist the passage of the resolution to investigate the Department of Justice and my official acts. But the resolution was held up in the Senate by its promoters in order that, day by day, they could take advantage of the immunity they abused in order to create a condition of suspicion, doubt and prejudice throughout the country."

The former Attorney General drew a contrast between the action of Senator Wheeler as Committee Prosecutor in the Daugherty investigation and the Montana Senator's action when he was himself accused in an indictment returned by a Federal Grand Jury in Montana.

He said that Wheeler, "who for weeks has been summoning irresponsible witnesses to retail gossip and rumor against me asked for trial by a Senate committee in advance of his trial in the courts."

"An effort is made by Wheeler and his friends," Mr. Daugherty continued, "to make it appear that this regular proceeding of the court is a 'frame-up' against a Senator whose conduct of the so-called investigation of me and my office could be described by no other name."

Mr. Daugherty's friends and admirers who crowded the hotel ballroom and balconies interrupted his address many times to applaud and broke into wild demonstrations when he declared that he had given up his Cabinet post rather than contribute to "a treasonable cause."

Seated at the table with Mr. Daugherty were a number of life long Democrats and many others were scattered through the audience. Mrs. Harding, widow of the late President, sent the following telegram from Washington which was read:

"Will those who tonight are tendering Mr. Daugherty tribute of friendship and good will, permit me to join them in spirit? Memories of many years, marked by unannounced incidents of loyal friendship for Mr. Harding and myself, inspire in me an abiding confidence and sincere affection."

April 24, 1924

ASSAILS HULL HOUSE.

Illinois American Legion Head Calls It a Hotbed of Communism.

Special to The New York Times.

CHICAGO, Nov. 10.—Hull House and its founder, Jane Addams, were attacked before 600 members of the Illinois Federation of Women's Clubs today, when Captain Ferre Watkins, Commander of the Illinois Department of the American Legion, branded the Halsted Street Settlement as a hotbed of communism, and charged that the Communist "pinks" were trying to sell out America to international schemers for their own personal advantage.

"We don't fear the acknowledged radicals," said Captain Watkins. "The danger lies in organizations like the Women's International League for Peace, in the churches, the schools and the women's clubs.

"This person, Jane Addams, told in a public meeting how she hoped through influence at the White House to strip the uniforms from our Cadets at West Point, to deprive our colleges of military training and leave America undefended.

"We of the Legion, who hate war as no other organization does, demand that willingness to defend the flag shall no longer be regarded as an out-growth of savagery and the mob instinct."

CHICAGO, Nov. 10 (AP).—Miss Jane Addams declared tonight that the whole statement of Captain Watkins was so "utterly false, unwarranted and absurd" that she would not even take the trouble to deny it. She did, however, deny that she had made the statement that she "hoped through influence at the White House to strip the uniforms from our cadets at West Point, deprive our colleges of military training and leave America undefended."

November 11, 1926

AMERICAN COMMUNISTS NOW NUMBER ONLY 5000

Outpouring at Katovis Funeral the Result of a Call for a Demonstration—Splits in Party Encouraged—Some Present Slogans and Activities

By LOUIS STARK.

TUESDAY'S Communist funeral for Steve Katovis, killed by a policeman's bullet in the course of a strike of vegetable clerks, brought an outpouring of thousands of Communists and sympathizers that focused attention upon the Communist party, of which Katovis was a member.

Demonstrations are a policy with Communists. The word "demonstrate" appears frequently in their party propaganda, and even their enemies admit that they usually make an effective manifestation. The Katovis funeral was no exception. "Workers of the World, Unite" was the inscription on the red-draped coffin, decorated with red carnations and wreaths of red roses.

Borne on the shoulders of Young Communists wearing black and red arm bands, the coffin was carried out of the Workers Centre at 26 Union Square into the presence of a vast throng of which the police were no inconsiderable part. To many in the crowd that filled Union Square the funeral was an exotic incident even in a metropolis that furnishes a great variety of public processions. They heard some thousands of men and women, many in their teens and the majority under 30, shouting revolutionary slogans, singing revolutionary songs.

The vast and intricate machinery of mobilization responsible for the gathering was not apparent. But the leaders who returned to 26 Union Square after the funeral read with glowing eyes the page one stories in afternoon newspapers which they took as testimony to the effectiveness of their untiring efforts during many sleepless nights. For the Communists had mobilized almost their entire strength in New York for the Katovis cortège.

Demonstration Ordered.

For days the party press had called for mass demonstrations, first at the City Hall and then at the funeral. Shop nuclei, sectional meetings, housewives' sections, all "fractions" of the party in all radical unions and all unemployed members had been urged and entreated to flock to Union Square. "Young Pioneers," the Communist Boy Scouts, members of Communist Youth societies, sport club members, high school boys and girls, were mobilized for the occasion.

The discipline made evident at the funeral was imposed by a party modeled after the Communist party in Russia. Here it has the same slogans, the same intraparty quarrels, the same polemics and the same "theses" that are published in the official party press in Moscow. With one difference: the two factions here which have in the last few years been "cleansed" from the party, are, thanks to the American guarantee of free press, able to keep up (finances permitting) an opposition press. Here are found organs of the Trotsky adherents and also of the Lovestone group which calls itself the majority, despite possession of the official machinery of the Communist party of the U. S. A.

In the United States the Communist parties have passed through a complicated development. Hardly was one formed before there was a split. According to James Oneal, author of "American Communism," there have been more Communist parties in this country than in any other in the world. There were twelve between 1919 and 1921 or four for each of the three years. In the splitting process there has been on an average a new Communist party every ten months. Splits were defended as a necessity, for "the more you split the clearer and stronger you become."

The anti-Red raids of Attorney General Palmer in 1919 drove the party "underground" and the various branches became secret societies. The legal sections of the party flourished above ground as "literary clubs," and several years later when the Federal Government ban was removed the underground party became the officially recognized Communist party.

From a membership of 35,000 in its heyday the party has dwindled to about 5,000, including that of the two groups which have split off in the last year or two. In 1923 the party had 20,000 members, nine daily papers and twenty-one weeklies. The membership was largely alien and split into sixteen foreign language federations—"a modern Babel," as one of the Moscow representatives reported.

The Communist Party of the U. S. A., the official title, is part of the Communist International or Comintern. No effort is made to conceal the relationship. Orders to hew to the line of the Comintern are published in the party press, and American members who "deviate" from the "line" are compelled to "go to Canossa" and recant, just as in Soviet Russia. In the case of the members in this country, publication of "error" in the party press is usually sufficient to clear one's self.

Danger of Expulsion.

Differences with the theses of the Comintern mean expulsion, as in the case of Jay Lovestone, "the American Stalin," and a group of important leaders who were supreme in the local party but who "erred" by adhering to the view of "exceptionalism," which holds that America is developing according to its own economic laws and is relatively exempt "from the growing world crisis of capitalism."

Workers who join the Communist party pledge themselves to an iron discipline. They may be called at any time to take part in demonstrations, to hold meetings of shop or street nuclei, to hand out literature at meetings or to assume one of a hundred or more duties.

The basis of organization is the workshop, where the units are called nuclei. All the nuclei compose a factory group. The various groups are formed into sections. The principle of organization is called "democratic centralism," by which is meant that "the higher committees of the party are elected by and base themselves on the lower units and are responsible to conventions and congresses elected by these lower units."

In seeking to control the policies of non-Communist organizations such as trade unions, the small Communist group forms what is known as a "fraction." This "fraction" usually meets in advance of the entire group and agrees upon a plan of action at the meeting. In this way many non-Communist organizations are subjected to control by Communist "fractions" under direction of the higher party authorities exemplified in the Central Executive Committee.

The Fields of Action.

Despite all setbacks and reorganizations, the Communist party, through affiliated union and relief organizations, is active in the textile regions of New England and the South, in the coal fields of Illinois and Pennsylvania, among the shoe workers and furniture workers in New York and in some of the large automobile centres.

Spurred on by zeal for the Communist goal, the members stand at factory gates, pass out their leaflets, hold meetings, urge workers to join their party and go up and down the country agitating. From time to time new phrases, coined in Moscow to renew the faith of laggards or to castigate further the enemies of communism, reach this country and are adopted without hesitation. A month after the phrase "social Fascists," invented to describe the anti-Communists, first appeared in the Moscow press, it was published in the Communist publications of the entire world.

At present the "depressed industrial situation" is the rallying cry of the world Communist forces. The Communist International has set Feb. 26 as the day which shall be the culmination of mass demonstrations "against unemployment and for unemployment relief and social insurance." On that day there will be street meetings in the capitals of Europe and in many cities in this country.

In the United States the Communist attack is leveled against capitalists and capitalistic institutions, against the Socialists and the American Federation of Labor. To the Communist the Socialist is "the third party of the bourgeoisie," or the party of "social fascism." The American Federation of Labor is held to consist of "misleaders." Characterizations of the owners of wealth are many and picturesque.

Despite their lack of numbers the young leaders in the Communist unions have thrown themselves into their tasks with zeal. Undaunted by lack of large funds, they manage to continue carrying "their message to the people." In the South, where they have been active in attempting to organize the textile workers, the Communist leaders lived with the operatives, studied their needs, talked organization and incessantly kept up a barrage of arguments against the American Federation of Labor.

The Southern mill worker, the Illinois miner and the New England factory worker are being propagandized with the thesis that the world is now witnessing the general decay of capitalism, characterized by a crisis in what they call imperialism. Every speaker, every pamphlet stresses the era of "speed-up."

Special attention is being devoted to organization work among negroes. Racial equality is preached to Southern mill workers, and to those who question such a course as quixotic the Communist will reply that experience has amply proved that even in the South the working people do not object to including negroes in their trade unions. They say that when a white mob kidnapped some white union leaders in Gastonia several months ago it was the textile workers who secreted a negro organizer in one of their homes and kept him until it was safe to spirit him out of town. In the North the slogan "social equality" is carried out at dances and parties where whites and blacks ignore the color line.

The "Innocents Clubs."

Since 1921 the Communists have formed many auxiliary and supplementary organizations through which to approach the masses indirectly with the program of the Comintern. These organizations have names which do not identify them as Communist to the layman and they are known among the Communists as "innocents clubs," because the non-Communist members are unaware of the purpose in fostering them. Such organizations may have as their ostensible purpose the furtherance of bicycle riding, sports, China famine relief or relief to political prisoners.

One of the strange anomalies in the situation is the existence of three parties, each claiming to be the only genuine Communist party. The party of Lovestone, calling itself the "majority," now contains most of the old well-known leaders like Benjamin Gitlow, Bertram D. Wolfe, C. S. Zimmerman, Herbert Zam and Jack Rubinstein. The attack of this group on the Communist party of the U. S. A. is based on the latter's attitude that the workers in the United States are ready for revolution.

"The workers in the United States are not Communists," says Gitlow. "They have not yet developed to the most elemental stages of class consciousness."

The Communist League of America, adhering to the Trotsky formula of world revolution, attacks both the Lovestone group and the Communist party of the U. S. A., now led by W. Z. Foster and William Weinstone.

To overcome its loss of membership the Communist party is now engaged in a campaign for new members and its latest figures claim 3,081 new recruits out of a quota of 5,000, the goal. As the funeral cortège of Katovis wound through the streets Tuesday, cards were distributed among the bystanders inviting them to join the Communist party.

February 2, 1930

'RED SCARE' PROTEST ISSUED BY LIBERALS

100 Writers, Educators and Artists Warn of Dangers in 'Hysteria' and 'Persecution.'

SEE CIVIL RIGHTS AT STAKE

Statement Says 1,600 Have Been Wrongfully Arrested in 2 Months—Aid of Press Asked.

A protest against the imprisonment of men and women for expressing their political opinions, coupled with a warning that "Red-baiting" is rapidly becoming a permanent condition, was voiced in a statement issued yesterday by the John Reed Club, 102 West Fourteenth Street. The protest was signed by more than 100 writers, educators and artists.

Those who indorsed the statement, which contained an appeal to the press to awaken the public to the dangers of such hysteria, included H. L. Mencken, Sherwood Anderson, Professor Franz Boas, Carl Van Doren and John Sloan. In their declaration they maintained that the "Red scare" was sweeping the country and threatening the complete destruction of civil liberties.

Survey Shows Many Arrests.

A survey by the club has revealed that more than 1,600 men and women have been imprisoned within the past two months in violation of their constitutional rights, according to the statement. Cases cited included those of W. Z. Foster and the other radicals to whom bail was denied after their arrest on misdemeanor charges in connection with the riot in Union Square on March 6, and the case of Carr and Powers, arrested for distributing leaflets demanding "work or wages" at a meeting in Atlanta, Ga. They have been charged with "inciting to insurrection" under a law passed soon after the Civil War and since inoperative, and face the death penalty if convicted under that charge, according to the statement, which continues:

"An Ohio court has actually sentenced two young girls to ten years in prison for distributing pamphlets. In California more than 900 unemployed were arrested for the crime of being out of work. In Chicago 137 are being tried for sedition for holding an indoor meeting to discuss unemployment. Milwaukee has jailed fifty-eight for participation in the March 6 unemployment demonstrations, and in the South workers are being sent to the chain-gang for organizing unions.

"To combat this persecution for political opinion, concerted protest is necessary. The people of the United States must be awakened to the threatened complete destruction of their civil rights. The John Reed Club has instituted a campaign to spread information about this situation and to cooperate with the International Labor Defense, which is providing relief and legal aid to political prisoners."

Names of the Signers.

A list of the signers follows:

L. Adohmyan
Sherwood Anderson
Emjo Basshe
Helen Black
Prof. Franz Boas
Alter Brody
Samuel Brody
Fritz Brosius
Jacob Burck
David Burliuk
Rev. R. B. Callahan
Walt Carmon
Ralph Cheyney
N. Cikovsky
Lydia Cinquegrana
Sarah N. Cleghorn
Ann Coles
Malcolm Cowley
Franz E. Daniel
Miriam A. DeFord
Adolf Dehn
Floyd Dell
L. A. De Santes
Babette Deutsch
Carl Van Doren
John Dos Passos
Robert W. Dunn
Max Eastman
Charles Ellis
Fred Ellis
Ernestine Evans
Kenneth Fearing
Sara Bard Field
Waldo Frank
Harry Freeman
Al Frueh
Hugo Gellert
Michael Gold
Floyd S. Gove
C. Hartley-Grattan
Horace Gregory
William Gropper
Rose Gruening
Carl Haessler
E. Haldeman-Julius
M. Haldeman-Julius
Ruth Hale
Jack Hardy
Mina Harkavy
Prof. S. R. Harlow
Charles Y. Harrison
Aline D. Hays
Arthur G. Hays
Lowell B. Hazzard
Josephine Herbst
Joan Herrman
Harold Hickerson
Grace Hutchins
Eitaro Ishigaki
Joseph Kaplan
Ellen A. Kennan
Rev. C. D. Ketcham
Rev. Frank Kingdon
I. Kittine
I. Klein
Alfred Kreymborg
Joshua Kunitz
Melvin P. Levy
Louis Lozowick
Grace Lumpkin
Norman Macleod
A. B. Magil
Jan Matuika
H. L. Mencken
Norma Millay
Harriet Monroe
Prof. Frank McLean
Scott Nearing
Alfred H. Neumann
Eugene Nigob
Joseph North
Harvey O'Connor
M. J. Olgin
Joseph Pass
Morris Pass
Nemo Piccoli
Harry A. Potamkin
John Cowper Powys
Juanita Preval
Walter Quirt
Burton Rascoe
Anton Refregier
Philip Reisman
Louis Ribak
Boardman Robinson
Anna Rochester
Anna Rosenberg
Julius Rosenthal
Martin Russak
Samuel Russak
David Saposs
E. A. Schachner
Isidor Schneider
Evelyn Scott
Edwin Seaver
Edith Segal
Esther Shemitz
William Siegel
Upton Sinclair
John Sloan
Otto Soglow
A. Solataroff
Walter Snow
Raphael Soyer
Herman Spector
Prof. J. M. Stalnaker
Genevieve Taggard
Eunice Tietjens
Carlo Tresca
Jim Tully
Louis Untermeyer
Joseph Vogel
Keene Wallis
Frank Walts
Prof. R. E. Waxwell
Rev. C. C. Webber
G. F. Willison
Edmund Wilson Jr.
Adolf Wolff
Charles E. S. Wood
Art Young
Stark Young
Avrahm Yarmolinsky
William Zorach

May 19, 1930

HOUSE BY 210 TO 18 VOTES RED INQUIRY

Orders Special Committee to Look Into Communist Propaganda in This Country.

AMTORG TO BE ONE TARGET

Ramseyer Charges 'Witch Hunting' and Warns Against Starting a 'Wild Goose Chase.'

Special to The New York Times.

WASHINGTON, May 22.—Ignoring protests against "witch hunting" and "starting on a wild goose chase," the House voted, 210 to 18, today for an inquiry into Communist activities in the United States, including the connections of the Amtorg Trading Corporation, agency of the Soviet Government.

The resolution directs Speaker Longworth to appoint a committee of five to investigate "Communist propaganda in the United States and particularly in our educational institutions, the activities and membership of the Communist party of the United States and all affiliated organizations and groups thereof, the ramification of the Communist International in the United States, the Amtorg Trading Corporation, The Daily Worker and all entities, groups or individuals who are alleged to advise, teach or advocate the overthrow by force or violence of the government of the United States or attempt to undermine our republican form of government by inciting riots, sabotage or revolutionary disorders."

The resolution does not limit the expenditures and authorizes the committee or any subcommittee to sit anywhere at any time and to report its findings to the House.

Ramseyer Leads Opposition.

Representative Ramseyer of Iowa, farm leader and son of Swiss immigrants, opposed the resolution when it was unexpectedly brought to the floor by the Rules Committee. Representative Michener of Michigan, in charge of the committee, refused to defer action, and Mr. Ramseyer made a point of no quorum and forced a roll-call for a little delay.

The resolution was introduced by Representative Fish of New York. Some changes were made by the Rules Committee, and when the resolution was finally reported it bore the name of Chairman Snell.

Mr. Ramseyer ridiculed the measure, saying it was for a "wild goose chase," and called upon the House to turn its thoughts to what he held to be the more serious forces which might be undermining the republic.

"These are economic forces," he declared, "and I don't want anything to distract the minds of the people from the great and fundamental economic conditions they are faced with now.

"We have large surpluses of things to eat, to wear and to shelter our heads, but unemployment is rife. Instead of going off witch hunting, why not create a committee of Congress to study why, in the midst of plenty, we are in the midst of want? Why not have a committee study unemployment? In all seriousness, why not address ourselves to these problems?

"I know it is easier to go off on this hunt, and the front pages of the papers will be filled with alleged disclosures, along with names of members of the committee. But it isn't the preaching of radicals that creates unrest among our people. The thing that brings about unrest and revolution is a distressed economic condition.

"We have a condition which we ought to face squarely and frankly. It's a bigger issue than prohibition, bigger than the tariff, and if the Tuesday's election in Pennsylvania indicated anything, it indicated that false issues will have no place in coming campaigns."

Representative Fish declared that "the gentleman from Iowa is not going to get any help from the Communists in settling these problems."

"Why not bring in the Wagner bills and pass them to relieve the unemployment situation?" asked Representative Cullen of New York.

Mr. Fish declared the trail of the Third International ran through the labor-troubled sections of the South.

"If you want to create jobs in America, deport every Communist," he shouted.

"Where are you going to send them?" broke in Chairman Johnson of the Immigration Committee. "We already have 1,000 Russians on the waiting list who can't be sent back to Russia."

"Let's deport them to some isolated island where they can practice communism to their hearts' desire," continued Mr. Fish. "Let's have this investigation and find who our enemies are."

"While you are in the deporting business," interrupted Representative Green of Florida, "why not include all people in America not of white blood."

Chairman Snell said that the Rules Committee, after hearing the testimony, did not feel that it could take the responsibility of blocking such an investigation. He had been convinced, he said, that an inquiry of some kind should be made. He had found that no Federal law provided any protection. The Department of Justice had absolutely no weapon at its disposal, he said, not even one of investigation.

"If there is nothing to this agitation, then we surely ought to find it out," he added. "The Amtorg people themselves want a chance to clear their reputation of the charges made concerning them recently in New York."

"Then, do I understand the Communists themselves want this investigation?" asked Mr. Ramseyer.

"I mean nothing of the kind," retorted Mr. Snell curtly.

"Is this resolution broad enough to include Fascism?" asked Representative Huddleston of Alabama.

"Include what?" asked Mr. Snell.

"Fascism, Fascism," answered the Alabaman.

"I don't know what that is, but I guess it is," answered the Rules Committee chairman.

"Is this resolution before us now, the Fish resolution after it had been hijacked in the Rules Committee?" asked Representative Schafer of Wisconsin.

"I don't understand the word," said Mr. Snell, dismissing the question.

Interest centred on the New York City delegation, to see how it voted. Representative Somers of Brooklyn was the only member of the delegation voting against the resolution.

May 23, 1930

ASSAIL RED INQUIRY VOTED BY THE HOUSE

La Guardia and O'Connor Declare Congress Had Better Attack Unemployment.

WHERE COMMUNISM FEEDS

Special to The New York Times.
WASHINGTON, May 23.—A renewal of the agitation for an inquiry into unemployment throughout the country and for government action in curing it followed today in the wake of the passage yesterday of a resolution calling for an investigation by a special House committee of Communist activities in the United States.

Representatives O'Connor of Oklahoma and La Guardia of New York declared that Congress had better address itself to the conditions upon which communism feeds than upon the doctrine itself.

"The best way to fight communistic propaganda is to put something in soup besides statistics," said Mr. O'Connor in a statement, which yesterday he was prevented from making on the floor because of the short debate on the resolution but which today he put into the Record.

"The whole investigation will be nothing but 'open shop' propaganda against the labor unions," he said today. "The investigation had better be directed toward finding out what can be done to relieve the widespread unemployment throughout this country."

The House Judiciary subcommittee plans to begin hearings as soon as possible on the two Wagner unemployment bills, already passed by the Senate, and seven other such measures introduced in the House.

"If the committee would report out the two unemployment bills which were passed by the Senate and the House were to consider them, I think that we could do considerable more to cut down the demand for Communistic propaganda," declared Mr. O'Connor. "The idle men of America are asking for jobs and we are authorizing an investigation.

"What we are doing here is to start a movement which will give this Communistic propaganda publicity the Communists could not buy for a million dollars."

May 24, 1930

ELIHU ROOT URGES NEW FEDERAL POLICE TO CURB RED INTRIGUE

Warns of "Assault by Secret Means Aimed at Destruction of Our Government."

SEES LACK OF PROTECTION

R. M. Easley, Who Reveals Views, Predicts Congress Inquiry Will Bring New Police Arm.

INQUIRY HERE TOMORROW

Labor and Socialist Group Calls It Attempt to Divert Attention From Unemployment.

The creation of a special Federal police force to combat Communist intrigue and propaganda, which, he charges, is directed by the Soviet Government, was urged in a letter by Elihu Root to Ralph M. Easley, executive secretary of the National Civic Federation, made public by Mr. Easley yesterday.

The establishment of a special police force against Communists will result from the Congressional inquiry of Communist activities now under way by a committee headed by Representative Hamilton Fish Jr., Mr. Easley predicted. He said that members of the committee as well as other members of Congress favored the formation of such a police force because the government now has no police to combat subversive activities.

The Congressional inquiry committee, which has already held hearings in Washington, will begin sessions here tomorrow at the local office of the Department of Justice, 370 Lexington Avenue.

While making no specific reference to the Soviet Government, Mr. Root in his letter to Mr. Easley, indicates that it is his belief that Moscow is actively engaged in an assault upon American institutions in the hope of provoking a Communist revolution in the United States. In deploring the fact that "the Federal Government has no police force available for our protection," Mr. Root referred to the situation, which since 1924 has deprived the Department of Justice of funds and personnel to ferret out the true nature and sources of Communist agitation. Nor has the State Department any agency at its command to perform this work, Mr. Easley said.

Root's Letter to Easley.

Mr. Root's letter to Mr. Easley follows:

"Thank you for your letter of June 18. I am glad you have succeeded in getting a start made at Washington in the direction of remedying the defect in our police service.

"There is undoubtedly a defect in our present organization for police purposes. It arises from the way in which our government has developed. General police power belongs to the States. The Federal Government is a government of enumerated powers, and special bodies of police officers have been created to aid in the exercise of those enumerated powers.

"Thus we have a body of police officers aiding in the enforcement of the customs laws of the United States; another body of police officers aiding in the enforcement of the Internal Revenue laws; another aiding in the enforcement of the laws against counterfeiting; another aiding in the enforcement of the prohibition laws, but we have no general Federal police officers, because the States and not the Federal Government exercise general police authority.

"Now we have reason to believe that an assault is being made by secret means, supported by the resources of a great empire aimed at the destruction of our system of government, and we find that the Federal Government has no police force available for our protection. Of course, such a force ought to be provided."

Sees False Sense of Security.

Mr. Easley, in discussing Mr. Root's letter, said:

"The facts which will be brought out during the hearings of the Congressional committee will undoubtedly result in so arousing the American people out of their false sense of security that they will demand the sorely needed remedial legislation. This legislation, however, will not be secured without overcoming the determinated opposition of all the Red forces backed by the so-called Left-wing liberals. Shrieking 'Revival of Red Hysteria,' 'Recrudescence of Palmerism,' 'Scotland Yard Heroics' and so forth, they will claim that 'it will be highly unconstitutional for the Federal Government to deal with such matters which are entirely within the jurisdiction of the States.'"

Mr. Root's letter, Mr. Easley said, should prove ample justification for the establishment of the proposed special police force. In this connection, Mr. Easley said that the American Government was the only government in the world that does not take special precautions to protect itself against destructive Communist activities.

Taking the opposite view from that of Mr. Easley, the Conference for Progressive Labor Action, representing a number of trade unions, the Socialist party and certain liberal elements, declared yesterday that the $50,000 which has been appropriated for the Congressional inquiry should be turned over toward relief of New York's unemployed.

A demand for such action was embodied in a telegram addressed to Representative Fish. The Congressional investigation was denounced by the conference as an attempt to divert public attention from the present unemployment situation and the alleged failure of the Hoover Administration to cope with it.

The telegram was signed by Louis F. Budenz, executive secretary of the Conference for Progressive Labor Action.

July 14, 1930

WOLL SAYS AMTORG, IN FEDERAL FAVOR, PLOTS REVOLUTION

Laxity on Visas Has Enabled Reds to Gain Rapidly Here, He Tells Fish Committee.

WARNS BUSINESS OF PERIL

Labor Leader Holds It Builds a Frankenstein Monster by Trade With Soviet.

TERRORISM IS CHARGED

Police Inspector Asserts Knives and Clubs Are Used by Communists to Coerce City's Workers.

Matthew Woll, vice president of the American Federation of Labor, charged yesterday before the Congressional committee investigating communism here that for the sake of helping American corporations to do business with Soviet Russia the American Government was jeopardizing the interests and safety of the United States by being too lenient with Communist agents and representatives of the Amtorg, the Soviet trading agency in this country.

Declaring that the Amtorg was operating as a channel of communication between Moscow and American Communists, Mr. Woll asserted "our government has winked with one eye and has been asleep with the other, while the agents of Moscow have come among us."

Sees Officials Duped by Reds.

Visas and permits enabling Soviet agents to reside and do their subversive work in this country are being extended by the authorities without due consideration of the dangers involved, while high government officials, "dined and wined by Communist agents," are lured into unwitting co-operation with emissaries of Moscow, Mr. Woll charged.

He asserted that this situation is due, among other things, to the activity of a certain law firm which makes it its business to facilitate the admittance and residence of Communist agents in this country.

Asserting that the Soviet Government was engaged in an open attempt to bring about the overthrow of the American Government, Mr. Woll told the committee, on the basis of what he termed information received by him from the police, that Communist agents were also being smuggled into the United States from rum ships.

Because of the leniency displayed by the Federal authorities, Mr. Woll said, the Soviet Government has been able to establish in this country a branch of its Ogpu or secret police and espionage organization, whose leaders direct the work of Communists here. He demanded that the government adopt a more determined course. Agents of the Amtorg, he urged, should be watched more closely, adding it would be even better if they were barred from the country altogether.

Mr. Woll's attack on the Federal authorities and on the Amtorg came in the course of his testimony dealing with Communist activities from 1917 to the present day.

Previous to Mr. Woll's testimony, Inspector John A. Lyons, head of the Federal Bureau of the Police Department, painted a vivid picture of organized Communist terrorism in the city. Like Mr. Woll, he advocated a more energetic policy on the part of the government, urging among other things the authorization of the Department of Justice to act as a clearing house of information on Communist propaganda. In substance he and Mr. Woll favored the idea that the status quo as it existed in 1925 with respect to the work of the Department of Justice be restored. Up to that time the department had both funds and authority to employ some of its equipment in keeping watch on Communists. Since the department has been deprived of that function, Inspector Lyons said, the Communist movement has made impressive strides. He also urged wholesale deportation of alien Communists.

Fish Opposes Secret Police.

In this connection, Representative Hamilton Fish Jr., chairman of the investigating committee, declared that due to what he termed Elihu Root's unfortunate formulation of his recent proposal for more direct activity on the part of the government against Communists, the impression has gone out that Mr. Root and members of the committee favored the creation of a special Federal police for this work.

"The committee has nothing of the sort in mind," Mr. Fish said. "Nor do we want to go as far as recommending any sort of sedition laws. We do not seek the establishment in this country of any secret political police, on the order of the Russian Cheka or Ogpu. All that I for one favor is simply that the Department of Justice be enabled to do what it has done in the past: namely, to employ some of its own agents in keeping watch on Communists and to have enough money to do it with. That is all, I believe, Mr. Root also had in mind."

Repudiation of the suggestion that he favored the creation of a special Federal police against the Communists along the line of plan attributed to Mr. Root, was made also by Charles G. Wood, Commissioner of Conciliation of the Federal Department of Labor, who testified before the Congressional committee on Wednesday. Mr. Wood said he did not favor any such plan, pointing out that while urging special legislation against what he termed the Communist menace, he refrained from making any specific suggestions. He will make these suggestions at an executive session of the committee.

Gompers Data Introduced.

Mr. Woll's attack on the Amtorg came after he had presented to the committee testimony covering 1,000 pages, heavily documented, which Samuel Gompers, the late president of the American Federation of Labor, had prepared for presentation to the Senate Committee on Foreign Relations in 1922. Mr. Woll said Mr. Gompers had been unable to present the evidence to that committee because Senator Borah, its chairman, had failed to give him an opportunity to do so. The presentation was to have been made in connection with hearings held by the committee on the question of Soviet recognition by the United States. Mr. Woll said he could not explain Senator Borah's attitude. Senator Borah has been an advocate of Soviet recognition.

While the Gompers documents comprised an exhaustive review of Communist activities here and abroad up to 1922, Mr. Woll's own testimony, also richly documented, carried the data forward to the present day, dealing largely, however, with what he termed the desperate efforts of the Communists to obtain control of the labor movement. These attacks, Mr. Woll said, have been beaten back successfully, although the labor unions were compelled to be on constant guard against Communist activity. He saw the greatest danger from Communism at the present time in the activities of the Communist party and its sympathizers outside the labor movement, in educational institutions, in the army and navy, in camps, schools, among the intellectuals and among the youth of the land.

"Why should the labor unions be compelled to bear the brunt of this work?" he demanded. "Why does not the government do its duty?" Agreeing with Representative Nelson of Maine that the American Federation of Labor was the first line of defense against Communism in this country, he urged nevertheless that the other activities of the Communists, including their work among the Negroes, should be the object of government attack.

"Instead," he said, "I am told that people in our governmental departments are dined and wined by Soviet agents, and I have heard similar statements regarding officers of the army and navy."

Members of the committee hastened to discount this charge, saying it had been brought before them before in executive session. Mr. Nelson added that testimony before the committee showed that the Communists were making no headway in the army and navy. The committee also excluded from the record unauthenticated letters received by Mr. Woll making various charges against the Amtorg and the Communist party. The letters were accepted by the committee as information. Some of them will be followed up, Chairman Fish said.

Urges Active Defense.

"It is my hope that out of this inquiry will grow some proper authorization for adequate defensive action by our government," Mr. Woll said. "There has been too much leniency, too little knowledge of the facts. I see no reason why we should deal with any particular gentleness with these gentlemen from Moscow. That they may spend part of their time making contracts by which money is paid to some of our corporations constitutes no justification for permitting them the hospitality of our free country. That is merely a form of bribing our national conscience."

Mr. Woll warned American capitalists doing business with Russia under the Soviet régime that they were "setting up a Frankenstein which may some day come to plague them."

He told the committee that, while the actual number of members of the Communist party may be relatively small, there were some 500,000 Communists and Communist sympathizers in the United States.

When asked to be more specific about the alleged activities of the Amtorg, its agents and of the Communist party, Mr. Woll said that he could be specific only about those aspects of the Communist movement touching on labor organizations and that it was the duty of the government to uncover the rest of the facts. He warned, however, that, while he favored the setting up of some specific government machinery for this task, he was opposed to the creation of any espionage organizations, which, he said, have been used unjustly against all labor organizations in the past.

Inspector Lyons reviewed the history of about a dozen Communist strikes in New York since 1925 and, with police records in hand, detailed the story of the experience of the police in fighting Communist violence. He charged that violence was an approved and accepted method of the Communists, who, he said, believe that "revolution is at hand."

The maintenance of strong arm squads for terrorization of non-Communist workers and employers, the organization of "knife mobs" for the shadowing and stabbing of workers, the threatening of workers and their families and a systematic, never halting campaign by the Reds to push themselves forward in industry, in schools, in the army and navy constituted the details of Inspector Lyons's story.

He estimated the number of Communists in New York as between 15,000 and 20,000, saying this represented a considerable growth since 1925. In recent years the Communists have had considerable success among the Negroes, he said. He also charged that the Communists import professional gangsters to help conduct their campaign of violence.

In reply to questions from members of the committee he said it would be advisable for the police of various cities to coordinate their anti-Communist activity and to have the Department of Justice act as a clearing house. So far as the native Americans among the Communists are concerned, he said, they were merely engaged in "running a racket which gives them a living." He estimated that 85 per cent of the Communists are Russians and only a small fraction are Americans.

"The Communists have become a serious police problem," he declared, "and although we have them under control we have to be on guard all the time. They have worked untold hardships to the workers themselves, particularly in the needle trades. If it were not for the relentless fight waged by the A. F. of L., they would have made considerable progress in New York industries and would have had the dress, fur and other needle trades in their hands."

As it is, he said, many plants have been driven out of the city by the activities of the Communists.

"If wholesale deportations occurred for one month the bottom would drop out of the Communist movement in this country," he asserted. He agreed, however, that it was impossible to deport Communists to Soviet Russia in the absence of diplomatic relations, and urged that Russians be kept out of the country altogether.

Inspector Lyons declined to discuss the Amtorg, saying former Police Commissioner Whalen would deal with that subject today.

Another witness yesterday was Justice Mitchel May of the Supreme Court in Brooklyn, who defended a decision given by him in a Communist injunction case, in which he held that an employer had the right to refuse to employ Communists "or any one singled out by the government as an enemy of the government."

July 18, 1930

PRIEST SAYS FORD AIDS COMMUNISM

Detroit Witness Attacks Failure to Employ Thousands After Calling for Workers.

OTHERS SCOUT MOVEMENT

Ten Witnesses Before Congressional Committee See No Peril in Red Activities.

Special to The New York Times.
DETROIT, Mich., July 25.—Henry Ford was charged today with responsibility for the spread of communism, in a statement made by a Detroit priest before the Congressional committee investigating Red activities in this country. The committee heard eleven witnesses today after shifting its sessions from New York.

The Rev. Charles E. Coughlin, pastor of the Shrine of the Little Flower Church, asserted that "the greatest force in the movement to internationalize labor throughout the world is Henry Ford."

Representative Fish, chairman of the committee, asked the witness to explain the basis for his reasoning. "A year ago, on the eve of the automobile show in New York," Father Coughlin continued, "Mr. Ford issued a statement that was printed on the front page of every daily newspaper in the United States that he required 30,000 more workers at his plant in Detroit. As a result of that statement more than 40,000 men who were out of work flocked to Detroit from Southern States, and while the weather was at zero, stood in front of the Ford plant trying to get those jobs. There were no jobs for them, and the only redress they had was to have the fire hose turned on them to drive them away."

Recalls Ford Peace Ship.

"Getting all these men here in that manner was not done on purpose, was it?" Mr. Fish asked.

"No. It was done through ignorance, just as the peace ship was sent to Europe through ignorance by the same man who didn't know when the War of Independence was fought," Father Coughlin replied.

The priest added that Mr. Ford's money was helping the Soviet Government in Russia and he referred to the $13,000,000 contract Mr. Ford signed with Soviet representatives.

Of the eleven witnesses before the committee today only Father Coughlin seemed apprehensive over Communistic activities. He predicted that a revolution was near.

Most of the forenoon was devoted to listening to Caesar J. Scavarda, Flint Police Chief, tell of the recent strike difficulties in his city, said to have been caused by Communist influence. Other witnesses included N. R. Dougherty, personnel director of General Motors Corporation, and James E. Ferber, secretary of the Flint Manufacturers Association.

Estimates on Number of Reds.

Charles T. Winegar, Commissioner of Public Safety of Hamtramck, informed the committee that although persons of fifty-seven different nations were employed by him, and that the suburb is peopled with huge numbers of foreigners, he knew of only one bona fide Communist, George Kristalsky, a recent candidate for Mayor, and now a candidate for the Legislature.

"The whole spirit of the community is against communism so far as I have observed," the commissioner said. "In fact, more persons own their homes in Hamtramck than in any other city of its size in the country," he declared.

Estimates of the number of Communists in Detroit varied from 1,500 to 5,000. These included active members of the party as well as sympathizers. All the witnesses were of the opinion that at least 90 per cent of all these persons were foreigners. Unemployment tends to increase the interest in such movements, all believed.

Thomas C. Wilcox, who was formerly in charge of the local Department of Justice agents, told of his activities with Communists here in 1920, when 827 persons were arrested, following several demonstrations. Of this number 234 were deported, he said, and the remainder freed.

July 26, 1930

SAY REDS AGITATE IN CHICAGO SCHOOLS

Witnesses Before Fish Committee Assert Literature Has Been Distributed Among Students.

PROF. LOVETT IS ACCUSED

Special to The New York Times.
CHICAGO, July 28.—Evidence that Communist propaganda was being conducted in the Chicago public schools was presented today to the Congressional committee investigating communism in this country.

N. E. Hewitt, representative of the American Intelligence Vigilantes, said there were thirty-five Communist students in the Cregier High School. William J. Page, principal of the Brown Elementary School, said that on four occasions during the last year groups of six or eight Communist sympathizers, children of Jewish origin, were found in the schoolyard with circulars. Clarence Debutts, principal of Tuley Junior High, and Mary E. Tobin, principal of Cragin High School, told of Communist literature being discovered among the children and brought copies of it to the committee.

Mr. Hewitt also told of Communist propaganda among the Negroes of Chicago and of the origin of the American Negro Labor Congress as a branch of the Red party. He said that there were 238 Negro Communists in the United States, and in addition 1,100 in the Labor Congress, 900 in the Harlem Red League, and 2,000 in other groups.

Representative Oscar De Priest testified that while some efforts were being made among his people, the movement was not making much headway.

"They never will be able to muster more than 5 per cent of my race," he said.

Puts Membership at 15,000.

Mr. Hewitt told the committee headed by Representative Fish that the present Communist membership in this country is about 15,000. There is a movement now under way, he said, to place American-born leaders in charge in this country. He placed the Chicago membership at 1,150. He said he had found evidences of communism in the universities, and named David Gordon, a student at the University of Wisconsin, as one leader.

Mr. Hewitt said he believed that the Congressional investigation would drive the Red movement under ground, but that it would continue to function under the name of the Trade Union League. It received much aid, he said, from such organizations as the Civil Liberties League and from such men as Professor Robert Morse Lovett of the University of Chicago and Professor Holston E. Warne of the University of Pittsburgh.

He said the Communists had begun the work of organizing among farmers through headquarters in South Dakota.

"Pinks" Blamed for Fund Supply.

Major Walter Furbeshaw, representing the Illinois Steel Company, gave the committee much documentary evidence of Communist activity which he had collected. He said he thought the Communist funds came from "Pinks" in this country. The party membership, he said, was seven aliens to three American citizens. He figured the party's membership at 100,000.

Harry A. Jung, representing the National Clay Products' Association, was one of the chief witnesses of the day. He estimated the Red membership at 30,000.

"Communism is now a menace in America," he said, "but it will become one if it is not liquidated, to use a Communist term. Immigration and deportation laws should be strengthened to deal with Communists. The United States should compel all aliens to register."

The government of Soviet Russia was characterized as a machine held together by terrorism by Morris Gordin, who once carried the Red banner in the United States and who previously acted as State prosecutor and press agent for the Soviet Government.

Relating his experiences when he returned to Russia from the United States and was made a State prosecutor, he said:

"I had an illumination. I imagined that they had a free press and free speech. I soon learned that I was to keep still. I found the politicians just as bad as in America. They told me I was a fine orator, but did not know how to pronounce the death sentence. * * *

"I studied there at the University of Moscow and my conclusions forced me to a total negation of communism and its doctrines. I determined to return to the United States and try to undo some of the work I had done there."

July 29, 1930

FISH REPORT ASKS OUTLAWING OF REDS AS NATIONAL MENACE

House Is Told That 500,000 Communists Agitate for Political and Economic Overturn.

14 REMEDIES PROPOSED

Suppression of Party Is Sought by Canceling of Citizenship and Deporting Aliens.

AMTORG LINK NOT PROVED

But Labor Inspection in Russia Is Urged—Minority View Warns of "Hysteria"—First Bill Put In.

Special to The New York Times.

WASHINGTON, Jan. 17.—Declaring that 500,000 to 600,000 Communists, organized under leaders in twenty divisions of this country, with headquarters in New York City directed from Moscow, were agitating for the overthrow of the American political and economic systems, the Fish committee, in its report on eight months of investigation, submitted to the House today, made fourteen recommendations for legislation to combat communism.

It was recommended that Congress take immediate steps to outlaw the Communist party in America, canceling the citizenship of its members; to deport all alien Communists, to prevent further naturalization of Communists, to bar Communist publications from the mails and to prosecute Communists or "other persons, organizations, newspapers, &c.," for spreading false rumors for the purpose of starting runs on banks.

The report also suggested that the Treasury Department request, through the State Department, permission to send inspectors into Soviet Russia to investigate the alleged production of lumber and pulpwood by convict and forced labor for export to the United States, and that Congress give immediate consideration to a complete embargo on importation of manganese from the Soviet Union.

First Bill Against Reds Offered.

The committee report, a voluminous document, and the recommendations were signed by Chairman Hamilton Fish and Representatives Carl G. Bachmann, Republican, of West Virginia; Edward E. Eslick of Tennessee and Robert S. Hall of Mississippi, Democrats.

Representative Bachmann at once introduced a bill to amend the naturalization act by including "alien Communists" among those who may be excluded or expelled under that law. Soon after the report was filed it was learned that committee members would introduce bills to carry out the other recommendations.

An individual report was filed by Representative John E. Nelson, Republican of Maine, the fifth member of the committee, whose principal contention was that there was no cause for "hysteria" or the question of communism, which, he said, could best be met with economic and social justice for American workers.

Mr. Nelson made six recommendations, including greater care by consular officers in the selection of immigrants and issuing of immigration visas; resumption by the Department of Justice of its activities of following up radical movements; adequate appropriations to the Department of Labor for deportation activities; strengthening of deportation statutes to rid the country of criminal aliens; constant and careful inspection by the postoffice authorities of radical publications, and encouragement and support of organized labor.

"Financing World Revolution."

The committee report dealt not only with evidence of communism found in this country, but also with the history of the whole movement, particularly in Russia, and the Soviet five-year plan for industrialism which if successful, would make the Soviet Union into a great money making machine that "may finance communism in world revolution."

The committee admitted failure to develop anything, under the rules of evidence, to connect the Amtorg Trading Corporation with any "sub-versive" activities in the United States, but characterized its officers as "Communists and revolutionists" and stated that among its activities was the handling of a "visa business," incident to the entry of several hundred Communists into this country annually through the law firm of Simpson, Thacher & Bartlett.

The report added that "it is stated that Thomas D. Thacher, a member of this law firm and now Solicitor General of the United States, organized Amtorg as a New York corporation.

The majority group of the committee late yesterday considered requesting the Labor Department to refuse further extension of temporary stays of four high Amtorg officials, Peter A. Bogdanoff, Andrew C. Mamaev, Feodor M. Ziavkin and Gregory B. Grafpen, and to start deportation proceedings against Louis Bebritz, editor of the Hungarian daily Uj Elore. These recommendations, incorporated in one draft of the report, were stricken out today.

Text of the Recommendations.

The fourteen recommendations urged by Representative Fish and three other members of the committee are as follows:

(1) Enlarging the authority of the bureau of investigation of the Department of Justice for the purpose of investigating and keeping in constant touch with the revolutionary propaganda and activities of the Communists in the United States, and to provide for additional appropriations for skilled agents to devote their entire time to investigating and preparing reports on the personnel of all entities, groups, individuals who teach or advocate the overthrow of the government of the United States by force and violence.

(2) Strengthening immigration laws to prevent the admission of Communists into the United States and providing for immediate deportation of all alien Communists.

(3) Provide for additional appropriations to the Bureau of Immigration for vigorous handling of deportation cases.

(4) Amend the naturalization laws so as to forbid the naturalization of a Communist.

(5) Amend the naturalization laws so as to cancel the United States citizenship of a Communist.

(6) Deny re-entry to the United States to an alien who has visited Russia to secure training in communistic doctrines.

(7) Amend the postoffice laws to declare non-mailable all newspapers, magazines, pamphlets, circulars, &c., published, written or produced, advocating revolutionary communism.

(8) Amend interstate commerce laws to prohibit transportation of newspapers, magazines, pamphlets, circulars, &c., advocating revolutionary communism.

(9) Enactment of Federal law to

prosecute Communists or other persons, organizations, newspapers, &c., in the spreading of false rumors for the purpose of causing runs on banks.

(10) Restriction of or elimination of the use of secret codes or ciphers with any government with which the United States has no diplomatic relations, and its trade agencies.

Would Send Agents to Russia.

(11) In view of the fact that the Soviet Government is under the control and direction of the Communists, that the Treasury Department request, through the State Department, permission to send inspectors or agents to investigate the prison camps and the pulpwood land timber-cutting districts of Soviet Russia, and report back regarding the alleged production of lumber and pulpwood by convict labor, in order to intelligently and properly enforce the provision of the tariff act of 1930, section 307, which reads as follows:

"All goods, wares, articles and merchandise mined, produced or manufactured wholly or in part in any foreign country by convict labor or/and forced labor or/and indentured labor under penal sanctions shall not be entitled to entry at any of the ports of the United States, and the importation thereof is hereby prohibited, and the Secretary of the Treasury is authorized and directed to prescribe such regulations as may be necessary for the enforcement of this provision."

The difficulty in administering the law has been to prove that certain shiploads of pulpwood and lumber are specifically produced by convict labor.

Up to now the Treasury and Labor Departments have been unable to prove the use of convict labor in connection with any specific cargoes and the recent regulations requiring a certificate of origin and good character on each shipment to the effect that convict labor is not used is not sufficient for the protection of free American labor and industry.

If the Soviet Government should refuse such a reasonable request as sending American inspectors to investigate the use of convict labor in the production of lumber and pulpwood when approximately a thousand Russian engineers and Soviet subjects are roaming about at will in the United States, gathering all kinds of information in our factories, mills and mines then the committee recommends that the Treasury Department prohibit the entry of Soviet pulpwood and lumber until such time as the agents of the Treasury Department are permitted by the Soviet Government to make a thorough investigation and report.

(12)—That the Treasury Department should request through the State Department permission to send inspectors or agents to investigate the use of forced or indentured labor in Soviet Russia in order to intelligently and properly enforce the provision of the tariff act of 1930, Section 307, which reads as follows: "The provisions of this section relating to goods, wares, articles and merchandise mined, produced or manufactured by forced labor or/and indentured labor, shall take effect on Jan. 1, 1932; but in no case shall such provisions be applicable to goods, wares, articles or merchandise so mined, produced or manufactured, which are not mined, produced or manufactured in such quantities in the United States as to meet the consumptive demands of the United States. Forced labor, as herein used, shall mean all work or service which is exacted from any person under the menace of any penalty for its nonperformance and for which the worker does not offer himself voluntarily." [See trade and commerce section.]

(13)—That immediate consideration be given by the Congress to the placing of an embargo on the importation of manganese from Soviet Russia.

For Outlawing of Party.

(14)—That the Communist party of the United States of America, section of the Communist International, be declared illegal, or any other counterpart of the Communist party, advocating the overthrow of our republican form of government by force and violence, or those affiliated with the Communist International at Moscow, be declared illegal; and that the executive authority of each State and the Legislature thereof be informed of the revolutionary principles and objectives of the Communist party of the United States of America, section of the Communist International, and be requested to take appropriate action to have said party excluded from or denied recognition as a political entity.

Hon. Charles Evans Hughes, now Chief Justice of the Supreme Court of the United States, in a 500-page memorandum submitted to the Senate, Jan. 21, 1924, in his capacity as Secretary of State, devoted many pages to the Workers' (Communist) party programs regarding "force and violence" and is quoted in part as follows:

It will be seen that the question of whether Communist programs contemplate the use of force and violence has been passed upon by every class of tribunal which could pass upon it, namely, Federal and State courts, administrative tribunals and legislative committees of both Federal and State Governments, and in every case the result has been in support of the position that force and violence are inseparable from Communist programs.

Mr. Hughes stated further, in the same report that: "It is believed that the evidence presented by the Department of State establishes the unity of the Bolshevik organization, known as the Communist party, so-called Soviet Government, and the Communist International, all of which are controlled by a small group of individuals, technically known as the political bureau of the Russian Communist party; second, the spiritual and organic connection between the Moscow group and its agents in this country—the American Communist party and its legal counterpart, the Workers party. Not only are these organizations the creation of Moscow, but the latter has also elaborated their program and controlled and supervised their activities. While there may have existed in the United States individuals, and even groups, imbued with Marxist doctrines prior to the advent of the Communist International, the existence of a disciplined party equipped with a program aiming at the overthrow of the institutions of this country by force and violence is due to the intervention of the Bolshevik organizations into the domestic political life of the United States."

"Party" Termed a "Misnomer."

There is a sharp distinction between the right to advocate in an academic way any doctrine we like, and the right, which is not a right under any reasonable interpretation of our Constitution, to preach and plan the overthrow of our republican form of government by force and violence.

One of these programs is to appeal to public opinion; the other, in the case of Communists in the United States, is a military plan of revolution, directed from abroad by a foreign government.

While the Communists call themselves a party, they are not in the American sense a party at all, and this word is a misnomer, for the reason that Communists openly disavow the purpose of accomplishing their ends by parliamentary methods.

Nor are they seeking or expecting to win the approval of a majority of the people, any more than in Russia, where 150,000,000 people are governed by 1,500,000. The Socialist Government of Kerensky in Russia was overthrown by a mere handful of Communists, an insignificant number as compared with those today affiliated with the Communist party in the United States.

All the Communists in the United States expect to do is to collect into their organization enough fanatical, desperate men and women to strike at strategic points—such points as they mention in their pronunciamentoes as key industries—and to inaugurate a reign of terrorism and bring about an armed uprising.

It is self-evident that the Communists and their sympathizers have only one real object in view, not to obtain control of the government of the United States through peaceful and legal political methods as a political party, but to establish by force and violence in the United States and in all other nations a "Soviet Socialist republic," to which they often refer in their literature as a "dictatorship of the proletariat." These facts have been repeatedly substantiated at the hearings of the committee.

All of which is respectfully submitted.
HAMILTON FISH JR., Chairman.
CARL G. BACHMANN.
EDWARD E. ESLICK.
ROBERT S. HALL.

Extent of Red Movement.

The Communist movement started in the United States about September, 1919, at Chicago, according to the Fish committee's report, and since that time had grown into a "thoroughly and highly organized and extremely active" group, made up of between 500,000 and 600,000 members and active sympathizers, including those engaged in its "youth movement" activities. The committee places the dues-paying Communists in the United States at not over 12,000, but points out that this does not indicate their real strength.

The whole movement, according to the report, is directed from Moscow and carried on in the United States through an organization in New York. It is alleged to be promulgated through fifty-eight known unions, leagues and societies, named in the report, made up of people of twenty-six nationalities, besides Americans.

From evidence submitted and from information in the foreign-language press the committee estimates that the composition of the Communist membership of foreign origin in the United States, on membership strength and not on percentage, is as follows: Jews, Russians (Slavs), Lithuanians, Hungarians, Finns, Czechoslovaks, Ukrainians, Yugoslavs, Poles, Germans, Scandinavians, Italians, Mexicans, Greeks, Rumanians, Armenians, Portuguese, Spanish, South Americans, English, Irish, Scotch, French, Estonians, Lettish, Chinese, Japanese.

Their propaganda is said to emanate from twelve daily newspapers, thirty regularly published weekly, semi-weekly and monthly publications, and sixteen other irregularly circulated publications, all with a combined circulation in this country of an estimated 350,000.

Two of the last named class of publications are said to be published in Moscow, one in Berlin and ten in New York. Five of the daily papers, according to the list, are published in New York, and fifteen of the weekly, semi-weekly and monthly papers.

Purposes and Measures.

The report sets out that the Communist scheme in the United States is founded on the fundamental purpose of overthrowing the American system of government and economic organization, and the uprooting of the established religions.

The report says that a definite programs for furthering the organization in America was drawn up at the Red International of Labor Unions held in Moscow in July, 1921, and William Z. Foster, later Communist candidate for President, was placed at the head of the "American section" to carry it out.

The aim is described as primarily "to organize all the class-conscious workers in America, and to have them carefully drilled in methods of procedure as set forth specifically in resolutions passed at this congress, * * * the forming of minority groups in the unions and trade groups in the United States, and boring from within by opposing the

83

conservative officials in the established labor organizations."

Centring in New York City.

"The chief centre of all Communist activities, including political, is in New York City," the report goes on. "The Daily Worker, the official organ of the party, was founded in Chicago but moved to New York in 1925, when headquarters were transferred there, obviously to be in closer touch with the Communist International and its agents arriving from Russia.

"The central committee (formerly central executive committee), with headquarters in New York City, dominates the policies of the Communist party in the United States, although the real control is through the Communist International at Moscow.

"The central committee is composed of approximately twenty-eight members, of whom a smaller group of fourteen constitutes the political committee, which in turn is divided into the secretariat, a small executive committee of seven members, of which William Z. Foster is the recognized leader."

Districts and Leaders Listed.

Stating that the list of organizers is "constantly changing" and consequently needed to be "carefully checked," the report charts the organization of the country by twenty districts with the leader of each district, so far as known, as follows:

outstanding successes in open agitation among workers.

The Gastonia strike, in which a chief of police was killed, was termed the most successful from the standpoint of the Communists themselves. However, the principal strategy and aim of the Communists, the report said, was "the penetration and capture of the American Federation of Labor, with the object of turning it into a mass revolutionary institution for the overthrow of the Government of the United States and the building of a Soviet régime in its stead."

School, College and Negro Work.

The Youth Movement of the Communists has been only partly successful, according to the report, with most of the success in and around New York City. Their agitation has failed in most public schools, the report continues, and has been "negligible" in colleges and universities, with the exception of those situated in large industrial cities.

"It is apparent that there are quite a number of active Communists in New York University, having their own Communist Club, but it would be difficult to ascertain with any accuracy their numbers or how far their activities are carried on in that university," the report states. "Communists were also found to have infiltrated into the Universities of Chicago, Wisconsin, Washington, California, Harvard and Columbia."

Stating that the Communists "for years have looked hopefully toward the Negro as an element where they might gain recruits," the report adds:

units in universities and colleges are more fertile fields for Communistic agitations, the report continues:

"The evidence presented to the committee of Communist attacks against military training in schools and colleges is extensive and has led to considerable agitation in some of the big universities."

"Opposition to military training in educational institutions provides fertile fields for inflammatory speeches and articles by young Communists who pose as favoring eternal peace, while advocating civil war and world revolution."

Undecided on Amtorg's Status.

Taking up trade between the United States and Russia, the report goes into the wheat situation and reiterates the charge that the Amtorg Trading Corporation had been carrying on extensive short-selling operations on the Chicago Board of Trade, primarily for the purpose of depressing the American wheat market and causing discontent among grain growers.

The report also repeats the charges of dumping in America of Russian lumber and pulpwood, oil, manganese and manufactured goods, made or mined by convict labor, all for the purpose of disorganizing American markets.

The report represents the committee as being somewhat undecided as to the status of the Amtorg Trading Corporation. Though the concern has Communists as officials, it is admitted that "under the rules of evidence we find that is not sufficient legal evidence in the record to prove the connection of the Amtorg Trading Corporation as a body corporate, with subversive activities."

The report says that "it is stated" that Judge Thomas D. Thacher, present Solicitor General of the United States, was the lawyer who organized Amtorg. It further stated that the "visa business" of Amtorg, by which several hundred Russians are alleged to enter the country annually, is handled by the law firm of Simpson, Thacher & Bartlett.

"When a Russian desires to come to the United States a telegram is sent to Amtorg, and Amtorg then writes to Simpson, Thacher & Bartlett, and these attorneys inform the American consul at Berlin that the man is all right," the report adds. "One witness states that no one could get a visa unless he had the approval of this firm of lawyers."

Financial Structure of Amtorg.

The report says that Amtorg has built up a credit with American banks and business interests amounting to $80,000,000 and quotes "financial journals" to the effect that Soviet Russia owes American business interests $170,000,000. It states further that the capital investment of the trading corporation is only $2,000,000.

"Its business is conducted largely on a credit basis and the commerce to America from Russia is only about one-third of the amount of the purchases in the United States," the report states. "In case of failure of the Soviet Government, or the repudiation of that government, Amtorg's ability to pay would be gone."

The report charges that Amtorg officials sought to evade the inquiry of the Fish committee and offers testimony and records as circumstantial evidence that high officers of the corporation helped finance Communist activities in this country.

It sets out that Peter A. Bogdanov, chairman of the board of Amtorg, began his career as a revolutionist when a student 18 years of age, and since then has held high official posts in the Soviet Government.

The report also says that Mark Lubinsky, a naturalized American citizen, was sent on a mission to Mexico by Amtorg, was arrested and later deported from that country.

"Both the present chairman of the board and the business manager of Amtorg were not only Communists but revolutionists," the report continues.

"They now say they are not Communists. A man does not ordinarily cease to be a Communist and become a non-Communist simply by saying so.

"These high officials hold their

POLITICAL ACTIVITIES.

Dist. No.	District Organizer.	Headquarters.	States Included.
1	Nat Kaplan or Roy Stephens	Boston	Massachusetts, Rhode Island, Maine, Vermont, New Hampshire.
2	Israel Amter	New York City	New York City, Yonkers, New Jersey (Hudson and Essex Counties).
3	Emil Gerardos	Philadelphia	Washington, D. C.; Delaware, Eastern Pennsylvania, Western New Jersey.
4	A. Mills or J. Donald	Buffalo	Northwestern New York, Erie, Pa.
5	Pat Devine or Max Salzman	Pittsburgh	Western Pennsylvania.
6	J. Adams or Herbert Benjamin	Cleveland	Ohio.
7	Jack Stachel	Detroit	Lower Michigan, Indianapolis.
8	Bill Gebert	Chicago	Northwestern Indiana, St. Louis, Illinois, Lower Wisconsin.
9	Karl Reeves	Minneapolis	Minnesota, Wisconsin.
10	David Gorman or Paul Cline	Kansas City, Mo.	Missouri, Iowa, Texas, New Mexico.
11	Alfred Knutson (Northern Agricultural.)	Bismarck, N. D.	North Dakota, Montana, South Dakota, Kansas.
12	Sidney Bloomfield	Seattle	Washington, Oregon.
13	William Simons	San Francisco	California, Nevada, Arizona.
14	Unknown or unassigned (Southern Agricultural).		
15	Peter Chaunt	New Haven	Connecticut.
16	Jennie Cooper or M. H. Powers	Charlotte, N. C.	North Carolina, South Carolina, Virginia.
17	Tom Johnson	Birmingham	Alabama, Tennessee, Louisiana, Georgia.
18	Fraternal		
19	William Dietrichs	Denver	Colorado.
20	?	Butte	?

In addition to the district organizers, the report states, the party has many national organizers who travel from place to place, making speeches and staging demonstrations and holding themselves in readiness to take charge of Communist strikes.

"Some Success" Despite A. F. of L.

The committee took occasion in this section of the report to pay a tribute to the late Samuel Gompers, former president of the American Federation of Labor, and William Green, present head of the organization, who, the report said, had refused to compromise with the Communist elements in the various unions under their banner and had stood in the "front-line trenches between Americanism and Communism."

"If it were not for the fact that the American Federation of Labor, under the patriotic leadership of William Green and his predecessor, Samuel Gompers, has refused to compromise with the Communists in the United States, who have been trying to bore from within in order to gain control of the labor unions, communism would be a serious threat to American industry," the report declares.

The Communists have had some success, however, according to the report, not only in promoting certain strikes, but in almost breaking several of the unions affiliated with the American Federation of Labor. The textile strikes at Passaic, N. J.; New Bedford, Mass., and Gastonia, N. C., were cited as

"Up until this time, the Communist efforts to interest and line up the Negroes in this country has not met with great success, although a considerable number of Negroes employed in the Northern industrial centres have joined the movement. In the South efforts among the Negroes have not been very fruitful, although some little headway has been made in certain sections."

The report says that active agitation is still going on among the Negroes, however, and every year a number of American-born Negroes are sent to schools in Russia, "where they are indoctrinated by the Communists and then appointed to membership in the Negro department of the National Office."

Agitators Whipped at Army Posts.

Declaring that little headway has been made by the Communists in the army and navy, the report discloses that adults found distributing Communist literature in army posts are usually taken in hand by the soldiers and whipped.

It is further revealed that the Navy Code and Signal Section has been engaged for five months in trying to decode more than 3,000 messages exchanged between the Amtorg Trading Corporation, the Soviet fiscal agency in the United States, organized in New York, and the government at Moscow, but the code seems to have been so perfect that no headway has been made.

Asserting that the National Guard, the Citizens' Military Camps and the Reserve Officers' Training Corps present positions as political appointments. They represent the Russian Government control and they are dictated to by Communists. Only by word of mouth have they ceased to be Communists."

The committee dismissed in a paragraph the documents presented by former Police Commissioner Grover A. Whalen of New York purporting to show connection between Amtorg and Communist activities in this country.

"The committee heard all the evidence offered or that it could obtain relating to the so-called Whalen documents," the report says. "Some of the evidence apparently indicated the genuineness of these documents, but measured by the rules of evidence and the burden of proof resting on the proponents of the documents we find that the testimony failed to establish the genuineness of the so-called 'Whalen documents.'"

Praise for New York Police.

At the conclusion of the report the committee complimented the police of New York for their handling of Communist demonstrations, saying:

"The public should not overlook the fact that the police are human beings, and are carrying out orders to resist or break up Communist demonstrations when staged in defiance of the law.

"Often rough-house tactics prevail and Communist women and children insult and spit on the police and scratch and bite them. There has been too much denunciation of the police for alleged brutality by 'pinks' and metropolitan papers.

"The committee believes that the American public owes a debt of gratitude to the police of New York, Chicago and many other metropolitan centres for affording protection against the lawless and revolutionary activities of the Communists, and in safeguarding foreign consulates from insults and mass Communistic demonstrations."

The individual report submitted by Representative Nelson of Maine sets forth his personal conclusion that Communist agitation in America is but a part of a passing phase in human progress. He traces the development of the whole idea from the time of Plato to the present and concludes that there is no occasion for "hysteria."

He favors some stricter laws in dealing with the subject, but contends that "our best defense against the red shirt of the Communist and the black shirt of the Fascist is the blue shirt of the American working man."

"Modern scientific and industrial progress has created new social and economic conditions never contemplated by the founders of this republic," Mr. Nelson states.

"There is a chasm between the new life and the old ideas. We perhaps need a new attitude of thought and a more liberal approach to some of our problems.

Goal of "Economic Freedom."

"After all, a social system finds its final sanction human happiness and social welfare in the achievement of economic freedom for the individual through the elimination of economic poverty.

"The crisis that American industry and American labor are facing today speaks in no uncertain terms of something wrong in our social and industrial system, of that which calls for further and deeper study of causes, effects and cures. Out of such study much good may eventuate. Bolshevism was born out of a social and political chaos that can never obtain here in America.

"The solution of this problem lies in the wisdom of our legislators and in the unselfishness of our industrialists. In proportion as we work out economic justice here in America and so order our social system that labor shall share in the economic life of the nation as fully and as fairly as it now shares in its social and political life, in just that proportion will radicalism fall of its own inanition and the threat of communism cease to disturb us."

January 18, 1931

ASKS LAWS TO CURB FOREIGN AGITATORS

Committee in Report to House Attacks Nazis as the Chief Propagandists in Nation.

STATE DEPARTMENT ACTS

Checks Activities of an Italian Consul—Plan for March on Capital Is Held Proved.

Special to THE NEW YORK TIMES.

WASHINGTON, Feb. 15.—Stringent legislation to prevent the spread of revolutionary propaganda in the United States was recommended to Congress today by the special House committee which has been investigating alleged un-American activities.

Recounting in its final report evidence of Fascist, Nazi and Communist propaganda sponsored from abroad, as well as native movements such as the Silver Shirts, the committee, headed by Representative McCormack of Massachusetts, proposed that all foreign propagandists be compelled to register with the State Department.

It also urged that their sojourn in the United States be subject to the pleasure of the Secretary of State, and offered several other suggestions for controlling revolutionary propaganda.

The report included statements that diplomatic and consular agents of officially friendly foreign governments had engaged in propaganda favorable to their own forms of government as substitutes for the form now in existence in the United States.

Plan for "March" Recalled.

It also alleged that definite proof had been found that the much publicized Fascist march on Washington, which was to have been led by Major Gen. Smedley D. Butler, retired, according to testimony at a hearing, was actually contemplated.

The committee recalled testimony by General Butler, saying he had testified that Gerald C. MacGuire had tried to persuade him to accept the leadership of a Fascist army.

The State Department announced today that it was investigating for the committee alleged Fascist activities of an Italian Vice Consul in Detroit. Giacomo Ungarelli, the official concerned, was quoted in Detroit as saying that he had spread "informative facts," not propaganda, designed to familiarize Italian children born in this country with the language, traditions and present form of government of Italy.

In addition, the State Department will investigate reports of religious propaganda activities, beyond the scope of official duties, by a Mexican consular officer at San Bernardino, Calif.

The House committee's report said Fascist efforts in the United States had no connection with any similar activity in a European country, and the Communist movement in this country was termed not sufficiently strong numerically "to constitute a danger to American institutions at the present time." Communist agitation was declared widespread, however.

Nazi Record Is Traced.

The bulk of the report was taken up with a recital of the committee's findings concerning Nazi propaganda and organization in the United States since Chancellor Hitler's party has come into effective power in Germany.

The committee's conclusions were reached after hearings in Washington, New York, Chicago, Los Angeles, Asheville, N. C., and Newark. The committee includes, besides Chairman McCormack, Representatives Dickstein of New York, Kramer of California, Jenkins of Ohio, Taylor of Tennessee, and Guyer of Kansas.

An effort to continue the committee's activities until Jan. 3, 1937, was temporarily blocked on the floor today. Mr. Kramer asked unanimous consent to consider a resolution to that effect, and several members jumped to their feet to ask him questions about its findings.

Representatives Blanton of Texas and Martin of Massachusetts made formal objection, and the matter was dropped for the present.

The committee's legislative recommendations were as follows:

1. That all publicity, propaganda, or public relations agencies, or agents or agencies representing in this country a foreign government, foreign political power, or foreign industrial organization, must register with the Secretary of State, declaring details of their employment.

2. That the Secretary of Labor be empowered to shorten or terminate the sojourn in this country of any visitor engaging in the promotion or dissemination of propaganda, or carrying on political activity in the United States.

3. That treaties be negotiated with foreign countries by which they would receive back immigrants of their nationality who might become subject to deportation under our laws.

4. That it be made unlawful to advise, counsel or urge any member of the military or naval forces of the United States, including reservists, to disobey laws or regulations.

5. That Federal Attorneys throughout the country be empowered to proceed against witnesses who refuse to appear, testify, or produce records before any lawful congressional committee.

6. That it be made unlawful for any person to advocate changes in the manner that incites to the overthrow or destruction by force and violence of the government of the United States, or of the republican form of government guaranteed by the Constitution.

The committee's report set forth the history of Nazi efforts and organization and propaganda in this country, starting with the arrival of Kurt Georg Wilhelm Luedecke as a traveling representative for a German commercial house.

Mr. Luedecke admitted, the committee said, that he used his commercial position "as a smoke screen behind which to disseminate his propaganda in the United States in an effort to gain adherents and financial support for the Nazi movement."

Individuals and groups finally founded a society called "Teutonia," which was changed to the "Friends of New Germany" after Herr Hitler became Chancellor of Germany.

The report went on to say that Heinz Spanknoebel "usurped" the leadership of this organization as well as that of the Stahlhelm, a German veterans' organization, and of the United German Societies of New York.

His sway lasted until he was indicted in 1933 by a Federal grand jury for having failed to register as the agent of a foreign country. He fled the country and is still a fugitive.

Spanknoebel's successor was Fritz Gissibl, according to the report, although Reinhold Walter, an American citizen, became nominal head of the Nazi group in this country soon afterward. The committee learned that Gissibl remained the real directing force.

"This committee found indisputable evidence," the report continues, "to show that certain German Consuls in this country violated the pledge and proprieties of diplomatic status and engaged in vicious and un-American propaganda, paying for it in cash in the hope that it could not be traced."

The report also charged that Dr. Hans Luther, German Ambassador, requested a German steamship company to transport some American citizens to and from Germany free of charge that they might

The Birth of H.U.A.C.

write and speak favorably of the Nazi regime.

Carl Byoir and Associates and Ivy Lee-T. J. Ross were mentioned as American publicity concerns that accepted money for work of a propaganda nature in favor of Nazi Germany.

On the Byoir contract, it was alleged, "the first payment on the contract, amounting to $4,000, was made by Dr. Kiep, former German Consul General in New York City, in cash."

Dr. Otto H. F. Vollbehr, rare book dealer, testified that he spent many thousands of dollars of his own money to distribute "propaganda" to the American public, although warned by Ambassador Luther not to "mix in American politics."

"This committee condemns the establishment and the propaganda of the Nazi principles in this country," the report said. "We are unalterably opposed to any individual or any group of individuals seeking to bring about discord among the people of this country, either as a reprisal or as a means of changing our form of government."

Native Fascist organizations mentioned by the committee included the Order of '76, the Silver Shirts and the American Vigilante Intelligence Federation.

February 16, 1935

U. S. PROTESTS TO THE SOVIET OVER REDS' ACTIVITIES HERE; WARNS OF THE CONSEQUENCES

COMMUNIST PARLEY CITED

State Department Acts on Basis of Speeches Before International.

PLEDGES HELD VIOLATED

Litvinoff Letter to Roosevelt at Time of Recognition Is Quoted in the Note.

Special to THE NEW YORK TIMES.

WASHINGTON, Aug. 25.—The State Department, through Ambassador William C. Bullitt at Moscow, lodged with the Soviet Government today a "most emphatic protest" against "flagrant violation of the pledge given by the Government of the Union of Soviet Socialist Republics with respect to non-interference in the internal affairs of the United States."

The protest was based upon official reports of the proceedings of the congress of the Communist International, which concluded its sessions in Moscow last week, and was in the form of a note. It said the United States "anticipates the most serious consequences" if the Soviet Government does not halt the activities deemed to be a violation of the pledge.

The note was delivered by Ambassador William C. Bullitt to the Soviet Vice Commissar for Foreign Affairs, Nikolai Krestinsky. It cited the pledge signed in November, 1933, by Maxim Litvinoff, Soviet Foreign Commissar, that his government would restrain organizations from "propaganda having as its aim the bringing about by force of a change in the political or social order of the whole or any part of the United States."

Note Approved by Roosevelt.

While no comment was made by the State Department in issuing the note, beyond a statement by R. Walton Moore, Assistant Secretary of State, to the effect that it had the personal approval of President Roosevelt, officials privately warned against interpreting the move as a prelude to the discontinuance of diplomatic relations between the two countries.

For some time officials here have believed that the disclosures made by American Communists during the congress in Moscow, showing propaganda activity in this country in the name of the Communist party, were grounds for a protest, but they awaited the close of the gathering and the receipt of official reports from the United States Embassy in Moscow before drafting the note.

On the basis of the official reports, they found the "flagrant violation of the pledge," given at the time President Roosevelt recognized the Soviet Government.

Citation from Litvinoff Letter.

Attention was called to that part of the Litvinoff letter that agreed on behalf of the Soviet Government not "to permit the formation or residence on its territory of any organization or group and to prevent the activity on its territory of any organization or group, or of representatives or officials of any organization or group which has as an aim the overthrow or the preparation of the overthrow of, or the bringing about by force of a change in the political or social order of the whole or any part of the United States, its territories or possessions."

Speakers at the Communist congress included, among the American Communists, William Z. Foster, chairman of the Communist party of the United States; Earl Browder, its general secretary; James W. Ford, a member of its central committee and a sectional organizer in Harlem; Gilbert Greening, known also as Gil Green, secretary of the Young Communist League of the United States, and Samuel Dardeck, or Darcy, a district organizer in San Francisco.

While the State Department's note confined itself to a general statement that "interference in the internal affairs of the United States" formed the basis for its protest, which was considered surprisingly strong, it was generally believed that the utterances of these and other American speakers, claiming credit for Communist party activities in fomenting political and labor troubles here, were at the root of the matter.

Some typical statements of the kind, which probably influenced its official thought, as reported in the newspaper Pravda, follow:

Mr. Browder: The influence of the Communist party "has even penetrated into those movements which up to now have continued to exist within the framework of the bourgeois parties, as for example the creation by Upton Sinclair of the EPIC movement."

Mr. Dardeck: "We began to convince the workers not only to enter the American Federation of Labor, but to become its active and leading members. The stream of those entering into the federation was great."

Mr. Browder: "In the United States, there are ripening conditions for a wide anti-Fascist popular movement, the central nucleus of which will be the party of the united front."

Mr. Browder: "In a few of the more important strike battles, particularly in the general strike of workers in San Francisco, to the Communist party belonged the leadership, the decisive influence."

A resolution of recommendations to the executive committee of the Communist International urged it "sympathetically to assist in the creation and education of cadres and real Bolshevist leaders in Communist parties in order that the parties, on the basis of decisions of the congresses of the Communist International and the plenums of the executive committee of the Communist International, in times of a sharp turn of events could quickly and independently find the correct solution of political and tactical problems of the Communist movement."

August 26, 1935

Ousting of Reds in WPA Is Near; Widespread Agitation Revealed

Investigators Lay Frequent Strikes, Stoppages and Protests to Communist 'Cells' Entrenched Among 220,000 Workers—

The dismissal of a score of Communists, leaders of Communist "cells" in various parts of the WPA organization in this city, may be expected shortly as a beginning of a drive to stop subversive activity and the fanning of discontent among WPA employes, it was learned yesterday.

The dismissals, it was declared by a high WPA official, will be based on evidence obtained by the Intelligence Department of the WPA in an investigation ordered by General Hugh S. Johnson, who retired yesterday as Works Progress Administrator.

It was declared that the investigation revealed systematic activity by Communist "cells" designed to provoke dissatisfaction, stoppages and strikes with a view to crippling WPA operation and stimulating Communist sentiment among the 220,000 employes.

According to information unearthed by the intelligence department, whose report will be among the first things to be considered by Victor F. Ridder, the new administrator, the activities of the Communists in this direction have reached large proportions. Evidence has been obtained that Communists are taking the lead in many of the delegations and organizations of WPA employes who are constantly making protests to relief officials, putting forth demands and keeping the employes in a state of excitement and tension.

Before leaving his post as administrator General Johnson had made it known that a stop would be put to these activities and that careful watch would be kept on all persons that might fairly be characterized as acting in violation of legitimate collective bargaining. It was learned that the general preferred to leave action to Mr. Ridder, since the report of the intelligence department was submitted only a few days ago and additional evidence was being awaited.

October 16, 1935

20,000 HEAR THOMAS POINT WAY TO REDS

Socialist Leader, at Debate, Sees United Front Feasible if 'Good Faith' Is Shown.

BROWDER URGES HARMONY

Meeting in Garden Looked On as Rapprochement of Left-Wing Faction and Communists.

More than 20,000 Communists and Left Wing Socialists fraternized in Madison Square Garden last night, where a debate was staged on the merits of their respective doctrines by Earl Browder, Communist chieftain, and Norman Thomas, Socialist leader. Mr. Browder returned recently from Moscow, where he attended the congress of the Communist International.

The Socialists and Communists joined in singing the "International," the "Red Flag" and "Solidarity Forever." At one point Mr. Thomas led in the singing.

The huge crowd in the Garden cheered the appeals of both Mr. Browder and Mr. Thomas for unity,

but Mr. Thomas added a number of strong reservations to his appeal. While Mr. Browder hailed the meeting as speeding "the way toward the goal of united action by the Communist and Socialist parties," Mr. Thomas insisted that the Communists must show greater evidences of "good faith" before a genuine united front was possible.

At the end of the debate he expressed satisfaction with the sincerity displayed at the meeting and congratulated "Comrade" Browder.

"I favor the maximum possible amount of joint action by all who are opposed to war or fascism," Mr. Thomas said. He added that, pending development of "an inclusive, intelligent, aggressive Socialist party" as an instrument for the creation of a more comprehensive Farmer-Labor party, he welcomed "all possible cooperation in the fight against fascism in America." He said he would not exclude Communists from such a Farmer-Labor party "provided they prove sincerity and good faith."

The meeting marked the first mass rapprochement between Communists and Socialists in this city. This gained added emphasis from the fact that it was presided over by Leo Krzycki, national chairman of the Socialist party. Mr. Krzycki is also a vice president of the Amalgamated Clothing Workers of America.

In urging a united front between the Communists and Socialists, Mr. Browder declared that through such united action they "could play a big part in strengthening the forces of the industrial union bloc led by John L. Lewis" in the American Federation of Labor. The Amalgamated Clothing Workers, Mr. Krzycki's organization, is a member of the bloc.

While admitting that there were still disagreements between the two parties, Mr. Browder complimented Mr. Thomas for what he termed his advanced position as contrasted with that of the so-called "old guard" Socialists, in control of the organization in this State and city.

Mr. Thomas, however, suggested that "Mr. Browder was not qualified" to be a judge as to the factional conflict in the Socialist party."

The "old guard" kept away from last night's debate, in accordance with a rule of the party against participation of members in any kind of joint action with Communists. Mr. Thomas entered the debate in defiance of charges brought against him before his party's grievance committee for violating party discipline, and has announced that he will not appear before the committee.

In seeking to obtain Mr. Thomas's unqualified support of the "united front," Mr. Browder pointed to a previous declaration by Mr. Thomas that "to make Socialists swear that they can never conceive of any circumstances that will justify armed insurrection, or to compel Socialists to affirm a blind belief in a romantic parliamentarism is complete and unsocialist folly." Mr. Browder considered this good Communist doctrine.

Last night Mr. Thomas took a strong stand in favor of democracy against dictatorship.

"On the most fundamental differences which still remain between us Communists and the Socialist party we are not faced any more with an unbridgeable chasm," Mr. Browder said. "Comrade Thomas in his writings narrowed down this gulf when he abandoned the dogmatic affirmation that the Communist answer can never be accepted."

While agreeing that there has been a narrowing of the gulf of which Mr. Browder spoke, and declaring that "past grievances" should not be permitted to stand in the way of cooperation between the two parties, Mr. Thomas declared that in the face of what he termed the destructive record of the Communists "we are justified in asking for proof of sincerity of the changed position of the Communists." He wanted "to be shown" and expressed strong skepticism as to the Communist aim. Nevertheless, he said he was hopeful of ultimate unity, provided the Communists prove themselves fit for it.

Algernon Lee, city chairman of the Socialist party and leader here of the "Old Guard," issued the following statement last night:

"The verbal contest between Norman Thomas and Earl Browder in Madison Square Garden was in reality what we expected it to be—a love feast. Whether it served the cause of socialism and organized labor is more than doubtful, but there can be no doubt as to its service to the Communist party."

November 28, 1935

COMMUNIST STRENGTH VARIES

Party Which Seeks to Play a Part in American Campaign Now Claims 50,000 Members

By JOSEPH SHAPLEN

The injection of the issue of communism into the race between the major parties—an issue which President Roosevelt called a "false" one—has served to direct attention both to the strength of the Communist party in the United States and to

its strategy during this campaign.

Measured by its party membership in ratio to the population of the country, the Communist party of the United States is probably the weakest of all Communist parties functioning outside Russia. On Aug. 5, 1935, Earl Browder, as gen-

eral secretary of the Communist party, reported to the Seventh Congress of the Communist International in Moscow that the party in this country numbered 30,000 members, as compared with 10,000 in 1930. William Z. Foster, another Communist leader and the party's candidate for President in 1924, 1928 and 1932, reported, in addition, a membership of 8,000 in the League of Communist Young.

These are the last official Communist figures available. Recent unofficial claims vary between 45,-000 and 50,000.

The Communist movement began

functioning politically in this country in 1919. It made its first appearance in the national arena in the Presidential election of 1924, when Mr. Foster, candidate of the Workers Party, as the Communists then called themselves, polled 33,-361 votes out of a total vote of 29,022,261.

Four years later Mr. Foster received 48,770 votes, the total vote cast being 36,879,414.

In the 1932 election, after three years of depression offering conditions most fertile for the growth of radicalism, Mr. Foster's vote was 102,991 out of a total of 39,816,522 votes cast. This year a larger vote is sought, with Mr. Browder as the Presidential candidate.

On the basis of figures cited by Mr. Browder, it is evident that the party membership fluctuates widely. Writing in The Party Organizer, for May-June, 1934, official publication of the Central Committee of the Communist party of the United States, the party's general secretary said:

"Since 1930 we recruited 49,050 members. Together with the membership of 7,545 in 1930, this makes a total of 56,595 (March 1934). However, the actual dues-paying membership in the first quarter of 1934 averaged somewhat over 24,000—a gain of about 16,500 in the last three years. For the same period 33,000 members dropped out of the party."

In a table appended to his article, Mr. Browder revealed fluctuations in the party membership between the years 1931 to 1933, inclusive,

ranging from 50 to 77 per cent. "In this period we recruited 43,-426 members and increased the number of dues-paying members by only 15,197." Mr. Browder explained. "In the last six months of 1933 there has been a steady decrease in fluctuation, reaching the comparatively low figure of 53 per cent."

Communist Strategy

The Communists' strategy and tactics in the present campaign are in keeping with the Communist world strategy as laid down at the last Comintern congress. A perusal of recent press cables from Moscow and of the official record of the proceedings of the Comintern congress will reveal that the victory of Hitlerism in Germany, the weakening of the Communist movement in a number of countries and the threat of aggression against Soviet Russia emanating from Germany had brought Moscow to the view

that the old Communist policy of bitter opposition to capitalist democracy and all non-Communist labor and political elements had to be abandoned, for the time being at least; that the exigencies of Soviet foreign policy and Soviet national interests, as well as the interests of the Communist movement abroad, required cooperation, wherever such cooperation could be obtained, with all non-Communist democratic elements outside of Russia. Preservation of "the remnants of bourgeois democracy" became a new Communist slogan.

In embarking upon this new course, the Communist International, as the resolutions of its seventh congress show, in no way abandoned the ultimate aims of communism, namely establishment of proletarian dictatorships in other countries.

Results in France

In France the new strategy found expression in the united front be-

tween the Socialists and Communists and participation of the Communists in the Popular Front, which now controls the French Government. In other democratic countries, however, the Communists have been unable to make headway with their new "line."

In the United States the Communists, while appealing for votes for Mr. Browder, have subjected Governor Landon to greater attack than Mr. Roosevelt. This, in the view of some observers, is because Moscow fears that the election of a President more conservative than Mr. Roosevelt may lead to complications embarrassing to Soviet Russia—perhaps the withdrawal of Soviet recognition—and because in the event of a clash between Soviet Russia and Japan a liberal government in the United States would be more desirable than a conservative one from Moscow's point of view.

October 18, 1936

SMITH LINKS REDS WITH ROOSEVELT

President Is Preparing Way for Communist Conquest, He Says in Albany 'Swan Song.'

'DOWN WITH GOD' SPREAD

By F. RAYMOND DANIELL
Special to THE NEW YORK TIMES.

ALBANY, Oct. 31.—In the city where as Governor for four terms he rose to the eminence of Democratic nominee for President, Alfred E. Smith tonight accused Franklin D. Roosevelt of preparing the way for a Communist-controlled America and urged his fellow-Democrats to vote for Alfred M. Landon "to suppress class warfare

and revolution" in this country.

He spoke before a crowd of 3,500 in Harmanus Bleecker Hall under the auspices of the Independent Coalition of American Women and his words were broadcast over the nation in one of the most extensive radio hook-ups of the 1936 campaign.

As he put it at the beginning of his address, he stood "almost in the shadow" of the Capitol where as Governor he had "made Democratic history."

His speech was a bitter arraignment of the present leadership of the Democratic party and an appeal to Democrats to follow him this year into Mr. Landon's camp to purge their party of those who would deliver it to the radicals, as he said had been done in the Farmer-Labor alliance in Minnesota.

Asserting that the American Labor party, supporting President Roosevelt and Governor Lehman in New York, should be a warning to Democrats here, he declared that the President himself, surrounded by Republicans and "crack-

pots," had boasted at Yale that he had sometimes voted for Republicans.

In what was his last speech of this campaign and what his friends said probably was the former Governor's "swan song," his last appearance in a national election, Mr. Smith charged that taxpayers' money was being used under the New Deal "to train young men to go out and preach communism, to preach the gospel of 'down with property, down with capital, down with government, down with church, yes, down with God.'"

His audience cheered the former Governor's every charge of radicalism to the New Deal.

"Planting Seed of Communism"

Mr. Smith made it clear that he did not regard President Roosevelt as either a Socialist or a Communist, but he implied that he believed the man whom he helped make Governor of New York in 1928 had been affected by "some certain kind of foreign 'ism,'" which he said, was "crawling over this country."

What its "first name" would be when it was christened, Mr. Smith asserted, he had no idea, but the "sin" of it was, he said, that "it is here and he (the President) don't seem to know it."

"There is one thing that everybody admits," Mr. Smith continued. "Before you can have either Socialism or Communism you must prepare the country, you must till the soil and you must sow the seed, and, in all the history of the advances of Communism, how has the soil been tilled and how has the seed been planted?

"By arranging class against class, by starting people against each other, by leading large numbers of a community to believe that there is some hidden and unseen power that is attempting to crush them down to the earth. We call it class hatred."

Comintern Conquest Charged

Mr. Smith told his audience, which was about two-thirds Republican and one-third Democratic, that the Communists were supporting Mr. Roosevelt "because they are entirely satisfied with his administration in that it gives promise by the united front of the farmer and the laborer as dictated from the Comintern in Moscow to conquer America and countries like America that have constitutional law by peaceful means rather than by bloodshed in the beginning."

November 1, 1936

HIGH COURT UPSETS OREGON SENTENCE OF A COMMUNIST

Special to THE NEW YORK TIMES.

WASHINGTON, Jan. 4.—In one of the most striking rulings of recent years, the Supreme Court today, in a unanimous opinion written by Chief Justice Hughes, upset the conviction and seven-year jail

sentence of Dirk de Jonge, Oregon Communist, accused of violating the State's Criminal Syndicalism Law.

The court strongly asserted that the right of peaceable assembly was as fundamental as the constitutional guarantees of freedom of speech and freedom of the press.

The justices denounced the conviction of de Jonge merely for assisting in the conduct of a Communist meeting, which, it was shown, was orderly and lawful and at which neither criminal syndicalism nor unlawful conduct was urged.

The State Supreme Court in up-

holding de Jonge's conviction, emphasized that the sentence was not because he expressed incendiary sentiments at the meeting but because the Communist party, under whose auspices the gathering was held, was an advocate of criminal syndicalism. To this the Supreme Court replied:

"The holding of meetings for peaceable political action cannot be proscribed. Those who assist in the conduct of such meetings cannot be branded as criminals on that score."

"While the States are entitled to protect themselves from the

abuse of the privileges of our institutions through an attempted substitution of force and violence in the place of peaceful political action in order to effect revolutionary changes in government," the decision said, "none of our decisions go to the length of sustaining such a curtailment of the right of free speech and assembly as the Oregon statute demands in its present application."

Under the Oregon law severe penalties are imposed upon any one who "assists in conducting any assemblage, or persons, or any organization, or any society, or any group which teaches or advocates the doctrine of criminal syndicalism."

The scope of this law and the wide definitions under it of "criminal syndicalism" attracted the close attention of the court when the case was argued on Dec. 9. Maurice E. Tarshis, State Attorney General, conceded that if the Communist party had called a meeting to discuss almost any sort of a political question, those assisting in conducting the meeting could be found guilty under the law.

Chief Justice Hughes remarked in his opinion upon the latitude allowed under the statute. Emphasizing his words as he read, he commented:

"However innocuous the object of the meeting, however lawful the subjects and tenor of the addresses, however reasonable and timely the discussion, all those assisting in the conduct of the meeting would be subject to imprisonment as felons if the meeting were held by the Communist party."

De Jonge, the Chief Justice said.

was deprived by the indictment of showing that the meeting was orderly and lawful and was not called to advocate either criminal syndicalism or sabotage.

"His sole offense," Mr. Hughes added, was that he had "assisted" in the conduct of a meeting, lawful, but held under the auspices of the Communist party.

The conclusions expressed in the Hughes opinion dealt with the elemental privilege of peaceable meetings for lawful discussions.

The rights of free speech, free press and peaceful assembly may, he said, be abused by press or assembly in order to incite to violence and crime.

"The people, through their Legislatures, may protect themselves against that abuse. But the legislative intervention can find constitutional justification only by dealing with the abuse. The rights themselves must not be curtailed. The greater the importance of safeguarding the community from incitements to the overthrow of our institutions by force and violence, the more imperative is the need to preserve inviolate the constitutional rights of free speech, free press and free assembly in order to maintain the opportunity for free politi-

cal discussion, to the end that government may be responsive to the will of the people and that changes, if desired, may be obtained by peaceful means. Therein lies the security of the republic, the very foundation of constitutional government.

Peaceable Assembly Held No Crime

"It follows from these considerations," the Chief Justice continued, "that, consistently with the Federal Constitution, peaceable assembly for lawful discussion cannot be made a crime. The holding of meetings for peaceable political action cannot be proscribed. Those who assist in the conduct of such meetings cannot be branded as criminals on that score. The question, if the rights of free speech and peaceable assembly are to be preserved, is not as to the auspices under which the meeting is held, but to its purpose; not as to the relations of the speakers, but whether their utterances transcend the bounds of the freedom of speech which the Constitution protects.

"If the persons assembling have committed crimes elsewhere, if they have formed or are engaged in a conspiracy against the public peace and order, they may be

prosecuted for their conspiracy or other violation of valid laws. But it is a different matter when the State, instead of prosecuting them for such offense, seizes upon mere participation in a peaceable assembly and a lawful public discussion as the basis for a criminal charge.

"We are not called upon to review the findings of the State court as to the objectives of the Communist party. Notwithstanding those objectives, the defendant still enjoyed his personal right of free speech and to take part in a peaceable assembly having a lawful purpose, although called by that party.

"The defendant was none the less entitled to discuss the public issues of the day and thus in a lawful manner, without incitement to violence or crime, to seek redress of alleged grievances. That was of the essence of his guaranteed personal liberty."

The justices held the Oregon statute "repugnant" as applied to the de Jonge trial, and sent the case back to the State courts, where the conviction may be set aside or a new trial ordered.

January 5, 1937

HAGUE URGES EXILE OF 'REDS' TO ALASKA TO BAR REVOLUTION

Charges C. I. O. Seeks Control of Labor to Stir Uprising as in Russia and Spain

ACCUSES ERNST AS CHIEF

Jersey Mayor Would Suppress Civil Liberties of All Who Fight Government

By RUSSELL B. PORTER
Special to The New York Times.

NEWARK, N. J., June 14.—Declaring he did not believe in civil liberties for any one working for the overthrow of the government, Mayor Frank Hague advocated today a concentration camp in Alaska for native "Reds," deportation from the United States of alien radicals and suppression of free speech and other constitutional rights for all in this category.

The Mayor also included advocates of Fascist or Nazi revolutions among his candidates for exile. He urged other public officials throughout the United States to follow his lead in his war against Communists and all "subversive" elements.

The Mayor testified for more than

four hours on the second day of his appearance as a witness in the suit brought by the C. I. O. and the American Civil Liberties Union before Federal Judge William Clark for an injunction against repressive measures by the Jersey City authorities and police. He will return to the stand tomorrow morning.

Mayor Hague was a self-assured, confident witness, apparently without a doubt as to the correctness of his views and the moral righteousness of his fight against the "Reds." At the beginning of his testimony he was a trifle nervous, closing and unclosing his leather case for eyeglasses, which he used when reading documents, but after a few minutes he became completely composed.

Exhibits Power of "Boss"

For the most part he sat back relaxed with his long fingers clasped in front of him and spoke in a low but clear and measured tone, like one explaining something persuasively but patiently.

At critical periods he displayed the dominating personality that has helped make him Democratic leader of New Jersey and "boss" of Jersey City, by leaning forward in his chair, with his hawk-like features and pale blue eyes intense, with sharp-pointed gestures of his index finger, and by aggressively pounding in his points in arguments with opposing counsel.

He even overruled John A. Matthews, his special counsel, at times when the latter attempted to interpose legal objections to C. I. O. questions, and the Mayor insisted on answering. Once Mr. Matthews asked the Court to direct him not to answer. This time the Mayor obeyed. He used the first-person pronoun frequently and sometimes referred to himself in the third

person, saying "Mayor Hague" did this or that, as if conscious and proud of his power.

Dean Spaulding Frazer of Newark Law School, chief counsel for the plaintiffs, who subpoenaed the Mayor and made him their "star" witness against himself as chief defendant, conducted the questioning in a way that gave the Mayor free rein to expound his theory of government in the treatment of minorities.

In the little fencing between lawyer and witness that went on the Mayor held up his end well, but there was small dispute about facts. In the main the examination consisted of the clash of two philosophies, Dean Frazer suggesting by his questions that the Mayor was violating the constitutional guarantees of free speech, free press and free assembly, and abviously seeking proof of this from the Mayor's own lips by letting him talk freely, and the Mayor insisting that Americanism and law and order, not free speech and constitutional rights, were the issue.

Charges Reds Exploit Labor

In a crowded court room, where Hague sympathizers at times applauded his appeals to patriotism and laughed at his jests, Mayor Hague amplified the charges he began last Friday against the C. I. O., the A. C. L. U and allied organizations as communistic.

Today he charged that Communists behind the C. I. O. were trying to get control of the American labor movement in an effort to bring about a "Red" revolution similar to those in Russia, Spain and Mexico. Pointing his finger at Morris L. Ernst, who sat at the C. I. O. counsel table, the Mayor declared Mr. Ernst was the real leader of this revolutionary attempt and that John L. Lewis, who he reiterated was the only C. I. O. leader not a Communist, had merely "assumed" command to save his position as head of the United Mine Workers. Many of the C. I. O. rank and file, he said, were "loyal Americans," but had been coerced by thousands into joining, especially in the United Automobile Workers,

through fear for their lives.

The Mayor declared his belief that the Communists had hoped to win their revolution through the American Labor party, but that this political movement had failed. Predicting that the American Labor party would be "wiped out," he said it was "afraid" to enter a ticket in New Jersey elections and challenged it to do so, to let the voters decide between "100 per cent Americans" and "Reds."

Against this background, he insisted, he was justified in taking the C. I. O. threat of an "invasion" of 3,000 men into Jersey City on last Nov. 29 as an "uprising" against the government, and in refusing permits for street meetings thereafter to the C. I. O. and its sympathizers under the local ordinance that gives the police discretionary power to refuse such permits when there is danger of riot, bloodshed or public disturbance.

He said the people of Jersey City were so strongly aroused against the C. I. O. and its allies by this and subsequent "threats," made in the press and on the radio by Mr. Ernst, Roger N. Baldwin, director of the A. C. L. U., and others, as to cause additional risk of violence and give further reason for denial of permits under the terms of the ordinance.

The Mayor said the citizens were still in such a frame of mind as to make it dangerous to permit C. I. O. meetings and speeches and that he intended to continue to forbid them. As justification of his policy, he cited the riot in Newark a week ago last Saturday night, when Norman Thomas, Socialist leader, to whom the Jersey City police had refused to issue a permit was pelted with eggs and howled down by a mob. The Mayor said the Newark authorities had been "foolish" to grant a permit to Mr. Thomas in view of objections by war veterans and American Federation of Labor leaders. His policy, he declared, prevented such public disorders.

Mayor Hague's beliefs about deportations and concentration camps were stated in reply to questions by Dean Frazer, who asked whether he thought people who believed in the doctrines of Stalin, Hitler and

Mussolini should "go back where they came from." The Mayor replied they should not "go back," but "be driven back" if they came here to oppose this government, and if they were born here, should be sent to a camp in Alaska.

He said, however, that he did not believe in the use of castor oil or rubber hose against such persons, but only "lawful procedure." In making his attack on the American Labor party as a Communist adjunct, he said many of its members had been "misled," but would "wake up to the fact."

Admits He Decides Policies

Although the Mayor reiterated that he had been misquoted by "hostile" Newspaper Guild reporters, whose affiliation with the C. I. O. he emphasized, in the "me—right here" statement last December concerning who decided when there was danger of an "invasion," he admitted he never had issued a denial of the statement and that it was true that he made such decisions.

He admitted that fewer than 200, instead of 3,000, actually participated in the C. I. O. "invasion" last November, but insisted that the police had the right to assume that a big crowd was coming, in view of published statements by William J. Carney, C. I. O. regional director at Newark, and to take the necessary action to prevent disorder. He said they had to let everybody know there was "law and order" in Jersey City.

Mayor Hague admitted that when Dean Frazer applied in December for a permit for an A. C. L. U. street meeting to petition the City Commission to modify its ordinances on public meetings, distribution of circulars and the like, this was a proper purpose for a meeting, but asserted that in view of the Nov. 29 "uprising" the city had to be careful to prevent disorder and protect life and property. Protests from veterans' and civic organizations, he added, caused the city to decide it was time to "suppress these meetings for the present."

The Mayor admitted that the crowds of veterans, members of political clubs, civic organizations and others who gathered in Journal Square and Pershing Field on three occasions to prevent speeches by Mr. Thomas and Representatives O'Connell and Bernard had had no permit, but said they were "private citizens" and there was "no necessity" for a permit in such a case.

He said Messrs. Thomas, Baldwin, O'Connell, Bernard, Carney, Ernst and others to whom permits were denied were objectionable as "Reds," and defined a "Red" as a "Communist." He admitted that Mr. Thomas and Mr. Baldwin had spoken and the Socialist and Communist parties had held meetings in Jersey City without causing disorders, but said all these instances were before the Nov. 29 "uprising" had stirred up "unrest." Moreover, he said, their prior speeches were mostly at indoor meetings, where it was comparatively easy for the police to keep order.

The Mayor seized on evidence that he had formerly granted permits to Socialists and Communists to declare that "Mayor Hague never opposed free speech prior to this trouble," and that he wanted the country to know this.

Mayor Hague disagreed with Dean Frazer's suggestion that the veterans and others who objected to the C. I. O. and A. C. L. U. meetings would have remained quiet and refrained from violence if the Mayor had publicly appealed to them. He said they were too much incensed and that he saw no occasion for him to try to calm them. Asked if he did not think it was his duty to do so, he replied that it was his duty to do what was most beneficial to the city.

Dean Frazer asked if he did not think it the duty of the police to protect people who tried to express views disapproved by the people of the city, but the Mayor replied that it depended on what they were. Asked what his attitude would be if some one advocated nazism, the Mayor said the city never opposed public utterances by any one, that objections came from the people.

The C. I. O. lawyer then read from an opinion by Vice Chancellor Bigelow of New Jersey in a case in which a permit had been denied to the American Friends of New Germany in Union City, near Jersey City, because the meeting was to be for the purpose of advocating nazism. The Vice Chancellor had held that the law did not forbid advocating unpopular doctrines and that it was the duty of the police to protect the lawful assembly of those advocating them and to arrest any lawless elements that resorted to riot against them.

Asked if he would observe that ruling, the Mayor replied that he would "ignore any Vice Chancellor's order" if the circumstances constituted a threat to life and property. He said no one could restrict him when there was danger of any one losing his life.

Questioned about his denial of civil rights, which he admitted in the case of Communists, saying that the man who claimed them usually had "a Russian flag under his coat," the Mayor asserted that he had been in Russia and found that a man who spoke against the government would be shot. He said he did not believe in that, but did think all public officials should "suppress" them by withholding the right to hold public meetings.

Asked if he thought every one who asserted the constitutional rights of free speech, free press and free assemblage should be suppressed, the Mayor retorted that he should be asked if he believed in "an organized mob" causing disorders and producing conditions like those in Spain.

Dean Frazier inquired if he thought the leaders of the local C. I. O. unions, as well as the national leaders, were Communists. Mayor Hague replied they were selected by the national leaders to "browbeat people" into joining the unions.

Questioned as to whether he thought C. I. O. leaders were Communists even if they belonged to other political parties, the Mayor replied that they were "anything that is beneficial to themselves," while "waiting for the day" when communism would come in this country, and had mistakenly believed this day had dawned with the formation of the American Labor party.

Recalls Jersey City Strikes

Although he said last Friday that there had been no labor trouble in Jersey City before the C. I. O. seamen's strike in 1936-37, the Mayor admitted today there had been strikes and other troubles with labor unions, including A. F. of L. unions, in his city before then. He said some of these were caused by gangsters and racketeers who had got control of certain unions.

He admitted he had announced publicly that "the nightstick must prevail," but explained that this referred to breaking up gangs of "thugs" that operated when labor racketeering was "at its height." He said he would order the use of "nightsticks" again if gangsters regained power in labor unions.

He admitted that one especially serious A. F. of L. strike occurred long before the C. I. O., but said this happened because Theodore Brandle, former head of the iron workers, had broken an agreement to take a pay reduction of $16 to $14 a day for his men on the Pulaski Skyway construction. He added that this was the real cause of the break between him and Brandle, long his associate.

The Mayor also said some of the pre-C. I. O. strikes had occurred because "foreign" elements came in from New York and Brooklyn and attempted mass picketing, "which we do not allow."

Questioned about a complaint made on behalf of the A. F. of L. Central Labor Union of Hudson County in 1936 against alleged violations of civil rights by the Hague police in handling labor disputes, the Mayor replied that the letter of complaint had been drafted by Morris Isserman, whom he identified as a "noted Communist" lawyer. He said "Reds" had seized power in A. F. of L. unions at that time, but were ejected when the unions realized it.

The Mayor refused to admit that at the time of the seamen's strike the strikers belonged to A. F. of L. unions, arguing that Harry Bridges, West Coast C. I. O. leader, came to New York to lead the strike and sent some of his "strong-arm men" to Jersey City, two of whom were arrested and sent to prison for fourteen years.

The Mayor declared he had done as much for labor as any public official in the country and was not opposed to organized labor, but he also believed that "the man who provides the payroll" should be protected, that labor must function legally and that the rank and file of labor should be safeguarded from "dishonest" leaders.

Asked about his advertising program to attract new industries, he said several hundred companies had come to Jersey City in the last few years. He said companies were investigated to find whether they had had labor troubles and if so were told they were not wanted. He said he thought employers who paid only $6 to $8 a week wage, as C. I. O. witnesses have testified some in Jersey City have done, should be "put in State's prison."

Dean Frazer read from an opinion by Chief Justice Hughes holding the Oregon criminal syndicalism law unconstitutional. Asked if he considered the Chief Justice a "Red," the Mayor replied he did not, but that the situation was entirely different.

Tomorrow Mr. Ernst is expected to take up the examination of the Mayor before he is turned over to his own counsel for further questioning.

June 15, 1938

MAPS WIDE INQUIRY INTO PROPAGANDA

House Group Will Have Aid of All Investigating Agencies of the Government

HEARINGS DUE ABOUT AUG. 1

Special to THE NEW YORK TIMES.

WASHINGTON, June 18.—The investigation by a special House committee of the diffusion within the United States of subversive and un-American propaganda of foreign as well as of domestic instigation will be in many respects different from any other investigation ever made by a committee of Congress.

Representative Martin Dies of Texas, chairman of the committee, said today that he would remain in Washington to press plans for the start of the hearings, probably about Aug. 1. Representatives of the committee will assemble data and interview witnesses in various cities.

Every investigating agency of the government, including the Federal Bureau of Investigation and the Postal Inspection Service, is directed under the authorizing resolution to aid the committee in getting evidence and in preparing the agenda which will govern the proceedings.

Awaits Field Reports

"It will require six or seven weeks," Mr. Dies declared, "to assemble the basic information which will guide the committee in its efforts to get the facts bearing on the un-American activities the committee will investigate. Agents of the committee, including the G-men and operatives of other Federal investigating units, will go into the field immediately and their reports will largely determine the course the investigation will take.

"This is not going to be any 'shooting in the dark' inquiry. We want the facts only and when the hearings start we will know where to go to get them. While the hearings will probably not be open to the general public, this does not say they will be star-chamber proceedings. Newspaper men will not be barred from any of the hearings and the proceedings will be disclosed in the newspapers day by day without restriction of any kind.

"Owing to the very nature of the investigation I think this is the best way to conduct these hearings. We do not want any person or persons to use these proceedings for demonstrative purposes either for or against the alleged propaganda activities which are to be the subject of the inquiry.

"The hearings will probably start on the Pacific Coast, probably Los Angeles or San Francisco, and will end somewhere in the East—just where, I am not now in a position to say."

Scope of Committee's Task

Under the terms of the resolution the committee's task is threefold:

1. To investigate the extent, character and objects of un-American propaganda activities in the United States.

2. To investigate the diffusion within the United States of subversive and un-American propaganda that is instigated from foreign countries or of a domestic origin and which attacks the principle or the form of government guaranteed by the United States Constitution.

3. To investigate all other questions in relation thereto that would aid Congress in any necessary remedial legislation.

The committee has the power to subpoena witnesses and the resolution stipulates that "every person who, having been summoned as a witness, or any subcommittee thereof, wilfully makes default, or who, having appeared, refuses to answer any question pertinent to the investigation, shall be held to the penalties provided by Section 102 of the Revised Statutes of the United States."

In addition to Mr. Dies, the members of the committee are Representatives Arthur D. Healey of Massachusetts, Harold G. Mosier of Ohio, J. Purnell Thomas of New Jersey, John J. Dempsey of New Mexico, Noah M. Mason of Illinois and Joseph H. Starnes of Alabama. Representatives Mason and Thom-

as are Republicans, the others Democrats.

The resolution does not specify any group to be investigated. It is so drawn as to cover all un-American or subversive activities, whether of Nazi, Fascist, Communist or other origin. The activities of certain Nazi organizations in the country will be vigorously investigated, the inquiry to cover the financing of such organizations, the leadership and the number of aliens in the membership.

June 19, 1938

COMMUNISTS RULE THE C.I.O., FREY OF A.F.L. TESTIFIES; HE NAMES 284 ORGANIZERS

BROPHY IS ACCUSED

Sit-Ins and Mass Picketing Declared Used in Plot for Revolution

LA FOLLETTE IS CRITICIZED

His Committee Works in Close Cooperation With Communists, Witness Says

Special to THE NEW YORK TIMES.

WASHINGTON, Aug. 13.—John P. Frey, vice president of the American Federation of Labor, told the Special House Committee Investigating Un-American Activities in the United States today that Communists held many key positions in the C. I. O.

He listed 284 alleged Communist party members who were or are on the C. I. O. payroll. He listed about sixty others as C. I. O. leaders who, he said, were either members of the Communist party or were lending their support to Communist propaganda within the C. I. O.

He added that next week he would offer 230 more names to bring his list of Communist party

members who were active C. I. O. workers to about 500.

He declared that the program of the C. I. O. had the "hearty endorsement of the Communist party" and that violent disturbances in connection with the strikes in the steel and automobile industries were fostered by Communist leaders.

The sit-down strike and mass picketing had been used by Communists, he charged, as front line trenches in which to train members "for the day when the signal for revolution is given."

He asserted that Communist efforts to gain a foothold in the ranks of organized labor in America were unsuccessful until John L. Lewis organized the Committee for Industrial Organization and that since then communism had become a definite factor in the American labor movement.

Alleges Senate Group Link

He charged that the Senate Civil Liberties Committee, of which Senator Robert M. LaFollette of Wisconsin is chairman, had worked in close cooperation with Communists in Cleveland, and that Coleman Taylor of that city, a C. I. O. organizer and "a Communist party spokesman," had been "in constant communication" with investigators for the LaFollette Committee.

Vincent Favorito, described as a "star witness" for the committee in its investigation of the "Little Steel strike," was, Mr. Frey charged, a member of the communist party.

Among the sixty C. I. O. officials whom he described as either Com-

munists or supporters of Communist propaganda were John Brophy, C. I. O. director; Francis Gorman, president of the United Textile Workers; Morris Muster, president of the United Furniture Workers of America; George Woolf, president of the Fish and Cannery Workers International Union; Harold Pritchett, a Canadian, who is president of the International Woodworkers of America, and Michael J. Quill, president of the Transport Workers Union.

Also Professor Donald Henderson, formerly of Columbia University, and now president of the United Cannery, Agricultural Packing and Allied Workers of America; Julius H. Klyman, vice president of the American Newspaper Guild, and Joseph Curran, president of the National Maritime Workers Union.

He said that William Gebhert, a member of the Central Committee of the Communist party, had been active in the C. I. O. campaign to organize workers in the steel industry.

Comparison of Policies

Mr. Frey prefaced his testimony with a declaration of A. F. of L. policy in its battle with the C. I. O.

"The American Federation of Labor," he said, "has believed in evolutionary instead of revolutionary methods. It has believed that labor, through voluntary association in trade unions, must build up the structure of protection step by step and stone by stone.

"The leaders of the American Federation of Labor have been convinced, from the study of history, that the evolutionary and educational method is the only constructive one. It has been applying these methods for over fifty years, and the record of accomplishment is impressive.

"The Communists heap ridicule upon the progress made by the American Federation of Labor. They jeer at its constructive evolutionary methods. They preach revolution. Within the last two or three years they have seized every sit-down strike, every mass picketing venture, as a means of stimulating their revolutionary tactics.

"The sit-down strike and mass

picketing have been used by the Communists in our country as a training camp in which Communists can become familiar with the tactics they are to apply when their revolutionary program is put into action. The sitdown strike and mass picketing have been used as front line trenches in which the mass revolutionists of the future are to receive experience and training to equip them for the day when the signal for revolution is given.

"The American Federation of Labor in its structure, its policy and its methods has been made to conform as closely as possible to the principles underlying our American form of government and our American institutions of human liberty.

"Because of its understanding of American institutions and methods it vigorously set itself in opposition to the theories and apparent purposes of socialism. As a result the Socialists' attempts to determine the policies of the American Federation of Labor met with complete failure. The American Federation of Labor learned its lessons in the practical and sometimes costly school of experience.

"As the success of the Communist party in any country depends primarily upon its ability to infiltrate into the national trade union movements and control their policymaking, the American Federation of Labor has vigorously defended its affiliated unions from Communist propaganda and Communists boring from within. Because of this the Communist party made no real progress in the United States.

"It failed to secure a foothold in an American trade union movement until the C. I. O. was organized. Since then the Communist party has become a definite factor in the American labor movement.

"In connection with the evidence indicating Communist activities within the C. I. O., it must be said, in all fairness to the majority of the membership, that they are not Communists and that they are opposed to communism. In many local instances these members of the C. I. O. have arisen in revolt against the Communist leadership which had secured control.

"The C. I. O. is not yet a Communist organization, so far as the great majority of the rank and file is concerned. The fact seems to be that the C. I. O. membership unwittingly became a carrier for the virus of communism because of the attitude of its leadership."

August 14, 1938

Peace League Here 'Born' In Moscow, Witness Says

J. B. Matthews, Once Leader in Movement, Tells Dies Committee It Is Part of Communist 'Front'—Testifies on College Links

Special to THE NEW YORK TIMES.

WASHINGTON, Aug. 20.—The American League for Peace and Democracy was directly linked with Moscow today before the House Committee on un-American activities in testimony by J. B. Matthews of Washington, N. J., who said he was the first head of the American League Against War and Fascism, its predecessor.

The league "was born in Moscow" in 1933, he testified, and the person mainly responsible for the organization was Henri Barbusse, the French Communist, who subsequently toured the United States under the auspices of the league and died in the Kremlin, at Moscow, soon after his return from the United States.

Mr. Matthews, who said he had turned against communism, also testified as to the organization of Communist student movements in the United States—the financing of the Communist party and its allied or affiliated organizations; the unemployed councils, formed and controlled by Communists, now operating, he said, under the name of the Workers' Alliance, and other organizations and movements which, he declared, were definitely a part of the Communist "front" in the United States.

The American League for Peace and Democracy now claims a membership in the United States of about 4,000,000 persons, said Dr. Matthews, and the extent of its influence is better measured "by the fact that it recently obtained the endorsement of the Solicitor General of the United States."

Mr. Matthews did not name the Solicitor General, who at the present time is Robert H. Jackson, the Acting Attorney General.

The American Youth Congress, which is at this time host to the World Youth Congress in convention at Vassar College, is nothing less than one of the many "united fronts" which are part of the Communist program in the United States, the witness said.

There are about fifty American delegates to the congress, and of them, Mr. Matthews declared, about thirty-five are Communists.

In his examination by members of the committee, Mr. Matthews said that many prominent persons whose names are published as sponsors of this or that "red-tinted" organization had no idea what it was they were sponsoring when they agreed to stand before the public as "background" for the organization in question.

As a worker for the Communist cause, the witness said, he had approached personally many promi-

nent persons and asked them to become members of or to serve as a sponsor or in other honorary capacities for organizations organized as part of the Communist "front."

"They would sign without any knowledge at all as to the real character or mission of the organization they were identifying themselves with," he testified.

"If the wife of the President of the United States gets up at a meeting of the League for Peace and Democracy and makes a speech, by so doing she adds to the influence of that organization. Is not that a fact?" asked Representative Mason of Illinois.

"The question answers itself," replied Mr. Matthews.

Mr. Matthews was asked to name the members of the National Advisory Committee of the American Youth Congress.

He read a long list of names which included those of Bishop Ralph D. Cushman of the Methodist Church, former Governor Hoffman of New Jersey, President Henry Noble MacCracken of Vassar College, William Allen White of The Emporia Gazette, Miss Mary K. Woolley of Mount Holyoke College, Miss Lillian D. Wald of the Henry Street Settlement, Archibald MacLeish, editor of Fortune; Philip Murray, chairman of the C. I. O. Steel Workers Organizing Committee; Jerome Davis, president of the American Federation of Teachers; Professor Edmund de S. Brunner of Columbia University, Philip Schiff of the Madison House, Mary Van Kleeck of the Russell Sage Foundation, Rabbi Sidney E. Goldstein of the Free Synagogue, Governor Benson of Minnesota, Ruth O. Blakeslee, chief of the division of policies and procedure of the Social Security Board; Professor Paul H. Douglas of the University of Chicago and Jeremiah T. Mahoney, president of the Amateur Athletic Union.

"When I convinced Governor Hoffman the congress was Communist-inspired he resigned," said Mr. Matthews. He did not know if any of the others had resigned.

Describes Split in Russia

Mr. Mason, after a reference to reports that many persons holding high Federal positions in Washington are members of the league, asked Mr. Matthews this question:

"Is there a direct connection between Moscow and the league?"

"Yes," Mr. Matthews replied.

"The league," he went on, "is the most ambitious and influential of all the 'united fronts' in the United States. The decision to set it up was actually made in Moscow.

"Hitler's rule spelled the disastrous defeat of the Communist movement in Germany. It also marked the complete failure of the foreign policy of the Communist International in other countries of the world.

"The substance of that Soviet policy was the baiting of Social Democrats, Socialists, Liberals and the so-called reformists among trade

unionists. Moscow declared that these, rather than the Fascists, were the chief enemies of communism. They were dubbed 'Social Fascists' and were everywhere attacked and slandered.

"The result of that policy had left the Communists a weak and isolated sect. In Germany, the Communist party faced annihilation. In France, Great Britain and the United States it had no substantial influence.

Asserts Stalin Sought Aid Here

"Moscow foresaw a military showdown with Hitler," the witness continued. "It was to be a death struggle between the Fascist dictator and the Communist dictator.

"Stalin began to feel the need for powerful allies in that coming conflict. How should he get these allies among the unfriendly capitalist powers? He summoned the Communist leaders of the world to Moscow. They deliberated, and out of their deliberations came the decision to set up the Popular Front in France.

"But France was farther developed along the road to the final class struggle than was the United States. Sooner or later the Communists must set up a Popular Front in the United States, but first they decided to set up the American League. The prelude to an American Popular Front! Earl Browder brought back the word from Moscow. And I was chosen by Browder and his colleagues in the Communist party to head the new organization.

"The actual management of the affairs of the American League was turned over to Donald Henderson, former Columbia University professor. Henderson had publicly declared his membership in the Communist party a year or two before when he resigned from the Socialist party and while he was still an instructor in economics at Columbia University.

"Henderson was later assigned by the Communist party to agitational work among farmers. He is now the head of the C. I. O. union for farmers. He has lately been active among the pecan workers of Texas. He is now the head of the United Cannery, Agricultural, Packing and Allied Workers of America, which is affiliated with the C. I. O.

"These facts dispose, once and for all, of the question of whether or not the American League was launched by the Communist party," Mr. Matthews declared. "Nevertheless, there are numerous participants in this Communist united front who are still fooled into thinking that it is an independent agency for peace and democracy. The Communist party plans it that way.

"An amusing instance of the public's 'innocence' regarding the true nature of the American League occurred at one of the national gatherings of the organization. Meeting in Cleveland, the Communists and their fellow-travelers, with a small sprinkling of 'innocents,' were welcomed by the local Jewish rabbi. The rabbi walked right into a faux pas by urging that the task of the American League be broadened to include a fight against communism as well as against war and fascism.

"The Cleveland rabbi may be excused for his error when other prominent churchmen, who know better, nevertheless declare publicly that the American League is not controlled by the Communist party.

"The secretary of the Church League for Industrial Democracy, affiliated with the Protestant Episcopal Church, has been a member of the national executive committee of the American League from its very beginning. And yet he has been publicly quoted recently as

denying the Communist origin and control of the American League.

Link With Church Cited

"It passes belief, but his church organization actually shares a field organizer with the American League.

"When a Communist manoeuvre is skillful enough to establish any kind of a connection between the Protestant Episcopal Church and the Communist party, it is hardly to be wondered at that we were able to fool thousands of others about the character of the league."

"How is the League financed?" asked Representative Starnes of Alabama.

"In three ways," Mr. Matthews answered, "the first being what we call the 'nickel, dime and quarter drive,' the driving being against the 'innocents.' The nickels, dimes and quarters are garnered in at meetings, the money being dropped into tin cans or anything else handy.

"The second way is to give a dinner for the so-called upper middle class—the 'pink intellectuals.' At some of these banquets I have known as much as $2,000 to be collected.

"The third way was to get Mr. Corliss Lamont [son of Thomas W. Lamont, the banker, and prominent in the radical movement in New York] to sign a note which I would endorse. If that did not work we communicated with Earl Browder and the money was sent to the proper person by messenger. I don't know where Browder got the money, but it possibly came out of a fund made available for such emergencies. Whether it was of Moscow origin or not I am not prepared to testify."

Chairman Dies asked Mr. Matthews to give the facts, as he knew them, about the alleged Communist student movement.

"I was among the national sponsors of the Student Congress Against War held at the University of Chicago, Dec. 27-29, 1932," the witness said. "I was one of the speakers at this congress and also a discussion leader for one of its subdivisions.

"The congress was organized by the National Student League, which was at that time the Communist party's agency on American college campuses. The leader of the Student Congress Against War and also of the National Student League was Donald Henderson.

"Students of other political persuasions, Socialist, pacifist and liberal, participated in the Chicago congress, but we encountered no difficulty whatever in obtaining the adoption of a set of resolutions which conformed completely to the 'line' of the Communist party.

"On numerous other occassions I made speeches under the auspices of the National Student League. In the Spring of 1933, Columbia University refused to renew, for the following academic year, its teaching contract with Donald Henderson, who had been an instructor in economics in the university.

"For a number of weeks that Spring we conducted open air protest meetings in front of Columbia University at which we endeavored to make Henderson's 'dismissal' into an issue of academic freedom," the witness went on.

"The fact was, as Henderson explained to me, that he had deliberately neglected his Columbia classes with a view to forcing the issue of his 'dismissal' from the university.

"It was the Communist party's plan to invest Henderson with the stature of an academic martyr and thereby obtain for him a kind of publicity which would be useful in a larger party service then contemplated.

"In the Fall of 1935 the National Student League and the Student League for Industrial Democracy (Socialist in its complexion) were merged to form the present American Student Union.

"As a member of the board of directors of the League for Industrial Democracy I voted for this merger. The American Student Union thus became the broader 'united front' movement among American college students.

"The outstanding event in the academic year of the American Student Union is its annual 'anti-war strike' on college campuses—an event in which more than 150,000 students have participated on a single occasion.

Example of "United Front"

"In the Spring of 1935 I was the principal speaker for the 'anti-war strike' on the campus of the University of Virginia at Charlottesville. There I found that the affair was entirely under the direction of the student members of the Communist party.

"Closely associated with the American Student Union and deriving much of its impetus and direction from it is the American Youth Congress.

"The congress is an excellent example of the methods and purposes of the Communist party's 'united front.' Among the organizations

which have been persuaded to endorse the Youth Congress and to participate in its Communist-guided work, we find numerous groups of Christian young people, such as the National Council of Methodist Youth and the Christian Youth Conference of North America.

"Among the individuals sponsoring the Youth Congress, as members of its so-called National Advisory Committee, we find, in addition to the usual left-wingers who appear frequently on 'united front' committees, the names of Ralph S. Cushman, Bishop of the Methodist Episcopal Church; Harold G. Hoffman, Governor of New Jersey, and Henry Noble MacCracken, president of Vassar College.

"Ostensibly these organizations and individuals are associated with the youth organization which is dedicated to peace as one of its major goals. Actually they are being made the innocent dupes of a carefully contrived Communist manoeuvre.

Points to College Session

"At this very moment, the American Youth Congress is host to a so-called World Youth Congress meeting on the campus of Vassar College. This World Youth Congress at Vassar is nothing more nor less than one of these 'united front' manoeuvres dedicated to forwarding the aims of the foreign

policy of the Soviet Union. Any one who denies this demonstrable fact is either the unfortunate victim of deceit or a willful deceiver. The resolutions which are assured of adoption at this World Youth Congress will follow faithfully the current 'line' of the Communist party and will express the same purpose of 'giving the world proletariat still more time to rally its forces for the final overthrow of capitalism.' "

Next Mr. Matthews discussed briefly the origin of the Workers Alliance.

"Prior to the organization of the Workers Alliance of America the Communist party," he said, "maintained its own rigidly controlled groups for the unemployed, which were known as Unemployed Councils. Under the auspices of this group a 'hunger march' on Washington was staged in 1933. I worked with the group on sundry matters of arranging its descent upon the nation's capital.

"I was likewise frequently a speaker for the Unemployed Leagues, supported by the left wing Socialists, which were subsequently merged with the Unemployed Councils to form the Workers Alliance of America. In the Fall of 1933 I strongly urged that merger and personally brought David Lasser and Herbert Benjamin, its two leaders, together on the platform of the

United States Congress Against War."

Linked With Foreign Groups

Just before the committee adjourned until Monday Representative Starnes asked Mr. Matthews if he could not give more evidence to support his assertion that the League for Peace and Democracy is of Moscow origin.

"I may say," he answered, "that simultaneously with the organization of the League Against War and Fascism in the United States there was organized a league of the same name in Canada, one in France and one in England. When they changed the name to the League for Peace and Democracy in the United States they did the same thing, at the same time, in Canada, England and France. In all these countries it is Peace and Democracy now."

Asked why he had identified himself with the Communist movement, Mr. Matthews answered that, like thousands of other Americans, when he left college he was what he described as "a sentimental idealist." No one can become involved in the Communist movement, he said, without his eyes being opened eventually to the fact that the evils of the left wing are greater than those in the camps opposed by the Communists.

August 21, 1938

RED GROWTH SWIFT, MATTHEWS ASSERTS

'United Front' Gain in Nation in Last Few Years Has Far Outrun Hopes, He Says

---

POINTS TO NEW DEAL AIMS

Likens Some to Those of Communists — Alleges Plans to Absorb Democratic Party

---

Special to THE NEW YORK TIMES.

WASHINGTON, Aug. 22.—The "united front" movement of the Communist party had made more progress in the United States in a few recent years than had been hoped for in fifty and the movement continued in full swing, James B. Matthews of Washington, N. J., former president of the American League Against War and Fascism, testified today before the Special House Committee to Investigate Un-American Activities in the United States.

Mr. Matthews, who began his testimony Saturday, declared that major aims in the American program of the Communists were the disruption if not the absorption of the Democratic party, the control of labor unions and the placing of

persons of Communist views or sympathies in responsible government positions.

In answer to a question, the witness said it was clear that certain immediate objectives of the Roosevelt Administration were very little different from objectives of the Communist party.

It was a matter of "pride and boasting" in Communist party circles, he testified, that the Communist party had "its friends, and sympathizers situated strategically in every important institution in this country—government agencies, newspapers, magazines, the churches, women's clubs, trade unions, universities and colleges and in industry."

Definitions Held Different

The Communist party, he added, had no interest in peace, job security or civil liberties as those things are understood by the average American.

"They are," he asserted, "the temporary ideas and ideals which the Communist party utilizes for its objective of bringing about class war, almost universal insecurity, and the complete abolition of civil liberties."

Manoeuvres in America to impress "the gullible" that the Communist party was in favor of peaceful methods of accomplishing its objectives were wholly false, he said.

"The principle which is unalterable in communism," he continued, "is that violence, in which Communists take the offensive against the bourgeoisie, is necessary for the setting up of the dictatorship of the proletariat."

In a prepared statement the witness said:

"There are four orders of individuals who make up a Communist united front. We used all of them in the work of the American League.

"First, there are the Communist party members. Sometimes their

membership is secret, but often it is openly acknowledged. Party members invariably occupy strategic positions of control.

"Second, there are the fellow travelers who as a rule go along as faithfully as if they were actually party members. Usually these are middle class intellectuals—professors, 'stooges' and clergymen, and even Congressmen.

"Stooges" and "Innocents"

"Third, there are the 'stooges.' These are persons of prominence whose names have considerable publicity value. They are the real decoys whose names do the work of covering up the Communist control of the united front.

"Finally, there are the innocents, so called by the Communists themselves. The innocents are supposed to make up the overwhelming number of the adherents to the united front. The chief object of the united front is to draw the innocents gradually closer and closer to the Communist party until they are at last completely under its influence.

"The party members do most of the hard work. The fellow travelers are the go-betweens who bring the Communist world and the capitalist world together. The stooges are the necessary camouflage for the united front manoeuvre. The innocents are the fodder for revolution, although some of them are prospective party members as well.

"It was easy to get party members and fellow travelers in order to start the American League. They were to be had for the asking. It required long and patient work to get the stooges. The first half dozen such decoys were the hardest to get. After that the decoys decoyed each other.

"There was great jubilation in the headquarters of the American League on the occasion when we were able to list as a speaker one of the nationally prominent officers of the General Federation of Women's Clubs. Every additional stooge or

decoy made it twice as easy to get another.

Tells of "Almost Perfect Trick"

"We had an almost perfect trick for silencing any critics who suspected or knew the Communist nature of our united front. All we had to do was to cry 'red baiting.'

"This cry of red baiting is the best trick ever invented, short of a firing squad, for making short work of anybody who dares to object to Communist theories or practices. If he isn't effectively silenced, he is at least thoroughly discredited in that vast flock of citizens who like to think of themselves as liberals.

"A twentieth century American 'liberal' would rather face the charge of slapping his grandmother than to be accused of red baiting. And so the cry of red baiting enabled us to carry on the work of Moscow in this country with little or no molestation from knowing critics."

Concerning "boring-in" tactics of the Communists to get a foothold in American labor organizations, Mr. Matthews said that, except in a few isolated instances, not much progress had been made in the American Federation of Labor. It was a different story, he added, in the case of the Committee for Industrial Organization.

"It was not very long ago when John L. Lewis, head of the C. I. O., was the man most hated by the Communist leaders in this country," he declared. "Today they are hanging to his coattails.

Names Some "Red Unions"

"In most cases A. F. of L. trade unions were more difficult to enroll in the united front. In those days, five years ago, the Communists had set up their own Red unions under an international body with headquarters in Moscow.

"Among these red unions which were participating in the newly formed American League were the National Textile Workers Union, the National Mine Workers Union, the Marine Workers Industrial Union, the Needle Trade Workers Industrial Union.

"Their presence in our united front was all the proof that A. F. of L. unions generally needed to establish the Communist control of the American League. There were, however, a few A. F. of L. unions in which Communists were effectively boring. Although they constituted an insignificant numerical minority in these unions, the 'planted' Communists were instructed by the party to introduce resolutions of affiliation with the American League. A number of these resolutions were adopted, although the union membership generally had no idea of what they were doing.

"When I complained repeatedly to Donald Henderson that we were making such slight progress in enrolling A. F. of L. unions, he reminded me that my work was to enroll the members of middle-class organizations and that the Communist party would take care of the trade unions.

Reports "Sabotage" Plans

"He assured me that the Communists already had several strategic men in important plants and industries where they would be in a position to sabotage vital processes in the event of war—just in case the United States should become involved in a war against the Soviet Union.

"In this connection Henderson was especially boastful of a revolutionary nucleus in submarine plants in Connecticut and of the work of Harry Bridges in the shipping industry on the West Coast. They were, Henderson claimed, secretly allied with the American League.

"The one dramatic event at our United States Congress Against War was the appearance on the platform of a fully uniformed soldier of the United States Army. Those were days before the Communist party had donned the mask of 100 per cent American patriotism.

"Earl Browder had made the most careful plans for the soldier to appear as a symbol of the insurrectionary 'fraction' of the Communist party within the army. Flying squadrons were placed in readiness to block all aisles of the hall in the event of an attempted arrest of the soldier by Secret Service men. Other committees of comrades were deputized to take care of all news photographers, with instructions to

smash their cameras if they insisted on making pictures of the soldier as he addressed the congress."

The American League was financed by a four-fold method, the witness said.

Reviews Alleged Financing

"First, there was the nickel-dime-and-quarter drive upon the innocents," he proceeded. "Next came the money-raising banquets for the upper middle class, with Henri Barbusse, John Strachey or Lord Marley as speaker. When these were insufficient, money was borrowed on notes signed by Corliss Lamont, and finally, in a pinch, we got Browder on the telephone and had him send over cash from the party chest, which was regularly stocked from Moscow.

"When one of our publicity stories included the name of Corliss Lamont there was a rule that his family connections with the house of Morgan should be given appropriate emphasis. Marley's lordship was equally useful to our cause.

"It was recognized at the outset and at all times subsequently that only so-called imperialist war was to be opposed by members of the American League as such. Other kinds of war were admissible. The question frequently arose in our meetings as to the attitude of the American League toward a war by certain powers upon the Soviet Union.

"The answer was always two-fold: if the United States joined in an attack upon the Soviet Union, the American League's first and only loyalty was to the Soviet Union, and to the end of fulfilling this loyalty efforts would be made to cripple the basic industries of the United States and bring about this country's defeat, including mutiny in the army; if, on the other hand, the United States should side with the Soviet Union, then the American League would wholeheartedly support the United States, and the war would not be called an imperialist war, but rather class war on an international scale. Outright pacifists who abjured all wars, including class war, were to be exposed and fought."

"Let's go back to labor for a moment," interrupted Representative Mason of Illinois. "I ask you if you have any knowledge of any C. I. O. organizers being members of the Communist party?"

"I do," replied Mr. Matthews.

"Will you supply the committee with the names?"

"I will. I recall in the case of Harry Bridges that we were told that if he was landed he could be used to paralyze shipping on the Pacific Coast. The plan was also to get Communists in the Electric Boat plant, which is one of the principal yards building submarines for the United States Navy.

"Henderson assured me that the Communists had men in certain other industrial plants where they would be of service in event of an emergency or a war. The scheme was to sabotage these plants in the event the United States took sides against the Soviet in a war.

"There also was a plan to cause disturbances in the armed forces of this country when it opposed the Soviet cause in war."

Asked if he had the names of officials of the government who are Communists or in sympathy with communism, Mr. Matthews said he had not completed the list and wanted to check it before filing it with the committee.

Questioned concerning alleged Communist infiltration of industrial plants, newspaper offices and other business fields, Mr. Matthews asserted that Communists on the staff of THE NEW YORK TIMES published a paper called "The Better Times." Until recently, he added, Communists in the Scripps-Howard organization also published a paper, as did Communists employed on Hearst newspapers.

"Indifferences" Called a Help

The Communist party, he testified, relied heavily upon the carelessness or indifference of thousands of prominent citizens in lending their names to its propaganda purposes.

"The French newspaper Ce Soir, which is owned outright by the Communist party, recently featured hearty greetings from Clark Gable, Robert Taylor, James Cagney, and even Shirley Temple," he said, "while the League of Women Shoppers, Communist supported, boasts the membership of Miriam Hopkins and Bette Davis.

"No one, I am sure, will assert that these persons are Communists. Yet there are thousands in the United States who unwittingly permit the use of their names to further the cause of communism."

Asked if "Charley McCarthy" was included in the Hollywood list, the witness replied that it was not necessary, since there were plenty of "Charleys" in Hollywood who were not made of wood.

Mr. Matthews said that when he resigned in 1934 as chairman of the American League Against War and Fascism, now the American League for Peace and Democracy, he was succeeded by Dr. Harry F. Ward of the Union Theological Seminary, who is still chairman of the organization.

"It is relatively easy to identify the professional 'united fronters' or stooges who are doing the cover-up work for the Communist party in the 'united front' manoeuvres," he went on. "Any person in this class is almost certain to bob up at a number of places in the whole manoeuvre."

Moves Ascribed to Mangold

"Take, for example, Mr. William P. Mangold, who is one of the editors of The New Republic. Mr. Mangold is, and has been for several years, the treasurer of the American League for Peace and Democracy. The same Mr. Mangold recently appeared in the nation's capital as the representative of the North American Committee to Aid Spanish Democracy, where he succeeded in obtaining the signatures of sixty members of Congress of the United States to a greeting to be forwarded to the Loyalist government of Spain."

Heywood Broun, newspaper writer, took the chair to deny that he was a Communist. He said he was for the C. I. O. and the Spanish Loyalists, against Fascism and for peace and democracy. He was replying to a statement made by Mr. Matthews Saturday that Mr. Broun told him he quit the Socialist party to be free to work with Communists.

When Mr. Broun declared that the investigation "would get nowhere," Chairman Dies banged his gavel and told him he was excused.

The committee heard briefly the testimony of several workers on the Federal Theatre Project in New York. They supported testimony given Saturday and yesterday that Communists are active in the organization and that the Workers Alliance, which is alleged to be largely Communistic, had a major voice in the administration of the project.

The committee will end its hearings in Washington tomorrow and in a week will divide into three subcommittees to hold hearings in the East, the Middle West and the Pacific Coast.

August 23, 1938

PROBERS: A Suggestion

After several weeks of reading news reports of the sessions of the House committee on un-American activities, it seems to me that the investigators themselves should do a bit of testifying. First, what definition of "American activities" are they using? Logically one must be acquainted with the thesis before attempting to discover antitheses. Secondly, what action do they expect to take after having discovered the sources of "un-American" activities? Other such investigations in history have been followed by repression. It is not inconceivable that this "investigation" may become an inquisition.—RICHARD E. KERESEY JR., Montclair, N. J.

August 28, 1938

HITS CHURCH GROUP AS RADICALS' AID

Professor Graebner Tells Dies Committee Federal Council 'Meddles in Politics'

WASHINGTON, Dec. 9 (AP).—Representatives of the D. A. R. and the Lutheran Church proposed to the Dies committee today that the United States protect itself from subversive elements by developing its "Americanism" and by throwing the light of publicity on foreign influences.

Mrs. Henry M. Robert Jr., president of the Daughters of the American Revolution, urged that the government bring to every citizen "an appreciation" of the advantages of life in the United States.

"The first step is to provide the great American public with a concise definition of Americanism," she said. "The second essential is a primer of Americanism."

Professor Theodore Graebner, philosophy teacher at Concordia Theological Seminary of the Lutheran Church at St. Louis, advocated informing the public as to the "meaning of nazism, fascism, sovietism, and opening their eyes to the extent which this evil has attained."

Says Russia Broke Promise

He said Russia had broken its promise to make no efforts from Moscow to spread "Marxian socialism" in the United States, and added:

"If we applied the Soviet standards of what constitutes the right of the State, we should have long ago shipped every unnaturalized Russian out of the country with Leningrad as his destination."

Professor Graebner asserted that religious leadership had become infected with political radicalism and outright bolshevistic communism to an appalling extent.

Questioned by committee members about his criticism of some religious groups, he charged that the Federal Council of Churches had "meddled incessantly in political affairs, invariably sponsoring the ideals of radical groups."

Mrs. Robert recommended an immediate campaign by the Federal Office of Education, directed primarily toward the youth of the nation, to spread the "real meaning of America and with concrete reasons why life in this nation, even with all of its imperfections, is more satisfying than elsewhere."

"One reason for the rapidity and completeness of the growth of the political systems that would now supplant ours," Mrs. Robert said, "is the fact that there was immediately placed, in the hands of children, and youth, simple statements of reasons why the new system was believed to be better.

"The United States of America never wants government control of education and never a minister of propaganda. At this moment, however, when need for defense is generally recognized, this great people can surely build or encourage the building of its educational defense."

Other recommendations in the program advocated by Mrs. Robert included support for the proposal by Chairman Dies to require incorporated political organizations to file annual reports with Congress; declaration of the Communist party as outside the definition of an American political party, and that it "be known for what it is, a dues-paying society under a program dictated by the Third International in Moscow."

The witness also recommended that aliens ineligible for permanent residence in this country because of their political beliefs "be denied visas for speaking tours for the promotion of propaganda." She urged deportation of aliens attempting to break down American institutions and the annual registration of all aliens.

December 10, 1938

RED LINK IS DENIED BY LIBERTIES UNION

Baldwin Also Sends Disavowal to Dies Committee

The American Civil Liberties Union disavowed any connection with the Communist party in an affidavit sent yesterday to Representative Martin Dies, chairman of the House Committee on Un-American Activities. In a separate affidavit Roger N. Baldwin, director of the union, denied that he had ever belonged to the Communist party and said he was opposed to many of the party's principles and tactics.

The affidavits were prepared at the invitation of Robert E. Stripling, secretary of the Dies committee, who assured the Civil Liberties Union that they would be included in the official record of the committee.

"The American Civil Liberties Union has never been a front or part of a united front for the Communist party," the organization's affidavit said. "The American Civil Liberties Union has no direct or indirect connection with any political movement.

"The American Civil Liberties Union has no connection with any other organization except when co-operating on some particular issue or case involving a question of civil liberties. It has no official connection, as testified to by certain witnesses, with the International Labor Defense, the Workers Defense League or the American League for Peace and Democracy."

The management of the union is vested in a board of directors and a national committee of seventy, only one of whom is a Communist, the affidavit declared.

The union's sworn statement was signed by John Haynes Holmes, vice chairman; B. W. Huebsch, treasurer, and Mr. Baldwin. In his personal affidavit Mr. Baldwin describes himself as "a pacifist, wholly disbelieving in any philosophy, program or movement committed to the use of violence in any form."

January 5, 1939

Denies New Republic Is 'Red'

Bruce Bliven, managing editor of The New Republic, has filed a sworn statement with the Dies committee denying allegations that the magazine is a Communist weekly. The affidavit specifically denied testimony before the committee by Harper Knowles and Ray Nimmo, and added: "The New Republic is not and never has been a Communist organ of any kind, directly or indirectly. It is and always has been devoted to the discussion and defense of American ideals."

January 12, 1939

WITH NEW GRANT, DIES PLANS 'REAL' INQUIRY

Fairness Pledged When Controversial Committee Renews Its Hearings On Un-American Activities

By FREDERICK R. BARKLEY

WASHINGTON, Feb. 11.—When the House last week, by the vote of 344 to 35, gave the so-called Dies committee 100,000 and ordered it to go ahead for another full year with its inquiry into un-American activities it climaxed one of the most remarkable episodes in Congressional history.

The committee originally was created last May with an appropriation of $25,000, and ordered to make a final report at the beginning of the present Congress, which it did. Its legal life ended at 12 o'clock noon on Jan. 3 along with that of the Congress which created it.

The committee report admitted that criticism and ridicule of the committee had been widespread. While it did not refer to President Roosevelt's indictment of its "flagrantly unfair and un-American attempts to influence an election" (against Frank Mur hy, then Governor of Michigan) it did note that it had been the butt of similar attacks by Secretaries Ickes and Perkins, as well as numerous other high-ranking government officials and "radical" writers.

It admitted also, at least by inference, a failure to operate under "a strictly nonpartisan attitude and policy" in a section of the report which had to be added as the price of the signatures of two members who had previously publicly criticized it for such alleged failure. And the committee chairman, Representative Martin Dies of Texas, has publicly admitted that the investigation was not a "good" one, that "screwball witnesses" were heard and that some decent Americans may have been unfairly "smeared."

Request for Renewal

In view of all this criticism, it might have appeared to be the utmost presumption for the committee to ask, as it did, for its reconstitution for two more years and with six times its original fund. The fact was, however, that, as the party leaders soon learned from returning members, the Dies exposures had caught the imagination of the country. The Gallup poll reported that 74 per cent of those questioned favored continuing the inquiry. The party leaders found an almost unanimous sentiment among members that it would be politically unsafe for them to vote contrary, even if they had little respect for what the committee had done and less for how it had done it.

Admitting the soundness of many of the attacks on the committee, Mr. Dies had a plausible answer. He insisted on the impossibility of making a thorough and high-grade investigation with the sum the committee had had available. He pointed to the refusal of Government departments and agencies to lend investigators and clerks as had been done for other committees, like the La Follette Civil Liberties inquiry. He referred to "misrepresentations" made against the committee.

Administration's Stand

Why Administration leaders took the position they did toward the committee never has been authoritatively explained. In some quarters it is suggested the reason was a suspicion that Mr. Dies planned to operate under the inspiration of Vice President Garner, a fellow-Texan, in an effort to discredit leftist elements in the party. The Congressman denies this in toto.

Elsewhere the idea is advanced that the New Deal would have been antagonistic to such an inquiry under any one's direction because of fear that it might expose communistic—or, probably more exactly, socialistic—infiltrations into the Administration.

A third conclusion has been that the inquiry was feared because it might expose (as it did) Communist infiltration into some of the constituent unions of the C. I. O., to which the Administration was felt to be obligated because of its political and financial support in 1936.

Although the testimony heard by the committee was often unsubstantiated or discredited, it did show, shorn of its irrelevancies, an apparent spread of communistic sympathies and of Communist party activity in the country, largely through so-called "front" organizations; and an active Nazi movement which did not appear to be making much headway except among some German-Americans. It showed Communist infiltration into labor, social, liberal and even church organizations, and it showed,

furthermore, the existence of a large number of organizations, mostly apparently one-man "paper" outfits, which were, nevertheless, spreading a vast amount of racial propaganda.

But the inquiry, the committee held, "only scratched the surface." It did not go far enough, it was asserted, to justify recommending legislation to Congress, which would require two years' more probing, including several months to consider what legislation to recommend.

Most of Plea Granted

And because of the fears or curiosity aroused throughout the country, Mr. Dies got most of what he asked for. The leaders did manage to cut the extension of life down to a year, so that the committee will at least not be functioning on its present life-lease in the next national campaign. They also reduced the amount asked to $100,000 and eliminated the second request for departmental aid; the committee must go ahead solely on its own funds. Furthermore, they have put on the committee a third New Dealer, and an ardent one, Representative Voorhis of California, to fill a vacancy. To this Mr. Dies had assented in advance.

And now, the Texan says, he is going to conduct a "real investigation," if the other committee members agree to his plans. These involve hiring two or three "good lawyers" and ten or twelve expert investigators, whom he hopes to recruit from among former Justice Department G-men.

Furthermore, he asserts, he hopes the committee will revert to his original plan of questioning all witnesses in executive sessions.

"Of course, the public may want open hearings," the chairman added. "We'll have to feel our way. But we are going to try to be absolutely fair, to avoid smearing any one.

"I think what the public wants is an accurate picture. We've got a good outline now, and the thing to do is to fill it in. There are 300 or 400 organizations which should be probed and I'd like to start on them. But it will be a month or

THE COMMITTEE MAKES ITSELF KNOWN

Eiderman in The Washington Post

The Dies group now has funds to continue for another year.

two before we can get to work. The committee hasn't met and we haven't got the money yet, and we didn't get enough, either. We'll have to ask for more before Summer.

"And I don't think the department heads or the columnists are going to open their mouths about us this time," Mr. Dies concluded triumphantly. "We've proved this job should be done."

February 12, 1939

ROOSEVELT OPENS TAX FILES TO DIES

WASHINGTON, May 15 (Æ).—The Treasury made public today an executive order signed by President Roosevelt, directing that income tax files be opened to auditors of House Committee on Un-American Activities. A few days ago Chairman Dies demanded the right to examine the returns of a number of alleged fascist and communist leaders.

Mr. Dies said tonight that his investigators would study Federal income tax returns to determine whether certain individuals were paying taxes on money derived from radical or fascist activities.

The committee chairman, gratified that this power had been accorded to him, said tonight it would be used with care.

"It will not be used except where we already have information and leads, regarding specific individuals," he said.

In cases where the committee determined by subpoenaing bank accounts and other records that persons were profiting from subversive activities, he continued, the committee would look up the income

tax returns to make sure such income had been reported.

President Roosevelt last Summer accused the committee of receiving hearsay testimony and using improper methods in prosecuting its inquiry. Secretary Perkins and Secretary Ickes also exchanged words with the committee chairman.

Mr. Dies, at the same time, charged that Administration officials hampered committee activities.

Mr. Dies said today that when hearings are resumed, they would, among other things, "show that the testimony before was absolutely genuine." He realized, he added, that the committee had made "hon-

est mistakes," but asserted that in future proceedings it would profit from them and satisfy the previous criticism of "honest liberals." The hearings, he added, would be "dignified and judicial."

Some weeks will elapse before hearings are begun again, Mr. Dies said, as the committee investigators are engaged now in "doing spadework," and assembling facts preliminary to actual testimony. He expects to take the committee to numerous cities, including Los Angeles, Pittsburgh, New York, Chicago and Birmingham for hearings after Congress adjourns.

May 16, 1939

LIBERTY PLEA MADE BY MRS. ROOSEVELT

Speakers at the ninth annual New York Herald Tribune Forum on Current Problems who had vigorously warned of Communist-Nazi-Fascist "termites" boring from within yesterday heard Mrs. Franklin D. Roosevelt explain that she

was "not afraid of meeting and talking with a Communist" if she could talk of democracy.

Some 5,000 delegates, representing women's organizations, civic groups, national societies and schools and colleges in virtually every State, crowded the grand ballroom of the Waldorf-Astoria Hotel to hear Mrs. Roosevelt and other speakers discuss the general theme, "The Challenge to Civilization."

John Lord O'Brian, veteran head of war emergency, Department of

Justice, during the World War, declared "it would be a great mistake for public officials to encourage private citizens to go searching for spies" during the present European war tension. J. Edgar Hoover, director of the Federal Bureau of Investigation, who followed him, urged all Americans to inform the FBI of "any suspected act of sabotage, espionage, or neutrality violation," but not to develop their efforts into "a witch hunt."

Dr. James Bryant Conant, presi-

dent of Harvard University, in the keynote address of the opening session of the forum, devoted to the sub-topic "The Home Front," discussed "A Free Classless Society: Ideal or Illusion?" Among other things, he said:

"As much as I mistrust the new social order proffered to us by the advocates of the class struggle, so much do I also suspect the freedom that would remain when the nation was governed by the extremists of the right.

"I am perfectly frank to admit

that from my point of view the sort of individual liberty which has been characteristic of this country is a prime requisite for a satisfactory type of civilization. I should put this first on my list of desirables. The freedom of the mind which goes with the political freedom of the United States is more important to me than many other ends for which society might strive. The Bill of Rights and academic freedom go hand in hand. Dislike of governmental tyranny and hatred of restraints on man's intellectual powers are close allies.

"It is for that reason that I dread the possibility of this country's becoming more intensely class conscious and more highly stratified. For, in that event, it seems extremely probable that over the horizon will loom as a model either Germany or Russia. I suspect that the United States cannot respond with vigor to today's challenge to civilization unless through education, social mobility may be once again achieved."

Calling the Forum to order, Ogden Reid, president of The New York Herald Tribune, expressed gratification at the "large and representative attendance." He explained that the forum activities were not designed to advocate any particular program.

Mrs. Ogden Reid, vice president of The New York Herald Tribune, was presented by her husband as chairman of the Forum. Mrs. Reid said she had prayed for weeks that the neutrality issue would be settled in Washington so that "we could know where we stand."

The question of "Termites in America," was first touched on by Edna St. Vincent Millay, Pulitzer Prize poet, who asked why there should be anything un-neutral in repeal of the embargo. The topic was also discussed by Stanley High, writer and lecturer, and Mr. Hoover.

Deportation of resident aliens and abolition of both the German-American Bund and American Communist party had been advocated, when Mrs. Reid presented Mrs. Roosevelt and suggested that "no one who works hard enough will

ever grow old." Mrs. Roosevelt's subject was, "Humanistic Democracy—The American Ideal." In defining the American ideal, Mrs. Roosevelt declared that there should be an opportunity for the education of every child in the country in so far as the child was able to take that opportunity, but that we fell far short of that ideal.

She further asserted that every child should have the chance to come into the world at least healthy and strong, but that we fell short of that ideal because many mothers were without adequate food or medical care. Mrs. Roosevelt finally insisted that every one should have an opportunity to earn a living under decent working conditions, but that she was afraid that we fell short of that ideal.

Warns of Check on Freedom

Referring to the attacks that had been launched against the Communist, Nazi and other groups, Mrs. Roosevelt told members of the Forum that she believed they were not much surprised, adding:

"I think it important that we beware lest in suppressing them we suppress some of our own freedom. We should try to understand what are the objectives of democracy and work for these. We should take the trouble to defend the liberties we believe are inherent in democracy. It's not enough to say we believe in the Sermon on The Mount without trying to live up to it.

"We've heard a great deal about termites. I believe I agree with most of it. But we should make up our minds what we are going to do about it and not just use catch phrases."

Mrs. Roosevelt declared that true democracy did not exist in this country any more than it existed in other countries.

"I'm not afraid of meeting a Communist or talking with a Communist," Mrs. Roosevelt added. "I'm interested in working for democracy. I'm interested in working to make this land a country where we do not live under fear, but where we work to make life worth while."

Backs Dies Committee

Mr. High maintained that "insecticide is efficacious" for the body politics, that it was good political housekeeping to know how to use it, adding: "That's why I'm

for the Dies committee. He added: "Mr. Dies, himself, may not be quite the finest bloom from the hothouse of Texas politics. But he's certainly a handyman with the flit-gun."

Mr. O'Brian held that German spies and propaganda had failed in the end during the World War because of "one factor which they had underrated"—the "intelligence and integrity of the individual American."

"Placed in a new dilemma by the war now abroad, we can safely assume that our law-enforcing agents and the integrity and competence of the high officials of our government will amply protect our interests," he continued. "As private citizens, we can best help the situation by keeping a sane point of view, avoiding distrust and endeavoring to keep American public opinion alive to the underlying moral implications of the great struggle in Europe."

Mr. Hoover, who was presented by Mrs. Reid as one who had taken "glamor from the gangsters and given it to our G-men," declared that "foes within our gates, like termites, have sought by every scheming means to inculcate their alien ideas into our social order, fouling our cradle of liberty." After citing the possibilities of sabotage by such criminals, Mr. Hoover said:

"Every hour of the day must be devoted to the support of law and order. Dedication to this effort is true Americanism. You can help by being ever alert in order that any suspected act of sabotage, espionage or neutrality act violation, designed to undermine internal defense, can be called to the attention of the Federal Bureau of Investigation.

Vigilante Bands Decried

"This cooperation should be limited, however, to passing on to the proper officials all questionable facts or rumors which may come one's way. Bands of vigilantes, no matter in what manner they act, or what high ideals they proclaim, are un-American, unpatriotic, and subversive of the very things the nation now has the most need of preserving. The FBI is receiving complaints of espionage, sabotage, and neutrality violations at the rate of 214 daily."

Professor Sidney Hook of New York University emphasized that

the problem of dealing with the country's enemies becomes "acute when an anti-democratic minority invokes the protection of the Bill of Rights with the declared purpose, once it has power, of denying to others those very rights it now demands for itself."

Benjamin Stolberg, writer on labor problems, discussing "Communism in American Labor," insisted that Communists had "lost almost all their influence" in the American Federation of Labor and that they must contend with "a growing opposition" in the C. I. O.

Cites Labor's Stand

"It should be remembered," declared Matthew Woll, vice president of the American Federation of Labor, "that the American labor movement is the only movement in the world that has consistently and effectively repudiated both communism and socialism. Labor has been steadfast to the principles of democracy. It was labor that first sounded the note of warning against communism, fascism and Nazism."

After Elizabeth Knaust, former employe of the German Propaganda Ministry, who is seeking American citizenship, and C. J. Friedrich, Professor of Government at Harvard University, had addressed the forum, Mrs. William Brown Meloney, editor of This Week Magazine, was heard by the forum members in an address broadcast from the studio of Lowell Thomas, her neighbor in Pawling, N. Y.

Mrs. Meloney suggested that Hitler had come into power because his faith had inspired confidence and allegiance. She warned that "the American people are losing strength through lack of faith," adding:

"At this point in history we may be the final custodians of freedom. How dare we be afraid that freedom will die? The chief menace America need fear is our own indolence, our own carelessness in shielding this priceless gift. How dare we have less faith in freedom than the Nazis of Germany have in regimentation?"

The forum will continue in session this afternoon at 1:45 o'clock. Leopold, King of the Belgians, is scheduled to speak to the Forum over the radio tomorrow night.

October 25, 1939

---

563 FEDERAL AIDES PUT IN 'RED FRONT'

Protests Fly as Dies Committee Gives Out List From Files of the Peace League

By CHARLES W. HURD
Special to THE NEW YORK TIMES.

WASHINGTON, Oct. 25—Publication by the House Committee Investigating Un-American Activities today of 563 names of Federal employes purported to be members of the American League for Peace and Democracy, in conjunction with a statement labeling this a Commu-

nist "front" organization, aroused sharp controversy within and without Congress.

Representative Dies of Texas, chairman, won a majority of the committee to support of his effort to publish the names, but only over the protests of Democratic Representatives Voorhis of Texas and Dempsey of New Mexico.

A subsequent effort by Representative Thorkelson, Republican, of Montana, to insert the list in the Congressional Record by unanimous consent of the House was balked by Representative Coffee, Democrat, of Kansas, who precipitated a debate which became lively despite the fact that only about forty members were present.

The list was made available for the early editions of afternoon newspapers, but by this evening challenges were being made both by persons named in it, by the

league itself, and by members of the committee which issued it.

Many Denials Made

Many of those named said in response to inquiries that they were not and never had been members of the league. Others as definitely challenged the committee statement that the league either fostered or abetted communism.

And the Dies committee itself could not agree whether the list, which was among records obtained from the league's local headquarters, included members only or a combination of members and persons on the league's mailing list.

As prepared for issuance to reporters the committee's list was headed:

"American League for Peace and Democracy
"Washington, D. C.
"Membership and Mailing List."

However, a pencil was used to de-

lete the words "and mailing" from the heading before the list was distributed.

Representative Dempsey declared that he knew "that some of the persons on that list are not Communists" and described the committee's action in voting to release the list, action taken in his absence, as "most damnable."

Among names on the list were those of Oscar Chapman, Assistant Secretary of the Interior; Louis Bolch, member of the Maritime Labor Board; Edwin S. Smith, member of the National Labor Relations Board, and Mordecai Ezekiel of the Agricultural Adjustment Administration.

Other high-ranking members or former members of Federal departments and bureaus listed were Nathan Witt, executive secretary of the Labor Board; Lincoln Fairley, senior economist for the WPA; L.

C. Vass, former WPA statistical expert; Milton Cohen, former WPA attorney; Merrill G. Murray, director of the Analysis Division of the Social Security Board; Ward B. Freeman, coordinator engineer, and Foster Adams, chief research statistician for the REA; Willard W. Beatty of the office of Indian Affairs of the Interior Department; Robert Marshall, administrative officer of the Forest Service; Helen Wood, director, and George S. Wheeler, economist of the Wage-Hour Division of the Department of Labor, and Milton Kramer, principal attorney for the Railroad Retirement Board.

With the list the Dies committee issued the following statement:

"As a result of testimony which has been presented to our committee at intervals for more than a year it has been established conclusively that the American League for Peace and Democracy was organized and is controlled by the Communist party. More than a year ago the committee pointed this fact out in connection with the Washington branch of the American League for Peace and Democracy, which is largely composed of government employes.

Cites "Branding" of League

"On Jan. 3, 1939, the committee unanimously adopted a report in which the American League for Peace and Democracy was branded as a Communist front organization. With few exceptions, the government employes who are members of the local branch of the league continued their affiliation with the league in so far as this committee is informed. The committee, therefore, feels that these government employes have been fully apprised of the true nature and purpose of the league and have been given ample opportunity to sever their connections with it.

"From the files of the local branch of the League it is made clear that nuclei have been established in different government agencies.

"We feel that the country is entitled to this information since many of these employes hold key positions in the government. The committee has not hesitated to make public the names of private citizens who have been charged with Communist or Fascist activities and we can see no justification for making an exception in the case of government employes. In fact there is more reason for making public the names of government employes than in the case of private citizens."

Statement by Lamberton

A formal response for the league was issued by Harry C. Lamberton, chairman of the Washington branch, as follows:

"The action of the Dies Committee in publishing a list of members and individuals on the mailing list of the Washington branch of the American League, with their salaries, together with the utterly false statement that the American League is a Communist-front organization, is an outrageous violation of civil liberties. Certainly it can serve no possible public purpose.

"The Washington branch of the American League for Peace and Democracy has made it plain on numerous occasions, and has tried its best to get an opportunity to make plain to the Dies Committee, that it is not a Communist-front organization. The league is a democratically controlled organization, responsible only to its membership, and owes no allegiance either directly or indirectly to any other organization or individuals.

"The league some weeks ago furnished the Dies Committee with a detailed list of all of its activities since its organization in Washington. These activities can by no stretch of the imagination be characterized as un-American. On the contrary, they are aggressively American.

"When I testified Monday before the Dies Committee, I asked to be allowed to make a full presentation of our program. This opportunity was denied me. Instead, Chairman Dies has continued his tactics of attempting to vilify and intimidate government employes.

Lays "Effrontery" to Dies

"Most recently he has called upon members of the league to resign. In plain language, this means that Chairman Dies has the effrontery to ask government employes not to belong to organizations of which he personally disapproves."

Some members of the committee who joined in publishing the list were quick to say that they did not mean to label members of the league as Communists, these including Representatives Casey of Massachusetts and Starnes of Alabama, but these statements did not mollify Mr. Dempsey.

He argued his contentions at the end of a brief session of the committee this morning, arousing particularly Representative Mason, Republican, of Illinois, who had put the motion for publication of the names.

"I'm afraid," Mr. Dempsey said, "that, in doing this, we not only release the names of some members, but those who contributed to Spanish refugees and are not members at all."

"The action was taken and that settles it," Mr. Mason retorted.

Representative Voorhis said that he was "in accord" with Mr. Dempsey, but felt that he should abide by the wishes of the majority of the committee, to which Mr. Dempsey replied that, while he opposed Communists in the government, "I am not for smearing a lot of American citizens."

When Representative Thorkelson first tried to insert the list in the Congressional Record he was dissuaded by Representative Rich, Republican, of Pennsylvania, and on a subsequent attempt Mr. Coffee balked him.

Defends League Members

In the House debate, which immediately followed these moves, Representative Voorhis declared that he was "convinced" the league was "substantially dominated by Communists," but that he also knew "the vast majority of

the people who joined are no more Communists than the gentleman from Montana."

Representative Hook, Democrat, of Michigan, suggested that the government "get a real list of Communists instead of the phoney list we have now."

When Mr. Thorkelson finally was able to speak he caused another uproar by stating that he, after reading the remarks of Mrs. Franklin D. Roosevelt at The New York Herald Tribune Forum yesterday, he had decided that she "evidently thinks we shouldn't hunt members of these subversive organizations."

Mr. Coffee took the floor later to ask the House to "repudiate" the committee for "an unwarranted intrusion on American rights."

"The committee is guilty," he added, "of being engaged in un-American activities, the very thing it was appointed to smoke out."

Action Assailed by League

The action of the Dies committee in making public a list of governmental employes was assailed here yesterday in a statement from the national office of the American League for Peace and Democracy, 79 Fifth Avenue, as "a dictatorial attempt on the part of Mr. Dies to intimidate government employes and officials from the exercise of basic lawful freedom."

The statement declared it evident that Mr. Dies and his committee "plan to smash any and every organization which has supported the progressive principles of the New Deal Administration."

It added:

"Long after Mr. Dies's name has been forgotten the 600 names of the members of the American League for Peace and Democracy in Washington will stand as a testimonial to the courage of Americans who refuse to be intimidated by this twentieth century inquisition. No American is safe so long as the Dies committee is permitted to defy the American Bill of Rights. The American League for Peace and Democracy will continue to expose the enemies of peace and democracy in the United States."

October 26, 1939

PRESIDENT ASSAILS ISSUE OF 'RED LIST'

'Sordid Procedure,' He Says —Dies in Address Backs Publishing of Names

Special to THE NEW YORK TIMES.

WASHINGTON, Oct. 27—Publication by the House Committee to Investigate Un-American Activities of a list of purported members of the local branch of the American League for Peace and Democracy was declared today by President Roosevelt to be a "sordid procedure."

His description was given at a press conference in response to a

question as to his opinion on the action by the committee, which was taken on Wednesday on the ground that the league is a Communist "front."

The President replied that he was not sufficiently acquainted with the details to discuss this "sordid procedure," but when reporters asked if they might quote his description he said they might.

[Later in the day Representative Martin Dies, chairman of the committee, defended the action of the committee in an address given before the annual convention of the New York City Federation of Women's Clubs in New York. While refusing to enter into a controversy with the President, Mr. Dies said that "government employes who belong to organizations controlled by a foreign power ought to be exposed."]

The President's remark served principally, for the time being, to accent Republican efforts in the House to make a direct issue of the alleged Communist control of

the league in the political campaigns next year.

In carrying forward this program, Representatives Mason of Illinois and Hoffman of Michigan took the floor today to suggest courses of action to clear this alleged "Communist influence" from the government.

Mr. Mason, who started the movement to publish the league list, called on Federal employes to resign from the league or resign from government positions.

Hoffman Would Stop Pay

Mr. Hoffman introduced a bill to forbid payment of government salaries to persons "belonging to any organization which is affiliated with any organization which advocates the overthrow of the government by force, or which is controlled in whole or in part by any foreign government or any agency of any foreign government."

The speeches and the bill were predicated upon a complicated argument embodied yesterday by

Chairman Dies in a letter requesting the Attorney General to proceed against the league for alleged violation of American laws requiring the registration of agents of foreign governments.

Chairman Dies, Mr. Mason and other committee members maintain that evidence taken by the committee shows the league to have been an agent of the Communist party, although possibly an unwilling one as far as many members were concerned.

On the basis of that decision, the committee published the names of 563 persons who are or have been on the government payroll.

The list was made public as "a membership list." Many of the persons so named denied they were members. Others defended the league against the reports of Communist control.

Mr. Mason told the House, in which were about a score of members, that the President's description "undoubtedly is his opinion," but, he added:

"It is not my opinion, and neither do I believe it to be the opinion of the great majority of the nation.

"The publication of this list at my insistence is the culmination of a campaign of 'moral suasion' that the committee has conducted for more than a year for the purpose of securing:

"1. The resignation of the innocent government employes that are members of the local chapter, and

"2. The resignation from government service of those members who are not innocent, but who sympa-thize with and are willing to aid the Communists in their efforts to overthrow the very government they are working for, and if the resignations from the government service are not forthcoming, then to separate them forcibly from the public payroll."

Representative Mason indicated that forced dismissal could be accomplished by Congress only through legislation affecting appropriation bills, and this conclusion was believed to have prompted the introduction of Mr. Hoffman's bill.

Mr. Hoffman made it clear that his bill was aimed directly at the league, although it was drafted in general terms.

In the midst of this debate, Representative Dempsey of New Mexico, a committee member who fought to stop publication of the league list, placed in the Record a letter from a woman named in the list who, he said, had been subjected to demands for her resignation from a teaching position because of this publication.

The woman, Mr. Dempsey said, "had never even heard of the league."

The action of the committee was denounced by Mr. Dempsey as "assassinating character."

October 28, 1939

WARNING SOUNDED ON 'WITCH-HUNTING'

62 Americans Sign Protest Against Alleged 'Efforts to Create War Hysteria'

CITE THE COMMUNIST PARTY

Sixty-two Americans, including educators, scientists, writers and artists, endorsed a statement "In Defense of the Bill of Rights," made public yesterday by Dashiell Hammett, author. Declaring that the Bill of Rights must apply equally to all Americans, the statement protested against efforts "to create war hysteria and to incite witch hunts." It charged that certain forces want to deprive the Communist party of its minority rights as the first step toward the destruction of all civil liberties in America.

The endorsements were obtained by a "self-constituted" committee composed of Mr. Hammett, Gordon W. Allport, Professor of Psychology at Harvard; Professor Franz Boas, anthropologist; Theodore Dreiser, novelist, and Professor Harold C. Urey of Columbia, Nobel prize winner in chemistry.

Regarding the situation in this country as the committee sees it and the Communist party, the statement said:

"We recognize the following blunt facts: 1, that the Dies committee is talking openly of the suppression of dissident groups, and that in this it has secured the support of influential newspapers throughout the country; 2, that open incitement to vigilante activity against labor, against minority radical groups, against national and religious groups is increasing in this country; 3, that various discriminatory and repressive measures against the foreign-born have been passed by the House of Representatives and have become law in many States.

"We recognize particularly that serious efforts are being made to silence and suppress the Communist party.

"We have before us the example of many European countries where suppression of the Communist party was but a beginning, followed by a campaign against trade unions, cultural groups, Jews, Catholics, Masons, and ending with the destruction of all freedom. It is in our own interest, therefore, and in the interest of those rights for which America has struggled these many years that we raise our voices in solemn warning against denying to the Communists, or to any other minority group, the full freedom guaranteed by the Bill of Rights."

Among the signers were Professors Joseph Warren Beach of the University of Minnesota, Hadley Cantril, Princeton University; Irving Fisher, Yale University; Richard Foster Flint, Yale University; Robert S. Lynd, Columbia University; Kirtly F. Mather, Harvard University; Clyde R. Miller, Columbia University; Wesley C. Mitchell, president of the American Association for the Advancement of Science; O. H. Mowrer, Yale University; Gardner Murphy, Columbia University; Harold C. Urey, Columbia University, and J. Raymond Walsh of Hobart College.

December 14, 1939

RED MENACE CALLED GREATER THAN NAZISM

Voters Hold It Better Field for Inquiry, Survey Shows

The activities of Communists in the United States are considered a more important field of investigation than those of the Nazis, according to a survey of the American Institute of Public Opinion, of which Dr. George Gallup is director.

The announcement of the institute, made public yesterday, said:

"The survey shows that a majority of voters—over two-thirds of those polled with opinions—believe it is more important for the Dies committee to investigate Communist activities than Nazi activities at the present time. The growing apprehension over Soviet activity in the United States is signalized by the fact that less than a year ago the public felt Nazi efforts warranted more attention from the Dies committee than Communist efforts. Today, twice as many want the Dies group to turn the spotlight on American Communists as on American Nazis.

"The survey, which reached a cross-section of voters in all walks of life, put the following issue to those polled:

"'Which of the following do you consider more important for the Dies committee to investigate—Communist activities in this country, or Nazi activities in this country?'

"Those with opinions divided as follows:
Communist activities 70%
Nazi activities 30%

"Approximately one voter in every four familiar with the committee's work expressed no opinion.

"The Dies Committee is seeking an appropriation in the present session of Congress to continue its investigation of foreign 'isms.' With many New Deal leaders critical of the committee's work some observers believe a fight is in store when the appropriation comes up.

"Institute studies of public opinion show that the majority of voters are on the side of the committee, for 75 per cent of those with opinions in a recent poll said they favored continuing the committee another year."

January 5, 1940

DIES CLEARS FOUR ACCUSED AS REDS

He Defends Cagney, Bogart, March and Dunne After Hearing Movie Folk

SAN FRANCISCO, Aug. 20 (UP) —James Cagney, Humphrey Bogart and Fredric March, movie performers, and Phillip Dunne, screen writer, are not, and never have been, sympathetic with the Communist movement, Chairman Martin Dies of the House committee investigating un-American activities said today.

Mr. Dies made the statement a few minutes after concluding a hearing with Mr. Cagney, screen "tough guy," who flew here from Massachusetts by way of Los Angeles to deny charges previously filed with Mr. Dies.

Mr. Dies, who has been conducting secret hearings into alleged West Coast subversive activities, said that he would report his opinion to the full committee.

Although the Representative said he believed that Messrs. Bogart, Cagney, March and Dunne were patriotic Americans, he added there are "numerous actors and screen people, out of humane motives, who have made contributions to, and let their names be used by, certain organizations which the Dies committee has unanimously found to be organized under Communist leadership."

Mr. Cagney, supported by fifty World War veterans who rallied to his aid under leadership of William Wilson, past State commander of the Veterans of Foreign Wars, said that he had been questioned by Mr. Dies about various contributions he had made during recent years, "including money I gave to aid women and children in the Salinas lettuce strike and other San Joaquin Valley strikes."

Mr. Cagney said that he told Mr. Dies of contributions of money and services to the motion picture relief fund, the Hollywood Guild, the Scottsboro Boys' Defense Fund, community chest "and other organizations whose work I have never considered un-American."

Charges that Hollywood is permeated with communism are "so exaggerated they are ridiculous," Mr. Cagney declared in an interview after the one-hour hearing.

Mr. Dies did not say whether he would question other movie actors at his secret hearings in San Francisco.

August 21, 1940

ROOSEVELT WARNS DIES HIS METHODS ENDANGER JUSTICE

President Tells Chairman He Imperils Efforts to Prevent Subversive Acts

TASK UP TO EXECUTIVE

'Red Paper' Given Out by Committee Charges Communist Plan to Sabotage Defense

President Warns Dies

Special to THE NEW YORK TIMES.

WASHINGTON, Nov. 27 — President Roosevelt warned Martin Dies, chairman of the House Committee investigating un-American activities, today that his methods might "defeat the ends of justice."

In a telegram of reply to one Mr. Dies had sent him Monday from his home in Orange, Texas, Mr. Roosevelt cautioned him against infringing upon constitutional functions of the executive branch of the government by interfering with "administrative duties in relation to illegal activities." He emphasized that the President was solely responsible for executive action.

Mr. Dies had called on the government to make an end of Communist instigated strikes and urged closer coordination of government investigating bodies.

The reply was sent to the Representative last night after the White House had received an acceptance from him to an invitation to confer with the President on Friday on defining the bailiwicks of the various agencies fighting subversive influences.

The President's message supported the attitude of Attorney General Jackson. The latter, in a statement on Saturday, criticized what he said were attempts by the House committee to undermine public confidence in the Federal Bureau of Investigation by implying that the FBI was not active enough in suppressing subversive Communist activities.

Communists testifying before the Dies Committee have refused to answer questions regarding evidence, on the ground that facts were obtained illegally. Mr. Dies has insisted that he could not obtain secret papers by other means.

THE PRESIDENT'S MESSAGE

The President's telegram read as follows:

I have received your telegram from Orange, Texas.

You are correct in saying that there should be the closest harmony between your committee of the House and all administrative departments in the investigation of fifth-column activities in this country.

There can be no constitutional objection to the investigation of such activities and a report thereon and recommendations thereon by a committee of the House of Representatives.

It is, however, clear that the Constitution of the United States lodges the executive responsibility in the hands of the President and that, therefore, continuing administrative duties in relation to illegal activities lie in the executive branch of the government and not in the legislative branch.

As soon as this distinction is clearly recognized, there is no reason why there should not be complete harmony between your committee and the executive branch of the government.

Warns on Harm to Justice

I know that you will also see the point when I suggest that in the regular conduct of administrative work of this nature, carefully laid plans for the obtaining of further information, which may lead to the breaking up of subversive activities, may be severely handicapped or completely destroyed by premature disclosure of facts or of suppositions to the public, or by hasty seizure of evidence which might with a little more patience be obtained in a manner to be admissible in court, or by the giving of immunities to witnesses before Congressional committees as to matters revealed by their own testimony.

Such action may defeat the ends of justice.

If you agree, as I am sure you do, that this is a proper division of functions, any difficulties as to detail in applying these general principles can be worked out in conference between the executive department or departements affected and your committee.

The Attorney General will be glad to arrange for the holding of such conference at your convenience.

November 28, 1940

DIES CHARGES 1,124 IN FEDERAL POSTS HELP COMMUNISTS

He Sends Biddle a List Which Does Not Include Those on Defense Work

Special to THE NEW YORK TIMES.

WASHINGTON, Oct. 19—A list of 1,124 names of Federal employes alleged to be Communists or affiliates of subversive organizations was sent tonight to Attorney General Biddle by Representative Dies, chairman of the Committee on Un-American Activities.

In an accompanying letter Mr. Dies said that the list did not include persons in the new defense agencies, which would be submitted later. None of the names was made public.

The list was sent to Mr. Biddle on his request to the committee for information upon the membership of Federal workers in subversive organizations, or "such employes' advocacy of the overthrow of the government."

Mr. Dies reminded the Attorney General that two years ago the committee made public a list of 563 Federal employes who belonged to the American League for Peace and Democracy. This organization, Mr. Dies said, was one of "the front organizations" of the Communist party.

Fears "New Western Front"

The Representative also told Mr. Biddle that early last month he sent to President Roosevelt "a partial compilation of evidence bearing on the subversive activities and connections of various employes of the Office of Price Administration" and added that he assumed "that your department has received that evidence from the White House." Among those named in this connection was Leon Henderson, Price Administrator, who vigorously denied the accusation.

Mr. Dies said in his letter that "the very grave danger exists that our government, by its aid to Russia on the Eastern Front, has opened up for Stalin a new Western Front right here in the capital of America."

"I trust," he said, "that your investigation will be both thorough and prompt, and then followed up by appropriate action.

"The retention on the Federal payroll of several thousand persons who, to put the matter mildly, have strong leanings toward Moscow will confirm the widely held suspicion that a large and influential sector of official Washington is utilizing the national emergency for undermining the American system of democratic government."

Representative Dies submitted a breakdown of the 1,124 workers "in order that you may see at a glance how completely the Communists, their fellow travelers and their sympathizers have permeated the entire structure of the Federal Government."

It was as follows:

"Department of Agriculture, 207; Bituminous Coal Consumers Counsel, 1; Board of Tax Appeals, 2; Civil Service Commission, 15; Department of Commerce, 70; District of Columbia Government, 46; Employes Compensation Commission, 2; Executive Office of the President, 9; Federal Communications Commissiou, 2; Federal Loan Agency, 19; Federal Power Commission, 5; Federal Reserve System, 7; Federal Security Agency, 145; Federal Trade Commission, 1; Federal Works Agency, 72; General Accounting Office, 6.

"Government Printing Office, 11; Department of Interior, 45; Interstate Commerce Commission, 10; Department of Justice, 20; Department of Labor, 98; Library of Congress, 25; Maritime Commission, 1.

"Maritime Labor Board, 3; National Archives, 4; National Capitol Park and Planning Commission, 1; National Labor Relations Board, 49; National Resources Board, 1; Navy Department, 40; Postoffice Department, 2; Railroad Retirement Board, 27; Securities and Exchange Commission, 44; State Department, 12; Tariff Commission, 6; Treasury Department, 56; Veterans Administration, 15; War Department, 45."

"Without exception," Mr. Dies wrote, "the evidence upon which this list has been compiled is taken from original documents. These documents are available for the inspection and study of your agents, just as they have been available to all agents of the Federal Government for the past three years.

"By way of further comment upon the seriousness of the problem which faces your department in its investigation of those who have allowed themselves to become the tools of subversive organizations, may I point out that the accompanying list of more than 1,000 Federal Government employes is not composed solely of those who are employed at clerical jobs of a more or less routine nature.

"The list includes a large number of those who are in executive and policy-making positions. For example:

"Five receive salaries of $10,000 a year or more, eight of $9,000, seven of $8,000, twenty-four of $7,000, twenty-five of $6,000, fifty-five of $5,000, ninety-six of $4,000 and 153 of $3,000 a year.

"The evidence which I am submitting to you, Mr. Attorney General, indicates that there is a new influx of subversive elements into official Washington.

"It must, of course, be apparent to all that our present foreign policy of all-out aid to Russia is one that makes it very easy for Communists and their sympathizers to pose as the most ardent patriots."

October 20, 1941

FBI EXONERATES FEDERAL WORKERS ACCUSED BY DIES

Biddle Tells Congress Inquiry It Ordered Has Brought Only 36 Employe Dismissals

13 OTHERS 'DISCIPLINED'

Many 'Had Not Even Heard' of Groups Linked to Them— Texan Attacks Biddle

By C. P. TRUSSELL
Special to THE NEW YORK TIMES.

WASHINGTON, Sept. 2—Attorney General Biddle told Congress in a report today that thirty-six Federal employes had been discharged during the last year and that thirteen others had been disciplined for activities associated with alleged subversive organizations, but he declared that "sweeping charges of disloyalty in the Federal service" had not been substantiated in the $100,000 F. B. I. investigation ordered by Congress.

A large part of the complaints, 2,095 completed cases involving alleged connections with forty-seven organizations ruled to be subversive, were "clearly unfounded," and "never should have been submitted for investigation in the first instance," Mr. Biddle stated.

This, the Attorney General reported, was "conspicuously true" of a list of 1,121 names submitted at F. B. I. request last October by the Special House (Dies) Committee on Un-American Activities.

"Hundreds of employes, for example, have been alleged to be 'subversive' for no better reason than the appearance of their names on the mailing lists of certain organizations," Mr. Biddle said. "Upon investigation it develops that a large number had not even heard of the organizations with which they were said to be affiliated."

Dies Accuses Attorney General

Representative Dies, chairman of the House committee, in a statement issued later, called the Biddle report political and accused the Attorney General of favoring employment by the government of persons admittedly members of organizations which he himself had branded as subversive.

Of the 1,100 persons named by the Dies committee, Mr. Biddle re-

ported, only two had been dismissed from Federal service. Thirty-four dismissals, he said, had resulted from investigations of complaints coming from other sources.

In one other case on the Dies list, the Attorney General reported, administrative action other than dismissal, such as reprimand or transfer from national defense employment—it was not stated which in this instance—was taken. Twelve cases of "other disciplinary action," he said, had followed investigation of complaints from other quarters.

With his communication to Congress the Attorney General also submitted detailed reports from the F. B. I. and from the Interdepartmental Committee on Investigations which was established last April to advise and assist in the inquiry. Members of this committee are Edwin D. Dickinson, special assistant to the Attorney General; Francis C. Broen, solicitor of the Federal Deposit Insurance Corporation; Herbert Gaston, assistant secretary of the Treasury, and Wayne C. Taylor, Under-Secretary of Commerce. Until he resigned as Under-Secretary of the Interior in June, John J. Dempsey, a former member of the Dies Committee, was chairman of the interdepartmental body.

3,479 Cases Weighed in Inquiry

On complaints from all sources, these reports stated, the F. B. I. considered 3,479 cases up to last Aug. 22, the date of last check-up. After eliminating persons no longer employed by the Federal Government and others not coming within the scope of the Congressional order, 1,814 investigations were ordered and 1,494 completed, with reports transmitted to the heads of the employing departments and agencies, it was stated.

In each case, the reports said, the decision as to the taking of disciplinary or other action, or no action at all, rested wholly with the head of the employing agency or department involved.

In the cases on the Dies list, it was stated that 767 investigations had been ordered after eliminations had been made from the list of 1,121 for duplications and persons not falling within the inquiry's investigation (persons no longer employed by the government, civilian employes of the War and Navy Departments, etc.). By Aug. 22, the reports stated, 601 investigations had been completed and reports forwarded to the employing units.

69 Still Under Investigation

Of the rest of the cases, the reports stated, ninety-seven of those involved were found to be no longer employed by the government. Sixty-nine cases still are

under investigation. In 498 of the cases upon which F. B. I. reports were made to the employing agencies, it was decided, Mr. Biddle said, that there was no basis for further administrative action.

In submitting the 1,121 names, Mr. Biddle told the Congress, Representative Dies had asserted in an accompanying letter: "The evidence which I am submitting to you, Mr. Attorney General, indicates that there is a new influx of subversive elements into official Washington."

Stating that in 1,178 completed cases the employing department or agency heads had found no basis for action against the employes involved, Mr. Biddle reported:

"In view of the manner in which all investigations have been conducted and having regard for the attention which the departments and agencies have given to investigative reports, these figures [referring to all he had presented] may fairly be said to demonstrate that the government is not 'infiltrated' with Communists, Bundists or Fascists."

Dies Replies in Statement

Mr. Dies, in a statement issued through the committee, said:

"In plain English, Mr. Biddle's report means that he favors the employment of people in the government who are admittedly members of organizations such as the American League for Peace and Democracy, the German-American Bund, the Kyffhauser Bund, American Youth Congress, International Labor Defense, National Federation for Constitutional Liberties and others which even Mr. Biddle has pronounced subversive.

"I am sure that the great majority of the American people who are far more interested in winning the war than the November elections do not agree with Mr. Biddle. This is the only issue involved in the controversy."

Even more critical of the investigation which the Congress demanded than was the Attorney General, the Interdepartmental Committee on Investigations reported that the results achieved "have been utterly disproportionate to resources expended."

"The futility and harmful character of a broad personnel inquiry have been too amply demonstrated," it continued. "We respectfully urge that the project be reorganized promptly to exclude all but matters clearly pertinent to the vital problem of internal security."

Says Many Are Harassed

More than 2,000 government employes, the committee stated, had been and were being "needlessly" harassed by investigations which did not require disciplinary action, and a large staff of agents had been diverted from "more useful employment."

"It is now possible to report that the overwhelming majority of the investigated cases have been investigated because the subject's name appeared on the 'active indices' of one or more 'Communist

front organizations,' " it stated, adding:

"It is to be noted that there is no law forbidding membership or participation in a front organization. At most, such membership or participation is some evidence of affiliation with the subversive organizations for which the organization provides a front.

"It was disclosed in most instances that the employe's name had been used for solicitation for mailing-list purposes without his knowledge or consent or that employe's name had been handed down by an earlier front organization to a later front organization without his knowledge or consent, or that employe's name had been added to the lists because he had agreed to sponsor what appeared to him to be meritorious causes in no respect incompatible with his patriotic duties as a citizen, made nominal financial contributions or attended occasional meetings, or that employe had knowingly permitted his enthusiasm for what appeared to him to be worthy causes to override any concern he may have felt about being associated in such causes with known Communists, or, finally, that employe had been active in left-wing employe unions whose thinking had approximated closely the Communist-party line in certain important respects."

Anonymous Sources Stressed

Some of the disclosures noted, the interdepartmental committee reported, might be thought "indicative of irresponsibility ill becoming a government employe," but, it added:

"It is not often that such disclosures can be said to require dismissal from the Federal service.

"The nature and scope of the project have been such as to require a method of reporting information gathered from anonymous sources which is satisfactory neither to the employing departments or agencies, the employes investigated, nor the Federal Bureau of Investigation."

These situations, the committee conceded, might not be subject to criticisms as they developed during a trial period. It urged, however, that steps be taken to reorient the whole investigative program. It made these recommendations:

Investigations of Federal employes should be restricted hereafter to those instances in which there is substantial reasons for suspecting that there has been a violation of law requiring prosecution or dismissal from Federal service.

The Justice Department should exercise "the greatest care" in determining prima facie cases for investigation, upon the basis of preliminary investigation where necessary, to the end that all unnecessary embarrassment to employes and waste of investigative resources may be avoided.

Urges Comprehensive Inquiries

The investigations ordered should be made "comprehensive and thorough, unhampered by artificial classification of organization as within or without the scope of the investigative project," and that the identity and credibility of informants be sufficiently reported to enable employing departments or agencies to take such prompt and decisive action as internal security may require in each instance.

The employing departments and agencies should be encouraged to provide adequate and fair procedures for the disposition of individual cases, including opportunity to be heard in all cases in which disciplinary action may be recommended.

A permanent interdepartmental board or committee should be established to provide advisory review for individual cases upon request of either the employing department or agency or the employes.

Noting that the Congressional directive for the investigation neither defined "subversive organizations" nor indicated standards to be applied, Attorney General Biddle reported, the investigation turned to authority in judicial decisions, administrative rulings and the legislative history for classifying the Communist party and its affiliates and the German-American Bund as "subversive organizations within legislative intent."

"Subversive" Groups Put at 47

Much difficulty, Mr. Biddle stated, was encountered in determining procedure with respect to various "front" organizations. Finally, however, the reports brought out, the list of "subversive" organizations was increased to forty-seven as the investigation proceeded. The reports did not list these organizations, but designated twelve as Communist or Communist-front organizations, two as American Fascist organizations, eight as Nazi organizations, four as Italian Fascist organizations and twenty-one as Japanese organizations.

Of the 3,479 cases considered, the FBI report brought out 2,290 government employes were alleged to have been affiliated with Communist organizations or "fronts," 968 with German organizations, eleven with Italian groups, thirteen with Japanese organizations, and 149 with unclassified un-American bodies.

Upon completion of an investigator's report in each case handled by the FBI, the summation to Congress stated, the employe involved was invited to appear for an interview at an office of the FBI.

"At this interview," the explanation continued, "the bureau agent in charge informed the employe of the purpose of the investigation, stated further that questions would be based upon information received by the investigator, and advised the employe that he might answer questions if he desired and further that he would be given an opportunity to make whatever statement he might like to have incorporated in the record.

"It was made clear in each instance that the interview was primarily for the employe's benefit and that it was not to be regarded as a hearing. After the conclusion of the interview he was given an opportunity to read, correct and sign the transcript."

All statements, it was emphasized, were made under oath.

September 3, 1942

NAMES COMMITTEE ON SUBVERSION

President Creates Group of 5 Within Department of Justice to Consider Complaints

WILL ADVISE AGENCIES

Order Applies Only to Allegations Made Against Employes of the Executive Branch

Special to THE NEW YORK TIMES.

WASHINGTON, Feb. 6—An interdepartmental committee of five members to serve as an advisory and coordinating agency in all matters pertaining to the investigation and disposition of complaints of subversive activity on the part of employes of the executive branch of the government was established within the Department of Justice by President Roosevelt today by an executive order.

The order followed assertions made on the floor of the House on Monday by Representative Dies, chairman of the House Committee on Un-American Activities, that there were numerous government employes, several of whom he named, who were "irresponsible, unrepresentative, crackpot and radical bureaucrats," or who had Communist affiliations.

Whether the establishment of the committee was connected with the allegations of Mr. Dies was not revealed. The executive order was given out by the White House without comment.

The committee is composed of Herbert E. Gaston, Assistant Secretary of the Treasury in charge of customs, narcotics and the Secret Service; Francis C. Brown, solicitor of the Federal Deposit Insurance Corporation and special counsel to the Alien Property Custodian; Oscar L. Chapman, Assistant Secretary of the Interior, and John Q. Canno Jr., legal adviser of the Civil Service Commission.

The committee is not empowered to take action concerning the War or Navy Departments, unless requested to do so by them. It is directed to originate measures looking to a fair and prompt disposition of complaints, consider complaints upon request of the Department of Justice and recommend to that department "appropriate policies to govern the investigation of complaints."

The committee will receive all reports made by the FBI on complaints and advise government departments and agencies concerning the procedures for determining action on them; review cases upon its own initiative and transmit its recommendations to the employing department or agency and give advisory opinions to departments or agencies after having been requested by them to review a record.

The executive order directs departments and agencies to refer complaints to the F. B. I. for information and investigation. The departments and agencies also are required to report the procedures followed and action taken on all cases referred to them by the committee. In turn, the committee must report to the F. B. I. the action taken by the employing agency.

Attorney General Biddle reported to Congress last September that thirty-six Federal employes had been discharged the previous year and thirteen others had been disciplined for activities associated with alleged subversive organizations but that "sweeping charges of disloyalty in the Federal service" had not been substantiated.

Of those discharged the previous year, only two had been on a list of 1,100 names furnished by the Dies committee, Mr. Biddle said.

February 7, 1943

Dies Predicts End Of His Committee

By The United Press.

JASPER, Texas, May 22—Representative Martin Dies, informed of the Moscow action to dissolve the Communist International, said tonight the move would probably result in the dissolution of his Congressional Committee to Investigate Un-American Activities.

Mr. Dies said he could not estimate when his committee would conclude its work, but added:

"I believe it will enable us to wind up our work at an early date so that we can make a final report to the House."

The action "makes it unnecessary to enact legislation which we have recommended outlawing the (American) Communist party," he said, adding: "That is exactly what I have been advocating for five years."

May 23, 1943

Communists Disband Party in U.S.; Back Roosevelt for Fourth Term

The Communist party of the United States, after an embattled quarter century on the political scene, dissolved itself yesterday as a political party and was immediately reconstituted as a non-party organization with a political mission.

The mission, according to Earl Browder, general secretary, will be to work with the majority of the American people for "a more democratic and progressive America" both during and after the winning of the war and for the establishment of lasting peace. To this end, said Mr. Browder in his keynote speech at the Communists' national convention here, the group was willing to shelve its aim of making the United States a socialist nation "because there does not exist now in our country an actual or potential majority support for such a program."

The four-day convention, attended by 402 delegates and alternates from forty-four States, is being held at the Riverside Plaza Hotel, 253 West Seventy-third Street.

The transition from party to association occurred at 11 A. M. when, to the cheers of several hundred spectators, the delegates held aloft their blue credential cards in support of Mr. Browder's resolution to disband the party. The session, by the same act, was transformed into an organizing convention for the "new" group that will take the name Communist Political Association.

Mr. Browder, the party's Presidential candidate in 1936 and 1940, urged the re-election of President Roosevelt. The convention later adopted a resolution calling for "the continuance of Roosevelt's leadership, and the election of a victory Congress."

The wording of the resolution and of the association's constitution, which is to be adopted today, made it clear that the Communists, while not putting a national ticket into the field under the hammer and sickle emblem—or its hammer and hoe variant—intend to campaign actively in national and local elections. Article 1 of the new constitution provides for "organized participation in the political life of the country."

The change in the Communist organization's structure came on Mr. Browder's fifty-third birthday and the delegates stood and sang "Happy Birthday to You." They also sang "We Shall Not Be Moved."

May 21, 1944

LEADERS AT COMMUNIST CONVENTION HERE

William Z. Foster, national chairman; Earl Browder, general secretary, and Robert Minor, national committeeman, at yesterday's session in the Riverside Plaza Hotel.
The New York Times

WORLD WAR II

WASHINGTON ALERT TO 'FIFTH COLUMN'

White House and the Congress Sound a Warning Against Sabotage and Treason

NEW STRENGTH FOR FBI

By FRANK L. KLUCKHOHN

WASHINGTON, June 1—Defense of any country these days must include protection against treason, sabotage and subversive foreign propaganda. The United States recognizes this and is preparing to suppress "Fifth Column" activities.

It is really only in recent weeks that full recognition of the part a "Fifth Column" can play has dawned in Washington. President Roosevelt himself went so far as to indicate that, with all its failings, the Dies Committee on Un-American Activities has provided useful information on "Fifth Column" activities.

In Washington it is said that the "Fifth Column" includes not only organized elements, like the Communists and the Nazis, which criticize the established political and economic system of this country and say a new one is needed, but those which put partisan and personal considerations above those of national well-being and safety.

It is believed in Washington, however, that the chief danger of a blow from within comes from the Nazis and the Communists, both of which are well organized and vocal.

Dies Committee Helps

Considerable evidence has been adduced by the Dies committee to show that many Communist leaders in this country have acted as agents of Moscow; that they have attempted, with a degree of success, to influence opinion in this country on world affairs for the benefit of foreign governments.

The Nazi leaders, including Fritz Kuhn, now in Sing Sing Prison, have attempted to hide behind the laws of democracy and claim that they and their organizations are "purely American," but they make patent a sympathy for the Hitler system and ideology.

Official Washington is not inclined to minimize the "Fifth Column" danger, but neither is it disposed to become hysterical about it. It is felt that national recognition of the danger and unity of purpose and belief in our system are the most efficient protection.

The Administration trusts the laborer and expects him to beware of those who would sabotage their country; it expects the more reactionary among the men of wealth to realize that Hitlerism, like Stalinism, destroys their class. It believes that Americans as a whole, with our system of universal education, will know what is fundamentally Americanism and what isn't, and uphold the former.

Last September the President assigned to the Federal Bureau of Investigation, under J. Edgar Hoover, the task of dealing with all espionage, sabotage and "Fifth Column" activities in the United States.

More G-Men

Additional G-men to the number of 150 were added to the FBI force of 763 agents for the exclusive purpose of suppressing the "fifth column," and 100 more are to be added July 1. Whereas only $1,455,000 in addition to regular appropriations was given to Mr. Hoover's agency for this extra work during the present fiscal year, the special sum of $2,488,000 was voted for next year by Congress.

In all, an estimated force of 2,000 to 2,500 Federal agents of various departments is said to form the "sixth column" combating the activities of the "fifth." The principal Federal agencies working closely with the FBI on the problem are the Army and Navy Intelligences and their volunteer reserves (the exact number of these agents has not been revealed), the Secret Service, with its 375 employes, and the Immigration Service.

The "extra" and regular FBI

force is supposed to see that factories producing essential war materials are satisfactorily manned and protected, to discover plots against the safety of the States and to forestall or arrest espionage agents of foreign powers.

The FBI has compiled a list of those regarded as potential or active enemies of the State from such varying sources as the Immigration Service, the Army and the Navy, and the Dies committee, information which is carefully scrutinized, judged and, where necessary, investigated. The FBI also checks the fingerprints of each man enlisting in the Army, Navy and Marine Corps.

Must Do Other Work

It must be noted, however, that the FBI says that it is employing most of its regular men on routine tasks and not in combating the "fifth column." In some quarters the number of official agents fighting the hidden danger as a full-time job is considered inadequate.

There are already on the statute books numerous laws dealing with seditious conspiracy, espionage and sabotage and these give the FBI considerable legal power. The recent transfer of the Immigration Service from the Labor to the Justice Department, which houses the FBI, should assist the G-Men, it is felt, although the move was not made primarily for defense purposes.

New laws intended to plug the gaps in existing legislation for dealing with "Fifth Column" activities are in the process of being formulated.

The most far-reaching new measure, requiring the registration and finger-printing of aliens, already has passed the House and is expected to be approved by the Senate. It would enable the government to keep a check on aliens. It is estimated that there are

G-MAN

Times Wide World

J. Edgar Hoover's staff has been enlarged to fight "Fifth Column" activities in this country.

3,500,000 to 4,000,000 aliens in the United States, and all those who failed to comply with the projected law would be deported. Aliens would even be required to inform the government of a change of address.

Congress has been asked by Robert H. Jackson, the Attorney General, to enact legislation requiring the registration of all types of firearms in this country. The Attorney General explained that such legislation as he asked would keep subversive groups from arming themselves.

Although numerous other measures have been introduced, and one Representative has even suggested that aliens be sent to concentration camps, it is unlikely that Congress will act upon them.

Representative Celler of New York has introduced a bill which, in the opinion of observers, has an outside chance of passage. It would permit the FBI to tap wires in counter-espionage work.

The Senate passed the La Follette Civil Liberties Bill which contains a prohibition against employment by the government of any Communists or Nazis, but, because of widespread opposition to other provisions of the measure, the bill is expected to have extremely rough sledding in the House.

The relief bill prohibits WPA jobs for Nazis or Communists but leaves it to the administrator to determine who these are.

Query Being Prepared

The Civil Service is preparing to include a query in sworn applications for employment as to whether the Federal job applicant is "a member of any political party or organization which advocates the overthrow of our constitutional form of government in the United States."

Critics assert that altogether too small a force is being employed to combat the "Fifth Column" in this country and that steps being taken against it are too mild. On the other hand, there are complaints of infringement of legal rights.

It is not only in this country that

ATTORNEY GENERAL

Times Wide World

Robert H. Jackson is asking for registration of all firearms.

the government is keeping watch. The increasing activity of Nazi and Communist "fifth column" elements in Brazil, Uruguay, Mexico and other parts of Latin America is carefully observed by Washington, which has its own attachés and information agents in all countries to the south.

In order to cooperate with the armies of Latin-American countries in their preparations to meet any situation that may develop, including the danger from the "fifth column," United States military missions are maintained in Brazil, Argentina, Guatemala, Colombia, Nicaragua and Chile. The Navy maintains missions in Brazil and Colombia and "advisers" in Argentina and Peru.

June 2, 1940

ROOSEVELT SIGNS BILL TO LIST ALIENS

President Says It Carries No Stigma for the Loyal and Aims to Protect Nation

POST FOR OWEN D. YOUNG

Special to The New York Times.

WASHINGTON, June 29—The first peace-time requirement that all aliens in the United States submit to registration and finger-printing became law today when President Roosevelt signed the legisla-

tion to that effect passed by Congress just before the week's recess for the Republican convention at Philadelphia.

Meanwhile the White House made known that President Roosevelt had enlisted the services of Owen D. Young to aid in coordinating the programs of the National Youth Administration and Civilian Conservation Corps for training technicians for second-line defense.

Mr. Young, former chairman of the board of the General Electric Company, will bring his widely recognized organizing ability into play to assist Sidney Hillman, C. I. O. official, who is in charge of youth training for the Defense Advisory Commission. Stephen Early, secretary to the President, said that Mr. Young would serve in a temporary capacity on a dollar-a-year basis.

President Explains Law

President Roosevelt issued a statement explaining the extent of the

new statute regarding aliens which read as follows:

"The Alien Registration Act of 1940, which I have just signed, should be interpreted and administered as a program designed not only for the protection of the country but also for the protection of the loyal aliens who are its guests. The registration and identification of approximately three and one-half million aliens who are now within our borders does not carry with it any stigma or implication of hostility toward those two, while they may not be citizens, are loyal to this country and its institutions.

"Most of the aliens in this country are people who came here because they believed and had faith in the principles of American democracy, and they are entitled to and must receive full protection of the law. It is of the utmost importance to the security of the country that the program of alien control shall be carried out with a high sense of responsibility. It would be unfortunate if, in the course of this regulative program,

any loyal aliens were subjected to harassment.

Asks For Cooperation

"The only effective system of control over aliens in this country must come from the Federal Government alone. This is as true from a practical point of view as it is from a legal and constitutional point of view. Since Congress, by the act, has attempted to provide a single and uniform method of handling this difficult problem of alien registration in this country, it seems to me that attempts by the States or communities to deal with the problem individually will result in undesirable confusion and duplication.

"I ask that citizens and non-citizens alike cooperate with a full sense of the responsibilities involved so that we may accomplish this task of registration smoothly, quickly and in a friendly manner, our aim being to preserve and build up the loyalty and confidence of those aliens within our borders who desire to be faithful to its principles. With those aliens who are disloyal and are bent on harm to the country, the government, through its law enforcement agencies, can and will deal vigorously."

Ban on Reds and Bund Urged

Mr. Roosevelt, by executive order, had previously transferred the Bureau of Immigration and Naturalization from the Labor Department to the Justice Department. This change provoked considerable controversy in Congress, but it was approved. The Congressional opponents feared that the work of supervising aliens would be confided to J. Edgar Hoover and the Federal Bureau of Investigation, but this was denied by Attorney General Jackson and the President.

At the F. B. I.'s graduating exercises today William Green, president of the American Federation of Labor, called upon Congress to outlaw the Communist party and the German-American Bund on the ground that these organizations engage in "tratorous activities" contrary to the interests of the nation's safety and defense.

Mr. Green said that the United States was "inviting danger" in permitting such organizations to operate "openly or secretly." He held it is self-evident that "the various brands of totalitarianism which have engulfed Continental Europe — whether their label be Nazi, Communist or Fascist—are hostile to America and to everything which Americans hold dear."

In addition to President Roosevelt's statement on signing the Alien Registration Statute, the Administration gave further indication of its attitude toward the problem of aliens and spies in a speech made by Attorney General Jackson before the New York State Bar Association at Saranac Lake tonight.

June 30, 1940

ALIEN ORDER BILL SIGNED

New Law Requires Revolutionary Organizations to Register

WASHINGTON, Oct. 18 (UP)— President Roosevelt signed legislation tonight requiring foreign controlled organizations and groups advocating the overthrow of government by force to register with the Department of Justice.

The measure, sponsored by Representative Voorhis of California, met little opposition in either house of Congress. The State and Justice Departments aided in its preparation. Violators are subject to a fine of $10,000, or imprisonment of five years or both. Persons filing false statements may be fined $2,000 and imprisoned for five years.

While pledging rigid enforcement of the law, Justice Department officials tonight declined to say what organizations they expect it to reach.

Information on several organizations, compiled by the Dies Committee on un-American activities, by the labor and other Federal departments, is available to justice officials.

October 19, 1940

MICHIGAN LISTS 10,000 AS FIFTH COLUMNISTS

New Police Unit Keeps Check on Possible Saboteurs

Special to THE NEW YORK TIMES.

DETROIT, Feb. 7—Nearly 10,000 potential fifth columnists have been identified and placed under surveillance, State police revealed today.

Cataloguing of 9,374 suspects has been done in the first five months of work by a new division set up "to combat subversive activity," Commissioner Oscar G. Olander said. "The list is growing every day," he added.

Files on suspected fifth columnists are being formed as a part of the State's effort to cooperate in the national defense program. The list includes not only the names and addresses of potential fifth columnists but the manner in which they might seek to commit sabotage in time of war, Commissioner Olander said.

Mr. Olander said that the new division, organized in August, had men at each State police post and that an interchange of information in anti-espionage work had been effected between the State police and the Royal Canadian Mounted Police along 650 miles of the border.

Suspects are catalogued by name and by county. The new division has listed all vital places to be protected in an emergency, including public utilities, water supplies, bridge tunnels and medical facilities, he added.

"The investigation has extended to 115 amateur radio operators in the State who can be enlisted for emergency communication service," Mr. Olander said.

He said that 186 meeting places for supects were under surveillance and 85 cases of suspected sabotage were investigated at the request of Federal authorities.

The State police have checked 1,095 industrial plants for alien workers or workers of doubtful loyalty, systems of plant production and similar data, he said.

February 8, 1941

DEFERS JAPANESE INQUIRY

Dies Shelves Spy Investigation at Request of Roosevelt

WASHINGTON, Sept. 21 (U.P.)— Chairman Martin Dies of the House committee investigating un-American activities, said last night that President Roosevelt had asked him to defer an investigation of Japanese espionage on the West Coast and that he would comply.

Presumably the request was made because the inquiry might affect adversely the progress of Japanese - American diplomatic conversations, Mr. Dies said. The chairman said that the committee would "defer to the Administration's wishes."

Mr. Dies said that the inquiry would have revealed many sensational facts, and one committee member described the potential Japanese espionage organization in America as "greater than the Germans ever dreamed of having in the Low Countries." He said that it would be a "tremendous force to reckon with in event of war."

This committee member said that the situation in the San Francisco area was "critical," with the Mare Island Navy Yard and many industrial establishments grouped in a relatively small area which would be sabotaged effectively.

September 22, 1941

ALIEN CAMPS MADE ENCLOSED PRISONS

Fences, Towers, Floodlights, Alarm Systems Installed at Three Detention Forts

24-HOUR ARMED PATROL

WASHINGTON, Jan. 11 (AP)— Wartime precautions have changed the Immigration Service's three detention camps into virtual prisons, with protective and alarm systems regarded as foolproof, an official disclosed today.

Prior to the war the camps at Fort Lincoln, N. D., and Fort Missoula, Mont., were fenced in and patrolled by men carrying sidearms. The camp at Fort Stanton, N. M., where 410 members of the Columbus crew are held, was not even fenced.

The coming of war with the Axis changed that. Here is the new picture:

Fort Stanton has been enclosed.

All three camps are patrolled twenty-four hours daily by automobile and horse-mounted guards, all armed with submachine guns and gas guns. The fences are floodlighted at night and twenty-four watches are maintained in towers, the watchers armed with high-power rifles.

The guard forces have police dogs trained by the Federal Bureau of Prisons in patrol, attack and trailing.

An alarm-blockade system originally established at Fort Missoula has been set up at the other camps. Upon report of an escape, every road, railway and important trail within 150 miles can be blockaded almost instantly through a pre-arranged program of warnings.

Fort Missoula now has 1,100 Italians and 660 Japanese. Fort Lincoln has 422 Germans.

Conditions inside the three camps have not changed since the freezing of foreign funds last Summer threw the burden of upkeep on this government. Prior to that the aliens got extra funds from their embassies. Now they have the same diet and recreational routine as Federal prisoners.

January 12, 1942

ORDERS ALIENS OUT OF ZONES ON COAST

Biddle Acts on Request of War Department Against Japanese, Germans and Italians

FIRST STEP IN CALIFORNIA

Special to THE NEW YORK TIMES.

WASHINGTON, Jan. 29—All Japanese, German and Italian alien enemies are being ousted from vital areas in San Francisco and Los Angeles, on the recommendation of the War Department, Attorney General Biddle said today.

The official announcement, which said that all enemy aliens must be out of the coast industrial cities by Feb. 24, indicated that this was just the beginning of a movement to remove all potential fifth columnists from a wide area.

In addition to these two main areas, the Attorney General said that an additional twenty-seven safety regions will be designated tomorrow, and it is understood that eventually enemy aliens will be restricted in their movements in other parts of the country.

Mr. Biddle said that he did not know how many aliens would be affected by the order, but added that most of those in the prohibited San Francisco area were employed in industries, while most of those in Los Angeles were classified as residents.

Action in Other Areas

In advising Mr. Biddle that action should be taken in these areas at once the War Department said that further areas in other States also would be designated. These would make up the Western defense command and take in parts of Oregon, Washington, Montana, Idaho, Utah and Nevada.

This is only one of several important moves to guard the nation's security from possible internal attack. Directly after the Japanese bombing of Pearl Harbor most suspicious enemy aliens were taken into custody. Subsequently all other enemy aliens were ordered to register with the police, and in certain areas they were required to hand over to the police all firearms and cameras.

The prohibited San Francisco area, designated as Area No. 19 by the War Department, includes a part of a waterfront and in general the embarcadero from Pier 46 to Pier 14, and the entire waterfront from China Basin to the Presidio reservation boundary line.

Area No. 33 in Los Angeles is a rectangle which includes the municipal airport and is bounded by the shoreline on the west, Rosecrans Avenue on the south, Western Avenue on the east, and Manchester Avenue on the north.

January 30, 1942

DIES GROUP FAVORS SHIFTING JAPANESE

Would Move All on West Coast 500 Miles or More Inland and Intern Them

WASHINGTON, Feb. 8 (AP)—The House Committee on Un-American Activities has decided tentatively to propose that all Japanese in Pacific Coast States be removed at least 500 miles inland and interned.

This recommendation is contained in a first draft of a 1,000-page report which the committee has prepared on subversive Japanese activities. The report, which is expected to be made public within two weeks, is still subject to revision, but in its present form it states:

"The United States has been and still is lax, tolerant and soft toward the Japanese who have violated American hospitality.

"Shinto temples still operate, propaganda outlets still disseminate propaganda material, and Japanese, both alien and American citizens, still spy for the Japanese Government—all constituting an ever-dangerous menace to the peace and security of the people and of the defense industries, particularly on the Pacific coast."

Information in the committee's possession, said Representative Dies of Texas, chairman of the committee, indicates that recent Department of Justice moves designed to close Pacific areas to Japanese have not been fully effective and that the Japanese have taken advantage of "protection of civil rights" to promote systematic espionage such as prepared the way for the attack on Pearl Harbor Dec. 7.

The proposed report says that the "focal point" of the Japanese fifth column in the United States is in Southern California, and adds:

"The Japanese Government's use of its fifth column in the Philippines and in Hawaii is a sample of what the United States can expect from the Japanese fifth column located on our Pacific Coast when the time comes for that fifth column to strike. That time will be decided by the Japanese High Command."

February 9, 1942

WEST COAST WIDENS MARTIAL LAW CALL

California's Attorney General Goes on Record for Step in Modified Form

DEMAND BY LOS ANGELES

FBI Raids Net 38 Japanese, Guns, Radios, Ammunition and Signal Devices

By LAWRENCE E. DAVIES
Special to THE NEW YORK TIMES.

SAN FRANCISCO, Feb. 11—Calls for a solution of the West Coast's Japanese problem through a declaration of martial law grew in volume today, with Earl Warren, California's Attorney General, going on record in favor of this step, at least in a modified form.

As an aftermath of raids on Japanese colonies in widely separated sections of the Coast, in which were seized large quantities of contraband material such as fifth columnists might find useful, both Federal and State officials met here with Lieut. Gen. John L. DeWitt, head of the Western Defense Command, to discuss the problem of measures against sabotage and espionage.

Mayor Fletcher Bowron of Los Angeles, who has been urging the evacuation of all Japanese—citizens and aliens alike—from the Coast's combat zone, outlined for General Dewitt what he described as "the reaction of a big majority of the people of Los Angeles."

"Positive Safety" Is Assured

The Mayor was advised, according to Thomas C. Clark, coordinator of enemy alien control for the Far West, that the War Department and the Department of Justice would take all steps necessary "to bring positive safety to the West Coast."

Mayor Bowron said he hoped that the situation could be handled "without martial law." His views, as expressed earlier, were that American-born Japanese presented a more serious problem than the aliens, and that they should be moved inland to do useful farm work. Whether this could be achieved without a Presidential proclamation was another matter.

Attorney General Warren, presenting what he termed his personal opinion and not necessarily that of the conferees, declared that "in view of the circumstances the problem becomes a military problem rather than one in civil government."

While General DeWitt and the others were in session here the Los Angeles County Civil Defense Council was preparing a resolution to ask that the Army declare martial law and remove enemy aliens from coastal areas to inland concentration camps. There they would be permitted to engage in "productive agricultural labor."

Frame Internment Resolution

A council subcommittee urged further that "all native-born citizens of Japanese descent not selected for Army service shall likewise, with their dependents, be invited to take residence and occupation in such internment areas." This was along the line of Mayor Bowron's suggestion earlier in the week.

By tonight, at the end of two days of raids by Federal agents and police in the Monterey Bay region, thirty-eight Japanese had been rounded up and brought to this city. Agents of the FBI listed, as their "best catch," Koyo Tamanaka, a so-called Buddhist priest, who was arrested in a temple at Salinas with two of his colleagues. They said he formerly was a minor police official in Tokyo.

The Monterey Bay raids, according to the FBI office here, yielded 60,839 rounds of rifle ammunition, 18,907 rounds of shotgun ammunition, thirty-one shotguns, rifles and revolvers, eighty-four knives, a dozen binoculars, twelve cameras, nine radio-receiving sets, and more than a score of assorted signal devices and other articles, part from the stock of a sporting goods store operated by an alien Japanese.

In this city Joseph P. DiMaggio, Sr., father of three baseball stars, all of whom are American citizens, took out his first citizenship papers the day, along with Mrs. DiMaggio. They live, however, outside the "prohibited" fishermen's wharf area, so that Attorney General Biddle's recent order will not require them to move.

John Majus, 36 years old, a ship's carpenter, who was arrested yesterday by the FBI on a sabotage charge, pleaded guilty and was held in Oakland for the grand jury. Majus was accused of sawing a steering rod on the freighter Calmar while it was in dock at Alameda.

February 12, 1942

ARMY GETS POWER TO MOVE CITIZENS OR ALIENS INLAND

President's Order Is Designed Primarily to Allow Round-Up of West Coast Japanese

---

OFFICERS CAN NAME AREAS

Habeas Corpus Is Still a Right, but, Says Biddle, Courts Can See Military Urgency

---

By LEWIS WOOD
Special to THE NEW YORK TIMES.

WASHINGTON, Feb. 20—President Roosevelt in a drastic move authorized the Secretary of War today to eject any or all citizens or aliens from designated military control areas.

Primarily aimed at Japanese residents on the Pacific Coast, the order could assure a mass evacuation from the Western seaboard to inland States, and could be applied as well to regions all over the country.

Officials intimated, however, that even in the West Coast situation there would be no mass removals at present, and said that the order would not be applied elsewhere than on the Pacific Coast, nor at this time to citizens of German or Italian descent.

Widest discretion was granted by the Executive order to military commanders to prescribe military areas from which "any or all persons" could be excluded. As yet no areas have been announced, but the Army, if it chose, could designate the entire State of California, seat of airplane and other key national defense industries. In that State 60,000 Japanese -Americans reside, in addition to about 38,000 Japanese aliens.

The order was issued under the broad war powers of President Roosevelt, Attorney General Biddle announced, and at the request of Secretary Stimson, after joint conferences between the War and Justice Departments.

Rigorous' as was the Executive order, Mr. Biddle denied that it amounted to martial law.

"It is not identical with martial law," the Attorney General said. "Martial law means the abolition of civil rights, and here no civil processes, including the right to seek a writ of habeas corpus, have been suspended.

"But," he added instantly, "in my judgment the courts would say 'This is a military matter and we will not go behind it.'"

The order followed a mounting flood of protests from the West Coast against the presence there of second-generation Japanese, a fact considered by the Far Westerners to be dangerous to the national safety.

Until today the government control of persons of Japanese and other Axis descent was confined to those of alien status. It was exercised by the Department of Justice. The inclusion of citizens, however, throws control of the entire situation to the Army, which will determine which persons must move and will evacuate all who do not leave voluntarily.

Other Agencies Will Help

The order authorizes the Secretary of War to provide transportation, food, shelter and other accommodations for ejected persons, and the military commanders will lay down rules for those permitted to remain.

Every Federal agency of any character is directed to assist in furnishing medical aid, hospitalization, food, clothing, transportation and other necessaries. After the evacuation is completed, enterprises such as the Department of Agriculture, Social Security and Farm Security will assist in finding jobs or settling the individuals on other lands.

As yet no special areas have been announced, but in various instances the zones will duplicate those laid down by the Department of Justice as "barred" or "restricted" to aliens. These, for the most part, centered around industrial plants, water works, hydroelectric plants and other vital points.

Mr. Biddle, when asked for a precedent for the Executive order pointed out that President Wilson said during the World War that "nobody could move in the air without a permit," and that even before the present war President Roosevelt limited the movements of American citizens on the sea. These precedents, Mr. Biddle asserted, could be used when it is sought to control the movements of citizens on land.

In view of the comparatively limited personnel, facilities and money of the Justice Department, it was necessary that the Army undertake the task of removals from the areas, Mr. Biddle stated. He said it was "perfectly obvious" that his department could not cope with the job, since there were only 350 Federal Bureau of Investigation agents on the entire West Coast.

The Attorney General said, however, that he knew of no other instance when this country had set up a plan which could involve a mass evacuation.

"The move has been taken largely for the protection of the Japanese themselves," he stated. "And I think we are going to have complete cooperation from the Japanese."

In every instance, he went on, the Department of Justice has followed the suggestions of the War Department in meeting the alien problem on the West Coast. He said that since the work of alien control was passing to the Army in that region, Thomas C. Clark, one of the ranking assistants to the Attorney General, would return to California tonight and would be in complete touch with Major Gen. John L. DeWitt, commanding the area.

Alien Japanese, Germans and Italians in California number 109,-000 as of the 1940 alien registration act. In Oregon there are 8,400 and in the State of Washington, 13,000.

February 21, 1942

EVACUATION AREA SET FOR JAPANESE IN PACIFIC STATES

Zone Averaging a Depth of 100 Miles Is Included in Military Area No. 1

WITH A SLICE OF ARIZONA

By LAWRENCE E. DAVIES
Special to THE NEW YORK TIMES.

SAN FRANCISCO, March 3—Practically a quarter of a million square miles of the Western coastal region, an area almost as large as the entire Japanese Empire, was set apart today by Lieut. Gen. John L. De Witt, Western Defense Commander, as a military zone from which all Japanese, American citizens as well as aliens, must move.

Starting at the Canadian border, the 2,000-mile-long "evacuation line" will force Japanese to vacate about two-thirds of Washington, two-fifths of Oregon, far more than half of California to the west of the Sierras and the southern two-fifths of Arizona.

General De Witt's proclamation, issued under authority of a Presidential order, was the blow which aliens and Japanese-Americans had been expecting for more than two weeks. The proclamation did not actually order an evacuation and the general said that "immediate compulsory mass evacuation" of all Japanese and other aliens from the coast was "impracticable." But he left no doubt that every person of Japanese lineage must get out of the region defined under orders to be issued "eventually."

Cites Gain to Early Movers

"Those Japanese and other aliens who move into the interior out of this area now," he added, "will gain considerable advantage and in all probability will not again be disturbed."

There was no official announcement as to how much time would be allowed for voluntary evacuation, but some estimates put the "deadline" at around April 15. Japanese-American leaders begged for further information as to resettlement plans, so that they might give proper advice to an estimated 100,-000 persons of Japanese ancestry who will be affected by the later moving orders.

Officials in charge of resettlement were understood to be planning a registration and reception center for the Japanese in California's Owens Valley, now owned by the city of Los Angeles. Already materials are being assembled there and buildings are being fabricated. The first unit, it is said, will house between 5,000 and 10,000 and eventually perhaps 50,000 persons can be taken care of in that Southern California area, east of the Sierras.

General De Witt said the Federal Government was "fully aware" of the problems involved, particularly with respect to "property, resettlement and relocation" of the groups to be affected.

"Since the issuance of the Executive order," he went on, "all aspects of the various problems have been subjected to careful study by appropriate agencies of the Federal Government. Plans are being developed to minimize economic dislocation and the sacrifice of property rights. Military necessity is the most vital consideration, but the fullest attention is being given the effect upon individual and property rights."

The man in whom the President reposed full authority to set up military zones and exclude citizens and aliens alike as a precaution against fifth column activities declared that the evacuation would be carried out as "a continuing process."

To simplify procedure General De Witt set up these five classes:

107

Class 1—All who are suspected of espionage, sabotage, fifth column or other subversive activity.

Class 2—Japanese aliens.

Class 3—American-born persons of Japanese lineage.

Class 4—German aliens.

Class 5—Italian aliens.

"Persons in Classes 2 and 3," General De Witt explained, "will be required by future orders to leave critical points within the military areas first. These areas will be defined and announced shortly. After exclusion has been completed around the most strategic areas, a gradual program of exclusion from the remainder of Military Area No. 1 will be developed."

Next on the list for evacuation after the Japanese aliens and American-born Japanese, the General indicated, would be the German and I an aliens, but persons 70 years old or more would not be required to move except when individually suspected. The families, including parents, wives, children, sisters and brothers, of Germans and Italians in the armed forces would not be moved unless for some specific reason.

General De Witt pointed out that persons in Class 1 were being seized daily by agents of the Federal Bureau of Investigation and other intelligence services.

His "Proclamation No. 1," after setting up Military Area No. 1 along the 2,000-mile front in Washington, Oregon, California and Arizona, defined Military Area No. 2 as the remaining parts of those States. The coastal area extends on an average about 100 miles inland, but in Washington and in parts of California the width is much greater.

Inland States May Get Some

General De Witt's language indicated that persons who moved from Area 1 to Area 2 would not be further disturbed. This presumably will be good news to the Governors of a group of inland States who had protested against any influx of Japanese from the coastal areas; still it does not necessarily mean that California, Oregon and Washington will retain all, for study is being given to the idea of letting some go to the interior for farm jobs.

The general already has indicated that he will not pay much attention to other States' protests if they are against the interests of security and "military necessity."

Military Area No. 1, from which all Japanese and some German and cludes most of the leading cities of Italian aliens will be moved, in the four States, although Spokane, Wash., lies outside its boundaries.

Eastern Border of Area

Its eastern border begins, on the north, where United States Highway 97 intersects the international boundary line between this country and Canada. Thence it runs south along Highway 97 to a projection of United States Highway 10-A near the junction of the Columbia River with the Wenatchee River. It roughly follows the Columbia to a point two miles south of Maryhill, Wash., where Queen Marie of Rumania dedicated a museum some fifteen years ago, and then extends south along United States Highway 97 through Oregon into California to a point where this road, projected, intersects United States Highway 99.

The line then proceeds southward to the vicinity of Red Bluff, running near Auburn, Mariposa, Raymond, Coarse Gold, Fresno, Visalia, Exeter and Ducor. Near Isabella, in Southern California, it turns eastward, eventually following United States Highway 66 across the Colorado River to a point near Topock, Ariz. The line runs through or near Yucca, Signal, Congress Junction, Phoenix and Florence Junction to the Arizona-New Mexico line.

This, in a general way, shows the extent of Military Area No. 1. It is divided by the Army, however, into two zones. The western boundary of Military Zone A-1 runs roughly three miles off the coast from all continental parts of the United States, plus the Farallon and Santa Barbara Islands, and its eastern boundary is from thirty-five to eighty miles inland. Zone B includes all of Military Area No. 1 lying outside Zone A-1.

"Prohibited" Areas Designated

In addition, General De Witt's first proclamation designated "prohibited" regions within Military Area No. 2, which he labeled "Zones A-2 to A-99." He did not explain his reasons for dividing Military Area No. 1, apparently leaving the explanation to future proclamations.

The zones in Military Area No. 2, however, are all in the vicinity of defense plants, communication centers, dam sites, power houses and the like, many of which already were "prohibited" areas under an order of Attorney General Francis Biddle.

Thus, General De Witt's procla-

mation appeared to leave the eastern parts of Oregon, Washington and California and Northern Arizona open for resettlement of persons required to leave Military Area No. 1, with such resettlement forbidden, however, in the military zones established in that area.

"Such persons or classes or persons as the situation may require," he said, "will by subsequent proclamation be excluded from all of Military Area No. 1 and also from such of those zones herein described as Zones A-2 to A-99, inclusive, as are within Military Area No. 2.

"Certain persons or classes of persons who are by subsequent proclamation excluded from the zones last above mentioned may be permitted, under certain regulations and restrictions to be hereinafter prescribed, to enter upon or remain within Zone B.

"The designation of Military Area No. 2 as such does not contemplate any prohibition or regulation or restriction except with respect to the zones established therein."

Notice of Moving Required

General De Witt warned that any Japanese, German or Italian or any person of Japanese ancestry now resident in Military Area No. 1, who changed his place of habitual residence was required to obtain and executive "a change of residence notice" at any postoffice within the four States.

"Such notice must be executed not more than five days or less than one day prior to affecting any such change of residence," he stated; "nothing contained herein shall be construed to affect the existing regulations of the United States Attorney General which require aliens of enemy nationalities to obtain travel permits from United States Attorneys and to notify the Federal Bureau of Investigation and the Commission of Immigration of any change in permanent address."

General De Witt said further that the designation of prohibited and restricted areas by Attorney General Biddle on Dec. 7 and 8 and regulations prescribed by him were "hereby adopted and continued in full force and effect."

As the proclamation defining new military areas was issued at the Presidio, FBI agents and police seized sixty-nine crates of skyrockets and colored flares in the home of George Makamura, an alien Japanese who lived a few yards from the seashore at Santa Cruz.

"Arsenal" Fills Jail Storage

The arsenal of fireworks, described as of "the most powerful

type," more than filled all storage space in the Santa Cruz jail. The crates were the size of large office desks. The raiders saw in the flares a potentially dangerous signalling system.

Illegal cameras were found in possession of Joe Moreno, also of Santa Cruz, who had failed to register as an alien. Police in Oakland seized Carlo Lenandrino, 35, an alien Italian itinerant, who, they declared, "cussed the United States" when arrested.

Japanese families, leaving some restricted areas in advance of formal orders from the Army, were reported wandering about California districts uncertain where they should go.

This subject of destination was the theme of a statement given out by Mike Masaoka, national secretary and field executive of the Japanese-American Citizens League, with a membership of 20,000. He said:

"We trust that our government will treat us as civilian citizens who are voluntarily cooperating in national defense and not as military wards.

"The Japanese-American Citizens League is interested in a positive constructive program of resettlement for the evacuees so that they may continue to contribute on the production lines to the inevitable victory of the democratic forces. With this purpose in mind, we are instructing the sixty-five chapters of our organization in 300 communities to call meetings immediately in their localities to discuss methods by which they can correlate their energies and cooperate extensively in the evacuation process."

The statement urged that an opportunity be given to American-born Japanese "to collaborate in the work and planning of resettlement."

The Committee on National Security and Fair Play, headed by Dr. Henry F. Grady, a former Assistant Secretary of State, said in a statement that there appeared to be "only three methods of caring for the evacuees: either allow them to settle where they can work freely and produce; or set up supervised work projects; or support them in whole or in part at public expense."

Some officials are understood to be hopeful that Owens Valley can be turned into a highly productive agricultural area by the Japanese and that vocational schools and workshops can be established, making it adaptable to rehabilitation of United States soldiers after the war.

March 4, 1942

JAPANESE BEGIN EVACUATION TREK

By LAWRENCE E. DAVIES

Special to THE NEW YORK TIMES.

MANZANAR, Calif., March 23— The vanguard of 112,000 Japanese, aliens and American-born, who

must evacuate the West Coast combat zone rolled up the Owens Valley by motor convoy this evening to temporary new homes.

The first 500 to arrive, weary but gripped with the spirit of adventure over a new pioneering chapter in American history, drove the 230 miles from the outskirts of Los Angeles in their own cars, paced by highway patrolmen and Army jeeps.

A similar number came by train to the Lone Pine, where buses and

trucks met them to carry the evacuees and their possessions the last ten miles to a new reception center rising as if by magic at the foot of snow-capped peaks.

Tonight Arthur Hirano, Japanese steward, who in the early depression years managed two restaurants in the "Fifties" in New York City, fed the hungry newcomers a tasty dinner—beef stew, steamed rice, string beans, canned apricots, bread, jelly, and peas. Their exclamations for the most

part were divided between the food and the view.

Hirano himself, who came into the valley on Saturday, voiced what seemed to be a widely held opinion when he declared:

"This is a wonderful place. We didn't expect such fine treatment."

Strike Is Threatened

The first arrivals came, however, amid rumblings of a threatened strike by A. F. L. building trade workers who, since Wednesday afternoon, have erected thirty-eight prefabricated buildings, including barracks or apartments, a headquarters structure, a 150-bed hospital and a mess hall.

By tomorrow night thirty-eight more are scheduled for completion. Union carpenters warned, however, that if Japanese evacuees were put to work on the job they would lay down their tools.

It was late at night before the last of the Japanese had been transported into the new reception center, registered by a group of young women secretaries of Japanese ancestry, fed and assigned to apartments. They were to sleep on metal Army cots, covered with straw ticks. They brought their own bedding and they soon will begin to make their own furniture in workshops to be set up in the area.

The first contingent, exclusively of men, some single and some married, but with the families of the latter to follow in a few days, began assembling long before daylight near the Pacadena Rose Bowl, scene of many a great football game.

By 6:15 A. M. the convoy was nearly ready. It included 188 Army and civilian trucks, jeeps, peeps, and private cars, mostly in the moderately priced group and only a few of ancient vintage. There were also road repair trucks and an ambulance. Fifteen minutes later the vanguard moved away and the whole procession soon was in motion, with an Army peep spaced between every ten Japanese-driven machines.

A few sad friends and relatives gathered to bid their menfolk good-bye. Most of the faces showed little or no emotion, but conversations on every side emphasized the adventurous nature of the evacuation movement.

B. O. Yagi, who claimed the distinction of driving the oldest car in the convoy, a 1928 Ford roadster, is a graduate of the Agricultural Division of the University of California, but he has been a broccoli farmer at Santa Maria and aspired to do the landscaping work around the Owens Valley buildings.

George Wakamoto, 38, a carpenter, left his family behind temporarily in Los Angeles, but, as his light truck pulled away, spectators noticed sticking out from under a tarpaulin part of a tricycle he was taking to Owens Valley for the future use of his son, Charles, age 3.

Another evacue, Mike Nishida, 28, who has raised celery and berries on a truck farm near Torrance for seven years, was making the trip as a first lap of a journey into the Army. He had orders to report for induction in a month at Lone Pine, but, he explained, "I'm going up there to do any job they put me on in the meantime."

The center eventually will accommodate at least 10,000 and will cover part of a 6,000-acre tract leased by the Federal Government from the City of Los Angeles.

20,000 for Arizona
Special to THE NEW YORK TIMES.
WASHINGTON, March 23 — Twenty thousand alien and citizen Japanese will be moved to the Colorado River Indian Reservation at Parker, Ariz., in the first extensive relocation of Japanese evacuated from West Coast military areas.

The colonization plan has been worked out by the newly created War Relocation Authority, the United States Indian Service, the Indians who own the land, and the War Department.

March 24, 1942

Kansas Bars Japanese
TOPEKA, Kan., April 1 (Æ)— Governor Ratner today ordered Kansas highway patrolmen to turn back any Japanese trying to enter the State. "We don't want them here," he said.

April 2, 1942

DECIDES SETTLING OF COAST EVACUEES

By LAWRENCE E. DAVIES
Special to THE NEW YORK TIMES.
SAN FRANCISCO, April 14— West Coast Japanese, numbering 105,000, who have waited to be moved from military area No. 1 under Army supervision, are to be settled in communities of 5,000 or more population on lands now owned or to be purchased by the Federal Government, under a policy announced today by Milton S. Eisenhower, director of the War Relocation Authority.

This appeared to confirm the growing impression that, for this season at least, inland farm operators who had hoped to have groups of Japanese do their farm work under Army guard were going to be disappointed.

The evacuees at the relocation centers, American citizens as well as Japanese nationals, will at all times be under the protection of military police. Man power needs in the armed services, it was understood, precluded the assignment of soldiers to guard small groups of Japanese on inland farms.

Mr. Eisenhower asserted that every relocation center must provide work opportunities throughout the year for the available workers to be located there and that every center must be situated at a "safe distance" from strategic works. The centers will be located on public lands "so that improvements at public expense become public, not private, assets."

Three types of work will be carried on at each relocation center, public work, such as land subjugation, food production and the production of war goods.

At the Owens Valley reception center first steps have been taken to make the population self-sufficient in foodstuffs.

The Authority is exploring the possibilities of manufacturing at the centers articles requiring much hand labor which are needed by the Army or Navy or which otherwise contribute to war needs. A thousand Japanese fishermen, evacuated from Terminal Island at Los Angeles might, it was suggested, weave nets used for camouflage. Manufacture of cartridge belts and gloves for the Navy is under consideration. Manufacturers who have long employed Japanese having voiced interest in transferring their plants to points near the relocation centers.

The evacuation of Los Angeles zones was completed during the day. The 2,500 evacuees went to the Santa Anita assembly center.

April 15, 1942

ARMY TO DIM SHORE; ALL OF EAST TO BE NEW MILITARY AREA

Establishment at an early date of an Eastern Military Area along the entire Eastern seaboard, with the Army taking immediate control over dimming of shore lights and regulation of enemy aliens, was announced here yesterday by Lieut. Gen. Hugh A. Drum, commanding general of the Eastern Defense Command and First Army.

The order, described as "an important and necessary adjunct to the defense of our Eastern seaboard," will set up the machinery for complete and effective Army control over any threats to "the national defense and security."

When put into effect completely, it will set up in sixteen Eastern States, from Maine to Florida, and the District of Columbia, a military area similar to that created by the Western Defense Command on the Pacific coast, where 112,000 Japanese are being evacuated to inland points. General Drum's statement, however, made it clear that no "mass evacuation" is being contemplated on the Eastern seaboard, and that "regulation or control of conduct is the keynote of the plan."

The order also means, in effect, that, as far as the Army is concerned, the honeymoon of waiting for completely satisfactory voluntary cooperation by civilian authorities and localities in regard to dimming out shore lights is at an end. From now on, shore lights, which are an aid to enemy submarines in picking off shipping along the Atlantic coast, will be dimmed out or else the Army will take steps to enforce its orders.

As a token of the Army's intentions on the shore light problem General Drum's announcement was followed immediately by a statement from Major Gen. Irving J. Phillipson, commanding general of the Second Corps Area, who will be in charge of enforcement in New York, New Jersey and Delaware. General Phillipson observed that, through cooperation of State and local authorities, an "effective dimming" of shore lighting, "with certain exceptions," already had been accomplished. The Army soon will make public "more comprehensive regulations" and "it is hoped" that the necessity for "enforced blackouts" may be avoided, he said. However, he warned, if the new regulations prove ineffective "complete blackouts may be necessary."

In New York City Mayor La Guardia took notice of the new Army order when he acknowledged that General Drum will be in "supreme command," and expressed the hope that shore localities will cooperate in dimming lights in order to avoid "very drastic penalties."

General Drum emphasized in his order that the new plan will not interfere at all "with the lives of the great mass of loyal Americans," but he warned that it is "the determination of the military authorities" to stop any enemy sympathizer, whether alien or "disloyal American," from doing anything that might harm the United States. The Federal Bureau of Investigation and other Federal agencies will assist in execution of the military orders. he said.

The following States will be included in the Eastern Military Area: Maine, Vermont, New Hampshire, Massachusetts, Connecticut, Rhode Island, New York, New Jersey, Delaware, Pennsylvania, Virginia, Maryland (also the District of Columbia), North Carolina, South Carolina, Georgia and all of Florida east of the Apalachicola River. This takes in most of Florida, as the Apalachicola River is near the extreme western boundary of the State, about parallel with the Alabama State line.

General Drum, whose headquarters are at Governors Island, will b in command of the entire military area. Control of the area will be carried out under him by the commanding generals of the four existing corps areas in the territory. In this corps area General Phillipson, whose headquarters also is at Governors Island, will be in charge. The other commanders are:

Major Gen. Sherman Miles, commanding general, First Corps Area, with headquarters at Boston. His territory takes in all the New England States.

Major Gen. Milton A. Reckord, commanding general, Third Corps Area, with headquarters at Baltimore. His territory in Pennsylvania, Virginia, Maryland and the District of Columbia.

Major Gen. J. P. Smith, commanding general, Fourth Corps Area, with Headquarters at Atlanta. His area includes North and South Carolina, Georgia, Florida, Alabama and Tennessee, but Alabama, Tennessee and the part of Florida west of the Appalachicola are not included in the Eastern Military Area.

General Drum's statement gave no indication how soon the complete plan would be in operation, stating only in a prefatory note that the Eastern Military Area would be established "at an early date." It explained that the area was being set up under a Presidential executive order of Feb. 19, 1942, empowering military commanders designated by the Secretary of War to take such steps "whenever the designated commander deems such action necessary or desirable."

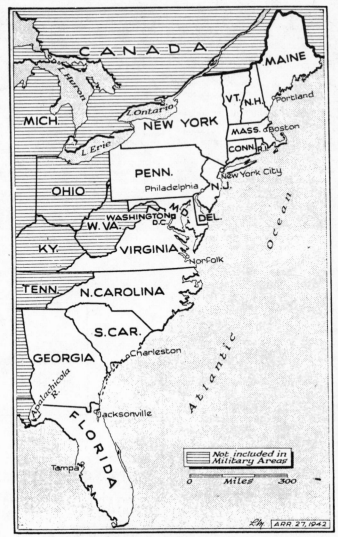

In sixteen States from Maine to Florida and in the District of Columbia the Army takes immediate control of the dimming of shore lights and the regulation of enemy aliens. Florida, west of the Apalachicola River, is not included.

"The object of prescribing a military area is to facilitate control so as to prevent subversive activities and aid being given the enemy, such as by lighting along our coasts," the general's statement said.

Control is to be decentralized within the various corps areas and "will be maintained primarily by means of a system of definitely described zones," it was explained. State and local officials "will be requested to assist." A zone, generally, will embrace a public utility, a military, naval or civil installation, a commercial or defense facility, a territorial region, a strip of coastline or waterfront or any other strategic point.

Emphasizing that regulation and control of conduct and movements of enemy aliens and any other persons suspected of subversive activities, rather than wholesale evacuations, was the plan, the statement said:

"The fundamental policy embodied in the plan is not to interfere in any manner whatever with the lives of the great mass of loyal Americans in the States included in the military area, or with the economic life of the area, but it does express the determination of the military authorities to prevent any enemy sympathizer, whether alien enemy, alien of other nationality or disloyal American, if any exist, from committing any act detrimental to the national security. Those persons whose conduct reflects their patriotic motives will not be affected by this administration."

Enforcement will be accomplished by application of penalties provided by law. These include "exclusion from the area, internment of aliens, prosecutions * * * and evacuations." While "mass evacuation is not contemplated," there may be evacuations "by selective processes applicable to enemy aliens or to any other persons deemed dangerous to remain at large within the area or within its zones."

April 27, 1942

OUR 'TOLERANCE' IN WARTIME HAILED

Civil Liberties Union Calls Forbearance 'Remarkable' After Pearl Harbor

EVACUATION IS SCORED

Removal of Japanese From the Pacific Coast Held Invasion of Citizens' Rights

The Government and people of the United States demonstrated a "remarkable wartime tolerance" in the six months following the Japanese assault on Pearl Harbor, the American Civil Liberties Union declared in its annual report, made public yesterday.

Under the title of "The Bill of Rights in War," the report contained a balance sheet listing twenty-eight developments as "favorable" from the standpoint of civil liberties and twenty-three as "unfavorable."

The evacuation of Japanese from the Pacific Coast without examination of their loyalty and without distinction between aliens and citizens was put first among the items classified by the union as "unfavorable."

"No such invasion of the liberties of American citizens on the basis of racial origin has ever before been undertaken in war or peace," the report said, "and it is to be explained only by the sectional fears and prejudices arising out of the extraordinary circumstances of the war."

Evidence that the Roosevelt Administration was determined to resist pressure to curb civil rights was seen in its refusal to approve anti-labor legislation, its prosecution of violators of minority rights, its encouragement of measures to minimize race prejudice in war industries and its "reasonable application" of newspaper and radio censorship codes.

The general attitude of the public, according to the report, continued "favorable to criticism of the conduct of the war, to the discussion of war and peace aims and to the rights of minorities."

The Dies committee and the Rapp-Coudert committee in this State were criticized for confining their investigations to cases of alleged communism and for stirring up "confusion and prejudice without either legislative or criminal action."

The report commended the Supreme Court for some of its decisions but maintained that its record for the year constituted "a setback to civil liberties." The ruling to which principal exception was taken upheld the right of cities to require licenses for the sale of non-commercial literature.

President Roosevelt was praised for combatting discrimination in the employment of aliens, Negroes and Jews; for commuting the sentence of Earl Browder, Communist leader, and for making official the celebration of Bill of Rights Day last Dec. 15.

The union noted with approval Attorney General Biddle's handling of the problem of conscientious objectors and the internment of enemy aliens. It also commended him for pushing investigations of peonage in the South and of mob violence against Jehovah's Witnesses.

On the other hand, the Attorney General was censured for his deportation order against Harry Bridges, California C. I. O. director; for prosecuting members of the Socialist Workers party in Minneapolis under the sedition laws; and for seeking to extend the legal bases for revoking the citizenship of naturalized persons.

June 28, 1942

BIDDLE DESCRIBES FIGHT ON SABOTAGE

Says No Single Large-Scale Act of Damage Occurred in First Six Months of War

9,405 ALIENS ARRESTED

1,200 Persons Convicted of Subversive Activities, Most of Them in Draft Cases

Special to THE NEW YORK TIMES.

WASHINGTON, July 4—No single large-scale act of sabotage was committed in this country in the first six months of the war, Attorney General Francis Biddle announced today as plans proceeded for the trial of eight captured Nazi agents next week.

Armed with explosives and money, the invaders might well have caused serious damage had they not been quickly captured by the Federal Bureau of Investigation.

Ten sentences have been imposed for sabotage, Mr. Biddle revealed, but these, he added, involved no aggravated cases, the majority "stemming from acts of spite and malicious mischief." One saboteur received a ten-year prison term, while the rest were sentenced to terms ranging from ninety days to four years.

In the six months almost 1,200 individuals were convicted of various subversive and disloyal activities and were sentenced to serve up to twenty years. Most convictions came from violations of the Selective Service Act, but there were forty-eight for espionage and nine for acting as agents for hostile foreign powers.

Preventive Work Stressed

In February identification certificates were issued to almost 1,000,000 enemy aliens. The cases of 3,853 enemy aliens were disposed of by internment or parole. Denaturalization proceedings were brought against 65 persons. The FBI arrested a total of 9,405 allegedly disloyal alien enemies, including 4,764 Japanese, 3,120 Germans and 1,521 Italians.

"Through preventive work by the FBI and other branches of the Department of Justice much hostile activity which might be normally expected in wartime failed to materialize," Mr. Biddle remarked.

"For example there has not been perpetrated to date any single large-scale act of sabotage. No serious depredations by organized fifth columnists have occurred. And there has been a drastic falling off in the activities of those publications and organizations which hover on the fringe of sedition and disloyalty.

"No false sense of security should be derived from these facts. The threat to our internal security deepens with each day that the war continues, as evidenced by the desperate attempts of the Nazis to land saboteurs along our coasts. But it is reassuring to know that the defenses which we have erected against these threats have, so far at least, proved effective."

Convictions Are Varied

The espionage convictions, Mr. Biddle noted, included those of Frederick Joubert Duquesne and his thirty-three Nazi confederates sentenced in Brooklyn, and of Anastase Vonsiatsky and Otto Willumeit in Hartford. Wilhelm Kunze, Bund leader and member of this group, was said today to have been arrested in Mexico.

Nine paid propagandists of Germany or Japan have been convicted under the Foreign Agents Registration Act, notably Laura Ingalls and George Sylvester Viereck. Eight others were convicted before Pearl Harbor.

Sedition charges resulted in two convictions, one acquittal and five persons yet to stand trial. George W. Christians, organizer of the Crusader White Shirts, was sentenced to five years and a $5,000 fine; Christian Loeffler, a naturalized German living in Detroit, was sentenced to six years for discouraging Army enlistments.

William Dudley Pelley, organizer of the Silver Shirts and publisher of The Galilean, will be tried as a seditionist this month. Under indictment are Robert Noble and Ellis O. Jones of Los Angeles, and Elmer J. and Jack F. Garner of Wichita.

Moreover, Max Stephan, a Detroit restaurant keeper, has just been convicted of treason in aiding Peter Krug, a Nazi lieutenant who escaped from a Canadian prison camp.

Cooperating with the Post Office Department, the Department of Justice has succeeded in bringing about suspension of publications such as the Coughlin-organized Social Justice; Publicity, published by the Garners at Wichita; X-ray, published by Court Asher at Muncie, Ind., and the Philadelphia Herold, a German language newspaper. As a result, several other defeatist papers have voluntarily gone out of business.

As part of the departmental campaign against subversive influences, Federal grand juries are conducting intensive investigations in Washington, Chicago and Los Angeles.

July 5, 1942

F. B. I. BIDS PUBLIC HELP HUNT SPIES

But Hoover, in Offering Six Rules for the Cooperation, Sounds Some Warnings

INVITES ALL INFORMATION

Declares Anything Suspicious Should Be Reported, Even if It Seems to Be Trivial

North American Newspaper Alliance.

WASHINGTON, Sept. 6—Rules to guide the average citizen in helping the war against spies, saboteurs and a potential fifth column have been formulated by J. Edgar Hoover, head of the Federal Bureau of Investigation and the nation's chief spy hunter.

"There are more than 150,000 police officers throughout the country working hand in hand on this job with 4,300 agents of the F. B. I.," Mr. Hoover said in an interview. "Their efforts are coordinated on a national scale. But they can't have too much help on a job of this nature.

"A spy or a saboteur or an enemy propagandist has to work among people. He can't hide out in a forest and get his work done. Policemen can't be everywhere. But the American people are. Americans are everywhere in this country of ours and if they follow these few simple rules, the enemy is going to have a lot of trouble getting his work done."

Advice to the Public

The proper procedure, as outlined by Mr. Hoover, is as follows:

1. Report to the F. B. I. field office nearest your home any person or situation you know of personally that may be of possible danger to our national security.

2. Do not attempt to evaluate your information. What may seem trivial to you may fit into the intricate pattern of a case being investigated by the F. B. I. from coast to coast. The F. B. I. would rather receive a thousand unfounded reports than miss one that is worthwhile.

3. Do not take any action yourself and play amateur detective. Your efforts may warn the person or persons in question and nullify months of investigation by the G-men.

4. If you do report something questionable, do not become agitated if nothing is apparently done about the information you furnished. You may rest assured that it is being given attention. Newspaper headlines do not convict foreign agents. It is sometimes better to keep known agents under surveillance until all the members of a particular ring have been identified and their sources of information ascertained. Premature disclosure may permit many dangerous individuals to elude apprehension. In the famous Duquesne spy case the F. B. I. worked for almost two years, but in the end thirty-three espionage agents of the German Government were sentenced in Federal Court at Brooklyn.

Warns Against Gossip

5. Do not accept gossip or rumor and do not pass it on to your friends or neighbors. One method found most effective by the Axis nations consists of circulating wild rumors which tend to create hysteria among the civilian population. By passing unfounded stories along you may cause irreparable injury to innocent people, add unnecessarily to the burden of the F. B. I. and delay the war effort.

6. Do not be suspicious of persons merely because they have foreign sounding names. While a small percentage of aliens have turned traitor to the land of their adoption, the majority are loyal and dependable, who embrace the United States as a refuge from oppression. The persecution of minority groups also recruits fifth columnists and is one of the things we are fighting.

September 7, 1942

FAR WEST FINISHES MOVING JAPANESE

'Ghost Cities' Left as the Last Go From Assembly Places to Ten 'Duration' Centers

YOUNG MISS OLD CONTACTS

By LAWRENCE E. DAVIES

SAN FRANCISCO, Oct. 31—Sixteen "boom towns" populated wholly by persons of Japanese ancestry during the Summer and early Fall have now become "ghost cities." As they mushroomed on race tracks and county fair grounds of Washington, Oregon, California and Arizona, their thousands of 100-by-25-foot wooden barracklike buildings offered temporary shelter for more than 100,000 Japanese evacuees, removed from their coastal homes by the Army in a forced population movement unparalleled in American history.

This week-end the last step in the West Coast's evacuation program, dictated by "military necessity," is being completed. Sixteen temporary assembly centers, each of which was home to from 250 to 19,000 persons, were used until permanent centers in the interior could be prepared for use. Now, except for a few thousand residents who migrated to the Middle West and East when voluntary evacuation was permitted, all the West Coast's Japanese population is living at ten carefully selected agricultural sites, designed for occupancy for the duration of the war.

Situation Is Eased

The exposed West Coast undoubtedly feels better with the Japanese removed. Thousands of them lived in militarily strategic areas. Many of them were aliens. Many of the American-born had been educated in Japan. Even those white residents who swore that their own Japanese house boy was loyal to America would not vouch for others. And the temper of Filipinos and long-time white critics of industrious Japanese farmers made the further presence of Japanese in some areas dangerous to the Japanese themselves.

So, wholly aside from those agricultural operators and wholesale produce merchants who have been competing with the Japanese for years and are glad to have them out of the way, the Coast is relieved over not having to worry about its Japanese population for the duration of the war.

What of the Japanese themselves? How are they reacting to their new life? More specifically, how are the American citizens, who constitute the majority of the evacuees, adjusting themselves to the new environment? The experience is much more difficult emotionally for them than for their elders, mostly aliens, who had more reason to expect some sort of protective custody in time of war and who apparently are favorably impressed with their treatment.

Two Groups Together

To prevent the breakup of families and scattering of community members, aliens, or Issei, and American-born, or Nisei, were moved together to the centers. It is not uncommon for Issei to taunt the American citizens with these words: "Of what use is your American citizenship now? We're all in here together and you have no more rights than we."

The Nisei, at least those loyal to America, are fearful that their own children may become Nipponized by their wartime experience. This fear rises to the point where, in some of the centers, there is great reluctance of parents and children alike to have the pupils sign up for schoolroom classes taught by Japanese, no matter how competent.

Without much fanfare, 9,000 evacuees have left the centers for temporary outside employment, as volunteers to help save the sugar beet crop. Hostility against them in some areas has been marked. A special appeal to patriotism was made when the Army let down the bars to enable evacuees to work inside Military Area No. 1 picking long-staple cotton, vital for Army purposes.

Local Attacks Made

About 300, including well-to-do former wholesale merchants and professional men, signed up. But local officials in the cotton area went on the radio and accused the evacuees of sabotage. Fearful, some of the volunteers backed out.

Steadily, but without much publicity, evacuees are leaving the centers for permanent private jobs in the interior of the country.

To get this permission they must first have the jobs, then they must be acceptable to their prospective adopted communities. In all cases they are "processed" by intelligence services. It is the hope of some persons concerned over the post-war Japanese problem in this country that thousands of the evacuated citizens may by then be re-established in new homes and communities.

November 1, 1942

BAN ON JAPANESE LIFTED ON COAST

Army Area Chief Permits All Proved Loyal to Return to Three States After Jan. 2

By LAWRENCE E. DAVIES
Special to THE NEW YORK TIMES.

SAN FRANCISCO, Dec. 17 — Mass exclusion of persons of Japanese ancestry from West Coast States was ended today by Maj. Gen. H. Conger Pratt, Western commander, in a proclamation effective on Jan. 2.

On that date the thirty-month exile of more than 100,000 men, women and children from their old homes in Washington, Oregon and California will cease.

Their resettlement, however, will be a gradual process and several thousand of them presumably will continue to be blocked off from the coastal military area through individual Army exclusion orders issued against those known to be pro-Japan in their sympathies or whose presence on the coast is adjudged dangerous to the war effort.

Army Expects No Trouble

General Pratt announced that the restrictions, imposed originally by Lieut. Gen. John L. DeWitt in the early war months when this coast momentarily feared Japanese raids, were being lifted because "existing military necessity does not justify control over American citizens who have been determined not to be potentially dangerous."

He said at a press interview at his Presidio headquarters that he hoped those evacuees who chose to come back might do so "without undue incident." Emphasizing that he expected "no trouble other than verbal of any magnitude," he voiced confidence that nothing would develop to "require Army intervention."

The evacuees had been "screened thoroughly" and all of those permitted to come back to the coast, he promised, would be "either loyal or harmless."

Small Ratio Likely to Return

Of the 110,000 or so evacuated from Coast States 32,800 have left relocation centers for jobs and homes in the East and Middle West. There are 18,700 at the Tule Lake (Calif.) camp for disloyal evacuees and 61,000 still living in the eight centers operated by the War Relocation Authority.

How many of these will be drawn back to Coast States is anybody's guess, although some WRA officials doubt that more than 10 per cent will have the courage or desire to go in view of expressions of some West Coast organizations and publications.

Gov. Earl Warren of California, however, called upon "all Americans" to comply "loyally, cheerfully and carefully" with the decision of the Western Defense Command to revoke the exclusion orders. He instructed chiefs of police, sheriffs and public officials throughout California to develop uniform plans to prevent intemperate actions and civil disorder.

Majority Found to Be Loyal

General Pratt told newspaper men that when General Dewitt excluded the Japanese citizens and aliens neither the military nor civilian agencies possessed the data to enable them to determine which should be evacuated and which

should be permitted to remain.

"But during the last two years a vast quantity of information pertaining to the history and activities of all persons of Japanese ancestry, both citizens and aliens, has been assembled," he went on.

"This material has been the subject of exhaustive study and as a result it is now possible to consider persons of Japanese ancestry on an individual basis rather than as a group.

"I consider it of great importance that the people of the West Coast understand and appreciate that the most careful scrutiny of the vast amount of information now available has led to the conclusion that the great majority of Japanese have severed all connections with Japan and are prepared to assume the responsibilities of their situation as Americans.

"However, this same scrutiny has clearly revealed that there are still a considerable number of persons of Japanese ancestry, both in the citizen and in the alien group, who continue to give their loyalty to Japan, who do not wish to be Americans and who are willing to sacrifice themselves to advance the interests of Japan.

"Military necessity requires that such individuals shall continue to be excluded and that those requiring control shall be adequately controlled."

Dealing With Individuals

General Pratt explained that the individual exclusion plan to be applied called for about thirty officers, with many clerical assistants, to visit all of the WRA centers, examine records and talk with some of the evacuees.

With the information already at hand, he felt that by Jan. 2 the Army would have built up an exclusion list which would require only a minimum of changes in the future.

Nevertheless, he said, any person who found his name on the list would have the right of appeal with counsel to boards of three officers each, all of "comparative senior rank," which would submit recommendations to the command-

ing general.

"If any of these committees says there is doubt about any specific person, out he stays," the General continued.

"I want to emphasize that the Japanese who are on the excluded list are placed there by the Army. The remainder, therefore, under the dates set forth, will resume their normal duties as citizens of the United States.

"We have a number of names on the tentative exclusion list who have sons and daughters in the service. In a case of that kind unless the father definitely is against the United States, or says he does not want his son in the service, we will remove the name from the list."

It already has been announced that about 15,000 persons of Japanese ancestry were serving in the American armed forces, divided between mainland and Hawaiian residents. About 2,500 have been inducted into the Army from the relocation centers, which have also had about 1,200 volunteers.

It is understood that yesterday 105 relatives, including mothers, fathers, wives and sisters of the Japanese-American soldiers were released from the center at Poston, Ariz., so that the soldiers fighting abroad could be notified for Christmas.

General Pratt said identification cards would be prepared and made available for any evacuee, except those on the excluded list, resettle or visit on the West Coast.

Stating that the Army's "main hope" was that there would be "no immediate influx," he continued:

"We are going to help the War Relocation Authority and it is going to help us. We believe those who do return to the Coast will not be in too great a hurry to do so. We know what the housing situation is and we know the transportation situation.

"At any rate, we believe the people of these States will see the justice of what is being done if they stop to think about it."

December 18, 1944

Supreme Court Upholds Return Of Loyal Japanese to West Coast

By LEWIS WOOD
Special to THE NEW YORK TIMES.

WASHINGTON, Dec. 18 — The constitutionality of the wartime regulations under which American citizens of Japanese ancestry were evacuated from Pacific Coast areas in 1942 was upheld by a vote of 6 to 3 in the Supreme Court today, but in another decision the court ruled unanimously that Japanese-Americans of unquestioned loyalty to the United States could not be detained in war relocation centers.

The Supreme Court rulings came only twenty-four hours after the Army announcement that exclusion of Japanese-Americans from the West Coast would be ended Jan. 2. They came also at about the time

Secretary Ickes declared in a statement that he did not foresee a "hasty mass movement" of evacuees back to the West Coast.

Justice Hugo L. Black wrote the majority opinion on the evacuation question, which involved the 1942 order of Maj. Gen. John L. De Witt as applied to Fred Toyosaburo Korematsu.

Upholding the order as "of the time it was made and when (Korematsu) violated it," he deplored compulsory exclusion, but said that Korematsu was excluded because we were at war with Japan, adding:

"When under conditions of mod-

ern warfare our shores are threatened by hostile forces, the power to protect must be commensurate with the threatened danger.

"We are unable to conclude that it was beyond the war powers of Congress and of the Executive to exclude those of Japanese ancestry from the West Coast area at the time they did."

Justices Owen J. Roberts, Frank Murphy and Robert H. Jackson all entered dissents on the ground that the majority finding violated the Constitution.

The unanimous opinion regarding confinement in war relocation centers was written by Justice Willian O. Douglas in the case of 22-year-old Mitsuye Endo, held at Topaz, Utah. Without going into constitutional issues, Mr. Douglas held that, as Miss Endo's detention was not related to espionage or sabotage, she must be released. He noted that she was a concededly loyal citizen and stated:

"Loyalty is a matter of the heart and mind, not of race, creed or color."

As in the case of Miss Endo, no question has been raised concerning the loyalty of Korematsu, native American. Accused of remaining in a military zone after his exclusion was ordered, he was convicted and sentenced to serve five years, but was placed on probation.

In upholding the exclusion order, Justice Black said that the court was "not unmindful of the hardships" which it imposed on a large group of American citizens.

"But," he stated, "hardships are part of war, and war is an aggregation of hardships. All citizens alike, both in and out of uniform, feel the impact of war in greater or lesser measure."

Pressing public necessity may sometimes justify the existence of restrictions on a racial group, but "racial antagonism never can," Justice Black remarked.

He pointed out that in the Hirabayashi case of several months ago the Supreme Court had held that a curfew applied properly to the program controlling Japanese-Americans.

"We upheld the curfew order as an exercise of the power of the Government to take steps necessary to prevent espionage and sabotage in an area threatened by Japanese attack," he said.

Steps to Prevent Sabotage

"In the light of the principles we announced in the Hirabayashi case, we are unable to conclude that it was beyond the war power of Congress and the Executive to exclude those of Japanese ancestry from the West Coast area at the time they did. True, exclusion from the area in which one's home is located is a far greater deprivation than constant confinement to the home from 8 P. M. to 6 A. M., the curfew hours.

"Nothing short of apprehension by the proper military authorities of the gravest imminent danger to the public safety can constitutionally justify either. But exclusion from a threatened area, no less than curfew, has a definite and close relationship to the prevention of espionage and sabotage."

Justice Black declared that it was wrong to "cast this case into outlines of racial prejudice," for, he contended, Korematsu was not excluded "because of hostility to him or his race," but because of the war circumstances. He pointed out that while many persons of Japanese origin were loyal to the United States, 5,000 refused to swear allegiance and several thousands sought repatriation to Japan.

In one of the dissents, Justice Jackson said the majority seemed to be "distorting the Constitution to approve all that the military may deem expedient." He asserted that he could not determine on the evidence whether General De Witt's orders were reasonable cautions.

Challenges Constitutionality

"But even if they were permissible military procedures," he commented, "I deny that it follows that they are constitutional. If, as the court holds, it does follow, then we may as well say that any military order will be constitutional and have done with it."

Justice Roberts declared that the "indisputable facts exhibit a clear violation of constitutional rights." He held also that Korematsu was faced by two orders, one, not to remain in the zone unless in an assembly center; two, not to leave the zone.

Justice Black held for the majority, however, that only the exclusion order was the issue.

Justice Murphy charged in his dissent that the exclusion of all Japanese, alien and non-alien, from the West Coast, "goes over the 'very brink of constitutional power' and falls into the ugly abyss of racism."

"No reasonable relations to an immediate, imminent and impending public danger is evident," he said, "to support this racial restriction which is one of the most sweeping and complete deprivation of constitutional rights in the history of this nation in the absence of martial law."

Justice Felix Frankfurter agreed with the majority, but said independently:

"To find that the Constitution does not forbid the military measures now complained of does not carry with it approval of that which Congress and the Executive did. That is their business, not mine."

State Civil Service Employe

The detention program was challenged by Miss Endo, a Civil Service employe of the California State Government at Sacramento, who appealed from a denial of a writ of habeas corpus. She contended that the resettlement of evacuated Japanese-Americans had been depriving her of her rights as an American citizen.

"We are of the view that Mitsuye Endo should be given her liberty," said Justice Douglas. "In reaching that conclusion we do not come to the underlying constitutional issues which have been argued. For we conclude that, whatever power the War Relocation Authority may have to detain other classes of citizens, it has no authority to subject citizens who are concededly loyal to its leave procedure."

Justice Murphy, in a concurrence, asserted that the whole program of detention was unauthorized and only "another example of the unconstitutional resort to racism inherent in the entire evacuation program."

This "racial discrimination," he argued, was "utterly foreign to American ideals and traditions."

Also concurring, Justice Roberts said that, just as in the Korematsu case, the court sought to avoid constitutional issues.

Plans Outlined by Ickes

Secretary Ickes, in his statement, said that, under the Army order of yesterday, the War Relocation Authority would "intensify its efforts" to relocate loyal West Coast evacuees in other parts of the country, but would also assist those who "prefer to exercise their legal and moral right of return" to the West Coast.

He stated also that the WRA would work toward early liquidation of its centers. None would be closed in less than six months, he added, but it was hoped to close all inside of a year.

He called on State and local officials, especially on the West Coast, and public and private agencies, including church and welfare groups, and the American Legion and other veterans organizations "to aid these people and by so doing to show their devotion to the American principles of charity, justice and democracy."

December 19, 1944

FBI'S HIDDEN STRUGGLE AGAINST SPIES CONTINUES

Trial of Enemy Agents at Governors Island Reveals Enemy Activity

By SAMUEL A. TOWER

WASHINGTON, Feb. 10 — The trial of William Curtis Colepaugh and Erich Gimpel, accused by the Government of being enemy agents, before a military commission on Governors Island this week, has a sharp reminder of the constant, hidden struggle between the Federal Bureau of Investigation, responsible for the internal security of the United States and the espionage system of Germany and Japan.

The submarine which brought over the two men hovered close to the shores of Maine for about a week, submerged in daylight hours and coming up at night, then it moved in to land its human cargo. Over a period of several weeks the men were able to make their way down the coast, unnoticed and unhampered, before the FBI finally caught up with them in the New York area.

The FBI knew that the men were coming—that is the meaning of the word "finally." More than 1,000 Federal agents were mobilized as a reception committee. There were G-men waiting for them at every port along the Atlantic Coast. Other G-men were moving through every town and hamlet of the Eastern seaboard, eliciting information and tracking down leads.

J. Edgar Hoover, FBI chief, discloses that his bureau is aware of the identity of the students at the Nazi schools for espionage and sabotage, and of the movement of enemy spies toward this country. Details must remain secret for security reasons, but he indicates that "we have our own media of information about Axis spies and their connections. Noting that the two latest arrivals were given elaborate instructions by their teachers on the necessity of keeping out of the way of the FBI, Mr. Hoover points out that enemy agents, cut off from their connections, become "lone wolves in a community and are spotted."

J. EDGAR HOOVER

Associated Press

He leads fight against Nazi spies and attempts at sabotage.

This state of preparedness by Federal agencies for undercover enemy attacks stands out as the chief difference between our approach in the present war and in the first World War. The problem of the spy and his companion, the saboteur, for whom he is generally the forerunner, remains basically the same, of course, as it has been down through the centuries.

In the days before and during American participation in the first World War, the FBI was passing through its embryonic stages. It was made up of some 200 young lawyers, without training in counter-espionage, and who relied on their luck and ingenuity.

As Mr. Hoover puts it, "they were handed a badge, sworn in and sent out on the job."

Another problem of the last war centered around the establishment by the Germans of an integrated spy organization, composed of enemy diplomatic officials, aliens and American employes, which was organized both for sabotage, like the great Kingsland fire or the Black Tom explosion, and espionage or war activities, with propaganda work to stir up labor troubles and retard production as a sideline.

According to the FBI, the leader, Capt. Franz von Rintelen, for a time a dashing figure in his financial and social circles, was the last great master spy.

Overzealous Public

The third major difficulty in the intelligence activities of the first World War was an overzealousness on the part of the public, which almost reached the point of unrestrained vigilante action against a suspected individual. The situation is effectively described by John Lord O'Brian, in 1917 a special assistant to the Attorney General, who tells of one patriotic organization, with good intentions, carrying full page advertisements "offering in substance to make every man a spy-chaser on the payment of a dollar membership fee." He summarizes it in this way:

"There was no community in the country so small that it did not produce a complaint because of failure to intern or execute at least one alleged German spy."

All of these problems—counter-activity by the Government, thorough enemy preparedness and restraint of the public enthusiasm of amateur spy hunting, were present in this war. In addition, new difficulties were encountered in the greater number of nationalities represented by the Axis, compared with the Central Powers, and in the development of new communication methods such as radio and microfilm and improvement in fast transportation.

Profiting from the lessons of the last war, a number of actions were initiated in preliminary form during the years when only the shadow of war appeared. The FBI began the compilation of data of potential espionage activity and undertook a plant protection survey to guard against sabotage.

Registration of aliens was ordered. Channels of information through diplomatic offices were eliminated with the closing of consulates. Within forty-eight hours, when war came, 16,000 enemy aliens were arrested, of which 4,000 were ultimately interned. The public was educated to transmit "tips" to the professional handling of the FBI, which was placed in complete charge of security within our borders.

The bureau itself went on a wartime footing, increasing its personnel to the point where there are now 2,000 agents, from 600 in 1939. The student body of the National Police Academy, conducted by the FBI for State and local officers, was doubled.

Good Record

The results of these measures, in addition to others which can be disclosed only after the war, have been that there has been no case of foreign-directed sabotage and that espionage activity has been kept under control. All the cases of sabotage investigated by the FBI have thus far been caused by spite, thoughtlessness and prankishness.

"SO YOU THOUGHT HE'D GONE HOME LONG AGO!"

Hutton in The Philadelphia Inquirer

There have been about 100 convictions for espionage obtained by the Department of Justice so far. Many of those convicted were "small fry," who received little notice, but there have been about a dozen major "catches."

Probably the most important espionage case took place before the war, in June, 1941, when thirty-three members of a German spy ring, headed by Fritz Joubert Duquesne, noted Nazi spy, were trapped by the FBI and sent to prison. The elimination of this organization, which had extended ramifications, placed a decisive check in German espionage operations, from which it has found it difficult to recover.

The Nazis have been unable to recruit agents in this country, and like the Japanese, who are not able to use their citizens as spies, they have been forced to attempt espionage with English-speaking agents who are smuggled in.

Despite the success of American counter-measures, the FBI chief is gravely concerned over manifestations of public overcomplacency and overconfidence.

Plans for Future

The FBI knows at the present moment of a particular number of German agents who are receiving special training before being sent to the United States and the Western Hemisphere, according to Mr. Hoover. Further German and Japanese intelligence systems work in cooperation, he points out, so the war's end in Europe will not mean an end to German espionage.

Notwithstanding our successes, Mr. Hoover warns that the danger of enemy espionage is always present, and that there is "no assurance that we are going to be as successful tonight or tomorrow."

February 11, 1945

CHAPTER 3

Necessary Vigilance or Witch Hunt?

Senator Joseph McCarthy studies a copy of the *Daily Worker*.

Courtesy The New York Times

Un-Americanisms Are Defined by Brookings; Would Check Holders of Subversive Views

WASHINGTON, March 30 (AP)— The Brookings Institution recommended to the Committee on Un-American Activities today that it investigate those who attack "the principle of the form of government as guaranteed by our Constitution."

In a report to the committee the institution added that the committee should be mainly concerned with the rights of individuals assured by the Constitution.

The committee had requested the organization to prepare an analysis of replies they received from scores of prominent Americans asked to define "un-American activities." Mrs. Franklin D. Roosevelt was among those who replied, but her views were not made public.

The report laid down what it regarded as the consensus of the replies:

"1. It is un-American for any individual or group by force, intimidation, deceit, fraud or bribery to prevent or seek to prevent any person from exerci-ing any right or privilege which cannot constitutionally be denied to him either by the Federal Government or by a State government.

"2. It is un-American for any individual to advocate, to conspire or to attempt to bring about a change in the form of government in the United States without following the processes prescribed for that purpose by the Constitution.

"3. It is un-American for any person (secretly) to conspire by any methods, constitutional or otherwise, to overthrow or attempt to overthrow a government of law and to substitute therefore a government vested with complete discretionary power.

"4. It is un-American for any person with the primary intent to advance the interests of a foreign nation or association to take action clearly and definitely against the interests of the United States.

"5. In time of war or threatened war, it is un-American for any person with the intent to interfere with the successful preparation for or prosecution of war."

March 31, 1945

REDS HERE RETURN TO SOCIALIST AIMS

New Constitution Liquidates Policies Browder Advocated in Recent Times

A new constitution of the Communist party of the United States, expressing the party's desire to lead the working people of the country in "the establishment of socialism by the free choice of the American people," was published yesterday in The Daily Worker.

The document put the official taboo on the policies advocated during the last nineteen months by Earl Browder, deposed head of the party, who in a speech Jan. 10, 1944, in Madison Square Garden said the party would not raise the issue of socialism in the post-war period so as not to weaken national unity.

The new constitution, which was adopted at a national convention held here two weeks ago, was in most respects similar to the constitution the party had before it became the Communist Political Association, but its preamble lays greater emphasis on the need for friendly international relations than the old one.

"Overthrow" Policy Disclaimed

Like the old party constitution, the new document explicitly denounced any effort to overthrow the American form of Government against the will of the majority of the people, a policy the Communists have been accused of sponsoring despite statements to the contrary by their protagonists.

In Section 2 of Article IX, the new constitution declared: "Adherence to or participation in the activities of any clique, group, circle, faction or party which conspires or acts to subvert, undermine, weaken or overthrow any or all institutions of American democracy, whereby the majority of the American people can maintain their right to determine their destinies in any degree, shall be punished by immediate expulsion."

The preamble said that the party "upholds the achievements of American democracy and defends the United States Constitution and the Bill of Rights against its reactionary enemies, who would destroy democracy and popular liberties."

Besides expressing the party's opposition to racial and religious oppression and Jim-Crowism, the preamble said the Communists struggle "for the complete destruction of fascism and for a durable peace."

On the subject of international relations, the preamble declared: "The Communist party holds as a basic principle that there is an identity of interest which serves as a common bond uniting the workers of all lands. It recognizes further that the true national interests of our country and the cause of peace and progress require the solidarity of all freedom-loving people and the continued and ever closer cooperation of the United States."

The constitution listed the national convention as the highest national authority of the party, the State convention as the highest State authority, and gives national and State committees the right to direct policy in the interim periods.

It set up a schedule of dues of 35 cents a month for members earning under $25 weekly; $1 monthly for members earning from $25 to $60 weekly; $2 for members earning more than $60 weekly and ten cents monthly for unemployed.

Fifty per cent of the proceeds, the constitution specified, is to go to the national body, 20 per cent to local clubs and the remaining 30 per cent is to be divided among the respective city, county and State organizations in accordance with decisions of State conventions.

August 8, 1945

NEW 'DIES' COMMITTEE OFF ON SAME BOISTEROUS FOOT

By ANTHONY H. LEVIERO

WASHINGTON, Oct. 6—Councilman Benjamin Davis of New York City, who is a Negro and a Communist, stood defiantly before the House Committee on Un-American Activities recently and declared that, as a Negro, he could expect no consideration from Representative Rankin of Mississippi. Another angry witness, Earl Browder, deposed head of the Communist party, bluntly told the committee that it had no constitutional right to question him about his political views.

These incidents focus attention on the committee, and a question that is being asked in the capital is whether it will follow the same course as its much-criticized predecessor, the Dies committee.

The question is pertinent and significant, for the committee is now a permanent one, cloaked with the same prestige and status as the Naval Affairs and other hard-working legislative agencies.

Inquiry in Hollywood

The committee is presently engaged in a three-point program. It is investigating the reconstituted Communist party; it has an agent in Hollywood, inquiring into alleged subversion there; and it is digging into affiliates of Japan's Black Dragon Society in this country. Under discussion for possible early investigation is Gerald L. K. Smith, the head of the America First party. About a dozen other lines of investigation are also being considered.

One point of view expressed here is that the committee's program is not so touchy a subject as its methods. If the committee would revamp its inquisitorial technique, it is suggested in some quarters, it can investigate allegations of subversion in the political right, left, or middle without any clamor from press and public.

One step suggested as a help in building up public confidence in the committee is to give its witnesses the right of direct testimony. The old and the new committees have ignored this form of legal procedure. In this respect the Committee on Un-American Activities is much different from other Congressional committees.

At the hearing of the Un-American Activities group, however, Ernie Adamson, the committee's counsel, shot questions at Mr. Browder the moment he sat in the witness chair. Placed in the pan, the witness sizzled. Until adjournment the sharp-witted Communist engaged in acrimonious debate with committee members. They failed to draw any new facts out of him, either about the old or the new Communist party.

It is conceivable that, had Mr. Browder been given the chance to tell his story in his own words, the committee might have got a fairly straight story, or at least a clear statement of the reasons why Mr. Browder could not or would not express his views.

In at least a part of the membership of the new committee observers see a possibility for a restrained, more judicial approach to the task of investigating subversive action. One official closely identified with the committee has asserted that the members are "above average" and cited the fact that all the Democratic members except Representative Wood are chairmen of other committees. This latter statement was offered as evidence that the committee possesses more maturity and experience than did the one headed by Mr. Dies.

Representative Mundt of South Dakota, a member of the old as well as the new committee, was the author recently of a magazine article in which he reported the comments of 100 prominent persons whom he had invited to write a definition of "un-American activities." There were almost as many definitions as there were letters.

October 7, 1945

Budenz Names the 'Secret Head' Of Communists in United States

Louis Budenz, former editor of The Daily Worker, yesterday named Gerhard Eisler, ex-member of the Germna Communist party central committee, as the person to whom he referred last Sunday as the secret chief agent of the Communist party in the United States. Eisler, he said, is now using the name of Hans Berger.

Mr. Budenz renounced the Communist party last year. He became a Catholic and is now assistant professor of economics at Fordham University. In a radio address in Detroit last Sunday, he charged that American Commu-

nists took orders from a secret agent of the Kremlin in this country and said that he could identify him.

Mr. Budenz refused to go into details regarding Berger because he will be a witness late in November in Washington before the House Committee on un-American Activities, which invited him to testify. There under oath, Mr. Budenz said, he will tell all ne knows about Berger, and produce documentary proof to support his accusation that Berger is the chief Communist in this country. Mr. Budenz added he did not know if

Berger is in New York at present, or in some other part of the country.

Berger is described as one of the leading if not the top figure in the American Communist party. His orders are supposed to be followed implicitly, Mr. Budenz said. Mr. Budenz in his address on Sunday made the point that the Communist International ostensibly dissolved during the war and is not supposed to function in this country. According to Mr. Budenz, it does exist in the United States, and its representative here is Berger.

"He never shows his face," Mr. Budenz continued. "He does not appear in official Communist buildings. Very few Communist leaders here ever see him. They all, however, follow his orders or suggestions. His signature on an article or suggestion makes it official. The

average rank-and-file American Communist, however, never heard of him."

Mr. Budenz also said that Berger is a brother of Ruth Fischer, a former Communist expelled in 1925 from the party on orders from Moscow. She is anti-Communist now and publishes a mimeographed bulletin here exposing Communist activities.

Berger is said to be well known to Federal agents. Federal Bureau of Investigation agents said Berger at one time was on the news staff of The Daily Worker and contributed articles to various Communist publications in the United States.

Berger is an Austrian by birth. He was a member of the German Communist party's central committee and an agent of the Comintern from 1919 until the time it was supposed to have been dissolved.

October 18, 1946

All Communists Here Are Spies, Budenz, Once Red, Tells Hearing

By SAMUEL A. TOWER
Special to THE NEW YORK TIMES.

WASHINGTON, Nov. 22—Louis F. Budenz, a former leader in the American Communist party, asserted today that every Communist in the United States was "a part of a Russian fifth column" operating entirely in behalf of the Soviet Union.

In testimony before the House Un-American Activities Committee, Mr. Budenz charged further that the Soviet Government was engaged in "a war of nerves" against this country, similar to that waged by Adolf Hitler, "but with Soviet variations."

This war of nerves, he maintained, could result "in military conflict between the two countries, in which the leaders of the American Communist party would be loyal to Russia."

A belief that representatives of the NKVD, the Russian secret police, were at work in the United States was expressed by Mr. Budenz, a member of the Communist party for ten years and formerly managing editor of the party's organ in this country, The Daily Worker.

After telling the committee that representatives of the secret police had been here in 1936 and 1937 and that he had had dealings with them in those two years, Mr. Budenz was asked by Representative J. Parnell Thomas, Republican, of New Jersey:

"Are they still here?"

"It would be a surprise to me if they were not," the witness replied.

The 55-year-old former Communist, a native of Indianapolis, now is an assistant professor of economics at Fordham University. He

recently held a similar position at Notre Dame University. He renounced communism and rejoined the Catholic Church last year.

The Communist movement, he told the committee, was "a conspiracy to set up world dictatorship under the control of the dictatorship in the Kremlin." It was "a quisling movement," he added, designed "to set up a Soviet dictatorship, which means overthrow of the Government of the United States."

In charting a conspiracy on behalf of the Soviet Union, Mr. Budenz maintained, the movement operated through a Communist underground in this country linked up with the regular Communist party and making use in varied degrees of "different types of Communist-front organizations."

He said that members of the party referred to various organizations used as a front as "softheaded, soft-hearted" liberals.

Eisler Not Questioned

Mr. Budenz was the only witness at the hearing. The committee postponed, probably until after the opening of Congress, questioning of Gerhard Eisler, identified by Mr. Budenz as one of the most influential figures in the American Communist movement.

In attendance among the audience, however, Mr. Eisler distributed to newsmen a statement accusing the committee of "continuing to play with my person a detestable game," and adding:

"Apparently the Un-American Activities Committee preferred not to question me and to prolong my forced stay in this country in order to have in the person of a German anti-Fascist refugee an object for its red-baiting propaganda."

The committee has issued a subpoena upon Mr. Eisler requiring his continued presence in this country, the legality of which was questioned by the witness, who said

TELLS OF COMMUNISM

Louis F. Budenz
Associated Press Wirephoto

that he "had no business being in this country."

According to Mr. Budenz, Gerhard Eisler, also referred to as Hans Berger, is "the equivalent to the representative of the Communist International, the chief communications officer of the Comintern who brings and directs the party line."

Such Communist leaders as Earl Browder or William Z. Foster "have no political life except as transmitted by Eisler," the witness declared. "Eisler-Berger can dictate to Browder and Foster."

Mr. Budenz challenged the validity of the Comintern's dissolution, maintaining that it "exists in fact if not in form and instructions still go from Moscow to parties in various countries."

A party leader of varying political hue is "always kept on

ice and pulled out when policy changes," he asserted, citing the case of the allegedly deposed Earl Browder, "who has been put on ice and made head of the Communist book trust and now can write for THE NEW YORK TIMES or appear on the radio as an ex-Communist."

In Mr. Budenz's view Mr. Browder was deposed as a symbol of a changed point of view toward the Teheran Agreement, held by the Communists to be "merely a diplomatic gesture toward peace."

Apparently expecting trouble, almost a score of Capitol policemen marched into the large committee room at the beginning of the hearing, but no disturbances occurred, and they remained as the greater part of the audience, outnumbering the sparse group of other listeners.

Mr. Budenz's three and a half hours of testimony was repetitious and disjointed and he asked the committee's permission to return at a later date with exact notes on "Communist infiltration into the schools, the movies, the radio and the press."

"We will give you all the time you want, if it takes from now to Christmas or this time next year," replied Representative John E. Rankin, Democrat, of Mississippi.

Party Retorts to Budenz

Eugene Dennis, general secretary of the Communist party, replying here last night to the testimony of Mr. Budenz, said:

"Mr. Budenz performed true to color, as a renegade and provocateur. His 'testimony' is as valid as that of a Goering or a van der Lubbe in the Reichstag trial.

"Every progressive American will understand this and will judge Budenz, the Un-American Rankin Committee and the Department of Justice accordingly."

In reference to alleged violation of passport regulations, he said:

"The allegations of this turncoat are as preposterous as they are false. The only thing true about the remarks of Budenz is that I have 'passed for an Irishman.' I, as an American of Irish descent, am an Irish-American of working-class origin."

November 23, 1946

PRESIDENT ORDERS INQUIRY ON DISLOYAL JOBHOLDERS; COMMUNISTS FIRST TARGET

FBI WILL AID STUDY

In Unprecedented Step Heads of Departments Must Back 'Purge'

REVIEW BOARD IS CREATED

It Will Hear Final Appeals of All Workers or Applicants Marked For Job Elimination

By WALTER H. WAGGONER
Special to THE NEW YORK TIMES.

WASHINGTON, March 22 — President Truman, by executive decree, ordered into effect today an elaborate and unprecedented program of security and precautions against Federal employment of any person who, on "reasonable grounds," can be judged disloyal.

The Presidential Order called for an immediate investigation of the loyalty and intentions of every person entering civilian employment in any department or agency of the Executive Branch of the Government.

Present job holders who have not already been checked for loyalty will be scrutinized by the Federal Bureau of Investigation, and their fate will rest on the decision of department heads held "personally responsible" for the character of their subordinates.

Although they were not singled out in the order, Communists and Communist sympathizers would be the first targets of the President's prescribed loyalty standards, it was indicated.

There have been repeated allegations in Congress that Communists held Federal posts, and many attacks have been made on the Administration for not ridding itself of them.

Charges Made By House Group

The House Civil Service Committee charged this week that only nine persons had been discharged from Government jobs as Communists since July 1, and promised a "full-scale investigation" of additional suspected employes.

Mr. Truman called for this sweeping program on the recommendation of his six-agency Temporary Commission on Employe Loyalty, which he named by Executive Order on last Nov. 25.

The President received the Commission's thirty-eight-page report on Feb. 20. Its publication had been held up, according to Charles G. Ross, White House press secretary, so that Mr. Truman could "study it and give time for the preparation of an Executive Order which carries out and implements the recommendations of the Commission."

Introducing his order, the President stated that every Government employe "is endowed with a measure of trusteeship over the democratic processes which are the heart and sinew of the United States."

It was of vital importance that all Federal employes be of "complete and unswerving loyalty" to this country, he continued, adding that the presence of any disloyal or subversive persons "constitutes a threat to our democratic processes."

Major Provisions of Order

Other major provisions of the ruling, in summary form, are as follows:

1. A "central master index" will be compiled of the records of all persons who have undergone loyalty checks by any agency or department since Sept. 1, 1939.

2. An over-all "Loyalty Review Board" will be set up in the Civil Service Commission, consisting of three "impartial" officers or employes of the commission. The board will review cases as an authority of final appeal for employes recommended for dismissal on grounds of disloyalty.

3. One or more three-member loyalty boards will be named by the head of each department or agency to hear cases within the agency itself.

4. The Attorney General will list all "totalitarian, fascist, communist or subversive" groups and organizations, and those which have a policy of "advocating or approving the commission of acts of force or violence to deny other persons their rights" under the Constitution, or "seeking to alter the form of government of the United States by unconstitutional means."

5. Should "derogatory information" with regard to loyalty standards of any job applicant be uncovered, a "full field investigation," utilizing all the Government's resources, will be conducted.

Maximum Protection Sought

"Maximum protection must be afforded the United States against infiltration of disloyal persons into the ranks of its employes," said the President, "and equal protection from unfounded accusations of disloyalty must be afforded the loyal employes of the Government."

The President's program, although ordered into effect immediately, requires funds, which have not yet been appropriated. It is widely felt, however, that if Congress will authorize any additional expenditures, a loyalty program such as the President has set forth will be provided with funds.

In the meantime Mr. Truman instructed the Secretaries of War and Navy and of the Treasury, so far as the Treasury Department relates to the Coast Guard, to continue to enforce and maintain "the highest standards of loyalty within the armed services."

Files to be Made Available

The government's total resources will be mobilized to carry out the President's ruling. In addition, investigation of a job applicant may include reference to the files of the FBI, the Civil Service Commission, military and naval intelligence authorities, any other "appropriate government investigative or intelligence agency," the House Committee on Un-American Activities, and state and local law enforcement agencies.

Also considered as potential sources of information relating to a person's loyalty are the schools and colleges attended by the applicant, his former employers, references given on his application, and any other source not specified or excluded in the order.

Names of persons giving information about an applicant or employe under investigation may be withheld under the terms of the order. The investigating agency must, however, supply sufficient informatioin to enable the department involved to make "an adequate evaluation" of the statements.

The investigator must also advise the agency requesting the information in writing that "it is essential to the protection of the informants or to the investigation of other cases that the names of the informants not be revealed."

Condemned Activities Listed

The specific "activities and associations" condemned in the President's program are:

Sabotage, espionage, or trying or preparing for either;

Knowingly associating with spies or saboteurs;

Treason or sedition, or the advocacy of either;

Advocacy of revolution, force, or violence to change the constitutional form of the American Government;

Intentional, unauthorized disclosure to any person, "under circumstances which may indicate disloyalty to the United States," of documents or information of a confidential or nonpublic character obtained by the person making the disclosure as a result of his Government position;

Performing his duties, whatever they are, or in any way acting in a manner which better serves the interests of a foreign Government than the United States;

Membership in or affiliation with any of the groups designated by the Attorney General as "totalitarian, Fascist, Communist, or subversive."

The first step in eliminating present employes suspected of disloyalty will be the submission to the FBI of the personnel rolls of all departments or agencies covered by the order.

The FBI will then check each name against its records of persons against whom there is already a body of evidence pointing to disloyalty. Suggestions of disloyalty by any employes will be returned to the department.

Departments will make their own investigations of suspected employes or request investigation by the Civil Service Commission.

Job applicants will be investigated first by the Civil Service Commission if they are entering positions which it covers, or, if they are not, by the department or agency in which they are seeking employment.

March 23, 1947

WOULD PROSECUTE COMMUNIST PARTY

Thomas Urges Clark to Act —Says Red Group Fails to Register as Foreign Agent

WASHINGTON, April 1 (U.P.)—Chairman J. Parnell Thomas of the House Un-American Activities Committee asked Tom C. Clark, Attorney General, today to begin prosecution of the Communist party and its officials for failure to register as foreign agents and for seeking overthrow of the Government.

He said in a letter to Mr. Clark that the committee's hearings on bills to curb or outlaw the party had established "beyond any doubt" that it was an agent of a foreign government.

He recalled the testimony of J. Edgar Hoover, director of the Federal Bureau of Investigation, that the party "is a fifth column if there ever was one."

Mr. Thomas did not name Russia but, in a report to Congress Monday, the committee stated that party members acted on direct orders from Moscow.

The Justice Department said that Mr. Clark was studying the request.

As the House Administration Committee, meanwhile, approved the group's request for $50,000 to expand its inquiry into subversive activities, committee officials said that newsreels and broadcast recordings would be used in an attempt to prove that a subpoena was served on Eugene Dennis, general secretary of the Communist party. He was escorted from the committee room by police last week after he refused to give his "real name."

The newsreels are reported to show that he brushed the subpoena aside after it was put on his arm. He was summoned to appear again April 9.

TEXT OF THOMAS LETTER

The text of Mr. Thomas' letter was as follows:

You will recall that on Oct. 7, 1946, I wrote to you and requested that you prosecute the Communist party of the United States and its officers for violation of the McCormack Registration Act (52 Statutes 631), which required that "every person who is an agent of a foreign principal shall * * * register with the Secretary of State," and the Voorhis Act (54 Statutes 1201), which requires that "every organization subject to foreign control which engages in political activity * * * shall be required to register with the Attorney General."

(The Voorhis Act further provides that "every organization, the purpose or aim of which or one of the purposes or aims of which is the establishment, control, conduct, seizure, or overthrow of a government or subdivision thereof by the use of force, violence, military measures, or threats of any one or more of the foregoing * * * shall be required to register with the Attorney General.")

The Committee on Un-American Activities today filed with the House of Representatives a report entitled "The Communist Party of the United States as an Agent of a Foreign Power."

I am enclosing herewith copies of this fifty-six-page report, which to my mind establishes beyond any doubt that the Communist party of the United States is now, and has been since its inception, an agent of a foreign government, and I respectfully request that you take immediate steps to prosecute the Communist party and its officials for failure to comply with the McCormack Act and the Voorhis Act.

Hoover's Testimony Stressed

The Committee on Un-American Activities has just completed a full week of public hearings on certain legislative proposals which seek to curb or outlaw the Communist party.

The committee has had before it a number of very competent and qualified authorities on this subject, including your director of the Federal Bureau of Investigation, J. Edgar Hoover, and it was the unanimous opinion of all these authorities who appeared before the committee that the Communist party and its agents are acting in the interest of a foreign government.

I call your attention to the following quotation from Mr. Hoover's statement before the committee:

"The Communist party of the United States is a fifth column if there ever was one. It is far better organized than were the Nazis in occupied countries prior to their capitulation.

"They are seeking to weaken America just as they did in their era of obstruction when they were aligned with the Nazis. Their goal is the overthrow of our government.

"There is no doubt as to where a real Communist's loyalty rests. Their allegiance is to Russia, not the United States."

I am sure you will agree with me, Mr. Attorney General, that from those very statements of Mr. Hoover, there is very little question but that the Voorhis Act and the McCormack Act should apply in the case of the Communist party and its officers, and I again urge you to take prompt action against this fifth column within our midst, and that they be prosecuted to the full extent of the law.

April 2, 1947

State Department Bars All Of 'Risky' Loyalty From Staff

Special to THE NEW YORK TIMES.

WASHINGTON, Oct. 7—The State Department promulgated today a sweeping set of security principles in order to safeguard itself as "a vital target for persons engaged in espionage or subversion of the United States Government."

These spell out the rules the Secretary of State will observe in exercising the wide powers given him through the rider placed in an appropriation bill by Senator Pat McCarran, Democrat, of Nevada.

The Secretary is empowered to discharge any employe considered a risk against the interests of the United States, and under his new authority a number already have had their services terminated.

The security principles declare that no person should be employed who constitutes "a security risk." It includes within that definition anyone who "is a member of, affiliated with, or in sympathetic association with the Communist, Nazi or Fascist parties."

Such persons will be observed by the department's Personnel Security Board of three men, which is headed by Conrad Snow, and which will review cases for final recommendation to the Secretary of State.

The investigation, both of employes and of applicants for positions, has been in progress for months. Since the first of the year, twelve have had their services terminated. Three on reconsideration have been permitted to resign without prejudice. The latter, therefore, may still be employed by other branches of the Government. The others cannot. No names have been disclosed.

Altogether some 4,000 cases of employes and applicants have been examined, according to officials. In addition, a number, said to be less than 100, have been permitted to resign without prejudice before investigations were completed. Some fifty applicants have been turned down or had their cases put in "pending status."

Although the powers available are sweeping, Hamilton Robinson, director of the Office of Controls, said at a news conference that there would be no "witch hunting," while at the same time every effort would be made to safeguard the department.

Unlimited power of the sort contained in the McCarran rider, he said, carries equally grave responsibility that the power be used fairly and justly. The essential problem, he added, was to protect the security interests of the department without violating the civil rights of any individual.

Rejecting either extreme, he said, the security program would be applied with sound, objective judgment by reasonable men.

Yet, he declared, in the State Department the balance must weigh somewhat more heavily in favor of security considerations than in the case of some other, though not all, government agencies; and in cases of reasonable doubt the reasonable doubt must be decided in favor of the Government.

This thesis is set forth in the text of the security principles, which includes the procedure under which the Personnel Security Board will hear cases before an employe is discharged. The board will reach its decisions by ballot and on majority vote.

Following is the text of the "security principles."

I. Security principles of the Department of State

A. The Department of State, because of its responsibility for the conduct of foreign affairs, is a vital target for persons engaged in espionage or subversion of the United States Government. Due to this fact and because of the great number of highly classified communications which pass through the department, the security of which is essential to the maintenance of peaceful and friendly international relations, it is highly important to the interests of the United States that no person should be employed in the department who constitutes a security risk.

B. The Secretary of State has been granted by Congress the right, in his absolute discretion, to terminate the employment of any officer or employe of the Department of State or of the foreign service of the United States whenever he shall deem such termination necessary or advisable in the interests of the United States. Accordingly, in the interest of the United States, the Department of State will immediately terminate the employment of any officer or employe of the Department of State or of the foreign service who is deemed to constitute a security risk.

Security Risk Defined

C. As used herein an officer or employe constitutes a security risk when he falls into one or more of the following categories: when he is——

1. A person who engages in, supports or advocates treason, subversion, or sedition, or who is a member of, affiliated with, or in sympathetic association with the Communist, Nazi or Fascist parties, or of any foreign or domestic party, organization, movement, group or combination of persons which seeks to alter the form of government of the United States by unconstitutional

means or whose policy is to advocate or approve the commission of acts of force or violence to deny other persons their rights under the Constitution of the United States; or a person who consistently believes in or supports the ideologies and policies of such a party, organization, movement, group or combination of persons.

2. A person who is engaged in espionage or who is acting directly or indirectly under the instructions of any foreign government; or who deliberately performs his duties, or otherwise acts to serve the interests of another government in preference to the interests of the United States.

3. A person who has knowingly divulged classified information without authority and with the knowledge or with reasonable grounds for the knowledge or belief that it will be transmitted to agencies of a foreign government, or who is so consistently irresponsible in the handling of classified information as to compel the conclusion of extreme lack of care or judgment.

4. A person who has habitual or close association with persons believed to be in categories 1 or 2 above to an extent which would justify the conclusion that he might through such association voluntarily or involuntarily divulge classified information without authority.

5. A person who has such basic weakness of character or lack of judgment as reasonably to justify the fear that he might be led into any course of action specified above.

Link to "Fronts" a Risk

D. In the determination of the question whether a person is a security risk the following factors, among others, will be taken into account together with such mitigating circumstances as may exist.

1. Participation in one or more of the parties or organizations re-ferred to above, or in organizations which are "fronts" for, or are controlled by, such party or organization, either by membership therein, taking part in its executive direction or control, contribution of funds thereto, attendance at meetings, employment thereby, registration to vote as a member of such a party, or signature of petition to elect a member of such a party, to public office or to accomplish any other purpose supported by such a party; or written evidences or oral expressions by speeches or otherwise, of political, economic or social views;

2. Service in the Government or armed forces of enemy countries, or other voluntary activities in support of foreign Governments;

3. Violations of security regulations;

4. Voluntary association with persons in categories C (1) or C (2);

5. Habitual drunkenness, sexual perversion, moral turpitude, financial responsibility or criminal record.

In weighing the evidence on any charges that a person constitutes risk the following considerations will obtain:

1. A former course of conduct or holding of beliefs will be presumed to continue in the absence of positive evidence indicating a change, both in course of action and conviction, by clear, overt and unequivocal acts.

2. There will be no presumption of truth in favor or statements of the witnesses in any hearing on security risk, but their statements will be weighed with all the other evidence before the hearing board, and the conclusion will be drawn by the board.

3. If a reasonable doubt exists as to whether the person falls into one of the categories listed in Paragraph I C, the department will be given the benefit of the doubt, and the person will be deemed a security risk.

II. Hearing procedure of the Personnel Security Board

A. Before any officer or employee of the Department of State or of the foreign service of the United States is summarily removed, under the provisions of the Department of State Appropriation Act, 1948, as a security risk, he shall be granted a hearing before the Personnel Security Board.

B. The officer or employe shall be served with a written notice of such hearing, at least fifteen days before such hearing is to take place, and in any event in sufficient time to enable him to prepare for and attend such hearing.

C. So far as possible, without jeopardizing national security, such notice shall state the charges made against him, as fully and completely as, in the discretion of the office of controls (CON) security considerations permit. The officer or employe shall be informed in the notice of his privilege to reply to such charges in writing before the date set for said hearing, to appear before said board personally at said hearing, to be accompanied, if he so desires, by counsel or representative of his own choosing, and to present evidence in his own behalf, through witness or by affidavit.

Evidence to Be Confidential

D. Evidence on behalf of the Department of State shall be presented to said board by CON in advance of said hearing, and shall not be presented at said hearing. For security reasons the officer or employe, his representative or counsel, cannot be permitted to hear or examine such evidence, which shall be classified as confidential or secret, as the case may be.

E. At said hearing the chairman of the board shall preside; the officer or employe shall be permitted to appear personally, and either by himself, his representative or counsel of his own choosing, to present evidence in his own behalf, through witness or by affidavit. The officer or employe and his witness shall not be sworn except on their express request. Members of the board may ask such questions of him and his witness as they may desire, but he and his witness shall not be required to answer. A stenotypist record will be made of the testimony.

F. After the record of the hearing has been reduced to writing, the board will convene in executive session to reach a decision. In its consideration the board shall be governed by the security principles of the Department of State. After examination of the evidence and following any desired discussion the vote shall be by ballot, and the decision will be by majority vote. The vote by each member will be recorded, with any statement which he may desire to make as to his reasons therefor.

G. The finding of the board will be either that (1) the board finds insufficient evidence on which the adjust the officer or employe a security risk; or that (2) the board finds the officer or employe to constitute a security risk. In the event of a finding of insufficient evidence the board may in its discretion recommend further or continued investigation of specific points on which they consider the record inadequate, or may recommend that the case be closed. The findings of the board shall be accompanied by a brief analysis of the evidence, and an indication of the reasons of the board for its decision. The record will be classified as secret and transmitted to the Secretary of State, with a copy to the Office of Controls.

October 8, 1947

Hollywood Is a Main Red Center, Adolphe Menjou Tells House Body

By GLADWIN HILL
Special to The New York Times.

LOS ANGELES, May 15 — Adolphe Menjou, a veteran actor, told a House Un-American Activities subcommittee today that "Hollywood is one of the main centers of Communist activity in America."

He asserted that this was so because motion pictures "are our greatest medium of propaganda, and it is the desire and wish of the masters of Moscow to use this medium for their purpose—which is the overthrow of the American Government."

Representative J. Parnell Thomas of New Jersey, chairman of the committee, who relayed Mr. Menjou's formally recorded opinions to reporters after a closed hearing, said that the actor agreed to appear in Washington June 16 when the full committee would continue the inquiry into alleged commu-nistic activities in Hollywood and elsewhere.

Mr. Thomas said that Mr. Menjou and Jack Warner, a producer, who also testified today, provided the committee with names of Hollywood Communists.

"We have now hundreds of names, prominent names," the chairman asserted, "and they are mostly writers. It is my opinion, based on the testimony we have received, that the film industry itself can clean house if it will have the will to do so."

"I think the Un-American Activities Committee is doing an excellent job here," Mr. Warner testified, "and I am happy to have had the opportunity to cooperate with its members."

Both names and Communist party membership numbers of Hollywood individuals were fur-nished by Rupert Hughes, a leader of the conservative writing faction in Hollywood, Mr. Thomas reported.

Mr. Hughes, outside the hearing room, said that the Screen Writers Guild, which he helped found, was "lousy with Communists."

"They began to take over the guild in 1937," he asserted. "They've been powerful in Hollywood for years, both secretly and openly. They've attacked me and anything else that ever opposed them."

After the hearing Mr. Menjou said to reporters:

"What I can't understand is how there are so many millionaires who are for Communism.

"There are lots of them in Hollywood—at least half a dozen red directors and some red actors. The Communist movement in Hollywood has reached serious proportions. They are out to soften up the United States just as the Nazis did in Norway."

A veteran of World War I who speaks a number of languages, including Russian, Mr. Menjou has been in Hollywood for twenty-seven years.

Leo McCarey, a producer, after conferring with the committee for a half hour, said:

"I only came down because I was glad of an opportunity to co-operate with the committee."

The alleged holders of party membership numbers were believed likely to have been a group of some fifteen individuals who were listed with the numbers in an "exposé" some months ago by a Hollywood film trade paper.

Mr. Thomas announced that Victor Kravchenko, former Communist who wrote the book "I Chose Freedom," had been called as a witness.

His eventual appearance before the committee was arranged four weeks ago at a "secret and highly important" conference in Washington, Mr. Thomas said, and was advanced when it was learned that he was in Los Angeles.

After Mr. Kravchenko talked with the committee, Mr. Thomas telegraphed Tom C. Clark, Federal attorney general, that he had subpoenaed the writer for appearance in Washington June 26.

Stating that a threat had been made to bomb or burn the home of Mr. Kravchenko's Beverly Hills host, L. R. Brooks, the chairman asked that the Federal Bureau of Investigation be assigned to the matter and to the protection of Mr. Kravchenko as a "friendly" witness until his Washington appearance.

May 16, 1947

FILM MEN ADMIT ACTIVITY BY REDS; HOLD IT IS FOILED

Sam Wood Lists Writers by Name as Communists and Says Group Seeks Rule

SOME CONTRACTS DROPPED

Jack Warner Tells Congress Inquiry Ousted Workers Had Un-American Views

By SAMUEL A. TOWER
Special to THE NEW YORK TIMES.

WASHINGTON, Oct. 20—While they conceded the presence of a core of persons of "un-American" or reputed Communist leanings in the film industry, principally among screen writers, three Hollywood producers asserted today that Communist efforts to penetrate the movies had been checkmated in their productions and that the bulk of the industry was overwhelmingly patriotic.

The three producers, Louis B. Mayer, president of Metro-Goldwyn-Mayer; Jack Warner, vice president of Warner Brothers, and Sam Wood, an independent, were the first day's witnesses as the House Committee on Un-American Activities opened an inquiry into "alleged Communist influence and infiltration in the motion-picture industry."

In the course of the testimony, Mr. Wood, president of the Motion Picture Alliance for the Preservation of American Ideals, a recently-formed Hollywood organization, denounced a group of screen writers and directors specifically by name as unquestioned Communists, serving, in his view, as "agents of a foreign power." He maintained that "a tight disciplined group of Communist party members and party-liners" had been and still was endeavoring to gain control of the industry.

Rejects Move for Quashing

Mr. Warner, carefully shunning the term "Communist," testified that Warner Brothers had failed to renew the contracts of almost a dozen writers because they held what he considered "un-American" views.

Mr. Mayer acknowledged the presence of two or three reputed Communists in his company, but stated that the reports were not proved, that nothing subversive had ever been contributed by them and that M-G-M, through examination and re-examination of its productions, had never put out any movies containing anything alien to American doctrines.

The committee refused to take up a motion to quash the subpoenas that it had issued against nineteen Hollywood figures, directing them to appear as witnesses.

The motion was brought before the committee by Robert W. Kenny, former Attorney General of California, and Bartley C. Crum, San Francisco attorney, acting in conjunction with four other lawyers in behalf of the group of nineteen, some of whom were subsequently named by the producers. Representative J. Parnell Thomas, Republican, of New Jersey, the committee chairman, directed the two attorneys, who presented their motion as the hearings began, to make it next week, when their clients would be summoned to testify. In the meantime the committee took the brief under consideration.

Wood Lists Several Names

Mr. Wood, an independent producer and director of thirty years' experience in the industry, has made such films as "For Whom the Bell Tolls," "Saratoga Trunk," "Kitty Foyle" and "Ivy." He asserted that the Communists and their sympathizers, although "a small proportion," were constantly seeking to gain control of segments of the industry and to spread their influence either by pro-Communist contributions or by touches inimical to the United States.

Speaking as a member of the Screen Directors Guild, he charged John Cromwell, Irving Pichel, Edward Dymtryk, Frank Tuttle and another whose name he could not recall with trying to "steer us into the red river."

Under questioning as to the activities of screen writers, he alleged that Dalton Trumbo, Donald Ogden Stewart and John Howard Lawson held Communist leanings.

"Is there any question in your mind that Lawson is a Communist?" he was asked.

"If there is I haven't any mind," he replied.

While wholeheartedly in favor of uprooting "the conspiratorial group" seeking to subvert the screen, Mr. Wood warned of the danger of censorship in such efforts, along with the danger of violation of freedom of expression.

"Those people are so well organized that they would go to town and put their people in control of the censorship," he said.

In response to a question about financial contributions to the Com-

UN-AMERICAN COMMITTEE OPENS ITS HEARINGS ON THE MOTION PICTURE INDUSTRY

Jack L. Warner as he testified yesterday

Louis B. Mayer (right) talking to Eric Johnston

munist cause in Hollywood, Mr. Wood stated that "substantial" contributions were made, calling attention to a recent rally at which Katharine Hepburn, the actress, appeared and $87,000 was raised. This money "didn't go to the Boy Scouts," he added.

Mr. Warner, emphasizing that anything subversive was culled from his studio's productions, admitted that there had been some infiltration into the movie capital of individuals whose outlook he regarded as "un-American."

Despite repeated questions by Robert E. Stripling, the committee's chief investigator, he steadfastly avoided the term Communist, submitting that he had encountered, principally among his writers, those seeking to incorporate into film productions ideas that he regarded as "un-American."

The producer's testimony of last Spring, taken in Hollywood by a subcommittee under Chairman Thomas, was read. In this Mr. Warner stated that he had failed to take up the contracts, because of lack of sympathy with their views, of Irwin Shaw, Clifford Odets, Alvah Bessie, Gordon Kahn, Guy Endore, Howard Koch, Ring Lardner Jr., Robert Rosson, Emmett Lavery, Albert Maltz, Sheridan Gibney, Julius and Philip Epstein, John Wexley, Dalton Trumbo and John Howard Lawson.

In his testimony today Mr. Warner declared that he had reconsidered and that he felt, in retrospect, that the names of Messrs. Endore, Gibney and J. and P. Epstein should be deleted from the list.

He stood by his previous testimony that 95 per cent of those holding "un-American" views were writers. He reiterated that he had never seen a Communist, to his knowledge, and explained that his attitude toward the writers was based on what he regarded as "slanted" lines and writing that "I consider un-American doctrine."

Mr. Mayer told the committee that the Communists were unable

to get "a single thing" in M-G-M productions because they were checked and rechecked by himself, his readers, his editors and his producers.

Asked if there were any Communist writers in his studio, he testified that he had heard three mentioned in this category, Dalton Trumbo, Donald Ogden Stewart and Lester Cole, but that he had never seen any Communist propaganda in their work.

Mr. Mayer observed that M-G-M counsel had informed him that the studio, if it attempted to discharge an employe for communism, would have to prove it or be liable for damage suits. In response to questions he said that he would not employ anyone holding a dues card from the Communist party.

Along with Mr. Warner and Mr. Wood, Mr. Mayer favored action to make the Communist party an illegal organization.

The M-G-M head then read a spirited statement defending his studio and the industry and particularly the production of the film, "Song of Russia," which committee representatives described as containing Communist propaganda.

"Like others in the motion picture industry," he declared, "I have maintained a relentless vigilance against un-American influences. If, as has been alleged, Communists have attempted to use the screen for subversive purposes, I am proud of our success in circumventing them.

"The motion picture industry employs many thousands of people. As is the case with the newspaper, radio, publishing and theater business, we cannot be responsible for the political views of each individual employe. It is, however, our complete responsibility to determine what appears on the motion picture screen.

"The Communists attack our screen as an instrument of capitalism. Few, if any, of our films, ever reach Russia. It hates us be-

cause it fears us. We show too much of the American way of life, of human dignity, of the opportunity and the happiness to be enjoyed in a democracy.

"More than any other country in the world, we have enjoyed the fullest freedom of speech in all means of communication. It is this freedom that has enabled the motion picture to carry the message to the world of our democratic way of life."

While acknowledging that the criticized movie, "Song of Russia," was friendly to Russia, Mr. Mayer emphasized that it was produced in an effort to aid the war, at a time when the Russian situation at Stalingrad was desperate and our national leaders were pleading for all-out support for our wartime ally.

Differing with the star of the movie, Robert Taylor, who has testified before the subcommittee that the picture was "Communist propaganda," Mr. Mayer contended that the final script of the film was little more than a musical boy-and-girl romance featuring a Russian setting and the music of Tchaikovsky.

Because the script of the movie was changed to eliminate references to Soviet farm collectivism— "I don't preach any ideology except Americanism and I don't even preach that, I let it speak for itself"—Mr. Mayer explained that the late Frank Knox, then Secretary of the Navy, had put off Mr. Taylor's enlistment in the Navy to allow him to complete the delayed film.

Reminding the committee of a number of films produced by M-G-M to support the war effort, including "Mrs. Miniver," which "was rushed into release at the urgent request of the United States officials to meet the rising tide of anti-English feeling that followed the fall of Tobruk," Mr. Mayer recalled further:

"The United States Army Signal Corps made 'The Battle of Stalin-

grad,' released in 1943, with a prologue expressing high tribute from President Roosevelt, our Secretaries of State, War and Navy, and from Generals Marshall and MacArthur."

After Mr. Mayer had read reviews of "Song of Russia" from THE NEW YORK TIMES, The New York Herald Tribune, The Washington Post and other newspapers, describing the film as a harmless musical film containing more things American than Russian, the committee's chief investigator summoned Ayn Rand, Russian-born novelist and author of a recent best-seller, "The Fountainhead," to the stand.

The novelist, who testified that she had left Russia in 1926 and was under contract to write film productions, denounced "Song of Russia" as a vehicle of Communist propaganda full of distortions and inaccuracies and an outright falsification of Russian life as she knew it.

Mr. Warner asserted that "there is not a Warner Brothers picture that can fairly be judged to be hostile to our country, or communistic in tone or purpose," and cited many movies produced by that studio furthering the American way of life and ideals. He similarly rejected committee allegations that the studio's production of "Mission to Moscow" contained Communist propaganda.

It followed faithfully the book written by Joseph E. Davies, former Ambassador to Russia, he stated when challenged as to its accuracy, and added that it was designed to further our war effort by encouraging Russia at a time when it was feared the Soviet Union might withdraw from the war.

Mr. Thomas, opening the hearings, read a statement asserting that "there is no question that there are Communists in Hollywood" and said his committee was trying to determine the "extent" of penetration.

October 21, 1947

79 IN HOLLYWOOD FOUND SUBVERSIVE, INQUIRY HEAD SAYS

Evidence of Communist Spying Will Be Offered Next Week, Thomas Declares

By SAMUEL A. TOWER
Special to THE NEW YORK TIMES.

WASHINGTON, Oct. 22—Actors, writers and others in Hollywood were named today as members of the Communist party or as Communist sympathizers. The accusations were by Robert Taylor, screen actor, and by other movie figures

as the inquiry of the House Committee on Un-American Activities into the extent of Communist penetration into the film industry went into its third day.

At the same time the movie industry, reacting to a persistent committee criticism that no anti-Communist pictures were being made, charged through its counsel, Paul V. McNutt, that suggestions concerning films to be made represented "one method of censorship" and did "violence to the principle of free speech."

The committee chairman, Representative J. Parnell Thomas, asserted that the committee would produce at coming sessions evidence that "at least 79" persons in Hollywood had been engaged in subversive activity.

To Reveal Data on Spying

After a noon executive session the committee announced that it

would present next week evidence of Communist espionage activities, with a surprise witness, in developing further yesterday's testimony that confidential data on an Army supersonic plane had fallen into Communist hands through a Hollywood literary agent.

Mr. Taylor, arriving to appear at the afternoon session, was greeted with an audible "ah" by the spectators, mostly women, who filled the hearing chamber. Outside the chamber there was a mob scene as those unable to get in swirled and pushed against Capitol police.

The actor, a native of Nebraska, drew a laugh by his reply to the first question, how long he had been an actor?

"I have been employed as an actor since 1934," he said.

In his testimony he declared at one point:

"I personally believe the Com-

munist party should be outlawed. If I had my way they'd all be sent back to Russia."

When this drew loud applause from the audience, following a lesser burst earlier, Chairman Thomas reprimanded the spectators and requested no further demonstrations.

Rise in Activity "Indicated"

Mr. Taylor asserted that there had been "more indications" of Communist activity in Hollywood in the past four or five years, but guarded and qualified his testimony when committee interrogators sought specific data on activities and individuals. He testified that, as a member of the Screen Actors Guild, he had come to believe that there were actors and actresses "who, if not Communists, are working awfully hard to be so" and whose philosophy and tactics seemed closely akin to the Communist party line. This group constituted what he called "a disrupting influence."

Asked for names, he mentioned Howard Da Silva and Karen Morley as "the only two I can think of at the moment," adding, "I don't know whether they're Communists."

At another point, queried about Hollywood writers, Mr. Taylor mentioned Lester Cole as "reputedly a Communist, I wouldn't know personally."

The handsome actor declared that the film, "Song of Russia," was, in his view, Communist propaganda and that he had objected "strenuously" to playing in it.

He added, however, that the industry at that time was producing a number of movies designed to strengthen the feeling of the American people toward Russia and that many of the points to which he objected had been eliminated in the final script.

He rejected any suggestion that the movie had been made at the instigation of the Government. He reported that he attended a five-minute meeting of Metro-Goldwyn-Mayer executives, producing the film, and Lowell Mellett, then heading the motion picture division of the Office of War Information. At this meeting, he stated, it developed that the Government approved of the movie's production.

Also taking the opportunity to correct any impressions that he had been compelled to act in the movie, the witness said:

"If I ever gave the impression that I was forced to make the picture—I wasn't forced, because they can't force you to make any picture."

Mr. Taylor asserted that he had not knowingly worked with a Communist and would not do so. Along with 99.9 per cent of the industry, he stated, he regarded the Communist segment as "the rotten apple in the barrel."

Robert W. Kenny, counsel for Mr. Cole, slated to be a witness later, circulated a communication to the press that Mr. Cole, whom Mr. Taylor had said he suspected of communism, was one of the authors of Mr. Taylor's forthcoming movie, "The High Wall."

"This is difficult to reconcile with Taylor's statement that he would not work on any picture with anyone he suspected of 'communistic tendencies,'" the Kenny note said.

After twenty-five minutes on the stand, during which he assured the committee that the motion picture industry would make anti-Communist films "when the time comes, and it may not be long," the star made his departure, accompanied by applause and the shouts of "Hurray for Robert Taylor" from a middle-aged woman wearing a red hat.

Ex-Communist Heard

Another witness today was Howard Rushmore, a member of the Communist party from 1936 to 1939, former movie critic of the Daily Worker, Communist newspaper, and now a writer for the New York Journal-American.

He stated that he broke with the

AT THE UN-AMERICAN HEARING YESTERDAY

Robert Taylor and Representative J. Parnell Thomas in conference
The New York Times (by Tames)

party because of differences over the film "Gone With the Wind," which he found partly praiseworthy while the party line dictated outright condemnation and boycott.

He told the committee that a party objective was to gain control of propaganda vehicles, including films, that Communist leaders received "regular information" about pictures and scripts and that the party sought to organize "letter and telegram campaigns" against movies it opposed.

During his party membership, he said, John Howard Lawson, a film writer subpoenaed for appearance later, was "in direct charge of activities in Hollywood." He described Mr. Lawson as a "top sergeant" under a V. J. Jerome, heading the party's cultural operations and in turn under the representative of the Communist International.

In response to questions the witness said that the Daily Worker regarded Charlie Chaplin and Edward G. Robinson, screen actors, as "what we call in the newspaper business sacred cows, people you treat favorably."

"I don't know whether or not he is a Communist," he said of Mr. Robinson, "but for ten years he has been joining front organizations and is still doing it."

He declared that Mr. Robinson was a sponsor of the American Committee for the Protection of Foreign Born, "a front organization," along with Albert Waltz, a writer; Mr. Da Silva, Herbert K. Sorrell, Hollywood labor figure; Mr. Kenny, who is a former At-

torney General of California and counsel for a number of prospective witnesses, "and a number of others."

He testified that he had seen Clifford Odets, playwright and movie author, at the office of The Daily Worker, that Mr. Lawson "referred to Lionel Stander as a perfect example of how a Communist should not act in Hollywood" and that writers Alvah Bessie, Albert Maltz and Michael Blankford had been sent to Hollywood under party direction.

In the course of telling of "thousands" raised by party workers in Hollywood, he quoted Joe North, whom he described as editor of the New Masses, Communist magazine, as complaining over the refusal of John Garfield, actor, to contribute with the words: "That's what happens to our comrades when they get to Hollywood."

Another witness, Morrie Ryskind, stage and screen writer, declared that the Screen Writers Guild, under the leadership of Emmett Lavery and Gordon Kahn, was Communist-controlled.

He and Max Kahn had neighboring homes, but relations were strained, he stated, observing that each was nice to the other's children and "our dogs are very good friends." He acknowledged that labeling his neighbor as a person with communistic leanings "will not increase neighborly relations."

He asserted that Lester Cole was unquestionably a Communist.

"You would have to be deaf, dumb and blind not to notice Communist penetration," he declared. He listed as Communist objectives

front organizations "for suckers" and control of the guilds and crafts in the industry.

He described as such a front organization the League Against War and Fascism, tracing its name changes to the League for Peace and Democracy and "probably now called League to Get Americans Out of Greece and Henry Wallace in the White House."

An M-G-M executive, James K. McGuinness, in charge of scripts for the studio, asserted that ten or fifteen top-flight writers were Communists, including some at M-G-M. He related that there had been apparently Communist-inspired protests against a studio production, "Tennessee Johnson," on the ground that it reflected upon Negroes.

The protest was signed by five Hollywood writers who, in his opinion, "have consistently followed the Communist party line in every twist and turn." He named these as Donald Ogden Stewart, Hy Kraft, Richard Collins, Ring Lardner Jr., and Jules Dassein. He also linked the names of Mr. Lawson and Mr. Bessie with communism.

The executive testified that Communists in the story end were able to put forward their sympathizers and block opponents and that the name of Hollywood was invaluable in bolstering attendance and financial aid for Communist-front organizations.

In the course of defending such criticized movies as "Mission to Moscow," "Song of Russia," and "North Star," as pro-Soviet rather than pro-Communist, Mr. McGuinness was asked by the chairman and other committee members questions along this line:

Has the industry the will to make anti-Communist movies? Why haven't they been made? Why couldn't the studios produce such films and circulate them through schools, like the patriotic wartime pictures?

Referring to this line of questioning, Mr. McNutt, special counsel for the industry, declared himself "shocked to see the violence done to the principle of free speech during the hearings this morning."

"How would your editors like to be told what should be put on the editorial page?" he exclaimed to the crowd of reporters encircling him.

In a statement repeating his extemporaneous remarks, Mr. McNutt declared:

"It became perfectly apparent, during the chairman's questioning of Mr. McGuinness, that the purpose was to try to dictate and control, through the device of the hearings, what goes on the screens of America.

"Free Screen" Fight Promised

"This is no concern of any Congressional committee. It is the concern solely of those who produce motion pictures.

"You don't need a law to impair the constitutional rights of free speech. It can be done by intimidation and coercion. That is the way of totalitarian regimes which we all hate.

"We shall fight to continue a free screen in America. We fought for it when freedom of speech was challenged before a Senate committee in 1941. The industry asserted then its right to choose the material to be used on the screen. It emphatically reasserts that right today and accepts the full responsibility for screen content."

In addition to promising to introduce into the hearings "complete records' on the seventy-nine personalities the committee regarded as subversive, Mr. Thomas

told reporters that along with developments in the supersonic plane testimony given yesterday the committee planned to present additional evidence of a Communist espionage network.

Another Name Is Added

Robert Stripling read into the record a telegram from Sam Wood, an independent movie director and witness two days ago, who added

the name of Lewis Milestone to a list of directors that he had informed the committee he regarded as sympathetic to the Communist movement.

Representative Emanuel Celler, Democrat, of New York, attacked the committee's inquiry as "Donnybrook Fair proceedings" to make "all true Americans blush with shame."

"If Chairman Thomas sought,"

he said, "to strike terror into the minds of the movie magnates, he succeeded. They were white-livered.

"One vital aspect of these antics must be kept in mind. Today it is the motion pictures. Tomorrow it may be the newspapers or the radio. The threat to civil liberties is a real one."

October 23, 1947

Hollywood Communists 'Militant,' But Small in Number, Stars Testify

By SAMUEL A. TOWER
Special to THE NEW YORK TIMES.

WASHINGTON, Oct. 23—Three Hollywood stars, leaders in the Screen Actors Guild, stated today that their profession contained a "militant, well-organized, well-disciplined minority" of Communist leanings. They declared that the group was tiny and had made no headway.

The three actors, Robert Montgomery, George Murphy and Ronald Reagan, joined another stellar figure, Gary Cooper, in giving their views on communism in Hollywood before the House Committee on Un-American Activities, conducting an inquiry into the degree of Communist infiltration in the film industry.

Another group of Broadway and Hollywood artists, professing their belief "in constitutional democratic government," disclosed after the hearing that its members had banded together to form the Committee for the First Amendment of the Constitution, to oppose the inquiry on the grounds that it "stifled" the "free spirit of creativeness" and violated the constitutional right of free expression by investigating individual political beliefs.

In an informal news conference in the hearing chamber, John Garfield, actor, and Paul Draper, dancer, acting as spokesmen, listed among the Hollywood members of the new committee Paulette Goddard, Henry Fonda, Gregory Peck, Van Heflin, Myrna Loy and Burgess Meredith; and among the members from Broadway George S. Kaufman, Moss Hart, Olin Downes, music critic of THE NEW YORK TIMES, and Louis Calhern, actor.

Mr. Reagan, present president of the Screen Actors Guild, along with two past presidents, Messrs. Montgomery and Murphy, described to the committee the tactics allegedly used by Communist adherents in the acting profession, but declared that a "very small minority," less than 1 per cent,

belonged to that group and that its efforts to gain control had been completely frustrated.

While making plain their aversion to the Communist movement they stressed the necessity for applying democratic procedures in combating it. In contrast to some of their Hollywood colleagues they indicated an unwillingness to label Hollywood personalities as Communists on mere hearsay without conclusive evidence.

There was a long drawn-out "ooooh" from the jam-packed, predominantly feminine audience as the tall Mr. Reagan, clad in a tan gabardine suit, a blue knitted tie and a white shirt.

Moves in Other Fields Cited

Mr. Reagan stated that there was in his field, as in virtually every labor organization, at least a small group which had followed policies usually associated with the Communist party. He added that within "the bounds of democracy we have done a pretty good job in blocking their activities" and have been "eminently successful" in keeping them from "their usual tactics of running an organization by minority."

"The best thing to do in opposing those people is to make democracy work," he declared in response to committee questions as to anti-Communist steps and the desirability of outlawing the Communist party, adding:

"I abhor the Communist philosophy but more than that I detest their tactics which are the tactics of a fifth column.

"However, as a citizen, I hope that we are never prompted by fear or resentment of communism into compromising any of our democratic principles in order to fight them.

"As Jefferson said it better than I, if the people know all of the facts they will never make a mistake."

"Character Assassination" Hit

Preceding Mr. Reagan was his predecessor in the Guild's presidency, the veteran actor, Mr. Montgomery, 43 years old, who created a stir in the crowd as he appeared, conservatively attired in a double-breasted brown suit.

In response to questions he described the behavior pattern of the Communist fringe as a policy

TESTIFYING BEFORE HOUSE GROUP IN CAPITAL

Robert Montgomery

Ronald Reagan

Gary Cooper

Fred Niblo Jr.
The New York Times (by Tames)

of confusing issues by long and protracted discussion and "character assassination."

"We have had in the Guild, as have other unions, a very militant, very small minority, well-organized and well disciplined," he related.

He added that this minority was "never successful under any circumstances at any time" in dominating Guild policy.

In common with his Guild colleagues he thought the production of anti-Communist films would be "helpful."

Another former president of the Actors Guild, bespectacled, 36-year-old George Murphy, actor and dancer, followed Mr. Montgomery on the stand. He wore a double-breasted blue suit, white shirt and blue tie speckled with red.

Mr. Murphy echoed the views of his colleagues that there was "constant irritation" from a small group and maintained that there were in Hollywood "an awful lot of good, honest, liberal people who are being used" by the Communist fragment, "less than 1 per cent."

Action by Congress Proposed

As did his associates, Mr. Murphy said he regarded himself as "not qualified" to answer questions about banning the Communist party, although he and they said they viewed the movement as operating in behalf of a foreign government. He held that Federal agencies should disclose information about Communists and that the decision on outlawing them was one for Congress and the Government.

The audience, obviously stirred by the personal appearance of the screen celebrities, demonstrated only once, at a point where Mr. Montgomery asserted:

"I give up my job to fight a totalitarianism called fascism. I am quite willing to give it up again to fight a totalitarianism called Communism."

Before terminating their brief testimony, the three leaders in the Actors' Guild asserted that the great preponderance of the industry, and not just a segment, was fighting all "isms."

The 46-year-old Mr. Cooper, in a gray double-breasted suit, light blue silk tie and white shirt, appeared at the afternoon session.

In his testimony, Mr. Cooper said that he had rejected a number of scripts because they contained what he regarded as subversive ideas, though he was unable to recall any titles. He said that he had encountered communistic doctrines at various gatherings.

As examples of what he considered "un-American" expressions, he submitted statements made to him that the Constitution of the United States was 150 years out of date and that this country would have a more efficient government without Congress. At the latter the crowd and the committee members laughed.

Mr. Cooper acknowledged that statements distributed by the Communist party in Italy and Yugoslavia which described him as a Communist here, a leader in the class struggle and a mourner of the brutal assassination of a fellow-actor on Broadway were evident and ridiculous fabrications. The actor reported slain was still alive, Mr. Cooper said.

Gulping as he heard himself described as a Communist leader addressing a horde of 90,000 followers in Philadelphia, the tall, former cowboy drawled:

"An audience of 90,000 is a little tough to disregard, but it is not true."

After ten minutes on the stand, Mr. Cooper left and was succeeded by Leo McCarey, veteran screen director, responsible for such hits as "Going My Way" and "The Bells of St. Mary."

Replying to questions about the success of these films in Russia, Mr. McCarey remarked that they had not brought in "one ruble from Russia" because "I think we have a character in them that they don't like."

"Who, Bing Crosby?" he was asked.

"No, God," replied the director.

Mr. McCarey felt that there was some Communist propaganda in some pictures through repulsive characterizations of bankers and similar figures, but he took issue with suggestions that the industry put out anti-Communist movies, contending that the screen's primary role was entertainment and that, because of its international audience, more enmity would be produced by a display of partisanship.

Richard Macaulay and Fred Niblo Jr., two writers, were earlier witnesses and contended that the Screen Writers Guild was Communist-controlled.

Mr. Macaulay offered the committee a list of members of the Writers Guild of whom he said he was certain or "morally certain" that they were Communists or followers of the party line.

The names submitted by Mr. Macaulay were:

Alvah Bessie, Lester Cole, Gordon Kahn, Howard Koch, Ring Lardner Jr., John Howard Lawson, Waldo Salt, Samuel Ornitz, Robert Rossen, Dalton Trumbo, Guy Endore, Hugo Butler, Maurice Rapf, Michael Blankfort, Donald Ogden Stewart, John Wexley, R. MacDougall, John Collier, Abraham Polensky, Henry Myers, Marian Spitzer, Paul Trivers, William Pomerance, Richard Collins, Albert Maltz, Melvin Levy, Harold Buchman and Clifford Odets.

Mr. Niblo, describing the Writers' Guild as the "sparkplug and spearhead" of Communist activities in Hollywood, also designated some of the above as adherents of the movement, but added that "I can't prove that any more than Custer could prove the people massacring him were Indians."

In executive session the committee drew up plans to conclude its hearing of witnesses sympathetic to its inquiry early next week and to introduce at that time a "surprise" witness and thereafter to summon for testimony witnesses opposing the inquiry, beginning with the writer, John Howard Lawson.

"No official, high or petty, can proscribe what can be considered orthodox," said Mr. Garfield at his impromptu news conference to declare the opposition of his group to the committee's investigation.

Mr. Draper asserted that the group's objective was to see "that the spirit of free creativeness is not stifled by individual ambition of Congressional committees."

Mr. Garfield distributed copies of the following statement drawn up by the Hollywood branch of the Committee for the First Amendment:

"We the undersigned, as American citizens who believe in constitutional, democratic government, are disgusted and outraged by the continuing attempts of the House Un-American Activities Committee to smear the motion-picture industry.

"We hold that these hearings are morally wrong because any investigation into the political beliefs of the individual is contrary to the basic principles of our democracy. Any attempt to curb freedom of expression and to set arbitrary standards of Americanism is in itself disloyal to both the spirit and the letter of our Constitution."

In addition to those Hollywood personalities already named the signatures on the statement were stated to include:

Ava Gardner, Dorothy McGuire, Eddie Cantor, Norman Corwin, Cornel Wilde, Marsha Hunt, Paul Henreid, Barry Sullivan, Sheppard Strudwick, William Wyler, Anatole Litvak, Jerry Wald, Norman Krasna, John Huston, Philip Dunne, Doris Nolan, Sheridan Gibney, Richard Conte, Julius Epstein, Philip Epstein, John Houseman and Collier Young.

In the Broadway group of the committee, in addition to those named, Messrs. Draper and Garfield listed the following:

Agnes de Mille, Jerome Chodorov, Irwin Shaw, Godhard Lieberson, Hugh Marlowe, Philip Loeb, Leonard Bernstein, Harold Rome, Daniel Saidenberg, Cheryl Crawford, Paul Stewart, and Richard Watts Jr., drama critic of The New York Post.

"So far as we know there are no Communists in our group," committee spokesmen declared. "The committee is certainly and absolutely not a Communist front."

October 24, 1947

Ten Film Men Cited for Contempt In Overwhelming Votes by House

By JAY WALZ
Special to THE NEW YORK TIMES.

WASHINGTON, Nov. 24—The House approved overwhelmingly today citations for contempt of Congress against ten Hollywood personalities who refused last month to tell the Committee on Un-American Activities whether they were members of the Communist party.

The first of the cases, against Albert Maltz, a writer credited with "Destination Tokyo," resulted in a vote of 346 to 17 for the citation, thus turning the case over to the United States Attorney for prosecution. One Republican and the sole American Labor member of the House voted with fifteen Democrats in opposition.

The second case, that of Dalton Trumbo, another motion-picture writer, was decided in a standing vote of 240 to 15. The remaining eight cases were handled in rapid-fire order without debate and by voice vote. These concerned Samuel Ornitz, John Howard Lawson, Ring Lardner Jr., Lester Cole and Alvah Bessie, writers; Herbert Biberman, a director-producer; Edward Dmytryk, director, and Robert Adrian Scott, a writer and producer.

Attorney General Tom C. Clark said tonight that he had asked the United States District Attorney, Morris Fay, to prosecute the ten witnesses accused of contempt, adding that "the authority of the Congress must be maintained."

A court conviction of contempt of Congress carries a maximum punishment of one year in jail and a $1,000 fine.

Chairman J. Parnell Thomas of the House committee brought in the unanimous recommendation of the Un-American Activities group that the ten "hostile" witnesses be cited, and told House members that the men had utterly defied the committee in its effort to delve into subversive activities in this country.

Each of the cases was introduced with the presentation by Mr. Thomas of a formal report of the witness' appearance before the committee. These reports, as presented to the House, contained quotations from their testimony showing that none had answered directly the question: "Are you now, or have you ever been, a member of the Communist party?"

Some had also declined to state, on constitutional grounds, whether they belonged to the Screen Writers Guild.

When the witnesses declined direct answers to these questions, they were excused from the witness stand without further testimony. Most of the witnesses, described by the committee as "hostile" or "unfriendly," had come with prepared statements, which

Chairman Thomas refused to let them present.

Leading off the debate on Mr. Maltz's case, Mr. Thomas promised that his committee had staged "only the beginning" of a drive against Communists in the motion-picture industry. He said it was "ridiculous" for the ten witnesses and their supporters to think that the committee had no right to inquire into their political affiliations.

"The Constitution was never intended to cloak or shield those who would destroy it," he said. He added that the Communist party was in no sense a political party, but "a conspiracy to overthrow the Government of the United States."

"We have been called to Washington to sit in special session to appropriate billions of dollars to stop the floodtide of communism from sweeping all of Europe," Mr. Thomas continued. "What a paradox if that same Congress cannot inquire into the activities of a Communist conspirator in the United States, whose first allegiance is to a foreign government."

Mr. Thomas and fellow committee members insisted throughout the afternoon that the contempt citations were based on the refusal of the witnesses "to answer the most pertinent question that we could ask."

The committee chairman declared, however, that the ten witnesses had not been picked at random, but were subpoenaed "because our investigation had disclosed that they were Communists or had long records of Communist affiliation and activities."

Opponents of the citations contended vigorously that Mr. Thomas' committee had conducted its inquiry illegally by violating the constitutional rights of free speech and thought.

Representative Herman Eberharter, Democrat, of Pennsylvania, who was first to speak against the citations, said the House had the choice of supporting either the Thomas committee, or free speech.

"We cannot do both," he said.

The Pennsylvanian added that he felt the committee was trying not to destroy a subversive threat, but to control the motion-picture industry. If Congressional committees were to try men, they should do it "in the American tradition," he said, holding that the men facing citation had not received rights from the committee which they would have received in a trial court.

Representative Chet Holifield, Democrat, of California, who also voted against the citations, said the House, in upholding the Un-American Activities Committee, was "treading on dangerous grounds," and was stepping into a 'quicksand which will engulf our liberties."

Representative Vito Marcantonio, American Laborite of New York, attacked the Thomas committee's procedure as unconstitutional.

Representative Helen Gahagan Douglas, Democrat, of California, announced that she was introducing a bill to modify drastically committee procedures "to adequately safeguard individual rights."

Committee supporters, however, contended that committee procedures in the recent hearings had been both constitutional and fair.

Representative Richard B. Vail, Illinois Republican, said each of the ten witnesses had conducted himself "in full accord with standard Communist practice long established."

Representative Claude I. Bakewell of St. Louis was the only Republican who voted against citing Mr. Maltz.

The fifteen Democrats were Representatives Eberharter, Holifield and Douglas, Emanuel Celler of New York, Arthur G. Klein of New York, John A. Blatnik of Minnesota, Sol Bloom of New York, John A. Carroll of Colorado, F. R. Havenner of California, Walter B. Huber of Ohio, Frank M. Karsten of Missouri, Thomas E. Morgan of Pennsylvania, Joseph L. Pfeifer of New York, Adam C. Powell Jr. of New York and George G. Sadowski of Michigan.

On the only roll call vote taken, 209 Republicans and 137 Democrats favored citing Mr. Maltz for contempt.

Accused Group Makes Reply

HOLLYWOOD, Calif., Nov. 24 (AP)—The ten screen personalities cited by the House issued a joint statement expressing the opinion that "the Thomas-Rankin committee succeeded today in having the Congress cite the Bill of Rights for contempt."

"Nevertheless," the statement added, "the people and the press of the country have expressed almost unparalleled opposition to this committee, which pretends to defend America by calling the Ku Klux Klan an acceptable organization. This opposition will ultimately determine the issue.

"The next test is in the office of the Attorney General. Since there is no expectation that the Supreme Court will uphold the Thomas committee, it is hoped that the Attorney General will stand with the Constitution and will refuse to permit the citation to proceed to the courts.

"We are gratified that seventeen members of Congress were not stampeded by the irresponsible lies and charges with which Thomas and Rankin attempted to justify these citations.

"The assertion that a Congressional committee can act as prosecutor, judge and jury, and thus destroy a citizen's character and livelihood, threatens every teacher, writer, publisher, scientist, and every church and trade union member in America.

"We are confident that these seventeen votes in Congress reflect the increasing determination of the American people to abolish this corrupt committee. The United States can keep its constitutional liberties or it can keep the Thomas committee. It can't keep both."

November 25, 1947

Movies to Oust Ten Cited For Contempt of Congress

Major Companies Also Vote to Refuse Jobs to Communists—'Hysteria, Surrender of Freedom' Charged by Defense Counsel

The motion picture industry, in an action unprecedented in American industrial fields, voted unanimously yesterday to refuse employment to Communists and to 'discharge or suspend without compensation" the ten Hollywood figures who have been cited for contempt of Congress.

This step was taken at the end of a two-day meeting of fifty leaders in the industry at the Waldorf-Astoria Hotel. Virtually the entire industry was represented, including the major studios and the independents, through the Motion Picture Association of America, the Association of Motion Picture Producers and the Society of Independent Motion Picture Producers.

In a statement issued by Eric Johnston, president of the first two of these groups, and Donald M. Nelson, president of the independents, it was declared that the new policy was "not going to be swayed by hysteria or intimidation." It promised that an atmosphere of fear in Hollywood would not be created and innocent persons would be protected.

The groups also called on Congress to enact legislation to help all American industry "rid itself of subversive, disloyal elements." They declared that Hollywood has produced nothing "subversive or un-American" and defended the work and loyalty of the industry during war and peace.

The film executives' action brought immediate protests from the chief counsel of the ten men n Washington, from the men themselves in Hollywood and from liberal groups. Mr. Johnston's statement was denounced as "hysteria" and a proof that the film industry has been "stampeded into surrendering" its freedom.

Yesterday's decision here followed similar steps taken by separate companies in the film industry. Last Thursday Twentieth Century-Fox decided to dispense with the services of acknowledged Communists or of any employes who refused before any Congressional committee to answer questions as to whether they were Communists. Two weeks ago RKO-Radio Pictures announced it would not employ "known Communists."

Text of Statement

The text of yesterday's statement follows:

"Members of the Association of Motion Picture Producers deplore the action of the ten Hollywood men who have been cited for contempt of the House of Representatives. We do not desire to prejudge their legal rights, but their actions have been a disservice to their employers and have impaired their usefulness to the industry.

"We will forthwith discharge or suspend without compensation those in our employ, and we will not re-employ any of the ten until such time as he is acquitted or has purged himself of contempt and declares under oath that he is not a Communist.

"On the broader issue of alleged subversive and disloyal elements in Hollywood, our members are likewise prepared to take positive action. We will not knowingly employ a Communist or a member of any party or group which advocates the overthrow of the Government of the United States by force or by any illegal or unconstitutional methods.

"In pursuing this policy, we are not going to be swayed by hysteria or intimidation from any source. We are frank to recognize that such a policy involves dangers and risks. There is the danger of hurting innocent people. There is the risk of creating an atmosphere of fear. Creative work at its best cannot be carried on in an atmosphere of fear. We will guard against this danger, this risk, this fear.

"To this end we will invite the Hollywood talent guilds to work with us to eliminate any subversives; to protect the innocent; and to safeguard free speech and a free screen wherever threatened.

Help of Congress Asked

"The absence of a national policy, established by Congress with respect to the employment of Communists in private industry, makes our task difficult. Ours is a nation of laws. We request Congress to enact legislation to assist American industry to rid itself of subversive, disloyal elements.

"Nothing subversive or un-American has appeared on the screen. Nor can any number of Hollywood investigations obscure the patriotic services of the 30,000 loyal Americans employed in Hollywood who have given our Government invaluable aid in war and peace."

Mr. Johnston was reluctant to amplify the statement, saying, "It speaks for itself, it's very clear." When asked whether the phrase, "We will not knowingly employ a Communist," referred to both present and future employes, he declared:

"That phrase is perfectly clear. 'Not employ' means you are not going to have some one in your employment. I assume that's what the language means."

Asked about the distinction between discharging and suspending without pay the ten cited for contempt, Mr. Johnston said:

"That is a legal matter, having to do with the statutes of the State of California. I believe that our purpose is to suspend, not to discharge."

One of the Hollywood executives attending the meeting was Dore Schary, vice president in charge of production for RKO, who had told the House Committee on Un-American Activities during the Hollywood investigation that he would not discharge an employe because he was a Communist.

"The decision was unanimous," Mr. Schary said after yesterday's meeting. "What I told the Un-American Activities Committee was my own personal view. However, I also stated that the ultimate policy would have to be made by the president of RKO. That policy has now been established. As an employe of the company, I will abide by the decision."

Others attending the meeting were former Secretary of State James F. Byrnes and Paul V. McNutt, among the industry's counsel; Nicholas M. Schenck, president of Loew's, Inc.; Barney Balaban, president of Paramount Pictures; J. Cheever Cowdin, chairman of the board of Universal Pictures; Jack Cohn, vice president of Columbia Pictures; Spyros Skouras, president of Twentieth Century-Fox; Nate Blumberg, president of Universal; Harry Cohn, president of Columbia; Ned Depinet, executive vice president of RKO; Samuel Goldwyn and Walter Wanger, independent producers, and many others important in the industry.

The ten men cited for contempt were Albert Maltz, Dalton Trumbo, Samuel Ornitz, John Howard Lawson, Ring Lardner Jr., Lester Cole and Alvah Bessie, all writers; Herbert Biberman, a director-producer; Edward Dmytryk, a direc-

AFTER VOTING TO REFUSE EMPLOYMENT TO COMMUNISTS

Leaders of the motion picture industry at the Waldorf-Astoria Hotel yesterday. Left to right, front: Gradwell G. Sears, president of United Artists; Barney Balaban, president of Paramount; Eric Johnston, president of the Motion Picture Association of America; Nicholas M. Schenck, president of Loew's, and Jack Cohn, vice president of Columbia. Left to right, rear: Ned Depinet, executive vice president of RKO; Nate Blumberg, president of Universal, and Sam Schneider, vice president of Warner Brothers.

The New York Times

tor, and Robert Adrian Scott, a writer and producer.

Their chief counsel, Robert W. Kenny, said yesterday in Washington that the announcement, along with the statement by Chairman J. Parnell Thomas of the Un-American Activities Committee that he would publish a list of films containing Communist propaganda, "proves that any appeasement by the motion-picture industry is only an invitation to further attack."

"To surrender to the demand for discrimination against individuals means that the real objective of the committee — censorship — has been attained," Mr. Kenny declared.

"The ten witnesses who upheld the proposition that the Thomas committee had no right to invade the realm of ideas, whether manifested by speech, writing or association are truly the defenders of a free screen—not Mr. Johnston and his associates. Despite the producers' willingness to abandon them at this time, only by the defense these men are presenting can a free and prosperous film industry be maintained. The Thomas committee does not respect the Bill of Rights, but the Producers Association goes one step further and apparently takes the position that a man is guilty until he is proven innocent.

"I am confident the courts will rule in our favor. The Constitution is the same document that it always was despite the present hysteria."

Mr. Thomas, according to The Associated Press, called the executives' action "a constructive step and a body blow to the Communists." He added that, while the committee would help the film industry in every way to oust the Communists, "our hearings and exposures will continue."

Another protest came here from Dr. Harlow Shapley of Harvard University, chairman of the Arts, Sciences and Professions Council of the Progressive Citizens of America. He telegraphed to Mr. Johnston that "to yield to hysteria by establishing blacklists and purges would be a betrayal of the trust of the American people."

November 26, 1947

FILM RED INQUIRY ASSAILED AS UNFAIR

The Council of The Authors League of America issued a protest yesterday against the recent Hollywood investigation by the House Committee on Un-American Activities, charging that it represented an "immoderate, uncontrolled and radically harmful form of censorship" against the entire profession of writing.

By impugning an individual's character, the House committee has, in effect, made his entire life's work suspect, thereby achieving a

fatal form of censorship, the league's statement said.

Council members, headed by Oscar Hammerstein 2d, president, also condemned the motion-picture industry for having "cravenly submitted to this censorship" by blacklisting the ten Hollywood writers and directors cited by Congress for contempt.

"The intent of censorship," the statement said, "is to deny to the individual author (and his publisher or producer) the right to distribute and sell a product of his intelligence and his art. In the past this has commonly operated only against a work already produced and issued to the public, and only to one work at a time. The author so censored has had the opportunity to oppose and re-

fute these specific accusations of censorship in courts of law.

"Here, however, we are faced with a different form of censorship. Here the man himself is proclaimed suspect, and the committee has avoided, as probably fatal to its whole malign project, the necessity of impugning the author's works in detail.

"Indeed, the whole corpus of a man's work, past and future, is thus declared suspect. It is obvious that any who buy and use the work of that author are thereby clearly warned that they may be adjudged collaborators with a citizen so arbitrarily declared to be subversive and may thus themselves be subject to the same calumny and suspicion, opened to the same grave yet unproven

charge of conduct contrary to the interests of their country.

"There has thus been established a method and a principle of censorship fiercely unfair, basically undemocratic and deeply un-American."

Signers of the statement included John Hersey, vice president; Peter Lyon, secretary; Arthur Schwartz, treasurer, and thirty-six council members, among them Franklin P. Adams, Maxwell Anderson, Russel Crouse, Paul Gallico, Arthur Garfield Hays, Lillian Hellman, Christopher LaFarge, Howard Lindsay, Henry F. Pringle, Elmer Rice, Richard Rodgers, Rex T. Stout, John Vandercook and Kurt Weill.

December 5, 1947

90 GROUPS, SCHOOLS NAMED ON U. S. LIST AS BEING DISLOYAL

Clark Cites Communist Party, 'Totalitarians, Fascists' to Guide Federal Agencies

3 NEW YORK SCHOOLS HIT

These Are Among 11 Classed as Adjuncts of Soviet—Klan and Film Body Accused

By LEWIS WOOD
Special to THE NEW YORK TIMES.

WASHINGTON, Dec. 4—A list of about ninety organizations of questioned loyalty to the United States, prepared under direction of Attorney General Tom C. Clark, was made public tonight by the special board now examining the loyalty of Federal Government employes.

The groups were designated by the Attorney General as "totalitarian, fascist, Communist, or subversive." In preparing the long calendar, Mr. Clark followed the Executive Order of President Truman, who set up the loyalty board some weeks ago.

Out of the long list, thirty-three associations were, with few exceptions, named for the first time, in addition to eleven schools which the Attorney General designated as adjuncts of the Communist party.

Included in the thirty-three groups were organizations such as the Communist party and its divisions; the Ku Klux Klan; Hollywood Writers Mobilization for Defense; Veterans of the Abraham Lincoln Brigade, and the National Council of American-Soviet Friendship.

Three of the schools which Mr. Clark held to be communistic are in New York City: George Washington Carver School, Jefferson School of Social Science, School of Jewish Studies.

The list compiled by Attorney General Clark is now being circulated by Seth W. Richardson, chairman of the loyalty board, to the heads of various Government departments and agencies, so it can be ascertained whether any Government employes are members of the organizations.

However, the mere fact of membership will not be proof of disloyalty. Quoting President Truman on this point, Mr. Richardson said his board agreed with the President that membership was simply one piece of evidence which might or might not be helpful in reaching a conclusion on a particular case. And Mr. Clark strongly stated:

"Guilt by association has never been one of the principles of our American jurisprudence. We must be satisfied that reasonable grounds exist for concluding that an individual is disloyal. That must be the guide."

Attorney General Clark told Mr. Richardson that the list was drawn up as the result of FBI investigation, the recommendations of Department of Justice officials, and "my subsequent study of the recommendations of all."

The Attorney General said also that the list did not represent a complete or final docket.

"For example," he wrote, "a number of small and local organizations are not listed. As to many organizations not named, the presently available information is insufficient to warrant a final determination as to their character.

"Others, presently innocuous, may become the victims of dangerous infiltrating forces and, as a consequence, become proper subjects for designation. New organizations may come into existence whose purposes and activities are in conflict with loyalty to the United States."

Further Lists May Come

Further lists would be submitted if investigation warranted such action, he stated.

The loyalty board was set up by an executive order of President Truman, also requiring the Department of Justice to supply the board with:

"The name of each foreign or domestic organization, association, movement, group or combination of persons which the Attorney General, after appropriate investigation and determination, designates as totalitarian, fascist, communist, or subversive, or as having adopted a policy of advocating or approving the commission of acts of force or violence to deny others their rights under the Constitution of the United States, or as seeking to alter the form of government of the United States by unconstitutional means."

Opening witnesses appeared today before the District of Columbia grand jury now investigating the cases of the ten Hollywood writers and executives who refused to tell the House Un-American Activities Committee whether they were members of the Communist party.

December 5, 1947

Groups Called Disloyal

Special to THE NEW YORK TIMES.

WASHINGTON, Dec. 4—The list of questionable groups submitted by Attorney General Clark today contained the names of forty-seven organizations or associations first disclosed on Feb. 5, 1943. Many of these have expired, but the original list also contained the following names:

American League Against War and Fascism.
American Patriots, Inc.
American Peace Mobilization.
American Youth Congress.
Communist Party of U.S.A.
Congress of American Revolutionary Writers.
Michigan Federation for Constitutional Liberties.
National Committee for Defense of Political Prisoners.
National Federation for Constitutional Liberties.
National Negro Congress.
Protestant War Veterans of the U.S.A., Inc.
Silver Shirt Legion of America.
Washington Book Shop Association.
Washington Committee for Democratic Alliance.
Workers Alliance.

Next, the Attorney General presented the "additional" thirty-three organizations. In some instances, there were repetitions of names on the former list, such as those of the Ku Klux Klan and Communist party.

Names on the New Listing

The newly disclosed list includes:
American Polish Labor Council.
American Youth for Democracy.
Armenian Progressive League of America.
Civil Rights Congress and its affiliated organizations, including:
Civil Rights Congress for Texas.
Veterans Against Discrimination of Civil Rights Congress of New York.
The Columbians.
Communist Party, U. S. A., formerly Communist Political Association, and its affiliates and committees including:
Citizens Committee of the Upper West Side (New York City).
Committee to Aid the Fighting South.
Dennis Defense Committee.
Labor Research Association, Inc.
Southern Negro Youth Congress.
United May Day Committee.
United Negro and Allied Veterans of America.
Connecticut State Youth Conference.
Council on African Affairs.
Hollywood Writers Mobilization for Defense.
Hungarian-American Council for Democracy.
International Workers Order, including People's Radio Foundation, Inc.
Joint Anti-Fascist Refugee Committee.
Ku Klux Klan.
Macedonian-American People's League.
National Committee to Win the Peace.
National Council of American-Soviet Friendship.
Nature Friends of America (since 1935).
New Committee for Publications.
Photo League (New York City).
Proletarian Party of America.
Revolutionary Workers League.
Socialist Workers Party, including American Committee for European Workers' Relief.
Veterans of the Abraham Lincoln Brigade.
Workers Party, including Socialist Youth League.

The Eleven Accused Schools

"Your attention is also directed to certain organizations which are operated as schools," Mr. Clark wrote to Mr. Richardson. "While, of course, I am not of the view that any institution of learning, devoted to the advancement of knowledge, is subversive, it appears that these organizations are adjuncts of the Communist party."

These were named as follows:
Abraham Lincoln School, Chicago, Ill.
George Washington Carver School, New York City.
Jefferson School of Social Science, New York City.
Ohio School of Social Sciences.
Philadelphia School on Social Science and Art.
Samuel Adams School, Boston, Mass.
School of Jewish Studies, New York City.
Seattle Labor School, Seattle, Wash.
Tom Paine School of Social Science, Philadelphia, Pa.
Tom Paine School of Westchester, N. Y.
Walt Whitman School of Social Science, Newark, N. J.

December 5, 1947

U.S. LOYALTY CHECK TO SHIELD ACCUSERS AND SOURCES OF FBI

Cross-Examination Forbidden in Most Cases Under Rules Announced by Board

'WITCH HUNT' BAN PLEDGED

Government Rights Held Same As a Private Employer's— Privacy Assured Suspects

By WILLIAM S. WHITE
Special to The New York Times.

WASHINGTON, Dec. 27—The new Loyalty Review Board laid down today its standards for testing the loyalty of employes of the Government and promised that "the program shall not degenerate into a witch-hunt."

In a statement by Chairman Seth W. Richardson, it was acknowledged at the same time that certain adopted procedures, specifically one denying to accused persons the right to confront their accusers, had raised "grave considerations."

In the "great majority of cases," it was made known, the board will permit neither confrontation, cross-examination nor a disclosure to the accused of the sources of the evidence against him.

Hearings will be private. An accused may be accompanied by his attorney, but he will not be permitted at any time to inspect any report against him by the Federal Bureau of Investigation, which will do substantially all the investigative work involved.

There will be no provision for publication of final action against an employe.

Strong Objections Made

Mr. Richardson, in his statement and in a news conference, made no secret of the fact that the board had approached some of these limitations with great anxiety, an anxiety directed particularly against the denial of the right of cross-examination.

Objections, it was added, had been put forward strongly—so strongly, in fact, that the board had been urged by "responsible persons" to drop the whole program rather than permit "a situation which ought to, and does, give rise to most serious questions in the mind of the general public."

Against all this, it was stated, the board had been confronted with the dual facts that it must depend upon the Federal Bureau of Investigation for the whole foundation of its investigative work and that the bureau had insistently demanded that its work be kept in confidence.

Thus, Mr. Richardson said in summary, his colleagues and he had the alternatives of following the FBI recommendations or simply advising the Civil Service Commission "that in our opinion the proposed loyalty program as planned should not be permitted to function."

Three Authorities Set Up

The whole procedure rests first on individual governmental agencies, each of which will operate loyalty boards; regional loyalty boards of the Civil Service Commission to function in the cases of applicants for, rather than incumbents in, Government jobs, and finally upon the Loyalty Review Board itself as the final authority.

The review board will have only recommendatory power to the Government departments for the discharge of a person. It will not have the power of subpoena.

Mr. Richardson, elaborating on the board's reasoning on the question of a suspected employe's rights, continued:

"After the most careful consideration we have concluded that the objection to non-confrontation and no cross-examination, while important, is not essentially controlling.

"In the first place, the board is of the opinion that legally the Government is entitled to discharge any employe for reasons which seem sufficient to the Government, and without extending to such employe any hearing whatsoever.

"We believe that the rights of the Government in that respect are at least equal to those possessed by private employers."

He pointed out that in the mechanism now being put in operation an accused employe had two appeals—first to the head of the agency for which he worked, from an adverse decision of the initial agency loyalty board, and then to the national board.

Mr. Richardson stressed also that the test for removal of an employe, under the terms of a Presidential order, was "whether on all the evidence in the record, reasonable grounds exist for belief that the person involved is disloyal."

Mere past membership in an organization branded as subversive by the Department of Justice would not in itself be enough for an employe's ouster, he said, but would simply be "one piece" in the mosaic of evidence, all of which had to be considered.

Agents Warned on "Opinions"

Moreover, he added, there were other important qualifications—for instance, advocacy of whatever change in our form of Government or economic system, "however far-reaching such a change might be," would not, under the board's definition, be disloyalty, unless unconstitutional means for bringing about such a change were involved.

Also, FBI agents had been specially trained and put under specific instructions that their reports on a man's loyalty were to be accompanied by no "opinions, recommendations or conclusions," and that they were not to act in any sense as prosecutors.

With all the designed safeguards, he added, the board felt that "the Government might justly carry on the proposed loyalty program, even though an affected employe may have had neither confrontation nor cross-examination of evidence sources."

"If further experience shall change our minds in this regard, we shall not hesitate to so report," he declared.

Within the scope of the inquiry, at least in theory, Mr. Richardson said, are approximately 2,000,000 Federal employes. Civilian workers for the Army, he added, "are not in our bailiwick—at least not yet." He was uncertain whether the Atomic Energy Commission would want to make use of the board's services.

December 28, 1947

PRESIDENT ORDERS AGENCIES TO BAR DATA ON LOYALTY

Issues Directive to Officials to Disregard Congressional and Court Subpoenas

By ANTHONY LEVIERO
Special to The New York Times.

WASHINGTON, March 15—President Truman directed all Federal departments today to disregard court and Congressional subpoenas and other demands for confidential information gathered in the investigation of the loyalty of Federal employes.

Ordering that all such requests be referred to him, the Chief Executive assumed personal responsibility for disposal of each demand in keeping with "the public interest."

His directive came as the culmination of a long skirmish with Congress involving the prerogatives of the executive and legislative branches of the Government in the recent loyalty and other Congressional inquiries.

The President's action raised the possibilities of a show-down. It was taken in the face of a pending Republican-sponsored bill that would compel the executive branch to give up any data on demand of Congress.

Earlier Decisions Recalled

In support of his position, Mr. Truman cited the decisions of several Presidents, from Washington to Taft. He also mentioned opinions of the Attorney General and of the Supreme Court.

Court subpoenas have not been involved in the recent inquiries, and the President did not mention them in his memorandum to all officers and employes of the executive branch. The White House made it clear, however, that such writs were included in the scope of his directive in a long background statement giving the legal basis for his action.

"The new directive indicates that this policy is to be applied even where a 'subpoena or demand' has been received," the statement said. "Subpoenas issued by courts and Congressional committees are to be 'respectfully declined' but are at the same time to be referred to the President, who will determine in the public interest the nature of the response to be made in the particular case.

"The President thus takes responsibility for informing the court or Congressional committee concerning the extent of the confidential information, if any, which can properly be furnished."

The Commerce Department recently refused to yield to a House Un-American Activities subcommittee a confidential report clearing Dr. Edward U. Condon, director of the National Bureau of Standards, of suspicion that he had subversive contacts with Communists.

It was as a result of the Condon case that a bill was introduced to deprive the President of the power to withhold confidential data of the executive branch. Today Representative John McDowell, Republican of Pennsylvania, proposed that Congress grant the presiding officer of the Senate and the Speaker of the House the power to obtain secret documents from any Government agency.

Last December the Administration took the position that it could not, under the law, disclose the names of traders in the commodity markets without an act of Congress. Thereupon Congress passed a resolution authorizing the disclosure, and subsequently the Senate Apropriations Committee conducted an inquiry which resulted in the listing of many hundreds of traders who speculated in grains.

TEXT OF TRUMAN ORDER

The text of Mr. Truman's directive was as follows:

The efficient and just administration of the Employe Loyalty Program, under Executive Order No. 9835 of March 21, 1947, requires that reports, records and files relative to the program be preserved in strict confidence.

This is necessary in the interest of our national security and welfare, to preserve the confidential character and sources of information furnished, and to protect Government personnel against the dissemination of unfounded or disproved allegations. It is necessary also in order to insure the fair and just disposition of loyalty cases.

For these reasons, and in accordance with the long established policy that reports rendered by the Federal Bureau of Investigation and other investigative agencies of the executive branch are to be regarded as confidential, all reports, records, and files relative to the loyalty of employes or prospective employes (including reports of such investigative agencies) shall be maintained in confidence, and shall not be transmitted or disclosed except as required in the efficient conduct of business.

Any subpoena or demand or request for information, reports, or files of the nature described received from sources other than those persons in the executive branch of the Government who are entitled thereto, by reason of their official duties, shall be respectfully declined, on the basis of this directive and the subpoena or demand or other request shall be referred to the Office of the President for such response as the President may determine to be in the public interest in the particular case.

There shall be no relaxation of the provisions of this directive except with my expressed authority.

This directive shall be published in the Federal Register.

March 16, 1948

8 SCIENTISTS ASSAIL THOMAS COMMITTEE

'Smear Tactics' That Drive Best Men From U. S. Service Imperil Nation, They Say

Eight of the country's leading atomic scientists charged yesterday that the Thomas un-American Activities Committee was endangering national security through its "objectionable smear tactics." These tactics, they held, were driving the most competent scientists out of Government service at a dangerous rate.

In telegrams to President Truman and Governor Dewey the scientists pleaded that the Government's atomic energy program be taken out of partisan politics.

The signers were Dr. Karl T. Compton, president of the Massachusetts Institute of Technology; Dr. Harold C. Urey, Professor of Nuclear Physics at the University of Chicago and Nobel Prize winner in 1934; Dr. George B. Pegram, Professor of Physics and dean of the graduate faculties at Columbia University; Dr. Philip M. Morse, Professor of Physics at M. I. T. and former director of the Brookhaven National Laboratories; Dr. Thorfin R. Hogness, director of the Institute of Radiobiology and Biophysics at Chicago; Dr. John C. Warner, Professor of Chemistry and dean of the graduate school at Carnegie Institute of Technology; Dr. Charles C. Lauritsen, Professor of Physics at California Institute of Technology, and Prof. Harrison Brown, Professor of Nuclear Chemistry at Chicago.

All Worked on Atom Bomb

All the signers played prominent roles in the development of the atomic bomb.

Of more than 150 senior American scientists mentioned in the Smyth report who were actively engaged in the wartime projects, fewer than 10 per cent now are working full-time on government atomic research, and an equally small percentage is devoting even part-time to Government work, the telegrams said, adding:

"With the greatest respect to those relatively few excellent men who are now attempting to carry out adequate programs, we are forced to the conclusion that the combined full-time personnel of highly capable scientists and engineers in the various laboratories is on the verge of reaching a dangerously low level."

The scientists emphasized that they were not condemning reasonable activities to combat espionage, but declared that not even successful spying by well-trained enemy agents could jeopardize our security more effectively than the atmosphere created by the Thomas Committee.

Atomic energy was a young man's business during the war, the message declared. It cited as an example the Plutonium Project in 1944, at the peak of the research activities, when 60 per cent of the scientists were under 30 years old, 80 per cent under 35, and 90 per cent under 40.

"It is among these younger men that our nation must expect to find its leadership in atomic energy research during the coming years," the telegrams said. "But few of these men remain in Government service to assume leadership.

"Many have not remained because they have found it increasingly difficult to reconcile themselves to Government employment on secret projects where they are looked upon by groups such as the Un-American Activities Committee as men not to be trusted, where they must subject themselves to the possibility of irresponsible smears that may ruin them professionally for life. In many cases the men prefer to work elsewhere for considerably lower salaries on research programs completely unconnected with our atomic endeavors."

Three Give Interview

The sending of the telegrams yesterday morning was announced at an afternoon interview by Professor Morse, Dean Pegram and Professor Brown, representing the eight scientists. The eight men acted as individuals—"a few representative men who can speak with authority, yet freely, now that none of us is connected any longer with the Government," said Professor Brown, who was assistant director of chemistry at the Oak Ridge laboratories from 1943 to 1946.

No specific course of action was recommended in the telegrams, the spokesmen said.

"We are only hoping for the bringing of reasonableness into the proceedings," Professor Brown explained. "Once our leaders understand the situation and how grave it is, there will be a chance to do something. There is a frightening lack of understanding at present. Members of the Thomas Committee have no conception of what is secret and what is not secret."

The Atomic Energy Commission is "in no way to blame for the unfortunate situation that now exists," the telegrams declared, but the commission "has been needlessly hampered because atomic energy has unfortunately become a 'political football'; as a result, the commission has had to adjust its own workings to the atmosphere created by the Thomas Committee."

This unhealthy atmosphere is being created by the committee "in spite of its best intentions," the telegrams declared. They attacked Representative J. Parnell Thomas for published articles that were "masterpieces of insinuation," and said the attack this spring on Dr. Edward U. Condon was "so repugnant that it will be years before the damage can be undone."

The texts of the telegrams were identical, except that in the final sentences the President was called on to "investigate this situation and then direct your powers in an attempt to secure a remedy," while the Republican nominee was urged, "as a possible successor to the Presidency, to make yourself aware of this situation."

September 7, 1948

Scientists Form Group to Help Research Men in Loyalty Tests

Special to THE NEW YORK TIMES.

PRINCETON, N. J., Oct. 17—The Federation of American Scientists has set up a scientists' committee on loyalty problems, Prof. Henry De Wolf Smyth, chairman of the department of physics at Princeton University, announced today.

The federation was spurred into action by a general feeling among scientists that "persecution" of atomic scientists had created a serious situation, Professor Smyth, author of the Smyth report on atomic energy, said.

Fifty-three scientists at various universities are sponsors of the committee, which will function semi-autonomously, he said. They included Harold C. Urey, Chicago; Harlow Shapley, Harvard; Robert S. Milliken, Chicago; Glenn T. Seaborg, California, Anton J. Carlson, Chicago; Richard Courant, New York; Kirtley F. Mather, Harvard, and Robert M. Yerkes, Yale.

The committee, with offices at Princeton, will provide information and legal advice to individual scientists faced with clearance problems, Professor Smyth said. It will also try to bring about a clearer public understanding of the issues involved in loyalty and clearance problems, he said.

The committee will not "defend" scientists under investigation but will seek to obtain full and fair hearings by Government agencies and Congressional committees and fair treatment in the press, he explained.

The membership of the committee is as follows:

W. A. Higinbotham, Brookhaven National Laboratory, chairman; A. S. Wightman, Princeton, secretary; D. R. Hamilton, Princeton, treasurer.

Also David Bohm, Princeton; Roy Britten, Princeton; R. R. Bush, Princeton; Albert Einstein, Institute for Advanced Study; L. P. Eisenhart, Princeton; S. A. Goudsmit, Brookhaven National Laboratory; M. Stanley Livingston, Massachusetts Institute of Technology; Stuart Mudd, University of Pennsylvania; H. D. Smyth, Princeton; Lyman Spitzer Jr., Princeton Observatory; Oswald Veblen, Institute for Advanced

Study, and Irving Wolff, RCA Laboratories, Princeton.

Professor Smyth told about the committee at a press conference attended by Mr. Wightman, who is a teaching assistant in his department; Mr. Bush, an instructor in it, and Mr. Hamilton, associate professor of physics at Princeton.

The prospectus of the committee was released. It said that since the war, the problems of secrecy and loyalty clearance procedures for scientists had become pressing, affecting the future of science and the lives of scientists.

Pointing out that some scientific and technical information must be classified and protected from falling into unauthorized hands, as the activities of the Canadian spy ring showed, it continued:

"The appplication of clearance procedures used to date has caused some grave and wholly unnecessary injustices to many scientists and, as a result, the difficulties of Government laboratories in employing new scientific personnel have been enhanced.

"In nearly all cases, the doctrine of guilt by association seems to have been carried to absurd lengths. And it is significant that 'associations' have been the principal, or perhaps entire, basis for loyalty action. Although the question may be raised ... to whether scientists who have agreed to do secret work should be afforded the complete freedom in their social lives enjoyed by other citizens, we do believe that, in any case, restrictions imposed should be made clear before a person begins secret work.

"Moreover, we believe that no restrictions of any sort should be placed on scientists doing unclassified work. The increasingly prevalent practice of 'black-listing' a man who was once refused clearance, thereby preventing him from obtaining employment for completely unclassified work elsewhere, shauld be combatted."

October 18, 1948

RED 'UNDERGROUND' IN FEDERAL POSTS ALLEGED BY EDITOR

IN NEW DEAL ERA

Ex-Communist Names Alger Hiss, Then in State Department

WALLACE AIDES ON LIST

Chambers Also Includes Former Treasury Official, White— Tells of Fears for His Life

By C. P. TRUSSELL
Special to THE NEW YORK TIMES.

WASHINGTON, Aug. 3 — An "underground" Communist organization, led by men at key posts of government and operating to infiltrate the whole establishment with its party members, was described to the House Committee on Un-American Activities today by an admitted former Communist, Whittaker Chambers, who said he served as a courier for the group.

Mr. Chambers, now a senior editor of Time magazine, swore that this organization, which he viewed as a forerunner of the Soviet spy rings testimony of which has shaken Washington recently, had these leaders:

Alger Hiss, former director of special political affairs in the State Department, executive secretary of the Dumbarton Oaks conversations and secretary general of the San Francisco Conference at which the United Nations charter was written. Mr. Hiss accompanied President Franklin D. Roosevelt to Malta and the Yalta conference in 1945 and the following year was a principal adviser to the American delegation at the first session of the United Nations General Assembly at London. He is now president of the Carnegie Endowment for International Peace, in New York.

Donald Hiss, a younger brother of Alger Hiss, who held posts in the State and Agriculture Departments.

Former NLRB Secretary Named

Nathan Witt, former general secretary of the National Labor Relations Board, who resigned in 1941 after eight years of service. He is now practicing law in New York.

Lee Pressman, who held posts as assistant general counsel in the Agricultural Adjustment Administration under appointment by former Secretary Henry A. Wallace; general counsel for the Works Progress Administration by appointment of the late Harry L. Hopkins, and general counsel of the Resettlement Administration under Rexford G. Tugwell. Later Mr. Pressman was general counsel for the Congress of Industrial Organizations and the CIO's Steelworkers' Organizing Committee. He is now associated with Mr. Wallace's Progressive party.

John J. Abt, who from 1933 to 1935 was chief of litigation for the AAA, an assistant general counsel for the WPA in 1935, chief counsel for the Senate (La Follette) Civil Liberties Investigating Committee in 1936 and 1937 and special assistant to the Attorney General in 1937 and 1938. Mr. Abt was accused last Saturday by Miss Elizabeth T. Bentley, confessed courier for the alleged Soviet spy ring, as being a member of the "Perlo group" of that organization.

War Production Board Aide

Victor Perlo, formerly with the War Production Board, the alleged head of one of several espionage groups about which Miss Bentley testified.

Charles Kramer, also described as Charles Kravitzky, who was identified as counsel to special Senate labor problems committees under the chairmanships of Senators Claude Pepper of Florida and Harley M. Kilgore of West Virginia. Mr. Kramer was said by committee attachés to be now associated with the Progressive party.

Henry Collins, formerly in the Agriculture Department, at whose apartment the meetings of the organization described by Mr. Chambers were said to have been held.

Meanwhile William W. Remington, formerly with the War Production Board and now in the Department of Commerce, told a Senate committee that he had never given confidential information to Miss Bentley, whose revelations inspired the current Congressional inquiries.

Testimony that he had knowledge of some aspects of the atomic bomb project brought from the witness a statement that he "did not give it to Miss Bentley or mention it to a single soul." He asserted that what he knew was "nothing very much."

As Mr. Chambers testified before the House group, dramatically at first as he told of risks in quitting Communist affiliation and discipline, and later with great calm, the name of Harry Dexter White, former Assistant Secretary of the Treasury, was brought into his story. Mr. White was named by Miss Bentley as one of those who had supplied "information" to the espionage organization. She explained that she never had received information from him direct. The former assistant secretary, in informal rebuttal, has described her testimony concerning him as "fantastic" and "shocking."

Today, Mr. Chambers described him as a willing and cooperative "fellow traveler" with the group of which he testified and, as it was asked whether Mr. White was a Communist party member, added:

"I cannot say whether he was a member. But he certainly was a fellow traveler so far within the fold that his not being a party member would have been a mistake on both sides."

"But," interposed Representative F. Edward Hebert, Democrat, of Louisiana, "Mr. White has called the charges against him 'fantastic' and 'shocking.'"

"After my testimony," Mr. Chambers responded, "he will have to find some more adjectives."

Once Feared for His Life

Mr. Chambers, a quiet, heavy-set man who spoke so softly that at times committee members requested him to repeat what he had said, explained that his was an old story, although it had not come into the open before. He joined the Communist party in 1924, he said, and in 1937 "repudiated Marx's doctrines and Lenin's tactics." For a year, he added, he lived in fear of personal harm being done him. He slept during the day, hidden out, and at night stayed awake with a gun handy. He had told his story "to the Government," Mr. Chambers continued, and had "sound reason for supposing that the Communists might try to kill me."

Although he had given his story to the State Department "almost exactly nine years ago"—two days after Hitler and Stalin signed their pact—nothing had been done about it, Mr. Chambers said.

To get the story to the Government, he added, he went to the White House. Through Isaac Don Levine, editor of Plain Talk, he said, the late Marvin McIntyre, then a secretary to President Roosevelt, was told that he was willing to talk. Mr. McIntyre, the witness testified, referred him to A. A. Berle, then Assistant Secretary of State. Mr. Berle is now the head of the Liberal party of New York, which was formed in 1944 when the American Labor party was taken over by the Left Wing.

"When I told Mr. Berle my story," Mr. Chambers said to the committee, "he indicated great excitement. He said, 'we absolutely must have a clear Government service, as we are faced with a possibility of war.'

"I was surprised, a long time afterward, when I checked up, that nothing had been done about it.

"I went to Washington and reported to the authorities that I knew about the infiltration of the United States Government by Communists. For years international communism, of which the United States Communist party is an integral part, had been in a state of undeclared war with this republic.

"I regarded my action in going to the Government as a simple act of war, like the shooting of an armed enemy in combat. I was one of the few men on this side of the battle who could perform this service.

"The heart of my report consisted of a description of the apparatus to which I was attached. It was an underground organization of the United States Communist party developed, to the best of my knowledge, by Harold Ware, one of the sons of the Communist leader known as 'Mother Bloor.'

"I knew it at its top level, a group of seven or so men, from among whom, in later years, certain members of Miss Bentley's (alleged wartime espionage) organization were apparently recruited.

"The head of the underground group at the time I knew it was Nathan Witt. Later, John Abt became the leader. Lee Pressman was also a member of this group, as was Alger Hiss who, as a member of the State Department, later or-

ganized the conference at Dumbarton Oaks, San Francisco, and the United States side of the Yalta conference.

"The purpose of this group at that time was not primarily espionage. Its original purpose was the Communist infiltration of the American Government. But espionage was certainly one of its eventual objectives. Let no one be surprised at this statement. Disloyalty is a matter of principle with every member of the Communist party.

"The Communist party exists for the specific purpose of overthrowing the Government, at the opportune time, by any and all means, and each of its members, by the fact that he is a member, is dedicated to this purpose."

Mr. Chambers contended that the Washington group, while apparently functioning in the pattern of Harold Ware, was really in the hands of one "J. Peters," who, he said, used many party names. He identified this functionary as being a former member of the Russian agricultural commissariat who had come into this country by means of an illegal passport.

The witness also said that Peters had explained to him "how easy it was to get false passports." The system, he added, was to have Communist party researchers pos-

ing as genealogical students seeking information at the New York Public Library pick out the names of American babies born on convenient dates and use their names and birth records for passport procurement. Peters, he said, got into the country under the name of "Isadore Boorstein," and added that he also was known as "Goldberg," which Mr. Chambers had heard was the "real name."

As committee attention focused on Alger Hiss who, when he left the State Department late in 1946, was described by Dean Acheson, Undersecretary, as one who had served "with outstanding devotion and ability," Mr. Chambers said he had "tried to get Mr. Hiss away from the Communists," but had failed."

Mr. Chambers said that he went to the Hiss home at what he viewed as "a considerable personal risk." While he awaited the return of Mr. Hiss, he testified, Mrs. Hiss attempted to make a telephone call which he assumed was "to other Communists." He said that she "hung up" as he approached closely enough to hear what might be said.

"When Hiss came home," he told the committee, "I tried to persuade him to break away from this group. He cried when we separated, but he said something about 'the party line' and wouldn't break with the party."

Mr. Chambers testified that he also had endeavored to call Mr. White, the former Assistant Secretary of the Treasury and its former director of monetary research, away from association with the group he accused. He asserted that "developments" had indicated that he had "failed."

Mr. White, according to Mr. Chambers, had been picked by the group as one who might "go places" in the administration and thus aid the infiltration movement. What the Communist organization was looking for, he said, was a group of "the elite" in government, that would encourage Communist infiltration.

"So it was decided," Mr. Chambers testified, "to add people who were not previously in the apparatus. One was Mr. White."

"These," he said, "were an elite group which, it was believed, would rise to posts in Government and thus make their positions more valuable to the party."

"Would you say," asked Representative Hebert, "that Mr. White was an unwitting dupe?"

"I would hardly say 'unwitting'," Mr. Chambers answered.

"Did he know what he was being used?" Mr. Herbert persisted.

"I would scarcely say 'used'," Mr. Chambers said. "He was willing."

August 4, 1948

TRUMAN CALLS SPY INQUIRIES A REPUBLICAN 'RED HERRING'

PRESIDENT IS BLUNT

Says FBI, Grand Jury Had All Information Now Being Revealed

'WIDE OPEN BREAK' SEEN

Mundt Tells of 'Mystery Witness'—Hiss Makes a Denial —Uranium Sent to Soviet

By C. P. TRUSSELL
Special to THE NEW YORK TIMES.

WASHINGTON, Aug. 5—President Truman denounced today the Congressional investigations into alleged Soviet spy rings and Communist infiltration into the American Government. He said that they were a "red herring" designed to

detract public attention from the snubbing by the Republican-controlled extra session of his program to curb inflation.

Mr. Truman, responding to questions at a news conference, delivered this and further castigation of the inquiries during a day which brought the following developments.

Alger Hiss, former State Department official and a key man in the organization of the United Nations, appeared as a volunteer witness before the House Committee on Un-American Activities.

He has been accused by Whittaker Chambers, an admitted former Communist and now a senior editor of Time Magazine, of being a leader of a pre-war Communist underground organization set up to put party members at key points throughout the Federal establishment.

Hiss Denies Communist Link

This organization, Mr. Chambers has indicated, was a forerunner of the alleged wartime Soviet spy ring. The latter was described in

previous testimony by Miss Elizabeth T. Bentley, a confessed courier for the ring.

"I am not and never have been a member of the Communist party," Mr. Hiss testified. "I do not and never have adhered to the tenets of the Communist party. I am not and never have been a member of any Communist 'front' organization. I have never followed the Communist party line directly or indirectly. To the best of my knowledge none of my friends is a Communist."

Later, Representative Karl E. Mundt of South Dakota, acting chairman of the House Investigating Committee, announced that "the whole spy case" was likely to be "broken wide open" next week.

He said that a new and important witness had been located, a man in "splendid position to know what he is talking about." A special subcommittee, its members unidentified, left tonight for an undisclosed destination. At this location, the evidence will be taken in secret, then the case will be publicly exposed, Mr. Mundt added.

Says Russia Gets U. S. Uranium

The evidence in the hands of this witness, he said, would implicate a second person. Between the two, he asserted, the whole story of spy rings would be forced into the open. As far as he knew, Mr. Mundt said, the main mystery witness was not a present or former Government official. He added that he did not know whether he was a Communist, a former one, or never was one.

Even before the House Committee started to take testimony today, Representative John McDowell, Republican, of Pennsylvania, chairman of a special subcommittee, asserted that 1,300 pounds of uranium compound had been shipped to Russia "at the height" of American experiments with the atomic bomb.

Giving a progress report on his subcommittee's work, Mr. McDowell said that two shipments of the uranium compound were made to the Soviet Union in 1943 "after tremendous pressure on all phases of our Government from known Russian agents and others who had worked themselves into positions of importance."

The shipments, one of 1,000 pounds and the other of 300 pounds, Mr. McDowell said, were made from "a small and obscure airfield" at a point in this country, which he did not identify.

Mr. McDowell added that his subcommittee also had "established almost beyond question" that during the war there were shipments to Russia of heavy water, a substance employed in atomic research.

Testifying formally before the committee, Representative Fred E. Busbey, Republican of Illinois, urged that the Civil Service Commission be investigated. He called that agency "a spawning ground" for Communist infiltration into the Federal Government.

He cited case histories which, he argued, were examples of instances where the Commission, either by action or non-action, had prevented the ouster of Communists from Federal service.

His principal target was Nathan Gregory Silvermaster, who spent twelve years as a Government employe and was a witness before the House committee yesterday. Mr. Silvermaster was accused by Miss Bentley of being at a key post in the alleged Soviet wartime spy ring of Washington. He refused to answer any questions concerning her charges on the ground that his responses might be self-incriminatory.

An investigation of Henry A. Wallace, Progressive party candidate for the Presidency, was demanded by Representative John E. Rankin, Democrat, of Mississippi, a committee member. He urged that Mr. Wallace be called in "to tell us why these Communists who were plotting the overthrow of the Government were placed in key positions in his [Commerce] department at a time when our young men were fighting and dying on every battle front in the world for the protection of this country."

Mr. Busbey urged that Mr. Wallace be investigated also in connection with his first functions in the New Deal Cabinet as Secretary of Agriculture. He emphasized that many of those who had been cited as leaders of the pre-war "Communist infiltration ring" had served in the Agricultural Adjustment Administration.

Truman Issues Statement

President Truman, answering questions at his news meeting, laughed at a declaration by Mr. Mundt that a Communist spy ring was operating in Washington "right now." He said that he believed this ring was in Mr. Mundt's mind. To go further in denouncing the inquiries, Mr. Truman released a formal statement, in which he stated:

"No information (obtained in the course of 'certain Congressional investigations now under way') has been revealed that has not long since been presented to a Federal grand jury (in New York, where twelve top Communist leaders were indicted recently on the charge of conspiracy to overthrow the government of the United States).

"No information has been disclosed in the past few days by Congressional committees that has not long been known to the Federal Bureau of Investigation.

"The Federal grand jury found this information insufficient to justify indictment of the Federal employes involved.

"All but two of the employes involved have left the Federal Government and these two have been placed on involuntary leave.

"The public hearings now under

PRINCIPALS AT CONGRESSIONAL HEARING IN WASHINGTON

Elizabeth T. Bentley, a capital policeman, William L. Marbury and Alger Hiss listening to testimony given yesterday by Representative Fred E. Busbey of Illinois before the House Committee on Un-American Activities. Hiss, earlier on the stand, denied under oath that he had ever been a member of the Communist party.

way are serving no useful purpose. On the contrary, they are doing irreparable harm to certain persons, seriously impairing the morale of Federal employes, and undermining public confidence in the Government."

The charges made by Mr. Chambers on Tuesday have rocked Washington. Cited with Mr. Hiss as leaders of the underground movement which had sought to fill the Government with Communists at key posts, were:

Donald Hiss, Alger Hiss' younger brother, formerly holding posts in the State and Agriculture Departments; Nathan Witt, former general secretary National Labor Relations Board; Lee Pressman, who left government work to be general counsel for the CIO; John J. Abt, Victor Perlo, Charles Kramer and Henry Collins, who had held Federal posts. Mr. Chambers testified that the meetings of this underground group were held at the apartment of Mr. Collins.

Today Mr. Alger Hiss swore to the following statement:

"As a State Department official I have had contacts with representatives of foreign governments some of whom undoubtedly have been members of the Communist party, as for example representatives of the Soviet Government. My contacts with any foreign representative who could possibly have been a Communist have been strictly official.

"To the best of my knowledge I never heard of Whittaker Chambers until in 1947, when two representatives of the FBI asked me if I knew him and various other people, some of whom I knew and some of whom I did not know.

"I said I did not know Chambers. So far as I am aware, I have never laid eyes on him, and I shoud like to have the opportunity to do so.

"I have known Henry Collins since we were boys in camp together. I knew him again when he was at the Harvard Business School, while I was at Harvard Law School, and have seen him from time to time since I came to Washington in 1933.

"Lee Pressman was in my class at Harvard Law School, and we were both on the Harvard Law Review at the same time. We were also both assistants to Judge Jerome Frank on the legal staff of the AAA. Since I left the Department of Agriculture I have seen him only casually and infrequently.

"Witt and Abt were both members of the legal staff of AAA. I knew them both in that capacity. I believe I met Witt in New York a year or so before I came to Washington. We were both practicing law in New York at that time.

"Kramer was in another office in the AAA and I met him in that connection.

"I have seen none of the last three except most infrequently, since I left the Department of Agriculture.

"I don't believe I know Victor Perlo.

"Except as I have indicated, the statements about me made by Mr. Chambers are complete fabrications. I think my record in the Government and since (Mr. Hiss is now president of the Carnegie Endowment for International Peace) speaks for itself."

This volunteered statement by Mr. Hiss seemed to stun the investigating group. Mr. Mundt confessed that, as a long-time investi-

gator, he had not found sworn declarations quite as diametrically opposite as those of Mr. Chambers and Mr. Hiss.

Both, he told the committee and the spectators who crowded the big House Office Building Caucus Room, were witnesses of apparently unimpeachable integrity.

But, Mr. Mundt added, one of them had not told the truth.

Later, after the committee had met in executive session, Mr. Mundt said that the whole staff of committee investigators had been assigned to "check" the testimony of one against the other, and to run down what developed into a foundation for seeing which was giving accurate testimony.

If there was found a ground of perjury against either, Mr. Mundt said, the committee would make a citation to the Attorney General for prosecution.

Meanwhile, in New York, Mr. Chambers was quoted as saying:

"Mr. Hiss has seen fit to deny under oath that sworn testimony which I gave before the House committee. I have no change whatever to make in my testimony concerning him."

Committee members believed that there might be possibility of a case of mistaken identity. Robert E. Stripling, chief committee investigator, showed Mr. Hiss a photograph of Mr. Chambers. Mr. Hiss looked at it and said that it might be identified as that of many persons, including even Mr. Mundt, the acting chairman. He said he wanted to face his accuser and indicated surprise that he was not in the hearing room, ready to make the identification.

August 6, 1948

HISS AND CHAMBERS MEET FACE TO FACE; CLASH IN TESTIMONY

Both Stand by Their Stories, and House Body Head Says One Faces Perjury Trial

---

OLD AUTO HAS A BIG ROLE

Federal Ex-Aide, Charged With Giving Car to Reds, Denies It, Calls Accuser a Liar

---

By C. P. TRUSSELL
Special to THE NEW YORK TIMES.

WASHINGTON, Aug. 25—The sworn testimony of Alger Hiss, former high official in the State Department, and Whittaker Chambers, who has accused him of leadership in a pre-war "elite" Communist underground, remained in sharp and bitter conflict tonight after many hours of facing each other in public before the House Committee on Un-American Activities.

As the hearing opened to "a standing room audience," Representative J. Parnell Thomas of New Jersey, the committee chairman, told the two witnesses that "certainly one of you will be tried for perjury."

When Mr. Chambers, confessed former Communist party paid functionary, took the stand he charged that Mr. Hiss, as "a rather romantic Communist" in 1936, had given an old Ford automobile to the Communist party for use in organizational work.

This car, a 1929 Model A, about which the Hiss-Chambers controversy has waged for weeks, had a major role today in the committee's effort to find out who was telling the truth and who had committed perjury.

Mr. Hiss has said that for sentimental reasons he had kept the old car, long after he had bought a new Plymouth, because he had purchased the Ford just before his marriage. He also testified that he had given Mr. Chambers, whom he has admitted knowing as "George Crosley," the use of it in 1935 and had "thrown it in" when he rented Mr. Chambers an apartment which he was leaving for a house.

Chambers Denies Rental Pact

Mr. Chambers testified that there was no rental agreement when he took over the apartment.

"Why?" asked Representative Richard M. Nixon, Republican, of California.

"We were Communists together," Mr. Chambers replied. "It was just the usual party arrangement. There was to be no payment of rent."

Mr. Hiss has testified that Mr. Chambers was still about $120 in arrears on his 1934-35 rent and also owed him about $25 to $30 in small loans. Mr. Chambers said that he had received money from Mr. Hiss, but that it was in dues to the Communist party.

Mr. Hiss remained steadfast in denying that he was or ever had been a Communist or had reason to know whether any of the alleged associates named in the so-called underground named in were or had been members of the party.

Mr. Hiss called his accuser "a self-confessed liar, spy and traitor," and "questioned his sanity," and whether he had been treated for "a mental illness."

In reply, Mr. Chambers said that, "I have never been treated for a mental illness," and "I have never been treated in a mental institution."

Prosecutor to Get Record

When the hearing adjourned tonight the committee halted public hearings for the present. The group will meet in executive session tomorrow. Members indicated that Messrs. Hiss and Chambers would not be recalled, at least for public questioning, and that the transcript of the public and closed hearings, as it concerned them, would be sent to the office of George Morris Fay, Federal district attorney here.

Earlier, when Mr. Chambers was questioned about the Hiss roadster, he said:

"Mr. Hiss at that time was a rather romantic Communist. There was a rigid rule of the underground that there should be no communication between it and the open Communist party.

"Mr. Hiss insisted that his old car be given to the local chapter of the party so it would be turned over to some poor Communist for organizational work. I was opposed to this and so was Mr. Peters."

"Who was Mr. Peters?" asked Representative Nixon.

"J. Peters was the head of the Communist underground for the United States," Mr. Chambers said. "He was my immediate superior in my work in Washington as a courier for the group."

Mr. Peters, who also is known as "Alexander Stevens" and "Isadore Boorstein," is scheduled to appear before immigration authorities in New York next Monday for a hearing on deportation proceedings instituted against him last October.

The House committee plans to have an investigator ready with a subpoena for Mr. Peters when he appears at the New York hearing.

Mr. Chambers said that Mr. Hiss was finally permitted to give his old car to the open party.

Earlier testimony has shown that this was nearly a year after the record indicated that Mr. Chambers held possession of the Hiss roadster. Mr. Hiss said that he had no recollection of the disposition of the car. He conceded that it might have "bounced back," but he recalled no details.

As the crowd which packed the big caucus room of the Old House Office Building listened, Robert E. Stripling, chief committee investigator, read to Mr. Hiss what Mr. Chambers had said about the automobile in testimony taken in executive session two weeks ago. Mr. Chambers repeated it this evening.

Louis J. Russell, a committee investigator, told of tracing the old car to the Cherner Motor Company here. The vehicle, he said, had been transferred to the concern on July 23, 1936, and on the same day was transferred to a William Rosen of 5403 Thirteenth Street, Washington. The certificate of transfer to the Cherner Company, he asserted, was signed by "Alger Hiss."

Mr. Stripling stressed that three officials of the Cherner Company testified in closed session yesterday that they had no record of the deal.

Mr. Russell reported there was no William Rosen living at the Thirteenth Street address at the time of the transfer. Nor, he added, did the real estate records disclose that a William Rosen had ever lived at that address.

A photostatic copy of the certificate of transfer, taken from the original in the files of the District of Columbia Division of Vehicles and Traffic, was produced.

"Handwriting experts have testified," Mr. Russell added, "that the signature appearing on the back of this document, called 'Assignment of Title,' was written by Alger Hiss."

Mr. Hiss was recalled to the stand and handed the document. He examined it, then said:

"Mr. Stripling, it certainly looks like my signature to me. Do you have the original document?"

"No, I do not," the chief investigator answered.

Mr. Hiss: "This is a photostat. I would prefer to have the original."

Mr. Stripling: "The original document cannot be removed from the Department of Motor Vehicles. They keep it in their possession."

Wants Original Document

Representative Thomas then asked:

"Well, Mr. Hiss, can't you tell from the photostat what this signature is? Whether it is your signature or not?"

Mr. Hiss: "It looks like my signature to me, Mr. Chairman."

Mr. Thomas: "Well, if that were the original, would it look any more like your signature?"

Mr. Hiss: "I think if I saw the original document I would be able to see whether this photostat is an exact reproduction of the original document. I would just rather deal with originals than with copies. The reason I asked was

that we have not been able to get access to the original. I just wondered what had happened to it."

Mr. Stripling: "Do you recall signing the assignment, Mr. Hiss?"

Mr. Hiss: "I do not at the moment recall signing this."

Mr. Stripling (designating other writing on the document): "Is this your handwriting? There is written here, 'Cherner Motor Company, 1781 Florida Avenue, Northwest.' Did you write that?"

Mr. Hiss: "I could not be sure from the outline of the letters in this photostatic copy. That also looks not unlike my own handwriting."

Mr. Stripling told Mr. Hiss that the committee had called in W. Marvin Smith, who notarized the certificate's signature, and resumed:

"Mr. Smith is an attorney in the Department of Justice in the Solicitor General's office. He has been employed there for thirty-five years. He testified that he knew Mr. Hiss. He does not recall notarizing this particular document, but he did testify that this was his signature."

"I know Mr. Smith," Mr. Hiss said.

Mr. Nixon: "It would not be likely that he would have notarized your signature unless you would have been there?"

Mr. Hiss: "It certainly would not."

Mr. Nixon: "In other words, you would not want to say now that you question the fact that Mr. Smith might have violated his oaths as a notary in notarizing a forged signature?"

Mr. Hiss: "Definitely not."

Mr. Nixon: "Then, as far as you are concerned, this is your signature?"

Mr. Hiss: "As far as I am concerned, with the evidence that has been shown to me, it is."

Representative F. Edward Hebert, Democrat, of Louisiana, asked:

"Mr. Hiss, now that your memory has been refreshed by the development of the last few minutes, do you recall the transaction whereby you disposed of that Ford that you could not remember this morning?"

"No," Mr. Hiss responded, "I have no present recollection of the disposition of the Ford, Mr. Hebert."

"In view of the refreshing of your memory?" Mr. Hebert persisted.

"In view of that, and in view of all other developments," said Mr. Hiss.

The committee, Mr. Stripling announced, was seeking for questioning two William Rosens, one in California and the other in Detroit.

The search for Mr. Rosen was made more intense by previous testimony given by Mr. Chambers in executive session. This testimony ran at one point as follows:

"The Communist party had in Washington a service station, that is, the man in charge or owner of the station was a Communist, or it may have been a car lot. The owner was a Communist. I never knew who he was or where he was.

"It was against all the rules of the underground organization for Hiss to do anything with his old car but trade it in, and I think this investigation has proved how right

HISS AND CHAMBERS FACE EACH OTHER AT CONGRESSIONAL HEARING

A dramatic moment at yesterday's session of the House Committee on Un-American Activities in Washington when Alger Hiss (standing, left) former State Department official and Whittaker Chambers (standing, right), a former Communist, were asked to rise at the same time by the Committee Investigator, Robert Stripling (in white suit).

The New York Times (Washington Bureau)

the Communists are in such matters.

"But Hiss insisted that he wanted that car turned over to the open (Communist) party so it could be of use of some poor organizer n the West or somewhere * * *

"Peters knew where this lot was and he either took Hiss there or he gave Hiss the address and Hiss went there and, to the best of my recollection of his description of that happening, he left the car there and simply went away, and the man in charge of the station took care of the rest of it for him. I should think the records of that transfer would be traceable."

Before leaving the witness chair Mr. Hiss offered the suggestion that Mr. Chambers make his accusations outside of a "privileged" Congressional hearing and thus make himself subject to a suit for slander or libel.

He insisted again in his testimony today that he had known Mr. Chambers only as "George Crosley," a freelance magazine writer whom he met in his office when he was legal assistant to the Senate (Nye) Munitions Investigating Committee in 1934.

Mr. Chambers repeated that Mr. Hiss knew him, despite close association during 1934 and 1935 and later, only as "Carl," a paid hand of the Communist party. Mr. Chambers is now a senior editor of Time magazine. Mr. Hiss is president of the Carnegie Foundation for International Peace.

As he neared the close of his testimony Mr. Hiss was permitted to read into the record a 7-page letter which he had written to the committee yesterday. In it he called Mr. Chambers "a liar, spy and traitor" and raised a question of his sanity.

He also called on the committee to ask Mr. Chambers a series of

questions which he had prepared. Committee members did. The questions and answers ran as follows:

"Where do you reside?" Mr. Hiss had said he had been unable to find this out.

Chairman Thomas ruled that Mr. Chambers need not answer this on the ground that it would provide information for the Communist party, with which Mr. Chambers said he broke in 1937 after serving it from 1924.

"List the various places where you have lived since 1930, indicating the length of time you have lived at each place and the name you have used at that place."

Mr. Chambers said he was living in New Jersey in 1930 and was there perhaps more than a year. He went to live with his mother on Long Island for another year. Then he occupied the apartment of Mr. Hiss on Twenty-eighth Street N. W., Washington, and, after leaving it, went back to Long Island. Later he moved to Baltimore, where he lived for a couple of years, and from Baltimore "fled from the Communist party and went into hiding for about six months."

"Then," he stated, "I felt I must try to come above ground and establish an identity. I was a faceless man."

He added that he bought a house on St. Paul Street in Baltimore and from that house moved to his present address, which he did not disclose.

As to names, he said, he was known as "Carl" and never as "George Crosley."

Employment Record Asked

"Give your complete employment record during your membership in

the Communist party and since your resignation from the Communist party stating the name of your employer, your occupation and your compensation."

Mr. Chambers said that while a Communist he "last worked for the party" editing and writing for the Daily Worker and the New Masses. From the Communist party, he added, he went to Time Magazine, hired as a writer through a friend, Robert Cantwell.

"Give a complete bibliography of your writings under any and every name you have used."

Mr. Chambers said that he never had written any books, but that he had translated some, among them a novel about the Spanish Civil War.

"Have you ever been charged or convicted of a crime? Give full particulars as to where, when and for what."

"Never," Mr. Chambers answered.

"Have you ever been treated for a mental illness? If so, where, when and by whom?"

"I have never been treated for a mental illness period," Mr. Chambers asserted. "I have never been in a mental institution. Any one on Time can tell you that."

Mr. Hiss had said previously that a former employe of Time Magazine had "reported" that Mr. Chambers had been in such an institution. That and another indirect report he had received, he added, prompted this question.

"When, where and to whom were you married? Have you any children? Where does your wife now reside?"

Mr. Chambers said that he was married to his "first and only wife," and that he had two children. He did not say where his wife was living.

"Describe the circumstances under which you came in contact with the committee and make public all written memoranda which you have handed to any representative of the committee."

Mr. Stripling said at this point that Mr. Chambers had not got in touch with the committee. He added that the committee sent two investigators to interview him and that a subpoena was issued without any prior knowledge on Mr. Chambers' part.

Fond of Hiss, He Says

Mr. Chambers repeated that in 1937 he ad gone to Mr. Hiss' home to urge that he, too, break with the Communist party.

"Did you feel any risk in going?" asked Mr. Nixon.

"Yes," the witness said. "I was afraid of an ambush."

"Why did you want to get Mr. Hiss away from the party?" Mr. Nixon asked.

"I was very fond of Mr. Hiss. He was my closest friend—certainly my closest friend in the Communist party."

Mr. Nixon asked whether he had a motive for accusing Mr. Hiss.

"Motive?" asked Mr. Chambers. "This story of 'old grudge, of hatred' has been going around. I don't hate Mr. Hiss. We were close friends. But we got caught in the tragedy of history. Mr. Hiss represents the concealed enemy we are all fighting and I am fighting. I am testifying against him with remorse and pity. But in this moment of historic jeopardy at which the nation now stands, so help me God, I could not do otherwise."

"You have heard Mr. Hiss' testimony today. What is your reaction to that testimony?" Mr. Hebert asked.

"Mr. Hiss is lying," Mr. Chambers said.

"You think his testimony is pure fabrication from whole cloth?" Mr. Hebert asked.

"I'd say 80 per cent fabrication," Mr. Chambers replied.

Mr. Hiss said that he was handicapped in his testimony since he was compelled, because of a lack of records, to deal in off-the-cuff recollections.

Mr. Hiss recollected that he had "thrown in" the old car with the oral arrangement for letting Mr. Chambers have his Twenty-eighth Street apartment when he moved into a house on P Street. Committee members said that the weight of other testimony had shown that Mr. Hiss had released the car to Mr. Chambers much later. The new Plymouth which Mr. Hiss bought, it was held, was purchased, according to title records, some five months after he said he had let Mr. Chambers have his "second and older car."

Representative Karl E. Mundt, Republican, of South Dakota, asked the witness:

"Would you like to have this committee believe, Mr. Hiss, actually believe, that you cannot remember how you finally disposed of an automobile that had such a sentimental attachment to you?"

Mr. Hiss: "Mr. Mundt, I have already testified that my recollection is that I let Crosley have the use of it. I may have let him have complete disposition. He may be the person who disposed of it."

In this connection, Mr. Hiss said that his signing of the "assignment of title" document may have been a casual closing out of technical disposition of the car; that he might have been asked to do this, might have done it and then forgotten it. At least, he insisted, it was not in his present recollection.

August 26, 1948

HOUSE BODY SAYS SPY RINGS STILL EXIST IN GOVERNMENT; SCORES WHITE HOUSE TACTICS

TRUMAN, CLARK HIT

Administration's Failure to Yield Data Called Menace to Security

LAWS TO CURB REDS ASKED

Un-American Committee Also Questions Hiss' Veracity— 'Interim Report' Is Made

By JOHN D. MORRIS
Special to THE NEW YORK TIMES.

WASHINGTON, Aug. 28—The House Committee on Un-American Activities reported today that it had definitely established the wartime existence of "numerous Communist espionage rings" in the Federal Government.

It expressed the belief that "such groups are still operating within the Government" and said the public would never know all about them if the White House had not obstructed its investigation.

It called on Attorney General Tom C. Clark to enforce present anti-espionage laws "without regard to partisan or political considerations because the very security of the nation is at stake." It said the Attorney General's past failures were largely responsible for the growth and power "of the Communist conspiracy."

Legislation was recommended to strengthen the laws and legally meet the "new challenge" of recalcitrant witnesses before the committee who refused to answer questions, taking refuge in the Fifth Amendment to the Constitution.

With respect to the contradictory sworn testimony of Alger Hiss and Whittaker Chambers regarding their alleged connection with a pre-war Communist "underground," the committee questioned Mr. Hiss' veracity, expressing confidence in that of Mr. Chambers.

Report Takes 7,000 Words

All of this was contained in a fifteen-page, 7,000-word printed "interim report" on the committee's investigation of alleged Communist underground activities.

One phase of the inquiry evolved from Mr. Chambers' testimony of the existence in the Nineteen Thirties of an "apparatus" which aimed to put Communists into key Federal posts and thus influence Government policy. Mr. Chambers, now a senior editor of Time magazine, said he had been a paid functionary in this organization and accused Mr. Hiss, then a Government official and now president of the Carnegie Endowment for International Peace, of having been a Communist and an active member of the "underground" group.

The other principal phase of the committee's investigation concerned Mrs. Elizabeth T. Bentley's account of a wartime Communist espionage ring which she said had obtained information for Russia from Government officials. Mrs. Bentley said she was a courier for the ring.

The Hiss-Chambers controversy, which has been the main focus of recent hearings, was somewhat overshadowed in the committee's report by its criticism of President Truman, who had called the inquiry a "red herring," and of Attorney General Clark.

President's Order Assailed

The committee said it had been "hampered at every turn by the refusal of the executive branch of the Government to cooperate in any way with the investigation due to the President's loyalty freeze order."

It referred to Mr. Truman's directive prohibiting executive agencies from giving Congress data of loyalty investigations of Federal employes.

"Not only have the executive agencies refused to turn over to the committee the loyalty files of the suspected members of the spy rings but they have even gone so far as to refuse to turn over the employment records of these individuals," the committee said.

"The committee can see no excuse whatever for such arbitrary action since it is obvious that turning over employment records would in no wise involve disclosing sources of information or confidential data.

"The committee has proceeded to obtain information in every way possible and eventually will see that it is presented to the public, but the committee deplores the fact that the executive branch of the Government will in no way aid the committee in its efforts to protect the national security from those who are doing everything they can to undermine and destroy it."

The Attorney General, the committee said, should not only enforce present laws vigorously but also give Congress recommendations for strengthening them "at the earliest possible date." Mr. Clark promised to do this "at an early date" as long ago as Feb. 5, the report said.

For its own part, the committee called for enactment of the Mundt-Nixon Communist Control bill, which the House passed and the Senate shelved in the last regular session, and recommended other legislation to tighten present espionage laws, force the transmission to Congress of loyalty data, curb immigration of Communists and penalize government officials for providing security information to foreign powers, friendly or enemy, in peace or war.

Hiss Testimony Discussed

The report devoted considerable space to its reasons for questioning the veracity of Alger Hiss and expressing confidence in that of Whittaker Chambers.

"Hiss," the committee said, "will be given every opportunity to reconcile the conflicting portions of his testimony, but the confrontation of the two men and the attendant testimony from both witnesses have definitely shifted the burden of proof from Chambers to Hiss, in the opinion of this committee.

"Up to now, the verifiable portions of Chambers' testimony have stood up strongly; the verifiable portions of the Hiss testimony have been badly shaken and are primarily refuted by the testimony of Hiss versus Hiss, as the complete text of the printed hearings will reveal."

The committee said that Mr. Hiss' "vague and evasive testimony" regarding the disposition of his 1929 Ford roadster "raises a doubt as to other portions of his testimony."

"In this connection," it added, "it should be observed that on 198 occasions Hiss qualified his answers to questions by the phrase 'to the best of my recollection' and similar qualifying phrases, while Chambers, on the other hand, was for the most part forthright and emphatic in his answers."

August 29, 1948

138

Hiss Sues Chambers for Slander; Calls Communist Charge 'False'

In an attempt to clear himself of the charge that he was a member of the Communist party, Alger Hiss, former high State Department official, filed a slander action yesterday in Federal Court against his accuser, Whittaker Chambers, now a senior editor of Time magazine.

Although the suit, charging defamation of character and asking damages of $50,000, was filed in the Maryland District Court, the complaint was given out here by Mr. Hiss, now president of the Carnegie Endowment for International Peace. Mr. Chambers, an avowed former Communist, lives in Carroll County, Md.

The complaint alleged that the "untrue, false and defamatory" accusations were made in a radio broadcast on Aug. 30 and were a repetition of Mr. Chambers' testimony in five appearances before the House Committee on Un-American Activities.

Mr. Hiss denied the charge under oath when he was called by the committee and dared his accuser to repeat it at a public forum where Mr. Chambers would not be immune from legal action.

Mr. Chambers did repeat it. A transcript of the broadcast was incorporated in Mr. Hiss' complaint. It reportedly contained several statements that the plaintiff as-

serted "damaged his professional reputation and office, brought him into public odium and contempt and caused him great pain and mental anguish."

The contents of the broadcast, Mr. Hiss charged, were designed to show him as disloyal and unfaithful to the United States, that he had betrayed his duty and had sworn falsely to oaths of office upon assuming various Government posts.

Asked at that time if he thought Mr. Hiss would sue for slander and libel, Mr. Chambers said, "I do not think so."

At his fourth appearance before the House committee, Mr. Chambers met Mr. Hiss in a dramatic confrontation. Both men were firm on flatly contradictory stories and ended by directly calling each other liars.

The Hiss-Chambers controversy held the spotlight of the House group's investigation into pre-war and wartime Communist activity through most of last month. Mr. Chambers charged in public and private hearings that among other things Mr. Hiss was a member of an "elite" Communist group whose objective it was to work Communists into key Government jobs. The magazine editor repeated that in the broadcast, Mr. Hiss complained also.

BALTIMORE, Sept. 27 (AP)—Whittaker Chambers issued a three-sentence comment on Alger Hiss' suit from his Westminster home. Mr. Chambers said:

"I welcome Mr. Hiss' daring suit. I do not minimize the audacity or the ferocity of the forces which work through him. But I do not believe that Mr. Hiss or anybody else can use the means of justice to defeat the ends of justice."

September 28, 1948

HOUSE UNIT SEIZES FILMED U. S. SECRETS AT CHAMBERS' HOME

Vital State Department Data Reportedly Fed to Red Spies Bared in Row With Hiss

FEDERAL JURY MAY ACT

Committee Declares Evidence of Big Network Is 'Definite' —Hearings to Be Resumed

By W. H. LAWRENCE
Special to THE NEW YORK TIMES.

WASHINGTON, Dec. 3—The House Committee on Un-American Activities declared tonight that it had "definite proof of one of the most extensive espionage rings in the history of the United States" and that it possessed "microfilm copies of documents of tremendous importance" which had been removed from the State Department for transmission to "Russian Communist agents."

The committee said that the evidence was taken from Whittaker Chambers, senior editor of Time magazine and declared former Communist underground agent, who has been engaged in a running controversy, involving alleged slander and perjury, with Alger Hiss, former high-ranking State Department official.

STUDYING MICROFILMS IN CAPITAL

Robert E. Stripling (seated), chief investigator for the House Committee on Un-American Activities, looking over microfilms found in a hollowed-out pumpkin on a Maryland farm. The others, left to right, are Robert Gaston, Donald Appell and C. E. McKillips.

Associated Press Wirephoto

Mr. Hiss, who is now president of the Carnegie Foundation for International Peace in New York City, has filed a $75,000 slander suit against Mr. Chambers in Baltimore.

Hiss Claims Credit

[The Associated Press quoted Mr. Hiss as saying in a statement issued in New York:

["During the course of examination by my counsel of Mr. Chambers in the libel action which I have brought against him in Baltimore, Mr. Chambers produced certain documents which I consider of such importance that I directed my attorneys to place them at once before the Department of Justice.

["This has been done, and I have offered my full cooperation to the Department of Justice and to the grand jury in the further investigation of this matter."]

The committee announcement was made by Robert Stripling, its chief investigator, who issued a statement in the name of Representative Karl Mundt, Republican, of South Dakota, recently elected to the Senate, who is in his home state, but who announced his intention to reassemble the committee as soon as possible.

Mr. Stripling, in making Mr. Mundt's statement public, said that some of the microfilmed documents turned over to the committee would have permitted cracking of a United States secret code if placed side by side with the coded originals.

All Dated Before War

He said that none of the documents microfilmed was dated after the year 1938, but that he had a stack of papers, developed from the film, about three feet high.

Mr. Stripling said that Mr. Chambers had not volunteered the data but that it had been taken, under subpoena, at the Time editor's home in Westminster, Md., last night.

The committee investigator described two of the documents. One, he said, was a report signed "Bullitt," obviously referring to William C. Bullitt, former Ambassador to Russia and to France, who reported to the department his conversations with a Chinese official, formerly in Moscow, regarding the prospects of Russia's entrance into the Chinese-Japanese war.

Another concerned a statement handed to the German Ambassador by "Mr. Welles," an obvious reference to Sumner Welles, formerly Under-Secretary of State.

The Mundt statement said that the committee had posted a twenty-four-hour guard over its new evidence, which included "conclusive proof * * * that secret documents of direct significance to our national security were fed out of the State Department by a member of the Communist underground to Whittaker Chambers, who at that time was operating as one of the Washington contacts for the Communist underground operating in America."

It did not name the member of the "Communist underground" who supplied the documents to Mr. Chambers, but it did say that the purpose of their removal from State Department offices was "transmittal to Russian Communist agents."

The House committee's statement was made public a few hours after Attorney General Tom C. Clark told reporters at the White House that the Department of Justice had "new information" regarding the Hiss-Chambers case.

It was indicated that this material might be placed before a Federal grand jury in New York next week. Attorney General Clark and Justice Department officials declined to discuss it in any way.

Mr. Stripling said that Representative Mundt spoke for the entire House Committee on Un-American Activities in the following statement:

"Documents secured by subpoena last night from Whittaker Chambers indicate that a final conclusion is imminent in the long discussed Hiss-Chambers espionage case with which the House Committee on Un-American Activities has been concerned since before the the special session of the Eightieth Congress.

"There is now in the possession of the committee, under twenty-four-hour guard, microfilmed copies of documents of tremendous importance, which were removed from the offices of the State Department and turned over to Chambers for the purpose of transmittal to Russian Communist agents.

Documents Sought Ten Years

"These documents are of such startling and significant importance, and reveal such a vast network of Communist espionage within the State Department, that they far exceed anything yet brought before the committee in its ten-year history.

"Those microfilms have been the object of a ten-year search by agents of the United States Government, and provide definite proof of one of the most extensive espionage rings in the history of the United States.

"On the basis of evidence now before the committee, it appears that conclusive proof has been established that secret documents of direct significance to our national security were fed out of the State Department by a member of the Communist underground to Whittaker Chambers, who at that time was operating as one of the Washington contacts for the Communist

underground operating in America.

"As the chairman of the subcommittee handling this entire matter, I shall proceed to Washington as soon as possible. I have radioed Congressman [Richard M.] Nixon [Republican. of California] to fly back to Washington, if possible. and am getting in touch with other members of the subcommittee to ascertain the earliest possible date for a public hearing. The evidence before us is so shocking that I do not feel justified in delaying action a day longer than required."

The Hiss-Chambers controversy, which has brought about not only the $75,000 damage suit but also demands that one or the other be indicted for perjury. has concerned Mr. Chambers' charge that Mr. Hiss was a member of a pre-war "Communist apparatus" operating in Washington. Mr. Hiss has categorically denied the assertion.

Mr. Hiss entered the service of the State Department in 1936 as an assistant to an Assistant Secretary of State and thereafter held posts in the Office for Far Eastern Affairs and the Office of Special Political Affairs until January, 1945, when he became director of the latter office and held that position until 1947.

Outgrowth of Libel Suit

Before the House committee acted tonight. Attorney General Clark had indicated that the new evidence had been discovered in Baltimore while depositions were being taken in Mr. Hiss' suit against Mr. Chambers.

Although the un-American Activities Committee now is very much of a "lame duck" group because it is under Republican lead-

ership and so many of its members were defeated in the elections last month. Representative Mundt, who moves to the Senate in January, said that "the evidence before us is so shocking that I do not feel justified in delaying action a day longer than required."

In the November elections, control of Congress passed from the Republicans to the Democrats and this means the retirement of Representative J. Parnell Thomas of New Jersey as chairman. Since the election Mr. Thomas has been indicted on charges of conspiracy to defraud the Government and of making false payroll claims against the Government.

Representatives John McDowell of Pennsylvania and Richard B. Vail of Illinois, Republican members of the committee, were defeated for re-election.

Mr. Stripling said in response to a question that the Justice and State Departments had not been consulted about the microfilmed evidence, and added in response to another inquiry that the committee would have to decide what it wished to do if the Justice Department requested them.

Presumably the "new information" mentioned by Attorney General Clark will be presented to the same Federal grand jury which indicted twelve top Communist leaders and which is scheduled to end its term of service Dec. 18.

Nobody at the Justice Department would go beyond Mr. Clark's statement, but it was understood there had been lengthy conferences concerning presentation of the matter to the grand jury.

December 4, 1948

Microfilms in Pumpkin At the Chambers Farm

Special to The New York Times.

WASHINGTON, Dec. 3— Microfilms which the House Un-American Activities Committee described as definite proof of an extensive espionage ring were produced from a hollowed-out pumpkin, Robert E. Stripling, the committee's chief investigator, said tonight.

He said that when investigators talked with Whittaker Chambers under subpoena last night at his farm near Westminster, Md., Mr. Chambers led them to a spot behind the farmhouse. There he showed them a pumpkin. He then lifted a cut-out lid and pulled out the microfilms.

December 4, 1948

CHAMBERS SAYS HISS PASSED U. S. DATA TO HIM FOR RUSSIA

NKVD AGENT NAMED

Colonel Bykov Identified in Libel Suit Testimony as Russian Contact

HISS' WIFE IS IMPLICATED

Accuser Says She Typed Copies of Stolen Papers—House Unit Delays Public Hearings

By C. P. TRUSSELL
Special to THE NEW YORK TIMES.

WASHINGTON, Dec. 6—Sworn testimony by Whittaker Chambers, confessed courier for a pre-war Communist underground, that Alger Hiss, as a State Department official, slipped him "restricted" documents for delivery to a Russian agent was made public by the House Committee on Un-American Activities today.

The Soviet agent was identified in this testimony as Col. Boris Bykov. Committee members said that Colonel Bykov was the principal agent in the United States for NKVD, the Russian secret police, during the period covered by the Chambers allegations. This was in 1937 and 1938.

Mrs. Hiss, wife of the former Federal official who is now president of the Carnegie Endowment for International Peace, also was involved in the Chambers testimony. It was alleged that she typed copies of documents brought home by her husband for delivery to Mr. Chambers.

Jury at Work Year and Half

The testimony was taken from Mr. Chambers, now a senior editor of Time magazine, in preparation for his defense against a $75,000 suit for libel filed in Baltimore by Mr. Hiss. Mr. Chambers had accused Mr. Hiss of being a leader in the "elite" Communist underground.

Mr. Chambers was scheduled to be a principal witness at a public hearing by the House committee tomorrow. This was to reopen, and perhaps bring to a conclusion, the puzzling Hiss-Chambers case before the committee.

However, a special Federal grand jury in New York, which has been investigating communism and espionage for a year and a half, reconvened suddenly. The first principal witnesses it called were Messrs. Chambers and Hiss. The House committee postponed the public hearing.

As in the case of the House committee, the New York grand jury's attention focused on new evidence.

In the pre-trial testimony taken for the libel suit at Baltimore, it developed that Mr. Chambers had produced documents that had not been brought to light before. Then, at 1 A. M. Friday, Mr. Chambers led Robert E. Stripling, chief investigator for the committee, to a hollowed-out pumpkin on his farm in Maryland.

Material Taken From Files

In the pumpkin shell were tiny rolls of microfilm which, investigators said, recorded enough important State, Navy and Army documents to make a pile, when reproduced on enlarged scale, two or three feet high.

The Chambers testimony disclosed by the committee today did not concern the films. Representative Richard M. Nixon, Republican, of California, a committee member, explained that it dealt with other documents which Mr. Chambers had in his possession and involved official business of the Government which, in some manner, had escaped from files of "restricted" interchange.

The new charges against Mr. Hiss by Mr. Chambers were included in a pesotion said by Mr. Nixon to have been made during an interrogation of him by William L. Marbury of Baltimore, counsel for Mr. Hiss.

Representative Nixon did not read the entire transcript but he emphasized that the whole had been made a part of the committee's official record.

At a news conference that drew a record assembly of reporters, Mr. Nixon read from Mr. Chambers' testimony as follows:

" 'Sometime in 1937—about the middle of the year—J. Peters (accused previously by Mr. Chambers as the "real head" of the alleged Washington underground and now facing deportation proceedings) introduced me to a Russian who identified himself under the pseudonym Peter. * * * The Russian, Peter, was one Colonel Bykov. * * *

" 'Colonel Bykov was extremely interested in the Washington apparatus (Mr. Chambers had previously described the alleged underground as "an apparatus") * * * In August or in the early fall of 1937, I arranged a meeting between Alger Hiss and Colonel Bykov. For that purpose Mr. Hiss came to New York, where I met him. * * *

Flow of Data "Fairly Consistent"

" 'Colonel Bykov * * * raised the question of procuring documents from the State Department and Mr. Hiss agreed.' "

At this point, Representative Nixon interjected, Mr. Marbury, Mr. Hiss' counsel asked: "What?"

" 'Mr. Hiss agreed,' " Mr. Nixon repeated as he read from the transcript, and then continued: " 'Following that meeting, Alger Hiss began a fairly consistent flow of such material as we have before us here.' "

Representative Nixon emphasized that there was no evidence that the exhibits before the pre-trial testimony-taking group had been passed on to Soviet agents. Under questioning, he said that the Chambers testimony was claiming only a similarity between the material found in his possession and and that which he swore he had passed on to Colonel Bykov before he broke with communism in 1938.

The "similar" documents, Mr. Nixon said, were "restricted," "important," and, in some cases, contained military information.

Continuing the reading from Mr. Chambers' testimony, Representative Nixon quoted:

" 'Following that meeting, Alger Hiss began a fairly consistent flow of such material as we have before us here. The method was for him to bring home documents in his brief case which Mrs. Hiss usually typed.' * * *

Notes Ascribed to Hiss

" 'There occasionally came to Mr. Hiss' knowledge certain things, or he saw certain things, or he saw certain papers which he was not able to bring out of the department for one reason or another, either because they merely passed through his hands so quickly or because he thought it inadvisable.

" 'But notations in his handwriting are notes of such documents, such information, which he made and brought out in that form.' "

Representative Nixon said that the committee, among its exhibits, had three documents which had been written by hand. He said, too, that a Government handwriting expert had studied them and had declared, "conclusively and without qualification" that the penmanship was that of Mr. Hiss.

A reporter asked whether such a document might have been something which Mr. Hiss had summarized for State Department files and possibly could have been removed from the files by some one else.

"I have read the record carefully," Mr. Nixon said, "and it is apparent that the form and content of these documents were obviously not intended to simply be a part of the State Department records."

Nixon Assails Justice Department

With the breaking up, by the New York grand jury, of the committee's plans to open public hearings tomorrow, a subcommittee suddenly left for New York in late afternoon.

Mr. Nixon said the subcommittee, comprising himself and Representative John McDowell, Republican, of Pennsylvania, would question "two important" witnesses in New York during the night. Mr. Stripling, the chief investigator, accompanied them.

A committee investigator, William A. Wheeler, previously had taken copies of committee exhibits to the New York grand jury, which in its initial indictments several months ago cited twelve top Communist officials on charges of conspiring to overthrow the American Government.

In making public the new charges by Mr. Chambers, Representative Nixon, who flew back to Washington in a Coast Guard plane from a ship at sea to handle the new developments, was highly critical of the Department of Justice in the Hiss-Chambers case.

"The committee," Mr. Nixon said, "is concerned over the apparent lack of interest by the Department of Justice in getting to the crux of this case. It seems to be trying frantically to find a method which will place the blame of possession of these documents on Mr. Chambers.

State Department Intervenes

"This is a situation that is not debatable. Mr. Chambers admits possession of the documents. He is prepared to take the consequences of having them, if consequences come.

"The real issue which concerns the committee, and should concern the Department of Justice, is to determine who in the State Department furnished this information to Mr. Chambers."

Later, Mr. Nixon observed, as further questions were pressed on him:

"Mr. Chambers has made his record. He also has made his bed and will have to lie in it."

Conferring with the committee today were representatives of the Department of State and of the office of the United States Attorney for the District of Columbia. They were cautious in discussing the meetings.

The representatives of the State Department—Samuel D. Boykin, director of the Office of Controls, and Donald L. Nicholson, chief of the Division of Security, emphasized, however, that they had appeared at their own request and sought permission to evaluate the evidence documents as to their possible effect on national security.

December 7, 1948

HISS INDICTED FOR PERJURY IN COMMUNIST SPY INQUIRY

TWO COUNTS IN BILL

Turning Over of State Papers to Spy Courier in 1938 Is Alleged

HEARINGS TO BE CONTINUED

Conviction Could Mean Ten Years in Prison — Accused Persists in Denial

By RUSSELL PORTER

Alger Hiss, former State Department official, was indicted by a Federal grand jury yesterday on two counts of perjury.

The grand jury charged that Mr. Hiss lied when he testified before it that neither he nor his wife ever turned over any State Department documents to Whittaker Chambers, self-styled courier for a Communist spy ring, and that he never saw Mr. Chambers after Jan. 1, 1937.

After examining the evidence presented to it, the grand jury held that Mr. Hiss saw Mr. Chambers in February and March, 1938, and turned over to him "secret, confidential and restricted" documents and other papers in violation of Federal law.

Mr. Hiss denied last night that he had committed perjury. In a statement issued through the office of his lawyer, Edward C. McLean, the defendant said:

"My testimony before the grand jury was entirely truthful."

Arraignment Today Probable

United States Attorney John F. X. McGohey told reporters that Mr. Hiss would be notified through his attorney to appear in Federal court for arraignment, probably this morning.

If convicted, Mr. Hiss would be subject to penalties of five years in prison and $2,000 fine on each of the two counts in the indictment.

The indictment was handed up to Federal Judge John W. Clancy by the same special grand jury that recently indicted twelve American Communist leaders on charges of conspiracy to "teach and advocate" the forcible overthrow of the United States Government.

This grand jury has been sitting for eighteen months and yesterday was the last day of its existence. It was recalled two weeks ago to investigate new charges made by Mr. Chambers in defending himself against a $75,000 libel suit brought by Mr. Hiss.

Mr. Chambers' original charges against Mr. Hiss before the House Committee on Un-American Activities did not charge espionage, but alleged that Mr. Hiss and his brother, Donald, also a former State Department official, were members of a pre-war Communist underground "apparatus" in Washington.

Papers Shown in Libel Case

After Mr. Chambers repeated his charges on the radio without Congressional privilege and was sued for libel, he produced in a Baltimore court a number of documents to support his charges. Then he turned over to House Committee investigators a number of microfilm copies of additional documents, which he took from a hollowed-out pumpkin on his farm near Baltimore the night of Dec. 2.

Mr. Chambers then charged that Mr. Hiss had turned over to him at various times, particularly in early 1938, various State Department documents for transmission to a Soviet spy ring.

The grand jury met nine days in the last two weeks on the new Chambers revelations. Among the witnesses were Mr. Chambers, Mr. Hiss, his wife, Priscilla, his brother Donald, and several other persons named by Mr. Chambers. Mr. Chambers and Mr. Hiss have been before the Grand Jury every day.

Yesterday Mr. Hiss and Mr. Chambers left the grand jury room on the fourteenth floor of the Federal Court Building about the same time, shortly before the indictment was handed up. As usual, Mr. Chambers slipped down a back stairway to a lower floor to avoid reporters, and Mr. Hiss walked out to the corridor where reporters were waiting.

When Mr. Hiss took an elevator from the fourteenth floor, however, it stopped at the eleventh floor to take on Mr. Chambers. The latter turned his back on Mr. Hiss, and the two rode downstairs without saying a word.

Then, at 5:37 P. M., the grand jury filed out of its room into elevators that took the eighteen members present down to Judge Clancy's court room on the third floor.

Judge Clancy took his seat on the bench at 5:45 o'clock. Thomas J. Donegan, special assistant to the Attorney General, who has been presenting the evidence, announced that the grand jury was ready to make its report.

Jerome Blumauer, acting foreman of the jury, a plastics manufacturer, of 205 West Eighty-eighth Street, then handed up the indictment to Judge Clancy.

Jury's Work Is Praised

Mr. McGohey and Mr. Donegan both commended the grand jury for the amount of time they had devoted to their duties in the last eighteen months.

At the suggestion of one of the jurors, Mr. Donegan read a statement from the jury that it had been unable to complete its investigation of all the matters that had come before it, and that unfinished matters would receive the attention of a successor grand jury that will be impaneled today.

Judge Clancy then discharged the grand jury with the thanks of the court, saying that in recognition of its unusually arduous work its members would be released from grand jury duty for the next five years if they wished.

Copies of the indictment were made public by Mr. McGohey after court adjourned. Mr. McGohey pointed out that the indictment showed that Mr. Hiss had made his allegedly false statements under oath at yesterday's session of the grand jury. He said the Government had the two witnesses needed to prove its case and would produce them in court when the case was tried.

He declined to say whether the statute of limitations-barred prosecution of the alleged abstraction of the documents from State Department files.

Mr. McGohey said the new grand jury would start work right away, continuing the investigation of Communist espionage charges. The new grand jury, he said, will be briefed on the testimony taken by the old one. If necessary, he added, some of the same witnesses who have testified before the old jury will be called before the new one.

A panel of 100 persons from whom the new grand jury will be selected will report at 10:30 A. M. today to Judge Clancy. The panel includes business executives, merchants, salesmen, consultants, housewives and authors. Twenty-three members will be selected, and sworn in by Judge Clancy.

Kilpatrick on the Panel

John Reed Kilpatrick, president of the Madison Square Garden Corporation, and Harry Scherman, book publisher, of the Book of the Month Club, are on the panel.

In addition to the Chambers charges, the new grand jury will look into charges made by Miss Elizabeth T. Bentley, a former Communist agent, before the House committee. Abraham George Silverman, a former Government economist, named by Miss Bentley, was on the grand jury floor yesterday. So was Henry Julian Wadleigh, former Government economist, named by Mr. Chambers.

Mr. Chambers told reporters yesterday that when he talked in 1939 with A. A. Berle Jr., former assistant Secretary of State, he gave Mr. Berle the names of Communist members of the Washington underground "apparatus," and also the name of Col. Boris Bykov, alleged head of one of the Soviet spy rings to whom Mr. Chambers gave information.

He also said he had named a Washington dentist believed to be in active contact with the Soviet spies, a metallurgist with a high laboratory position in the United States Steel Corporation, and a civilian employe of the Aberdeen, Md., proving grounds. He said he had urgently warned Mr. Berle of the need for getting this man out of Aberdeen promptly.

Mr. Berle has said that the information given by Mr. Chambers in 1939 was not as specific as that which he has given this year.

Attorney General Tom Clark said last night that he was "not surprised" at the indictment. Mr. Clark, who was attending a dinner at the Waldorf-Astoria Hotel, predicted Mr. Hiss would be brought to trial some time next month.

He was asked whether the indictment would affect President Truman's characterization of the House committee's investigation as a "red herring."

"I don't think it will alter it," Mr. Clark replied.

In Washington, Representative R. M. Nixon of California, a member of the House committee, said the indictment was a vindication of the committee's activities. He said the committee would continue with the investigation of other leads, including facts given by Mr. Chambers regarding others besides Mr. Hiss.

"Despite criticism from all sources from the President down," said Mr. Nixon, "the indictment establishes beyond doubt the justification for committees of Congress investigating in this field."

December 16, 1948

142

WHAT IS AMERICANISM?

One holiday gift the American people might like to have would be a return to sanity and fair dealing in the present crusade against acts, associations and thoughts which a committee of Congress has taken upon itself to define as "un-American." The committee in question will not long exist in its present form. Nevertheless, it has had a long career, it has had widespread support and it represents a tendency which will not be abruptly cut off when the Eighty-first Congress organizes.

This committee has recently dug up some evidence. It has established through the testimony of two former Communists, and through films belatedly and reluctantly produced by one of those former Communists, that unauthorized persons some years ago were receiving copies of secret State Department documents. If there was a Communist "apparatus" in our Government before the Second World War, or during it, or after it; if those guilty are found and convicted; and if successful spying on our state secrets is thus terminated the committee will have rendered a service.

But this committee, in its long history under the present and previous chairmanships, has rendered a grave disservice, too. Nothing that it has achieved or can achieve can wipe this stain off its record. It has made accusations without giving the accused a hearing; it has brought accused individuals into hearings and then allowed them no proper opportunity to present their cases; it has impeached men's characters and ruined their careers on flimsy grounds; it has set up preposterous standards of what is "American" and what is not. Within the week, on hearsay evidence, its acting chairman contributed his bit to the obituaries on a man whose superior officers in the State Department found to be a good and faithful servant of the American people, dead in what is believed to be a tragic accident; the acting chairman published a charge that the dead man, now past all answering, had been a part of the Communist "apparatus" in the State Department.

This committee legitimately exists for one purpose, and one purpose only: to gather facts which may be useful to our national Legislature in framing laws. It does not legitimately exist to cross-examine people as to their beliefs; to damn them by their associations; to tell free American citizens to what organizations they may belong or may not belong, to what causes they may subscribe and to what causes they may not subscribe; to erect a golden calf of a circumscribed "Americanism" to which all must bow down.

It is time that we re-examined our concept of Americanism. Certainly we must say at the beginning that no good American will betray official secrets to a foreign government, or put the interests of that government ahead of those of his own country; or conspire to bring about a violent revolution. A good American respects the democratic process. His principles are those of the Bill of Rights and the Gettysburg Address.

But the principles of a good American do not bind him to adhere to any political party, or to any set of economic views; they do not bind him to be right of center; they do not require him to choose his friends according to the dictates of a committee of Congress; indeed, if he is an intelligent man, they impel him to the fullest possible inquiry in all fields of political and economic thought. The good American makes up his own mind and is guided by his private conscience.

We have come dangerously near in this country to a substitution of official character assassination for judicial process. We have come dangerously near to a censorship over the press, the radio, the motion picture and the drama. No doubt some misguided characters in those agencies have been "un-American" by the most exact definition. But which is the more "un-American": to meet an outrageous or unpopular idea in open battle and beat it or to suppress those who hold it? We think the American people know the answer. We think they will support any needed federal legislation to prevent treason or conspiracy, but we think, also, they will steadfastly oppose any legislation or any administrative or legislative action which restricts the citizen's right to say what he chooses, write and print what he chooses and associate with such friends as he chooses. For this is the very essence of Americanism.

December 26, 1948

LOYALTY CHECKS HELD EXCESSIVE

Prof. Emerson, D. M. Helfeld of the Yale Law School See Conflict With Basic Rights

By KALMAN SIEGEL

Comparing the Government's loyalty program to those of Nazi Germany and Fascist Italy, an article in the Yale Law Journal published today declared that the current loyalty check not only was unnecessary, but was making the Federal Government an example of repression for the whole nation.

Admitting that any government must always be able to protect itself against dangerous activity within its own ranks, the authors contended that existing legislation and administrative regulation afforded adequate protection against "actions" of public employes that were dangerous to the Government.

The article, a 143-page report of a comprehensive study of loyalty among Government employes, was written by Prof. Thomas I. Emerson of the Yale University Law School, and David M. Helfeld, a graduate fellow at the law school.

Professor Emerson is a former general counsel of the Office of War Mobilization who joined the Yale faculty in 1946 after holding important Government legal posts since 1933. He is also a national committeeman of the Progressive party. Mr. Helfeld, an alumnus of City College here, received his LL. B. from Yale last June.

The Journal announced that William J. (Wild Bill) Donovan, former director of the Office of Strategic Services, was preparing a second article on the loyalty program representing a different viewpoint. It is scheduled for publication later this year.

See Blow to Freedoms

In essence, Professor Emerson and Mr. Helfeld declared, the loyalty program was an aggressive effort to weed out the potentially disloyal, and was designed to remove from Government service individuals whose ideas, associations and legal activities indicate that they may in the future engage in conduct injurious to the Government.

Specifically, the authors pointed out, it is this latter characteristic of the loyalty program that conflicts with basic American traditions of freedom of speech and belief, and necessitates "a large staff of secret police, the maintenance of a master file of 'derogatory information,' investigations and hearings that probe into every corner of a man's life for information on opinions, associations and personal habits."

Denying that a need for a general loyalty check involving all Federal employes existed, the authors said that "no concrete showing of immediate and widespread danger, adequate to outweigh the price that must be paid in the loss of democratic values, has thus far been presented to the country."

Neither the hearings before the House Committee on Un-American Activities nor the Government's loyalty checks, in which 200 to 250 out of more than 2,000,000 employes will have been found disloyal, indicates a "serious problem," according to Professor Emerson and Mr. Helfeld.

For the great mass of Federal employes, they held, the existing criminal statutes, plus the normal disciplinary powers of a Government agency, were sufficient to meet any present or immediately foreseeable danger.

The authors proposed, however, a positive program of screening for Federal employes dealing directly with "vital and highly secret matters of national defense," primarily in the Defense and State Departments and the Atomic Energy Commission.

Expressing doubt that a loyalty program was "advisable under present conditions" for the limited number of persons occupying policy-making positions, the article declared that such employes must conform to the policies of their superiors, and overt acts of espionage, sabotage or conspiracy on their part could be dealt with by customary methods of detection and punishment. However, the authors said, the "present temper of Congress, and perhaps of the country, seems to demand some action" with respect to those in policy-making positions.

For this reason, the authors said, they would consider whether, in the case of the policy-making employes, standards and procedures could be developed "which might assure a greater measure of protection and at the same time avoid some of the worst pitfalls of the current program."

The proposed program, it was emphasized, would not allow screening out of Federal employes or applicants "who advocate or believe in political, economic or social changes accomplished by peaceful, legal and democratic means."

"If we succumb to the fears and passions of those who shun the new ideas and seek to postpone inevitable change by repressive measures, we shall deal a crippling blow to all democratic institutions and values," the authors said.

Under the proposed program of screening the following standards

143

would disqualify persons for Government service: (1) "Personal advocacy of the overthrow or change of government by violent or other illegal means; and (2) membership in an organization after such organization has been found, in accordance with appropriate procedures including court review, to advocate the overthrow or change of government by violent or other illegal means."

Proof that a particular individual falls within the ban, the authors held, should be based on direct evidence, and "membership" should not be limited to actual card-holding, but should include participation in the activities or management of the organization regardless of formal status.

To administer the proposed program, Professor Emerson and Mr. Helfeld suggested that the Loyalty Review Board, "assuming that it

continues to be staffed with men of liberal and tolerant tendencies," should maintain affirmative supervision of administration of the program.

Sharply Critical of FBI

In a second suggestion on administration, the authors were sharply critical of the Federal Bureau of Investigation, maintaining that the "FBI and other professional investigating agencies should be subject to a greater degree of 'civilian' control." They held that there were signs that the FBI was "moving dangerously" in the direction of developing into "a grave and ruthless menace to democratic processes."

In their critical appraisal, Professor Emerson and Mr. Helfeld stressed that this nation's history "has been marked by a never-ending struggle between the ideal of

freedom in political expression and the efforts of temporarily dominant groups, particularly in periods of crisis, to demand rigid political orthodoxy." Such a period of crisis exists now in the matter of political and civil rights, they said.

Administration of the present loyalty program has violated Anglo-American traditions of procedural fairness by failing to provide for complete notice of the charges and for full disclosure of the evidence upon which the decision was reached, the authors held.

Other findings were that the program failed to provide for judicial review; that there has been no "satisfactory" definition of loyalty or disloyalty formulated by Federal legislation, or executive agency or the courts; that the operation of the program placed the

average Government worker under "constant pressure to conform to the conventional and the safe," thus placing him in fear of exhibiting the very qualities most sought after by competent administrators in private industry as well as government.

Also that the program in effect place "a veto power on Government employment in the hands of the FBI; that no procedural limitations were placed upon the Attorney General's power to designate an organization or group as subversive, and that no precedent was available in foreign experience outside the totalitarian states for a system of loyalty surveillance similar to the United States program.

January 17, 1949

HOOVER ANSWERS ATTACKERS OF FBI

FBI Chief Asserts Pages of Yale Law Journal Were Used to 'Misrepresent the Truth'

WASHINGTON, March 19 (UP)—J. Edgar Hoover, director of the Federal Bureau of Investigation, charged today that the pages of the Yale Law Journal had been used to "distort and misrepresent the truth" about his organization.

The February issue of the Journal, just off the press, contained Mr. Hoover's sharp complaint. His remarks were in response to a December Journal article in which Prof. Thomas I. Emerson of Yale collaborated with David M. Helfeld in an attack on FBI investigation methods.

Professor Emerson and Mr. Helfeld particularly challenged the FBI's investigation of the loyalty of Government employes, which is carried out under orders of President Truman and Congress.

Some of the charges leveled by

Professor Emerson and Mr. Helfeld at the FBI and Mr. Hoover's replies:

Professor Emerson and Mr. Helfeld—FBI methods include the use of paid informers.

Mr. Hoover—This is correct. How else is it possible to secure certain types of information? The most important espionage case in American history was solved through the services of a paid informant of the FBI. By the same token, how could the FBI in certain loyalty investigations report that the Federal employe had issued to him a membership card of the Communist Political Association No. 35985, Communist membership card No. 83987, Communist party dues book No. 79298, Communist registration card No. 67202, Communist card No. 79418 without having paid informants?

Professor Emerson and Mr. Helfeld—Although the FBI denies that it taps telephones, instances of that practice have been reported and it is widely believed in Washington that many telephones are in fact tapped.

Mr. Hoover—I challenge the authors to come forward with one single instance wherein a telephone was tapped in the investigation of a Federal employe loyalty program case. It is no secret that the

FBI does tap telephones in a very limited type of cases with the express approval in each instance of the Attorney General, but only in cases involving espionage, sabotage, grave risks to internal security, or when human lives are in jeopardy. This is never done in the investigation of the loyalty of Federal employes. This unsubstantiated statement by the authors typifies their obvious efforts to discredit the work of the FBI in loyalty cases.

Professor Emerson and Mr. Helfeld—The FBI and other professional investigating agencies should be subjected to greater degree of "civilian" control. The FBI, in particular, operates on a completely independent basis, acknowledging little or no responsibility to anyone outside its own organization. Inevitably such an institution develops an ingrown tradition of militant police methods. A secret police established to investigate the loyalty of American citizens can develop into a grave and ruthless menace to democratic process. There are signs that the FBI is moving dangerously in this direction.

Mr. Hoover—Any doubts that I have had about the authors' sincerity or competence to write on this subject from the standpoint

of knowledge of the various ramifications of the loyalty program were completely resolved by the above statement. I realize, of course, that largely it is the opinion of the authors, which they have every right to express; however, I find such opinions most frequently expressed in the pages of The Daily Worker, the publication of the Communist party, and at least I would expect a higher plane of objectivity in the pages of The Yale Law Journal.

Professor Emerson and Mr. Helfeld charged that the efficiency rating of FBI investigators tended to depend on how much unfavorable information they could dig up on the persons under investigation. They implied that Mr. Hoover made that a matter of policy so he would have something to show Congress for the money annually voted to run the FBI.

"This statement is a libel," Mr. Hoover replied, "upon the integrity of every member of the FBI as well as of Congress."

Professor Emerson formerly was in the legal department here of the National Labor Relations Board and later was with the Office of Price Administration.

March 20, 1949

Jackie Robinson Terms Stand Of Robeson on Negroes False

By C. P. TRUSSELL
Special to THE NEW YORK TIMES.

WASHINGTON, July 18—Jackie Robinson, Brooklyn Dodgers' star, dealt in blunt philosophy about Negroes, communism and racial discrimination today as he appeared before the House Committee on Un-American Activities to dispute a declaration by Paul Robeson, singer and actor, that Negroes would not fight against Russia.

Mr. Robinson, first of his race

to be signed by the major leagues, called the Robeson statement silly and untrue. He contended, however, that statements and activities by others also were confusing American thought, resulting in "a

terrific lot of misunderstanding on this subject of communism among the Negroes." And, he added, "it's bound to hurt my people's cause unless it's cleared up."

The witness told the committee and a crowded hearing room that "I don't pretend to be an expert on communism or any other kind of political 'ism.'" He said college, the war and trying to make good with the Dodgers have "been enough to keep me busy without becoming an 'expert'—except on base stealing."

But he did ask to be put down as "an expert on being a colored American, with thirty years of experience at it." He said he had

not been "fooled" because he had had opportunities.

"I know that life in these United States can be mighty tough for people who are a little different from the majority, in their skin color or the way they worship their God, or the way they spell their names," he declared.

The fact that a Communist denounces "injustice in the courts, police brutality and lynching when it happens," he said, did not "change the truth of his charges." However, he contended, "a lot of people try to pretend that the whole issue is a creation of Communist imagination."

"Negroes were stirred up long before there was a Communist party," he said, "and they'll stay stirred up long after the party has disappeared—unless Jim Crow has disappeared by then as well * * * We can win our fight without the Communists, and we don't want their help."

Mr. Robinson said his testimony might divide his fans, hurting his box-office standing.

"And so it isn't very pleasant for me to find myself in the middle of a public argument that has nothing to do with the standing of the Dodgers in the pennant race—or even the pay raise I am going to ask Mr. Branch Rickey for next year," he asserted.

The witness had been asked to discuss the Robeson statement concerning Negroes and possible war with Russia. If Mr. Robeson made the statement, he said, "it sounds very silly to me."

"But," Mr. Robinson added, "he has a right to his personal views, and if he wants to sound silly when he expresses them in public, that's his business and not mine. He's still a famous ex-athlete and a great singer and actor."

31 Months in Service

Mr. Robinson, a World War II veteran with thirty-one months' service, said he understood there were "some few" Negroes who were members of the Communist party and that they would be likely to act "just as any other Communists would" in the event of war with Russia. This, he held, would be true of Communists of other minority and majority groups. There were Negro pacifists, too, he said, and they would act like pacifists of any color.

"And most Negroes—and Italians and Irish and Jews and Swedes and Slavs and other Americans——" he added, "would act just as all these groups did in the last war.

"They'd do their best to help their country stay out of war; if unsuccessful, they'd do their best to help their country win the war —against Russia or any other enemy that threatened us."

What he was saying, Mr. Robinson emphasized, was not as a defense of the Negro's loyalty. Any loyalty that needed defense, he observed, "can't amount to much in the long run."

What he was trying to "get across," he said, was this: That the American public was "off on the wrong foot" when it began to think of radicalism in terms of any special minority group.

He said that it was such thinking that "gets people scared because one Negro, addressing a Communist group in Paris, threatens an organized boycott by 15,000,000 members of his race."

Negroes and others have too much invested in the country's welfare "for any of us to throw it away because of a siren song sung in bass," Mr. Robinson declared.

But that, however, did not mean that the fight against race discrimination was going to stop. It meant, instead, he said, that "we're going to fight it all the harder because our stake in the future is so big."

Committee members appeared to be impressed. As Mr. Robinson completed his statement a voice from the audience shouted, "Amen."

July 19, 1949

FIVE KEY QUESTIONS IN THE HISS TRIAL

Whittaker Chambers.   Alger Hiss.

The second perjury trial of Alger Hiss begins this Thursday. As in the first trial, which ended last July in a hung jury, attention centers on the conflicting testimony of two men—Mr. Hiss, 44, a former officer in the State Department, and Whittaker Chambers, 48, onetime Communist underground agent and senior editor of Time Magazine. The chief matters in dispute between Mr. Hiss and Mr. Chambers are these five questions:

(1) What was Mr. Hiss' relation, if any, to Mr. Chambers' Communist apparatus?
(2) What was the relationship between Mr. Hiss and Mr. Chambers?
(3) Did Mr. Hiss ever transmit any Government secrets to Mr. Chambers?
(4) What is the history of certain papers in Mr. Chambers' possession?
(5) Why and when did the Hiss-Chambers relationship of the Thirties end?

Mr. Chambers has made certain accusations on those five questions; Mr. Hiss has answered them. These are the accusations and the answers:

I: THE APPARATUS

That Chambers belonged to a Communist underground apparatus during the Thirties is widely accepted as fact. The question is: What was Hiss' relation, if any, to that apparatus?

THE ACCUSATION: "I had come to Washington as a functionary of the Communist party. * * * I was to head an underground apparatus * * * [which] I knew * * * at its top level, a group of seven or so men. * * * A member of this group was Alger Hiss. * * * I was introduced to him [in the summer of 1934] by Harold Ware and Jay Peters [members of the underground]. * * * [Hiss] knew me by the party name of Carl."

THE ANSWER: "I am not and have never been a member of the Communist party. * * * I met [Chambers] either in the latter part of December, 1934, or early in January, 1935. * * * I met him in my office in the Senate Office Building, where I was employed as counsel to the [Nye] Munitions Committee. * * * He represented himself as a free-lance writer for magazines. He said that his name was George Crosley. * * * [I never] knew him as Carl."

II: THE RELATIONSHIP

Hiss and Chambers disagree on how often they saw each other during their acquaintance of the Thirties; on why Chambers was allowed to use an apartment of Hiss' at Twenty-eighth Street, Washington, for some weeks in 1935, and on whether Hiss gave Chambers a 1929 Ford roadster of little value once or lent him money to buy a better car. These issues are part of the larger question: What was the relationship between Hiss and Chambers?

THE ACCUSATION: "I stayed overnight frequently at his [Hiss'] home [and] made it a kind of headquarters. * * * My relationship with Alger Hiss * * * transcended our formal relationship. * * * He was the closest friend I ever had in the Communist party."

Mrs. Chambers, in support of her husband: She saw Mr. and Mrs. Hiss "on many occasions. * * * They called me 'Lisa' and called my husband 'Carl.'" She once left her baby with Mrs. Hiss for ten days.

In 1935 Hiss let him (Chambers) use an apartment rent free for six weeks. In 1936 Hiss gave an old Ford roadster he owned to the Communist party. In November, 1937, Hiss lent him (Chambers) $400 to buy a car. (A Washington bank official produced records showing that Mrs. Hiss withdrew $400 on Nov. 19, 1937, from an account held jointly with Hiss.)

THE ANSWER: He saw "Crosley" at his office and had lunch with him once or twice early in 1935. During his entire relationship with "Crosley" he saw him only a dozen times or so. "We talked about * * * general matters. * * * [He] spent some time in my apartment."

Mrs. Hiss, in support of her husband: She saw Mrs. Chambers only a few times and never called her by her first name. As for taking care of Mrs. Chambers' baby, "Nothing of that kind ever happened."

In 1935, after moving to a new home, he (Hiss) sublet his old apartment at cost to "Crosley." "Crosley" never paid the rent. In August, 1935, he turned his worthless old Ford over to "Crosley" because he (Hiss) had bought a new Plymouth. He made a few small loans to "Crosley" but never one of $400. He spent $400 in 1937 to furnish a new house.

III: THE SPY LINK

The most serious charge made against Hiss is that he brought secret State Department documents to Chambers for ultimate delivery to Colonel Bykov, a Russian espionage agent. The Government could not prosecute Hiss for espionage because of the statute of limitations. When Hiss denied the charge, he was accused of perjury. The question has not yet been conclusively answered: Did Hiss transmit any Government secrets to Chambers?

THE ACCUSATION: "In [early] 1937 * * * I met Mr. Hiss in a cafeteria on Chambers Street. * * * We entered the Prospect movie theatre [in Brooklyn]. * * * Colonel Bykov soon came out of the audience and I introduced him to Mr. Hiss. * * * Bykov asked if Mr. Hiss would be willing to procure * * * documents [from the State Department]. Hiss said, 'Yes.'"

Beginning "soon afterwards," Hiss brought secret State Department documents home. Chambers met Hiss there, photographed the papers and turned the photographs over to Colonel Bykov. Hiss brought papers home at first every two weeks; later, every night.

THE ANSWER: At his first public trial Hiss was asked this question by his attorney: "Mr. Chambers has testified that on one occasion * * * you went with him out into some remote part of Brooklyn to a moving picture theatre house and * * * met a man named Bykov. * * * Is there a word of truth in that?" Hiss answered: "There is not a word of truth in it."

Hiss was asked this question by the grand jury: "At any time did you * * * turn any documents of the State Department * * * or copies * * * over to Whittaker Chambers?" He answered: "Never." The indictment of Hiss charges that his answer was perjured.

IV: THE PAPERS

In November, 1948, Chambers produced certain State Department papers which, he said, had been passed to him by Hiss. Forty-seven of these papers, dated January, February and March, 1938, were introduced as evidence in the first Hiss trial. Of these, forty-three were typewritten summaries of State documents. Four were handwritten memoranda.

The dispute with regard to the typewritten papers centers on a battered old Woodstock owned by Mrs. Hiss in the Thirties. The typewriter was a vital piece of evidence in the first trial. The dispute with regard to the handwritten papers centers on the issue of for whom Hiss wrote them. The question, then, is: What is the history of these papers?

THE ACCUSATION: "The [usual] method was for him [Hiss] to bring home documents * * * which Mrs. Hiss * * * typed." The Government introduced four personal letters typed by Mrs. Hiss on the old Woodstock, the latest dated May 25, 1937. A typewriting expert testified that these letters and the forty-three typewritten papers in evidence had been typed on the same machine.

As for the handwritten documents, "Notations in his [Hiss'] handwriting are notes of * * * documents which he was not able to bring out of the department." Government experts in the first trial said the handwriting on the four handwritten papers in evidence was the same as certain samples of Hiss' handwriting.

THE ANSWER: If the papers in evidence were typed on the old Woodstock (the Government expert's testimony was not disputed), someone else must have typed them. The reason is that Mrs. Hiss gave the Woodstock to a servant in December, 1937—a time prior to the dates on any of the papers in evidence. (The servant's testimony in court tended to confirm this story.)

The handwriting on the four handwritten papers is admittedly his (Hiss'). They were the sort of memoranda he frequently prepared for his State Department superior, Francis B. Sayre; when Mr. Sayre had read them, they were thrown away. Someone else must have passed the discarded memos along to Chambers.

V: THE RELATIONSHIP'S END

The views on the reasons for the end of the Hiss-Chambers relationship parallel the disputed views of what that relationship was. The importance of the time of the relationship's end is this: Chambers says Hiss passed him papers in 1937 and 1938 (the papers in court were dated January, February and March, 1938); Hiss denies even seeing Chambers after 1936. The indictment challenges this denial along with Hiss' denial of ever passing any papers. Thus this dual question is debated: Why and when did the Hiss-Chambers relationship end?

THE ACCUSATION: "In 1937 I resolved to break with the Communist party. * * * Toward the end of 1938 I tried to break away from the Communist party a number of people. * * * I went to Mr. Hiss. * * * He said it was a pity that I had broken with the party. * * * He cried when we separated * * * but he absolutely refused to break."

That was the last time he saw Hiss. To prove that he had seen him in the two years previous, he (Chambers) can list several specific occasions when they met: In August, 1937, when he and the Hisses drove to New Hampshire to see a play; in December, 1937, when the Hisses came to his house in Baltimore; on Dec. 31, 1937, when he and his wife went to the Hisses' home for a New Year's Eve party.

THE ANSWER: "Sometime in [May or June] 1936 * * * he [Chambers] again requested a small loan. * * * I finally decided * * * that I had been a sucker and he was a sort of deadbeat. * * * I told Mr. Chambers that I had become convinced that he would not repay the sums he owed me * * * and that I thought any further contacts had best be discontinued."

That was the last time he saw Chambers. He did not see him on the specific occasions listed by Chambers. (Several witnesses have testified that Hiss was elsewhere at those times.) Hiss was asked by the grand jury: "Can you definitely say that you did not see him [Chambers] after Jan. 1, 1937?" Hiss answered: "Yes." The second count in the indictment of Hiss charges that his answer was perjured.

—J. ANTHONY LEWIS.

November 13, 1949

CHAMBERS ADMITS TESTIFYING FALSELY BEFORE GRAND JURY

Did Not Tell Truth on Activities With Soviet Agent and Hiss on Six Occasions, He Says

LIED TO HOUSE BODY, FBI

Psychiatrist Studies Witness —May Be Called to Stand as Expert by Defense

By WILLIAM R. CONKLIN

Six instances of false testimony were admitted yesterday by Whittaker Chambers as Lloyd Paul Stryker, defense counsel for Alger Hiss, continued to hammer at the character of the key witness for the second successive trial day.

The occasions included appearances before the New York Federal Grand Jury, the House Committee on Un-American Activities and the Federal Bureau of Investigation at which he did not tell the complete truth about dealings with a Soviet agent and Mr. Hiss.

Mr. Stryker continued his cross-examination of the ex-Communist agent, trying to tear down his story that he had received State Department documents from Mr. Hiss up to April, 1938.

Mr. Hiss is on trial before Federal Judge Samuel H. Kaufman and a jury in Federal Court on two counts of perjury. The Federal indictment is based upon testimony by Mr. Hiss that he never gave State Department documents to Mr. Chambers, and that he had not seen the 48-year-old former Communist after Jan. 1, 1937.

While Mr. Chambers resumed his testimony on the fourth day of the trial, Dr. Carl Binger, psychiatrist, studied his words and actions intently from a seat just behind the defense counsel table. Dr. Binger was brought in on Thursday by the defense under an agreement with Judge Kaufman that the purpose of his attendance would not be divulged. The psychiatrist is a Fellow of the New York Academy of Medicine and a member of the faculty of Cornell University Medical College in New York. He was accompanied to court by Louis S. Weiss, a lawyer.

After admitting their identities, both men refused to tell the press why they were in court. It was rumored that Dr. Binger might be called later by the defense as an expert to testify to his professional opinion of Mr. Chambers. Throughout yesterday's short court session, the psychiatrist studied the witness with the air of a man who has found an object of professional interest.

Mr. Stryker's questions on cross-examination were studded with such terms as "perjurer," "traitor," "liar," "criminal conspirator" and "atheist." When he asked whether Mr. Chambers had not lived with "One-Eyed Annie, a prostitute" in a "wretched dive" in New Orleans, the witness laughed for the first time in the trial.

"No, I did not," he replied loudly.

"Did you live in a New Orleans dive with a prostitute named Ida Dales?" Mr. Stryker pursued.

"Ida Dales is not a prostitute," the pudgy former senior editor of Time magazine replied. "I lived with her in New Orleans for about one year when I was 17."

"And did you not take her to your mother's home, this woman not your wife, and did she not live there with you?" Mr. Stryker asked. "And was the reason that your mother had lost one son and did not want to lose another? Was that the reason why she took this illicit mistress in?"

"That is correct," Mr. Chambers answered.

"Did you not testify elsewhere that you lived in 'a wretched kind of dive' on the lower end of Eienville Street in New Orleans, and that there was a girl named 'One-Eyed Annie' living there, and that she was a prostitute? Is that true?"

"Certainly," replied the witness. Turning to Judge Kaufman rather plaintively, he complained:

"I think the impression is being left that I lived with One-Eyed Annie."

When Mr. Stryker provided the opportunity with another question, the witness denied that he had lived with the woman of that name.

Admits Being Traitor

Turning to the fourteen years Mr. Chambers spent as a member of the Communist party between 1924 and 1938, the attorney asked:

"Is it not true that for those fourteen years you were a traitor to the United States and an enemy to your country?"

"That is right," the witness answered in undisturbed fashion.

"Is it true that every Communist party member is a potential spy, saboteur and actually an enemy to our system of government?" Mr. Stryker demanded.

"True," Mr. Chambers murmured.

"Have you not said that the Communist party in America is an integral part of international communism?" the attorney asked.

"Yes, it is," Mr. Chambers replied.

A slight wrangle developed over Mr. Stryker's effort to gain an admission that "every Communist was ipso facto an atheist." Mr. Chambers conceded that the statement was "true in a sense, but it needs amplification." The attorney drew the admission that Mr. Chambers' play "Play for Puppets," written while he was a student in Columbia College, was highly offensive to the Christian religion. The witness added that it represented his viewpoint of Christianity as "a sadistic religion."

The antagonists then developed the Communist-versus-Christian attitudes on matrimony. After Mr. Chambers had admitted that a tenet of communism was that marriage was "a bourgeois convention," Mr. Stryker asked:

"Then you believed that marriage was simply a bourgeois convention, and that what we know as holy wedlock was nothing more than an example of capitalistic reaction?" Mr. Stryker prodded.

"I can phrase it more aptly yet," the witness retorted tartly. "Communists believe that marriage is a middle-class convention. For their own purposes, they prefer to have party members live together outside marriage."

When Mr. Stryker applied the word "treason" to Mr. Chambers' activities, Thomas F. Murphy, Assistant United States Attorney, objected, saying that Mr. Chambers had not been guilty of treason "unless he gave aid and comfort to the enemy."

"He used the word 'traitor,' and admitted being one," Mr. Stryker shot back. "That's out of his own mouth."

Known by Other Names

The defense attorney developed that Mr. Chambers had been known at various times as Charles Adams, Charles Whittaker, Arthur Dwyer, Lloyd Cantwell and "Breen." In Thursday's testimony Mr. Chambers said also he was known as "Carl" and as "Crosley."

"So you sneaked around for fourteen years under all those false names, to deceive people about your real identity. Is that a fair statement?"

"I think it's a beautiful statement for your purposes," the witness replied with a malicious gleam in his eye. "I would say that I used false names."

Under further questioning Mr. Chambers admitted that he had not told the whole truth about his Communist activities with Col. Boris Bykov, Soviet espionage agent, and Mr. Hiss, on at least six occasions.

Mr. Stryker brought out that this circumstance applied to the New York Federal grand jury; the House Committee on Un-American Activities; the Federal Bureau of Investigation; former Assistant Secretary of State Adolf A. Berle Jr.; a "Mr. Murphy," security officer for the State Department, and the statement made in Baltimore by the witness in an examination before trial of a $75,000 slander suit brought against him by Mr. Hiss.

"And the reason you didn't tell these people about Colonel Bykov, and you, and Alger Hiss, was that your story was not true?" Mr. Stryker suggested.

"Certainly not," the witness snapped.

"Do you concede that lying can take many forms?" Mr. Stryker demanded.

"Oh yes," Mr. Chambers replied. "It's around us all the time."

"You testified that when you wrote for The Daily Worker you stole news from THE NEW YORK TIMES. . . ." Mr. Stryker began.

"I object to the word 'stole'" Mr. Murphy broke in. "The United States Supreme Court has ruled that it is not stealing."

"Well, then," Mr. Stryker pursued, "did you not think it was unethical to take news from THE NEW YORK TIMES, news which that paper had spent much effort and money to get?"

"No," the witness answered. "I did the same thing on Time."

"I had a high regard for Time up to now," the attorney observed. "Do you mean to say they do the same thing as The Daily Worker does?"

"It was a matter of rewriting," the witness said.

"And to give it the Communist party slant in the rewriting, wasn't that lying?" Mr. Stryker said.

"I used the word 'slant' yesterday," Mr. Chambers replied. "I should have said 'interpretation.' It was a matter of interpretation."

Commenting later on the reference to Time, Bernard Barnes, assistant to the president of Time magazine, said:

"We use every legitimate source of information that we can. Time is a' member of The Associated Press, has editorial offices in twenty-six cities in the United States and abroad, over 180 correspondents and string men, plus forty-eight researchers, all of them gathering and verifying news."

Mr. Chambers, a former senior editor of Time at $30,000 a year, resigned that position last Dec. 10 after he had disclosed his Communist party activity. After bringing out that that activity had brought him about $360 monthly at his peak, Mr. Stryker closed his cross-examination for the day.

The trial will resume at 10:30 on Monday in Room 1306 of the United States Court House in Foley Square. Each session this week has been packed, with standees in the hall awaiting admission.

June 4, 1949

FRANKFURTER, REED TESTIFY TO LOYALTY, INTEGRITY OF HISS

Defense Produces Typewriter U. S. Charges Wife Used to Copy Papers for Courier

MAID'S SON IDENTIFIES IT

Says He Got It on Moving Day —Mother Swears She Saw Chambers Only Once

By WILLIAM R. CONKLIN

Felix Frankfurter and Stanley F. Reed, associate justices of the Supreme Court of the United States, testified as character witnesses for Alger Hiss yesterday as his defense against Federal perjury charges shifted into high gear on its second day in Federal court.

Late in the day the defense produced the long-missing Woodstock typewriter once owned by Mr. Hiss and his wife, Priscilla, a focal exhibit in the trial. The Government contends that this typewriter was used by Mrs. Hiss in January, February and March, 1938, to copy forty-seven State Department documents for transmission to Whittaker Chambers, then a courier for a Communist spy ring.

The defense began to lay its groundwork yesterday for the claim that the Hisses had disposed of the typewriter well before January, 1938. It also expects to show that Mr. Hiss never saw Mr. Chambers after Jan. 1, 1937.

After calling the two members of the nation's highest court in the morning, the defense provided a striking contrast in witnesses. Following the two legal experts on the witness stand were the Hiss maid and her son, whose testimony showed scant grasp of legal procedure. While they were on, the jury and spectators laughed more than they have on any day since the trial began on May 31.

Recommended Hiss to Holmes

Justice Frankfurter, who took the stand as the eleventh defense witness on the trial's sixteenth day, engaged in a minor clash with Thomas F. Murphy, Assistant United States Attorney, who cross-examined him. The jurist, who lives in Massachusetts, testified that Mr. Hiss held an excellent reputation for loyalty to his Government, integrity and veracity. As a Harvard Law School professor when Mr. Hiss studied there between 1926 and 1929, the jurist said he had recommended Mr. Hiss as a law clerk to the late Supreme Court Justice Oliver Wendell Holmes.

On cross-examination Mr. Murphy asked Justice Frankfurter if he had not heard something about Mr. Hiss from Jerome Frank that "wasn't too good." While he said he could not answer "yes," Justice Frankfurter said he recalled that Judge Frank had discussed Mr. Hiss with him. Whatever the discussion was, he added, it had no bearing on loyalty or integrity.

"But you remember talking to Jerome Frank about it?" Mr. Murphy asked.

"No," the jurist replied, "I remember his talking to me."

"Then I assume that you talked to him when he talked to you," Mr. Murphy observed.

"Well, let us not fence," the Justice began. "All I meant to say was ——"

"Well, you were the one that started fencing with me, weren't you, Judge?" Mr. Murphy cut in. "I asked you whether you talked to Jerome Frank and you said Jerome Frank talked with you. Am I accurate?"

"I am trying to answer as carefully as I can with due regard to your responsibility and mine, and the jury's, and the responsibility of this case," Justice Frankfurter replied.

Denies Hearing of Betrayal

The jurist added that he would "deny unequivocally" that he had heard any question of Mr. Hiss' loyalty to the United States or that he had been "involved in the slightest betrayal of this country." Mr. Frank is now a judge of the United States Court of Appeals, Second Circuit, which covers New York, Connecticut and Vermont.

Following his colleague on the stand, Supreme Court Justice Reed told the jury of ten men and two women that he had never heard any question of Mr. Hiss' reputation for integrity, loyalty and veracity. So far as he knew, he said, Mr. Hiss bore a good reputation in those qualities. Should the Hiss case go to the United States Supreme Court on appeal, it was taken for granted in the courtroom that both Justice Frankfurter and Justice Reed would disqualify themselves as interested parties.

Other character witnesses for Mr. Hiss yesterday were Chief Judge Calvert Magruder of the United States Court of Appeals, First Circuit, Boston, who told the court that Mr. Hiss carried an "excellent" reputation; Gov. Adlai Stevenson of Illinois, who testified by deposition, and Gerard Swope Jr., general counsel for the International General Electric Corporation.

Turning to the Hiss family's servants in Washington, Edward C. McLean of defense counsel called Mrs. Claudie Catlett, 47-year-old housekeeper, and her son, Raymond Sylvester Catlett, who did odd jobs. Called by her nickname, "Clytie," Mrs. Catlett testified that she was making her first appearance in any court.

She testified that she had worked for the Hisses when they lived on P Street, on Thirtieth Street and on Volta Place. On one of the moving days, she said, the Hisses had given her an old typewriter as a toy for her children. She could not remember just when the typewriter was given to the children.

Mrs. Catlett testified that she had seen Mr. Chambers only once, when he called at 2905 P Street and announced himself as "Mr. Crosby." Earlier testimony had shown that the Hisses moved from P Street to Thirtieth Street on June 15, 1936, whereas Mr. Chambers had testified that he saw them fortnightly up to April, 1938.

The maid testified that "Mr. Crosby" was poorly dressed, "pretty shabby," and that she took a good long look at him because he appeared different from the usual Hiss visitors. She served tea in the parlor for the visitor and Mrs. Hiss, she said, and the caller departed after staying about one hour. She added that she had never seen Mrs. Chambers or her child, contradicting Mrs. Chambers' testimony that she was a frequent visitor.

When Mr. Murphy took her on cross-examination, Mrs. Catlett testified that she could not remember the date when the typewriter was given, or whether it was a standard or portable machine. Asked how many times she had been questioned by special agents of the Federal Bureau of Investigation, she said:

"I didn't keep the time on it, but they came plenty often."

She testified that she had seen a red rug rolled up in a closet at P Street, and that when the Hisses moved to Volta Place on Dec. 29, 1937, the rug was placed on the floor of the room occupied by Timothy Hobson, stepson of Mr. Hiss. A red Oriental rug has been described in previous testimony as a gift to Mr. Hiss from Mr. Chambers "in gratitude from the Soviet people for the work of American Communists." At one point in the cross-examination Mrs. Catlett referred to the FBI men and said:

"There were so many of 'em asking so many questions that I don't remember all I told them. I told the truth, and if it's right, I'll say it's right, and if it's wrong, I'll say it's wrong. When I

saw Mr. Chambers in Washington he asked me more questions than the FBI. He told me I was the one that made good mashed potatoes."

"Well, you do make good mashed potatoes, don't you?" Mr. Murphy asked.

"Anybody can mash potatoes," the witness snorted. "I never made any mashed potatoes for him. He was trying to make me believe that he was at the Thirtieth Street house, which he wasn't. The furniture he described and asked me about was in the P Street house."

Mr. Murphy brought out that Mrs. Catlett had told the FBI that she had been married twenty-seven years ago and lived at 542 North Tenth Street, Winchester, Va. Her son, Raymond, who followed her on the stand, said he was 27 years old.

"I did work for Mr. Hiss, such as cleaning up, washing the car, washing windows and waxing floors," the son began. "I didn't run no errands. I never saw Whit-

taker Chambers, Mrs. Chambers, or their child. One time when Mr. and Mrs. Hiss moved they gave me some clothes, some books and a typewriter."

"What kind of a typewriter was it?" Mr. McLean asked.

"Woodstock," the witness shot back. "It was broke. The keys were jammed and it couldn't type good. A wheel was broken and the ribbon wouldn't work."

After being shown the typewriter and testing a few keys, Mr. Catlett said:

"That's the typewriter."

When he began to recount how the typewriter had passed from one Catlett to another he found Mr. Murphy's questions confusing.

"I don't want to say something Mr. McLean said and then have some other man asking questions in back of me and getting me all crossed up," he protested. "I don't keep these papers, and I got no secretary to keep all these things down. I'm not a typist, but I can put my name down."

"What system do you use?" Mr. Murphy asked.

"Why, my fingers," the witness replied as the courtroom broke into laughter.

At another point when Mr. Murphy was pressing him, he asked:

"How can I keep your questions in my mind when somebody is going to ask me something else? I don't understand you—explain yourself. You're getting me all balled up."

"If I tell you that I do not want to confuse you, will you believe me?" Mr. Murphy asked.

"No," the witness answered shortly as Judge Samuel H. Kaufman rapped for order.

Despite questioning from Mr. Murphy and the judge, the witness could not fix the date when he got the typewriter. He will resume testifying when the trial goes into its seventeenth day at 10:30 this morning.

June 23, 1949

HISS GUILTY ON BOTH PERJURY COUNTS; BETRAYAL OF U.S. SECRETS IS AFFIRMED; SENTENCE WEDNESDAY; LIMIT 10 YEARS

JURY OUT 24 HOURS

Verdict Follows a Call on Judge to Restate Rulings on Evidence

CHAMBERS STORY UPHELD

Defendant Is Impassive—His Counsel Announces That an Appeal Will Be Taken

By WILLIAM R. CONKLIN

Alger Hiss, a highly regarded State Department official for ten of his forty-five years, was found guilty on two counts of perjury by a Federal jury of eight women and four men yesterday.

Nearly twenty-four hours after receiving the case, the jury reported its verdict at 2:50 P. M. The middle-aged jurors had begun their

deliberations at 3:10 P. M. on Friday after ten weeks of testimony in the second perjury trial.

By convicting Hiss on both counts, the jury found that he had betrayed his trust by passing secret State Department documents to Whittaker Chambers. The former courier for a Communist spy ring was the Government's key witness against the former official. The verdict meant that the jury believed Mr. Chambers and the corroborating evidence produced by the Government.

The convicted defendant faces maximum penalties of five years' imprisonment and a $2,000 fine on each count, a combined total of ten years and $4,000. Federal Judge Henry W. Goddard continued his bail at $5,000 and set Wednesday at 10:30 A. M. for sentencing. Sentence will be passed in the same thirteenth floor courtroom of the United States District Court where Hiss was tried.

Lapsing of Espionage Charge

The case of "The United States of America versus Alger Hiss" rested on a two-count perjury indictment. Thomas F. Murphy, Government prosecutor, had taxed Mr. Hiss with treason and espionage against his country. However,

any possible prosecution for espionage had been ruled out by a three-year statute of limitations, which conferred immunity after March, 1941.

Hiss was thus brought to trial on one count of perjury for denying that he ever gave secret documents to Mr. Chambers. The second count charged perjury for denying that he had seen the ex-Communist after Jan. 1, 1937. The Government contended that the documents were passed in February and March, 1938.

By its verdict the jury upheld the Government's contention that Priscilla Hiss, 46-year-old wife of the defendant, had typed copies of the documents for Mr. Chambers on the Hisses' Woodstock typewriter.

Mr. Chambers had told the jury that he had been a paid functionary of the Communist party in Washington and had collected secret information for Russia from 1935 to April, 1938.

Basis Laid for Appeal

Claude B. Cross and Edward C. McLean, defense attorneys, would not say at first whether they would appeal the verdict. They had established a basis for an appeal by taking exception to a part of the

charge of Judge Henry W. Goddard.

"There won't be any statement," Mr. McLean said. "I do not wish to discuss the possibility of an appeal now. There is just no statement." But later Mr. Cross said that "you can be sure the verdict will be appealed."

After the jury had convicted on both counts, Mr. Murphy asked that Hiss' bail of $5,000 be increased in conformity with the custom for "all convicted defendants." After Mr. Cross protested, Judge Goddard permitted Hiss to remain at liberty under the same bail. Mr. Cross said he would make some motions on Wednesday, the day set for sentencing.

Should defense attorneys file an appeal, it would act as an automatic stay of sentence. If an appeal should reach the United States Supreme Court, it was considered a foregone conclusion that Justices Felix Frankfurter and Stanley H. Reed would disqualify themselves. Both appeared at the first trial as character witnesses for Hiss, but were absent from his second trial.

In his first trial, which began on May 31 and ended on July 8, Hiss failed to win vindication from a jury. After hearing testimony for six weeks, the jury of ten men and two women deadlocked at eight to four for conviction. The second trial began on Nov. 17, took ten weeks and ended on its fortieth court day with the verdict.

United States Attorney Irving H. Saypol commended Mr. Murphy and his associates for the presentation of the Government's case.

"The verdict of the jury demonstrates that Mr. Murphy has vindicated justice," he said. "My personal and official commendations go to him and to the members of my staff, including Clarke S. Ryan, Assistant United States Attorney; Thomas J. Donegan, special assistant to the Attorney General, and the Federal Bureau of Investiga-

tion."

Asked for his comment, Federal Prosecutor Murphy said:

"My job was to present the facts to an American jury, and it was their job to decide the facts. By their verdict this issue has now been permanently decided. I want to take the opportunity to thank sincerely all the men who have worked so hard and so long with me on this case."

Final Instruction of Jury

The jury, scheduled to resume deliberations at 10 o'clock yesterday morning, arrived at 9:20. At 10:31 the jurors asked Judge Goddard to reread parts of his charge

on reasonable doubt, circumstantial evidence, corroborative evidence, and the relation of these factors to each other. They listened to the reading from 10:44 to 10:55 o'clock.

After luncheon, 12:55 to 2:08 P. M., the jury filed in with its verdict at 2:48. Two minutes later the verdict was on the record and Mr. Cross had polled the jury without changing the result. The jury was out a total of 23 hours 40 minutes, with 9 hours and 13 minutes spent in actual deliberations.

Hiss steadfastly refused comment on the outcome of the case, maintaining his silence until he left Foley Square with his wife in a

friend's car at 3:23 o'clock. Like his wife, he had taken the verdict stolidly.

Hiss is the plaintiff in a $75,000 libel suit filed in November, 1948, in Baltimore against Mr. Chambers. The suit is based on the fact that Mr. Chambers called Hiss a Communist on a nation-wide broadcast.

Judge Goddard in his charge to the jury said the outcome of the perjury trial might well affect the decision in the libel suit. The Baltimore action has been deferred pending the outcome of the perjury trial here.

January 22, 1950

ACHESON RENEWS DEFENSE OF HISS

Says He Won't Turn Back, Cites Bible Passage—Senators Criticize His Attitude

Special to THE NEW YORK TIMES.

WASHINGTON, Jan. 25—Secretary of State Dean Acheson told his news conference today that regardless of what the courts or other men might do he did not intend to turn his back on Alger Hiss, the former State Department official who was sentenced this morning to five years in prison for perjury.

Mr. Acheson, who proclaimed his friendship for Mr. Hiss a year ago before the Senate Foreign Relations Committee, said that it would be "highly improper" for him to discuss anything to do with the case itself, but he observed that each man who had worked with Hiss had upon his conscience "the very serious task of deciding what his attitude is and what his conduct should be."

As for himself, Mr. Acheson continued, he would be guided by the principles of charity recommended by Jesus on the Mount of Olives in the last judgment.

These remarks were made after Mr. Acheson was criticized by various members of Congress for his past associations and comments about Hiss. At the opening of his press conference this afternoon, the secretary was asked if he had any comment on the case.

Secretary Shows Emotion

After refusing to comment in any way on the evidence, the secretary edged forward in his chair and with some feeling made the following extemporaneous statement:

"I take the purpose of your question was to bring something other than that out of me. I should like to make it clear to you that, whatever the outcome of any appeal which Mr. Hiss or his lawyer may take in this case, I do not intend to turn my back on Alger Hiss.

"I think every person who has known Alger Hiss or has served

with him at any time had upon his conscience the very serious task of deciding what his attitude is and what his conduct should be. That must be done by each person in the light of his own standards and his own principles.

"For me, there is very little doubt about those standards or those principles. I think they were stated for us a very long time ago. They were stated on the Mount of Olives and if you are interested in seeing them you will find them in the Twenty-fifth Chapter of the Gospel according to St. Matthew, beginning at Verse 34."

This passage of Scripture referred to the prophecy that those who were merciful to men in trouble shall be welcomed on the judgment day into "life eternal" and those who were indifferent to the misery of others "shall go away into everlasting punishment."

The Biblical passage reads as follows:

34 Then shall the King say unto them on his right hand, Come, ye blessed of my Father, inherit the kingdom prepared for you from the foundation of the world:

35 For I was an hungred, and ye gave me meat: I was thirsty, and ye gave me drink: I was a stranger, and ye took me in:

36 Naked, and ye clothed me: I was sick, and ye visited me: I was in prison, and ye came unto me.

37 Then shall the righteous answer him, saying, Lord, when saw we thee an hungred and fed thee? or thirsty, and gave thee drink?

38 When saw we thee a stranger, and took thee in? or naked, and clothed thee?

39 Or when saw we thee sick, or in prison, and came unto thee?

40 And the King shall answer and say unto them, verily I say unto you, Inasmuch as ye have done it unto one of the least of these my brethren, ye have done it unto me.

41 Then shall he say also unto them on the left hand, Depart from me, ye cursed, into everlasting fire, prepared for the devil and his angels:

42 For I was an hungred, and ye gave me no meat: I was thirsty and ye gave me no drink:

43 I was a stranger, and ye took me not in: naked, and ye clothed me not: sick, and in prison, and ye visited me not.

44 Then shall they also answer

him, saying, Lord, when saw we thee an hungred, or athirst, or a stranger, or naked, or sick, or in prison, and did not minister unto thee?

45 Then shall be answer them, saying, verily I say unto you, Inasmuch as ye did it not to one of the least of these, ye did it not to me.

46 And these shall go away into everlasting punishment: but the righteous into life eternal.

Incident Year Ago Recalled

Mr. Acheson took much the same position when he came before the Foreign Relations Committee just a year ago last week to be confirmed as Secretary of State. At that time he was asked whether he knew Hiss and replied that he did. When he was pressed for a statement of his feeling about Hiss, he remarked that his friendship was not easily given nor was it easily withdrawn.

Later, in a secret meeting of the Foreign Relations Committee, it was suggested to him that this statement might raise questions in the minds of some people that he would place personal friendship above the security of the Department of State. Consequently, it was proposed that he might agree to a statement which would remove any such doubts.

Mr. Acheson replied that he was perfectly willing to make a statement of his opposition to communism and of his determination to maintain the security of the department, but that no job, not even that of Secretary of State, would induce him to desert a friend who was in need and who was entitled to an assumption of innocence until he was finally proved guilty.

The first public reaction to Mr. Acheson's statement this afternoon was again critical of the Secretary of State. Senator Joseph R. McCarthy, Republican, of Wisconsin, told the Senate about Mr. Acheson's remark and characterized it as "a fantastic statement."

Senator Homer E. Capehart, Republican, of Indiana, took the floor after Senator McCarthy's observations and said he was more proud than ever that he had voted against Mr. Acheson's confirmation as Secretary of State.

Senator Karl E. Mundt, Republican, of South Dakota, who was reviewing the Hiss case in the Senate while Mr. Acheson was talking to the press, said that he was not surprised by Mr. Acheson's re-

marks, and observed that the Secretary of State could not be regarded as an objective witness in view of his close friendship for Hiss.

Senator Mundt, who was formerly a member of the House Un-American Activities Committee, which originally investigated charges that Hiss had collaborated with former Soviet agents, criticized President Truman for describing the House committee's investigation as a "red herring." He said that the committee had "suffered severely from obstructionist tactics" of the Executive branch of the Government during the Hiss case.

In his criticism of the executive branch for failing to give certain information to the Government he was joined by Senators Bourke B. Hickenlooper of Iowa, Homer Ferguson of Michigan, and William F. Knowland, of California, all Republicans.

Mundt Asks 5 Questions

In his summary of the Hiss case, Senator Mundt urged the Senate to devote "careful and thoughtful consideration" to these five questions:

1. What impact and influence did Alger Hiss have on his associates in the State Department in the formation of our present foreign policy and in international commitments?
2. Why should not the Republican party not assume a greater responsibility in the formation of foreign policy, so that such agreements as were made at Yalta will never again be repeated?
3. Why should the statute of limitations not be expanded, so that "men like Alger Hiss and Henry Julian Wadleigh" cannot buy immunity from punishment merely by the lapse of three short years?
4. Why should the so-called Mundt-Nixon bill outlawing the Communist party not be passed by the Congress?
5. Why should the Congress not continue to support the House un-American activities committee in its efforts to "stand guard at all times to help expose and detect those who would destroy our way of life by subversion and conspiratorial treachery?"

January 26, 1950

Text of Acheson's Statement on Hiss

WASHINGTON, Feb. 28 (AP)—
Following is the text of Secretary of State Dean Acheson's statement on Alger Hiss:

I have been asked to explain the statement which I made in regard to Alger Hiss on the 25th of January in the light of various criticisms which have been leveled at it; such as that it impugned proceedings before a United States court; that it should not have been made; that it condoned the offense for which Mr. Hiss was tried; and so forth.

First, I stated, as clearly as I could, that I would not discuss in any manner whatever the charges against Mr. Hiss, since those charges were then, as they are now, before a court. This is a principle of the most fundamental importance.

No one who was brought up in the law, as I was, by Mr. Justice Brandeis and Mr. Justice Holmes, can have the faintest doubt of the transcendent importance of practicing this principle in the strictest possible way. I have been a member of the bar for thirty years. I have never departed from this principle and I never expect to do so.

Therefore, I did not in my former statement, nor shall I now, discuss the charges in this case in any way, either directly or indirectly. The duty of passing upon them rests with the court, and the court should not be, in any manner whatever, embarrassed or prejudiced in performing this duty.

Second, I have been asked why I did not let the matter rest with what I have just said. There seemed to me public and private reasons why this could not be done.

At the time of my confirmation the Senate committee before which I appeared inquired of me regarding my relations with Mr. Hiss. This is clearly indicative of the committee's belief that the matter was relevant to my fitness for the office.

Disagrees With View

Many of those who have criticized my statement give further ground for this belief. It has been charged, for instance, that what I said indicates that I am not qualified for the office which I hold. I do not agree with this view, but it surely indicates that some persons believe that my views in this matter are relevant to the question of my fitness for the office and that, therefore, the public is entitled to know my views.

At any rate, the question which was put to me was directed toward bringing them out, and the issue was, therefore, presented whether I should state them or withhold them.

There were also personal reasons for stating my attitude. One must be true to the things by which one lives. The counsels of discretion and cowardice are appealing. The safe course is to avoid situations which are disagreeable and dangerous. Such a course might get one by the issue of the moment, but it has bitter and evil consequences.

In the long days and years which stretch beyond that moment of decision one must live with one's self; and the consequences of living with a decision which one knows has sprung from timidity and cowardice go to the roots of one's life. It is not merely a question of peace of mind, though that is vital; it is a matter of integrity of character. This is the most fundamental of all considerations.

For these reasons it seemed, and it still seems, to me that there was no alternative to saying what I said.

Third. The attitude which one, who has known and worked with Mr. Hiss, will take toward him in his deep trouble is a matter for the individual conscience to decide. It isn't a matter which a court, or public opinion, or the Government can decide for one. That is fundamental, not only under our institutions of personal liberty and responsibility, but under the Christian ethic.

It is not true, for instance, in the Soviet Union. There, all those who have known or worked with a person who has been even charged with the offenses with which Mr. Hiss has been charged must flee from him as from the plague, if they would preserve even the safety of their lives. But that is not true of us; and, indeed, that difference between us and the Soviet Union goes to the very root of the issues which so deeply divide the free world from the Communist world.

Turning then to my personal attitude toward Mr. Hiss, I said that it would be founded upon the principles as stated by Christ in the passages which I cited from the Gospel according to St. Matthew. These passages represent the tradition in which I have been bred, going back beyond the limits of memory.

Mr. Hiss is in the greatest trouble in which a man could be. The outcome of his appeal can have little bearing upon his personal tragedy. The court of appeals can either affirm the conviction and sentence, in which case he must go to prison; or, if it finds error in the proceedings below, it can reverse the judgment of the court and remand the case for still another trial in conformity with its opinion. It is in regard to a man in this situation that I referred to Christ's words setting forth compassion as the highest of Christian duties and as the highest quality in the sight of God.

If there is anything in what I have said which casts doubt upon the proceedings of a United States court, I fail to see it. And I do not believe that any fair mind, brought up in the principles which I have discussed, would differ from me. What I have said has nothing whatever to do with the decision of the jury or with the correctness of the rulings of the trial judge. It would be equally valid whether the conviction is affirmed or reversed.

Fourth. Similarly, what I have said would not, I believe, carry to any fair mind the implication that I was condoning the offenses with which Mr. Hiss was charged and of which he has been convicted. It seems fantastic in the light of the facts of my life, which have been a matter of most public record, that any such insinuation should be made.

Over the past thirty years I have repeatedly served the United States, and have done so almost continuously for the past ten years. No one can be found to say that I have not done this faithfully and to the best of my ability. Few can doubt that on all of these occasions there were far easier and more profitable courses open to me. So far as public avowals of loyalty are concerned, I have on numerous occasions taken the most solemn oath of allegiance and loyalty to my country and to its Constitution.

But for the benefit of those who would create doubt where none existed, I will accept the humiliation of stating what should be obvious, that I did not and do not condone in any way the offenses charged, whether committed by a friend or by a total stranger, and that I would never knowingly tolerate any disloyal person in the Department of State.

March 1, 1950

11 COMMUNISTS CONVICTED OF PLOT; MEDINA TO SENTENCE THEM FRIDAY; 6 OF COUNSEL JAILED IN CONTEMPT

VERDICT IN 7 HOURS

By RUSSELL PORTER

Eleven top leaders of the Communist party of the United States were found guilty yesterday of criminal conspiracy. They were convicted of secretly teaching and advocating, on secret orders from Moscow, overthrow of the United States Government and destruction of American democracy by force and violence.

The verdict was returned in the Federal Court House on Foley Square by a jury of four men and eight women, including two Negroes. They spent seven hours in actual deliberations.

Federal Judge Harold R. Medina approved the verdict as "amply supported" by the evidence. He remanded the defendants to jail pending imposition of sentence at 10:30 o'clock next Friday morning.

He also adjudged six members of defense counsel, including Eugene Dennis, the party's general secretary, acting as his own counsel, guilty of forty different criminal contempts during the trial. The judge sentenced counsel to terms varying between thirty days and six months in jail, beginning Nov. 15.

Arguments of Verdict Set

The maximum penalty for each defendant in the conspiracy case is ten years in prison and $10,000 fine.

Defense counsel announced they would appeal both the conspiracy verdict and the contempt sentences. They can appeal both cases to the United States Circuit Court of Appeals and finally to the United States Supreme Court. Judge Medina fixed Friday, Oct. 28, for arguments before himself on defense motions attacking the verdict.

The defendants in the conspiracy trial are members of the party's American Politburo or national board. Their trial, which began on Jan. 17, was one of the longest criminal trials on record, lasting just two days under nine months.

Judge Medina submitted the case to the jury at 3:53 o'clock Thursday afternoon. Unable to

Are You Now Or Have You Ever Been...?

CONVICTED COMMUNISTS HANDCUFFED AND ON THEIR WAY TO JAIL

Defendants line up before leaving the Federal Courthouse for House of Detention. They are (left to right) Henry Winston, Eugene Dennis, Jacob Stachel, Gilbert Green, Benjamin J. Davis Jr., John B. Williamson, Robert G. Thompson, Gus Hall, Irving Potash, Carl Winter and John Gates.

The New York Times (by Ernest Sisto)

reach an immediate verdict, the jury was locked up for the night at 10:20 P. M., under the protection of deputy Federal marshals.

Yesterday morning the jury was taken by bus from the Knickerbocker Hotel, 120 West Forty-fifth Street, where it spent the night, to the court house. It returned to the jury room, behind the first-floor court room, and resumed its deliberations at 9:30 A. M.

Note From Jury to Judge

Judge Medina mounted the bench at 10:09 A. M., opened court, and immediately took a recess. At 11:10 A. M. Mrs. Thelma Dial, Negro foreman of the jury, sent a note from the jury room to Judge Medina in his chambers.

At that moment a few lawyers, newspaper men and spectators were lounging in the court room, reading newspapers, drinking coffee, or talking aimlessly. They knew nothing of the note to the judge.

This calm was broken by a sudden stir in the court room and a rise in tension. Strange faces began to appear as deputy marshals, summoned from other parts of the court house, hurried in. United States Attorney John F. X. McGohey, who headed the prosecution, arrived with his staff of young lawyers.

Defense lawyers and eight of the defendants, who had been pacing in the corridor, smoking one cigarette after another, came in. They were followed by their wives, relatives and friends. Newspaper reporters rushed in.

Deputy marshals brought in three of the defendants, sentenced earlier in the trial for contempt of court, from the detention pen behind the court room. All eleven defendants sat down in a row of chairs just inside the railing between the court and the spectators.

The defendants held themselves tense and looked at one another with questions in their eyes. A dozen deputy marshals filed in and stood up in a row behind the defendants.

Whispers spread through the court room: first, "the jury's coming in" and then "it's a verdict." The woman deputy marshal in the special jury guard appeared inside the rear door leading from the judge's chambers and the jury room. Then came the familiar knock on the door, and the cry "All rise!" with which the judge's gray-haired bailiff always announces his approach.

At 11:24 o'clock the judge in his black robe mounted the bench and in solemn tones said to William Borman, clerk of the court:

"You may bring in the jury."

Looking stern, the judge leaned back in his high-backed chair, under the American flag and the great seal of the United States, and waited for the jury.

The deep silence in the high-

ceilinged court room was broken by the sound of voices coming from the corridor to the jury room. At 11:25 Mrs. Jane Schultz, Juror No. 5, led the jury into the court room.

The jurors came in one by one and sat down in the red upholstered chairs in the jury box they had occupied for so many weeks. None of them smiled. None of them looked at the anxious, searching faces of the defendants.

Rendering of the Verdict

In a deeply serious manner, as if conscious of the importance of their task and of their participation in a historic moment, they turned their gaze toward Judge Medina, who sat with his hands clasped before him and a brooding look on his face.

"Shall I proceed, Your Honor?" asked the clerk.

"Yes," replied the judge, in a tone that gave that one simple word profound significance.

"Will the jurors kindly answer as their names are called," the clerk said, and then read the twelve names one after the other, each juror answering "here."

"Madam Foreman," said the clerk, turning to Mrs. Dial at the end of the jury box nearest to the bench, "have you agreed upon a verdict?"

Mrs. Dial, a slight, smartly dressed young woman, stood up facing the judge, and holding a piece of paper in her hand.

"We have," she replied, in a faint voice that shook just a little.

"How say you?"

"The jury finds each of the de-

fendants guilty," said Mrs. Dial, reading the verdict in a voice that was barely audible in the press section.

It was then 11:26 o'clock.

Polling and Thanking of Jury

There was a slight stir, a subdued murmur in the court room.

Judge Medina directed that the jury be polled separately as to each defendant. Then the clerk asked the following question twelve times, each time naming each of the eleven defendants, once of each juror:

"You say you find the defendants Eugene Dennis, John B. Williamson, Jacob Stachel, Robert G. Thompson, Benjamin J. Davis Jr., Henry Winston, John Gates, Irving Potash, Gilbert Green, Carl Winter and Gus Hall guilty as charged?"

"I do!" repeated each of the twelve jurors, one after the other.

Judge Medina then thanked the jurors and said they deserved the thanks of the entire country for the "patience and careful attention" with which they had performed their duties. He also requested them not to discuss any phase of the trial or their deliberations with anyone, specifically mentioning "relatives, friends, members of the press, magazine writers or curious persons."

"Whatever you might say," he explained, "would be subject to misinterpretation, repetition and change, and might do irreparable harm to the administration of justice."

He then dismissed the jury and it filed out of the court room at 11:35 o'clock.

152

Judge Medina watched them go. Then the usual pleasant look on his face changed to a hard, determined gaze as he turned to face defense counsel, brushed away some papers from in front of him, and said in a stern voice:

"Now I turn to some unfinished business. The following will kindly rise!"

He called out the names of six defense counsel — Harry Sacher and Eugene Dennis of New York, Richard Gladstein of San Francisco, George W. Crockett Jr. of Detroit, Louis F. McCabe of Philadelphia and Abraham J. Isserman of Newark, N. J.

One at a time, one after the other, as they used to get up to bait him during the trial, the six men rose as their names were called and stood in a row, waiting silently for him to speak.

Reading slowly in a clear, strong voice, Judge Medina then adjudged all six in criminal contempt, and imposed sentences as follows:

Six months—Sacher, Gladstein and Dennis.

Four months—Crockett and Isserman.

Thirty days—McCabe.

As the first six-month sentence was announced a gasp came from the Communists and their sym-

pathizers among the spectators, but there was no further sound until the judge finished and asked if counsel had any motions to make.

Each of defense counsel then protested against the sentences. Most of them shouted angrily at the judge, denouncing him and attacking him with the same charges and in the same manner that had caused him to adjudge them in contempt.

Judge Medina interrupted one of their tirades and said:

"Let these contempt adjudications be notice to you and all who may be tempted to follow your example that there is power in the judicial system of the United States under its Constitution and there are laws to protect and maintain the dignity of the court and the orderly administration of justice."

When Sacher referred to "the price of liberty," the judge said:

"It isn't the price of liberty; it's the price of misbehavior and disorder. You continue in the same brazen manner you used throughout the trial, trying to make it appear you had never done any of these things."

McCabe was the only one who in any way apologized. He said that

if he had been guilty of failure "to observe the obligation I took to observe full fidelity to the court, I regret that."

Dennis Denounces Trial

In a weak, faltering voice contrasting with the boldness of his words, Dennis said:

"This trial, and the verdict, is an evil and an illegitimate product of a bipartisan conspiracy, of a conspiracy of men who want to destroy the Bill of Rights and peace, and I think that the adjudgment of counsel and the accompanying decision to remand the defendants without bail is in keeping with the sinister and police state character of this trial.

"I don't think any democratic-minded American, and people in other lands, will pass off lightly even the sentencing of the lawyers which took place today because this is just the first teeny fruits of the infamous verdict in this trial, but it will serve to alert and to arouse our people as to their stake in what has happened here.

"And I would say to your Honor, as in Nazi Germany, in Mussolini Italy, men also sat in high tribunals, also wore black robes and also handed down pro-Fascist decisions; but I would remind the Court that the people reversed

those verdicts and decisions just as our people will reverse the decisions and the verdict in this case, and the people's verdict will be for peace, for democracy and for social progress."

Judge Medina denied defense motions to allow the defendants bail in the conspiracy case and to stay execution of the contempt sentences.

Defense counsel told the court that they would file a motion for an arrest of judgment and a new trial in the conspiracy case.

The judge remanded the defendants in the conspiracy case to jail without bail and adjourned court at 12:35 P. M. until 10:30 A. M. next Friday when they will be sentenced.

Deputy marshals herded the grim-faced Communist leaders, who had remained silent and impassive all morning, through a rear door into the detention pen, after the prisoners had shaken hands with their lawyers and waved good-bye to friends and relatives in the courtroom.

Within an hour, they were handcuffed, put into a prison van, and taken to the Federal House of Detention.

October 15, 1949

COMMUNIST CASE TO PROVIDE TEST OF SMITH ACT

Supreme Court Decision Should Clear Up Some Long-Standing Doubts

By CABELL PHILLIPS
Special to THE NEW YORK TIMES.

WASHINGTON, Oct. 15—Irrespective of legal semantics, the purpose and effect of the Smith Act, under which eleven members of the Communist party of America were convicted in the United States District Court in New York this week, is to outlaw the Communist party in this country and to make active participation therein a crime punishable by fine, imprisonment or both.

Judge Harold R. Medina was careful to charge the jury, which had heard thirty-nine weeks of evidence and argument, that the Communist party "as such", was not on trial. This was true.

But the effect of the jury's verdict was to affirm that the eleven defendants conspiring through the instrumentality of the Communist party, did seek the forcible and violent overthrow of the Government. If this verdict is sustained on the expected appeal to the Supreme Court, it will, in the opinion of many legal experts, establish a precedent whereby active and knowledgable participation in Communist activity hereafter will become prima facie evidence of intent to overthrow the United States Government.

Government attorneys have long been seeking a clear-cut test of the Smith Act. They think they have it in the present case, and they are confident — with that

cautionary reserve with which most lawyers regard the august upper tribunal — that the conviction will be upheld when, finally, it is appealed to the Supreme Court. If so, they believe, they will be considerably less bedeviled by the "Communist stalemate" than they have been during the last ten years and more.

Scope of Statute

The Smith Act in reality is no more than Title One of an omnibus anti-subversive statute passed by Congress soon after the outbreak of the second World War. The over-all statute is known as the Alien Registration Act of 1940. Among other things, it broadened considerably the legal basis for the deportation of aliens, and it provided machinery for the finger-printing and identification of all aliens above the age of 14 living in, or coming to, the United States.

Title One — or the Smith Act part of the statute—is the only part, however, which is relevant to the case of the eleven Communists. And its teeth are long and sharp, so much so, indeed, that it frightens many thoughtful persons, the intensity of whose devotion to civil rights is matched only by the intensity of their hatred of

communism. Unscrupulously employed, they argue, it could become an instrument of anti-democratic persecution.

Here, in substance, is what the Smith Act does, making these things unlawful:

(1) To advise or counsel disloyalty or mutiny in the armed forces.

(2) To distribute any written or printed matter tending toward the same end.

(3) To advocate or teach the duty or desirability of destroying the Government "by force or violence."

(4) To print, publish or circulate any matter tending toward the same end.

(5) "To organize or help to organize any society, group or assembly of persons who teach, advocate or encourage the overthrow or destruction of any Government in the United States by force or violence; or to be or become a member of, or affiliate with, any such group, society or assembly of persons, knowing the purposes thereof."

Basis of Indictment

It was this last clause specifically which formed the basis of the conspiracy alleged in the indictment of the eleven Communists.

What principally distinguishes the Smith Act from other statutes relating to subversive activity of this character is (a) It is applicable in peace as well as in war (b) it makes advocacy and teaching of violent overthrow a criminal offense even if there is no overt act toward overthrow, and (c) it defines as a criminal offense membership in certain classes of organization. The nearest comparable law to it is one passed in 1861 (Title 18, Sect. 6, U. S. Code) which covers only deliberate conspiracy to overthrow the Government, not the advocacy or teaching of the desirability of such an act.

Fifth Column Fears

When the Smith Act was signed into law on June 28, 1940, the United States had already undergone its first shudders of nervous apprehension over the spreading of Hitler's war to American shores. The concept of the "fifth column" had just come into the public's consciousness. The terrifying accounts of the employment of this deadly and invisible weapon in the Sudetenland, Austria, France and the Low Countries dominated the newspapers and magazines.

The United States was in the throes, if not of a spy scare, at least of an acute spy consciousness in those days. Already the Federal Bureau of Investigation had broken up two or three espionage rings, the very size and boldness of which left many people shocked and incredulous. Charges were being hurled between the interventionists and the isolationists of "warmonger" and "appeaser."

America was in the grip of a war psychosis. The root of that fear was Nazi Germany, with which Communist Russia was then bound by the Ribbentrop-Molotov pact. The Smith Act was aimed at both the German-American Bund and the Communist party. The other provisions of the law were intended to guard against subversion and sabotage by German, Japanese and Italian aliens.

To date, five prosecutions have been brought by the Department of Justice under the Smith Act, including that of the eleven communists in New York. Excluding the current case, the most important one involved twenty-nine members of the Socialist Workers party, in Minneapolis. Eighteen of the group were found guilty and sentenced to terms of a year and a day to sixteen months in prison.

In two other cases, John K. Larremore of Los Angeles and Christian Loeffler of Detroit were sentenced to prison terms of two and six years, respectively.

The Pelley Case

A fourth case involving William Dudley Pelley and twenty-nine other defendants was dismissed "for lack of prosecution" after

Justus in The Minneapolis Star
"You can't fight ideas with a club."

Bimrose in The Portland Oregonian
"The blinding light to keep us free."

seven inconclusive months of argument and testimony in the Federal Court here.

The Socialist Workers party case was the only one of this group to reach the Supreme Court. The court's decision, however, did not come to grips with the central

enigma posed by the Smith Act—whether or not the Communist party does advocate the violent overthrow of the Government. It is the hope of the Department of Justice that this critical question will be met head-on this time.

The principal criticism of the Smith Act, and the chief argument put up by the defendants in the New York case, is that it violates the constitutional protections of free speech and assembly.

A good many thoughtful people, who have no interest whatever in saving the individual necks of the eleven Communist defendants, are concerned nevertheless that what we have forged is a two-edged sword; that if it can be used to cut down subversive enemies, it can also be used against persistent but non-violent dissidents. The wording of the statute, they argue, is dangerously broad and inclusive.

On the other hand, it is pointed out, without some such tough statute as this the country remains helpless against what has proved to be its deadliest peacetime enemy. Under existing laws, Communists—or any other brand of revolutionaries—enjoy virtual immunity while they go about their work of destruction.

October 16, 1949

HIGH COURT UPHOLDS GUILT OF 11 TOP U. S. COMMUNISTS; OTHER PROSECUTIONS ARE SET

DECISION IS 6 TO 2

Vinson Ruling Affirms Smith Act—Cites the 'Clear, Present' Peril

By JAY WALZ
Special to THE NEW YORK TIMES.

WASHINGTON, June 4 — The Supreme Court affirmed today in a 6-to-2 decision the convictions of the eleven United States Communist leaders on charges they advocated overthrow of the Government by force and violence.

Chief Justice Fred M. Vinson, announcing the Court's judgment, said the Communist defendants were "properly and constitutionally" convicted. They "intended to overthrow the Government of the United States as speedily as circumstances would permit," he added.

The ruling means that the Communist eleven must go to prison and pay the fines imposed on them by Judge Harold R. Medina in October, 1949, after a nine-month jury trial in New York. Judge Medina sentenced ten to jail terms of five years, one to three years and fined each $10,000.

The Communist leaders brought their appeal to the Supreme Court on a challenge of the constitutionality of the Smith Act, a Federal anti-subversive statute enacted by Congress in the early days of World War II. The law makes it a criminal offense to advocate or teach the overthrow of the Government by force or violence.

Majority Upholds Law

The court majority today rejected this challenge and upheld the law, as had the Court of Appeals in New York last August.

After the decision was announced Attorney General J. Howard McGrath noted in a statement that this was "a bad day for conspirators," and indicated that the Justice Department was ready for new actions against subversives. He pointed out, however, that the trial result did not outlaw the Communist party.

A separate action by the Court today has the effect of sending to jail also six defense counsel for the Communists in the New York trial. The tribunal issued an order refusing the six a review, which means that the six-month sentences given them by Judge Medina for contemptuous conduct will stand.

The eleven, all members of the Communist party's National Board in the United States, are: Eugene Dennis, John B. Williamson, Jacob Stachel, Robert G. Thompson, Benjamin J. Davis Jr., Henry Winston, John Gates, Irving Potash, Gilbert Green, Carl Winter and Gus Hall.

All except Thompson received five-year terms. Thompson got a three-year sentence in view of his war record in the Pacific.

Dennis Served Contempt Term

Dennis, who is general secretary of the Communist party in the United States, served ten months of a one-year sentence in a New York prison on conviction of charges of contempt of Congress. He was released last March 12. The contempt charge followed his refusal to answer questions when he was a witness before the House Un-American Activities Committee.

Pending appeal of their conspiracy case, the eleven leaders have been free on bond ranging from $20,000 to $30,000.

In a twenty-two-page 7,500-word majority opinion Chief Justice Vinson spoke for four justices (himself and Justices Stanley F. Reed, Harold H. Burton and Sherman Minton). Justices Felix Frankfurter and Robert H. Jackson each wrote separate concurrences running to forty-five and nineteen pages, respectively.

Justice Hugo L. Black dissented in three pages, and Justice William O. Douglas wrote thirteen pages in dissent. Justice Tom C. Clark, who was Attorney General during part of the Government action against the Communist leaders, did not participate.

The high court's decision was made public just before the nine justices laid aside their robes for the court's summer recess.

Chief Justice Vinson in his opinion reviewed carefully both the history of this case and the law. He said the court had decided that:

"Where there is doubt as to the intent of the defendants, the nature of their activities, or their power to bring about an evil, this Court will review the convictions with the scrupulous care demanded by our Constitution.

"But we are not convinced that because there may be borderline cases at some time in the future, these convictions should be reversed because of the arugment that these petitioners [the eleven Communists] could not know that their activities were constitutionally proscribed by [the Smith Act]."

Charged "Suppression of Ideas"

Counsel for the Communists had held the Federal law restricted constitutional guarantees of free speech and assembly and that the act was "too indefinite." During arguments before the high court last Dec. 4 lawyers for the defendants said prosecution of the Communist leaders represented "an unabashed suppression of political ideas that were thought dangerous."

They laid emphasis, too, on an argument that the convictions were against the "clear and present danger" doctrine enunciated by the late Justice Oliver Wendell Holmes. This was to the effect that the Government should not begin restricting free speech until danger was "clear and present."

Chief Justice Vinson said the argument that the Smith Act was "too vague" was not persuasive coming from persons who, a jury found, "intended" to overthrow the government fast as circumstances would enable them to do so. so.

"Their conspiracy to organize the Communist party and to teach and advocate the overthrow of the Government of the United States by force and violence created a 'clear and present danger' of an attempt to overthrow the Government by force and violence," said Mr. Vinson.

"We hold that [the appropriate provisions] of the Smith Act, do not inherently, or as construed or applied in the instant case, violate the First Amendment and other provisions of the Bill of Rights, or the First and Fifth Amendments because of indefiniteness," he added.

Jackson Chides Dissenters

Justice Jackson in his opinion concurring with the Vinson group, chided his dissenting colleagues for "lamenting * * * the injustice of conviction in the absence of some overt act."

"Of course, there has been no general uprising against the Government," said Mr. Jackson, "but the record is replete with acts to carry out the conspiracy alleged, acts such as always are held sufficient to consummate the crime where the statute requires an overt act."

Later, Mr. Jackson, conceding his belief that the Smith Act was constitutional and within the power of Congress to enact, added:

"I have little faith in the long-range effectiveness of this conviction to stop the rise of Communist movement. Communism will not go to jail with these Communists."

Justice Frankfurter, in the longest opinion of the case, a document of some 14,000 words, reminded that "constitutionality" of legislation is frequently confused with "wisdom" of a legislative act.

"In finding that Congress has acted within its power, a judge does not remotely imply that he favors the implications that lie beneath the legal issues," he observed. "The legislation we are here considering is but a truncated aspect of a deeper issue."

Sees Conspiracy's Object Clear

Mr. Frankfurter observed there is "no divining rod" by which to locate "advocacy," and sometimes it readily merged with "exposition of ideas."

"But there is underlying validity in the distinction between advocacy and the interchange of ideas, and we do not discard a useful tool because it may be misused," the Justice added.

"That such a distinction could be used unreasonably by those in power against hostile or unorthodox views does not negate the fact that it may be used equally against an organization wielding the power of the centrally controlled international Communist movement.

"The object of the conspiracy before us is clear enough," Mr. Frankfurter continued, "that the chance of error in saying that the defendants conspired to advocate rather than to express ideas is slight.

"Mr. Justice Douglas [in dissent] quite properly points out that the conspiracy before us is not a conspiracy to overthrow the Government. But it would be equally wrong to treat it as a seminar in political theory."

Black Sees "Prior Censorship"

Both Justices Black and Douglas, in their separate dissents, noted that the Communist eleven were not convicted on charges of conspiracy to overthrow, or try to overthrow the government. Such charges, had they been made, could have led to prosecution under the country's conspiracy laws.

"The indictment [in this case] is that they conspired to organize the Communist party and to use speech or newspapers and other publications in the future to teach and advocate the forcible overthrow of the government," said Justice Black.

"No matter how it is worded, this is a virulent form of prior censorship of speech and press, which I believe the First Amendment forbids. I would hold [the provision] of the Smith Act authorizing this prior restraint unconstitutional on its face and as applied.

"So long as this court exercises the power of judicial review of legislation, I cannot agree that the First Amendment permits us to sustain laws suppressing freedom of speech and press on the basis of Congress' or our own notions of mere 'reasonableness'. Such a doctrine waters down the First Amendment so that it amounts to little more than an admonition to Congress."

Douglas Questions Danger

Justice Douglas said the First Amendment, barring any abridgment of free speech in this country, did not mean that the Government need "hold its hand" until it was too late to save itself from a revolution.

"But the command of the First Amendment is so clear that we should not allow Congress to call a halt to free speech except in the extreme case of peril from the speech itself," Mr. Douglas said.

He expressed belief that all known facts of Communist activity in this country had bearing on the "likelihood that their advocacy of the Soviet theory of revolution will endanger the republic."

"But the record [in this case] is silent on the facts," Mr. Douglas continued. "If we are to proceed on the basis of judicial notice, it is impossible for me to say that the Communists in this country are so potent or so strategically deployed that they must be suppressed for their speech."

Justice Black observed that "public opinion being what it now is, few will protest the conviction of these Communist petitioners. There is hope, however, that in calmer times, when present pressures, passions and fears subside, this or some later court will restore the First Amendment liberties to the high preferred place where they belong in a free society."

In his statement after the decision Mr. McGrath said:

"Now that it is known that the Smith Act is valid, the department [of Justice] is able to proceed to give additional protection against those who seek to overthrow the Government by violence.

"This is a good day for loyal citizens and a bad day for the conspirators. I am proud of those who worked so hard and faithfully to achieve the result."

June 5, 1951

THE CRUCIBLE OF THE FIFTIES

Dewey Signs Bill to Oust Reds And 'Fellow-Travelers' in Schools

By LEO EGAN
Special to THE NEW YORK TIMES.

ALBANY, April 1—The Feinberg Bill directing the Board of Regents to purge the public school system of teachers and other employes who are Communists or "fellow-travelers" was signed today by Governor Dewey, without comment.

The State's Chief Executive acted on the bill, which passed the Assembly in the closing hours of the Legislature on Wednesday, without requesting the Regents or the Department of Education for any statement.

On the theory that it might have been asked for advice on whether the measure should be approved, the Department had started on a memorandum in opposition. This was abruptly dropped today when the Governor's approval of the measure was announced.

Another bill, introduced by Senator Charles V. Scanlan, Republican, of the Bronx, to bar the use of public buildings to any organization listed by the Attorney General of the United States as subversive, was vetoed. In a memorandum, the Governor said it represented an unconstitutional delegation of legislative power.

The Feinberg bill, which was put forward by Senator Benjamin F. Feinberg, the retired Senate Majority Leader, passed both branches of the Legislature by overwhelming votes.

It directs the Regents to promulgate a list of subversive organizations, and makes membership in any organization so listed the grounds for removal or refusal to appoint. In preparing the list, the Regents may take into account the list made by the Federal Department of Justice.

In a declaration of policy, the new law finds officially that Communists and "fellow - travelers" have infiltrated the teaching system, and that existing statutes designed to dislodge them are not being adequately enforced. It also finds, officially, that propaganda dissemination by Communists in classrooms is frequently so subtle as to defy detection, and continues:

"It is essential that the laws prohibiting persons who are members of subversive groups, such as the Communist party and its affiliated organizations, from obtaining or retaining employment in the public schools, be rigorously enforced.

"To this end, the Board of Regents, which is charged primarily with the responsibility of supervising the public school system in the state, should be admonished, and directed to take affirmative action to meet this grave menace and to report thereon regularly to the Legislature.",

Substantive provisions of the new law provide:

"1. The Board of Regents shall adopt, promulgate and enforce rules and regulations for the disqualification, or removal of superintendents of schools, teachers, or employes in the public schools in any city or school district of the state who violate the provisions of Section 3021 of this article (relating to employment of members of subversive organizations) or who are ineligible for appointment or retention in any office or position in such public schools on any of the grounds set forth in Section 12-A of the Civil Service Law, and shall provide therein appropriate methods and procedure for the enforcement of such sections of his article and the Civil Service Law.

"2. The Board of Regents shall, after inquiry and after such notice and hearing as may be appropriate, make a listing of organizations which it finds to be subversive in that they advocate advise, teach, or embrace the doctrine that the Government of the United States, or of any state, or of any political sub-division thereof, shall be overthrown or overturned by force, violence or any unlawful means; or that they advocate, advise, teach or embrace the duty, necessity or propriety of adopting any such doctrine, as set forth in Section 12-A of the Civil Service Law.

"Such listings may be amended and revised from time to time. The board, in making such inquiry may utilize any similar listings or designations promulgated by any Federal agency or authority authorized by Federal law regulation or executive order, and, for the purposes of such inquiry, the board may request and receive from such Federal agencies, or authorities, any supporting material or evidence that may be made available to it.

"The Board of Regents shall provide, in the rules and regulations required by Subdivision 1 hereof, that membership in any such organization included in such listing made by it shall constitute prima facie evidence of disqualification, or appointment to, or retention in, any office or position in the public schools of the state."

The law also reques the Regents to submit a special report on the action it takes under the new provisions by Feb. 15 of each year.

As to the other bills today Governor Dewey vetoed one that would have permitted court attendants, who are lawyers, to practice law in courts other than the one in which they are employed. He approved a bill authorizing Monroe County to hold a referendum this fall on the question of substituting a gross receeipts tax on the existing sales tax.

April 2, 1949

Charges of Freedom Curbs Rising in Nation's Colleges

By BENJAMIN FINE

A record number of academic freedom cases involving college faculty members who charge they were dismissed or that promotion was denied because of their political activities has arisen during the past year.

The American Association of University Professors, said to be "swamped" with complaints, is conducting investigations to determine whether the teachers have just cause for complaint. The most noted case, and the one that is expected to set the pattern for nearly all of the others, is the inquiry being made into the situation at the University of Washington. Three faculty members, two of them avowed Communists, were dismissed after a trial conducted by university officials.

According to Dr. Ralph E. Himstead, general secretary of the association, the aftermath of the Henry A. Wallace Presidential campaign is still being felt on the academic level. To date, eight professors or faculty members, from eight institutions of higher learning in this country, have complained that they have been dismissed because they openly supported Mr. Wallace or were active in the Progressive party.

The association has been informed of a number of other situations in which teachers have had difficulties because of their support of Mr. Wallace. However, these cases have not come to the association officially, and therefore no investigations will be made.

For the most part those dismissed for Wallace activities did not have tenure. Many were on probationary status, and they have been informed that their contracts would not be renewed for the coming year. Moreover, it is difficult to prove the exact reason for the dismissals. In a number of controversial cases the college presidents maintain that the contracts were not renewed because of "lack of competence" or some other general reason, while the educators charge that their outspoken political activities were behind their dismissal.

In the opinion of Dr. Himstead, the tension caused by the "cold war" is responsible in large measure for the unprecedented strain being put on academic freedom. Many college administrators are concerned lest they be accused of harboring Communists or fellow-travelers on their campuses, and therefore act against those professors who appear to be too far left of center.

A study indicates that few college or university presidents would retain known Communist professors on their campuses. The administrators are convinced that members of the Communist party cannot do an adequate teaching job.

However, the danger to academic freedom lies in the "in-between" zone, responsible educators emphasized. Because of the present tensions, it is sometimes difficult for a college head to resist the community pressures, particularly if a member of his faculty has been active in unpopular political causes. Thus far the only out-and-out dismissal on Communist grounds has been that at the University of Washington. In other instances the evidence may point strongly to Communist sympathy, but other grounds for dismissal are utilized.

Curbs Advanced by States

But it has not been solely on the higher levels that the issue of academic freedom is being challenged today. Many states have passed legislation or now have bills before them that would bar Communist or subversive teachers from the classroom. In most instances the teaching profession has lined up against such proposed measures, charging that by singling out one group the measures were of a discriminatory nature.

Three new trends in legislation have become apparent in the last year or two:

Dismissal of teachers on grounds of disloyalty is now authorized by Kansas, Massachusetts and Pennsylvania.

Teachers are forbidden to join certain organizations, usually designated as subversive, in Maryland, New Jersey and New York.

Investigations or check-ups on the loyalty of teachers are authorized in Maryland and New York.

Many school leaders see in this trend the forerunner of the type of "witch hunt" that took place after World War I. They fear that the freedom of teachers to express themselves or to be free citizens of the community may be endangered by restrictive legislation. Many who oppose the measures are known anti-Communists; they maintain that the teaching profession is endangered by the action taken against teachers generally.

The National Commission for the Defense of Democracy Through Education, an influential group within the National Education Association, deplored "the constantly increasing legislation appearing in the various states which impugns the integrity of the teaching profession by requiring teachers to take oaths other than those required by all officeholders." In a recent resolution the commission said:

"We view with alarm the danger to the many loyal teachers resulting from the investigations of teachers by committees of the state legislatures. These are reminiscent of the witch-hunting of the 'Twenties. These legislative enactments are loosely drawn, and are frequently used to curb the proper rights of teaching which the democratic processes demand."

Self-Policing Is Favored

At its meeting in Chicago last month the Department of Higher Education of the NEA likewise condemned the legislation that has been passed limiting the teachers' activities and singling them out for special investigation. The academic discipline of a teacher suspected of subversive behavior or "adherence to organizations which might corrupt his integrity," the department said, should be undertaken by the profession itself.

"The Department of Higher Education of the National Education Association condemns legislative actions which restrict freedom of learning and freedom of lawful association and by implication make the American teacher suspect by virtue of his calling," the educators declared.

Under the Feinberg law, passed by the recent session of the New York State Legislature, the Board of Regents is requested to draw up a list of subversive organizations, membership in which would be cause for dismissal from the teaching position. The board has appointed a special committee to develop the administrative plans necessary for this action. In announcing this action, Chancellor William J. Wallin commented:

"The Board of Regents is fully alive to its responsibilities under the Feinberg act dealing with subversive activities of those in the public school system and is determined in carrying out the law not to tolerate any so-called witch hunt."

The Illinois Legislature is considering a bill that would amend the school code concerning teachers. Any teacher could be dismissed for "advocating in his teaching any doctrine to undermine the form of government of this state or of the United States by force and violence."

Vigorous opposition has been voiced in Illinois to the school measures under consideration.

Many top-flight educators in that state have warned that the academic freedom of the teaching profession would be seriously curtained if the bills were passed.

On the college and university levels, the number of cases involving the question of academic freedom has grown to a record height. The American Association of University Professors serves as the clearing house for the higher education profession. This association, founded thirty-five years ago, has a membership of 35,000. Although it does not have any actual authority to force a college to reinstate a teacher judged to be dismissed unjustly, it does have tremendous influence through its power to put the administration of an institution on the censured list, or "blacklist." Such a listing is considered to be a smirch on the good name of the institution.

The association does not reach its conclusions hastily. It usually takes three to six months, sometimes longer, to reach a decision. At present the association has under investigation, or is preparing to investigate, the eight colleges that are charged with dismissing faculty members because of political grounds.

Other cases, in the general field of tenure and academic freedom, are expected to reach the association soon. In some instances the faculty member does not appeal to the association, but puts up a fight himself, or, to avoid publicity, resigns and gets a post on another campus.

Summary of Major Cases

Below is a brief summary of the most important cases involving academic freedom that have taken place in recent months:

1. University of Washington: Three professors were dismissed, two for Communist party membership and one for "neglect of duty" to the university.

This is the first case to reach the association that deals directly with the Communist issue. A committee has been appointed to study the voluminous records in the case and to decide whether the professors were unjustly discharged. Everyone in the education profession recognizes the importance of this case. No matter what decision is reached, the repercussions will be severe. Many college presidents have indicated that they are awaiting the association's verdict before they take action against suspected Communists on their own campuses.

Members of the committee making the inquiry include Dr. William T. Laprade, Duke University, chairman; Edward C. Kirkland, Bowdoin College; Ralph H. Lutz, Stanford University; J. M. Maguire, Harvard; Quincy Wright, University of Chicago, and George Pope Shannon and Dr. Himstead, representing the professors' association. Several meetings have been held thus far, with others scheduled during the coming summer months. It is expected that the final decision will be reached early this fall, at which time the report will be published in the AAUP bulletin.

2. Oregon State University: Dr. Ralph Spitzer, an Associate Professor of Chemistry, has been dismissed for supporting the genetics teachings of Lysenko, the Russian Communist, who advocates the theory that acquired characteristics can be inherited. In dismissing Dr. Spitzer, Dr. A. L. Strand, the president, said that "any scientist who has such poor power of discrimination so as to choose to support Lysenko's genetics against all the weight of evidence against it is not much of a scientist or has lost the freedom that an instructor or investigator should possess."

This case is now under inquiry by the AAUP. It is not known when a decision will be reached, but Dr. Himstead explained that a thorough investigation would be made of all the factors entering the situation. An attempt will be made to determine whether the principles of academic freedom have been violated.

Spoke for Wallace Cause

3. Evansville College, Evansville, Ind.: Prof. George Parker was dismissed on April 10, 1948, because, the college announced at the time, "his activities both on and off the campus * * * put an end to his usefulness to the institution." Professor Parker served as chairman of the Vanderburgh County Citizens for Wallace Committee and spoke in behalf of Mr. Wallace's candidacy.

The AAUP has completed its investigation and will make its report public soon. This is the first of the so-called Wallace cases that has been completed. Although the findings are to be kept secret until the official report is released, it is known that the academic committee of the AAUP is not satisfied with the explanations of the dismissal offered by Dr. Lincoln B. Hale, president of Evansville. If the committee finds Evansville guilty of violating the principles of academic freedom the decision may have serious repercussions on the other cases dealing with similar issues of political activity.

"In considering the application of the principles of freedom to the facts in the case of Professor Parker and in kindred cases it is important that we keep in mind the purpose of these principles," a spokesman for the AAUP asserted. "The purpose of the principles of freedom, both constitutional and academic, is to encourage freedom —freedom of thought, of inquiry and of expression. Those who believe in the principles of freedom understand this salient fact. They also understand that implicit in the principles of freedom is the right of others to express views with which they may not be in accord and which they may regard as unwise or even dangerous."

4. Olivet College, Olivet, Mich.: Although this case has not come before the association, it has attracted considerable attention in academic circles. Last summer Dr. Aubrey L. Ashby, the president, discharged a professor and his wife, the college librarian. The professor, Dr. T. Barton Akeley, was discharged for "ultra-liberal views." Last January five faculty members, including Tucker P. Smith, Socialist candidate for Vice President, were discharged. Subsequently ten more faculty members resigned, making a total of seventeen who were dismissed or left voluntarily. This was more than half of the original number of thirty.

Alumni groups of the college, as well as educational and professional organizations, have taken up the cudgels for the discharged professors. A new institution to be known as Shipherd College, headed by Dr. Alvin S. Johnson, president emeritus of the New School for Social Search, is planned for this fall, as a "secession" from Olivet. The issue of academic freedom has been raised by students and faculty members of the college.

5. University of New Hampshire: Prof. John E. Rideout, who served as State Progressive party chairman, has resigned his teaching post in the English Department. The university announced that Professor Rideout had accepted a professorship at Idaho State College, although his contract was not due to expire for another year.

At the same time, Dr. G. Harris Daggett, Assistant Professor of English, said he might "be forced to resign to save my career." Dr. Daggett was chairman of the local Progressive committee. Recently the students circulated a petition asking the board of trustees to reconsider its decision withholding Dr. Daggett's promotion. The board acted on the petition, but upon reconsideration again voted to deny the promotion.

6. Yale University: John M. Marsalka, assistant professor of history and Russian studies at Yale, was denied reappointment. In appealing to the American Association of University Professors, Professor Marsalka called himself a victim of "thought control" and State Department "pressure." He has been an organizer of the People's (Wallace) party in Connecticut and its 1948 candidate for Congress from the Third District. He recently invited Dmitri Shostakovich, the Soviet composer, to speak at Yale University, only to have his plans canceled by the university authorities.

In his letter to the AAUP Professor Marsalka charged the Yale authorities with "the violation of my traditional university rights of academic freedom." He added that "it is not only my future teaching career that is an issue, not only my civil liberties and academic freedom that have been violated, but it is the civil liberties and academic freedom of students and faculty at Yale and elsewhere that are at stake." Officials at Yale said that his left-wing associations had nothing to do with his contract not being renewed. It was stated that they were dissatisfied with his teaching.

Othter instances are cited by educators to indicate that the question of academic freedom is imperiled in some quarters. In March Dr. Harold J. Laski, a member of the Executive Committee of the British Labor party and a professor at the University of London, was barred from making two lecture appearances on the campus of the University of California at Los Angeles. Several colleges have barred communist or left-wing speakers from appearing on their campuses.

Last month the University of Chicago and Roosevelt College were investigated by a special legislative committee for alleged Communist activities. Educational leaders at both institutions vigorously denied any Communist taint, and defended their faculty and student body. In his statement before the Subversive Activities Commission on April 21, Dr. Robert M. Hutchins, Chancellor of the University of Chicago, said in part:

"It has sometimes been said that some members of the faculty belong to some so-called 'Communist-front' organizations. The University of Chicago does not believe in the un-American doctrine of guilt by association. The fact that some Communists belong to, believe in, or even dominate some of the organizations to which some of our professors belong does not show that those professors are engaged in subversive activities. All that such facts would show would be that these professors believed in some of the objects of the organizations."

More recently the question of Communist students receiving scholarships or fellowships from the Atomic Energy Commission has raised considerable discussion. The issue came up when it was discovered that Hans Freistadt, an avowed Communist and part-time physics instructor at the University of North Carolina, had received an AEC fellowship. Subsequently the university announced that Mr. Freistadt had been dismissed from his position as of June 1. It appears certain that Congress will put curbs on the granting of fellowships to Communists in the future.

In an interview with this writer Dr. Himstead expressed the view that the "cold war" was responsible in great measure for the increased number of cases dealing with academic freedom. He said the association attempts to follow the principles of freedom consistently, regardless of the public pressures of the moment.

According to Dr. Himstead and others reached in the study, the ideological warfare has made many college presidents and boards of trustees uneasy. Dr. Himstead said that "the principle of academic freedom is under greater fire than at any time in our thirty-five-year history."

The American Association of University Professors, according to its spokesman, appeals to the university to settle the cases on the basis of reason. Each case is thoroughly explored before any decision is reached.

Basically, the challenge to academic freedom in this country comes from the fear that Communists or fellow-travelers are gaining power in the schools and colleges. Responsible educators are convinced that the overwhelming majority of teachers and professors are loyal, conscientious public-spirited American citizens. Few among the teaching profession can be classified as "subversive" or disloyal to the democratic ideals of this country, they say; laws exist to oust those who are subversive or disloyal without weakening the traditional American principles of academic freedom.

A belief that the American people's "good common sense" would halt abuses of academic freedom was voiced by Dr. Ralph McDonald, secretary of the Department of Higher Education of the National Education Association. Dr. McDonald declared that an attack on freedom of inquiry was an attack on the American way of life and the democratic form of government.

May 29, 1949

EDUCATORS WARN ON LOYALTY OATHS

Board, Including Eisenhower and Conant, Decries Loose Talk of 'Red' Teachers

By MURRAY ILLSON

The Educational Policies Commission, whose membership includes Gen. Dwight D. Eisenhower, president of Columbia University, and James B. Conant, head of Harvard University, declared last night that state laws requiring special loyalty oaths of teachers were a menace to educational freedom.

In a statement issued here after three days of closed meetings in the Westchester Country Club, Rye, N. Y., the commission also called upon citizens to "condemn the careless application of such words as 'Red' and 'Communist' to teachers and other persons who merely have views different from those of their accusers."

The commission, on which twenty leading educators are serving, was established in 1935 by the National Education Association and the American Association of School Administrators to develop long-term policies for American education. Seventeen of the members, including Dr. William Jansen, New York Superintendent of Schools, took part in formulating last night's statement.

Unable to be present were Alonzo G. Grace, former head of the United States Military Government's Division of Educational and Cultural Relations in Germany; George A. Selke, chancellor of the University of Montana, and Andrew D. Holt, president of the NEA, who arrived too late to participate.

Alertness for "Freedom"

In issuing the statement, the educators explained that they wished "to re-emphasize and expand certain recommendations" that the commission had made public on June 8 in a declaration titled "American Education and International Tensions."

That pronouncement, which was subtitled "Meeting the Threat of Totalitarianism," took the position that while pupils should have the opportunity to learn about Communism and other forms of totalitarianism, the advocacy of such doctrines "should not be permitted in American schools." The commission also recommended that "members of the Communist party of the United States should not be employed as teachers."

Last night's amplified statement pointed out that while the commission still adhered "to its previously stated position concerning the non-employment of members of the Communist party as teachers, it wished also to emphasize again that citizens should be especially alert at this time to defend the essential need of their schools for freedom of teaching and learning."

Noting that "the news of an atomic explosion in the Soviet Union" had intensified "a major problem of the American people," the commission observed that the schools of the nation could "be of substantial assistance" in helping to deal with this problem. In line with this the educators said:

"State laws requiring special oaths for teachers, or laying down detailed prescriptions for the school curriculum, or establishing uniform tests and criteria of loyalty impair the vigor of local school autonomy and thus do harm to an important safeguard of freedom in education."

"The schools should continue with vigor their programs for giving young citizens a clear understanding of the principles of the American way of life and a desire to make these principles prevail in their own lives and in the life of their country. Educational programs should develop a greater measure of national unity among the many groups in the population of the United States.

"The schools should also try to help resist exaggerated fears which tend to rise in periods of heightened tensions. While the dangers of atomic warfare should not be concealed, they should be calmly faced. Anxieties that accompany a sense of danger must not be permitted to impair civil liberties or to lower our efficiency.

"The schools should help strengthen national defense and individual morale by promoting health, fostering confidence and courage, by developing skills and habits of sustained and purposeful work, and by guiding students in their search for moral values."

According to the statement, the commission intends to issue a leaflet to "assist teachers and other citizens to adapt their local school programs to meet the needs created by new developments in the international situation."

October 9, 1949

HUNDREDS NAMED AS RED APPEASERS

California's Tenney Committee Lists Actors, Musicians and Others as 'Line' Followers

SACRAMENTO, Calif., June 8 (AP)—The State Senate Committee on Un-American activities today listed numerous motion-picture personages, writers, musicians and other prominent individuals as having "followed or appeased some of the Communist party line program over a long period of time."

Several hundred persons were named in the committee's fifth biennial report.

Among them were Pearl S. Buck, Charles Chaplin, Lester Cole, Norman Corwin, Bartley Crum, Howard da Silva, Helen Gahagan Douglas, Hans Eisler, Lion Feuchtwanger, Lillian Hellman, Katharine Hepburn, Lena Horne, Dashiell Hammett, Danny Kaye, Gene Kelly, Robert W. Kenny, Ring Lardner Jr., Carey McWilliams, Dr. Thomas Mann, Fredric March, Burgess Meredith, Karen Morley, Clifford Odets, Dorothy Parker.

Also Gregory Peck, Paul Robeson, Edward G. Robinson, John Rogge, Artie Shaw, Frank Sinatra, Lionel Stander, Johannes Steel, Donald Ogden Stewart, Anna Louise Strong, Gloria Stuart, Senator Glen H. Taylor, Henry A. Wallace, Orson Welles, Prof. Haakon M. Chevalier, Paul Draper, Muriel Draper, John Garfield, Canada Lee and George Seldes.

The names were a part of a 709-page document, a report that the committee said was not intended as an exposé but rather as "a statement of the problem posed by the march of world communism in a period of cold war and irreconcilable conflict between two utterly contradictory concepts of government."

Four Counter-Steps Urged

The committee suggested these steps:

(A) Legislation to control and prevent subversive activity.
(B) Continuous investigation and exposure of subversive activity.
(C) "Prompt and consistent" law enforcement against subversive activity.
(D) Adoption of a broad, community-wide approach to "a clear understanding of the American heritage in contrast with the brutal, inhumane and treacherous doctrines of Marxism-Leninism-Stalinism."

Robert W. Kenny, former California Attorney General who has announced that he will oppose Jack Tenney—chairman of the Senate Committee on Un-American Activities—for the post as State Senator from Los Angeles County, declared:

"Apparently Mr. Tenney thinks it's un-American for anyone to run against him. He never did me the honor of putting me on his lists, so I announce I am going to unseat him."

Frank Sinatra declared:

"This unfair and unjustified attack gives every American a good reason to be critical of the Tenney committee. This statement is the product of liars, and liars to me make very un-American leaders.

"And furthermore, if they don't cut it out, I'll show them how much an American can fight back —even if it's against the state— if the American happens to be right.

"And I'm right, not Left, Mr. Tenney."

Comment By Others Accused

Other comment by persons mentioned in the California report was given in dispatches as follows:

Gregory Peck: "I have been denying these allegations for several years and will do so once more. I am not now and never have been associated with any Communist organization or supporters of communism."

Artie Shaw: "I don't understand what they are talking about. I don't think they do either. I have never traveled in a Stalinist orbit, unless that orbit includes the United States."

Carey McWilliams: "Like many liberals who are members of the Democratic party, I have developed a remarkable indifference to the slanders of Senator Jack Tenney."

John Huston: "The Tenney report is yet another example of that Senator's vicious campaign to smear the names of his betters in loyalty and obedience to the principles of our democracy."

A studio spokesman said that Katharine Hepburn "refused to dignify Mr. Tenney's un-American accusation with a reply."

Gene Kelly: "I don't know what Mr. Tenney is talking about. I am not a Communist, never was a Communist and have no sympathy with Communist activities. The only line I know how to follow is the American line."

June 9, 1949

TRUMAN DECLARES HYSTERIA OVER REDS SWEEPS THE NATION

By ANTHONY LEVIERO
Special to THE NEW YORK TIMES.

WASHINGTON, June 16—This country is experiencing a wave of hysteria as a result of current spy trials and loyalty inquiries, President Truman suggested today, but he asserted emphatically that we were not going to hell.

The President likened the current situation created by the conflict with communism to the troubled atmosphere engendered in the early days of the Republic by the alien and sedition laws. He also recalled what he characterized as the crazy activities of the Ku Klux Klan after World War I, and said that every great crisis brought a period of public hysteria.

The present feeling would subside as similar situations had died out after past periods of stress, Mr. Truman contended.

The Chief Executive did express confidence, however, that the hysteria had no part of his Executive Department in its grip. He gave assurance that if this ever happened he would root it out.

The country had not gone to hell in the Washington-Adams-Jefferson era and it would not now, President Truman asserted.

The views of the Chief Executive were elicited during his weekly news conference which today took longer than usual as correspondents tried to inquire into the whole wide range of the espionage-loyalty field.

Noteworthy in the long discussion was the coolness the President indicated toward J. Edgar Hoover, who for many years has been the director of the Federal Bureau of Investigation.

For instance, when he was asked whether Mr. Hoover had his confidence, the President replied obliquely that Mr. Hoover had done a good job. He denied, however, that the FBI chief had submitted his resignation.

In summary form, some other views expressed by Mr. Truman were:

No comment to a suggestion that an inquiry on the scale of the Roberts Pearl Harbor investigation be made of the FBI and its practices.

Contempt for an investigation of school textbooks undertaken by the House Committee on Un-American Activities.

President's Views Implied

While he has withheld confidential loyalty reports from Congressional committees, Mr. Truman said he would not attempt to do this with the judiciary where, as in the Judith Coplon spy case, the requirement was a fair trial.

The President's views were mostly implied rather than explicit. That was because they were not voluntary declarative statements but answers to questions. His meaning was none the less clear. In the detailed report that follows the questions are given verbatim and in the order in which they occurred, while the President's answers are given indirectly, as required by White House rules.

The discussion was started by Frederic W. Collins of The Providence Journal with this question:

"Mr. President, my paper has suggested editorially that you appoint a special commission, something like the Roberts Pearl Harbor committee, to make a thorough inquiry into FBI practices and to make a report to you not for publication—a quiet, closed study of the FBI."

Did you ever hear of anything like that in Washington, the President answered, laughing. The allusion to the fanfare of inquiries on Capitol Hill was obvious.

"Do you think such a study might be valuable?" came back Mr. Collins.

No comment, replied Mr. Truman.

Questions on other topics followed and then came this one:

"The House Un-American Activities Committee has suggested that schools and colleges send in a list of their school books, and California University has asked for an oath from its faculty. Do you see in these developments any threat to educational freedom in this country?"

Mr. Truman said he thought the question was pretty well answered in a cartoon in the Washington Post this morning. The cartoon by Herbert L. Block ridiculed the inquiry.

"Mr. President, an awful lot of fine people are being branded as Communists, Reds, subversives and what not these days at any number of trials, hearings, the situa-

tion in the Army and things of that sort. Do you have any word of counsel you could give on this rash of branding people?"

Yes, yes, he had given it once before, said Mr. Truman. He suggested that the reporters read the history of the Alien and Sedition Acts in the Seventeen Nineties, under almost exactly the same situation. They would be surprised at how parallel the cases are when they had read how they came out.

Questions on two other topics ensued as newsmen went after their particular stories and then came this follow-up question:

"Mr. President, regarding the alien and sedition laws, how can we apply their lesson to the problem of today?"

Just continue to read your history through the Jefferson Administration and you will find out that the hysteria subsided and that the country did not go to hell at all, and it isn't going to now, Mr. Truman replied.

[The Alien and Sedition Acts had their origins in two main causes: The possibility of war with France developed and three Alien Acts were passed by Congress to deal with naturalization, deportation, imprisonment or banishment of aliens. While they were rarely applied they scared many Frenchmen into leaving this country. The Sedition Act was inspired by the violent partisanships of the press of the times. In the face of strong public opinion, the law was used relatively few times by the Federalists against Jeffersonian Republican editors.]

"Mr. President, the first thing Jefferson did was to release eleven newspaper publishers from prison," observed a reporter.

Jefferson made a mistake on that, Mr. Truman said, but not seriously. He laughed. Then he went on to say that Jefferson not only had done that but had released a Federal judge, if he was not mistaken.

"What was that date?"

It began in John Adams' Administration and went over into Jefferson's—it was in the Seventeen Nineties, Seventeen Ninety-sevens and Seventeen Ninety-eights, he thought, said Mr. Truman.

"Do you think hysteria is causing this, and that it is fit for a country that is as strong and powerful as this country?"

Such things happened after every great crisis, after every great war, Mr. Truman replied. It had happened after the first World War, he went on, when the Ku Klux Klan went out to clean up the country. They tried to do crazy things. Out in Indiana they tried

to clean up and they made a mess of things.

"Are you confident that no part of your executive branch is gripped by this hysteria?"

He was, and he would clean it out if it were, the Chief Executive said.

"In the case of Gordon Clapp [chairman of the Tennessee Valley Authority characterized as "unemployable" by the Army] you stepped in quickly to straighten that out. Do you intend to step in if an executive is involved in one of these cases?"

Certainly, he always did that, that was not new at all, said Mr. Truman.

"Did J. Edgar Hoover submit his resignation?" He had not, said Mr. Truman.

"Do you confer with Mr. Hoover from time to time?"

He makes reports from time to time and he conferred with him through the Attorney General, the President responded.

"Mr. President, there has been a lot of smoke around Mr. Hoover for the last several days; could you go further and clear that situation up?"

There was nothing for him to clear up, the President said.

"There is no idea that Mr. Hoover has any intention of resigning?"

He had never heard of it, he had just answered that, and he knew nothing about it, Mr. Truman said.

"Does Hoover have your confidence?"

Hoover has done a good job, was the answer.

"You said last week that all these investigations just amounted to a lot of headline hunting."

That was all, Mr. Truman answered before the reporter finished the question with this: "Does that include Hoover?"

You could make your own assay on that situation as well as he could, the President said.

"Is your Administration giving any thought to providing protection to Executive papers?"

Every effort had been made to protect them, the President replied, but it was not the policy of the Executive to interfere with the judiciary when it is trying to give a person a fair trial.

"Would it be helpful if there were a law on the subject?"

That would relieve the executive from having to make a decision, was Mr. Truman's opinion.

"Do you think it might be a good thing to clear out of the files of the FBI all unsubstantiated allegations that persons are Reds, subversives and things like that?"

No comment, Mr. Truman said.

June 17, 1949

M'Carthy Charges Spy for Russia Has a High State Department Post

By HAROLD B. HINTON
Special to THE NEW YORK TIMES.

WASHINGTON, Feb. 20—Senator Joseph R. McCarthy, Republican, of Wisconsin, told the Senate tonight that an individual who once passed highly secret United States information to a known Soviet agent in an important European listening post now was "one of our foreign ministers."

He said the case was no secret at the State Department, but he refused all suggestions from the floor that he name the individual. According to his account, the White House and the State Department prepared some information to be sent to another Government, but before it left Washington it showed up in Moscow.

This individual at the important European listening post was shadowed, he continued, and was seen to speak to a Soviet agent. The agent was followed in turn, until he entered the Soviet Embassy.

The major portion of the State Department file on this individual, he declared, was removed about two years ago from the usual repository and put in the safe of an unspecified "high official" of the department.

Mr. McCarthy gave details of

this and several others of the eighty-one cases he said he had unearthed, but refused to give any names. Senator Scott W. Lucas of Illinois, the Majority Leader, said several times that the Wisconsin Senator owed it to the Senate and to the public to make known the names of the men against whom he was making such grave charges.

Point Raised on Quorum

In declining, Mr. McCarthy contended that public revelation of names might embarrass activities of investigative agencies. He volunteered to give the names to Mr. Lucas confidentially, in his own office, or to turn them over to an executive session of any appropriate committee of the Senate.

Senator William Langer, Republican, of North Dakota, supported this position. He said that the Judiciary Committee, of which he is a member, never gives out the names of subversives it discovers without the consent of J. Edgar Hoover, director of the Federal Bureau of Investigation.

As the exchanges between Mr. McCarthy and Mr. Lucas grew more acrimonious, the former suddenly made the point that no quorum was present. Most of the Senators, having been assured there would be no important vote tonight, had left for their homes.

When only thirty-four Senators answered the quorum call (it requires forty-nine to constitute a quorum) Mr. Lucas moved to adjourn, but his motion was defeated, 18 to 16. The sergeant-at-arms then was instructed to find enough Senators to make a quorum.

It took about thirty-five minutes for the quorum to be rounded up. Then the Senate heard Mr. McCarthy through his eighty-first case. It finally recessed at 11:43 P. M.

Mr. McCarthy charged that there was a sizable fifth column of Communists in the State Department, adding that Republicans and Democrats must unite to root them out. He said that President Truman did not know the situation, depicting the Chief Executive as "a prisoner of a bunch of twisted intellectuals telling him only what they want him to know."

Of the eighty-one cases he knows he said there were three that are really "big." He said he could not understand how any Secretary of State could allow them to remain in his department.

Shadowing Is Related

The three most important cases, he said, were those of the "Foreign Minister" already mentioned, an individual now working in the office of an Assistant Secretary of State, and a "top official" of the Office of International Education, which handles the broadcasts of the Voice of America.

One he mentioned, as a member of the group "trying to take over the Democratic party and the Government," was alleged to be now employed in the office of an Assistant Secretary of State.

He said this individual had been shadowed and had been in contact with members of a Soviet espionage group. He also intervened, Mr. McCarthy said, on behalf of two Communists who were engaged and later discharged, although they had access to secret information during their employment. Both men associate with Soviet espionage agents, he said. He expressed the belief that the individual was still in the State Department.

Another individual he mentioned was born in Flushing, N. Y., in 1903 and was employed by the Office of Strategic Services from 1942 to 1945, when he transferred to the Office of Research and Intelligence of the State Department. (Mr. McCarthy said that Communists trying to infiltrate the department set their sights on this

unit, on the Voice of America and on the Office of Far Eastern Affairs as their prime targets.)

The State Department's own reports, Mr. McCarthy said, describe this individual as a member of a number of Communist-front organizations and as an associate of known Communists. His superiors in the department, he added, have described him as overly sympathetic to Russia and as blaming on the capitalists all current troubles with the Soviet Union.

Leftist Union Mentioned

A woman in the Division of Special Services, according to Senator McCarthy, was provided with top secret clearance, although she was known to be a "pink" and a member of the United Public Workers of America, a union expelled from the Congress of Industrial Organizations last week for alleged Communist domination.

Another individual he cited as cleared for access to top secret information was described as a member of the Young Communist League and of four organizations on the Attorney General's list of Communist-front bodies. This individual, according to the Senator's records, now declares he has changed his views.

He told the Senate of another individual who was refused security clearance by the State Department and then obtained a job in the office of the Secretary of Defense.

"What do you suppose he's doing now?" Mr. McCarthy asked the Senators. "He's a speech writer at the White House. I am doing President Truman a favor by telling him this. He wouldn't have this individual there if he knew it."

A former analyst from the Office of Strategic Services, who joined the Military Assistance Program intelligence service of the State Department in 1945, was said to be a close friend of a Commu-

nist and to be a regular reader of The Daily Worker. This individual has stated, according to Mr. McCarthy's information, that "the Communists should take over in this country."

A man he described as "a foreign reserve officer" in the Information and Cultural Program of the State Department went to the Soviet Union in 1947, he said, as a member of a trade union delegation later disavowed by the American Federation of Labor. This individual has been cited a number of times in The Daily Worker, and Chicago police files listed him as a Communist as early as 1930, Mr. McCarthy said.

Questioned by Lehman

At one point, Senator Herbert H. Lehman, Democrat - Liberal, of New York, asked Mr. McCarthy whether he did not consider it his duty, "as a Senator and as a citizen" to reveal the names involved in the cases he was citing either to the State Department or to the Senate in an executive session.

Mr. McCarthy replied that the information had been available to the State Department for some time. He recalled that, after he had made his original charges in a speech at Wheeling, W. Va., last Thursday, President Truman had called him a liar at a press conference.

"The only way to clean out the State Department," he said, "is not by laws but by the cooperation of the President."

Senator Lucas promised to lend all possible assistance to obtain for Mr. McCarthy a hearing under oath before any appropriate committee of the Senate.

"Then Senator thinks this should be a trial of the man digging up the Communists," Mr. McCarthy retorted, "and not of the Communists themselves."

February 21, 1950

Truman Brands M'Carthy Charges as False; Won't Yield Loyalty Files Even to Subpoena

Special to THE NEW YORK TIMES.

WASHINGTON, Feb. 23—President Truman today branded as false the charges of Senator Joseph R. McCarthy, Wisconsin Republican, that there are card-carrying Communists in the State Department.

Furthermore, he reaffirmed his policy of last year, expressed in an executive order, that the executive branch of the Government would not surrender loyalty files to Congress, even under subpoena.

Mr. Truman recalled a statement of Andrew Jackson apropos of the subpoena threat: "The Chief Justice of the Supreme

Court has made his decision; now let's see him enforce it."

Yesterday the Senate unanimously directed its Foreign Relations Committee to investigate Mr. McCarthy's charge that there were or recently had been fifty-seven Communists in the State Department. The resolution included an order to subpoena loyalty files and Mr. Truman's allusion to Jackson was related to this order.

Mr. Truman said in his news conference that he had told the Foreign Relations Committee that

he would cooperate to disprove the false charges.

Mr. Truman recalled today that the Federal courts had upheld the right, ever since the early days of the Republic, to withhold records of the executive branch from the legislative branch.

This evening Mr. McCarthy made this retort to the President:

"I do not think the Senate will allow the President to get away with his boyish thumbing of his nose at all the Senators who represent the forty-eight states."

February 24, 1950

McCarthy Says Miss Kenyon Helped 28 Red Front Groups

By WILLIAM S. WHITE
Special to THE NEW YORK TIMES.

WASHINGTON, March 8—Sworn charges that Dorothy Kenyon, a recent State Department official at the United Nations, had been "affiliated with at least twenty-eight Communist-front or-

ganizations" were made today by Senator Joseph R. McCarthy, Republican of Wisconsin.

[In New York, Miss Kenyon called Senator McCarthy "an unmitigated liar." She declared that she had "never had anything to do with any Communist

fronts" and that she had never heard of most of the organizations to which the Senator charged she had belonged.

[Miss Kenyon, a former Municipal Court Justice, added that "Senator McCarthy is a coward to take shelter in the cloak of Congressional immunity."]

Appearing under oath as the first witness before a Senate investigation into his accusations that "at least fifty-seven" Communists were or recently had been

in the State Department, Senator McCarthy struck also at Philip C. Jessup, United States Ambassador at Large.

He accused Dr. Jessup, as a "gentleman now formulating top flight policy in the Far East," of an "unusual affinity for Communist causes," and as a sponsor of the American Russian Institute, an organization found subversive by the Attorney General.

Mr. McCarthy asserted also that the wife of the Secretary of State himself, Mrs. Dean Acheson, was listed in records of the House Committee on Un-American Activities as a sponsor of the Washington branch of the Congress of American Women.

This organization, too, the Senator testified, had been branded as subversive by the Attorney General. He made no accusation against Mrs. Acheson, however, beyond implying that she had been duped.

"There is no length," he declared, "to which these purveyors to treason (the Communists) will not go to bring into their fold the names of misguided men and women who are influenced by a glib story of social or economic improvement."

At his regular press conference this afternoon, Secretary Acheson commented with a smile on the fact that Mrs. Acheson's name had been mentioned.

He had telephoned her, he said, and asked her what she had been up to. She had first replied, he went on, that she never heard of the Congress of American Women but had recalled that it had been merged with a shoppers' league to which she had belonged.

Mr. Acheson said his wife recalled having once paid the league two dollars for membership, and maybe even twice. Looking over the list of sponsors of the organization, the Secretary went on, Mrs. Acheson observed that it sounded rather like the Social Register.

As to the inquiry in general, Mr. Acheson observed, in serious tones, that it had only begun and that the State Department would cooperate with it.

Accusations against Miss Kenyon and, briefly, against Dr. Jessup, were the salient charges offered by Senator McCarthy in opening his case before the investigators, a Senate Foreign Relations subcommittee headed by Senator Millard E. Tydings, Democrat of Maryland.

The inquiry had not been under way for fifteen minutes before the bitterest of wrangling had broken out between its three Democratic members and its two Republican members.

Dorothy Kenyon
Associated Press

Amid it all, Senator McCarthy refused Democratic demands that he state at the outset whether he knew the name of the anonymous "high State Department official" whom he earlier had accused on the Senate floor of successfully putting on "pressure" to restore the job of a State Department employe discharged as a security risk.

The Senator on Feb. 20 had said that the employe was "flagrantly homosexual," and had been dismissed on Feb. 19, 1946, but was reinstated on April 1, 1946. The reinstatement, the Senator asserted, was made through the intervention of a "high official" who caused accusing witnesses to repudiate their affidavits against the discharged man.

Tydings Draws Protests

Before Mr. McCarthy had a chance to begin his prepared presentation to the subcommittee, Senator Tydings, with the backing of Democratic associates, insisted that he first say whether he proposed to make a charge against "the high State Department official," and whether he could name that official.

Republican members of the subcommittee shouted protests. Senator Henry Cabot Lodge Jr., of Massachusetts, contended that Mr. Tydings was following "an amazing procedure," was breaking the continuity of the McCarthy testimony and denying the witness "the ordinary courtesy of being allowed to tell his own story in his own way."

Referring to Senator Tydings' promise that the hearing was to be "neither a witch hunt nor a whitewash," Senator Bourke B. Hickenlooper, Republican of Iowa, cried out:

"A label may have to be attached to this thing if proceedings go on like they are now!"

Mr. Tydings retorted that he, too, had "a label" in mind for the Republicans.

Senator McCarthy promised that the incident of the "high State Department official" would be fully handled tomorrow, when, he said, he would be prepared to bring forth the data.

Later, he told reporters he did not know the name of the official, but asserted it was in the files and could be found by the subcommittee.

Opportunity to Reply Planned

Senator Tydings contended that if such an official had sought, as Mr. McCarthy had charged on the Senate floor, to have persons repudiate affidavits against an employe discharged for security reasons, it was "a matter of the highest importance."

The thing should be pursued at once, Mr. Tydings added, so that if Senator McCarthy was correct the official could be suspended and removed from possible further access to State Department files.

To this, Senator Lodge responded that Mr. McCarthy had first made his accusation more than two weeks ago and that precautionary action should have been taken then by the Administration.

After the hearing had recessed for the day, Senator Tydings announced that Miss Kenyon and every other accused person would have opportunity to answer in public.

So disputatious was the session

TELLS NAMES

Senator Joseph R. McCarthy testifying before a Senate Foreign Relations subcommittee in Washington yesterday.
Associated Press Wirephoto

that at noon, when the hearing was adjourned until tomorrow, Senator McCarthy had not finished reading the first of many papers he will offer. In the meantime, he had given its text to the press.

In this situation, he proposed that the entire manuscript be put into the record of today's session. Mr. Tydings rejected this, saying that the subcommittee could not permit the transcript to indicate that testimony had been taken unless it had been given. Senator McCarthy then put into the record of the Senate itself the full document.

In it, Mr. McCarthy brought up the name of Miss Kenyon at the outset. The latest official registry, he asserted, indicated that she still was employed by the State Department at $12,000 a year — specifically as a member of the United States Mission to the United Nations serving on the Commission on the Status of Women and on commissions of the Economic and Social Council.

The State Department said later that Miss Kenyon's only connection with the department had been her post at the United Nations and that her term there had expired last December.

As his first exhibit, Senator McCarthy handed the subcommittee a clipping from The Daily Worker, the New York Communist newspaper, stating that Miss Kenyon in 1940 had signed a manifesto that war hysteria was "being whipped up by the Roosevelt Administration."

Senator Brien McMahon, Democrat of Connecticut, objected that Mr. McCarthy's authority, The Daily Worker, had "a genius for

misrepresentation" and that the subcommittee ought to have the original document, the petition itself.

Next, Senator McCarthy offered an exhibit that, he said, "fully" documented Miss Kenyon's association with the National Council of American-Soviet Friendship, which, he said, had been found subversive by the Attorney General.

Senator Tydings, asserting that "every rule of evidence" required that "all and not merely selected parts" of a document be put in evidence, proceeded to read aloud the entire list of persons represented in the exhibit as sponsors of the council.

These included, apart from "the well-known Communists" whom Mr. McCarthy had mentioned, such names as those of Senator Tydings' father-in-law, Joseph E. Davies, former Ambassador to Moscow, and former Republican Senator Arthur Capper of Kansas and the incumbent Democratic Senators James E. Murray of Montana, Claude Pepper of Florida and Elbert D. Thomas of Utah.

The Democrats, and particularly Senator McMahon, likewise pressed Senator McCarthy to state at what date the American Russian Institute, an organization to which he had linked both Miss Kenyon and Dr. Jessup, had been found subversive.

They demanded especially to know whether the stigmatization of the organization had occurred after Miss Kenyon's alleged sponsorship of it.

Senator Makes Charges

Mr. McCarthy testified that he had no investigative staff of his own and thus could not supply the date. Every "front" organization, he added, had a "fine" name attached to it. But, he asserted, the case of Miss Kenyon was one of repeated association with "more than a score" of front organizations and with such "known pro-Communists" as Ben Gold and Paul Robeson, and Irving Potash, "who is one of the eleven convicted Communist conspirators."

Miss Kenyon, Senator McCarthy told the subcommittee, had "collaborated" with Messrs. Gold and Robeson in 1948 in welcoming to the United States "the red Dean of Canterbury," Dr. Hewlett Johnson, whereas the State Department itself had refused to admit him to this country this year.

"The Communist activities of Miss Kenyon," Mr. McCarthy asserted, were "not only deep-rooted, but extend back through the years."

"It is inconceivable," he went on, "that this woman could collaborate with a score of organizations dedicated to the overthrow of our form of government by force and violence, participate in their activities, lend her name to their nefarious purposes, and be ignorant of the whole sordid and un-American aspect of their work."

As the hearing started Mr. Tydings said all witnesses would be sworn.

"It is an excellent idea," replied Mr. McCarthy. "I don't want anyone to take advantage of any immunity—whether it be a Senator or the Secretary of State."

March 9, 1950

MISS KENYON CITES PATRIOTIC RECORD TO REFUTE CHARGES

Denies at Senate Hearing She Has or Ever Has Had Tie of Any Kind With Communism

M'CARTHY NAMES 4 MORE

Says Dr. Shapley, J. S. Service, Prof. F. L. Schuman and an Ex-Diplomat Are Pro-Reds

By WILLIAM S. WHITE
Special to THE NEW YORK TIMES.

WASHINGTON, March 14—Dorothy Kenyon, a former member of this country's mission to the United Nations, denied under oath today "any connection of any kind with communism or its adherents."

Repudiating at a Senate investigation charges made against her by Senator Joseph R. McCarthy, Republican of Wisconsin, Miss Kenyon offered documentary evidence that in 1939 she had publicly denounced the Stalin-Hitler pact and that as recently as 1949 she had been violently attacked by Soviet propaganda.

Miss Kenyon appeared this afternoon before the inquiry, which is being conducted by a Senate Foreign Relations subcommittee, in the absence of her accuser, Senator McCarthy. In the morning session the Wisconsin Senator had attacked five more persons and had handed in the names of twenty-five others for "further investigation."

The five assailed by Senator McCarthy this morning were Gustavo Duran, former State Department official; Dr. Harlow Shapley, Harvard astronomer; Dr. Frederick L. Schuman of Williams College; John Stewart Service, State Department official, and an unidentified man, who, the Senator said, was formerly connected with the State Department.

Recalls White Committee Service

Miss Kenyon testified that she was publicly urging American aid for Britain and France against the Nazis before the German invasion of Russia, while the Communists were then demanding isolation from the war, and that she had been one of the original members of William Allen White's Committee to Defend America by Aiding

the Allies.

The only Republican subcommittee member present, Senator Bourke B. Hickenlooper of Iowa, declared from the bench that there was not "the least evidence." or "the least belief" on his part, that she had been "in any way subversive or disloyal."

Mr. Hickenlooper argued, however, over the sardonic cries of the Democrats, that in his interpretation Senator McCarthy had not charged her with subversion.

The Democrats retorted that the Senate resolution ordering the investigation, on the basis of Senator McCarthy's original accusations that "at least fifty-seven Communists" were or recently had been in the State Department, directed an investigation of those charged with being "disloyal." If Mr. McCarthy was not charging disloyalty, they said, he could not have brought the case before the subcommittee's forum.

McCarthy's Charges Cited

They pointed also to the fact that Senator McCarthy, in testifying last week, had asserted that Miss Kenyon had been "affiliated with at least twenty-eight Communist front organizations" and that her "Communist activities" were "deep rooted" and extended "back through the years."

Miss Kenyon, who termed herself "an independent, liberal, Rooseveltian Democrat," conceded

REPLIES TO SENATOR M'CARTHY

Dorothy Kenyon before Senate Foreign Relations subcommittee in Washington yesterday.
The New York Times (by George Tames)

that her name might have been used, "even at times with my consent, in connection with organizations that later proved to be subversive but which at the time seemed to be engaged in activities or dedicated to objectives that I could and did approve."

But never, she swore, had she been knowingly identified with any organization, or person, holding subversive views.

She acknowledged, in a long cross-examination by Senator Hickenlooper, that she had been in one way or another associated at one time with some of the organizations on Senator McCarthy's list that had perhaps later been declared subversive by the House Committee on Un-American Activities or the Attorney General.

It was possible, she said, that she had been a "sucker," a word attributed to her in a newspaper interview, as to some of the organizations that had used her name. It was also possible, she said, that her interest in "little people and civil liberties" had made "enemies" for her.

Miss Kenyon, dressed in black and wearing a black hat, by implication offered to submit to cross-examination by Senator McCarthy himself, saying that she was "ready to answer the questions the members of this subcommittee, or anyone permitted by the subcommittee, may care to ask."

Mr. McCarthy, however, did not attend the afternoon session at which Miss Kenyon was heard.

He left at the noon recess, having previously stated that he could attend no afternoon sessions. He refused the demand of the subcommittee chairman, Senator Millard E. Tydings, Democrat, of Maryland, that he submit at once the names of the eighty-one "cases" of doubtful loyalty or habits who, he had stated, were or had been in the State Department.

In this charge, made on the Senate floor in February, Mr. McCarthy distinguished them from the fifty-seven persons he asserted actually were Communists.

Mr. Tydings said that this was a "baffling" refusal. He contended that the subcommittee could not proceed to demand or subpoena the State Department and other loyalty files of accused persons until Mr. McCarthy gave the names.

Senator McCarthy retorted that Mr. Tydings already had "plenty to go on," with the names already put in the record and with the twenty-five additional names that he had handed up privately this morning. He would provide the names of the eighty-one "cases" mentioned, he said, as soon as he had "time to document them."

His new accusations asserted that:

1. Mr. Duran, a State Department official who resigned in October, 1946, engaged in Soviet activities in the Spanish civil war, according to American military intelligence. Mr. McCarthy said Mr. Duran was now an official of the United Nations. The office of the United Nations Secretary General, Trygve Lie, had declined to give information about Mr. Duran, Mr. McCarthy asserted, but the available data indicated that he was now working in the International Refugee Organization program.

2. Dr. Shapley, appointed to a United Nations post by the State Department, had been connected with Communist front organizations.

3. A former State Department official, whose name he withheld, was reported in the Washington police files to be homosexual and had been allowed to resign from the State Department in 1948 only to find employment in a "most sensitive" place, the Central Intelligence Agency. Mr. McCarthy gave this name privately to the subcommittee. It was an "important" case, he asserted, because perverts were officially considered to be security risks because they were "subject to blackmail."

4. Mr. Service, a State Department official, and now a member of the United States diplomatic mission in Calcutta, India, "where he is helping determine the all-important policy of our Government toward India," was a "bad security risk." He said Mr. Service had "Communist affiliations."

5. Professor Schuman, "a highly placed lecturer with the Department of State," and a consultant on Far Eastern Affairs, was a sponsor of Communist fronts. Mr. McCarthy charged that Mr.

Duran, on the authority of American military intelligence reports known to the State Department, had been active during the Spanish civil war in "secret Soviet operations in the Spanish Republican Army," and had been a "regional head of the Russian secret police."

Mr. Duran, Mr. McCarthy went on, after resigning from the State Department "under intense Congressional pressure" in 1946, had gone to the United Nations with what was indicated by "a confidential report" to have been the backing of "a member of the present Presidential Cabinet."

Senator McCarthy put in exhibits indicating that Col. Wendell G. Johnson, United States military attaché in Madrid, on June 4, 1946, had sent to the State Department and other agencies a report stating, on the authority of an anti-Franco Spaniard, that Mr. Duran as commanding officer of an international brigade in Spain had ordered the execution of two men without justification.

In December of 1943, Mr. McCarthy testified, Lieut. Edward J. Ruff, assistant United States military attaché in the Dominican Republic, had officially declared himself convinced that Mr. Duran was a Communist.

The Senator offered a Dec. 21, 1943, memorandum signed with the typed name of Spruille Braden, then Ambassador to Cuba, backing Mr. Duran for State Department foreign service work and calling him "not a Communist but a liberal of the highest type."

Finally, he quoted excerpts from a book by Indalecio Prieto, former Minister of Defense for the Spanish Republic, to the effect that Soviet agents had forced Mr. Duran upon him to be an official of the Spanish "S. I. M.," which the Senator termed a secret police group.

Shapley Appointment Noted

Of Mr. Shapley, Senator McCarthy testified that he had been appointed to the National Commission for the United Nations Educational, Scientific and Cultural Organization by the "predecessor" of Secretary of State Dean Acheson, Gen. George C. Marshall.

Dr. Shapley had not been dismissed by Secretary Acheson, Mr.

McCarthy went on, although he had been "prominent in the affairs" of the "Scientific and Cultural Conference for World Peace" held in New York in 1949 and "denounced by Mr. Acheson himself as 'a sounding board for communistic propaganda.'"

As to Mr. Service, Senator McCarthy told the subcommittee that he had information that the Loyalty Appeals Board of the Civil Service Commission ten days ago had returned to the State Department "the file of Mr. Service with the report that they did not feel they could give him clearance."

Mr. Service's "Communist affiliations," Mr. McCarthy testified, were "well known," but, after four or five investigations concerning his loyalty, he remained "one of the small, potent group of 'untouchables' who year after year formulate and carry out the plans for the Department of State."

The Senator asserted that Mr. Service and five others interested in the magazine Amerasia had been arrested in 1945 on charges of espionage for the "theft" of secret Government papers but had not been prosecuted.

Amerasia, Mr. McCarthy continued, shortly had opened attacks upon the then Under Secretary of State Joseph C. Grew, leading to his dismissal in favor of Mr. Acheson, because Mr. Grew had wanted to take a hard line in prosecuting the espionage charges.

Mr. Grew, the Senator added, also had opposed "the clique which favored scuttling Chiang Kai-shek and allowing the Communist element in China to take over."

Mr. McCarthy's main charge against Dr. Schuman was that he was "one of the closest collaborators in and sponsors of Communist-front organizations in America," and that if he was not "a card-holding member of the Communist party the difference is so slight that it is unimportant."

Mr. McCarthy testified that Dr. Schuman also had supported Henry A. Wallace for President in 1948 and had been associated in one way or another with the following organizations, all of which, the Senator said, had been cited as subversive by the Attorney General or the House or California State un-American activities committees:

American Committee for the Protection of Foreign Born, American Council on Soviet Relations, American League for Peace and Democracy, American Russian Institute, American Slav Congress, Civil Rights Congress, Committee for Boycott Against Japanese Aggression, Friends of the Soviet Union, African Aid Committee, National Conference of American Policy in China and the Far East.

Senator Hickenlooper's cross-examination of Miss Kenyon was prolonged but level in tone.

Mr. Hickenlooper went to many of the organizations that Miss Kenyon herself had mentioned in her prepared statement. Often, her response was that she could not recall any such association. Again, she said, here and there, that perhaps she had made a speech before one of them.

Once or twice, when Senator Hickenlooper handed her a photocopy of a letterhead of an organization, she observed that she was "in good company" at the time.

Miss Kenyon conceded that in a recent speech in Troy, N. Y., she had stated that the then current perjury trial of Alger Hiss, the former State Department official, was "a product of hysteria created by the House Committee on Un-American Activities." She still stood on that opinion, she said in effect.

She testified also that in the same speech she had said that "in the present temper of the country" it was doubtful that Hiss could obtain a fair trial and that there was "not a shred" of direct evidence against him save from Whittaker Chambers and from "documents that went back to Mr. Chambers."

In saying that he saw no evidence of disloyalty on her part, Senator Hickenlooper told Miss Kenyon that he thought Senator McCarthy had meant only to "suggest that your membership in organizations at least later termed subversive was a matter for concern so far as security risks go in the State Department."

Miss Kenyon retorted that she

was "trying to keep her temper," but that Mr. McCarthy had charged her with "a great deal more than that."

Miss Kenyon in Flat Denial

What the State Department should do, she added, in her case, or any case, was to "look at the record in the round and all the activities of the subject." To brand any organization subversive short of a court hearing. she asserted, was in itself a "violation of civil rights," as was "guilt by association."

Miss Kenyon, in her direct statement denying Senator McCarthy's charges, declared that she had had no warning that they were coming and that they had "seriously jeopardized, if not destroyed," the professional and personal reputation she had acquired in a lifetime.

Her answer to Mr. McCarthy was summarized in this passage:

"I am not and never have been a Communist. I am not and never have been a fellow-traveler. I am not and never have been a supporter of, or member of, or a sympathizer with any organization known to me to be, or suspected by me of being, controlled or dominated by Communists.

"As emphatically and unreservedly as possible, I deny any connection of any kind or character with communism or its adherents. If this leaves anything unsaid to indicate my total and complete detestation of that political philosophy, it is impossible for me to express my sentiments. I mean my denial to be all-inclusive."

She testified that in 1940 she was in the forefront of an effort in the American Labor party to keep it from "Communist domination" and that when this effort had failed she had left the party.

As a final item in her defense, her counsel read into the record a statement signed by thirteen New York lawyers, including John W. Davis, a former Presidential candidate, and Robert P. Patterson, a former Secretary of War, asserting of their "own knowledge" that she "never had the slightest sympathy with communism in any of its forms."

March 15, 1950

Acheson 'Welcomes' Inquiry; G.O.P. Shuns 'Red' Charges

By WILLIAM S. WHITE
Special to The New York Times.

WASHINGTON, March 22—Secretary of State Dean Acheson declared today that his department welcomed the current Senate investigation of charges by Senator Joseph R. McCarthy of Wisconsin that Communists had infiltrated the agency.

Senator McCarthy himself renewed the attacks, as Republican leadership of the Senate after a meeting of the party's policy committee made it known that the McCarthy accusations were not to be a matter of party policy. But Senator Robert A. Taft, highest ranking member of the committee, said that while Mr. McCarthy's charges were "not a matter of party policy," he (Mr. Taft) had personally urged the Wisconsin Senator to press his charges.

Secretary Acheson's comment on the investigation was made at a news conference as reporters asked about the man "connected with the State Department" whom Senator McCarthy had labeled "the top Russian espionage agent" in the United States.

Mr. McCarthy had, meanwhile, called upon President Truman to "put up or shut up" on the issue of turning over to the investigators the private files on the man, whose name has not been publicly made known.

Finally, Representative Richard M. Nixon, Republican of California, who as a member of the House Committee on Un-American Activities had a leading part in the committee inquiry that led at length to Alger Hiss' conviction for perjury, accused the Republicans and Democrats alike of playing politics in the McCarthy investigation.

Mr. Nixon appealed to President Truman to take it out of the hands of the Senate and "out of the realm of partisan politics" by appointing an impartial nonpolitical commission to make an inquiry.

"If the investigation continues on its present course, with charges and counter-charges being made for political purposes, the only party that will gain any advantage is the Communist party," Mr. Nixon said.

John Stewart Service, State Department foreign service officer, whose loyalty has been questioned by Senator McCarthy, is returning from Japan to testify before the Senate investigators, and is scheduled to reach here on Friday.

Mr. Acheson's comments on the McCarthy investigation at his press conference all were in answer to questions. He supported the assertion of Ambassador at Large Philip C. Jessup that Senator McCarthy's charges were harming this country's foreign relations, by raising doubts in foreign offices as to this country's unity and the status of its representatives.

But, said the Secretary, the trouble with continuing statements on that point was that they might make the people think that the State Department did not want the inquiry to go on. The reverse was true, he asserted, and the Department welcomed the investigation.

Senator McCarthy's demand upon President Truman was made in a press conference in the afternoon. Referring to the man he had called "the top Russian espionage agent" in this country, Mr. McCarthy asserted:

"I have given (to the investigating subcommittee) the name of that case and have told of the importance of obtaining the files. It is up to the President to put up or shut up. Unless the President is afraid of what the files would disclose he should hand them over."

Senator McCarthy added that he considered Ambassador Jessup "sincere and well-intentioned but completely fooled" and under the domination of Prof. Owen Lattimore of the Johns Hopkins University, Baltimore, who has been termed by the Senator a State Department consultant on Far Eastern affairs.

Dr. Jessup, the Senator asserted, was "the voice of Lattimore."

"Everything that Jessup has done so far in the East," he added, "has been a case where the voice is Jessup's but the hand is Lattimore's."

The chairman of the investigating subcommittee, Senator Millard E. Tydings, Democrat of Maryland, conferred during the morning with Peyton Ford, chief assistant to the Attorney General, and John E. Peurifoy, Deputy Under-Secretary of State, on the question of a disclosure to the subcommittee of the loyalty files.

Senator Tydings said afterward that Mr. Peurifoy "wanted very much," subject to President Truman's ultimate decision, to hand over the State Department documents, but that Mr. Ford was extremely reluctant in the case of Federal Bureau of Investigation files.

The F. B. I., Mr. Tydings added, hoped to be able to stand on its policy of never revealing the sources of its information, lest future sources be "dried up."

Nevertheless, the Senator added, he thought "very good progress" was being made toward obtaining all the data. He hoped, he said, for a final decision from President Truman before this week was out.

Mr. Peurifoy told reporters that the man Senator McCarthy claimed to be the "top Russian espionage agent" did not now work in the State Department and never had been in its employ.

March 23, 1950

Texts of Truman Letters on Loyalty Files

KEY WEST, Fla., March 28 (AP) —Following is the text of President Truman's letter today to Senator Millard E. Tydings, Democrat of Maryland, chairman of the Senate subcommittee investigating charges of communism in the State Department:

Hon. MILLARD E. TYDINGS
United States Senate
Washington, D. C.

Dear Senator Tydings:

This is in reply to your letter of March 2, 1950, in which you asked for the production before your subcommittee of the investigative files relating to Government employes who are or have been employed in the Department of State, and against whom charges of disloyalty have been made before your subcommittee by Senator McCarthy. The question raised by your request is one of grave concern, and I have given very careful consideration to the response contained herein.

In March of 1948, I issued a directive to all officers and employes in the Executive Branch of the Government, directing that all reports, records, and files relating to the employe loyalty program be kept in strict confidence, even in instances where subpoenas were received.

As you know, this directive was clearly within the power of the President, and I issued it only after the most careful consideration and after I had satisfied myself beyond any doubt that any other decision would have resulted in the collapse of the loyalty program.

At that time I issued a release in which I pointed out the long-standing precedents regarding the production of confidential files and the reasons for my decision.

Jackson Letter Recalled

I referred, among other things, to a letter from former Attorney General Robert H. Jackson, dated April 30, 1941, to the chairman of the House Committee on Naval Affairs, declining to furnish that committee with certain reports of the Federal Bureau of Investigation, which letter was written with the approval and at the direction of President Roosevelt.

That letter forcefully pointed out the serious consequences that would have resulted from compliance with the request of the House Naval Affairs Committee. Among others things, Attorney General Jackson stated:

"Moreover, disclosure of the reports would be of serious prejudice to the future usefulness of the Federal Bureau of Investigation. As you probably know, much of this information is given in confidence and can only be obtained upon pledge not to disclose its sources.

"A disclosure of the sources would embarrass informants — sometimes in their employment, sometimes in their social relations, and in extreme cases might even endanger their lives. We regard the keeping of faith with confidential informants as an indispensable condition of future efficiency.

"Disclosure of information contained in the reports might also be the grossest kind of injustice to innocent individuals. Investigative reports include leads and suspicions, and sometimes even the statements of malicious or misinformed people.

Even though later and more complete reports exonerate the individuals, the use of particular or selected reports might constitute the grossest injustice, and we all know that a correction never catches up with an accusation.

These three elements—the serious prejudice to the effectiveness of the Federal Bureau of Investigation as an investigative agency, the resulting embarrassment and danger to confidential informants, and injustice and unfairness to innocent individuals—led me to the inescapable conclusion that the single most important element in an effective and at the same time just and fair loyalty program was the preservation of all files in connection therewith in the strictest confidence. I cannot over-emphasize this point.

Views of F. B. I. Director

During the last month, I have been re-examining with utmost care this entire problem, and in this connection I have asked the Attorney General, the director of the Federal Bureau of Investigation, and Mr. Seth Richardson, chairman of the Loyalty Review Board, to give their careful consideration to this matter.

They have unanimously advised me that disclosure of loyalty files would be contrary to the public interest, and would do much more harm than good. The Attorney General has outlined the very serious consequences that would result from any such disclosure. The director of the Federal Bureau of Investigation stated:

1. The public disclosure of F. B. I. reports will reveal investigative procedures and techniques. If publicized, criminals, foreign agents, subversives, and others would thus be forewarned and seek ways and means to carry out their activities, thus avoiding detection and hampering the efficiency of an investigative agency.

The underground operation of criminals and subversives already are most difficult of detection, and I do not believe the security of the nation would be furthered by applying any additional shackles to the F. B. I.

2. For the last twenty-five years, the F. B. I. has represented to the American public that the F. B. I. would maintain their confidences. To make public F. B. I. reports would be to break confidences, and persons interviewed in the future might be even more reluctant to furnish information.

In recent months, on numerous occasions, some citizens, shirking their responsibilities, have refused to furnish information on the grounds that it might be misused, and have gone so far as to decline to furnish information, even in application investigations, claiming they would do so only if forced by a subpoena.

3. A public disclosure of F. B. I. reports would reveal the identity of sources of information, and in some cases, at least, would place in jeopardy the lives of confidential sources of information.

4. Disclosure of information contained in F. B. I. reports might result in an injustice to innocent individuals who find themselves entwined in a web of suspicious circumstances, which can be explained only by further investigation, and disclosures might be made under circumstances which would deny the aggrieved the opportunity to publicly state their positions.

5. A public disclosure could warn persons whose names appear in F. B. I. reports of the investigation, and serve as an effective means of enabling them to avoid detection, to approach witnesses, to bring about the destruction of evidence, or permit them to flee the country.

6. Public disclosure of F. B. I. reports could contribute to blackmail of persons investigated, or could result in degrading persons who have made a mistake or fallen prey to false propaganda.

7. Disclosure might reveal highly restricted information vital to the national security and of considerable value to a foreign power.

8. F. B. I. reports set forth full details secured from a witness, and if disclosed, could be subject to misinterpretation, quoting out of context, or used to thwart truth, distort half-truths, and misrepresent facts.

Complete Inquiry Backed

It is my desire, however, that the charges of disloyalty made before your subcommittee be given the most thorough and complete investigation, and it is my purpose to cooperate with your subcommittee to the greatest extent possible, bearing in mind at all times my responsibility to take care that the investigative activities and efficiency of the Federal Bureau of Investigation and other investigative agencies remain unimpaired; that innocent people—both those under investigation and those who have provided information—not be unnecessarily injured, and that the effectiveness of the employe loyalty program as a whole not be interfered with.

I am, therefore, asking Mr. Seth Richardson, chairman of the Loyalty Review Board, to have the board arrange for a complete and detailed review, as soon as possible, of the cases in which charges of disloyalty have been made before your subcommittee (including cases heretofore reviewed by the board), and am asking him to give me a full and complete report after review.

This review will include reports of loyalty investigation made by the Federal Bureau of Investigation, and the files of the State Department and the Civil Service Commission relating to these cases, as well as all other evidence of disloyalty made available to the Loyalty Review Board, including, of course, any evidence produced before your subcommittee.

Upon receipt of Mr. Richardson's report, I will advise your subcommittee further.

For your information I am attaching hereto a list of the members of the Loyalty Review Board.

Sincerely yours,
HARRY S. TRUMAN.

MEMBERS OF LOYALTY REVIEW BOARD

Seth W. Richardson, chairman; Davies, Richberg, Beebe, Busick and Richardson, 100 Vermont Avenue, N. W., Washington 5, D. C.

George W. Alger: Alger, Andrew and Rohlfs, 55 Liberty Street, New York 5, N. Y.

John H. Amen; Amen, Gans and Butler, 17 East Sixty-third Street, New York 21, N. Y.

John Kirland Clark, 72 Wall Street, New York 5, N. Y.

Clem W. Collins; Collins, Peabody and Schmit, First National Bank Building, Denver 2, Col.

Harry W. Colmery, National Bank of Topeka Building, Topeka, Kan.

Edwin Angell Cotterell, the Haynes Foundation, 2324 South Figueroa Street, Los Angeles 7, Calif.

Dr. Burton L. French, 402 East Church Street, Oxford, Ohio.

Dr. Meta Glass, Ipsissima, Farmington, Charlottesville, Va.

Paul M. Hebert, 1854 Blouin Avenue, Baton Rouge, La.

Garrett S. Hoag; Foley, Hoag and Eliot, 10 Post Office Square, Boston 10, Mass.

Wilbur La Roe Jr., Room 743, Continental Building, Washington 4, D. C.

Laurence F. Leen, president, Occidental Life Insurance Company, Raleigh, N. C. (also president, Peninsular Life Insurance Company, Jacksonville, Fla.).

Brunswon McChesney, Professor of Law, Northwestern University, 357 East Chicago Avenue, Chicago 11, Ill.

Dr. Arthur W. MacMahon, Professor of Political Science, Columbia University, New York 27, N. Y.

Murray Seasongood; Paxton and Seasongood, 1616 Union Central Building, Cincinnati 2, Ohio.

Henry L. Shattuck; Shattuck and Brooks, 10 Milk Street, tenth floor, Boston, Mass.

Andrew Steers, president, Metropolitan Building Company, 105 Cobb Building, Seattle 1, Wash.

James F. Twohy, 326 Adelaide Drive, Santa Monica, Calif.

Leonard D. White, Professor of Public Administration, Department of Political Science, University of Chicago, Chicago 37, Ill.

Letter to Richardson

HON. SETH W. RICHARDSON
Chairman, Loyalty Review Board
United States Civil Service Commission, Washington, D. C.

Dear Mr. Richardson:

I am enclosing herewith a copy of a letter which I am sending to Senator Tydings, with reference to the investigation now being conducted by the subcommittee of the Senate Committee on Foreign Relations of Government employes who are or have been employed in the Department of State and against whom charges of disloyalty have been made. I believe the letter is self-explanatory.

In accordance with the letter, I would appreciate it if the Loyalty Review Board would arrange for a complete and detailed review, as soon as possible, of the cases in which charges of disloyalty have been made before Senator Tyding's subcommittee.

This review should include cases which have heretofore been reviewed by the board, and should include a review of reports of loyalty investigations made by the Federal Bureau of Investigation and files of the State Department and the Civil Service Commission relating to such cases, as well as a review of all other evidence of disloyalty made available to you, including of course any evidence produced before the subcommittee.

Would you please furnish me with a full and complete report after completion of the board's review?

Sincerely yours,
HARRY S. TRUMAN.

March 29, 1950

LATTIMORE NAMED AS 'TOP SOVIET SPY' CITED BY M'CARTHY

Far Eastern Expert Is Called State Department Adviser Accused Before Senators

NOW ON U. N. TRIP IN EAST

Truman Decides Files Policy— Loyalty Head Backs Secrecy —Stimson Scores Charges

By JAY WALZ
Special to THE NEW YORK TIMES.

WASHINGTON, March 26—Owen Lattimore, who has served as a State Department adviser on the Far East, was identified tonight as the man described by Senator Joseph R. McCarthy of Wisconsin as being Russia's top espionage agent in the United States.

The name, given privately to Senate investigators examining charges by Mr. McCarthy of Communist infiltration of the State Department, was mentioned publicly tonight by a radio commentator, and members of the Senate group said the identification was correct.

Mr. McCarthy had mentioned Mr. Lattimore's name in the early stages of the current investigation, but in a less specific way. At a public hearing the Wisconsin Republican listed Mr. Lattimore among four persons at the State Department he regarded as poor security risks.

Enlarged on Charge Later

When, however, Mr. McCarthy later told the investigators of a man in the State Department he said was the top-ranking Soviet spy in this country, he gave no name until the subcommittee went into closed session. He has not given the name publicly, although members of the subcommittee gave it privately to a number of newspaper men. The radio commentator who named Mr. Lattimore was Drew Pearson.

[From Key West came word that President Truman and other high officials had decided on the Administration's position on releasing loyalty files—a position to be set forth Monday. Henry L. Stimson sharply attacked the "noisy antics" of critics of the State Department.]

Seth W. Richardson, chairman of the President's Loyalty Review Board, today endorsed the Federal Bureau of Investigation's position against handing over any confidential files to Congressional investigating committees. He said that if the F. B. I. had to give up secret data its work "would stop."

Mr. McCarthy was not available for comment tonight on the naming of Mr. Lattimore and Senator Millard E. Tydings, chairman of the investigating body, a subcommittee of the Foreign Relations Committee, declined to say anything about the case.

"This is not a one-man subcommittee, you know," he said when asked if Mr. Lattimore were the man. He would have to talk to his colleagues before deciding whether to name the person publicly, he added.

Lattimore in Afghanistan

Mr. Lattimore is in Afghanistan on a mission for the United Nations, and has not discussed any of the McCarthy charges. Mrs. Lattimore could not be reached tonight, but she earlier had flatly denied the public charges that Senator McCarthy had directed against her husband. Similar denials were issued by associates at Johns Hopkins University, where Mr. Lattimore heads the Walter Hines Page School of International Relations.

Last fall Mr. Lattimore took part in a two-day meeting of a citizens' round-table conference on foreign policy at the State Department.

The record shows that Senator McCarthy has had Mr. Lattimore on his mind during much of the current investigation into the extent of communism in the State Department. After listing the Johns Hopkins professor as a man with a "pro-Communist record," Senator McCarthy brought up the name again when Philip C. Jessup, Ambassador at Large, came before the subcommittee to deny similar charges.

Senator McCarthy said that to know everything in Dr. Jessup's record the Senators would have to look into the complete files of Owen Lattimore.

"I am sure the files will prove * * * beyond a doubt that Jessup is a dangerously efficient Lattimore-front," said Mr. McCarthy.

Mr. McCarthy told members of the Tydings committee that he considered the case, now identified as Lattimore's, as the most important on his list. He said he would be willing to let his general charge against the State Department stand or fall on the basis of this one.

But, according to Senator Tydings, Mr. McCarthy had produced no "primary evidence" to support his accusation. Instead, he urged the subcommittee members to get at the confidential files in the State Department and the Federal Bureau of Investigation.

Whether the files in this case, or others brought forward by Mr. McCarthy, will be made available has become a subject of great controversy and Senator Tydings said today that he hoped to be able to announce the solution tomorrow. The Federal Bureau of Investigation, and the Administration generally, have insisted that such secret files cannot be released even to Congressional groups without destroying information sources of the F. B. I.

However, Mr. Tydings and colleagues of his subcommittee conferred with J. Edgar Hoover, director of the F. B. I., on Friday on the case of the "top espionage agent," and obtained from him an "analysis" of the case. The question whether the Senators might inspect the files of this and other cases at first hand was not settled, however. Both Mr. Hoover and J. Howard McGrath, Attorney General, are expected to give their reasons for reluctance in handing over secret data when they appear before the subcommittee in public meeting tomorrow.

The State Department, in discussing this "top" case, without naming Mr. Lattimore, has denied that the person involved was ever an employe of the department. Mr. Tydings said he was told that the man involved had never been connected with the State Department except once when he was associated with a mission outside the United States for about four months.

Mr. Lattimore, 49 years old, was

165

a member of the Japanese Reparation Commission in 1945-46. A Harvard graduate, he has been a student of Far Eastern affairs since the early Nineteen Twenties. He served as political adviser to Chiang Kai-shek in 1941-42, and was Deputy Director of the United States Office of War Information from 1942 to 1944.

Author of Many Books

Mr. Lattimore, born in Washington, D. C., is the author of a number of books on Far East subjects. He began his writing career as a newspaperman in Tientsin in 1921, after attending schools in the United States and England. Throughout the Nineteen Twenties he traveled and lived in many parts of China, and in 1929 undertook research in Manchuria for the Science Research Council.

He continued his studies under the Guggenheim Memorial Foundation from 1931 to 1933, and then conducted research in Peiping for the Institute of Pacific Relations. From 1934 to 1941, he edited the magazine Pacific Affairs.

Mr. Lattimore's books include "Manchuria: Cradle of Conflict" (1932); "Inner Asian Frontiers of China" (1940); "The Making of Modern China," in collaboration with Mrs. Lattimore, (1944); "Solution in Asia" (1945), and "Pivot of Asia," just published.

He was employed by the Chinese Government as a political adviser to Generalissimo Chiang Kai-shek in 1941 on the recommendation of President Roosevelt. His job was to facilitate United States aid to the Chinese Government in the period just prior to American entrance into the war. Later, while serving in the Office of War Information in 1944, he accompanied Vice President Henry A. Wallace on a special mission for President Roosevelt to China and Siberia.

Mrs. Lattimore is the former Eleanor Holgate, whose father was at one time acting president of Northwestern University. She and Mr. Lattimore were married in 1926 in China and their honeymoon was a trip by horseback, camel and sled through Chinese Turkestan and Mongolian back country. The Lattimores have one son, David.

Mr. Lattimore is now in Afghanistan as one of four members of a United Nations mission to find out what technical aid could best serve the country.

Senator Tydings said today that he expected to clear up tomorrow the controversy over whether his subcommittee should have confidential files in its investigation of State Department employes.

Messrs. Hoover and McGrath, it was strongly indicated, would be closely examined tomorrow on the question of the secret files, which the F. B. I. and the Administration generally have insisted must be held from public view.

Mr. McCarthy has told the subcommittee the files contain the proof of his charges, and has persisted in demands that they be made available for examination.

Senator Tydings, who has sent a letter to President Truman with a general request for all the files involved, indicated in a radio talk today that he expected some definite decision by tomorrow night.

Mr. Richardson, whose board is the last appeal for Government employes confronted with disloyalty charges, told a television audience that the F. B. I. must have the full confidence of its informants. That confidence would be destroyed as soon as any files were released, he said.

Mr. Richardson said that under the Government's loyalty program some 2,800,000 persons had been checked, with about 150 to 175 being dismissed from Federal service because they were regarded as loyalty risks.

"But there has not been one single instance where espionage has been charged," said the board chairman.

Senator McCarthy, in public remarks that precipitated the present investigation, said there were fifty-seven card-carrying Communists in the State Department, and has outlined eighty-one cases of State employes who he says are involved with Communists either by affiliation or association.

In closed session, Senator McCarthy gave the name of the man he describes as Russia's top Soviet agent in the United States, and today Senator Tydings called upon Senator McCarthy to prove his statement that this man has, or once had, a desk in the State Department.

"Nobody in the department seems to know where it is," Senator Tydings said in a radio talk broadcast by Maryland stations.

"I'd be grateful if Senator McCarthy would tell me the room and the place where this desk is."

Mrs. Esther C. Brunauer, whom Mr. McCarthy presented as Case 47, will appear before the subcommittee tomorrow morning. The Wisconsin Senator said Mrs. Brunauer, currently employed in the State Department, held Communist-front memberships and associations that "seriously questioned her security status."

Haldore Hansen, another employe in the department whom Mr. McCarthy said had "pro-Communist proclivities," will appear before the subcommittee on Tuesday. He asked for the opportunity to testify because of "humiliations" that had been brought upon him as a result of the charges.

March 27, 1950

LOYALTY HEAD SAYS 3 YEARS' WORK NETS 'NOT A SINGLE SPY'

Richardson Tells Senate Unit 10,000 Inquiries Failed to Show Any in U. S. Service

STATE DEPARTMENT CLEAR

So Asserts Its Security Chief in Reply to McCarthy Charge— Lattimore on Stand Today

By WILLIAM S. WHITE
Special to The New York Times.

WASHINGTON, April 5 — The highest official in the loyalty program swore today that 10,000 full field investigations in three years of screening had produced "not one single case" of espionage anywhere in the Federal Government's ranks.

Moreover, he added, no evidence even "directing toward espionage" had been found by the Federal Bureau of Investigation, either in these field inquiries concerning persons about whom some specific question had been raised or in a more general consideration of "3,000,000 files."

This was the testimony of Seth W. Richardson, chairman of the Loyalty Review Board, before a Senate subcommittee which is investigating Senator Joseph R. McCarthy's charges of heavy Communist infiltration of the State Department. Mr. Richardson is a Republican who served as an Assistant Attorney General in the administration of Herbert Hoover.

Mr. Richardson, himself, mentioned the case of Judith Coplon, who was convicted of taking secret files from the Department of Justice. But he said that neither suspicion nor detection of her activities had arisen from the loyalty program, but rather from the internal operations of the Department of Justice itself.

Brig. Gen. Conrad E. Snow (Reserve), chairman of the State Department's own Loyalty Security Board, a body subordinate to that of Mr. Richardson, told the subcommittee:

"If there are any Communists in the State Department, the Loyalty Security Board is uninformed of their existence." General Snow described himself as "Republican all my life."

Senator McCarthy, a Republican of Wisconsin, had asserted in a Senate speech Feb. 20 that "at least fifty-seven Communists" were or recently had been in the department.

Since then, he has declared himself willing to "stand or fall" in his entire campaign on his accusations against Prof. Owen Lattimore of Johns Hopkins University, whom the Senator had accused of being a Communist and "top Soviet agent" while serving as a State Department consultant on Far Eastern affairs.

As the subcommittee prepared to hear tomorrow Professor Lattimore's rebuttal under oath, in what all regarded as a moment of climax for the whole Senate investigation, he was denounced by Senator William F. Knowland, Republican of California.

Senator Knowland in a statement to the press asserted that Professor Lattimore, in a recently published advisory memorandum to the State Department which was made seven months ago, had in effect recommended that Japan be allowed to fall into "the orbit of international communism."

Professor Lattimore, Mr. Knowland added, had "consistently and insistently played an important part in the undermining of the Republic of China" in its struggles with its Communist antagonists.

"Professor Lattimore and others he has influenced in the Far Eastern Division of the State Department," Senator Knowland added, "have made a mighty contribution to the débâcle which has taken place in China."

Senator McCarthy, for his part, declined at noon today the request of the subcommittee's chairman, Senator Millard E. Tydings, Democrat of Maryland, that he turn over any additional information against the persons he accused.

Having previously stated that he would hand in to the subcommittee nothing that might disclose the source of his information or affidavits, Mr. McCarthy had been asked by Mr. Tydings to give up any data that would make no such disclosures.

Tydings Does Nothing, He Says

In the first of a series of letters exchanged during the day, Senator McCarthy retorted that he found it "difficult to understand the urgency of this request for further information in view of the fact that you [Senator Tydings] have done absolutely nothing with the great wealth of material turned over to you during the past five weeks."

While he was not ready now to turn in further data, Mr. McCarthy went on, he felt "reasonably certain" that if a firm date was fixed for their testimony he would be able to produce certain witnesses, not yet identified, whom he had mentioned in attacking Professor Lattimore.

"If you will give me your solemn promise that they will be heard on such date as you set," Senator McCarthy continued, "I shall undoubtedly be able to arrange for the appearance of some, if not all, of those witnesses.

"I am sure, however, that they will object to having their names made public unless they are assured they will actually be subpoenaed to testify. In other words, they would not be willing to be badgered and heckled unless the subcommittee is going to make use of their testimony.

"If you will set some date next week for such appearances and will hand me subpoenas, I shall attempt to contact them [the witnesses] over the week-end and serve the subpoenas."

Mr. Tydings first replied to this with the comment: "That response of Senator McCarthy's speaks for itself." Later, he fixed Thursday of next week for hearing any witnesses Mr. McCarthy brought forward.

Senator McCarthy then sent a second letter to Senator Tydings, asking to be allowed to cross-examine Professor Lattimore when he testifies tomorrow.

Mr. Tydings at once denied this permission, offering to allow Mr. McCarthy to put questions to Professor Lattimore through members of the subcommittee, but recalling that those whom the Wisconsin Senator had attacked from the stand had had no opportunity to cross-examine him.

Mr. McCarthy again attacked Ambassador-at-large Philip C. Jessup, asserting that if he had been permitted to examine that official in his appearance before the subcommittee he would have inquired "about the Communist funds received by Mr. Jessup at the time his publication was so clearly following the Communist party line."

This referred to accusations made some time ago on the Senate floor—and repudiated by Dr. Jessup — that the Ambassador through a connection with the American Council of the Institute of Pacific Relations had conducted a "smear campaign" against Chiang Kai-shek, leader of the China Nationalists, to which money from Communist sources had been contributed.

Mr. Richardson, in his testimony

before the subcommittee, defended the loyalty program as one that had raised, rather than lowered, the morale of Federal employes because long inquiries by the Federal Bureau of Investigation had found "anything wrong with less than one-twentieth of 1 per cent" of their colleagues.

He announced that in proceeding as directed by President Truman to review the loyalty files of all persons accused by Senator McCarthy, he was calling on the Senator, and the subcommittee as well, to come forward with all "relevant evidence" in their possession.

The board's investigation, he said, would encompass only those charged with disloyalty, and not those accused of being bad security risks, a category in which many of Mr. McCarthy's accusations had rested.

The review was being thus limited, Mr. Richardson said, by the terms of the President's request for it and by the fact that the subcommittee's own mandate from the Senate did not mention security risks but only those charged with disloyalty.

The ultimate findings, he added, would be turned over to the President alone.

Describing the whole of the loyalty procedure, Mr. Richardson testified that his board, which is to the departmental boards what the Supreme Court is to the inferior courts, had restored to their federal positions 124 persons whose departmental boards had sought to oust as suspected of disloyalty or indiscretion.

These reversals, he went on, in

no case involved a finding of the State Department Loyalty Security Board, which General Snow had just stated had standards of greater rigor than elsewhere in the Government.

The review board, Mr. Richardson said, was a part-time body of twenty-six men active in the law, education and business which was paid "only when it works," and he thought its members were about "evenly divided between the Democratic and Republican parties."

As to the fact that no trace of espionage had been found, Mr. Richardson said that after the loyalty program was instituted by the President in 1947 there was "an immense increase in resignations" from the Federal service. This no doubt could be explained, in part at least, he observed, "by the fact that there were some people who didn't care to meet the test of the F. B. I."

The board had been responsible to date, he disclosed, for the dismissal from the Federal payroll of 182 persons. This, it was made clear, did not reflect the total of those discharged as presumably disloyal or security risks in the last three years, but only those upon whose cases the board itself had adversely passed.

General Snow, head of the State Department Loyalty Security Board, testified that under procedures first approved by Gen. George C. Marshall, as Secretary of State, and supplemented in the general loyalty program of President Truman, he and his associates always "gave the Government the

benefit of the doubt" in cases before them.

The board, he said, had never been reversed on appeal to Mr. Richardson's higher body, nor had the State Department ever rejected one of its recommendations for the ouster of an employe.

Asked by Senator Bourke B. Hickenlooper, Republican of Iowa, whether membership by a State Department official in organizations that might later have been declared subversive was not "significant," General Snow asserted that this was not necessarily so.

Donald L. Nicholson, chief of the State Department's division of security, presented graphs and other matter to show how its screening process operated. He testified that in many matters the State Department had the help of the F.B.I.'s investigative machinery as well as that of its own permanent investigative branch.

He testified that no person who came to the State Department as a consultant or lecturer could have access to any secret document and that no such person was "processed" by the investigators "because there would be no reason for it."

Professor Lattimore has been described by the State Department as substantially in the category of an occasional lecturer and visitor. The subcommittee was informed by General Snow that to be termed "a security risk" did not suggest disloyalty "or any kind of guilt," but only that the person so labeled might let out unauthorized secret information.

April 6, 1950

LATTIMORE DENIES HE WAS EVER A RED; TYDINGS CLEARS HIM

Professor Tells Senate Inquiry McCarthy Is 'Willing Tool' of 'China Lobby' in U. S.

CHAIRMAN BACKS WITNESS

Says F.B.I. File Bared Nothing —Accused Expert Testifies He Never Met Acheson

By WILLIAM S. WHITE
Special to The New York Times.

WASHINGTON, April 6 — Prof. Owen Lattimore swore today that he was not and never had been a Communist, a Communist sympathizer or a Communist agent.

He took this "solemn oath," he said, in full awareness that "perjured or mistaken testimony could

be used for entrapment."

He denounced his accuser, Senator Joseph R. McCarthy, Republican of Wisconsin, as "the willing tool" of an "implacable" pro-Nationalist China lobby which was seeking by intimidation to silence all in the United States, including the State Department itself, who were opposed to further aid to the Chiang Kai-shek regime.

Then, at the end of a long and bitter day before a Senate investigating subcommittee, he was in effect absolved by its chairman, Senator Millard E. Tydings, Democrat of Maryland, of Mr. McCarthy's charges.

"Nothing to Show" Party Tie

From the bench, Mr. Tydings told Professor Lattimore:

"Your case has been designated by Senator McCarthy as his No. 1 case [in his accusations of heavy Communist infiltration of the State Department]. As chairman I think I owe it to you and to the country to tell you that four members of this subcommittee recently had a complete summary of your loyalty file read to us in the presence of Mr. J. Edgar Hoover, head of the Federal Bureau of Investigation.

"At the conclusion of the reading it was the unanimous opinion of all members of the subcommit-

tee and of all others in the room that there is nothing in the files to show you have ever been a Communist or ever have been connected with espionage.

"So that the F. B. I. file puts you completely, up to this moment at least, in the clear."

Senator McCarthy said of this to reporters:

"Either Tydings hasn't seen the files, or he is lying. There is no other alternative."

Told of this, Mr. Tydings observed:

"I'll let my reputation for accuracy stand. It is significant that no member of the subcommittee contradicted the statement when I made it."

Senator McCarthy had said he would "stand or fall" on the Lattimore case in his whole drive against the State Department, and today, when asked about this statement, he said:

"I am retracting nothing. I intend to prove everything right down the line."

Senator Tydings emphasized that those present when the Lattimore file was summarized included one of the two Republican members of the subcommittee, Senator Henry Cabot Lodge Jr., of Massachusetts. The non-members present, he said,

were J. Howard McGrath, Attorney General; Peyton Ford, First Assistant Attorney General, and Mr. Hoover.

Witness Calls Record Clean

Senator Bourke B. Hickenlooper, Republican of Iowa, asked Mr. Lattimore if he would object to having his complete file turned over to the investigators, and the Far East consultant replied:

"As far as I am concerned, my record is open and clean and I do not mind any form of fair investigation that would help me prove it."

But, in referring to the fact that President Truman had ordered all loyalty data to be kept in confidence, Mr. Lattimore added:

"As an individual it would not be fair for me to ask special treatment apart from the regular procedures. If I asked for the file, it would be asking a favor, and that I refuse to do."

He challenged Senator McCarthy to repeat his accusations outside of Congress, and thus without immunity from libel suit.

To this Mr. McCarthy replied, to reporters, that he would not repeat his charges unless the loyalty files were obtained so that they could be "tested in a libel action." These charges were that the Johns

THEY CAME FACE TO FACE IN WASHINGTON YESTERDAY

Hopkins professor was a Communist, "the top Soviet agent" in the United States and the "architect" of a Far Eastern policy that had "betrayed" Nationalist China to the Communists.

Pictured by Senator McCarthy as a dominating influence over Secretary of State Dean Acheson's Far Eastern policy, Mr. Lattimore testified that he had never even met Mr. Acheson, thus corroborating a recent statement of the Secretary that to the best of his recollection he did not know the professor.

Actually, Professor Lattimore declared, State Department policy on the Far East had run almost exactly counter to his own ideas in many major matters, and he was of all Far Eastern experts "the least consulted."

He agreed that in an advisory memorandum to the State Department last August he had recommended against further help to the China Nationalists, but declared that in this he was convinced that advancing more money would tend to aid the Communists rather than otherwise.

As to the fact that in the mid-forties he had supported the notion of admitting Chinese Communists into the Nationalist Government, he asserted that in this he was following the lead of such men as Gen. George C. Marshall.

Professor Lattimore, who sat all day under the hot glare of floodlights, attacked Senator McCarthy as one who had told "base and contemptible" lies and had prepared his evidence by "perverse and twisted" quotations out of context.

He used as an illustration a letter from which Mr. McCarthy had quoted excerpts on the Senate floor. The latter had summarized the document on the floor with assertions to the effect that it showed that Professor Lattimore, as an official of the Office of War Information, in 1943 had "directed" a colleague, Joseph Barnes, to discharge all Chinese Nationalist employes and recruit Communists.

Abe Fortas, Professor Lattimore's chief counsel, read the whole letter into the record. It included the following:

"In the circumstances, we have to be extremely careful about our Chinese personnel. While we need to avoid recruiting any Chinese Communists, we must be careful not to be frightened out of hiring people who have loosely been accused of being Communists."

Nationalist "Lobby" Is Hit

As to his charge that Senator McCarthy was the "tool" of a pro-Chiang lobby, Mr. Lattimore asserted that the Senator had used accusations "exactly similar" to those which had been distributed earlier by William J. Goodwin.

Mr. Goodwin, the professor continued, was "registered both as a lobbyist and the agent of a foreign power, namely, the Nationalist Government of China," and was being paid about $36,000 a year "plus some expenses."

The "fanatical group" that Senator McCarthy was serving, as "instrument or dupe," was using "methods to intimidate persons like me and even officials of the United States Government from expressing views that are contrary to their

Prof. Owen Lattimore testifying

Senator Joseph R. McCarthy listening

The New York Times (by George Tames)

own," Professor Lattimore asserted.

"Their weapon of intimidation," he went on, "is McCarthy's machine-gun—namely, accusation of disloyalty and traitorous conduct.

"I get a certain amount of wry amusement out of the fact that some of these people are acknowledged ex-Communists. Perhaps that status gives them a special right to criticize those who do not happen to be Communists, ex or otherwise.

"Certainly it provides them with ideal training and unique skill for the kind of vilification and distorton that the so-called China lobby is conducting through the instrumentality of the Senator from Wisconsin.

"I believe that both capitalism and political democracy have immense vitality and adaptability. If they fail to survive, I believe it will be because of dogmatic or uninformed men who insist on policies of coercion, repression and inequality—not because of inherent defects in capitalism and democracy.

"If the people of this country can differ with the so-called China lobby or with Senator McCarthy only at the risk of the abuse to which I have been subjected, freedom will not long survive.

"If officials of our Government cannot consult people of diverse views without exposing themselves to the kind of attack that Senator McCarthy has visited upon officers of the State Department, our governmental policy will necessarily be sterile.

"It is only from a diversity of views freely expressed and strongly advocated that sound policy is distilled. He who contributes to the destruction of this process is either a fool or an enemy of his country."

Mr. Lattimore paused at this point, raised his voice, stared at Senator McCarthy, and added:

"Let Senator McCarthy take note of this."

There was applause in the room. Senator McCarthy himself, who attended the morning session but did not return this afternoon, had protested the subcommittee's refusal to let him cross-examine Professor Lattimore.

Professor Lattimore, who is head of the Walter Hines Page School of International Relations at Johns Hopkins University, was cross-examined at length by Senator Hickenlooper, who said twice that he was approaching the matter "with no preconceptions."

The witness agreed that he had recommended that this country make no attempt to help hold Formosa, the last stronghold of the China Nationalists, and the Republic of Korea from the Communists. Senator Hickenlooper sought to show that this paralleled the policies urged by the Communists.

Professor Lattimore asserted in substance that he had taken those views quite independently of the Communists. He still believed, he said, that aid to "corrupt and brutal" forces in China's Nationalist regime and to the "police state" officials of Korea simply would "push" the oriental peoples,

in their "disgust," farther into Soviet hands.

"The fact simply is," he added, "that the position in Formosa is untenable. To have to give it up later, in conditions where every potty little Communist committee can crow over us, would be very humiliating."

Asked who had recommended him to be political adviser to Chiang Kai-shek in 1941, Professor Lattimore replied that he did not know but that Lauchlin Currie, then a White House assistant to President Roosevelt, had first telephoned him about the mission.

Trip With Wallace Recalled

In accompanying the then Vice President Henry Wallace to China in 1944, the witness said, he was acting as an official of the Office of War Information and assumed that his assignment came from President Roosevelt.

He said in another connection that he had returned with the view that he could not support Mr. Wallace politically and that he had not done so when the former Vice President ran for President on a third party ticket in 1948.

Professor Lattimore began his forty-two page prepared manuscript, to which was added many pages of excerpts from prominent persons who had written in his behalf, by saying that Mr. McCarthy's conduct had been "unworthy of a Senator or an American."

"He has violated it [his office]," Professor Lattimore went on, "by impairing the effectiveness of the United States Government in its relations with its friends and allies, and by making the Government of the United States an object of suspicion in the eyes of the anti-Communist world and undoubtedly the laughing stock of the Communist Governments.

"He has violated it by instituting a reign of terror among officials and employes in the United States Government, no one of whom can be sure of safety from attack by the machine-gun or irresponsible publicity in Joseph McCarthy's hands.

"He has without authorization used secret documents obtained from official Government files.

"He has vilified citizens of the United States and accused them of high crime, without giving them an opportunity to defend themselves.

"He has refused to submit alleged documentary evidence to a duly constituted committee of the Senate.

"He has invited disrespect to himself and his high office."

"Can't Have It Both Ways"

Professor Lattimore went on then to take up one by one the accusations Senator McCarthy had made against him.

The Senator, the witness said, had quoted a witness to the effect that Professor Lattimore was not a Communist in 1936 but had elsewhere quoted two anonymous "red generals" as having "particularly mentioned Owen Lattimore" in a discussion about espionage in that same year.

"Now," Professor Lattimore added, "I suggest that the Senator can't have it both ways. He and his informants should make up their minds whether I was or was not a Communist in 1936."

Speaking of Senator McCarthy's attacks on the Institute of Pacific Relations, with which Professor Lattimore served, the witness declared that these were almost identical with old and "thoroughly discredited charges" made by Alfred Kohlberg of New York and circulated by Mr. Goodwin.

Referring to Senator McCarthy's statement that he had information that Professor Lattimore had been a leader in "pro-Russian student uprisings" in China, the witness denied this categorically. He offered supporting statements from Nelson T. Johnson, a former Ambassador to China, and T. L. Yuan, formerly head of the Chinese National Library.

As to another McCarthy statement, he declared he "had no connection with Amerasia after 1941, four years before the arrests in the case."

This was a reference to arrests in 1945 of some of the persons connected with that magazine on charges of unlawful possession of government documents.

When he came to Mr. McCarthy's most specific charge, Professor Lattimore told the subcommittee:

"The Senator states that a witness will testify that I was a member of the Communist party, a member over whom they had disciplinary powers.

"I do not know the name of this alleged witness.

"With full and complete realization of the serious implications and consequences of what I am to say; having in mind the advice of counsel that a member of the Communist party may presumably decline on constitutional grounds to state whether he is or has been a member of the Communist party; realizing the possibility that perjured or mistaken testimony may be used for purposes of entrapment—whether innocent or not—I make to you on my solemn oath the following statement:

"I am not and never have been a member of the Communist party. I have never been affiliated with or associated with the Communist party. I have never believed in the principles of communism nor subscribed to nor advocated the Communist or Soviet form of government either within the United States, in China, in the Far East or anywhere in the world.

"I have never consciously or deliberately advocated or participated in promoting the cause of communism anywhere in the world."

Professor Lattimore quoted Soviet denunciations of him as a "learned lackey of imperialism."

As to foreign policy, he asserted that American military support to the Chiang regime on Formosa might make it easy for the Chinese Communists to invite the Russians to come into the Communist mainland with air bases which would remain as a permanent threat to this country.

He went on:

"Accordingly, it is my view that the major American effort must be in one of the other two directions: namely, to encourage a nationalism, even if it is Communist nationalism, capable of standing up to the Soviet Union and maintaining independence in its dealings with us, or to encourage in every possible way the conditions that will make possible the survival of a so-called third force, a democratic group within China, that can change the character of the government.

"It seems to me that our long-term objective should clearly be the latter.

"But it may be that in the short run, while working at this long-term objective, our first objective will have to be to avoid closing the trap on the Chinese, so that they feel they have no alternative but Russia—even if it means temporizing with Titoism.

"Now, gentlemen, my analysis of this may be partly or wholly wrong. But if anybody says that it is disloyal or un-American, he is a fool or a knave."

Senator Tydings said the subcommittee's next meeting would be held behind closed doors Tuesday.

April 7, 1950

PRESIDENT OPENS 81 LOYALTY FILES TO SENATE INQUIRY

He Agrees to Release Records of State Department on Some Accused by McCarthy

F. B. I. DATA HELD BACK

Senator Asserts New Witness Says Russia Received Atomic Secrets Before Hiroshima

By WILLIAM S. WHITE
Special to The New York Times.

WASHINGTON, May 4—President Truman has agreed to open to Senate investigators the State Department's loyalty files on eighty-one persons accused by Senator Joseph R. McCarthy in his campaign alleging Communist penetration of the department.

This was announced late today by Senator Millard E. Tydings, Democrat of Maryland, chairman of a subcommittee that is making the inquiry.

Mr. Tydings asserted that by detailed personal research he had established, and had so reported to the President, that the Wisconsin Republican's eighty-one cases were identically those investigated some three years ago by four committees of the Republican-controlled Eightieth Congress without an adverse finding against any departmental employe.

In view of the fact that such confidential data already had been examined by Congressional bodies, Senator Tydings added, Mr. Truman had decided that the present disclosure would set no precedent and accordingly had reversed his consistent refusals to turn over the files.

Senator Kenneth S. Wherry of Nebraska, the Republican floor leader, asserted for his part that the President had been "afraid" to face the people on his coming Western tour while refusing to surrender the dossiers.

McCarthy Widens Charges

A few hours beforehand, Senator McCarthy had greatly broadened his accusations. He asserted that a witness called by him, Frank Bielaski, was even then testifying in secret before the Tydings subcommittee that State Department personnel six months before the atomic bomb was dropped on Hiroshima had aided in "collecting and transmitting" the weapon's secrets to the Soviet Union.

The witness himself, a security officer for the wartime Office of Strategic Services, told reporters, during a hiatus in his testimony in closed session, that there was "an atomic aspect to it."

When a copy of Mr. McCarthy's statement as to what he would say was shown to Mr. Bielaski he commented that he considered it an "enlargement." He also indicated a reservation particularly to the word "transmitting" in the reference to atomic information and the Soviet Union.

Mr. Bielaski added, however, that "the evidence of which I have knowledge" fully established "the seriousness of the whole matter."

"Without regard to McCarthy, or the evidence I've given the subcommittee," he went on, "of my own knowledge there is something to it."

Senator Tydings declined to comment on what had been asserted by Senator McCarthy, except to say that "surmises" were hampering the investigation, to recall that Mr. McCarthy had not been in the room, and to assert that no one except those present was in a position to give an "accurate" account of what had gone on.

He appealed to the public to withhold judgment until the inquiry had been completed.

President Truman's decision to give access to the State Department files did not meet all Senator McCarthy's present demands. The latter has been insisting on a disclosure also of Federal Bureau of Investigation and civil service dossiers.

On this point, Senator Tydings would say only this to reporters:

"Go back to the Congressional Record of Feb. 20 and see what McCarthy was demanding."

This was the day that Mr. McCarthy first attacked the eighty-one anonymously on the Senate floor, and made them the basis of his campaign. Since then, he has given in public the names of ten of the persons he has accused.

With "one or two exceptions," Mr. Tydings said, data about these ten would be found in the files covering the eighty-one.

There probably would be no dossier on Prof. Owen Lattimore, Senator Tydings added, "since he never was an employe of the State Department."

Senator McCarthy has stated that he would "stand or fall," in all his accusations, on the case of Mr. Lattimore, whom he has called a Communist, a "top Soviet agent" and, as a State Department consultant, the "architect" of a policy that "betrayed" the Chinese Nationalists to the Chinese Communists.

Coincident with Mr. Tydings' announcement about the files, President Truman himself told reporters that he had observed no special concern among the people of the country about the subject of communism.

The people, Mr. Truman said in answer to questions at his news conference, were always uneasy about organizations that advocated the overthrow of this Government, but his mail and the like did not reflect any unusual rise in this fear.

As to Mr. McCarthy, the President said he would not comment on anything the Senator had to say, for it was not worthy of comment.

Mr. Bielaski, who is now head of the Research and Security Corporation in New York, a concern engaged in investigations and publicity work, testified specifically concerning the so-called "Amerasia case." This involved the arrest in 1945 of six persons connected with the magazine Amerasia on charges of the theft of highly confidential government documents.

Among those arrested were John S. Service, a present State Department employe whose loyalty has been questioned by Senator McCarthy, and Emmanuel S. Larsen, then but not now a departmental employe.

Mr. Service was cleared and restored to duty. Mr. Larsen was fined $500. Philip Jaffe, editor of Amerasia, was fined $2,500. Andrew Roth, then a lieutenant in Naval Intelligence; Mark Julius Gayn, a writer, and Kate Louise Mitchell, an editor of Amerasia, were cleared.

With this history for the background, Senator McCarthy issued this morning a statement, which

had been prepared before Mr. Bielaski took the stand at the subcommittee inquiry, that the testimony of the witness would be as follows:

1. That Mr. Bielaski, as a security officer for the Office of Strategic Services, had led a raid on Amerasia on March 11, 1945, and found "reports which showed that six months before the atomic bomb was dropped on Hiroshima the people who operated Amerasia, with the assistance of State Department presonnel, were collecting and transmitting to Soviet Russia the secrets of the atomic bomb."

2. "That top secret State Department reports were found in the Amerasia office.

3. "That an extremely secret report marked 'For Delivery by Officer-Messenger Only to Director of Naval Intelligence' was found in the Amerasia office.

4. "That reports were found in the Amerasia office showing that the interlocking directors of Amerasia and the Institute of Pacific Relations were undermining the Chinese Nationalist Government and were collecting minute details of the anti-Communist armies.

5. "That reports were found in the Amerasia office which dealt with the intimate family relationships of the family of Generalissimo Chiang Kai-shek.

"Espionage Operation So Great"

6. "That the immensity of this espionage operation was so great and the number of stolen secret documents so large that Mr. Bielaski took away fifteen copies which were never even missed by Amerasia personnel before the F. B. I came back to conduct the raid three months later.

7. "That Mr. Bielaski had difficult gaining entrance to the Amerasia office because crews were working all night in its huge photo lab photographing secret Government documents.

8. "That the scope of this operation was such that when the F. B. I. agents raided the office three months later, the documents seen there by Mr. Bielaski were no longer there, they having been copied, removed and replaced by others."

Senator McCarthy gave this summary, of what he said Mr. Bielaski would testify, in a letter addressed to Senator Tydings accusing the Democratic majority of the subcommittee of hearing in open sessions witnesses on the State Department side and in closed session those "who are striving to expose Communists in government."

"Compelled" to Tell the People

He had therefore "felt compelled," Mr. McCarthy went on, to "give the American people" an account of the testimony that Mr. Bielaski was going to present in executive session. He asked also that the subcommittee call as witnesses Maj. Gen. William J. Donovan, head of the Office of Strategic Services, and Archbold Van Beuren, a former official of the agency.

Coincidentally, in returning to Mr. Service, the Senator asserted that the State Department was giving to that official access to material, to be used in his forthcoming loyalty review, that it had denied to the Senate investigators.

The New York Herald Tribune of this morning had carried a Washington dispatch which also stated that material was being made available to Mr. Service's counsel that was being denied to the Senate — specifically, documents that were being declassified and heretofore had been restricted or confidential.

The State Department gave out the text of a letter to Whitelaw Reid, editor of The Herald Tribune, asserting that the headings on this and a previous article had raised

a "natural" inference that the departmental Loyalty Security Board "is either not going forward with the hearing on the case, or is giving Mr. Service's counsel some unfair or illegitimate advantage."

"Neither of these inferences," said the letter, which was written by the board's chairman, Brig. Gen. Conrad E. Snow, "is justified by the facts."

There had been no "indefinite postponement" of the Service hearing, which was "a serious matter and must cover in detail all charges," General Snow wrote.

"The board has an obligation to give him the fullest opportunity to prepare and present his defense," the statement said later.

Tydings Cites Truman Attitude

Mr. Tydings, in disclosing that President Truman was going to allow the subcommittee to see the State Department files, declared that he had actually "got the go-ahead yesterday" from Mr. Truman. He had never "lost hope," he said, that the President ultimately would surrender the data, and had conferred with him about it five or six times.

President Truman, the Senator added, personally had always wanted to turn over the data, but had decided originally not to do so because J. Edgar Hoover, head of the Federal Bureau of Investigation, had so "strongly opposed" any such disclosure.

When he was able to show the President that the dossiers on the eighty-one persons in question had already been examined by committees in the Eightieth Congress, before the present loyalty program was set up, Mr. Tydings asserted, Mr. Truman consented, because no precedent would be involved.

May 5, 1950

Seven G.O.P. Senators Decry 'Smear' Tactics of McCarthy

Attack Led by Mrs. Smith of Maine, Who Also Scores Democratic 'Whitewash'

By WILLIAM S. WHITE
Special to THE NEW YORK TIMES

WASHINGTON, June 1—Seven Republican Senators denounced and repudiated today the tactics of their party colleague, Joseph R. McCarthy of Wisconsin, in his campaign to try to prove Communist penetration of the State Department.

Led by the Senate's only woman member, Margaret Chase Smith of Maine, they issued a "Declaration of Conscience" that accused "certain elements" of a design for "rid-

ing the Republican party to victory through the selfish political exploitation of fear, bigotry, ignorance and intolerance."

They attacked the Democrats as well, specifically accusing the Truman Administration of lacking leadership, of giving "contradictory grave warnings and optimistic assurances," of "complacency" toward communism, of "oversensitiveness to rightful criticism" and of "petty bitterness against its critics."

The other signers of the declaration were Senators Irving M. Ives of New York, a close political associate of Governor Dewey; Charles W. Tobey of New Hampshire, George D. Aiken of Vermont, Robert C. Hendrickson of New Jersey, Edward J. Thye of

Minnesota and Wayne L. Morse of Oregon.

This revolt among the avowedly liberal Republican wing of the Senate against the encouragement given to Senator McCarthy by the party hierarchy came in the midst of an effort by other Republicans to force a full-scale public investigation of the Amerasia case of 1945.

Taking the lead in this drive, Senator William F. Knowland, Republican of California, asserted that grave, "unanswered questions" remained concerning the disposition of the case, which involved the unlawful possession in wartime of secret Government documents.

Mr. Knowland accused the Democratic - controlled investigating subcommittee, which is studying the Amerasia incident as a part of Senator McCarthy's general charges, of "star chamber" proceedings and giving the impression of a "whitewash."

Amerasia, a now defunct magazine that dealt with Far Eastern affairs, was a "'transmission belt" between the Communists and the

State Department, Senator Knowland asserted.

Mrs. Smith read the "Declaration of Conscience" from the floor, as Senator McCarthy sat white and silent hardly three feet behind her. She accompanied the reading with a speech, in which she rebuked Mr. McCarthy, though not by name.

Mr. McCarthy heard her out, then left as she was being congratulated by several colleagues. One of these, Senator H. Alexander Smith, Republican of New Jersey, said that he found nothing in her words "with which I do not wholeheartedly agree."

The whole episode was profoundly comforting to the long-harassed Democrats. Senator Millard E. Tydings, Democrat of Maryland, chairman of the subcommittee investigating the McCarthy charges, offered no direct objection to Mrs. Smith's strictures on his own party. He called her speech "temperate" and "fair" and an act of "stateswomanship."

Asked at his afternoon press conference about the address, with special reference to Mrs. Smith's assertion that she would not like to see the Republicans win on "calumny," President Truman replied, with a broad smile, that he would not want to say anything that bad about the Republican party.

Text of the Declaration

The declaration issued by the seven Senators was as follows:

We are Republicans. But we are Americans first. It is as Americans that we express our concern with the growing confusion that threatens the security and stability of our country. Democrats and Republicans alike have contributed to that confusion.

The Democratic Administration has initially created the confusion by its lack of effective leadership, by its contradictory grave warnings and optimistic assurances, by its complacency to the threat of communism here at home, by its oversensitiveness to rightful criticism, by its petty bitterness against its critics.

Certain elements of the Republican party have materially added to this confusion in the hopes of riding the Republican party to victory through the selfish political exploitation of fear, bigotry, ignorance and intolerance. There are enough mistakes of the Democrats for Republicans to criticize constructively without resorting to political smears.

To this extent, Democrats and Republicans alike have unwittingly, but undeniably, played directly into the Communist design of "confuse, divide and conquer."

It is high time that we stopped thinking politically as Republicans and Democrats about elections and started thinking patriotically as Americans about national security based on individual freedom. It is high time that we all stopped being tools and victims of totalitarian techniques—techniques that, if continued here unchecked, will surely end what we have come to cherish as the American way of life.

Senator Margaret Chase Smith
The New York Times (Washington Bureau)

Mrs. Smith told the Senate at the outset that there was now "a national feeling of fear and frustration that could result in national suicide and the end of everything we Americans hold dear." There was no definite leadership now, she argued, either in the White House or Congress. "I speak as briefly as possible," she said, "because too much harm has already been done with irresponsible words of bitterness and selfish political opportunism.

"The United States Senate has long enjoyed world-wide respect as the greatest deliberative body in the world. But recently, that deliberative character has too often been debased to the level of a forum of hate and character assassination sheltered by the shield of Congressional immunity.

"It is ironical that we Senators can in debate in the Senate di-

rectly or indirectly impute to any American, who is not a Senator, any conduct or motive unworthy or unbecoming an American—and without that non-Senator American having any legal redress against us—yet if we say the same thing in the Senate about our colleagues, we can be stopped on the grounds of being out of order.

"I think it is high time that we remembered that we have sworn to uphold and defend the Constitution. I think it is high time that we remembered that the Constitution, as amended, speaks not only of the freedom of speech, but also of trial by jury instead of trial by accusation.

"Whether it be a criminal prosecution in court or a character prosecution in the Senate, there is no practical distinction when the life of a person has been ruined.

"Those of us who shout the loudest about Americanism in making character assassinations are all too frequently those who, by our own words and acts, ignore some of the basic principles of Americanism—the right to criticize, the right to hold unpopular beliefs, the right to protest, the right to independent thought.

"The American people are sick and tired of being afraid to speak their minds lest they be politically smeared as 'Communists' or 'Fascists' by their opponents. Freedom of speech is not what it used to be in America. It has been so abused by some that it is not exercised by others.

"The American people are sick and tired of seeing innocent people smeared and guilty people whitewashed. But there have been enough proved cases to cause nation-wide distrust and strong suspicion that there may be something to unproved, sensational accusations."

The country, Mrs. Smith asserted, was "being psychologically divided by the confusions and the suspicions that are bred in the Senate to spread like cancerous tenacles of 'know nothing, suspect everything' attitudes.

"Today we have a Democratic

Administration that has developed a mania for loose spending and loose programs. History is repeating itself—and the Republican party again has the opportunity to emerge as the champions of unity and prudence.

"The record of the present Democratic Administration has provided us with sufficient campaign issues without the necessity of resorting to political smears. America is rapidly losing its position as a leader of the world simply because the Democratic Administration has pitifully failed to provide effective leadership.

"The Democratic Administration has greatly lost the confidence of the American people by its complacency to the threat of communism here at home and the leak of vital secrets to Russia through key officials of the Democratic Administration. There are enough proved charges to make this point without diluting our criticism with unproved charges.

"Surely, these are sufficient reasons to make it clear to the American people that it is time for a change and that a Republican victory is necessary to the security of this country. Surely, it is clear that this nation will continue to suffer as long as it is governed by the present ineffective Democratic Administration.

"Yet to displace it with a Republican regime embracing a philosophy that lacks political integrity or intellectual honesty would prove equally disastrous to this nation. The nation sorely needs a Republican victory. But I don't want to see the Republican party ride to a political victory on the Four Horsemen of Calumny—Fear, Ignorance, Bigotry and Smear.

"I don't want to see the Republican party win that way. While it might be a fleeting victory for the Republican party, it would be a more lasting defeat for the American people."

June 2, 1950

Excerpts from Text of Majority Report on Charges by Senator McCarthy

WASHINGTON, July 17 (P)—
Following are textual excerpts from the findings and recommendations of the Democratic majority of the Senate Foreign Relations subcommittee set up to investigate charges by Senator Joseph R. McCarthy, Republican of Wisconsin, that Communists have infiltrated the State Department:

Findings and Conclusions

Despite his denials on the Senate floor, publicly and before this subcommittee, that he made the statement, we find on the evi-

dence that Senator Joseph R. McCarthy, on Feb. 9, 1950, at Wheeling, W. Va., said:

"Ladies and Gentlemen: While I cannot take the time to name all the men in the State Department who have been named as active members of the Communist party and members of a spy ring, I have here in my hand a list of 205; a list of names that were made known to the Secretary of States as being members of the Communist party and who, nevertheless, are still working and shaping policy in the State Department."

Our investigation establishes that the foregoing allegations are

false and, particularly, that Senator McCarthy had no such list as alleged and that there is not one member of the Communist party or of a "spy ring" employed in the State Department known to the Secretary of State or other responsible officials of that department.

We find that on Feb. 20, 1950, at Salt Lake City, Utah, Senator McCarthy said:

"Last night I discussed the Communists in the State Department. I stated that I had the names of fifty-seven card-carrying members of the Communist party."

Our investigation establishes

that Senator McCarthy at no time has had the names of fift--seven card-carrying members of the Communist party in the State Department and that during the course of a four months' investigation he has been unable to produce competent evidence or to indicate where such evidence is obtainable concerning one member of the Communist party, card-carrying or otherwise, who is employed in the State Department.

We find that on the evening of Feb. 11, 1950, at Reno, Nev., Senator McCarthy again spoke on the question. As reported in The Nevada State Journal:

"Senator McCarthy, who had first typed a total of 205 employes of the State Department who could be considered disloyal to the United States and pro-Communists, scratched out that number, and mentioned only 'fifty-seven card-carrying members' whom Acheson [Secretary of State Dean Acheson] should know as well as members of Congress."

We find that in making a speech on the Senate floor on Feb. 20, 1950, Senator McCarthy read what purported to be the speech delivered by him at Wheeling, W. Va.; that the purported speech as read to the Senate was identical with the speech delivered at Wheeling except that he withheld from the Senate the statement actually made, as set forth in Conclusion 1 above, and substituted in lieu thereof the following:

"I have in my hand fifty-seven cases of individuals who would appear to be either card-carrying members or certainly loyal to the Communist party, but who nevertheless are still helping to shape our foreign policy."

The substitution of the foregoing terminology constituted a misrepresentation of the true facts to the Senate.

We find that in making his speech on Feb. 20, 1950, which occasioned the passage of Senate Resolution 231, Senator McCarthy left the unmistakable inference that he had but recently obtained from unrevealed sources in the State Department the information which he was presenting to the Senate.

Our investigation establishes that the material presented in this speech was data developed in 1947 by the Republican controlled Eightieth Congress; and that representations indicating it had recently come from "loyal" State Department employes misled and deceived the Senate.

We find that the information presented to the Senate on Feb. 20, 1950, by Senator McCarthy, concerning "eighty-one" individuals identified by him only by numbers, was a colored and distorted version of material developed by investigators of the House Appropriations Committee in 1947 during the Eightieth Congress.

To the extent that the information was colored and distorted and the source thereof concealed the Senate was deceived.

We find that four separate committees of the Eightieth Congress, controlled by Senator McCarthy's own party, formally considered the same information relative to the "eighty-one" individuals, as that utilized in the Senator's speech, and did not regard such information as sufficiently significant to prepare a report relative to the matter or to cite a single employe of the State Department as disloyal. * * *

We find that Senator McCarthy failed to cooperate with the subcommittee or to supply further information concerning the "eighty-one" individuals mentioned in his speech of Feb. 20, 1950, after having assured the Senate that he would "be willing, happy, and eager to go before any committee and give the names and all the information available."

Our investigation establishes that the only logical reason for the Senator's noncooperation and failure to supply further informa-

tion was the fact that he had no information to supply.

We find that Senator McCarthy asserted the proof to sustain his charges against the "eighty-one" individuals would be found in the loyalty files concerning them.

Our review of these files reveals that they do not contain proof to support the charges.* * * Amazingly, despite Senator McCarthy's insistence that the loyalty files would prove his case and the clamor that the files be opened after the President made the files available to us, Senator Hickenlooper [Senator Bourke B. Hickenlooper, Republican of Iowa, a member of the committee] read only nine of the files and Senator Lodge [Senator Henry Cabot Lodge Jr., Republican of Massachusetts, also a member of the committee] only twelve.

Our investigation reveals that the loyalty program is of indispensable value in protecting both the employe and the security of the Federal service and that it is being efficiently administered, specifically:

(a) That the F. B. I.'s loyalty investigations are comprehensive and conclusive with respect to the facts.

(b) That the State Department's Security Division is efficiently operated by highly qualified personnel.

(c) That the Loyalty ad Security Board of the State Department is made up of high-type individuals of unquestioned loyalty, integrity and sound judgment.

(d) That the Loyalty Review Board provides an effective and salutary control over the functioning of the loyalty program.

Our conclusions with respect to each of the individuals publicly charged by Senator McCarthy are being restated as follows:

(a) Esther Caukin Brunauer

* * * The evidence against Mrs. Brunauer, under impartial examination, reduces itself to the fact that she was a member of one organization five years before it was cited as a Communist front, and that in 1934 and 1936, over fourteen years ago, she participated in two meetings sponsored by a pro-Soviet organization of which she was not a member * * *.

The conclusion is inescapable, on the basis of our inquiry, that there is no evidence that Mrs. Brunauer is disloyal, a Communist sympathizer or a security risk.

(b) Gustavo Duran

Duran was employed in the State Department from Jan. 30, 1943, to Oct. 3, 1946, when he resigned. In view of the fact that his employment in the department ceased before the loyalty program was instituted, we do not feel that a discussion of him is merited in our report * * *

(c) Haldore Hanson

It is clear from the evidence concerning Hanson, that he is not "one of the most strategically important officers in the entire State Department" as charged by Senator McCarthy, and that he will not be in charge of the expenditure of hundreds of millions of dollars under the Point Four program * * *

On the basis of our record and the results of the FBI investi-

gation as indicated by the Loyalty Board's action, we do not find Haldore Hanson to be disloyal, or a man with pro-Communist proclivities or a mission to communize the world.

(d) Philip C. Jessup

The facts before us fail completely to establish that Philip C. Jessup has "an unusual affinity for Communist causes" or is a "dupe" of anyone.

His connections with the Institute of Pacific Relations do not in any way reflect unfavorably upon him when the true character of the organization is revealed. Of the many thousands of dollars received by the institute as contributions, only a few thousand dollars are shown to have come from Communist contributors. Many prominent men of unquestioned loyalty and integrity have been instrumental in the management of the organization and in making financial contributions to it. It is noteworthy that only the California Committee on Un-American Activities has cited the American Council of the institute as a Communist front, and that was done in its 1948 report, two years after Dr. Jessup had resigned.

Senator McCarthy also charged that Dr. Jessup opposed an attempt to investigate the Institute of Pacific Relations to determine if it were Communist-controlled. It had been shown that this reference is to an attempt made by Alfred Kohlberg to wrest control of the institute. The dispute was primarily a private feud between the controlling group and the faction supporting Kohlberg which resulted in overwhelming defeat for Kohlberg and his faction. While we do not pass on the merits of the contest, it is apparent that this is a correct explanation of the incident in contradiction of the erroneous interpretation given it by Senator McCarthy.

We also cannot find any evidence to support the allegation that Dr. Jessup was in control of the publication Far Eastern Survey or that that magazine took part in a "smear campaign" against Chiang Kai-shek * * *

Only a casual review of the record is required to demonstrate the erroneous and misleading character of the charge that Dr. Jessup has been affiliated with five Communist-front organizations * * *

* * * This subcommittee feels that the accusations made against Dr. Philip C. Jessup are completely unfounded and unjustified and have done irreparable harm to the prestige of the United States.

(e) Dorothy Kenyon

The evidence before this subcommittee fails to establish that Dorothy Kenyon is a Communist or an otherwise disloyal person. It is apparent that she was less than judicious in joining certain organizations during the late 1930's and early 1940's. Significantly, however, though her name has been associated in one manner or another with twenty different cited organizations, she was found to be connected on but one occasion with an organization after it was cited as subversive. Moreover, many of the alleged associations were denied or explained. In other cases, she had a great deal of distinguished company * * *

* * * We do not find that aer employment in the past by the State Department is evidence of the fact that that department has employed disloyal persons.

(f) Owen Lattimore

We find that Owen Lattimore is not now and never has been in any proper sense an employe of our State Department. His connection with that department in any capacity has been at most peripheral and that on a most sporadic basis.

Far from being the "architect of our Far Eastern policy," we find that Mr. Lattimore has had no controlling or effective influence whatever on that policy.

His views have but been among those of hundreds of others that have gone into the cauldron from which emerges the source material that the policy makers of our State Department employed in making their judgments.

We find no evidence to support the charge that Owen Lattimore is the "top Russian spy" or, for that matter, any other sort of spy. Even the testimony of Louis F. Budenz, if given the fullest weight and import, could establish no more than that the Communists used Lattimore to project a propaganda line anent China. We have every confidence that were Mr. Lattimore an espionage agent the efficient F B I would long since have taken action against him.

Owen Lattimore is a writer and a scholar who has been charged with a record of pro-communism going back many years. There is no legal evidence before us whatever to support this charge and the weight of all other information indicates that it is not true. For the greater portion of his life Mr. Lattimore has made studies concerning Mongolia, a land little known to most Americans. These studies have brought him physically into contact with peoples whose lives have been influenced and conditioned, to a lesser degree, by Sino-Russian influences. In making his studies, Mr. Lattimore has found it necessary perforce to come into contact with and study these influences.

We find absolutely no evidence to indicate that his writings and other expressions have been anything but the honest opinions and convictions of Owen Lattimore. Similar opinions and convictions vis-a-vis the Far East are entertained by many Americans about whom no conceivable suggestion of Communist proclivities could be entertained. We do not find that Mr. Lattimore's writings follow the Communist or any other line, save as his very consistent position on the Far East may be called the Lattimore line.

* * * Perhaps, in many of his contacts, Mr. Lattimore has not exercised the discretion which our knowledge of communism in 1950 indicates would have been wise, but we are impelled to comment that in no instance has Mr. Lattimore on the evidence before us been shown to have knowingly associated with Communists. The convenient theory suggested to us that he must have known has not yet become the criterion for judging a private citizen in this country * * *

In our view, the Lattimore case affords an opportunity to reaffirm this nation's determination to protect its citizens when they, not as minions or agents of a foreign power or subversive group but as independent researchers, writers and speakers, express freely their honest views and convictions * * *

(g) Frederick L. Schuman

Our inquiry establishes that Dr. Frederick L. Schuman has never been an employe of the State Department. In fact, his one and only connection with the department in any way was to deliver a one-hour lecture, without remuneration, at the Foreign Service Institute on June 19, 1946.

(h) John Stewart Service

We have carefully considered the evidence and conclude that John Stewart Service is neither a disloyal person, a pro-Communist, nor a security risk. We have been particularly impressed with the frankness and cooperativeness of Mr. Service in his appearances before us. Many questions with hidden implications have been asked him about events that transpired many years ago. Never did he seek to avoid answering on the ground he could not remember but always gave this subcommittee the benefit of any recollection he might have. In addition, he waved his immunity and voluntarily appeared before the grand jury in August of 1945. After hearing all the facts, the grand jury unanimously voted not to indict Mr. Service. We could not fail to be impressed also by the almost continuous scrutiny to which he has been subjected during the last five years. He has been cleared four times by either the State Department Personnel Board or the State Department Security and Loyalty Board.

While not condoning it, we recognize that it was an accepted practice for State Department officials to impart some types of classified information to writers in order to give them background information for their articles. John S. Service was in an unusual position in China and, in accordance with General Stilwell's wishes [Gen. Joseph W. Stilwell], he maintained relations with the representatives in China of the American press in order to brief them on political and quasi-military developments in the China theater.

He appears to have been allowed a greater freedom in contacts with the press than would an officer in a similar position in Washington. It should also be emphasized that both Mark Gayn and Philip Jaffe were considered reputable newsmen and writers by the public in the spring of 1945 when Service first met them. Mark Gayn was known for his articles in Collier's and the Saturday Evening Post and had also worked for Time and Fortune.

Mr. Service was unaware of the changes in the editorial board of Amerasia and still considered it an impartial authority on Far Eastern affairs. Because of the limited number of writers specializing on China, it was natural that he would expect experts in that field, like Gayn and Jaffe, to show a greater interest in his material than the average writer. In addition, it is undisputed that Mr. Service was seeing other

correspondents during this same period.

We must conclude that Service was extremely indiscreet in his dealings with Gayn and Jaffe, a fact which he himself readily admits. Perhaps the State Department's administration process was at fault in failing to brief its employes coming into Washington on short consultations on how they should treat the press during their stay. But we cannot and do not conclude that his indiscretion in the Amerasia matter is sufficient to brand an otherwise competent and loyal employe of seventeen years' service as disloyal, pro-Communist, or a security risk.

(i) Harlow Shapley

Our inquiry establishes that Dr. Shapley is not an employe of the Department of State in any real and proper sense * * *
Within the proper purview of our inquiry, no consideration need be given the charges made against Dr. Shapley.

(j) John Carter Vincent

While not among the nine individuals charged before us, Senator McCarthy has had a great deal to say reflecting upon the loyalty of Mr. John Carter Vincent, the American Minister to Switzerland. He referred to Mr. Vincent, who was No. 2 among the so-called eighty-one cases, as (1) a big Communist tremendously important to Russia, as (2) a part of an espionage ring in the State Department, and (3) as one who should "not only be discharged but should be immediately prosecuted."

In passing, it should be stated that we have carefully reviewed the loyalty file concerning Mr. Vincent, and the McCarthy charges are absurd. The file does not show him to be disloyal or a security risk.

Relative to the Amerasia case * * * We find there is not one shred of evidence to support the unwarranted charge that the Amerasia case was "fixed" in any manner; and that responsible prosecutive officials had absolutely a free rein in handling the case in their best judgment.

We find that three bodies have now investigated the Amerasia case (1) a committee of the House of Representatives in 1946 (2) a special grand jury in New York City in 1950, and (3) this subcommittee, and that each inquiry has established that the case was not improperly handled either by the F. B. I. in the investigation or the Department of Justice in the prosecution.

While the investigation by the F. B. I. failed to establish foreign-inspired or directed espionage, the Amerasia case represents a disgusting and inexcusable effort to obtain unlawfully classified documents of the United States Government.

A companion consideration, in contemplation of future security, is our finding that the system and method of classification existing at the time was ridiculous. Documents clearly were classified in a haphazard and juvenile fashion with an almost total disregard as to whether the information contained in the documents was of a character warranting classification. This practice clearly had the effect of vitiating the significance of doc-

ument: warranting classification * * *

This subcommittee has been subjected to an organized campaign of unwarranted and unfair vilification without parallel in the history of Congressional investigations. This vilification included repeated charges that we were attempting to "whitewash" the State and Justice Departments * * *

The subcommittee, unfortunately, has been burdened in its work by reason of the failure of the two minority members to attend subcommittee sessions with any degree of regularity. Out of thirty-one sessions, the senior Senator from Iowa [Senator Hickenlooper] attended only twenty-six sessions and the junior Senator from Massachusetts [Senator Lodge] only twenty-two. Significantly, a substantial percentage of those absences occurred during our consideration of the Amerasia case.

Additionally, we were confronted with the extremely anomalous situation of the minority members being unable to agree on whether the sessions should be public or executive. Senator Hickenlooper insisted on public sessions; Senator Lodge insisted that "the show be taken off the road" and all hearings be in executive session * * *

The job of getting the facts concerning disloyal persons and protecting the Government against foreign penetration belongs essentially to the FBI. Inherent in the charges that have been made is the suggestion that the FBI has not done its job well. We do not find this to be true; on the contrary, all evidence points to the fact that the FBI is fully capable of discharging its responsibility now and in the future, as it has in the past.

We are fully satisfied that the FBI and the security staff of the State Department are eminently qualified to ferret out individuals who may be disloyal in the State Department, and that the responsible officials of that department possess the character, integrity, ability and loyalty to take appropriate corrective action in any instance where the facts as developed by investigation indicate the necessity therefor.

We have found that the complaint of Senator McCarthy concerning disloyalty in the State Department, which precipitated our investigation, is false and have fully assured ourselves that the existing agencies and facilities for meeting the problem of security are doing their jobs efficiently and conscientiously. Having made this finding on the basis of the evidence before us, the suggestion that we continue further to "investigate" in the abstract becomes absurd * * *

Inquiries of the character impressed upon us are justified only where evidence exists that our duly constituted agencies of Government have failed to discharge their duty. We find, despite irresponsible representations to the contrary, that absolutely no such evidence existed as a predicate for our inquiry and that after an intensive investigation there is still no such evidence.

We feel that one of the most reprehensible aspects and unfortunate results of unwarranted charges of the type made in this matter is the actual injury done

to the true fight against communism. Such charges, being unproved and not subject to proof, have the effect of dulling the awareness of our people to the menace of communism, unnecessarily embarrass and expose the methods and techniques of our intelligence agencies charged with protecting our security, interfere with and compromise their confidential investigations, destroy the effectiveness of confidential informants, and inevitably give basis for ridicule of those who fight communism with truth, the only weapon with which it can be destroyed.

At a time when American blood is being shed to preserve our dream of freedom, we are constrained fearlessly and frankly to call the charges, and the methods employed to give them ostensible validity, what they truly are: A fraud and a hoax perpetrated on the Senate of the United States and the American people.

They represent perhaps the most nefarious campaign of half-truths and untruth in the history of this Republic. For the first time in our history, we have seen the totalitarian technique of the "big lie" employed on a sustained basis.

The result has been to confuse and divide the American people, at a time when they should be strong in their unity, to a degree far beyond the hopes of the Communists themselves, whose stock in trade is confusion and division. In such a disillusioning setting, we appreciate as never before our Bill of Rights, a free press and the heritage of freedom that has made this nation great

Recommendations
1

While the charges which resulted in Senate Resolution No. 231 have clearly not been sustained upon investigation, it is believed that their inevitable effect, considering the treatment given them by certain segments of the press and radio, has been to disturb the faith of some American citizens in the security of the State Department, one department in which their faith today should and must be strong and secure.

We believe that our findings and conclusions flow naturally from the evidence developed incident to an intensive investigation and are true and judicious; yet we feel that human nature being what it is, particularly in an election year, some Americans may question the findings of any investigative body that may have any degree of political complexion, as, of course, is true of any Congressional committee.

With this in mind, together with the memory of repeated charges, however unwarranted, concerning the loyalty program throughout the Government service as a whole, we make the following recommendation:

(a) That the President of the United States favorably consider the appointment of a commission, in the nature of the Hoover Commission, to make a thorough and comprehensive study of the loyalty program throughout the

Federal service with a view to determining its adequacy to meet the requirements of security at this critical juncture of our international relations:

(b) That this commission be composed of twelve high-minded and public-spirited individuals* * *

II

It is recommended that a joint committee of the House and Senate be appointed to make a careful study of the immunity from civil suit by reason of statements made by them on the floor of either House before Congressional committees.

Our experience in this investigation indicates that this privilege extended us should not become a license for the character assassination of American citizens.

It is believed that from such a study it may be possible to evolve legislation which is designed to preserve this immunity without prejudice to the historic and necessary reasons therefor and at the same time insure that it does not become a shield to perpetrate injustice and fraud.

III

We earnestly recommend that all committees of the Congress exercise the utmost restraint in conducting public hearings relative to proceedings involving questions of the loyalty of a particular individual and that the same be held only in instances of compelling necessity in the public interest or in instances where an individual has been charged publicly and requests a public hearing to present his defense.

By reason of the inveterate practice of Congressional committees to receive evidence and information that are not admissible by legal standards, it is sincerely believed that public hearings involving the loyalty of an individual offer many opportunities for grave injustice to the individual for which there is no redress.

IV

The existing statute relative to immunity from criminal prosecution which is accorded a witness by reason of his testimony before a committee of the Congress has, in practical effect, been declared invalid by the Supreme Court in the case of United States v. Bryan (70 S. CT. 724 (1950); rehearing denied 70 S. CT. 1018 (1950).

Two witnesses have appeared before us and refused to testify, claiming their privilege against self-incrimination under the Fifth Amendment to the Constitution. While contempt citations have been recommended in the case of each of these individuals, it is apparent that even if they are convicted for contempt, we have still been deprived of testimony on matters deemed material to our inquiry.

Such a situation tends to threaten the very foundation of the immemorial prerogative of the Congress to conduct investigations and hearings. It is accordingly recommended that the appropriate committee of each branch of Congress conduct an immediate study with a view to developing a statute which will provide the necessary immunity where testimony is material to an inquiry and at the same time not be a vehicle to be employed by unscrupulous individuals seeking to escape punishment for crimes committed.

V

It is recommended that the State Department take immediate and continuing steps to acquaint the American people with its world-wide security program. We have been greatly impressed with the high caliber of State Department personnel charged with responsibility for security, both in Washington and abroad

We believe the American people would like to know and are entitled to know of the excellent strides which the department has taken to meet the peculiar and manifold problems entailed by the global disposition of its employes, activities and installations.

VI

The Amerasia case revealed that during the last war (1) there was a complete lack of common sense or good judgment shown in the classifying of documents and dispatches and (2) the system, at least at that time, for keeping records which would serve to determine the location of classified material was manifestly inadequate. While it is understood that studies have been made in the Executive Branch of the Government to correct this situation, it is recommended that the President, through the National Security Council or otherwise, determine that such studies have resulted in corrective instructions that have been appropriately implemented * * *.

Respectfully submitted,
MILLARD E. TYDINGS, *Chairman*.
THEODORE FRANCIS GREEN.
BRIEN MCMAHON.

July 18, 1950

Summary by Senator Lodge on Minority's Report on Communism

WASHINGTON, July 17 (AP) — Following is Senator Henry Cabot Lodge's own summary of his 20,000-word minority statement as a Republican member of the Senate Foreign Relations subcommittee set up to investigate charges by Senator Joseph R. McCarthy that Communists have infiltrated the State Department:

1

The investigation must be set down as superficial and inconclusive. The proceedings often lacked impartiality; the atmosphere was too often not that of seeking to ascertain the truth. The subcommittee's record is a tangle of loose threads, of witnesses who were not subpoenaed, of leads which were not followed up.

2

The fact that many charges have been made which have not been proven does not in the slightest degree relieve the subcommittee of the responsibility for undertaking a relentlessly thorough investigation of its own. Senate Resolution 231 carefully did not direct the subcommittee to concentrate on proving or disproving the charges made by one individual. On the contrary Senate Resolution 231 gave the subcommittee a broad directive covering the whole question of disloyalty.

There, nevertheless, was a distinct tendency throughout the investigation to give a far greater amount of time to proving or disproving individual charges than was given to the over-all problem of ferreting out disloyal persons and protecting the Government against foreign penetration. In my view, the emphasis was faulty in this respect.

3

The loyalty files which I read were in such an unfinished state as to indicate that an examination of each file would be a waste of time. There were many instances in those files which I read where hostile and serious allegations were made about the employe concerned, but which in so far as the files were concerned, were left unexplained.

Assuming an average of ten witnesses per file, which is a modest estimate, a thorough study which would establish the credibility of persons making statements and would track down all leads would mean a total of 800 persons to be examined. This is obviously a job which is beyond the reach of any Congressional committee and would probably take a commission of trained men a good six months.

4

The incomplete character of the investigation becomes apparent when one considers the almost endless number of questions which have not even been asked by the subcommittee, samples of which are:

What officials were responsible for placing [Alger] Hiss and [Julian] Wadleigh in the State Department?

What person or persons were primarily responsible for sponsoring for employment of ninety-one sexual perverts who were in the State Department and were reported as having been dismissed as of Jan. 1, 1947?

Were those State Department officials who opposed United States recognition of Soviet Russia and who thereafter warned against any appeasement of the Soviet regime in any way discriminated against by the State Department?

How did Communists use American visas to gain entry into the United States?

What are the facts with reference to the release of two Soviet spies, Gaik Badalovich Ovakimian and Mikhala Nickolavich Goran?

What State Department officials were responsible for advising that the Soviets would allow free elections in Poland, Czechoslovakia, Hungary, Rumania and the other satellite countries?

What are the facts regarding the so-called F. B. I. chart showing that on July 12 there were ten Communists in the State Department?

5

An important element of strength in our system of government is that our "checks and balances" give us as a people the opportunity to criticize ourselves. When this general truth is applied to the ferreting out of disloyalty in the State Department it becomes obvious that the asset which a Congressional committee has, of being independent of the Executive, is accompanied by at least three serious drawbacks:

(1) The members of a Congressional committee clearly lack enough time.

(2) The tools which the Congressional committee has, which are essentially the tools of publicity and development of facts for the use of public opinion, are precisely the implements which cannot be used effectively when it comes to tracking down disloyal persons in the Government departments and which require long, patient detective work which obviously no Congressional committee is in a position to do.

(3) The setting up of a Congressional committee on a majority-minority basis inescapably introduces political considerations into a subject where they very definitely have no place at all.

The result of all these drawbacks has been that the work of the subcommittee has in its end results tended to besmirch the reputations of innocent persons, hamper the work of the Government investigative agencies, impair the position of the United States before the world, reflect unjustly on the many excellent persons in the State Department, discourage other excellent persons from entering the service of the State Department, and, after all these misfortunes, end up with only a most superficial and inclusive finding.

6

Where a Congressional investigation has the advantage of being independent of the executive, the FBI, the security personnel of the State Department and the loyalty boards have advantages which the Congress has not got, to wit: the time to do the work, the technical expertness, and the tools which are needed.

But they are under the executive and it is a basic American instinct that it is not human nature to expect an impartial audit of the executive by the executive. Obviously, therefore, there should be an official group of persons who had the time and the technical expertness and the tools, who were as proficient in their way as the FBI is in its way, and which would be at the same time as independent of the executive as is Congress.

7

I, therefore, favor a bipartisan commission of eight persons, two of whom would be Senators, three to be appointed on behalf of the majority, three on behalf of the minority, to be chosen from a panel to be appointed by the President and to function under the seal of secrecy, making a public announcement of the findings well after the forthcoming election, thereby taking the whole matter out of politics and getting a clean ending to the whole business, let the chips fall where they may.

This business will never end at all, cleanly or otherwise, if the practice of having the majority party investigate the majority continues to hold sway. Nor will satisfactory results be obtained if the minority investigated the majority. The investigation must be nonpolitical.

8

History indicates that Congress acting through investigating committees often acts incompetently. But Congress in the past has evolved and now employs competent men to do its legislative drafting, to make studies of internal revenue taxation and other expert matters. This evolution should continue. Where foreign governments proceeding in secrecy with trained men have achieved splendid results in rooting out espionage, we, with our circus-like proceedings, have bagged only a corporal's guard.

9

In 1945 there was a very serious failure in high places to sense the new realities of the world situation.

(a) This reflected itself in the rapid disintegration of our armed forces whereby the United States in a few short months lost the position of world influence which it had built up through the sacrifice of its fighting men, for it cannot be doubted that if our national leaders in 1945 had clearly stated the need for maintaining adequate armed forces, this disintegration would never have happened.

(b) This awareness of the world situation resulted in the failure to punish adequately those involved in the Amerasia case, and at a time when the nation was at war.

(c) It reflected itself in the case of the State Department in a real negligence about security which reached a climax in late 1945 and early 1946, when over 4,000 persons who had been employed by the F. E. A., O. W. I., O. S. S. and other wartime agencies were transferred to the State Department by a stroke of the pen and without any screening whatever. It is here that a large number of persons managed to get into the State Department who should never have been there at all.

The fact that these transfers occurred has been stated under oath in executive session on the record by those State Department officials having direct responsibility for personnel and security. It cannot, therefore, be dismissed as a partisan or political assertion. This was a negligent act for which we have paid heavily ever since.

10

In the Amerasia case, no satisfactory answer was obtained to the question as to why the criminal division of the Department of Justice failed to prosecute [Philip J.] Jaffee, [Emmanuel S.] Larsen and [Andrew] Roth with vigor, imagination, resourcefulness and enthusiasm. No satisfactory answer was also found to the question why the Department of Justice failed to take advantage of the precedent which it had itself established in similar circumstances in the past.

11

Interviews with a representative cross-section of the security officers showed that no one knew of anyone now in the State Department who was a Communist or whose personal habits were such as to make him a target for blackmail.

12

There are many fine people in the State Department and there are the essential elements of a good security system if it is invigorated and developed. The men who are currently administering the program, from Deputy Under-Secretary [John E.] Peurifoy on down, are running the program in a conscientious manner.

13

Aliens employed in American establishments abroad, some 3,000 in number, should be replaced as rapidly as possible by Americans, giving first priority to those in clerical positions.

14

There should be more agents in the United States and more security officers overseas.

15

The policy should constantly be: Give the Government the benefit of the doubt whenever a personnel question arises.

16

The Loyalty Board should be set up by statute.

17

Loopholes should be blocked to prevent unsatisfactory individuals from going from one sensitive agency to another.

18

A complete revaluation of all State Department personnel in accordance with up-to-date personnel procedures should be undertaken by the commission which is here proposed.

19

It is surely not beyond the bounds of American ingenuity to devise a constitutional method relentlessly to ferret out disloyalty without doing injury to innocent individuals or to the interests of the whole American people in their relations with foreign countries.

* * *

Mr. Lodge also had this to say in past of Owen Lattimore and John S. Service:

* * * The subcommittee's investigation included perusal of the summary of the F. B. I. file on Mr. Lattimore as of March 24, 1950; testimony by all the witnesses whose names are a matter of public record; private cross-examination of Louis F. Budenz, and letters from the last four Secretaries of State bearing on Lattimore's relationship to the State Department.

The subcommittee, however, was denied access to the so-called "raw" F. B. I. file for reasons which are to me understandable, but it did see a summary. We also were denied the benefit of cross-examination in this case conducted by counsel representing the minority, and the opportunity to question in private Mr. Lattimore, J. Edgar Hoover, and those who had presided over the China desk in the State Department and had been United States Ambassadors to China during the period when it was asserted that Mr. Lattimore was the "top architect" of United States foreign policy in the Far East.

Whatever conclusions are to be announced in this case, therefore, must be based both on hearsay evidence and on incomplete investigation, and are inescapably tentative. This is regrettable both from the standpoint of Mr. Lattimore and from the standpoint of the country.

In these circumstances, the only possible conclusion is that the investigation which the subcommittee conducted, and which was, as has been set forth above, definitely limited in its character, not only failed to prove the allegation that Mr. Lattimore was a Communist; it also clearly failed to prove the charges that he was either "the architect of our Far Eastern policy" or "one of the top Communist agents in this country."

* * *

* * * I believe that [John Stewart] Service in the Amerasia case was most indiscreet in his associations, which were entered into in an apparently rapid, thoughtless, and undiscriminating manner. Service was a trusted official of the Government, and this imposed upon him a far greater responsibility for discretion than that imposed upon persons in a less responsible position.

He should certainly not have associated himself with these people without first having made very sure that such association would not endanger the United States or embarrass him or his superiors. He could, it would seem, at least have sought to ascertain the truth about those whom he was seeing so often— during that period. There is no proof of disloyalty and no rumor against his character.

Furthermore, it is evident that Service has a remarkable knowledge of Chinese language and culture. But it must be set down that in the Amerasia case he showed himself to be gullible and indiscreet and that he completely failed to understand the human and political realities which he was confronting.

July 18, 1950

Text of McCarthy Reply

WASHINGTON, July 17 (Æ) — Following is the text of Senator Joseph R. McCarthy's statement on the majority report of a Senate Foreign Relations subcommittee which investigated charges of Communists in the Federal Government:

The Tydings-McMahon report is a green light to the Red fifth column in the United States.

It is a signal to the traitors, Communists, and fellow travelers in our Government that they need have no fear of exposure from this Administration. It is public notification that we will officially "turn our back" on traitors, Communists, and fellow travelers in our Government.

The most loyal stooges of the Kremlin could not have done a better job of giving a clean bill of health to Stalin's fifth column in this country. At a time when American blood is staining the Korean valleys, the Tydings-McMahon report gives unlimited aid and comfort to the very enemies responsible for tying the hands and shooting the faces off some of our soldiers.

In its dying gasp the Tydings-McMahon half of the committee is attempting to give birth to the most evil fraud that has ever besmirched and dishonored the good name of the United States Senate.

If allowed to succeed, this fraud will maintain in power those who will extend the trail of blood from the valleys of Korea, across the sands of Iran, to the streets of Berlin. It comes at a time when honest people were waiting and hoping for honest answers to the questions of why the terror of communism which has engulfed vast areas of the world has succeeded in spreading the filth of its fifth column into our way of life.

Instead the Tydings-McMahon half of the committee has degenerated to new lows of planned deception. The result of their work is a clever, evil thing to behold. It is gigantic in its fraud and deep in its deceit. It camouflages the facts and it protects Communists and fellow travelers in our Government.

July 18, 1950

U. S. Reds Go Underground To Foil F. B. I., Hoover Says

540,000 Communists and Followers Seek Our Atomic, Military, Industrial Secrets, He Tells Closed Senate Unit Session

By The United Press.

WASHINGTON, June 8—J. Edgar Hoover, director of the Federal Bureau of Investigation, warned Senators two months ago that unprecedented numbers of Communists were seeking United States atomic, military and industrial secrets.

Mr. Hoover's hitherto secret testimony last April 3 before a Senate Appropriations subcommittee was disclosed today.

It was revealed that he had asked for more agents to ferret out a "potential 'fifth column' of 540,000 people" including 54,000 known Reds and nearly 500,000 sympathizers who, he said, were more active now than Nazi and Fascist operatives ever had been during World War II.

He said the Communists have gone underground, use "double talk," and have instituted their own "loyalty" purge to make the F. B. I.'s check on them more difficult. They are even checking their thirteen-member Central Committee, he added, and have set up no fewer than forty-nine "loyalty" boards of their own.

He said that in addition to secret codes and destruction of membership records, the spy leaders have set up "investigating committees" in every state—as well as a special three-man subcommittee to keep tabs on the party's executive committee.

Some spies, he said, hide behind "diplomatic passports." In some instances they "may very well be employed as a clerk or in some minor capacity in a foreign establishment" but actually give orders to higher-ups, he testified.

He said the F. B. I. must expand its work to "preserve our internal security" in event of emergencies. Mr. Hoover testified that Soviet sympathizers were after information on atomic research, radar, jet propulsion, coastal maps, military airports, biological warfare and industrial resources.

Mr. Hoover said the job of dealing with native-born Communists and sympathizers was much more difficult than the wartime job of curbing Nazi agents, because the espionage laws were intended mainly to deal with aliens.

"There is less likelihood for a native-born citizen to attract suspicion than there is for an alien, because he blends into the very background which he would destroy," he explained.

Mr. Hoover, who said the Reds also were stirring up civil rights agitation in the South, lashed out at the National Lawyers Guild which, he said, had allowed itself to be used as a sounding board for Communist actions. He accused the Guild of having tried to oust him from his job since 1940.

Mr. Hoover appeared before the subcommittee to request increased appropriations for a larger F. B. I. administrative and investigative staff. He said part of the money was needed to handle "internal security" cases.

The "orbit of Communist control," he explained, has increased from one-seventh of the world's population in 1917 to one-third of the world's population today.

"The intensification of communism and underground activity in the United States has increased proportionately," he said. "If we are to preserve our internal security in times of emergency, it is incumbent that the identities of those who work against the peace and security of America be established."

Mr. Hoover said the Communists had launched an all-out drive to infiltrate heavy industry and communications. A partial breakdown of its 54,174 members reflects the party's concentration on heavy centers of population, he said.

He added that New York State has 25,000 Communists; California 6,977; Illinois 3,361; Pennsylvania 2,876; Ohio 2,834; Michigan 1,250; Massachusetts 1,022; Nevada 23; Wyoming 10; Tennessee 27; Alabama 141 and New Hampshire 43.

"Even though there are only 54,174 members of the party, the fact remains that the party leaders themselves boast that for every party member there are ten others who follow the party line and who are ready, willing and able to do the party's work," he said.

"In other words, there is a potential fifth column of 540,000 people dedicated to this philosophy."

The recent conviction of the eleven Communist leaders in New York has driven the party into concentrated underground activity, Mr. Hoover said, and no party cards were issued in 1949 or 1950. Maintenance of membership records also has been discontinued, he testified.

"To counteract the F. B. I.'s penetration of the Communist party its leaders have established a far-reaching and vigorous loyalty program of its own, calling for the establishment of investigating committees in each state and a thorough investigation of each member of the party as to personal history, activities, associations, contacts and length of membership," he said.

He said the F. B. I. had "good sources of information" and "good representation in the party in varying positions of trust," but that it was more difficult to penetrate the party today than formerly.

"Those in the party exercise greater caution and investigation of party leaders requires more ingenuity," he explained. "Public meetings are maintained at an absolute minimum," he said, and a courier system has been established to protect confidential communications.

"Surplus Secreted for Future"

"Secret printing facilities and supplies have been secreted for future underground operations, and transfers of party members from one district to another are now controlled through the use of an elaborate identification system," Mr. Hoover testified.

As proof of F. B. I. efficiency, Mr. Hoover noted that seven of its confidential party informants had been revealed during the trial of the top party leaders and said "we had more available if they were necessary."

Forty-eight per cent of the party membership, he continued, is in "the basic industry of this country, as in this manner they would be able to sabotage essential industry in vital defense areas in the event of a national emergency."

Mr. Hoover said the Communists recently had stepped up their activities in the steel, heavy machinery, mining communications, transportation, electrical and maritime industries.

But he said the "most amazing" thing to him was the way they have been able to infiltrate the legal profession—an apparent reference to the Lawyers Guild.

"It is regrettable," Mr. Hoover said, "that any association of lawyers will permit itself to be used and parrot the Communist party line."

He said the Communists also had made "special efforts" to penetrate the communications field. To this end, he said, they established special courses in radio writing, acting and directing.

"One front group boasts of having thousands of monitors in every section of the country who will take up a letter writing campaign against any commentator who disagrees with what they advocate," he said.

June 9, 1950

PRESIDENT PLEDGES ACTION ON TRAITORS

By LEWIS WOOD
Special to THE NEW YORK TIMES.

WASHINGTON, July 27—The Federal Government moved further today to tighten protection against subversive elements in the emergency.

President Truman promised that steps would be taken to deal with traitors and saboteurs. He asserted, however, that he wanted no repetition of the harsh Alien and Sedition Laws of 1798.

A few hours later, J. Edgar Hoover, director of the Federal Bureau of Investigation, made public seven suggestions, following the President's recent call for law enforcement agencies, patriotic organizations and individuals to report suspicious activities to the F. B. I.

Mr. Hoover warned that the F. B. I. desired "facts," without resort to "rumors, hysteria or witch hunts." He cautioned, too, against "private investigations" or arrests too hurried to permit tracing those who worked with spies.

President Truman's statement was made at his weekly news conference. His remarks came when he was asked if he would discuss pending legislation to curb aliens and subversive persons, in the light of his warning to the nation this week to watch for spies and saboteurs.

No Alien and Sedition Mood

Mr. Truman replied that the country should be very careful in times like these to avoid getting into the Alien and Sedition mood of 1798. The Bill of Rights was still a part of the Constitution, and a most important part, the Chief Executive added.

He went on to say that this did not mean that the Government would overlook any opportunities to see that traitors and saboteurs would be taken care of properly.

The Alien and Sedition Acts, around which raged a great controversy, placed severe restrictions on aliens. They authorized the President to deport or imprison foreigners considered dangerous and curtailed the freedom of the press.

Mr. Hoover's seven suggestions on reporting information:

"1. The F. B. I. is as near to you as your telephone. The first page of every telephone book in the country lists the nearest office of the F. B. I. You can communicate with the F. B. I. by telephone, letter or call at our nearest office.

"2. Feel free to furnish all facts in your possession. Many times a small bit of information might furnish the data we are seeking. * * *

"3. The F. B. I. is interested in receiving facts, we are not interested in what a person thinks but what he does which undermines our internal security. Avoid reporting malicious gossip or idle rumors.

"4. Do not circulate rumors about subversive activities, or draw conclusions from information you furnish the F. B. I. The data you possess might be incomplete or only partially accurate. By drawing conclusions based on insufficient evidence grave injustices might result to innocent persons.

"5. Once you have reported your information to the F. B. I. do not endeavor to make private investigations. This can best be done by trained investigators who have access to data acquired over the years on individuals engaged in subversive activities.

"Hysteria, witch-hunts and vigilantes weaken internal security. Investigations involving internal security require care and pains-

taking effort. We all can contribute to our internal security by protecting the innocent as well as by identifying the enemies within our midst. In cases involving espionage it is more important to identify spies, their contacts, sources of information, and methods of communications than to make immediate arrests.

"6. Be alert. The greatest defenders against sabotage are the loyal American workmen who are producing the materials and weapons for our defense. They can be the sentinels of defense in every walk of life.

"7. The forces which are most

anxious to weaken our internal security are not always easy to identify. Communists have been trained in deceit and secretly work toward the day when they hope to replace our American way of life with a Communist dictatorship. They utilize cleverly camouflaged movements, such as some peace groups and civil rights organizations, to achieve their sinister purposes. While they as individuals are difficult to identify—the Communist party line is clear. Its concern is the advancement of Soviet Russia and the Godless Communist cause. It is important to learn to know the enemies of the American way

of life."

The pending legislation to curb Communists and others, referred to at the President's news conference, consists principally of two proposals. One is the Mundt-Ferguson Communist-control bill, now on the Senate calendar. This would impose severe restrictions upon Communist or Communist-front organizations. The other is the Hobbs bill, passed by the House a week ago. In effect, this would assure internment of subversives who cannot now be deported because of the international situation.

July 28, 1950

FOURTH AMERICAN HELD AS ATOM SPY

New Yorker Seized Here Got Los Alamos Bomb Data for Soviet Ring, F.B.I. Reports

Special to THE NEW YORK TIMES.

WASHINGTON, July 17—The Federal Bureau of Investigation today arrested Julius Rosenberg, 32 years old, a New Yorker, on charges of spying for Russia. He was the fourth American held within the past few months in connection with the passing of United States atomic secrets to the Soviet Union.

Rosenberg was arrested in New York, where he resides at 10 Monroe Street with his wife and two children, Michael, 7, and Robert, 3. He is an electrical engineer who operates Pitt Engine Products, Inc., at 370 East Houston Street, New York.

The announcement of the arrest was made jointly by J. Howard McGrath, the Attorney General, and J. Edgar Hoover, director of the Federal Bureau of Investigation.

Mr. Hoover described Mr. Rosen-

berg as "another important link in the Soviet espionage apparatus" that included Dr. Klaus Fuchs, British atomic scientist, Harry Gold, Philadelphia biochemist, Alfred Dean Slack, Syracuse scientist, and David Greenglass, former United States Army sergeant.

All of the above have been arrested in recent months. Dr. Fuchs, is now serving a sentence in a British prison for giving the Russians secrets he acquired while in the United States as a member of a British atomic mission. The arrests of the others followed a visit by F. B. I. agents to England, where they interviewed Dr. Fuchs.

Rosenberg was held in $100,000 bail after his arraignment tonight before Judge John F. X. McGohey in the Federal District Court for the Southern District of New York.

The charge was conspiracy to commit espionage. Technically it was conspiracy to violate Section 32 A (Espionage Act), Title 50 of the United States Code.

Mr. Hoover related that Rosenberg recruited Greenglass to make secret technical information on the atomic bomb available both to Gold and Rosenberg in 1945.

Mr. Hoover said that Rosenberg gave Greenglass specific information on the type of atomic data the Russians desired.

The F. B. I. investigation revealed, Mr. Hoover said, that Rosenberg made himself available to

Soviet espionage agents "so he could do the work he was fated for" and "so he might do something to help Russia."

According to Mr. Hoover, Rosenberg early in 1945 gave Greenglass, while the latter was on furlough in New York, one half of an irregularly cut jello box top. The other half of the top was given by Rosenberg to Harry Gold in Albuquerque, N. M. This was done so Gold could identify himself to Greenglass.

When Gold and Greenglass met in June of 1945 Greenglass was paid $500 by Gold, who got it from his Soviet superior, Anatoli A. Yakovlev, vice consul of the Soviet Consulate in New York. Mr. Yakovlev, who was recently indicted for espionage by a Federal grand jury in Brooklyn, returned to Russia several years ago.

Greenglass Is Arrested

Greenglass, Mr. Hoover said, turned over to Gold secret information he had secured from the atomic bomb project at Los Alamos, where Greenglass was stationed as a soldier.

After Dr. Fuchs and Gold were arrested in February and May, respectively, Greenglass was warned by Rosenberg to leave the country. The F. B. I. said that he instructed Greenglass to obtain a passport to Mexico. He was then told to make his way to Switzerland and report to the Czechoslovakian Embassy there.

However, Greenglass was ar-

rested shortly after he got those instructions from Rosenberg.

The F. B. I. director said that the gravity of Rosenberg's offense was accentuated by the fact, that he, an American-born citizen, "aggressively sought means to secretly conspire with the Soviet Government to the detriment of his own country."

Rosenberg was born in New York on May 18, 1918, and took his B. S. degree in electrical engineering from the City College in February of 1939.

After working for various electrical engineering firms in Manhattan and Brooklyn he was employed as a junior engineer in the signal service of the War Department's general depot in Brooklyn on Sept. 3, 1940.

Rosenberg later transferred to the signal corps, working as an assistant engineering inspector in the Philadelphia and New Jersey areas.

In February of 1943 he was promoted to associate engineering inspector and continued in this position until suspended on Feb. 9, 1949.

His suspension was by the Secretary of War on recommendation of his commanding officer. The later action came on the basis of information that Rosenberg was a member of the Communist Party.

Mr. Hoover said that Rosenberg made numerous unsuccessful efforts to be reinstated. He later purchased and operated the Pitt Engine firm.

July 18, 1950

Text of President's Message Vetoing the Communist-Control Bill

WASHINGTON, Sept. 22 (UP)— Following is the text of President Truman's message vetoing the Communist-control bill:

I return herewith, without my approval, H.R. 9490, the proposed Internal Security Act of 1950.

I am taking this action only after the most serious study and reflection and after consultation with the Security and intelligence agencies of the Government. The Department of Justice, the De-

partment of Defense, the Central Intelligence Agency, and the Department of State have all advised me that the bill would seriously damage the security and intelligence operations for which they are responsible. They have expressed the hope that the bill would not become law.

This is an omnibus bill containing many different legislative proposals with only one thing in common: they are all represented

to be "anti-Communist."

But when the many complicated pieces of the bill are analyzed in detail, a startling result appears.

H.R. 9490 would not hurt the Communists. Instead, it would help them.

It has been claimed over and over again that this is an "anti-Communist" bill—a "Communist-control" bill. But in actual operation the bill would have results exactly the opposite of those in-

tended.

It would actually weaken our existing internal security measures and would seriously hamper the Federal Bureau of Investigation and our other security agencies.

It would help the Communists in their efforts to create dissension and confusion within our borders.

It would help the Communist propagandists throughout the

177

world who are trying to undermine freedom by discrediting as hypocrisy the efforts of the United States on behalf of freedom.

Seven Objections Listed

Specifically, some of the principal objections to the bill are as follows:

1. It would aid potential enemies by requiring the publication of a complete list of vital defense plants, laboratories and other installations.
2. It would require the Department of Justice and its Federal Bureau of Investigation to waste immense amounts of time and energy attempting to carry out its unworkable registration provisions.
3. It would deprive us of the great assistance of many aliens in intelligence matters.
4. It would antagonize friendly governments.
5. It would put the Government of the United States in the thought control business.
6. It would make it easier for subversive aliens to become naturalized as United States citizens.
7. It would give Government officials vast powers to harass all of our citizens in the exercise of their right of free speech.

Legislation with these consequences is not necessary to meet the real dangers which communism presents to our free society. Those dangers are serious, and must be met. But this bill would hinder us, not help us in meeting them.

Fortunately, we already have on the books strong laws which give us most of the protection we need from the real dangers of treason, espionage, sabotage and actions looking to the overthrow of our Government by force and violence. Most of the provisions of this bill have no relation to these real dangers.

One provision alone of this bill is enough to demonstrate how far it misses the real target. Section 5 would require the Secretary of Defense to "proclaim" and "have published in The Federal Register" a public catalogue of defense plants, laboratories, and all other facilities vital to our national defense—no matter how secret.

I cannot imagine any document a hostile foreign government would desire more. Spies and saboteurs would willingly spend years of effort seeking to find out the information that this bill would require the Government to hand them on a silver platter.

There are many provisions of this bill which impel me to return it without my approval, but this one would be enough by itself. It is inconceivable to me that a majority of the Congress could expect the Commander-in-Chief of the armed forces of the United States to approve such a flagrant violation of proper security safeguards.

This is only one example of many provisions in the bill which would in actual practice work to the detriment of our national security.

I know that the Congress had no intention of achieving such results when it passed this bill. I know that the vast majority of the members of Congress who voted for the bill sincerely intended to strike a blow at the Communists.

"Outweighed by Others"

It is true that certain provisions of this bill would improve the laws protecting us against espionage and sabotage. But these provisions are greatly outweighed by others which would actually impair our security.

I repeat, the net result of this bill would be to help the Communists, not to hurt them.

I therefore most earnestly request the Congress to reconsider its action. I am confident that on more careful analysis most members of Congress will recognice that this bill is contrary to the best interests of our country at this critical time.

H. R. 9490 is made up of a number of different parts. In summary, their purposes and probable effects may be described as follows.

Sections 1 through 17 are designed for two purposes. First, they are intended to force Communist organizations to register and to divulge certain information about themselves — information on their officers, their finances, and, in some cases, their membership.

These provisions would in practice be ineffective, and would result in obtaining no information about Communists that the F.B.I. and our other security agencies do not already have. But in trying to enforce these sections, we would have to spend a great deal of time, effort, and money — all to no good purpose.

Second, these provisions are intended to impose various penalties on Communists and others covered by the terms of the bill. So far as Communists are concerned, all these penalties which can be practicably enforced are already in effect under existing laws and procedures. But the language of the bill is so broad and vague that it might well result in penalizing the legitimate activities of people who are not Communists at all, but loyal citizens.

Thus the net result of these sections of the bill would be: No serious damage to the Communists, much damage to the rest of us. Only the Communist movement would gain from such an outcome.

Sections 18 through 21 and Section 23 of this bill constitute, in large measure, the improvements in our internal security laws which I recommended some time ago. Although the language of these sections is in some respects weaker than is desirable, I should be glad to approve these provisions if they were enacted separately, since they are improvements developed by the F. B. I. and other Government security agencies to meet certain clear deficiencies of the present law.

But even though these improvements are needed, other provisions of the bill would weaken our security far more than these would strengthen it. We have better protection for our internal security under existing law than we would have with the amendments and additions made by H.R. 9490.

Sees Injury to Government

Sections 22 and 25 of this bill would make sweeping changes in our laws governing the admission of aliens to the United States and their naturalization as citizens.

The ostensible purpose of these provisions is to prevent persons who would be dangerous to our national security from entering the country or becoming citizens. In fact, present law already achieves that objective.

What these provisions would actually do is to prevent us from admitting to our country, or to citizenship, many people who could make real contributions to our national strength. The bill would deprive our Government and our intelligence agencies of the valuable services of aliens in security operations.

It would require us to exclude and to deport the citizens of some friendly non-Communist countries. Furthermore, it would actually make it easier for subversive aliens to become United States citizens. Only the Communist movement would gain from such actions.

Section 24 and Sections 26 through 30 of this bill make a number of minor changes in the naturalization laws. None of them is of great significance—nor are they particularly relevant to the problem of internal security. These provisions, for the most part, have received little or no attention in the legislative process. I believe that several of them would not be approved by the Congress if they were considered on their merits, rather than as parts of an omnibus bill.

Section 31 of this bill makes it a crime to attempt to influence a judge or jury by public demonstration, such as picketing. While the courts already have considerable power to punish such actions under existing law, I have no objection to this section.

Sections 100 through 117 of this bill (Title II) are intended to give the Government power, in the event of invasion, war, or insurrection in the United States in aid of a foreign enemy, to seize and hold persons who could be expected to attempt acts of espionage or sabotage, even though they had as yet committed no crime.

It may be that legislation of this type should be on the statute books. But the provisions in H. R. 9490 would very probably prove ineffective to achieve the objective sought, since they would not suspend the writ of habeas corpus, and under our legal system to detain a man not charged with a crime would raise serious Constitutional questions unless the writ of habeas corpus were suspended

Furthermore, it may well be that other persons than those covered by these provisions would be more important to detain in the event of emergency. This whole problem, therefore, should clearly be studied more thoroughly before further legislative action along these lines is considered.

In brief, when all the provisions of H. R. 9490 are considered together, it is evident that the great bulk of them are not directed toward the real and present dangers that exist from Communism. Instead of striking blows at communism, they would strike blows at our own liberties and at our position in the forefront of those working for freedom in the world. At a time when our young men are fighting for freedom in Korea, it would be tragic to advance the objective of communism in this country, as this bill would do.

Because I feel so strongly that this legislation would be a terrible mistake, I want to discuss more fully its worst features—Sections 1 through 17, and Sections 22 and 25.

Most of the first seventeen sections of H. R. 9490 are concerned with requiring registration and annual reports, by what the bill calls "Communist-action organizations," and "Communist-front organizations," of names of officers, sources and uses of funds, and, in the case of "Communist-action organizations," names of members.

The idea of requiring Communist organizations to divulge information about themselves is a simple and attractive one. But it is about as practical as requiring thieves to register with the Sheriff. Obviously, no such organization as the Communist party is likely to register voluntarily.

Under the provisions of the bill, if an organization which the Attorney General believes should register does not do so, he must request a five-man Subversive Activities Control Board to order the organization to register. The Attorney General would have to produce proof that the organization in question was in fact a "Communist-action" or a "Communist-front organization."

To do this he would have to offer evidence relating to every aspect of the organization's activities. The organization could present opposing evidence. Prolonged hearings would be required to allow both sides to present proof and to cross-examine opposing witnesses.

To estimate the duration of such a proceeding involving the Communist party, we need only recall that on much narrower issues the trial of the eleven Communist leaders under the Smith Act consumed nine months. In a hearing under this bill, the difficulties of proof would be much greater and would take a much longer time.

The bill lists a number of criteria for the board to consider in deciding whether or not an organization is a "Communist-action" or "Communist-front" organization. Many of these deal with the attitudes or states of mind of the organization's leaders.

It is frequently difficult in legal proceedings to establish whether or not a man has committed an overt act, such as theft or perjury. But under this bill, the Attorney General would have to attempt the immensely more difficult task of producing concrete legal evidence that men have particular ideas or opinions. This would inevitably require the disclosure of many of the F. B. I.'s confidential sources of information and thus would damage our national security.

Decision Could Be Appealed

If, eventually, the Attorney General should overcome these difficulties and get a favorable decision from the board, the board's decision could be appealed to the courts. The courts would review any questions of law involved, and whether the board's findings of fact were supported by the "preponderance" of the evidence.

All these proceedings would require great effort and much time. It is almost certain that from two to four years would elapse between the Attorney General's decision to go before the board with a case, and the final disposition of the matter by the courts.

And when all this time and effort had been spent, it is still most likely that no organization would actually register.

The simple fact is that when the courts at long last found that a particular organization was required to register, all the leaders of the organization would have to do to frustrate the law would be to dissolve the organization and establish a new one with a different name and a new roster of nominal officers.

NECESSARY VIGILANCE OR WITCH HUNT?

The Communist party has done this again and again in countries throughout the world. And nothing could be done about it except to begin all over again the long dreary process of investigative, administrative, and judicial proceedings to require registration.

Thus the net result of the registration provisions of this bill would probably be an endless chasing of one organization after another, with the Communists always able to frustrate the law enforcement agencies and prevent any final result from being achieved. It could only result in wasting the energies of the Department of Justice and in destroying the sources of information of its F. B. I. To impose these fruitless burdens upon the F. B. I. would divert it from its vital security duties and thus give aid and comfort to the very Communists whom the bill is supposed to control.

Unfortunately, these provisions are not merely ineffective and unworkable. They represent a clear and present danger to our institutions.

In so far as the bill would require registration by the Communist party itself, it does not endanger our traditional liberties. However, the application of the registration requirements to so-called Communist-front organizations can be the greatest danger to freedom of speech, press and assembly, since the Alien and Sedition Laws of 1798. This danger arises out of the criteria or standards to be applied in determining whether an organization is a Communist-front organization.

There would be no serious problem if the bill required proof that an organization was controlled and financed by the Communist party before it could be classified as a Communist-front organization. However, recognizing the difficulty of proving those matters, the bill would permit such a determination to be based solely upon "the extent to which the positions taken or advanced by it from time to time on matters of policy do not deviate from those" of the Communist movement.

This provision could easily be used to classify as a Communist-front organization any organization which is advocating a single policy or objective which is also being urged by the Communist party or by a Communist foreign government.

In fact, this may be the intended result, since the bill defines "organization" to include "a group of persons * * * permanently or temporarily associated together for joint action on any subject or subjects." Thus, an organization which advocates low-cost housing for sincere humanitarian reasons might be classified as a Communist-front organization because the Communists regularly exploit slum conditions as one of their fifth-column techniques.

It is not enough to say that this probably would not be done. The mere fact that it could be done shows clearly how the bill would open a Pandora's box of opportunities for official condemnation of organizations and individuals for perfectly honest opinions which happen to be stated also by Communists.

The basic error of these sections is that they move in the direction of suppressing opinion and belief. This would be a very dangerous course to take, not because we have any sympathy for Communist opinions, but because any governmental stifling of the free expression of opinion is a long step toward totalitarianism.

There is no more fundamental axiom of American freedom than the familiar statement: in a free country, we punish men for the crimes they commit, but never for the opinions they have. And the reason this is so fundamental to freedom is not, as many suppose, that it protects the few unorthodox from suppression by the majority. To permit freedom of expression is primarily for the benefit of the majority, because it protects criticism, and criticism leads to progress.

We can and we will prevent espionage, sabotage, or other actions endangering our national security. But we would betray our finest traditions if we attempted, as this bill would attempt, to curb the simple expression of opinion.

This we should never do, no matter how distasteful the opinion may be to the vast majority of our people. The course proposed by this bill would delight the Communists, for it would make a mockery of the Bill of Rights and of our claims to stand for freedom in the world.

Silencing Effect Seen

And what kind of effect would these provisions have on the normal expression of political views? Obviously, if this law were on the statute books, the part of prudence would be to avoid saying anything that might be construed by someone as not deviating sufficiently from the current Communist propaganda line. And since no one could be sure in advance what views were safe to express, the inevitable tendency would be to express no views on controversial subjects.

The result could only be to reduce the vigor and strength of our political life—an outcome that the Communists would happily welcome, but that free men should abhor.

We need not fear the expression of ideas—we do not need to fear their suppression.

Our position in the vanguard of freedom rests largely on our demonstration that the free expression of opinion, coupled with government by popular consent, leads to national strength and human advancement. Let us not, in cowering and foolish fear, throw away the ideals which are the fundamental basis of our free society.

Not only are the registration provisions of this bill unworkable and dangerous, they are also grossly misleading in that all but one of the objectives which are claimed for them are already being accomplished by other and superior methods — and the one objective which is not now being accomplished would not in fact be accomplished under this bill either.

It is claimed that the bill would provide information about the Communist party and its members. The fact is, the F. B. I. already possesses very complete sources of information concerning the Communist movement in this country. If the F. B. I. must disclose its sources of information in public hearings to require registration under this bill, its present sources of information, and its ability to acquire new information, will be largely destroyed.

It is claimed that this bill would deny income tax exemptions to Communist organizations. The fact is that the Bureau of Internal Revenue already denies income tax exemptions to such organizations.

It is claimed that this bill would deny passports to Communists. The fact is that the Government can and does deny passports to Communists under existing law.

It is claimed that this bill would prohibit the employment of Communists by the Federal Government. The fact is that the employment of Communists by the Federal Government is already prohibited and, at least in the Executive Branch, there is an effective program to see that they are not employed.

"Could Be Easily Evaded"

It is claimed that this bill would prohibit the employment of Communists in defense plants. The fact is that it would be years before this bill would have any effect of this nature—if it ever would. Fortunately, this objective is already being substantially achieved under the present procedures of the Department of Defense, and if the Congress would enact one of the provisions I have recommended—which it did not include in this bill—the situation would be entirely taken care of, promptly and effectively.

It is also claimed—and this is the one new objective of the registration provisions of this bill—that it would require Communist organizations to label all their publications and radio and television broadcasts as emanating from a Communist source. The fact is that this requirement, even if constitutional, could be easily and permanently evaded, simply by the continuous creation of new organizations to distribute Communist information.

Section 4(a) of the bill, like its registration provisions, would be ineffective, would be subject to dangerous abuse and would seek to accomplish an objective which is already better accomplished under existing law.

This provision would make unlawful any agreement "to perform any act which would substantially contribute to the establishment within the United States" of a foreign-controlled dictatorship. Of course, this provision would be unconstitutional if it infringed upon the fundamental right of the American people to establish for themselves by Constitutional methods any form of government they choose. To avoid this, it is provided that this section "shall not apply to the proposal of a Constitutional amendment."

If this language limits the prohibition of the section to the use of unlawful methods, then it adds nothing to the Smith Act, under which eleven Communist leaders have been convicted, and would be more difficult to enforce. Thus, it would accomplish nothing. Moreover, the bill does not even purport to define the phrase, unique in a criminal statute, "substantially contribute." A phrase so vague raises a serious Constitutional question.

Sections 22 and 25 of this bill are directed toward the specific questions of who should be admitted to our country, and who should be permitted to become a United States citizen. I believe there is general agreement that the answers to those questions should be: We should admit to our country, within the available quotas, anyone with a legitimate purpose who would not endanger our security, and we should admit to citizenship, any immigrant who will be a loyal and constructive member of the community.

Those are essentially the standards set by existing law. Under present law, we do not admit to our country known Communists, because we believe they work to overthrow our Government, and we do not admit Communists to citizenship, because we believe they are not loyal to the United States.

The changes which would be made in the present law by Sections 22 and 25 would not reinforce those sensible standards. Instead, they would add a number of new standards, which, for no good and sufficient reason, would interfere with our relations with other countries and seriously damage our national security.

Section 22 would, for example, exclude from our country anyone who advocates any form of totalitarian or one-party government. We of course believe in the democratic system of competing political parties, offering a choice of candidates and policies. But a number of countries with which we maintain friendly relations have a different form of government.

Until now, no one has suggested that we should abandon cultural and commercial relations with a country merely because it has a form of government different from ours. Yet Section 22 would require that. As one instance, it is clear that under the definitions of the bill the present government of Spain, among others, would be classified as "totalitarian."

As a result, the Attorney General would be required to exclude from the United States all Spanish business men, students, and other nonofficial travelers who support the present government of their country. I cannot understand how the sponsors of this bill can think that such an action would contribute to our national security.

Moreover, the provisions of Section 22 of this bill would strike a serious blow to our national security by taking away from the Government the power to grant asylum in this country to foreign diplomats who repudiate Communist imperialism and wish to escape its reprisals.

It must be obvious to anyone that it is in our national interest to persuade people to renounce communism, and to encourage their defection from Communist forces. Many of these people are extremely valuable to our intelligence operations. Yet under this bill the Government would lose the limited authority it now has to offer asylum in our country as the great incentive for such defection.

In addition, the provisions of Section 22 would sharply limit the authority of the Government to admit foreign diplomatic representatives and their families on official business. Under existing law, we already have the authority to send out of the country any person who abuses diplomatic privileges by working against the interests of the United States. But under this bill a whole series of unnecessary restrictions would be placed on the admission of diplomatic personnel.

This is not only ungenerous, for a country which eagerly sought and proudly holds the honor of being the seat of the United Nations, it is also very unwise, because it makes our country appear to be fearful of "foreigners," when in fact we are working as hard as we know how to build mutual confidence and friendly relations among the nations of the world.

Section 22 is so contrary to our national interests that it would actually put the Government into the business of thought control by requiring the deportation of any alien who distributes or publishes, or who is affiliated with an organization which distributes or publishes, any written or printed matter advocating (or merely expressing belief in) the economic and Governmental doctrines of any form of totalitarianism.

This provision does not require an evil intent or purpose on the part of the alien, as does a similar provision in the Smith Act. Thus, the Attorney General would be required to deport any alien operating or connected with a well-stocked bookshop containing books on economics or politics written by supporters of the present Government of Spain, of Yugoslavia, or any one of a number of other countries.

Section 25 would make the same aliens ineligible for citizenship. There should be no room in our laws for such hysterical provisions. The next logical step would be to "burn the books."

This illustrates the fundamental error of these immigration and naturalization provisions. It is easy to see that they are hasty and ill-considered. But far more significant—and far more dangerous—is their apparent underlying purpose.

Instead of trying to encourage the free movement of people, sub-

ject only to the real requirements of national security, these provisions attempt to bar movement to anyone who is, or once was, associated with ideas we dislike, and in the process, they would succeed in barring many people whom it would be to our advantage to admit.

Such an action would be a serious blow to our work for world peace. We uphold—or have upheld till now, at any rate—the concept of freedom on an international scale. That is the root concept of our efforts to bring unity among the free nations and peace in the world.

The Communists, on the other hand, attempt to break down in every possible way the free interchange of persons and ideas. It will be to their advantage, and not ours, if we establish for ourselves an Iron Curtain against those who can help us in the fight for freedom.

Gives Community Advantage

Another provision of the bill which would greatly weaken our national security is Section 25, which would make subversive aliens eligible for naturalization as soon as they withdraw from organizations required to register under this bill, whereas under existing law they must wait for a period of ten years after such withdrawal before becoming eligible for citizenship. This proposal is clearly contrary to the national interest, and clearly gives to the Communists an advantage they do not have under existing law.

I have discussed the provisions

of this bill at some length in order to explain why I am convinced that it would be harmful to our security and damaging to the individual rights of our people if it were enacted.

Earlier this month, we launched a great Crusade for Freedom designed, in the words of General Eisenhower, to fight the big lie with the big truth. I can think of no better way to make a mockery of that crusade and of the deep American belief in human freedom and dignity which underlies it than to put the provisions of H. R. 9490 on our statute books.

I do not undertake lightly the responsibility of differing with the majority in both Houses of Congress who have voted for this bill. We are all Americans; we all wish to safeguard and preserve our constitutional liberties against internal and external enemies. But I cannot approve this legislation, which instead of accomplishing its avowed purpose would actually interfere with our liberties and help the Communists against whom the bill was aimed.

This is a time when we must marshal all our resources and all the moral strength of our free system in self-defense against the threat of Communist aggression. We will fail in this, and we will destroy all that we seek to preserve, if we sacrifice the liberties of our citizens in a misguided attempt to achieve national security.

There is no reason why we should fail. Our country has been through dangerous times before,

without losing our liberties to external attack or internal hysteria. Each of us, in Government and out, has a share in guarding our liberties. Each of us must search is own conscience to find whether he is doing all that can be done to preserve and strengthen them.

No considerations of expediency can justify the enactment of such a bill as this, a bill which would so greatly weaken our liberties and give aid and comfort to those who would destroy us. I have, therefore, no alternative but to return this bill without my approval, and I earnestly request the Congress to reconsider its action.

HARRY S. TRUMAN
The White House,
Sept. 22, 1950

September 23, 1950

A Correction

Through an error in composition in the text of President Truman's message vetoing the Communist-control bill, as it appeared in yesterday's NEW YORK TIMES, the President was misquoted as saying: "We need not fear the expression of ideas—we do not need to fear their suppression." What the President actually said was: "We need not fear the expression of ideas—we do need to fear their suppression."

September 24, 1950

RED BILL VETO BEATEN, 57-10, BY SENATORS

CONGRESS RECESSES

Action Follows 22-Hour Debate That Precedes Vote to Override

RETURN SET FOR NOV. 27

By C. P. TRUSSELL
Special to THE NEW YORK TIMES.

WASHINGTON, Sept. 23—After a twenty-two hour continuous battle, the Senate completed today the overriding of President Truman's veto of the long-controverted anti-Communist bill and or-

dered that it be made the law of the land.

Congress then adjourned to Nov. 27, the Senate quitting at 5:23 P. M., and the House at 4:17 P. M.

By a vote of 57—10, the Senate rejected the President's contentions that the proposed statute was unconstitutional at many points, would help, not hurt, communism, and that it would prove to be a great Congressional mistake to seek to curb espionage and sabotage the way the bill proposed.

To upset the President's decision by twelve votes more than the two-thirds majority required to override Presidential disapproval, twenty-six Democrats, including Senator Scott W. Lucas of Illinois, the majority leader, joined thirty-one Republicans to administer this White House defeat.

The House of Representatives

voted 286—48 yesterday, without debate, and as soon as the veto message had been read to it, to repass the legislation, the President's position notwithstanding. The House vote to override the veto was sixty-three in excess of the required two-thirds.

These rejections of Presidential appeal, coming on the verge of a two-month recess of Congress for campaigning, almost set a record.

The bill had two programs that underwent the brunt of debate and decision. One called for control of communism by forcing the registration and reporting of activities by Communist-action organizations and their "fronts." It was conceded that many patriotic innocents had been drawn into the "front" groups.

A second program called for the summary apprehension and detention in concentration camps of Communists or others suspect of becoming spies or saboteurs in the event of a declaration of war, an insurrection or an invasion to help a foreign enemy.

All through last night and until 2 P. M. today, a group of seven Senators, with Senator Hubert H. Humphrey, Democrat of Minnesota, as anchor man, fought steadily to turn the tide of previous voting tests on the bill.

In the course of his repeated appearances at the lectern, Mr.

Humphrey conceded that this group was facing a licking. Making no such concessions, the other members of this band included Senators Paul H. Douglas of Illinois, Frank P. Graham of North Carolina, Estes Kefauver of Tennessee, Herbert H. Lehman of New York and James E. Murray of Montana, Democrats, and William Langer, Republican of North Dakota.

A little after 5 A. M. today, Mr. Langer, a roaring and desk-beating debater viewed as the "Terrible-tempered Mr. Bang" of the Senate, collapsed after some five hours of floor-holding. Doctors said it was exhaustion, nothing worst. Stretcher-bearers took him to an ambulance bound for the Naval Medical Center at near-by Bethesda. He was reported to be "all right" this afternoon, but unable to return to the Senate in time to vote.

Decisive Tests on Bill

There had been three decisive voting tests on the measure in the Senate. On Sept. 12 it voted 70—7 for passage of the program which Mr. Truman denounced from top to bottom yesterday in what was viewed widely in Congress as perhaps his "strongest" message.

To support his arguments against the legislative prescriptions—not, he emphasized, against its objectives—the President had signed a letter to all members of Congress, urging them to refrain from voting until they had studied his objections thoroughly.

After the first test, the Senate had voted 51—7 on Tuesday to pass the final draft of the legislation, as worked out by Senate-House managers. Today it followed up with the 57-10 vote to write the programs into law in the face of White House opposition.

A re-checking of Senate roll calls indicated that in all three tests, not more than twelve of the ninety-six Senators had voted directly to kill the proposed legislation.

These were Senators Dennis Chavez of New Mexico, Douglas, Graham, Theodore F. Green and Edward L. Leahy of Rhode Island, Humphrey, Kefauver, Harley M. Kilgore of West Virginia, Lehman, Murray and Glen H. Taylor of Idaho, Democras, and Mr. Langer.

At 2 P. M. today the group that had fought to sustain the veto through the night and morning rested its case. What might have been taken as a rebuttal by men confident of the results to come lasted an hour and a half.

Senator Pat McCarran, Democrat of Nevada, chairman of the Judiciary Committee and handler of the bill in the Senate. rounded up the Presidential complaints against the measure, point by point. He said he would not express himself as bluntly as he wished to, for fear he might say something that would not be proper to say in the light of disagreement with the Chief Executive.

He did observe, however, on the point of Presidential contention that some provisions of the bill would put unnecessary restrictions on admitting foreign diplomats to the United States:

"Any schoolboy could read this bill and see that aliens of diplomatic status are specifically exempt unless their entry would endanger the public security."

Mr. McCarran disagreed with the President's principal complaint, about a clause which Mr. Truman asserted would of itself impel him to veto the whole bill. It prescribes a listing in the Federal Register of defense plants from which Communists should be barred as officers or employes.

Truman's View of Section

Mr. Truman viewed this section as a virtual guidebook for spies and saboteurs, a listing of militarily sensitive spots which subversives otherwise would have to work in secret for years to obtain. This section, Senator McCarran held, would not require the publication of a complete list. Atomic and other secret installations, he said, could be withheld from the list.

It appeared that the fight over the legislation was not finished. Tonight Jerry O'Connell, a former member of the House from Montana and now chairman of the National Committee to Defeat the Mundt (anti-Communist) Bill, said a repeal of the measure would be sought when Congress returned in November.

Mr. O'Connell figured in Senate debate today. Senator Karl E. Mundt, Republican of South Dakota and co-author of the controversial bill, declared that Mr. O'Connell had been described by Louis Budenz, a former Communist, in Congressional hearings as having followed the Communist "party line" to the satisfaction of that party.

Senator Mundt said also that Mr. O'Connell had been "moving around in the shadowy darkness and twilight, almost within spitting distance" of the Senate's temporary chamber, "pulling his wires" during the all-night fight.

Views on Enforcement

In reaction to the enactment, Department of Justice sources intimated that its provisions would not be enforced in instances viewed as "endangering national security." It was pointed out that Congress had enacted "authorizations" and "directives" but had not yet provided the funds to carry them out.

President Truman had indicated such a reaction yesterday in his veto message to Congress. He struck particularly at a clause that called for a public listing of defense plants from which Communists would be barred as officers or employes.

"It is inconceivable to me," he stated, "that a majority of the Congress could expect the Commander in Chief of the armed forces to approve such a flagrant violation of proper security safeguards."

He viewed such a listing as a guidebook for spies and saboteurs.

The President challenged the constitutionality of the measure at many points.

There might be a "strike" within the executive branch against the provision calling for the deportation of "subversive aliens." Some aliens that could be listed in this classification, it was said, include former diplomats who resigned from their posts when their countries were forced behind the Iron Curtain. They have been invaluable sources of security information, it is reported.

Under the new law Communist organizations are required to identify their officers and members, even under their aliases. The Communist "fronts" would register only their officers. Both sets of organizations would be called on to report periodically on receipts and use of their finances.

The President held that this provision was like trying to require thieves to register with the sheriff. He said it would not work. He predicted that it would take years of court action to force such registrations, and then not without risk of falsified reporting that might ensnare more patriots than traitors.

September 24, 1950

U.S. OPENS ROUND-UP OF 86 AS ALIEN REDS; BOARD IS APPOINTED

Party Workers Are Accused of Engaging in Propaganda —20 Arrested So Far

TRUMAN IMPLEMENTS ACT

Appoints Richardson Head of Subversive Control Panel — Communists Don't Register

By WILLIAM S. WHITE
Special to THE NEW YORK TIMES.

WASHINGTON, Oct. 23 — The Department of Justice began today a country-wide round-up of eighty-six persons accused of being alien Communists especially active in propaganda work for the party.

[Twenty arrests had been made up to late Monday night, according to The Associated Press.]

The department's drive was started under the Internal Security Act of 1950, which President Truman implemented today by naming the bipartisan Subversive Activities Control Board. He put a Republican, Seth W. Richardson, at its head.

The board is required by the so-called McCarran anti-subversive law, which Congress passed over the President's veto.

The department's drive on the eighty-six aliens was aimed at deporting them wherever the country of origin would accept them, and failing that to put them under the six-month detention provided in the security act.

If after six months deportation still is impossible, the aliens will be subject to indefinite surveillance by the Immigration Service.

Reds Refuse to Register

Today was the last day for Communist organizations to register voluntarily with the Department of Justice under the act, and they carried out their threat to refuse to do so.

[At national headquarters of the Communist party in New York, a spokesman said Monday that the party leadership was unconcerned about passage of the registration deadline.

["We stand on everything we've said previously," he said. "We don't fit the bill. We're not foreign controlled. We're not a conspiracy. We'll join with the growing number of people working to repeal it as a menace."]

Under the terms of the law, the department must now appeal to the Subversive Activities Control Board. The board must hold hearings and permit the accused associations the right of counsel and of cross-examination, before making a finding of record as to whether or not they are subversive. From any board conclusion, an appeal may be carried to the Federal Supreme Court.

Fines, Imprisonment Possible

The officers of the Communist party, Federal officials said, had a duty under the law to register the party today, but that as individuals they could free themselves from personal liability by coming forward with a registration for it within ten days.

A department spokesman told reporters that the case against known Communist organizations would necessarily have to be a comprehensive one, rather like making a major prosecution in court. It thus would involve a great deal of paper work that would take much time.

For failure to register, after a final determination that it is subversive and after exhaustion of all appeals, an organization may be fined $10,000 a day and its responsible officers—the four top ones in each case—may be imprisoned for five years.

On the subversive control board with Mr. Richardson, who is retiring as chairman of the Federal Loyalty Review Board, the highest appeals body in the program by which the Government tests the loyalty of its employes, President Truman appointed the following:

For two-year terms — Peter Campbell Brown of New York and Charles M. La Follette of Virginia.

For one-year terms—David J. Coddaire of Massachusetts and Dr. Kathryn McHale of Indiana.

Mr. Richardson's tenure as chairman will run for three years. Along with all his associates, he will receive $12,500 a year, and like them, he must give up all private employment.

Like Mr. Richardson, Mr. Coddaire, a Boston and Haverhill, Mass., attorney, is a Republican.

Mr. La Follette, though once a Republican member of Congress from Indiana, was formerly executive director of Americans for Democratic Action, an organization that supported Mr. Truman strongly in 1948 and, like him, strongly opposed enactment of the McCarran Act. Mr. La Follette, however, was not an official of the A. D. A. when it attacked the law.

Mr. Brown, a Brooklyn lawyer and at present a special assistant to the Attorney General, J. Howard McGrath, is a Democrat. Dr. McHale, an educator and psychologist of Logansport, Ind., is a sister of Frank McHale, Democratic National Committeeman for Indiana.

Mr. Richardson, though an orthodox Republican and a former

181

The Crucible of the Fifties

assistant Attorney General in the Hoover Administration, has often been denounced by those Republicans who accuse the Truman regime of "softness" toward communism.

The function of the Loyalty Review Board is to referee the findings of loyalty or disloyalty among personnel of the executive branch of the Government, but the Subversive Activities Control Board has the whole country for its jurisdiction.

Any organization believed by the Attorney General to be subversive and refusing, as the Communist groups have done, to register with him, may be brought by him before the latter board for its determination of whether it is a "Communist-action" group, a "Communist-front" group, or neither.

The board thus is the most important single agency for the enforcement of the McCarran act.

That law was assailed during the day in Federal District Court here by Ralph A. Powe, a Washington lawyer who said that he was acting for 107 persons living in thirty-two states.

Mr. Powe offered a petition seeking an injunction to restrain the Attorney General from enforcing the act and challenging its constitutionality. He was not permitted to file the case because the street addresses of some of the 107 plaintiffs were not listed. He said that he would rectify that error and go into court again within three days.

The Justice Department was stressing more than any other current activity its movement against alien Communists. It identified "the top men" among the eighty-six as follows:

Arrested in New York—Franjo, or Frank, Borich, or Boric, 50, of Yugoslavia, who was officially said to have been here since 1913 as a labor organizer and to have been active in the National Miners Union. The department identified this union as an affiliate of "the red international of labor unions."

Arrested in Pittsburgh—Vincent, or Vinko, Kemenovich, 51, of Yugoslavia, also described as associated with the National Miners Union.

Arrested in Chicago—Moses Resnikoff, 64, of Russia, identified as a member of the International Workers Order.

Carl Sklar, 49, native of Poland, described as an organizer for the United Packinghouse Workers, C. I. O.

Vincent Andrulis, or Vincent Andrulewicz, 60, of Lithuania, identified as editor of the newspaper Vilnis, which the department called an alleged Communist organ.

Arrested in Seattle — Erneso Mangaoang, 48, native of the Philippines, business agent of the International Cannery Workers Union.

Boris Sassieff, a Seattle book store operator and a native of Russia.

Arrested in Los Angeles—David Hyun, 33, a native of Korea and a citizen of China, alleged to be a member of the executive board of the Communist party in Hawaii.

Harry Carlisle, 52, of Britain, former owner of The Western Worker in San Francisco, described as active in an "anti-war congress"

HEADS CONTROL BOARD

Seth W. Richardson
The New York Times (Washington Bureau)

and a lecturer on Marxist theory in Hollywood in 1948.

Solomon Sholnick, alias Frank Carlsa, 37, of Poland, identified as associated with the Young Communist League and the Communist party.

Arrested in San Francisco— Nathan Yanish, alias Noyach Yanishevsky, 41, of Russia, member of the Friends of the Abraham Lincoln Brigade, which fought in the Spanish Civil War, against whom a deportation action had been pending since 1946.

Ernest Otto Fuchs, alias Fox, 44, of Germany, active in maritime unions. (He is not related to Klaus Fuchs, the convicted German-born atomic scientist imprisoned in England for espionage.)

Arrested in St. Paul, Minn.— John Peter Warhol, 40, native of Czechoslovakia, identified as a state officer of the International Workers Order in 1942 and honorably discharged from the United States Army in 1946.

Arrested in St. Louis—Antonia Sentner, 43, native of Yugoslavia.

Arrested in Croton-on-Hudson, N. Y.—Alexander Bittelman, 60, native of Russia, a writer identified as a former national Communist party committee man.

[In New York, the Immigration Service arrested Harry Yaris, Andrew Dmytryshyn and George Pirinsky.]

Each of the arrested aliens had been in the United States for years—one of them, Mr. Resnikoff, since 1903.

About 3,600 aliens in the United States have been ordered deported, but remain here because their countries of origin will not take them back. The intention of the Justice Department's campaign of arrests is to use the six months detention provision of the McCarran act to spur unwanted aliens to greater efforts toward their own repatriation.

New Attack by McCarthy

During the day, one of the Administration's most persistent

critics on the issue of its attitude toward communism, Senator Joseph R. McCarthy, Republican, of Wisconsin, returned to the assault.

Mr. McCarthy, in a statement published in the Congressional Record, which gives members of Congress immunity from libel suits for declarations made there, asserted:

"The ranks of American scientists have been infiltered to an alarming degree by the Communist enemies of the United States."

He said that the Atomic Energy Commission had "ignored" the problem or treated it "far too lightly." He attacked Prof. Kirtley Mather of Harvard as having been "affiliated with upward of forty Communist front organizations."

The Senator accused the American Federation of Scientists of being "heavily infiltrated with Communist fellow-travelers." He said that W. A. Higenbotham, a member of the Brookhaven Laboratory staff of the Atomic Energy Commission, had served as chairman of the federation.

Others attacked by Senator McCarthy for alleged associations of one kind or another with Communist or subversive organizations or causes included Lyle Borst, an atomic scientist; Prof. Philip Morrison of Cornell University; Prof. Harold C. Urey of the University of Chicago, a Nobel Prize winner, and Prof. Linus Carl Pauling of the California Institute of Technology.

Mr. McCarthy's charges were denounced in several quarters. Dr. Howard Meyerhoff of the Association for the Advancement of Science, termed them "utterly irresponsible."

Commented Dr. Clifford Grobstein of the Federation of American Scientists: "McCarthy is right in one thing. Higenbotham is chairman of our federation. The rest is fantastic nonsense."

Gordon Dean, chairman of the Atomic Energy Commission, issued this statement:

"Since the Atomic Energy Commission assumed office on Jan. 1, 1947, no person employed by the commission or its contractors nor any of the commission's consultants or advisers has ever been arrested or indicted much less convicted of any act of disloyalty. It is deplorable that statements of the type made by Senator McCarthy tend to undermine confidence in the atomic energy program in defiance of the facts of a security record which speaks for itself."

Pauling Calls Peace His Aim

PASADENA, Calif., Oct. 23 (AP) —Doctor Pauling said in reply to Senator McCarthy:

"I have been working in support of the international policy that would lead to peace and avert an atomic war, and I assume that is what the Senator is referring to."

Comment on Charges Refused

A spokesman for the Atomic Energy Commission's Brookhaven staff said here yesterday that Doctors Higinbotham and Borst had no comment on the McCarthy assertions.

Urey Replies to Senator
Special to THE NEW YORK TIMES.

CHICAGO, Oct. 23—Replying to Senator McCarthy's charges, Chancellor Robert Maynard Hutchins of the University of Chicago said today:

"I should think Senator McCarthy would want to prove some of the charges he already has made before making any more."

Professor Urey answered the Senator as follows:

"As usual, Senator McCarthy doesn't know his facts. Up to the end of the war I worked on the atomic bomb. Since 1945 I have had nothing to do with secret work or the A. E. C.

"One very good reason I haven't is that there are too many ignorant politicians of the McCarthy kind who hide behind immunity to abuse and slander those engaged in secret research. Long ago I decided life is too short to spend one's time defending himself and at the same time trying to do scientific research."

Called "Wild Allegations"
Special to THE NEW YORK TIMES.

BOSTON, Oct. 23—Prof. Kirtley F. Mather of Harvard asserted tonight that Senator McCarthy and the rest of the country "may rest at ease since I have never been engaged by the Atomic Energy Commission or the Manhattan District Project for any work dealing with atomic energy, or any other project under Government auspices connected with security."

He added that the Wisconsin Republican's "wild allegations and irresponsible charges dealt out so liberally under Senatorial immunity against libel have been so discredited that they no longer have any meaning."

As for Mr. McCarthy's charges that he was "a Communist, fellow traveler or fifth columnist," Professor Mather said, "they are just as false as those he has made against other people, including Owen Lattimore."

Fears McCarthy's Approval

ITHACA, N. Y., Oct. 23 (AP)— Professor Morrison said that "I belong to no subversive organizations and I maintain my right to write, speak and act independently and publicity, whatever Senator McCarthy thinks."

Professor Morrison said he was pleased to find himself named in "such pleasant company," and that he was "not disturbed that Senator McCarthy is on the other side."

"When Senator McCarthy approves of my activities I shall have reason to be concerned about my patriotism," he added.

The professor listed some organizations to which he belonged, and said he was "most active" in the American Physical Society, American Society of Bacteriologists, Phi Beta Kappa, Sigma XI (honorary science research society), the Federation of American Scientists, the American Federation of Teachers, A. F. L., the American Labor party and the National Council for Arts, Sciences and Professions.

October 24, 1950

HIGH COURT UPHOLDS SELF-INCRIMINATION AS PLEA IN RED CASE

Contempt Conviction of Woman Who Balked at Queries by Federal Jury Is Reversed

OPINION IS FAR-REACHING

Unanimous Decision, Written by Justice Black, Is Based on Fifth Amendment

By LEWIS WOOD
Special to THE NEW YORK TIMES.

WASHINGTON, Dec. 11—The Supreme Court unanimously ruled today that witnesses before Federal grand juries might refuse to answer questions concerning their alleged Communist affiliations if they pleaded possible self-incrimination.

The effect of the undivided opinion was considered far-reaching, and experts of the Department of Justice were studying its import. The finding, however, did not disturb the power of courts to punish persons declining to answer questions of Congressional committees on the ground that their free speech guarantee had been violated.

The high court opinion, written by Justice Hugo L. Black, reversed a sentence of one year imposed on Mrs. Patricia Blau of Denver for contempt of court. She told a Denver grand jury that to answer questions on alleged Communist affiliations would tend to incriminate her under the ten-year-old, anti-subversive Smith Act.

"Prior decisions of this court," Justice Black wrote, "have clearly established that under such circumstances, the Constitution gives a witness the privilege of remaining silent. The attempt by the courts below to compel petitioner (Mrs. Blau) to testify runs counter to the Fifth Amendment as it has been interpreted from the beginning."

Aaron Burr Case Cited

The Fifth Amendment provides that "no person . . . shall be compelled in any criminal case to be a witness against himself."

For its precedents, and as Justice Black said, "from the beginning," the Supreme Court went back 143 years to a ruling by Chief Justice John Marshall in the Circuit Court for the Virginia District in the case of Aaron Burr. This was during the trial of Burr for treason after his ill-fated dream of empire.

In contrast to the usual Supreme Court document, the Black opinion was remarkably short—in fact only about two pages. Justice Tom C. Clark, former Attorney General, did not participate.

Three persons originally appealed this case to the Supreme Court, Mrs. Blau, her husband, Irving Blau, and Jane Rogers. All declined to answer the grand jury's questions, and the pleas of all were argued before the Supreme Court simultaneously. The Court, however, did not pass on any except the case of Mrs. Blau today.

When she appealed, Mrs. Blau noted that eleven high Communist leaders had been convicted in New York. The case of these men was argued a week ago before the Supreme Court, which now has under consideration their attack on the validity of the Smith Act making it criminal to teach or advocate the violent overthrow of the Government.

Smith Act Mentioned

In sustaining Mrs. Blau's refusal to answer on the ground of possible self-incrimination, Justice Black said that the provisions of the Smith Act made her future prosecution far more than a "mere imaginary possibility." He added:

"She could reasonably fear that criminal charges might be brought against her if she admitted employment by the Communist party or intimate knowledge of its workings."

The decision was sure to affect the scope of future Federal grand jury investigations and possibly in enforcement of some phases of the McCarran Anti-Subversion Act. It may affect, too, the contempt-of-Congress cases against persons who have refused to reply to questions on their Communist connections on self-incrimination grounds.

In this group are Earl Browder, former Communist party leader in the United States; Frederick Vanderbilt Field, millionaire left-wing supporter, and Philip Jaffe, former editor of Amerasia Magazine. All were indicted recently for refusing to answer questions during the Senate's investigation of Senator Joseph McCarthy's charges of Communist infiltration in the State Department. All await trial.

The three contempt convictions, including Mrs. Blau's, grew out of a loyalty inquiry by the Federal grand jury in Denver. The investigation concerned Government employes who were accused of making false statements in connection with loyalty oaths. In pressing the investigation, the grand jury tried to obtain the names of officers of the Communist party in Colorado as well as books and data revealing the membership.

Mrs. Blau refused to give the names of the officers, to say if she had ever been hired by the party, or to describe any of the books and records of the organization.

As a result she was convicted and later sentenced to one year imprisonment. Jane Rogers, according to the Government charges, admitted that she had been party treasurer, but would not say to whom she had given the records. Irving Blau would not answer questions concerning his wife's "whereabouts," or if he were connected with the party. Jane Rogers was sentenced to four months and Mr. Blau to six months.

Party Seen Put First

In a final appearance before the grand jury, Mrs. Blau declined to answer any inquiries, pleading again that "any testimony which I may give which associates myself with any leaders of the Communist party will therefore incriminate myself."

When the case was argued in the Supreme Court, the Government asked the justices to sustain the contempt convictions. Justice Department lawyers held that the three witnesses were "primarily concerned with preserving the secrecy of Communist party records, rather than concealing their own participation in party activities."

Up to now, the Supreme Court has sustained a number of contempt of Congress convictions, the defendants in which based their pleas on free speech violations. Lately a number of cases affecting the theory of self-incrimination have reached the lower courts and will eventually find their way to the Supreme Court.

December 12, 1950

M'CARTHY'S INFLUENCE IS GREATER IN THE 82D

Republicans Bow to Political Success As the Senator Plans New Campaign

By WILLIAM S. WHITE
Special to THE NEW YORK TIMES.

WASHINGTON, Jan. 6—There was a time, only a few months ago, when many Republicans in the Senate quietly arranged matters in the daily routine so as never to pass close to the desk of their colleague, Joseph R. McCarthy of Wisconsin.

With a seeming casualness they avoided any public friendliness. If Mr. McCarthy was a member of the historic club, he was a rather lonely one. The point of the snubs was never lost; but it never showed in the dark, heavy, almost perpetually smiling face of the junior Senator from Wisconsin.

The desk of Senator McCarthy of Wisconsin is not, these days, avoided very often by his Republican associates. "McCarthyism," be it an incomparable epithet, is simply today a very considerable force in the Congress of the United States.

And it seems to be here to stay. Senator McCarthy himself, against whom a half-dozen of his colleagues once issued a "declaration of conscience," is, by any standard, the most politically powerful first-term Senator in this Congress. This is the fact of the case. (He came here from the 1946 elections and is still, officially, a freshman.)

Lessons Not Lost

The man who pursued the highest member of the American Cabinet, Secretary of State Dean Acheson, now finds that the Republican membership of Congress officially has demanded Mr. Acheson's head.

The man who in the late campaign pursued across country the two most formidable Democratic fighters in the Senate—Scott W. Lucas of Illinois and Millard E. Tydings of Maryland—now surveys a scene in which both are retired to private life.

The lessons of these matters have not been lost, in this first week of the new Congress, on the Republicans. Nor have the Democrats ignored Mr. McCarthy, as so long they had tried to do.

Deference to McCarthy

A consensus of Congress, reluctantly or not arrived at, is this:

(1) Essentially, Senator McCarthy beat Senator Tydings in Maryland, though the successor to the office was the new Republican Senator, John M. Butler.

(2) Senator McCarthy contributed a heavy part, if not perhaps the decisive part, to the defeat of Senator Lucas of Illinois.

(3) The newly elected Republican Senator from Idaho, Herman Welker, owes much to Mr. McCarthy.

(4) The newly elected Republican Senator from Utah, Wallace

F. Bennett, is at least unconsciously and unwittingly a beneficiary of Mr. McCarthy's strenuous and unprecedented campaign against the alleged Communists in Government.

The Republicans have responded to all this with an obvious new deference to Mr. McCarthy. For in the hard, objective books of the politicians, there is beside his name an entry of success.

The Senate Democrats, for the first time as a group, have made a response of their own. In their pre-Congress caucus of this week they decided to put a reservation about the seating of Senator Butler, upon Mr. Tydings' claim that he had been pictured in doctored documents circulated by Butler partisans as a friend of the Communists. This action was the first occasion that Democrats of the right, center and left had come together without a break on the issue of Senator McCarthy's activities.

The Democratic tactic that required Mr. Butler to be sworn in "without prejudice" to a possible future effort to expel him had a significance beyond Senator Butler.

There was little real Democratic feeling that Mr. Butler could be ousted; indeed, there was by no means, at this stage, any unanimity that he should be. The unanimity was upon a different matter: that at least some sort of demonstration had to be made to discourage in future the type of representations that had been made about Senator Tydings—including a "composite" photograph that appeared to show him in friendly conversation with the deposed American Communist leader, Earl Browder.

Lesson of Tydings Case

There ran through the caucus—and this on the authority even of some of the most entrenched right-wing Southern Democratic patriarchs who participated—a general expression of fear that what had happened to Mr. Tydings, with all his standing in the Senate, could happen to any other man in the Senate.

"For whom does the bell toll? It tolls for thee," said a powerful Senator as later he summarized the decision of the caucus.

The Democrats, in brief, had achieved at last a solid front against the manifestations of "McCarthyism," something they had not done in all the months before.

Senator McCarthy, for his part, is busy now, quite unconcerned with this possible collision with a force that never yet has he met in its full strength, with plans for future investigations of alleged communism in government.

He has it in mind that these should involve not simply the State Department but should encompass as well the Commerce Department, the Department of Agriculture, and an agency that is uniquely the President's own, the Bureau of the Budget.

Whether these inquiries actually are to come off in any full-scale way and by what agency of the Senate will be determined, in all probability, by a series of circumstances quite unrelated in themselves.

In the event of major war, Republican thrusts of this sort at the Administration almost certainly would be stilled or deferred. As to mechanics, Senator Pat McCarran, Democrat of Nevada, author of the Subversive Control Act, is now preparing to set up an investigating subcommittee of the Senate Judiciary Committee, of which he is chairman, of almost limitless scope.

Senator McCarthy has the highest regard for Senator McCarran; indeed, he welcomed the formation of the subcommittee. Nevertheless, Mr. McCarthy himself is a member of the standing Senate group that is normally charged with the Senate's investigative functions, a body with the rather unlikely name of the "Committee on Expenditures in the Executive Departments."

McCarthy's View

Senator McCarthy, though by no means deprecating Senator McCarran—whose hostility to many Administration programs and notions is not outmatched by that of any Republican—would not like to see the Executive Expenditures Committee altogether lose the jurisdiction.

In sum, the air of Congress may be assumed to be at least latently full of "McCarthyism," however defined, all through the life of this Congress—in a spectacular way, if foreign events permit, and, in any case, in a pervasive way.

January 7, 1951

Senate Unit to Push Again Today For Its Own 'Un-American' Inquiry

By C. P. TRUSSELL
Special to THE NEW YORK TIMES.

WASHINGTON, Jan. 16 — The Senate Judiciary Committee was scheduled to move again tomorrow to create within its own membership a Senate counterpart of the House Committee on Un-American Activities.

The extent to which it succeeds rests largely with the Senate Committee on Rules and Administration, which has jurisdiction over the funds with which special groups of the Senate operate.

A principal function of the new investigating panel would be to watch the administration and enforcement of the Internal Security Act of 1950. This is the omnibus anti-subversive statute that the Eighty-first Congress enacted over the veto of President Truman. Senator Pat McCarran, Democrat of Nevada and chairman of the Judiciary Committee, was the principal sponsor of the act.

Fields of Investigation

In December the Senate approved the organization of the panel and its investigation in these fields:

1. The administration, operation and enforcement of the new act, which calls for registration of Communist-action organizations and their "fronts" and registration of aliens.
2. Administration, operation and enforcement of other laws relating to espionage, sabotage and the protection of the internal security.
3. The extent, nature and effects of subversive activities in the United States, its Territories and possessions. This would include but not be limited to espionage, sabotage and infiltration by persons who are or may be under the domination of a foreign government, Communist organizations or any movements seeking to overthrow the Government of the United States by force.

Question Raised

Before the Senate action was taken the Judiciary Committee approved the resolution to establish the special group unanimously. The measure went to the Committee on Rules and Administration for approval of $100,000 of operating funds.

Senator Carl Hayden, Democrat of Arizona, chairman of the Rules group, explained to the Senate that a question had been raised concerning the resolution's proposal for watchdog operations over specific statutes. It was contended that the Judiciary Committee already had such authority.

However, the Rules group recommended a $10,000 fund and made it available only until Jan. 31, to give the committee an opportunity to review it after the present Congress came in. Senator McCarran decided to hold the project in abeyance pending a fresh start.

The Judiciary Committee was scheduled to take up tomorrow a resolution calling for additional funds, perhaps to make up the entire $100,000. Prompt approval was predicted. Then the matter will be up to the Rules group. Senator McCarran said he anticipated no trouble. He expected to name the personnel of the investigating group and put it to work soon, he said.

January 17, 1951

TRUMAN SHARPENS LOYALTY STANDARD

Special to THE NEW YORK TIMES.

WASHINGTON, April 28—President Truman tightened Federal loyalty regulations today by authorizing the denial of Federal jobs to anyone about whose loyalty to the United States Government there was "reasonable doubt."

Hitherto, "reasonable grounds" for believing a person disloyal were required for such action, which had been interpreted as meaning evidence of present loyalty, regardless of the past, would qualify one for Federal employment. Under the new standard the background of a person could provide "reasonable doubt."

An executive order issued by the President at the request of Robert Ramspeck, chairman of the Civil Service Commission, established the severer standard.

Similar pleas for such a standard had been made before by Hiram Bingham, chairman of the Loyalty Review Board, and his predecessor, Seth W. Richardson, who is now head of the Anti-Subversive Control Board created by the McCarran Anti-Subversive Act, which requires among other things the registration of Communists.

The text of the new rule follows:

"The standard for the refusal of employment or the removal from employment in an executive department or agency on grounds relating to loyalty shall be that, on all the evidence, there is a reasonable doubt as to the loyalty of the person involved to the Government of the United States."

President Truman had been reluctant to establish the new rule until the proposal could be studied by the Commission on Internal Security and Individual Rights that he created to survey the whole controversial problem of Federal employe loyalty. But this group has been unable to function because of red tape since its first meeting on Lincoln's birthday.

While they are part-time and temporary Federal employes, the members of the commission, headed by Fleet Admiral Chester W. Nimitz, contended that they could not act until they were exempted from Federal statutes that prohibit Federal employes from filing claims against, or having business relationships with, the Government. These laws affect members whose business concerns or law firms have defense contracts or are likely to be engaged in claims involving this Government.

Recommendation Is Withheld

Consequently the commission withheld a recommendation on the "reasonable doubt" issue and decided to cease functioning in a formal way until Congress provided relief.

Mr. Ramspeck, recently appointed to the Civil Service Commission, called attention to the impasse affecting the commission in a letter of April 16 requesting the President to authorize the "reasonable doubt" provision.

Mr. Ramspeck referred to the previous request on Feb. 13 that Mr. Bingham had made and added: "The Civil Service Commission is informed that this matter was referred to the Commission on Internal Security and Individual Rights for consideration. The Civil Service Commission is now informed that the Commission on Internal Security and Individual Rights has adjourned pending action by the Congress on a proposed enactment to relieve the members * * * from the sections of the criminal code which prohibit the prosecution of claims against the Government by an employe of the Government."

Mr. Ramspeck said that the desired exemption was pending before the Senate Judiciary Committee and that "it will be some time before this matter is considered by the Judiciary Committee." The committee is reported to be cool toward the idea of granting the exemption.

Backlogs Are Cited

"Backlogs are being created in the agency and regional loyalty boards due to the increased employment in Government and the high rate of turnover caused by the establishment of new agencies in the Government," Mr. Ramspeck continued, "and also to the fact that many of the lower boards are looking forward to and are anticipating early action on the resolution of the Loyalty Review Board amending the standard in Executive Order 9835 [which had prescribed the original disloyalty standard]."

Demand for the tighter standard increased after the conviction last February of William W. Remington, former Department of Commerce employe, for perjury for concealing his past Communist party membership. Two years before, the Loyalty Review Board, then headed by Mr. Richardson, had cleared him of a disloyalty charge.

Critics of the old standard contended that they were required to find a suspect guilty of present disloyalty. They contended they were unable to disqualify anyone whose background aroused suspicions although his present character appeared proper. Thus they felt that Communists who have gone underground in recent years had a loophole in the original standard which permitted them to remain in Government employ.

April 29, 1951

LARRY PARKS SAYS HE WAS COMMUNIST

Actor Testifies He Quit in '45 —Gale Sondergaard and Da Silva Will Not Answer

By The United Press.

WASHINGTON, March 21 — Larry Parks, motion picture actor, admitted today that he once belonged to the Communist party but two other Hollywood players— Howard Da Silva and Gale Sondergaard—refused to testify to possible Red activities on the ground that it might incriminate them.

The three were lead-off witnesses at the revival of the House Committee on Un-American Activities' 1947 communism-in-Hollywood hearings. Representative John S. Wood, Democrat of Georgia, committee chairman, said that contempt citations would be considered against Mr. Da Silva and Miss Sondergaard.

Mr. Parks, who at first pleaded with the investigators not to force him to "crawl through the mud to be an informer" on other film figures, later went behind closed doors to give them the names of "four or five" Hollywood Communists he had known.

Committee members said afterward that Mr. Parks was "very cooperative" and they were not considering contempt action against him. Mr. Parks, the first Hollywood witness to admit ever being a Red, said he drifted into the party in 1941 and drifted out again in 1945.

Report Names Were Known

He said there is a very great difference in being a Communist

now and being a Communist in 1945. Committee members said the names he provided in closed session already were known to the group. They said the hearings will be resumed April 10.

Conviction of contempt of Congress carries a maximum penalty of one year in jail and a $1,000 fine on each count.

Frank S. Tavenner Jr., committee counsel, conducted the questioning of Mr. Parks, star of "The Jolson Story," and of the other two witnesses.

Mr. Da Silva was featured in the original Broadway production of the musical "Oklahoma." Since 1940 he has appeared in such films as "They Live by Night," "The Lost Week-end," and "Unconquered."

Miss Sondergaard is well known to movie fans for her portrayal of villainesses. She won Hollywood's first Academy award in 1936 for the best performance by a supporting actress in her role in "Anthony Adverse." She also played featured roles in "Anna and the King of Siam" and in "The Life of Emile Zola."

Mr. Da Silva, an actor since 1929, answered a few nonpolitical questions, but on advice of his attorneys refused to discuss any possible relations he might have had with communism. He based his refusal on the constitutional ground that to reply might lead to his prosecution.

Ten Hollywood writers, actors and directors who similarly refused to answer the committee's questions in 1947 were sent to jail. But unlike Mr. Da Silva they did not base their refusal on the ground of possible self-incrimination.

The Supreme Court ruled recently that witnesses in certain investigations cannot be jailed for refusing to answer questions if they plead self-incrimination. Some Federal district courts have held this applies to witnesses before

Larry Parks telling the House Committee on Un-American Activities that he was a member of the Communist party ten years ago, but later resigned.

The New York Times (Washington Bureau)

Congressional committees.

Miss Sondergaard refused to reply when asked if she had held Communist party card number 46943 for 1944 and number 47328 for 1945.

Mr. Parks said he joined the party in 1941, when he was 25 years old because it was "the most liberal of the parties." He said he left it in 1945 from a "lack of interest—of not finding the things I thought I would find."

Asserting that his confession probably would wreck his Hollywood career, he pleaded almost tearfully with the committee not to force him to be an informer.

"It's not sportsmanlike, it's not

American justice," he said. He compared the committee's earlier hint of a contempt citation to Nazi practices under Hitler.

Mr. Da Silva, a native of Cleveland, refused to reply when asked if he had held office in the New York chapter of the Civil Rights Congress, labeled a Communist front by the Justice Department. He would not say whether he ever was a Communist, or whether he ever tried to recruit persons into the party.

Mr. Da Silva said under the Constitution he was not compelled to answer questions "designed to drive" him from the acting profession.

185

Miss Sondergaard, deeply tanned and wearing a black and white checked suit, agreed that Congressional committees should investigate subversive activities but said "this committee is doing incriminating work."

In refusing to answer other questions, she reminded the committee she is the wife of Herbert Biberman "who recently came out of prison for defending the First Amendment." The First Amendment provides for freedom of speech, religion, press and assembly. Biberman was one of the "Hollywood Ten" jailed for contempt as a result of the committee's 1947 hearings.

Under Mr. Tavenner's questions. Mr. Parks said he did not believe that persons who are members of a conspiracy to overthrow the Government should have power in unions or where they could influence the writing of movie scripts or the course of cinema stories.

Under questioning, Mr. Parks admitted there were Communists in the Actors Laboratory, a school and "showcase" for actors. He said he was honorary treasurer of the group but testified that he knew of no attempt by Communists to gain control of the organization.

He told the committee he considered it "an impossibility" to slant movie scripts toward com-

munism and said anything that in individual films probably was a mistake in judgment.

He testified that he knew Lionel Stander, an actor, but did not recall attending any Communist meetings with him.

Mr. Parks said he attended only ten, twelve or fifteen Communist party meetings during his five years of party membership and contributed only about $50 or $60 to the party, perhaps because he is "a close man with a dollar."

The actor said he never had been ordered to try to influence American thinking along Communist lines through his screen or stage roles, and added: "If you go to the movies, it is almost evident

that this was not done."

Mr. Parks, who was born in Olathe, Kan., grew up in Joliet, Ill. He said he acquired his beliefs and convictions from his home, a Protestant church and the public schools.

He added that he is opposed to anti-semitism and believes that "every Negro child has the same right to food and shelter and education and opportunity and dignity that was granted me at birth."

He said that he remained a registered Democrat while a Communist, still is a Democrat and votes the straight party ticket.

March 22, 1951

LILLIAN HELLMAN BALKS HOUSE UNIT

Says She Is Not Red Now, but Won't Disclose if She Was Lest It Hurt Others

WASHINGTON, May 21 (UP)— Lillian Hellman, stage and screen writer, refused to say today whether she ever had belonged to the Communist party because her testimony "would hurt innocent people in order to save myself."

"I cannot and will not cut my conscience to fit this year's fashions," she told the House Un-American Activities Committee.

Miss Hellman, who wrote such hit plays as "The Children's Hour," "The Little Foxes" and "Watch on the Rhine," testified she was not a Communist now but refused to say whether she had belonged to the party in the past.

She declined to say whether she

was a party member three or more years ago because her answers might be "self-incriminating."

In a letter to the chairman, Representative John S. Wood, Democrat of Georgia, Miss Hellman had offered to "answer all questions about myself" if the committee agreed not to name other persons with whom she had associated in the past. The author wrote that she would have to refuse to answer any questions about herself if her request was not accepted.

Mr. Wood announced that the committee could not permit a witness to set forth terms for testifying or be "placed in the position of trading with a witness."

When Frank S. Tavenner Jr., the committee's counsel, asked Miss Hellman if she was "acquainted" with Martin Berkeley, a screen writer, she stopped testifying.

"I refuse to answer on grounds it might incriminate me," she said.

Mr. Berkeley, at committee hearings on the West Coast last year, testified that Miss Hellman had attended a 1937 meeting in his Hollywood home when the Communist party's "Hollywood Section" first was organized.

Miss Hellman told Mr. Tavenner she would have to stand on the

statements in her letter when he asked her if she ever attended any Communist party meetings at Mr. Berkeley's Hollywood home.

Letter is Quoted

Miss Hellman made public here yesterday a letter she had sent on Monday to Mr. Wood. In it the author declared:

" * * * I am ready and willing to testify before the representatives of our Government as to my own opinions and my own actions, regardless of any risks or consequences to myself.

"But I am advised by counsel that if I answer the committee's questions about myself, I must also answer questions about other people and that if I refuse to do so, I can be cited for contempt. My counsel tells me that if I answer questions about myself, I will have waived my rights under the Fifth Amendment and could be forced legally to answer questions about others.

"This is very difficult for a layman to understand. But there is one principle that I do understand: I am not willing, now or in the future, to bring bad trouble to people who, in my past association with them, were completely innocent of any talk or any action that

was disloyal or subversive.

"I do not like subversion or disloyalty in any form, and if I had ever seen any I would have considered it my duty to have reported it to the proper authorities. But to hurt innocent people whom I knew many years ago in order to save myself is, to me, inhuman and indecent and dishonorable.

"I cannot and will not cut my conscience to fit this year's fashions, even though I long ago came to the conclusion that I was not a political person and could have no comfortable place in any political group.

" * * * I am prepared to waive the privilege against self-incrimination and to tell you anything you wish to know about my views or actions, if your committee will agree to refrain from asking me to name other people. If the committee is unwilling to give me this assurance, I will be forced to plead the privilege of the Fifth Amendment at the hearing."

The Fifth Amendment to the Constitution says "No person * * * shall be compelled in any criminal case to be a witness against himself, nor be deprived of life, liberty or property without due process of law * * *."

May 22, 1952

Arthur Miller Admits Helping Communist-Front Groups in '40's

But Playwright Denies Being Under 'Discipline'—To Wed Marilyn Monroe Soon

By ALLEN DRURY
Special to The New York Times

WASHINGTON, June 21— Arthur Miller, playwright, disclosed today a past filled with Communist-front associations and a future filled with Marilyn Monroe. He said he would marry the film star before July 13.

The 40-year-old dramatist, a Pulitzer Prize winner, told the House Committee on Un-American Activities that he had signed

many appeals and protests issued by Red front groups in the last decade. But he denied that he ever had been "under Communist discipline." He risked a possible contempt citation by refusing to give the committee names of those he had seen at Communist-run meetings.

Mr. Miller revealed his plans to marry Miss Monroe during a recess in the committee hearing. He said they would be wed before she left for England on July 13 to make a film with Sir Laurence Olivier.

In response to questions by Richard Arens, committee counsel, the playwright testified that

"in those days"—referring principally to the late Nineteen Forties—"I did sign a lot of things." He said he was not denying that he had also joined in sponsoring many Communist-backed causes.

He said that in recent years he had "ceased issuing statements right and left except where I personally was involved."

"I found I was getting tangled up in too many thing I didn't want to defend 100 per cent," he said.

Mr. Miller was questioned about two passport applications he made. One, in 1947, was granted. The second, in March, 1954, was rejected by the State Department.

He said he was awaiting department action on an application for a passport to England. He wants to go there to be with Miss Monroe and to arrange for production of his play, "A View from the Bridge."

A department press officer, Joseph W. Reap, said that action on this application was being held up because the department had some "derogatory information" about the playwright that "must be answered by an affidavit."

"We have asked him through his attorney," Mr. Reap said, "to make an affidavit concerning past or present membership in the Communist party. We have not received it yet."

Mr. Arens asked Mr. Miller a series of questions concerning Communist-front activities.

Youth Festival Mentioned

These included sponsorship of a world youth festival in Prague in 1947; a signature on a 1947 statement against the outlawing of the Communist party; a signature on a statement defending Gerhart Eisler before he fled this country to become a top Communist official in East Germany; statements attacking the Committee on Un-American Activities; statements supporting relief work in Red China, and statements opposing the Smith Act.

The Smith Act forbids teaching or advocating the overthrow of the United States Government by force and violence.

Mr. Miller said he had no memory of most of these things, but that he would not deny them. He said he was opposed to the Smith Act because he feared it

might involve placing limitations on "advocacy." He said this would get "smack into the middle of literature."

Artists, he said, must have the right to express themselves freely.

Mr. Arens asked Mr. Miller whether he signed an application to join the Communist party in 1939 or 1940. The playwright said he had signed an application for what he thought

was "a study course" on Marxism, but did not know the exact nature of the application.

He also testified that he had attended Communist party writers' meetings four or five times. He refused to name persons he had seen there.

Mr. Miller won the Pulitzer Prize in 1949 for his play "Death of a Salesman." He won acclaim also in 1947 for "All My Sons," and in 1953 he produced

"The Crucible," a story of the persecution of persons accused of witchcraft in Salem in 1692.

The playwright returned to New York last week after obtaining a divorce in Reno, Nev., from his wife of fifteen years, Mary Grace Slattery Miller. They have two children.

June 22, 1956

Viewing the Miller Case Abroad
TO THE EDITOR OF THE NEW YORK TIMES:

I have just read in the French newspaper Le Monde that the United States Congress has decided to prosecute the famous writer Arthur Miller for not giving the names of people who belonged with him to a "subversive" organization.

I certainly do not want to interfere with American internal policies, and though I lived for some years in the United States I am trying to consider this case purely from a foreign viewpoint. I believe that such a story, largely publicized outside the United States, more than counterbalances all the effects of American generosity. I am afraid that the immense "reservoir of goodwill" toward America is now drying up fast.

I must confess that it is very difficult for me to defend the American cause before anyone (non-Communist, of course) who has never lived in the United States. For "local" stories—the Montgomery racial case, for instance—I can try to explain the state of mind of the poor Southern white people. But it is practically impossible to "justify" such a case as that of Arthur Miller, which, rightly or wrongly, people interpret as a result of Senator McCarthy's hysteria.

I become sadder each day when I discover that the irresponsible actions of a few politicians can give such a bad image of the American people, who are so kind-hearted, friendly and generous—and of their country, which is still the land of freedom in spite of narrow-minded people who do nothing but help the Communist cause.

GILBERT B. MELESE.
Sèvres, France, July 26, 1956.

August 8, 1956

College Freedoms Being Stifled By Students' Fear of Red Label

By KALMAN SEIGEL

A subtle, creeping paralysis of freedom of thought and speech is attacking college campuses in many parts of the country, limiting both students and faculty in the area traditionally reserved for the free exploration of knowledge and truth.

These limitations on free inquiry take a variety of forms, but their net effect is a widening tendency toward passive acceptance of the status quo, conformity, and a narrowing of the area of tolerance in which students, faculty and administrators feel free to speak, act and think independently.

A study of seventy-two major colleges in the United States by THE NEW YORK TIMES showed that many members of the college community were wary and felt varying degrees of inhibition about speaking out on controversial issues, discussing unpopular concepts and participating in student political activity, because they were fearful of:

1. Social disapproval.
2. A "pink" or Communist label.
3. Criticism by regents, legislatures and friends.
4. Rejection for further study at graduate schools.
5. The spotlight of investigation by Government and private industry for post-graduate employment and service with the armed forces.

Such caution, in effect, has made many campuses barren of the free give-and-take of ideas, the study found. At the same time it has posed a seemingly insoluble problem for the campus liberal, depleted his ranks and brought to many college campuses an apathy about current problems that borders almost on their deliberate exclusion.

A number of the nation's leading educators held that such a developing unwillingness to pursue free inquiry, fostered by pressures that promote prejudice and fear, struck a body-blow at the American educational process, one of democracy's most potent weapons, and that it was a long step toward defeating one of the basic purposes of the university.

But at the same time it also gave new impetus to a small but growing resistance to conformity and stimulated a new appreciation of America's free heritage.

Convinced that adolescence was a normal period of rebellion and a time when the young student challenged accepted doctrines, the educators maintained that the student's continued exploration of new horizons was "a normal symptom," a part of the process of growing up and of developing critical faculties and the ability to evaluate. The latter, in their option, was a virtual "must" in today's market of conflicting ideologies.

A little more than a fortnight ago, Earl J. McGrath, United States Commissioner of Education, told a group of educators in New York:

"Education for life in the world community of nations * * * begins in the school and on the campus in which democratic respect for personal and social differences is nourished."

The campus study revealed in the main a growing restrictive atmosphere, and that while there were few instances of reprisal or overt action against free expression, there was considerable evidence of self-censorship.

Controversies Skirted

Discussions with student leaders, teachers and administrators—in most instances names were withheld for fear of reprisal or criticism—disclosed that this censorship, wariness, caution and inhibition largely took these forms:

1. A reluctance to speak out on controversial issues in and out of class.
2. A reluctance to handle currently unpopular concepts even in classroom work where they may be part of the study program.
3. An unwillingness to join student political clubs.
4. Neglect of humanitarian causes because they may be suspect in the minds of politically unsophisticated officials.
5. An emphasis on lack of affiliations.
6. An unusual amount of serio-comic joking about this or that official investigating committee "getting you."
7. A shying away, both physically

187

and intellectually from any association with the words, "liberal," "peace," "freedom," and from classmates of a liberal stripe.

8. A sharp turning inward to local college problems, to the exclusion of broader current questions.

Part of the wariness and apathy —the latter is a marked characteristic on many college campuses— is not solely a product of current "hysteria," or as a majority of students and faculty put it, "the pressures generated by Senator Joseph McCarthy of Wisconsin."

While this was an important contributing factor, they said, it stemmed also from the "times," the probable inevitability of the draft, the fear and uncertainty in national life and a fatalistic and frustrated conviction that little can be done in the college area to alter international developments.

Other Factors Noted

Other contributing factors toward decreased liberal activity were a mature awareness of the true nature of communism, with the result that it has lost much of its former fascination, and the feeling that under present conditions a firm, unswerving allegiance to established concepts is in the national interest and should be accepted.

How much each contributed, however, was almost impossible to assess.

According to the study, municipal colleges and large state universities in large cities felt the impact of the pressures most, with lesser state universities, large private colleges, smaller private institutions and denominational colleges following.

The concern with the problem shown by educators is apparent in this comment from Dr. Alvin Eurich, president of the University of the State of New York:

"Freedom of inquiry, thought and speech are indivisible human rights in a democracy. In recent months justifiable fear of communism has set in motion unjustifiable behavior denying these very principles. Such extreme counteractions are as dangerous as communism itself, because they seek to deny to our citizens the freedoms for which our nation was originally founded.

Stresses Importance of Inquiry

"We as educators are concerned daily with these attitudes creeping onto the college campus. There has been much discussion of loyalty and academic freedom for professors. An exact parallel to this issue is academic freedom for the student. Nowhere is it more important to cherish and protect freedom of inquiry, thought and speech than on college campuses— the training grounds for some 2,-500,000 future citizens who must understand the values and responsibilities of democracy."

Some random examples taken from the study turned up these indications of repressionism and inhibition on the college campuses:

At the City College of New York, a student leader said he was "extremely reluctant" to express any opinions that might be considered left-wing, even when asked to write a theme in class on a political issue.

A student editor held that his fellow-students were unwilling to speak out, particularly in engineering, where, he said, "the wrong word at the wrong time might jeopardize their futures." He said agents of the Federal Bureau of Investigation were constantly inquiring about students applying for Government jobs, and that some graduate schools, with Government-classified projects, were extremely reluctant to accept students who had committed themselves to an unpopular point of view.

"It Can Only Be Felt"

The current issue of one of the undergraduate papers at the college explored another phase of the problem in this way: "The willingness of instructors to express their own honest viewpoint has been slowly ebbing. Evidence in support of this statement cannot be given in black-and-white. It can only be felt in the classroom."

At Queens College, Dr. Harold Lenz, dean of students, declared that students were now more afraid of controversial issues and speakers than in previous years. A student editor declared that the students "were playing it safe."

Student leaders at Hunter College reported that students were fearful of signing petitions, because they were reluctant to get their names on "any list." Letters to the editor of the undergraduate paper, they said, in explaining the greater caution, now open with "It appears that," rather than with the "I think," and "I believe," of years ago.

A number of the teachers offer qualifying apologies during their lectures, particularly when they move from the black-and-white realm of the textbook, to analysis and interpretation, saying, "Don't get me wrong," and "Don't think I'm a Communist."

Dean Millicent C. McIntosh of Barnard told of a meeting with dormitory students recently. She said she summoned the girls because some had indicated that speakers at a political institute had skimmed over vital issues and made only "patriotic speeches."

"Obscurantism" Noted

The dean said she found some girls held that anything identified with peace, freedom of speech or negotiation to resolve differences was suspected of Communist influence.

"Girls are becoming afraid to advocate the humanitarian point of view," Dean McIntosh declared, "because it has been associated with communism. The most fearless will not be influenced, but the middle group is made to feel the confusion and fear involved in the 'obscurantism' that is, Mc-Carthyism."

The president of the college's political association noted that she had found a definite emotional reaction to anything verbally tinged with ultra-radicalism. The president of the Liberal Action Club, which has no set platform or outside affiliation, reported that students were fearful of joining any political clubs on the campus, because they were afraid that such affiliations would hurt them in Government work.

In the college placement office, Miss Ruth Houghton, director, said the word "liberal" was "a poisonous word" to many would-be employers, who conceived of the "liberal girl" as an "obstructionist" and "organizer against employer interests."

At Columbia University, responsible student spokesmen said a generally good record on academic freedom for faculty and students was slowly being marred by the national "hysteria." Prof. Robert S. Lynd, sociologist, said students were "pretty apprehensive and cautious," but the precise difficulty and the reasons for the wary attitudes were difficult to identify.

Vassar Situation Similar

At Vassar, the evidence was repeated by the leaders of liberal clubs, who said fear of future reprisal was the motivating factor that kept their club rolls small. They pointed to a recent anonymous letter to the editor of The Miscellany News, one of the two undergraduate papers on the campus, in which the writer noted that she did not now belong to, nor did she intend to join any political association on the campus. The decision, she said, involved careful thought on her and her parents' part.

"In today's world of 'witch hunting,' 'subversive actions' and 'pink tinges,' such factors as these must be taken into consideration by every student," the writer declared. "It is particularly important if the student might some day want a position with the Government."

At Rutgers, several student leaders told this story that pointed up the problem:

A number of students who were asked to sign the widely publicized, anti-Communist Crusade for Freedom Scroll refused, because they were suspicious of the words "crusade" and "freedom" and unsure of the sponsors. After the scroll was explained, a few came into the fold, but others remained adamant, maintaining that they didn't want their names on any suspicious lists.

At Yale University, as a result of a recent campus incident, The Daily News, student newspaper, explored the problem in a long editorial in which the editors declared:

"We cannot believe that the American people will indefinitely tolerate this control over youthful lives by looming up before them the spectre of the 'loyalty check.' We cannot believe that this virtual blockade of the marketplace of ideas to young men can go on for a lifetime.

"And yet, despite hope, we see the sky growing darker, the night of thought-conformity closing in. We see college men growing more and more docile, more and more accepting the status quo, paralyzed by the fear of their futures, radicalism snuffed out where it should flame the brightest."

Leaders See "Reticence"

At New York University, a group of student leaders reported "a reticence" on the part of their classmates to express liberal viewpoints for fear of reprisal in graduate school, thus failing to take advantage of a liberal policy on student and faculty freedom.

At the University of Michigan, Dean Erich A. Walter explained that students were quite obviously more careful in their affiliations, recognizing that Federal security officers were making careful checks of the memberships of liberal organizations.

Student leaders also reported a shrinking of the numbers and membership rolls of campus liberal organizations.

Students at the University of California were also pictured by their leaders and faculty as being increasingly more careful about choosing their associations and committing themselves to actions they might later regret.

Student leaders here and at many other colleges and universities also cited the social disapproval factor as an important inhibiting influence, indicating that in many respects the college community had ceased to be an arena for divergent views.

Several student leaders at the University of North Carolina asserted that students with radical views were not accepted socially as formerly. John Sanders, retiring student body president, explained:

"The liberal traditions of the university are still intact. I do not feel that there has been any particular increase in restriction of student expression over the past year by the university administration.

"We, however, are not by our academic status isolated from the prevailing climate of opinion. The growing fear of new ideas and of different ideas, largely a consequence of the McCarthy witchhunts, has had its effect on students, as on citizens everywhere."

Henry Bowers, newly elected president of the student body, believes that students with radical opinions are discouraged "only through social action." He added that "the academic freedom of the administration has been limited by the inclusion of a non-Communist oath."

John R. Harris, assistant attorney general for the student body, said that while the student newspaper was free to say what it pleased, there was an atmosphere on the campus, "as in most of the country, which tends to equate criticism with disloyalty and liberalism with communism."

At the University of Wisconsin, John Searle, president of the student body, pointed to the rejection of Max Lerner, newspaper columnist, as a lecturer; the refusal to permit an instructor to take part in a debate with a Catholic professor on "Scholastic Sociology vs. Scientific Sociology," and to a general tagging of the student board as "subversive" because it had issued a statement opposing the views of Senator McCarthy.

George Rucker, president of Students for Democratic Action at the University of Oklahoma, said the lack of opposition to a recently enacted loyalty oath law in that state has been "nothing short of tragic in its evidence of the extent to which fear reigns in our nation." Student reaction, he added, has been on the whole "appallingly apathetic."

Mr. Rucker said that the faculty, which is "almost completely in intellectual opposition to the oath, has done nothing about it."

Article Is Withdrawn

At the University of Nebraska, a faculty member advised a student who had completed an article for publication critical of the McCarran (National Security) Act that such an article might damage his reputation. The article was withdrawn. Student spokesmen cited the case of a woman student who informed a faculty member that her name had been put on a Communist-front mailing list, and faculty members called in the F. B. I. to investigate.

They reported that a student who submitted an article comparing modern subversive investigations with witch trials was told that it could not be printed because it was too controversial.

They also noted that the university organization to which all foreign students belonged halted programs on political and international issues when students from Asia and elsewhere were accused of being communistic.

At six Midwestern campuses—Iowa State, Indiana University, Purdue, Oberlin, Kenyon, Washington University—college and university authorities, deans and student leaders said they detected greater caution on the part of students. Students, it was reported, were aware of the increased activity of the F. B. I. and other investigative units. Political expression appeared to have faded on these campuses in the last year and a half.

Purdue students, according to Paul Schule, head of the Student Union Board, were more willing to express and explore liberal ideas when in intimate groups, or fraternity, sorority or small dormitory bull sessions.

"McCarthyism" Prevalent

"But in public and off campus," Mr. Schule continued, "McCarthyism, or call it what you will, is disgustingly prevalent. Students fear being tagged by others who might say of their views, 'This is the same as something (left-wing line) else.'"

Similar evidence was reported at Ohio State University, Bryn Mawr College, the University of Colorado, Haverford College, and to a lesser degree at Princeton, Stanford and perhaps twenty to thirty other colleges.

In New England's privately endowed colleges—Williams, Bowdoin, Amherst, Smith, Wellesley—left-wing liberalism has been ebbing for some time, even before Senator McCarthy began his drive to rid the State Department of what he termed Communist influence.

The reluctance to speak out on controversial issues for fear of reprisal has caused more of a ripple than a wave in this area, with the chief sufferers seniors who are thinking of Government jobs after graduation.

Harvard showed the greatest effects of the current pressures in the New England area, although these were compared to effects in colleges elsewhere. Student and faculty spokesmen here said that organizations still were willing to speak out in a nonconformist vein, but individuals tended to be more reticent.

The pattern at the bulk of other private New England schools, which reportedly have never seen much political activity, remained virtually unchanged.

Catholic Schools Different

At the country's leading Catholic colleges, deans and students explained that any pressures toward conformism were virtually nonexistent because student and faculty thinking and action were consistent with the Catholic point of view.

At Manhattanville and Fordham, students reported that the current pressures had resulted in a more militant Catholicism, and in a growing awareness of social and economic problems with which most of the colleges were now dealing. They said that rare expressions of extreme liberalism might bring social disapproval and "constructive criticism."

The sameness of background and belief almost erased the area of debate on most controversial issues of the day, but did not preclude discussion. Similar views were expressed at Georgetown University, Holy Cross College, Loyola University and Notre Dame University.

May 10, 1951

MARSHALL U. S. FOE, M'CARTHY CHARGES

Republican Asserts General Is Part of Conspiracy Seeking American Defeat by Russia

By HAROLD B. HINTON
Special to THE NEW YORK TIMES.

WASHINGTON, June 14—Senator Joseph R. McCarthy, Republican of Wisconsin, charged in the Senate today that there existed a conspiracy, with which he associated Dean Acheson, Secretary of State, and General of the Army George C. Marshall, Secretary of Defense, to weaken the United States for its conquest by the Soviet Union.

He described President Truman as the captive of the alleged conspiracy, calling him a man who "is only dimly aware of what is going on."

Mr. McCarthy held the floor for three hours, during which he was able to read only a portion of his prepared speech of 60,000 words. He inserted the remainder in The Congressional Record.

His principal target was General Marshall, who, Mr. McCarthy declared, ever since 1942 had sponsored major policies identical with those advocated by the Kremlin. He charged "a conspiracy so immense, an infamy so black, as to dwarf any in the previous history of man."

"I do not believe that Mr. Truman is a conscious party to the great conspiracy," Mr. McCarthy declared, "although it is being conducted in his name."

Pentagon Sends "Reply"

Senator McCarthy drew his material from his own analysis of the testimony before the Senate committees investigating the recall of General of the Army Douglas MacArthur, the State Department's White Paper on China and from a number of books he described as "friendly" to General Marshall.

They included the memoirs of Winston Churchill, Fleet Admiral William Leahy, former Secretary of State Cordell Hull, the late Henry L. Stimson, former Secretary of War, and the writings of Robert Sherwood, author, Jonathan Daniels, former White House Press Secretary; Hanson Baldwin, military editor of THE NEW YORK TIMES, and others.

The Defense Department during the day sent to the Senate Press Gallery excerpts in praise of General Marshall and taken from books and speeches by the same authors used by Mr. McCarthy.

Starting with the spring of 1942, when General Marshall was Chief of Staff of the Army, Senator McCarthy traced the major policy decisions with which the present Secretary of Defense has been connected, purporting to show that in each case the secretary's recommendations ran parallel to the wishes of Russia.

McCarthy Cites Charges

The Senator declared that General Marshall sided with Russia in arguing for an Allied invasion of France to strike against the German forces from the west, rather than from the south of Europe, as advocated by then British Prime Minister Winston Churchill, in World War II.

Mr. McCarthy said General Marshall also served the purposes of the Soviet Union by:

1. Opposition to the invasion of Italy and the conquest, advocated by Mr. Churchill, of the Balkans before Russian troops could get there.
2. Advocacy of the "enticement" of the Soviet Union into the war against Japan, with the subsequent concessions President Roosevelt made at the Teheran and Yalta conferences.
3. Refusal to demand a corridor of access to Berlin, leading to the Soviet blockade that was broken by the airlift.
4. Creation of the China policy that resulted in that country's conquest by the Chinese Communists.
5. Establishment of the Thirty-eighth Parallel as the dividing line in Korea.
6. Exclusion of Western Germany, Spain, Greece and Turkey from the armed forces supporting the North Atlantic Treaty Organization.

"If Marshall is innocent of guilty intention," Senator McCarthy demanded, "how could he be trusted to guide the defense of this country further?

Outlines the 'Conspiracy'

"We have declined so precipitiously in relation to the Soviet Union in the last six years," Mr. McCarthy said. "How much swifter may be our fall into disaster with Marshall at the helm?"

He described the "great conspiracy" to which he had referred at the outset of his speech as a move "to diminish the United States in world affairs, to weaken us militarily, to confuse our spirit with talk of surrender in the Far East and to impair our will to resist evil."

"To what end?" he asked, and answered his own question: "To the end that we shall be contained, frustrated and finally fall victim to Soviet intrigue from within and Russian military might from without."

June 15, 1951

MANY FOUND WARY OF JULY 4 PETITION

Wisconsin Reporter Says 111 of 112 Balked at Document Cited by Truman

MADISON, Wis., July 28 (AP)—The refusal of 111 persons, of 112 asked, to sign a "petition" containing quotations from the Declaration of Independence and the Bill of Rights was described today by a reporter for The Madison Capital Times.

The incident, which occurred here on the Fourth of July, was cited by President Truman today in his Detroit speech as illustrative of the effects of "all these lies, and smears and fear campaigns."

President Truman said the refusal of signatures indicated that the persons approached were afraid the petition was "some kind of a subversive document, and that they would lose their jobs or be called Communists."

John Hunter, the reporter, said that as an assignment for his paper he took the printed petitions to Vilas Park on July 4.

Mr. Hunter said his purpose was to "find out if McCarthyism had made the people so afraid that they would not sign a patriotic document." The newspaper, he said, had reference to the charges by Senator Joseph R. McCarthy, Republican of Wisconsin, of Communist influences in Government.

The petitions, Mr. Hunter explained, were headed "Preamble to the Declaration of Independence and the Bill of Rights." He added that the printed matter under the title contained the preamble, the first six of ten Constitutional amendments, known as the Bill of Rights, and the Fifteenth Amendment to the Constitution.

Mr. Hunter said that during the same afternoon the Madison Chapter of the American Peace Crusade was circulating mimeographed pamphlets asking for the removal of American troops from Korea and asking Congress to make "no more laws taxing the working man to pay for a rich man's war in Korea."

Mr. Hunter's story in the July 5 issue of The Capital Times said "several" persons asked to sign his petitions "mistook" it for the Peace Crusade pamphlet.

July 29, 1951

TWO U.S. DIPLOMATS UNDER SUSPENSION ON SECURITY COUNT

By ANTHONY LEVIERO
Special to THE NEW YORK TIMES.

WASHINGTON, July 12—The State Department disclosed today the suspension of Oliver Edmund Clubb, director of the Office of Chinese Affairs, and John Paton Davies Jr., member of the department's policy planning staff, pending hearings of security charges against them.

Suspension of the two high-ranking career diplomats since June 27 was an outgrowth of the postwar controversy over Far Eastern policy and of the charges by Senator Joseph R. McCarthy, Wisconsin Republican, and others that the State Department has become the refuge of Communist spies and sympathizers.

In disclosing its action, the State Department emphasized that the loyalty of the two officials was not in question in any way. The charges bear not on disloyalty but on "security", which may mean no more than that they were indiscreet in expressing their views or in their associations with persons considered to be Communist sympathizers.

The department also emphasized that the suspensions and forthcoming hearings before its Loyalty Security Board carried no presumption that the two officials, who have served long in the Far East, were guilty of misconduct or that they were a security risk.

Davies Hearing July 23

Mr. Davies will receive a hearing before the Loyalty Security Board July 23 and Mr. Clubb July 31. Mr. Davies is a controversial figure who has been attacked and defended by persons in high places, most recently in the recent investigation of the dismissal of General of the Army Douglas MacArthur.

Regardless of whether the departmental board clears the officials or finds substance in the charges, their cases will go up to the Federal Loyalty Review Board, highest agency in the governmental loyalty surveillance system.

Michael McDermott, State Department press officer, who made the announcement, also disclosed that a number of others had been suspended in a review of the background of 500 employes. He explained that the re-examination of the 500 cases was a result of the recent tightening by President Truman of the loyalty standard.

Mr. McDermott declined to say who the other suspended employes were. He disclosed the suspension of Mr. Clubb and Mr. Davies only because they had leaked out and he was confronted with questions.

As in all Federal loyalty cases, the accused are informed of the charges but are not told who their accusers are.

Mr. Davies, who is a son-in-law of Henry F. Grady, United States Ambassador to Iran, made this statement tonight:

"I welcome the opportunity that the loyalty board of the State Department is giving me to answer the malicious and irresponsible charges made against me. I am confident that I shall be able to dispose of, once and for all, the contemptible accusations which have added immeasurably to my burdens as a loyal Government worker."

Mr. Clubb declined to say anything for the time. Mr. Clubb, as a Class One Foreign Service officer, is the highest official yet called before the departmental board. Only the class of career minister is higher. Mr. Davies is a Class Two officer.

Mr. Clubb is 50 years old and Mr. Davies is 43. Both are married. Mr. Clubb was born in St. Paul, Minn., and was educated there in the public schools, in the University of Minnesota, where he was graduated in 1927, and in the California College in China, where he took his Master's degree in 1940.

He served in the Army during the First World War and entered the foreign service in 1928, serving in many positions in China and a period as consul at the Far Eastern Russian port of Vladivostok.

Mr. Davies was born in Kiating, China, of American parents, and was educated at the Shanghai-American School, Yenching University in Peiping and at Columbia University, where he received his Bachelor of Science degree in 1931.

He was appointed to the foreign service in 1931 and like Mr. Clubb served in many places in China and as second secretary and consul in Moscow in 1945. He became a member of the policy planning staff, one of the highest policy-making bodies in the department, on July 1, 1950.

Mr. Davies served a tour in the United States Embassy in Moscow. Lieut. Gen. Walter Bedell Smith, then the Ambassador, wrote of him in his book, "My Three Years in Moscow":

"The chancery officer next in seniority to Kennan was John Davies, for years a Far Eastern specialist. Born in China, and with long service there, he was extremely valuable in interpreting trends and events in that area, and I found him a very loyal and very capable officer of sound judgment. His beautiful and talented wife, herself the daughter of an Ambassador and former Assistant Secretary of State, worked in the chancery, as did almost all the embassy wives."

Senator McCarthy said tonight that last year he had handed the name of Mr. Davies to a Senate Foreign Relations subcommittee investigating his charges of Communist penetration of the State Department. The name was not made public at the time, and Senator McCarthy said he did not recall the specific nature of the accusation he had made.

He also said he had a file on Mr. Clubb last year but felt he did not have enough material to warrant an investigation.

Mr. Davies was one of four career diplomats accused in 1945 by the then Ambassador to China, Maj. Gen. Patrick J. Hurley, of favoring the Communists over the Nationalists.

In the so-called White Paper on China, issued by the State Department in August, 1949, in defense of its China policy, are a number of memoranda by Mr. Davies among the annexes.

In an extract dated Sept. 17, 1943, Mr. Davies said:

"It is perhaps not too early to suggest that Soviet policy will probably be directed initially at establishing frontiers which will insure Russian security and a rehabilitation of the U.S.S.R. There is no reason to cherish optimism regarding a voluntary Soviet contribution to our fight against Japan, whether in the shape of air bases or the early opening of a second front in Northeast Asia.

"The Russians may be expected to move against the Japanese when it suits their pleasure, which may not be until the final phases of the war—and then only in order to be able to participate in dictating terms to the Japanese and to establish new strategic frontiers."

On Nov. 15, 1944, Mr. Davies gave his views on the effort to bring the Chinese Communists into a coalition government with the Nationalists. To accomplish that purpose, never achieved, President Truman sent General of the Army George C. Marshall, now Secretary of Defense, to China. Mr. Davies wrote in part:

"We should not now abandon Chiang Kai-shek. To do so at this juncture would be to lose more than we could gain. We must for the time being continue recognition of Chiang's Government. But we must be realistic. We must not indefinitely underwrite a politically bankrupt regime. And, if the Russians are going to enter the Pacific war, we must make a determined effort to capture politically the Chinese Communists rather than allow them to go by default wholly to the Russians.

"Furthermore, we must fully understand that by reason of our recognition of the Chiang Kai-shek Government as now constituted we are committed to a steadily decaying regime and severely restricted in working out military and political cooperation with the Chinese Communists.

"A coalition Chinese government in which the Communists find a satisfactory place is the solution of this impasse most desirable to us. It provides our greatest assurance of a strong, united, democratic, independent and friendly China—our basic strategic aim in Asia and the Pacific.

"If Chiang and the Communists reach a mutually satisfactory agreement, there will have been achieved from our point of view the most desirable possible solution. If Chiang and the Communists are irreconcilable, then we shall have to decide which faction we are going to support.

"In seeking to determine which faction we should support we must keep in mind these basic considerations: power in China is on the verge of shifting from Chiang to the Communists. If the Russians enter North China and Manchuria, we obviously cannot hope to win the Communists entirely over to us, but we can through control of supplies and postwar aid expect to exert considerable influence in the direction of Chinese nationalism and independence from Soviet control."

July 13, 1951

WEDEMEYER BARS BLAMING ADVISERS

By WILLIAM S. WHITE
Special to THE NEW YORK TIMES.

WASHINGTON, Sept. 19—Lieut. Gen. Albert C. Wedemeyer, a wartime commander of the China theatre, asserted today that had he followed his State Department political advisers "communism would have run rampant over China more rapidly than it did."

General Wedemeyer, now a New York corporation executive retired from the Army, testified before the Senate Internal Security subcommittee that is investigating the Institute of Pacific Relations as part of its inquiry to determine whether pro-Communist influences shaped United States policy in the Far East.

He declared himself unwilling "categorically" to accuse his former State Department staff associates as disloyal.

He said in substance, however, that memoranda handed in by three of them, John Davies, John S. Service and Raymond Ludden, were against the policy of the United States, as he interpreted it, to give aid to the China Nationalists and not the China Communists. American policies generally, however, he added, were not "clearly enunciated" in those days —the period around 1944.

He testified that he could not recall having received any report or proposals from a fourth State Department man, John Emerson.

Applauded by Spectators

"If I had followed some of the advice of those advisers," General Wedemeyer said, "in my judgment I would not have been carrying out my directive in following the policy of my country."

The general, whose name has often been invoked by Republican critics of the Administration's actions in Asia, left the stand with this declaration to the subcommittee, which is headed by Senator Pat McCarran, Democrat of Nevada:

"I have been following the work of this committee. I commend both the Democratic and Republican members for what I believe is an objective investigation. Don't pay any attention to the smear campaign, please, being instituted by those very same forces you are investigating."

There was applause among the spectators.

General Wedemeyer's testimony against Mr. Service, Mr. Davies and Mr. Ludden was based on the assertion that they tended to "play up" the shortcomings of the Chiang Nationalist regime of Generalissimo Chiang Kai-shek and to overstate the capabilities of the Communist leaders in pursuit of an "idea" to give more aid to the Communists "in lieu" of aid to the Nationalists.

Testimony in June Recalled

He would not state "categorically," he said under questioning, that the proposals of the Service-Davies-Ludden group were pro-Communist.

In appearances in June before the two combined Senate committees that investigated the recall of General MacArthur, testimony about which he was not asked today, General Wedemeyer declared that Mr. Service, Mr. Davies and Mr. Ludden had been no more critical of the Chinese Nationalist Government in the period of the mid-forties than he himself had been as late as 1947 in a speech to the Nationalist leaders themselves.

Today, General Wedemeyer put the responsibility on Henry L. Stimson, a Republican and Secretary of War in the Roosevelt Administration, for having placed Mr. Service and his associates in the China theatre, first oh the staff of the late Gen. Joseph W. Stillwell.

He had regarded them at that time, he said, as "very bright and keen" and loyal to him personally and to the United States.

At the time, he testifted, "I did not express any disapproval of these men—I had none."

"What is your opinion now?" asked Senator Homer Ferguson of Michigan. "Were they disloyal to this Government and its policy?"

"I can't answer that question, sir," replied General Wedemeyer. "I honestly can't say. But if I had followed their advice communism would have run rampant over China more rapidly than it did."

Davies Report Is Quoted

Robert Morris, the subcommittee's counsel, read into the record an excerpt from a State Department loyalty proceeding, in which Mr. Service subsequently was cleared, in which it appeared that the State Department career man had disavowed any interest in the Institute of Pacific Relations, apart from "being a subscriber to some of its magazines."

Another excerpt indicated that in the proceeding an exhibit had been offered indicating that Mr.

Service had paid $15 in membership dues to the institute for the year ended in February, 1951.

An excerpt from one of Mr. Davies' reports, on Nov. 15, 1944, indicated that he had written:

"We should not now abandon Chiang Kai-shek. We must for the time being continue recognition of Chiang's government.

"But we must be realistic. We must not indefinitely underwrite a politically bankrupt regime. And, if the Russians are going to enter the Pacific war, we must make a determined effort to capture politically the Chinese Communists, rather than allow them to go by default wholly to the Russians. * * *

"A coalition government in which the Communists find a satisfactory place is the solution of this impasse most desirable to us. It provides our greatest assurance of a strong, united, democratic, independent and friendly China—our basic strategic aim in the Pacific."

September 20, 1951

John S. Service Is Ousted; Diplomat's Loyalty 'Doubted'

By WALTER H. WAGGONER
Special to The New York Times.

WASHINGTON, Dec. 13—The State Department dismissed John Stewart Service tonight on the advice of the Government's top loyalty agency that there was "reasonable doubt" as to the foreign service officer's loyalty.

The Civil Service Commission's Loyalty Review Board found that Mr. Service, a career diplomat ror eighteen years, had raised doubt as to his loyalty by making "intentional and unauthorized disclosure" of classified documents. It said it had uncovered no evidence that Mr. Service had been a member of the Communist party or of any other organization which had been listed as subversive by the Attorney General.

The Loyalty Review Board, set up by President Truman last year to be the final arbiter of loyalty questions, reversed the State Department's own Loyalty Security Board, which six times had found Mr. Service free of any suspicion of disloyalty. The Review Board is headed by Hiram Bingham, former Republican Senator from Connecticut.

Mr. Service has been working in the State Department's Office of Operating Facilities, an administrative and housekeeping unit without access to classified material, since being recalled from India for investigation in March, 1950.

"Amerasia" Case Cited

That investigation and an almost continuous inquiry into charges against Mr. Service since then had been provoked by Senator Joseph R. McCarthy, Republican of Wisconsin, who made the foreign service office one of the targets of his attacks against what he called Communists in the State Department.

The principal basis for the Loyalty Review Board's unfavorable decision was Mr. Service's role in the so-called Amerasia case of 1945, when classified official reports were made available to the magazine of that name.

The Loyalty Review Board's letter telling Secretary of State Dean Acheson that its findings stated only that "reasonable doubt" had been raised as to Mr. Service's loyalty.

In its announcement tonight, however, the State Department included also the opinion of its own Loyalty Security Board, which, in 8,500 words, set down the reasons for having cleared Mr. Service on six previous occasions.

It found that Mr. Service had "clearly committed two serious indiscretions" by turning over classified reports and other information to Philip J. Jaffe, Russian-born American citizen who was co-editor of Amerasia.

The department's loyalty unit, nevertheless, concluded that the material made available by Mr. Service contained nothing "harmful to the national security" and that it did not form a basis for finding Mr. Service disloyal.

Amerasia, now defunct, was published in New York. It dealt with Far Eastern affairs. Six persons were arrested after raids on its offices revealed secret documents. Mr. Jaffe was fined $2,500, and Emmanuel S. Larsen, an alleged associate, $500 on charges of possessing secret Government documents. The other defendants were

cleared. Later Senator McCarthy charged a "whitewash."

The State Department's announcement of Mr. Service's dismissal said the decision by the President's Loyalty Review Board "is based on the evidence which was considered by the department's board and found to be insufficient on which to base a finding of 'reasonable doubt' as to Mr. Service's loyalty or security."

Service Issues Statement

Mr. Service, on learning of the board's action, issued this statement:

"The Loyalty Review Board's decision is a surprise, a shock and an injustice. I am not now and never have been disloyal to the United States.

"The board expressly states that is does not find me disloyal. What is has done is base a 'reasonable doubt' on a single episode which occurred six and a half years ago which has been freely admitted by me and known to all responsible quarters since that time and for which I have been tried and unanimously acquitted at least nine times.

"That episode involved discussing normal and proper background information with a journalist whom I believed and had every reason to believe at the time to be nothing more than the editor of a reputable, specialist magazine dealing with the Far East.

"The selected background information which I gave him did not adversely affect or even deal with the national interests of the United States, nor did it come within the meaning of regulations defining the classifications 'secret and confidential.'

"The information involved was known, or at least available to, all of the American correspondents in China. The only thing that kept these facts about China from an uninformed American public was a foreign censorship. The same information had been used repeatedly by me, with official approval, in discussing the situation in China with other writers and researchers in the United States.

"I am confident that my record of eighteen and a half years' service to the American Government

John S. Service
Associated Press

and the testimony of the many people who have worked with me during that period will support me in my conviction that there is no doubt of my loyalty."

Was Cleared Seven Times

Altogether, Mr. Service had been cleared of disloyalty charges seven times since the Amerasia case. The chronology of those inquiries follows:

In August, 1945, a grand jury investigation of the Amerasia case cleared Mr. Service with a "no true bill," in effect finding that the charges of having transmitted classified material to unauthorized persons had not been substantiated.

The State Department's Loyalty Security Board, under the direction of Gen. Conrad E. Snow (Reserve), a New Hampshire Republican, then cleared Mr. Service on these dates: Jan. 18, 1949; March 1, 1950; Oct. 6, 1950; March 7, 1951; June 11, 1951; and, after the standards had been changed from "reasonable grounds" for finding a person disloyal to "reasonable doubt" of his loyalty, finally on July 31, 1951.

The State Department's loyalty unit submitted its final report on Mr. Service to the Loyalty Review Board Sept. 4, for what is known as a "post-audit," or review. On Oct. 9 the Civil Service Commission Board again took up the case and returned its verdict today.

In effect, the State Department this evening stood by its favorable decisions. Its announcement called attention to the fact that the department's loyalty unit, "while censuring Mr. Service for indiscretions, believed that the experience Mr. Service had been through as a result of his indiscretions in 1945 had served to make him far more than normally security conscious."

Mr. Service denied repeatedly that he ever had been a Communist or friendly to communism. The report of the Loyalty Review Board appeared to support him on that point.

The foreign service officer also had won the respect and friendship of his associates and superiors holding influential posts in the State Department.

In a statement replying to Senator McCarthy, John E. Peurifoy, then Deputy Under Secretary of State and now Ambassador to Greece, declared on March 16, 1950: "Here, in the person of Jack Service, we have an able, conscientious, and—I say again, as I've already said many times before—a demonstrably loyal foreign service officer, a veteran of seventeen years with the department, and one of our outstanding experts on Far Eastern affairs."

On that occasion Mr. Peurifoy bitterly reported that orders had gone out to Mr. Service, en route to a new assignment as First Secretary in the United States Embassy in India, to return to Washington "to face another 'loyalty probe.'"

China Career Examined

The report of the Loyalty Review Board, dated yesterday, reviewed Mr. Service's career in China in 1944 and said that "we have in the file no sufficient evidence to support a doubt on the question of loyalty."

It stated similarly that a review of the entire file "also satisfied us that no reasonable doubt concerning the employe's loyalty arises from his activities while assigned to the staff of General MacArthur in Tokyo."

In connection with Mr. Service's participation in the Amerasia case, set down in some detail in the agency's report to the State Department the Civil Service Commission loyalty board found its ground for "reasonable doubt."

"To say that his course of conduct does not raise a reasonable doubt as to Service's own loyalty," the board concluded, "would, we are forced to think, stretch the mantle of charity much too far.

"We are not required to find Service guilty of disloyalty, and we do not do so, but for an experienced and trusted representative of our State Department to so far forget his duty to his trust as his conduct with Jaffe so clearly indicates, forces us with great regret to conclude that there is reasonable doubt as to his loyalty. The favorable finding of the Loyalty Security Board of the Department of State is accordingly reversed."

Was Born in China

Mr. Service, born in China of American parents forty-two years ago, joined the United States foreign service in 1933 at the age of 24 as clerk in the United States Consulate in Yunnanfu.

He remained in China for the diplomatic service until May, 1945, when he was assigned to the State Department here. Then he was named political adviser to General MacArthur in September of that year; was moved to Wellington, New Zealand, in July, 1946; returned briefly to the State Department in 1948; went to Calcutta as counselor in November, 1949; and was then assigned as counselor of the embassy in New Delhi, a post he never reached.

Mr. Service is married and has three children.

'Good,' Says McCarthy

LOS ANGELES, Dec. 13 (UP)— When Senator McCarthy heard in Los Angeles of the discharge, he exclaimed: "Good, good, good!"

In a statement, Senator McCarthy said:

"It should be remembered that when I forced the recall of Service from the Far East * * * the State Department issued a press release calling Service one of their most valued and trusted experts. * * *

"It should be remembered that the Tydings committee gave Service a completely clean bill and called my evidence fraud and a hoax.

"And it should be remembered that the Gillette committee even now is spending tens of thousands of dollars to decide if McCarthy should be expelled from the Senate because he exposed Service and other members of his group in the State Department."

December 14, 1951

The Black Silence of Fear

If we are afraid of ideas, Justice Douglas says, we will imperil our power and prestige.

By WILLIAM O. DOUGLAS

THERE is an ominous trend in this nation. We are developing tolerance only for the orthodox point of view on world affairs, intolerance for new or different approaches. Orthodoxy normally has stood in the path of change. Orthodoxy was always the stronghold of the status quo, the enemy of new ideas—at least new ideas that were disturbing. He who was wedded to the orthodox view was isolated from the challenge of new facts.

The democratic way of life rejects standardized thought. It rejects orthodoxy. It wants the fullest and freest discussion, within peaceful limits, of all public issues. It encourages constant search for truth at the periphery of knowledge.

We as a people have probably never lived up to that standard in any of our communities. But it has been an ideal toward which most of our communities have strived. We have over the years swung from tolerance to intolerance and back again. There have been eras of intolerance when the

WILLIAM O. DOUGLAS, an Associate Justice of the United States Supreme Court, adapted this article from a recent address.

views of minorities have been suppressed. But there probably has not been a period of greater intolerance than we witness today.

To understand this, I think one, has to leave the country, go into the back regions of the world, lose himself there, and become absorbed in the problems of the peoples of different civilizations. When he returns to America after a few months he probably will be shocked. He will be shocked not at the intentions or purposes or ideals of the American people. He will be shocked at the arrogance and intolerance of great segments of the American press, at the arrogance and intolerance of many leaders in public office, at the arrogance and intolerance reflected in many of our attitudes toward Asia. He will find that thought is being standardized, that the permissible area for calm discussion is being narrowed, that the range of ideas is being limited, that many minds are closed to the receipt of any ideas from Asia.

This is alarming to one who loves his country. It means that the philosophy of strength through free speech is being forsaken for the philosophy of fear through repression.

That choice in Russia is conscious. Under Lenin the ministers and officials were encouraged to debate, to advance new ideas and criticisms. Once the debate was over, however, no dissension or disagreement was permitted. But even that small degree of tolerance for free discussion that Lenin permitted disappeared under Stalin. Stalin maintains a tight system of control, permitting no free speech, no real clash in ideas, even in the inner circle. We are, of course, not emulating either Lenin or Stalin. But we are drifting in the direction of repression, drifting dangerously fast.

WHAT is the cause of this drift? What are the forces behind it? It is only a drift, for certainly everything in our tradition would make the great majority of us reject that course as a conscious choice.

The drift goes back, I think, to the fact that we carried over to days of peace the military approach to world affairs. Diplomacy, certainly in our relations with Asia, took a back seat. The military approach conditioned our thinking and our planning. The military, in fact, determined our approach

The heart of the American tradition—"Our real power is our spiritual strength, and that spiritual strength stems from our civil liberties."

to the Asians and their problems. That has been a great tragedy in Asia. And the tragedy to us at home has been about as great.

MILITARY thinking continued to play a dominant role in our domestic affairs. The conspiratorial role of Soviet communism in the world scene was apparent to all who could read This conspiratorial role of Soviet communism was, of course, backed by Russia's military strength. We, therefore, had to be strong in a military sense to hold off Russia. But we soon accepted the military role as the dominant one. We thought of Asia in terms of military bases, not in terms of peoples and their aspirations. We wanted the starving people of Asia to choose sides, to make up their minds whether they were for us or against us, to cast their lot with us and against Russia.

We did not realize that to millions of these people the difference between Soviet dictatorship and the dictatorship under which
they presently live is not very great. We did not realize that in some reigons of Asia it is the Communist party that has identified itself with the so-called reform program, the other parties being mere. instruments for keeping a ruling class in power. We did not realize that the choice between democracy and communism is not, in the eyes of millions of illiterates, the critical choice it is for us.

We forgot that democracy in many lands is an empty word; that the appeal is hollow when made to illiterate people living at the subsistence level. We asked them to furnish staging grounds for a military operation whose

outcome, in their eyes, had no perceptible relation to their own welfare. Those who rejected our overtures must be Communists, we said. Those who did not fall in with our military plans must be secretly aligning with Russia, we thought. This was the result of our military thinking, of our absorption in military affairs. In Asia it has brought us the lowest prestige in our existence.

THE military effort has been involving more and more of our sons, more and more of our budget, more and more of our thinking. The military policy has so completely absorbed our thoughts that we have mostly forgotten that our greatest strength, our enduring power is not in guns, but in ideas. Today in Asia we are identified not with ideas of freedom, but with guns. Today at home we are thinking less and less in terms of defeating communism with ideas, more and more in terms of defeating communism with military might.

The concentration on military means has helped to breed fear. It has bred fear and insecurity partly because of the horror of atomic war. But the real reason strikes deeper. In spite of our enormous expenditures, we see that Soviet imperialism continues to expand and that the expansion proceeds without the Soviets firing a shot. The free world continues to contract without a battle for its survival having been fought. It becomes apparent, as country after country falls to Soviet imperialistic ambitions, that military policy alone is a weak one; that military policy alone will end in political bankruptcy and futility. Thus fear mounts.

FEAR has many manifestations. The Communist threat inside the country

has been magnified and exalted far beyond its realities. Irresponsible talk by irresponsible people has fanned the flames of fear. Accusations have been loosely made. Character assassinations have become common. Suspicion has taken the place of good-will. Once we could debate with impunity along a wide range of inquiry. Once we could safely explore to the edges of a problem, challenge orthodoxy without qualms, and run the gamut of ideas in search of solutions to perplexing problems. Once we had confidence in each other. Now there is suspicion. Innocent acts become tell-tale marks of disloyalty. The coincidence that an idea parallels Soviet Russia's policy for a moment of time settles an aura of suspicion around a person.

Suspicion grows until only the orthodox idea is the safe one. Suspicion grows until only the person who loudly proclaims that orthodox view, or who, once having been a Communist, has been converted, is trustworthy. Competition for embracing the new orthodoxy increases. Those who are unorthodox are suspect. Everyone who does not follow the military policymakers is suspect. Everyone who voices opposition to the trend away from diplomacy and away from political tactics takes a chance. Some who are opposed are indeed "subversive." Therefore, the thundering edict commands that all who are opposed are "subversive." Fear is fanned to a fury. Good and honest men are pilloried. Character is assassinated. Fear runs rampant.

Fear even strikes at lawyers and the bar. Those accused of illegal Communist activity—all presumed innocent, of course, until found guilty—have difficulty getting reputable lawyers to defend them. Lawyers have talked with me about it. Many are worried. Some could not volunteer their services, for if they did they would lose clients and their firms would suffer. Others could not volunteer because if they did they would be dubbed "subversive" by their community and put in the same category as those they would defend. This is a dark tragedy.

FEAR has driven more and more men and women in all walks of life either to silence or to the folds of the orthodox. Fear has mounted—fear of losing one's job, fear of being investigated, fear of being pilloried. This fear has stereotyped our thinking, narrowed the range of free public discussion, and driven many thoughtful people to despair. This fear has even entered universities, great citadels of our spiritual strength, and corrupted them. We have the spectacle of university officials lending themselves to one of the worst witch hunts we have seen since early days.

This fear has affected the youngsters. Youth has played a very important role in our national affairs. It has usually been the oncoming generation—full of enthusiasm, full of idealism, full of energy—that has challenged its elders and the status quo. It is from this young group that the country has received much of its moral power. They have always been prone to question the stewardship of their fathers, to doubt the wisdom of traditional practices, to explode clichés, to quarrel with the management of public affairs.

Youth—like the opposition party in a parliamentary system—has served a powerful role. It has cast doubts on our policies, challenged our inarticulate major premises, put the light on our prejudices, and exposed our inconsistencies. Youth has made each generation indulge in self-examination.

BUT a great change has taken place. Youth is still rebellious; but it is largely holding its tongue. There is

the fear of being labeled a "subversive" if one departs from the orthodox party line. That charge—if leveled against a young man or young woman —may have profound effects. It may ruin a youngster's business or professional career. No one wants a Communist in his organization nor anyone who is suspect.

And so the lips of the younger generation have become more and more sealed. Repression of ideas has taken the place of debate. There may not be a swelling crowd of converts to the orthodox, military view. But the voice of the opposition is more and more stilled; and youth, the mainstay in early days of the revolt against orthodoxy, is largely immobilized.

This pattern of orthodoxy that is shaping our thinking has dangerous implications. No one man, no one group can have the answer to the many perplexing problems that today confront the management of world affairs. The scene is a troubled and complicated one. The problems require the pooling of many ideas, the exposure of different points of view, the hammering out in public discussions of the pros and cons of this policy or of that.

There are few who know first hand the conditions in the villages of Asia, the South Pacific, South America, and Africa. There are few who really know the powerful forces operating from the grass roots in those areas— forces that are reflected in the attitudes of the men who head up the Governments in those countries. But unless we know those attitudes, we cannot manage intelligently. Unless we know, we will waste our energies and our resources. Unless we know, we are not in position to win even political alliances of an enduring nature. Unless we are eager to know, unless we invite a flood of information on these problems, unless we encourage every avenue of approach to them, we will live and act in ignorance.

There are those who think

that our present policy toward Asia will lead to disaster—for us. There are those who believe that in Asia we are fast becoming the symbol of what the people of Asia fear and hate. There are those who believe that the most effective bases we can get in Asia are bases in the hearts of Asia's millions, not bases on their lands. There are those who believe that we must substitute a political for a military strategy in Asia; that when there is a cease-fire in Korea, we must make a political settlement with Red China; that if we apply to China the attitude we are now brilliantly exploiting in Yugoslavia, we can manage to make Soviet imperialism crumble.

THERE are those who are deeply opposed, many of whom put that issue beyond the pale of discussion. There are even some who make the crucial test of one's loyalty or sanity his acceptance or rejection of our present policy toward Asia.

The question of our Asian policy illustrates the need for a wide range of free public discussion. Asia poses probably the most critical issues of the day. Certain it is that if Asia, like China, is swept into the political orbit of Soviet Russia, the Soviets will then command or be able to immobilize

——*the bulk of the people of the world*
——*the bulk of the wealth of the world.*

If that happens, it is doubtful if we, with all our atomic bombs, could even win a war.

THE great danger of this period is not inflation, nor the national debt, nor atomic warfare. The great, the critical danger is that we will so limit or narrow the range of permissible discussion and permissible thought that we will become victims of the orthodox school. If we do, we will lose flexibility. We will lose the capacity for expert management. We will then become wedded to a few techniques,

to a few devices. They will define our policy and at the same time limit our ability to alter or modify it. Once we narrow the range of thought and discussion, we will surrender a great deal of our power. We will become like the man on the toboggan who can ride it but who can neither steer it nor stop it.

The mind of man must always be free. The strong society is one that sanctions and encourages freedom of thought and expression. When there is that freedom, a nation has resiliency and adaptability. When freedom of expression is supreme, a nation will keep its balance and stability.

OUR real power is our spiritual strength, and that spiritual strength stems from our civil liberties. If we are true to our traditions, if we are tolerant of a whole market place of ideas, we will always be strong. Our weakness grows when we become intolerant of opposing ideas, depart from our standards of civil liberties, and borrow the policeman's philosophy from the enemy we detest.

That has been the direction of our drift. It is dangerous to the morale of our people; it is destructive of the influence and prestige of our counica that is losing its human- our resiliency, much of our inventive genius. The demands of orthodoxy already have begun to sap our strength— and to deprive us of power. One sees it from far-off Asia. From Asia one sees an America that is losing its humanity, its idealism, and its Christian character. From Asia one sees an America that is strong and rich and powerful, and yet crippled and ineffective because of its limited vision.

When we view this problem full face we are following the American tradition. The times demand a renaissance in freedom of thought and freedom of expression, a renaissance that will end the orthodoxy that threatens to devitalize us.

January 13, 1952

LATTIMORE CALLS SENATORS' INQUIRY ON CHINA 'STACKED'

By WILLIAM S. WHITE

Special to THE NEW YORK TIMES.

WASHINGTON, Feb. 26—Prof. Owen Lattimore of Johns Hopkins University accused the Senate Internal Security subcommittee today of suppression and distortion of evidence and of welcoming "stacked" testimony that was destroying innocent men and jeopardizing this country.

The chairman, Senator Pat McCarran, Democrat of Nevada, retorted with the charge that Mr. Lattimore was "not at all out of line with the general procedure of the Communist party," the subcommittee.

"The witness," Senator McCarran added, "must be responsible for the full gravity of his remarks."

Appearing before the forum in which for nearly a year he had been under running attack, Professor Lattimore denounced his judges, Chairman McCarran and the members of the subcommittee, in terms rarely heard in the history of Congressional investigations.

He declared in substance that

the subcommittee, in its inquiry to determine whether "subversive forces" had softened United States policy toward the Chinese Communists, was so determined to find evil that it had given shelter to "a nightmare of outrageous lies, shaky hearsay and undisguised personal spite."

All this and more he charged under oath, while denying that he ever had been any sort of Communist or pro-Communist, in a 17,500-word statement filed with the subcommittee.

He came to the witness stand with this formidable document at 2:30 P. M. At the day's adjournment at 5 P. M. he had read eight sentences of it, so vehement and prolonged had been the cross-examination from the investigators' bench.

At that hour he declared himself so fatigued that his mind was "in a maze."

His attorney, Abe Fortas, had appealed to the subcommittee "in the name of humanity" to allow Professor Lattimore to finish reading at least a single section of his prepared statement before further interrogation.

"No human being," cried Mr. Fortas, could make an orderly presentation under such circumstances where his lawyer, as was the case here, could not come to his aid unless he specifically sought such aid.

Subcommittee members made it plain that they did not propose to let Professor Lattimore put in the whole document, with its bitter attacks upon them, until they had challenged it almost line by line.

Refuses to Retract Charges

Here matters were left for the night. In the meantime Professor Lattimore persistently had refused to retract or to modify what he had said in his paper about the subcommittee. He had spoken, he said, "because I am an innocent man."

The subcommittee, he complained, had cross-examined him for two and a half hours while he was reading a total of some 300 words of his statement whereas many accusing witnesses who had appeared had not been cross-examined at all. This, he asserted, was a measure of the subcommittee's procedures.

Senator McCarran's denunciation of Professor Lattimore came at the very opening of the hearing. Mr. Lattimore and his attorneys already had given out his statement to the press, stipulating that it was to be released at 2:30 P. M., the hour of the meeting.

The subcommittee members, Mr. McCarran had known in advance that "we would be the targets of invective and disparaging remarks."

He recalled that "for many months" Federal Judge Harold R. Medina, in trying the Communist leaders in New York, had "sat enduring all kinds of condemnatory remarks and insulting expressions."

"This subcommittee," Senator McCarran went on, "could exercise its rights. We could deny that [the Lattimore] statement the right to become a part of the record.

"We realize this is a country of free speech and that is one of our great heritages and we propose to see to it that it is carried out here today. Notwithstanding the insulting and offensive remarks that appear in the statement by the witness, he may proceed with his statement, with the understanding that from time to time as he goes along, counsel for the committee will interrogate him."

The first of these interruptions came in the first sentence of Professor Lattimore's reading.

In his prepared statement, he accused the subcommittee of loosing "a reign of terror" against Foreign Service officers of the United States, against the inquiring mind in general and against all who would not agree with a "China Lobby" that was trying to take control of this country in behalf of the Chinese Nationalist regime of Generalissimo Chiang Kai-shek.

He said flatly and defiantly that he had no hope at all that the subcommittee was going to give him a fair hearing or would "fairly appraise the facts."

He defended the State Department itself, and especially its small group of experts on China, and the Institute of Pacific Relations, a privately financed research group that had been accused by some witnesses of a past Communist bias and had been credited with great influence on the department.

He said as a former editor of the Institute it never occurred to him in the late Thirties to "set up a private F. B. I. or security screening to determine the exact political affiliation" of Institute staff members or contributing writers, just as this had not occurred to such publications as the Saturday Evening Post.

"If it was (Communist) party strategy to infiltrate the Institute of Pacific Relations," he went on, "I did not suspect it. Nor, as a matter of fact, did Senator [Homer] Ferguson [Republican of Michigan and a member of the subcommittee], who was a member of and contributor to the Institute of Public Relations from 1936 to 1944.

"Maybe a few Communists or pro-Communists did work for the Institute of Pacific Relations," Professor Lattimore continued. "I suppose that a few worked for the United States Government, too, and for some of our leading papers and great corporations. It does not follow that this made them Communistic or that their other employes and executives were infected with the virus."

"The impression has been assiduously conveyed in your proceedings," he told the subcommittee, "that I am a Communist or a Communist sympathizer or dupe; that I master-minded the Institute of Pacific Relations; that the Institute of Pacific Relations and I master-minded the Far Eastern experts of the State Department; and that the State Department 'sold' China to the Russians.

"Every one of these is false—utterly and completely false."

Professor Lattimore recalled that he already had sworn a denial to charges by Senator Joseph R. McCarthy, Republican of Wisconsin, that he was a "Soviet agent."

Denies Any Link With Reds

"Now I want to make my position clear," he said. "I am not interested in fine or technical distinctions. I am not interested in graduations or degrees of disloyalty. I have no use for fancy, legalistic distinctions.

"I am none of these things and I have never been: I am not and have never been a Communist, a Soviet agent, a sympathizer or any other kind of promoter of communism or Communists' interests, and all of these are nonsense."

Accusing the subcommittee of deliberate unfairness, Professor Lattimore declared it was a "shocking" fact that not one of the witnesses who had testified

Associated Press Wirephoto

The Johns Hopkins University professor talking with his wife while awaiting the start of yesterday's hearing in Washington.

against him had ever been asked in cross examination "a question that would test his motives or his reliability."

He asserted, for example, that Robert Morris, the subcommittee's counsel, had ignored past evidence that reflected upon one of the principal Lattimore accusers, Louis F. Budenz, the recanted former Communist who used to be editor of the party newspaper The Daily Worker.

Moreover, Professor Lattimore charged, Mr. Morris had "sedulously kept out of sight" other material evidence concerning Mr. Budenz of which the attorney had been directly aware of in his former capacity as co-counsel for the 1950 Senate investigation of Senator McCarthy's charges.

Mr. Budenz, Professor Lattimore asserted, had received "borrowed immunity" from the subcommittee and thus "admonished, drilled, and exhorted to take heart and fear not," had finally made a direct accusation of a Lattimore connection with a Communist cell.

In the previous inquiry, that conducted by the then Senator Millard E. Tydings, Democrat of Maryland, Mr. Budenz had "backed away" from any charge so flat, Mr. Lattimore asserted.

He turned then to Chairman McCarran, saying that Mr. McCarran had "already publicly proclaimed that he had prejudged" the Institute of Pacific Relations, having given it as his "curbstone opinion" that the Institute "was taken over by Communist design."

"It sounds almost as if the curbstone from which the distinguished

Senator delivered this opinion had been imported from one of the countries in which accusation is accepted as conclusive of guilt," Professor Lattimore observed.

Often he spoke in this satirical vein. He referred to Harold E. Stassen, one of his detractors, as a "roadshow McCarthy" and a "perpetual Presidential candidate."

He called Senator McCarthy "the Wisconsin Whimperer."

He asserted that the subcommittee had always leaned mainly on former Communists, those who had spent their lives "in the Communist school of lies, deceit and intrigue," and had operated in "a murky atmosphere of pretended plots and conspiracies."

As an editor of the Institute of Pacific Relations, he declared, his work actually had leaned more to the Right than the Left.

Apart from the "regurgitation" of old charges made against him by Senator McCarthy, he went on, the subcommittee had produced through witnesses a "ludicrous mishmash" suggesting that the Lattimore views toward defeated Japan were pro-Communist because they involved what was called a hard attitude toward the Emperor.

The fact was, said Professor Lattimore, that others, including Senator Richard B. Russell, Democrat of Georgia, and Fleet Admiral William F. Halsey Jr., had "wanted to be more drastic" with the Emperor than had the witness.

But he added:

"On the subject of Japan, I don't want to be misunderstood. If the

195

price of gaining your approval is that I forget the stab in the back at Pearl Harbor, that I forget the barbarous depredations of Japan in China and other countries, and that I subscribe to Emperor worship, then the price is one that you will not get from me."

One of the major sections of Professor Lattimore's prepared presentation of fifty typewritten pages—these exclusive of several sheets of appendices—was his argument that the subcommittee was endangering this country's security by making Foreign Service men afraid to report objectively what was happening abroad.

'The personal damage that has been done to me by the way in which this subcommittee has allowed malicious testimony to be stacked against me,'" he said, "is probably beyond repair. But much more important is the damage that has been done to my country, the country of which I am only one private citizen, and the damage that has been done to the conduct of the foreign policy of our country."

The "mistakes of the past" as to China, he said, should be analyzed, but the victory of the Communists was not due either to "treachery or incompetence," and the "attribution of personal guilt for the mere purpose of providing political scapegoats is not civilized or democratic behavior, however widespread it may be among primative groups of men."

The subcommittee, he went on, had been directly attacking "irreplaceable" State Department experts and "impairing the confidence of the nation and our foreign allies in our State Department."

"Sacrificed to the hysteria" of the time, he said, had been three able Foreign Service officers, John Stewart Service, O. Edmund Clubb and John Carter Vincent.

He recalled that Mr. Service recently had been dismissed on an ultimate finding of "reasonable doubt" of his loyalty, and that Mr. Clubb had resigned after being cleared.

Mr. Vincent, professor Lattimore declared, had been removed from his speciality, the Far East, and assigned to a post in Tangier "because in the prevailing temper the Administration dares not return him to work where he belongs and is needed."

The Russians in 1939 had "walked into a booby trap" in Finland, Professor Lattimore asserted, because Soviet agents had been afraid to report the truth about the Finns and wanted to report only what Moscow wanted to hear.

February 27, 1952

U. S. HAS NEVER GOT M'CARTHY RED DATA

Justice Department Says He Has Not Acted—Replies to Benton Ouster Query

Special to THE NEW YORK TIMES.

WASHINGTON, Dec. 18 — The Department of Justice has stated that Senator Joseph R. McCarthy has never turned over to it for possible prosecution any of his principal "cases" of alleged Communists in Government.

It has declared, moreover, that Mr. McCarthy, a Wisconsin Republican, has not yet offered to hand in his files against persons whom for nearly two years he has been attacking as high in an alleged conspiracy against the country.

These statements were made in an exchange of correspondence with Senator William Benton, Democrat of Connecticut, that Mr. Benton made public today.

Senator McCarthy, whose expulsion from the Senate is being sought by Senator Benton, was not available for comment.

Mr. Benton gave out the following series of the questions he had put in writing and the answers given to him by Assistant Attorney General James M. McInerney:

Q.—Does or does not Senator McCarthy's claim to have evidence that 205 (more or less) employes of the United States Government are "card-carrying Communists" or "members of a spy ring" or "conspirators to turn the world over to communism" raise the question as to whether any such people are not subject to criminal prosecution * * * if there is any valid evidence against them?

A.—Obviously, under the public law you cite, such persons would in fact be subject to prosecution, assuming the existence of the several factors set forth.

Q.—Is not the indicated procedure for any citizen (and most assuredly for a Senator) who believes he has evidence that a felony is being committed to report this evidence to the appropriate law-enforcement agencies? A.—It is certainly the duty of every individual possessing information or evidence with respect to the commission of a crime to report the same to the proper authorities.

Q.—Is it or is it not an indicated procedure for Senator McCarthy to present his evidence to United States Attorney Morris Fay of the District of Columbia for presentation to any Federal grand jury. * * * Aren't they [Federal grand juries] even empowered to subpoena Secretary Acheson or Senator McCarthy?

A.—If an individual within the District of Columbia believes he has evidence involving breaches of Federal law in the District of Columbia then—as I stated above—it is his duty to report same to the proper authorities, and in this instance the proper authority would be the United States Attorney for the District of Columbia. * * * Grand juries are, of course, empowered to subpoena any witness they deem necessary regardless of whether he holds public office or not.

Q.—Can you inform me whether Senator McCarthy has ever volunteered to submit the evidence he claims to have on felonious disloyalty on the part of employes of the United States Government to the Department of Justice or to any United States Attorney?

A.—Like thousands of other citizens in the United States, Senator McCarthy has on occasion made information available to the Department of Justice. He did not turn over to the Justice Department his files on cases which he has named publicly; most of these were old cases already investigated by the Government. He has, however, turned over items of information which have come to him through mail or otherwise.

Q.—If he has not so volunteered, is he not, under our laws, derelict in his duty as a citizen (and most assuredly as a Senator)? A.—I believe this question has been answered by the answers to the previous questions.

Q.—If he does not volunteer, could not any Federal grand jury which so desired, in view of Senator McCarthy's public claim to possess pertinent information, subpoena him and demand it? A.—I believe this question also has been answered by the answers to the previous questions.

December 19, 1951

TEXTBOOK CENSORS ALARM EDUCATORS

By BENJAMIN FINE

A growing censorship of school and college textbooks in this country is causing America's leading educators serious concern.

Widespread attacks have been made in recent months on schoolbooks and other reading materials. The attacks have been based on the grounds that the texts contain subversive passages or have been written by authors suspected of un-American views.

In some instances librarians have been persuaded to remove textbooks or not to order materials that might create a controversy in the community. Self-appointed committees are being organized in many areas to "screen" the books used by colleges or by the general population. Books that have been in use for years suddenly become suspect when an unfavorable review appears in print.

Book-burning, such as took place in Sapulpa, Okla., does not often occur, but the end result is just as serious when books charged with being subversive, or written by suspected authors, are removed from school or library shelves. A vigorous protest against "the poisoning of America's historic spirit of freedom" has been lodged by leading educators and others concerned over the trend.

This situation is disclosed by a nation-wide study of book censorship conducted by THE NEW YORK TIMES. Data obtained from the forty-eight state commissioners of education have been supplemented by interviews with many of the nation's educational spokesmen.

Manifestations of Tendency

The censorship is usually conducted in the name of a patriotic organization or committee, set up to protect the community against subversive literature. At other times the attacks come from individuals, who stir up a controversy by airing their views in print.

Most state education departments report that they have legally constituted committees to screen books for subversive leanings or other unfitness. It is the growing number of voluntary censorship groups that is causing deep concern.

A summary of THE TIMES findings, based on the nation-wide reports, follows:

1. A concerted campaign is under way over the country to censor school and college textbooks, reading materials and other visual aids.

2. Voluntary groups are being formed in nearly every state to screen books for "subversive" or un-American statements. These organizations, not accountable to any legal body, are sometimes doing great harm in their communities.

3. Librarians are intimidated by outside pressures in their choice of books and other materials. Unwilling to risk a public controversy, they meekly accept the requests of the self-appointed censorship groups.

4. Several textbooks and other materials have already been removed from school or college libraries and are effectively on "the blacklist."

5. The attacks on the "subversive" school texts appear to be part of a general campaign against public schools and other educational institutions.

That the attacks on books and the growing censorship are creating alarm in educational circles is evident by the reaction of prominent educators. Many regard them as heralding even greater assaults upon the principles and traditions of American democracy. They see in the censorship trend a negation of America's historic role of the protection of free speech and press..

According to Dr. David K. Berninghausen, for many years chairman of the American Library Association's Committee on Intellectual Freedom, these anti-intellectual onsets loom as a major threat to society.

Librarian at Cooper Union, Dr. Berninghausen has for several years collected data on the attempts at library censorship. He declared yesterday that "the volunteer educational dictators" that are censoring textbooks had created a serious problem for all who believe in free discussion and the flow of ideas of all types.

These "dictators," he indicated, confuse teaching with indoctrination and are ready to condemn anyone as subversive who fails to endorse their particular beliefs.

"Copying the Nazis or the Communists in thought control techniques in communications and education is not the way to meet our problem," he said. "The antidote to authoritarianism is not some form of American authoritarianism. The antidote is free inquiry.

"And the future of free public education depends upon the willingness of good citizens to hold to our traditional freedom to pursue truth where and how we will. If we allow our schools to become the tool of any group which seeks to control our minds, if we choose indoctrination over education, the whole human species will suffer."

Congress Librarian's Warning

A sharp attack against "the poisoning of the historic spirit of America" was made by Dr. Luther H. Evans, Librarian of Congress. He warned against "the strong and ugly movement" for the destruction of our great freedom. A situation exists, he added, where the shrillest and most fear-ridden defenders of the Bill of Rights are themselves making specious arguments for its abridgment in spirit.

"The American public library is one of the great bulwarks of liberty and democracy in this great land," declared Dr. Evans. "It must remain a place where citizens can go to learn what is to be said for and against all of the proposals made on the great public issues of the day, issues which they either must face or must forfeit the claim of being good citizens.

"The drawing of lines against the study of this or that proposal, on the ground that it would poison the minds of the people, is abhorrent to the spirit on which this country is founded. Such a setting up of forbidden zones of thought must be fought to the death."

Tied to Fight on Public Schools

In the opinion of Dr. Earl J. McGrath, United States Commissioner of Education, "the intense and widespread attacks on textbooks" represent a threat to the American system of education. This onslaught is all the more serious, he said, because it is part of the fight against the public schools.

The controversy over textbooks, he added, must be viewed from the perspective of the long fight for freedom of expression and freedom to learn. And this vital question must be asked: "Shall the minds of men be shackled?"

The educators generally agree that the citizens should be concerned with what is taught in the public schools or colleges. But, they insist, this interest should be honest, and not based on self-interest or a desire to exploit the present fear of communism for selfish ends.

This point of view is best expressed by Dr. Virgil M. Rogers, Superintendent of Schools, Battle Creek, Mich., and president of the American Association of School Administrators.

In these difficult days of world tensions, he said, it is not surprising that American citizens are concerned about what is being taught in the public schools where textbook and teacher are the most influential forces in the educational experiences of pupils.

It is of the utmost importance, he added, that citizens work through the elected or appointed boards of education, the school administration and the local parent-teacher associations in making their approaches to the schools.

"Unfortunately, occasionally individuals or small groups become excited and forget the democratic process and make unwarranted assaults upon teachers, the schools, the school board or the administration," Dr. Rogers observed.

"These forces must be met by the intelligent citizens of our several communities keeping in close touch with education. The educational forces should keep them involved in the planning and policy making as we work toward a stronger America."

According to Dr. Richard B. Kennan, executive director of the National Education Association's defense commission, the teaching profession welcomes any review of books for public school use that is fair, objective, intelligent and based on generally understood criteria.

Book Test by Fair Review

The present danger lies, he warned, in the possibility that some local school authorities, owing to outside pressures or influences, may relinquish their traditional responsibility for determining what shall be taught in the schools to remote, centralized special interest agencies.

"Such abrogation of local autonomy in school control would be a loss of most serious consequences," Dr. Kennan declared.

In its study, "The Freedom of the Public School Teacher," the National Education Association emphasized pressure groups that try to influence the selection of textbooks and teaching materials. Some are not local groups but are organized over a wider territory. Not all are honestly concerned with improving the schools, the association said, in urging that the profession oppose those whose chief aim is to make trouble.

Complaints against textbooks come from three major sources, Dr. Hubert C. Armstrong, director of the Public Education Association, observed. He summarized them this way:

"First, the ultra or super-patriots who for the most part are plain, ordinary, uninformed, good-hearted American citizens. They get greatly aroused about books they haven't read—if someone else tells them they are dangerous or subversive. I remember an American Legion post that got quite excited about the Rugg books and were about to raid the schoolhouse when the principal prevailed upon them to read the books first. This delayed the whole process, led to a lot of discussion and the books weren't burned, after all.

"Second, a group composed of organized minorities, usually racial or religious, who find passages which they feel are prejudicial. What they don't quite see is that once they give in to the principle of censorship or banning, they have opened the gates to anyone else who may wish to use it against them.

"Third, there are full-time complainers like the Zolls [Allan A. Zoll] and the Crains [Lucille C. Crain] who are zealous to make the literary world over in their own images. They seem to be sources of very unhealthy attitudes in a democratic society, for they are so grim that they frighten a good many people. I feel we ought to have informed minds rather than inflamed ones."

Evidence of the growing attacks on textbooks, and the way they mushroom, can be found in the concerted drive against "subversive" material. The case against Frank A. Magruder's "American Government" is a good illustration. One of the most widely used texts in its field, in use for many years, it was attacked in The Educational Reviewer as having socialist or communist overtones. The review was broadcast nationally by a well-known radio commentator.

Things began to happen fast. The book was banned in Houston, Texas. It was dropped as a text in Little Rock, Ark., although retained as a reference work. Georgia banned it, although state officials offered to sell the 30,000 copies in stock to neighboring states.

The book was attacked in Washington, D. C. and in the State of Washington. One school district banned the use of the book, although about two weeks ago the same board authorized the use of the 1952 edition (revised to meet some of the complaints) as a supplemental text.

In Florida a Committee for American Action vigorously spearheaded the Magruder attack. The Virginia Education Department had to answer a charge that the Magruder text advocated world government. But the Superintendent of Public Instruction, Dr. Dowell J. Howard, took this position: "We must teach about other forms of government if our children are to appreciate democracy."

The list of states and communities where the Magruder book has been under fire covers wide areas. Concern over its use is reported in Jackson, Mich., and in Montana and Alabama.

Yet, upon a thorough reading of the book, the school boards and educators give it a clean bill of health. They maintain there is nothing subversive about it, nothing contrary to the American ideals and traditions. But public pressures have been formed to force it out of schools and colleges.

Another illustration might be cited. Arkansas reports that in recent months a fifth-grade history text, a series on health and a high school civics text have been under question. According to Dr. H. T. Steele, supervisor of the Arkansas division of free textbooks, the attacks came from an "overzealous" group. Sentences of the history book were taken out of context. The State Board of Education had the text thoroughly examined by a responsible dean of history, who reported that it contained no subversive teaching.

The attack on the health series held that the texts advocated socialized medicine. Again, the education board cleared this series. The high school civics text was attacked on the grounds that it discussed the theories of Communism. The book was taken off the basal list of the high schools in the state and placed on a supplemental list. Now the teachers are demanding that the book be returned to its former place.

May 25, 1952

PRESIDENT VETOES IMMIGRATION BILL AS DISCRIMINATORY

By ANTHONY LEVIERO
Special to THE NEW YORK TIMES.

WASHINGTON, June 25—President Truman today vetoed the McCarran-Walter Immigration and Nationality Bill with some of the strongest language he has used in recent messages to Congress.

While the President invoked the Bible and the Constitution to denounce the measure as an abdication of this country's moral leadership in the struggle for world peace, Senator Pat McCarran, Nevada Democrat, assailed his veto as "un-American" and conforming to Communist doctrine.

Tonight the lines were being drawn for a final battle over the bill of more than 300 pages. Into the measure went more than three years of study by Congressional committees. It would codify the immigration laws that have accumulated during the last three decades. But Mr. Truman denounced the bill as a step backward that would intensify "the repressive and inhumane aspects" of present immigration procedures.

By retaining the present national origins quota system, said Mr. Truman, the bill would deprive this country of the growth in manpower needed to maintain "the strength and vigor of our economy." He called for a re-examination of immigration policies and practices to fit the needs of the second half of the twentieth century.

The President's Proposals

Mr. Truman made three proposals for Congressional action:

1. The creation of a bipartisan commission of outstanding Americans that would examine immigration policy with the aim of bringing it "into line with our national ideals and our foreign policy." This group would consist of four members named

by the President, four by the Vice President in behalf of the Senate and four by the Speaker of the House.

2. The enactment of legislation removing racial barriers against Asians, for failure to do so "can only have serious consequences for our relations with the peoples of the Far East." Mr. Truman said this could be accomplished by Senate passage of H. R. 403, already passed by the House.

3. The enactment of the program that Mr. Truman sent to Congress from Key West in March, which would admit 300,000 immigrants to the United States over a three-year period, thus alleviating overpopulation in Europe and aiding refugees from Soviet despotism.

Tomorrow the House of Representatives is expected to vote on the veto and the Senate plans to act later this week if the House overrides. Proponents of the bill will seek to muster the two-thirds majority of those voting that will be necessary to override the President.

The Administration, combating week-end absenteeism in Congress, will try to rally all available members who would vote to sustain President Truman on a question that fits into the framework of his civil rights objectives. Mr. Truman has already sounded the call for an uncompromising civil rights fight, and his message today cited what he considered many discriminations against Southern and Eastern European and Asiatic peoples.

The vote on the veto is expected to be close and the President's supporters are expected to press hard for acceptance of the three alternative proposals, or at least for the national commission. The program for 300,000 immigrants has received a cool reception.

The House passed the McCarran-Walter bill by a vote of 203 to 53, and therefore Administration adherents were not too hopeful of sustaining the veto there. In the Senate the bill had passed by a voice vote on June 11, when less than a score of members were on the floor. But in earlier tests an effort to substitute a more liberal bill was defeated by a vote of 51 to 27, while an attempt to pigeonhole the bill by sending it back to committee was defeated by 44 to 28.

The verbal duel between the President and Senator McCarran revived the controversy that has marked the course of the bill through Congress for months.

Raking over the bill in one of his longest and most detailed messages to the present session, Mr. Truman discussed the advantages it offered but said he found these too few against the many disadvantages which he discussed with asperity.

He said the bill was inhumane; would discriminate in favor of the English, the Irish and the Germans and against Southern and Eastern Europeans and Asians; would limit the certain rights of first-generation Americans; unreasonably invade the privacy of citizens returning from abroad; overrule the Supreme Court and other Federal courts in some instances; impinge on the prerogatives of the Executive Branch of the Government, and in some respects was "worse than the infamous Alien Act of 1798."

"The idea behind this discriminatory policy was, to put it badly," said Mr. Truman, "that Americans with English or Irish names were better people and better citizens than Americans with Italian or Greek or Polish names. It was thought that people of West European origin made better citizens than Rumanians or Yugoslavs or Ukrainians or Hungarians or Balts or Austrians.

"Such a concept is utterly unworthy of our traditions and our ideals. It violates the great political doctrine of the Declaration of Independence that 'all men are created equal.' It denies the humanitarian creed inscribed beneath the Statue of Liberty proclaiming to all nations, 'Give me your tired, your poor, your huddled masses yearning to breathe free.'

"It repudiates our basic religious concepts, our belief in the brotherhood of man, and in the words of St. Paul that 'There is neither Jew nor Greek, there is neither bond nor free * * * for ye are all one in Christ Jesus.' "

Senator McCarran declared the veto was "one of the most un-American acts I have witnessed in my public career." He said Mr. Truman had disregarded the advice of the State and Justice Departments, the Central Intelligence Agency, the Immigration and Naturalization Service and hundreds of patriotic organizations.

Mr. Truman "has adopted the doctrine that is promulgated by The Daily Worker," continued the chairman of the Senate Judiciary Committee, recalling the attacks on the bill made by the Communist newspaper. He said the veto, if sustained, would waste three years of committee work that had cost two-thirds of a million dollars.

June 26, 1952

CONGRESS ENACTS IMMIGRATION BILL OVER TRUMAN VETO

Senate, 57-26, Follows House on Overriding President— Law Effective in 6 Months

By C. P. TRUSSELL
Special to THE NEW YORK TIMES.

WASHINGTON, June 27—The Senate today joined the House of Representatives in overriding President Truman's veto of the McCarran-Walter immigration bill, and thus wrote the measure into law. The Senate's vote was 57 to 26.

The bill, designed to codify and overhaul immigration and naturalization statutes enacted piecemeal through many generations, will become effective six months from today. It represents the first complete redrafting of such laws since 1798.

Mr. Truman had called the bill infamous. He said the measure, the result of more than three years of Congressional committee work, smacked of thought control. He held its bad points far outweighed the good and would injure the country's international position.

The fifty-seven votes to override were one more than the two-thirds majority required to kill a veto. A switch of two votes would have sustained the President's action. Yesterday the House gave seventeen votes more than a two-thirds majority to the motion to override. The vote was 278 to 113.

Party Lines Shattered

As in the House, party lines were shattered in the Senate. Voting to override were twenty-five Democrats, mostly from the South, but including Senator Ernest W. McFarland of Arizona, the majority leader. Thirty-two Republicans voted to override.

Eighteen Democrats voted to sustain the veto. Eight Republicans joined them.

Five of the Senate's aspirants for Presidential nominations were not present. They were Senator Robert A. Taft, Republican of Ohio, and Senators Estes Kefauver of Tennessee, Richard B. Russell of Georgia, Brien McMahon of Connecticut and Robert S. Kerr of Oklahoma, Democrats.

Senators Kefauver and McMahon were announced as favoring upholding the veto.

Debate before the vote was limited but bitter.

Senator Pat McCarran, Democrat of Nevada, principal sponsor of the bill and chairman of the Judiciary Committee, accused the President of making "unfounded and untrue" statements in his veto message. He also declared that "a person or persons" in the President's office had dealt in "chicanery" in futile attempts to break down State Department endorsement of his bill.

McCarran Makes Plea

The President, Mr. McCarran held, had vetoed the bill although recommendations that he sign it had been made by all other Federal agencies that would be concerned with its administration and enforcement, including the Federal Bureau of Investigation, the Central Intelligence Agency and the Immigration and Naturalization Service. The Senator said the principal issue was internal security at a critical time.

"In God's name, in the name of the American people, in the name of America's future," he declared, "let us override this veto."

The opposition, led by Senators Hubert H. Humphrey of Minnesota, Herbert H. Lehman of New York, William Benton of Connecticut, Blair Moody of Michigan, Paul H. Douglas of Illinois and John O. Pastore of Rhode Island, all Democrats, appeared stunned by the result of the voting, for it had expected the veto to be sustained.

Senator Lehman contended that the bill would make immigration "a myth" by "reducing it to a trickle," in violation of the American spirit of welcoming worthy foreigners.

Senator Humphrey said the measure would bar anyone from Poland and "slam the door" on most immigrants from other Baltic countries. Senator Moody argued that overriding the veto would be "a blow for Stalin," by discriminating against entry of persons seeking to escape from Iron Curtain countries.

The measure retains the quota system of immigration based on national origins. Mr. Truman criticized that system bitterly in his veto message.

Under the system, immigration quotas are assigned to countries in a ratio comparable to that of the various groups of foreign origin in this country's population in 1920. Since the heaviest immigration before 1920 came from Great Britain, Ireland, Germany and other Northern European lands, opponents of the measure argued it would discriminate against immigrants from Southern and Eastern Europe.

Senator Pastore said today the bill was "born in bigotry, founded in hate, and sought to reaffirm the discriminations devised in the present national origin quota system." Senator Benton warned that "more than one seat in this chamber is going to change hands, based on this vote alone."

Today's overriding of a Presidential veto was the first since Oct. 20, 1951. The issue then was contribution by the Government of $1,600 toward the purchase of an automobile for every veteran of World War II or of the Korean fighting who had been blinded or had lost a limb. It was the first enactment over veto on major legislation since 1947, when Congress enacted the Taft-Hartley labor law.

Applause broke out in the House today when it was announced that the Senate had concurred in overriding the veto of the McCarran-Walter bill. The co-author of the measure was Representative Francis E. Walter, Democrat of Pennsylvania.

June 28, 1952

Provisions of Immigration Law

Special to THE NEW YORK TIMES.
WASHINGTON, June 27—The McCarran-Walter bill to overhaul the country's immigration and naturalization laws, which Congress has written into law despite President Truman's veto of Wednesday, puts the permissable annual immigration at 154,658. This is 308 more than now can be admitted. Other provisions of the law:

1. The present national origin system of quotas for entry on the basis of ratios of foreign-born to United States population in 1920 is retained.

2. The Pacific area receives a total quota of 2,000 immigrants a year. The quotas of independent islands and trusteeships are 100 each, with Japan having a limit of 185. Thus, present racial barriers to immigration are removed.

3. A prospective immigrant, regardless of where he was born, must enter subject to the quota of the area of original nationality of either parent. Without this provision, proponents of the bill argued, the United States might be "flooded" with Orientals now living in nonquota Latin-American countries.

4. The present bar to naturalization of many people of Oriental birth will be wiped out, permitting about 88,000 persons living in the continental United States and Hawaii to become citizens. About 85,000 of them are estimated to be Japanese. Previous legislation had cleared the way for Chinese, Indians and Filipinos to become United States citizens.

Stiffens Exclusion Law

5. Law on the admittance, exclusion and deportation of aliens found to be dangerous to national security or general law and order is stiffened.

6. A system of selective immigration, under which top priority will be given to those having superior education or skills needed in this country, is introduced.

7. The grounds for exclusion of aliens are broadened, based on the findings of the Senate's investigation into interstate crime.

8. Decisions against aliens are subject to review.

9. Foreigners married to women who are United States citizens may come into the country without regard to quotas. Service men may bring foreign brides home.

10. Certain members of families that have established footholds in this country are exempt from literacy tests for entry.

11. The "hodge-podge" of existing immigration, naturalization and nationality law is clarified by codification.

June 28, 1952

SENATE UNIT CALLS LATTIMORE AGENT OF RED CONSPIRACY

Report of Investigation Group Says He Has Been 'Conscious Instrument of Soviet' Plot

PERJURY ACTION SOUGHT

Official of State Department at Bonn Also Accused— Charges Denied by Both

By C. P. TRUSSELL
Special to THE NEW YORK TIMES.

WASHINGTON, July 2 — Prof. Owen Lattimore, specialist in Far Eastern affairs and formerly an occasional consultant to the State Department, was accused by a Senate investigating subcommittee today of having been "a conscious articulate instrument of the Soviet conspiracy."

Reporting on conclusions drawn from an eighteen-month inquiry into the Institute of Pacific Relations, in which Professor Lattimore was a top figure, the investigators recommended that the Justice Department call a grand jury to determine whether Professor Lattimore, who is a member of the faculty at the Johns Hopkins University at Baltimore, and John Paton Davies Jr., a State Department official, should face perjury charges.

Mr. Davies, now Deputy Director of Political Affairs for the United States High Commissioner at Bonn, Germany, was cleared by the Loyalty Security Board of charges made against him last autumn while he was a member of the State Department's policy planning staff.

Professor Lattimore and Mr. Davies promptly denied the allegations in the 226-page report to the Senate.

Attorney General James P. McGranery said that "upon receipt of the report the matter will be given prompt consideration" by the Justice Department.

Policy Declared Swayed

The inquiry report charged that Professor Lattimore and John Carter Vincent, former head of the State Department's Far Eastern Affairs Division and now American diplomatic representative at Tangier, were influential in bringing about a change in United States policy in 1945 favorable to the Chinese Communists. Mr. Vincent also has been cleared in loyalty board inquiries.

During the period 1945-49, the report alleged, persons associated with the Institute of Pacific Relations were instrumental in keeping United States policy "on a course favorable to Communist objectives in China." In 1949, it added, members of the "small core" controlling the institute were influential in "giving United States Far Eastern policy a direction that furthered Communist purposes."

Holding that a principal objective of the institute was to influence American public opinion, the report stated that the net effect of this phase of its operations served Communist interests, while the interests of the United States were adversely affected.

The report emphasized that the highest officers and trustees, as well as most of the rank and file of the institute, had lent their funds, time and prestige to what they had believed to be noble purposes and were not aware of the pro-Communist activities.

McCarran Addresses Senate

The investigation was conducted by a special subcommittee of the Senate (Judiciary) Subcommittee on Internal Security. Its conclusions and recommendations were approved by the main subcommittee and also the full committee. Senator Pat McCarran, Democrat of Nevada, heads both the full committee and the subcommittee and was a member of the investigating group.

Mr. McCarran, addressing the Senate this afternoon, reviewed the findings and added:

"I am convinced, from the evidence developed in this inquiry, but for the machinations of the small group that controlled and activated the I. P. R., China today would be free and a bulwark against the further advance of the Red hordes in the Far East."

Through activities of the Institute of Pacific Relations, Senator McCarran contended, the American Government had been "infiltrated by persons whose allegiance is with Communist Russia."

"Our official secrets have been bared to agents of the Soviet," he went on. "Loyal and sincere men have been driven from their diplomatics posts, and, under the cloak of public office, messages have been written and words spoken that have tended to weaken this nation's position in world affairs."

The subcommittee report said the institute had been financed as an objective research organization since its birth in 1925 largely by constributions from American industrialists, corporations and foundations that could only lose by siding with communism. Through the years contributions averaged about $100,000 a year, of which 48 per cent were made by the Rockefeller Foundation and the Carnegie Corporation, the report asserted, adding:

"The I. P. R. has been considered by the American Communist party and by Soviet officials as an instrument of Communist policy, propaganda and military intelligence. The I. P. R. disseminated and sought to popularize false information, including information from Soviet and Communist sources * * *.

"I. P. R. officials testified falsely before the * * * subcommittee concerning the relationship between I. P. R. and the Soviet Union."

Perjury Charges Detailed

The subcommittee contended that Professor Lattimore had testified falsely, as follows:

¶By swearing that Outer Mongolia was an independent country until after World War II, when he knew in 1936 that it was controlled by Russia.

¶By swearing that he did not know that one Ch'ao-Ting Chi, a functionary in the institute with whom he worked, was a Communist.

¶By not telling the truth about his associations with Frederick Vanderbilt Field, wealthy New Yorker long under investigation as an alleged Communist, and his knowledge of the Field record.

¶By not admitting that he knew that the author of articles published in an institute magazine, of which he was editor, was a Communist.

¶By not giving an accurate account, under oath, of his association with Catesby Jones, a Johns Hopkins graduate student, who was alleged to have attended and reported investigation hearings "on assignment" from Mrs. Lattimore.

Mr. Davies was accused of having given false testimony in denying that he had recommended to the Central Intelligence Agency that it employ a group of persons for highly sensitive operations who allegedly were Communists or pro-Communists.

A previous investigation by the State Department into this charge had been dismissed.

Other Recommendations Made

The Judiciary Committee, in filing the report, also recommended:

¶That Congress enact "an adequate" statute to permit Congressional investigating committees or subcommittees to grant immunity from prosecution to witnesses having vital information concerning conditions requiring correction but who refuse to testify on constitutional grounds that their testimony might incriminate them.

¶That the Justice Department and the Judiciary Committee study the espionage laws together and work out legislative plans to deal most effectively with present-day security problems.

¶That the Senate's Committee on Government Operations, having general investigative jurisdiction, determine what legislation was needed to require departments and agencies of the Executive Branch to make available to Congressional inquiry groups material from their files.

¶That consideration be given to investigation by appropriate agencies of:

(a) Possible Communist infiltration of and influence upon the Treasury Department and other agencies forming and administering fiscal and monetary policies and affairs.

(b) The role of Alger Hiss, former State Department official now serving a prison sentence for perjury in testimony concerning leakage of secret official information to a Communist spy ring, in foreign affairs and formulation of United States foreign policy, and his influence on personnel decisions in the State Department.

(c) The extent to which persons actively associated with the "pro-Communist core" of the Institute of Public Relations had been employed in any governmental agency, and the activities and influence of persons still so employed.

(d) The extent to which contributions by American charitable scientific and education foundations had aided Communist or pro-Communist activity in the country.

Professor Lattimore had been under Congressional investigation, off and on, since 1950. In that year another Senate group, a subcommittee of the Foreign Relations Committee, went into the I. P. R. charges made by Senator Joseph R. McCarthy, Republican of Wisconsin.

The professor called them "moonshine." The subcommittee, headed by former Senator Millard E. Tydings, Democrat of Maryland, dismissed the charges as "a fraud and a hoax." Mr. McCarthy charged a "whitewash." Last year the McCarran group picked up the investigation again.

'UNTRUE,' LATTIMORE SAYS

Charge Supported by No Creditable Evidence, Professor Asserts

Special to THE NEW YORK TIMES.

BALTIMORE, July 2—Professor Lattimore said the Senate subcommittee's charge was "untrue and is supported by no creditable evidence."

The professor issued a written statement after he had spent several hours in conference with Thurman Arnold of the Washington law firm of Arnold, Fortas and Porter. The statement follows:

"I have already denied under oath any sympathy for or any participation in Soviet activities. The new suggestion made by the McCarran committee that I was a conscious and articulate instrument of the Soviet conspiracy is untrue and is supported by no creditable evidence.

"The further suggestion of the committee that I committed perjury or indeed that I had anything to commit perjury about is as fantastic and as inane as the recent report that I was trying to leave the country without a passport.

"I have been living for more than two years in the full glare of public investigations that have gone into every aspect of my life and opinions. However, I am quite prepared to assist any inquiry that may be considered necessary by any responsible authority.

"It is a matter of great regret to me that the transcript of my testimony before the committee which bears on its face, I believe, the refutation of these charges, has not yet been made available to the press by the committee.

"I am convinced that when this long record has been read and studied no reasonable man can place any credence in any of the charges against me."

The State Department apologized to Professor Lattimore last week for a stop order to prevent him from leaving on any trip behind the Iron Curtain. The tip on which that order was based turned out to be a hoax.

In Washington, meanwhile, Acting Secretary of State David Bruce said he hoped the State Department never again would embarrass an American citizen as it did in the case of Professor Lattimore.

Mr. Bruce said the department should only take action when it had considered all the evidence in a particular case. He declined, however, to indicate what specific policy changes might be called for.

Davies Denies Perjury

BONN, Germany, July 2 (Æ)—"I certainly deny allegations of perjury," Mr. Davies said.

He declined to discuss what he said in his testimony before the subcommittee.

"This was about a year ago—in July or August, I think," he said, adding:

"The State Department has all the facts on the matter. Any comment should come from the State Department."

Mr. Davies came to Germany last fall shortly after being investigated and cleared by the State Department's Loyalty Security Board.

Institute Aide Issues Denial

William L. Holland, secretary general of the Institute of Pacific Relations, issued an emphatic denial yesterday of the McCarran subcommittee's charges against the research agency.

"Only by disregarding overwhelming evidence to the contrary, in the form of the I. P. R.'s voluminous publications and the opinions of qualified experts who have known its work long and intimately, could the subcommittee have reached the fantastic conclusion that 'the net effect of the I. P. R. activities on United States public opinion has been pro-Communist and pro-Soviet,'" he declared.

Mr. Holland said it had always been recognized that "a few Communists" might have tried to use the institute for their own purposes, "but concrete evidence of the I. P. R.'s record shows that if such attempts were made, they failed."

July 3, 1952

F.B.I. Says Overthrow by Violence Is Stalin Policy for Red Rule Here

Special to THE NEW YORK TIMES.

WASHINGTON, July 29—Overthrow of the United States Government by force and violence and not by peaceful methods is now Premier Joseph Stalin's key to Communist ascendancy in this country, a Federal Bureau of Investigation report released today declared.

The report was issued by Senator Pat McCarran, Democrat of Nevada, as chairman of the Senate Internal Security subcommittee. Senator McCarran said he had persuaded the F. B. I. to make the report available because "there have been some persons who tried to tell us the Communists were not dangerous; that they had no plans for an armed revolution in this country."

The report, described by J. Edgar Hoover, F. B. I. director, as a "monograph based primarily on the writings of Communist leaders," was compiled by his agency and until now has been classified as confidential material.

"The purpose of this brief paper," the report states in its opening sentence, "is to set forth documentary proof that the Communist party in the United States, teaches and advocates the overthrow and destruction of the United States Government by force and violence."

The report quotes toward this end from the writings of William Z. Foster, chairman of the party in this country, and from the writings and speeches of Marx, Engels, Lenin and Stalin. The report quotes Premier Stalin as writing in 1939:

"The proletarian revolution is impossible without the forcible destruction of the bourgeois state machine and the substitution for it of a new one."

At another point the report quotes Premier Stalin as explaining:

"The dictatorship of the proletariat is not a mere change of government, but a new state, with new organs of power, both central and local; it is the state of the proletariat, which has risen on the ruins of the old state, the state of the bourgeoisie."

The report concludes that both Stalin and Lenin have rejected finally the argument sometimes resorted to by United States Communists that Marxist doctrine provides latitude for the installation of Communist-type socialism in the United States and Britain without resort to violence.

The report points out also that the Communist party "line" is "continually calling for changes and improvements in the political, economic and social order," many of which might be considered as "reforms." It adds that the Communist party despises the "reformist" approach as opposed to the "revolutionary" one.

"Reforms are a means, not an end," the report says. "They serve as a 'cover' under which illegal work can be conducted. They serve to weaken the capitalist regime and prepare the way for the revolution."

The report then goes on to quote Premier Stalin as having written, in a work entitled "Foundations of Leninism," published in 1939 in New York, by International Publishers, the following:

"To a revolutionary, the main thing is revolutionary work and not reforms; to him reforms are by-products of the revolution. That is why, with revolutionary tactics under the bourgeois regime, reforms are naturally transformed into instruments for disintegrating this regime, into instruments for strengthening the revolution, into a base for the further development of the revolutionary movement.

"The revolutionary will accept a reform in order to use it as an aid in combining legal work with illegal work, to intensify, under its cover, the illegal work for the revolutionary preparation of the masses for the overthrow of the bourgeoisie."

July 30, 1952

McCarran Inquiry Unit Says Pro-Reds Rule Radio Guild

By C. P. TRUSSELL
Special to THE NEW YORK TIMES.

WASHINGTON, Aug. 27 — A Senate investigating subcommittee charged today that the Radio Writers Guild, whose members produce some 90 per cent of the scripts broadcast by radio networks, had permitted a minority band of pro-Communists to control the organization for the last nine years.

The Internal Security subcommittee, a group of the Senate Judiciary Committee, released testimony taken in closed hearings to the effect that:

¶Through control of the organization, a subordinate group of the Authors League of America, pro-Communists were enabled to form guild alliances with Communist-front groups and help finance their activities with funds provided mostly by dues paid by anti-Communists.

¶Employment blacklists were maintained against anti-Communists who fought the controlling group.

¶Through what was called the "Jack Goodman Group," liaison was established with alleged pro-Communists in key positions in prominent book publishing houses.

¶From about 1937 to 1950, the Actors Equity Association was dominated by pro-Communists and used not only for trade-union but political purposes. The situation in that organization was described as being "improved" but "still critical."

Release of the subcommittee report and testimony immediately brought a denial from the Radio Writers Guild headquarters in New York. The organization stated that it never had aligned itself with or supported any Communist or pro-Communist group and emphasized that in compliance with the Taft-Hartley Act its officers had signed non-Communist affidavits.

"This attack upon [the guild] and some of its individual members," the statement added, "is the latest in a two-year series of reports by a self-admitted minority group to rule or ruin this organization."

At the same time, Welbourn E. Kelley of New York, a founder of the guild and a principal witness for what was called the anti-Communist faction, made public a copy of a letter of complaint to the investigating group.

Mr. Kelley asserted that all of the statements he had made in closed session did not appear in the transcripts made public today. He said he had used the term "pro-Communist" at the request of subcommittee counsel. What he meant, he said, was "left wing," but he had complied with the subcommittee instructions in belief that his testimony would remain confidential.

"I respectfully ask," Mr. Kelley continued, "that the statements made by me which somehow were omitted from the records now be made a part of that record—namely, that I cannot say of my own knowledge that any member of the Guild is a Communist."

Investigator Replies

At subcommittee headquarters. Donald D. Conners Jr., an investigator, said:

"There was an off-the-record discussion in which Mr. Kelley was instructed that the subcommittee was not interested in receiving opinions of witnesses that any individual was a left-winger, or left-of-center, or a radical, because we were seeking information about Communists, not about radicals."

"Communists and Communism are terms that have definite meaning," Mr. Conners continued, "whereas the terms left-winger, left-of-center or radical are only relative terms which do not necessarily mean the same thing to all people."

The transcript of the Kelly testimony, Mr. Conners said, was verbatim and complete as made public.

The investigation was made over more than a year, with hearings in Washington and New York, by a unit of the Internal Security subcommittee of the Senate Judiciary Committee. Senator Pat McCarran, Democrat of Nevada and chairman of the full subcommittee and of the Judiciary Committee, was a member of the unit, as were Senator James O. Eastland, Democrat of Mississippi, who headed the unit, and Senator Arthur V. Watkins, Republican of Utah.

One hundred and twenty-six printed pages of testimony were made public. The testimony linked members of the alleged pro-Communist faction with radio programs followed in millions of American homes.

"The 1,200 to 1,500 members of the Radio Writers Guild who have allowed less than 100 pro-Communists to take over their organization," Senator McCarran said, "must share equally in responsibility for the subversive activities of those few whom they permit to use the name and power of the organization. Nor can the parent organization, the Authors League, be absolved from blame, so long as it allows such a situation to exist."

Testimony Aimed at Two

Testimony was aimed sharply against two radio writers described as prominent in their field and in the guild. They were Robert C. Lyon Jr., known professionally as Peter Lyon, and Millard Lampell, both alleged to have "notorious records of affiliation with Communist fronts and causes."

Both appeared as witnesses. They declined, on constitutional grounds of possible self-incrimination, to answer questions concerning communism or organizations that had been cited officially as being "subversive."

Witnesses for what they described as the anti-Communist faction in the guild testified that the opposing minority faction easily obtained control because anti-Communist members were reluctant to participate in guild business activities.

The "cooperative" witnesses, besides Mr. Kelley, were Vincent W. Hartnett, who had training as a naval intelligence officer; Ruth Adams Knight, author of a dozen books, and Paul R. Milton. All are radio script writers.

Miss Knight was asked how a pro-Communist writer could get Communist propaganda into a radio script in view of the editing and monitoring of radio programs.

'Constant Derision' Cited

"You would find, I am sure, if you examined the work of these people," Miss Knight replied, "a constant derision of the capitalistic system, and a constant derision of the average citizen. * * * There is no such thing in their scripts as a decent banker and a decent lawyer. The thing is subtle * * * it is scorn and it is contempt * * *. It is that attitude expressed that is the undetermining thing with the simple people who listen to radio [but] who would turn off outright Communist propaganda."

Mr. Kelley, the subcommittee report said, cited as leaders of the pro-Communist group the following:

"Peter Lyon, Sam Moore, Jule Font, Robert Cenedella, Abram Ginnes, George Fass, Leon Meadow, Morton Green, Jim Hart, Philo Higley, Ernest Kinoy, Dave Kogan, Joe Liss, Ira Marion [identified in testimony as being president of the Radio Writers Guild while the investigation was on], Sig Miller, Norman Ober, Arnold Perl, Addie Richton, Howard Rodman, Lillian Schoen, Lynn Stone, and Tex Wiener."

Mr. Kelley, in his letter, which was sent to Senator McCarran, referred to his testimony specifying twenty-two writers as "active leaders" in the guild "from the standpoint of pro-Communist group."

Step Called 'Mistake'

"I am extremely sorry that I allowed myself to make this mistake," Mr. Kelley wrote. "I have no doubt that these people will be harmed, an intention furthest from my mind. Therefore I respectfully ask that the statements made by me which somehow were omitted from the records now be made part of that record—namely, that I cannot say of my own knowledge that any member of the guild is a Communist."

Mr. Kelley asserted that the testimony released in the report "does not reflect a true picture of all that I said, nor does it include the premise on which my testimony was given." He declared that "I do not wish to deny any of my testimony as printed," but added that at one point Richard Arens, staff director for the subcommittee, called the discussion off the record and "gave me to understand that anything I said was confidential."

Mr. Kelley said he was then requested by Mr. Arens not to refer to a certain guild faction as "left wing," which Mr. Kelley had been doing, but to call the two factions "pro-Communist and anti-Communist" for the purpose of clarification.

"I demurred at this," said Mr. Kelley, "stating that there were people in the 'left-wing' faction for whom I had the greatest respect, and who in my opinion were neither Communist nor pro-Communist; however, I agreed to use he terms requested on the assumption that what I had to say was in confidence and would remain so."

The so-called "Jack Goodman Group" was mentioned by Mr. Hartnett, who testified:

"There is a certain group functioning, which I will call the Jack Goodman Group.

'This group, my sources indicate, includes, among others, Angus Cameron, editor of Little, Brown & Co., famous Boston publishing firm; Kenneth McCormick, executive editor of Doubleday & Co., New York publishing firm; Jack Goodman, an editor of Simon & Schuster, New York publishers; Joseph Barnes, former New York Herald Tribune correspondent, who is now an assistant to Jack Goodman at Simon & Schuster and a teacher at Sarah Lawrence College at Bronxville, N. Y., and Millard Lampell.

"This group of highly placed writers and publishers is in a position to exert a synchronized and powerful influence for communism or pro-Communist causes throughout a large segment of the publishing field."

The testimony concerning Actors Equity Association also was given by Mr. Hartnett.

Witnesses reluctant to answer all subcommittee questions insisted that the scripts they wrote had to receive final approval from program sponsors.

Wrote for U. S. Agencies

Mr. Lyon testified he had written scripts during World War II for the Office of War Information, the Coordinator of Inter-American Affairs and the Treasury Department in war bond drives.

He denied that he also had written for The Daily Worker, the official Communist party publication in the United States, under the name Peter Ivy, as had been charged by witnesses.

Mr. Lampell testified, as did Mr. Lyon, that he had written scripts for some of the best-known radio programs. In addition, he wrote, produced and directed official Air Force radio programs. His scripts, he said, also helped to sell war bonds, and through them, he added, he won official military citations.

One group of his scripts, Mr. Lampell testified, was published in book form, with royalties going to the Air Force Convalescence Fund.

Mr. Lampell emphasized that he also was author of a radio script that was produced by the United States Steel Corporation, and of a cantata, "Morning Star," which was commissioned by Mrs. Ogden Reid, publisher of The New York Herald Tribune, for the opening of that newspaper's annual forum in 1947 and which was narrated by Robert Montgomery, movie star and news commentator and vigorous foe of communism.

The Crucible of the Fifties

'Mr. Lyon, who was out of town, could not be reached for comment yesterday, but his attorney, Benedict Wolf of 160 Broadway, said:

"I have just talked with Mr. Lyon by phone and he has authorized me to say that he is not a member of the Communist party. The reasons for availing himself of the Fifth Amendment [in the hearings] were personal and sufficient."

It could not be learned, what radio and television programs, if any, Mr. Lyon was now writing. He is a freelance writer and not normally engaged with a regular weekly or daily assignment.

Mr. Lampell declined to comment on the subcommittee report, saying he had not read it. He added that for the last three years he had been writing fiction mainly, not radio and television scripts.

Some of the organizations with which Mr. Lyon and Mr. Lampell were linked in the subcommittee hearings are the same groups with which they were identified in Red Channels, a privately printed anti-Communist publication issued in June, 1950.

None of the writers who testified in the hearings is now an officer in the Radio Writers Guild, although some have been in the past. Guild headquarters said that Mr. Hartnett, a radio writer and producer, had never been a member of the group.

August 28, 1952

EISENHOWER SCORES PRESIDENT ON REDS; SUPPORTS M'CARTHY

In Tour of Wisconsin, General Asserts He Backs Senator's Aims Not His Methods

DENOUNCES 'VIGILANTISM'

Says Administration Tolerated Penetration by Communists —Asks Fight on 'Treason'

By W. H. LAWRENCE
Special to The New York Times.

MILWAUKEE, Oct. 3—Gen. Dwight D. Eisenhower today coupled a call for the re-election of Senator Joseph R. McCarthy, Wisconsin Republican, with a fierce attack upon Democratic Administrations for tolerating Communist penetration of the Government and "treason itself."

He told a Green Bay, Wis., audience this morning that the purposes Senator McCarthy and he had "of ridding this Government of the incompetents, the dishonest and above all the subversive and the disloyal are one and the same" and that they differed only over "methods."

And tonight, in a nation-wide broadcast, he said the future of the country belonged to courageous men and not to "those who have sneered at the warnings of men trying to drive Communists from high places—but who themselves have never had the sense or the stamina to take after the Communists themselves."

Omits Defense of Marshall

The Republican Presidential nominee warned, however, that "we would have nothing left to defend if we allowed ourselves to be swept into any spirit of violent vigilantism" and that we must, therefore, respect freedom in combating communism.

While he significantly failed to demonstrate any great enthusiasm at having Senator McCarthy aboard his special campaign train, General Eisenhower did bow to the Wisconsin Senator's urging and eliminate from his Milwaukee speech tonight a defense of his old friend and chief, General of the Army George C. Marshall, who has been one of Senator McCarthy's targets.

General Eisenhower informed Senator McCarthy at their Peoria, Ill., conference last night that he intended to include in his denunciation of communism tonight a defense of General Marshall from some of the attacks made upon him.

'Whole Decades Poisoned'

Senator McCarthy, it was said, told the Republican nominee that he had no particular objection to General Eisenhower's saying anything that he wished to say, but that he believed a defense of General Marshall probably could be made better before another audience.

And tonight in Milwaukee, General Eisenhower said that a national tolerance of communism as a credo that believed in "economic democracy" had "poisoned two whole decades of our national life" and insinuated itself into our schools, our public forums, some of our news channels, some of our labor unions "and—most terrifyingly—into our Government itself."

"What did this penetration into government mean?" the general said, continuing:

"It meant contamination in some degree of virtually every department, every agency, every bureau, every section of our Government. It meant a Government by men whose very brains were confused by the opiate of this deceit.

"These men were advisers in a foreign policy that—on one side of the world—weakly bowed before the triumph in China of Communists hailed as 'agrarian reformers.' On the other side of the world this policy condoned the surrender of whole nations to an implacable enemy whose appetite for conquest sharpened with every victory.

"This penetration meant a domestic policy whose tone was set by men who sneered and scoffed at warnings of the enemy infiltrating our most secret counsels.

"It meant—in its most ugly triumph—treason itself."

McCarthy Is Heckled

Speaking to the crowd of 8,500, which only partially filled the 13,700-seat Milwaukee arena, before General Eisenhower arrived, Senator McCarthy thanked the Wisconsin voters for his overwhelming Sept. 9 primary victory.

There were a few hecklers in the crowd, and Senator McCarthy was interrupted by other members of the audience shouting, "Throw them out." He quieted the audience by saying "Don't worry about one or two troublemakers in the crowd—I'm used to troublemakers."

General Eisenhower was introduced in Milwaukee by Gov. Walter Kohler. Sitting on the platform was Thomas E. Coleman, Madison industrialist and floor manager for Senator Robert A. Taft at the Chicago convention, who insisted that he had really retired from politics. He was aboard the Eisenhower special in Michigan on Wednesday and during the Wisconsin stops today.

Derides 'Silly Game' Charge

Without mentioning him by name, General Eisenhower sharply criticized Gov. Adlai E. Stevenson of Illinois, the Democratic Presidential nominee, for allegedly minimizing the Communist threat. Referring to a recent message by Governor Stevenson to the Veterans of Foreign Wars' convention in Los Angeles, he said "an Administration Democrat grandly declared that Communists in our national life were 'not very important' and that we should not waste time chasing 'phantoms.'"

He also asserted "the same man dismissed the quest for Communists in our Government as a kind of silly game being played in the bureau of wildlife and fisheries."

"Such comedy touches," General Eisenhower said, "do little to relieve the tragic knowledge that we have been for years the gullible victims of Communist espionage experts. These experts in treason have plundered us of secrets involving our highest diplomatic decisions, our atomic research. Tragically, we do not know how much more our security may have been jeopardized."

The problems of combating communism and the exact manner in which he should urge Senator McCarthy's re-election were very much on General Eisenhower's mind as he stumped through Wisconsin today in quest of its twelve electoral votes that went Democratic in 1948. His five rear-platform appearances drew crowds totaling about 20,000 before he reached Milwaukee.

But he deviated at one stop—at Neenah—and held out the possibility that a Republican Administration might reduce over-all taxes paid by citizens by as much as 55 per cent. He said that "National Tax Freedom Day" now fell on May 19, because the average family worked from Jan. 1 up until that date "for the Government" and that "none of the money" earned in that period went into its own pocket or for its own maintenance.

Calling for the election of a Republican President and Congress he said that "when you get that kind of a Government, you will begin to push National Tax Freedom Day back toward the first of the year."

"We will get it back into March and we will get it back into February and back into a decent place," General Eisenhower said.

The "McCarthy problem" began for the Eisenhower staff last night in Peoria, when Senator McCarthy turned up at the last stop in Illinois along with Governor Kohler —without, it was understood, the advance knowledge of General Eisenhower.

'Differences' Are Cited

The general and Senator McCarthy had a long talk, and afterward the Wisconsin Republican confined his remarks to the statement that it had been "very very pleasant."

Senator McCarthy and Governor Kohler boarded the Eisenhower "Look - Ahead - Neighbor" special train to ride into Wisconsin with General Eisenhower, and the general's assistants made no secret of their problem as to how the McCarthy endorsement could be handled without alienating important Eisenhower supporters who would have liked him to repudiate or ignore the Wisconsin Senator.

Attempts by photographers to get General Eisenhower to pose in the rear car with Senator McCarthy were turned down.

At the first stop this morning in Green Bay, Senator McCarthy was introduced amid loud cheers from the crowd of about 3,000 persons and left the rear platform before General Eisenhower appeared.

It was at that stop that General Eisenhower made his only direct personal call for Senator McCarthy's re-election.

He said that the "positive program" he was offering to the United States required "strong party strength," and for that reason he was calling in every state for the election of the entire Republican ticket because "they must be a part of the team if we are to accept responsibility and to be the party of performance."

"It is, of course, well known, ladies and gentlemen, to you and to many others that there have been differences of opinion, sometimes on important matters, between me and other people in the Republican party," General Eisenhower said. "Indeed, it would be a miracle if there were not.

202

"The differences between me and Senator McCarthy are well known to others. But what is more important, they are well known to him and to me and we have discussed them," the general added. He continued:

"I want to make one thing very clear. The purposes that he and I have of ridding this Government of the incompetents, the dishonest and above all the subversive and the disloyal are one and the same.

"Our differences, therefore, have nothing to do with the end result that we are seeking. The differences apply to method.

"This is the pledge that I make: If I am charged by you people to be the responsible head of the Executive Department, it will be my initial responsibility to see that subversion and disloyalty are kept out of the Executive Department.

"We will always appreciate and welcome Congressional investigation but we certainly will not depend upon it to unearth and show where subversion exists and then after it is shown be indifferent and complacent about rooting it out. The responsibility will rest squarely on the shoulders of the executive, and I hold that there are already ample powers in the Government to get rid of these people if the Executive Department is really concerned with doing it.

"We can do it with absolute assurance that American principles of trial by jury, of innocence until proof of guilt, are all observed, and I expect to do it. So I pledge you that it will be my responsibility to be vigilant, to keep that Executive Department clean, and I make the same pledge to the Congress of the United States."

McCarthy Introduces General

The next scheduled stop was Appleton, which is Senator McCarthy's home town, and there had been speculation all through the night as to whether Senator McCarthy would introduce the Republican nominee there.

Senator McCarthy said he was not sure whether he would make the introduction. Some Eisenhower staff members indicated that the Senator probably would, and others said that he would not. Just five minutes before the train reached Appleton, a party official said that Senator McCarthy would introduce Governor Kohler and the Governor would introduce General Eisenhower.

But when the train came to a halt before a crowd of 6,000 to 7,000 persons, it was Senator McCarthy who came bouncing out of the rear car onto the rear platform to introduce General Eisenhower as "a man who is an outstanding general, who was an outstanding administrator in Europe, and who will make an outstanding President."

Before the home town crowd General Eisenhower made no reference whatever to Senator McCarthy. He confined himself instead to saying the crowds he had seen on his campaign were determined to clean out the mess in Washington "and they are going to clean it out by sending to Washington a great team in the Senate, in the Congress, in the Executive Departments, of the finest people we can draw from this whole United States to give you honesty, integrity, fairness and friendliness to try to help you and not to boss you."

"For that purpose, you need every single man we have got on the ticket here in Wisconsin from the Governor himself through the Senate and the House," General Eisenhower added. "Please give us the whole works, and we will do the job, we promise you."

After this address, the Wisconsin Senator was asked if he was satisfied with the endorsement General Eisenhower had expressed.

Senator McCarthy said that he was satisfied with General Eisenhower's endorsement, that he was sure both of them would carry Wisconsin, and that General Eisenhower would be elected and would make "a good President."

He declined to discuss the differences between himself and General Eisenhower, saying that he would leave that up to the Republican nominee.

In his Milwaukee speech tonight, General Eisenhower said that "freedom must defend itself with courage, with care, with force and with fairness."

"To defend freedom, in short, is —first of all—to respect freedom," he continued. "That respect demands another, quite simple kind of respect—respect for the integrity of fellow citizens who enjoy their right to disagree. The right to question a man's judgment carries with it no automatic right to question his honor."

Strictest Tests Promised

But General Eisenhower went on to say that "the Bill of Rights contains no grant of privilege for a group of people to join together to destroy the Bill of Rights" and that a group like the Communist party "cannot be allowed to claim civil liberties as its privileged sanctuary from which to carry on subversion of the Government.

"At the same time, we have the right to call a spade a spade," he said. "That means, in every proved case, the right to call a Red a Red."

He said that while every political voice had a right to be heard, "let each voice be named and counted." He would require every person or organization distributing political literature through the mails to disclose both its source of funds and its membership. Every political organization, he said, should be compelled to make public its finances, membership and affiliations.

He promised to apply the strictest tests of loyalty and patriotism to Federal employes, whose employment, he said, is a privilege and "not a right."

It was announced today that General Eisenhower had changed his itinerary to permit active campaigning tomorrow in South Dakota and North Dakota, which had not been included in the original plans for this trip. He will leave his train at Duluth, Minn., tomorrow, and fly to St. Cloud, Minn., for a noontime speech, to Brookings, S. Dak., for a midafternoon speech, and into Fargo, N. Dak., for a late afternoon speech. He will reboard his train at Fargo for the long Sunday ride to the Pacific Northwest.

October 4, 1952

STEVENSON AVERS RIVAL AND DULLES HAD FAITH IN HISS

Charges Republicans Failed to Disavow Official Even After He Was Indicted

STRIKES BACK AT CRITICS

Governor Asserts Eisenhower Must Be 'Responsible' for 'Lies' of G. O. P. Drive

By W. H. LAWRENCE
Special to THE NEW YORK TIMES.

CLEVELAND, Oct. 23 — Gov. Adlai E. Stevenson of Illinois charged tonight that Gen. Dwight D. Eisenhower and his foreign affairs adviser, John Foster Dulles, "demonstrated a continued personal faith" in Alger Hiss even after Hiss had been indicted for perjury in connection with espionage aimed to benefit the Soviet Union.

The Democratic Presidential nominee struck back at the Republican candidate and his advisers in a full-length, nationally broadcast and televised defense of his own character deposition given at the Hiss trial. This has been made a campaign issue by Senators Richard M. Nixon of California, the G. O. P. Vice Presidential candidate, and by Joseph R. McCarthy of Wisconsin.

Governor Stevenson asserted he had never testified as to the guilt or innocence of Alger Hiss and added that he had repeatedly declared he "never doubted the verdict of the jury which convicted him."

Testified on Court Order

He said he had simply testified that Hiss' reputation for character was "good" in response to an order of the court, and that he could not have done less as a lawyer and as a citizen.

He accused the Republicans of attempting to "beguile the voters by lies and half truths" and said that these tactics, for which General Eisenhower himself must assume full responsibility, are "spiritual treason against our institutions, for they are surely doing the work of their enemies."

"I would suggest to the Republican crusaders that if they were to apply the same methods to their own candidate, General Eisenhower, and to his foreign affairs adviser, John Foster Dulles, they would find that both these men were of the same opinion and more so," Governor Stevenson said in reference to his own deposition as to Hiss' character.

"The facts are that the General and Mr. Dulles both demonstrated a continued personal faith in Alger Hiss in circumstances which imposed on them as circumstances never did on me—the obligation to make a searching examination of his character and background."

He said that Mr. Dulles was chairman of the board of trustees of the Carnegie Endowment for International Peace when Hiss was selected as its president, and that at this time, Mr. Dulles had received from a Detroit lawyer a letter offering to provide "evidence that Hiss had a provable Communist record."

He read to the audience in the Cleveland arena this excerpt from Mr. Dulles' reply to this offer:

"I have heard the report which you refer to, but I have confidence that there is no reason to doubt Mr. Hiss' complete loyalty to our American institutions. I have been thrown into intimate contact with him at San Francisco, London and Washington. * * * Under these circumstances I feel a little skeptical about information which seems inconsistent with all that I personally know and what is the judgment of reliable friends and associates in Washington."

General Eisenhower, he went on, was elected to the board of trustees of the Carnegie Foundation in May, 1948, at a meeting at which Hiss was re-elected president, and Governor Stevenson commented that "this was months after I had seen Hiss for the last time."

Hiss Indicted for Perjury

Later, after Hiss had been indicted by a Federal grand jury on charges of perjury in connection with the testimony of Whittaker Chambers, a self-admitted spy for Russia, that Hiss had passed secret State Department documents to him, Governor Stevenson pointed out that the Carnegie board gave the accused official a three-month leave of absence "with full pay so that he might defend himself."

"The General was not present at the meeting. But I do not find that he ever voiced disapproval of this concrete expression of trust and confidence," the Illinois Governor continued. "In May of 1949, the month in which I gave my deposition, and again in December, 1949, after the first trial of Alger Hiss, the board of trustees, of which General Eisenhower was still a member, again voted to reject Hiss' resignation as a trustee.

"Alger Hiss, General Eisenhower and Dulles continued as fellow members of the board of trustees until after the conviction of Alger Hiss."

Governor Stevenson said he had brought these facts before the public "not to suggest that either General Eisenhower or John Foster Dulles is soft toward Communists or even guilty of the bad judgment that the General's running mate charges against me."

"I bring them out only to make the point that the mistrust, the innuendos, the accusations which this crusade is employing, threatens not merely themselves, but the integrity of our institutions," he declared.

Puts Responsibility on General

Again and again, Governor Stevenson emphasized that General Eisenhower himself must accept full responsibility for the kind of campaign being conducted by Senators Nixon and McCarthy, and recalled that only last week, in New York, the General had asserted the decisions in this campaign "have been and will be mine alone."

He called attention to the forthcoming national broadcast by Senator McCarthy in these words:

"Next Monday night, for example, the junior Senator from Wisconsin is going to make a highly advertised speech—the man who said last week that, if he were put aboard my campaign train with a club, he might be able to make a good American out of me.

"Now plainly I have no concern about what the junior Senator from Wisconsin as such has to say about me. As an isolated voice it would be unimportant. But he has become more than the voice of a single individual who thinks the way to teach Americanism is with a club.

"He appears next Monday night on nation-wide radio and television as the planned climax of the Republican campaign—as the very voice of the wing of the Republican party that lost the nomination but won the nominee. You will hear the voice of the Senator from Wisconsin, with the permission and the approval of General Eisenhower."

Governor Stevenson referred to Senator Nixon as the "brash young man who aspires to the Vice Presidency" and denied a recent charge by the Californian that he had testified incorrectly when he denied having seen Hiss between March 1946 and the fall of 1947.

Senator Nixon asserted that Mr. Stevenson, before he became Governor, had introduced Hiss to a Chicago audience on Nov. 12, 1946.

This claim was untrue, Governor Stevenson said, because the official records made it clear that on that date "I was in official attendance as a delegate to the United Nations in New York, and was not in Chicago at all."

Reaffirming that it was his duty to testify honestly that so far as he knew Hiss' reputation had been good when he knew him, Governor Stevenson compared his action with that of Senators Robert A. Taft and John W. Bricker, both of Ohio, who appeared in court to give character references for Representative Walter Brehm of Ohio when he was on trial on charges of unlawfully receiving political contributions from his employes.

Representative Brehm was convicted after Senator Taft testified that his reputation was "excellent beyond question" and Senator Bricker said his reputation was "very, very good."

"It is obvious," the Governor said, "that my testimony in the Hiss case no more shows softness towards communism than the testimony of these Republican leaders shows softness towards corruption."

October 24, 1952

M'CARTHY TERMS STEVENSON UNFIT

Senator Accuses Governor of Sympathy With and Aid to Communist Cause

By RICHARD J. H. JOHNSTON
Special to THE NEW YORK TIMES.

CHICAGO, Oct. 27 — Senator Joseph R. McCarthy, Republican of Wisconsin, charged tonight that Gov. Adlai E. Stevenson of Illinois, Democratic Presidential candidate, was unfit to serve in the nation's highest office because of his associations and advisers.

The Senator accused Governor Stevenson of sympathy with and, on occasions, of assistance to the Communist cause. He said he was performing "this unpleasant task because the American people are entitled to have the coldly documented background of this man who wants to be President."

The Senator spoke in the grand ballroom of the Palmer House at a $50-a-plate "McCarthy Broadcast Dinner," arranged by a committee headed by Gen. Robert E. Wood, chairman of the board of Sears, Roebuck & Co. The dinner was attended by 1,150 persons. The speech was carried on nation-wide television and radio networks.

Mr. McCarthy asserted that he was giving "the facts on the evidence in the case of Stevenson vs. Stevenson." Mr. McCarthy then reviewed virtually all of his previous charges concerning alleged association between Governor Stevenson and Communists or Communist sympathizers.

Declaring that he was prepared to document these charges, Mr. McCarthy waved aloft a handful of newspaper clippings and other documents.

Senator McCarthy charged that Governor Stevenson through his personal manager, Wilson W. Wyatt, and his speech writers, Arthur Schlesinger Jr., Bernard DeVoto, James Wechsler, Archibald MacLeish and others, had aligned himself with the Leftists.

Archibald MacLeish s a Pulitzer Prize poet and professor at Harvard University. He formerly was Librarian of Congress and formerly Assistant Secretary of the Navy. Arthur Schlesinger Jr., as associate professor of history at Harvard, is a Pulitzer Prize winner in history. Bernard DeVoto is an author and historian, and James Wechsler is the editor of The New York Post.

The Senator said he was delivering his speech "a full week before Election Day" to enable Governor Stevenson "to explain it — if he can."

For the most part, he offered as sources for his charges against Stevenson speech writers' references to newspaper stories.

"Perhaps the most revealing article written by Stevenson's speech writer [Mr. Schlesinger] appeared in THE NEW YORK TIMES on Dec. 11, 1949, on page 3 * * *" Senator McCarthy said.

"I quote, he says, 'I happen to believe—I happen to believe that the Communist party should be granted the freedom of political action and that Communists should be allowed to teach in universities.'"

The prepared text, which Senator McCarthy released to the press, continued the quotation with "so long as they do not disqualify themselves by intellectual distortions in the classroom." Senator McCarthy dropped the qualifying clause when he delivered the speech.

It was taken from a book review by Professor Schlesinger that appeared in the Book Review section of THE NEW YORK TIMES.

Much of the Senator's "documentation" was lost to the radio and television audience when his half-hour of broadcast time expired about the mid-point of his speech. He finished the speech, however, for his ballroom audience.

Among the charges Senator McCarthy made were:
1. That Governor Stevenson in the summer of 1943, while working for the State Department, received the task of formulating post-war policy in Italy. Mr. McCarthy said that Gen. Walter Bedell Smith, head of the Central Intelligence Agency, had written a book in which the general called that policy an attempt to "connive" to bring Communists into the Italian Government.
2. That Governor Stevenson was on the policy-forming committee of the World Citizenship Association, an organization, Senator McCarthy said, that advocated a "super-world government."
3. That Governor Stevenson was a member of the Institute for Pacific Relations, which was investigated by the Senate committee. The Wisconsin Senator charged that Alger Hiss, now serving a sentence for perjury, and Frank Coe, who the Senator said had been named under oath before Congressional committees seven times as a member of the Communist party, once recommended Governor Stevenson as a delegate to a conference of the Institute for Pacific Relations.
4. That, despite Governor Stevenson's denials, he "invited, sought out and brought" Hiss to speak at Northwestern University Nov. 12, 1946, and that the Governor later defended his deposition on Hiss' loyalty by saying, "I said his reputation was good. I did not say his reputation was very good." The Democratic Presidential candidate .has asserted that it was his duty as a lawyer to give testimony in reply to a court order. This view has been upheld by a group of lawyers and opposed by another lawyer group.
5. That Stevenson as Governor of Illinois vetoed the so-called Broyles bill aimed at outlawing the Communist party and requiring loyalty oaths of teachers and state employes.
6. That Governor Stevenson said he was not a member of the Americans for Democratic Action although an A. D. A. publication of February, 1952, listed him as a charter member.

Within the five minutes before his air time expired, Senator McCarthy was interrupted twice by disturbances in the rear of the ballroom. One man shouted, "That's not so," when the Senator said that Governor Stevenson was a member of the World Citizenship Association, whose purpose, he charged, was "to fly the flag of a super-world government over the Stars and Stripes."

The man was ejected.

Two minutes later another person attempted to interrupt Senator McCarthy while he was talking about the discovery of "over 200,-000 astounding documents" of the Institute for Pacific Relations in a Massachusetts barn.

The Senator drew prolonged applause and loud boos when he denounced the World Citizenship Association and declared that Governor Stevenson was a member of the association's policy-forming committee.

In the portion of his speech that followed his broadcast time, Senator McCarthy cited an editorial that appeared in The Daily Worker, official organ of the Communist party.

"I hold in my hand a photostat of the Daily Worker of Oct. 19, 1952," the Senator said. "That is only eight days old. They damn Eisenhower and what they call 'Eisenhowerism' from hell to breakfast.

"They refer, and I quote, to 'their hatred of Eisenhowerism' and they go on to say that they do not like Stevenson so well, but that if Communists want to vote for Stevenson—okay, vote for him—but be sure if you do that, vote for no one else on the Democratic ticket—elect local Progressive party candidates and pile up a big vote for those Communist candidates who are in the field."

Red Paper Issues Denial

A spokesman of The Daily Worker said last night:

"We are backing Vincent Hallinan and Mrs. Charlotta Bass, Pro-

gressive party candidates for President and Vice President. We are not backing Governor Stevenson. However, we cannot speak for the Communist party."

The statement on the backing of Mr. Hallinan and Mrs. Bass was verifiable by many editorials of recent date in The Worker. In

Sunday's issue The Worker Magazine stated:

"There is only one way to vote against the death-dealing policies of Eisenhower and Stevenson. Cast your ballot for Vincent Hallinan and Mrs. Charlotta Bass on the Progressive ticket."

A story by George B. Charney

in The Worker yesterday stated:

"The most clear-headed peace votes will be cast nationally for the Progressive party candidates, Vincent Hallinan and Mrs. Charlotta Bass. That vote must be fought for right down to the wire."

October 28, 1952

2 SENATORS BID U. N. OUST 'SPIES' OR GO

At Security Hearing Here They Warn the World Body to Help Purge Itself or Quit U. S.

By CHARLES GRUTZNER

Two members of the Senate Judiciary Committee suggested yesterday that the United Nations be ousted from its New York headquarters unless the international organization rid itself of "spies and saboteurs."

Senator Willis Smith, Democrat of North Carolina, declared angrily at the close of an all-day hearing in the Federal Court House on Foley Square:

"It is up to the United Nations to help us purge it of spies and saboteurs, and if that can't be done, the United Nations ought not to be allowed to sit in America."

"Senator, I agree with you heartily," said Senator Pat McCarran, Democrat of Nevada, the committee chairman, who sat with Senator Smith as an internal security subcommittee investigating subversion among United States employes of the United Nations.

Comment on Lie Resignation

Senator McCarran renewed his criticism of the United Nations secretariat after the hearing ended for the day, by saying he believed that disclosures made by the subcommittee and others it was about to make had been the reason why Trygve Lie announced his resignation as Secretary-General.

The subcommittee, which will resume its public session today at noon, questioned yesterday five witnesses, one of whom contended that she had switched her citizenship from American to Russian simply by obtaining a Russian passport, although she was born in the United States of naturalized parents.

The witness, who said she never used the Soviet passport after receiving it in 1949, was Olga Michka, a $3,500-a-year clerk and typist employed in the United Nations since 1946. Miss Michka, a green-eyed blonde, said she had been suspended last Thursday without pay after she had been questioned by a Federal grand jury

here and subpoenaed by the McCarran committee. Miss Michka gave her age as 33 years and her address as 65-08 223d Place, Bayside, Queens.

Miss Michka, under questioning by Robert Morris, subcommittee counsel, told a story of a family divided by loyalties between the "old country" and the United States. Her parents came here from Russia. She and a brother were born in Chicago. The father preferred American ways, the mother longed to go back to Russia, and the family finally split up.

Miss Michka testified that she had applied as long ago as 1939 for a Russian passport, intending to make a trip with her mother to Russia. When she started working for the United Nations, she did not mention the passport application because no passport had been granted. She spoke and read Russian and was assigned to the radio news section, typing from dictation scripts for United Nations broadcasts to the U.S.S.R.

Thought She Became Russian

When the U.S.S.R. finally issued a Russian passport, Miss Michka said, she "took it for granted that made me a Soviet citizen." She said she did not report this to the personnel bureau at the United Nations because she thought it "made no difference" in the type of job she held. She denied that she had tried to conceal anything.

Senator McCarran interposed that it made a difference in loyalties whether a United Nations employe was a United States or Soviet citizen.

"When you take the oath of the United Nations," said the witness, "you don't pledge loyalty to any country. You pledge loyalty to the United Nations. I have nothing against the United States and I have nothing against the Soviet Union. I have never done anything to hurt America."

Senator McCarran said Congress should do something quickly if it were true "that the Soviets can make Russian citizens by handing out passports promiscuously."

Charles Recht, attorney for Miss Michka, and Mr. Morris said the question of dual citizenship seemed involved and that Miss Michka's status was a problem that had not yet been solved.

In Washington, a State Department official said he did not think Miss Michka automatically lost her American citizenship when she received a Russian passport. Without committing the department formally, he said he believed she would have to renounce her United States citizenship outside this country to an American diplomatic officer, then comply with whatever Soviet laws applied to Russian naturalization.

Miss Michka said she had been told her job suspension was for "defrauding the United Nations." She said she had been listed as a United States national for income tax purposes, had paid income

taxes here right along and had been reimbursed by the United Nations for her tax payments, according to standard procedure of the international organization.

Mr. Morris expressed indignation that Miss Michka had been "charged to the United States quota" of jobs in the United Nations Secretariat even after she received a Soviet passport and presumably Russian citizenship.

U. N. Spokesman Disagrees

A United Nations spokesman pointed out last night that Mr. Morris was mistaken in his assumption. Of 4,500 jobs in the United Nations organization, only 1,344 professional and high-ranking posts are apportioned by quota among member nations. The lower ratings, most of which are filled here, are not charged against any nation. Miss Michka's was not a quota job.

Miss Michka testified that after she received a Russian passport she renewed it annually, although she never went abroad. She told of several visits to the Russian consulate here and the embassy in Washington. She said in reply to the Senators' questions that she had never discussed anything but the passports on those visits, which last about fifteen minutes, and had paid her own way when she went to Washington. Her last visit to the embassy was in September, she said.

Miss Michka was not asked by the committee whether she was or had ever been a member of the Communist party, but three other witnesses were asked and refused, on the ground of possible self-incrimination, to answer one or both those questions.

Helen Kagen-Pozner of 898 Third Avenue, seeking reinstatement as translator in the Russian verbatim reporting group after her employment was ended last July, refused to answer both questions about Communist affiliation but replied with a loud "No!" when Senator Smith asked if she was "connected with the Russian espionage system here."

Leon Elveson of 2802 Olinville Avenue, the Bronx, $3,700-a-year clerk in the Security Council library, said he was not now a Communist and had not been one on June 1, but refused to answer the question as related to earlier dates.

Mrs. Peter Guest of 511 East Twentieth Street, who was never a United Nations employe but whose husband is editor in the documents control division of that organization, balked at both questions about Communist affiliation and refused, also on constitutional grounds, to answer Mr. Morris' query whether she was a half-sister of Robert G. Thompson, convicted Communist leader who is a fugitive from justice.

The day's other witness, who was not asked if she was or ever had been a Communist, was Joyce Campbell, program officer of the

United Nations International Children's Emergency Fund.

Witness Spars With Senator

It was Mrs. Kagen's frequent recourse to her constitutional right to refuse to answer questions that might tend to incriminate her that led to Senator Smith's strongest criticism of the United Nations secretariat. The day's last witness, she started calmly enough, saying she was born in Russia and became a United States citizen in 1931. She explained that she also used the name Kagen-Pozner, having added her maiden name after she and Mr. Kagen were divorced.

After balking at a few questions, Mrs. Kagen was asked by Senator Smith:

"If you were not a Communist, would you feel ashamed to admit you were not a Communist?"

"I refuse to answer on the ground that might tend to incriminate me," the witness droned.

"If you were back in Russia," Senator Smith demanded, "do you think you would be as fairly treated as here?"

Mrs. Kagen phrased her refusal to answer in the now familiar words.

"Do you want to go back to Russia where you came from?" Senator Smith asked, his exasperation increasing.

Again the answer was the same.

"Are you connected with the Russian espionage system here?" asked the Senator, shouting by this time.

The witness varied her reply with a loud "No!"

"You know there is a Russian espionage system here?" Senator Smith pressed. Mrs. Kagen said she would not answer, for the same reason as before, but added "and without any implications."

Senator Smith said he would draw implications, and expected the public would, from the witness' refusal to answer such a question. Mrs. Kagen said she had received no specific reason for the termination of her United Nations job, which was a temporary listing.

Mr. Morris said it had been his purpose to learn from the witnesses about the procedures in the United Nations on dismissals and appeals therefrom and on the influence of the United Nations Association, an employe organization, but that the recalcitrance of witnesses was making that difficult.

It was then that Senator Smith uttered his warning that there should be no place here for the United Nations headquarters unless the secretariat cooperated in getting rid of "spies and saboteurs." Senator McCarran asserted there was "an implication of guilt" in the recourse by the witness to her Constitutional right against self-incrimination.

November 12, 1952

U.N. Chief Counsel Dies in 12th-Floor Leap; Lie Lays Act to Strain of Fighting 'Smears'

Secretary General Says Aide Sought Justice for Those Accused of Subversion

By THOMAS J. HAMILTON
Special to THE NEW YORK TIMES.

UNITED NATIONS, N.Y., Nov. 13—Secretary General Trygve Lie declared today that the suicide of Abraham H. Feller, General Counsel of the United Nations, resulted from overwork in defending United States members of the Secretariat "against indiscriminate smears and exaggerated charges."

Mr. Lie said that the death of Mr. Feller was "an irreparable loss to the United Nations and to me personally." He added that he had made Mr. Feller his representative in the twin investigations by the McCarran Senate Internal Security subcommittee and a Federal grand jury into "subversive affiliations" by United States employes of the the United Nations.

Three members of the Senate Internal Security subcommittee issued a joint statement last night through Robert Morris, special counsel to the committee, describing Mr. Lie's statement as "irresponsible."

They declared that the subcommittee was "charged with the duty of determining whether any United States citizen working at the United Nations posed a threat to our national security" and that the "shocking effect" of the hearings had been in the refusal of United Nations officials to deny under oath "their participation in the Communist conspiracy."

The statement, according to Mr. Morris, came from Senators James O. Eastland, Democrat of Mississippi; Homer Ferguson, Republican of Michigan, and Willis Smith, Democrat of North Carolina. Mr. Morris said he had been unable

Associated Press
Abraham H. Feller

last night to reach Senator Herbert O'Conor, Democrat of Maryland. Senator Pat McCarran, Democrat of Nevada, and chairman of the committee, is en route to South American on the liner Uruguay.

Mr. Lie said that Mr. Feller's death was the result of "a prolonged and serious strain" and that the general counsel had been held in "deep admiration and affection" by the whole Secretariat.

"He had worked tirelessly day and night under my direction to uphold due process of law and justice in the investigations against indiscriminate smears and exaggerated charges," Mr. Lie continued. "This placed him under a prolonged and serious strain. The terrible tragedy of his death today is the result."

Mr. Lie described Mr. Feller as "a great and loyal international civil servant and a great and loyal American." Recalling seven years in which Mr. Feller had been at his side as "one of my closest and most trusted advisers," Mr. Lie observed:

"He has made many important contributions to the cause of peace and to the development of the United Nations as the defender of peace that will live in the history of our times."

Dr. Bunche Scores 'Pressure'

Speaking in Philadelphia last night, Dr. Ralph Bunche, director of the Department of Trusteeship of the United Nations, denounced Americans who bring pressure upon the United Nations as unable to understand that such an international body cannot serve the exclusive national interests of any member state.

Dr. Bunche was alluding to the Senate Internal Security subcommittee, although he did not mention it or any other group by name. He eulogized Abraham Feller to his audience, the American Philosophical Society, as "a distinguished legal scholar and brilliant public official" and "a great and loyal American."

Members of the Secretariat, of all ranks, praised Mr. Feller's work for the United Nations, but their feeling of indignation against the McCarran subcommittee was even stronger than their grief.

It is their belief that the subcommittee has not confined itself to a search for employes guilty of espionage or of subversive activities, or for members of the Communist party, but actually is on the trail of all with a Left Wing or New Deal background.

As for the grand jury, United Nations officials said that its proceedings had been nominally kept secret, but that there had been "leaks" to newspapers that had resulted in unfounded suspicion of some members of the Secretariat who had been called to testify.

The dislike here of the McCarran subcommittee is strengthened by the fact that it has overlooked few United States employes of the United Nations who were ever in the slightest degree associated with Alger Hiss, now serving a five-year term for swearing falsely that he had never given classified State Department documents to Whittaker Chambers.

Two recent events had tended to sadden Mr. Feller. One was the

defeat of Gov. Adlai E. Stevenson of Illinois, the Democratic candidate for President, and the other was the resignation of Mr. Lie last Monday which, according to United Nations officials, was partly due to worry over the McCarran subcommittee, although the Soviet Union's refusal to recognize him as Secretary General was the principal reason.

Close associates of Mr. Feller said that he had appeared very depressed for the last month, particularly so this week. He had not been to his office since Mr. Lie's resignation, although he came here Tuesday and talked briefly with friends among delegates and correspondents.

The McCarran subcommittee abruptly suspended its sessions here yesterday until January. One usually well-informed source said tonight he believed that instructions to that effect must come from Gen. Dwight D. Eisenhower, the President-elect, or from someone close to him, and that in any event the subcommittee's investigation of the United Nations would not be continued under the new Administration.

A high United Nations official, who is an American, said tonight that the work of weeding out American communists from the secretariat had been proceeding smoothly and efficiently until the McCarran subcommittee began its hearings in New York last month, on the day that the General Assembly opened its 1952 session. He said that the subcommittee had greatly interfered with this work.

As a result of the retirement of Dr. Ivan E. Kerno, the Assistant Secretary General for legal affairs, Mr. Feller recently had become head of the United Nations Legal Department. He was already one of the two or three closest advisers to Mr. Lie in the Secretariat.

Mr. Feller's work for the United Nations had resulted in numerous attacks by Communist publications. Pravda, in an article published Feb. 21, 1951, said that Mr. Feller decided all matters in the legal department and that Mr. Feller and Andrew W. Cordier, Mr. Lie's executive assistant, were "agents of the American State Department" and "American stooges" who "plan in the machinery of the Secretariat various behind-the-scene actions connected with the American aggression in Korea."

November 14, 1952

U.N. PANEL INSISTS THAT LIE DISCHARGE ALL DISLOYAL AIDES

By A. M. ROSENTHAL
Special to THE NEW YORK TIMES.

UNITED NATIONS, N.Y., Nov. 30—The dismissal from the United Nations staff of all active members of the United States Communist party or other organizations officially declared subversive was recommended today by a special three-man legal panel set up by Secretary General Trygve Lie.

In a report to Mr. Lie made public here, the panel took the position that the United States, as host to the United Nations, had the right to call for the ousting from the staff of all Secretariat members whom it considered disloyal or subversive.

Active membership in the Communist party or current participation in other "activities regarded as disloyal" should constitute bars to continued United Nations employment, the report said. The panel also told the Secretary General that staff members found to have engaged in subversive work in this country in the past, but who claimed to have dropped out, should be suspended pending confidential hearings by a new staff board.

Secretariat members, the report declared, should not be allowed to protect their jobs by refusing to answer questions on the grounds that the answers might incriminate them. Pleading of the constitutional privilege against self-incrimination created "a suspicion of guilt" and was ground for dismissal, according to the panel.

The report suggested, too, that refusal of the United States to grant passports to American employes of the United Nations should lead to an investigation as to the fitness of the person involved to continue on the United Nations staff.

The recommendations of the panel were written to cover not only United States nationals but also all members of the Secretariat except those who came from Communist countries. But it was emphasized that to keep their places on the United Nations staff in the United States, Communists from the Soviet world must not take part in activities regarded as subversive by the United States Government.

Mr. Lie set up the panel on Nov. 7 to advise him on the legal problems growing out of anti-Communist inquiries conducted by a Federal grand jury in New York and by the Senate Subcommittee on Internal Security headed by Senator Pat McCarran, Democrat of Nevada. The panel's recommendations are not binding on Mr. Lie, but may form the basis of future United Nations staff policy.

The findings of the panel were praised by Senator Alexander Wiley, Republican of Wisconsin, as "constructive and helpful." Senator Wiley, a member of the United States delegation at the current session of the General Assembly, said the report would "clear up a lot of misconceptions" and "clear the cobwebs out of some heads."

He had been named by the United States delegation to try to work out changes in the staff regulations that would give Mr. Lie the power to dismiss any employee judged to be subversive, whether or not he had "a permanent contract" with the United Nations.

The Senator said that the panel's report was so satisfactory that it eliminated the need for regulation changes. The report itself said that the Secretary General already had the power to oust any staff member for disloyalty or subversive activities and opposed altering the regulations.

All member governments will get copies of the fifty-page report. It will probably become the center of debate when the Assembly's Administrative and Budgetary Committee takes up staff problems. All sixty members of the United Na-

tions have seats on the committee and Senator Wiley is the United States Representative.

The unanimous report was signed by the panel's three members as experts in their own right, not as official representatives of their countries. They were:

William DeWitt Mitchell of the United States, who was Attorney General under former President Herbert Hoover.

Sir Edwin Herbert of Great Britain, senior partner of Sydney Morse & Co., London, and wartime director of Britain's Postal and Telegraph Censorship.

Prof. Paul Veldekens of Belgium, a member of the bar of his country's Supreme Court and Professor of Law at the Catholic University of Louvain.

Mr. Lie's decision to appoint the panel to advise him came after more than a dozen members of the staff—all United States nationals—had been dismissed or suspended because of their refusal to answer questions put to them by the Senate subcommittee concerning alleged subversive activities.

Several times in the report, the panel made the point that there should be no "dictation" of staff policies from member governments. The independence of the Secretary General and the fact that his sole responsibility is to the General Assembly should be recognized, the jurists declared.

From the beginning of its work the panel was faced with the fact that a general pronouncement against the employment of "disloyal" persons might be used not only against United States Communists but also against staff members from other countries—anti-Communist Czechs, anti-Tito Yugoslavs, anti-Perón Argentines, for example.

The jurists decided that there was a special relationship between the "host country" and the United Nations, especially important to the United States but capable of being applied to other countries where staff members of the United Nations were working on missions or in its regional offices.

Because of the international character of the staff, the report said, it is "wholly desirable" that the United Nations employ nationals of Communist countries. And just as Soviet-bloc citizens must not carry on subversive activities in this country, the report declared, it would be wrong for the United Nations to station in Iron Curtain lands employes who would **work against the Communist regimes**

The only organization identified by name in the report was the Communist party in the United States—which does not make United States citizenship a prerequisite for membership. The re-

port, therefore, did not specify what other groups could be called "subversive," but an authoritative source said the panel meant to include all organizations promoting the forcible overthrow of the United States Government.

The report indicated that the final responsibility for dismissals rested with the Secretary General. It was held to be his duty to start inquiries when informed of allegedly disloyal employes or when the employes themselves admitted that they took part in subversive activities in the past.

To help him judge individual cases, the report suggested that the Secretary General, after consulting groups representing Secretariat members, appoint an advisory panel consisting of two senior officials and an independent chairman.

The Secretary General should refuse to make public evidence submitted against employes, aside from taking the advisory panel into his confidence, the report said.

The jurists also submitted a legal analysis in support of their statement that existing staff regulations were broad enough for the Secretary General to dismiss on the grounds of breach of contract or serious misconduct any employe judged guilty of subversive activities.

December 1, 1952

LODGE ASKS F. B. I. FOR SECURITY TEST OF U.S. AIDES IN U.N.

New Envoy, in First Official Action, Calls on Hoover for Investigation of Employees

SEES COOPERATION OF LIE

Ex-Senator Says He Does Not Expect Protests When the Assembly Meets Feb. 24

By THOMAS J. HAMILTON
Special to The New York Times.

UNITED NATIONS, N. Y., Jan. 26—Henry Cabot Lodge Jr., in his first official action as United States representative to the United Nations, asked J. Edgar Hoover, director of the Federal Bureau of Investigation, today to make a full field investigation of the 144 members of the delegation who were serving under him.

He sent a request also to Mr. Hoover "that there be made" an investigation of all 1,680 Americans on the United Nations payroll.

Mr. Lodge said the investigations would be "more a question of

security risks than disloyalty—you can be loyal and still be a bad security risk."

He made public his letters to Mr. Hoover at a press conference immediately after he had presented his credentials to Secretary General Trygve Lie and had paid courtesy calls on Mr. Lie's principal assistants. Mr. Lodge was appointed by President Eisenhower to succeed Warren R. Austin of Vermont, also a former Republican Senator.

Customary Washington Procedure

Mr. Lodge did not explain why he had sent the letters direct to Mr. Hoover, for under customary Washington procedure a request from a member of the State Department to someone in the Justice Department would have been sent by Secretary of State John Foster Dulles to Attorney General Herbert Brownell Jr.

A spokesman for the United States delegation said later that he did not know whether President Eisenhower or Mr. Dulles had authorized Mr. Lodge to make the request. He stated, however, that Mr. Lodge, in addition to his United Nations duties, was a foreign policy adviser to President Eisenhower entitled to attend Cabinet meetings.

Between thirty and forty members of the United States delegation are in a professional category, the rest holding positions as clerks, chauffeurs, and the like. Mr. Lodge had asked for an F. B. I. investigation of himself the day he was

The New York Times (by Fred J. Sass)

TAKES OVER U. N. POST: Henry Cabot Lodge Jr., new chief United States delegate to the United Nations, presenting his credentials yesterday to Trygve Lie, Secretary General.

appointed to the United Nations post with the rank of Ambassador.

Asked today why a recheck of the United States delegation was necessary since all its members had previously been cleared by the F. B. I., Mr. Lodge said that "in view of all the things that have

happened I think it's a good thing to do—in justice to them."

The text of his letter to Mr. Hoover follows:

"I request that you undertake, as soon as possible, a full field investigation of all the employes to the United States Mission to the

United Nations, and that you will let me have this report on each person as soon as it is completed."

The letter to Mr. Hoover regarding United States employes of the United Nations did not specify who should make the investigation, but requested that Mr. Hoover submit to Mr. Lodge "a report on each case as soon as it is completed."

Differs From Truman Order

He did not say how such employes should be investigated, but his letter appeared to set up a different procedure, in the following respects, from that laid down in former President Truman's Executive Order of Jan. 9:

¶Mr. Lodge made no distinction between the 345 United States employes of the United Nations in the better-paid professional or language positions and the remainder,

who are clerks, chauffeurs, and the like. Mr. Truman's Executive Order called for a full field investigation of the former, but said that unless "derogatory" information about the remainder was uncovered, the investigation should be limited mainly to information already available in Federal agencies.

¶Under the Executive Order this preliminary or "inter-agency" investigation is to be carried out by the United States Civil Service Commission, to which the United Nations is to submit the names and addresses of United States employes. The results of cases warranting a full field investigation are to be reported to the commission's regional loyalty boards. Mr. Lodge's letter, however, requested that the reports be submitted directly to him, and left the impression with some that he expected the F. B. I. to make the investigations.

¶The Executive Order said the investigations were to determine whether there was "reasonable doubt" of the loyalty to the United States of its employes of the United Nations, whereas Mr. Lodge emphasized the question of "a bad security risk."

Denies Any Inconsistency

Mr. Lodge denied, however, that the procedure he laid down was inconsistent with the Executive Order, saying that the findings by F. B. I. would be submitted to the Civil Service Commission.

Mr. Lodge said also that Mr. Lie had promised to cooperate in the spirit of the Executive Order and of the United States request that the United Nations not take on any more American employes until the security procedures were worked out. Reminded that Mr. Lie had not replied to this request, Mr. Lodge declined to elaborate.

Asked whether he expected

United States policy regarding American members of the United Nations to produce protests when the General Assembly reconvened on Feb. 24, Mr. Lodge said he did not. He added that he did not think anyone could seriously challenge the right of the United States "to investigate its citizens on American soil."

Regarding United States employes of the United Nations on whom the State Department had submitted adverse reports, thirty-six have been discharged, two have resigned, and one has retired. United Nations officials have explained that their failure to take action on the remaining seven resulted from their belief that the information submitted by the State Department was inadequate or inconclusive.

January 27, 1953

HOUSE UNIT STUDIES ROCKEFELLER FUND

Foundation Head Says 'Batting Average' Is Good on Grants Totaling $470,000,000

By JOHN D. MORRIS
Special to THE NEW YORK TIMES.

WASHINGTON, Dec. 9 — The $321,000,000 Rockefeller Foundation came under Congressional scrutiny today in connection with its extension of financial aid to some organizations and individuals criticized by Senate and House committees investigating subversive activities.

Explanations given by Dean Rusk, president, and other officials appeared to be accepted as satisfactory by members of a special House committee before whom they appeared. The committee, headed by Representative E. E. Cox, Democrat of Georgia, is seeking to determine whether tax-exempt foundations have contributed to the promotion of un-American causes.

Mr. Rusk was examined specifically about grants to organizations listed as subversive by the Attorney General and to individuals and

organizations "criticized or cited" by the House Committee on Un-American Activities or the Senate Judiciary Subcommittee on Internal Security.

He testified that no group on the Attorney General's list ever had received Rockefeller aid. Two organizations and twenty-three individuals criticized or cited by one or the other Congressional committee have benefited from grants aggregating less than $3,000,000 since 1926, according to Mr. Rusk's listing.

Sees Good 'Batting Average'

The foundation feels, he said, that it has made a good "batting average" in view of the fact that it has made 28,753 grants aggregating $470,000,000 since its establishment forty years ago.

He also observed that "some of the most eminent, distinguished Americans in American public life" had been listed by the House committee. He maintained that grants to only about eight of the twenty-three individuals mentioned could even now, with the benefit of "hindsight," be regarded as mistakes.

Of the grants questioned, $1,885,359 went to the Institute of Pacific Relations from 1926 to 1950. The institute has been criticized by the Senate subcommittee, headed by Senator Pat McCarran, Democrat of Nevada, on grounds that staff members had engaged in subversive activities and the organi-

zation was "considered by the American Communist party and by Soviet officials as an instrument of Communist policy, propaganda and military intelligence."

Mr. Rusk said that if the "grave questions" raised by the subcommittee had been brought up at the time of the grants without satisfactory answers, further aid by the Rockefeller Foundation would have been precluded.

He described as "very remote" the prospect of additional Rockefeller money going to the institute now.

Grant to China Aid Group

Mr. Rusk also acknowledged a $7,500 grant to the China Aid Council in 1948 as an "unavoidable and calculated risk," even though the council had been cited by the Un-American Activities Committee in 1942. The money was for what was regarded as a worthwhile project—the translation of western literature into the Chinese language—though some of the translators participating were known to be "Left Wing."

Among the twenty-three "criticized or cited" individuals benefiting from the Rockefeller Foundation grants was Prof. Owen Lattimore of Johns Hopkins University, formerly an official of the Institute of Pacific Relations, who was castigated by the McCarran subcommittee.

Professor Lattimore received $1,500 to attend an institute con-

ference at New Delhi in 1949 as the result of what Mr. Rusk called "a misunderstanding." Seven other applications for grants "for or on behalf of" Professor Lattimore were rejected, Mr. Rusk testified.

Grants to individuals that Mr. Rusk conceded were questionable in the light of information now available included $25,684 from 1934 to 1939 for research by Frédéric Joliot-Curie, the French nuclear scientist, now an active Communist. The fund head placed in the same category grants of $6,050 from 1933 to 1936 to Dr. Oscar Lange for economic studies. Dr. Lange later became a diplomatic representative of the Communist Government in Poland.

Another such grant was $8,250 in 1940 to Hans Eisler, Austrian composer then in the United States for research on music in film production. Eisler left the country later while deportation proceedings were pending. He is a brother of Gerhart Eisler, formerly a top United States Communist and now an official in the Soviet Zone of Germany.

John D. Rockefeller 3d, chairman of the foundation's board, told the committee that the foundation was "not a matter of perpetuity." The policy of its founder, his grandfather, the late John D. Rockefeller, was that "when it has the opportunity to expend its funds," he said, "it should do so."

December 10, 1952

Cohn, Veteran Investigator at 25, Will Aid McCarthy in Inquiries

Counsel-Designate to Senate Subcommittee Helped Prosecute the Atomic Spies— Served as Saypol's Assistant

Special to THE NEW YORK TIMES.

WASHINGTON, Jan. 2—Roy M. Cohn, who was one of the witnesses Tuesday before the Judiciary subcommittee of the House of Representatives, will take his place soon in the Washington scene on

the other side of the table when he becomes chief counsel for the Senate investigating subcommittee to be headed by Senator Joseph R. McCarthy, Republican of Wisconsin.

Mr. Cohn, as an Assistant United States Attorney for the Southern District of New York, served as confidential assistant to Myles J. Lane, United States Attorney, until early September. At that time he was assigned by James P. McGranery, Attorney General, to work under William E. Foley, chief of the Internal Security Section of the Department of Justice.

In this position Mr. Cohn assisted the Senate Internal Security subcommittee, headed by Senator Pat McCarran, Democrat of Nevada, in its investigation of Communist infiltration into the United States personnel of the United Nations.

Although Mr. Cohn's professional career as an Assistant

United States Attorney has been relatively brief, he is something of a veteran in investigations. As a confidential assistant to Irving H. Saypol, then United States Attorney, Mr. Cohn handled investigations ranging from stamp and currency counterfeiting to traffic in narcotics.

At that time he had only recently passed his twenty-first birthday and was a constant source of astonishment to underworld characters. They invariably spent the first minutes of interviews with him overcoming the feeling they were victims of a practical joke in being quizzed by a person who seemed to be a schoolboy.

The astonishment in those early

days was shared by young Mr. Cohn and the characters he dealt with. The higher echelons of the crime world held the fascination for him that a first detective thriller holds for a teen-ager.

He was particularly impressed by the artistry of the counterfeiters, especially the stamp forgers. He entertained visitors by showing them the real stamps and the counterfeit, and explaining the difficulty of detecting the false issue.

Mr. Cohn proved his point beyond doubt one day when he got the false and the real stamps mixed and spread momentary consternation by sending out some personal mail from the United States Courthouse with counterfeit stamps.

Newspaper men on the Federal Building run in the early days of Mr. Cohn's investigations were constantly bombarded with reports of the "biggest," "most sensational" and "world-wide" vice rings in past or contemporary crime annals. The reporters usually were amused at the youthful investigator's enthusiasm. The net result, however, was that Mr. Cohn established a basis of confidence and goodwill between himself and the press that he has continued to maintain.

The investigating committee counsel-designate was born in New York, Feb. 20, 1927. He is the son of Justice Albert Cohn of the Appellate Division of the New York Supreme Court. He received his

law degree at the Columbia University Law School at the age of 19 and had to wait the two years until he reached his majority to take the bar examinations.

From his role as an investigator and all-around "trouble-shooter" for the United States Attorney's office, Mr. Cohn quickly took on additional duties until he was participating in some of the office's top cases. He assisted in the successful prosecution of Julius and Ethel Rosenberg, who are now under sentence of death for atomic espionage. He also worked on the William Remington perjury trial and the perjury indictment of Prof. Owen Lattimore.

Mr. Cohn, who is of medium height and stocky build, goes light

on forensics in the courtroom but assumes an aggressive manner that is at once effective to his own cause and a source of irritation to opposing counsel. "Brash kid" was one of the more genteel descriptions the opposition had for him in his early days at the bar.

Mr. Cohn's rapid rise is attributed to any number of things but principally to his determination and his great energy. He is a hard worker and tops off a long day by teaching at the New York Law School at 224 William Street. He is active in numerous organizational and civic affairs, particularly in Jewish philanthropies.

January 3, 1953

M'CARTHY POSES AN ADMINISTRATION PROBLEM

By WILLIAM S. WHITE
Special to THE NEW YORK TIMES.

WASHINGTON, Feb. 21—The Eisenhower Administration, after one month and one day in office, is now faced with the necessity of making an accommodation with Senator Joseph R. McCarthy or colliding heavily with the most feared and powerful investigator in Congress.

The Wisconsin Republican's search for alleged Communist influences in the State Department has not relaxed at all with the departure of the Democratic Truman Administration and its Democratic Secretary of State, Dean Acheson.

The vast, sprawling establishment now headed by the Republican John Foster Dulles has been and apparently will be under very heavy fire and for an indefinite duration.

Three times this week Mr. McCarthy has forced the State Department to reverse itself on internal operating procedures.

Three Reversals Forced

(1) The department has now issued an order that its Voice of America, the current subject of Senator McCarthy's inquiries as head of the Permanent Senate Investigating subcommittee, may no longer use in any circumstance in its overseas information and propaganda programs the writings of any "controversial" author accused of being Communist or pro-Communist.

Such writings in some peculiar circumstances—where, for example, a known Communist had nevertheless said something deemed helpful to this country's objectives and harmful to Russian objectives—had been permissible in the past under a policy suggested by a citizens committee that included three university presidents and a professor at Catholic University here.

The theory had been that where a broadcast was beamed to Communists, in an attempt to shake their allegiance, good words about the American scene by a man the

His Wide Swings Are Hitting Dulles And the State Department Routine

hearers nevertheless knew to be a Communist might be helpful.

(2) The State Department has canceled a directive that lasted two days, by which it had authorized employes to refuse to talk, if they chose, to investigators for Mr. McCarthy's or other such groups in the absence of a Senator himself.

Net Effect

(3) The Department has yielded to McCarthy demands and has agreed to reinstate John E. Matson, a departmental security agent who had cooperated with the McCarthy committee, to his old job.

Mr. Matson had testified that the department's personnel files were in "a deplorable condition" and shortly afterward he had been transferred to what Senator McCarthy called a "beat-pounding" post. Mr. Matson's superior, John W. Ford, had declared the transfer essential to maintain morale because the filing room had got so afraid of Mr. Matson that it could not do its work properly.

Mr. Ford notwithstanding, Mr. Matson now goes back to the old job despite attacks on the "accuracy" of his testimony by Mr. Ford.

The effect of all this was dual. First, there was plain notification to State Department officials that they would be quite unwary to refuse any information to any of Mr. McCarthy's agents and extremely unwary to take any disciplinary action against any employe cooperating with Mr. McCarthy.

Second, Senator McCarthy, who already had entered the investigative field into State Department files, was given an unexampled entree into the workings of the department—an entree he never was able to approach in the Truman-Acheson days.

There was therefore nothing to

suggest that he could not now proceed unimpeded anywhere in all the State Department area called "foggy bottom." No greater series of victories by a Congressional body over a senior Executive department in so short a time is recalled here.

All this was accomplished in a single week of a single phase of Senator McCarthy's projected investigations—that is, the "Voice" inquiry—and he says that this alone may well run several months.

Moreover, roughly parallel investigations, with which Mr. McCarthy is in the closest touch, are going on over a wide field and their central theme is the American diplomatic establishment. For example, the Senate Internal Security subcommittee, headed by Senator William E. Jenner, Republican of Indiana, has been looking into the loyalty of American citizens working in the United Nations.

This loyalty, in the view of politicians, is an inescapable responsibility of the State Department, notwithstanding the fact that the employment itself is in a sense international or supra-national.

Senator McCarthy's position is certainly a more powerful one than it was in the Democratic days, since he unquestionably is receiving a degree of State Department

ONE VIEW OF SENATE INVESTIGATIONS

I DON'T KNOW WHO *BUILT* THIS CONTRAPTION... ....BUT I KNOW WHO'S GOING TO *TAKE IT APART!*

The Voice of America

Berryman in The Washington Star

cooperation that he did not receive then.

His method of procedure is, moreover, immeasurably more satisfactory from his standpoint. Never before was he more than an arm-swinging outsider trying to fight his way in; now he has both the apparent and the subtle place that goes with a committee chairmanship. He is on the inside now and in the last analysis could hardly be restricted short of a decision at the top of the Eisenhower Administration.

Senate chairmanships, by long custom, give a long writ to the holder. There is no effective Senate way, short of cutting off his operating funds, to halt the project of a Senator in that position of power—and in this case the Rules Committee, which has charge of such funds, is in the control of an old McCarthy friend, Senator Jenner.

Department's Reaction

Too, the Senate's attitude toward Senator McCarthy is now, if anything, more mixed than it ever was before.

While there is no effort here to judge the rights and wrongs of the issue itself, some of Mr. McCarthy's disclosures about the Voice of America — particularly those dealing with alleged waste as distinguished from alleged subversion—have to some extent interested Senators who have been among his old critics.

Too, the State Department's conduct thus far of its case before him has not seemed to some more or less disinterested Senators to have been impressive.

Finally, there is the fact, though it is not often mentioned, that Mr. Dulles is by no means the beau ideal of a good many Republican Senators of the isolationist or near-isolationist wing. They look upon him not of course as a Communist or anything of that sort but as a rather doubtful and possibly dangerous leader.

There is no doubt that some among this group are not anxiously studying ways to help Mr. Dulles succeed as Secretary of State—and this could be said in the case of President Eisenhower as well.

What may be done about all this is one of Washington's most interesting riddles—a riddle in which the Administration itself is completely enigmatic. Senate action to attempt to restrain Senator McCarthy is certainly no closer than it ever was—and it never was on any visible horizon. He has demonstrated enormous political influence, and not only in his own state. He has reached his point of power, in the committee and hierarchial sense, in a perfectly ordinary way against which there could be no logical Senate challenge.

Even if these things were not true—and they are profound political realities—the whole tradition of the Senate gives the utmost freedom to members, in speech, in action, in whatever they may choose to do. And there is the ever-present fear, even among those who toy more or less idly with the notion of somehow trying to discipline Mr. McCarthy, that the responsibility would be a heavy one, not only in the sense of Senate tradition but also if events should prove Mr. McCarthy to be right about some of his caveats, as the Committee on Un-American Activities at length turned out to be right about Alger Hiss.

Thus, from any viewpoint and in any viable scheme of things, the responsibility for putting a check on Senator McCarthy, if it should be decided that he should be checked, seems always to return to the White House.

President Eisenhower is not a member of the Senate, and presumably need not greatly concern himself with all its inner attitudes. And it is the Administration of the President, and not primarily of the Republican Senate or Congress, that is under Mr. McCarthy's not too gentle scrutiny.

Relation to White House

And while the Republicans as a party seem demonstrably to owe Senator McCarthy a great deal—since by objective standards he seems to have had some hand in the election of at least eight Republican Senators in the last two years — President Eisenhower's own debt is debatable if not non-existent.

For while the Republicans barely carried Congress, General Eisenhower swept the country and he carried Wisconsin by a bigger vote than Senator McCarthy did.

And it is, of course, no secret that President Eisenhower is not one of Mr. McCarthy's greatest admirers—the campaign itself demonstrated that the President's association with the Senator was not the most cordial.

At all events, the position is clear: If the Administration does not attempt to act against Senator McCarthy no one will. The opinion of disinterested Senate observers is that if any attempt were made by that body to chastise Senator McCarthy there would hardly be eight votes for it—if it ever came to a vote at all.

February 22, 1953

Text of the Academic Freedom Policy Adopted by Universities

Following is the text of a statement on "The Rights and Responsibilities of Universities and Their Faculties," issued yesterday by the Association of American Universities:

I

Role of the University in American Life

For three hundred years higher education has played a leading role in the advancement of American civilization. No country in history so early perceived the importance of that role and none has derived such widespread benefits from it. Colleges moved westward with the frontier and carried with them the seeds of learning. When the university idea was transplanted from Europe, it spread across the nation with extraordinary speed. Today our universities are the standard bearers of our whole system of education. They are the mainstays of the professions. They are the prime source of our competence in science and the arts. The names of their graduates crowd the honor rolls of two world wars and of the nation's peacetime affairs. By every test of war and peace they have proved themselves indispensable instruments of cultural progress and national welfare.

In the United States there is a greater degree of equality of opportunity in higher education than anywhere else in the world. A larger proportion of Americans study in universities and colleges than any other people. These universities have shown, and continue to show, greater responsiveness to the needs of our society than their European counterparts. They have equipped our people with the varied skills and sciences essential to the development of a pioneer country. They have imparted the shape and coherence of the American nation to formless immigrant groups. American ideals have been strengthened, the great cultural tradition of the West has been broadened and enriched by their teaching and example.

Modern knowledge of ourselves and of our universe has been nurtured in the universities. The scientific, technological, medical and surgical advances of our time were born in them. They have supplied intellectual capital as essential to our society as financial capital is to our industrial enterprise. They have more than justified the faith of the public in our distinctive system of higher education. They have proved themselves dynamic forces of American progress.

II

The Nature of a University

A university is the institutional embodiment of an urge for knowledge that is basic in human nature and as old as the human race. It is inherent in every individual. The search that it inspires is an individual affair. Men vary in the intensity of their passion for the search for knowledge as well as in their competence to pursue it. History, therefore presents us with a series of scholarly pioneers who advanced our knowledge from age to age and increased our ability to discover new knowledge. Great scholars and teachers drew students to them, and in the Middle Ages a few such groups organized themselves into the first universities.

The modern university, which evolved from these, is a unique type of organization. For many reasons it must differ from a corporation created for the purpose of producing a salable article for profit. Its internal structure, procedures and discipline are properly quite different from those of business organizations. It is not so closely integrated and there is no such hierarchy of authority as is appropriate to a business concern; the permanent members of a university are essentially equals.

Like its medieval prototype, the modern American university is an association of individual scholars. Their effectiveness, both as scholars and as teachers, requires the capitalizing of their individual passion for knowledge and their individual competence to pursue it and communicate it to others. They are united in loyalty to the ideal of learning, to the moral code, to the country and to its form of government. They represent diversified fields of knowledge; they express many points of view. Even within the same department of instruction there are not only specialists in various phases of the subject but men with widely differing interests and outlook.

Free enterprise is as essential to intellectual as to economic progress.

A university must, therefore, be hospitable to an infinite variety of skills and viewpoints, relying upon open competition among them as the surest safeguard of truth. Its whole spirit requires investigation, criticism and presentation of ideas in an atmosphere of freedom and mutual confidence. This is the real meaning of "academic" freedom. It is essential to the achievement of its ends that the faculty of a university be guaranteed this freedom by its governing board, and that the reasons for the guarantee be understood by the public. To enjoin uniformity of outlook upon a university faculty would put a stop to learning at the source. To censor individual faculty members would put a stop to learning at its outlet.

For these reasons a university does not take an official position of its own either on disputed questions of scholarship or on political questions or matters of public policy. It refrains from so doing not only in its own but in the public interest, to capitalize the search for knowledge for the benefit of society, to give the individuals pursuing that search the freest possible scope and the greatest possible encouragement in their efforts to preserve the learning of the past and advance learning in the present. The scholar who pursues the search on these terms does so at maximum advantage to society. So does the student. To the scholar lie open new discoveries in the whole field of knowledge, to his student the opportunity of sharing in those discoveries and at the same time developing his powers of rational thought, intelligent judgment and an understanding use of acquired knowledge. Thus essential qualities of learning are combined with essential qualities of citizenship in a free society.

To fulfill their function, the members of university faculties must continue to analyze, test, criticize and reassess existing institutions and beliefs, approving when the evidence supports them and disapproving when the weight of evidence is on the other side. Such investigations cannot be confined to the physical world. the acknowledged fact that moral, social and political progress have not kept pace with mastery of the physical world shows the need for more intensified research, fresh insights, vigorous criticism and inventiveness. The scholar's mission requires the study and examination of unpopular ideas, of ideas considered abhorrent and even dangerous. For, just as in the case of deadly disease or the military potential of an enemy, it is only by intense study and research that the nature and extent of the danger can be understood and defenses against it perfected.

Scholar's Silence Assailed

Timidity must not lead the scholar to stand silent when he ought to speak, particularly in the field of his competence. In matters of conscience and when he has truth to proclaim the scholar has no obligation to be silent in the face of popular disapproval. Some of the great passages in the history of truth have involved the open challenge of popular prejudice in times of tension such as those in which we live.

What applies to research applies equally to teaching. So long as an instructor's observations are scholarly and germane to his subject, his freedom of expression in his classroom should not be curbed. The university student should be exposed to competing opinions and beliefs in every field, so that he may learn to weigh them and gain maturity of judgment. Honest and skillful exposition of such opinions and beliefs is the duty of every instructor; and it is equally his privilege to express his own critical opinion and the reasons for holding it. In teaching, as in research, he is limited by the requirements of citizenship, of professional competence and good taste. Having met those standards, he is entitled to all the protection the full resources of the university can provide.

Whatever criticism is occasioned by these practices, the universities are committed to them by their very nature. To curb them, in the hope of avoiding criticism, would mean distorting the true process of learning and depriving society of its benefits. It would invite the fate of the German and Italian universities under fascism and the Russian universities under communism. It would deny our society one of its most fruitful sources of strength and welfare and represent a sinister change in our ideal of government.

III
The Obligations and Responsibilities of University Faculties

We must recognize the fact that honest men hold differing opinions. This fundamental truth underlies the assertion and definition of individual rights and freedom in our Bill of Rights. How does it apply to universities? In the eyes of the law, the university scholar has no more and no less freedom than his fellow citizens outside a university. None the less, because of the vital importance of the university to civilization, membership in its society of scholars enhances the prestige of persons admitted to its fellowship after probation and upon the basis of achievement in research and teaching. The university supplies a distinctive forum and, in so doing, strengthens the scholar's voice. When his opinions challenge existing orthodox points of view, his freedom may be more in need of defense than that of men in other professions. The guarantee of tenure to professors of mature and proven scholarship is one such defense. As in the case of judges, tenure protects the scholar against undue economic or political pressures and ensures the continuity of the scholarly process.

There is a line at which "freedom" or "privilege" begins to be qualified by legal "duty" and "obligation." The determination of the line is the function of the legislature and the courts. The ultimate interpretation and application of the First and Fourteenth Amendments are the function of the United States Supreme Court; but every public official is bound by his oath of office to respect and preserve the liberties guaranteed therein. These are not to be determined arbitrarily or by public outcry. The line thus drawn can be changed by legislative and judicial action; it has varied in the past because of prevailing anxieties as well as by reason of "clear and present" danger. Its location is subject to, and should receive, criticism, both popular and judicial. However much the location of the line may be criticized, it cannot be disregarded with impunity. Any member of a university who crosses the duly established line is not excused by the fact that he believes the line ill-drawn. When the speech, writing, or other actions of a member of a faculty exceed lawful limits, he is subject to the same penalties as other persons. In addition, he may lose his university status.

No Endorsement of Views

Historically the word "university" is a guarantee of standards. It implies endorsement not of its members' views but of their capability and integrity. Every scholar has an obligation to maintain this reputation. By ill-advised, though not illegal, public acts or utterances he may do serious harm to his profession, his university, to education and to the general welfare. He bears a heavy responsibility to weigh the soundness of his opinions and the manner in which they are expressed. His effectiveness, both as scholar and teacher, is not reduced but enhanced if he has the humility and the wisdom to recognize the fallibility of his own judgment. He should remember that he is as much a layman as anyone else in all fields except those in which he has special competence. Others, both within and without the university, are as free to criticize his opinions as he is free to express them; "academic freedom" does not include freedom from criticism.

As in all acts of association, the professor accepts conventions which become morally binding. Above all, he owes his colleagues in the university complete candor and perfect integrity, precluding any kind of clandestine or conspiratorial activities. He owes equal candor to the public. If he is called upon to answer for his convictions, it is his duty as a citizen to speak out. It is even more definitely his duty as a professor. Refusal to do so, on whatever legal grounds, cannot fail to reflect upon a profession that claims for itself the fullest freedom to speak and the maximum protection of that freedom available in our society. In this respect, invocation of the Fifth Amendment places upon a professor a heavy burden of proof of his fitness to hold a teaching position and lays upon his university an obligation to re-examine his qualifications for membership in its society.

In all universities faculties exercise wide authority in internal affairs. The greater their autonomy, the greater their share of responsibility to the public. They must maintain the highest standards and exercise the utmost wisdom in appointments and promotions. They must accept their share of responsibility for the discipline of those who fall short in the discharge of their academic trust.

The universities owe their existence to legislative acts and public charters. A state university exists by constitutional and legislative acts, an endowed university enjoys its independence by franchise from the state and by custom. The state university is supported by public funds. The endowed university is benefited by tax exemptions. Such benefits are conferred upon the universities not as favors, but in furtherance of the public interest. They carry with them public obligation of direct concern to the faculties of the universities as well as to the governing boards.

Legislative bodies from time to time may scrutinize these benefits and privileges. It is clearly the duty of universities and their members to cooperate in official inquiries directed to those ends. When the powers of legislative inquiry are abused, the remedy does not lie in non-cooperation or defiance; it is to be sought through the normal channels of informed public opinion.

IV
The Present Danger

We have set forth the nature and function of the university. We have outlined its rights and responsibilities and those of its faculties. What are the implications for current anxiety over Russian communism and the subversive activities connected with it?

We condemn Russian communism as we condemn every form of toltalitarianism. We share the profound concern of the American people at the existence of an international conspiracy whose goal is the destruction of our cherished institutions. The police state would be the death of our universities, as of our Government. Three of its principles in particular are abhorrent to us: the fomenting of world-wide revolution as a step to seizing power; the use of falsehood and deceit as normal means of persuasion; thought control—the dictation of doctrines which must be accepted and taught by all party members. Under these principles, no scholar could adequately disseminate knowledge or pursue investigations in the effort to make further progress toward truth.

Appointment to a university position and retention after appointment require not only professional competence but involve the affirmative obligation of being diligent and loyal in citizenship. Above all, a scholar must have integrity and independence. This renders impossible adherence to such a regime as that of Russia and its satellites. No person who accepts or advocates such principles and methods has any place in a university. Since present membership in the Communist party requires the acceptance of these principles and methods, such membership extinguishes the right to a university position. Moreover, if an instructor follows communistic practice by becoming a propagandist for one opinion, adopting a "party line," silencing criticism or impairing freedom of thought and expression in his classroom, he forfeits not only all university support but his right to membership in the university.

"Academic freedom" is not a shield for those who break the law. Universities must cooperate fully with law-enforcement officers whose duty requires them to prosecute those charged with offenses. Under a well-established American principle, their innocence is to be assumed until they have been convicted, under due process, in a court of proper jurisdiction.

Unless a faculty member violates a law, however, his discipline or discharge is a university responsibility and should not be assumed by political authority. Discipline on the basis of irresponsible accusations or suspicion can never be condoned. It is as damaging to the public welfare as it is to academic integrity. The university is competent to establish a tribunal to determine the facts and fairly judge the nature and degree of any trespass upon academic integrity, as well as to determine the penalty such trespass merits.

As the professor is entitled to no special privileges in law, so also he should be subject to no special discrimination. Universities are bound to deprecate special loyalty tests which are applied to their faculties but to which others are not subjected. Such discrimination does harm to the individual and even greater harm to his university and the whole cause of education by destroying faith in the ideals of university scholarship.

V
Conclusion

Finally, we assert that freedom of thought and speech is vital to the maintenance of the American system and is essential to the general welfare. Condemnation of communism and its protagonists is not to be interpreted as readiness to curb social, political, or economic investigation and research. To insist upon complete conformity to current beliefs and practices would do infinite harm to the principle of freedom, which is the greatest, the central, American doctrine. Fidelity to that principle has made it possible for the universities of America to confer great benefits upon our society and our country. Adherence to that principle is the only guarantee that the nation may continue to enjoy those benefits.

March 31, 1953

ACADEMIC FREEDOM ISSUE AT COLUMBIA

Professors' Chapter Criticizes Stand Taken by University on Communist Teachers

The Columbia University chapter of the American Association of University Professors issued a statement yesterday in which it defended the right of Communists to teach and attacked the investigations of American educational institutions as "unnecessary and unwise."

The statement was accompanied by a note saying it had been adopted because of "strong dissatisfaction" over the recent policy declaration of the Association of American Universities on academic freedom.

The professors' group asserted that the policy statement, to which the administration of Columbia University adhered, was "a wholly inadequate formulation" of the rights and responsibilities of universities and their faculties, and that "by accepting the essential assumptions of current Congressional committees investigating education the statement in effect surrenders basic principles of academic freedom."

The declaration illustrated sharply on the local level the conflict between the position of university professors and the administrative officials of universities on whether or not members of the Communist party should be permitted to teach.

The statement of the Columbia chapter held, as did earlier resolutions of the national organization and the chapter at Princeton University, that professional competence and personal integrity alone should be the basic test of fitness to teach.

The Association of American Universities, the national organization of university administrations, held, however, that membership in the Communist party "extinguishes the right to a university position."

The Columbia group, which was dormant for ten years before last February, adopted the statement unanimously Tuesday night at a meeting that was attended by about thirty of the 250 members of the chapter. The statement was held up for release pending the adherence of members who were not present at the meeting, Ernest Nagel, Professor of Philosophy and president of the chapter, said.

April 17, 1953

New Security Plan Issued; Thousands Face Re-Inquiry

Eisenhower Program Discards Truman Idea of Loyalty Distinction—Review Boards Dropped—McCarthy Is Enthusiastic

By ANTHONY LEVIERO
Special to THE NEW YORK TIMES.

WASHINGTON, April 27 — The Eisenhower Administration today announced a new, stricter security program for Federal employes, discarding the dual Truman system that had made a distinction between loyalty and security.

The new program will go into effect May 27 with the aim of assuring that all employes of the Executive Branch of the Government are "reliable, trustworthy, of good conduct and character, and of complete and unswerving loyalty to the United States."

President Eisenhower stated this aim in the preamble of a five-page Executive Order that will subject all present and future employes to a character scrutiny based on seven specified standards of conduct.

The outright traitor and a tipsy Federal employe, talking about his work in a bar, alike are subject to dismissal under the new program. The tipsy employe might receive a chance in another, less sensitive Federal job. Essentially, the Truman system did the same thing, but the traitor would be branded disloyal and the loose-talking drinker would be labeled a security risk.

Under the new system no provision is made for a distinction between disloyalty and borderline or misconduct cases, unless department heads, who will have the final adjudication authority, indicate it.

The new program will require a new investigation of many thousands of employes previously investigated, as well as many more thousands who have had no security check. The Truman system had started as a loyalty program, requiring a finding of disloyalty as a cause for dismissal.

Then came the case of William W. Remington, former Commerce Department economist, in which the Loyalty Review Board on Feb. 10, 1949, decided that a finding of disloyalty against him would be "a travesty of American justice." Subsequently, Remington was convicted in Federal court for perjury in lying about his Communist associations.

That case caused a sharp change in the loyalty program. It was modified to add the "security" aspect, to permit the dismissal of any person about whom there was reasonable doubt of loyalty or who had been indiscreet in his associations or conduct.

Under the first or loyalty phase, only persons in "sensitive" jobs were investigated. That left many thousands of uninvestigated persons in Federal employ and some of these were able to transfer to sensitive agencies such as the State and Defense Departments without being investigated.

The new system requires an investigation of any employe not previously investigated and of all new applicants for positions. Usually the investigation for non-sensitive jobs involves a name check in Federal personnel files and, if this turns up derogatory information, the case is referred to the Federal Bureau of Investigation for what is called a full-field investigation, which may take three to nine months.

Under the old system there were 18,901 cases that had gone through the full-field inquiry as a result of adverse data, and the President's order today specified that these cases should be "re-adjudicated." In addition, there are 1,831 full-field investigations now in process that developed out of adverse data.

It should be stressed that many Federal employes were required to submit automatically to full-field investigation because they held highly important positions involving national security, and not because of derogatory information. The order did not call for a re-investigation of these persons.

Discarded with the old system are the Loyalty Review Board of the Civil Service Commission and the regional boards consisting of leading citizens unconnected with the Federal service. Replacing this "court of appeals" outside the Federal service will be "hearing boards" consisting of three Federal officials who are not employes in the same department as an accused person.

Held 'Move Workable'

These comparative features of the new and old systems were brought out in an hour-long press conference held by Herbert Brownell Jr., the Attorney General, in the office of James C. Hagerty, White House press secretary. With Mr. Brownell were the Deputy Attorney General, William P. Rogers, Bernard M. Shanly, acting special counsel of the President, and Philip Young, chairman of the Civil Service Commission.

"We believe this machinery is much more workable and therefore an employe's case can't be dragged along for several years," Mr. Brownell said.

Asked why he thought so, Mr. Brownell replied: "Because the standards and rules are much more explicit."

In opening the news conference, Mr. Brownell reminded the press of President Eisenhower's views in his Message on the State of the Union. The President had said he desired a security program that would make certain that the nation's security was "not jeopardized by false servants," that would clear the air of unreasoned suspicion, rumor and gossip, and to make it unnecessary for "another branch of the Government" to police the Executive Branch.

The reference to "policing" by another branch was understood to mean that the President desired to reduce to a minimum the investigations of Federal loyalty by Congress and the resultant quarrels.

The new security program won approving comments from the three leading investigators in Congress — Senator Joseph R. McCarthy, Republican of Wisconsin, chairman of the Senate Government Operations Committee and long the chief investigator of loyalty in the State Department; Senator William E. Jenner, Republican of Indiana, chairman of the Senate Internal Security subcommittee, and Representative Harold H. Velde, Republican of Illinois, chairman of the Un-American Activities Committee of the House of Representatives.

Recognizing their interest in the loyalty and anti-Communist field, President Eisenhower invited the three investigators to the White House this morning to take part in his usual Monday morning conference with Congressional leaders.

McCarthy Approves

General Eisenhower reviewed the new program for the committee chairmen and afterward Senator McCarthy said:

"I think it is a tremendous improvement over the old method. Altogether it represents a pretty darn good program. I like it. It shows that the new Administration was sincere in the campaign promises to clean house."

When Senator Robert A. Taft, Senate Majority Leader, and Speaker Joseph W. Martin Jr., were asked what they thought of it, Speaker Martin replied, "We didn't have any vote but I heard no criticism."

A prime source of dispute has been Congressional efforts to get carte blanche to examine loyalty files, and Presidents since Washington have resisted this.

There was nothing explicit in the President's order denying access to the records to persons outside the Executive Branch. Asked about this, Mr. Brownell said the privacy of the files had been preserved by a provision of the Executive Order that stated that they shall be "maintained in confidence."

This provision requires that loyalty information shall belong to the investigating agency that developed it but, "subject to considerations of national security," may be retained by the department concerned. It may be passed on to other executive departments or agencies if the investigating agency, normally the Federal Bureau of Investigation, is willing.

Criteria of Security

Seven numbered criteria for security were established by the President, but actually the total was twelve, because the first point had five subdivisions. All five subdivisions of Point No. 1 dealt with problems of behavior involving trustworthiness, misrepresentations, criminal and immoral acts, including drug addiction and sexual perversion, insanity or neurological disorder, and susceptibility to coercion.

The other six points dealt directly with loyalty, including acts of sabotage, espionage and treason; association with saboteurs, spies, traitors, seditionists, anarchists or revolutionists; advocacy of force to overthrow the Government; membership in any organization that was totalitarian, Fascist, Communist or subversive; intentional, unauthorized disclosure of information relating to national security; performing one's work in a manner that would serve the interests of another Government in preference to United States interests.

The new system stresses the authority of department heads. When derogatory information is turned up against an employe, his chief may decide the case is insubstantial and put him back to work; or, if adverse but with ameliorating circumstances, transfer him to a nonsensitive job, pending final

adjudication; or suspend him.

A suspect who is suspended or placed temporarily in a nonsensitive job then receives a hearing before a three-man board chosen by his chief from a roster of Federal officials maintained for the purpose by the Attorney General. After a hearing, this board makes recommendations and the case goes back to the department chief, who may accept or reject the recommendations.

No Judicial Review

Under the old system, the department head made the final decision, too, but he could be influenced by two boards. First, a suspect received a hearing before a board drawn from his own department.

The case was then reviewed by a panel drawn from the lists of lawyers, educators and other selected citizens of the Loyalty Review Board. The recommendations of the Loyalty Review Board were not binding but were usually accepted. The board will complete the cases it now has in process.

Neither the old system nor the new provides any form of judicial review. Any employe who felt he was dismissed unfairly would have no recourse beyond his department head unless he could find a basis for litigation. The President's order made clear, however, that working for the Government was a privilege and not a right.

It appeared from a reading of the order and of the twelve pages of a sample of security regulations

sent to all departments and agencies by the Justice Department that an accused person under the new system—as under the old—might be dismissed on the basis of a case initiated after accusations from anonymous accusers.

The sample regulations state that rules of evidence are not binding on the hearing boards, but that they should take into consideration the situation when the accused "is handicapped by the nondisclosure to him of confidential information or by lack of opportunity to cross-examine confidential informants."

When Mr. Brownell was asked if it was not correct that a person could be dismissed without ever knowing his accusers, he replied:

"Only if you assume bad faith on the part of everybody involved."

In his order the President specified that the Civil Service Commision and the National Security Council should keep the new system under review in order to eliminate deficiencies that appear, as well as any tendency "to deny to individual employes fair, impartial and equitable treatment at the hands of the Government, or rights under the Constitution and laws of the United States or this order."

Bingham Approves

Hiram Bingham, former Republican Senator from Connecticut and chairman of the Loyalty Review Board, declared of the new system:

"It puts into effect some of the

things I tried to get President Truman to put into effect. I asked the former President several times to go beyond the field of loyalty and allow us to get rid of people we thought were undesirable and unsuitable but not disloyal. He never would allow us to do that. So far as it extends the dismissal authority it is excellent.

"I am sorry that there is no appeal allowed from the decisions of the heads of sixty departments. I have been in the program for two and a half years and have found that people who make decisions in departments on firing do not always do so justly. We have reversed a good many cases where the lower boards have found people to be ineligible.

"I think it is a mistake to extend the character of 'sensitive' to such agencies as the Department of Agriculture, the Post Office Department, the Interior Department, etc. There are hundreds of thousands of jobs in such agencies which are not sensitive and where employes should be allowed to appeal.

"Because of this extension people can be put out because somebody doesn't like them. There are 1,500,000 people who are in agencies which are not sensitive and their rights of appeal have been taken away.

"I think there should be appeals allowed to nongovernmental bodies like the Loyalty Review Board, not composed of Government employes."

April 28, 1953

Excerpts From Testimony of Wechsler Before McCarthy Inquiry

WASHINGTON, May 7 (AP)— Following are excerpts from the transcript of the testimony of James A. Wechsler, editor of The New York Post, which was released today by the Senate Investigations subcommittee headed by Senator Joseph R. McCarthy, Republican of Wisconsin:

THE CHAIRMAN [Senator McCarthy].—I may say the reason for your being called today is that you are one of the many authors of books whose books have been used in the information program in various libraries, and we would like to check into a number of matters. Mr. Cohn [subcommittee counsel] will do the questioning.

MR. COHN.—Mr. Wechsler, can you tell us how many books you have written?

MR. WECHSLER.—I have written four books.

Q.—Will you give us their titles? A.—I wrote a book called "Revolt on the Campus."

Q.—And the approximate year? Was that '34? A.—I wrote a book or was co-author of a book called "War, Our Heritage," in 1937. I was author of a book called "War Propaganda and the United States," or co-author, again, in 1940. And I was author of a book called "Labor Baron," the biography of John L. Lewis, that

was published, I believe, in 1945.

Q.—Now I will ask you this, Mr. Wechsler. Were you a Communist when you wrote any of these books, any of these four books? A.—Well, let me say this is all a matter of record, but I will repeat. I was a member of the Young Communist League at the time that I wrote "Revolt on the Campus" and at the time that I wrote "War, Our Heritage." In connection with both the other books, at the time that they were published, I was a vigorous anti-Communist, as the content of the books would demonstrate.

Q.—You say the content would show that in both cases? A.—No question about it.

Q.—Now, how about the content in the case of the first two books? A.—Since I have said that at the time I wrote them I was in the Young Communist League, I would hardly contend they were anti-Communist books.

Q.—Well, did they follow the Communist line? A.—Obviously, yes.

THE CHAIRMAN.—May I interrupt, Mr. Cohn? Mr. Wechsler, do you have any other people who are members of the Young Commnist League, who were or are members of the Young Communist League, working for you on

your newspaper?

MR. WECHSLER.—Well, Senator, I will say that I am going to answer that question, because I believe that it is a citizen's responsibility to testify before a Senate committee whether he likes the committee or not.

Q.—I know you do not like this committee. A.—I want to say that I think you are now exploring a subject which the American Society of Newspaper Editors might want to consider at some length. I answer the question solely because I recognize the capacity for misstatement or misinterpretation of a failure to answer. I answer it with the protest signified. To my knowledge, there are no Communists on the staff of The New York Post at this time.

Q.—The question was: Do you have anyone working on The New York Post who were or are members of the Young Communist League or of the Communist party?

A. Oh, I believe that there are. I couldn't give you the number. I believe that there are former members of the Young Communist League on The New York Post. * * * I know of one. Mr. Cohn knows of him too. He is a man named Kempton. And I should like to say that he would

be very glad to discuss his position the same as I am discussing mine here. He is the only one, to my knowledge, who was a member of the Young Communist League.

Q.—I think we should have the record clear whether Mr. Wechsler objects to our asking him questions as to whether he has Communists working on his paper or members of the Young Communist League. We consider that rather important.

You see, your books, some of them, were paid for by taxpayers' money. They are being used, allegedly, to fight communism. Your record, as far as I can see it, has not been to fight communism, as far as I know. Your paper, in my opinion, is next to and almost paralleling The Daily Worker. We are curious to know, therefore, why your books were purchased. We want to know how many Communists, if any, you still have working with you.

Have you been making attacks upon J. Edgar Hoover in the editorial columns of your paper?

A.—Sir, The New York Post has, on a couple of occasions, carried editorials critical of the Federal Bureau of Investigation. We do not regard any Government agency as above criticism. I assume your committee

213

doesn't either. We have at the same time taken very strongly the position that the charge that the F. B. I. is a Gestapo or a Fascist agency was an unfounded, unwarranted charge.

Q.—Have you ever, in your editorial columns, over the last two years, praised the F. B. I.? A.—Well, sir, I would have to go back and read our editorials for the last two years. I did not understand that I was being called down here for a discussion of Post editorial policy. I have tried to say to you what we have said editorially about the F. B. I.

Q.—Is your answer that you do not recall at this time any praise of the F. B. I., but you do recall editorializing against the F. B. I.? A.—The statement that I made was not a criticism of the F. B. I. The statement I made was an attitude toward the F. B. I., which was that it was an agency that did not deserve to be above criticism, but that neither was it an agency which deserved to be denounced as it has been denounced in some quarters as a Fascist-Gestapo agency, and so on. That is my attitude toward the F. B. I. * * *

Q.—Have you consistently criticized the chairmen of the House Un-American Activities Committee, whose task it is to expose Communists, or have you ever found one of them that you thought was a pretty good fellow, that you praised, or that you could praise as of today—a chairman?

A.—Well, if you are asking me my position on the activities of the Velde Committee [the House Un-American Activities Committee] my answer is that I have been editorially critical of those activities, as have many other newspapers.

Q.—The principal villains in your book are those in the Congress who have gone about the job of exposing Communists. Is that correct; or is that an unfair statement? A.—No, Senator, that is not correct. If I may, since you have asked the question, we have repeatedly taken the position that The New York Post is as bitterly opposed to Joe Stalin as it is to Joe McCarthy, and we believe that a free society can combat both.

Q. And you are opposed to Bill Jenner, too. [Senator William E. Jenner, Republican of Indiana and chairman of the Senate Internal Security subcommittee]. You think he is a dangerous man. A.—Senator, I give you a priority in this field.

SENATOR [HENRY M.] JACKSON [Democrat of Washington]—As I take it, your position publicly and in written articles has been on an anti-Communist basis, and on basic Communist issues you have been anti-Communist, including such matters as the Nazi pact and action taken by the Soviet after World War II?

MR. WECHSLER.—Yes, sir. There is no question about it.

Q.—What was your position on Greek-Turkish aid? Did you have anything on that? A.—I became editor of The Post in May, 1949. At that time one of the great issues which the Communists were fighting in America was the Marshall Plan. I was a vigorous supporter editorially of the Marshall Plan. I was a vigorous supporter of the Truman Doctrine. This is editorially; these are matters that are on the record. I would be happy to submit to this committee every editorial written since I became editor.

THE CHAIRMAN.—Mr. Wechsler, let me ask you this. If you or I were a member of the Communist party, and we wanted to advance the Communist list, perhaps the most effective way of doing that would be to claim we deserted the party, and if we got in control of the paper, use that paper to attack and smear anybody who actually was fighting communism. Now, without saying whether you have done it, you would agree that would be a good tactic, would you not?

MR. WECHSLER.—Senator, perhaps I have some more knowledge on this than you do. I don't know of cases in which the Communist party undertook that activity. I would doubt very much that because you have an ex-Communist on your staff—that he was an agent of the Communists working within your committee.

Q.—I may say, Mr. Wechsler, there is a big difference between the ex-Communist on our committee and your ex-communism, either real or alleged. Mr. Rushmore has testified before a very sizable number of committees. He has cooperated with the F. B. I. He has given all the information, complete information, on the Communists that he has worked with on The Daily Worker. There is no doubt about his anti-communism and his being a real ex-Communist. He does not spend his time, you see, trying to smear and tear down the people who are really fighting communism.

[The reference was to Howard A. Rushmore, who is research director for the McCarthy subcommittee. A spokesman for The New York Journal-American said Mr. Rushmore was on leave from that paper, for which he is a reporter.]

A.—Senator, let's face it. You are saying that an ex-Communist who is for McCarthy is a good one and an ex-Communist who is against McCarthy is suspect. I will stand on that distinction.

Q.—Do you feel that a committee such as this has the right and duty to check the books by Communist authors on the information program shelves? A.—Sir, I believe that the expedition of your associates was one of the most absurd and fantastic wastes of taxpayers' money in history, because I do not believe that the presence of one book on one shelf is going to be a decisive issue in the battle against Communist ideas. I would say that The New York Post has been not alone in suggesting that the journey did more to enable the Communists to ridicule us than anything that has happened in many years.

Q.—Will you get back to my question? We are not talking about one book. We are talking about tens of thousands of books. A.—I am sure the committee has the right to do so. I would question whether the committee was exercising great wisdom in its selection when it did so.

Q.—As I recall, and I may misquote this, because I do not read your sheet, I understand that you have been disturbed by the "unfair treatment" witnesses rereceived before this committee. Do you feel you were unfairly treated? A.—Why, Senator, I question the basic nature of this proceeding. Of course I do.

Q.—You feel you are unfairly treated? A.—I regard this proceeding as the first in a long line of attempts to intimidate editors who do not equate McCarthyism with patriotism.

Q.—You have not been intimidated, have you? A.—Senator, I am a pretty tough guy. I am fully aware that this is a proceeding designed to smear The New York Post. I recognize that, Senator. We are both grown up. But this is a free country, and I am going to keep fighting.

Q.—So will The Daily Worker and every other Communist line paper. I feel that you have not broken with Communist ideal. I feel that you are serving them very, very actively. Whether you are doing it knowingly or not, that is in your own mind. I have no knowledge as to whether you have a card in the party. A.—Senator, I should like to say before you leave that under the standards you have established here this afternoon, the only way that I would in your view prove my devotion to America and the validity of my break with communism would be to come out in support of Senator McCarthy. This I do not plan to do.

(Mr. Wechsler, who first appeared before the committee on April 24, resumed his testimony May 5 at which, at the committee's direction, he presented a list of persons he had known to be Communists. He asked that the list not be made public. He continued):

I therefore felt I had no alternative except to submit this list so that the true issue at stake in this proceeding could not be distorted.

From the moment Senator McCarthy summoned me to Washington, it has been my conviction that he has raised grave questions of freedom of the press worthy of full investigation by the American Society of Newspaper editors. I do not propose to allow anyone to cloud that issue.

THE CHAIRMAN.—If the American Society of Newspaper Editors does comply with your request—which I doubt—I hope they extend their investigation to the lack of ethics and the lack of truth in the newspaper which you edit. I also hope they investigate your abuse of freedom of the press and your low ethical standards as a newspaper man.

Can I ask you this question: If you were not a newsman, if you were a lawyer or a banker, and you had written books that were on the information shelves, if we had the information that at one time at least you were so important in the Communist movement that you were on the national committee for the Young Communist League, if we found that you had gone to Moscow under the direction of the Young Communist League and came back and then announced that both you and your wife had decided to break with the Communist party, and if the committee, either rightly or wrongly, decided that there was no change in your public activities after this alleged break, and let us assume you are not a newspaper man, do you think we would then have the right to call you and try to find out what your works were being used for?

MR. WECHSLER.—Senator, it is for the Senate of the United States in the last analysis to determine the scope of any inquiry, and I stand on that position.

I believe Senator McCarthy instituted this whole proceeding as a reprisal against a newspaper and its editor for their opposition to the methods of this committee's chairman. In short, I believe I have been called here by Senator McCarthy, not because of anything I wrote or did fifteen or eighteen years ago—none of which I have ever concealed—but because of what my newspaper has said about the committee's chairman in very recent times.

The fact that a book I wrote was reportedly found in an Information Service Library overseas hardly warrants this large-scale examination—especially in view of my known hostility to communism over so many years. Incidentally, I have not yet even been told which book it was or where it was found, but Senator McCarthy has been quoted publicly as saying it was my book on John L. Lewis—a book which contains a full chapter describing the destructive operations of Communists in the labor movement.

SENATOR [STUART] SYMINGTON [Democrat of Missouri].—Getting back to the fundamentals, you were a member of the Communist party or the Young Communist League?

MR. WECHSLER.—League.

Q.—You thought that was the right thing to be. You were very young, and then you changed, and you became very anti-Communist because you thought it was the wrong thing to be as a good American? A.—I appreciate the summary, Senator.

Q.—Are those facts? A.—That is right.

Q.—I want to say that you have been the most forthright witness formerly interested in the Communist party, or a member of it, that we have had before this committee.

THE CHAIRMAN.—I may say that perhaps the only reason you say that, Senator, is that you have not been here to hear all of the testimony.

SENATOR SYMINGTON.—I have to answer that if you had told me the day before he came that he was to testify I would have been here.

MR. WECHSLER.—I want to show that there is no question that you have submitted to me that I have refused to answer to the best of my ability. * * *

THE CHAIRMAN.—We both recognize that it is the Communist line to denounce the people who really broke with the party and testified against their former comrades, that the party line is to denounce them as traitors and smear them as much as possible.

MR. WECHSLER.—No question about that. I read similar denunciation of myself.

Q.—I believe that is recognized as the party line. That is one of the reasons why we are curious about the State Department buying your works because we found that The New York Post has been, I think, the leader—next to The Daily Worker and a few others such as The Compass, which is no longer in existence—the leader, in denouncing very vigorously and intemperately without regard to the truth at all, I think without exception, every man who has ever broken with the Communist party and appeared as a witness against spies and traitors.

I believe The Post may have, with one exception. Your testimony was that you did not make such attacks on Whittaker Chambers. I have not searched the papers to find out whether you did or not. I would like to ask you this question, Mr. Wechsler:

You say you broke with the party, you went to Moscow, you came back and you said you broke. Did the tone of your writings change at that time? Did you then find any anti—that is, former Communists who were testifying against, Communists in whom you could find some good counter to what the Young Communist League preached? Was there any overt act that would convince anybody reading your books, looking for something to put in the Voice of America, to show that you had changed?

A.—I suggest that my articles on the Hiss case, which I intend to introduce as exhibits, would answer that question.

Q.—It is easy to write anti-Communist articles, the easiest thing in the world to get up and say communism is bad. The hard thing is to do a thing like [Louis] Budenz, get up and testify against your former comrades to see that they are deported or sent to jail. [Mr. Budenz, a Fordham professor, is a former member of the Communist party National Committee and a former managing editor of The Daily Worker.]

In the book of the Young Communist leaders you say that man is a traitor. In your book he is still a traitor according to your writing.

A.—Senator, that is not a true statement. I have never made such a comment on Louis Budenz.

Q.—Mr. Wechsler, you have just said that the Communist line was to, I believe, preach that every man who broke with the Communist party was a—"traitor" or something along that line—and there was no good in any man that broke with the party. We find that you, whose books are being used to fight communism, still follow that same theory apparently. If not, will you tell us what former member of the party, who has come up and testified against his former comrades, you have ever found any good in?

A.—I have mentioned Whittaker Chambers, who is perhaps the most celebrated witness.

Q.—You have objected strenuously to your being called. Let me ask you this, if you were not a newspaper man and you were a lawyer or banker and if your books were discovered in the information program libraries and if we found that you were so high in the Communist movement, in the National Committee of the Young Communist League, if we found that you claimed to have broken with the Communist party in 1937 but since then have been quite consistently attacking anyone who hurts individual Communists * * * —and waging a rather constant attack on the various chairmen and members of Committee, would you think it was improper to call you, if you were not a newspaper man?

A.—You are asking me for comment on the scope of this inquiry. I think first of all I would take the editorial position that I believe there are more sinister problems to deal with than the books that may be on the shelves overseas. But let me add even more emphatically that I have not been told which book of mine it was that has been found.

Q.—Yes, you have. You were offered one chapter in the record. That was from one of the books. We have told you very clearly that we do not have the record of the number of your books and which of your books are on the shelves. We are now attempting to find out whether the two books which you wrote, which I believe you said followed the Communist party line while you were a member of the Young Communist League, were on the shelves.

A.—Senator, I believe that the question of whether a man is called obviously would depend, for one thing, on the content of the book. At this late date in this proceeding you acknowledged to me that your staff, after a trip to Europe, is unable to tell me what books were found there.

Associated Press

James A. Wechsler, editor of The New York Post, whose testimony before Senate Permanent Investigations subcommittee was released yesterday.

Q.—We know that some of your books are on the shelves. We do not know how many.

SENATOR SYMINGTON.—They have not been able to tell you what books are on the shelves?

MR. WECHSLER.—No, sir. At the last hearing I presented for the record a book called "Labor Baron" which is an biography of John L. Lewis. It is that book that I believe Senator McCarthy said had been found in the library overseas. That book includes a lengthy chapter discussing Communist infiltration in the labor movement and exposing it.

MR. COHN.—I think the record ought to be clear on this. The author's index indicates Mr. Wechsler's books are in use. That is for certain. Exactly which of them, it is a practical impossibility at this point to know.

MR. WECHSLER.—But that is a rather crucial question, Mr. Cohn. Two of the books I wrote when I was an anti-Communist.

SENATOR SYMINGTON.—Do you think you are being persecuted by this committee?

MR. WECHSLER.—I believe the object of this proceeding was, as I stated, a reprisal against The Post for its fight against the chairman of this committee. I believe I would not be here if I were not the editor of The Post and I did not engage in such a fight.

THE CHAIRMAN.—Did you feel, Mr. Wechsler, that it is your status as a newspaper man which gives you some special immunity or do you feel we have the same right to call newsmen as we have lawyers and doctors?

MR. WECHSLER.—I ask no special immunity. I say only that I believe I am here because I am a newspaper man and because of what I have done as a newspaper man.

Q.—You would say if you were not a newspaper man, if you had this record of being so high in the Communist party, if the State Department informed us that your books were being used, would you say then that we would have the same right to call you as any other witness?

I ask you that because you have been shouting that this is interfering with freedom of the press. It puts me in mind of so many people screaming that their right to scream has been denied. I have not found that your right to scream has been denied you at all.

I have not found that your

right to distort and twist the news has been interfered with since you have been here. I may say again, just so you need not go out and say McCarthy intimated that Wechsler is still a member of the party or McCarthy insinuated you were valuable to the Communist movement. I may say that your purported reformation does not convince me at all.

I know if I were head of the Communist party and I had Jim Wechsler come to Moscow and I discovered this bright man, apparently a good writer, I would say, "Mr. Wechsler, when you go back to the United States, you will state that you are breaking with the Communist party, you will make general attacks against communism, and then you will be our ringleader in trying to attack and destroy any man who tries to hurt and dig out the specific traitors who are hurting our country."

You have followed that pattern.

SENATOR JACKSON. — His whole behavior has been inconsistent since he left the Young Communist League with anything that would be in line with the Communist program.

SENATOR McCARTHY.—Have you been reading his paper?

SENATOR JACKSON.—Sure I have.

SENATOR McCARTHY.—Are you not aware of the fact that Wechsler has been the ring leader in trying to assassinate the character of anyone who deserts the party and testifies against his former comrades? It is all right in Wechsler's philosophy to allegedly desert the party and do nothing about it?

He has been the chief ring leader in smearing the head of every Un-American Activities Committee. There has been no change in his writings since he admits he was active in the Communist movement as far as I can see. And then and now Mr. Wechsler does from time to time cuss out communism generally, the easiest, the safest thing in the world to do.

SENATOR SYMINGTON. — What came up is this, that based on the way the chairman looks at it—and I cannot agree with him about it—if you have not denounced all the Communists around you, then you are automatically not really leaving the party. You might carry it a little further and say that the cleverest thing of all would be to do all those things which people would not suspect that you would do in order to come in with the crowd and yet maintain your position in the Communist party.

MR. WECHSLER.—Let me say as I conclude, I think I have indicated to you the nature of the fantasy in which I find myself. I do not claim that all the acts of my life have been acts of superior and unquestioned wisdom. I do assert on the basis of a record and a public record and a record of activity that I have nothing to hide and that I yield to no one on the issue of fighting communism in the manner that I believe to be the effective way of fighting it.

THE CHAIRMAN.—Would you like to tell us any Communists that you have fought who have not been previously exposed?

MR. WECHSLER.—Senator, I have tried to indicate to you just a moment ago that in all my coverage of the Wallace movement, which was in my judgment the most serious threat in recent years of Communist strength in America, I was continually exposing it as a Communist operation. Now, I say that with some

emphasis because that, if I may say, Senator, is before you had undertaken this crusade.

[The reference was to the 1948 Presidential campaign, on the Progressive party ticket, of former Vice President Henry A. Wallace.]

Q.—Did you think there was danger of the Wallace party winning the election or did you think that there was danger of the Wallace party taking enough votes so that the old Acheson crowd would be kicked out and exposed? A.—I thought there was very grave danger of the Wallace party getting enough votes so that the world would be confused as to the nature and solemnity of American resistance to Communist aggression because it was Mr. Wallace's position at that time that there was no real threat from the Russians.

Q.—Now, Mr. Wechsler, let us be a bit frank here, if I may. You are talking of this as a shining example of your fight against communism. Is it not the truth that you knew that the Wallace party had no possible chance of winning that election, but that you were afraid if they picked up enough of the votes of the type that you appealed to, the left-wingers, the party liners, that perhaps it would mean a defeat and an exposure of the old Acheson crowd that had been so thoroughly infiltrated by Communists?

A.—Senator, the Communists up and down the line were supporting Wallace. If you are accusing me of a subjective conspiracy to elect a Democratic President, we have certainly widened the scope of this inquiry and that perhaps affects other Senators on this committee.

Q.—We are not talking about a Democrat or Republican. But when you get up and tell us that your attack upon Wallace proves how anti-Communist you are, that does not ring too true there.

A.—Senator, it is clear to me that nothing that I say will be acknowledged by you to be a valid point. I have been guilty, as I freely acknowledge, of criticizing you pretty hard. I stand by that criticism.

Q.—I have not questioned you about that criticism. A.—You have referred numerous times about my criticism of the committee. I think it is your basic belief that the only test of patriotism, as I said before, is the attitude of the newspaper editor toward the operations of your committee in this field. I cannot and do not meet that test and do not propose, if I may say so, to try to meet it.

I want to say in all earnestness that I regard this as a very serious thing not merely because of what I consider to be the press issue, but because I have been known as an anti-Communist for many years. I say to you this proceeding against me is going to make it less likely that some young kids somewhere will break with communism. If I can be brought before this proceeding fifteen years later and subjected to this brainwashing, all I can say is that there are going to be a lot of people who are going to say, "How do you possibly win back a place in decent democratic society?"

Q.—You refer to brainwashing, you feel that the questions that have been asked you are unfair, that you have been browbeaten? A.—I have said many times in the hearing, Senator, that I believe I am here because of our editorial policy.

'Refuse to Testify,' Einstein Advises Intellectuals Called In by Congress

By LEONARD BUDER

Dr. Albert Einstein, in a letter made public yesterday, said that every intellectual called before a Congressional investigating committee should refuse to testify, and "must be prepared for jail and economic ruin, in short, for the sacrifice of his personal welfare in the interest of the cultural welfare of his country."

He declared that "it is shameful for a blameless citizen to submit to such an inquisition," and that "this kind of inquisition violates the spirit of the Constitution."

The world's foremost physicist made his views known in an exchange of correspondence with a New York teacher of English who is facing dismissal from the school system because of his refusal to testify before the Senate Internal Security subcommittee. The teacher, William Frauenglass of James Madison High School, made public Dr. Einstein's letter, which bore the postscript that it need not be considered confidential.

Reached by telephone at his home in Princeton, N. J., Dr. Einstein confirmed the letter, which was read to him. He said, in response to a question, that he would refuse to testify if called before a Congressional committee.

Mr. Frauenglass, a high school teacher for more than twenty-three years, wrote to Dr. Einstein on May 9 and referred to a statement the scientist had made recently in which he described himself as "an incorrigible nonconformist" in a "remote field of endeavor" that no Senatorial committee had as yet felt impelled to tackle.

The Brooklyn teacher then related that on April 24 he had been called before the Senate subcommittee as a result of lectures he had given six years earlier at an in-service course for teachers arranged by the Board of Education. The course, on "Techniques of Intercultural Teaching," was criticized by a committee witness as being "against the interests of the United States."

"On principled constitutional grounds I refused to answer questions as to political affiliations," Mr. Frauenglass wrote, noting that he now faced dismissal under Section 903 of the City Charter. This section vacates the positions of city employes who refuse to answer official questions by pleading the protection of the Fifth Amendment to the Constitution.

"A statement from you," the teacher's letter said, "would be most helpful in rallying educators and the public to meet this new obscurantist attack."

Scientist Explains Views

Dr. Einstein's reply, dated May 16, was as follows:

Dear Mr. Frauenglass:

Thank you for your communication. By "remote field" I referred to the theoretical foundations of physics.

The problem with which the intellectuals of this country are confronted is very serious. The reactionary politicians have managed to instill suspicion of all intellectual efforts into the public by dangling before their eyes a danger from without. Having succeeded so far they are now proceeding to suppress the freedom of teaching and to deprive of their positions all those who do not prove submissive, i. e., to starve them.

What ought the minority of intellectuals to do against this evil? Frankly, I can see only the revolutionary way of non-cooperation in the sense of Gandhi's. Every intellectual who is called before one of the committees ought to refuse to testify, i. e., he must be prepared for jail and economic ruin, in short, for the sacrifice of his personal welfare in the interest of the cultural welfare of his country.

This refusal to testify must be based on the assertion that it is shameful for a blameless citizen to submit to such an inquisition and that this kind of inquisition violates the spirit of the Constitution.

If enough people are ready to take this grave step they will be successful. If not, then the intellectuals of this country deserve nothing better than the slavery which is intended for them.

Sincerely yours,
A. EINSTEIN.

P. S. This letter need not be considered "confidential."

First Letter Revised

Mr. Frauenglass said yesterday that Dr. Einstein also mentioned in the letter that intellectuals should not seek the protection of the Fifth Amendment in refusing to testify. However, the teacher said that Dr. Einstein agreed to his request to delete this statement, and sent him another copy without such mention.

The teacher added that on Monday morning he had traveled to Princeton, and although he did not have an appointment, was permitted to see Dr. Einstein. He said he had told the scientist of his intention to make public the letter, and he quoted Dr. Einstein as saying that he was prepared to go to jail if he should be called before an investigating committee.

June 12, 1953

STORY OF THE ROSENBERGS: TWO LINKS IN ATOMIC CONSPIRACY

Chain of Evidence, Starting With the Arrest of Fuchs, Tied the Couple to the Soviet Espionage Ring

By A. H. RASKIN

The execution of Julius and Ethel Rosenberg on Friday night brought to an end a case that has stirred more worldwide interest than any American judicial proceeding since the Sacco-Vanzetti trial a quarter of a century ago. The Rosenbergs were sentenced to death for a new kind of crime in a new age—the age of atomic destruction. What follows is a narrative of the Rosenbergs' story as it was developed at their trial.

THE EARLY LIFE

The depression brought Julius and Ethel Rosenberg to communism, and communism brought them to one another. Born on Manhattan's poverty-ridden East Side, they embraced the Communist movement in their 'teens while millions of Americans were out of work and Franklin D. Roosevelt was struggling to put a splintered economy back into one piece.

Julius was a skinny, sallow youth, whose parents hoped he would become a rabbi but who found the faith of his fathers less satisfying than the faith that took its inspiration from the Kremlin. Ethel, two years his senior, was a plain-faced girl, petite without being pretty. They met while both were students at Seward Park High School. She got a job as a stenographer after graduation; he went on to City College but became so engrossed in Communist activities that he "flunked out" in 1937. He resolved to give more attention to his classes, was reinstated at the college and won his degree in electrical engineering in February, 1939. A few months later Julius and Ethel were married.

He bounced from one engineering job to another until he got a civil service appointment as a junior engineer in the Army Signal Corps on Sept. 3, 1940. That was the period of the Hitler-Stalin pact, when the Communists in this country were doing everything they could to obstruct our preparedness program, but there was no testimony that reflected adversely on Julius Rosenberg's performance of his job.

BEGINNING OF THE PLOT

After Pearl Harbor, with the United States and Russia established as wartime allies, Julius began to brood over the reluctance of our Government to entrust all its military secrets to the Soviet Union. He decided that the Russians were entitled to know everything we knew and that it was his responsibility to help them get any information they could not get through established channels of military or diplomatic communications.

His first big opportunity to help the Russians came in August, 1944, when the Army assigned Ethel's brother, David Greenglass, to work on the atomic bomb at Los Alamos, N. M. It was a full year before the first bomb was dropped on Hiroshima, and everything about the project was shrouded in deepest secrecy. Even Greenglass had no idea of what he was working on. He had been drafted in April, 1943, and had spent most of his time before he came to Los Alamos at the Aberdeen Proving Ground in Maryland. He had been a machinist before he got into uniform, and he was put to work in a machine shop at Los Alamos. All he knew about the significance of his job was that everything about the project was highly classified.

News From His Wife

David's first inkling of what it all meant came from a surprising source—his wife, Ruth. She went out to visit him in November, 1944. It was their second wedding anniversary, but their talk was not of marital affairs. Ruth told David she had had dinner a few days before with the Rosenbergs in their Knickerbocker Village apartment.

The conversation ran along a startling line. The Rosenbergs disclosed that they had joined the Communist underground — they were shunning open association with the party's activities, staying away from its meetings and not

216

buying The Daily Worker. The explanation, as Ruth relayed it to David, was that "Julius has finally gotten to the point where he is doing what he wanted to do all along, which was that he was giving information to the Soviet Union."

After Ruth had gulped down the notion that Julius was a Russian spy, he dished up an even more formidable mouthful for her to swallow. He told her that her husband was working on the atomic bomb and he urged her to rush out to New Mexico and bring back facts about the bomb for transmission to the Russians. Ruth's first response was that she would not ask David to cooperate, but she changed her mind when the Rosenbergs insisted that he would want to help and that the least she could do was pass the request on. Julius gave her $150 to pay for her trip.

GREENGLASS' ROLE

David was no more enthusiastic about the proposal than Ruth had been when he first heard it. He was frightened and hostile to the idea, but Julius' influence was strong, even with a continent between them. The G. I. thought over Julius' argument that Russia was fighting side by side with the United States and was not getting data she ought to have. After a sleepless night, David told his wife he would supply the information Julius wanted about the physical layout at Los Alamos, the number of people working there and the names of the key scientists supervising the project.

Rosenberg had instructed Ruth not to make any notes. She memorized David's answers and carried them back to New York. In January David came home himself on a twenty-two day furlough. Julius asked him to turn over everything he knew about the bomb that might be of value to the Soviets. Working from memory, David made sketches of a high-explosive lens, for which he had made molds in his New Mexico machine shop. (The lens is a curve-shaped high explosive used to set off the chain reaction that detonates the bomb.)

Greenglass had taken his duties seriously. He was able to supplement his sketches with a mass of technical material about the bomb and how it worked. He had wandered all over the top-secret "tech area" at Los Alamos, listening avidly to everything he could hear and questioning people "without their knowing it" to get a clearer idea of what they were doing. Julius was jubilant when David delivered his information. He said the sketches were "very good," and he got out a portable typewriter so Ethel could type up the data on the workings of the bomb. It took twelve pages to get it all down.

CONTACT WITH RUSSIANS

What did Julius do with the material he got from David? According to the Greenglasses, he had microfilming equipment concealed in a hollowed-out section

Associated Press
Ethel and Julius Rosenberg, key figures in the atomic spy case.

on the underside of a console table that had been given to him by the Russians. Whenever he had a message or microfilm to turn over, he would leave it in the alcove of a movie theatre. When a personal meeting seemed in order, he would leave a note in the alcove, then rendezvous with his contacts in little-frequented spots on Long Island. Greenglass testified that on his furlough visit to New York Rosenberg had arranged to have him meet a Russian, whose name David never learned, on First Avenue, between Forty-second and Fifty-seventh Streets.

When David went back to his post, he took Ruth with him. He also took $200 Julius had given him for his sketches, and plans for supplying still more information to Julius' Russian friends. The first plan had been for Ruth and a woman named Anne Sidorovitch to exchange handbags in a Denver movie house, but this plan was scrapped in favor of a more ingenious one Julius thought up. He gave Greenglass an irregularly cut section of a Jello package and told him to have his information ready for transmission to a courier who would present the matching part of the package as identification.

Dealing With Harry Gold

The courier was Harry Gold, a Swiss-born biochemist, who had been a member of the Communist spy ring since 1935. He had no direct dealings with Rosenberg and he never made his identity known to Greenglass. Gold's contact was Anatoli A. Yakovlev, Soviet Vice Consul in New York. He ordered the courier to undertake a double-barreled mission to New Mexico at the beginning of June, 1945.

One part of Gold's task was to go to Santa Fe and get data from Dr. Klaus Fuchs, a high-ranking British atomic scientist, from whom Gold had obtained vital ma-

terial before. The other part was to visit Greenglass in Albuquerque. Gold objected that the trip to Greenglass might jeopardize what seemed to him the much more important job of contacting Fuchs, but Yakovlev insisted that he do both. At a meeting in a restaurant at Forty-second Street and Third Avenue, the Soviet diplomat gave Gold a note with Greenglass' name and address and the recognition signal, "I come from Julius." Along with the note went the companion half of the Jello panel Rosenberg had cut out for David.

In Albuquerque, on the morning of June 3, Gold went through the prescribed ritual of recognition signal and panel presentation. Greenglass walked across the parlor and fished the matching section out of his wife's pocketbook. The pudgy-faced courier sat down and introduced himself as "Dave from Pittsburgh."

Paid $500

Before departing with a fresh set of drawings and explanatory material from Greenglass, Gold gave the G.I. an envelope containing $500. The money came from Yakovlev. Two days later, Gold met the Russian on Metropolitan Avenue in Brooklyn and handed him two manila folders. One marked "doctor" contained the information the spy had got from Fuchs; the second marked "other" contained the Greenglass offering. Two weeks later Yakovlev told Gold that the material had been sent to the Soviet Union right away and that the data from Greenglass had proved "extremely excellent and very valuable."

Russian as Co-Conspirator

The indictment that led to the Rosenbergs' death named Yakovlev as a co-conspirator, but he never came to trial. He left the United States on Dec. 27, 1946, and vanished behind the Iron Curtain.

Rosenberg did not confine his professional interest to atomic information, according to the evidence at his trial. He confided to Greenglass that he had stolen the proximity fuse while he was working at the Emerson Radio Company on a Signal Corps project. He simply slipped the fuse into the brief case in which he had brought his lunch, and gave it to the Russians. His Communist ties cost him his civilian job with the Signal Corps on Feb. 9, 1945, even though he protested to his commanding officer that he had never belonged to the party. But neither his dismissal nor the end of the war brought a close to his career as a spy. In 1947 he told David about a fantastic "sky platform" that might be used as a launching site for guided missiles. He was well ahead of the public in learning that American scientists had solved the mathematical problems involved in the use of atomic energy for planes.

In June, 1948, he urged a City College classmate, Max Elitcher, not to give up a job as an electrical engineer in the Navy Bureau of Ordnance in Washington because the spy network needed a contact in the Navy Department. Elitcher spurned his advice. A month later, Elitcher was with another classmate, Morton Sobell, an electronics and radar expert, who worked on the classified Government contracts, when Sobell drove to Rosenberg's home with a 35mm film can filled with secret information. Tried with the Rosenbergs, Sobell drew a thirty-year jail sentence.

END OF THE ROAD

Rosenberg knew that the end of the road was in sight for him when the British announced the arrest of Klaus Fuchs in February, 1950. He warned Greenglass that Gold would be taken into custody soon and he recommended that David leave the country before he found himself behind bars, too.

When the F. B. I. jailed Gold on May 23 of that year, Rosenberg went into high gear. He gave Greenglass $1,000 and promised that the Russians would supply as much more as was needed to get David, his wife and their two small children out of the United States. The escape had been planned in elaborate detail. The family was to slip into Mexico on a tourist card; David was to send a letter to the Soviet ambassador's secretary, signing himself "I. Jackson" and saying something complimentary about the Russian position in the United Nations; then he was to take up a stance at a specified time beside a statue of Columbus in Mexico City. He was to have a finger in a guidebook and, when a man approached, he was to say:

"That is a magnificent statue. I am from Oklahoma, and I never saw anything like it." To which the man was to reply: "There are much more beautiful statues in Paris." Then the man was to give David money and passports that would carry the Greenglasses to an eventual haven in Czechoslovakia.

Preparations for Flight

The thought of fleeing with a two-week-old infant did not appeal to David and Ruth, but they pretended to fall in with the plan. Rosenberg gave them another $4,-000, wrapped in brown paper. They later used the money to pay for David's lawyer at the spy trial. In the meantime, the Rosenbergs were making preparations of their own to get out of the country. They had passport pictures taken, but they were still here when Julius was arrested on July 17, 1950. Ethel was arrested less than a month later.

The only one who did leave after Fuchs and Gold had been apprehended was Sobell. He flew to Mexico City on June 21 with his wife and two children, leaving a brand new automobile in the garage of his Flushing home and giving no notice to his employer. He was deported from Mexico at the request of Federal authorities and arrested as he crossed the border at Laredo, Tex.

THE AFTERMATH

The Government has indicated that the death of the Rosenbergs will not end the story of their espionage. William Perl, one of America's foremost experts on jet propulsion, has been sentenced to a five-year prison term for falsely swearing that he did not know Rosenberg or Sobell, and the Justice Department says it is now in a position to link Perl to the spy network.

The Rosenbergs steadfastly denied throughout their trial that they had anything to do with espionage. They denied everything the Greenglasses and Gold swore to — meetings, money, microfilm, knowledge about the atomic bomb. They refused to answer questions about membership in the Communist party or the Young Communist League on grounds of possible self-incrimination, but swore that they were loyal to the United States.

Case of the Defense

The defense sought to convince the jury that David Greenglass had perjured himself in a deliber-ate effort to save his wife at the expense of his sister. Efforts also were made to get across the idea that Greenglass was personally unstable and unreliable, that he had been coached by the F. B. I., and that he had a grudge against Julius Rosenberg because of a business row they had when they were partners in a New York machine shop after the war. Greenglass, now serving a fifteen-year sentence for his part in the conspiracy, has assured his mother and elder brother that all his testimony was the truth and that he could not have shielded his sister without lying. Ruth Greenglass was not indicted for her part in the plot.

The echoes of the case will be heard as long as the "cold war" goes on. The legal point that split the Supreme Court will be tortured by a million amateur experts. The evidence that brought the jury's verdict and the judge's sentence will be lost in endless clouds of emotion, much of it politically generated.

June 21, 1953

Books of 40 Authors Banned By U. S. in Overseas Libraries

By MILTON BRACKER

Several hundred books by more than forty authors have been removed from the shelves of United States libraries abroad in connection with at least six confidential State Department directives between Feb. 19 and June 21, according to a survey covering twenty capitals conducted by correspondents of THE NEW YORK TIMES.

No single specific instruction covered all the withdrawals. Of sixteen authors whose names were listed by Washington, the nearest to a common factor appeared to be refusal to tell Federal investigators about Communist affiliation.

Other works—whose authors were not mentioned per se—in many instances involved criticism of United States policy in the Far East. In other cases, the banning was apparently based on the interpretation given to one or more of the directives by library officials in the individual capitals.

In only one case—Tokyo—"many" such books and periodicals were acknowledged to have been "burned or scrapped for pulping." This occurred in the earliest phase of the purging of the shelves. The directive of May 15 to all embassies emphasized that books withdrawn from the information centers *"will not repeat not be destroyed but stored pending further instructions."*

In Washington exactly a month after this directive, John Foster Dulles, Secretary of State, said that eleven books literally had been burned, without specifying where the fires had been set. Unofficial reports at the time mentioned Sydney, Australia, and Singapore.

But in connection with the survey, Gillespie Evans, a veteran of public affairs work in the Middle East and South America who now directs the library in Sydney, told THE TIMES:

"During more than a year in which I have been in charge of the information service in Australia, no books have been burned and we have received no instructions to burn books."

In general, it was indicated that the undesirable volumes simply had been removed from the reach of the public and stored, crated or otherwise hidden away pending final word from Washington on their disposition.

Officials Are Reluctant

Library officials showed varying degrees of reluctance to discuss the directives that had governed them. In one case or another, they told inquirers the instructions were "classified," "restricted," "confidential," "secret" and "entirely internal." And in fact the final directive— received in some cases on Saturday morning—demanded complete secrecy on the whole subject.

But correspondents learned that the first communication, dated Feb. 19, impressed some of its recipients as extremely loose. In one case, library personnel felt it would have involved a screening by local embassy personnel of hundreds of thousands of books and more than 1,000,000 periodicals.

On March 17 the matter was clarified to an extent by a directive that said:

"* * * matter produced by Communists or their agents or sympathizers should be used with great care [in information work] and when responsible persons judge them (sic) to be an effective way —an unquestionably effective way —to confound international communism with its own words, to expose its fallacies and refute its doctrines."

At the same time, with particular reference to periodicals, the State Department ordered the withdrawal of "any individual issues containing any material detrimental to United States objectives."

"Periodicals which repeatedly publish international Communist propaganda," the communication continued, "have no place in the program and cannot be used."

The question of periodicals was taken up further in the directive of May 15, cited below.

Limitations Are Defined

The March directive went on to remind that the works of "all Communist authors, any publication continually publishing Communist propaganda and questionable material lending undue emphasis to Communist personalities and their statements" should be banned from all public libraries and information centers of the United States Information Service.

It added that "for purposes of this instruction, authors who obviously follow the Communist line or participate in Communist front organizations will be considered Communists and their works banned."

On April 28, adding guidance— presumably after further queries from aides abroad—the State Department called for the removal of works by authors who cited the Fifth Amendment to avoid telling Congressional groups their political affiliations. This plainly gave the overseas personnel at least one absolute yardstick by which doubtful books could be measured.

The Fifth Amendment to the Constitution states that a witness need not give information against himself.

On May 13, the previous directive was in effect repeated with specific reference to those authors who had appeared before the Senate Permanent subcommittee on investigations headed by Senator Joseph R. McCarthy, Republican of Wisconsin, on behalf of whom two agents had previously toured some foreign libraries looking over the shelves.

"Their books will be immediately removed from information center library collections if contained therein," it was ordered.

Key Directive in May

Then, dated May 15, came the key directive—an airgram to the effect that all such books must be stored rather than destroyed pending further orders. This message also went further into the matter of periodicals, saying:

"No periodicals now being sent by the Department to information center libraries are known to 'repeatedly publish international Communist propaganda' and no existing United States Information Service financed subscriptions are being canceled except by field request at the expiration of present subscriptions."

Librarians were instructed to notify Washington of any individual periodicals withdrawn for what appeared to be security reasons.

Only one of the directives specifically listed authors. It included

218

sixteen names, without mention of any of their specific works. The nearest to a common denominator was plainly the fact that most of those listed had refused at one time or other to tell Federal investigators, often the McCarthy subcommittee, if they were or had been Communists. The sixteen were:

James S. Allen (Sol Auerbach), Herbert Aptheker, Millen Brand, Earl Browder, Howard Fast, Philip S. Foner, Helen Goldfrank (Helen Kay or Kolodny), William Gropper, Dashiell Hammett, Donald Henderson, Julius H. Hlavaty, William Marx Mandel, Lawrence K. Rosinger, Morris U. Schappes, Bernhard J. Stern and Gene Weltfish.

Interpretations Varied

Whereas such a list, plus the directive about witnesses invoking the Fifth Amendment, obviously lightened the task of the librarians abroad, it was apparent from various individual reports that interpretations still varied from capital to capital on such works that were not specifically covered by word from Washington.

For instance, Whittaker Chambers' "Witness"—the story by the man who exposed Alger Hiss and more than any other, led to his conviction—was removed from the shelves of the Abraham Lincoln Library in Buenos Aires. So was an anthology of humor, in which Washington Irving was represented—because Edwin Seaver had edited the volume.

At a televised hearing of Senator McCarthy's group in Washington March 26, Mr. Seaver admitted that a former sympathy with communism had been reflected in his early writing. He added that if at present he were fighting communism through a Governmental information program, he would not have selected such books to further it.

A similar position was taken at the same hearing by the poet, Langston Hughes, whose books have been removed from some embassies also.

Works by Walter Duranty, Owen Lattimore and Theodore H. White were removed from the libraries in Berlin—but not disturbed in Vienna. Other writers, whose works were taken out of circulation in some embassies but left alone in others, included:

John Abt, Paul B. Anderson, Bert Andrews, Alan Barth, Thomas A. Bisson, Joseph R. Davies, Vera Micheles Dean, Foster Rhea Dulles, Lillian Hellman, Stefan Heym, Annalee Jacoby, Corliss Lamont, Kenneth Scott Latourette, Richard E. Lauterbach, Charles A. Madison, Agnes Smedley, Edgar Snow, Clarence K. Streit, Walter White, Harold M. Vinacke.

Probably the single theme most nearly common to the works of writers on that list was criticism of American policy in the Far East —the books by Miss Jacoby, a coauthor with Theodore H. White of "Thunder Out of China," Mr. Latourette and Miss Smedley, for examples.

Spokesmen at many of the libraries noted that there was in effect a standing instruction that would cover the withdrawal of a book unsuited to the furtherance of United States objectives by reason of a local political situation. For example, the Cairo library would not stock a book unqualifiedly enthusiastic about Israel. But this policy was regarded as apart from that now being applied in implementation of the controversial directives since last February.

June 22, 1953

EISENHOWER SCORES ATTACK ON CLERGY; M'CARTHY AIDE OUT

President Replies to 3 Clerical Leaders' Protest on Matthews' 'Reds and Churches' Article

HE CALLS IT DEPLORABLE

White House Action Interpreted as Shot at Senator and Investigations Group

By C. P. TRUSSELL
Special to THE NEW YORK TIMES.

WASHINGTON, July 9—In what was construed widely here as a direct shot by President Eisenhower at Senator Joseph R. McCarthy, Republican of Wisconsin, and his Senate Permanent Subcommittee on Investigations, the President stated today that he agreed fully with a protest by churchmen that a recently published attack on Protestant clergymen was unjustified and deplorable.

This evening, Senator McCarthy accepted the resignation of the subcommittee's new executive staff director, J. B. Matthews, author of the attack, which appears in the July issue of The American Mercury magazine. Its opening sentence stated that "the largest single group supporting the Communist apparatus in the United States today is composed of Protestant clergymen."

Mr. Matthews also said that "at least 7,000" Protestant clergymen had served "the Kremlin's conspiracy."

Although the article was written before Mr. Matthews became head of the subcommittee staff on June 22, a majority of the seven-member subcommittee demanded that Mr. Matthews be ousted from his $11,600-a-year position. The majority consisted of three Democrats and one Republican.

Mr. Matthews was Mr. McCarthy's appointee. The appointment had been made without consultation with the subcommittee.

Vote Blocked Previously

Senator McCarthy previously had blocked a vote on the question of Mr. Matthews' dismissal, holding that as chairman he had power to hire and discharge staff members who did not have a "professional" rating. He rated the staff director as a nonprofessional and "temporary" employe.

President Eisenhower's action was understood to have been taken after considerable consideration at conferences that resulted in conclusions that it was time for the President to act.

President Eisenhower's sharp position was set out in his reply to a telegram today from the three national co-chairmen of the Commission on Religious Organizations of the National Conference of Christians and Jews. The President's reply was apparently immediate. The President did not mention Mr. Matthews or Senator McCarthy in his reply to the clergymen.

A White House aide, asked whether the speed of response was significant, said "time runs out on these things, you know."

Those who signed the telegram to the President were Msgr. John A. O'Brien of the University of Notre Dame; Rabbi Maurice H. Eisendrath, president of the Union of American Hebrew Congregations, and the Rev. Dr. John Sutherland Bonnell, pastor of the Fifth Avenue Presbyterian Church of New York. Their telegram and the President's reply were made public by the White House.

Attack Called 'Deplorable'

"The sweeping attack on the loyalty of Protestant clergymen and the charge that they are the largest single group supporting the Communist apparatus is unjustifiable and deplorable," the religious leaders said.

The President began his reply with this statement:

"I want you to know at once that I fully share the convictions you state."

President Eisenhower asserted "such attacks portray contempt for the principles of freedom and decency" and went on:

"And when these attacks—whatever their professed purpose be—condemn such a vast portion of the churches or clergy as to create doubt in the loyalty of all, the damage to our nation is multiplied.

"If there be found any American among us, whatever his calling, guilty of treasonous action against the state, let him legally and properly be convicted and punished. This applies to every person, lay or clergy."

July 10, 1953

McCarthy Broke Security On Manual, Army Charges

By C. P. TRUSSELL
Special to THE NEW YORK TIMES.

WASHINGTON, Sept. 11—Senator Joseph R. McCarthy was accused, in effect, today by a Department of the Army spokesman of having violated the anti-espionage law by making public Wednesday a "restricted" military intelligence document that the Wisconsin Republican denounced as being "95 per cent Communist propaganda."

Convictions under this law could bring fines up to $10,000 and imprisonment up to ten years. No such prosecution was expected, however, in this new controversy between Mr. McCarthy and Executive departments.

The seventy-five page document, giving the conclusions from studies of psychological and cultural traits in Soviet Siberia, indicated it was designed to supply intelligence officers information useful in war.

Distribution was limited to 100 copies among the Far East Command, other Pacific areas and the Pentagon. The volume was put out from Tokyo last year.

When Senator McCarthy re-

219

leased seventy of the seventy-five pages Wednesday he admitted that he did not know whether the book had been "declassified." Yesterday he said that he had been informed by an Army spokesman that it had been "declassified" before he made it public. Today the Army said it had "declassified" the document yesterday only as "a result of prior disclosure."

The Army held that if the Senator had made public the concluding pages, there would have been proof that its findings led to anti-communistic conclusions.

Senator McCarthy said his committee had not been in possession of the final pages and so had not withheld them, as was indicated in the Army's formal retort.

In another development today, the Senate Permanent Subcommittee on Investigations, which Mr. McCarthy heads, took testimony from John Lautner, an admitted former long-time high functionary of the Communist party, concerning alleged infiltration of the United Nations by United States Communists.

Mr. Lautner, expelled as "disloyal" by the Communist party in January, 1950, after twenty years, is now in the Criminal Division of the Department of Justice. He was a Government witness in all the trials resulting in the convictions of top Communists accused of conspiring to teach the overthrow of the Government by force and violence.

Mr. Lautner, who testified that his "trial" for party disloyalty, held in a cellar in Cleveland, had been accompanied by threats of death, said the party had concentrated upon getting employment for its members not only with the United States delegation but also with those from Iron Curtain countries for better information on how Communists here could follow the party line.

Witness Names Others

Questions and answers brought out these charges:

¶That Eugene Wallach, one of the twelve American United Nations employes whose appeal from

Associated Press wirephoto
John Lautner

dismissal because of refusal to say whether they were Communists, has caused the United Nations' administrative tribunal to recommend a new hearing, was a Communist placed in "a technical capacity" at the United Nations Secretariat.

¶That Joel Remes, an American with a long Communist record as a high functionary, had joined the Polish delegation.

¶That Joe Starobin, a former editor of The Daily Worker, the Communist organ, had served as the liaison officer between the United Nations and the United States Communist party up to 1949, when he went to Europe. Mr. Starobin, Mr. Lautner said, was reported recently to be active in Indo-China.

The subcommittee will open hearings in New York Monday to pursue the investigation into Communist infiltration in the United Nations.

On the Army's intelligence doc-

ument the department's statement contended that an understanding by intelligence officers, in occupation duty, requested "a realistic insight into the attitudes, reaction patterns and social tendencies" of the Soviet citizen.

"The problem here," it stated, "is not to demonstrate the political injustice and economic tyranny of the Bolshevik Government, but to illumine the Russian in his existing Soviet habitat * * *. The most valuable material for this study derives from repatriated Japanese war prisoners."

The statement added:

"It is obvious that the necessary instruction of officers and men in this field cannot proceed without attempting to enter the mind and thought processes of the Soviet citizen. To understand the mind of the Soviet citizens it is essential to consider the Communist propaganda which plays an important role in shaping that mind."

The Army statement quoted from pages of the document that it held refuted Senator McCarthy's allegation that the document was riddled with Communist propaganda. The quotations included these:

Col. R. S. Bratton, retired, who wrote the preamble to the document, was reported in Honolulu, where he is living, to have offered to testify before the McCarthy subcommittee if the Army asked him to.

Senator McCarthy commented on the Army statement that "neither the Army nor any other branch of the Government is going to hide dishonesty, corruption or communism by putting a 'restricted' or 'secret' label" on a document.

"This subcommittee," he added, "has been very careful to not release anything that would jeopardize the security of this country. We have leaned backwards on that."

Sees Pattern Repeated

WASHINGTON, Sept. 12 (AP)—Senator McCarthy commented further:

"I find that unfortunately the Army today is doing what they did under the old Truman Administration. The pattern is the same.

"The document is 95 per cent Communist propaganda. Two or 3 or 5 per cent is a slap on the wrist for communism. Whenever they are called to task, they quote the small per cent that lightly condemns communism."

Remes on Polish Payroll
Special to THE NEW YORK TIMES.

UNITED NATIONS, N. Y., Sept. 11 — Official Polish sources confirmed tonight that Mr. Remes was on the payroll of Poland's United Nations delegation.

A member of the delegation said that Mr. Remes was employed as a "documentation clerk" but refused further information. The delegation member said the United Nations "knew about Mr. Remes."

The Indian delegation commented, meanwhile, on testimony by Mr. Lautner that an Indian delegate had spoken before a secret Communist meeting in New York. An Indian delegate countered: "Absolute nonsense."

Starobin a U. N. Correspondent

UNITED NATIONS, N. Y., Sept. 11 (AP)—The Joe Starobin mentioned at the hearing today apparently is Joseph R. Starobin, former United Nations correspondent of The Daily Worker.

Mr. Starobin covered the United Nations regularly until the end of the Paris session of the General Assembly late in 1951. After that he visited a number of countries, including Russia and Red China.

Pierre Courtade, foreign editor of the Paris Communist newspaper L'Humanité, attended sessions of the Assembly at Lake Success in 1950, but has not been back at the United Nations since then.

Before M. Courtade's 1950 visit the United States refused him a visa, but finally gave it after representations by the French Government. He was restricted to the New York area.

September 12, 1953

EISENHOWER MOVES TO OUST U. S. AIDES WHO BALK INQUIRY

Fights Self-Incrimination Plea —Brownell Asks Law, Seeks Part in Immunity Decision

By LUTHER A. HUSTON
Special to THE NEW YORK TIMES.

WASHINGTON, Oct. 14—President Eisenhower today made the refusal of Federal employes to testify before Congressional committees on the ground of possible self-incrimination a basis for their

dismissal from their Government jobs.

His Executive Order was directed at those charged with disloyalty or other misconduct.

[In another move on the loyalty front, at the state level in Albany the State Civil Service Department announced a program requiring all persons seeking appointment or promotion to any state job to list present or past membership in any group designated subversive by the United States Attorney General.]

Later, in an address to the National Press Club, Herbert Brownell Jr., Attorney General, said the Executive Order was "in accord with my opinion that a Government employe who claims privilege in a Congressional investigation may be too much of a risk to be retained in Government service."

"In my mind," Mr. Brownell declared, "there is no room in Federal service for an employe who refuses on the ground of privilege to answer a Congressional committee's inquiry dealing with his loyalty or other conduct affecting the nation's security.

"There is no law that requires the Government to sit supinely by until the suspected employe has been convicted of disloyalty or other similar misconduct inconsistent with the interests of national security before it can separate him from the Government service."

Legislation to Be Sought

Mr. Brownell further disclosed that the Department of Justice would seek legislation at the next session of Congress to compel witnesses who sought the protection of the Fifth Amendment to testify if they received a grant of immunity from criminal prosecution.

The Fifth Amendment, which provides that no person shall be required to give testimony against himself in any criminal proceeding, has been the refuge of large numbers of witnesses summoned before Congressional committees and grand juries inquiring into subversion and other crimes.

The courts have held repeatedly that this amendment gave witnesses in legislative inquiries, grand jury proceedings or court trials the constitutional right to refuse to answer questions, Mr. Brownell stated. He then asked whether the country could afford to "permit these wrongdoers to destroy the institutions of freedom by hiding behind the shield of this constitutional privilege."

"It is my opinion," the Attorney General said, "that the interests of justice and the nation's safety will best be served, without loss or impairment of constitutional privileges, if the testimony of witnesses can be compelled, upon grant of immunity from criminal prosecution."

The President's Executive Order was an amendment to the order he had issued April 27 prescribing security requirements for Government employment. That order made character, suitability and numerous other factors the qualifications for determining whether a person should be retained or engaged for a Government job. Today's order, according to James C. Hagerty, White House press secretary, was designed to close another loophole in the Government's security machinery.

In the immunity legislation that

Mr. Brownell will recommend he will ask that the Attorney General be made a participant in decisions who shall receive immunity from a Senate or a House of Representatives committee. To leave that power solely in the hands of the committees, Mr. Brownell said, "might subject members of Congress to undue pressures for granting immunity to criminals who are ineligible to receive it."

Mr. Brownell pointed out that the Attorney General, as the chief legal officer of the Government, had the responsibility for prosecuting persons charged with criminal offenses against the Federal laws. "This responsibility must be coupled with adequate authority to permit its discharge," he asserted. "It would seem to be inadvisable for others who may lack

immediate knowledge of a criminal's background and propensities to provide immunity for such a person."

To permit the Attorney General to participate in immunity decisions would not, he declared, impair 'the investigatory power of Congressional bodies.

Measures are pending in the Senate and the House, Mr. Brownell said, that would seek to compel the testimony of witnesses in exchange for immunity from prosecution. One of them, however, does not extend the immunity to witnesses before Congressional committees, but only in grand jury proceedings and court trials.

A Senate bill and a companion measure in the House would grant immunity to persons summoned to testify at Congressional inquiries

at the discretion of the committee in question. Mr. Brownell felt that these bills could achieve their purpose better if the Attorney General shared in the granting of immunity.

Congress, he asserted, could easily be embarrassed "by impeding or blocking prosecutions planned by the Department of Justice on any matter even incidentally testified to." Witnesses might gain immunity from prosecution for more serous crimes through Congressional action by agreeing to give evidence or to produce documents in less vital matters into which the legislative bodies were inquiring.

October 15, 1953

BROWNELL ASSERTS TRUMAN PROMOTED A SPY AND KNEW IT

Says in Address That F. B. I. Filed Two Detailed Reports on Harry Dexter White

By RICHARD J. H. JOHNSTON
Special to THE NEW YORK TIMES.

CHICAGO, Nov. 6 — Attorney General Herbert Brownell Jr. said today that former President Truman had promoted an official to a high Government post in 1946 despite a report by the Federal Bureau of Investigation that the man was spying for Russia.

Mr. Brownell identified the spy as the late Harry Dexter White. The recipient of the F. B. I. report, addressed to Mr. Truman, he said, was Maj. Gen. Harry H. Vaughan, then a brigadier general, who was Mr. Truman's military aide.

Mr. Brownell told an audience of 1,200 persons attending a luncheon meeting of the Executives Club of Chicago in the Palmer House:

"I can now announce officially, for the first time in public, that the records in my department show that White's spying activities for the Soviet Government were reported in detail by the F. B. I. to the White House by means of a report delivered to President Truman through his military aide, Brig. Gen. Harry H. Vaughan, in December of 1945.

"In the face of this information and incredible though it may seem, President Truman subsequently, on Jan. 23, 1946, nominated White, who was then Assistant Secretary of the Treasury, for the even more important position of executive director for the United States in the International Monetary Fund."

Truman Replies by Phone

Mr. Truman, reached by telephone in Missouri, later replied:

"I know nothing about any such F. B. I. report. I talked with General Vaughan a little while ago and he said he knew nothing about it either, and he said that if such a report had been prepared it should have been delivered to the Attorney General's office."

"As soon as we found White was disloyal we fired him," Mr. Truman said. "The Republicans need some headlines to offset what happened to them last Tuesday."

[In Washington, James C. Hagerty, the White House press secretary, disputed Mr. Truman and said Mr. White had "resigned." The Associated Press quoted Mr. Truman as countering that "people are sometimes fired by being allowed to resign."

[There were indications that the incident was the start of an Administration campaign on the "Reds-in-Government" issue.

[A Senate subcommittee subpoenaed General Vaughan to testify. The general, now retired, said he had never heard of Mr. White.]

Mr. Brownell had led up to his charge by declaring:

"It is a source of humiliation to every American that during the period of the Truman Administration the Communists were so strikingly successful in infiltrating the Government of the United States.

"The failure of our predecessors to defend the Government from Communist infiltration left the new Administration a necessary but very difficult task."

'Delusion' is Charged

The Attorney General added that the problem had been inherited by the Republican Administration because of "the unwillingness of the non-Communists in responsible positions to face the facts and a persistent delusion that communism in the Government of the United States was only a 'red herring.'"

He then declared he would cite "the case of Harry Dexter White."

He traced the education and professional career of Mr. White from the latter's first Government em-

ployment in 1934, through his service as executive director for the United States in the International Monetary Fund. Recounting Mr. White's Government positions from 1934 through 1944, Mr. Brownell declared:

"Notwithstanding all this, Harry Dexter White was a Russian spy. He smuggled secret documents to Russian agents for transmission to Moscow. Harry Dexter White was known to be a Communist spy by the very people who appointed him to the most sensitive and important position he ever held in Government service."

The Attorney General continued:

"The F. B.–I. became aware of White's espionage activities at an early point in his Government career and from the beginning made reports on these activities to the appropriate officials in authority.

"But these reports did not impede White's advancement to the old Administration."

Declaring that "a number of these facts have been made public before," Mr. Brownell also said:

"As soon as White's nomination [to the International Monetary Fund] for this sensitive post became public, the F. B. I. compiled a special and detailed report concerning Harry Dexter White and his espionage activities.

"As you know, the F. B. I. was not allowed to make these facts public, but merely to present its findings confidentially to higher authorities. With respect to the authenticity of the information, the F. B. I. had this to say, and I quote from the report:

"'This information has been received from numerous confidential sources whose reliability has been established either by inquiry or long established observation and evaluation. In no instance is any transaction or event related where the reliability of the sources of information is questionable.'"

Senate Approval Recalled

The second summary of Mr. White's activities, Mr. Brownell said, was handed to General Vaughan for delivery to Mr. Truman on Feb. 4, 1946.

Mr. White had been appointed to the International Monetary Fund post less than two weeks earlier, on Jan. 23, 1946. The appointment came before the Senate Banking and Currency Committee for approval during the first week of February.

In spite of the second report to

the White House, Mr. Brownell declared, "the Senate Banking and Currency Committee was permitted to recommend White's appointment on Feb. 5, in ignorance of the report. The Senate itself was allowed to confirm White on Feb. 6 without the Senate being informed that White was a spy."

The full text of the F. B. I. report could not be made public at the time nor now "without compromising important sources of information and otherwise adversely affecting the public interest," he conceded. "But there certainly was no reason why the Senate could not be informed of the established fact that White was a spy."

The first report was "in the White House" for almost six months and the second "conclusively documenting his espionage activities" for nearly three months, Mr. Brownell said. Nevertheless, he charged, Mr. Truman accepted Mr. White's resignation as Assistant Secretary of the Treasury with "regret." He also said that the President told Mr. White in a letter that his new position you will add distinction to your already distinguished career with the Treasury."

Mr. Truman's letter to Mr. White was written April 30, 1946. The next day, Mr. White entered his new post.

Mr. White's resignation from this job was accepted by the White House on April 8, 1947. Mr. Truman then wrote that he was accepting the resignation with "sincere regret and considerable reluctance."

Mr. White died in 1948, after denying that he had been a Communist or that he had engaged in espionage. He had been identified at a Congressional hearing by Elizabeth Bentley, a former Communist courier, as a member of the United States Communist apparatus.

Mr. Brownell told his audience today that the White case was "illustrative of why the present Administration is faced with the problem of disloyalty in Government."

He declared that the Republican Administration had embarked early on a drive to weed out subversives.

The Attorney General was introduced to the luncheon meeting by Illinois' Republican Governor, William G. Stratton.

November 7, 1953

Texts of Truman Letter and Velde Reply

Following are the texts, as supplied by The Associated Press, of a letter by Former President Truman to Representative Harold H. Velde rejecting a subpoena and of a statement issued in Washington by Mr. Velde, chairman of the House Committee on Un-American Activities:

Truman Letter

Dear Sir:

I have your subpoena dated Nov. 9, 1953, directing my appearance before your committee on Friday, Nov. 13, in Washington. The subpoena does not state the matters upon which you seek my testimony, but I assume from the press stories that you seek to examine me with respect to matters which occurred during my tenure of the Presidency of the United States.

In spite of my personal willingness to cooperate with your committee, I feel constrained by my duty to the people of the United States to decline to comply with the subpoena

In doing so I am carrying out the provisions of the Constitution of the United States; and am following a long line of precedents, commencing with George Washington himself in 1796. Since his day, Presidents Jefferson, Monroe, Jackson, Tyler, Polk, Fillmore, Buchanan, Lincoln, Grant, Hayes, Cleveland, Theodore Roosevelt, Coolidge, Hoover and Franklin D. Roosevelt have declined to respond to subpoenas or demands for information of various kinds by Congress.

Authority Is Cited

The underlying reason for this clearly established and universally recognized constitutional doctrine has been succinctly set forth by Charles Warren, one of our leading constitutional authorities, as follows:

"In this long series of contests by the Executive to maintain his constitutional integrity, one sees a legitimate conclusion from our theory of government. * * * Under our Constitution, each branch of the Government is designed to be a coordinate representative of the will of the people. * * * Defense by the Executive of his constitutional powers becomes in very truth, therefore, defense of popular rights—defense of power which the people granted to him.

"It was in that sense that President Cleveland spoke of his duty to the people not to relinquish any of the powers of his great office. It was in that sense that President Buchanan stated the people have rights and prerogatives in the execution of his office by the President which every President is under a duty to see 'shall never be violated in his person' but 'passed to his successors unimpaired by the adoption of a dangerous precedent.' In maintaining his rights against a trespassing Congress, the President defends not himself, but popular government; he represents not himself but the people."

President Jackson repelled an attempt by the Congress to break down the separation of powers in these words:

"For myself I shall repel all such attempts as an invasion of the principles of justice as well as of the Constitution, and I shall esteem it my sacred duty to the people of the United States to resist them as I would the establishment of a Spanish Inquisition."

Points to House Report

I might commend to your reading the opinion of one of the committees of the House of Representatives in 1879, House Report 141 March 3, 1879, Forty-fifth Congress, Third Session, in which the House Judiciary Committee said the following:

"The Executive is as independent of either house of Congress as either house of Congress is independent of him, and they cannot call for the records of his actions, or the action of his officers against his consent, any more than he can call for any of the journals or records of the House or Senate."

It must be obvious to you that if the doctrine of separation of powers and the independence of the Presidency is to have any validity at all, it must be equally applicable to a President after his term of office has expired when he is sought to be examined with respect to any acts occurring while he is President.

The doctrine would be shattered, and the President, contrary to our fundamental theory of constitutional government, would become a mere arm of the Legislative Branch of the Government if he would feel during his term of office that his every act might be subject to official inquiry and possible distortion for political purposes.

If your intention, however, is to inquire into any acts as a private individual either before or after my Presidency and unrelated to any acts as President, I shall be happy to appear.

Yours Very Truly,
HARRY S. TRUMAN.

Velde Statement

Former President Harry S. Truman today notified the House Committee on Un-American Activities that he does not intend to respond to the subpoena issued by the committee for his appearance on Friday in connection with the case of Harry Dexter White, former Assistant Secretary of the Treasury, and later director of the International Monetary Fund.

I regret very much that Mr. Truman evidently does not intend to answer several pertinent questions which the committee desired to ask him, respecting his relationship with Harry Dexter White, described last week by Attorney General [Herbert] Brownell [Jr.] as a "spy" for the Soviet Union. These questions are in the minds of millions of American citizens today, and are not of a nature to be easily put aside with indeterminant references to freedom of religion and education.

The committee wished to ask several pertinent questions of Mr. Truman, questions which are entirely proper in the light of recent charges made, and questions to which answers may properly be required of any American citizen.

It is alleged that Mr. Truman, while President of the United States, received from the Federal Bureau of Investigation an adverse report on Harry Dexter White, which report indicated that White was releasing confidential information to Soviet agents. The committee wished to determine whether Mr. Truman actually had received this report personally, prior to the issuance by him of a strong letter of recommendation on White's behalf.

If Mr. Truman did not personally receive the report in time to alert the Senate committee, then acting on the White confirmation, the committee wanted to ascertain why the report did not come to the personal attention of President Truman, and what individuals or individual was responsible for what must be considered a dangerous dereliction of duty.

The personal loyalty of Mr. Truman has not been put in question but the collective security of the people of the United States was certainly jeopardized by failure on the part of some responsible authority in the previous Administration in failing to alert the Senate of the United States and the American people as to the nature of White's alleged activities, particularly in the face of written memoranda made available to a number of high Administration officials by the single agency of Government charged with the collection and evaluation of data respecting the loyalty of Federal public servants.

Mr. Truman's refusal to elaborate upon his knowledge of the White case leaves the entire matter in limbo. The committee has no intention of attempting to force the cooperation of those who, although shielded by an uncertain and ill-defined immunity, have a continuing and sacred duty to cooperate in all respects where the public safety and the public welfare are concerned.

November 13, 1953

WHITE CASE: WHAT'S ON THE RECORD

Present Controversy Traces Back to the Chambers Papers

By A. H. RASKIN

The trail that led to last week's explosions over Harry Dexter White has been twisting through various Government departments for fourteen years.

It started on Sept. 2, 1939, a day after the Nazi-Soviet pact had emboldened Hitler to unleash his forces against Poland. On that day Whittaker Chambers went to the home of Assistant Secretary of State Adolf A. Berle Jr. in Washington and gave him the names of people he said he had known as transmitters of Government secrets to the Soviet Union. Chambers was a Communist spy who had become disenchanted with the party in April, 1938. When he met Mr. Berle, he was on the staff of Time magazine.

The list of names Mr. Chambers reeled off included a dozen Federal jobholders. The most prominent were Alger Hiss and his brother, Donald, both rising young officials in the State Department, and Nathan Witt, executive secretary of the National Labor Relations Board.

The name of Harry Dexter White did not appear in the list. Mr. Chambers said later that he left it out because he hoped he had induced Mr. White to abandon all connection with Communist activities.

White's Name Added

No one in authority in Washington took the Chambers information very seriously. It was not until two years later that two special agents for the Federal Bureau of Investigation came to see him in New York and he repeated to them the list of names he had given Mr. Berle. But this time he added the name of Mr. White. Pearl Harbor came along; the United States and Russia were wartime allies. The Chambers data seemed forgotten.

A Vassar graduate named Elizabeth T. Bentley brought his story back to life. She had succeeded Mr. Chambers as courier for the Soviet secret service. No one ever told her his name. All she knew was that he was a man who had 'gone sour.' After six years in the underground Miss Bentley "went sour," too.

In the summer of 1945, as the war was ending, she decided to tell all to the F. B. I. She made her first contact with the bureau in New Haven, Conn., but the story she unfolded was so bizarre that the F. B. I. manifested little interest at the start. However, its skepticism evaporated when she marched into the New York office and turned over $2,000 in $20 bills she had just got from a Russian she knew as Al.

F. B. I. Memorandum

At that point in November, 1945, the F. B. I. went into high gear to get Miss Bentley's story and fit it together with that told by Mr. Chambers. Its efforts resulted in the preparation of the now famous memorandum of Nov. 25, which is generally believed to be the first of the two documents Attorney General Herbert Brownell Jr. was referring to when he charged that Former President Truman knew Mr. White was a spy at the time he was transferred from his post as Assistant Secretary of the Treasury to a newly created job as United States Executive Director of the International Monetary Fund.

The F. B. I. memorandum ran to about seventy-five pages, and only a small part of it ever has been made public. This part identified Miss Bentley's open-handed Russian friend, Al, as Anatole Gromov, First Secretary of the Soviet Embassy in Washington, and described him as the probable head of the N. K. V. D. in North America.

Miss Bentley said she had regularly turned over to him and to other Soviet agents classified information she gathered from Federal employes in the capital. The most important of the espionage groups with which she dealt, Miss Bentley told the F. B. I., was headed by Nathan Gregory Silvermaster, now a New Jersey builder but then a ranking economist in the Treasury Department. Among those she listed as members of the

Silvermaster group were Mr. White and Lauchlin Currie, Administrative Assistant to the President from 1939 until shortly after the death of Franklin D. Roosevelt in 1945.

Second F. B. I. Report

The first F. B. I. report, which went to the White House Dec. 4, 1945, put no special focus on Mr. White. He was one of eighty people named by Miss Bentley, thirty-seven of whom were in the Government. No official information about what was in the second report has been disclosed, but it apparently contained everything the F. B. I. could pull together from wire taps and other sources that bore on Mr. White's loyalty. It was delivered to the White House twelve days after Mr. Truman had nominated Mr. White for the Monetary Fund post. Two days later, unaware of either F. B. I. report, the Senate confirmed the appointment.

Thirteen months later, in March, 1947, Mr. White resigned under circumstances that still await clarification. Mr. Truman sent him a laudatory letter when he quit. But, after the Brownell speech nine days ago, the former President said: "As soon as we found out White was disloyal, we fired him." The Democrats say he was kept on by arrangement with F. B. I. so the G-men could keep him under scrutiny and get additional

data on the spy ring's operations. The Republicans say their checks with the F. B. I. indicate that there is no support for this explanation.

Grand Jury Action

In any event, the F. B. I. assigned scores of men to explore the leads it got from Miss Bentley and Mr. Chambers. By the middle of 1947, the Justice Department felt that a special grand jury should be impaneled in New York to consider whether the evidence that had been collected was sufficient to justify indictments against Mr. White, Mr. Hiss and other persons named by the two couriers.

The grand jury had not found the evidence against Mr. White substantial enough to warrant an indictment up to the time he died on Aug. 16, 1948. At that point it abandoned its inquiry into his possible connection with the spy apparatus.

Three months after Mr. White's death the first documentary support of the Bentley-Chambers charges popped out of a pumpkin on Mr. Chambers' Maryland farm.

The documents included eight pages of handwritten notes by Mr. White, as well as a great many notes that were later identified in the Hiss perjury trials as having been written on the Hiss typewriter. The documents were

turned over to the Justice Department on Dec. 3, 1948. Twelve days later the special grand jury in New York indicted Mr. Hiss for having lied when he told it he had never passed classified papers to Mr. Chambers.

Congressional Hearings

The public had no knowledge that either Mr. White or Mr. Hiss was under suspicion until the end of July, 1948, when House and Senate committees investigating subversive activities called Miss Bentley to testify in Washington. Mr. Chambers followed her in the witness chair. When they got through, all the names were in the record. Several of those named, notably the Hiss brothers, Mr. White and Lauchlin Currie, denied unreservedly that they had had any part in the Russian spy apparatus. However, most took refuge in the Fifth Amendment and refused to answer questions put to them by Congressional committees on the ground of possible self-incrimination.

Only one of those accused of being a spy has confessed. He is Henry Julian Wadleigh, who admitted at the Hiss trials that he had channeled more than 400 papers into Soviet hands in 1936 and 1937 while he worked as an economic analyst for the State Department.

November 15, 1953

EIGHT CARTOON OBSERVATIONS ON THE CASE OF HARRY DEXTER WHITE

Roche in The Buffalo Courier-Express

"Political tornado."

Herblock in The Washington Post

At the Department of Justice.

"Active ingredient."

White in The Akron Beacon-Journal

"Me?"

Little in The Nashville Tennessean

"Clean-up casualty."

Jensen in The Chicago Daily News

"Let's look at the record."

Page in The Louisville Courier Journal

"More digging to do?"

Carmack in The Christian Science Monitor

"Time out for unpredictable weather."

Hutton in The Philadelphia Inquirer

TRUMAN ACCUSES BROWNELL OF LYING; SEES OFFICE DEBASED IN WHITE CASE; SAYS G. O. P. EMBRACES 'M'CARTHYISM'

ADDRESS TO NATION

Ex-President Cites F.B.I. Inquiry as Reason He Kept White in Job

By W. H. LAWRENCE

Special to The New York Times.

KANSAS CITY, Nov. 16—Former President Truman charged tonight that Herbert Brownell Jr., the Attorney General, had "lied" about the Harry Dexter White case.

Mr. Truman accused Mr. Brownell of "shameful demagoguery" and of degrading the administration of justice for "cheap political trickery."

He denounced as "false" and "phony" charges that he had promoted Mr. White, a Treasury Department official, to a high and sensitive post in 1946 after he knew that Mr. White was a spy for the Soviet Union.

The incident, the former President declared, was a demonstration that the Eisenhower Administration as a whole had "fully embraced, for political advantage, McCarthyism," and he told Americans to fight "this evil at every level of our national life."

Mr. Brownell will have his chance to reply at 2 P. M. tomorrow when he appears before the Senate Internal Security subcommittee investigating his charges.

In a broadcast over all major radio and television networks, the former President defended his retention of Mr. White in a position on the International Monetary Fund as essential to a full inquiry by the Federal Bureau of Investigation into charges of espionage that had been made against Mr. White and others. He said that Mr. White was "separated" from Government service promptly when the necessity for secrecy concerning the intensive investigation by the F. B. I. had ended.

Does Not Mention Letter

He made no mention of the flattering letter he had written Mr. White when he accepted his resignation in 1947.

The former President said that Mr. Brownell "lied to the American people" when he said he had had no intention of impugning the loyalty of any high official of the previous Administration.

Mr. Truman declared that "up to now no Administration has ever accused a former President of disloyalty." He said such a charge resembled those made in Communist countries against officials of previous governments.

For the attack upon him, he placed most of the blame upon Mr. Brownell. But he went on from there to attack the Eisenhower Administration as a whole, saying:

"It is now evident that the present Administration has fully embraced, for political advantage, McCarthyism. I am not referring to the Senator from Wisconsin. He is only important in that his name has taken on a dictionary meaning in the world.

"It is the corruption of truth, the abandonment of the due process of law. It is the use of the big lie and the unfounded accusation against any citizen in the name of Americanism or security. It is the rise to power of the demagogue who lives on untruth: it is the spreading of fear and the destruction of faith in every level of our society."

Mr. Truman observed caustically that "in Communist countries, it is the practice when a new government comes to power to accuse outgoing officials of treason, to frame public trials for them, and to degrade and prosecute the key officials of the previous government."

Reviews White Case

The former President, seated at a desk in front of the American flag in a huge television studio at station WDAF-TV here, offered to his vast viewing and listening audience a detailed defense of his handling of the White case. Mr. White, he noted, for many years had been an official of the Treasury Department and was an Assistant Secretary of the Treasury when, in early 1946, he was nominated to be a member of the Board of Executive Directors of the International Monetary Fund.

"As best I can now determine," Mr. Truman said, "I first learned of the accusations against White early in February, 1946, when an F. B. I. report specifically discussing activities of Harry Dexter White was brought to my attention. The February report was delivered to me by General Vaughan [Maj. Gen. Harry H. Vaughan, Military Aide] and was also brought to my personal attention by Secretary of State [James F.] Byrnes. This report showed that

Associated Press Wirephoto

LIGHTS, CAMERA: Mr. Truman shown just before going on the air with a nation-wide television broadcast last night.

serious accusations had been made against White, but it was pointed out that it would be practically impossible to prove those charges with the evidence at hand."

He said the information came too late to stop Senate confirmation of Mr. White's nomination for the Monetary Fund job, and so he requested the advice of Mr. Byrnes and of Fred M. Vinson, who then was Secretary of the Treasury and later became Chief Justice of the United States.

"Secretary of the Treasury Vinson consulted with Attorney General Tom Clark and other Government officials," the former President continued. "When the results of these consultations were reported to me, the conclusion was reached that the appointment should be allowed to take its normal course. The final responsibility for this decision, of course, was mine.

"The reason for this decision was that the charges which had been made to the F. B. I. against Mr. White also involved many other persons. Hundreds of F. B. I. agents were engaged in investigating the charges against all those who had been accused It was of great importance to the nation that this investigation be continued in order to prove or disprove these charges and to determine if still other persons were implicated.

"Any unusual action with respect to Mr. White's appointment might well have alerted all those persons involved to the fact that the investigation was under way and thus endanger the success of the investigation."

Mr. Truman carefully did not

225

name the "other Government officials" with whom Messrs. Vinson and Clark had conferred. Close associates have said that one was J. Edgar Hoover, F. B. I. director, and that Mr. Hoover interposed no objections. Republicans, on the other hand, have said that Mr. Hoover will deny that he approved the plan.

The former President said that, while it was decided not to expose Mr. White by dismissing him at once, he and his Cabinet did decide not to go forward with an earlier plan of supporting him to the top managerial position in the Monetary Fund—the job of managing director.

He recounted how the F. B. I. had kept up its search for law violations, and in 1947 took its work before a Federal grand jury in New York, which failed to indict Mr. White. Mr. White died in 1948.

At all times, Mr. Truman insisted that Mr. Brownell's charges against him really were charges of disloyalty, and he said the Attorney General had "deceived his chief [President Eisenhower] as to what he proposed to do." But Mr. Truman declared also that the charges of disloyalty against him also were a reflection on one of his principal advisers, the late Chief Justice Vinson.

Mr. Brownell, in a speech in Chicago on Nov. 6, said that "Harry Dexter White was known to be a Communist spy by the very people who appointed him to the most sensitive and important position he ever held in Government service."

Charges Political Motive

"I do not mind too much for myself or for those members of my cabinet who are alive, for we are able to defend ourselves," Mr. Truman declared. "But I deeply resent these cowardly insinuations against one who is dead."

He said the political motivation of the attack upon him should be clear to everyone, and that the Republican Attorney General worked closely with the Republican National Committee in timing its exploitation and in the hope of political game.

"No election is worth so much," Mr. Truman added.

The former President declared that Mr. Brownell had "made the Justice Department the headquarters for political skulduggery."

Mr. Truman began his speech with an explanation of why he had declined to honor a subpoena for his testimony by the Un-American Activities Committee of the House of Representatives, and why he chose to tell his story voluntarily over a radio and television network.

He said when the committee first summoned him, it was an appealing suggestion to him that he might use that group "as a forum to answer the scurrilous charges which have been made against me." He said he finally decided he could not accept because the separation and balance of powers among the three indpendent branches of government—the Legislative, the Executive, and the judicial—was fundamental.

He said it was essential that no President or former President be required to appear before Congressional committees to explain their acts. Otherwise, he said, "the office of the President would be dominated by the Congress, and the Presidency might become a mere appendage of Congress."

Constitutional Oath Cited

When he became President, he said, he took an oath to preserve, protect and defend the Constitution, and "I am still bound by that oath as long as I live."

"When I was in office, I lived up to that oath—and I believe I passed on to my successor the great office of President of the United States with its integrity and independence unimpaired," he declared. "Now that I have laid down the heavy burdens of that office, I do not propose to take any step which would violate that oath or which would in any way lead to encroachments on the independence of that office."

In reviewing the White case generally, Mr. Truman conceded he had made a few misstatements of

fact when Mr. Brownell first raised the charges, but he explained why.

"It is not possible to recall eight years later the precise day or the precise document which may have been brought to my attention," he said. "In fact, when Mr. Brownell first made his charges. I was unable to remember the precise documents to which he referred, just as President Eisenhower was unable to remember that he had met with Harry Dexter White and Secretary of the Treasury [Henry] Morgenthau [Jr.] in 1944."

One of Mr. Truman's first statements was that he had got rid of Mr. White as soon as he discovered he was disloyal. Tonight he said that his "recent off-hand comment concerning his resignation was in error" but "the fact" was that Mr. White was separated from Government service as soon as the need for secrecy about the F. B. I. investigation had ended.

Before he began his talk the former President appeared tense, but as he spoke any tension vanished. Mr. Truman wore a blue suit, a white shirt and blue tie. In his lapel was his American Legion pin.

The President, who spoke about seven minutes less than the allotted half hour, said early in his talk that he was here to set the record straight. He said he was glad he was talking from the "show-me" State of Missouri to "show you the truth."

Mr. Truman prepared his important broadcast in painstaking detail, working on the speech until late afternoon. He worked in a tiny private office in the small suite he has engaged in the Federal Reserve Bank Building here as a place to write his memoirs.

The door to the inner office was locked and staff members had to use a key as they entered. Closeted with Mr. Truman were Charles Murphy, a Washington lawyer who was his counsel at the White House, and William Hillman, author of the Truman biography, "Mr. President."

After the speech had been writ-

ten, Mr. Truman drove fifteen miles to his Independence, Mo., home for a brief rest and dinner.

Later, accompanied by Mrs. Truman, her brother, George Wallace, and his wife, he drove back to the Kansas City television studios. His chauffeur for the night was Thomas J. Gavin, City Councilman here who gained fame as Mr. Truman's alternate at the Democratic National Convention last year when he cast the then President's vote for the nomination of Adlai E. Stevenson of Illinois. Members of the Truman family watched the broadcast from a glass-enclosed booth in the studio.

The Brownell charge was based on F. B. I. reports prepared after its agents had interrogated Miss Elizabeth Bentley and Whittaker Chambers, both confessed former spies for the Soviet Union. These reports have not been made public and Mr. Brownell has said that they cannot be made public in full.

Wide Political Repercussion

But President Eisenhower, at a news conference last week, said his Attorney General ought to make public evidence in support of his charges. Presumably Mr. Brownell will do that in his testimony before the Senate subcommittee tomorrow.

The case has had and will continue to have major political repercussions. The Republicans believe that they have an issue here that will wreck mounting Democratic hopes of capturing control of Congress in 1954. The Democrats dispute this, contending that the people "will not eat warmed-over spy" when they are concerned with other grave issues at home.

The two principal antagonists are not strangers. Mr. Brownell master-minded the Presidential campaign of Governor Dewey of New York, the Republican nominee in 1948, when Mr. Truman, cast throughout the race in the role of under-dog, won an upset victory.

November 17, 1953

REPORTERS POLLED ON 'M'CARTHYISM'

When Eisenhower Leaves Issue Up to Press 80 News Men Are Canvassed

TRUMAN CHARGE WEIGHED

By ANTHONY LEVIERO
Special to The New York Times.

WASHINGTON, Nov. 18—President Eisenhower indignantly bounced back to the press today the question whether his Administration had embraced "McCarthyism," as former President Truman charged in a speech Monday

night.

He was ready to take the verdict of the reporters on this issue, said President Eisenhower, addressing the 179 men and women who attended his weekly news conference this morning.

The press made no reply then, but the Washington Bureau of The New York Times polled at least eighty of the news men and women afterward. The prevailing opinion that turned up was that the former President's charge could not be sustained against his successor but that it applied to his Administration or to Herbert Brownell Jr., the Attorney General.

"It is now evident," Mr. Truman contended in his nation-wide television speech in the Harry Dexter White case, "that the present Administration has fully embraced, for political advantage, McCarthyism. I am not referring to the Senator [Joseph R. McCarthy] from Wisconsin. He is only important in that his name has taken on a dictionary meaning in the world.

"It is the corruption of truth, the

abandonment of the due process of law. It is the use of the big lie and the unfounded accusation against any citizen in the name of Americanism or security. It is the rise to power of the demagogue who lives on untruth; it is the spreading of fear and the destruction of faith in every level of our society."

That was the definition of "McCarthyism" made by former President Truman. This morning Robert Clark of the International News Service put this question to the President:

"President Truman has charged that your Administration has now embraced McCarthyism. Do you have any comment on that?"

President's Face Flushes

President Eisenhower stepped back from his desk in the Indian Treaty Room of the Old State Department Building where he holds his news conferences. His face flushed and the President stared at Mr. Clark for a moment. His movement, his demeanor and then his words bespoke indignation.

He was ready to take the verdict of the reporters on that, said the President. His words were sharp and clear, but the question had been missed by several persons in the crowded room. Several voices said they had not heard the question.

The question was whether this Administration had embraced something called McCarthyism, the President said. To start with, he added, this was a term that he did not particularly understand, but his answer was that he was ready to take the judgment of this body on whether there was any truth in such a statement.

That was the final comment by the President today on the inflammatory issue that flared up recently when Mr. Brownell contended in a Chicago speech:

"Harry Dexter White was known to be a Communist spy by the very people who appointed him."

The comments of the correspondents who were polled went beyond the White case in suggesting why they believed the Administration had embraced McCarthyism. The evidence they cited may be summarized as follows:

¶The policy of the State Department of giving personnel and security control to Scott McLeod who has exercised his authority in a way that pleased Senator McCarthy.

¶The President's failure to support Harold E. Stassen, then Director of the Mutual Security Agency and now head of the Foreign Operations Administration, when he protested the action of Senator McCarthy in his investigation of Greek shipping operations to Red China. Mr. Stassen asserted that the Senator had tended to assume foreign policy functions that belonged to the Executive branch of the Government.

¶The distribution by the Republican National Committee of a report by the Senate Internal Security subcommittee, entitled, "Interlocking Subversion in Government Departments," of which about 150,000 copies were distributed to individuals and groups. The committee acknowledged that it had distributed 50,000 copies of the report to party workers.

The committee issuing this report is headed by Senator William E. Jenner, Republican of Indiana, who has charged in the Senate that Gen. George C. Marshall, former Army Chief of Staff, former Secretary of State and of Defense, "was a living lie" and a "front for traitors."

¶The use of Senator McCarthy and his activities by the National Committee in political rallies.

¶The failure with some exceptions on the part of the Administration to speak out in opposition to McCarthy or to challenge his tactics.

Several of The New York Times reporters polled their colleagues, promising to report them anonymously. News men and women known to be friendly as well as reporters opposed to the Administration were questioned. Some returned a blunt "no" or a "yes." Others were sharp or sarcastic, and some weighed their words.

Among those polled was a cross-section of those who attend the White House news conferences: reporters for daily newspapers, for press associations, for magazines, for radio and television, the trade

publications, foreign correspondents, and editorial columnists.

A few reporters, remembering the reaction to the poll taken of the views covering General Eisenhower during his political campaign, declined to comment. In the campaign poll a majority of the reporters indicated they favored Adlai E. Stevenson, the Democratic candidate, over President Eisenhower. They were criticized for indicating their views while engaged in factual reporting.

Representative of many of the responses from reporters to The Times poll was the following:

"I believe I would say that the President has not embraced McCarthyism at all, personally. I do think that Brownell went so far in his accusation as to utilize, even if unwittingly, the McCarthy techniques."

Other reporters' comments follow:

"Yes—but I think McCarthyism is distasteful to President Eisenhower if only what McCarthy said about General Marshall."

"I don't think it has. It is not a fair conclusion that he (the Administration) embraced McCarthyism at all.

"Seems to me obvious that he has not embraced McCarthyism but he does not want to denounce McCarthyism. I personally think that Brownell does not like McCarthyism and while he did act in a McCarthy-like way I think he does not intend to follow up that way."

"I don't think it is, particularly in the sense that Truman used the word."

"No."

"I'd vote yes, that they have embraced it."

"I don't think Ike has embraced McCarthyism. I think he sought to stave it off wherever he had a good case but he could have spoken out more strongly against it on a number of occasions."

Distinctions Pressed

"No, I don't think the Administration has. Awful lot of Congressmen have and intend to for the next campaign. If by McCarthyism we mean reckless charges, I certainly don't think the Administration has embraced it. McCarthy has personally collided with Administration in a number of instances, but Administration didn't

knuckle under to him."

"Eisenhower personally has not. As far as rest of Administration is concerned, I'm not sure."

"I would say Eisenhower himself has not adopted McCarthyism. But people in his administration have in that they have helped the Senator at most every turn. They have accommodated McCarthy at his various hearings, and some in the Administration are trying to out-McCarthy McCarthy."

"I think that the President doesn't realize it but members of his Cabinet have done it for the Administration."

"I don't like the word. McCarthyism means a lot of different things to different people. I don't know what it means myself."

"The Harry Dexter White case and the completion by the Administration of the investigation and prosecution of those in the Communist apparatus that operated in the Truman Administration is a far cry from embracing McCarthyism."

"I don't think it is."

"It doesn't seem to me that Ike himself is embracing McCarthyism but he hasn't gone out of his way to repudiate it either."

"It would appear from the innuendos of Brownell in Chicago that the Administration has endorsed McCarthyism. This coming from a Cabinet officer rather than just a Republican in Congress ties directly into the Administration."

"I am afraid it looks like it has * * * and it disturbs me very much."

"I don't think the Administration has embraced what Mr. Truman meant by 'McCarthyism.' A lot depends upon what you mean by McCarthyism. If you mean that the Administration is out to injure innocent persons the answer is NO. I do believe, however, that the Administration is out to root out Communists in the Government whether they hold office in the last Administration or in the present one."

Battle in Party Foreseen

"It strikes me that there is the difference between the Eisenhower Republicans and the just plain Republicans. It is now a battle as to who is going to win. Ike hasn't found a way to bring both ends together. Brownell in

his speech certainly drifted from the Eisenhower Republicans but was brought back into line by Ike."

"Administration has neither embraced McCarthyism or Trumanism because I believe they are the same thing—both based on demagoguery. Brownell made very dignified presentation of the facts. If anything his speech was an understatement."

"Yes, I think the Administration people have caught up McCarthyism. While the President himself may not realize the fact, what his Administration is doing certainly smacks of 'McCarthyism.' A further point is that if the Attorney General is permitted to dip into confidential Government files for political purposes he has a potent weapon that McCarthy never had."

"I don't think the Administration has embraced McCarthyism, but it is up to the President to explain his Administration."

"If you look back to Brownell's address in Chicago, and consider the charges he made, and that he wrote the last six pages of his speech himself, and that he geared his speech with the White House, the Republican National Committee and the Jenner Committee, and the timing after the election, I would say yes, certain people in his Administration have embraced McCarthyism. The President has disavowed it. The proof will come in the next several months. The material submitted by Mr. Brownell yesterday was devastating (against Mr. Truman) but Hall (Leonard Hall, chairman of the Republican National Committee) said that communism will be the main issue."

"I'd be more inclined to call it Brownellism than McCarthyism. It's Tweedledum and Tweedledee."

"I'd answer it the same way the President did. I don't know what McCarthyism is."

"I'd say no. I'd say that Ike has been told to play ball with McCarthy and that he is doing just that. But Ike himself despises McCarthy and hates that part of his political job which calls for him to cooperate with the Senator."

November 19, 1953

Text of Senator McCarthy's Speech Accusing Truman of Aiding Suspected Red Agents

Following is the text of a radio and television address last night by Senator Joseph R. McCarthy, as recorded and transcribed by The New York Times:

Good evening, fellow Americans. Last Monday night a former President of the United States, while attempting to explain away his promotion of a Communist spy, made a completely untruthful attack upon me. Tonight I shall spend but very little time on Harry Truman. He is of no more im-

portance than any other defeated politician.

Trumanism, however, becomes an issue in so far as it is embraced by the Democrat party.

Now, the other night, Truman defined what he calls "McCarthyism." The definition was identical, word for word, comma for comma, with the definition adopted by the Communist Daily Worker, which originated the term McCarthyism. And yesterday, yesterday the National Committee of the Communist party

issued a 1,000-word statement condemning Attorney General Brownell and lauding Truman for his attack upon me.

This statement by the Communist party was signed by William Z. Foster, national chairman of the Communist party, Elizabeth Gurley Flynn and Pettis Perry—all three of whom have been indicted for Communist conspiracy against this country. I am sure they will not applaud my speech tonight.

Trumanism can perhaps best be

defined as the placing of your political party above the interest of the country, regardless of how much the country is damaged thereby. It is the theory that no matter how great the wrong, it is right if it helps your political party.

Trumanism also in effect says to the head of a household if you catch a criminal looting your safe, kidnapping your children and attacking your wife, do not dare turn the spotlight on him, do not get rough with him, do

227

The Crucible of the Fifties

not call the police, because if you do, the criminal will have you arrested for disturbing the peace.

Now as to Mr. Truman's speech the other night, let us very briefly examine the unusual series of statements made by him explaining his promotion and retention of a Communist spy.

STATEMENT NO. 1—After Attorney General Brownell first revealed the fact that Truman had promoted a man known as an espionage agent, the first newspaper report quoted Truman as saying he had never read any of the derogatory material about White.

STATEMENT NO. 2—When Truman was confronted with the fact that the F. B. I. report had been placed in his hands, then he was quoted as saying that he fired White as soon as he discovered White was disloyal.

STATEMENT NO. 3—Then later, when confronted with the fact that White had not been fired, Truman answered, "White was fired by resignation." Now just what that means, I frankly don't know.

STATEMENT No. 4—Next Truman was confronted with the letter over his own signature commending this Communist spy in the most glowing terms. And let me quote Truman. Here's what he said. Here's Harry Truman speaking. He says: "I am confident, Mr. White, that in your new position you will add distinction to your already distinguished career."

STATEMENT No. 5—Truman finally came up with the excuse that while he had read the F. B. I. report which branded White as a spy, that he kept White on and promoted him to a higher job to help the F. B. I. in its investigation of a spy ring.

As to this one, I'd like to call upon the testimony of J. Edgar Hoover, a man whose truthfulness has not even been questioned by the Communist party, believe it or not. On Page 136 of the hearings, here's what J. Edgar Hoover says. He says:

"At no time was the F. B. I. a party to an agreement to promote Harry Dexter White and at no time did the F. B. I. give its approval to such an agreement. Such an agreement on the part of the F. B. I. would have been inconceivable."

Well, there you have it! But after having been caught five times red handed, Truman comes up with the grand daddy of them all. Here's what he says. He says: "Oh, but it's all McCarthy's fault." He says—all the fault of McCarthyism, and isn't that nasty McCarthy an awful man.

Well, I guess there's no reason —there's no reason on earth, why this fight to expose and remove Communists and traitors from positions of power should be a contest between America's two great political parties. Certainly the millions of loyal American Democrats love America just as much.

They hate and despise Communist traitors just as much as the Republicans do. Certainly there's no division along party lines among the mothers and fathers and wives of the 140,000 Korean casualties whose miseries have come to them from the trickeries, the betrayals, of an administration whose foreign policy was so carefully shaped by the Alger Hisses, the Harry Dexter Whites, the Owen Lattimores, the Dean Achesons, the John Carter Vincents.

We should keep in mind that

The New York Times

REPLIES TO TRUMAN: Senator Joseph R. McCarthy, shown last night at television microphone just before opening attack on former President Truman in the Harry Dexter White case.

as of tonight, as of tonight we are engaged in a war which was declared in 1914 by Lenin, repeatedly reaffirmed by Joe Stalin, and approved two-and-a-half weeks ago by high officials of the Kremlin. It is the Communist war against free men.

Now, when that first Communist declaration of war was made 105 years ago, you could number the active Communist leaders on the fingers of both hands. At the time Truman became President, the number of people under Communist domination was 180,000,-000. During his term as President, the figure increased from 180,000,000 people to 800,000,000 people. Now this represents, my good friends, the greatest victory of any brutalitarian dictatorship since time first commenced to run.

Why? Is it because Communist slavery is more attractive than the clean fresh air of freedom? Certainly not. Then why?

The pattern of Communist conquest has been the same in every country over which the stygian blackness of Communist night has descended. Always first the infiltration of key posts in Government by Communist traitors and then the creeping paralysis of fear to speak out and expose the traitors.

This fear has been engendered and nurtured not only by Communists, but also by the phoney, deluded, fuzzy-minded liberals in whose book it is a mortal sin ever to expose or criticize a Communist. Of course, of course, it's perfectly proper for a Communist to scream lies and vituperations at anyone who hurts the Communist cause. Thus, my good friends, the picture has been in Hungary, Czechoslovakia, Rumania, and every other nation taken over by the black death of communism. Thus the picture has been in our country also.

In connection with Communist

infiltration of our government let me give you, if I may, very briefly, another case in which Truman intervened in behalf of a communist agent.

On April 13, 1950, George Shaw Wheeler who had been working for the United States Government in Europe, deserted to the Communist cause. At that time he denounced what he called, and I quote, the "Gestapo methods" of the United States. He stated that he was going to stand "proudly with the Soviet regime." Wheeler then disappeared behind the Iron Curtain.

Now what does Truman have to do with this? As early as 1944 the Civil Service Commission Loyalty Board had found Wheeler disloyal because of Communist and espionage activities.

Listen to these dates, if you will. On Oct. 4, 1944, Harry Truman, candidate for Vice President, wrote a three-page letter to the Civil Service Commission denouncing the commission in the strongest language for having ordered the dismissal of Wheeler. That was in 1944. In October of 1945, Harry Truman, as President, the Civil Service Commission then reversed itself and ordered Wheeler reinstated.

And, of course, as you know, Wheeler is now behind the Iron Curtain, having admitted that he was an espionage agent.

Now add to this, add to this picture of Glasser, Silvermaster, Ullman, Kaplan and all the rest named in F. B. I. reports of Communists, Communists who were kept in high positions of power with access to vital secrets by the Truman Administration and you have some small portion of the sordid picture.

My fellow Americans there is nothing accidental about this picture. It is a pattern of deliberate Communist infiltration.

Impossible, you say? Yes. Unbelievable? Yes. But there you

have it. It is all a matter of cold record. And the most amazing and disturbing thing about this incredibly unbelievable picture is that as the danger of this nation is slowly and laboriously exposed, instead of an admission of guilt, or stupidity, cheap politicians from coast to coast join the chorus of the Communist Daily Worker and shout, "Oh, isn't this McCarthyism an awful thing? Isn't it terrible to dig out these Communists?"

Now how many American young men have died and how many will die because of stupidity, blindness and treason no one will ever know. But what answer do we get when it is exposed? The leader of the Democrat party— Harry Truman—in the most intemperate language condemns Attorney General Brownell for giving the American people the facts.

He then, of course, proceeds to damn McCarthy, drawing very heavily upon his repertoire of dirty names because I took some part in the exposure of the Communist infiltration of his administration.

I would not be concerned about what a discredited politician has to say, except that his leadership on the Communist issue is being followed by so many Democrats.

I would like to briefly review some of the work of our committee. This may furnish a key to the bitterness of the Truman Democrats—I emphasize Truman Democrats—toward my work which they prefer to call McCarthyism.

Now for a glance at a few excerpts from the testimony before our committee. On Nov. 19, 1953, we were investigating Communist infiltration and potential espionage and sabotage in the huge General Electric plant. Defense officials freely stated that if enemy agents were to sabotage General Electric facilities it would deal a crippling blow to our defense attempts. The first witness before the committee, Henry Archdeacon.

The question—Mr. Archdeacon were you engaged in espionage over the past few weeks? This question was asked less than a week ago.

Answ.—I decline to answer that question on the basis that it might tend to incriminate me.

Then I asked him, "as a matter of fact you have been giving to the Communist party complete detailed information on everything going on at the General Electric plant. Is that correct?"

Answer—I decline to answer on the basis of the Fifth Amendment.

Question—Just one further question. If we were to have a war with Communist Russia and if the Communist party ordered you to sabotage, to blow up the facilities at General Electric, this defense plant, would you disobey that order of the Communist party?

Listen to this answer: "I decline to answer that question on the ground that my answer might tend to incriminate me."

Well this morning, less than twelve hours ago, a witness, Joseph Levitsky, appeared before our committee. Levitsky had until very recently been working in the tele-communications, a lab which was handling secret radar work dealing with the defense of this nation.

He refused under the Fifth Amendment, on the grounds of self-incrimination, to tell whether, during the last thirty days, he had been engaged in a conspiracy to commit espionage and whether during July of this year he had attempted to get people from the Evans Signal Corps Laboratory to commit espionage.

A few months ago, we were investigating espionage in the Government Printing Office, which handles secret material for every department of Government—that includes, Army, Navy, the Air Corps, Secret Service, atomic energy, on down the line.

One of the witnesses before the committee was Edward Rothchild. The F. B. I. had given the Truman Administration detailed reports upon him and his wife. Reports to the effect they were Communists, that she was an important officer in the Communist party, that Communist meetings were held in their home, and that he had been engaged in stealing Government secrets, including secret codes from the printing office. He was before our committee on Aug. 10 of this year.

Now let me quote a few questions and answers, if I may:

Question—Is it a fact, Mr. Rothchild, that you have access to secret and confidential material?

Answer—Yes.

Up until today?

Answer—Up until this moment, Mr. Senator.

Question—Are you a member of the Communist party as of this moment?

Answer—Under the Fifth Amendment, I decline to answer.

Question—Did you ever steal a secret code book from the Government Printing Office?

Answer—Again a refusal to answer under the Fifth Amendment.

Question—Were you engaged in espionage against the United States on Aug. 9, 1953?

Answer—I refuse to answer—Fifth Amendment.

Well, to get rid of a Communist handling secret material is, of course, important. But it is even more important to discover how a Communist could hold a job handling secrets which affected the lives and deaths of 160,000,000 American people for ten, fifteen, twenty years.

So, we went into that. So, we called the men on the mis-named Loyalty Board. I think their testimony gives, perhaps as clearly as any other, the reason why the Truman Democratic Administration was crawling with Communists.

The secretary of the Loyalty Board was asked the question why they did not call witnesses whom the F. B. I. could furnish. The answer: Listen to this: That was not our practice, Mr. Senator.

Then I asked the secretary of the Loyalty Board this question, Is it true that in the Rothchild hearing, you only called witnesses who were suggested by Rothchild. Is it the usual practice to hear only the witnesses whom the accused wants you to hear?

Answer—This is by the chairman of the Loyalty Board: Yes, Mr. Senator, that has been the practice.

Next question—Let me ask you this. Does your board operate under the rule that membership in the Communist party is not sufficient to bar a worker?

Answer—that is true.

Well, my good friends, this gives you some of the picture why the Communists, the fellow-travelers, the Truman-type Democrats, who place party above country, scream so loudly about McCarthyism, why their hatred and venom knows no bounds.

Now, a few days ago—a few days ago, I read that President Eisenhower expressed the hope that by election time in 1954 the subject of communism would be a dead and forgotten issue. The raw, harsh, unpleasant fact is that communism is an issue and will be an issue in 1954.

Truman's diatribe against those who expose Communists is the best proof of that.

I would also like to remind those very well-meaning people, who speak about communism not being an issue, that communism is not isolated from the other great evils which beset us today.

For example, when a Harry Dexter White, by his manipulations through the Treasury Department, undermines the money system of Nationalist China; when a Lauchlin Currie, on White House stationery, countermanded the orders to ship vast amounts of captured German equipment to China, to be used in her war against the Communists; when the Communists, and fellow travelers, in policy-making positions, sold out our friends to our enemies, with the result that 620,000,000 disappeared behind the Iron Curtain—that is, between 1945 and 1953—when they were doing all of those things, they were making necessary a huge tax burden upon the American people—a tax burden necessary to build up our defenses.

They were, in effect, signing the draft call for the hundreds of thousands of young men who've been called to military duty. They were setting the stage for future wars; they were signing the death warrants of unknown numbers of Americans. Therefore, my good friends, practically every issue which we face today, from high taxes to the shameful mess in Korea, is inextricably interwoven with the Communist issue.

Now Democrat office-seekers from the Atlantic to the Pacific have been proclaiming that McCarthyism is the issue in this campaign. In a way, I guess, it is, because Republican control of the Senate determines whether I shall continue as chairman of the investigating committee.

Therefore, if the American people agree with Truman, they have a chance to get rid of me as chairman of the investigating committee next fall by defeating any Republican up for election.

If the American people, on the other hand, believe in the necessity of digging out and getting rid of the type of Communists who have been before our committee; if they believe, as I do, that treason, dishonesty and stupidity should be exposed wherever and whenever found, regardless of the party label, then their answer is to keep the Republicans in power so we may continue to clean out the Augean stables.

But now, now let's take a look at the Republican party. Unfortunately, in some cases, our batting average has not been too good. Before looking at some of the cases in which our batting average is zero, let me make it clear that I think that the new Administration is doing a job so infinitely better than the Truman Acheson regime that there is absolutely no comparison.

For example, the new Administration in the first ten months in office has gotten rid of 1,456 Truman holdovers who were all security risks. And over 90 per cent of the 1,456 security risks were gotten rid of because of Communist connections and activities or perversion. Fourteen hundred and fifty-six, I would say, an excellent record for the time President Eisenhower has been in office.

However, let us glance at a few cases where we struck out. For example, we still have John Paton Davies on the payroll after eleven months of the Eisenhower Administration.

And who is John Paton Davies? John Paton Davies was (1) part and parcel of the old Acheson-Lattimore - Vincent - White - Hiss group which did so much toward delivering our Chinese friends into Communist hands; (2) he was unanimously referred by the McCarran Committee to the Justice Department in connection with a proposed indictment because he lied under oath about his activities in trying to put—listen to this—in trying to put Communists and espionage agents in key spots in the Central Intelligence Agency.

A question which we ask is: Why is this man still a high official in our department after eleven months of Republican Administration?

Now let us examine the failure of my party, if we may, to liquidate the foulest bankruptcy of the Democrat Administration.

On Sept. 12, 1953, the Chinese Communists announced that they would not treat as prisoners of war American fliers who were shot down during the Korean war over Manchuria. On Sept. 10, 1953, the Army announced that some 900 American young men known to have been prisoners of the Communists in Korea were still unaccounted for. Unaccounted for as of tonight, my good friends.

Well, why do I bring this situation up tonight in telling about the Republican party? The Republican party did not create the situation, I admit. We inherited it. But we are responsible for the proper handling of the situation as of tonight. Now what are we going to do about it? Are we going to continue to send perfumed notes, following the style of the Truman-Acheson regime?

Or are we going to take the only position that an honorable nation can take—namely, that every uniformed American packs the pride and the honor and the power of this nation on his shoulder.

Millions of people in my radio and television audience tonight will recall that even in grade school your hearts beat a bit faster and you felt a great surge of pride when you heard in song this was the land of the free and the home of the brave.

But let me ask you, how free are we? How free are we when American aviators fighting under the American flag at this very moment, on Nov. 24, 1953, are being brainwashed, starved or murdered behind an Iron or Bamboo Curtain. How brave are we—how brave are we when we do not use all the power of this nation to rescue those airmen and the 900 other military men who have been unaccounted for for months.

I realize, of course, the low ebb to which our honor has sunk over the past twenty years. But it is time that we, the Republican party, liquidate this blood-stained blunder of the Acheson-Truman regime. We promised the American people something different. It is up to us now to deliver—not next year, next month—let us deliver now, my good friends.

How are we going to do it? Once a nation has allowed itself to be reduced to a state of whining, whimpering appeasement, the cost of regaining national honor may be very high. But we must regain our national honor regardless of what it costs. Now I know it is easy to talk in general terms about what can be done. Let us be specific.

As you know, we have been voting billions of dollars each year to help our allies build up their military and economic strength, so that they can help in this day to day struggle between the free half of the world and the Communist slave half. If that money we give them is being used for that purpose, then it is well spent. If not, then those allies are defrauding us.

How does that affect you? As of today, some money was taken out of your paycheck and sent to Britain. As of today, Britain used that money from your paycheck to pay for the shipment of the sinews of war to Red China.

What can we do about that? We can deal a death blow to the war-making power of Communist China. We can, without firing a single shot, force the Communists in China to open their filthy Communist dungeons and release every American. We can blockade the coast of China, without using a single ship, a single sailor or a single gun.

In this connection I want to point out that Lloyds of London the outfit that keeps track of shipping, according to their records the shipments to Red China for this year have increased over 1,500 per cent over what they were last year.

Now what can we do about it? We can handle this by saying this to our Allies: If you continue to ship to Red China, while they are imprisoning and torturing American men, you will get not one cent of American money.

If we do that, my good friends, this trading in blood-money will cease. No question about that.

Now, I see time is running out. Let me remind you that when the smoke-screen of false political righteousness is raised against McCarthyism by Harry Truman, or anyone else singing in his choir of defeat, remember that he, Truman, stands on his record as an individual and as a President. He promoted Harry Dexter White, Russian spy. He fired Gen. Douglas MacArthur, one of the greatest living Americans.

In conclusion I would like to quote as well as I can remember Abraham Lincoln, who when discussing the only way this nation could ever be destroyed said: "All the armies in Europe, all the armies of Europe and Asia combined, with all the wealth of the world in their military chests, with a Bonaparte for a commander, in a trial of a thousand years, could not place one foot upon the Blue Ridge Mountains; could not take one drink from the Ohio River.

As Lincoln said: From whence then will danger come? If this nation is to be destroyed, it will be destroyed from within, if it is not destroyed from within, it will live for all time to come.

November 25, 1953

Eisenhower Staff Interprets McCarthy Speech as Attack

Top White House Aides Feel That Senator, Who Got Air Time to Reply to Truman, Used It to Criticize Administration

By JAMES RESTON
Special to THE NEW YORK TIMES.

WASHINGTON, Nov. 25—Top White House staff members were hopping mad today about Senator Joseph R. McCarthy's TV-radio speech last night.

They would not comment officially, but unofficially they made these points about the Wisconsin Senator's performance:

¶He received time on the air to criticize former President Truman and ended up by criticizing President Eisenhower as well.

¶He sought to make himself, rather than President Eisenhower's legislative program, the central issue in the 1954 Congressional campaign.

¶He distorted the John Paton Davies case, although he knew the facts in that case as well as did Under Secretary of State W. Bedell Smith, who gave them to him under oath.

¶He demonstrated more clearly than ever before that he was not prepared to follow the President's lead either in fighting the Communists at home or in the strategy against them in Communist China.

One White House aide described the speech as "a declaration of war against the President."

Others put their criticism more mildly, but there seemed to be general agreement that the speech marked one more crisis in the stormy relations between the White House and the junior Republican Senator from Wisconsin.

There are some Republicans in this city who want to see Senator McCarthy emerge as the symbol of the Republican party, but President Eisenhower and his White House aides are not among them.

They concede that the Wisconsin Senator beat them to the draw in demanding time to answer Mr. Truman's blast at the Eisenhower Administration a week ago last Monday. Mr. Truman's charge was that the Eisenhower Administration had embraced "McCarthyism," which he went on to define in terms derogatory to Mr. McCarthy.

However, Mr. Truman's charge was primarily against the Eisenhower Administration and there was some feeling at the White House that General Eisenhower should have been given the privilege of deciding who was going to answer for his Administration.

What upset the White House staff, though, was that Senator McCarthy used part of the time to play up the issues he knew President Eisenhower was trying to play down, to support policies he knew the President opposed and to distort facts that the Eisenhower Administration had taken considerable trouble to set straight.

Here are specific cases in illustration of their points:

¶Communists-in-Government Issue. President Eisenhower said last week that he hoped this problem would have been dealt with so effectively that it no longer would be an issue in the 1954 election campaign.

Last night Senator McCarthy said:

"A few days ago I read that President Eisenhower expressed the hope that by election time in 1954, the subject of communism would be a dead and forgotten issue. [President Eisenhower was referring not to "the subject of communism," but to the Communists-in-Government issue.] The raw, harsh fact is that communism is an issue and will be an issue in 1954 * * *

"I would also like to remind those very well-meaning people who speak about communism not being an issue that communism is not isolated from the other great evils that beset us today."

¶The Eisenhower record. The President has been emphasizing that the record of his party will be the main issue in 1954 and that no man could decide what the issues would be. Last night, Senator McCarthy attacked some aspects of that record, and said this:

"Now Democrat office seekers from the Atlantic to the Pacific have been proclaiming that McCarthyism is the issue in this campaign. In a way, I guess it is, because Republican control of the Senate determines whether I shall continue as chairman of the investigating committee.

"Therefore, if the American people agree with Truman, they have a chance to get rid of me as chairman of the investigating committee next fall by defeating any Republican up for election."

His point here was that, with the Senate now divided with forty-eight Democrats to forty-seven Republicans and one Independent (Senator Wayne Morse of Oregon, who votes with the Republicans on controlling the administrative machinery of the Senate), the net loss of one Republican seat in the 1954 Senate race would enable the Democrats to organize the upper chamber and take over the committee chairmanships.

Mr. McCarthy continued:

"If the American people, on the other hand, believe in the necessity of digging out and getting rid of the type of Communists who have been before our committee; if they believe as I do, that treason, dishonesty, and stupidity should be exposed wherever and whenever found, regardless of party label, then their answer is to keep the Republicans in power so we may continue to clean out the Augean stables."

¶The John Paton Davies case. Senators McCarthy and Pat McCarran, Democrat of Nevada, have been attacking the Eisenhower Administration for retaining Mr. Davies, a Foreign Service officer, on the government payroll.

On several occasions they have charged that Mr. Davies, now United States chargé d'Affaires in Peru, recommended putting Communists in key spots in the Central Intelligence Agency, and Under Secretary of State Smith finally went before them and declassified some top secret information in order to set this charge straight.

Permitted to Testify

He told them that a decision had been taken to use some Communists as counter-espionage agents and that Mr. Davies had been asked to recommend several men who might handle the job.

While this information still was classified top secret, and Mr. Davies was not permitted to let it be known that the C. I. A. was using some Communists as counter-espionage agents, Mr. Davies was asked about this and said he knew nothing about it.

Later Under Secretary Smith agreed to allow Mr. Davies to discuss the espionage plan with the Senators and he so did in Mr. McCarthy's presence.

Nevertheless, Mr. McCarthy last night gave the impression, not that Mr. Davies was engaged in a counter-espionage plan in which Communists would be used to trap other Communist spies, but that Mr. Davies actually was trying to help the Communist cause.

Here is what he said:

"Let me make clear that the new Administration is doing a job so infinitely better than the Truman-Acheson regime that there is absolutely no comparison * * * However, let's glance at a few cases where we struck out. For example, we still have John Paton Davies on the payroll after eleven months of the Eisenhower Administration.

"And who is John Paton Davies? John Paton Davies was (1) part and parcel of the old Acheson-Lattimore-Vincent-White-Hiss group which did so much toward delivering our Chinese friends into Communist hands; (2) he was unanimously referred by the McCarran Committee to the Justice Department in connection with a proposed indictment because he lied under oath about his activities in trying to put—listen to this—in trying to put Communists and espionage agents in key spots in the Central Intelligence Agency."

The White House aide knows all about this case. They know that Mr. McCarthy knows the facts in the case, and they feel that he distorted the facts in order to make it appear that the Eisenhower Administration was soft on a man who actually had tried to damage his country by putting Communists into the C. I. A. This did not increase the Senator's popularity at 1600 Pennsylvania Avenue.

The Democrats are glad to see a rift in the Republican ranks, and intend to do what they can to widen it, and Senator McCarthy's friends now see him, not so much as an ally of the President as a rival and maybe even as a successor.

KANSAS CITY, Nov. 25 (AP)—Former President Truman said at his office this morning he would have no comment on Senator McCarthy's speech. "I didn't even listen to it. I was asleep," he said.

November 26, 1953

V. F. W. in Norwalk Is Turning in 'Reds'

By DAVID ANDERSON
Special to THE NEW YORK TIMES.

NORWALK, Conn., Jan. 26—The names and addresses of residents of this city whose records or activities are deemed to be "communistic" by the local post of the Veterans of Foreign Wars are being forwarded by it to the Federal Bureau of Investigation.

It was learned today that a special committee, formed of men "from all walks of life," had been created to sift the suspects. The procedure calls for the submission of data on all likely persons and, when the weight of such testimony impresses the committee, it is sent on to the Federal authorities.

Charles J. Post, Connecticut state commander of the organization and a member of the Mulvoy-Tarlov-Aquino Post here, defended the practice as designed to "wake up our own people in this town."

"There is nothing fly-by-night about it," he explained. "We have more or less been alerted by the national organization to keep our community active and wise. I wouldn't say that we received a directive to do this; it's not exactly that. But it is the sort of thing that's being done in other towns across the country."

The post commander, Albert A. Beres, owner of the White Bridge service station on Five Mile River Road in Darien, said that the policy underlying the campaign was one laid down in a resolution at the V. F. W. encampment of 1926 in El Paso, Tex. It charged the membership with the duty of reporting any persons believed to be engaged in subversive activity.

"I cannot tell you whether I have personally turned in the names of Norwalk people," continued Mr. Beres. "But you can say that sources close to the officials of the V. F. W. have done so.

"You must understand that we aren't judges. A man with a tendency to be leftist may be all right. It doesn't mean that every name turned in is of a Communist or subversive person, for lots of good Americans might have been pushed into such activities long ago. If a man has a clear conscience, why should he worry?"

Mr. Beres resented the imputation around Norwalk at this time that the veterans were "guys snooping behind bushes, watching houses, and acting like totalitarians." News of the turn-in policy became public when it was announced as a feature designed to spark the membership drive carried on this week in Norwalk as it is throughout the nation.

Both Mr. Beres and Mr. Post were enthusiastic over the recruiting prospect, for the post had a record high of 350 paid-up members on Jan. 10. It is now hoped to reach 500 this year.

A sharp counterattack against the veterans' organization has been started in Connecticut by the state branch of Americans for Democratic Action. A display advertisement in The Norwalk Hour, over the signatures of Alfred Baker Lewis of Greenwich, Devere Allen of Wilton and Donald M. Douglas, also of Wilton, says:

"The veterans of foreign wars themselves are un-American. For the post does not allow the people so suspected a chance to answer the charges and clear themselves before they are smeared, and does not tell the public what tests are used to determine whether or not their fellow-citizens are doing things not related to a strong America.

"If any reader feels as we do, that such secret smears are un-American, please get in touch with one of the undersigned, and we will be glad to send you more information about the truly liberal and truly effective anti-Communist measures we stand for, in contrast to the police state methods of secret smears that are too often being adopted lately."

January 27, 1954

BROWNELL PLANS ANTI-SPY DIVISION

New Security Unit to Handle Treason, Sabotage Cases, Supplementing F.B.I. Work

Special to The New York Times.

WASHINGTON, May 4—Attorney General Herbert Brownell Jr. will announce soon the establishment of a Division of Internal Security in the Department of Justice.

It will handle cases involving espionage, treason, sabotage, Federal employe loyalty or security risks and subversive activities —in fact, all court proceedings dealing with matters affecting the internal security of the United States and its possessions.

The division will be headed by an Assistant Attorney General, bringing to eight the number of Assistant Attorneys General. It will be the first new division set up in the department in a number of years.

Justice Department officials would not comment today upon plans formulated in recent weeks. However, Mr. Brownell may disclose details of the plan in an address scheduled for this week-end.

Reflects Official Concern

The decision to create a Division of Internal Security reflects the concern over such problems that has been manifested by Mr. Brownell and his associates since the Eisenhower Administration came into office. The Attorney General has said in several public statements and addresses that stamping out subversive activities was a major problem of law enforcement.

Some of the procedures established to deal with internal security matters have been widely criticized. This was particularly true of an order issued in April, 1953, that established basic security standards for Federal employes.

The fact that the line of demarcation between actual subversion and lesser security risks was not finely drawn gave rise to much of the criticism. Many felt that persons denied Government employment or dismissed from it might be branded as disloyal when they were "security risks" solely because of personal habits or indiscreet associations.

Mr. Brownell, however, has held to his position that the Administration's internal security program is fair.

It was understood that the new division would supplement the work of the Federal Bureau of Investigation. Internal security investigations now constitute a substantial part of the workload of the F. B. I., which will continue to operate as in the past.

Prosecution of cases developed by the F. B. I., however, would be a function of the new division, it was understood. Presumably its aim would include tightening the enforcement of internal security laws and expediting such cases through the courts.

May 5, 1954

OPPENHEIMER LOSES APPEAL TO A.E.C., 4 TO 1

CLEARANCE DENIED

By JAMES RESTON

Special to The New York Times.

WASHINGTON, June 29—Dr. J. Robert Oppenheimer, the man who directed the making of the first atomic bomb, today lost his long fight for reinstatement as an adviser to the Government.

The Atomic Energy Commission announced this afternoon that it had voted 4 to 1 to deny him further access to secret Government information.

Three members of the commission—Rear Admiral Lewis L. Strauss, Chairman; Joseph Campbell and Eugene M. Zuckert—voted against him (1) because of "proof of fundamental defects in his character"; and (2) because his association with known Communists "extended far beyond the tolerable limits of prudence and self-restraint."

One other member, Thomas E. Murray, concurred in this judgment but went beyond it. Unlike the commission's Special Security Clearance Board (the Gray board), which voted 2 to 1 against clearance but praised Dr. Oppenheimer's loyalty and discretion in handling atomic secrets, Mr. Murray condemned him for failing to show "exact fidelity" and "obedience" to the Government's security regulations. Mr. Murray concluded: "He was disloyal."

Dr. Henry DeWolf Smyth, the senior member of the commission, wrote the lone dissent.

"I agree with the 'clear conclusion' of the Gray board," he said, "that he is completely loyal, and I do not believe he is a security risk."

Further Plea Unlikely

Dr. Oppenheimer could still appeal to President Eisenhower, but this is thought unlikely.

The decision was announced by the A. E. C. at 4 P. M. Representative W. Sterling Cole, Republican of upstate New York and chairman of the Joint Congressional Atomic Energy Committee, announced the decision on the floor of the House during the foreign aid debate. It was greeted by a smattering of applause.

[In a statement issued in New York Tuesday night, Dr. Oppenheimer said that Dr. Smyth's dissenting opinion "says what needs to be said." He refrained from commenting directly on the commission's decision, but said:

["Our country is fortunate in its scientists, in their high skill and their devotion. I know that they will work faithfully to preserve and strengthen this country. I hope that the fruit of their work will be used with humanity, with wisdom and with courage. I know that their counsel when sought will be given honestly and freely. I hope that it will be heard."]

Many Roles End

The situation now is as follows:

Dr. Oppenheimer's contract as a consultant to the A. E. C. ends tomorrow and will not be renewed. He no longer will be called upon, as he has been in the past, to advise the National Security Council on such things as continental defense; the Defense Department on its new weapons program; the State Department on international control of atomic energy.

Though he is in possession of most of the secrets of the atomic and hydrogen bomb programs, he will be placed, more or less permanently, behind the "blank wall" that was put between him and classified information last Dec. 3 on the personal order of President Eisenhower.

Finally, it was generally assumed that, because his reliability, character and loyalty to the security regulations of the Government had been officially challenged, he would resign as Director of the Institute for Advanced Studies at Princeton, N. J., and be refused clearance on all allied Government atomic projects.

The majority opinion (Strauss-Campbell-Zuckert) differed from the Gray board's majority (Gordon Gray, president of the University of North Carolina, and Thomas A. Morgan, former president of the Sperry Corporation) in two main respects.

It did not attest to his loyalty or discretion, as the Gray board majority had done; and it did not condemn him for his role in opposing the development of the hydrogen bomb in 1949.

In fact, all the commissioners emphasized that they had not reached their conclusions on the basis of anything he had said or done, or failed to say or do, in the controversy over that weapon.

The commission majority pointed out that it had a duty under the Atomic Energy Act of 1946 to reach a determination as to the "character" and "associations" of A. E. C. employes as well as on their "loyalty."

The majority then made these statements:

¶"On the basis of the record before the commission * * * we find Dr. Oppenheimer is not entitled to the continued confidence of the Government and of this commission because of the proof of fundamental defects in his 'character.' * * *

¶"In respect to the criterion of 'associations,' we find that his associations with persons known to him to be Communists have extended far beyond the tolerable limits of prudence and self-restraint which are to be expected of one holding the high positions that the Government has continuously entrusted to him since 1942. * * *

¶"A Government official having access to the most sensitive areas of restricted data and to the innermost details of national war plans and weapons must measure up to exemplary standards of reliability, self-discipline and trustworthiness. Dr. Oppenheimer has fallen far short of acceptable standards."

The New York Times
Lewis L. Strauss

The commission majority members listed six incidents that persuaded them of fundamental defects in Dr. Oppenheimer's character:

¶He admitted he had lied to a military intelligence officer (Col. Borist T. Pash) who was trying to get a straight story about a Soviet agent who had sought secret information from Dr. Oppenheimer.

¶He told the Gray board he would not have asked for the employment of one Giovanni Rossi Lomanitz at Los Alamos if he had known that Lomanitz was an active Communist who had given information to an unauthorized person. On Aug. 26, 1943, however, he had told Colonel Pash that he did not know that Lomanitz was a Communist and that he (Lomanitz) had given out information to an unauthorized person.

¶In 1943 he testified that he did not know Rudy Lambert, a Communist party functionary, but recently under oath he testified that he had seen Lambert at least half a dozen times before 1943 and knew he was a Communist.

¶In 1949 he testified before the House Un-American Activities Committee about the Communist party membership of Dr. Bernard Peters and later wrote a letter to The Rochester Times-Union which, in effect, contradicted that testimony.

¶He testified before the Gray board that the General Advisory Committee of the A. E. C. had been "surprisingly unanimous" in its recommendation against the hydrogen bomb program, but did not testify that one of the members of the committee had in fact written him a letter—before the General Advisory Committee met—favoring production of the hydrogen bomb.

¶Finally, in 1950, he told an agent of the Federal Bureau of Investigation that he had not known Joseph Weinberg to be a member of the Communist party, but on Sept. 12, 1943, he told another Government official that

Weinberg was a Communist party member.

"The catalogue does not end with these six examples," the majority said. "The work of military intelligence, the Federal Bureau of Investigation and the Atomic Energy Commission—all at one time or another have felt the effect of his falsehoods, evasions and misrepresentations."

"Chevalier Incident" Cited

There was reason for believing, however, that the so-called "Chevalier incident" was more damaging to Dr. Oppenheimer's fight for reinstatement than any other. Indeed, it can be stated on fairly reliable authority that at least one of the commission members who voted against reinstatement would have switched but for this incident.

In the Chevalier incident, Dr. Oppenheimer was questioned in 1943 by Colonel Pash, Col. John Lansdale Jr., and Lieut. Gen. Leslie R. Groves, all officials at Los Alamos, about the attempt to obtain information from him on the atomic bomb project in the interest of the Soviet Government.

He waited eight months before mentioning the occurrence to the proper authorities. Thereafter for almost four months he refused to name the individual (Haakon Chevalier) who approached him.

Moreover, on Feb. 25, 1950, Dr. Oppenheimer tried to help Chevalier to get a United States passport.

Later that year Chevalier stayed with Dr. Oppenheimer for several days at the latter's home. In December, 1953, Dr. Oppenheimer visited with Chevalier privately on two occasions in Paris, and lent his name to Chevalier's dealings with the United States Embassy in Paris on a problem that, according to Dr. Oppenheimer involved Chevalier's clearance.

Late Associations Scored

The majority seemed to forgive the scientist for his earlier Communist associations, but it was clearly critical, as was the Gray board and Dr. Smyth, the lone dissenter, of his continuing this association right up until December of 1953.

Incidentally, there is one aspect of this visit with Chevalier that is not mentioned anywhere in the testimony but is known to have worried some of the commissioners. This was that, though Dr. Oppenheimer was not sure, even in 1953, that Chevalier was not a Communist, he visited him in Paris and took the chance that, like many other nuclear scientists, he might have been forced at gun-point into a plane and taken behind the Iron Curtain.

Dr. Oppenheimer scoffs at this possibility, pointing out that the United States Government knew where he was, but others here cite this prospect as evidence that he was casual about security matters that affected not only his own safety but the safety of the country.

In his dissent from the positions taken by the other four commissioners, Dr. Smyth looked to the future rather than to the past.

Because Dr. Oppenheimer was one of the most knowledgeable and lucid physicists in the United

States, Dr. Smyth observed, his services could be of great value to the country in the future. Therefore, he argued, the only question before the Atomic Energy Commission was whether there was a possibility that Dr. Oppenheimer intentionally or unintentionally would reveal secret information to persons who should not have it.

"To me," he said, "this is what is meant within our security system by the term 'security risk.' Character and associations are important only in so far as they bear on the possibility that secret information will be improperly revealed.

"In my opinion the most important evidence in this regard is the fact that there is no indication in the entire record that Dr. Oppenheimer has ever divulged any secret information."

Dr. Smyth took up the six incidents catalogued against the scientist by the majority and sought to show that these did not justify what he called the "severe" decision of the majority.

There was a marked contrast in the estimates of the commissioners about the effect on the commission of the loss of Dr. Oppenheimer.

Dr. Smyth said that failure to employ a man of such great talents might impair the strength and power of the country, but Commissioner Campbell, relying on the judgment of the general manager, felt that Dr. Oppenheimer was not "indispensable."

He observed that the Atomic Energy Commission was absolutely vital to the survival of the nation; that the security regulations were intentionally severe; that no violations could be countenanced and that, "where responsibility is highest, fidelity should be most perfect."

"The American citizen in private life, the man who is not engaged in governmental service," he said, "is not bound by the requirements of the security system. However, those American citizens who have the privilege of participating in the operations of Government, especially in sensitive agencies, are necessarily subject to this special system of law.

"Consequently, their faithfulness to the lawful Government of the United States, that is to say, their loyalty, must be judged by the standard of their obedience to security regulations. Dr. Oppenheimer was subject to the security system which applies to those engaged in the atomic energy program. The measure of his obedience to the requirements of this system is the decisive measure of his loyalty to his lawful Government. No lesser test will settle the question of his loyalty. Dr. Oppenheimer did not meet this decisive test. He was disloyal."

Commissioner Murray was sharply critical of Dr. Oppenheimer's judgments about the hydrogen bomb project. He asserted flatly that the scientist's political and technical reasons for producing the bomb had "been proved wrong." He defended Dr. Oppenheimer's right to put forward "moral reasons" against producing the hydrogen bomb, but observed that he (Oppenheimer) was no "expert in morality."

It was not on this ground, however, that he reached the stark conclusion: "He was disloyal." He put the main test on the question of the scientist's "obedience" to the security regulations of the Government. Commissioner Murray put it this way:

"The American citizen recognizes that his Government, for all its imperfections, is a government under law, of law, by law; therefore, he is loyal to it.

Furthermore, he recognizes that his Government, because it is lawful, has the right and the responsibility to protect itself against the action of those who would subvert it.

"The cooperative effort of the citizen with the rightful action of American Government in its discharge of this primary responsibility also belongs to the very substance of American loyalty. This is the crucial principle in the present case."

Commissioner Zuckert, whose

term on the commission will end tomorrow, said it was "a source of real sadness" to him that his last act as a public official should involve the denial of clearance to a man who had made "a substantial contribution to the United States."

This thread of "sadness" ran through his separate opinion. As long as there were human emotions like love of family or human feelings like pain, he observed, everyone was to some degree vulnerable to influence, and thus

a potential risk in some degree to our security.

"But," he concluded, "when I see such a combination of seriously disturbing actions and events as are present in this case, then I believe the risk to security passes acceptable bounds. All these actions and events and the relation between them make no other conclusion possible in my opinion than to deny clearance to Dr. Oppenheimer."

June 30, 1954

THE COMMUNIST CONTROL ACT

The bill depriving the Communist party of legal rights is an emphatic expression on the part of Congress that communism in this and every other country is "an instrumentality of a conspiracy" on behalf of the Soviet Union. With this judgment we believe practically every loyal American would agree. Yet the question remains whether we hurt communism or whether we hurt ourselves more by passing a measure such as this, and by passing it in the manner in which this one was stampeded through Congress.

The bill that has now become known as "the Communist Control Act of 1954" was promoted as a political coup by so-called Democratic "liberals" headed by Senator Humphrey of Minnesota, who is running

for re-election this fall. The Democrats had been goaded for months, even years, by Republican demagogues charging them with "twenty years of treason" and the like; and this time they apparently decided that they could out-demagogue the Republicans. In the present atmosphere, the Democrats reasoned, they would get credit for being more anti-Communist than the Republicans because they were proposing legislation superficially even more anti-Communist than anything the Republicans had come up with. The Administration resisted this bill in the form in which it was passed twice by the Senate and endorsed by the House; and in hasty conferences the measure was modified and brought somewhat more into conformity with our other laws and institutions.

We think there is much to be said

for removing the Communist party from the ballot and depriving it of legal rights; but we think the pros and cons ought to have been discussed more fully and in a more rational atmosphere. There is no doubt that this bill, even as amended, raises many constitutional and practical questions. While the bill does accurately record the contempt and hatred of the American people for comm—'sm, it still will not destroy the idea of communism in the minds of those persons who, believe in it. And we do not think that the country is in such imminent danger of being taken over by Communist subversion that frantic and ill-considered legislation adopted in circumstances such as this is either necessary or desirable.

August 21, 1954

Text of Eisenhower Statement on Red Control Bill

DENVER, Aug. 24 (AP)—Following is the text of President Eisenhower's statement today on the signing of legislation to outlaw the Communist party and penalizing Red-infiltrated labor unions:

I have today signed S. 3706, An Act to Make Illegal the Communist Party and to Prohibit Members of Communist Organizations from Serving in Certain Representative Capacities.

The American people are determined to protect themselves and their institutions against any organization in their midst which, purporting to be a political party within the normally accepted meaning, is actually a conspiracy dedicated to the violent overthrow of our entire form of government. The American people, likewise, are determined to accomplish this in strict conformity with the requirements of justice, fair play and the Constitution of the United States. They realize that employment of any other means would react unfavorably against the innocent as well as the guilty, and in the long run would distort and damage the judicial procedures of our country. The whole se-

ries of bills that the Administration has sponsored in this field have been designed in just this spirit and with just these purposes.

The new law which I am signing today includes one of the many recommendations made by this Administration to support existing statutes in defeating the Communist conspiracy in this country. Administratively, we have in the past nineteen months stepped up enforcement of laws against subversives. As a result, forty-one top Communist leaders have been convicted, thirty-five more are indicted and scheduled for trial, and 105 subversive aliens have been deported.

Cites New Laws

The new laws enacted in this session of the Congress provide to the F. B. I. and the Department of Justice much more effective weapons to help destroy the Communist menace. They include the following:

1. Last week I signed a bill granting immunity from prosecution to certain suspected persons in order to aid in obtaining the conviction of subversives. Investigation and prosecution of crimes involving national security have been seriously hampered by witnesses who have invoked

the constitutional privilege against self-incrimination embodied in the Fifth Amendment. This act provides a new means of breaking through the secrecy which is characteristic of traitors, spies and saboteurs.

2. Congress has passed a bill providing for the loss of citizenship by those advocating the overthrow of our Government by force and violence. In carrying out the Administration's recommendation that any citizen who knowingly and actively participates in the Communist conspiracy to overthrow the Government by force and violence should be regarded as renouncing his allegiance to the United States and forfeiting his right to citizenship, the Congress has reinforced our historic concept that citizenship is a right only of those who bear true faith and allegiance to the United States and its free institutions. This bill to which I shall presently give my approval adheres closely to our standards of due process of law and provides that the loss of citizenship shall become effective only upon conviction by a court of competent jurisdiction.

3. My approval has already been given to the bill which carries out the recommendation by

this Administration increasing the penalty for harboring or concealing any person who is a fugitive from justice. There are at the present time five Communist leaders who have been indicted or convicted under the Smith Act who are fugitives from justice. This bill serves notice that any person who assists such fugitives in any way to conceal their whereabouts will be subject to severe penalty.

4. My approval has already been given to a bill designed to serve as an effective additional deterrent to wilful bail jumping by making such act a crime subject to severe penalty.

5. The Congress has passed, and I shall approve, a bill to include within the definition of sabotage, acts involving the use of radio-active, biological and chemical agents not presently covered by the law.

6. The foregoing bill also includes a provision for the death penalty for persons found guilty of peacetime espionage.

7. I have already approved a bill requiring "Communist-action" or "Communist-front" organizations, which must register under the Internal Security Act, to submit full information regarding printing equipment in

233

their custody or control.

8. I shall shortly sign a bill preventing the payment of annuities by the United States to former officers and employes who have been convicted of certain criminal offenses. This act includes those who have made false statements regarding past or present membership in the Communist party.

Defines Present Law

In addition to the foregoing measures enacted by the Eighty-third Congress, the bill which I have signed today further carries out an important part of the recommendations made by this Administration. It creates within the framework of the Internal Security Act of 1950 a new category entitled, "Communist-infiltrated organizations."

This provision will enable the Administration to assist members of those few labor organizations which are dominated by Communists, to rid themselves of the Communist control under which they have been forced to operate.

In the final days of the session, the Congress added to this measure certain clauses denying to Communists all rights, privileges and immunities which they have under the Federal Government. These provisions also subject members of the Communist party or its front organizations, having knowledge of their revolutionary aims and objectives, to their provisions and penalties of the Internal Security Act. The full impact of these clauses upon the enforcement of the laws by which we are now fighting the Communist conspiracy in this country will require further careful study. I am satisfied, however, that they were not intended to impair or abrogate any portion of the Internal Security Act or the criminal statutes under which the leaders of the Communist party are now being prosecuted and that they may prove helpful in several respects.

The Congress has thus enacted a substantial portion of the Administration's recommendations to strengthen our internal security laws.

In order to provide aggressive administration and enforcement of the foregoing measures, I have already strengthened the mechanism for carrying out more effectively our entire anti-Communist program by the creation of the Division of Internal Security in the Department of Justice.

We have made great progress in the past year and a half in prosecuting the leadership of the Communist conspiracy. I am proud that in this battle against the subversive elements in this country we have been able to preserve the rights of the accused in accordance with our traditions and the Bill of Rights. The Eighty-third Congress has added effective new legal weapons to assist us in our fight to destroy communism in this country.

August 25, 1954

Provisions of the Bill

DENVER, Aug. 24 (AP)—Following are the main provisions of the bill signed by President Eisenhower today to outlaw the Communist party:

[1]

Congress finds and declares that "the Communist party of the United States, although purportedly a political party, is in fact an instrumentality of a conspiracy to overthrow the Government of the United States."

[2]

The Communist party, or any of its successors whose object is to overthrow the Government, is denied "any of the rights, privileges and immunities attendant upon legal bodies created under the jurisdiction of the laws of the United States."

[3]

Whoever "knowingly or willfully becomes or remains a member" of the Communist party or any other organization aimed at the forcible overthrow of the Government, with knowledge of the organization's purpose, shall be subject to the penalties provided for members of "Communist-action" groups under the 1950 Internal Security Law.

Under the Internal Security Act, members of organizations found by the Subversive Activities Control Board to be "Communist-action" groups are ineligible for non-elective Federal jobs, jobs in defense plants and for passports.

In addition, if they fail to register with the Attorney General, they may be imprisoned for five years and fined $10,000.

[4]

The bill sets out fourteen criteria that juries may consider in determining membership or participation in the Communist party. However, these criteria are neither conclusive nor exclusive.

[5]

Labor unions or business organizations found to be Communist-infiltrated are deprived of their legal standing before the National Labor Relations Board for collective bargaining purposes. Determinations are to be made by the Subversive Activities Control Board on petition of the Attorney General. Findings are subject to court review.

To be found "Communist-infiltrated" a labor union or other organization must:

¶Be "substantially directed, dominated or controlled by an individual or individuals" who are working for the world Communist movement or have been within the past three years.

¶Be "serving" or, within three years, have served as a means for "giving of aid or support to" the world Communist movement or as a means for "the impairment of the military strength of the United States or its industrial capacity to furnish logistical or other material support required by its armed forces."

August 25, 1954

McCARTHYISM FADES

Tumultuous Issue

McCarthy vs. Eisenhower

Four years and nineteen days ago the junior U. S. Senator from Wisconsin—a former judge and Marine veteran, then a relatively obscure figure on Capitol Hill—stood before a Republican audience in Wheeling, W. Va. Joseph R. McCarthy said: "* * * I have here in my hands a list of 205 [the Senator in his book has since said he used the figure fifty-seven]—a list of names that were made known to the Secretary of State as being members of the Communist Party and who nevertheless are still working and shaping policy in the State Department."

The Wheeling speech opened one of the most extraordinary chapters in U. S. political history. In the years since, the very name McCarthy has come to symbolize an issue of great force. The Senator has charged the Democratic Administrations with a record of "twenty years of treason." Now armed with broad investigating power in a Republican Congress, he has challenged the Eisenhower Administration on many fronts, contending that it needs prodding to get Communists out of Government.

The McCarthy question has deeply divided and enflamed American opinion. On the one hand are those who cheer the Senator on with the cry that "McCarthy knows how to handle these Reds." On the other hand are those who deplore him as a demagogue who is imperiling American liberties.

Last week Washington rocked with the most tumultuous controversy so far between Senator McCarthy and the Eisenhower Administration. The controversy grew out of a relatively narrow question— why the Army allowed a dental officer, whom it suspected of being a Communist, to leave the service with an honorable discharge. It gathered heat rapidly the week before last when the Senator scathingly rebuked Army personnel involved, and Secretary of the Army Robert T. Stevens moved for a showdown on the question of Executive versus Legislative authority.

At the beginning of last week Mr. Stevens seemed to be looking forward to the showdown with confidence. Then something happened. There were reports that Republican professionals were cautioning against the effect of an open row in the party in an election year. In midweek, the Secretary and the Senator came to what was called an "understanding." But its terms were widely interpreted as a "surrender," and a wave of shock went across the nation. The intensity of the reaction set in motion efforts in the White House and on the Hill to salvage the Secretary's position. Thursday he issued a statement claiming that he had not yielded, and President Eisenhower backed him up "100 per cent." But Senator McCarthy stuck to his guns also.

Thus at the week-end it appeared that a battle had been fought but the war would go on. In Congress Republican leaders talked of restraints on the Senator's investigative tactics. There were doubts that the party professionals, who have regarded Mr. McCarthy as a campaign asset, would be eager to curb him seriously. But at the same time the feeling was that the President would now be under pressure to draw a firmer line on Mr. McCarthy's incursions into the fields of Executive authority and Presidential leadership. In the apparent hope of giving full play to these conflicting forces within the G. O. P. most Democrats, all during last week's furor, were conspicuously silent.

The Setting

These are the facts in the case that led to the McCarthy-Army controversy last week:

In October, 1952, Dr. Irving Peress, a dentist from Queens in New York City, was notified he would be drafted under the medical draft law. He applied for and got a reserve commission as a captain. On Oct. 28 he was given a standard questionnaire on, among other things, his loyalty. In the space provided for answers on loyalty he claimed the privilege under the Fifth Amendment of refusing to answer. Army regulations did not then require complete answers.

On Jan. 3, 1953, Peress was called to active duty. A month later his refusals to answer were noted and the Army started a loyalty investigation as required by Army regulations. In June, 1953, as a result of the investigation, the Commandant at Camp Kilmer, N. J., where Peress was stationed, recommended that he be dismissed. The Army says that, in accordance with procedure, the case was referred to the Army personnel board, which notified Peress of the evidence against him and invited his reply. Many weeks passed in the interchange of communications. When Peress again cited the Fifth Amendment, the Army studied what to do next. In a separate action in October, 1953, Peress was promoted to major under automatic provisions of the law requiring advancement of medical men according to age and professional experience.

On Dec. 3, the McCarthy committee opened an investigation of Peress. On Dec. 30, the Army decided to discharge him. On Jan. 18 orders were sent to Peress' Kilmer commandant—now Brig. Gen. Ralph W. Zwicker—for his honorable discharge at his own pleasure within ninety days.

On Jan. 30, Senator McCarthy questioned Peress at a hearing in New York. Peress refused to answer most questions, citing the Fifth Amendment. The Senator demanded that Peress be held in the Army for court-martial. On Feb. 2, at Peress' own request, he was honorably discharged.

The discharge incensed Mr. McCarthy. He wrote Secretary Stevens demanding that the officers involved in the Peress promotion and discharge be investigated for possible court-martial. Mr. Stevens conceded that the Peress case had revealed defects in Army procedure, promised vigorous action if an inquiry disclosed anything irregular in the promotion and discharge, but argued that there had been no grounds for a court-martial of Peress. The Senator termed the answer "double-talk" and called a new hearing ten days ago.

After wrangling with other Army officials, the Senator questioned General Zwicker in secret session. The record of that session was made public last Monday. It showed that the Senator hammered at the general on the questions of why Peress was honorably discharged and who ordered it, that the general replied repeatedly that he had to obey orders and was forbidden, under a Presidential directive, dating back to the Truman Administration, to reveal details of loyalty investigations. The Senator's tone grew sharp. Among the things he said to General Zwicker were:

General, let's try and be truthful. * * * I cannot help but question either your honesty or your intelligence. * * * Don't you give me that double-talk. * * * Anyone with the brains of a five-year-old child can understand that question. * * * Any [general] who says, 'I will protect another general who protected Communists' is not fit to wear that uniform * * *.

The Senator wound up by ordering General Zwicker and the Adjutant General to appear the following Tuesday. But when word of the Zwicker questioning reached Mr. Stevens, he reacted sharply. He ordered the two officers not to appear Tuesday and said he would testify himself.

Out of the Peress case there had now emerged two main issues and two conflicting points of view. In the McCarthy view the main issue was why Peress was promoted and then honorably discharged despite the fact that the Army for many months had evidence that he was a Communist. The Senator insisted on the right of a Congressional committee to get all the facts.

The Army view was that the main issue was the Senator's tactics in "abusing" and "humiliating" a loyal officer and pillorying him and other officials for carrying out their orders. As to Peress, the Army contended that honorable discharge was the quickest way to get him out of the service. At the same time, Army officials acknowledged privately that the Peress case "looked bad" and was hard to defend—regulations or no regulations.

The Big Week

Thus was the stage set for what was widely billed as "The Show-

down" between Senator McCarthy and the Administration. This was the tumultuous week:

SUNDAY

At the White House (the President was still on his golfing holiday in California) the staff was reported to be worried. There was little zest for the approaching battle. A New York Times correspondent sent this description of White House thinking:

"Stevens, of course, would want to talk about Zwicker. But McCarthy was going to talk about Peress, and being chairman, he would ask the questions, and the Secretary would have to answer them. By the time another Senator got a chance to ask about Zwicker, TV time would have been dominated by the Peress discussion."

On the Hill, Republicans were equally worried. They did not relish a public Republican brawl over communism—the issue that was to be used against Democrats. Thus there was growing feeling at both ends of Pennsylvania Avenue that perhaps a compromise could be found.

MONDAY

At a Washington Birthday celebration at Valley Forge, Senator Karl E. Mundt of South Dakota, a member of the McCarthy committee, talked with Secretary Stevens on a possible patch-up. In Washington, Senator Everett M. Dirksen, another committee member, with the same idea in mind, asked Senator McCarthy to postpone the Stevens hearing until Thursday. Senator McCarthy was willing. He had another iron heating. He summoned Mrs. Annie Lee Moss, an Army employe.

TUESDAY

Mrs. Mary Markward, a former F. B. I. under-cover agent, told the McCarthy subcommittee that an Annie Lee Moss had been on Communist party lists until 1945. Senator McCarthy said that Mrs. Moss was employed as a "code clerk" in the Army message center in the Pentagon, and decoded "top secret" messages. The Army said that Mrs. Moss was merely a "relay machine operator" who fed perforated tape from receiving to transmitting machines; that the coded messages on the tape were unclassified, and that Mrs. Moss had no access to codes or the cryptograph room.

The Moss case gave added impetus to the feeling among Republicans that the McCarthy-Stevens bout should be canceled. According to reports, White House officials, in talking to Mr. Stevens, conveyed the impression that an accommodation should be sought, but there was no suggestion that he yield on principle. In any event, a luncheon was arranged with the Republican members of the committee for Wednesday. The three Democratic members were not invited.

WEDNESDAY

Just before noon Secretary Stevens met with H. Struve Hensel,

McCarthyism Fades

Defense Department General Counsel, for a run-through on the questions Senator McCarthy would likely fire at the Secretary the next day. When he left, Mr. Stevens said nothing about his upcoming luncheon.

The luncheon—fried chicken—was held in the Capitol Hill office of the Senate Republican Campaign Committee. All the Republican members of the subcommittee were present—Senators McCarthy, Mundt, Dirksen, and Charles E. Potter of Michigan. The meeting lasted two hours.

The Senators, it was reported later, put tremendous heat on Mr. Stevens. According to accounts by his friends, the Senators told him that a public row would jeopardize the party's chances in November, that it would fuzz up the Communist issue, and that he owed it to the party to retreat.

For his part, Mr. Stevens was reported to have asked assurances that Army witnesses would not be mistreated in the future. He later insisted these assurances were given. Two of the Senators supported his account. Senator McCarthy denied that he made any promise.

At 2:55 the doors were opened. Reporters and photographers poured in. Mr. Stevens was poker-faced. Senator McCarthy sat beside him, all smiles. Mr. Mundt read a "Memorandum of Understanding." It was short—only five paragraphs. It made no mention of treatment of witnesses or other concessions. This was the critical paragraph:

There is complete agreement * * * that the Secretary of the Army will order the Inspector General to complete the investigation * * * in the Peress case as rapidly as possible; and he will give the committee the names of everyone involved in the promotion and honorable discharge of Peress; and that such individuals will be available to appear before the committee.

When Mr. Stevens returned to the Pentagon, he found Roger M. Kyes, Under Secretary of Defense, Gen. Matthew B. Ridgway, Army Chief of Staff, and H. Struve Heusel in his office. He told them he had got what he went for—a promise of fair treatment. General Ridgway shook his hand warmly. The meeting disbanded. But soon after, one of the officials secured the text of the memorandum. Another meeting was called—without Mr. Stevens. It was agreed that the Secretary was in trouble.

Mr. Stevens did not have to wait long to taste the ashes. It was reported to him that Senator McCarthy had told a reporter that Mr. Stevens could not have surrendered "more abjectly if he had got down on his knees." Then the late editions of the afternoon papers hit the streets. Across the nation, the headline verbs were: "SURRENDERS," "CAPITULATES," "RETREATS."

Mr. Stevens was reported "steaming mad" at the press interpretation. He contended that there had been no surrender. He leaked a statement which he had intended to read at the hearing. It said: "I am here today to defend an officer of the United States Army * * * who was humiliated at a hearing before this committee * * *. I feel that the integrity of the entire Army is involved."

On Wednesday night Mr. Stevens called James C. Hagerty, the White House Press Secretary for guidance. He also called several Senators. They told reporters later that he was sobbing, and said he would have to resign because he had "lost standing" at the Pentagon.

THURSDAY

Overnight things had come to a boil. The New York Times headline read: "STEVENS BOWS TO M'CARTHY." Across the country, editorials were protesting the "surrender" in angry words. The Administration had made "a public display of the white feather" (Los Angeles Daily News). It had ordered an "ignominious retreat" (Nashville Tennessean). The "disgraceful cave-in" was not Secretary Steven's responsibility alone—"It goes back to the President" (Washington Post). "[McCarthy's] assault * * * was a supreme test of the ability of men in high office to meet a threat which in other parts of the world has been fatal to liberty itself. They have failed to meet that test" (New York Herald Tribune). Even the pro-McCarthy Chicago Tribune rebuked the Senator: "It seems to us that Sen. McCarthy will better serve his cause if he learns to distinguish the role of investigator from the role of avenging angel."

And the wits of Washington were up early. One said: "The Secretary didn't mean to surrender to the Senators; he merely thought they wanted to look at his sword." An old Western gag was revived—"Then inserting our nose between his teeth, we had him."

The feeling of the Army was vividly portrayed by the remark of a senior staff officer at the Pentagon: "Private David Schine is the only man in the Army today with any morale." (Private Schine, until drafted, was on the McCarthy committee staff.)

Plainly something had to be done to offset the reaction. But the White House staff still hoped to keep the President aloof from the fray. At Vice President Nixon's suggestion, it was reported, President Eisenhower sent for Senator Dirksen. A draft of a statement was given to the Senator. It made the points that Mr. Stevens had not surrendered and that the committee would give assurances that witnesses were to be treated with respect henceforth. The President asked Mr. Dirksen's help in getting the four Republican members to issue the statement.

Mr. Dirksen went back to the Hill. All day the Senators fussed over the language of the statement while the White House waited. Senator McCarthy objected to any language intimating that witnesses had been abused. Finally they agreed.

About 4 P. M. Vice President Nixon brought the Senators' amended version to the White House. A conference was assembled in the East Wing. Present were the Vice President, Mr. Kyes, Mr. Stevens, Sherman Adams, White House chief of staff, and several other Pentagon and White House officials. The President, who often finds release from tension in exercise, was practicing chip shots on the South Lawn.

The Senators' statement was not acceptable to Mr. Stevens. At 5:30 the meeting broke up. A smaller group then met for thirty minutes with the President in the second floor study. It was decided that Mr. Stevens should issue his own statement. He also carried his point—which he had been fighting for since the night before—that he must have the President's full support. A statement was drawn up. The President approved it.

In Hagerty's Office

At 6:15, reporters were admitted to Mr. Hagerty's office. Mr. Kyes, who as late as that afternoon, was reported as saying that Mr. Stevens had no other course but to resign, was standing beside the Army Secretary. Mr. Stevens began reading in a steady voice:

I did not at that meeting [recede] * * * from any of the principles upon which I stand. * * * I shall never accede to [Army personnel] * * * being browbeaten or humiliated. * * * From assurances which I have received from members of the committee, I am confident they will not permit such conditions to develop in the future.

When Mr. Stevens returned to the Pentagon, his staff applauded him. Mr. Stevens was smiling broadly. He said: "We've certainly got a Commander in Chief. He stepped right up and hit a home run."

Up on the Hill, Senator McCarthy said Mr. Stevens had made a "completely false statement" about the assurances. He denied there had been any abuse. But, he said, he had made it clear to Mr. Stevens that if witnesses "are not frank and truthful * * * they will be examined vigorously to get the truth."

Now the issue was joined.

FRIDAY

Republicans began moving in behind the President. Senators Mundt and Potter said Mr. Stevens rightly claimed that assurances had been given against the abuse of witnesses. A meeting of the Senate Republican Policy Committee, hastily summoned by Chairman Homer Ferguson, unanimously voted a study of the rules for investigating committees. Republicans made no secret of the fact that the study had grown out of the latest McCarthy fracas and was aimed at curbing one-man inquiries.

Senator McCarthy himself mixed soft and tough talk. He said: "Eisenhower said he was against browbeating witnesses—I am too." But he said he was going to continue exposing Communists "even if it embarrasses my own party." He had no objection to the rules study. He wanted the Democrats to attend hearings.

February 28, 1954

236

PRAISE POURS IN ON MURROW SHOW

C. B. S. Says Responses Are 15 to 1 in Favor of Critical Report on McCarthy

By VAL ADAMS

Television viewers across the country continued to voice their reaction in ever mounting numbers yesterday to Edward R. Murrow's critical report on Senator Joseph R. McCarthy.

The Columbia Broadcasting System, which televised the report Tuesday night in the "See It Now" show, said late yesterday that it had received 12,348 telephone calls and telegrams so far in response to the program.

"This is the largest spontaneous response we have ever known," the network added.

Mr. Murrow's report was based largely on filmed excerpts from speeches and investigations conducted by the Wisconsin Republican Senator. The commentator accused him of using half-truths as a staple item and said Senator McCarthy's "primary achievement has been in confusing the public mind as between internal and the external threats of communism."

The network said that among the tabulated responses here, 11,567 persons favored Mr. Murrow's comments and 781 disapproved, a ratio of about 15 to 1.

Survey of Stations

The response made to individual television stations carrying the program also was generally favorable. A survey of stations brought the following comments:

WTOP-TV, Washington — "Received 466 telephone calls, with 454 endorsing program. Program brought the quickest, most instantaneous reaction we've received since telecast made by [then] Senator Richard M. Nixon during the Republican campaign."

WCAN-TV, Milwaukee — "Received upward of 400 telephone calls, every one of them complimentary to program."

WCAU-TV, Philadelphia—"Received eighty-eight calls praising the program and three in protest."

WDTV, Pittsburgh—"Received forty-two phone calls. About twenty-five were pro-Murrow. Three expressed no opinions and remainder asked where they could write or wire Murrow."

KPIX, San Francisco—"Seventy-two callers supported Murrow and five dissented. Switchboard swamped and many calls could not be handled."

WBBM-TV, Chicago — "Received approximately 1,200 calls up to 3 P. M. Wednesday. Ratio breaks down 2 to 1 in favor of Murrow."

WKNB-TV, New Britain, Conn. —"About forty phone calls, all favorable. Station personnel have received hundreds of personal comments on Murrow's 'courage' and urging more programs like it."

Some viewers took their response directly to the Aluminum Company of America, sponsor of the program. Of some 200 phone calls received by the company here, the ratio was about 4 to 1 in favor of the telecast, according to Joseph Steel, public relations representative in the New York office.

Many Letters Written

It was learned that many viewers, unable to break through the jammed switchboards of the network and sponsor, had written letters expressing their opinions.

C. B. S. said it had received more than 1,000 requests to repeat the program, but had made no decision.

Mr. Murrow said on his program that an opportunity to speak on the program would be afforded Senator McCarthy if he "believes we have done violence to his words or pictures." This offer had nothing to do with the Senator's demands that C. B. S. and the National Broadcasting Company grant him time to answer charges made in a speech last week by Adlai E. Stevenson, Democratic Presidential candidate in 1952.

In Washington, Mr. McCarthy said he had not seen the Murrow show and that he was "inclined" to think he would accept the offer of time to reply.

The Senator will appear today on the program of Fulton Lewis Jr., at 7 P. M. over WOR and the Mutual Broadcasting System radio network. Mr. Lewis extended the invitation to Senator McCarthy because, as Mr. Lewis expressed it, of "the refusal of N. B. C. and C. B. S. to grant you time, and in view of Edward R. Murrow's distorted and slanted tirade against you."

Senator McCarthy also received another offer of free radio time from WGN, The Chicago Tribune station.

Meanwhile, the Radio, Newsreel, Television Working Press Association of New York protested in a wire to Senator McCarthy that he was discriminatory because he refused to accept C. B. S. and N. B. C. men at a news conference here Tuesday. At the conference, Senator McCarthy had said he would not talk or pose for C. B. S. and N. B. C. reporters.

March 11, 1954

H-BOMB HELD BACK, M'CARTHY ASSERTS

Asks Inquiry Into '18-Month Deliberate Delay' — He Replies to Murrow

By PETER KIHSS

Senator Joseph R. McCarthy charged last night that there had been an "eighteen-month deliberate delay" in American development of the hydrogen bomb. He demanded to know whether this was caused by "loyal Americans or traitors."

"If there were no Communists in our Government," the Wisconsin Republican exclaimed, in a nation-wide telecast, "why did we delay for eighteen months— delay our research on the hydrogen bomb, even though our intelligence agencies were reporting, day after day, that the Russians were feverishly pushing their development of the hydrogen bomb?

"Our nation may well die because of that eighteen-month deliberate delay. And I ask who caused it? Was it loyal Americans—or was it traitors in our Government?"

[In Washington, The United Press quoted Representative W. Sterling Cole, Republican of Up-state New York and chairman of the Joint Committee on Atomic Energy, as saying that the United States had taken "a long time" deciding to build the hydrogen bomb, "but that does not mean there was anything sinister necessarily."]

Senator McCarthy opened up his new proposed line of inquiry over the forty-two-station Columbia Broadcasting System network television program "See It Now." His twenty-five-minute time had been made available to him by commentator Edward R. Murrow for a reply to a March 9 program criticizing the Senator and his record.

Murrow Is Attacked

In last night's reply, Senator McCarthy charged that Mr. Murrow "as far back as twenty years ago was engaged in propaganda for Communist causes." Asserting the Communist newspaper The Daily Worker had praised Mr. Murrow while attacking himself, Senator McCarthy asserted that if the commentator was giving comfort to the nation's enemies, "he ought not to be brought into the homes of millions of Americans by the Columbia Broadcasting System."

The network issued an immediate statement in which it said that "C. B. S. subscribes fully to the integrity and responsibility of Mr. Murrow as a broadcaster and as a loyal American."

Mr. Murrow said he could not take responsibility for what any Communist publication could say about him, and charged in turn that Senator McCarthy had knowingly accepted Communist support as a 1946 candidate for Senator. He insisted he was opposed to the danger of Communist infiltration, but said it was his devotion to "justice, freedom and fairness" that set him apart from Senator McCarthy.

Senator McCarthy's main attack on Mr. Murrow was once again linked to the broadcaster's connection with the Institute of International Education, of which Mr. Murrow was assistant director from 1932 to 1935 and a trustee since 1937.

The Senator charged that the institute was "chosen to act as representative by a Soviet agency to do a job which would normally be done by the Russian secret police." He said the agency was "the Russian espionage and propaganda organization known as VOKS."

The institute, Senator McCarthy said, selected American students and teachers to attend a Moscow school. Many of those selected, he charged, were later exposed as Communists.

He named Isidor Begun, former Communist lobbyist in Albany, who was acquitted in 1952 of charges under the Smith Act against subversion, and David Zablodowsky, a former United Nations official who resigned after admitting he had worked with the Communist underground in 1936 although denying he was ever a Communist.

Mr. Murrow noted the institute had sponsored a 1934 summer session for American students at Moscow University, as it did for other schools in such countries as England, France and Germany. The only contact VOKS had with the group, he said, was in procuring living and travel facilities, since it was the Soviet bureau in charge of such matters for foreigners, he said.

After that session, he said, the Russians refused to have anything more to do with the institute. When the institute, at the request of the United States Government, tried to arrange for American students to visit Russia after World War II, Mr. Murrow related, it was attacked in European Communist publications as "the center of international propaganda for American reaction." He and John Foster Dulles, as trustees, Mr. Murrow said, were singled out for special attack.

Mr. Murrow observed that the institute is now the United States Government's contracting agency for various student programs abroad, and recalled its program had been endorsed by President Eisenhower in 1948.

Book Dedication Explained

On other charges by Senator McCarthy, Mr. Murrow denied he had ever been a member of the Industrial Workers of the World. He conceded the late Harold J. Laski, who he stressed was a British Socialist, as against Senator McCarthy's label of "Communist," had dedicated a book to him, but noted the dedication was explained as a tribute to his World War II broadcasts rather than an agreement with his ideas.

Senator McCarthy said Mr. Murrow had been favorably mentioned in a book by Owen Lattimore, who the Senator said was under indictment for perjury and had been attacked as a Communist sympathizer. Mr. Murrow noted the book said he had never met Mr. Lattimore, and was

237

based on his reporting, in line with the concept of innocence unless proved guilty.

Senator McCarthy depicted the work of his Senate Permanent Subcommittee on Investigations as equivalent to that of "watchdogs upon the activities of potential burglars." He said that in slightly more than a year, it had turned up eighty-four witnesses refusing to testify to Communist activity, with twenty-four witnesses of Communist backgrounds being discharged from jobs in which they handled confidential material.

His disclosure of Communists in the military forces, he said, had resulted in abolition of an appeals board which had cleared and ordered "Communists" reinstated, and brought orders to prevent recurrence of "the Major Peress scandal." This referred to the honorable discharge of an Army dentist who had refused to say if he was a Communist.

Newspaper files show that before President Truman on Jan. 31, 1950, ordered the Atomic Energy Commission to continue work on the hydrogen bomb, there had been reports that various officials urged one more attempt first to reach an atomic agreement with the Soviet Union.

Efforts by Strauss

Rear Admiral Lewis L. Strauss, then a commissioner and now chairman of the atomic agency, was reported pressing for the hydrogen development. The then chairman, David E. Lilienthal, was described in newspaper reports as favoring further control efforts first, while Dr. J. Robert Oppenheimer, chief consultant, was also reported in opposition to the development move.

Reactions by listeners were reported by C. B. S. to favor Mr. Murrow as against the Senator. The tallies were given as 2,012 to 977 telephone calls in New York in two hours while telegrams ran 686 to 274. The Chicago figures for one hour and a half were 454 to 147 telephone calls. Los Angeles reported 949 to 144. In Washington the report was 233 to 29 calls.

In its statement, C. B. S. said that in nineteen years in which Mr. Murrow had been associated with it, its management had become "fully aware of Mr. Murrow's passionate devotion to his country and to the fundamental principles upon which it is built."

The network added it also knew of "his equally passionate opposition to those who, either within or outside our boundaries, would subvert those principles." The statement noted Mr. Murrow had been acclaimed by high Government officials, and won more than fifty awards attesting to his integrity and accuracy.

At a press conference after the telecast Mr. Murrow said that he had not given "any thought" to the possibility of initiating legal action against the Wisconsin Senator for charges made against him last night. Speaking away from the Senate floor, Senator McCarthy does not enjoy Congressional immunity and could be conceivably open to a libel suit.

In reply to a question, Mr. Murrow said that he would have to read "with care" the transcript of the Senator's address before deciding on any legal steps.

Senator McCarthy's film had been in preparation since last Friday, with Roy M. Cohn, chief counsel to his subcommittee, as chief aide, and with others present during various stages, including Carl Byoir, public relations expert; Louis B. Mayer, Hollywood producer, and George E. Sokolsky, newspaper columnist.

The Fox Movietone News, retained by the Senator to make the film, said it would bill him for the cost, but it was not known whether he would seek to recover payment from C. B. S.

Strauss Has No Comment

WASHINGTON, April 6 (UP)— Admiral Strauss, said he did not hear Mr. McCarthy's remarks and therefore thought he should not comment.

Asked about the eighteen-month delay mentioned by Mr. McCarthy, Representative Chet Holifield, Democrat of California and a member of the Atomic Energy Committee, said, "I don't know what he's referring to."

Mr. Holifield said there were many considerations, such as the number of scientists available, peaceful use of atomic energy and what type of research to proceed with next. "It was quite complicated," he added. "But this is the first time I've ever heard Communists brought into it."

April 7, 1954

ARMY CHARGES M'CARTHY AND COHN THREATENED IT IN TRYING TO OBTAIN PREFERRED TREATMENT FOR SCHINE

STEVENS A TARGET

Report Quotes Counsel As Saying Secretary Would Be 'Through'

By W. H. LAWRENCE
Special to The New York Times.

WASHINGTON, March 11— The Army reported today it had been subjected to direct threats by Senator Joseph R. McCarthy and his chief counsel, Roy Cohn.

The threats, the Army said, had been made in an effort to obtain preferential treatment for G. David Schine, now a private in the Army but formerly an investigator for the McCarthy subcommittee.

In a thirty-four-page report sent to each member of Senator McCarthy's Permanent Subcommittee on Investigations and some members of the Armed Services Committee, the Army declared the Wisconsin Republican and Mr. Cohn first had sought a direct commission for Private Schine.

Failing in that, the report said, they had then demanded for him an assignment in the New York area so he could study alleged subversive material in West Point textbooks.

In the period between Oct. 15 and Nov. 3, before Senator McCarthy began his open fight with the Army, John G. Adams, Army Counsel, reported he had told Mr. Cohn that it would not be in the national interest to give preferential treatment to Private Schine.

"Mr. Cohn replied that if the national interest was what the Army wanted, he'd give it a little and then proceeded to outline how he would expose the Army in its worst light and show the country how shabbily it is being run," the report declared.

Threat to Stevens Cited

The report quoted Mr. Cohn as threatening on one occasion to "wreck the Army" and make certain that Robert T. Stevens was "through" as the Secretary of the Army. At another time, the report said, "Mr. Cohn stated to Mr. Adams that he would teach Mr. Adams what it meant to go over his head."

The report is expected to spur growing demands for Mr. Cohn's ouster.

Senator McCarthy made it clear in answer that he would accept battle with "one or two" in the Army high command on the Cohn-Schine case. He said he had instructed his own committee staff to pull out of its files everything bearing on the case and give them to him so they could be "made available to the American public."

"I don't like to do it," he told a New York Times correspondent. "The deeper I get into it, I'm convinced the Army as a whole is damn clean. What some people in the Army do doesn't mean the entire Army."

He said he had sought at a luncheon with Charles E. Wilson, Secretary of Defense, yesterday to get the Defense Department to send its investigators over to look at his files before completing the report "so it wouldn't be just Mr. Adams' version."

The Senator said he had not yet read the full report.

He left no doubt he would continue to fight for Mr. Cohn's retention as committee counsel, even if some Republicans deserted him on the issue.

Mr. Cohn was reached late tonight and asked for comment about the Army's report. He said that he had not seen it as yet.

"I can't comment if I haven't seen it," he said.

As recently as Jan. 22 Mr. Adams was called to a conference with Senator McCarthy at his apartment in Washington. The Senator on three occasions sought definite commitments from Mr. Adams that Private Schine would receive an assignment in New York City, the Army said.

"Senator McCarthy pointed out that the Army was walking into a long range fight with Mr. Cohn and that even if he was fired from the committee staff he would carry on his campaign against the Army thereafter from outside Washington," the report said.

The Army report was in the form of a narrative covering the period from mid-July, when Senator McCarthy first requested a commission for Mr. Schine, until the date of Feb. 17 when notice was served that Brig. Gen. Ralph W. Zwicker, Commanding General of Camp Kilmer, N. J., was wanted for testimony by the committee.

It was Senator McCarthy's treatment of General Zwicker on the witness stand that led to the latest controversy, which now involves not only the Army but the President as well.

Schine Called a 'Pest'

The narrative pictures Senator McCarthy as interested in preferential treatment for Private Schine at times and, at others, as angry both with Mr. Cohn and Mr. Schine.

In mid-October, for example, Mr. Adams reported that Senator McCarthy had told him that Mr. Schine was a photo-loving publicity seeker and "things had reached a point where Mr. Schine was a pest."

On that occasion he also expressed the hope that Mr. Schine's draft processing would proceed promptly.

However, on Nov. 6, at a Pentagon luncheon with Secretary Stevens, Senator McCarthy brought up his request for a New York assignment for Private Schine so he could study and report "on evidence of pro-Communist leanings in West Point textbooks."

A month later, on Dec. 9, Senator McCarthy again was annoyed, and told Mr. Adams that "the committee had no further interest in Private Schine and that he hoped that Private Schine would be treated the same as other soldiers."

He said he would advise committee staff members of this decision. He communicated both decisions to the Army in a letter dated Dec. 22.

"Mr. Cohn stated to Mr. Adams that he would teach Mr. Adams what it meant to go over his head," the report declared.

A month later, Mr. Adams advised Mr. Cohn that there were nine chances out of ten that Private Schine would receive an overseas assignment after he completed his training at Camp Gordon, Ga.

Mr. Cohn responded with threats to "wreck the Army," the report said, and make certain that Mr. Stevens was "through" as the Army Secretary.

The report begins with a dating of "mid-July." It recounts a conference between Maj. Gen. Miles Reber, Chief of the Army Legislative Liaison Office, and Senator McCarthy, at which the Senator requested a direct commission for Mr. Schine "on the basis of Schines' education, business experience and prior service with the Army Transportation Service."

The Senator said rapid action was necessary because Mr. Schine was about to be drafted.

During the conference, Mr. Cohn entered the room and re-enforced Senator McCarthy's request, the report declared.

On July 15, Mr. Schine himself got his physical examination.

Between July 15 and 30, the Army reached a decision that Mr. Schine was not qualified for a direct commission. On Aug. 1, according to the report, Mr. Cohn

asked officials to explore the possibilities of a reserve commission in the Air Force or the Navy for Mr. Schine. Subsequently he was notified that the answer was negative, the report said.

On Oct. 2, the document continued, Mr. Cohn and Francis Carr, Staff Director for the McCarthy sub-committee, met with minutes. They discussed the proposed investigation of Fort Monmouth, N. J., and at the same time asked an assignment to the New York area for Mr. Schine when he was inducted.

Secretary Stevens, at that time, said that fifteen days of temporary duty in New York for Mr. Schine might be arranged.

By mid-October, when the Monmouth investigation was in progress, Senator McCarthy told Secretary Stevens and Mr. Adams that Mr. Schine "was a nuisance," but added that he did not want Mr. Cohn to know of his views on Mr. Schine.

Between the period of Oct. 18 and Nov. 3, the report said that Mr. Cohn and Mr. Adams had talked on the telephone nearly every day about the New York assignment for Mr. Schine. It was then that Mr. Adams said it was not in the national interest to give him preferential treatment and Mr. Cohn snapped back his threat to give the Army "a little" national interest by exposing it "in its worst light."

On Nov. 3, Mr. Schine was inducted, but received a fifteen-day assignment on temporary duty to complete his committee work.

At this point, however, Senator McCarthy suggested reporters would wonder why Mr. Schine was on duty with the subcommittee rather than with the Army and suggested that the temporary assignment be canceled.

On Nov. 6, the Pentagon luncheon took place, where Secretary Stevens again was asked for a New York assignment for Private Schine.

'Leaving Post Every Night'

On Nov. 10, Private Schine reported to the Fort Dix, N. J., reception center, and on the following day Mr. Cohn and Mr. Carr called on the Commanding General, Cornelius J. Ryan, and requested an interview with Mr. Schine, the report added.

On Nov. 12, Mr. Schine got his first week-end pass. He had other passes for varying durations on Nov. 17, Nov. 19, Nov. 23, Nov. 25, and Nov. 28.

On Dec. 8, General Ryan complained to Mr. Adams by telephone that the "matter of handling" Private Schine was "becoming increasingly difficult because the soldier was leaving the post nearly every night."

General Ryan said, according to the report, that Private Schine usually returned "very late at night."

Mr. Adams told General Ryan that "from that moment forward Private Schine was no longer available for committee business on weekdays." He added, however, that the Army would honor its original commitment that he be available on week-ends.

On Dec. 9, Mr. Cohn again brought up with Mr. Adams the treatment of Private Schine and his prospective assignment and

The New York Times

FIGURE IN THREATS: G. David Schine, for whom Senator Joseph R. McCarthy and Roy M. Cohn interceded, according to Army report.

Mr. Adams responded that "Private Schine was going to be handled the same as any other soldier."

Mr. Cohn broke off the conversation in the middle," the report went on, "turning his back on Mr. Adams in the Senate caucus room."

Mr. Adams went to Senator McCarthy on this matter Dec. 9, and it was at that time that the Senator declared the committee and its staff had no further interest in special treatment for Private Schine. This was followed by Mr. Cohn's warning to Mr. Adams that he would show him "what it meant to go over his head."

There was a luncheon at the Carroll Arms Hotel, across the street from the Senate Office Building, on Dec. 10, attended by Secretary Stevens, Senator McCarthy, Mr. Adams and Mr. Carr.

Mr. Carr said, the report continued that "Mr. Cohn was too upset to attend the luncheon because of the Private Schine situation and the Army's unwillingness to settle on Private Schine's future assignment."

Cut in Training Urged

Senator McCarthy at this time requested anew an immediate assignment in New York for Private Schine.

Mr. Stevens replied that sixteen weeks of basic training must be completed before a future assignment could be discussed. Senator McCarthy suggested several times, according to the Army report, that there were precedents for cutting the basic training to eight weeks and making the New York assignment at the end of that period.

On Dec. 11, Private Schine was informed at Camp Dix that he now would be required to perform duty on Saturdays as well as weekdays. Mr. Cohn promptly protested to Mr. Adams.

"During these conversations,

Mr. Cohn, using extremely vituperative language, told Mr. Adams that the Army had again 'double-crossed' Mr. Cohn, Private Schine and Senator McCarthy," the narrative continued.

"The first double-cross, according to Mr. Cohn, was when the Army had not given a commission to Schine after promising one to him; the second double-cross, according to Mr. Cohn, was that the Army had not assigned Private Schine immediately to New York; and another was that the Army canceled Private Schine's availability during weekends.

"The request that Private Schine perform duties on Saturday morning was a new double-cross."

Senator McCarthy came back into the picture on Dec. 17, saying he had just learned of the extent of the staff's intervention with the Army concerning Mr. Schine. The report went on to say that Senator McCarthy "wished to advise Mr. Adams thereafter to see that nothing was done on the committee's behalf with reference to Schine."

Still Another Request

But again the request was made for a New York assignment for Private Schine "to examine the textbooks at West Point and to report to the Secretary as to whether they contained anything of a subversive nature."

By mid-December, Army examiners had declared Private Schine physically unfit for infantry duty, and the decision had been reached to send him to the Provost Marshall General School at Camp Gordon, Ga., for training in the Criminal Investigation Division.

Private Schine got the usual pass for New Year's from Dec. 31 through Jan. 3.

On Jan. 9, Mr. Adams had gone to Amherst, Mass., to make a speech. There he received a telephone call from Mr. Carr, reporting that Mr. Cohn had been trying to reach him "to have Mr. Adams intercede with the commanding general at Fort Dix because Private Schine was scheduled for k.p. duty on the following day, a Sunday."

Two days later, Mr. Cohn again got in touch with Mr. Adams to inquire about the nature of Mr. Schine's probable duties at Camp Gordon and to request the name of an Army officer at the Georgia camp who could serve as a contact man "for the purpose of relieving Schine from his duties when necessary."

Mr. Adams was not receptive, according to the report, and Mr. Cohn "hung up the telephone after teling Mr. Adams he would not stand for any more Army double-crosses."

On either Jan. 13 or 14, Mr. Adams brought up the point that 90 per cent of all inductees got overseas duties, and that, therefore, the chances were nine out of ten that Private Schine would go overseas after finishing his training at Camp Gordon.

It was after this conversation that Mr. Cohn made his reported threat to "wreck the Army" and force Mr. Stevens out as Army Secretary.

On Jan. 16 Private Schine completed his training at Fort Dix and received the usual two weeks' leave before reporting to Camp Gordon.

It was during this period also that Senator McCarthy was demanding that the Army make available to him as witnesses twenty members of former loyalty-security boards who had reinstated suspended personnel at Fort Monmouth. The Army was refusing the request, on ground that it could not make such witnesses available under current Presidential directives.

Long Conference Held

On Jan. 22 Mr. Adams went to Senator McCarthy's apartment for an appointment that lasted from 8:30 P. M. to 11:15 P. M. Here the conversation involved both the demand for the loyalty-security board personnel as witnesses and a New York assignment for Private Schine.

It was at this meeting, the report said, that the Senator warned of the long-range possibilities of the fight that Mr.

Cohn might make on the Army, in or out of Washington.

Senator McCarthy said that Mr. Cohn had contact with important press elements that would help him wage this fight. These alleged contacts were not named.

On Feb. 4 Mr. Carr telephoned Mr. Adams that Senator McCarthy was very angry about the honorable discharge granted to Maj. Irving Peress, the dental officer who had refused to answer any questions about his alleged

Communist activities.

Mr. Carr told Mr. Adams, according to the report, that the "situation had reached the point where the Senator was no longer willing to discuss matters either with the Secretary or Mr. Adams."

The narrative ended with the Feb. 16 telephone call requesting that General Zwicker be made available for testimony.

STEVENS SWEARS M'CARTHY FALSIFIED, LAYS 'PERVERSION OF POWER' TO HIM; SENATOR IMPUGNS GENERAL'S MOTIVES

HEARING IS STORMY

Gen. Reber Asserts Cohn Put Pressure on Him to Commission Schine

By W. H. LAWRENCE
Special to The New York Times.

WASHINGTON, April 22—The Secretary of the Army testified under oath today that Senator Joseph R. McCarthy had falsified in his charges against Army officials and about his efforts to get preferential treatment for Pvt. G. David Schine.

The appearance of Robert T. Stevens, Secretary of the Army, to back up his accusations of "perversion of power" against the Wisconsin Republican came near the end of the opening day of public, televised and often stormy hearings before the Senate Permanent Subcommittee on Investigations.

New and special rules failed to restrain Senator McCarthy from interrupting witnesses and other Senators whenever he wished on what he called "points of order."

He suggested that one Army witness, Maj. Gen. Miles Reber, might have been motivated in his testimony by "the fact that your brother [Samuel Reber, former acting United States High Commissioner for Germany] was allowed to resign [from the State Department] when charges that he was a bad security risk were made against him as a result of

Principal Witnesses at the McCarthy-Army Inquiry

Secretary Robert T. Stevens

Associated Press Wirephotos

Maj. Gen. Miles Reber

the investigations of this committee."

After a prolonged wrangle about the relevance of this question to the current inquiry, Senator McCarthy withdrew it. Then General Reber, pounding his hand in his fist as he talked to the Army's counsel, Joseph N. Welch, asked the subcommittee for special permission to answer it anyway.

"I do not know and have never heard that my brother retired as a result of any action of this committee," General Reber said. "The answer is positively no to that question."

Later, General Reber said that "as I understand my brother's case, he retired, as he is entitled to do by law upon reaching the age of 50."

"I know nothing about any

security case involving him," he added.

A State Department spokesman in response to inquiries later said simply that "Mr. Reber retired voluntarily on July 31, 1953."

That clash with General Reber and other events of the day made it clear that Senator McCarthy will use every weapon at his command—and they are numerous—in this case in which he is one of the accused as well as accuser.

He clashed frequently with Ray H. Jenkins, special counsel for the inquiry, about argumentative questions and occasionally was overruled, but not before he had made his point to millions of television viewers across the land.

While all principals to the dispute were accorded rights of cross-examination equal to subcommittee members, Senator McCarthy held the microphone longer and more frequently than any other Senator, and was the only accused person who interrupted proceedings while others were talking.

Several times he admonished Senator Karl E. Mundt, South Dakota Republican, and acting committee chairman, to give him undivided attention.

Only three witnesses were heard during the total of four hours and eight minutes the committee sat during morning and afternoon sessions today. They were Secretary Stevens, General Reber, and Walter Bedell Smith, Under Secretary of State and a retired Army general.

They painted a picture of extraordinary efforts made by Senator McCarthy and Roy M. Cohn, his chief counsel, first to get a commission and when that was unsuccessful to get other favors for Private Schine, who, until he was drafted, was an unpaid consultant for the McCarthy subcommittee.

Secretary Stevens testified that during an inspection tour at Fort Monmouth, N. J., Mr. Cohn, angered because he had been excluded from a secret laboratory, said:

"This means ware * * * Don't they think I am cleared for classified information? I have access to F. B. I. files when I want them * * * They did this on purpose just to embarrass me. We will really investigate the Army now."

Smith Surprise Witness

General Reber said that there was nothing improper in any of the few approaches Senator McCarthy had made to him for a commission for Mr. Schine, but that Mr. Cohn had telephoned him so frequently about the matter that he felt he was under "unusual pressure" to get a favorable answer.

He said he had assumed that Mr. Cohn had been acting for Senator McCarthy as well as in his individual capacity as a close friend of Mr. Schine.

General Smith was a surprise witness in mid-afternoon, and he disclosed that Mr. Cohn had carried to him his fight for a commission for Mr. Schine after the Army had turned him down on the ground he was not qualified.

General Smith said, however, that he did not regard Mr. Cohn's actions as improper.

Both General Smith and Secretary Stevens testified that Mr. Cohn had mentioned to them the possibility of getting the Central Intelligence Agency—one of the McCarthy committee targets—to intervene in behalf of commissioning Mr. Schine. Secretary Stevens said that he had reached Allen W. Dulles, C. I. A. Director, who refused to give Mr. Schine a job.

As General Smith told it, Mr. Cohn asked him, as a former C. I. A. Director, whether that agency "could not arrange to have Mr. Schine commissioned, as he had investigative experience."

"I replied that C. I. A. drew a few commissioned personnel by detail from the armed services, but gave them additional training and required a longer tour of duty," General Smith said. "However, I offered to telephone Mr. Allen Dulles * * * and ask about the possibilities.

"Mr. Cohn said that I need not do this. The C. I. A., he said, was too juicy a subject for future investigation, and it would not be right to ask them to get Mr. Schine commissioned and then investigate the organization later."

It remained for Secretary Stevens, however, to state the Army case against Senator McCarthy and his associates bluntly and fully.

As to their efforts to get favors for Private Schine, both before and after he was refused a commission, Secretary Stevens said that during the fourteen months he has been civilian head of the Army "there is no record that matches this persistent, tireless effort to obtain special consideration and privileges for this man."

"The Schine case," he said, "is only an example of the wrongful seeking of privilege, of the perversion of power. It has been a distraction that has kept many men from the performance of tasks far more important to the welfare of this country than the convenience of a single Army private."

He said that Senator McCarthy's charge that he sought to "blackmail" the committee out of investigating alleged Communists in the Army was "absolutely false." He said he had never suggested, as Senator McCarthy and his associates formally charged, that they drop their inquiry into the Army and "go after" the Navy and Air Force.

The long-awaited public airing of the Army-McCarthy controversy began shortly after 10:30 o'clock this morning in the high-ceilinged, marble-walled caucus room on the third floor of the Senate Office Building.

Mundt Defines Issues

It was jammed to capacity with more than 400 spectators, more than 100 news and radio reporters, and a dozen motion-picture and television cameras.

Senator Mundt began by defining the issues as "grave and serious" and said the Republicans and Democrats on the subcommittee, fully cognizant that they were "on the spot," were determined to "make a full and impartial effort to reveal that which is true and to expose that which is false."

"The reputations, the actions and perhaps the integrity of responsible public officials are being challenged in these hearings," Senator Mundt said. "Under these circumstances, it is right and proper that each of us at this end of the committee room considers himself in a sense to be on trial to the extent that all of us have the obligation to do our best to enable justice and equity to prevail throughout these unprecedented hearings."

Speaking for the three Democrats, Senator John L. McClellan of Arkansas declared that "the charges and accusations are so diametrically in conflict, as I see it, that they cannot possibly be reconciled." The committee, he said, has "an arduous and difficult task, one that is not pleasant to contemplate, but it is a job that must be done."

Senator McClellan pledged on behalf of the Democrats every cooperation with the Republicans to make the hearings "impartial, fair and thorough, to the end that that which is true may be revealed and that which is false may be exposed, without regard to any personalities that may be involved."

Because Senator McCarthy surrendered both the chairmanship and membership on the subcommittee for the duration of the inquiry to which he is a party, he was seated at the end of the twenty-six-foot-long table and not in the center spot where he customarily presides.

As Senator Mundt rapped for order with a glass ashtray, he was flanked by Mr. Jenkins on his right and Senator McClellan to his left. On Mr. Jenkins' right were three Republican Senators —Everett M. Dirksen of Illinois, Charles E. Potter of Michigan and Henry C. Dworshak of Idaho. To Senator McClellan's left were the two other Democrat Senators —Stuart Symington of Missouri and Henry M. Jackson of Washington.

Opponents to Switch Seats

Beyond the Democrats sat three Army officials — Secretary Stevens seated between Lieut. Gen. Lyman Lemnitzer, Deputy Chief of Staff for Plans, and Maj. Gen. Robert N. Young, Assistant Chief of Staff for Personnel.

And beyond them, at the end of the table, sat Senator McCarthy with Mr. Cohn on his right and Francis P. Carr, committee staff director, on his left.

Tomorrow, and on alternate days, the Army group and the McCarthy trio will change places so each contesting side will have equal opportunities to be brought into focus by the television cameras carrying the proceedings throughout the nation.

While the new rules were designed to provide absolute equality for Senator McCarthy and his accusers from the Army, the Wisconsin Republican was the first to take advantage of his rights within seventeen minutes after the proceedings got under way.

Raising what he called a point of order, he challenged the right of Secretary Stevens and John G. Adams, counselor of the Army, to describe their specifications against him as being filed on behalf of "the Department of the Army."

"I may say, Mr. Chairman, that I have heard—may I have the attention of the chair—may I say, Mr. Chairman, that I have heard from people in the military all the way down from generals, with the most upstanding combat records, down to privates recently inducted, and they are very resentful of the fact that a few Pentagon politicians, attempting to disrupt our investigations, are naming them-

selves the Department of the Army," Senator McCarthy declared.

He got nowhere with his legal objection, but he did get his chance to make a speech denouncing Messrs. Stevens and Adams and to declare they had no right "to attempt to make this a contest between me and the Army."

General Reber, wearing a single ribbon on his khaki uniform to signify that he was the winner of the Distinguished Service Medal, was the first witness called by Mr. Jenkins.

It was in his capacity as chief of the Army's Office of Legislative Liaison that he first was called to Senator McCarthy's office in July, 1953, to discuss a speedy commission for Mr. Schine before he was drafted.

McClellan Demands Ruling

It was near the end of his testimony and long cross-examination that Senator McCarthy first interjected the name of General Reber's brother, Sam, and suggested the general might be biased because Messrs. Cohn and Schine had a run-in with Sam Reber in Germany during their much discussed European journey last year.

On the first occasion of his mention of Sam Reber, Senator McCarthy did not go into the issue of whether he had been under "security risk" charges and indeed he did not raise this controversial question at all until after he had said at one stage that he had no further questions to ask General Reber.

Senator McCarthy's tactics exasperated Senator McClellan, who called for a ruling on the materiality of the Sam Reber question "because we may be trying members of everybody's family involved before we get through."

Mr. Jenkins, a tall raw-boned veteran trial lawyer from east Tennessee and self-styled "Taft Republican," dominated the proceedings of the committee, except on the occasions when Senator McCarthy took over.

In his cross-examination of General Reber, Mr. Jenkins indicated strongly that he believed Senator McCarthy had succeeded where the Army had failed in rooting out "Communists and those with Communistic leanings" at Fort Monmouth.

This still is one of the more controversial investigations ever undertaken by Senator McCarthy, sitting as a one-man subcommittee, and Secretary Stevens denied again today the subcommittee had turned up any evidence of "current espionage," as the Wisconsin Republican frequently claimed.

Addressing himself to General Reber, Mr. Jenkins asked this question:

"Taking into consideration the vital work in which they [Senator McCarthy and Mr. Cohn] told you that Schine was engaged, I believe you say that you did not regard the efforts of Senator McCarthy as being improper in any respect in his efforts to get some, shall we say, preferential treatment for Schine so that he could assist in carrying on this investigative work of the Senate, is that right?"

General Reber responded that he did not consider the number

of telephone calls received from Senator McCarthy were extraordinary, but added that "I do not believe I said anything about the propriety of those calls."

Asked if he felt if Mr. Cohn's activities in behalf of Mr. Schine were "improper" in the light of of the importance of Mr. Schine's work, General Reber said:

"I felt that in view of the position of the committee staff that I was being put under definite pressure because I know, sir, that there is a specific proviso whereby an individual who is considered to be sufficiently important to the national safety, health and interest, that he should remain on his then current duties, that individual can be exempted from Selective Service."

General Reber said in response to another query that no such application had been made on behalf of Mr. Schine.

General Smith was subjected to a minimum of cross-examination at the request of Mr. Jenkins, who said he had interrupted a busy work day as Acting Secretary of State and was preparing to go abroad.

Secretary Stevens had interrupted the reading of his own twenty-five-page prepared statement in order to allow General Smith to make his brief appearance this afternoon so that he would be free to continue his preparations for the Geneva conference.

The Army Secretary resumed reading his statement after General Smith had left the room and finished it just as the committee reached its adjournment time.

He will be the first witness tomorrow, with Mr. Jenkins leading off the questioning, followed by Senator Mundt and the other committee members who will be limited to ten minutes each a round.

Then the Army Counsel, Mr. Welch, and Senator McCarthy and his associates will get an equal ten minutes opportunity for questioning.

April 23, 1954

Calls Monitored Often in Capital; Hearing Revives Evidence Issue

Special to THE NEW YORK TIMES.

WASHINGTON, April 23—The monitoring of telephone calls in Washington officialdom is regarded as standard operating procedure.

Secretaries and other office assistants often listen in on telephone conversations and make notes, but there is no official gauge on how widespread the practice is. It was highlighted today in the McCarthy-Army hearing.

Frequently officials or members of Congress will let it be known that a secretary is on the line by asking that he or she get certain material or arrange for the caller to see the proper person. While the practice is considered to be confined mainly to top officials, it also extends to lower echelons. Some Government press officers have their calls monitored.

The practice exists in almost all departments of the Government, including the Departments of State, Justice, Commerce and Agriculture, and in the Pentagon. Members of Congress also have members of their staff as the third party on the line.

There is no legal ban on such monitoring or note-making but, as developed in the McCarthy-Army hearing, such transcripts may not be admitted as evidence in court without the consent of the person on the other end of the telephone. This provision is contained in Section 605, entitled "Unauthorized Publication of Communications," of Public Law 416. The law was passed by Congress in 1934.

The use of mechanical devices to record telephone conversations is illegal under Federal law without the sounding of an intermittent warning signal. In most cases this is an audible "beep." It is not known whether the devices are employed widely in Washington.

In 1951, however, the late Senator Charles W. Tobey, New Hampshire Republican, stirred President Truman to anger by recording two telephone conversations with the President. Mr. Truman called the incident "outrageous." The calls were in regard to an investigation of the Reconstruction Finance Corporation.

At that time Senator Tobey said: "It is no secret that recorders are installed in United States Senators' offices when requested for the purpose of taking records of telephone calls, or to dictate speeches and to have accurate records on file."

He said that the device had been "a great help to me, and so often I utilize this machine to make sure I have an accurate record on file, and oftentimes for dictation to be transcribed later.

"When the President called, as so often is done when calls from conversation was recorded in the important people come in, the customary manner in a desire to be sure of the facts."

Senator Joseph R. McCarthy once sought to use a tape recorder in a pre-trial session of his $2,000,000 libel-slander suit against former Senator William Benton of Connecticut, a suit that the Wisconsin Republican recently dropped.

Senator McCarthy installed the machine in a Senate hearing room, but Mr. Benton refused to answer while the recorder was operating. Mr. McCarthy said he wanted to insure an accurate account of the proceedings in the event Mr. Benton gave perjured testimony.

The Wisconsin Senator sought a court order for the use of the recorder but was turned down by Judge Walter Bastian in the Federal district court here.

For several years there have been efforts to get legislation to admit to Federal courts wiretapped evidence against alleged spies, traitors and saboteurs in the interest of national security.

The Eisenhower Administration succeeded on April 9 in getting a measure on wiretapped evidence through the House. The Administration, however, wanted the complete control of such evidence in the hands of the Attorney General. The House, by a vote of 221 to 166, decided that while the Attorney General could certify that specific evidence was needed by the interception of communications, a Federal court judge would have to rule on whether wires could be tapped.

The measure now is before the Senate Judiciary Committee. It carries a "retroactive" feature that would permit the use of material already gathered to bring to trial suspects now free. This material could be used with the approval of the Attorney General.

The Supreme Court has ruled on the inadmissibility of evidence obtained by wiretapping, but has not held that wiretapping by Federal officers was illegal without disclosure.

Following is the text of Section 605 of Public Law 416, which is involved in today's dispute:

TEXT OF THE LAW

Sec. 605. No person receiving or assisting in receiving, or transmitting, or assisting in transmitting, any interstate or foreign communications by wire or radio shall divulge or publish the existence, contents, substance, purport, effect, or meaning thereof, except through authorized channels of transmission or reception, to any person other than the addressee, his agent, or attorney, or to a person employed or authorized to forward such communication to its destination, or to proper accounting or distributing officers of the various communicating centers over which the communication may be passed, or to the master of a ship under whom he is serving, or in response to a subpoena issued by a court of competent jurisdiction, or on demand of other lawful authority;

And no person not being authorized by the sender shall intercept any communication and divulge or publish the existence, contents, substance, purport, effect or meaning of such intercepted communication to any person;

And no person not being entitled thereto shall receive or assist in receiving any interstate or foreign communication by wire or radio and use the same or any information therein contained for his own benefit or for the benefit of another not entitled thereto;

And no person having received such intercepted communication or having become acquainted with the contents, substance, purport, effect, or meaning of the same or any part thereof, knowing that such information was so obtained, shall divulge or publish the existence, contents, substance, purport, effect, or meaning of the same or any part thereof, or use the same or any information therein contained for his own benefit or for the benefit of another not entitled thereto;

Provided, that this section shall not apply to the receiving, divulging, publishing, or utilizing the contents of any radio communication broadcast, or transmitted by amateurs or others for the use of the general public, or relating to ships in distress.

April 24, 1954

WELCH ASSAILS M'CARTHY'S 'CRUELTY' AND 'RECKLESSNESS' IN ATTACK ON AIDE

EXCHANGE BITTER

Counsel Is Near Tears as Crowd Applauds Him at Finish

By W. H. LAWRENCE
Special to The New York Times.

WASHINGTON, June 9—The Army-McCarthy hearings reached a dramatic high point today in an angry, emotion-packed exchange between Senator Joseph R. McCarthy and Joseph N. Welch, special counsel for the Army.

Irritated by Mr. Welch's persistent cross-examination of Roy M. Cohn, Senator McCarthy suddenly injected into the hearings a charge that one of Mr. Welch's Boston law firm associates, Frederick G. Fisher Jr., had been a member of the National Lawyers Guild "long after it had been exposed as the legal arm of the Communist party."

Mr. Welch, almost in tears from this unexpected attack, told the Wisconsin Republican that "until this moment, Senator, I think I never really gauged your cruelty or your recklessness." He asked Senator McCarthy if any "sense of decency" remained in him.

"If there is a God in heaven, it [the attack on Mr. Fisher] will do neither you nor your cause any good," Mr. Welch declared.

Spectators Break into Applause

The crowded hearing room burst into applause for Mr. Welch as he abruptly broke off his conversation with Senator McCarthy. Mr. Welch refused to address any more questions to Mr. Cohn, counsel to the McCarthy subcommittee, and suggested to Senator Karl E. Mundt, South Dakota Republican who is acting committee chairman, that he call another witness.

Senator McCarthy thereupon was called and took the stand on the thirtieth day of the hearing.

Senator McCarthy had interrupted Mr. Welch's cross-examination of Mr. Cohn to denounce Mr. Fisher. He asserted, despite contradictions by Senator Mundt, that Mr. Welch had tried to get Mr. Fisher employed as "the assistant counsel for this commit-

tee" so he could be in Washington "looking over the secret and classified material."

Senator Mundt said Mr. Welch never had recommended Mr. Fisher or anyone else for a subcommittee job. Mr. Welch explained that he had planned to have Mr. Fisher, a leader in the Young Republican League of Newton, Mass., as one of his own assistants in this case until Mr. Fisher told him that he had belonged to the National Lawyers Guild while at Harvard Law School "and for a period of months after."

The violent, unforseen character of Senator McCarthy's attack seemed to upset Mr. Cohn, himself, whose facial expressions and grimaces caused Senator McCarthy to comment: " I know Mr. Cohn would rather not have me go into this."

Senator Mundt has daily cautioned the audience to refrain from "audible expressions of approval or disapproval" of the proceedings on pain of being expelled from the hearing room. But he made no effort to control or admonish the crowd that applauded Mr. Welch's retort to Senator McCarthy.

Disputes Obscure the Issues

The McCarthy-Welch exchange, and another hot battle between Senators McCarthy and Stuart Symington, Missouri Democrat, served to divert attention from the basic issues in this controversy.

The Army initially charged that Senator McCarthy and Mr. Cohn had sought by improper means to obtain preferential treatment for Pvt. G. David Schine, who until he was drafted, was an unpaid committee consultant.

Senator McCarthy and Mr. Cohn, in turn, have charged that the Army held Private Schine as a "hostage" and tried to "blackmail" the committee out of investigating the Army.

Other highlights of the day were:

¶The Senate Permanent Subcommittee on Investigations, hearing the dispute, formally requested the Adjutant General of New York to authorize a delay in the military training of Mr. Cohn, who has been ordered to report to Camp Kilmer, N. J., this week-end for a two-week duty with the National Guard. Senator McCarthy had said a recess would be necessary during Mr. Cohn's training because it would be unfair to continue in his absence. Acting for the Army, Mr. Welch suggested that a delay be requested, and the subcommittee approved his proposal.

¶Mr. Welch's cross-examination of Mr. Cohn cast doubt on how much work Private Schine did for the McCarthy subcommittee during periods he was on authorized leave from Fort Dix,

Associated Press Wirephoto

NEAR TEARS: Joseph N. Welch, special counsel for Army, holds a handkerchief to his face in a hallway outside hearing room, where he wept after an exchange with McCarthy.

N. J., to work on committee business.

¶Mr. Welch chided Mr. Cohn and, inferentially, Senator McCarthy because they had not immediately notified Robert T. Stevens, Secretary of the Army, early in his tenure in office that they had received a Federal Bureau of Investigation report about alleged Communists at Fort Monmouth, N. J. He brought out that while Senator McCarthy received the report last spring, it was not brought to Secretary Stevens' attention for several months. Mr. Cohn had testified "time was of the essence" in eliminating security risks.

¶Senator Symington offered to testify before the subcommittee, as demanded by Senator McCarthy, if the latter would agree in writing to testify under oath before a special Senate committee to be named by Vice President Richard M. Nixon on recommendation of Republican and Democratic leaders.

Senator Symington specified that Senator McCarthy agree to explain whether, among other things, it had been proper for him to accept $10,000 from the

Lustron Corporation for a pamphlet on housing, whether funds supplied to fight communism were diverted to Senator McCarthy's own use and whether he had violated state and Federal tax laws and banking laws over a period of years.

¶Charging that Senator Symington's offer demonstrated "how low an alleged man can sink," Senator McCarthy said he would give a firm commitment, but sign no letter, agreeing to testify before such a committee "if the Vice President or the Senate wants to appoint a committee to investigate these smears."

¶Calling the exchange's diversionary and "mid-morning madness," Senator Mundt tried to halt the personal feud between the two Senators, but not until Senator McCarthy had charged, and Senator Symington had denied, that Senator Symington, while in private industry, had dealt with a Communist, one William Sentner, and paid him money to settle a strike.

, When the hearings recessed today, Senator Mundt served notice that the Republicans would attempt at a closed-door session late tomorrow to fix a final time limit for the investigation to conclude.

The Army and McCarthy sides are willing to end the hearings after Senator McCarthy and his subcommittee staff director, Francis P. Carr, have testified fully and been cross-examined.

The Republican members and Senator McCarthy are seeking a specific date as a time limit, but Mr. Welch has thus far resisted that proposal. He has said he is willing instead to accept a stated number of turns in ten-minute cross-examination periods.

The Democrats, on the other hand, have been fighting against an arbitrary time limit, and have insisted that other witnesses whose testimony may be material to the controversy not be refused the right to appear.

Mr. Welch mixed humor with persistency in his cross-examination of Mr. Cohn early in the day. He made Senator McCarthy angry when he chided "these Communist hunters" for "sitting on a document for month after month" while they waited for committee hearings instead of telling Secretary Stevens about alleged Reds at Fort Monmouth.

He brought out that the altered F. B. I. report "purloined" from the Army's files had been given to Senator McCarthy last spring, but that not during March, April, May, June or July did Mr. Cohn or Senator McCarthy convey the information in it to Mr. Stevens.

The crowd in the room roared with laughter as Mr. Welch added:

"I think it is really dramatic to see how these Communist hunters will sit on this document when they could have brought it to the attention of Bob Stevens in twenty minutes, and they let month after month go by without going to the head and saying, 'Sic 'em, Stevens.'"

Angrily Senator McCarthy said Mr. Welch was being unfair.

"That may sound funny as all get-out here," Senator McCarthy said. "It may get a laugh. He knows it is ridiculous. He is wasting time doing it. He is trying to create a false impression.

"I would like to suggest that after this long series of ridiculous questions, talking about why he wouldn't go over to the Pentagon and yell out 'Sic 'em, Stevens,'

that Mr. Cohn should be able to tell what happened after the document was received. That is the only fair thing, Mr. Chairman."

The Symington-McCarthy exchanges, which have been increasing in bitterness in recent days, were indecisive again today, but Senator Symington demanded that the committee call James B. Carey, secretary of the Congress of Industrial Organizations, to tell it about the alleged labor negotiations between Senator Symington and Mr. Sentner. Senator Mundt said the issue was irrelevant to the hearings and that he was not disposed to summon Mr. Carey.

Just before Mr. Cohn was excused abruptly, Mr. Welch created something of a stir in the committee room by disclosing he had obtained hotel and night club records indicating Mr. Cohn's expenditures for dinners and parties in New York and Trenton at times when Private Schine was on leave from Fort Dix.

Some of them concerned the Stork Club, but Mr. Cohn swore that Private Schine had not been there during the time he was assigned to Fort Dix. Some of the other expenditures, he said, rep-

resented occasions when he had dined with Private Schine, and, on one occasion, when they had been accompanied by girls.

Calls Fisher a 'Fine Kid'

WASHINGTON, June 9 (UP)— After his denunciation of Senator McCarthy, Mr. Welch retired briefly to a near-by rest room during a recess. He appeared to be wiping his face.

"I'm close to tears," he told reporters.

"Here's a young kid with one mistake—just one mistake—and he tries to crucify him," Mr. Welch said, "I don't see how in the name of God you can fight anybody like that. I never saw such cruelty * * * such arrogance."

Mr. Welch said Mr. Fisher was "just a young kid starting out * * * a fine kid * * * I like him."

The Army lawyer strolled down a long corridor and back before returning to the hearing room.

During the recess, Senator McCarthy told reporters that "too many people can dish it out but can't take it."

June 10, 1954

ARMY-M'CARTHY VERDICTS PUT BLAME ON BOTH SIDES; WATKINS SILENCES SENATOR

COHN IS ASSAILED

Majority and Minority Hit Counsel—Stevens' 'Vacillation' Scored

By C. P. TRUSSELL
Special to The New York Times.

WASHINGTON, Aug. 31—The Army-McCarthy battle of charge and counter-charge that ran through thirty-six days of April-to-June televised hearings ended tonight with both sides sharing censure.

The Republican majority of Senator Joseph R. McCarthy's own panel, the Senate Permanent Subcommittee on Investigations, cleared the chairman of operating directly to force the Army to bestow special favors on G.

David Schine, the subcommittee's unpaid chief consultant, after Mr. Schine had been drafted.

However, the majority found that the Wisconsin Republican had permitted Roy M. Cohn, chief counsel of his investigating group, and perhaps others to make things uncomfortable for the Army if Mr. Schine did not get special privileges.

The three Democratic members in a minority report said Senator McCarthy "merited severe criticism" along with Mr. Cohn for actions in Mr. Schine's behalf.

Robert T. Stevens, Secretary of the Army, who faced many days of sharp questioning, was held by the Republicans of the subcommittee to have been "beyond reproach." However, to these words of comfort were added a criticism that Mr. Stevens had dealt in "placation," "appeasement" and "vacillation" in handling Mr. Cohn in particular.

The four Republicans who signed the majority report were Senators Karl E. Mundt of South Dakota, who served as chairman of the special investigation; Everett M. Dirksen of Illinois; Charles E. Potter of Michigan, and Henry C. Dworshak of Idaho.

The Democratic minority was composed of Senators John L. McClellan of Arkansas, Henry M. Jackson of Washington, and Stuart Symington of Missouri.

Senator Potter filed a separate report in which, speaking for himself, he was much more critical of all concerned than was the general tenor of the majority's findings. Senator Dirksen also filed an individual report saying the Army charges against Senator McCarthy had not been proved.

Senator McClellan, in a brief statement, said he was "gratified" that the Democratic members had been able to reconcile differences on minor points and submit a joint report, not separate and independent views. The

majority report ran to about 2,000 words, while the Democrats let theirs extend to about 7,800.

These reports released today had been culled from more than 1,000,000 words of testimony supplemented by supporting exhibits.

The Majority Points

The Republican majority of the special committee concluded:

¶That the charge of improper influence on behalf of Private Schine had not been established as a deliberate and personal act of Senator McCarthy, but that he should have displayed "more vigorous discipline in stopping any member of his staff" from attempting such a move.

¶That Mr. McCarthy appeared to have known about such activities and to have condoned them.

¶That Mr. Cohn was "unduly persistent and aggressive" on behalf of Mr. Schine without any curbs being applied by Senator McCarthy.

¶That the Fort Monmouth, N. J., inquiry, still largely in controversy, was not a part of a possible plan to get Army favors for Mr. Schine.

¶That Secretary Stevens and John G. Adams, Army Counsellor, did try to bring about a termination or deferment of the Fort Monmouth investigations in one backstage maneuver or another.

¶That when matters subject to Congressional investigation were apparent, the Army's spokesmen were "derelict" in not introducing immediate protest against the committee's alleged interest in and pressures for Mr. Schine.

Democrats Milder

The report of the Democrats seemed milder at many points

244

than those made jointly or individually by Republicans. The Democratic report held that Mr. McCarthy had "fully acquiesced in and condoned" the "improper actions" of Mr. Cohn.

"For these inexcusable actions," the report added, "Senator McCarthy and Mr. Cohn merit severe criticism" on the ground that they had sought preferential Army treatment for Private Schine.

The Democrats also rebuked Secretary Stevens and Mr. Adams for following the line of "appeasement."

It was the duty of Secretary Stevens, as the head of the Army, the Democrats contended, to report immediately any instance in which pressure had been invoked to urge the department to depart from its system of impartial treatment to all of its human components.

Herein, it was held, the Secretary "demonstrated an inexcusable indecisiveness."

The principal issues of the long and sensational inquiry were these:

¶Did Senator McCarthy, Mr. Cohn and Francis P. Carr, the subcommittee's executive director, use the investigating arm of the Senate in an effort to secure preferential treatment for Mr. Schine?

¶Did Mr. Stevens seek to use Mr. Schine as a means to halt or deter investigation of certain activities of the Army by the McCarthy subcommittee?

Two Discarded Issues

Other issues entered the picture. Senator McCarthy was accused of using "vehement language" and "browbeating" Brig. Gen. Ralph W. Zwicker, commandant of Camp Kilmer, as he questioned him in closed session.

One discarded issue was the propriety of Senator McCarthy's presentation as evidence of excerpts of a report by the Federal Bureau of Investigation—held to be "top secret"—for public view. Another was Mr. McCarthy's contention that employes or officials in executive departments should turn over to his committee information "in the public interest' that remained classified as matter still under security order.

The Republicans of the subcommittee held that these were extraneous matters, even though their importance might be great. As assigned to the specific Army-McCarthy dispute, they held such matters were beyond their jurisdiction and should be handled as routine of the investigations subcommittee when it returns to its assigned tasks.

On Future Investigations

The majority made several specific recommendations dealing with the conduct of committee personnel and with future procedures of Congressional investigations. Among them were:

¶That no unpaid staff members be used.

¶That committees adopt a rule against unauthorized contacts between staff members and policy-forming officials of the Executive Branch on matters not specifically involved in committee proceedings.

¶That hearings outside Washington be authorized by majority

Associated Press Wirephoto

BACK TO BACK: Senators Edwin C. Johnson and Joseph R. McCarthy as they appeared at end of yesterday's special Senate Committee hearing. They were principals in heated exchange.

vote and that at least two members attend.

¶That investigating committee chairmen supply members with a weekly summary of staff activities.

¶That a Senate Judiciary subcommittee study what data the Executive Branch is justified in denying Congress.

In his report Senator Dirksen alleged, in effect, that the Army never would have filed charges against the investigating group if Senator McCarthy had not served notice that he was going to subpoena members of the Army loyalty and screening board. Mr. McCarthy served this notice as he was investigating the case of Maj. Irving M. Peress, an Army dentist who received an honorable discharge after refusing to answer questions concerning alleged Communistic sympathies.

Senator Potter contended that while the subcommittee was investigating the Army, Mr. Cohn exerted his full pressures as chief counsel of the subcommittee to obtain favors for Private Schine. Senator McCarthy knew what was going on, he stated, but instead of stopping it, continued to praise and express confidence in Mr. Cohn and the work he was doing. That, he held, was giving Mr. Cohn a free rein.

Dirksen Cites Chronology

Mr. Dirksen focused on the Army's own "chronology of events," the basis of its twenty-nine charges against Senator Mc-

Carthy and members of his staff. The chronology covered more than a year, during which, the Senator contended, luncheons, dinners, prize fights, theatre tickets and other signs of harmonious companionship — not suspicion and recriminations—were the order of the day.

It was four months after Mr. Schine joined the subcommittee staff, Mr. Dirksen held, that the first alleged improper effort was made to obtain for him, as a prospective draftee, an Army commission. Mr. Schine did not get a commission, he said, but there was no complaint about Mr. Cohn's attempt to get him one.

Four hours later, Mr. Dirksen declared, the committee first began to formalize its inquiry to Fort Monmouth. Mr. Schine was drafted about a month after that.

Not until last January, Senator Dirksen emphasized, did the subpoena issue arise, accompanied by the first indication that the Army was to open fire on the subcommittee. At that time, the Senator said, the Army began compiling its "chronology," which developed into formal charges in April.

Senator Dirksen contended that the review of monitored telephone calls to, from and within the Pentagon "impels" a conclusion that Secretary Stevens "entertained no belief of improper means or influence on the part of Senator McCarthy or his staff."

One call in particular, the Senator stated, demonstrated that Secretary Stevens was "fully acquainted with every facet and angle of the Schine story." He declared that in this telephonic conversation Mr. Stevens had said: "* * * I don't have a lot of stuff so far as my contact with Joe or the committee is concerned."

Potter's Conclusions

Senator Potter concluded, in brief, that:

¶Secretary Stevens handled charge and counter-charge through days of questioning in a way suggesting "lack of competency," "bewilderment" and a record of "vacillation and appeasement" while under pressure for favors to be granted Mr. Schine. Meanwhile the Secretary strongly supported charges intending to defer or terminate investigations at Fort Monmouth, with the Schine case developments as weapons to fight off further inquiry.

¶Mr. Schine, lacking professional investigative training and being of "questionable value" to the subcommittee, knew of the imminence of his induction not long after Mr. Cohn had got him his post as a volunteer and unpaid chief consultant of the subcommittee.

¶Mr. Cohn's activities on the part of Mr. Schine impaired the effectiveness of legislative inquiries into the operations of the Executive Branch and subtracted from public confidence in Congressional investigations.

¶Mr. Carr, an F. B. I.-trained investigator, who became executive director of subcommittee programs, was junior to Mr. Cohn in service and appeared to be acceding to Mr. Cohn's wishes. Whatever protests he entered were "feeble."

¶Mr. Adams, the highest legal authority in the Department of the Army, appeared to share the Secretary's hope that the Fort Monmouth investigation could be deterred, and to act accordingly in his back-stage discussions with committee spokesmen.

McClellan's Statement

Senator McClellan in his statement commenting on the report said:

"Because of the highly controversial nature of the issues and the personalities involved, this has been one of the most unpleasant public services I have ever had to perform. Throughout the hearings and in writing this report, I have tried to be fair and just to all of the principles to this controversy. In considering and writing this report, there was present at times the natural inclination to say as little as possible, or to say more than might be necessary, or to so phrase it in language that might be susceptible of varied interpretations—in other words, to say a lot that might mean nothing.

"Speaking for the Democratic members of the subcommittee, however, we were able to reconcile such minor differences as may have existed among us, and it is gratifying to me that we have been able to submit a joint report and not separate and independent views. We have recorded our findings in terms we trust that are temperate and judicious and that are based upon and sustained by the record of the proceedings before us."

Three of the principals withheld comment this evening.

Senator McCarthy declared he would have nothing to say tonight.

Secretary Stevens left word at the Pentagon that he had "no comment at this time."

Mr. Adams said he planned to spend the evening at Griffith Stadium watching a baseball game between the Washington Senators and the Detroit Tigers.

"I will have nothing to say about the report, in whole or in part, until I've had an opportunity to read it," he declared.

People Judge, Says Cohn

Mr. Cohn issued the following statement last night:

"The American people have seen and heard what took place at these hearings. They are the jury. Their decision is what counts. And they have given me tremendous support in this controversy and in my work on the prosecution of Communists and spies.

"It is now apparent that anyone who associates himself with the cause of exposing atheistic Communist infiltration has to contend not only with the smears of Communists but with partisan politics as well."

Welch, St. Clair on Vacation

Special to The New York Times.
BOSTON, Aug. 31—Both Joseph N. Welch, Army counsel in the inquiry, and James D. St. Clair, his associate, were on vacation on Cape Cod. Neither could be reached immediately.

September 1, 1954

Excerpt From Speeches That Define G.O.P. and Democratic Positions

INTERNAL SECURITY

THE REPUBLICAN POSITION

NIXON: The previous Administration's lack of understanding of the Communist danger and its failures to deal with it firmly * * * [have] led to our major difficulties today. The previous Administration unfortunately adopted policies which were soft, vacillating and inconsistent in dealing with the Communist threat.

* * * The Eisenhower Adminis-
tration, with the solid backing of the Republican Eighty-third Congress, has finally put the Reds on the run in America. * * *

Laws have been passed [providing] more effective legal weapons to use against the Communist conspircy. * * * The Communists and their sympathizers have been driven from Federal employment * * * During the Truman years * * * the Communist Fifth Column made a shambles of our domestic security.

The Communist party is right when it says the 1954 elections are crucial in determining the path America will take. It has determined to conduct its program within the Democratic party * * * to infiltrate the Democratic party and to make its policies the policies of the Democratic party.

THE DEMOCRATIC POSITION

STEVENSON: As to the * * * Republican campaign theme, model C3K1—crime, corruption controls and Korea—well, I doubt that the market for yesterday's slogans is any better than the market for yesterday's newspapers * * *. President Eisenhower has begun to talk about Communists in Government and red herrings, after assuring us months ago that his Administration's record was the only issue.

It looks as though the Great Crusade, under the leadership of the Vice President, is going to end up * * * on the elevated note of subversion, perversion and denunciation of President Truman. I suppose that's what they call McCarthyism in a white collar. [They have] maligned and impugned the very loyalty of a former President of the United States—a man * * * who has done more to fight communism on all the fronts than all the Republican politicians put together —and I mean Harry S. Truman.

October 31, 1954

FORECAST ON 'NIXONISM'

Schlesinger Says It Will Take Place of McCarthy 'Tactics'

Arthur M. Schlesinger Jr., Professor of History at Harvard University, said here last night that "Nixonism, a kind of kidgloves McCarthyism, would replace the more ruthless tactics of Senator McCarthy" in Republican strategy in the next two years.

He discussed the political roles of Vice President Richard M. Nixon and Senator Joseph R. McCarthy, Wisconsin Republican, in an address before the New York Young Democratic Club at Freedom House, 20 West Fortieth Street.

Mr. Schlesinger, who was a speech writer in 1952 for Adlai E. Stevenson, Democratic candidate for the Presidency, said that, while the recent election had been "a kind of a liquidation of McCarthy, it has not made a definite pronouncement against Nixonism."

November 19, 1954

FINAL VOTE CONDEMNS M'CARTHY, 67-22, FOR ABUSING SENATE AND COMMITTEE; ZWICKER COUNT ELIMINATED IN DEBATE

REPUBLICANS SPLIT

Democrats Act Solidly in Support of Motion Against Senator

By ANTHONY LEVIERO
Special to The New York Times.

WASHINGTON, Dec. 2—The Senate voted 67 to 22 tonight to condemn Joseph R. McCarthy, Republican Senator from Wisconsin.

Every one of the forty-four Democrats present voted against Mr. McCarthy. The Republicans were evenly divided—twenty-two for condemnation and twenty-two against. The one independent, Senator Wayne Morse of Oregon, also voted against Mr. McCarthy.

In the ultimate action the Senate voted to condemn Senator McCarthy for contempt of a Senate Elections subcommittee that investigated his conduct and financial affairs, for abuse of its members, and for his insults to the Senate itself during the censure proceeding.

Lost in a day of complex and often confused parliamentary maneuvering was the proposal to censure Senator McCarthy for his denunciation of Brig. Gen. Ralph W. Zwicker as unfit to wear his uniform.

This proposal was defeated by a parliamentary device that avoided a direct vote on the merits of the issue. Inquiry among influential Senators indicated they considered the Zwicker proposal a dilemma they wished to avoid.

Amendment Substituted

They said they wished to censure because the facts warranted it. If they failed to do so, they believed large elements of the public would feel the Senate took notice of offenses only against itself and not against ordinary citizens.

But also if they did censure for this, then Senator McCarthy could exploit the decision, contending he was being punished for his effort to expose former

Maj. Irving Peress, the Army dentist who was promoted and honorably discharged, and who was denounced by Mr. McCarthy as a "Fifth Amendment Communist."

Mr. McCarthy's denunciation of General Zwicker, who was commanding officer at Camp Kilmer, N. J., when Dr. Peress was discharged, occurred when the Senator interrogated General Zwicker on the question of who had promoted Dr. Peress.

The direct test on the Zwicker issue was avoided by the substitution of the amendment to condemn Senator McCarthy for having insulted the Senate during his censure trial.

McCarthy Loses Three Tests

Thus in its final form the resolution of condemnation was in two parts, covering the offenses against the Elections subcommittee and its members in the first part, and against the Senate in the second. Three test votes were all lost by Mr. McCarthy before the final condemnation.

First was a motion to table the Zwicker proposal, made by Senator Styles Bridges, Republican of New Hampshire, the president pro tem of th Senate, who assumed the leadership of the effort to save Mr. McCarthy yesterday.

Such a motion, if it had succeeded, might have led to a situation that would have prolonged the debate.

But amid signs that the Zwicker issue would have tough sledding, Senator Wallace F. Bennett, Republican of Utah, served notice that if Mr. Bridges' move were defeated he would attempt to substitute for the Zwicker issue his amendment for abuse of the Senate. The significance of this was that an amendment by substitution would require no time out for debate.

Then the voting proceeded. The motion to table was defeated 55 to 33. Mr. Bennett's motion to substitute passed by 64 to 23 and in the next vote his amendment was adopted by the same tally.

The final vote placing Mr. McCarthy under moral condemnation by the Senate came at 5:03 P. M.

The moment of decision was

Associated Press Wirephoto

CONDEMNED ON TWO COUNTS: Senator McCarthy as he left the Senate floor last night after members adopted a resolution condemning his conduct. The vote was 67-22.

something of an anti-climax after days of emotional and bitter debate. It was punctuated by mocking laughter from the hard core of Mr. McCarthy's adherents.

The accused Senator was present, but he was not led to the bar of the Senate to hear any punishment. Instead Mr. Bridges arose from the coterie in the vicinity of Mr. McCarthy and asked Vice President Richard M. Nixon if the word "censure" appeared anywhere in the resolution in its final form.

Laughter from Senator William E. Jenner, Republican of Indiana, and one of Mr. McCarthy's most vociferous sup-

porters, resounded through the chamber. Senator McCarthy was grinning. Senator George W. Malone, Republican of Nevada, standing by Senator Jenner, was laughing, and so was Senator Herman Welker, Republican of Idaho, sitting beside Mr. Jenner, who all through the debate made the running defense for Mr. McCarthy.

Mr. Jenner guffawed loudly again as Mr. Nixon, after examining the text with a clerk, announced the word "censure" was absent. The document used the word "condemned" in each of its two parts, it was explained.

"Then it is not a censure resolution," said Mr. Bridges, who by virtue of his office presides over the Senate when Mr. Nixon is absent. He also asked if condemnation was censure.

Fulbright Reads Definitions

"The resolutoin does concern the conduct of the junior Senator from Wisconsin," replied the Vice President. "The interpretation must be that of the Senator or any other Senator."

Then Senator J. William Fulbright, Democrat of Arkansas, rose with Webster's International Dictionary before him and read definitions of condemn and censure amid general laughter. Senator Jenner, without asking for the floor said, "Let's do it over again. Let's do a retake."

Senator Bridges then remarked that this was "peculiar censure" to discover after all the time and expense of a special Senate session that the resolution did not contain the word "censure."

Senator Fulbright asserted that Senator Welker had attached a more serious meaning to "condemn" than to "censure." Earlier today in one of his impassioned speeches Mr. Welker had said, "You don't censure a man to death, you condemn him to death."

Senator Arthur V. Watkins, Republican of Utah, who was chairman of the special committee that recommended censure, then said that in the last censure proceeding, twenty-five years ago, the word "censure" was not used but that the resolution had stated that "such conduct is hereby condemned."

"The point I wanted to make," said Senator Watkins, "is that it is the historical word used in censure resolutions."

Then Mr. Jenner asked for the floor in the usual parliamentary way, this time, to remark, grinning, there was some confusion and "do you suppose we could do it all over again?"

Senator Welker rose to comment on definitions and referred to the censure proceedings as a "mock court."

Shortly afterward Senator McCarthy left. He had been in the Senate chamber only briefly, coming in after the final roll-call on the ultimate vote had started. He said "present" instead of voting on the issue that is bound to have a marked effect on his political career.

Later, outside the chamber, reporters asked him if he felt he had been censured.

"Well, it wasn't exactly a vote of confidence," replied Mr. McCarthy, who was still wearing his right arm in a bandage for the bursitis that had interrupted the censure proceedings for ten days.

"I'm happy to have this circus ended so I can get back to the real work of digging out communism, crime and corruption," he continued. "That job will start officially Monday morning. after ten months of inaction." He was referring to a coming inquiry into alleged Communists in defense plants.

He had referred to the session as a "lynch party"—one of the remarks for which he was condemned in the Bennett amendment—and was asked if he felt he had been "lynched."

"I don't feel I have been lynched," he replied.

He expressed his disappointment that the Democrats had voted "straight down the party line, even though they had declared before it started that this was to be a judicial proceeding."

Among Democrats the view was that he might have received a number of their votes if he had not condemned the whole Democratic party some months ago as "the party of treason."

Mr. McCarthy said after referring to the "circus" that he felt no different than he had last night. That is when he had referred to the censure proceeding as a "farce" and a "foul job."

Shouting objections, Senator Jenner opposed an amendment by Senator Edwin C. Johnson, Democrat of Colorado, and vice chairman of the censure committee, that would have placed the Senate on record in the censure resolution as being against communism and determined to investigate subversion relentlessly.

"You're not going to gild the lily now," shouted Senator Jenner. "The record has been made and you are going to stay with it."

He declared that the Democrats had permitted Communists to steal Government secrets through infiltration of the Government.

Senator Price Daniels, Democrat of Texas, then made an eloquent plea, proposing that the resolution be amended to state that the resolution should not be construed to limit the investigative powers of the Senate, especially as to any Communist conspiracy.

He said he wanted to do this to counter the McCarthy charge that the Communist party had reached into the Senate to make a censure committee "do the work of the Communist party."

"I want to make them [the Communists] unhappy and they will be unhappy if you will per-

mit this amendement to be adopted," said Mr. Daniels to Mr. Jenner. "We will be able to say to the world that the allegation is untrue that the Communist party instigated this."

Vice President Nixon ruled that under a consent agreement between the two parties neither the Johnson nor the Daniel amendment could be accepted because it was not germane to the issue of censure.

Flanders Retracts One Point

Toward the end of the Senate session, which adjourned sine die for this year at 7:10 P. M., Senator Ralph E. Flanders, Republican of Vermont, who had sponsored the original censure resolution, said he would stand by all the speeches he had made against Senator McCarthy except that he would like to apologize for a passage in a speech of last March, when he had likened Mr. McCarthy to Hitler.

He also asked unanimous consent to strike the passage from whatever volumes of The Congressional Record remained unbound, but Senator Welker made the single objection that prevented this.

Senators McCarthy, Welker and Jenner have threatened to file counter censure resolutions against Senators Flanders, Fulbright and Morse, who had filed the specifications for the McCarthy censure action. They gave no indication of their plans, and adjournment of the Senate tonight would compel them to wait until the next session.

But Senator Jenner threatened Mr. Flanders with a subpoena if he did not appear before some committee to testify about any relations he might have had with Owen Lattimore.

Mr. Lattimore is a former State Department consultant and professor at Johns Hopkins University who is under indictment on a charge of perjury in a Congressional hearing on his alleged Communist associations.

General Zwicker, now with combat troops in Japan, was criticized by a few McCarthy adherents today as an arrogant and evasive witness against the contrary evidence of the censure committee, which had called him as a witness.

He had a great many champions, though, even among some Senators who said they would not vote for censure in his case, though they deplored the treatment he had received.

Senator Herbert H. Lehman,

Democrat of New York, was among those urging censure in the Zwicker incident. The view of this group was that it would be notice to the country that the Senate was interested only in the offenses against itself but cared nothing of abusive treatment of ordinary citizens.

Senator A. S. Mike Monroney, Democrat of Oklahoma, declared that failure to censure on this count would be notice to the public that the Senate was "a privileged class." He asserted the Zwicker incident was a prime example of how Senator McCarthy indiscriminately abused heroes of the United States and Communists.

Senator Monroney also said failure to censure on this count would be notice that it was all right to place wire taps and intercept mail and telephone calls of teachers, professors, private citizens, whether it was constitutional or not, but that it was not all right to do so in the case of the ninety-six Senators.

It would also amount to saying, he added, that "We are sacrosanct, we are going to disregard the constitutional guarantees."

His allusion here was to the charge by Senator McCarthy that the Elections subcommittee that had investigated his conduct and finances in 1952 had kept a undercover watch on his mail and telephone calls.

Mr. McCarthy contended this was illegal, but the debate brought out yesterday that the subcommittee had been investigating the charge that Senator McCarthy was using money sent him by the public to fight communism to speculate on a commodity exchange.

Senator Charles E. Potter, Republican of Michigan, a Silver Star Army veteran who lost both legs in combat, said he also favored censure in the Zwicker case.

Senator Irving M. Ives, Republican of New York, defeated in the race for Governor in the recent election, kept silent on the McCarthy issue all through the debate, but voted against Mr. McCarthy.

However, whenever Senator Watkins made the pro forma motions to reconsider each vote—a technicality needed to make it final—Senator Ives each time made the necessary motion to table.

December 3, 1954

M'CARTHY BREAKS WITH EISENHOWER; RUES 1952 SUPPORT

By ANTHONY LEVIERO

Special to The New York Times.

WASHINGTON, Dec. 7—Senator Joseph R. McCarthy broke his long-deteriorating relations with President Eisenhower today.

He denounced the President for his "tolerance" of Chinese Communists who were holding American war prisoners, and for congratulating two Senators who had urged the censure of the

Wisconsin Republican.

Mr. McCarthy "apologized" to the American people for having urged the election of General Eisenhower in the 1952 campaign. He declared he had been "mis-

taken" in believing General Eisenhower would fight Communists vigorously at home and abroad. And he accused the President of a "shrinking show of weakness" toward Red China.

The attack by Mr. McCarthy, who was condemned only last Thursday for conduct unbecoming to a Senator, precipitated a political storm in the capital For his sounding board, Mr. McCarthy used a hearing of his own Senate Permanent Subcommittee on Investigations.

He did not participate in the hearing. He merely appeared briefly twice, and loosed his blast the second time. Then he left with his wife, and tonight they were reported on their way out of town for a week or ten days.

In this first formal statement since he was condemned by the Senate Mr. McCarthy assailed the President for congratulating Senator Arthur V. Watkins of Utah, chairman of the special committee that recommended his censure, and Senator Ralph E. Flanders of Vermont, who had sponsored the censure resolution, both Republicans.

While avoiding direct comment on the condemnation verdict of the Senate, President Eisenhower praised Mr. Watkins when he visited the White House on Saturday, for a "very splendid job." There has been no evidence that President Eisenhower indicated his feelings to Mr. Flanders.

Other political figures lashed at Mr. McCarthy or upheld him, but President Eisenhower abided by his policy of avoiding personal involvement in the McCarthy dispute.

The only reaction from the White House was to bring up to date the statistics of the Administration's fight on Communists at home and to reiterate the President's statement, made last week:

"Now, on our side we must make certain that our efforts to promote peace are not interpreted as appeasement or any purchase of immediate favor at the cost of principle, but we must, on the other hand, be steady and refuse to be goaded into actions that would be unwise."

Mr. McCarthy's frontal attack on the President and leader of the Republican party immediately revived speculation that he might seek to start a third party. A cryptic remark by Mr. McCarthy fueled the talk about the division of the Republican party.

He was asked if he would bolt the party and start a new one.

"I have no interest — at the present time—in a third party," Mr. McCarthy replied. What was new in his position were the words "at the present time."

"I intend to work in the Republican party," Mr. McCarthy declared. "I've said all I'd better say."

Some Republican leaders felt, however, that if Mr. McCarthy continued with what they regarded as extreme tactics he might lose whatever substantial support he has in and outside Congress and find himself politically isolated.

Notable in the flood of comments that followed his explosion was the fact that some of the Senators who had defended Mr. McCarthy against censure assailed him today.

Among them was Senator Eugene D. Millikin, Republican of Colorado, one of the deans of the Senate, who has great influence in party councils.

Another was Senator Barry Goldwater, Republican of Arizona, who had assumed an active role in trying to save the Wisconsin Senator from the condemnation that was expressed by a vote of 67 to 22.

Leonard W. Hall, the Republican National Chairman, scored Mr. McCarthy with this statement:

"Senator McCarthy has made a major error. Without attempting to evaluate his fight against communism, I regret to find him in what must be strange company to him, making personal attack on the President of the United States.

"The record of the Eisenhower Administration on the Communist menace both at home and abroad speaks for itself. I do not think it is necessary to remind the people that President Eisenhower was fighting the Communists quite a few years before Senator McCarthy made his maiden speech on the subject in the Senate."

Senator McCarthy had calculated the time and setting for his statement. His subcommittee held its first public hearing in several months, with the aim of exposing alleged Communists employed in the Bethlehem Steel Company's plant in Bethlehem, Pa.

At the scheduled time, 10:30 A. M., only Senators Karl E. Mundt of South Dakota, and Charles E. Potter of Michigan, both Republicans, were on hand with staff counsel. They went ahead. Reporters were told that something important would happen and they would receive a text.

At 10:37 Mr. McCarthy walked in with his wife. She sat with the audience and he with the committee, but he took no part

and Mr. Mundt continued to preside. Mr. McCarthy was still wearing a bandage on his arm for his bursitis and gave this as the explanation for not participating. At 10:50 A. M., Mr. and Mrs. McCarthy left, but they came back at 11:40 A. M.

By that time two witnesses, Joseph A. Pecucci, native of Italy, and John S. Szabo, native of Hungary, both naturalized, had invoked the Fifth Amendment to the Constitution against self-incrimination as they were questioned about alleged Communist party membership and associations.

Mr. McCarthy resumed his seat as Mr. Szabo took refuge in the Constitution again. Senator McCarthy interrupted as the committee counsel, James N. Juliana, was asking a question. He said:

"I hate to do this. I'd like to read a brief statement."

He then read it, declaring that exposure of Communists working on secret weapons might determine whether "the sons of American mothers may live or die." He said his statement might be "my temporary swan song as chairman of the investigating committee."

He emphasized "temporary." Controll of Congress will pass to the Democrats in January and with it the chairmanships of the committees.

Then Mr. McCarthy stated that the work of this committee had been held up about ten months and the President had "taken it upon himself to congratulate Senators Flanders and Watkins who have been instrumental in holding up our work."

He went on in this vein, making his "apology" for having supported the President in 1952. He referred to the unsuccessful efforts by his friends to persuade him to apologize in their effort to prevent censure, saying he felt rather that he should "apologize" to the American people for having supported General Eisenhower in 1952.

"Unfortunately," Mr. McCarthy concluded, "the President sees fit to congratulate those who hold up the exposure of Communists in one breath and in the next breath urges patience, tolerance and niceties to those who are torturing American uniformed men."

Senator Flanders referred to Mr. McCarthy's statement about the thirteen Americans being held prisoners by Red China. He added:

"I cannot help feeling that the statement given out is primarily a political one, using a sad and very difficult situation as its excuse. The junior Senator from Wisconsin has declared political war."

Senator Watkins had this to say:

"Senator McCarthy's attack on the President, Senator Flanders and myself shows him to be the same irresponsible McCarthy that the Senate by an overwhelming vote condemned last Thursday."

Senator Watkins also said the Eisenhower Administration had reason to be proud of its record "in ferreting out Communists and jailing the guilty." He said he agreed with the Administration's Asian policy.

Senator Watkins called attention to his own long record of exposing Communists as a member of the Senate Internal Security subcommittee. He said that if this record was not as well known as Mr. McCarthy's it was because his investigations "were carried out without any thought of self-aggrandizement."

At first the White House would not comment on the McCarthy blast. Then it reissued a statement of last June 2, listing the results of the prosecutions of Communists for advocating the otherthrow of the Government through violence, and the campaign to eliminate security risks. This statement said that the "Department of Justice and the Federal Bureau of Investigation are the principal agents of the Government in dealing with subversives."

It listed eight items, including conviction of fifty Communist party leaders and indictment of forty-nine; addition of sixty-two organizations to the Justice Department's official list of subversive organizations that now total 255; indictment of one person for treason; conviction of two for espionage and ten for making false statements to the Government; deportation of 129 alien subversives; orders for 410 to be deported; orders for denaturalization of forty-nine and the barring of 172 subversive aliens.

Senator Herman Welker, Republican of Idaho and chief defender of Mr. McCarthy in the censure debate:

"I hardly think it is necessary for the Chief Executive to be warmly congratulating anyone in this very unfortunate matter. In this political trial, and that is all it was, the ninety-six Senators were not the judges. The 160,000,-000 Americans were the judges of the trial of McCarthy which in my opinion blew up in the face of the author of Senate Censure Resolution 801 and those who offered amendments. McCarthy stands vindicated before the jury of the American people."

December 8, 1954

The McCarthy Phenomenon--and How It Waxed and Waned

SENATOR JOE McCARTHY. By Richard H. Rovere. 280 pp. New York: Harcourt, Brace & Co. $3.95.

By ANTHONY LEWIS

"LIAR," "barbarian," "seditionist," "cynic." Those are some of Richard H. Ro-

vere's words for Joseph Raymond McCarthy, United States Senator from 1947 until his death ten years later, and for a few of those years—again Mr. Rovere's language—"in many ways the most gifted dema-

gogue ever bred on these shores." This, then, is an appraisal without apology. If its judgments are uncompromising, they are also given without rancor, indeed with an air of almost sympathetic curiosity

about the phenomenon that was McCarthy.

Mr. Rovere writes The New Yorker's "Letter From Washington," our most cultivated and penetrating regular magazine commentary on the capital.

It is no surprise, therefore, that his book is a vividly written, sophisticated re-creation of a political episode whose manic qualities already begin to seem unbelievable.

It all happened so fast. Elected in the Republican landslide of 1946, Senator McCarthy was just another member of the Senate, unsung, and—so far as anyone knew—untalented. Then, in 1950, as the time for his re-election campaign approached, he sought an issue and found it. He made a speech accusing the State Department of harboring 205 (or eighty-one or fifty-seven; the number he used is disputed) Communists on its staff. To his own surprise, and for reasons that have never been sufficiently explained, a few newspapers played up the speech.

Before long Senator McCarthy had propelled himself to a position of extraordinary power. His vehicle was, in his words, "The issue of Communism in government." Democrats who opposed him were beaten at the polls, and others quaked. The Democratic Administration, spending its efforts on rear-guard action against his attacks, was reduced to political impotency. Then a Republican Administration took office and found Senator McCarthy at its heels, too. As chairman of the investigations subcommittee of the Committee on Government Operations, he badgered the Voice of America, the State Department, the Army. President Eisenhower, Mr. Rovere accurately concludes, "shared with McCarthy the command of many parts of the Government."

"He walked, then," Mr. Rovere says, "with a heavy tread over large parts of the Constitution of the United States, and he cloaked his own gross figure in the sovereignty it asserts and the powers it distributes. He usurped executive and judicial authority whenever the fancy struck him. It struck him

often."

Then, as suddenly, it ended. The misadventures of two assistants, Roy M. Cohn and G. David Schine, led to a showdown with the Army, then the Administration, then the Senate. His condemnation by the Senate in 1954, together with the Democratic election victory that fall, finished Senator McCarthy's power.

In impressionist style, Mr. Rovere gives the reader an image of the man and his works —and also focuses attention on some things that should be remembered.

He reminds us of a President who thought it best to do nothing while his party, his Government and his country were torn apart and who, only after the Senate condemned McCarthy, struck the Senator and his wife from the White House guest list. He reminds us that Senator McCarthy was applauded by many intellectual conservatives, that Senator Robert A. Taft was said to have told him: "If one case doesn't work, try another." He reminds us that as late as 1954 a Gallup Poll showed 50 per cent of Americans with a "favorable opinion" of McCarthy and 29 per cent "unfavorable."

All this is valuable, but one must also say that it is not enough. What the book lacks is detailed documentation and the thorough research that would be needed to give any fresh insight into Joseph R. McCarthy. Instead of painting with a broad brush the effects on Government morale, for example, it would be necessary to examine in detail what happened to a particular agency. Nor could any work on McCarthy be definitive without new material—disclosures by those involved—on his dealings with the Eisenhower Administration. The facts of his childhood, life and death would have to be explored more thoroughly.

This lack of factual support affects the persuasiveness of

Mr. Rovere's interesting theorizing on the meaning of the McCarthy episode.

He rejects the thesis that McCarthy simply rode the crest of a wave of discontent produced by Soviet foreign policy successes, the Korean war, disclosures of espionage in this country, and the like. Even given all those factors, Mr. Rovere argues, McCarthy had an extraordinary demagogic talent that brought the wave to flood. He does not attempt any hard explanation of what produced the talent in McCarthy, but he does suggest that the nationalizing of issues and of communications in this country may make it easier for All-American demagogues to arise in the future.

On the other hand, Mr. Rovere argues that our institutions withstood the McCarthy assault better than many have said. Congress and the Executive may have quavered, but the Supreme Court and most of the churches and universities and press resisted. This would be a more heartening conclusion if it were not true, as Mr. Rovere indicates, that only accidents of history and curious mistakes of his own brought on Senator McCarthy's destruction. But if there are shortcomings in the book, it does paint a portrait of Joseph R. McCarthy which the reviewer finds uncommonly sensitive and accurate.

One of the troubling problems for newspaper men covering Senator McCarthy was knowing how to handle a man who lied without shame, in fact with a kind of joy. Few newspapers had the resources to attempt to sift out the untruths, as Mr. Rovere says, and in any case it seemed—at least at first —a ticklish idea to examine a politician's truthfulness. But what should one do with a man who stood on the floor of the Senate, purporting to read ex-

cerpts from a letter by one of his targets, when it turned out later that he literally had made up the quotations? Or what about the tactic that Mr. Rovere graphically describes as the "multiple untruth," a statement or even a sentence so crammed with misstatements, misinterpretations and half truths that one despaired of untangling it?

Senator McCarthy deliberately took the part—and with evident appeal to much of his audience—of a vulgarian, loud, and often profane. The label seditionist fits a man whose instinct was to wreck, who attacked all in power whether of his own party or the opposition, who encouraged civil servants to leak secrets to him and tattle on their superiors.

The characterization of Senator McCarthy as a cynic will be challenged; it produced sharp dissent when Mr. Rovere made it in an Esquire magazine article, now part of this book. Vice President Nixon, for one, has been quoted as feeling that Senator McCarthy "believed what he was doing very deeply." That view is hard to reconcile, however, with the vivid memory of a Senator who snarled almost uncontrollably in a hearing room, then stepped outside and asked reporters puckishly, "How am I doing?" or with the fact that Senator McCarthy invariably gave up any line of attack as soon as headlines diminished.

Most reporters who knew him probably would agree with Mr. Rovere's central conclusion: that Joseph R. McCarthy was a man without principle, without policy, without any long-run goal, who lived for momentary notoriety and sought it by using the best available method to create "noise, confusion, tumult."

June 21, 1959

ROLE OF INFORMERS NOW UNDER INQUIRY

Matusow Case Raises New Questions About Ex-Communists as Witnesses

By ANTHONY LEVIERO
Special to The New York Times.

WASHINGTON, Feb. 5 — The Senate Internal Security subcommittee has undertaken the difficult task of determing what is believable from the lips of an admitted false witness.

Harvey Matusow, a former Communist and, since early 1952, a paid, professional witness, has now made public confession that he has been a colossal slanderer before Congressional committees

and the bar of justice. His repudiation of previous testimony has focused the attention of Congess and the Justice Department on a large and repugnant problem. In the pending investigation of the generation of informers a few of them may be pinned down with perjury indictments.

Matusow could serve as the archetype of the ex-Communist turned professional informer. His repudiation of testimony in Federal courts and before Congressional committees, coupled with the doubts cast on the credibility of Paul Crouch, another ex-Communist, laid open to attack the whole policy of employing professional informers whose reliability and motives can never fully be ascertained.

Task for Federal Agencies

Courts, Congressional committees, the Subversive Activities Control Board, and the Department of Justice are now undertaking the complex task of tracking back through Matusow's long and devious trail. While he is frank now in confessing perjurious sins, officials wonder whether he will switch again when he faces retribution. The Justice Department has used Matusow as a witness on six occasions, twice in court. It is understood that the Department of Justice plans to summon Matusow before a grand jury and indict him for perjury if the evidence warrants.

Perhaps the most important case in which the Justice Department used him was the one in New York City in which thirteen second-string Communist leaders were convicted of conspiracy to advocate overthrow of the Government. In that case Matusov has filed an affidavit admitting perjury. He sought to implicate Roy M. Cohn, former chief counsel of the McCarthy committee and prosecutor of the thirteen Communists, as one who prefabricated some of the evidence against them. Mr. Cohn has denied this.

Matusow has filed a similar affidavit in the Federal Court in El Paso, Tex., where his testimony helped convict Clinton Jencks, a labor leader.

Subpoena Issued

In the wake of Matusow's much publicized confessional press conference the other day in New York, related to the promotion of his book, "False Witness," the Senate Internal Security Subcommittee acted with understandable promptness in subpoenaing him.

Matusow had been a frequent and eager witness before this committee, naming many names, in the celebrated inquiry into the Institute of Pacific Relations,

KEY FIGURE

The New York Times

Harvey M. Matusow.

and the investigation of Communist infiltration of labor unions, youth movements and the like.

The Senate Permanent Investigations Subcommittee, formerly headed by Senator Joseph R. McCarthy, and now under the chairmanship of Senator John L. McClellan, Democrat of Arkansas, may have to act, too. Matusow has asserted that he gave hearsay information to the McCarthy committee, and he also charged that Mr. McCarthy supplied him with "false documents and materials" that he used in political campaigns against several Democratic Senators in 1952.

'Plant' Charged

The Congressional committees also will have to consider the contention of Representative Francis E. Walter of Pennsylvania, chairman of the House Un-American Activities Committee, that Matusow was really a Communist "planted" as a witness by the Communists to discredit Congressional investigations.

The Subversive Activities Control Board, whose mission is to determine which organizations are Communistic and to compel them to register as such, has had Matusow as a witness in four cases.

Like many others of his kind, Matusow volunteered as an informer to the Federal Bureau of Investigation. Both the Justice Department and the control board say that his testimony for the most part was corroborative of other evidence and seldom of itself decisive. Nevertheless, with his credibility damaged or destroyed, new trials may follow.

The F. B. I. is not the only Federal agency that uses informers. The Central Intelligence Agency, the Internal Revenue Bureau, the Customs Service and the Immigration Service employ them to get information on Communists, spies, narcotics peddlers, tax evaders and smugglers.

It should be noted that the F.B.I. in its difficult task of infiltrating the Communist party recruited loyal Americans to join the party for the conscious mission of keeping watch on it. This

'THIS COULD SPOIL THE WHOLE RACKET, MEN'

Herblock in The Washington Post and Times-Herald

group, appealed to on patriotic grounds, has performed commendable and reliable service and evidence given by its members has generally gone unshaken before grand juries and Federal courts.

It is with the army of turnabout informers for profit that the inquiries are concerned and it is expected that the agencies using them will be compelled by the force of public opinion to reexamine their policies on this.

The Government has had the most trouble with informers in the anti-Communist field because of the obvious difficulties of corroborating testimony about Communist party membership. In this field also informers of unstable character and suspect motives have turned up.

In recent months the names of a considerable number of paid informers used by the Immigration and Naturalization Service have come to light. This agency

uses them against deportable Communists and criminals. Among the most prominent in this group was Paul Crouch, a former Communist, to whom $9,675.50 was paid between July 1, 1952, and May 31, 1954, for his various appearances as a witness.

Crouch's credibility was attacked from various quarters, and the Justice Department has had him under investigation since early last summer.

Some Federal law enforcement officials and Congressional staff members assert that it is virtually impossible to get convictions without the use of informers. For a long time now this attitude has prevailed. But there are new chairmen in the committees of the new Congress and Matusow has posed the problem in a way that cannot be evaded.

February 6, 1955

Survey of 50 Loyalty Cases Implies Evaluation Flaws

By LUTHER A. HUSTON
Special to The New York Times.

WASHINGTON, Aug. 14—A study of what happens when employes face charges involving loyalty under the Government's personnel security program was made public today. The study was under the direction of Adam Yarmolinsky, Washington lawyer. It was financed by the Fund for the Republic, an independent non-profit corporation in New York concerned with the protection of civil rights. The fund is endowed by the Ford Foundation.

The study made no recommendations and did not evaluate the information assembled.

Among the charges against one employe was that "Communist art" hung on the walls of his home. It turned out that the art consisted of works by Picasso, Matisse, Renoir and other famous painters.

The study implied that inclusion in the charges of factors that did not involve national security, or did so only remotely, was a major problem. It alluded to lack of experience and judgment of security officers in evaluating information, incompetent or inexperienced hearing boards and inadequate defense by lawyers representing employes.

In a case where a man and wife had been jointly charged, the principal accusation against the wife was that she had "continued a sympathetic association with your husband." The wife replied that she had loved her husband for thirty years and wondered if the security officer was suggesting that she get a divorce.

Tragedies were disclosed, too. In the same husband-wife case, the husband, who had been described in the charges as "a trouble-maker, antagonizer and braggart," was so upset that he resigned his Government position. Ten days later he entered a mental hospital.

Mr. Yarmolinsky was once a law clerk for Associate Justice Stanley F. Reed of the Supreme Court. Dr. Robert M. Hutchins, former chancellor of the University of Chicago, is head of the Fund for the Republic, which granted $60,000 for the study.

The fund also is financing a study of the Federal loyalty-security program by the Association of the Bar of the City of New York. Dudley B. Bonsal, New York lawyer, is chairman of the association's study committee.

Other members of the association committee are Richard M. Bentley of Chicago, Frederick M. Bradley of Washington, D. C.; Henry J. Friendly of New York, former Judge Harold M. Kennedy of New York, Monte M. Lemann of New Orleans, John O'Melveny of Los Angeles, George Roberts of New York and Whitney North Seymour of New York.

Entitled "Case Studies in Personnel Security," the study was printed here by the Bureau of National Affairs, Inc., publishers of business news. It contained details of fifty cases. The study is still in progress and eventually will comprise 350 cases.

Questions ranged from "What do you think of female chastity" to whether the employe was interested in dianoetics, which is described by the dictionary as pertaining to "discursive reasoning."

The fifty cases came from fourteen cities. They dealt with Government civilian employes, industrial employes, military and port security personnel and employes of international organizations.

In each case publication was authorized by the employe concerned. In no cases were names of defendants disclosed, and in only a few were the employing agencies identified. Even the cities where the workers were employed were not revealed, nor were names of security officers, hearing board members or witnesses.

This was the first study of a substantial number of cases under the security program, but Mr. Yarmolinsky conceded that it presented "only part of the picture."

"While these cases do not, of themselves, support conclusive statements about the system, they make it possible for it to be examined in operation, at least to the extent that its operations are not classified," he said.

The missing element in the study is the Government's file. Confidential information obtained by the Federal Bureau of Investigation was the basis for most of the charges. Only in one case was this information partly revealed.

In several cases where clearance of the employe had been granted by agency hearing boards, the decision was reversed by department heads on the basis of confidential F. B. I. information.

Basis for Decision

By the Executive order and the law under which the security program was established, the final factor in a decision is whether it would be in the interest of national security to retain the employe.

"The crucial issue in these cases is very seldom a question of fact but rather a question of the judgment to be made on a set of given facts," Mr. Yarmolinsky said.

"In making these judgments, the boards seem frequently to have to rely on the testimony of confidential informers, or of reluctant witnesses whose appearance they cannot compel. The absence of cross-examination is most important where the absent witness expressed an opinion about the employe. Where the case does turn on a controversial question of fact, the lack of cross-examination may be crucial."

In thirty-six of the cases, no Government witnesses appeared. In five, one or two witnesses were questioned.

28 Cases Cleared

That charges often had been hastily or improperly drafted, or were based on trivial information, was indicated in that employes won clearance in twenty-eight of the cases. Clearance was denied in twenty cases. One employe resigned, and in another case no decision has yet been announced.

"The cases illustrate not only how the system works but where the points of friction seem to come," Mr. Yarmolinsky said. "They do not, by themselves, provide enough information to suggest ways of eliminating this friction, if indeed it can be eliminated in every instance, but some of the more persistent friction points can be identified by the following questions:

¶"Can any more effective procedure be developed to dispose of cases without formal charges where further investigation or evaluation would indicate that formal proceedings were unnecessary?

¶"Can greater selectivity be exercised in drawing charges against employes so as to elimi-nate so far as possible those charges which later prove to be baseless, and so as to distinguish somewhat among degrees of seriousness?

¶"Can any mechanism be devised to permit the employe to challenge the sufficiency of a particular allegation without having first to assume the burden of disproving it?

¶"To what extent, if any, can the questioning by the board be limited so as to avoid possible confusion between subversives, and persons who, though holding radical or unpopular views, do not endanger the security of the United States?

¶"Can anything be done to avoid the apparently substantial hardships that result from lengthy suspensions without pay during the pendency of these proceedings, and can anything be done to accelerate the process of decision following the hearing?

¶"Can any provision be made to compel the attendance of reluctant witnesses both for and against the employe, whose presence would not disclose security information?"

Indication of Burden

An indication of the burden imposed on the employe, even in cases where clearance eventually resulted, is that the average elapsed time between suspension and hearing in the fifty cases was nine months, and the average fee paid to lawyers $400. In several cases lawyers charged no fees.

In case No. 23, for instance, the accusations centered on the fact that the employe had written a thesis based on ma-terial obtained from the Institute of Pacific Relations, which had been investigated by Senate groups.

It was also charged that the employe knew Robert E. Sherwood and the late Louis Adamic, well-known authors, and Owen Lattimore. An indictment charging Mr. Lattimore with perjury for denying that he had been a promoter of Communist causes or a follower of the Communist line was dismissed recently by the Department of Justice.

This employe replied that he also knew President Eisenhower, who had bestowed on him an award of the Freedoms Foundation. He testified that the only political organization he had ever belonged to was the Republican party.

He was cleared and restored to duty after a thirteen-month suspension, for which he got full back pay.

An outstanding case was that of an expert geographer employed by the Department of the Army. The study said that he had been cleared on four separate occasions, once "in 1950 by a Senate subcommittee after charges by a United States Senator."

Nineteen specific charges were made against the geographer, ranging from association with Communists and Communist symphatizers to a display of "unreasonable sympathy toward Russia."

One of the questions asked at his hearing was, "Do you by nature get a sort of secret, personal satisfaction out of acting as an individualist?" The geographer acknowledged that he did.

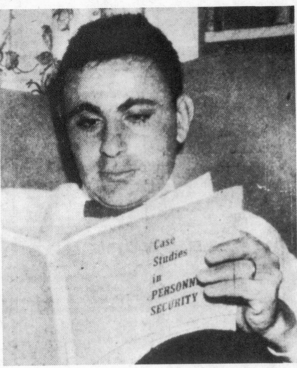

Associated Press Wirephoto

DIRECTOR OF LOYALTY STUDY: Adam Yarmolinsky, Washington lawyer, holds copy of report he edited. It is a study of cases under the Government security program.

He was also asked to define a reactionary. His answer was, "Somebody who wants to go backwards."

Nine and a half months after this employe had been suspended, he was cleared by the Secretary of the Army and reinstated with full back pay.

In another case a Negro semi-skilled Civil Service employe was cleared of charges of having been a Communist after it had been brought out at a hearing that he did not know what "proletariat" and "dialectical materialism" meant.

One employe held a night job in the Government printing office. The only witness for the Government was the agency security officer. Cross-examined, the officer said that one thing against the employe was that he had engaged in "left-wing talk."

Asked to define such talk, the officer said the employe had used the words "second-class citizen."

Counsel for the employe brought out that what the accused had said was that he would "rather be a second-class citizen in Mississippi than a first-class citizen in Russia."

The employe was cleared and reinstated.

August 15, 1955

BUCKLEY STARTING WEEKLY REVIEW

Critic of Yale and Defender of McCarthy Says It Will Counter 'Leftist' Trend

A Nov. 5 start for a new conservative weekly journal of opinion, The National Review, was announced yesterday.

William F. Buckley Jr., editor and publisher, said that $290,000 capital had been raised from 125 investors and that $160,000 had been lined up in circulation and advertising.

The editors include Mr. Buckley, author of "God and Man at Yale" and co-author of "McCarthy and His Enemies"; James Burnham, Willmoore Kendall, Suzanne La Follette, William S. Schlamm and Jonathan Mitchell.

Besides Mr. Buckley, directors are Peter W. Hoguet and Godfrey P. Schmidt, New York lawyers; Clarence Manion, former dean of the University of Notre Dame Law School; John William Rogers, Dallas newspaper man; Morrie Ryskind, playwright; Edwin S. Webster Jr., investment banker, and Gen. Albert C. Wedemeyer (retired).

A memorandum said the new magazine "hopes to change the nation's intellectual and political climate — which, at present, is preponderantly leftist."

Mr. Buckley said that it would contend that "appeasing the Soviet Union is suicidal" and that he believed the Eisenhower Administration had been conducting appeasement "for the past year and a half."

The first issue will print 50,000 copies, Mr. Buckley said, and go down to 25,000 in the third week. The magazine expects a loss of $210,000 in its first year and $100,000 in the second. It hopes to break even the third year and earn $100,000 the fourth. Mr. Buckley said he had invested $10,000 himself and had majority voting control.

Among regular features, he said, would be "a weekly survey of relevant misinformation and outright falsehoods published by the nation's influential reporters and commentators." This will be conducted by Ralph de Toledano, author of "Seeds of Treason."

October 14, 1955

U.S. Keeps Detention Camps Ready

Six Units Maintained for Emergency Could House Thousands

By LUTHER A. HUSTON
Special to The New York Times.

WASHINGTON, Dec. 26—The United States could intern 5,000 spies and saboteurs almost immediately in the event of war, an invasion or an insurrection. Thousands more could be put in detention camps as fast as they were rounded up.

Another Pearl Harbor would not catch the Government napping in matters of internal security to the extent that it was in 1941.

No one knows who would be detained, or how many. If there is a "pick-up list" it is super-secret. The Federal Bureau of Investigation, which probably would direct the "picking up," is notably reticent about such matters.

But there are six camps needing only about as much work as would be required to make the beds and light the fires ready to receive those deemed dangerous to security if a national emergency rises. This writer visited three of the camps in the last fortnight.

These camps were established under a national policy fixed by Congress when it passed the Internal Security Act of 1950. That act authorized the President, in

The New York Times   Dec. 27, 1955

Six camps (underlined) could be made ready almost immediately to hold 5,000 spies, saboteurs or other persons considered dangerous in case of a national emergency.

the event of invasion of the United States or its possessions, the declaration of war by Congress, or internal insurrection, to proclaim an "internal security emergency."

Powers Given Under Act

When such a proclamation is issued, the Attorney General is authorized to detain persons whom there is reasonable ground to believe might engage in, or conspire with others to commit, acts of espionage or sabotage. The law requires the Attorney General to provide places of detention for such persons.

In 1951 Congress appropriated money to place six camps on a standby basis. About $1,500,000 was spent to condition facilities that were taken over from other government services. For the most part they were Army or prisoner of war installations that had been abandoned after World War II. Some of them had deteriorated badly.

Prisoners from Federal penal institutions were transferred to the camps to do the restoration work. Roofs were repaired, plumbing made serviceable, some painting done and, at some of the camps, lumber and materials from abandoned buildings used to erect structures to replace buildings that had tumbled down.

Since the camps were renovated, no money has been appropriated by Congress for their maintenance. They are kept in repair and protected by the Federal Bureau of Prisons, a unit of the Department of Justice.

The six camps are at Allenwood, Pa., Avon Park, Fla., El Reno, Okla., Florence, Ariz., Wickenburg, Ariz., and Tule Lake, Calif.

Quarters for about 5,000 persons could be made ready almost immediately and barracks and other necessities could be expanded rapidly to take care of several times that number at the camps.

One Adjunct to Prison

For a time they were used as Federal prison camps and Florence is still so used. Four have now been closed and the one at Allenwood has become an adjunct of the United States penitentiary at Lewisburg, Pa. It could be "reactivated" to detain spies and saboteurs if a national emergency arose.

The camps at El Reno, Florence and Wickenburg were visited. El Reno might be a "ghost town" of the old west if it were not for a bright red fire engine outside the gates and a forbidding wire fence, ten feet high, that surrounds it.

There is nothing at any of the camps to suggest the "concentration camps" that horrified the free world in World War II. There are cold storage rooms, radio outlets, shower baths, steam tables to keep food warm, modern laundries, up-to-date hospital wards, heating plants and air conditioning.

Recreation Facilities

At Wickenburg there is a wide parade ground where prisoners could exercise. Prisoners were playing basketball at Florence. Wickenburg and Florence have libraries and game rooms for cards, chess or checkers. There were table tennis facilities in the barracks at El Reno.

There are no barbed wire barricades to halt those who might flee or searching lights to illuminate the land over which they might make a dash for freedom. Control towers arise at intervals outside the high woven-wire fences and they would be manned by armed guards if the camps were activated. Now, even at Florence where prisoners are housed, the towers are not manned and the gates are locked only at night.

At El Reno and Wickenburg the fences serve to keep thieves and vandals out, rather than dangerous persons in.

However, they are not luxury camps, where prisoners might loll on beds of ease and grow fat on rich food. Life could be mighty uncomfortable at any of the camps.

This would be especially true if they were filled or perhaps overcrowded. Disciplinary measures and security precautions would be necessary that could make prisoners uncomfortable and probably very unhappy.

The official viewpoint is that condition~ in the camps would be governed largely by the circumstances under which they were reactivated and the type of emergency with which the nation had to deal. The prisoners themselves, and their conduct would have something to do with the conditions, just as in other Federal penal institutions.

In the absence of evidence to the contrary and in the light of experience with American methods, the presumption must be that these camps would be humanely conducted, according to civilized rules and procedures.

If furor arose over the camps, it no doubt would derive from disagreement over who should be interned. Standards of what constitutes a menace to security are less clearly defined than those that govern humane conduct.

After Pearl Harbor, for instance, a great many Japanese were rounded up and interned, some in one of the camps still maintained. It later was acknowledged that not all of them were disloyal or a menace to national security.

Undoubtedly objections would arise over the detention of certain individuals if another national emergency arose. The Government's employe security program has been cirticized as unjust to hundreds who are not bona fide security risks. In the climate of a national emergency hundreds, perhaps thousands, could be sequestered in security camps who were not actual, or even potential, spies or saboteurs.

As in the last year, however, the official position probably would be that it is better to be safe than sorry. Those who now administer the detention camp program regard it as a precautionary measure and refuse to speculate on what might happen if it became necessary to populate the camps with enemies of national seecurity.

The Eisenhower Administration did not set up the program. However, it will continue to operate it on a stand-by basis in the hope that an active basis will not be necessary during this regime. Congress at any time could revise, expand or abolish the program.

There follows some details of the various camps:

THE FLORENCE CAMP

As Embry S. Osborn, the superintendent, was unlocking the door of one of the unoccupied barracks, a mild-looking old Indian came up and asked if he could enter.

"Why do you want to go in?" the superintendent asked.

"I've got some tools in there," the Indian replied.

After we had left the building Mr. Osborn said that the old Indian was in for a murder that had occurred during a drinking bout.

The elderly prisoner was doing time and proving very useful as a carpenter helping to keep the camp buildings in repair.

About 150 Federal prisoners are in the Florence Camp. Two-thirds of them are illegal immi-:rants. Others have been transferred from prisons to serve short terms, or finish terms due to expire soon. None is considered dangerous and the camp is a "minimum security" institution.

Anyone who wants to leave can walk past the gates if no one is looking. A few have done that. The catch is that where they would go is much more perilous than where they are.

If a fleeing prisoner goes a half mile one way he is in Florence, seat of Pinal County. If he goes any other way the desert is there to engulf him.

The Trail Is Clear

The desert can get terrifically hot and water is hard to obtain. Most prisoners are recaptured and usually they are glad to get back to the comforts of the camp.

A cleared area surrounds the camp fence and it is kept smooth so that tracks of a departing prisoner are visible. The direction of his flight is thus easy to determine.

The Arizona State Penitentiary is at Florence and bloodhounds are available to follow a fugitive. Sometimes, however, the dogs falter in the desert before the fugitives do. Tough men often can last long in the tough desert. But almost all are caught.

The guards at Florence do not wear guns. A small arsenal is at hand in Mr. Osborn's office, however, if needed to guard prisoners being transferred or for use in chasing fugitives.

Florence was set up during World War II for prisoners of war. At one time it housed 9,000, mostly Italians. These prisoners built a handsome stone shrine and erected an altar at which to worship. The shrine still stands outside the camp fence.

Many Germans also were kept in the camp near the close of the war.

Some Buildings Razed

As a prisoner of war camp it had more buildings than it has now. Many were torn down after the war, or allowed to deteriorate so they are no longer usable.

At present there are twenty-six buildings, all in good repair. In three days these buildings could be made ready to receive as many as 3,000 internees. Nineteen of the buildings are dormitories, in rows on each side of a main street. Four are warehouses where supplies for the present camp are stored and in which food and equipment for a full complement of occupants could be kept.

The camp has a chapel, a television room, a library and a well-equipped hospital. It is the only fully air-conditioned institution in the Federal prison system.

The mess hall seats 168 but construction is under way that will enlarge its capacity to 380. Cold-storage chambers have been built from surplus equipment, a modern pumping plant provides water, there is a completely equipped laundry, a barbershop and a modern shoe-repair shop. A sewage disposal system could serve 20,000 people.

Grows Some Food

Florence grows some of the food for the prisoners. About eighty acres outside the fence are cultivated. The camp has a "pork program," designed to build up a herd of swine to provide meat for the occupants. A combine was harvesting maize to feed the pigs just outside the gates.

Vegetables are grown and processed in a modern cannery.

Inside the fences are about forty acres. The entire camp contains 500 acres, leaving plenty of room for expansion.

Outside the camp there are barracks that cou.? be restored to accommodate between 500 and 600 persons. These might be used in an emergency to house women internees.

THE WICKENBURG CAMP

If spies and saboteurs who might be rounded up are given their choice they would be wise to choose Wickenburg. This camp was built as a glider training school for the Air Force during the war. Its buildings are of more substantial construction, its facilities more modern and its surroundings more attractive than the other Western camps.

It has been suggested that women internees might be kept at Wickenburg. It would house about 800.

There are eight dormitories inside a high wire fence that surrounds ten acres of land. A separate hospital could be provided as soon as medical supplies were obtained. Beds and mattresses are in warehouses, ready for immediate use. Venetian blinds are at some of the windows. Large picture windows in the dining room give a view of a hard-surfaced parade ground.

A completely equipped kitchen could be used as soon as the gas was turned on.

Wickenburg has a schoolroom, with blackboards and chairs. Glider students studied there when the camp was an Air Force facility.

For a time after the detention camp program was set up, Federal prisoners were kept at Wickenburg. It is now closed, with only a caretaker who reports to Mr. Osborn at Florence if anything goes wrong.

EL RENO CAMP

This camp was built solely for prisoners of war. Captured soldiers of Rommel's Afrika Korps were interned there. On the walls of the dingy barracks are pictures drawn by homesick Germans of scenes in their native country and sketches of regimental insignia. The Black Eagle of Germany predominates in these decorations, some of real artistic merit.

The prisoners were moved out in 1945, however, and since then the camp has been unoccupied.

There are twenty-nine buildings inside a fence that surrounds the camp proper. This is located on the old Fort Reno military reserve, once a cavalry remount station, of 8,000 acres.

Each of the buildings is about 100 feet long. Three iron stoves ranged down the middle would provide heat. An air conditioning unit at one end would help protect internees when the scorching Oklahoma sun beat on the roofs.

All the buildings are of frame construction, sheathed in plaster board. They are dull gray, with faded green roofs.

Near Federal Reformatory

What Oklahomans call a "norther" was blowing. The wind almost always blows and the few trees lean away from the prevailing wind. Cold winds in winter, hot winds in summer and a barren prairie provide a bleak aspect for this least attractive of the three camps.

The camp is situated across the road from the Federal Reformatory at El Reno, which houses more than 900 prisoners. Charles R. Hagen, warden of the reformatory, has charge of the camp. Prisoners keep it in repair.

Of the camps not visited, the best known is Tule Lake. This is located in northern California, near the Oregon border. During the war it housed about 20,000 Japanese. It was then the largest internee camp in the country.

After the Japanese were removed the camp was not kept up. Most of the buildings were torn down and it now has only about fifteen structures, that could be used to house spies or saboteurs.

Avon Park, originally a Federal prison camp, no longer is used to house prisoners. It is kept in repair by the Bureau of Prisons and probably could house 800 or 900 persons if a national emergency arose.

December 27, 1955

SENATE UNIT BIDS PUBLIC KNOW REDS

Handbook Says Alternative as Curb Would Be Secret Police Force of a Million

By DANA ADAMS SCHMIDT
Special to The New York Times.

WASHINGTON, Dec. 27—A Senate subcommittee said today that a public fully informed on Communist objectives and activities was the only alternative to a secret police force numbering up to a million men.

However, the subcommittee quickly rejected the idea of such a police force as "utterly contrary to our democratic traditions" because it would mean setting up "an enormous American Gestapo or MVD."

In "A Handbook for Americans," designed to give the public information about the Communist party, the Internal Security subcommittee of the Senate Committee on the Judiciary, said the Federal Bureau of Investigation fixed party membership at about 22,663. The handbook added, however, that the party had "at least ten times that number of sympathizers," and at times included "directly or in-

directly within its orbit, more than half a million individuals."

The handbook, made public today, also said that to get information of communism to the public much reliance must be placed upon data from ex-Communists.

On this basis, the subcommittee has compiled the 100-page handbook on "The Communist Party in the United States of America—What It Is, How It Works."

The handbook draws upon and carries further ground previously covered by the report of the House Committee on Un-American Activities about the Communist party of the United States as an agent of a foreign power, published in 1947, and findings since then by the Subversive Activities Control Board.

Similar topics have been covered by the following reports published by the House Committee on Un-American Activities: "100 Things You Should Know About Communism," 1951; "Colonization of America's Basic Industries by the Communist Party of the U. S. A.," 1954, and "The American Negro in the Communist Party," 1954.

The Senate subcommittee also published a report on interlocking subversion in Government departments, 1953.

An Army pamphlet on "How to Spot a Communist," prepared by the First Army and used by the Watertown, Mass., arsenal of the Ordnance Corps and the Continental Air Command, was withdrawn from circulation on June 15 after the American Civil Liberties Union had attacked it as a threat to free thought and expression.

The foreword of the handbook said "the average American is unaware of the amount of misinformation about the Communist party, U. S. A., which appears in the public press, in books and in the utterances of public speakers."

The chairman of the subcommittee is Senator James O. Eastland, Democrat of Mississippi.

The handbook found that ex-Communists had been useful in helping United States authorities collect reliable information about the Communist party.

"In the rare case of a Matusow," the handbook said, ex-Communists may be motivated by a mere desire for publicity. But in the cases of most former Communists who have given testimony against the party, it added, the motives are disillusionment, the conviction that the movement is anti-social and anti-American, and a desire to safeguard his country from "real and pressing danger."

Harvey A. Matusow is a turnabout Government witness who now faces prosecution for perjury.

Chain of Command Traced

For students of communism the newest aspect of the handbook is a chart tracing the Communist chain of command from the Politbureau in Moscow to the shop or community club of the party and local front organizations in the United States. The chart summarizes the opinions of numerous former Communists.

In an analysis of "What Makes a Communist Tick," the handbook finds that the inequalities of our social system

are not the cause of communism. Rather, it says that Communists are likely to be "mission-minded intellectuals * * * psychologically maladjusted individuals * * * neurotics * * * a vehicle for anyone with an axe to grind * * * and an attraction for adventurous spirits who thrive on the conspiratorial atmosphere of the party, secret meetings, the resort to aliases, the paraphernalia of illegality and opposition to constitutional authority."

Since Communists speaking openly as Communists could make little headway in this country, the subcommittee explained, the party works extensively through front organizations. Without them, it said, the Communist party would be "an isolated, insignificant sect."

Advising Americans how to recognize Communist fronts, it listed alphabetically eighty-two names ranging from Josephine Truslow Adams to Doxey A. Wilkerson as "the most active and typical sponsors of Communist fronts in the past."

In addition, it pointed out that "front" organizations could be recognized by whether they received publicity in Communist publications; whether speakers and entertainers employed were frequently associated with other Communist fronts or the Communist party; whether an organization cooperated with other fronts and the Communist party in election campaigns, May Day parades, peace campaigns, etc., and whether it cooperated with Communist-controlled unions.

December 28, 1955

U. S. Ends Fight to Shield Security Case Informers

By ANTHONY LEWIS
Special to The New York Times.

WASHINGTON, March 24—The Government has decided not to appeal to the Supreme Court a lower court decision condemning the use of "secret informers" in security proceedings. The determination against appealing, which became final today, marks a significant strategic retreat on the confrontation issue.

This is the controversial question of whether an accused security risk has a constitutional right to know and face his accusers or whether, as the Government has contended, informants' names must be kept secret in the interest of national security.

The opinion, which will now be left undisturbed, was handed down last October by the United States Court of Appeals in San Francisco, in the case of Parker v. Lester.

The court held that the Coast Guard's security program for maritime workers was unconstitutional because the seamen were not told the sources of the charges against them.

The decision was widely regarded as the strongest attack by any major American court on what the opinion called a "system of secret informers, whisperers and talebearers."

The Solicitor General, Simon E. Sobeloff, described the ruling as having "obvious far-reaching implications for the various governmental security program."

There has been intense interest among lawyers in the security field as to whether the Justice Department would petition the Supreme Court to review the case. Last January, as the closing date for a petition approached, Mr. Sobeloff sought and received a two-month extension from the court. The Solicitor General is in charge of the Justice Department's Supreme Court business.

The extended filing period expired today. It did not simply go by default. The decision not to appeal was made by Mr. Sobeloff after consultation with many other officials concerned, including Attorney General Herbert Brownell Jr., and with their concurrence.

Just last year, in the case of Dr. John P. Peters, the Justice Department took a vigorous position in the Supreme Court against any requirement for confrontation in security cases. Mr. Sobeloff broke with his colleagues in that case and refused to sign the brief. The court decided the Peters case on narrow

grounds, avoiding the confrontation issue.

The basic reason for avoiding a further test in the Parker case was apparently a feeling that the Government was not likely to win in the Supreme Court. The Parker case presented major difficulties for the Government because it involved not a Government job, as in the Peters case, but the right to private employment.

The Government always has argued that working for it is a "privilege, not a right." From that position it is contended that the Government worker is not entitled to the constitutional guarantee of "due process"—including confrontation of his accusers.

In the leading case, Bailey vs. Richardson, the Supreme Court split 4–4 on this contention, thus upholding a lower court decision for the Government.

But the courts often have held that private employment is a right protected by the due process guarantee. The Court of Appeals' opinion in the Parker case said: "The [seamen's] liberty to follow their chosen employment is no doubt a right more clearly entitled to constitutional protection than the right of a Government employe to obtain or retain his job."

Furthermore, in any court argument the Government would be charged with trying to extend the principle of secret informants potentially to all private employment, not just martime workers.

The port security program, which was challenged in the Parker case, covers about 500,-000 seamen and longshoremen. Under law they can work only if they have security cards issued by the Coast Guard.

Burden Upon Accused

If the local Coast Guard office has doubts about any maritime worker, it lifts his card and then holds a hearing at which the burden is on him to prove his right to get it back.

In the Parker case, a number of seamen whose cards had been lifted went to court and asked for an injunction against the security program. The names of informants were not disclosed and, in fact, the Coast Guard board members did not know the names.

District Judge Edward P. Murphy ordered the Coast Guard to give the seamen a general summary of the charges and testimony against them. But he specifically excluded any guarantee of confrontation, saying:

"The Federal Bureau of Investigation has uniformly insisted that practically none of [its] sources will continue to be available to it if proper secrecy and confidence cannot at all times be maintained with respect to the original source of the information."

The seamen went to the Court of Appeals for the Ninth Circuit and said that Judge Murphy's opinion did not go far enough. The opinion there was written by Judge Walter L. Pope, with Judge Thomas F. McAllister concurring.

Judge William Healy, dissenting, said that the confrontation issue should be left for the Supreme Court to decide.

The majority opinion said, in summary, that unless some kind of confrontation was required, the seamen might not really know the charges against them sufficiently to make a defense. The court said it might be possible to draft new Coast Guard security regulations qualifying "in some degree" the right of confrontation, but the present regulations were unconstitutional.

By not appealing to the Supreme Court, the Government avoids the risk of an adverse opinion that would carry even more weight. It is certain, nevertheless, that lawyers defending all kinds of security cases will be citing the Parker opinion given by the Court of Appeals from now on, especially because the opinion makes a broad attack on the whole institution of informants.

"It may be assumed," the court said, that its decision "will remove from the investigative agencies to some degree a certain kind of information and that, in the future, some persons will be deterred from carrying some of these tales to the investigating authorities.

"It is unbelievable that the result will prevent able officials from procuring proof * * *. But surely it is better that these agencies suffer from handicap than that the citizens of a freedom-loving country shall be denied that which has always been considered their birthright.

"Indeed it may well be that in the long run nothing but beneficial results will come from a lessening of such talebearing. It is a matter of public record that the somewhat comparable security risk program directed at government employes has been used to victimize perfectly innocent men.

"The objective of perpetuating a doubtful system of secret informers likely to bear upon the innocent as well as upon the guilty * * * cannot justify an abandonment here of the ancient standards of due process * * *.

"Furthermore, in considering the public interest in the preservation of a system under which unidentified informers are encouraged to make unchallengeable statements about their neighbors, it is not amiss to bear in mind whether or not we must look forward to a day when substantially everyone will have to contemplate the possibility that his neighbors are being encouraged to make reports to the F. B. I. about what he says, what he reads and what meetings he attends * * *.

"The time has not come when we have to abandon a system of liberty for one modeled on that of the Communists.'"

During the last two months the Coast Guard, in consultation with Attorney General Brownell and others, has been trying to draft new port security regulations in keeping with the Parker opinion. It is understood that a draft is near final approval.

March 25, 1956

HIGH COURT BACKS LAW ON IMMUNITY IN SECURITY CASES

Decides, 7 to 2, That U. S. Has Power to Force Balky Witnesses to Testify

FIRST TEST OF STATUTE

Defendant Held 1954 Rule Violated 5th Amendment— Douglas in Sharp Dissent

By LUTHER A. HUSTON
Special to The New York Times.

WASHINGTON, March 26—The Supreme Court upheld today the constitutionality of the Immunity Act of 1954.

This law gives the Government the right to compel a witness to testify in national security cases in exchange for immunity from prosecution.

This was the first test of the law to reach the tribunal. Justice Felix Frankfurter wrote the 7-to-2 opinion that affirmed the contempt conviction of William Ludwig Ullmann, a former Treasury Department offcial. Justices William O. Douglas and Hugo L. Black dissented.

Mr. Ullmann was sentenced to six months in prison after he had defied an order of Federal Judge Edward Weinfeld in New York to answer questions before a grand jury investigating espionage. Judge Weinfeld issued the order at the request of the United States Attorney General.

The defendant claimed the protection of the Fifth Amendment to the Constitution against being compelled to give testimony that might incriminate him. He challenged the Immunity Law as violative of his Fifth Amendment rights.

Ullmann Argument Rejected

A principal argument advanced by Mr. Ullmann was that even though he had been freed from the fear of Federal prosecution, there was still a very real possibility that he might be accused in state courts. He questioned the power of Congress to pass a law that immunized a witness from state prosecutions.

Justice Frankfurter rejected this argument. He held that Congress had such power in the interest of national security, saying:

"The Immunity Act is concerned with national security. It reflects a Congressional policy to increase the possibility of more complete and open disclosure by removal of fear of state prosecution. We cannot say that Congress' paramount authority in safeguarding national security does not justify the restriction it has placed on the exercise of state power for the more effective exercise of conceded Federal power."

Justice Douglas strongly disagreed. In his dissenting opinion, in which Justice Black concurred, Justice Douglas said:

"The critical point is that the Constitution places the right of silence beyond the reach of the Government. The Fifth Amendment stands between the citizen and his Government."

In deciding the Ullmann case, the high court reaffirmed a decision of sixty years ago, when it sustained an immunity statute of 1893.

This is the case known as Brown v. Walker in which Brown, auditor of a railroad company, was held in contempt for refusing to testify before a grand jury investigating charges that officials of the company had violated the Interstate Commerce Act.

"We reaffirm Brown v. Walker," Justice Frankfurter said. He added that the court could find "no distinction between the reach of Congressional power with respect to commerce and its power with respect to national security."

Again Justice Douglas disagreed. He said that the case, "decided by a bare majority of the court and now sixty years old, has no greater claim to sanctity than the other venerable decisions which history showed had outlived their usefulness or were conceived in error."

Mr. Ullmann was named by Elizabeth Bentley, a former Communist courier, as a member of a wartime espionage ring. The ring, she said, had been headed by Nathan Gregory Silvermaster, a former Government official.

Four Questions Raised

Since his retirement from the Treasury in 1947, Mr. Ullmann has been operating a construction business in partnership with Mr. Silvermaster. He lives in Harvey Cedars, N. J.

One of the charges was that he had photographed secret documents, intended for transmission to Moscow, in Mr. Silvermaster's Washington home where he lived at the time.

In the Treasury Department, Mr. Ullmann worked under Harry Dexter White, at that time director of the Monetary Research Division, as a senior economic analyst. Miss Bentley testified that Mr. White, who has since died, was a source of information for facts and material she transmitted to her Soviet spy chief.

Mr. Ullmann refused to answer questions about these and other alleged activities and associations when taken before the Federal grand jury.

Justice Frankfurter said that four major questions were raised by Mr. Ullmann's appeal. They were:

"Is the immunity provided by the act sufficiently broad to displace the protection afforded by the privilege against self-incrimination? Assuming that the statutory requirements are met, does the act give the district judge discretion to deny an application for an order requiring the witness to answer relevant questions put by the grand jury, and if so, is the court thereby required to exercise a function that is not an exercise of 'judicial power'? Did Congress provide immunity from state prosecution for crime, and if so, is it empowered to do so? Does the Fifth Amendment prohibit compulsion of what would otherwise be self-incriminating testimony no matter what the scope of the immunity statute?"

On the basis of Brown v. Walker, the court held today that a statute that compelled testimony, but exempted the witness against a criminal prosecution did not violate the Fifth Amendment's privilege against self-incrimination.

The language of the Immunity Act, Justice Frankfurter ruled,

makes it clear that the district judge does not have discretion to deny an application from the Attorney General for an order to compel a witness to testify.

As to the power of Congress to provide immunity from state prosecution, Justice Frankfurter said that "it cannot be contested that Congress has power to provide for national defense" and to make all laws necessary for the exercise of that power.

The constitutional protection of the Fifth Amendment, he added, "must not be interpreted in a hostile or niggardly spirit.

"Nothing new can be put into the Constitution except through the amendatory process. Nothing old can be taken out without the same process."

A "strict not lax observance" of the constitutional protection of the rights of the individual, Justice Frankfurter asserted, impelled the conclusion that the interdiction of the Fifth Amendment operated only where self-

incriminatory testimony was involved. When "immunity displaces the danger," he said, constitutional rights are preserved.

Justice Douglas, however, noted that the Immunity Act did not protect "disabilities created by Federal law that attach to a person who is a Communist." He named ineligibility for Federal employment in defense facilities, disqualification for a passport and the risk of internment as a few penalties.

"Any forfeiture of rights as a result of compelled testimony is at war with the Fifth Amendment," Justice Douglas said, adding:

"The guarantee against self-incrimination combined in the Fifth Amendment is not only a protection against conviction and prosecution but a safeguard of conscience and human dignity and freedom of expression as well. My view is that the fra-

mers [of the Constitution] put it beyond the power of Congress to compel anyone to confess his crimes."

The Fifth Amendment, Justice Douglas said, "was designed to protect the accused against infamy as well as against prosecution." The "concept of infamy," he asserted, was written into the amendment.

"There is great infamy involved in the present case," the justice said. "The disclosure that a person is a Communist practically excommunicates him from society."

Mr. Ullmann has been at liberty in $5,000 bond since his conviction.

His appeal was argued in the Supreme Court by Leonard B. Boudin of New York. Charles F. Barber, an Assistant Solicitor General, argued the case for the Government.

March 27, 1956

HIGH COURT LIMITS OUSTER OF 'RISKS' TO SENSITIVE JOBS

6-3 Ruling Holds President Violated Law in Extending Program to All Aides

CAIN HAILS THE DECISION

But Dissent Deplores End of 'Most Effective Weapon' Against Subversion

By ANTHONY LEWIS
Special to The New York Times.

WASHINGTON, June 11—The Supreme Court ruled today that only those Federal employes who held sensitive jobs could be dismissed as security risks.

By a 6-to-3 vote the court held that President Eisenhower had violated the law in setting up a security program applicable to all Government workers. It said a 1950 statute on which the President's program was based was intended to cover only positions "concerned with the nation's safety."

The decision was widely regarded as a major blow at the Administration's security regulations. Published statistics indicate that about half of the "risks" dismissed under the pro-

gram held non-sensitive positions.

The dissenting opinion said:

"We believe the court's order has stricken down the most effective weapon against subversive activity available to the Government."

The dissent was written by Justice Tom C. Clark and joined in by Justices Stanley F. Reed and Sherman Minton.

Final Session of Term

The decision was handed down in the court's final session of the term.

The court also took these actions:

¶It ruled, 5 to 3, that United States military courts had authority to try dependents of service men and other civilians who followed the armed forces overseas.

¶It dismissed, 4 to 3, Justice Department charges that E. I. du Pont de Nemours & Co. had illegally monopolized the cellophane market.

¶It held, 5 to 4, that the Government could refuse to suspend the deportation of an alien on the basis of confidential information even though his record was otherwise clear.

Approval of the decision in the security case was voiced by former Senator Harry P. Cain, Republican of Washington, a leading critic of existing security procedures. Mr. Cain, a member of the Subversive Activities Control Board, called the court's ruling "the best American good sense I have heard in a long time" and added:

"The court has affirmed what many of us have been saying—that it is neither sensible nor honest to apply the security system to non-security jobs."

The Justice Department had no official comment. But officials there saw these as among the possible consequences of the decision:

¶Persons dismissed from non-sensitive positions as security risks since the Eisenhower program began in 1953 may sue for reinstatement of their jobs. Or they may sue in the United States Court of Claims for back pay from the date of dismissal. Court of Claims rules permit recovery of pay for six years from the ouster.

¶Although virtually all present Government employes have been cleared in security checks, the President may revise his Executive order establishing the security program to make the language accord with the court decision.

¶Alternately, the Administration might vastly increase the number of Government jobs labeled "sensitive" and so hope to side-step the decision. Whether the court would accept such designations or review their validity is another question.

The court's ruling came on an appeal by Kendrick M. Cole, a former Federal Food and Drug inspector in New York. In 1953 he was accused of associating with persons "reliably reported to be Communists" and of attending meetings of the Nature Friends of America, a group on the list of organizations designated as subversive by the Attorney General.

Mr. Cole at first refused to reply to the charges, calling them "an invasion of my private rights." Two weeks later he said he had been sick and asked for a hearing. His request was denied, and Mrs. Oveta Culp Hobby, then Secretary of Health, Education and Welfare, dismissed him.

Mr. Cole appealed to the Civil Service Commission. As a veteran, he would ordinarily have been entitled to such an appeal

by the Veterans Preference Act. But the executive order establishing the security program barred Civil Service review of security dismissals.

The Executive order was based on a 1950 law permitting suspension and then dismissal of "security risks"—without appeal—in eleven sensitive Government units, such as the Departments of State and Defense. The act gave the President power to extend its provisions to other agencies as he deemed "necessary in the best interests of national security." The Executive order extended it to the entire Government.

Mr. Cole went to court and said he should have been given a Civil Service review. He had two main arguments:

That President Eisenhower had gone beyond the intent of Congress in extending the 1950 act to all Federal agencies and that in any event the act could not properly apply to any non-sensitive job like his.

The Government conceded that his position was neither sensitive nor policy-making.

The majority opinion, written by Justice John Marshall Harlan, dealt with the second of Mr. Cole's contentions and agreed with it. Joining with Justice Harlan were Chief Justice Earl Warren and Justices Hugo L. Black, Felix Frankfurter, William O. Douglas and Harold H. Burton.

Justice Harlan said the specifying of certain sensitive agencies in the 1950 act had indicated that it was aimed only at "those activities of the Government that are directly concerned with the protection of the nation from internal subversion or foreign aggression." He said the legislative history of the law buttressed this conclusion.

Justice Harlan agreed that genuinely disloyal employes would be undesirable in any Government job, regardless of sensitivity, but he held that many other existing laws provided ways to remove such employes without use of the tougher security risk procedures.

The dissent argued that the legislative history showed Congress had meant to permit inclusion of all Government agencies in the security program. Justice Clark noted that Congress had repeatedly voted appropriations to carry out the Eisenhower program.

"The President believed that the national security required the extension of the coverage of the act to all employes," Justice

Clark said. "That was his judgment, not ours. He was given that power, not us. By this action the court so interprets the act as to intrude itself into Presidential policy-making. * * *

"The court would require not only a finding that a particular person is subversive, but also that he occupies a sensitive job. Obviously this might leave the Government honeycombed with subversive employes."

The ruling reversed the United States Court of Appeals for the District of Columbia.

Mr. Cole's case was argued by

David L. Shapiro of New York City. The Government's side was argued by Donald B. Macguineas of the Justice Department.

Liberties Union Hails Ruling

Patrick Murphy Malin, executive director of the American Civil Liberties Union, welcomed the Cole decision yesterday as "tremendously important."

"The extension of the security program to millions of workers in non-sensitive positions has made the program a Pandora's box," he said adding that "em-

ployment status, reputation and personal life" of many in such posts had been "severely damaged."

Mr. Cole, 43 years old, a bachelor, has been working as a tree surgeon since discharge from his $4,950-a-year Federal position. He has been living in Hempstead, L. I., although he considers Needham, Mass., his home. He will receive back pay on reinstatement, minus his outside earnings.

June 12, 1956

25,000 BECLOUDED AS SECURITY RISKS

Bar Group Study Cites U. S. Total Since 1947 for Both Public and Private Jobs

---

2 PARTIES SHAPED CURBS

Federal Security Programs Took Root Before World War II and Then Grew

Federal security risk programs have left more than 25,000 Government or private employes under a cloud since 1947.

This was the indication yesterday from the most detailed statistics a special committee of the Association of the Bar of the City of New York could compile.

At least 9,394 persons have been dismissed from jobs or denied clearance. At least 15,928 more have had cases end with resignations or withdrawals while unfavorable marks remained on their records.

The programs grew out of the fear of subversion from many possible totalitarian conspiracies —Nazi, Fascist, Communist. Starting before World War II and intensified by the "cold war" and the Korean war, the security systems have been shaped by both Democrats and Republicans.

Overthrow Prohibited

The bar group's report noted that the Hatch Act—Aug. 2, 1939—made it illegal for Federal employes to belong to an organization advocating overthrow of the Constitutional form of Government. Appropriation acts since 1940 have prohibited pay for persons advocating overthrow of the Government by force or violence, or belonging to organizations so advocating.

In 1942 Congress appropriated

$200,000 for a Federal Bureau of Investigation check on Federal employes belonging to subversive organizations. This led to the Attorney General's list of organizations so designated.

On March 21, 1947, President Truman issued Executive Order 9835. This barred Federal jobs in the Executive Branch to any civilian when "reasonable grounds exist for belief that the person involved is disloyal to the Government of the United States."

Points to be considered included sabotage, espionage, treason and sedition—and also "sympathetic association" with organizations on the Attorney General's list.

The program was toughened when President Truman's Executive Order 10241 on April 28, 1951, made the criterion "reasonable doubt as to the loyalty of the person involved."

The present Federal employes' program rests on Public Law 733, enacted Aug. 26, 1950. This authorized payless suspensions and dismissals of civilian employes in eleven agencies and such others as the President might deem necessary "in the interest of national security."

On this basis President Eisenhower superseded the Truman program by Executive Order 10450 on April 27, 1953. Going beyond the question of loyalty, the new standard was whether employment was "clearly consistent with the interests of the national security."

Besides associations tending to disloyalty, the criteria were widened to include such points as reliability, misrepresentation, criminal or immoral acts, drunkenness, narcotic addiction, perversion, mental illness and susceptibility to pressure.

About seventy agencies set up programs. But last June 11 the United States Supreme Court ruled that under the 1950 law the Presidential order should not have covered non-sensitive jobs —those positions not "concerned with the nation's safety."

The Atomic Energy Commission, under the act creating it in 1946, has a separate security risk program both for its own employes and those of contractors with access to classified information.

The Department of Defense operates an Industrial Security Program imposed through defense contracts, covering contractors' employes with access to classified information.

A port security program was authorized by the Magnuson Act of Aug. 9, 1950. Under this the Coast Guard clears seamen on American vessels of 100 gross tons or more and longshoremen in restricted areas of American ports.

While all these programs empower Federal agency heads to make final decisions, an "advisory" program covers Americans who are present or prospective employes of the United Nations and other international organizations to which the United States belongs.

Aside from the specific security risk programs, Civil Service Commission regulations have evolved since the Lloyd-LaFollette Act of 1912.

Such regulations enable removals in case of "reasonable doubt" as to loyalty, as well as such other suitability criteria as delinquency, physical or mental unfitness, criminal or notoriously disgraceful conduct, drunkenness and false statements on appointment. Noncompetitive employes are not protected by Civil Service.

During the Eisenhower Administration, the bulk of security risk discharges have actually come under the Civil Service regulations.

The statistical record for the various programs, as gathered by the bar committee, follows:

EXECUTIVE ORDER 9835

4,756,705 persons were covered by "check" investigations and

-3,226 persons were referred to appropriate loyalty boards for consideration.

16,503 of those referred to boards were cleared.

560 of those referred to boards were removed or denied employment.

6,828 cases were discontinued because they "left the service or withdrew their application—1,192 after they had been sent interrogatories or charges."

569 processed by the Department of the Army solely under security laws.

EXECUTIVE ORDER 10450

2,346,710 persons employed by Executive branch June 30, 1954.

727,158 persons were subjected to security check in the two years from July 1, 1953 to June 30, 1955 (renewed check of most incumbents not required by Executive Order 10450).

1,016 suspensions under Executive Order 10450 in the two years from Oct. 1, 1953 to Sept. 30, 1955 (presumably the number of suspensions is about the same as number of charges issued, because charged employes almost always are suspended).

342 terminations under Executive Order 10450 procedures in the twenty-five months from May 28, 1953 to June 30, 1955.

37,450 total discharged from Federal service for all causes in the twenty-five months from May 28, 1953 to June 30, 1955.

3,241 terminations by Civil Service procedures but declared by department heads to be "because of security questions" in the twenty-five months from May 28, 1953 to June 30, 1955.

495,724 total resignations from Federal service in the twenty-five months from May 28, 1953 to June 30, 1955.

5,684 resignations from Federal service, where files contained adverse security information, in the twenty-five months from May 28, 1953 to June 30, 1955. (It does not appear how many of these persons were aware of this information).

ATOMIC ENERGY COMMISSION

503,810 persons were investigated, Jan. 1, 1947 to March 10, 1955.

5,532 of the 503,810 had their eligibility questioned.

1,622 of the 5,532 were cleared.

494 of the 5,532 were denied clearance.

3,416 of the 5,532 cases were not decided because of resignations prior to completion of cases and terminations or cancellations of clearance requests.

PORT SECURITY PROGRAM

427,182 seamen had sought clearance as of Dec. 31, 1955.

425,334 seamen granted clearance as of Dec. 31, 1955.

1,848 seamen denied clearance as of Dec. 31, 1955.

397,208 waterfront workers had sought clearance as of Dec. 31, 1955.

393,813 waterfront workers issued cards as of Dec. 31, 1955.

1,458 waterfront workers cleared but cards not applied for as of Dec. 31, 1955.

1,935 waterfront workers denied clearance as of Dec. 31, 1955.

DEFENSE DEPARTMENT INDUSTRIAL SECURITY

3,000,000 persons approximately encompassed in program, November, 1955.

20,000 plants cleared, June 25, 1950 to July 15, 1954.

500,000 employes cleared for access to top-secret, secret and confidential, June 25, 1950 to July 15, 1954.

688 persons refused clearance in four years up to July 15, 1954.

200 plants being cleared per month as of July 15, 1954.

4,000 employes being cleared per month as of July 15, 1954.

974 denials of clearance between July, 1949 and November, 1955.

INTERNATIONAL ORGANIZATIONS

5,469 cases of employes and applicants processed as of Feb. 16, 1956, by the International Organizations Employes Loyalty Board.

8,100 United States citizens now regular employes of international organizations in which the United States participates.

July 9, 1956

Eisenhower's Four Years

An Analysis of Policy on Loyalty And Problems in Red Investigations

By ANTHONY LEWIS
Special to The New York Times.

WASHINGTON, July 29—The issue of Communists in Government has been perhaps the most durable political commodity of the Republican party since World War II. Dwight D. Eisenhower used it freely in his 1952 campaign.

"When we find there have been Communists in Government," he said in Laporte, Ind., "and we get the answer 'red herring,' ladies and gentlemen, it is time to clean them out—not only the Communists and the people that have abused our trust * * * but the people that put them there. That is what we are going to do."

In his first State of the Union message, in 1953, President Eisenhower set out the dimensions of the problem more precisely:

"The safety of America and the trust of the people alike demand that the personnel of the Federal Government be loyal in their motives and reliable. * * * This security we must and we shall have. * * *

"The primary responsibility for keeping out the disloyal and the dangerous rests squarely upon the Executive branch. When this branch so conducts itself as to require policing by another branch of the Government, it invites its own disorder and confusion."

In effect the President had laid out two problems—to clear asserted subversives out of the Government and to end the disabling pressure of Congressional investigations of Communists.

The thesis—clearly General Eisenhower's strong personal belief at the time—was that the two problems were intertwined: If the Executive branch cleaned its own house, Congress would stop its investigations. In fact, this logic did not work.

The Administration applied security measures rigorously, often too rigorously for critics sensitive to the needs of individual liberty. But no measures were ever sufficient to head off the investigations.

THE SECURITY PROGRAM

The Truman Administration had separate loyalty and security programs. The first, which covered all Government employes, provided for dismissal of employes of whose loyalty there was a reasonable doubt. The second, for sensitive jobs only, provided for dismissal of em-

ployes whose habits might make them a risk to national security. Such habits might include drunkenness or homosexuality, not just subversive associations.

The loyalty standard was criticized from two sides. Civil libertarians called loyalty too vague and personal a matter to permit of fair judgment and said that a finding of disloyalty was so harsh as to tar a man for life. Persons concerned about subversive infiltration in government said hearing boards and officials were so reluctant to brand a man disloyal that they had refused to dismiss clearly suspect persons.

President Eisenhower attempted to meet these objections with a broad new program established three months after he took office. The loyalty standard was eliminated, and a security program covering personal habits, integrity and subversion was extended to all Government jobs. The theory was that it then would be easier to clean out unsuitable employes, while relieving those dismissed of the stigma of disloyalty.

Soon after the program got under way a series of publicized security cases illustrated shortcomings the Administration itself would admit later.

An early case to win notoriety was that of Milo J. Radulovich, an Air Force Reserve lieutenant who had been found to be a security risk because of Communist suspicions about his father and sister. The Air Force reversed the finding and restored Lieutenant Radulovich to the reserve rolls.

Weakness Exposed

The case illustrated a looseness of security charges that concededly was commonplace in the early days of the program. No discernible effort had been made to discover whether Lieutenant Radulovich himself had had any Communist views—the mere relationship had been enough.

Since then those administering the program have made efforts to cull out the foolish and the vague before charges were brought. More sophisticated security personnel have been trained. The Pentagon's industrial security program for defense workers has developed highly effective central screening of all charges before they are filed. The Army and Atomic Energy Commission formally have barred findings of suspect association unless the subject was shown to have shared the suspect views.

Another fault — the terrible

psychological and financial burden put on suspected security risks—was illustrated by the case of Abraham Chasanow, Navy Department employe. He was suspended without pay for fourteen months while under charges, found above suspicion by a hearing board and then summarily dismissed by an assistant secretary. Finally, after protests in the press, he was restored to duty with an apology from the Secretary of the Navy.

The case of Wolf Ladejinsky illustrated the dangers of decentralization in the Eisenhower program. He was cleared by the State Department, dismissed as a risk by Agriculture, then rehired after a public fuss by the Foreign Operations Administration.

Efforts to coordinate the program have been made since then through an interdepartmental committee, but no real centralizing power exists. A report by the New York City Bar Association has proposed an over-all security director.

A charge often made in the early days of the security program was that it was being used to remove employes for political purposes.

A contrary judgment was that there had been much less political use of the program than there might have been under any Republican President other than General Eisenhower.

Confrontation at Issue

Finally, the recurring issue of "confrontation" was debated. Administration officials took the view that there was no obligation to produce Government witnesses at security hearings, that the protection of confidential informants must be paramount. But in a letter to his departments in 1955 the Attorney General, Herbert Brownell Jr., urged that "every effort" be made to produce witnesses for cross-examination.

Administration officials have now moved toward acceptance of some form of limited guarantee of appearance of witnesses, before hearing boards if not the accused himself. The report of the New York Bar Association would provide subpoena power for the boards, pay witness fees and excuse only genuinely confidential informants from appearing at least before the boards.

As to the actual accomplishments of the security program in cleaning up the Federal payroll, opinions of course depend on point of view. The most important persons removed as "risks" —men such as J. Robert Oppenheimer and John Paton Davies— have had their attackers and defenders.

Again, the critics have said that the morale of Government employes had been badly disturbed by loose charges made under the program. The Administration's position was that unsuitable employes had been removed and that consequently the standards of the Government service had been raised.

But it is probably safe to as-

sume broad public acceptance of the program. Certainly a substantial majority of Americans —a much larger number than during the Truman Administration—believes our Government is well protected against infiltration by subversives.

The political clouds began forming around the program on Oct. 23, 1953, when a formal White House release carried the first statistics. The statement said that 1,456 Government employes had been dismissed—or had resigned under the security program since the Eisenhower Administration took over.

In the 1954 State of the Union message the President raised the total to 2,200. Subsequently it was increased to 6,926, then 8,008, and finally 9,600 before the statistics were halted. Republican politicians were quick to use the figures.

Dewey Talks of 'Traitors'

Gov. Thomas E. Dewey of New York spoke of a "Government infested with spies and traitors." In the next sentence of the speech he said the Administration had "discovered and dismissed" 1,456 security risks planted in the Government" by the Democrats.

And Vice President Richard M. Nixon, in a much-debated campaign speech in 1954, said:

"We're kicking the Communists and fellow-travelers and security risks out of the Government not by the hundreds but by the thousands."

After two years of Congressional investigations the Administration in effect conceded that its security figures had been misleading or false in virtually every respect, as follows:

¶More than 90 per cent of those numbered as "security risks," the Civil Service Commission said, actually had left the Government by regular civil service procedures—without hearings to test any security charges.

¶Many of the listed employes, perhaps most, had resigned without even knowing there had been any adverse information against them.

¶Through last Sept. 30, only 1,016 employes actually had been charged under the security program.

¶Of these, only 342 were dismissed under security procedures.

¶More than 50 per cent of the list of 9,600 employes had been hired by the Eisenhower Administration.

Never Disavowed"

The "numbers game," as the Democrats called it, was never disavowed publicly by the President or anyone else in the Administration. The practice was just quietly abandoned when it came under too heavy an attack.

The over-all record on the security program might be summarized as follows:

¶The Administration has carried out a strong program that has renewed public confidence in the integrity of Government personnel.

¶Procedural failings in the program have worked hardship and unfairness on the accused.

¶The program's administration has improved greatly in the last two years, but officials in charge believe changes, some requiring legislation, could bring much further improvement.

¶The Administration deliberately used misleading statistics about the program ror political purposes.

¶The political approach has damaged the President's asserted attempt to clear the air of "unreasoned suspicion."

CONGRESSIONAL
INVESTIGATIONS

President Eisenhower's expectation that a Republican Congress would not spend its time investigating and embarrassing the first Republican Administration in twenty years on the Communist issue soon was dashed.

In March, 1953, Senator Joseph R. McCarthy, Republican of Wisconsin, denounced as disloyal Charles E. Bohlen, the President's nominee to be Ambassador to Moscow. Joining in the attack was the late Senator Pat McCarran, Nevada Democrat.

The Executive branch stood firm. John Foster Dulles, Secretary of State, denounced the attack. The President praised Mr. Bohlen at a press conference. Before the issue was settled, a special two-man Senate committee reviewed a summary of the Federal Bureau of Investigation on Mr. Bohlen and "cleared" him. He was confirmed with only thirteen negative votes.

This might have set the pattern for a firm line in dealing with Congressional attacks on the Executive. Instead, over the many months, the country watched what many Administration officials now concede was a spectacle of Executive retreat before Congressional interference.

It is difficult from the relatively calm vantage point of 1956 to recall the atmosphere of 1953. The International Information Administration was Senator McCarthy's first broad target. He charged that thousands of books by "Communist authors" were in Government libraries overseas. He sent Roy M. Cohn and G. David Schine abroad to investigate the libraries. He charged that persons in the I. I. A. who had attacked Messrs. Cohn and Schine were security risks.

The Administration order was to "cooperate" with the Congressional investigators. I. I. A. employes were called by Senator McCarthy to public hearings on suspicion of subversion. These employes found they had no support from above and soon were forced out of their jobs.

President's View Confirmed

Robert J. Donovan's book, "Eisenhower: The Inside Story," documents the general belief that the President despised the Senator's tactics but was opposed personally and on political grounds to tangling directly with him.

General Eisenhower upheld the civil libertarian view in generalities. He told a Darthmouth College audience "Don't join the book-burners." But he took no action when, in the midst of the I. I. A.'s troubles, an overseas librarian actually burned some suspect books.

The crucial question is, what made the atmosphere change? More specifically, who was responsible for bringing Senator McCarthy to his present low estate as an almost ignored outcast?

Some Administration figures have talked about a conscious and successful policy of "letting McCarthy have enough rope and then hanging him when he made a mistake." The truth seems to be that the Senator himself, luck and politics had rather more to do with it.

The immediate cause of the start downhill was, it is commonly agreed, the urgings of Mr. Cohn on behalf of Mr. Schine after the latter became an Army private. But the fact is that almost no one in the Army or the White House wanted to make a stand on this issue.

So far as anyone knows now, it was John G. Adams, then Army counselor, who forced the decision. While controversy raged over the McCarthy investigations of communism in the Army, Mr. Adams temporized in the negotiations over Private Schine but finally drew the line. Most important, he told several newspapermen the story—in detail.

When Mr. Adams suggested breaking the story, White House staff members turned him down. Army and Defense Department officials apparently did the same. But at some point they learned that some of Mr. Adams' newspaper friends had the story, and they became convinced it would break into print anyway.

At these officials' request, Senator Charles E. Potter, Michigan Republican, wrote the Defense Department and asked for information on rumors about Private Schine. This produced the "chronology of events" leading to the thirty-six extraordinary days of the Army-McCarthy hearings.

The view of experts on public opinion was that Senator McCarthy severely damaged his public standing by his conduct in the televised hearings. The denouement was the Senate's vote, in a special session after the 1954 election, to censure him.

It should be noted that the two censure counts involved Senator McCarthy's behavior toward Senate committees, not toward the Executive. And it was Senator Ralph E. Flanders, Vermont Republican, who started the censure move—not, so far as is known, on White House inspiration.

Since the 1954 elections two major forces have worked to control Congressional Communist-hunting in the Executive.

First the Administration has worked affirmatively to develop good relations with most Republican members of Congress, using the prestige of the President to great political advantage. These tactics have succeeded in good measure in isolating and frustrating such extreme right-wing Republicans as Senators McCarthy, William E. Jenner of Indiana and Herman Welker of Idaho.

Second, the Democratic leadership in Congress has exercised a moderating and restraining influence of tremendous effect. It is a real question whether Senator McCarthy could have been successfully ignored, despite censure, if the Republicans had won the 1954 elections and he had remained a committee chairman. Democratic committees have continued investigating Communists, but largely not within the Administration.

The record might be summed up as follows:

¶In its early period the Administration allowed Congressional Communist investigations to disrupt its business and harm United States standing abroad.

¶This trend was checked in 1954 by a combination of circumstances in good part beyond the Administration's control.

¶Since then the Administration has worked shrewdly and effectively to channel Republican Congressional efforts to constructive ends.

¶At the same time Congressional Democrats have avoided baiting the Executive in investigations of communism.

¶Incursions into Executive responsibility are not a threat now, but no firm precedent has been set to deal with the problem if it recurs.

July 30, 1956

HIGH COURT BARS OUSTER FOR USING 5TH AMENDMENT

Orders City to Reinstate Dr. Slochower to the Faculty of Brooklyn College

By LUTHER A. HUSTON
Special to The New York Times.

WASHINGTON, April 9—The Supreme Court today denied New York City the right to dismiss a college professor for invoking the protection of the Fifth Amendment.

In a 5-to-4 ruling, the high court held that the "summary dismissal" of Dr. Harry Slochower, a teacher of German and literature at Brooklyn College for twenty-seven years, "violates due process of law."

[In New York, the president of Brooklyn College announced that Dr. Slochower would be reinstated on the faculty as the result of the court decision and then would be suspended on new charges of alleged "untruthfulness and perjury." It was estimated that Dr. Slochower would receive about $30,000 in back pay when he was reinstated.]

The Fifth Amendment to the Federal Constitution provides that no person shall be required to give self-incriminating testimony nor be deprived of life, liberty or property without due process of law.

Practice Is Condemned

"At the outset we must condemn the practice of imputing a sinister meaning to the exercise of a person's constitutional right under the Fifth Amendment," the majority opinion said.

"The privilege against self-incrimination would be reduced to a hollow mockery if its exercise could be taken as equivalent either to a confession of guilt or a conclusive presumption of perjury."

Dr. Slochower invoked the privilege against self-incriminating testimony when he was asked in September, 1952, at a Senate Judiciary subcommittee hearing, whether he had been a member of the Communist party in 1940 and 1941. On Oct. 6, 1952, he was dismissed under Section 903 of the New York City Charter.

That section provides for the automatic dismissal of any municipal officer or employe who refuses to answer any question regarding his official conduct on the ground that the answer might tend to incriminate him. Employes so discharged become ineligible to future election or appointment to municipal positions.

The law does not provide for notice, hearings, or opportunity to explain the refusal to answer the questions.

Dr. Slochower contended that the application of the Charter's provision to his case deprived him of due process of law. The Supreme Court agreed with him.

Justice Tom C. Clark delivered the opinion of the court. Chief Justice Earl Warren and Justices Hugo L. Black, Felix Frankfurter and William O. Douglas concurred.

The dissenters were Justices Stanley F. Reed, Harold H. Burton, Sherman Minton and John M. Harlan. Justice Harlan dissented on different grounds than the others and expressed his disagreement in a separate opinion.

Justice Clark said that "every city employee who invokes the Fifth Amendment" could be discharged if the interpretation of Section 903 in the Slochower case was universally applied.

"In practical effect the questions asked are taken as confessed and made the basis for the discharge," he said. "No consideration is given to such factors as the subject matter of the questions, the remoteness of the period to which they are directed, or justification for exercise of the privilege.

"It matters not whether the plea results from mistake, inadvertence or legal advice conscientiously given, whether wisely or unwisely. The heavy hand of the statute falls alike on all who exercise their constitutional privilege, the full enjoyment of which every person is entitled to receive."

New York has asserted that Dr. Slochower's refusal to answer would tend to prove him guilty of a crime or that he had falsely invoked the Fifth Amendment privilege to avoid answering and therefore committed perjury.

Justice Clark sharply rejected these contentions.

Justice Reed, in his dissent, disagreed with the assumption of the majority that "Section 903 as a practical matter takes the questions asked as confessed."

The city, Justice Reed said, "does have reasonable ground to require its employes either to give evidence regarding the facts of official conduct within their knowledge or give up the positions they hold."

"The fact that the witness has a right to plead the privilege against self-incrimination protects him against prosecution but not against the loss of his job," Justice Reed wrote.

Justice Harlan, in his separate dissent, asserted that the state did not violate due process when it made assertion of a claim of privilege grounds for discharge.

"I think that a state may justifiably consider that teachers who refuse to answer questions concerning their official conduct are no longer qualified for public school teaching, on the ground that their refusal to answer jeopardizes the confidence that the public should have in its school system," Justice Harlan said.

The Senate subcommittee was investigating subversive influences in the public schools throughout the country. Its chairman said it was not inquiring into the official conduct of city employes.

Dr. Slochower testified that he was not a member of the Communist party. It had been alleged in testimony before a committee of the New York Legislature that he had been a Communist in 1941.

Dr. Slochower said that he had answered questions of this committee and of a faculty board regarding his Communist affiliations in 1940 and 1941.

Justice Clark said that the New York Board of Education had "possessed the pertinent information for twelve years" to determine whether Dr. Slochower was qualified to continue in city employment. The questions asked by the Federal committee, he asserted, were propounded "for a purpose wholly unrelated to his college functions."

But the board had seized upon his invocation of the Fifth Amendment to "convert the use of Section 903 into a conclusive presumption of guilt."

"Since no inference of guilt was possible from the claim before the Federal committee the discharge falls of its own weight as wholly without support," Justice Clark concluded.

The case was argued in the high court last Oct. 17. Ephraim S. London of New York appeared for Dr. Slochower. Daniel T. Scannell, from the office of the Corporation Counsel, argued for the New York Board of Education.

April 10, 1956

HIGH COURT, RELEASING WATKINS, RESTRICTS CONGRESS ON PRIVACY; FREES 5 REDS IN SMITH ACT CASE

Judiciary Seen as Setting Limit on Other Branches

Supreme Court Declares Rights of Individuals Must Be Protected

By JAMES RESTON
Special to The New York Times.

WASHINGTON, June 17—The Supreme Court today warned all branches of the Government that they must be more faithful to the Constitutional guarantees of individual freedom.

Reasserting its ancient role as a defender of the Constitution and the Bill of Rights, the high court condemned the tendency to punish men for beliefs and associations, warned the Federal Executive to guard the constitutional freedoms of its employes, and sharply criticized the Congress for giving undefined and unlimited powers of investigation to Congressional committees.

Under the leadership of Chief Justice Earl Warren, the Supreme Court, which recently condemned the unrestricted use of secret Federal Bureau of Investigation documents in the courts, and forbade military trials for families of military personnel overseas, seemed to be curbing the power of the Executive and Legislative branches in their dealings with the individual.

During the last decade, the Supreme Court has been called upon to deal with a flood of cases dealing with the rights of aliens, ordinances affecting religious zealots, religion in the schools, Government employes and others affected by test oaths and loyalty proceedings, legislative investigations and direct restraints on Communists and others advocating forcible overthrow of the Government.

"A review of these decisions," John Lord O'Brien, the Washington constitutional authority, wrote in 1952, "establishes the disconcerting and perhaps startling fact that in no case has the court liberalized or extended the freedoms guaranteed by the Constitution.

"The general trend has been in the direction of sustaining, in the interest of national security, new restrictions upon those liberties."

The general view here tonight was that the significance of the recent decisions of the Supreme Court, and particularly of its principal findings today, was that this could no longer be said of the court as now constituted.

Today's majority opinions were studded with passages

Associated Press

Chief Justice Earl Warren

critical of the exercise of power by the Federal Government, and strong in the defense of the individual's rights.

Chief Justice Warren, speaking for the majority of the court in John T. Watkins vs. the United States, stated flatly that "we have no doubt that there is no Congressional power to expose for the sake of exposure." He conceded that the public is entitled to be informed of the workings of its Government but added:

"That cannot be inflated into a general power to expose where the predominant result can only be an invasion of the private rights of individuals."

Criticism by Warren

The Chief Justice criticized the broad range of inquiry followed in the Watkins case by the House Un-American Activities Committee, and condemned the House of Representatives for giving the committee such undefined power.

"The committee," he said, "is allowed, in essence, to define its own authority, to choose the direction and focus of its activities. In deciding what to do with the power that has been conferred upon them, members of the committee may act pursuant to motives that seem to them of the highest.

"Their decisions, nevertheless, can lead to ruthless exposure of private lives in order to gather data that is neither desired by the Congress nor useful to it * * *."

In turning free five of the convicted California Communist leaders, the court defended a man's right to advocate the forcible overthrow of the Government provided he did not advocate action to achieve that end.

"The essential distinction," Mr. Justice Harlan said for the court, "is that those to whom advocacy is addressed must be urged to do something, now or in the future, rather than merely to believe something."

As a result of these and other recent dramatic decisions, observers are now taking a new look at the balance of power on the court and of the court itself in its relation to the other two coordinate branches of the Government.

That the court is now playing a more powerful role on the most controversial issues of the day is generally assumed. It is not throwing out legislation passed by the Congress, as the Supreme Court did after the first flood of legislation in the first Roosevelt Administration, but it is asserting that the Legislative and Executive Branches of the Government and the lower courts must be more sensitive to procedures that may affect a citizen's liberties or good name.

Cardozo View Recalled

It is, in short, now defending that concept of "constitutionalism" best described by the late Mr. Justice Cardozo in these terms:

"The great ideals of liberty and equality are preserved against the assaults of opportunism, the expediency of the passing hour, the erosion of small encroachments, the scorn and derision of those who have no patience with general principles, by enshrining them in constitutions, and consecrating to the task of their protection a body of defenders. By conscious and subconscious influence, the presence of this restraining power, aloof in the background, but nonetheless always in reserve, tends to stabilize and rationalize the legislative judgment, to infuse it with the glow of principle, to hold the standard aloft and visible for those who must run the race and keep the faith."

Moreover, the feeling here is that the Eisenhower appointments to the court have established a new balance in which there is a reliable majority extremely sensitive to defense of civil liberties.

Justices Warren, Black, Doug-

las and Brennan seem to furnish the core of this majority, with Justices Harlan and Frankfurter often sustaining their judgments on civil liberties cases.

Some observers think they find in the opinions of Justices Frankfurter and Harlan a greater tendency to hesitate about making broad generalizations in this field. Nevertheless, they are usually in general agreement with the four mentioned above.

Justice Clark, a former Attorney General under President Truman, is generally found in dissent on this type of opinion, and is sometimes supported by Justice Burton. The other member, Justice Whittaker, has not been on the court long enough to indicate where he will be found in this increasingly apparent line-up.

June 18, 1957

Supreme Court Decision and Concurring and Dissenting Opinions in Watkins Case

WASHINGTON, June 17—Following are the texts of the Supreme Court decision and the concurring and dissenting opinions in the Watkins case:

Opinion of the Majority

Mr. Chief Justice Warren delivered the opinion of the court.

This is a review by certiorari of a conviction under 2 U.S.C. Section 192 for "contempt of Congress." The misdemeanor is alleged to have been committed during a hearing before a Congressional investigating committee. It is not the case of a truculent or contumacious witness who refuses to answer all questions or who, by boisterous or discourteous conduct, disturbs the decorum of the committee room.

Petitioner was prosecuted for refusing to make certain disclosures which he asserted to be beyond the authority of the committee to demand. The controversy thus rests upon fundamental principles of the power of the Congress and the limitations upon that power. We approach the questions presented with conscious awareness of the far-reaching ramifications that can follow from a decision of this nature.

On April 29, 1954, petitioner appeared as a witness in compliance with a subpoena issued by a subcommittee of the Committee on Un-American Activities of the House of Representatives. The subcommittee elicited from petitioner a description of his background in labor union activities. He had been an employee of the International Harvester Company between 1935 and 1953. During the last eleven years, he had been on leave of absence to serve as an official of the Farm Equipment

Workers International Union, later merged into the United Electrical Radio and Machine Workers.

Joined Auto Workers

He rose to the position of president of District No. 2 of the Farm Equipment Workers, a district defined geographically to include generally Canton and Rock Falls, Ill., and Dubuque, Iowa. In 1953, petitioner joined the United Auto Workers International Union as a labor organizer.

Petitioner's name had been mentioned by two witnesses who testified before the committee at prior hearings. In September, 1952, one Donald O. Spencer admitted having been a Communist from 1943 to 1946. He declared that he had been recruited into the party with the endorsement and prior approval of petitioner, whom he identified as the then district vice president of the Farm Equipment Workers. Spencer also mentioned that petitioner had attended meetings at which only card-carrying Communists were admitted. A month before petitioner testified, one Walter Rumsey stated that he had been recruited into the party by petitioner. Rumsey added that he had paid party dues to and later collected dues from petitioner, who had assumed the name, Sam Brown. Rumsey told the committee that he had left the party in 1944.

Petitioner answered these allegations freely and without reservation. His attitude toward the inquiry is clearly revealed from the statement he made when the questioning turned to the subject of his past conduct, associations and predilections:

"I am not now nor have I ever been a card-carrying member of the Communist party. Rumsey was wrong when he said I had recruited him into the party, that I had received his dues, that I paid dues to him, and that I had used the alias Sam Brown.

Denies Allegations

"Spencer was wrong when he termed any meetings which I attended as closed Communist party meetings.

"I would like to make it clear that for a period of time from approximately 1942 to 1947 I cooperated with the Communist party and participated in Communist activities to such a degree that some persons may honestly believe that I was a member of the party.

"I have made contributions upon occasions to Communist causes. I have signed petitions for Communist causes. I attended caucuses at an F. E. convention at which Communist party officials were present.

"Since I freely cooperated with the Communist party I have no motive for making the distinction between cooperation and membership except the simple fact that is the truth. I never carried a Communist party card. I never accepted discipline and indeed on several occasions I opposed their position.

"In a special convention held in the summer of 1947 I led the fight for compliance with the Taft-Hartley Act by the

F.E.C.I.O. International Union. This fight became so bitter that it ended any possibility of future cooperation."

The character of petitioner's testimony on these matters can perhaps best be summarized by the Government's own appraisal in its brief:

"A more complete and candid statement of his past political associations and activities (treating the Communist party for present purposes as a mere political party) can hardly be imagined. Petitioner certainly was not attempting to conceal or withhold from the committee his own past political associations, predilections and preferences. Furthermore, petitioner told the committee that he was entirely willing to identify for the committee, and answer any questions it might have concerning 'those persons whom I knew to be members of the Communist party,' provided that, 'to [his] best knowledge and belief,' they still were members of the party * * *."

Asked to Identify Names

The subcommittee, too, was apparently satisfied with petitioner's disclosures. After some further discussion elaborating on the statement, counsel for the committee turned to another aspect of Rumsey's testimony. Rumsey had identified a group of persons whom he had known as members of the Communist party, and counsel began to read this list of names to petitioner. Petitioner stated that he did not know several of the persons. Of those whom he did know, he refused to tell whether he knew them to have been members of the Communist party. He explained to the subcommittee why he took such a position:

"I am not going to plead the Fifth Amendment, but I refuse to answer certain questions that I believe are outside the proper scope of your committee's activities. I will answer any questions which this committee puts to me about myself. I will also answer questions about those persons whom I knew to be members of the Communist party and who I believe still are. I will not, however, answer any questions with respect to others with whom I associated in the past. I do not believe that any law in this country requires me to testify about persons who may in the past have been Communist party members or otherwise engaged in Communist party activity but who to my best knowledge and belief have long since removed themselves from the Communist movement.

"I do not believe that such questions are relevant to the work of this committee nor do I believe that this committee has the right to undertake the public exposure of persons because of their past activities. I may be wrong, and the committee may have this power, but until and unless a court of law so holds and directs me to answer, I must firmly refuse to discuss the political activities of my past associates."

Report Sent to House

The chairman of the committee submitted a report of petitioner's refusal to answer questions to the House of Representatives. H. R. Rep. No. 1579, 83d Cong. 2d Sess. The House directed the Speaker to certify the committee's report to the United States Attorney for initiation of criminal prosecution. R. Res. 534, 83d Cong., 2d Sess. A seven-count indictment was returned. Petitioner waived his right to jury trial and was found guilty on all counts by the court. The sentence, a fine of $100 and one year in prison, was suspended, and petitioner was placed on probation.

An appeal was taken to the Court of Appeals for the District of Columbia. The conviction was reversed by a three-judge panel, one member dissenting. Upon rehearing *en banc*, the full bench affirmed the conviction with the judges of the original majority in dissent. We granted certiorari because of the very important questions of constitutional law presented.

We start with several basic premises on which there is general agreement. The power of the Congress to conduct investigations is inherent in the legislative process. That power is broad. It encompasses inquiries concerning the administration of existing laws as well as proposed or possibly needed statutes. It includes surveys of defects in our social economic or political system for the purpose of enabling the Congress to remedy them. It comprehends probes into departments of the Federal Government to expose corruption, inefficiency or waste.

But broad as is this power of inquiry, it is not unlimited. There is no general authority to expose the private affairs of individuals without justification in

terms of the functions of the Congress. This was freely conceded by the Solicitor General in his argument of this case. Nor is the Congress a law enforcement or trial agency. These are functions of the Executive and Judicial departments of Government. No inquiry is an end in itself; it must be related to and in furtherance of a legitimate task of the Congress. Investigations conducted solely for the personal aggrandizement of the investigators or to "punish" those investigated are indefensible.

Duties of Citizens Cited

It is unquestionably the duty of a citizen to cooperate with the Congress in its efforts to obtain the facts needed for intelligent legislative action. It is their unremitting obligation to respond to subpoenas, to respect the dignity of the Congress and its committees and to testify fully with respect to matters within the province of proper investigation. This, of course, assumes that the Constitutional rights of witnesses will be respected by the Congress as they are in a court of justice. The Bill of Rights is applicable to investigations as to all forms of Governmental action. Witnesses cannot be compelled to give evidence against themselves. They cannot be subjected to unreasonable search and seizure. Nor can the First Amendment freedoms of speech, press, religion, or political belief and association be abridged.

The rudiments of the power to punish for "contempt of Congress" come to us from the pages of English history. The origin of privileges and contempts extends back into the period of the emergence of Parliament. The establishment of a legislative body which could challenge the absolute power of the monarch is a long and bitter story. In that struggle, Parliament made broad and varied use of the contempt power. Almost from the beginning, both the House of Commons and the House of Lords claimed absolute and plenary authority over their privileges. This was an independent body of law, described by Coke as lex parliamenti. Only Parliament could declare what those privileges were or what new privileges were occasioned, and by Parliament could judge what conduct constituted a breach of privilege.

In particular, this exclusion of lex parliamentia from the lex terrae, or law of the land, precluded judicial review of the exercise of the contempt power or the assertion of privilege. Parliament declared that no court had jurisdiction to consider such questions. In the latter part of the seventeenth century, an action for false imprisonment was brought by one Jay who had been held in contempt. The defendant, the Serjeant-at-Arms of the House of Commons, demurred that he had taken the plaintiff into custody for breach of privilege. The Chief Justice, Pemberton, overruled the demurrer. Summoned to the bar of the House, the Chief Justice explained that he believed that the assertion of privilege went to the merits of the action and did not

preclude jurisdiction. For his audacity, the Chief Justice was dispatched to Newgate prison.

Abuses of Power Recalled

It seems inevitable that the power claimed by Parliament would have been abused. Unquestionably it was. A few examples illustrate the way in which individual rights were infringed. During the seventeenth century, there was a violent upheaval, both religious and political. This was the time of the Reformation and the Establishment of the Church of England. It was also the period when the Stuarts proclaimed that the royal prerogative was absolute. Ultimately there were two revolutions, one protracted and bloody, the second without bloodshed. Critical commentary of all kinds was treated as contempt of Parliament in these troubled days. Even clergymen were imprisoned for remarks made in their sermons.

Perhaps the outstanding case arose from the private conversation of one Floyd, a Catholic, in which he expressed pleasure over the misfortune of the King's Protestant son-in-law and his wife. Floyd was not a Member of Parliament. None of the persons concerned was in any way connected with the House of Commons. Nevertheless, that body imposed an humiliating and cruel sentence upon Floyd for contempt. The House of Lords intervened, rebuking the Commons for their extension of the privilege. The Commons acceded and transferred the record of the case to the Lords, who imposed substantially the same penalty.

Pamphlet Author Hidden

Later in that century, during the reign of Charles II, there was great unrest over the fact that the heir apparent, James, had embraced Catholicism. Anti-Catholic feeling ran high, spilling over a few years later when the infamous rogue, Titus Oates, inflamed the country with rumors of a "Popish plot" to murder the King.

A committee of Parliament was appointed to learn the sources of certain pamphlets that had been appearing. One was entitled: "The Grand Question Concerning the Prorogation of this Parliament for a Year and Three Months Stated and Discussed." A Dr. Carey admitted to the committee that he knew the author, but refused to divulge his name. Brought to the bar of the House of Lords, he persisted in this stand. The House imposed a fine of £1,000 and committed the witness to the Tower.

A hundred years later, George III had managed to gain control of Parliament through his ministers. The King could not silence the opposition, however, and one of the most vocal was John Wilkes. This precipitated a struggle that lasted for several years until Wilkes finally prevailed. One writer sums up the case thus:

"He had won a victory for freedom of the press. He had directed popular attention to the royally controlled House of Com-

mons, and pointed out its unrepresentative character, and had shown how easily a claim of privilege might be used to sanction the arbitrary proceedings of ministers and Parliament, even when a fundamental right of the subject was concerned. It is one of life's little ironies that work of such magnitude had been reserved for one of the worst libertines and demagogues of all time."

1835 British Inquiry Cited

Even as late as 1835, the House of Commons appointed a select committee to inquire into "* * * the origin, nature, extent and tendency of the Orange Institutions." This was a political-religious organization, vehemently Protestant in religion and strongly in favor of the growth of the British Empire. The committee summoned the deputy grand secretary and demanded that he produce all the records of the organization. The witness refused to turn over a letter-book, which he admitted contained his answers to many communications upon Orange business. But it also contained, he said, records of private communications with respect to Orangeism. Summoned to the bar of the House of Commons, he remained adamant and was committed to Newgate Prison.

Modern times have seen a remarkable restraint in the use by Parliament of its contempt power. Important investigations, like those conducted in America by Congressional committees, are made by Royal Commissions of Inquiry. These commissions are comprised of experts in the problem to be studied. They are removed from the turbulent forces of politics and partisan considerations. Seldom, if ever, have these commissions been given the authority to compel the testimony of witnesses or the production of documents. Their success in fulfilling their fact-finding missions without resort to coercive tactics is a tribute to the fairness of the processes to the witnesses and their close adherence to the subject matter committed to them.

The history of contempt of the Legislature in this country is notably different from that of England. In the early days of the United States, there lingered the direct knowledge of the evil effects of absolute power. Most of the instances of use of compulsory process by the first Congresses concerned matters affecting the qualification or integrity of their members or came about in inquiries dealing with suspected corruption or mismanagement of Government officials. Unlike the English practice, from the very outset the use of contempt power by the Legislature was deemed subject to judicial review.

There was very little use of power of compulsory process in early years to enable the Congress to obtain facts pertinent to the enactment of new statutes or the administration of existing laws. The first occasion for such an investigation arose in 1827 when the House of Representatives was considering a revision of the tariff laws. In the Senate there was no use of a fact-finding investigation in aid of legislation until 1859. In the Legislative Reorganization Act the Committee on Un-American Activities is the only standing committee of the House of Representatives that was given the power to compel disclosures.

Power Used Sparingly

It is not surprising, from the fact that the Houses of Congress so sparingly employed the power to conduct investigations, that there have been few cases requiring judicial review of the power. The nation was almost 100 years old before the first case reached this court to challenge the use of compulsory process as a legislative device, rather than in inquiries concerning the elections or privileges of Congressmen. In Kilbourn v. Thompson, 103 U. S. 168, decided in 1881, an investigation had been authorized by the House of Representatives to learn the circumstances surrounding the bankruptcy of Jay Cooke & Company, in which the United States had deposited funds. The committee became particularly interested in a private real estate pool that was a part of the financial structure. The court found that the subject matter of the inquiry was "in its nature clearly judicial and therefore one in respect to which no valid legislation could be enacted." The House had thereby exceeded the limits of its own authority.

Subsequent to the decision in Kilbourn, until recent times, there were very few cases dealing with the investigative power. The matter came to the fore again when the Senate undertook to study the corruption in handling of oil leases in the Nineteen Twenties. In McGrain v. Daugherty, 273 U. S. 135, and Sinclair v. United States, 279 U. S. 263, the court applied the precepts of Kilbourn to uphold the authority of the Congress to conduct the challenged investigations. The court recognized the danger to effective and honest conduct of the Government if the legislature's power to probe corruption in the Executive Branch were unduly hampered.

Following these important decisions, there was another lull in judicial review of investigations. The absence of challenge, however, was not indicative of the absence of inquiries. To the contrary, there was vigorous use of the investigative process by a Congress bent upon harnessing and directing the vast economic and social forces of the times. Only one case came before this court, and the authority of the Congress was affirmed.

New Type of Inquiry

In the decade following World War II, there appeared a new kind of Congressional inquiry unknown in prior periods of American history. Principally this was the result of the various investigations into the threat of subversion of the United States Government, but other subjects of Congressional

interest also contributed to the changed scene. This new phase of legislative inquiry involved a broad-scale intrusion into the lives and affairs of private citizens. It brought before the courts novel questions of the appropriate limits of Congressional inquiry. Prior cases, like Kilbourn, McGrain and Sinclair, had defined the scope of investigative power in terms of the inherent limitations of the sources of that power.

In the more recent cases, the emphasis shifted to problems of accommodating the interest of the Government with the rights and privileges of individuals. The central theme was the application of the Bill of Rights as a restraint upon the assertion of Government power in this form.

It was during this period that the Fifth Amendment privilege against self-incrimination was frequently invoked and recognized as a legal limit upon the authority of a committee to require that a witness answer its questions. Some early doubts as to the applicability of that privilege before a legislative committee never matured. When the matter reached this court, the Government did not challenge in any way that the Fifth Amendment protection was available to the witness, and such a challenge could not have prevailed. It confined its argument to the character of the answers sought and to the adequacy of the claim of privilege. Quinn v. United States, 349 U. S. 155; Emspak v. United States, 349 U. S. 190; Bart v. United States, 349 U. S. 219.

First Amendment Claims

A far more difficult task evolved from the claim by witnesses that the committees' interrogations were infringements upon the freedoms of the First Amendment Clearly, an investigation is subject to the command that the Congress shall make no law abridging freedom of speech or press or assembly. While it is true that there is no statute to be reviewed, and that an investigation is not a law, nevertheless an investigation is part of lawmaking. It is justified solely as an adjunct to the legislative process. The First Amendment may be invoked against infringement of the protected freedoms by law or by lawmaking.

Abuses of the investigative process may imperceptibly lead to abridgment of protected freedoms. The mere summoning of a witness and compelling him to testify, against his will, about his beliefs, expressions or associations is a measure of Governmental interference. And when those forced revelations concern matters that are unorthodox, unpopular, or even hateful to the general public, the reaction in the life of the witness may be disastrous. This effect is even more harsh when it is past beliefs, expressions or associations that are disclosed and judged by current standards rather than those contemporary with the matters exposed. Nor does the witness alone suffer the consequences. Those who are identified by witnesses and there-

by placed in the same glare of publicity are equally subject to public stigma, scorn and obloquy. Beyond that, there is the more subtle and immeasurable effect upon those who tend to adhere to the most orthodox and uncontroversial views and associations in order to avoid a similar fate at some future time. That this impact is partly the result of non-Governmental activity by private persons cannot relieve the investigators of their responsibility for initiating the reaction.

The court recognized the restraints of the Bill of Right upon Congressional investigations in United States v. Rumely, 345 U. S. 41. The magnitude and complexity of the problem of applying the First Amendment to that case led the court to construe narrowly the resolution describing the committee's authority. It was concluded that, when First Amendment rights are threatened, the delegation of power to the committee must be clearly revealed in its charter.

A Difficult Accommodation

Accommodation of the Congressional need for particular information with the individual and personal interest in privacy is an arduous and delicate task for any court. We do not underestimate the difficulties that attend such an undertaking. It is manifest that despite the adverse effects which follow upon compelled disclosure of private matters, not all such inquiries are barred. Kilbourn v. Thompson teaches that such an investigation into individual affairs is invalid if unrelated to any legislative purpose. That is beyond the powers conferred upon the Congress in the Constitution. United States v. Rumely makes it plain that the mere semblance of legislative purpose would not justify an inquiry in the face of the Bill of Rights. The critical element is the existence of, and the weight to be ascribed to, the interest of the Congress in demanding disclosures from an unwilling witness. We cannot simply assume however, that every Congressional investigation is justified by a public need that overbalances any private rights affected. To do so would be to abdicate the responsibility placed by the Constitution upon the judiciary to insure that the Congress does not unjustifiably encroach upon an individual's right to privacy nor abridge his liberty of speech, press, religion or assembly.

Petitioner has earnestly suggested that the difficult questions of protecting these rights from infringement by legislative inquiries can be surmounted in this case because there was no public purpose served in his interrogation. His conclusion is based upon the thesis that the subcommittee was engaged in a program of exposure for the sake of exposure. The sole purpose of the inquiry, he contends, was to bring down upon himself and others the violence of public reaction because of their past beliefs, expressions and associations. In support of this argument, petitioner has marshalled an impressive array of

evidence that some Congressmen have believed that such was their duty, or part of it.

Congressional Power Limited

We have no doubt that there is no Congressional power to expose for the sake of exposure. The public is, of course, entitled to be informed concerning the workings of its Government. That cannot be inflated into a general power to expose where the predominant result can only be an invasion of the private rights of individuals. But a solution to our problem is not to be found in testing the motives of committee members for this purpose. Such is not our function. Their motives alone would not vitiate an investigation which had been instituted by a house of Congress if that assembly's legislative purpose is being served.

Petitioner's contentions do point to a situation of particular significance from the standpoint of the constitutional limitations upon Congressional investigations. The theory of a committee inquiry is that the committee members are serving as the representatives of the parent assembly in collecting information for a legislative purpose. Their function is to act as the eyes and ears of the Congress in obtaining facts upon which the full Legislature can act. To carry out this mission, committees and subcommittees, sometimes one Congressman, are endowed with the full power of the Congress to compel testimony. In this case, only two men exercised that authority in demanding information over petitioner's protest.

An essential premise in this situation is that the House or Senate shall have instructed the committee members on what they are to do with the power delegated to them. It is the responsibility of the Congress, in the first instance, to insure that compulsory process is used only in furtherance of a legislative purpose. That requires that the instructions to an investigating committee spell out that group's jurisdiction and purpose with sufficient particularity. Those instructions are embodied in the authorizing resolution. That document is the committee's charter. Broadly drafted and loosely worded, however, such resolutions can leave tremendous latitude to the discretion of the investigators. The more vague the committee's charter is, the greater becomes the possibility that the committee's specific actions are not in conformity with the will of the parent house of Congress.

1938 Resolution Quoted

The authorizing resolution of the Un-American Activities Committee was adopted in 1938 when a select committee, under the chairmanship of Representative Dies, was created. Several years later, the committee was made a standing organ of the House with the same mandate. It defines the committee's authority as follows:

"The Committee on Un-American Activities, as a whole or by subcommittee, is authorized to make from time to time investigations of (I) the extent, character, and objects of un-American propaganda activities in the United States, (II) the diffusion within the United States of subversive and un-American propaganda that is instigated from foreign countries or of a domestic origin and attacks the principle of the form of government as guaranteed by our Constitution, and (III) all other questions in relation thereto that would aid Congress in any necessary remedial legislation."

It would be difficult to imagine a less explicit authorizing resolution. Who can define the meaning of "un-American"? What is the single, solitary "principle of the form of government as guaranteed by our Constitution"? There is no need to dwell upon the language, however. At one time, perhaps, the resolution might have been read narrowly to confine the committee to the subject of propaganda. The events that have transpired in the fifteen years before the interrogation of petitioner makes such a construction impossible at this date.

Committee Supported Repeatedly

The members of the committee have clearly demonstrated that they did not feel themselves restricted in any way to propaganda in the narrow sense of the word. Unquestionably the committee conceived of its task in the grand view of its name. Un-American activities were its target, no matter how or where manifested. Notwithstanding the broad purview of the committee's experience, the House of Representatives repeatedly approved its continuation. Five times it extended the life of the special committee. Then it made the group a standing committee of the House. A year later the committee's charter was embodied in the Legislative Reorganization Act. On five occasions, at the beginning of sessions of Congress, it has made the authorizing resolution part of the rules of the House. On innumerable occasions, it has passed appropriation bills to allow the committee to continue its efforts.

Combining the language of the resolution with the construction it has been given, it is evident that the preliminary control of the committee exercised by the House of Representatives is slight or nonexistent. No one could reasonably deduce from the charter the kind of investigation that the committee was directed to make.

Core of the Inquiries

As a result, we are asked to engage in a process of retroactive rationalization. Looking backward from the events that transpired, we are asked to uphold the committee's actions unless it appears that they were clearly not authorized by the charter. As a corollary to this inverse approach, the Government urges that we must view the matter hospitably to the power of the Congress—that if there is any legislative purpose which might have been furthered by the kind of disclosure sought, the witness must be punished for withholding it. No doubt every reasonable indulgence of legality must be accorded to the

actions of a coordinate branch of our Government. But such deference cannot yield to an unnecessary and unreasonable dissipation of precious constitutional freedoms.

The Government contends that the public interest at the core of the investigations of the Un-American Activities Committee is the need by the Congress to be informed of efforts to overthrow the Government by force and violence so that adequate legislative safeguards can be erected. From this core, however, the committee can radiate outward infinitely to any topic thought to be related in some way to armed insurrection. The outer reaches of this domain are known only by the content of "Un-American activities." Remoteness of subject can be aggravated by a probe for a depth of detail even fartner removed from any basis of legislative action. A third dimension is added when the investigators turn their attention to the past to collect minutiae or remote topics, on the hypothesis that the past may reflect upon the present.

The consequences that flow from this situation are manifold. In the first place, a reviewing court is unable to make the kind of judgment made by the court in United States v. Rumely, supra. The committee is allowed, in essence, to define its own authority, to choose the direction and focus of its activities. In deciding what to do with the power that has been conferred upon them, members of the committee may act pursuant to motives that seem to them to be the highest. Their decisions, nevertheless, can lead to ruthless exposure of private lives in order to gather data that is neither desired by the Congress nor useful to it. Yet it is impossible in this circumstance, with constitutional freedoms in jeopardy, to declare that the committee has ranged beyond the area committed to it by its parent assembly because the boundaries are so nebulous.

More important and more fundamental than that, however, it insulates the House that has authorized the investigation from the witnesses who are subjected to the sanctions of compulsory process. There is a wide gulf between the responsibility for the use of investigative power and the actual exercise of that power. This is an especially vital consideration in assuring respect for constitutional liberties. Protected freedoms should not be placed in danger in the absence of a clear determination by the House or the Senate that a particular inquiry is justified by a specific legislative need.

Investigative Rules Cited

It is, of course, not the function of this court to prescribe rigid rules for the Congress to follow in drafting resolutions establishing investigating committees. That is a matter peculiarly within the realm of the legislature, and its decisions will be accepted by the courts up to the point where their own duty to enforce the constitutionally protected rights of individuals is affected. An excessively broad

charter, like that of the House Un-American Activities Committee, places the courts in an untenable position if they are to strike a balance between the public need for a particular interrogation and the right of citizens to carry on their affairs free from unnecessary governmental interference. It is impossible in such a situation to ascertain whether any legislative purpose justifies the disclosures sought and, if so, the importance of that information to the Congress in furtherance of its legislative function. The reason no court can make this critical judgment is that the House of Representatives itself has never made it. Only the legislative assembly initiating an investigation can assay the relative necessity of specific disclosures.

Absence of the qualitative consideration of petitioner's questioning by the House of Representatives aggravates a serious problem, revealed in this case, in the relationship of Congressional investigating committees and the witnesses who appear before them. Plainly these committees are restricted to the missions delegated to them, i, e. to acquire certain data to be used by the House or the Senate in coping with a problem that falls within its legislative sphere. No witness can be compelled to make disclosures on matters outside that area. This is a jurisdictional concept of pertinency drawn from the nature of a Congressional committee's source of authority. It is not wholly different from nor unrelated to the element of pertinency embodied in the criminal statute under which petitioner was prosecuted. When the definition of jurisdictional pertinency is as uncertain and wavering as in the case of the Un-American Activities Committee, it becomes extremely difficult for the committee to limit its inquiries to statutory pertinency.

Since World War II the Congress has practically abandoned its original practice of utilizing the coercive sanction of contempt proceedings at the bar of the House. The sanction there imposed was imprisonment by the House until the recalcitrant witness agrees to testify or disclose the matters sought, provided that the incarceration does not extend beyond adjournment. The Congress has instead invoked the aid of the Federal judicial system in protecting itself against contumacious conduct. It has become customary to refer these matters to the United States attorneys for prosecution under criminal law.

The appropriate statute is found in 2 U. S. C. Section 192. It provides:

"Every person who having been summoned as a witness by the authority of either house of Congress to give testimony or to produce papers upon any matter under inquiry before either House, or any joint committee established by a joint or concurrent resolution of the two Houses of Congress, or any committee of either House of Congress, willfully makes default, or who, having appeared, refuses to answer any question pertinent to the

question under inquiry, shall be deemed guilty of a misdemeanor, punishable by a fine of not more than $1,000 nor less than $100 and imprisonment in a common jail for not less than one month nor more than twelve months."

Court's Obligations Listed

In fulfillment of their obligation under this statute, the courts must accord to the defendants every right which is guaranteed to defendants in all other criminal cases. Among these is the right to have available, through a sufficiently precise statute, information revealing the standard of criminality before the commission of the alleged offense. Applied to persons prosecuted under Section 192, this raises a special problem in that the statute defines the crime as refusal to answer "any question pertinent to the question under inquiry." Part of the standard of criminality, therefore, is the pertinency of the questions propounded to the witness.

The problem attains proportion when viewed from the standpoint of the witness who appears before a Congressional committee. He must decide at the time the questions are propounded whether or not to answer. As the Court said in Sinclair v. United States, 279 U. S. 263, the witness acts at his peril. He is "* * * bound rightly to construe the statute." Id., at 299. An erroneous determination on his part, even if made in the utmost good faith, does not exculpate him if the court should later rule that the questions were pertinent to the question under inquiry.

Vice of Vagueness

It is obvious that a person compelled to make this choice is entitled to have knowledge of the subject to which the interrogation is deemed pertinent. That knowledge must be available with the same degree of explicitness and clarity that the due process clause requires in the expression of any element of a criminal offense. The "vice of vagueness" must be avoided here as in all other crimes. There are several sources that can outline the "question under inquiry" in such a way that the rules against vagueness are satisfied. The authorizing resolution, the remarks of the chairman or members of the committee, or even the nature of the proceedings themselves might sometimes make the topic clear. This case demonstrates, however, that these sources often leave the matter in grave doubt.

The first possibility is that the authorizing resolution itself will so clearly declare the "question under inquiry" that a witness can understand the pertinency of questions asked him. The Government does not contend that the authorizing resolution of the Un-American Activities Committee could serve such a purpose. Its confusing breadth is amply illustrated by the innumerable and diverse questions into which the committee has inquired under this charter since 1938. If the "question under inquiry" were stated with such sweeping and uncertain scope, we doubt that it would withstand an attack on the ground of vagueness.

That issue is not before us, however, in light of the Government's position that the immediate subject under inquiry before the subcommittee interviewing petitioner was only one aspect of the committee's authority to investigate un-American activities. Distilling the single topic from the broad field is an extremely difficult task upon the record before us. There was an opening statement by the committee chairman at the outset of the hearing, but this gives us no guidance. In this statement, the chairman did no more than paraphrase the authorizing resolution and give a very general sketch of the past efforts of the committee.'

Resolution Adopted

No aid is given as to the "question under inquiry" in the action of the full committee that authorized the creation of the subcommittee before which petitioner appeared. The committee adopted a formal resolution giving the chairman the power to appoint subcommittees "* * * for the purpose of performing any and all acts which the committee as a whole is authorized to do." In effect, this was a device to enable the investigations to proceed with a quorum of one or two members and sheds no light on the relevancy of the questions asked of petitioner.

The Government believes that the topic of inquiry before the subcommittee concerned Communist infiltration in labor. In his introductory remarks, the chairman made reference to a bill, then pending before the committee, which would have penalized labor unions controlled or dominated by persons who were, or had been, members of a "Communist-action" organization, as defined in the Internal Security Act of 1950. The subcommittee, it is contended, might have been endeavoring to determine the extent of such a problem.

This view is corroborated somewhat by the witnesses who preceded and followed petitioner before the subcommittee. Looking at the entire hearings, however, there is strong reason to doubt that the subject revolved about labor matters. The published transcript is entitled: Investigation of Communist Activities in the Chicago Area, and six of the nine witnesses had no connection with labor at all.

Doubts on Charges

The most serious doubts as to the subcommittee's "question under inquiry," however, stem from the precise questions that petitioner has been charged with refusing to answer. Under the terms of the statute, after all, it is these which must be proved pertinent. Petitioner is charged with refusing to tell the subcommittee whether or not he knew that certain named persons had been members of the Communist party in the past. The subcommittee's counsel read the list from the testimony of a previous witness who had identified them as Communists. Although this former witness was identified with labor, he had not

stated that the persons he named were involved in union affairs. Of the thirty names propounded to petitioner, seven were completely unconnected with organized labor. One operated a beauty parlor. Another was a watchmaker. Several were identified as "just citizens" or "only Communists." When almost a quarter of the persons on the list are not labor people, the inference becomes strong that the subject before the subcommittee was not defined in terms of communism in labor.

The final source of evidence as to the "question under inquiry" is the chairman's response when petitioner objected to the questions on the grounds of lack of pertinency. The chairman then announced that the subcommittee was investigating "subversion and subversive propaganda." This is a subject at least as broad and indefinite as the authorizing resolution of the committee, if not more so.

Pertinence Challenged

Having exhausted the several possible indicia of the "question under inquiry," we remain unenlightened as to the subject to which the questions asked petitioner were pertinent. Certainly, if the point is that obscure after trial and appeal, it was not adequately revealed to petitioner when he had to decide at his peril whether or not to answer. Fundamental fairness demands that no witness be compelled to make such a determination with so little guidance. Unless the subject matter has been made to appear with undisputable clarity, it is the duty of the investigative body, upon objection of the witness on grounds of pertinency, to state for the record the subject under inquiry at that time and the manner in which the propounded questions are pertinent thereto. To be meaningful, the explanation must describe what the topic under inquiry is and the connective reasoning whereby the precise questions asked relate to it.

The statement of the committee chairman in this case, in response to petitioner's protest, was woefully inadequate to convey sufficient information as to the pertinency of the questions to the subject under inquiry. Petitioner was thus not accorded a fair opportunity to determine whether he was within his rights in refusing to answer, and his conviction is necessarily invalid under the due process clause of the Fifth Amendment.

We are mindful of the complexities of modern government and the ample scope that must be left to the Congress as the sole constitutional depository of legislative power. Equally mindful are we of the indispensable function, in the exercise of that power, of Congressional investigations. The conclusions we have reached in this case will not prevent the Congress, through its committees, from obtaining any information it needs for the proper fulfillment of its role in our scheme of government. The legislature is free to determine the kinds of data that should be collected. It is only those investigations that are conducted by use of compul-

sory process that give rise to a need to protect the rights of individuals against illegal encroachment. That protection can be readily achieved through procedures which prevent the separation of power from responsibility and which provide the constitutional requisites of fairness for witnesses. A measure of added care on the part of the House and the Senate in authorizing the use of compulsory process and by their committees in exercising that power would suffice. That is a small price to pay if it serves to uphold the principles of limited, constitutional government without obstructing the power of the Congress to inform itself.

The judgment of the Court of Appeals is reversed, and the case is remanded to the District Court with instructions to dismiss the indictment.

It is so ordered.

Mr. Justice Burton and Mr. Justice Whittaker took no part in the consideration or decision of this case.

Frankfurter's Concurrence

Mr. Justice Frankfurter, concurring.

I deem it important to state what I understand to be the court's holding. Agreeing with its holding, I join its opinion.

The power of the Congress to punish for contempt of its authority is, as the court points out, rooted in history. It has been acknowledged by this court since 1821. Anderson v. Dunn, 6 Wheat. 204. Until 1857, Congress was content to punish for contempt through its own process. By the Act of Jan. 24, 1857, 11 Stat. 155, as amended by the Act of Jan. 24, 1862, 12 Stat. 333, Congress provided that, "in addition to the pains and penalties now existing" (referring of course to the power Congress itself to punish for contempt), "contumacy in a witness called to testify in a matter properly under consideration by either house, and deliberately refusing to answer questions pertinent thereto, shall be a misdemeanor against the United States." In re Chapman, 166 U.S. 661,672. This legislation is now 2 U.S.C. Section 192. By thus making the Federal judiciary the affirmative agency for enforcing the authority that underlies the Congressional power to punish for contempt, Congress necessarily brings into play the specific provisions of the Constitution relating to the prosecution of offenses and those implied restrictions under which courts function.

To turn to the immediate problem before us, the scope of

inquiry that a committee is authorized to pursue must be defined with sufficiently unambiguous clarity to safeguard a witness from the hazards of vagueness in the enforcement of the criminal process against which the due process clause protects. The questions must be put with relevance and definiteness sufficient to enable the witness to know whether his refusal to answer may lead to conviction for criminal contempt and to enable both the trial and the Appellate courts readily to determine whether the particular circumstances justify a finding of guilt.

While implied authority for the questioning by the committee, sweeping as was its inquiry, may be squeezed out of the repeated acquiescence by Congress in the committee's inquiries, the basis for determining petitioner's guilt is not thereby laid. Prosecution for contempt of Congress presupposes an adequate opportunity for the information that he has denied to Congress. And the basis of such awareness must be contemporaneous with the witness' refusal to answer and not at the trial for it. Accordingly, the actual scope of the inquiry that the committee was authorized to conduct and the relevance of the questions to that inquiry must be shown to have been luminous at the time when asked and not left, at best, in cloudiness. The circumstances of this case were wanting in these essentials.

Dissenting Opinion of Clark

Mr. Justice Clark, dissenting.

As I see it the chief fault in the majority opinion is its mischievous curbing of the informing function of the Congress. While I am not versed in its procedures, my experience in the Executive Branch of the Government leads me to believe that the requirements laid down in the opinion for the operation of the committee system of inquiry are both unnecessary and unworkable. It is my purpose to first discuss this phase of the opinion and then record my views on the merits of Watkins' case.

I

It may be that at times the House Committee on Un-American Activities has, as the Court says, "conceived of its task in

the grand view of its name." And, perhaps, as the Court indicates, the rules of conduct placed upon the committee by the House admit of individual abuse and unfairness.

But that is none of our affair. So long as the object of a legislative inquiry is legitimate and the questions propounded are pertinent thereto, it is not for the courts to interfere with the committee system of inquiry. To hold otherwise would be an infringement on the power given the Congress to inform itself, and thus a trespass upon the fundamental American principle of separation of powers. The majority has substituted the judiciary as the Grand Inquisitor and supervisor of Congressional investigations. It has never been so.

II

Legislative committees to inquire into facts or conditions for assurance of the public welfare or to determine the need for legislative action have grown in importance with the complexity of Government. The investigation that gave rise to this prosecution is of the latter type. Since many matters requiring statutory action lie in the domain of the specialist or are unknown without testimony from informed witnesses, the need for information has brought about legislative inquiries that have used the compulsion of the subpoena to lay bare needed facts and a statute, 2 U. S. C. Section 192 here involved, to punish recalcitrant witnesses. The propriety of investigations has long been recognized and rarely curbed by the courts, though Constitutional limtations on the investigatory powers are admitted. The use of legislative committees to secure information follows the example of the people from whom our legislative system is derived. The British method has variations from that of the United States but fundamentally serves the same purpose—the enlightenment of Parliament for the better performance of its duties. There are standing committees to carry on the routine work, Royal Commissions to grapple with important social or economic problems, and special tribunals of inquiry for some alleged offense in Government.

Cites Long History

Our Congress has since its beginning used the committee system to inform itself. It has been estimated that over 600 investigations have been conducted since the First Congress. They are "a necessary and appropriate attribute of the power to legislate * * *." McGrain v. Daugherty, 273 U. S. 135, 175 (1927).

The court indicates that in this case the source of the trouble lies in the "tremendous latitude" given the Un-American Activities Committee in the Legislative Reorganization Act. It finds that the committee is allowed, in essence, to define its own authority, (and) to choose the direction and focus of its activities." This, of course, is largely true of all committees within their respective spheres. And, while it is necessary that the "charter," as the opinion calls the enabling resolution, "spell out (its) jurisdiction and purpose," that must necessarily be in more or less general terms. An examination of the enabling resolutions of other committees reveals the extent to which this is true.

Permanent or standing committees of both Houses have been given power in exceedingly broad terms. For example, the committees on the armed services have jurisdiction over "common defense generally"; the committees on interstate and foreign commerce have jurisdiction over "interstate and foreign commerce generally"; and the committees on appropriation have jurisdiction over "appropriation of the revenue for the support of the Government." Perhaps even more important for purposes of are the broad authorizations given to select or special committees established by the Congress from time to time. Such committees have been "authorized and directed" to make full and complete studies "of whether *organized crime* utilizes the facilities of interstate commerce or otherwise operates an interstate commerce"; "of * * * *all lobbying activities* intended to influence, encourage, promote, or retard legislation"; "to determine the extent to which current literature * * * containing *immoral*, (or) *obscene* * * * matters, or placing *improper* emphasis on crime * * * are being made available to the people of the United States * * *." And "of the extent to which criminal or other *improper* practices * * * are, or have been, engaged in *the field of labor-management relations* * * * to the *detriment of the interests* of the public * * *." (Emphasis added in each example.)

Questions 'Latitude'

Surely these authorizations permit the committees even more "tremendous latitude" than the "charter" of the Un-American Activities Committee. Yet, no one has suggested that the powers granted were too broad. To restrain and limit the breadth of investigative power of this committee neccesitates the similar handling of all other committees. The resulting restraint imposed on the committee system appears to cripple the system beyond workability.

The court finds fault with the use made of compulsory process, power for the use of which is granted the committee in the Reorganization Act. While the court finds that the Congress is free "to determine the kinds of data" it wishes its committees to collect, this has led through the abuse of process the court says, to an encroachment on individual rights. To my mind, this indicates a lack of understanding of the problems facing such committees. I am sure that the committees would welcome voluntary disclosure. It would simplify and relieve their burden considerably if the parties involved in investigations would come forward with a frank willingness to cooperate. But every day experience shows this just does not happen. One needs only to read the newspapers to know that the Congress could gather little "data" unless its committees had, unfettered, the power of subpoena. In fact, Watkins himself could not be found for appearance at the first hearing and it was only by subpoena that he attended the second. The court generalizes on this critical problem, saying, "added care on the part of the House and the Senate in authorizing the use of compulsory process and by their committees in exercising that power would suffice."

Doubts Practicality

It does not say how this "added care" could be applied in practice; however, there are many implications since the opinion warns that "procedures which prevent the separation of power from responsibility" would be necessary along with "Constitutional requisites of fairness for witnesses." The "power" and "responsibility" for the investigations are, of course, in the House, where the proceeding is initiated. But the investigating job itself can only be done through the use of committees. They must have the "power" to force compliance with their requirements. If the rule requires that this power be retained in the full House then investigations will be so cumbrous that their conduct will be a practical impossibility. As to "fairness for witnesses" there is nothing in the record showing any abuse of Watkins. If anything, the committee was abused by his recalcitrance.

While ambiguity prevents exactness (and there is "vice in vagueness," the majority reminds), the sweep of the opinion seems to be that "preliminary control" of the committee must be exercised. The court says a witness' protected freedoms cannot "be placed in danger in the absence of a clear determination by the House or the Senate that a particular inquiry is justified by a specific legislative need."

Frankly I do not see how any such procedure as "preliminary control" can be effected in either house of the Congress. What will be controlled preliminarily? The plans of the investigation, the necessity of calling certain witnesses, the questions to be asked, the details of subpoenas duces tecum, etc.? As it is now, Congress is hard pressed to find sufficient time to fully debate and adopt all needed legislation. The court asserts that "the Congress has practically abandoned its original practice of utilizing the coercive sanction of contempt proceedings at the Bar of the House." This was to be expected. It may be that back in the Twenties and Thirties Congress could spare the time to conduct contempt hearings, but that appears impossible now.

'Greater Burden' Seen

The court places a greater burden in the conduct of contempt cases before the courts than it does before "the bar of the House." It cites with approval cases of contempt tried before a House of the Congress where no more safeguards were present than we find here. In contempt prosecutions before a court, however, the majority places an investigative hearing on a par with a criminal trial, requiring that "knowledge of the subject to which the interrogation is deemed pertinent * * * must be available (to the witness) with the same degree of explicitness and clarify that the due process clause requires in the expression of any element of a criminal offense." I know of no such claim ever being made before. Such a requirement has never been thought applicable to investigations and is wholly out of place when related to the informing function of the Congress. See Frankfurter, "Hands Off the Investigations," 38 New Republic, May 21, 1924, P. 329, 65 Cong. Rec. 90 80-9082. The Congress does not have the facts at the time of the investigation for it is the facts that are being sought. In a criminal trial the investigation has been completed and all of the facts are at hand. The informing function of the Congress is in effect "a study by the Government of circumstances which seem to call for study in the public interest." See Black, "Inside a Senate Investigation," 172 Harpers Magazine, Feb. 1936, PP. 275, 278. In the conduct of such a proceeding it is impossible to be as explicit and exact as in a criminal prosecution. If the court is saying that its new rule does not apply to contempt cases tried before the bar of the House affected, it may well lead to trial of all contempt cases before the bar of the whole House in order to avoid the restrictions of the rule. But this will not promote the result desired by the majority. Summary treatment, at best, could be provided before the whole House because of the time factor, and such treatment would necessarily deprive the witness of many of the safeguards in the present procedures. On review here the majority might then find fault with that procedure.

III

Coming to the merits of Watkins' case, the court reverses the judgment because: (1) the subject-matter of the inquiry was not "made to appear with undisputable clarity" either through its "charter" or by the chairman at the time of the hearing and, therefore, Watkins was deprived of a clear understanding of "The manner in which the propounded questions (were) pertinent thereto"; (2) the present Committee system of inquiry of the House, as practiced by the Un-American Activities Committee, does not provide adequate safeguards for the protection of the constitutional right of free speech. I subscribe to neither conclusion.

Background Is Listed

Watkins had been an active leader in the labor movement for many years and had been identified by two previous witnesses at the committee's hearing in Chicago as a member of the Communist party. There can be no question that he was fully informed of the subject-matter of the inquiry. His testimony reveals a complete knowledge and understanding of the hearings at Chicago. The chairman had announced that the committee had been directed "to ascertain the extent and success of subversive activities directed against these United States (and) on the basis of these investigations and hearings * * * (report) its findings to the Congress and (make) recommendations * * * for new legislation." He pointed to the various laws that had been enacted as a result of committee recommendations. He stated that "the Congress has also referred to the House Committee on Un-American Activities a bill which would amend the National Security Act of 1950" which, if made law, would restrict the availability of the labor act to unions not "in fact Communist-controlled action groups."

Chairman's Words Quoted

The chairman went on to say that "it cannot be said that subversive infiltration has had a greater nor a lesser success in infiltrating this important area. The hearings today are the culmination of an investigation * * *. Every witness who has been subpoenaed to appear before the committee here in Chicago * * * [is] known to possess information which will assist the committee in performing its directed function to the Congress of the United States."

A subpoena had been issued for Watkins to appear at the Chicago hearings but he was not served. After Watkins was served the hearing in question was held in Washington, D. C. Reference at this hearing was made to the one conducted in Chicago. Watkins came before the committee with a carefully prepared statement. He denied certain testimony of the previous witnesses and declared that he had never been a "card-carrying member" of the party. He admitted that for the period 1942-47 he "cooperated with the Communist party * * * participated in Communist activities * * * made contributions * * * attended caucuses at [his union's] convention at which Communist party officials were present * * * (and) freely cooperated with the Communist party * * *."

This indicated that for a five-year period he, a union official, was cooperating closely with the Communist party, even permitting its officials to attend union caucuses. For the last two years of this liaison the party had publicly thrown off its cloak of a political party. It was a reconstituted, militant group known to be dedicated to the overthrow of our Government by force and violence. In this setting the committee attempted to have Watkins identify thirty persons, most of whom were connected with labor unions in some way. While one "operated a beauty parlor" and another was "a watchmaker," they may well have been "drops" or other functionaries in the program of cooperation between the union and the party.

It is a non sequitur for the court to say that since "almost a quarter of the persons on the list are not labor people, the inference becomes strong that the subject before the subcommittee was not defined in terms of communism in labor." I submit that the opposite is true.

IV

I think the committee here was acting entirely within its scope and that the purpose of its inquiry was set out with "undisputable clarity." In the first place, the authorizing language of the Reorganization Act must be read as a whole, not dissected. It authorized investigation into subversive activity, its extent, character, objects, and diffusion. While the language might have been more explicit than using such words as "un-American," or phrases like "principle of the form of government," still these are fairly well understood terms. We must construe them to give them mean-ing if we can. Our cases indicate that rather than finding fault with the use of words or phrases, we are bound to presume that the action of the legislative body in granting authority to the committee was with a legitimate object "if (the action) is *capable* of being so construed." (Emphasis added.) People ex rel. McDonald v. Keeler, 99 N. Y. 463, 487 (1885), as quoted and approved in McGrain v. Daugherty, supra, at 178. Before we can deny the authority "it must be obvious that" the committee has "exceeded the bounds of legislative power." Tenney v. Brad-hove, 341 U. S. 367, 378 (1951). The fact that the committee has often been attacked has caused close scrutiny of its acts by the House as a whole and the House has repeatedly given the committee its approval. "Power" and "responsibility" have not been separated.

Explanation Is Cited

But the record in this case does not stop here. It shows that at the hearings involving Watkins, the chairman made statements explaining the functions of the committee. And, furthermore, Watkins' action at the hearing clearly reveals that he was well acquainted with the purpose of the hearing. It was to investigate Communist infiltration into his union. This certainly falls within the grant of authority from the Reorganization Act and the House has had ample opportunity to limit the investigative scope of the committee if it feels that the committee has exceeded its legitimate bounds.

The court makes much of petitioner's claim of "exposure for exposure's sake" and strikes at the purposes of the committee through this catch phrase. But we are bound to accept as the purpose of the committee that stated in the Reorganization Act together with the statements of the chairman at the hearings involved here. Nothing was said of exposure. The statements of a single Congressman cannot transform the real purpose of the committee into something not authorized by the parent resolution. See United States v. Rumely, 345 U. S. 41 (1953); Sinclair v. United States, 279 U. S. 263, 290, 295 (1929).

The court indicates that the questions propounded were asked for exposure's sake and had no pertinency to the inquiry. It appears to me that they were entirely pertinent to the announced purpose of the committee's inquiry. Undoubtedly Congress has the power to inquire into the subjects of communism and the Communist party. American Communications Assn. v. Douds, 339 U. S. 382 (1950). As a corollary of the Congressional power to inquire into such subject matter, the Congress, through its committees, can legitimately seek to identify individual members of the party. Barsky v. United States, 167 F. 2d 241 (1948). Cert. denied, 334 U. S. 843. See also Lawson v. United States, 176 F. 2d 49, 52-53 (1949), Cert. denied, 339 U. S. 934; United States v. Rosephson, 165 F. 2d 82, 90-92 (1947), Cert. denied, 333 U. S. 838.

The pertinency of the questions is highlighted by the need for the Congress to know the extent of infiltration of communism in labor unions. This technique of infiltration was that used in bringing the downfall of countries formerly free but now still remaining behind the Iron Curtain. The Douds case illustrates that the party is not an ordinary political party and has not been at least since 1945. Association with its officials is not an ordinary association. Nor does it matter that the questions related to the past. Influences of past associations often linger on as was clearly shown in the instance of the witness Matusow and others. The techniques used in the infiltration which admittedly existed here, might well be used again in the future. If the parties about whom Watkins was interrogated were Communists and collaborated with him, as a prior witness indicated, an entirely new area of investigation might have been opened up. Watkins' silence prevented the committee from learning this information which could have been vital to its future investigation.

Sees Reasons as Ample

The committee was likewise entitled to elicit testimony showing the truth or falsity of the prior testimony of the witnesses who had involved Watkins and the union with collaboration with the party. If the testimony was untrue, a false picture of the relationship between the union and the party leaders would have resulted. For these reasons there were ample indications of the pertinency of the questions.

V

The court condemns the long-established and long-recognized committee system of inquiry of the House because it raises serious questions concerning the protection it affords to Constitutional rights. It concludes that compelling a witness to reveal his "beliefs, expressions or associations" infringes upon First Amendment rights. The system of inquiry, it says, must "insure that the Congress does not unjustifiably encroach upon an individual's right to privacy nor abridge his liberty of speech, press, religion or assembly." In effect the court honors Watkins' claim of a "right to silence" which brings all inquiries, as we know, to a "dead end."

I do not see how any First Amendment rights were endangered here. There is nothing in the First Amendment that provides the guarantees Watkins claims. The amendment was designed to prevent attempts by law to curtail freedom of speech. Whitney v. California, 274 U. S. 357, 375 (1927). It forbids Congress from "making any law "abridging the freedom of speech, or of the press." It guarantees Watkins' right to join any organization and make any speech that does not have an intent to incite to crime. Dennis v. United States, 341 U. S. 494 (1951). But Watkins was asked if he knew named individuals and whether they were Communists. He refused to answer on the ground that his rights were being abridged. What he was actually seeking to do was to protect his former associates, not himself, from embarrassment.

Refers to Admissions

He had already admitted his own involvement. He sought to vindicate the rights, if any, of his associates. It is settled that one cannot invoke the Constitutional rights of another. Tileston v. Ullman, 318 U. S. 44, 46 (1943).

As already indicated, even if Watkins' associates were on the stand they could not decline to disclose their Communist connections on First Amendment grounds. While there may be no restraint by the Governmen of one's beliefs, the right of free belief has never been extended to include the withholding of knowledge of past events or transactions. There is no general privilege of silence. The First Amendment does not make speech or silence permissible to a person in such measure as he chooses.

Watkins has here exercised his own choice as to when he talks, what questions he answers, and when he remains silent. A witness is not given such a choice by the amendment. Remote and indirect disadvantages such as "public stigma, scorn and obloquy" may be related to the First Amendment, but they are not enough to block investigation. The Congress has recognized this since 1862 when it first adopted the Contempt Section, R. S. Section 103, as amended, 2 U. S. C. Section 193, declaring that no witness before a Congressional committee may refuse to testify "upon the ground that his testimony to such fact or his production of such paper may tend to disgrace him or otherwise render him infamous."

See also McGrain v. Daugherty, Supra, at 179-180; United States v. Josephson, 165 F. 2d 82, 89 (1947), Cert. Denied, 333 U. S. 838. See also Report on Congressional Investigations, Assn. of the Bar of the City of New York, 1948, 3-4.

We do not have in this case unauthorized, arbitrary, or unreasonable inquiries and disclosures with respect to a witness' personal and private affairs so ably and properly denounced in the Sinclair case, Supra, at 291-92. The inquiry is far different from the cases relied upon by the court.

Denies Thompson Analogy

There is no analogy to the case of Richard Thompson, involving the sermons of clergymen. It is not Floyd's case, involving criticism of the royal family. There is no resemblance to John Wilkes' struggle for a seat in Parliament. It is not Briggs, where the prosecutor sought to develop the national origin of policemen. It is not Kilbourn, involving a private real estate pool. Nor is it Quinn, Emspak, or Bart, involving the Fifth Amendment. It is not Rumely, involving the interpretation of a lobbying statute. Nor is this "a new kind of Congressional inquiry unknown in prior periods of American history * * * (I. E.) A broad scale intrusion into the lives and affairs of private citizens." As I see it only the setting is different. It involves new faces and new issues brought about by new situations which the Congress feels it is necessary to control in the public interest. The difficulties of getting information are identical if not more difficult. Like authority to that always used by the Congress is employed here and in the same manner so far as Congressional procedures are concerned. We should afford to Congress the presumption that it takes every precaution possible to avoid unnecessary damage to reputations. Some committees have codes of procedure, and others use the executive hearing technique to this end. The record in this case shows no conduct on the part of the Un-American Activities Committee that justifies condemnation. That there may have been such occasions is not for us to consider here. Nor should we permit its past transgressions, if any, to lead to the rigid restraint of all Congressional committees. To carry on its heavy responsibility the compulsion of truth that does not incriminate is not only necessary to the Congress but is permitted within the limits of the Constitution.

June 18, 1957

REDS STILL PLOT, HOUSE UNIT SAYS

Report Warns of Danger to U. S. Security Despite Talk of Party's Decline

Special to The New York Times.

WASHINGTON, Sept. 17—The House Committee on Un-American Activities urged Congress today to disregard assertions by the American Communist party that it was falling apart.

Despite talk of defections and disintegration, the investigating panel held, much dangerous work is being accomplished.

A report on findings during the recent Congress session warned that the country's security structure had been imperiled.

It spoke of dangers through the continued allegiance to "the conspiracy of international communism" by "a great number of Americans."

While the party appears to have shrunk, the committee said, more than 200 organizations of "independent" citizens have been dealing in "political subversion." These groups are "Communist-controlled in every instance," it declared.

They have been effective in creating impacts on Congress, state legislative bodies and other official groups through letters, petitions and other media of appeals calling for what the Communists want, it added.

Representative Francis E. Walter, Pennsylvania Democrat who heads the committee, said:

"The committee found that a prodigious campaign of political subversion, clandestinely directed by a nation-wide apparatus of Communist agents, menaces the entire security system of the United States.

The chief targets of the Communists, the report emphasized, are the Internal Security and the Immigration Acts. Mr. Walter is co-author of the immigration statute. President Eisenhower has called it discriminatory and recommended reforms.

In the last session Congress passed a bill, sponsored by Mr. Walter, that fell far short of what the President had recommended. The President signed it, but with disappointment.

Also under attack is the Smith Act, sponsored by Representative Howard W. Smith, Democrat of Virginia, the report said.

This act brought many convictions, but last spring the Supreme Court overruled them in a case involving several California Communists. It ruled that no proof had been brought that the defendants tried to overthrow the Government by force.

September 18, 1957

HOOVER SAYS F. B. I. KEEPS 90 WIRETAPS

WASHINGTON, May 18 (UP) —The Federal Bureau of Investigation is operating ninety telephone wiretaps across the country to keep watch on "internal security cases," its director, J. Edgar Hoover, said today.

He declared that, as a result of the last Communist convention, "the most rabid group of pro-Soviets in this country are in charge of the Communist party."

Despite occasional switches in the party line, he added, the Communist goal remains overthrow of the United States Government "by force and violence."

He said that some members had recently left the party, but that the "great bulk of them" had not renounced communism. They cannot be considered ex-Communists, he commented, because "they are not dedicated to the American way of life."

In an interview with Representative Kenneth B. Keating, Republican of upstate New York, filmed for use by New York State television stations, he asserted also that the F. B. I. would continue to crack down on subversive activities "despite the carpings of the professional do-gooders, the pseudo-liberals and the out-and-out Communists."

He said that crime in the country had reached "staggering proportions" since 1952, and juvenile delinquency had increased 55 per cent.

May 19, 1958

GROUP LISTS DATA ON 'SUBVERSIVES'

Business Men Aid Chicago Council, Which Claims a File of Million Names

By AUSTIN C. WEHRWEIN
Special to The New York Times.

CHICAGO, July 9 — The American Security Council is collecting here at the rate of 20,000 a month the names of individuals and organizations labeled as subversives.

The council is backed by a group of business men including Gen. Robert E. Wood, retired board chairman of Sears, Roebuck & Co.; Fred Lazarus Jr., board chairman of Federated Department Stores; Hughston M. McBain, retired board chairman of Marshall Field & Co., and Paul V. Galvin, board chairman, Motorola, Inc.

The stated purpose of the council, which maintains files with more than 1,000,000 names, is to gather and cross-index "factual information about Communist and other statist movements."

The council's leading staff members are former special agents for the Federal Bureau of Investigation. It publishes a monthly confidential news letter for its members and offers a number of special services.

Special Services Listed

Among the services are:

¶To assist member companies in making loyalty checks on employes when the Defense Department and other governmental agencies require the companies to make such checks as a condition for getting a Government contract.

¶To assist member companies in checking on "questionable" organizations asking for support or money.

¶To make material from the files and books available to certain member company executives and to outsiders, such as journalists that the council feels it can trust.

The council, by its own account, supplements the F. B. I. Its literature notes that the F. B. I. may not furnish information to industry on subversion.

However, the council president, John M. Fisher, national security coordinator for Sears, Roebuck and a former F. B. I. man in New York, said the council did not make "gum shoe" investigations of any individuals and had never used informers.

He said all reports were documented by material that would stand up in court. It is drawn from many sources, he said, including legislative investigations, newspaper clippings and political petitions.

The council has 175 member companies—100 more than it had Jan. 1. Among them are United States Steel, the Chicago Tribune, The Rockford (Ill.) Star, Illinois Central Railroad, Stewart-Warner Corporation, Acme Steel Company and Belden Manufacturing Company.

General Wood, Mr. McBain and Mr. Galvin have recently written letters to leading business men stating the council's aims and soliciting membership. The aim is to get 300 members by March 1, 1959, and 1,000 within the next five years.

Mr. Fisher said the council was also interested in groups such as the Ku Klux Klan.

He said each council report gave material found in the files.

"We don't," he asserted, "ever say a man is a Communist or not a Communist."

The council has a regular staff of eight persons and operates on an annual budget of $100,000. It was organized in 1955 as the Mid-American Research Library. The name was changed in 1956.

The operating director of the council is Robert J. Wilson, who, until last year, was director of security at Argonne National (atomic) Laboratory, at nearby Lemont, Ill.

July 10, 1958

269

HIGH COURT BACKS RIGHTS OF CONGRESS AND STATES IN SUBVERSION INQUIRIES

JUSTICES SPLIT 5-4

Contempt Conviction of Teacher Upheld in Federal Case

By ANTHONY LEWIS
Special to The New York Times.

WASHINGTON, June 8—The Supreme Court upheld in broad terms today the power of Congress and state legislatures to investigate alleged subversion.

By a vote of 5 to 4 the court affirmed the contempt conviction of Lloyd Barenblatt, a former instructor at Vassar College who refused to answer questions by a subcommittee of the House Un-American Activities Committee about Communist associations.

The majority rejected contentions by Barenblatt that the committee's entry into the field of education was unconstitutional, that its only purpose was an illegal one of "exposure for exposure's sake" and that the investigation discouraged free speech and association.

The court was divided precisely the same way in the closely related case of Willard Uphaus. It affirmed his contempt conviction for refusing to produce for a New Hampshire subversion inquiry guest lists of a summer camp he ran in that state.

Drama in the Court

It was a dramatic day in the courtroom. The justices sat until 5 P. M., past their normal closing hour, to read their opinions in several of the term's most controversial cases. They disposed of fourteen of fifty argued cases awaiting decision.

The Barenblatt case settled some big questions left unanswered two years ago by the court's landmark decision in the case of John T. Watkins, an organizer for the United Auto Workers.

The holding there was that a Congressional committee could not compel answers from a witness unless it made clear to him the subject of its inquiry and the pertinence of particular questions to that subject.

Many persons, including a large number in Congress, read the Watkins decision as a tight rein on Congressional investigations. Others saw it as a carefully limited procedural ruling and they were proved right today.

Barenblatt was questioned by the House committee in 1954. He refused to answer on the ground that the committee had no constitutional power to make him talk about associations, whether or not with alleged Communist persons and groups.

He was convicted of contempt, sentenced to six months in jail and fined $250. The Court of Appeals here upheld the conviction, but the Supreme Court sent the case back for reconsideration in the light of the Watkins case.

The Court of Appeals, by a vote of 5 to 4, again affirmed. It then held up a number of other Congressional contempt cases to see what the Supreme Court would say about Barenblatt. All those other cases are still pending.

Justice John Marshall Harlan wrote the majority opinion today. He was joined by Justices Felix Frankfurter, Tom C. Clark, Charles Evans Whittaker and Potter Stewart.

The power of Congress to investigate is limited by the Bill of Rights, Justice Harlan said. He explained that requirements of academic freedom, for example, would prohibit any committee from conducting a general inquiry into what a teacher was teaching.

He went on to say that the Supreme Court would be "alert" against any intrusion into "this constitutionally protected domain."

"But this does not mean that Congress is precluded from interrogating a witness merely because he is a teacher," he said.

"An educational institution is not a Constitutional sanctuary from inquiry into matters that may otherwise be within the Constitutional legislative domain merely for the reason that inquiry is made of someone within its walls."

The valid legislative purpose found by Justice Harlan in this situation was the Government's "right of self-preservation" against Communist attacks.

The opinion said the Supreme Court had "consistently refused to view the Communist party as an ordinary political party" and would have to "blind itself to world affairs" to do otherwise. It noted Congressional findings that communism seeks the overthrow of the Government.

Justice Harlan said an investigation could not be bound by the strict requirements of evidence needed for a criminal prosecution. Congress has a right to inquire step by step, he said, about matters leading up to attempts to overthrow the Government.

In this case, he said, the committee showed no design to control what is taught at universities or to intimidate or "pillory witnesses."

The majority specifically rejected contentions that the House committee was interested only in exposing alleged subversives to public obloquy. Justice Harlan said the court could not look into Congressmen's motives.

The issue of exposure was one ground of the principal dissent. It was by Justice Hugo L. Black and was joined by Chief Justice Earl Warren and Justice William O. Douglas. Justice William J. Brennan Jr. joined just that part of the Black opinion terming the inquiry "exposure purely for the sake of exposure."

Justice Black said "the court today fails to see what is here for all to see—that exposure and punishment is the aim of this committee and the reason for its existence." He added:

"I cannot believe that the nature of our judicial office requires us to be so blind."

He said the contempt conviction should not stand because the committee had taken over the function of the courts to "try witnesses and punish them because they are or have been Communists or because they refuse to admit or deny Communist affiliations."

Beyond this point, Justice Black argued broadly that the committee violated the First Amendment's guarantees of free speech and association.

It did so, he said, because witnesses are forced to expose their beliefs and associations and are subjected to "obloquy and public scorn" for them. He said the only effect can be to inhibit speech and association.

Justice Black rejected the majority's reliance on the nature of communism. He said all minority or unpopular views would be subject to harassment under the court's view.

He rejected also the majority view that public and private interests must be balanced. That, he said, was as if the First Amendment read:

"Congress shall pass no law abridging freedom of speech, press, assembly and petition unless Congress and the Supreme Court reach the joint conclusion that on balance the interests of the Government in stifling these freedoms is greater than the interest of the people in having them exercised."

But even on balance, Justice Black said, the majority did not weigh the interest "of the people as a whole in being able to join organizations, advocate causes and make political 'mistakes' without later being subjected to Governmental penalties for having dared to think for themselves."

"Ultimately," he concluded, "all the questions in this case really boil down to one—whether we as a people will try fearfully and futilely to preserve democracy by adopting totalitarian methods, or whether in accordance with our traditions and our Constitution we will have the confidence and courage to be free."

Close observers of the Supreme Court called the Barenblatt decision one of the most important of recent years.

They said it made plain the majority's unwillingness to restrain the substantive powers of Congressional inquiry. The decision thus restricted the Watkins case to a warning by the court that committees must have fair procedures.

The American Civil Liberties Union supported Barenblatt's appeal. Edward J. Ennis of New York argued for him and Philip R. Monahan for the Government.

Associated Press
CONVICTION UPHELD: Dr. Willard Uphaus, executive director of the New Hampshire World Fellowship Center. His contempt conviction was upheld yesterday by Supreme Court.

June 9, 1959

U. S. COMMUNISTS SURVEY A WEAKENED PARTY

By HARRY SCHWARTZ

About 250 persons, many of them gray haired, have spent much of the last three days crowded into the small ballroom of a Harlem hotel. This is the physical reality of the seventeenth national convention of the Communist party of the United States.

The dreary surroundings of the meeting spoke eloquently of the low state of American Communism's political fortunes. They supported strongly recent estimates that party's dues-paying membership is now down to a few thousand hard-core fanatics, a far cry from the 1945 peak of 75,000 to 85,000.

Even before the convention there were many evidences of the party's decline.

Its national English language newspaper is now only a weekly; The Daily Worker has been only a memory for almost two years. And even the weekly Worker, a sworn statement it has just published stated, had a circulation this last year that averaged less than 15,000.

Many of the former leaders and leading lights of the party have left it, as have a far greater number of obscure members. John Gates, Howard Fast and Doxey Wilkerson are among the better known figures who have left. And every reporter who has been concerned with the party in recent years knows numerous lesser lights.

Front Groups Fade

Many of the key fellow-traveler organizations and transmission-belt groups through which the party used to operate are now no more or are moribund. Gone is the International Workers Order, the insurance organization with comparatively large funds that offered interesting possibilities for party aid in bygone years. Gone too are the Progressive party and the American Labor party. The Jefferson School and other party schools in different cities have vanished. The list of such organizations which have passed into the abyss of history is at least in the hundreds. And except for a few isolated cases, the party's role in the trade unions today is insignificant.

The Communist party's own explanation of its decline here in the decade and a half tends to emphasize two factors: the "fascist terror" against Communists during the period of McCarthyism and the "leftist sectarianism" of party leaders in the past. The latter phrase is party jargon for the many mistakes it has made these past years.

A fuller and more objective explanation of that decline would seem to include the following factors:

(1) The party's best days were in the depression-ridden Nineteen Thirties and during World War II. During the war, sympathy here for the Soviet Union as a fighting ally against Germany and Japan was translated into comparatively high membership for the party.

Since World War II, the United States has enjoyed prosperity and nearly full employment, thus eliminating the economic base that existed in the Nineteen Thirties for Communist party strength. Politically, the "cold war" tensions between the United States and the Soviet Union put the party time and again into positions of obviously supporting a foreign power against the United States, a posture that disillusioned many of the innocents who had joined during the years of the war-time alliance.

(2) The Communist party here consistently misjudged the post-war American scene and it paid heavily for its errors. It anticipated a depression that would approach that of the Nineteen Thirties—an expectation yet to materialize. It thought that the outbreak of the Korean War signaled the beginning of World War III and of American fascism, and made haste to go partly underground and to get rid of independent members. Its tactics in the trade union field drove many of its former supporters out of the fold, while reducing to impotence or wiping out unions in which faithful party members tried to carry out the line as directed.

(3) The high level of anti-Communist feeling, as the menace of Communist aggression became ever more apparent, scared away the weak-hearted and those who could not face the community ostracism, loss of jobs, and other penalties Communist party membership has often carried with it since 1945.

(4) The culminating blow was Premier Khrushchev's speech in February, 1956, exposing some of Stalin's crimes. That speech destroyed the final illusions about the Soviet Union and about communism in thousands who had remained faithful through the hardest days of the cold war and despite all the legal and informal community sanctions against Communists.

Those who assembled last Thursday for the convention obviously had hope that the party would revive and once again become a power to be reckoned with in the United States.

In part their hopes are based upon the easing of tension between the United States and the Soviet Union. There seems little question but that Premier Khrushchev's visit here gave Communist morale in this country a boost and a hope of better days to come.

In addition, American Communists believe that the feats of the Soviet Union—its rocket successes in space, its rapid economic progress, and the like—are proving their case for them. Like Premier Khrushchev they believe such feats show the "superiority" of socialism over capitalism, and like him they believe that even in the United States such feats will convince many that the Soviet system is a desirable alternative to our own.

Only time can tell whether or not these hopes are well founded. But as the élite of the American Communist party have met these last three days they have demonstrated nothing more than the vast distance they have to go before they must again be considered a significant political force.

December 13, 1959

The Red Menace

THE COMMUNIST CONTROVERSY IN WASHINGTON: From the New Deal to McCarthy. By Earl Latham. 446 pp. Cambridge, Mass.: Harvard University Press. $7.95.

By PAUL SEABURY

AMONG the varieties of political violence in Churchill's "Terrible 20th" century, that of American Communism now seems rather mild—a sordid drama now commonly remembered in the vague catchwords of McCarthyism and witch hunts, treason and betrayal. The mortal victims of ideological warfare elsewhere in the world by now are numbered in the millions. But in the American aspect of this global experience the casualty lists are scanty.

The chief American Communists and their adversaries enjoyed the unheroic fate of dying, like Senator McCarthy, with their boots off, and not in prison cells, either. The dramatis personae of American Communism, as well as their scourges, were often victims of pitiless journalistic publicity and legal harassment. In the early 1950's, reputations and careers were broken, and many innocent as well as guilty men were driven from positions of prominence and influence. The American democratic process survived nevertheless.

IT is hard to see how there could be a fairer, more exhaustive historical analysis of the Communist problem in American politics and policies than that of Earl Latham's "The Communist Controversy in Washington." It is a late arrival in a series originally sponsored by the Fund for the Republic, and follows earlier studies of different aspects of the problem by authors such as Theodore Draper, Daniel Aaron, Nathan Glazer and Clinton Rossiter. Latham's work principally assesses the problem of Communist influence and power at the highest governmental levels and seeks to explain the dramatic importance of the Communist question in the early 1950's—an importance which, in Latham's judgment, it never deserved.

What kind of a conspiracy was there in Washington? Latham's analysis, which covers the span of time between 1930 and 1954, is probably as definitive a judgment as we will have for some time. One thing is clear: before 1936 (when the party obediently switched its line to conform with Soviet popular-front tactics) Communists were singularly unwilling to have anything to do with the Federal Government and the New Deal from the inside. To them, Roosevelt was indistinguishable from Mussolini.

Their targets lay outside the "establishment," involving agitation among the "masses." Collaboration with "social fascists" — i.e., liberals — was then heresy.

When the first Communist cells were formed inside the New Deal (most notably inside the Agricultural Adjustment Administration), Latham doubts that the party attached very much importance to them. He sees no pattern of strategic infiltration. Rather, these cabalistic groups were first composed of competent, aggressive professionals like Lee Pressman, called and attracted to Washington by able and loyal civil servants "responding to the requirements of the programs and of the service." As was certainly the case inside John L. Lewis's C.I.O. in Washington there was the interesting question of who was using whom—whether the New Deal, like the mass industrial unions, benefited unwittingly from the talents of individual Communists more

MR. SEABURY is professor of political science and Provost of the University of California at Santa Cruz.

than the party profited from the influence it thus obtained.

Furthermore, before the late 1930's it does not seem that either espionage or sabotage was a significant motive for Communist entry into the national Government. Soviet agents sought to recruit Americans, to be sure, but a principal purpose for this was to advance their cause outside the United States. However much stress Communist doctrine placed upon an American revolution, Soviet Russia had far more important *realpolitik* adversaries than the United States.

But after 1939, when war came, heavy stresses were put on the loyalty of American Communists in the Government. The Hiss-Chambers liaison between 1936 and 1938 had involved the purloining of Government documents. The more serious issues which later arose involved the abuse of office by clandestine Communists to further Soviet, rather than American, interests in world politics. When basic policy choices became substantial, the Communist problem, in Latham's analysis, became both more murky and important.

Take, for instance, Harry Dexter White, who by 1944 was one of Roosevelt's principal advisers on international monetary questions. He was other things, too: he drafted key elements in Hull's November 1941 "ultimatum" to Japan; next to Lord Keynes, he was the dominant figure at the Bretton Woods monetary conference in 1943; he helped devise the famous Morgenthau Plan for pastoralizing industrial Germany.

White also—according to significant accusers later—worked with Communists and with Soviet officials in a "buoyant and cooperative frame of mind." Was he a Communist party member? Even Whittaker Chambers said no. Had he delivered classified papers to unauthorized persons? Quite

possibly. Was he a Soviet "agent"? Even now we do not know.

Even were we to know much more, in this and other cases of alleged wartime espionage and infiltration, could we unravel the webs of mixed loyalties, disentangling those of White's activities which served Soviet, from those which served American, interests? In the White case, and in others, one

---

*A*MBITION, of course, played a strong role in the stimulation of the controversy over Communism in Washington . . . Congressmen in charge of sensational investigations enjoyed a notoriety which for some, doubtless, had rich psychic compensations and there was always the prospect of political reward. The prospect was always better than the reality.
—"The Communist Controversy in Washington."

---

has the impression that such arcane influence — the attempts to twist official policy this way or that on behalf of Soviet causes — at best had only marginal effects upon the larger landscape of policy. The wartime period, when Soviet and American interests briefly converged, was the context within which such influences flourished most significantly; but the convergence was not

something willed by Harry Dexter White, or even by Franklin D. Roosevelt.

Reading Latham's recital of these instances of presumptive pro-Soviet activity makes one freshly aware of the most poisonous qualities of Communist political style in American life — its clandestine behavior and its authoritarian structure. In Latham's analysis it becomes clear that these qualities developed far less as response to legal repression than as consequences of the party's own organizational doctrine.

The rigid separation of covert from overt political action occurred long before legal harassment against the party might have warranted secrecy as a prudent device for self-protection. But the operative norms of American democracy never have respected for long the right to clandestine political action; if Communists chose such behavior as their style, they could hardly have expected to be long immune from reprisals.

The central feature of Latham's thesis, however, is what he calls the "Communist question" in American politics. Why was it that this issue never became salient until the McCarthy period—after Communist influence in Government had reached its wartime high-point of strength?

From 1938 through 1952, Latham argues, an underswell of conservatism had quietly run beneath the surface of American life as reaction to New Deal reformism. Yet never during that time did a transfer of Presidential power constitutionally register this political fact of life.

The exigencies of war gave new lease of life to the New Dealers, if not the New Deal. Yet from 1938 to 1950 the popular margins of Democratic victories shrank. By 1946, the party of the New Deal was actually a minority in Congress.

The defeats of Landon, Willkie and Dewey intensified the frustrations of this conservative America, and it progressively embittered Republican leadership.

McCarthyism in Latham's view is not to be explained so much by sociological theorizing as by constitutional and political analysis. The issue of Communism was seized as a means of capturing and redressing political power in American society; it was the "cutting edge for the attack." "When McCarthy and the Communist issue had served their purposes, they both disappeared."

THIS thesis certainly is as impressive as earlier attempts to explain McCarthyism in terms other than those of the intrinsic problem of Communism itself. But, like sociological theories which preceded it, the thesis still seems incomplete and unsatisfying. The attempt to make the problem of American Communism a wholly American one draws too opaque a screen around the American political universe and underrates the impact of objective outside events. The Stalinization of Eastern Europe, the fall of Nationalist China and the Korean War all conspired to smash the wildly hopeful assumptions of Americans about the kind of world environment that victory in war would bring.

After all, the scapegoats for whom McCarthy scrounged were accused not so much of being reformers as they were of being associated with an international movement which by 1952 had done remarkably well for itself. To ascribe overriding importance, as Latham does, to internal political cycles underrates the impact that great historical events exert upon political behavior.

December 11, 1966

ECHOES OF AN ERA

---

52 Seized on Coast After Police Quell Riot at Red Inquiry

Special to The New York Times.

SAN FRANCISCO, May 13—Rioting disrupted a hearing by a House Un-American Activities subcommittee here today. The subcommittee is investigating alleged Communist activities in northern California.

In the domed and marbled rotunda of the City Hall, 200 persons, chiefly students, battled the police for thirty minutes before yielding to swinging clubs and high-pressure streams from fire hoses.

Twelve persons were injured in the fighting, eight of them policemen. Fifty-two men and women were arrested on charges ranging from assault with a deadly weapon to rioting, resisting arrest and disturbing the peace. One policeman was trampled and severely beaten with his own nightstick.

Subcommittee Assailed

Before the crowd gave way 400 policemen, seven ambulances and nine patrol wagons were called to the scene.

The demonstrators, chanting denunciations of the subcommittee, were protesting their exclusion from the already packed hearing room.

The rioting broke out as the subcommittee prepared to open

its afternoon session. Fifty-five policemen were on duty at the City Hall, assigned as a result of disturbances that occurred during yesterday's opening sessions. A dozen spectators and a witness had been expelled then.

This morning's session was without incident, except for noisemaking in the corridors that interfered with trial proceedings in City Hall courtrooms.

As the afternoon session prepared to convene in the chambers of the Board of Supervisors, crowds seeking admittance were informed that no seats were available. They were being held, according to a report that ran through the

throng, for holders of invitations issued by the committee's investigators.

Murmurs of discontent arose. Cries of "first come first served" went up. The police called for quiet and ordered the crowd back. The crowd moved forward. Fire hoses were unreeled. Demanding admittance to the hearing, the crowd surged forward and swept Ralph Schaumleffel, a policeman, from his feet.

As he went down, a demonstrator grabbed his club and began swinging at his head. The fire hoses were ordered into play. The crowd withdrew down the corridor to the head of the grand stairway leading from the ground floor and attempted to hold their ground against the drenching streams of water by sitting down.

Policemen moved in and began to drag tthem away.

"We won't move. We won't move," they chanted as they grabbed stair railings, clung to each other, and kicked at the police. Some sang "The Star-Spangled Banner." Others shouted "abolish the committee."

Taken to Patrol Wagon

At the end of a half hour, a dozen remained at the head of the stairs, and refusing to get to their feet were dragged step by step down to the waiting patrol wagons.

Harry Bridges, head of the Longshoremen's Union, arrived at City Hall in the midst of the rioting.

"This is a hell of a note — washing a bunch of kids down the steps like that," he commented.

Mayor George Christopher arrived shortly afterwad and addressed the crowd by loud speaker. Pickets outside the building booed.

"I don't want this to become a black day in the history of San Francisco," he said. "I urge you to obey the law."

He entered a building dripping with water, with floors slick and littered with debris.

Meanwhile, the subcommittee hearing resumed. About six routine witnesses were heard.

The subcommittee, with Representative Edwin E. Willis, Democrat of Louisiana, as chairman, will end its local sessions with two hearings tomorrow.

May 14, 1960

F. B. I. CHIEF SAYS REDS INCITE YOUTH

Finds College Students Led to Join in Disturbances All Over the World

By C. P. TRUSSELL
Special to The New York Times.

WASHINGTON, July 17 — J. Edgar Hoover reported today that Communists were attaining alarming success in inciting unsuspecting college youths throughout the world to join in outbursts of violence.

A highly disturbing factor, he said, is that while the students were doing it blindly, they were doing it effectively. He cited the riots in San Francisco last May, in which students played lead roles.

In a report to the House Commiteee on Un-American Activities, Mr. Hoover, the director of the Federal Bureau of Investigation, also recalled student uprisings in Uruguay that marred President Eisenhower's goodwill trip to Latin America. He mentioned also the riots in Japan, staged largely by students, that forced the cancellation of the President's visit to Tokyo.

Mr. Hoover called his report: "Communist Target—Youth."

"Particularly unfortunate," he asserted, "is the fact that many youth and student groups are totally unaware of the extent to which they can be victimized and exploited by Communists." A "sad proof," he said, was found in the Municipal Court at San Francisco last June 1, when Judge Albert A. Axelrod dismissed riot charges against sixty-two of the sixty-eight arrested after mob-violence during hearings by the House un-American Activities Committee.

He said that while there had been ample grounds for conviction in cases involving the sixty-two, mostly college students, the judge called them "clean-cut American students," and turned them loose. Fifty-eight of them promptly signed a statement declaring that they had not been "incited" or "misguided," but were following their "own convictions."

See Communist Line

Mr. Hoover contended that most of the students had actually followed a Communist line, laid down in months of planning, intended to discredit and possibly abolish the House committee and his agency itself.

These plans, the Hoover report indicated, included rehearsals of the defiance that subpoenaed witnesses would stage, and of disturbances to be created in the hearing room by planted agitators.

July 18, 1960

HIGH COURT BACKS HOUSE COMMITTEE IN CONTEMPT ISSUE

5-4 Rulings Support Power of Un-American Activities Group to Investigate

BLACK IN SHARP DISSENT

Finds Freedom Imperiled—Panel Critics Face Jail as Convictions Are Upheld

By ANTHONY LEWIS
Special to The New York Times.

WASHINGTON, Feb. 27—A bitterly divided Supreme Court upheld in broad terms today the investigating power of the House Committee on Un-American Activities.

By votes of 5 to 4 the court affirmed the contempt convictions of two critics of the House group who refused to testify about possible Communist affiliations. They were Frank Wilkinson of Los Angeles and Carl Braden of Louisville, Ky.

The dissenters charged that the court had opened the way for the House committee to intimidate its critics by investigating them. The majority said the mere fact that a man was a critic did not immunize him from inquiry if the committee had reason to think he had Communist affiliations.

Justice Hugo L. Black, in two passionate and despairing dissents, accused the majority of following "a constitutional doctrine that is steadily sacrificing individual control."

Finds Freedom Imperiled

"It is already past the time," Justice Black said, "when people who recognize and cherish the life-giving and life-preserving qualities of the freedoms protected by the Bill of Rights can afford to sit complacently by while those freedoms are being destroyed by sophistry and dialectics."

The majority opinions in both cases were written by Justice Potter Stewart. Joining him were Justices Felix Frankfurter, Tom C. Clark, John Marshall Harlan and Charles E. Whittaker.

Justice Black's dissents were joined by Chief Justice Earl Warren and Justice William O. Douglas. Justice Douglas wrote separate dissents in both cases, joined by the other two, and in the Braden case by Justice William J. Brennan Jr. In the Wilkinson case Justice Brennan wrote his own dissent.

40 Other Cases Pending

More than forty other contempt-of-Congress cases are now at various stages in the lower courts. While today's decisions do not necessarily mean that all these other witnesses will lose their legal fights, certainly their chances look dimmer.

The significance of the decisions is that a firm and consistent, albeit narrow, majority of the Supreme Court refuses to put tight legal or constitutional limitations on Congressional investigating committees.

The same five-man majority upheld the contempt conviction of Lloyd Barenblatt in 1959. That case in effect cut back on the sweep of the court's decision in 1957 in the case of John T. Watkins, when the court said a Congressional committee must inform witnesses of the purpose of its questions.

Justice Stewart went out of his way today to disassociate himself and the court from the House committee. In stating his Braden opinion in the courtroom he added at the end this comment, which did not appear in the printed text:

"Of course it is unnecessary for me to say that these opinions do not imply any personal views as to the wisdom or unwisdom of the creation or continuance of this committee."

The Wilkinson and Braden cases started the same day — July 30, 1958, in Atlanta. Both men appeared that day before a subcommittee of the House group, refused to answer questions and were cited for contempt. Upon conviction, each drew a year in prison.

Fought the Committee

Wilkinson, a former housing official in Los Angeles, had been campaigning against the Un-American Activities Committee and had gone to Atlanta to arouse opposition to it. He contended that he was subpoenaed only because he was such an opponent.

He was asked whether he was then a member of the Communist party. He declined to answer that or any other questions on the ground that Congress could not constitutionally inquire into such matters of beliefs and association.

Justice Stewart found that the committee had a legitimate legislative purpose—the investigation of Communist infiltration and propaganda in the South. And he said Congress had authorized such an inquiry.

He then rejected the argument that the committee was not authorized to investigate its own critics.

273

"We can find nothing to indicate," Justice Stewart said, "that it was the intent of Congress to immunize from interrogation all those (and there are many) who are opposed to the existence of the Un-American Activities Committee."

Justice Stewart also dismissed the contention that, whatever the general purpose of its Atlanta hearings, the committee had called Wilkinson only to "censure" him because he was a critic.

'Speculation Avoided'

He said the circumstances "do not necessarily lead to the conclusion that the subcommittee's intent was personal persecution." And in any case, he went on, "it is not for us to speculate as to the motivations of individual members of the subcommittee."

Finally, Justice Stewart said there was no constitutional barrier because Wilkinson was engaging in legitimate political activity. Congress, he said, has the right to look into Communist "manipulation and infiltration" of such activities.

Justice Douglas argued in his dissent that the committee had subpoenaed Wilkinson because he was a critic. And he said that the House resolution setting up the committee should be construed not to include such an investigation.

Unless "it is 'un-American' to criticize, impeach and berate the committee and to seek to have it abolished," Justice Douglas said, the House had given the committee no power to investigate its critics.

"If Wilkinson is to go to jail for criticizing the Un-American Committee," Justice Douglas added, when he stated his dissent in the courtroom, "I can think of a number of newspaper editors who should join him there."

He said that some newspapers had criticized the committee more strongly than Wilkinson had.

Justice Brennan in his dissent said that "the dominant purpose" of calling Wilkinson was "not to gather information in aid of law-making" but to harass him. He rejected that as not a valid legislative purpose.

Intimidations Foreseen

Justice Black's dissent was on constitutional grounds. He said the result of the committee's investigations—especially investigations of critics—would be to intimidate all who disagreed with it and perpetuate its own power.

"There are not many people in our society who will have the courage to speak out against such a formidable opponent," Justice Black wrote.

"If the present trend continues, this already small number will necessarily dwindle as their ranks are thinned by the jails.

"Government by consent will disappear to be replaced by government by intimidation because some people are afraid that this country cannot survive unless Congress has the power to set aside the freedoms of the First Amendment at will.

"I can only reiterate my firm conviction that these people are tragically wrong. This country was not built by men who were afraid and it cannot be preserved by such men."

Probable Cause Found

Justice Stewart emphasized in his opinion that the committee must have probable cause to call a witness. Here, he said, there was such cause, since another witness had identified Wilkinson as a Communist.

But Justice Black scoffed at this reasoning. He said many public officials, including Supreme Court justices, were called Communists these days. He suggested that the committee could always find some way to label as a Communist a person it wanted to investigate because he was a critic of the committee.

Braden, a former newspaper man, was once prosecuted for sedition in Kentucky in a case growing out of his part in moving a Negro family into a home in a white area of Louisville. He, too, contended he was subpoenaed only as a critic of the committee.

He refused to answer several questions. The only one considered by the court today was whether he was a Communist when he wrote a letter urging people to write to Congress against pending anti-sedition legislation.

Relied on Watkins Case

Braden argued that his refusal to answer should not be considered willful contempt because he had relied on the Watkins case in good faith. Justice Stewart dismissed that contention.

Justice Douglas' dissent went on that point, saying that Braden was entitled to rely on the Watkins decision since he had been questioned before the Barenblatt case had limited it. Justice Black again went on constitutional grounds.

Rowland Watts of New York argued for Wilkinson and Kevin T. Maroney for the Government in that case. Leonard B. Boudin of New York and John M. Coe of Pensacola, Fla., represented Braden, and J. Walter Yeagley argued for the Government.

Tonight Wilkinson issued a statement saying:

"We will not save free speech if we are not prepared to go to jail in its defense. I am prepared to pay that price."

February 28, 1961

BIRCH GROUP LISTS UNITS IN 34 STATES

Society Says It Has One to 100 Chapters in Each Area —Members' Total Secret

By United Press International.

At the start of 1961 the John Birch Society had organized one to 100 chapters in each of thirty-four states and the District of Columbia, according to its founder, Robert H. W. Welch Jr. of Massachusetts.

Still to be organized are Alabama, Alaska, Colorado, Delaware, Idaho, Maine, Maryland, Minnesota, Nebraska, Nevada New Jersey, Oklahoma, Pennsylvania, Rhode Island, Utah and Vermont.

"The John Birch Society is to be a monolithic body," said Mr. Welch, who is 61 years old, in a blue book of the organization's doctrine.

Its announced purpose is to fight and destroy communism within the United States. Its membership includes able and patriotic men.

But its methods, its specific aims and its judgments of some American leaders have led other able and patriotic citizens to denounce the society as going far beyond the tactics of the late Senator Joseph R. McCarthy, Wisconsin Republican.

When the society was founded in 1958, Mr. Welch, a retired candy manufacturer, announced that it would "operate under completely authoritative control at all levels. No collection of debating societies is ever going to stop the Communist conspiracy."

He hoped for 1,000,000 dedicated members to fight the forces of evil with "evangelical fervor."

Paul H. Talbert, Los Angeles insurance executive, who is a member of the society's governing council, estimated recently that it might have 100,000 members by the end of 1961, its third year.

Mr. Welch said he wanted to raise a million dollars from sources other than dues during the society's first year

"And even that amount," he remarked, "is an awfully small drop in the bucket, against what either the direct Communist propagandists or the Reutherite labor bosses are spending against us."

In his statement he referred to Walter P. Reuther, president of the United Automobile Workers, who is active in liberal political causes.

There is no public accounting of money or membership. Dues are $24 a year for men and $12 for women; life memberships are $1,000, either sex.

Appeals for voluntary contributions accompany virtually all mailings to members.

Mr. Welch has said he draws no salary. There are twenty-eight full-time employes at headquarters and the society is reported to be the largest single source of revenue for the Belmont (Mass.) post office next door.

In addition, thirty-five salaried persons work around the country as coordinators of member groups, and 100 work full or almost full time as volunteers.

Mr. Welch frankly has borrowed the Communist technique of setting up "front" groups for specific purposes. He acknowledges that another technique he advocates — the use of loaded questions to besmirch a suspect he cannot prove is a Communist—is "mean and dirty."

Chapters operate at widely different levels of secrecy. In North Dakota, meetings are announced on local radio stations and everyone's welcome.

The North Dakota organization, with about 400 members in nineteen chapters, was active in backing one of the society's proposals to outlaw the Federal income tax. The plan was approved by the state's lower house but killed in the state Senate.

In Dallas, Tex., a 32-year-old business man member of the society would not give his own name to an interviewer for publication.

"Most of our members in

Dallas are little people," he said, "just like I am. Most of these folks could not take a sustained smear attack. If it came along, they would probably be thrown out of their jobs. For that reason, the thing has been kept pretty quiet here. There are no real millionaires in Dallas in it as far as I know."

He estimated there were twenty chapters in Dallas and said he had heard there were 100 in Houston. Chapters are generally made up of twenty members.

There is no rule of thumb in Mr. Welch's book for members to determine on their own who is or who isn't a Communist, or Communist dupe.

"There are ways of sizing up both individuals and organizations in this battle which come only with experience, a knowledge of the interlocking pieces and personalities and a feel for the way the Communists work," says the "blue book."

"And while of course I can make mistakes too, I know from the way my opinion of various characters, formed independently, has then proved to coincide with the opinion of J. B. Matthews * * * that I have a fairly sensitive and accurate nose in this area. So we do not intend to be frustrated by indecisions of this nature."

Mr. Matthews is an associate editor of Mr. Welch's periodical, American Opinion, as well as the standard by which he checks his nose for Communists.

Mr. Matthews resigned in 1953 as chief investigator to Senator McCarthy's Senate Committee investigating communism. He resigned after the appearance in The American Mercury of Mr. Matthews' article asserting that clergymen were "the largest single group supporting the Communist apparatus" in this country.

John Birch had nothing to do with the society that bears his name. He was a young fundamentalist Baptist missionary from Georgia who served as an intelligence officer in China during World War II. He was killed by Chinese Communists ten days after the end of the war, the society says. He was 27 when he died.

Mr. Welch had not heard of Mr. Birch until after his death, but he did research on his life and wrote his life story.

Mr. Welch has memorialized Mr. Birch as "probably the first American casualty in that third world war, between Communists and the ever-shrinking 'free world,' which is still being waged against us."

And when he came to found an organization to fight Communists, he called it the John Birch Society.

Members Urged to Act

In Mr. Birch's name, members of the society are asked to write letters to Congressmen and others, and to operate in "front" organizations and through established community groups such as Parent-Teachers Associations and Chambers of Commerce.

Working through these groups,

the members are urged to press campaigns conceived as anti-Communist by Mr. Welch.

As well as striving for repeal of the Federal income tax, the society also seeks to impeach Chief Justice Earl Warren and to eliminate action in the churches for social legislation. It also opposes the North Atlantic Treaty Organization, foreign aid, the United Nations and any cultural or other exchanges with the Soviet Union.

In pressing his drive to expose all persons suspected of Communist affiliations — even though it might involve "mean and dirty" tactics—Mr. Welch has also urged his members to infiltrate suspected groups, to spy on persons in presumably respectable groups and to deluge newspapers with letters espousing the society's ideas.

Evidence that his exhortations to members have been effective may be seen in numerous newspaper editorials that denounced precisely what the society's members had accomplished.

On Feb. 26, for example, the publisher of The News Press in Santa Barbara, Calif., was moved to express his outrage against what the society was doing in his community. In a strongly worded editorial, the publisher, Thomas M. Storke, wrote:

"The News Press condemns the pressures on wealthy residents who fear and abhor communism, to contribute money to an organization whose leader has said that 'for reasons you will understand, there can be no accounting of funds.'

"The John Birch Society already has done a grave disservice to Santa Barbara by arousing suspicions and a mutual distrust among men of goodwill. The organization's adherents, sincere in their opposition to communism, do not seem to understand the dangers of the totalitarian dynamite with which they are tampering.

"The News Press challenges them: Come up from underground.

"And if they believe that in being challenged they have grounds for suit—let them sue. The News-Press would welcome a suit as a means of shedding more light on the John Birch Society."

It was widely assumed that the editorial referred in part to activities carried on by the society's members with the co-operation of Dr. Granville Knight, a Santa Barbara physician, who is on the society's twenty-six-man council. Several active chapters of the society, it was said, were studying communism at private meetings and looking around for Communists to expose.

Mr. Storke pointed out in his editorial that he was 85 and had spent his entire life in the community.

A little more than three weeks after Storke's editorial Chancellor Samuel B. Gould of the University of California at Santa Barbara, speaking at a university dinner, said that a "new type" of secret student organization had been set up

on the campus.

"Unless it is checked, can destroy the university, he said. Another official said "it was understood" Chancellor Gould referred to the Birch Society.

Mr. Gould said the organization to which he referred encouraged students to become informers and "take on the tasks of security agencies." He said the university and its officials "have been labeled and vilified in whispering campaigns, all purporting to prove that we are not only less than loyal to America but are downright subversive."

Congress was stirred to protest against the society's campaign against Chief Justice Warren. But it is the society's attack on the nation's churches that apparently has brought it to the attention of more communities—and has more bitterly divided those communities—than any of its other activities.

It is an attack that has been made for years by some religious fundamentalists and economic conservatives who see as both heresy and communism the preaching of a "social gospel" that attempts to apply Biblical teachings to current secular and political problems.

In Arizona, for instance, one of the society's "biggest" states, the American Council of Christian Churches, a Fundamentalist group, is vigorously campaigning against such "social gospel." The society is abetting the campaign in its own way.

In Santa Barbara, members of the First Presbyterian Church received through the mail a Birch Society "questionnaire" attacking its own church leadership and that of the National Council of Churches, a large group generally favorably inclined toward social legislation.

At Amarillo, Tex., Brig. Gen. William L. Lee, retired commander of the Amarillo Air Force Base, is head of the local Birch organization. He denied that the society had anything to do with the rumored circulation of a list accusing five prominent local men of being Communists.

But he acknowledged that the society was stirring up friction in local churches.

"We have documented proof that the National Council has been infiltrated by Communists and some of these ministers just won't listen to us," General Lee said. "Until we can convince them that the National Council has some Communist followers in it, there is going to be some friction."

Church Warfare Feared

Church leaders in Amarillo have said they are fearful that congregations may be split into warring camps.

The Birch group in Amarillo has been less successful in another campaign. The public library refused to yield to its demand that it call off a "great decisions" discussion series sponsored by the forty-two-year-old Foreign Policy Association.

At Wichita, Kan., the society has moved to battle in policy matters in the library and college. According to George H.

Lewis, assistant Professor of Economics at the University of Wichita and director of the Kansas Council for Industrial Peace, they "virtually control the Wichita Chamber of Commerce and seem to have a dominant influence in the state chamber organization.

"One of their major objectives in the state is to destroy collective bargaining," Dr. Lewis said. "They are preparing to push through some vicious anti-labor legislation during the next session."

The Birch Society was founded on Dec. 9, 1958, at Indianapolis, after Mr. Welch had delivered a two-day speech to eleven men he had invited to hear it.

That speech is today the "blue book" of the society, the official statement of its aims and methods. It is supplemented by monthly bulletins to members and the magazine American Opinion, which Mr. Welch founded before the society and of which he is editor.

The message and aim are:

"Less government, more responsibility and a better world."

Mr. Welch frankly views the social legislation of the twentieth century as the product of a sinister conspiracy to change the economic and political structure of the United States so that this nation can be merged with the Soviet Union without a fight.

"You have only a few more years," he told his listeners at Indianapolis. "We are living in such a fool's paradise as the people of China lived in twenty years ago."

"The danger is almost entirely internal," Mr. Welch said, "from Communist influences right in our midst and treason right in our Government."

Government Re 'Enemy'

Mr. Welch would repeal virtually all the social and economic legislation of the last 30 years.

"The greatest enemy of man is, and always has been, government," he said.

"We are not beginning any revolution in any technical sense," he said. "Yet our determination to overthrow an entrenched tyranny is the very stuff of which revolutions are made."

He has said that communism is being slipped over on the American people so gradually and insidiously that before long "they can no longer resist the Communist conspiracy as free citizens, but can resist the Communist tyranny only by themselves becoming conspirators against established government."

On Jan. 1, 1957, his biography says, Mr. Welch "gave up most of his business responsibilities—and most of his income —in order to devote practically all of his time and energy to the anti-Communist cause."

It was at that time that he gave up an executive post with the James O. Welch Company, a candy manufacturing concern, headed by his brother.

Physician Leads Anti-Red Drive With 'Poor Man's Birch Society'

Many in St. Louis Perturbed by Impact on City of Four-Day School Stressing Menace to American Way of Life

By CABELL PHILLIPS

Special to The New York Times.

ST. LOUIS, April 28—A "poor man's John Birch Society" has just completed a series of meetings here that has left many St. Louisans puzzled and vaguely troubled.

Last night, some 2,000 solemnly attentive men and women packed the Keil Auditorium in downtown St. Louis to hear two lectures on the menace of communism. The speakers were Dr. Fred C. Schwarz, national director of the Christian Anti-Communism Crusade of Long Beach, Calif., and Herbert A. Philbrick, former undercover agent in the American Communist party for the Federal Bureau of Investigation.

The occasion was the highlight of a four-day school on anti - communism that Dr. Schwarz has been conducting here this week, with Mr. Philbrick as a member of his ten-man faculty. Attendance at the thrice-daily sessions, held in a hotel, has ranged from 200 to 600 each.

Peril to Nation Seen

The theme of last night's meeting, as it has been of others in the series, was that the American way of life at every level—in the schools, in the churches, in government and in international affairs—was mortally threatened by "godless Communist ideology."

Dr. Schwarz said that the Communists had set 1973 as the date for their American takeover. He predicted that they would succeed unless ordinary men and women, "such as you sitting in this hall tonight," armed themselves with "the knowledge and the tools" to avert such a disaster.

The mildly derisive label of a poor man's Birch Society was applied to the anti-Communist project by a local newspaper man, who said that the school had made a greater impact on the city than he had expected.

"I frankly misjudged both the extent and the kind of appeal this thing would make," he said.

"We've had occasional operations of this sort here before," he said, "and they have created little more than a ripple of public interest. This one has not only drawn quite substantial crowds, but they seem to be a cut or so above the social and intellectual average of such turnouts."

The comparison with the John Birch Society, moreover, seems to be comparative rather than specific. Both groups have as their central aim the stirring up of a citizens' war against Communist subver-

sion. The Christian Anti-Communism Crusade, however, stops a good deal short of the vehement summons to retaliation advocated by Robert W. H. Welch Jr., the leader of the John Birch Society.

Dr. Schwarz, who is among other things, a Baptist evangelist, interlards his appeal with religious fundamentalism. His "action program" goes no further than to urge his students to set up anti-Communist schools and study groups of their own.

Any more positive methods they may want to pursue in fighting communism, he says, are their own business.

Many participants in the school said that backing "safe," conservative candidates for public office, and keeping an eye on local education officials were the surest ways of correcting the Communist evil.

While the Birch group aims its appeal at persons of wealth and community prestige, the Schwarz program appears to be designed for a less sophisticated, middle-class audience. This reporter, after attending several sessions of the Greater St. Louis School of Anti-Communism, as the current program is called, was struck by the large proportion of younger people.

Couples under forty, and boys and girls of college and high school age, were among the regular participants. Among the adults, proprietors of small businesses, salesmen, teachers, ministers and housewives active in community and neighborhood affairs seemed to predominate.

Aided by Area's Leaders

On the other hand, official sponsorship of the school is in the hands of persons who were not conspicuous in the student body. They are prominent leaders in business, industry and politics. The man chiefly responsible for bringing Dr. Schwarz and his team here is Richard H. Amberg, publisher of The St. Louis Globe-Democrat.

On the list of sixty sponsors appear the names of leading manufacturers, merchants, bankers, the Mayor and chief of police of St. Louis, the two United States Senators and two local directors of the John Birch Society. Gov. John M. Dalton officially proclaimed this "anti-Communism Week in Missouri."

The week's events in St. Louis, when viewed in a broader context, seemed symptomatic of a quickening right-wing movement that is appearing in

various guises in many parts of the country today.

But for all its diversity of aims and methods, the movement has certain things in common. Among these is a passionate anti-communism—a fear that communist doctrine is subtly infiltrating and destroying the American way of life. This is the motive power of the Christian Anti-Communism crusade.

Here in St. Louis the school has been conducted in the ballroom of the Ambassador Hotel, a modern outlying hotel facing Forest Park.

Promptly at 8:30 each morning, Dr. Schwarz, a crisp, energetic, self-confident Australian, who is a graduate physician as well as psychiatrist and lay preacher, raps his students to order. In a commanding, high-pitched voice, with an accent reminiscent of a London music hall, he warms them up with amusing cajolery and then he gives them a briefing on the film strip that will start off the morning's session.

One morning, the film was "Operation Abolition," prepared by the House Committee on Un-American Activities to tell its version of the student riot that marked a committee session in San Francisco last year.

According to the committee, and Dr. Schwarz, the riot was instigated and led by Communists as a stratagem to discredit the committee. Others contend the riot was a spontaneous reaction by the students to the police's handling of them.

"You will see here with your own eyes," Dr. Schwarz says with intensity, "just how a group of possibly innocent college students have been made the dupes of Communist strategy by trained Communist agitators.

"It is going on in colleges all over America, all over England, all over the free world."

Following the film, there is a brief period for questions and discussion. Then follow two hour-long lecture periods by Dr. Schwarz and one faculty member, with a brief coffee break in between. The afternoon and evening sessions, running about three hours each, follow much the same pattern. The "commencement ceremony," although no diplomas are awarded, is a dinner on the final night of the school.

The bulk of the course is a series of ten or a dozen lectures by Dr. Schwarz, based largely on his pamphleteering. It purports to give a scholarly history and analysis of the Communist movement and its tactics. Publicity releases from his office describe him as one of the world's leading authorities on the subject.

Varied Issues Discussed

Some of his topics are: "The Communist Party," "Communist Philosophy and Method of Violence," "Why Millionaires, College Professors and Ministers Become Communists," and "How to Debate with Communists and Fellow Travelers."

Supplementing this basic course are the lectures by the

faculty members. Only one or two of these are permanently connected with the crusade organization.

Others, such as Mr. Philbrick, come from the outside. But they regularly turn up at the various city-wide programs, such as those previously held in Los Angeles, Philadelphia and Dallas. Some of these lecturers and their subjects are as follows:

Fred Schlafly Jr., lawyer from Alton, Ill., "Is Communism Constitutional?" W. Cleon Skousen, a former F. B. I. agent now living in Salt Lake City, "Communism, Psychiatry and Crime." Robert Morris, formerly chief counsel for the Senate Internal Security subcommittee and now president of Dallas University, "America's Internal Security." Mr. Philbrick's topics here this week were "Cybernetic Warfare" and "Communism and Youth."

While there is a seeming diversity of subject matter in this catalogue, to the listener it all appears to be a variation on a single theme the duplicity, "demonic brutality" of communism and its steady, hidden erosion of "the moral fiber of America."

Often a point is driven home with a stark recitation of Communist atrocity. One speaker, for example described the agonies of a Marine prisoner in Korea whose fingers were broken by a Communist captor because he would not renounce his belief in "Christian democracy."

As the story ended, the speaker turned to his audience and whispered:

"Freedom doesn't belong to us; it is loaned to us by those who have paid the supreme price for it."

Charges that certain individuals or institutions are "soft on Communism" or have been duped into "serving the communist cause" were implied rather than directly slated by the speakers this reporter heard. It seemed apparent, however that most of the speakers were suspicious of the patriotism of some members of the Kennedy Administration and the United States Supreme Court, of large segments of the Protestant clergy, of the United Nations and of professors and the intellectual community in general.

Remarks and questions from the audiences indicated that such suspicions were widely held.

"Why can't we impeach Earl Warren, the Chief Justice?" one irate man asked a speaker during a coffee break.

Many of those who attended the sessions, however, said they believed that they had heard the truth about communism for the first time. They seemed more bitter about it than their teachers had been.

John Bommacito, an intense and intelligent young man employed in an advertising agency, said, for example:

"It's just shocking how little the people in this city know or care about all this. The business men are all asleep. I'm going to see to it that we have an anti-Communist cell, or whatever you want to call it," in the

Junior Chamber of Commerce.

A more skeptical view of the proceedings, however, was offered by a young Protestant minister, who had attended most of the meetings, but declined permission to use his name.

"This thing has all the elements of a brainwashing except that the victims are all ready and eager to be brainwashed," he said.

"What Schwarz and company does," he went on, "is to give them a vocabulary—a pretentious and fine sounding dialectic—to express something they are ready to believe in. I think it's a cockeyed vocabulary; it's so visceral, so blood-and-thunderish that it misses the real significance of the Communist danger. It drains off the energy we ought to be putting in the right places."

Dr. Schwarz arrived in this country in 1953 with, as he often says, only ten dollars in his pocket, but a great idea in his head.

He has built his organization into an enterprise with an annual turnover in excess of $380,000. This is derived from contributions, fees and income from publications. It is expended chiefly on such missionary work as he has carried on here this week, and some projects overseas.

The fees for the St. Louis school are $20 for the full course and $2 for single day or evening sessions. More than 1,100 persons registered.

Dr. Schwarz's rise to prominence was aided by an appearance in 1957 before the staff of the House Committee on Un-American Activities to give testimony on "the Communist mind." It was published in a fourteen-page booklet by the committee and now has a greater sale through the Government Printing Office, Dr. Schwarz says, than any item in the catalogue except the Constitution.

When he is not conducting schools, he is in almost constant motion around the country as a lecturer to school and civic groups, patriotic societies and at naval and air force installations.

He has speaking engagements in New York from May 8 to 12.

In private conversation Dr. Schwarz takes rather a dim view of the John Birch Society.

"There is always the temptation, in fighting communism, to try to form a totalitarian organization modeled on communism," he said the other day, relaxing shirt-sleeved in his hotel suite between sessions.

"Certainly, these people—these dedicated anti-Communists—want a leader.

"They want to be led; they want me to lead them. But I won't do it. If Bob Welch wants to do it he can; he's got a program of action and a lot of ready resolutions. But it's not my business."

"You know," he said, leaning forward with a grin, "I sometimes get the notion he follows me around the country, signing up the people after I've worked them up."

April 30, 1961

HIGH COURT PUTS CURB ON U.S. REDS IN 2 MAJOR CASES

BENCH IS SPLIT, 5-4

Registration Upheld— Members Liable to Criminal Charge

By ANTHONY LEWIS
Special to The New York Times.

WASHINGTON, June 5—The Supreme Court upheld today two of the Government's major legislative weapons against communism within the United States. Each decision was five-to-four.

The court sustained a section of the Internal Security Act of 1950 requiring "Communist-action" organizations to register with the Government. And it found constitutional the clause of the Smith Act of 1940 that makes it a crime to be an active member of a party advocating the violent overthrow of the Government.

[In New York, the national headquarters of the Communist party denounced the decisions as "a crushing blow at democracy and the Constitution." The party said it would continue to carry out its program.]

The decisions were the first definitive Supreme Court rulings on both these statutory provisions.

Scope of Rulings Limited

The court's opinions were carefully limited and did not give the Government a blank check in applying the two statutes. Nevertheless, the decisions were substantial victories for the Government—the most important legal victories it has had in the internal security field in many years.

Justice Felix Frankfurter wrote the opinion for the court in the Communist party registration case. Justice John Marshall Harlan wrote the opinions in two cases testing convictions under the Smith Act membership clause. He affirmed one but reversed the second for insufficient proof.

In each case, the two were joined in the majority by Justices Tom C. Clark, Charles E. Whittaker and Potter Stewart.

Chief Justice Dissents

Chief Justice Earl Warren and Justices Hugo L. Black, William O. Douglas and William J. Brennan Jr. dissented in whole or part in the party registration case. They dissented from the decision upholding the Smith Act conviction but concurred, for their own rea-

Justice Felix Frankfurter

The New York Times
Justice John M. Harlan

sons, in the reversal of the second conviction.

The registration case had been in the courts on and off for eleven years—since shortly after the passage of the Internal Security Act of 1950.

The act directs Communist-action and "Communist-front" organizations to register with the Attorney General. It defines the former as groups "substantially directed" by a foreign government "controlling the world Communist movement," and the latter as groups substantially controlled by Communist-action organizations.

Groups Were to Give Names

In registering, any group must supply the names of all officers and members within the last year. It also has to give an accounting of all money received and spent within a year, including the sources of funds.

Severe consequences follow registration. The registered group loses all tax exemptions and has to stamp all mail it sends:

"Disseminated by ———, a Communist organization."

Members of a registered group are barred from Government employment and are forbidden to use a United States passport or apply for one. Any naturalized citizen who joins a registered organization within five years of naturalization is in danger of losing his citizenship.

To decide whether an organization came within the definition of an "action" or "front" group, the statute created the Subversive Activities Control Board.

In 1950, the Attorney General began proceedings before the board against the Communist party. In 1953, the board decided that the party was controlled from abroad and hence was required to register as an action group.

This first order was set aside

by the Supreme Court because the board had relied on "tainted" evidence from demonstrated perjurers. A second order was set aside on other procedural grounds by the Court of Appeals here. The board then found again that the party must register.

Registration Approved

The Supreme Court upheld that registration order today. But a most important aspect about its decision was what it did not decide.

The court refused to consider now any of the legal consequences of registration—the loss of tax exemption, requirement for mail-stamping, denial of passports. It said that those were all "premature" and could be challenged later, if anyone tried to apply those sanctions to the party or its members.

Justice Frankfurter refused also to consider now a contention that, by the mere act of signing a registration statement, officers of the party would identify themselves and make themselves liable to punishment under the Smith Act. The argument was that this constituted forced self-incrimination in violation of the Fifth Amendment.

The majority opinion said a major purpose of the Smith Act of 1950 was "the public disclosure effected by registration," apart from the penalties in the statute. Hence Justice Frankfurter considered only the bare requirement of registration by the party.

The opinion did, however, pass on an argument by the party that forced disclosure of members' names would infringe on the freedom of association guaranteed by the First Amendment because it would discourage persons from joining the party.

Justice Frankfurter readily agreed that, in some circumstances, the names of an organization's members might not constitutionally be extracted from it. The court has so held in cases from the South involving the National Association for the Advancement of Colored people.

But Justice Frankfurter said there was all the difference between an organization with legal aims, such as the N. A. A. C. P., and one controlled from abroad and seeking illegal ends by secret means.

"When existing government," he said, "is menaced by a worldwide integrated movement which employs every combination of possible means, peaceful and violent, domestic and foreign, overt and clandestine, to destroy the Government itself—the legislative judgment as to how that threat may best be met consistently with the safeguarding of personal freedom is not to be set aside merely because the judgment of judges would, in the first instance, have chosen other methods."

The opinion rejected the argument that approval of registration here might allow Congress to make "any group which pursues unpopular political objectives" register.

Justice Frankfurter said that "nothing which we decide here remotely carries such an implication."

He noted that this statute was confined to foreign-controlled organizations working as part of a world movement.

Requirements Limited

The net effect of the majority opinion is to require the party to file a bare statement that it is registering. Party officers may refuse to sign the statement on the ground of the Fifth Amendment—and then test that issue out in court.

The majority indicated also that the registration statement would have to include the names of all members and officers within the last year and a financial statement. The court explicitly turned down First-Amendment objections to these requirements.

Justices Brennan and Douglas, in separate opinions, agreed with the majority that the court need not now face the consequences of registration. They agreed also that mere registration and disclosure of members' names did not violate the First Amendment.

"When an organization is used by a foreign power to make advances here," Justice Douglas wrote, "questions of security are raised beyond the ken of disputation and debate between the people resident here."

Backs Brennan's View

But these two dissenters thought that the court should consider now, and uphold, the contention that making officers sign the statement would violate their Fifth Amendment rights. Justice Douglas went further, arguing that the Fifth Amendment also barred forced disclosure of members' names by the party.

Chief Justice Warren thought the court should not reach constitutional questions. He said the subversive board's order should be set aside because of procedural flaws in its hearing and because it had used incorrect evidentiary standards.

The Chief Justice said, however, that since the majority rejected these non-constitutional arguments, he joined Justice Brennan in reaching and finding a violation of the Fifth Amendment as to the party officers' signing of the registration statement.

Justice Black alone considered the act as a whole, including all the penalties on the party and its members. He found it unconstitutional for a variety of reasons—as an act of outlawry, a bill of attainder, a denial of due process of law and a violation of the First Amendement.

Justice Black said it was impossible to read the Internal Security Act as a whole without concluding that it was a devious attempt to ban the Communist party. He said:

"The first banning of an association because it advocates hated ideas—whether that association be called a political party or not—marks a fateful moment in the history of a free country. That moment seems to have arrived for this country."

The first of two Smith Act cases decided today also has had a long legal history. It involved Junius Irving Scales, a former Communist leader in North Carolina, who has now left the party and is living in New York.

Scales was first convicted in 1955. The Supreme Court heard argument on his case in its 1956 term, then set the case down for reargument. The next term it sent the case back for a new trial on a procedural point. Scales was retried and again convicted. The Supreme Court heard argument two years ago, held the case last term and then had it argued again last October.

Scales' sentence was six years.

Limit on Speech Seen

The major constitutional attack on the membership clause asserted that it limited freedom of speech and association in violation of the first Amendment. The argument was that the statute covered not actual attempts at overthrow but membership in a group that merely advocated overthrow, however unlikely success seemed to be.

Justice Harlan indicated that this argument had been largely disposed of in the case of Eugene Dennis, decided by the Supreme Court on June 4, 1951—ten years and a day ago.

The Dennis case was a prosecution of Communist leaders under another Smith Act provision —for conspiring to advocate violent overthrow and organize a party to that end. The court, over the dissent of Justices Black and Douglas, found no infringement of the First Amendment.

"We can discern no reason," Justice Harlan wrote today, "why membership, when it constitutes a purposeful form of complicity in a group engaging in this same forbidden advocacy, should receive any greater degree of protection from the guarantees of [the first] amendment."

The membership clause is limited to persons "knowing the purposes" of the organization he joins. The Justice Department, to ward off constitutional attack, read two other limitations into the clause—and Justice Harlan accepted both of these today.

One was a requirement that, to be convicted, a person must be an "active" member of the group, not a "nominal" or "passive" member. The other limitation was that the member personally have a "specific intent to bring about violent overthrow."

Finds Requirements Met

Justice Harlan found that these various requirements had been met in Scales' case. Reviewing the evidence at length, he said the Government had proved that the party had engaged in illegal advocacy, that Scales had known about it, had intended to bring about revolution and had been an active party member.

The second Smith Act case concerned John Francis Noto of Buffalo. His conviction was reversed because, Justice Harlan found, the Justice Deparment had not proved the kind of advocacy by the Communist party that is covered by the Smith Act.

Justice Harlan drew on his own opinion in a case of 1957 setting aside a number of conspiracy convictions under the Smith Act. He said then, and repeated today, that the act covered only advocacy that is "incitement to action," not advocacy of the "mere abstract doctrine of forcible overthrow."

Distinction Is Renewed

"We held [in 1957], and we reiterate now," he wrote, "that the mere abstract teaching of Communist theory, including the teaching of the moral propriety or even moral necessity for a resort to force and violence is not the same as preparing a group for violent action and steeling it to such action."

The majority concluded that evidence of the latter kind of advocacy was insufficient in the Noto case.

Justice Harlan did not explicitly say that Noto should be retried, but Justice Department officials indicated that chances of any further effort to convict him under the membership clause were exceedingly slim.

Justice Douglas, dissenting in the Scales case, remarked that there was "no charge of any overt act to overthrow the Government by force and violence."

"Nothing but beliefs are on trial in this case," he said. "They are unpopular and to most of us revolting. But they are nonetheless ideas or dogmas or faith within the broad framework of the First Amendment.

"What we lose by majority vote today may be reclaimed at a future time when the fear of advocacy, dissent and non-conformity no longer cast a shadow over us."

Justice Brennan, joined by the Chief Justice and Justice Douglas, dissented on a non-constitutional ground.

Clause In Law Quoted

This was a clause in the Internal Security Act of 1950 saying that no one should be prosecuted for membership in the Communist party "per se." Justice Brennan said this clause had effectively foreclosed enforcement of the Smith Act's membership clause.

Justice Black, in a separate dissent, endorsed both the constitutional views of Justice Douglas and Justice Brennan's statutory ground.

In the Noto case these four concurred in reversal of the conviction for the reasons given in their Scales dissents. The Chief Justice and Justice Brennan also agreed with Justice Harlan that the evidence was insufficient.

The whole set of decisions should open the way for renewed enforcement by the Government of long-dormant internal security measures. For example, a large number of registration proceedings against alleged Communist front groups have been held in abeyance pending decision of the party registration case.

Attorney General Robert F. Kennedy had indicated that continuation of the Internal Se-

curity Division as a separate branch of the Justice Department would depend on the decisions in these cases. Some Congressmen have urged that internal security be brought within the Criminal Division for economy reasons and because of declining emphasis on the

subject.

In the Communist party case, J. Lee Rankin, then Solicitor General, argued for the Government. John J. Abt of New York and Joseph Forer of Washington represented the party.

John F. Davis argued for the Government in the Scales case

and Telford Taylor of New York for Scales. Mr. Davis and Kevin T. Maroney represented the Government in the Noto case, and Mr. Abt represented Noto.

June 6, 1961

Right-Wing Officers Worrying Pentagon

By CABELL PHILLIPS
Special to The New York Times.

WASHINGTON, June 17-- The Pentagon is having its troubles with right-wingers in uniform.

A number of officers of high and middle rank are indoctrinating their commands and the civilian population near their bases with political theories resembling those of the John Birch Society. They are also holding up to criticism and ridicule some official policies of the United States Government.

The most conspicuous example of some of these officers was Maj. Gen. Edwin A. Walker, who was officially "admonished" for his activities by the Secretary of the Army earlier this week.

General Walker's offense was in saying that a number of prominent Americans, as well as elements of the newspaper and television industries, were tainted with Communist ideology.

He did this in the course of a continuing effort that the general said was "designed to develop an understanding of the American military and civil heritage, responsibility toward that heritage and the facts and objectives of those enemies who would destroy it,"

General Walker was the commander of the Twenty-Fourth Infantry Division in Germany at the time.

Policy Set 3 Years Ago

In his anti-Communist effort General Walker was operating under a three-year-old policy of the National Security Council. This called for a mobilization of all arms of Government— military, diplomatic, civilian—in the "cold-war" struggle.

Where the general went wrong, apparently, was in confusing his own political inclinations with the Administration's strategy for fighting the "cold war."

High officials at the Pentagon have said that they hope this example will have a restraining effect on other military men whose zeal in the same cause has been creating mounting embarrassment for them.

"No other disciplinary actions are being considered now,'" said Arthur Sylvester, Assistant Secretary of Defense for Public

Affairs.

"It is no secret, however, that this sort of activity by representatives of the Defense Department has been a disturbing problem for us. We are trying to reach a more rational handling of this aspect of the 'cold war' effort than has been the case in the past."

The problem for the Pentagon arises out of the fact that a number of its higher ranking officers have participated in or publicly lent their support to a variety of so-called forums, schools, and seminars, ostensibly focused on the issues of national security. However, many of those groups—at least incidentally—are preoccupied with radically right-wing political philosophies.

Stress on Anti-Communism

The chief ingredient of these philosophies is often a militant anti-communism. The argument is that Communist subversion today is rife among the schools, the churches, labor unions, Government offices and elsewhere, and that this is a far greater threat to national survival than the international aspects of the Communist conspiracy.

In this argument, liberalism is equated with socialism and socialism with communism. Thus it opposes most welfare legislation, many programs for international cooperation such as foreign aid and disarmament conferences, and any effort by this Government to seek accommodations with the Soviet Union. Such activities are depicted as a playing into the hands of the Communists, and sometimes as stemming from Communist subversion.

As part of such indoctrination, citizens often are urged to form their own groups to "educate" others about the Communist menace and to be alert in discerning Communist influences in their neighborhoods, schools, newspapers and local governing bodies.

The genesis of this problem goes back to the so-called "cold war policy" evolved by the National Security Council in the summer of 1958.

That was a year of mounting international tensions when Communist power seemed to be on the rise around the world. Vice President Richard M. Nixon was then the victim of assaults by Communist mobs during a goodwill tour of South America; President Eisenhower dispatched Marines to Lebanon to fend off Communist political aggressions in the Middle East; Communist China stepped up its artillery attacks on Quemoy and Matsu.

President Eisenhower and his

top policy leaders decreed that the "cold war" could not be fought as a series of separate and often unrelated actions, as with foreign aid and propaganda. Rather, it must be fought with a concentration of all the resources of the Government and with the full understanding and support of the civilian population. It was decided, in particular, that the military should be used to reinforce the "cold-war" effort.

This was the substance of the still-classified "cold-war policy" paper of the National Security Council.

Its implementation in the Department of Defense was ordered through a series of directives and guidance papers, also classified, directed to the top civilian and uniformed authorities. These officials were told to take positive measures to alert the troops under their command and the public at large to the issues of national security and the "cold war."

How specific these directives were as to the particular tools and approaches to be employed in this effort cannot be learned. But commanding officers were supplied with literature and speech material and were required to report regularly on their "cold-war" activities.

However, it is known that commanding officers were allowed wide latitude in applying the directives within their commands.

Of the hundreds of military bases here and abroad, only a score have become involved in these programs to the point that they have caused alarm among the new civilian team in the Pentagon. Officials suspect, however, that the trend is somewhat more widespread than their reports currently indicate. They are quietly trying to find out how widespread it is.

A typical example about which they do know is a seminar labeled Project Action.

This was held at the Naval Air Station, Wold-Chamberlain Field, Minneapolis, on April 28 and 29 of this year. Capt. Robert T. Kieling is the commanding officer of the station. He was a co-sponsor of the program in collaboration with a committee of the Minneapolis-St. Paul Chamber of Commerce.

The official announcement described the program as follows:

"The purpose of Project Action is to inspire the citizens of this area to take an active part in the war against the danger that threatens our freedom and American way of life.

"The program of talks and presentations by nationally known leaders for the cause of democracy will bring to light

facts and figures concerning the rising crime rate, juvenile delinquency, drug addiction, the general degradation of morals, the complacent attitude toward patriotism and the tremendous gains the Communist conspiracy is making in this country * *

The United States Naval Air Station is making facilities available for the seminar at the request of the Twin Cities Council for American Ideals. Out-of-local-area participants are invited to take advantage of overnight accommodations on the air station. A nominal fee of 50 cents per person will be charged. The [seminar] fee of $7.50 includes two noon meals."

Approximately 500 persons from the upper Middle West attended the two-day program. Among the lecturers who addressed them were Dr. Gerhard Niemeyer, University of Notre Dame; Dr. Nicholas Nyaradi, Bradley University; Dr. B. N. Bengston, Maywood, Ill., and two defectors from the Soviet Union. Several films were shown and literature was distributed purporting to explain the nature of Communist subversion, with particular emphasis on its attack upon American morals.

Among the scores of letters concerning Project Action that reached the Pentagon in the following days was one from a newspaper editor. It said in part:

"Perhaps someone can clear up for us our lack of understanding as to just how co-sponsorship of such activities fits in with the Navy mission, or the over-all military mission, for that matter. It must be admitted that the local Project Action is politically partisan in a very real sense, although the partisanship is not of the party label type."

Another example of these political activities concerns Capt. Kenneth J. Sanger, commanding officer of the Sands Point Naval Air Station, Seattle, Wash. His activities over the last year have aroused a storm of controversy. Hundreds of letters, supporting and condemning him, have poured into the Pentagon and Congressional offices in recent weeks.

In pursuing what he describes as a program of "moral leadership," on and off base, Captain Sanger has made wide use of two controversial films, "Operation Abolition" and "Communism on The Map."

The first film was produced by the House Committee on Un-American Activities as a counter-weapon against those who sought last year to terminate its career. It depicts as Commu-

279

nist inspired and managed last year's student riots in San Francisco, where the committee held an inquiry. The message of the film is that Communist influence has infiltrated school life across the nation. Critics contend the film is distorted and misleading.

Film Made at College

The second film was produced at Harding College, Searcy, Ark. It shows the United States virtually engulfed in a world gone either Communist or socialist, including all of its NATO allies except Portugal. Among those whom the film narrator cites as responsible for this condition are President Franklin D. Roosevelt, for having recognized the Soviet Union, and Gen. of the Army George C. Marshall, for having "made possible" the Communist take-over of China.

These films and accompanying lectures by Captain Sanger and members of his "team" have been exhibited before hundreds of audiences, many of them composed of high school and college students, all over the northwest. Among the many letters condemning the program was one published in The Seattle Times of last March 22 from James I. Kimbrough, who wrote in part:

"My concern is not with Captain Sanger; my concern is with the concept which suggests that any branch of the armed forces is the appropriate vehicle for the dissemination to the civilian population, and particularly to our youth, of proper attitudes of patriotism and concern for our democratic ideals. This is the nut of the issue, not communism or anti-communism."

Among numerous other incidents that have been brought to the attention of the Defense Department is the "Fourth Dimensional Warfare Seminar"

held in Pittsburgh on April 15. Among those listed as giving "assistance and support" to the program were Lieut. Gen. Ridgely Gaither, Commanding General, Second Army, and Maj. Gen. Ralph C. Cooper, Commanding General Twenty-first Army Corps, and their respective staffs.

Several of the main speakers were highly critical of the Government's "cold war" policies.

One, for example, Admiral Chester Ward, retired, was reported in the local newspapers as having said that "some of the advisers now surrounding the President" have philosophies regarding foreign affairs "that would chill the average American." He mentioned by name in this connection, Adlai E. Stevenson, United States representative to the United Nations, and George F. Kennan, United States Ambassador to Yugoslavia.

Members of the seminar were given a list of eighteen points on "What You Can Do in the Fight Against Communism."

"This sort of thing, if carried far enough among susceptible people, can breed a wave of vigilantism and witch-hunting," one Pentagon official said. "Even Mr. Hoover of the F.B.I., whom nobody would call " 'soft on communism,' deplores these self-appointed counter-spies."

Left in Delicate Position

Civilian chiefs in the Pentagon find themselves in a delicate position with respect to this sort of activity in the higher uniformed echelons. They are disturbed by the right-wing views displayed by many of these officers. Yet, realistically, they cannot either ignore the threat of Communist subversion or be tagged, as one of them put it, "as being against anti-communism."

"The real problem," he went

on, "is one of proportion. Nearly every responsible official I know of thinks that the real war against communism has to be fought in the international arena as it's political, diplomatic, economic and in a limited sense, military. That, certainly, is the way the official policies of this Government are geared.

"When, as these fellows do, you change the target to looking for spies under the bed or in the P.T.A. you divert that much energy and support away from the main objective of the 'cold war.' And at the same time, you instill fear and distrust of our Government and its leader."

Reinforcing his point, he took from his desk a memorandum from Secretary of Defense Robert S. McNamara, which has been circulated as "guidance" throughout the services. In part, it said:

"After the President has taken a position, has established a policy, or after appropriate officials in the Defense Department have established a policy, I expect that no member of the department, either civilian or military, will discuss that policy other than in a way to support it before the public."

The dilemma of these officials is deepened by two other considerations.

One is that the experience of the servicemen captured by the Communists during the Korean War revealed a serious gap in the moral stamina and the patriotic dedication of a good part of American youth.

This has greatly alarmed many military men who believe that the nation must breed a tougher type of soldier if it is to survive in another war. To many schooled in the military discipline, there is a link between this moral and intellectual "softness" and certain social and political trends in

American life over the last two decades.

The other consideration is that under the so-called "cold war policy" evolved by the National Security Council in 1958, commanding officers were encouraged to help stimulate a widespread public awareness of the challenges and problems of national security. Inevitably, many interpreted the national peril in their own political terms, and, like General Walker, shaped their attacks accordingly.

The new civilian team in the Pentagon has begun a careful screening of the vast amount of printed and filmed material used by the services in their programs of troop indoctrination and community relations. The only positive step they have taken so far is to ban official use of the film "Communism on the Map," and to relegate "Operation Abolition" to a "when-asked-for" basis of availability.

"But this sort of screening doesn't directly affect General X if he wants to make a speech about communism in the schools or play footsie with the Birch Society people," an official explained. "Unless he gets 'way off base, like General Walker did, we can't discipline him.

"There is a big gray area here where the difference between right and wrong—between saying too much and not saying too much—is terribly hard to distinguish. Who is to tell a three-star admiral how right wing—or how left wing—his political outlook can be?

"Our best hope is that the extremists will begin to get the message themselves, as from General Walker and as from speeches of the secretaries, and use good judgment in what they say and do."

June 18, 1961

EVANGELIST ASKS PUSH ON U.S. REDS

Head of Christian Crusade Stresses Rightist Cause

By JOHN WICKLEIN
Special to The New York Times.

TULSA, Okla., Aug. 5—"Clean up communism internally and America's problem with communism internationally will be solved," a Right-Wing evangelist told his followers assembled in convention here tonight.

The evangelist, the Rev. Billy James Hargis, heads the Christian Crusade, which he calls the largest organization devoted exclusively to opposing domestic communism.

Year round, the Tulsa evangelist brings his message to

the people through daily radio and television talks, and public rallies across the country. He pitches no tents, but rides from auditorium to auditorium in an air-conditioned bus that has offices and sleeping quarters.

Last night his crusade's annual convention opened with a keynote address by Robert H. W. Welch Jr., founder of the ultra-conservative John Birch Society.

To clean up communism in America, Mr. Hargis indicated in an interview, means not only to root out communism, but also to clean up liberalism in Government and religion.

This, he declared, is because the liberals generally follow the Communist party line.

Do-Gooders Assailed

"We conservatives all agree on one thing—that our problem is almost entirely from internal subversion," he commented. In his prepared text he said:

"Were it not for the moral and financial support given in-

ternational communism by misguided do-gooders and outright traitors within this country, international communism would have died on the vine many years ago."

Mr. Hargis has attacked the administration of the National Council of Churches, because of its liberalism, as "one of the greatest threats to internal security that we have."

One of his brochures was used last year in a controversial Air Force manual as documentation for a charge that Communists had infiltrated the Protestant clergy.

Spokesman for the council responded by charging that Mr. Hargis was an opportunist capitalizing on the people's fears of communism for his own aggrandizement.

Mr. Hargis, a stocky, boyish looking teacher who turned 36 yesterday, disavowed any such implications.

"We're just as sincere in this as we can be," he said. "We don't want to be considered nuts or crackpots.

"I honestly feel that our movement has done a lot to hold back religious liberalism and political liberalism from running rampant in this country."

The Christian Crusade, he said, has grown to 100,000 in forty states since he incorporated it in 1950. Then he was pastor of a Disciples of Christ Church in Sapulpa, Okla.

Enjoyed Revivals

"I enjoyed holding revivals and evangelism is that type of work," he said, "and I decided to become an anti-Communist evangelist."

The movement's staff has grown to fifty, moving from a converted church to occupy the entire floor of a downtown Tulsa office building. This fall it expects to build a headquarters of its own on the outskirts of the city.

"My biggest break, so far as promotion is concerned, came in 1953," Mr. Hargis said. "I got the idea of ballooning Bibles into the Iron Curtain countries from West Germany.

The United States Government first confiscated the balloons, he said, but then gave its official approval—and the notoriety over the incident made Mr. Hargis a celebrity. Since then, the crusade has sent millions of scriptures aloft, he said, and will launch more this fall.

Mr. Hargis said his recorded anti-Communist and anti-liberal messages were reproduced by seventy radio stations from New England to the West Coast as public service features.

Most of his support, he said, comes from contributions from people who have been interested in the movement and its literature by the broadcasts.

Budget $75,000 Monthly

The crusade's budget runs to $75,000 a month, he said, about $25,000 each for printing, radio and administration. It mails 250,000 pieces of literature a month, he said. The literature includes pamphlets charging Communist influence in the Supreme Court, the councils of churches and the National Association for the Advancement of Colored People, and opposing racial mixing.

Stickers on cars around the convention hotel read "Impeach Earl Warren."

H. L. Hunt, the Texas oilman, has contributed to several of Mr. Hargis' projects, a spokesman said. "We intend to get other conservative millionaires to contribute to the crusade, without taking over the crusade for their pet ideas," he added.

Mr. Hargis is on the advisory board of the John Birch Society,

and his organization cooperates freely, though unofficially, with other conservative groups working in the same field.

"I feel all of us should do our work independently," the evangelist said. "I'm not interested in unifying all the anti-Communist groups. If we did, then the Communists would have only to knock over one organization, instead of 300 Right-Wing groups."

August 6, 1961

Minutemen Guerrilla Unit Found To Be Small and Loosely Knit

By GLADWIN HILL
Special to The New York Times.

LOS ANGELES, Nov. 11—The perils of the atomic age, apprehensions about the Soviet Union and contemporary currents of ultra-conservatism have combined to produce a strange organization known as The Minutemen.

Sketchy reports in recent weeks have conjured up an alarming picture of the movement, operating under the banner of patriotism, as a secret network of guerrilla bands, involving upward of 25,000 persons.

Pictures have been published of Minutemen on military maneuvers with weapons up to big-bore artillery pieces. There have been rumors of far-flung caches of guns, ammunition and other supplies and reports of numerous secret conclaves.

On Friday a regional Minutemen leader in southern Illinois was exonerated of charges of violating firearms laws.

On the same day another such leader in San Diego, Calif., was arrested on a technicality for questioning about the movement in that state.

Gov. Edmund G. Brown of California has denounced "guerrilla" movements and has mentioned an unconfirmed report of a plan among Minutemen to assassinate him.

The New York Times has made a nation-wide survey to find out the character and extent of the movement.

These are the principal findings, based on reports from all sections of the country:

¶The Minutemen is not an organization in an ordinary sense. It is a very loose federation of small units whose lack of structure casts doubt on its potential for growth.

¶While guerrilla warfare training is its foremost stated aim, the movement is essentially a catch-all group for persons with unfilled enthusiasms for almost anything from military drilling to spying on their neighbors.

¶Its supposed strength is based on uncorroborated claims. Responsible authorities throughout most of the country are unaware of any Minuteman activity. Intensive investigation has confirmed the existence of no more than a few hundred adherents.

¶The identities of only a handful of these—chiefly in southern California—have become known. A number of them are persons of questionable character and responsibility.

¶The chief import of the movement appears to be a disorganized sample of numerous right-wing movements dotting the country whose common denominator is "anti-communism."

¶Maneuvers of Minutemen have been observed only in southern Illinois and San Diego, involving no more than a few dozen persons in each case.

The movement's leader is Robert B. DePugh, 38 years old, of Norborne, Mo. He says he has held "guerrilla warfare seminars" in a number of cities, including Newark, N. J.; Philadelphia, Columbia, Ohio; Kansas City, Mo.; Omaha, Neb., and San Antonia, Tex.

Law enforcement authorities in these cities disclaim knowledge of any such meetings, and numerous other sources have seen no sign of them.

Chicago, Decatur and Champaign, Ill., are other places where Minutemen leaders have said they have units.

Usually Within the Law

Meetings studying guerrilla warfare generally do not violate the law, even if firearms are displayed, if there is no intent of producing public disorder. Federal and state laws throughout the country as a generality ban only possession of workable machine-guns.

Minutemen profess to be practicing for action if the country is "taken over" by an enemy and other public agencies are not functioning.

"We're only exercising our constitutional rights of freedom to bear arms, freedom of assembly and freedom of speech," says Mr. DePugh, a manufacturer of drugs and other compounds for animals.

He reports a national membership of 25,000 in forty states and "all major cities," with daily progress toward a goal of 1,000,000 by 1963.

An organization meeting, involving a dozen persons, was held in the Hilton Hotel in Denver, on Oct. 8. Three weeks before there was a published report of such a meeting in Omaha. But a number of other reported outcroppings of the movement have proved unfounded.

Guerrilla Action Optional

The discrepancy between claims and visible evidences may be largely due to the nature of the movement. Guerrilla practice is only one of its activities, and an optional one—like everything else in the movement.

Its program embraces almost every form of anti-Communist activity from preparing physically for enemy occupation to disseminating right-wing literature.

The movement is open to virtually anyone unconnected with a subversive organization. There are no restrictions as to age, sex or physical condition. There is no formal procedure for expelling members who prove undesirable; they are simply "isolated from vital information" and thereby ostracized.

"Even a felony record is not a bar to membershsip, if a person appears to be now a good citizen," Mr. DePugh said at Los Angeles this week.

Dues are optional, and there is no set program of activities. The movement is divided into autonomous "bands" of no more than fifteen members, which function independently of each other and, to a great extent, of any central organization.

About half the present units, Mr. DePugh says, were previously organized local lay militia groups that affiliated with The Minutemen. Thus the group in southern Illinois still maintains an identity as the Illinois Internal Security Force. The San Diego segment started as the Loyal Order of Mountain Men, led by a photographer of outdoor films.

Ten anonymous regional directors pass down manuals and literature to group leaders. But, Mr. DePugh says, there is no "chain of command" either upward or downward—on the theory that it is in the nature of guerrilla units to operate independently.

Secrecy of membership is maintained, he says, so that members—"many of them doctors, lawyers and professional people, and from all other walks of life"—will not be embarrassed by public "misunderstanding."

Primarily, the secrecy is to prevent the Communists from building a file of prime enemies in the event of a "take-over," he also says.

"I don't even know the members' names," Mr. DePugh says. "All we ask is the name and address of the unit leader—and this can be a pseudonym. I have no way of knowing exactly how many members we have, except that each group is supposed to have a minimum of five and a maximum of fifteen. So I strike an average of eight."

Recruit by Advertisement

Recruiting, now under way for about two years, is done initially through classified advertisements. A typical one recently invited readers to "Join the Minutemen" and described the group as:

"An organization of loyal Americans dedicated to the preservation of both national and individual freedom. Help put real strength into civilian defense. Pledge yourself and your rifle to a free America. For full details write 'Minutemen,' 613 East Alton, Independence, Mo.

This is only a mailing address, at a small building Mr. DePugh owns that is tenanted by a sign painting concern.

The Minutemen's centralized affairs are largely in his hat, his head, his modest home in near-by Norborne and in liaison, he says, he carries on with the nine other founders of the movement. Five of the nine have dispersed from the Independence area to other parts of the country.

They comprise its "executive council," and with 350 others who joined at their invitation, Mr. DePugh says, provide the modest financing for their literature distribution.

The Minutemen disclaim affiliation with any other organization—including a number of others with titular variants on the Revolutionary War name of Minute Men.

Mr. DePugh is non-committal about such other right-wing movements as the John Birch Society, to which he belongs and the Christian Anti-Communist Crusade headed by Dr. Fred C. Schwarz of Long Beach, Calif.

The Minutemen disseminate literature of such organizations, but concentrate mainly on their own, such as Mr. DePugh's monograph, "What's Wrong With Communism?"

He says this has been distributed in high schools to which Minutemen have access — the membership including persons as young as 15.

Asked about The Minutemen, a member of the Birch Society on the West Coast said:

"I think these people are idiots. There are a lot better ways of doing things."

Comments of public officials about The Minutemen movement included:

Utah's National Guard Adjutant, Brig. Gen. Maxwell E. Rich, who is organizing home-guard units following active-duty summons to the principal National Guard units, said:

"There's no need for guerrillas."

Arizona's Civil Defense Director, Col. Ralph Redburn: "We don't want any unorganized mobs in Arizona."

Melville Stark, civil defense director of Riverside County, Calif.:

"Such groups could be very dangerous if controlled by the wrong people. There's no reason for them to be independent of established public agencies."

The Federal Bureau of Investigation has a policy of not acknowledging inquiries in progress, but there are indications that its branches have Minutemen activities under surveillance.

A basic Minutemen tract lists the alternative Communist methods of "armed invasion," "internal revolution" and "non-violent political take-over."

"By getting secret Communists and their fellow-travelers elected or appointed to high Government posts," it says, "they can promote waste, inefficiency, delay preparations for war and turn our own foreign policy against us.

"What do you really know about the Congressmen from your district? The State Senator or State Representative? Could any of these men have been indoctrinated in Communist ideology at some time in their career?

"We must be willing to continue the fight for liberty even though we no longer have the legal support of established authority [and] prepare ourselves to take any action—no matter how brutal—that may be required to renew the protection of the United States Constitution for future generations.

"We must investigate, by means of our own secret memberships, the possible infiltration of Communist sympathizers into American organizations of government, business, labor, religion or education."

Thinks They Know Better

Asked about such intelligence operations, Mr. DePugh said this week:

"We're certainly not trying to compete with the Federal Bureau of Investigation or the Central Intelligence Agency. But on a local basis we feel we're in a better position to know our friends and neighbors than anybody else.

"A lot of people in this country are Communists without knowing it, themselves."

The Minutemen movement started, Mr. DePugh relates, as a result of a discussion among himself and nine friends on a duck hunt. They agreed that the nation's citizens were ill prepared for survival in the open in the event of Communist occupation of the country.

Mr. DePugh has contempt for the existing Federal civil defense organization, regarding it as largely as a group of jobholders. He favors citizens building inexpensive family bomb shelters but thinks they may be useless because the Russians will use "nerve gas and bacteriological warfare" before nuclear bombs.

Against this, he says, the organization is planning to mass produce for its members inexpensive "Minute masks"—plastic body-hoods with chemical-filled breathing tubes.

Mr. DePugh cites justification for the movement in President Kennedy's January remark that:

"We need a nation of Minute Men; citizens who are not only prepared to take up arms, but citizens who regard the preservation of freedom as a basic purpose of their daily life."

He also cites a statement of the House Committee on Un-American Activities in 1960 that "the American people cannot rely completely on this country's armed forces to protect themselves from Communist domination."

This was a reference to non-military aspects of communism.

The Minutemen came into prominence with a "guerrilla warfare seminar" at Shiloh, in southern Illinois, the week-end of Oct. 20. About twenty members attended.

Weapons ranging from ordinary rifles to 81-mm. mortars and 75-mm. recoilless rifles were involved.

Sheriff's deputies arrested Richard Albert Lauchli Jr., the chief supplier of the weapons and district Minutemen coordinator, on a fire arms violation charge. This was dismissed by a magistrate on Friday.

Mr. Lauchli, operator of a machine shop in near-by Collinsville, Ill., has been convicted of illegal possession of firearms and of the theft of arms from a Federal reservation.

Two Leaders in Dispute

The Shiloh publicity touched off public controversy between two San Diego unit leaders about their pre-eminence in the California picture. Their competing references to the existence of around 2.500 minutemen in California—uncorroborated by other evidence—apparently were the foundation for widespread reports of the organization's extent.

One of the men was William F. Colley, 40, free lance photographer.

According to official California state records, he was convicted in 1957 on three counts of sexual molestation of young children and put on ten year's probation with the proviso that he submit to orchibotomy (removal of reproductive powers).

The other man was Don Alderman, an alias for Troy Harold Houghton, 28.

According to state records, he has been in police custody fifteen times in the last eleven years, mostly in burglary cases. Other charges ranged from auto violations to suspicion of rape.

He was convicted in 1952 of tampering with a vehicle, and given a six-month suspended sentence. In 1957 he was convicted of indecent exposure and served two months of a six-month sentence. He was arrested on Friday on a charge of failing to report as a sex offender.

In the dispute over pre-eminence, Colley finally yielded to Alderman and withdrew from public attention.

Leader in California

Mr. DePugh spent last week in Los Angeles purportedly conferring with California unit leaders and addressing small gatherings, mostly in private. He said one had been a group of military reserve officers.

Alderman was with him most of the time, appearing with him at a news conference, and accompanying him to a meeting of civil defense persons in suburban Anaheim.

Mr. DePugh expressed great concern today that Alderman's arrest would greatly harm the movement.

The national Minutemen leader was invited to the Anaheim meeting by Kenneth E. Holloway, a junior high school teacher of history and English.

The teacher said he had had no previous contact with Mr. DePugh but was interested in what he had read about the movement:

"When I found out he was in Los Angeles I asked him to speak to our committee," said Mr. Holloway. "I thought he was very effective."

The teacher said, however, that he had not been impelled to join the movement immediately.

The coordinator of the Anaheim Citizens Civil Defense Committee, Charles E. Griffith, city personnel director, said of Mr. DePugh:

"His talk was particularly objectionable to me. They seemed to be appointing guerrilla committees without any regard for constituted authorities."

November 12, 1961

KENNEDY ASSERTS FAR-RIGHT GROUPS PROVOKE DISUNITY

By TOM WICKER
Special to The New York Times.

LOS ANGELES, Nov. 18 — President Kennedy spoke out tonight against the right-wing John Birch Society and the so-called Minutemen in a speech at a Democratic party dinner here.

The President mentioned neither group by name but left no doubt whom he meant.

[In Atlanta, Senator Barry Goldwater, Arizona Republican, attacked the "radicals in the White House." At a news conference he called President Kennedy "the wagon master" who is "riding on the left wheel all the time."]

The President, in his talk at the Hollywood Palladium, also made his first public response to Edward M. Dealey, publisher of The Dallas Morning News. Mr. Dealey attacked the President at a White House luncheon for "riding Caroline's tricycle" instead of being "a man on horseback."

Some 'Escape Responsibility'

"There have always been those fringes of our society who have sought to escape their own responsibility by finding a simple solution, an appealing slogan or a convenient scapegoat," Mr. Kennedy said.

Now, he continued, "men who are unwilling to face up to the danger from without are convinced that the real danger comes from within."

"They look suspiciously at their neighbors and their leaders," he declared. "They call for 'a man on horseback' because they do not trust the people. They find treason in our finest churches, in our highest court and even in the treatment of our water.

"They equate the Democratic party with the welfare state,

the welfare state with socialism and socialism with communism. They object quite rightly to politics' intruding on the military—but they are anxious for the military to engage in politics."

The President said he and most Americans "take a different view of our peril."

"We know that it comes from without, not within. It must be met by quiet preparedness, not provocative speeches," he continued.

The President warned the nation not to "heed these counsels of fear and suspicion."

"Let us concentrate more on keeping enemy bombers and missiles away from our shores and concentrate less on keeping neighbors away from our shelters," he said.

Mr. Kennedy chose a region in which the John Birch Society has some of its strongest support to make his third and sharpest attack on what he tonight called "the discordant voice of extremism."

In the first two speeches, at Chapel Hill, N. C., and Seattle, he also warned against left-wing and pacifist extremists. His remarks tonight were directed to far-right groups and individuals.

His comment about the "man on horseback" was obviously aimed at Mr. Dealey.

Just as obviously, the John Birch Society was his target when he spoke about persons' finding "treason in our finest churches" and in the Supreme Court. The Birch Society has as a cardinal point of its program the impeachment of Chief Justice Earl Warren.

The reference to "armed bands of civilian guerrillas" appeared to be directed at the Minutemen, individual groups of which are being organized and armed in some parts of the country. The organization is reported to be particularly strong in California.

Los Angeles is regarded almost as the heartland of the Birch Society. Two Republican Representatives from its urban districts, John H. Rousselot and Edgar W. Hiestand, are avowed members.

The President spoke in Phoenix last night and left there early this morning for Perrin Air Force Base in Texas on his way to the funeral of House Speaker Sam Rayburn.

One of his purposes in coming to California tonight was to unite the Democrats in an early send-off for the re-election campaign of Gov. Edmund G. Brown.

The President endorsed Governor Brown's candidacy in next year's gubernatorial election.

The $300,000 expected to come from tonight's $100-a-plate dinner will bring to more than $700,000 the amounts raised for the party by three Presidential appearances on his current swing through the West.

November 19, 1961

AID TO RIGHT WING LAID TO BIG FIRMS

Anti-Defamation Unit Holds They Donate Major Part of $14 Million Fund

By IRVING SPIEGEL

Some of the nation's "most public-spirited corporations and foundations" provide a major part of the $14 million a year that groups on the radical right have been spending in an "assault on democratic progress," the Anti-Defamation League of B'nai B'rith charged yesterday.

Dore Schary, the national chairman of the league, said his agency's survey showed that the financial support for these groups might rise to as much as $25 million this year.

In addition, he said, this year's figure will be increased by $1.5 million from "lunatic-fringe groups," which he defined as those that "include religious and racial bigotry in their extremist views."

Mr. Schary made his charges at a news conference at the league's headquarters, at 316 Lexington Avenue.

He explained that, in the league's view, the radical right is made up of those who ascribe alleged socialism to sinister plots in high places.

"The lunatic fringe," he continued, "while it cannot be classified as part of the radical right, and certainly not of its conservative supporters, nevertheless joins the bandwagon and adds the extra noxious ingredient of racial and religious bigotry."

Although there was no immediate comment from most of the major groups mentioned in the league report, the chairman of the board of the Gulf Oil Corporation was sharply critical of the survey. Other criticism was voiced by the president of Harding College and the public relations officer of the John Birch Society.

The league's findings are the result of a four-year survey by Arnold Forster, general counsel, and Benjamin R. Epstein, national director of the league. Their findings will be published by Random House on Oct. 9 as a book, "Danger on the Right."

Mr. Forster, co-author of the book, said that the radical right became a matter of concern to the league more than four years ago. The book, he said, was planned and written during the last year and was finished before Senator Barry Goldwater's nomination at the Republican National Convention.

In this connection, Mr. Schary, a playwright and producer, said that the book should not be considered an attack on the Republican party or Mr. Goldwater, but that its publication in book form before the election was a coincidence.

The report identified the radical right groups and their leaders as the John Birch Society, Robert H. W. Welch Jr.; the Christian Anti-Communist Crusade, Dr. Frederick C. Schwarz; Christian Crusade, the Rev. Billy James Hargis; Dan Smoot Report, Dan Smoot; Church League of America, Edgar Bundy; Conservative Society of America, Mr. Bundy and Phoebe and Kent Courtney; and the Liberty Amendment Committee of the U.S.A., Willis Stone.

The report did not identify any "lunatic-fringe" groups.

Mr. Schary said that the radical right was a "magnet for bigots" that rejected the "traditional tolerance and live-let-live tradition of our two-party system . . . it tends to see history as a conspiracy of evil and faithless men."

The survey listed as heavy contributors to radical right and conservative groups such corporations as Republic Steel, United States Steel, Gulf Oil and the Humble Oil and Refining Company.

These corporations, as well as foundations, the survey said, have made large donations to the National Education Program, which operates from Harding College, Searcy, Ark. Dr. George S. Benson is president of the college and director of the National Education Program.

Mr. Schary described the education program "as the largest producer of radical right propaganda in the country."

Contributions Cited

Mr. Schary said that "often the members and sometimes even the heads of these companies are not aware of the way to which their contributions are being used."

Gifts to right-wing groups, Mr. Schary said, are sometimes lumped with grants to schools, colleges, churches and other recipients "whose work is entirely free of any political connotation."

Through a five-year period up to 1963, the survey said, Republic Steel contributed $140,000 to Dr. Benson's "educational and propaganda activities"; United States Steel gave $33,000; Gulf Oil, $55,000, and Olin Mathieson Chemical Corporation, $57,000.

Sharp criticism of the league's report was made by William J. Whiteford, the chairman of the board of Gulf Oil, who pointed out that his corporation annually distributed more than $1.5 million to 600 universities and colleges "for the purpose of aiding them to carry out the large and increasing costly task of preparing our young people for the future."

Mr. Whiteford said that Harding College was a fully accredited institution "operating in an area where the educational opportunities and indeed all other kinds of opportunities are deficient."

"The fact that some of the people connected with this institution," he said, "have been vociferously anti-Communist is about as relevant as is the fact that some notorious Communists have been graduated by Harvard University to which Gulf also contributes, and indeed, in larger sums than it gives to Harding."

A spokesman for United States Steel said that no comment would be made until a study of the league's report had been made. Other corporations were not available for immediate comment.

Dr. Benson stressed over the telephone that "neither Harding College nor the National Education Program is associated with extreme literature or other materials" and "avoids being associated with bigotry and racism."

The educator also said that "Harding and the National Education Program were not anti-Jewish nor anti-colored," pointing out that there were Jewish and Negro students at the college.

"We are not," he said, "partisan in politics. We do not endorse political candidates or any political party."

He said that his college and the program "stand for the principles that made America the foremost nation in the world—faith in God, the constitutional government and private ownership of property."

At his home in San Marino, Calif., John Rousselot, the public relations director for the Birch Society, declined to make detailed comment on the survey, saying that he has not had an opportunity to read the report.

However, he said, "on the basis of previous experience in listening to comments of Dore Schary and his very sophomoric approach to the problems that face our nation, it would be perfectly understandable to learn that he has not yet learned the truth about the John Birch Society or any segment of the organized conservative movement in this country." He went on:

"We will now expect B'nai

B'rith to do an extensive, detailed study of the Communist criminal conspiracy and its internal and external threat to this country."

Dr. Benson's program, the survey said, also received support from foundations. The report listed the Sloan Foundation, with contributions of $600,-000; Armco Steel Foundation, $67,500; Allen-Bradley Foundation, $60,000; the Donner Foundation (now called the Independence Foundation), $38,000;

the Rosa Mary Foundation, $35,-000; the Texas Educational Association, $47,250; the Stockham Foundation, $25,000; the Houston Endowment, $20,000, and assorted other foundations with a "reported total of almost $175,000 over a period of years."

Financial support for the extremist groups, the report said, comes from 70 or more foundations, almost all tax-exempt; more than 100 business concerns and corporations; some 250 individuals who have contributed

at least $500 each, and "hundreds of thousands of one-to-five-dollar givers who have been frightened by the propaganda barrage and have succumbed to it."

The report listed the Allen-Bradley Corporation of Milwaukee, and Technicolor, Inc., a holding company whose subsidiaries include Eversharp, Inc., as contributors to the Christian Anti-Communism Crusade. Patrick Frawley Jr. was named as an official of Technicolor

"with radical right interests."

One of the largest individual contributors to extreme rightist causes, the survey said, was J. Howard Pew of Philadelphia of the Sun Oil interests.

Established in 1913, the Anti-Defamation League is devoted to combating anti-Semitism in this country and to the promotion of civil rights and civil liberties. It maintains 26 offices throughout the country.

September 20, 1964

EASTLAND CALLS WARREN PRO-RED

Says His Court Decisions Favor the Communists

By United Press International.

WASHINGTON, May 2 — Senator James O. Eastland, Democrat of Mississippi, said today that Chief Justice Earl Warren "decides for the Communists" whenever there is a clear-cut Supreme Court decision between them and the security of the United States.

Mr. Eastland, chairman of the Senate Judiciary Committee, made the charge during Senate debate on the Administration's literacy test bill.

Commenting on Mr. Eastland's charge, Senator Hubert H. Humphrey of Minnesota, the assist-

ant Democratic leader, said in a statement that "the Chief Justice is a great American and a courageous and learned judge."

In another comment, Senator Kenneth B. Keating, Republican of New York, said:

"However one may disagree with a specific decision of the Supreme Court, I do not consider that it serves a useful purpose to attack the character or motivation of the judge rendering the opinion."

Senator Eastland read to the Senate what he called a "box score" of each justice's votes in decisions that he said involved communism or subversion.

The tabulation, he said, measured votes against positions advocated by the Communist party or Communist sympathizers in the cases in question. The designations he gave were "pro" and "con." "Pro," Mr. Eastland said, meant "pro-Communist."

The box score read as follows:

Justice Hugo L. Black—102 pro, 0 con.

Justice Felix Frankfurter—69 pro, 34 con.

Justice William O. Douglas—97 pro, 3 con.

Justice Tom C. Clark—21 pro, 61 con.

Chief Justice Warren — 62 pro, 3 con.

Justice John Marshall Harlan—30 pro, 35 con.

Justice William J. Brennan Jr.—49 pro, 2 con.

Justice Charles Evans Whittaker, retired—12 pro, 30 con.

Justice Potter Stewart—6 pro, 14 con.

Senator Jacob K. Javits, Republican of New York, asked Senator Eastland whose criteria had been used in compiling the box score. Mr. Eastland said his staff had made the compilation, and added:

"Any lawyer with any sense could do it."

Mr. Eastland spoke on the seventh day of a Southern filibuster against an Administration-backed bill to outlaw literacy tests for voters. Under the bill, anyone with a sixth-

grade education would be eligible to vote in a Federal election.

The bill's supporters argue that some Southern registrars use unfair literacy tests to disenfranchise Negro voters. Southern opponents of the legislation argue that it is unconstitutional.

Mr. Eastland's "box score" dealt with cases before, as well as after Mr. Warren was named Chief Justice in 1953 by President Dwight D. Eisenhower.

Since Mr. Warren was appointed, Senator Eastland said, the high court has decided seventy cases involving communism or subversion.

"Forty-six of these decisions have sustained the position advocated by the Communists and twenty-four have been to the contrary," the Senator said.

"The Chief Justice of the United States, when there is a clear-cut decision between the Communist party and the security of the country, decides for the Communists," Mr. Eastland told the Senate.

May 3, 1962

6 CAMPS FOR REDS SET UP, THEN CLOSED

WASHINGTON, May 4 (AP) —The Government had six camps ready to confine American Communists in case of an emergency but they were abandoned or turned to other uses five years ago, the Justice Department reports.

The department's comment yesterday was in reply to charges of two alleged Communist party leaders, Benjamin Davis and Gus Hall, that the Government had "concentration camps" to confine what they termed "hundreds of thousands" of persons to be prosecuted under the 1950 Internal Security Act.

Mr. Hall and Mr. Davis have been indicted by a Federal

Grand Jury on a charge of failing to register as Communist party officials under the act. The Federal Bureau of Investigation estimates that there are 8,000 to 10,000 Communist party members in the United States.

The camps were at Avon Park, Fla., Allenwood, Pa., El Reno, Okla., Tule Lake, Calif., and Wickenberg and Florence Ariz.

The department said the Allenwood and Florence camps were being used to confine 550 minimum security Federal prisoners. The Wickenberg camp has been turned into a school. The Avon Park installation was converted into a state prison camp. The El Reno camp is being razed and the Yule Lake camp houses migratory workers.

May 5, 1962

$3,500,000 AWARD IS MADE TO FAULK IN LIBEL VERDICT

By JOHN SIBLEY

A State Supreme Court jury awarded $3,500,000 last night to John Henry Faulk, former radio and television entertainer, in his libel suit against Aware, Inc.; Vincent W. Hartnett, and the late Laurence A. Johnson.

In the suit, filed six years ago, Mr. Faulk charged that he had been dismissed by the Columbia Broadcasting System and blacklisted in the radio-television industry because of a pamphlet issued by Aware that linked him to a Communist conspiracy.

Mr. Faulk's lawyer, Louis Nizer, said that to his knowledge the verdict was the largest ever awarded in a libel action. Other lawyers agreed that it was by far the largest.

The verdict came at 11:40 P. M. after an eleven-week trial. The case had gone to the jury at 5:30 P. M., two hours after the panel was told that Mr. Johnson, a 73-year-old retired operator of supermarkets upstate, had died earlier this week in a Bronx motel.

One Motion Denied

The verdict specified compensatory damages of $1,000,000 against the three defendants jointly, and punitive damages of $1,250,000 each against Aware and Mr. Hartnett, who calls himself a "consultant" on communism.

Thomas A. Bolan, the defense lawyer, immediately moved to set aside the verdict against Aware and Mr. Hartnett as contrary to the weight of evidence and the law. Justice Abraham N. Geller denied this motion. Mr. Bolan then moved to set aside the awards as excessive. Justice Geller reserved decision on this, and directed both lawyers to submit briefs on the question.

Harry G. Liese, a lawyer whom Justice Geller had named earlier in the day as temporary administrator of the Johnson estate, then made identical motions and received the same rulings.

In his summation, Mr. Nizer had asked for a large award "to let the world know that in America we won't tolerate these private vigilante groups."

Mr. Nizer conceded last night that Mr. Faulk would not be able to collect the total amount awarded. He expressed confidence, however, that he could collect the $1,000,000 in compensatory damages from the Johnson estate. In this situation, all defendants are liable and the plaintiff may collect wherever he is able. Mr. Johnson was a multi-millionaire.

However, neither Mr. Hartnett nor Aware has substantial wealth, and it appeared doubtful they could pay more than a small fraction of the punitive damages.

Aware was incorporated in 1953 "to combat the Communist conspiracy in entertainment-communications." Its activities have dropped off since the middle Nineteen Fifties, but it still holds occasional meetings under its current president, Alexander C. Dick, a lawyer.

The award to Mr. Faulk was especially unusual because the punitive damages were more than Mr. Nizer had requested. He had asked the jury for $1,000,000 punitive damages against each defendant.

At 10:20 P. M. the jury returned to the courtroom to ask whether it could legally exceed the plaintiff's request. Justice Geller replied:

"The jury should weigh carefully the amounts requested by the plaintiff, although you are not bound by them. But the jury may not, because of Johnson's death, increase the amount of punitive damages which they would have awarded against Aware and Hartnett."

Confusion Over Death

The jury of eight men and four women divided 11 to 1 on the verdict. In a civil suit, a 10-to-2 verdict is sufficient. The dissenting juror, Miss Theresa V. Dermody, would not discuss her reasons.

As the jury foreman, Ralph R. Rosenfeld, read the verdict, an audience of about thirty-five spectators fell silent. When he finished, a loud gasp from Mr. Faulk's wife, Lynne, could be heard throughout the courtroom.

Yesterday was the Faulks' fourteenth wedding anniversary.

Mr. Faulk, appearing quietly elated, rose from the counsel table and warmly shook hands with each juror, including Miss Dermody. Miss Dermody approached Mr. Hartnett and exchanged a few words with him before she left the courtroom.

Mr. Nizer said he believed the largest previous libel award was in a case he also had handled. This was a verdict of $175,000 he helped win for Quentin Reynolds against Westbrook Pegler and others.

The trial was thrown into confusion during the closing hours Wednesday when news reached the courtroom that Mr. Johnson's body had been found. Positive identification of the body was made yesterday morning in the Jacobi Hospital morgue by Mr. Johnson's son-in-law, Donald J. Giancola of Syracuse.

Mr. Johnson is believed to have died of natural causes.

Justice Geller spent Wednesday night searching law books for a previous case in which a defendant had died after both sides rested their cases but before the jury began deliberating.

He could find none. Mr. Bolan contended Mr. Johnson should be removed from the case altogether.

Justice Geller rejected this contention, but granted a stay of execution until Oct. 1 of any award that might be made against the Johnson estate. This was to permit Mr. Bolan to ask the Appellate Division to remove Mr. Johnson's heirs from liability.

Mr. Bolan also made it clear he would appeal the over-all case on other grounds. During the trial, he had moved three times for a mistrial, on the ground that Justice Geller had received evidence that was legally inadmissable and prejudicial to the defendants.

The defense attorney had objected particularly to a parade of prominent actors, commentators, directors and producers who testified about the practice of blacklisting in the broadcasting industry.

These included David Susskind, Charles Collingwood, Kim Hunter, Mark Goodson, Garry Moore and Tony Randall.

Blacklisting Opposed

Mr. Faulk's trouble with Aware began late in 1955, when he was elected a director of the American Federation of Television and Radio Artists. He had campaigned on a "middle-of-the-road" slate that opposed communism and the blacklisting activities of Aware.

The Aware bulletin that attacked him as a principal spokesman of the slate was published on Feb. 10, 1956. It charged that he had been scheduled to entertain at a number of Communist-front affairs.

At the close of the defense's case, Justice Geller ruled that the defendants had not proved the truth of the accusations against Mr. Faulk. He ruled further that they could not plead the defense of fair comment, the only other complete defense in a libel suit in New York State.

Mr. Bolan was left with only one argument to present to the jury in his summation: that Mr. Hartnett, in compiling the material for the Aware bulletin, had relied in good faith on trustworthy sources.

Mr. Johnson did not appear in his own defense during the trial. Mr. Bolan presented a physician to testify that he was too ill to undergo cross examination.

A doctor selected by Mr. Nizer also examined Mr. Johnson and said he could testify without endangering his health.

Numerous witnesses testified that Mr. Johnson had threatened to remove from his stores the products of companies that sponsored or hired performers he regarded as pro-Communist. These were said to have included Mr. Faulk.

Mr. Hartnett, who spent several days on the witness stand, described his work as a "consultant" on the political backgrounds of figures in the broadcasting industry.

He was the principal author of "Red Channels," a 1951 book that listed entertainers with alleged pro-Communist affiliations. This volume, several witnesses said, became the blacklisting "Bible" for executives of the networks and advertising agencies in broadcasting.

Mr. Faulk was not listed in "Red Channels," although the events he was linked to in the Aware bulletin had occurred before its publication.

June 29, 1962

Pacifist Testifies Nazis And Reds May Aid Group

By HEDRICK SMITH
Special to The New York Times.

WASHINGTON, Dec. 13—The leader of an American women's pacifist movement told a Congressional committee today she would welcome Communists, Nazis, and Fascists to the movement to serve the cause of peace.

Mrs. Dagmar Wilson, founder of Women Strike for Peace, added that "unless everybody in the whole world joins us in this fight, then God help us."

She was the final witness called in three days of hearings by a three-member subcommittee of the House Committee on Un-American Activities.

The subcommittee has been investigating alleged Communist infiltration of peace groups, especially the Women Strike for Peace movement in the metropolitan New York-New Jersey-Connecticut area.

Her Answers Applauded

Mrs. Wilson, a well-known illustrator of children's books from Washington, told the committee she would "certainly not" take steps to purge Communists from the organization if it had been infiltrated as the committee suggested.

Asked if she would make the movement equally open to Nazis and Fascists, she replied: "If only we could get them on our side."

Her answers were roundly applauded by an audience of 500 persons, mostly women wearing emblems of Women Strike for Peace. Two busloads of women had come from New York City and another 19 had come by train from Chicago, Pittsburgh. Cleveland, Detroit and Ann Arbor, Mich.

Mrs. Wilson was one of three witnesses summoned today. The others were Dr. William Obrinsky of Staten Island, N.Y., and John W. Darr Jr., of New York.

Both men were asked about alleged Communist party membership and both refused to give the committee any information except their names and addresses.

Responses Evoke Laughter

Dr. Obrinsky, identified by the committee as founder of the Staten Island Community Peace Group, invoked the Fifth Amendment 33 times. Mr. Darr, chairman of the Greenwich Village Peace Center, said that he could not reply for reasons of conscience and because he felt the committee's questions violated his rights of free speech and association under the First Amendment.

But Mrs. Wilson, a pert and attractive brunette wearing a red dress, was clearly the favorite of the audience.

The audience stood and gave her strong applause when she was called to testify. One woman carrying an infant in orange rompers presented her with a bouquet of flowers and the hearing was interrupted for several minutes while photographers snapped her picture.

Frequently, both the audience and the committee were moved to laughter by her responses.

At one point, Alfred M. Nittle, the committee counsel, asked her is she had co-ordinated simultaneous demonstrations in 58 American cities on Nov. 1, 1961.

There were growing snickers and then a burst of laughter when Mrs. Wilson suggested that the spontaneity of the feminine peace movement was "hard to explain to the masculine mind."

The committee emphasized that it did not suspect Mrs. Wilson of Communist party membership or sympathies. But Mr. Nittle suggested that control of Women Strike for Peace had slipped from the 46-year-old housewife's hands.

He sought to prove that it had fallen under domination of the New York branch. And he contended that some of this group's leaders had been identified previously as Communists or, during this week's hearings, had refused to answer such questions about alleged Communist affiliations.

"Nobody is controlled by anybody in Women Strike for Peace," Mrs. Wilson commented.

Of the 11 witnesses summoned by the subcommittee to public hearings this week, nine refused to answer such questions and were applauded by the partisan audience.

After the hearing concluded, Mrs. Wilson said "the solid support of the women for those who took the Fifth (Amendment) is an indication that we are simply not concerned with personal points of view."

The committee formally thanked Mrs. Wilson for her co-operation. But after the hearing one member, Representative William Tuck, Democrat of Virginia, criticized her stand.

He told reporters he was "shocked to hear Mrs. Wilson state that she would encourage members of the Communist party to occupy positions of leadership in Women Strike for Peace."

A committee spokesman disclosed that a large number of letters had been received protesting the hearings, but he did not give the exact number.

About 70 of the women left the final hearings and marched 20 blocks to the White House. There, they marched for five minutes with signs reading, "End the Arms Race, Not the Human Race" and "Peace is American."

Seven members of Women Strike for Peace met last night with Arthur M. Schlesinger, Jr., a special assistant to President Kennedy. A spokesman said they sought an audience with the President to press for disarmament and an end to nuclear testing, but received no promises of such an appointment.

December 14, 1962

Keating Sings Out for Freedom of Hootennany

By WARREN WEAVER Jr.
Special to The New York Times

WASHINGTON, Sept. 26 — Unsupported by beard or banjo, Senator Kenneth B. Keating took to the Senate floor today to defend folk music against charges of Communist subversion.

With tongue in cheek, the New York Republican told his colleagues he had discovered that "the Communists have developed a new secret weapon to ensnare and capture youthful minds in America—folk music."

His source for this conclusion, Senator Keating said, was a resolution approved last month by the Fire and Police Research Association of Los Angeles, an organization consisting largely of firemen and policemen who collect information on various "social issues" during off-duty hours.

The association's directors had charged in the resolution that "certain of the hootennanies have been used to brainwash and subvert, 'n a seemingly innocuous but actually covert and deceptive manner, vast segments of young peoples' groups."

Examples Are Cited

The curious thing about Senator Keating's defense of folk music was that the more closely he examined a series of songs of his own choosing, the more evidence he seemed to find to support the Los Angeles association — and to make fun of it.

In an 1808 version of "Yankee Doodle," the Senator found Americans singing of plans to violate an embargo on French imports, an order that President Thomas Jefferson had made because it was curbing the local supply of brandy.

In "Darlin' Cory" and "Copper Kettle," Mr. Keating detected strong appeals to resist the lawful endeavors of revenue agents ("gonna tear your still house down") and tax collectors ("we ain't paid no whisky tax since 1792.")

The Senator spotted evidence of "this sinister folk music plot for disarmament" in these familiar spiritual lines:

Gonna lay down my sword and shield
Down by the riverside
And study war no more

Submits Lengthy Blacklist

But having examined his own evidence, the Senator found that he did not care for the conclusions. He added:

"And so now, to the list of subversive individuals, institutions and ideas, which includes the United Nations, the income tax, the Chief Justice of the United Sttes, the Girl Scouts of America, fluoridation of the water supply, the last four Presidents of the United States, beatniks, Harvard University, civil rights demonstrations, expenditures for mental health, the Arms Control and Disarmament Agency, coffee houses, every Secretary of State since William Jennings Bryan, professors of anthropology, back-door spending, metro government, Jews, Time Magazine, the Council on Foreign Relations, firearms registration, the Protestant clergy, the two United States Senators from New York plus between 77 and 83 of their colleagues and proposals for Federal aid to mass transportation— to this list we must now add, merciful heavens, American folk music!"

Senator Keating concluded that the Constitution "protects the right of everyone to sing out as well as speak out whenever the spirit moves him."

September 27, 1963

U.S. Balked by Court On Registering Reds

By ANTHONY LEWIS
Special to The New York Times

WASHINGTON, June 8—The Supreme Court left standing today a decision reversing the conviction of the Communist party for failing to register under the Internal Security Act.

The United States Court of Appeals here handed the decision down last Dec. 17. It held that the Government could not make the party register unless it proved that some individual, acting for the party, was willing to run the risk of self-incrimination.

The Supreme Court denied without comment today a Government petition for review of that decision. The result is another setback in the 14-year effort to enforce the Internal Security Act.

Today was a surprisingly light day at the Supreme Court. The Justices handed down a half-dozen opinions but did not deal with any of the major cases of great public interest that are awaiting decision.

First among these are six cases testing whether the districts in one or both houses of state legislatures must be substantially equal in population. The suits come from New York, Alabama, Maryland, Virginia, Delaware and Colorado.

In five sit-in cases the Court is considering the right of state law enforcement forces to punish persons protesting racial discrimination at privately owned places of business. Other cases present large issues of criminal law, obscenity and antitrust law.

Thirty argued cases are now awaiting decision in the Court, and the general expectation is that the Court will dispose of them before adjourning for the summer. The earliest date for ending the session is two weeks from today, June 22. But the Court may sit until June 29 or even later.

The requirement that the Communist party register under the act of 1950 was upheld by the Supreme Court in 1961. The party has steadfastly refused to comply.

In December, 1962, the party was indicted for violating the act and convicted by a jury. It was fined $120,000—a fine that was set aside by the Court of Appeals ruling.

Sanctions Applied

The difficulty in making the party register has not prevented various sanctions from coming into effect under the act of 1950. This has been so because the law applies certain penalties to organizations under orders to register, and their members, whether they comply or not.

Thus a provision of the law forbidding the issuance of passports to members of a party under orders to register has been invoked. The Supreme Court now has before it a case testing the constitutionality of this passport ban.

Nevertheless, the Government is evidently determined to complete the registration process if possible. Its petition for review in the Supreme Court said that the Court of Appeals decision would "seriously handicap the enforcement of the entire statute."

"The decision means," the petition continued, "that unless the Government can prove that volunteers will register the party, the act becomes totally inapplicable to the very organization most clearly within its terms.

"Moreover, the act probably cannot effectively be applied to Communist front organizations unless the Government similarly can prove the availability of volunteers."

The Court of Appeals opinion, by Chief Judge David L. Bazelon, relied on the fact that so many criminal laws were now aimed at the Communist party. He said:

"Mere association with the party incriminates."

Open to Prosecution

Any party official who filed a registration statement might therefore be opening the way to his own prosecution, Judge Bazelon said. And he held that officers could prevent that by invoking the Fifth Amendment's privilege against compelled self-incrimination.

The opinion said that some "volunteer" might be willing to submit the party's registration for it. But the court concluded that the Government must prove the existence of such a "volunteer."

The Government objected to having the burden of this proof put upon it. The party, it said, should have been made to show that no willing lawyer or agent was available.

The way is still open to the Government to try the party again for not registering and then attempt to offer the missing proof. Whether to do so will have to be decided now at the highest levels in the Justice Department.

If the Government lawyers decide that they cannot prove the existence of such a "volunteer," the effort to make the party register will presumably have to be abandoned.

June 9, 1964

The F.B.I. in American Life: Two Views of the Part It Plays

On these pages are two reviews, from widely divergent viewpoints, of a controversial book, "The F.B.I. Nobody Knows" by Fred J. Cook (436 pp., New York: The Macmillan Company, $5.95).

Mr. Kunstler, who defends the book, is a trial lawyer who has taught at New York University, served as counsel with the American Civil Liberties Union and the Southern Christian Leadership Conference, and written many books on crime and legal justice in America—most recently, the best-selling account of the Hall-Mills case, "The Minister and the Choir Singer."

Mr. Morris, who presents the case against the book, is a columnist and lawyer who has served as counsel for the U. S. Senate Internal Security Subcommittee, Municipal Court Justice for the City of New York and president of the University of Dallas, and written two books on Communist tactics, "No Wonder We Are Losing" (1958) and "Disarmament: Weapon of Conquest" (1963).

By WILLIAM M. KUNSTLER

THIS book has been a long time coming. After the open adulation of Frederick L. Collins's "The FBI in Peace and War," the press agentry of Don Whitehead's "The FBI Story," and the bouquets regularly tossed its way by politicians on the make, veterans' organizations and its own director, the Federal Bureau of Investigation has at last been put into proper perspective. For this admirable feat, veteran reporter Fred J. Cook will undoubtedly be stoned throughout the land.

To corral a sacred cow of this sanctity is to invite instant retaliation. No better example of such reaction exists than the case of industrialist Cyrus Eaton who, during a 1958 television interview, dared to classify the F.B.I. as "just one of scores of agencies in the United States engaged in investigating, in snooping, in informing, in creeping up on people." The words were scarcely out of his mouth when the House Un-American Activities Committee proclaimed that it intended to investigate him. Only the Cleveland millionaire's bold defiance saved him from a harassing Congressional inquisition.

Several months later, it became widely known that The New York Post was busily gathering material for an uninhibited study of the Bureau. Long before the series ever saw print, the public was alerted by no less figures than the national commander of the American Legion, Cardinal Cushing and Maryland's Senator John Marshall Butler that the newspaper intended to vilify J. Edgar Hoover. When these wholly unjustified attacks failed to deter the Post, one of its major advertisers was warned by Hoover himself that the proposed articles were, he felt, "a smear."

More recently, the Senate Internal Security Subcommittee turned its subpoena sights on the Pacifica Foundation. The latter, which operates listener-supported radio stations in New York and California, had aired interviews with two former F.B.I. agents who were highly critical of the Bureau's personnel policies. Barely a month later, seven Pacifica officials were ordered to appear before the Subcommittee in Washington.

These incidents—and they are not isolated — are significant because they underscore the fact that the F.B.I. has come to be considered all but infallible. When relatively mild reproof brings down the wrath of legislative investigating committees, when cardinals and congressmen join forces to prejudge newspaper articles even before they are written, when most Americans equate criticism of the Bureau with subversion or worse, then we must face up to the fact that we have, for the first time in our history, created the sacrosanct official. The next stage, Cook maintains glumly, is the police state.

Paradoxically, the F.B.I., whose immunity from criticism is the direct result of a monumental propaganda campaign spanning four decades, was born in secrecy. In 1908, Theodore Roosevelt's Attorney General, Charles J. Bonaparte, asked the Sixtieth Congress to approve the creation of a permanent detective force within the Department of Justice When his request was refused, Bonaparte waited until Congress had adjourned and then quietly established the very unit it had failed to authorize. Called the Bureau of Investigation (it was not to receive its present name until 1935), it quickly became a permanent Washington fixture.

From this surreptitious beginning, the agency has grown into a bureaucratic behemoth which employs almost 15,000 people and receives an annual appropriation of more than $130,000,000. According to the Congressional Record for June 13, 1963, it controls "almost 50 per cent of the entire personnel and appropriated funds for the Department of Justice as a whole." Only recently did Congress wake up to the sobering fact that this tremendous power was concentrated in the hands of one man who, as Senator Everett M. Dirksen put it, "is not legally required to be appointed by the President, nor is confirmation by the Senate required."

It is the extent of this power and the character of the man who wields it that frighten Fred Cook. While he is quick to recognize J. Edgar Hoover's very real accomplishments in building an efficient and apparently financially incorruptible organization, in establishing a central fingerprint file, and in stimulating the extensive use of technology in crime detection, he is just as quick to condemn the deliberate conversion of a government official into a national monument. "The phenomenon of universal praise," he declares, "can hardly be good for Hoover, for the bureau he heads or, for the American people."

It is not simply Hoover's carefully engineered publicity or unabashed credit-pirating that worries Cook. If that were all there was to the F.B.I. chief, there would be little need for another, even if considerably more realistic, book about him. The fact is, says Cook, that Hoover, secure in the conviction that he is above reproach, has become a prime architect of the political strategy of American reaction.

This is strong stuff indeed, but Cook has assembled a wealth of material to support his case. Starting with Hoover's key role in the infamous Palmer

Raids that punctuated World War I, he has methodically traced the director's steady right oblique toward the day when he would publicly bestow his blessing on the likes of Joe McCarthy. That this trend continues unabated is evidenced by the fact that, at this writing, he is lending aid and comfort to the Southern racists by giving respectability to their outlandish claims that the civil-rights movement is nothing more or less than a Communist plot to divide America.

"The pattern makes it clear," Cook states, "that, behind the scenes, loftily above the battle and unsmudged by the battle smoke, Hoover has been the heart and soul of the witchhunt era. His persistent overestimation of the threat of domestic Communism has been a major factor in creating a national mood of hysteria and unreason. His predilection for the use of such imprecise terms as 'fellow traveler' and 'pseudo liberal' has fostered the technique, so beloved by the right, of spattering with the treason label all liberal ideas and liberal opponents."

When Attorney General Harlan Fiske Stone named Hoover, then 29, to succeed the discredited William J. Burns as the Bureau's head in 1924, he was quite conscious of these dangers. "The Bureau of Investigation," Stone warned his new appointee, "is not concerned with political or other opinions of individuals. It is concerned only with their conduct and then only with such conduct as is forbidden by the laws of the United States. When a police system passes beyond these limits, it is dangerous to the proper administration of justice and to human liberty, which it should be our first concern to cherish."

According to Cook, Hoover has long since exceeded those limits. Under the classic guise of combating subversion, he has, by every means at his disposal, relentlessly pursued the

minds of those whose opinions are left of right. The result has been an age of conformity in which free discussion of vital issues has been inhibited by a genuine fear that the man on the fifth floor of Justice may not like what is being said. It was precisely this fearsome possibility that the Sixtieth Congress had in mind when it rejected the Roosevelt Administration's request for a new Federal detective force.

"The F.B.I. That Nobody Knows" cannot fail to be one of the most significant and widely discussed books of the year. Meticulously documented, superbly written and thoughtfully restrained, it will, hopefully, restore public inquiry to an area where, for too many quiescent years, it has been virtually nonexistent. And, in the process, it may pose the unsettling question as to why, in a hero-conscious nation, only a policeman has ever qualified as a demigod.

By ROBERT MORRIS

THE author here, to use a Navy expression, tries to blow the F.B.I. out of the water. He clearly charges that the F.B.I. framed Alger Hiss by "forgery by typewriter." He contends that the efforts of the executed Communist spies, the Rosenbergs, constituted "a fumbling amateurish type of endeavor that did not accomplish much." He insists that the Harry Dexter White case was a "ghoulish exhibition of the witch hunt." To Mr. Cook, John Dillinger was a minor hoodlum who was built into a legend by J. Edgar Hoover; the testimony of Elizabeth Bentley about Soviet espionage was "infinitely suspect"; the internal threat of Communism is "so negligible that it is a puny kitten" and F.B.I. concern in this area is the result of Mr. Hoover's "fixation" and "fetish" about the "Communist menace." He writes with especial horror of the cult of the "informer."

I spent many years with the United States Navy and the United States Senate working

in internal security. There are only a few ways of ascertaining Communist secrets and identities. The orthodox method is securing the sworn testimony of a witness who was a Communist and sat at the secret councils. This taking of testimony from eyewitnesses to an act is the essence of our judicial system.

If this direct testimony is to be rejected as the tattling of an "informer," then authorities must resort to the use of legal wiretapping and other electronic devices or to the planting of counteragents among the Communists to ascertain what they are doing. Every one of these possible sources of information receives the strong condemnation of Mr. Cook. Clearly, he does not want the F.B.I. learning what the Communists are doing.

Yet, when the author makes his case against the F.B.I., his prime source is what he himself would have to call an "informer." Jack Levine was an F.B.I. agent for almost 11 months, and his unsworn allegations and writings are the principal basis of Mr. Cook's case.

Mr. Levine resigned as an agent in August, 1961. He reapplied three weeks later and again in October and November of that year, expressing his "continued interest and loyalty to the bureau." Only after he was rejected, for "substandard work," did he commence his campaign against Mr. Hoover. The platform of his charges was a 38-page unsworn statement to Robert Kennedy's Criminal Division Chief, Herbert J. Miller Jr., who thereafter publicly called the Levine allegations "baseless."

Mr. Cook represents Mr. Levine, his source, as "moderate." "There was about him no suggestion of the wild-eyed fanatic," he writes. Yet he fails to tell his readers that on Dec. 11, 1962, Mr. Levine rushed down the aisle of a Congressional hearing investigating possible Communist infiltration

of "peace" strikes and denounced the proceeding as a "disgrace," for which act of moderation he was removed from the premises.

A prime target of Mr. Cook is the late Whittaker Chambers. Whittaker's gallant testimony has survived more crossexaminations and more challenges than any comparable effort in contemporary history. It has held up on every front. Mr. Cook's challenge completely omits the rather dramatic fact that, after the Hiss trials, Nathaniel Weyl came forward and acknowledged under oath that he, too, was in the famous Ware cell with Alger Hiss and had collected Communist dues from Hiss on scores of occasions.

In the Rosenberg case, which Mr. Cook calls the "crime-of-the-century myth," there has been a full and complete trial by our jury system. The sentencing judge, Irving R. Kaufman, did not consider the issue mythical. He said to the Rosenbergs, "I consider your crime worse than murder . . . [it] altered the course of history to the disadvantage of your country."

The publication of this book is an intensified effort to destroy the reputation of Mr. Hoover and the F.B.I., now almost the last security outpost in our land. It also serves the current campaign to rewrite the history of the 1950's.

Throughout the book is threaded the theme that there is no Communist menace and that the mountains of evidence produced, linking conclusively the fall of China and of Cuba to deliquencies in security, were the "right wing" fabrication of "demagogues." It was all a plot, with Mr. Hoover in the middle. In the plot, too, were the United States Senate, the House of Representatives, judges, attorneys general, government officials at all levels — a fantastic charge.

October 11, 1964

HIGH COURT LIMITS LAW TO REGISTER INDIVIDUAL REDS

By FRED P. GRAHAM
Special to The New York Times

WASHINGTON, Nov. 15 — The Supreme Court ruled today that individuals may invoke their constitutional privilege against self-incrimination and

refuse to register with the Government as members of the Communist party.

In an 8-to-0 opinion written by Justice William J. Brennan Jr., the Court held unenforceable orders of the Justice Department requiring two men to register under the Subversive Activities Control Act of 1950.

This would expose them to prosecution under other Federal laws "in an area permeated with criminal statutes," he said.

The opinion stopped short of declaring the registration provision unconstitutional because a party member could waive his

self-incrimination privilege and register. But its obvious effect will be to make the registration requirement unenforceable, it was widely agreed here.

[In New York, the leadership of the party hailed the decision as "a vindication," and said it would move immediately to enter candidates in the 1966 Congressional elections. Page 34.]

Might Waive Rights

Although the opinion did not directly concern the alternate provision of the act that requires the party itself to reg-

ister and list its membership, it seemed to leave that section hanging by a thread.

Presumably, if party officers register the party or authorize others to do so, they would forgo the same self-incrimination rights involved in today's decision.

Specifically involved in today's case were William Albertson of Brooklyn and Roscoe Quincy Proctor of Oakland, Calif. Both had been ordered to register as members of the party by the Subversive Activities Control Board.

The Court of Appeals for the

District of Columbia upheld the order. It ruled that the two men could not raise their self-incrimination plea before the board, but must wait until they were prosecuted for failing to register.

Liable to Prosecution

Critics of the law have argued that this places the individual on the horns of an unconstitutional dilemma.

But if he registers he forgoes a court decision on the self-incrimination privilege claim, and is subject to prosecution under the Smith Act and other antisubversive legislation.

Justice Brennan said, in effect, that an individual could not be forced to make such a choice.

The Smith Act of 1940 made it a crime to teach or advocate the overthrow of the Government by force or violence. Its author was Representative Howard W. Smith, Democrat of Virginia.

Although the Fifth Amendment declares that no person "shall be compelled in any criminal case to be a witness against himself," the men cannot be required to wait for a criminal trial to assert their constitutional rights, Justice Brennan said.

He pointed out that each day of failure to register carried a maximum five year prison sentence and a $10,000 fine.

Since the information now required by a registrant is skimpy—his organization and duties and offices in it and his aliases and place and date of birth—it is doubted here that the Justice Department could devise a form sufficiently innocuous to pass the Justices' scrutiny.

Justice Brennan said that the required information "might be used as evidence in or at least supply investigatory leads to a criminal prosecution."

The law includes an immunity section that says none of the information given by a registrant may be received in evidence in any criminal prosecution. But Justice Brennan said it did not afford full protection because it did not preclude the use of the data as a lead in an investigation.

Justice Tom C. Clark pointed out in a brief concurring opinion that as Attorney General in 1948 he warned in a letter to the Senate Judiciary Committee that the act might infringe on self-incrimination guarantees.

By prior agreement between the Government and the parties, the decision today dismisses the 42 other pending cases against alleged Communist party members for failing to register.

Today's decision was the latest in a series of setbacks the Subversive Activities Control Act of 1950 has experienced in the courts.

Last year the high court declared unconstitutional the section that allowed the State Department to deny a passport to a Communist. It also threw out proceedings against two alleged Communist Front organizations

for refusing to register, on the ground that the board's evidence—dating back to the late 1940's—was too stale.

In 1963 the Court of Appeals for the District of Columbia voided a $120,000 fine against the party for failing to register. It said the Government must prove the availability of a volunteer who could do so for party officers without forgoing his self-incrimination privilege.

Defense Lawyers Object

In a second trial of the party that is now in its second week here, the Government has offered proof that its informants within the organization have told Gus Hall, a party leader, that they would be willing to register the party for him.

But lawyers for the party have noted that he must authorize the volunteer to act for him and have contended that this would waive his self-incrimination rights.

The Justice Department has tried once to invoke the provision that requires "Communist-infiltrated" groups to register. It brought proceedings against the International Union of Mine, Moll and Smelter Workers, but a Federal District judge here threw the case out two weeks ago as being too stale.

During the 15-year history of the subversives control act the Justice Department has brought registration actions against the party itself, 22 alleged front organizations, and 44 individuals.

So far none has registered

with the board.

For the party, John J. Abt of New York argued the case decided today, and Kevin T. Maroney of the Internal Security Division of the Department of Justice argued for the Government.

The high court granted a hearing today to six officials of the Mine, Mill and Smelter Workers, who were convicted of falsely swearing they were not members of the Communist party.

They were convicted under a non-Communist oath provision of the Taft-Hartley Act that was replaced by a section of the Labor-Management Reporting Act of 1959. The substitute section was itself declared unconstitutional by the Supreme Court last June.

Eastland to Seek Changes

WASHINGTON, Nov. 15 (AP)—Senator James O. Eastland, chairman of the Senate Judiciary Committee, said that the Supreme Court's decision today "is not the first which has overthrown a provision of the law enacted by the Congress as protection against subversion.

"Either our Government has the power to protect itself against subversion, or it faces inevitable destruction."

Mr. Eastland, Democrat of Mississippi, said in a statement that he would ask his committee to meet early in the next session to "plug the gaps" in the subversion laws.

November 16, 1965

The Contempt Issue Overtakes the Klan

By FRED P. GRAHAM

Special to The New York Times

WASHINGTON, Sept. 17 — "Beatniks! Sex perverts! Tennis-shoe-wearing Communists!" hissed the Imperial Wizard of the United Klans of America last Wednesday afternoon.

Robert M. Shelton Jr. was not referring to the jury that had just convicted him of contempt of Congress—even though the jury included three Negroes.

Nor did he mean the House Committee on Un-American Activities, which had initiated the charges against him for refusing to produce subpoenaed Klan records.

The Wizard's invective was directed instead against the young radicals who had "spit epithets in the face of Congress" during recent Un-American Activities Committee hearings into critics of the Vietnam war.

Christian Gentleman

None of them had been cited for contempt by the committee, he pointed out, while he had behaved as a "Christian gentleman" and now faces a possible one-year prison sentence and $1,000 fine for contempt.

The Wizard's explanation for this made little sense (he claimed the Federal Government coddles "nigras," and "pinks," but few observers would include the House Committee on Un-American Activities in such a charge), but his complaint did raise an intriguing point.

The committee had charged him and six lesser Klan figures with contempt (they will be tried here next month), while pointedly avoiding a legal confrontation with the left. Why?

It was not that the committee lacked adequate justification to move against the "Vietniks." Two

war critics had simply ignored the committee's subpoenas, and two became so ill-mannered they were hauled bodily from the witness stand.

At one point, the committee members, momentarily losing their cool, did threaten to cite one witness for contempt. Delighted, he replied: "Do you wish to go for six on this?"

This was a backhanded reminder to the committee that it is in the throes of one of the most spectacular legal losing streaks in congressional history, and that a contempt citation might well become the committee's sixth consecutive Supreme Court defeat.

Actually, the committee's record in the past five years is even worse than that; 26 other contempt cases have failed in the lower courts, and no convictions have been upheld.

The battle began bravely for the

committee in 1946, shortly after it was created. Seventeen officials of the Joint Anti-Fascist Committee and the entertainment industry's famous "Hollywood Ten" simply refused to answer the committee's questions about their alleged Communist connections.

They claimed that the House of Representatives' rule that authorized the committee to investigate "un-American propaganda" was so broad that its investigations threatened the freedom of speech and association guaranteed by the First Amendment.

They lost in the lower courts, and the Supreme Court, not then ready to cross Congress over antisubversive investigations, affirmed the convictions.

For the next few years most witnesses who refused to talk relied on the Fifth Amendment's privilege against self-incrimination.

United Press International

IN CONTEMPT: Robert M. Shelton Jr., Imperial Wizard of the United Klans of America, shown here at a Klan rally, was convicted of contempt of Congress last week for refusing to produce Klan records for the House Committee on Un-American Activities.

This saved the witnesses from jail (75 were prosecuted for contempt and none were convicted), but the stigma of "taking the Fifth" became so strong that they began again to plead their First Amendment rights.

This paid off in 1957, when the Supreme Court sharply criticized the committee in *Watkins v. United States* and seemed almost ready to declare that its freewheeling mandate to probe "un-American propaganda" violates witnesses' freedom of speech.

The high Court retreated in 1959 when it upheld a committee contempt action in *Barenblatt v. United States,* but four dissenters— **Chief Justice Earl Warren and Justices Hugo L. Black, William J. Brennan Jr. and William O. Douglas—served notice that they would be prepared to crack down on the committee as soon as a fifth justice swung over to their view.**

They have been in the majority in all the committee's contempt cases since 1961, but the reversals have been on narrow (some critics say nit-picking) grounds.

Now many civil libertarians believe a majority of the Court is merely waiting for the right case in which severely to limit the committee's power to compel testimony, if not to declare the committee unconstitutional under the First Amendment. This explains the Vietnam war critics' bullying of the committee, many observers believe, as well as the members' forebearance.

Thus the Klan contempt cases might have offered an ironic forum for a legal showdown. The question as to whether the Klan, an indigenous institution born of Reconstruction, could be termed "un-American," placed in issue the constitutionality of the committee's mandate, and attorneys for the American Civil Liberties Union eagerly offered to assist in Mr Shelton's defense.

As Mr. Shelton put it this week, he turned them down on principle, saying that he considered the A.C.L.U. a "pink" organization.

But while the American left has become wise in the ways of constitutional litigation against the Un-American Activities Committee, the Klan indicated that it still has much to learn.

Mr. Shelton's attorney did not challenge the constitutionality of the Committee's broad authority, or claim that it had a chilling effect on free speech.

Instead, he contended that the subpoenaed papers were not relevant to any legitimate legislative purpose and that the language of the subpoena was overly broad.

The trial judge ruled against him on both points, and Mr. Shelton vowed to appeal, if necessary, to the Supreme Court, where the beatniks, if nothing else, know how to play the game.

September 18, 1966

U.S. DROPS FIGHT TO REGISTER REDS

Concedes Defeat After 2d Upset of a Conviction

By FRED P. GRAHAM
Special to The New York Times

WASHINGTON, April 3 — The Justice Department conceded tonight that the American Communist party could not be punished for refusing to register with the Government as an agent of the Soviet Union.

In a terse announcement by a department spokesman, the Government announced that it would not appeal to the Supreme Court a landmark lower court decision that had declared unconstitutional a central provision of the Internal Security Act of 1950.

The provision said that "Communist action" groups — agents of the Soviet — must register with the Government and provide the names of officers and members and financial data.

The legal battle to force the Communist party to register began in 1953, when the Subversive Activities Control Board ruled that the party was a Communist action group. This ruling was upheld by the Supreme Court on June 5, 1966.

'This Case Is Dead'

Today a Justice Department spokesman announced that the Government had let a 30-day deadline pass without appealing the March 3 decision of the Court of Appeals for the District of Columbia.

"This case is dead," the spokesman said.

The effect of the Justice Department action is to reduce the Internal Security Act to a shell, with the central provisions—those designed to force the Communist party and its "front" groups to register—admittedly unconstitutional.

The action came after years of litigation, in which the Communist party had twice been convicted and fined for refusing to register.

Both times the Court of Appeals here threw out the conviction.

Despite the decade and a half of litigation involving the registration provisions of the law, not a single individual or group ever registered with the Attorney General, as required by the act.

5th Amendment Plea

The Communist party's officers had refused to register the party, asserting that to do so would violate the Fifth Amendment guarantee against compulsory self-incrimination.

The party was indicted in December of 1961 for refusing to register and was convicted in December of 1962.

This conviction was overturned by the Court of Appeals here on the ground that the Government had not proved that there was a "willing volunteer" within the party who could register it without incriminating himself.

Again the Government indicted the party, and in a November, 1965, trial produced two agents of the Federal Bureau of Investigation who had been undercover party members and who had offered to register the party.

A jury found the party guilty and fined it $230,000.

In the meantime, a related legal issue was posed when the Government attempted to prosecute individual Communist party members for refusing to register in place of registration by the party.

Last fall the Supreme Court, in a historic ruling, declared that individual members could not be required to register. The Court said that to do so would violate their privilege against self-incrimination.

Last month a three-judge panel of the appeals court here relied heavily upon that Supreme Court decision.

In a unanimous opinion, written by Judge Carl McGowan, the appeals court said that Congress had "sought in effect to compel both disclosure by the party, and, at the same time, incrimination of its membership."

The court declared these provisions "hopelessly at odds" with the self-incrimination privilege.

The Justice Department spokesman said tonight that department officials had decided not to appeal after reviewing the Court of Appeals decision and the Supreme Court ruling of last year.

April 4, 1967

AGNEW RETRACTS CHARGE HUMPHREY IS 'SOFT' ON REDS

By HOMER BIGART
Special to The New York Times

ROCHESTER, Sept. 12—Gov. Spiro T. Agnew of Maryland took back today his charge that Hubert H. Humphrey was "soft on Communism."

The Republican Vice-Presidential candidate said he had erred in using the words that had become a familiar term during the days of Senator Joseph R. McCarthy and what Mr. Agnew called the "witch hunts" of the early nineteen-fifties.

His decision to retract, accompanied by a remark that "I've never been one to go 'the low road' in politics," came after Senator Everett McKinley Dirksen and Representative Gerald R. Ford, the Republican Congressional leaders, expressed disapproval of the Agnew remarks at a Washington news conference.

Unaware of Evidence

Both said they were unaware of any evidence that Mr. Humphrey was soft on Communism. Mr. Ford remarked that the Republicans had a lot of first-class issues — inflation, crime, lack of leadership—and "I don't think this one of soft on Communism should be pushed at this time." Senator Dirksen said pointedly, "I'm rather restrained in the statements I make."

Mr. Agnew said he had never been a "particular admirer" of the late Senator McCarthy.

He said he would never have applied the "soft on Communism" label to Mr. Humphrey, the Democratic Presidential candidate, had he known the "political history" of the phrase.

'Man of Great Integrity'

"If I'd known I'd be cast as the 'Joe McCarthy of 1968' I'd have turned five somersaults to avoid saying it," Mr. Agnew said.

Mr. Agnew called the Democratic standard bearer a "loyal American" and a "man of great integrity." He said his retraction had not been dictated by Richard M. Nixon, the Republican Presidential candidate.

Mr. Agnew said he had telephoned Senator Dirksen in Washington to apprise the Republican leader on "the full context the remark was made in."

Mr. Agnew told Mr. Dirksen he was provoked into making his charge at a meeting with newsmen in Washington Tuesday because Mr. Humphrey had called Mr. Nixon "a cold warrior and a hardliner."

He used the phrase as a rejoinder to Mr. Humphrey's "unwarranted remarks," he said, and meant it "in a comparison sense."

September 13, 1968

Unit on Un-American Activities Gets a New Name in House Vote

By MARJORIE HUNTER
Special to The New York Times

WASHINGTON, Feb. 18—The House voted today to give its Committee on Un-American Activities a new name and, some said, a chance to carve a new public image.

Renamed the House Internal Security Committee, the panel thus abandoned its old, familiar initials, H.U.A.C., and acquired a brand new set, H.I.S.C.

"A rose by any other name . . . ," longtime critics of the committee sputtered as they sought to block the name change in hopes of abolishing the committee entirely.

They failed, by a vote of 262 to 123. But while losing by a more than 2-to-1 margin, critics made their best showing in nearly 20 years of attempts to abolish the committee.

In previous years, opponents failed to muster more than 90 votes to abolish the committee.

Comic Strip Recalled

Scoffing at the contention that a name change would improve the committee, Representative Phillip Burton, Democrat of California, reminded colleagues of an Al Capp comic strip in which "the Dogpatch city council met to change the name of the skunk works to the Ozark Perfume Factory."

The smallest of all Congressional committees, the panel has had a turbulent career in its pursuit of Communists, educators, actors, peace leaders, Klansmen, alleged subversives and, most recently, instigators of the riots at last summer's Democratic National Convention.

First created in 1934 as a special committee to investigate the rise of "Hitlerism" in Germany, H.U.A.C. became a permanent House committee in 1945 and shifted its attention to ferreting out Communists or suspected Communists.

Its most famous investigation—the Alger Hiss case in 1948—helped to project Richard M. Nixon, then a young Congressman, into national prominence.

Through the years, the committee has been ardently liked by its supporters and violently disliked by its opponents, including civil libertarians protesting what they termed "witch-hunting."

After becoming chairman last fall, Richard H. Ichord, a Missouri Democrat, vowed to "improve the committee's image."

Urging the name change, Mr. Ichord noted that the committee's previous mandate to investigate "un-American propaganda" had been dropped.

"What is un-American?" he asked. "I, for one, am not capable to give it a definite meaning."

Even under the revised mandate, the committee is still authorized to investigate the extent, character, objectives and activities of groups seeking to establish a totalitarian dictatorship within the United States or to overthrow or alter or assist in the overthrow or alteration of the Government by force, violence, treachery, espionage, sabotage, insurrection or any unlawful means.

The committee is also authorized to investigate groups or individuals who incite or employ "acts of force, violence, terrorism or any unlawful means to obstruct or oppose the lawful authority of the Government of the United States in the execution of any law or policy affecting the security of the United States."

Final approval of the change in committee name came on a vote of 305 to 79 after opponents had failed to block consideration by the earlier vote of 262 to 123.

February 19, 1969

Court Voids Law on Urging Violence

Special to The New York Times

WASHINGTON, June 9 — Ohio's criminal syndicalism law, a prototype of the kind of antiradical statutes that were passed by a score of states during the post-World War I "red scare," was declared unconstitutional today by the Supreme Court.

The Court ruled in an unsigned opinion that the law violated the free speech guarantee of the First Amendment.

The statute makes it unlawful "by word of mouth or writing [to] advocate or teach the duty, necessity or propriety of crime, sabotage, violence or unlawful methods of terrorism as a means of accomplishing industrial or political reform."

for the first time to convict a Cincinnati Ku Klux Klan leader, Clarence Brandenburg.

'Revengence' Vowed

Brandenburg had invited a television cameraman to a Klan cross-burning ceremony, where he was filmed vowing "revengeance" against the nation's leaders and making slurring remarks about Negroes and Jews. The "organizational meeting" was later shown on local television.

His audience consisted of about a dozen Klansmen, some of whom were seen in the film to be brandishing firearms. Brandenburg was convicted and given one to 10 years in prison and a $100,000 fine.

In overturning the conviction, the Supreme Court noted that its recent cases had forbidden convictions against persons who merely advocated the moral propriety or necessity of using violence to overthrow the Government. It must appear that the speaker intended to

291

produce imminent lawless action and that violence was likely to result from his speech, the Court said.

The Ohio law was struck down because it permitted the conviction of persons who merely advocate violent attacks against the state as an idea, with no intention or capacity to accomplish it, the Court said.

Today's decision specifically overruled a 1927 decision, in which the Supreme Court upheld California's criminal syndicalism law, which closely resembles the Ohio law. The California law is also under attack in a case that is now under advisement before the Court.

New York's criminal syndicalism law, which predates the two others and differs from them in wording, is also being challenged before the Court.

New York and California recently revived their laws, after long years of disuse, to prosecute black nationalists who were said to be plotting insurrection. Officials of those states told the Justices that the black

militants' capacity to attempt insurrection was great enough to justify the use of these laws.

Allen Brown of Cincinnati argued for Brandenburg. Leonard Kirschner, assistant prosecuting attorney of Cincinnati, argued for the city.

June 10, 1969

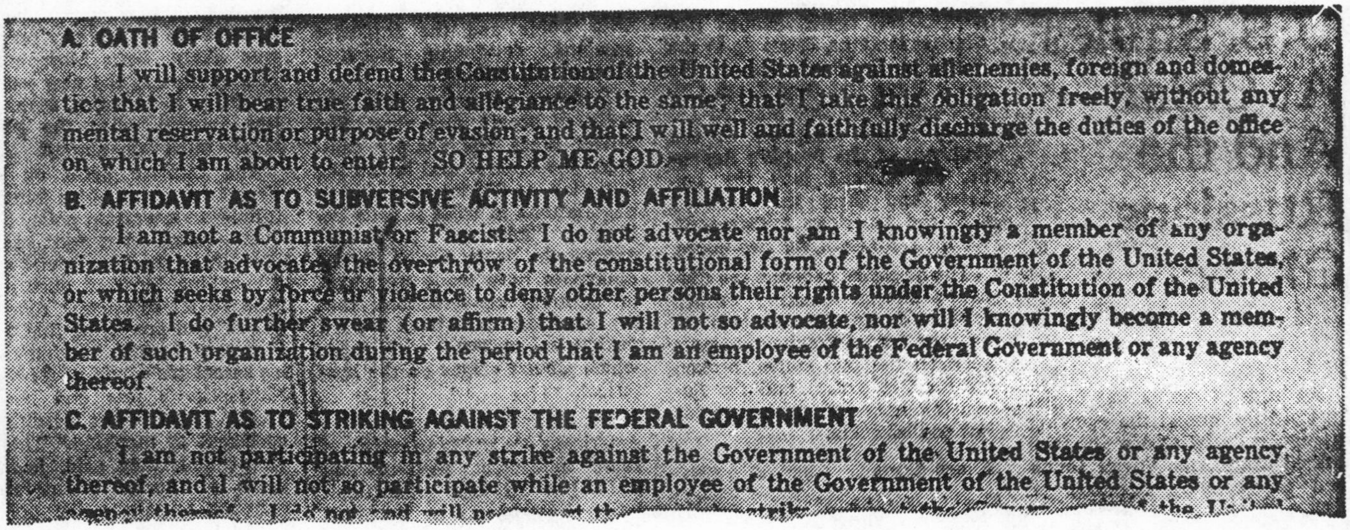

A. OATH OF OFFICE

I will support and defend the Constitution of the United States against all enemies, foreign and domestic; that I will bear true faith and allegiance to the same; that I take this obligation freely, without any mental reservation or purpose of evasion; and that I will well and faithfully discharge the duties of the office on which I am about to enter. SO HELP ME GOD.

B. AFFIDAVIT AS TO SUBVERSIVE ACTIVITY AND AFFILIATION

I am not a Communist or Fascist. I do not advocate nor am I knowingly a member of any organization that advocates the overthrow of the constitutional form of the Government of the United States, or which seeks by force or violence to deny other persons their rights under the Constitution of the United States. I do further swear (or affirm) that I will not so advocate, nor will I knowingly become a member of such organization during the period that I am an employee of the Federal Government or any agency thereof.

C. AFFIDAVIT AS TO STRIKING AGAINST THE FEDERAL GOVERNMENT

I am not participating in any strike against the Government of the United States or any agency thereof, and I will not so participate while an employee of the Government of the United States or any ...

As a result of court decisions seven months ago, and action by the Civil Service Commission last week, appointees to Federal jobs will no longer have to swear to section B of the loyalty oath shown here.

The Life And Death Of the Loyalty Oath

On June 4, 1969, a Federal Court in the District of Columbia declared invalid under the Constitution a statute embodying a loyalty oath that had been sworn to by millions of Federal employes. The statute requires employes to swear that they did not "advocate the overthrow of our constitutional form of government" or belonged knowingly to organizations that advocate overthrow. Mrs. Roma Stewart, a school teacher, had refused to subscribe to the oath on the ground that it was contrary to

her obligation as a citizen and objectionable as a matter of conscience.

Until last week the case had made no discernible impact on the practice of Federal agencies, which persisted in requiring prospective employes to sign the loyalty — or "test" — oath in plain disregard of the court decision and a directive of the Civil Service Commission that advised the departments of the new ruling. Then last Tuesday an official of the American Civil Liberties Union brought this situation to light and the oath was removed from circulation by the Civil Service Commission. An estimated 75,000 employes needlessly signed papers containing the oath.

This bureaucratic vignette aptly epitomizes the curious recent history of loyalty oaths, which are on the books of more than half the states and scores of municipalities, although most of them are as plainly unconstitutional as the Federal loyalty oath. State legislatures do not repeal these invalid oaths,

state attorneys general do not get around to issuing opinions declaring them to be void, and line officials—oblivious of the constitutional scene — perform their business as usual until a case is brought and the vulnerable oath is given the coup de grace. It is therefore not really surprising that the Federal oath persisted for seven months after the action of the Washington court.

There really was no doubt, moreover, that the Federal oath was invalid. In a series of cases beginning in 1961 the Supreme Court has ruled that teachers and other civil servants may not be required to swear, among other things, that they are not members of the Communist party; do not lend the party "aid," "support," "advise," "counsel," or "influence"; are not members of "subversive" organizations; or are not engaged in "seditious" activity.

Overlapping Theories

To achieve this result the Court has invoked a wide range of overlapping and sometimes confusing theories, which are

grounded in the clauses of the Constitution that outlaw Bills of Attainder (legislative acts that punish without judicial trial), Ex-Post Facto Laws (which impose punishment for acts lawful when committed), and above all protect the freedom of speech.

Thus, in Mrs. Stewart's case the oath was held to impair her free speech and association because it broadly applied to anyone who advocates overthrow of the government, and was not limited to those advocating overthrow by force and violence; because it applied to one who advocates overthrow in the distant future as well as the present or near future; because it applied to wholly passive members of organizations advocating overthrow; and because it applied to all Federal employes regardless of whether their post was at all sensitive.

But even this battery of reasons does not fully explain why test oaths have been stricken by the courts and are so widely detested. Their history is long and dishonorable. They were one of the chief devices used against the Huguenots in France, and against "heretics" during the Spanish Inquisition. English rulers used them to identify and outlaw Catholics, Quakers, Baptists and Congregationalists — groups then regarded as dangerous for political as well as religious reasons.

They were used in the United States after the Civil War against a Catholic priest suspected of sympathy with the rebels, and during the Second World War against Federal employes suspected of "subversive activity." They were much in vogue during the McCarthy period of the 1950's as a way of cleansing the Government of "security risks."

One attraction of loyalty oath programs to government has been their automatic operation; failure to take the oath usually means denial of a job despite all other qualifications without expensive enforcement procedures or drawn out legal proceedings characteristic of other security programs.

At the same time, this is a chief reason for their insidious quality — they require prospective employes to disavow that they have done or believed anything wrong, thereby shifting the burden from the government to the individual. Further, loyalty oaths penalize beliefs and associations rather than conduct, thereby inhibiting political activity which the First Amendment was designed to protect. Finally, test oaths run against the grain of many loyal individuals, who resent the assumption that the government can probe the inner workings of the mind.

A high point in the loyalty oath controversy occurred during the 1940's when West Virginia expelled from its public schools children who refused to salute the flag and pledge allegiance, because, as Jehovah's Witnesses, it was contrary to their religious principles. Overruling an earlier decision, the Supreme Court held that the state could not compel the children to take the oath. Justice Robert Jackson's opinion closed with the vivid and highly influential language:

"If there is any fixed star in our Constitutional constellation, it is that no official, high or petty, can prescribe what shall be orthodox in politics, nationalism, religion, or other matters of opinion or force citizens to confess by word or act their faith therein."

Relying on the implications of the Flag Salute Case, and the constitutional theories mentioned above, the Supreme Court has systematically voided test oaths since 1961.

But it has tolerated one exception. In 1968 it upheld a part of the New York Education Act that required prospective teachers in public colleges or schools to swear that they will support the Constitutions of the United States and New York. This so-called "affirmative" oath, to distinguish it from the disavowals required in other oaths, was challenged on the ground that it, too, interfered with freedom of belief and conscience. But the Court summarily rejected this claim, probably because it resembles so closely the oath of office of the President of the United States, which is set out in the Constitution itself.

Apart from this narrow exception, it seems clear, as the District of Columbia case shows, that the courts will look suspiciously on test oaths, and it is doubtful whether many will survive. This will be no great loss because, as Justices Hugo Black and William O. Douglas said while concurring in the Flag Salute Case: "Words uttered under coercion are proof of loyalty to nothing but self-interest. Love of country must spring from willing hearts and free minds."

—NORMAN DORSEN

Mr. Dorsen is a professor at New York University School of Law and is general counsel of the American Civil Liberties Union.

January 11, 1970

DETENTION CAMPS OPPOSED BY HOUSE

356-49 Vote Backs Repeal of a Never-Used Law for Holding Suspects in War

By MARJORIE HUNTER
Special to the New York Times

WASHINGTON, Sept. 13— The House voted today to repeal a never-used law that gives the Federal Government authority to put suspected spies or saboteurs into detention camps during time of war or insurrection.

The vote was 356 to 49. The bill now goes to the Senate, where quick approval is expected.

Although the detention law has never been used since its enactment in 1950, its existence has given rise in recent years to widespread fears, particularly among Negroes, that it might be used to establish concentration camps for black militants.

While describing such fears as unfounded, the Nixon Administration urged repeal of the law as a symbolic gesture of assurance.

In voting today to repeal the law, the House went even further than the Administration had first proposed. The House voted to ban establishment of such camps except by affirmative action of Congress.

This would prevent a President from setting up such detention camps under Executive order as President Franklin D. Roosevelt did in 1941, just after the Japanese attacked Pearl Harbor. At that time, approximately 112,000 Japanese-Americans, most of them born in the United States, were rounded up and placed in 10 "relocation centers."

The House fight for repeal of the detention law was led by Representative Spark M. Matsunaga, Democrat of Hawaii, a captain who was wounded twice in Italy as a member of the United States Nisei regiment during World War II.

He told the House that even while he was fighting for the United States, many of his Japanese-American relatives and friends were being detained in detention camps in this country.

"There is no place for concentration camps in the American scheme," he said quietly.

The law that Congress now seems ready to repeal was enacted during the Korean War, at the height of a wave of anti-Communism that seemed at times to approach hysteria. President Truman vetoed the bill, but a determined Congress overrode him.

'Reasonable Ground'

The law permits the establishment of detention camps to hold "each person as to whom there is reasonable ground to believe . . . probably will engage in . . . or conspire to engage in . . . acts of espionage or sabotage" in time of war, invasion or "insurrection in aid of a foreign enemy."

In 1952, the Government established six detention camps in Arizona, California, Florida, Oklahoma and Pennsylvania. They were never used, except for one, were later abandoned. The Pennsylvania camp is now used as a Federal maximum security prison.

During two days of spirited debate, opponents of outright repeal sought instead to retain the 1950 law but to limit its potential use in time of insurrection.

The proposed substitute was offered by Representative Richard H. Ichord, Democrat of Missouri, chairman of the House Internal Security Committee, formerly the House Committee on Un-American Activities.

Describing himself as a "civil libertarian," Mr. Ichord said he considered the detention of the Japanese-Americans in World War II "a black page in American history."

But he argued that outright repeal of the 1950 law would "prohibit the apprehension of saboteurs and espionage agents in time of war."

The Justice Department has said that there are numerous other laws dealing with espionage and sabotage and that the detention law is not needed.

The Ichord proposal was defeated, 68 to 22. The House also rejected—by votes of 272 to 124 and 292 to 111—two other moves by Mr. Ichord to strike from the bill the ban on creation of such detention camps by the President without Congressional approval.

Representative Emanuel Celler of Brooklyn, chairman of the House Judiciary Committee, compared Mr. Ichord's arguments to a cypress tree. "They are stately and tall and they bear no fruit," he said.

Also arguing for repeal, Representative Jim Wright, Democrat of Texas, reminded the House that when the law was enacted "hysteria ran like a fever in the American bloodstream, a symptom of a virus dominant in those years.'

He suggested that repeal would be a symbol," an expiation for sins committed before this law was ever enacted."

September 15, 1971

U.S. COMMUNISTS NOW OUT IN OPEN

They Find Signs of Thaw in the Public's Attitude

By The Associated Press

After 25 years, there are once more card-carrying Communists in the United States.

After years of meeting in secret for fear of exposure; of being called before Congressional committees; of suspecting that each new party recruit works for the Federal Bureau of Investigation, American Communism is, as the official line puts it, "showing the face of the party."

The membership cards, being issued for the first time since 1948, are the tangible proof that the Communists no longer think they would be best off if nobody knew who they were.

The reason for the Communist coming-out appears to be the fact that the thaw in international relations has convinced most Americans that the Communist conspiracy—so much a fact of life a decade or two ago—is no longer on the verge of overthrowing the United States. In the words of that period, few people now appear to be looking for Reds under their beds.

"You don't see the anti-Communists out with placards the way you did 10 or 15 years ago," says H. L. Richardson, a California State Senator, an author, a radio commentator and a one-time member of the John Birch Society.

"Maybe they're working within the Republican party, or have quit to join the American Independent party. Or maybe they've just thrown up their hands and say 'I'm going to enjoy myself before they come marching down the street.'"

Of the membership cards, Gus Hall, the party's general secretary, says, "The younger people wanted them. They're proud to be Communists."

Evidence of Change

Like the cards, the signs of the thaw are often more symbolic than anything else. But the symbols are the tangible evidence of a public mood evidenced by the following:

¶Joe L. Matthews, national commander of the always stanchly anti-Communist American Legion, visited the Soviet Union and Poland last winter. When he returned, he wrote an article in the legion's magazine that was glowing in its praise of veterans' facilities in the two countries. The legion has merged its Americanism division with the Division on Children and Youth, and the Americanism staff has been sharply reduced from a decade ago.

¶In Washington, the Subversive Activities Control Board has been phased out, and the House Un-American Activities Committee has been turned into the House Internal Security Committee. The committee has not held a hearing on Communism in more than two years.

¶The Internal Security Division of the Justice Department has been merged into a smaller department.

In California, where anti-Communist sentiment is still stronger than in most places, the State Senate's Committee on Un-American Activities was downgraded two years ago to a subcommittee on civil disorders. The impetus for the move came from James Mills, the Senate president pro tempore, after he found his name in the committee's files for having attended a meeting called by the International Longshoremen's and Warehousemen's Union.

The Communists see a noticeable difference in the way they are greeted when they travel and make speeches.

"There's no question that the atmosphere is so much better," Mr. Hall says. "It's a pleasure to present the party's position now. What's interesting is that you very seldom meet someone who is purposefully nasty. People disagree, but they are respectful."

Just about everyone who talks about the change in attitude sees its tangible origins in the events of the last decade: the war in Vietnam and the new relations with China and the Soviet Union.

But many people who have lived through the '40's and '50's, when every candidate for public office was bound to pay lip service to his opposition to Communism, sense that the reasons are more subtle.

Their consensus is that the clearest of those reasons are that a new generation has grown up unencumbered by the attitudes of their parents, that the attitudes of the parents themselves has been changed by events and that more people know more and fear less about Communism.

Dennis Carpenter, a former F.B.I. agent who is chairman of the California Senate's new civil disorders subcommittee, says, for example:

"A lot of people from my area have gone to Russia. They see what it's like over there, and they come back liking our system that much better. But they also see the people over there, and they see them as humans. I think leaving things to people is often a lot better than leaving them to governments."

Fred Kuszmaul, the American Legion's Americanism chairman, gives the same angle a reverse twist.

"Let's face it," he says. "The country can only benefit from the Brezhnev visit. The more the Russians can see what's in this country, the better off we are."

August 12, 1973

SUBVERSIVE LIST TO GET NEW STUDY

Saxbe Orders Investigation of Organizations and Laws to Check on Relevance

By LESLEY OELSNER
Special to the New York Times

WASHINGTON, April 3—Saying that a "new breed" of terrorist organizations had replaced the McCarthy-era "Communist-based" organizations as potential threats, Attorney General William B. Saxbe announced today that he had ordered a new study of the Justice Department's role regarding subversive activities.

He has ordered an investigation of the controversial Attorney General's list of subversive organizations and of the relevant internal security laws, he said, in order to determine whether there "should be such a list" and whether the present list, last revised in 1955, is "realistic."

The Justice Department, he said, is determined to "live up to" its duty to "protect the people from subversive activities, terrorism and so on," and to do "the best we can to know these organizations" which pose threats.

The Attorney General described his perceptions of the shift from the McCarthy era to the present day during a news briefing in his conference room, saying that the "worldwide trends are more towards terrorism" and that "we're dealing with a different type of person."

'The Jewish Intellectual'

He noted that during the McCarthy era "there was a great distrust of the intellectual," adding: "one of the changes that's come about is because of the Jewish intellectual, who was in those days very enamored of the Communist party."

"Some of these" were Americans, he said, and some foreign.

Mr. Saxbe, who is an Episcopalian, was strongly criticized by the leaders of two Jewish organizations for his comments.

"It is incredible that the Attorney General of the United States should make such an unfounded blanket charge accusing 'the Jewish intellectual' as a group of having been enamored of the Communist party," Benjamin R. Epstein, the national director of the Anti-Defamation League of 'B'nai B'rith, said in statement issued in response to a query about Mr. Saxbe's remarks.

"Mr. Saxbe's comment confirms A.D.L.'s newest findings about the insensitivity of otherwise responsible Americans to the harmful impact of false anti-Jewish stereotyping," he said.

Jacob Sheinkman, president of the Jewish Labor Committee, issued a statement this afternoon that concluded:

"The fitness of a man to hold high public office who engages in such insidious stereotypes must be seriously questioned. Saxbe's aspersions of the loyalty of American Jews is incompatible with his responsibilities as head of the Department of Justice."

A Different Communism

Mr. Saxbe said at his briefing that the growth of "Maoism" had brought about a "different kind of Communism." He said he looks at India, especially Behar and West Bengal, as a "battleground" of ideology between Maoists and "traditional Communists" and the socialists who are "more or less the Establishment." He said this could also be seen in "many African states."

The Attorney General's list of subversive organizations originated in the McCarthy era as a tool for making sure that Government employes met national security standards. The latest list, compiled in 1955 in accordance with an executive order, includes several hundred organizations, among them some which apparently no longer exist.

The director of the Federal Bureau of Investigation, Clarence M. Kelley, asked today about his views as to what should be done with the list, replied that "the subversive list has been abolished, of course, has not been continued."

He did not see any necessity for reviving it, and "there is no stimulation for this and none appears to be on the rise," he told a luncheon at the National Press Club.

April 4, 1974

Subversive List Abolished By Order of the President

WASHINGTON, June 4 (AP) —President Nixon has abolished the list of subversive organizations maintained by the Attorney General that was used to screen applicants for Government jobs, the White House and Justice Departments announced today.

Mr. Nixon signed an Executive order doing away with the list that was created in 1947 by President Truman.

Attorney General William B. Saxbe said he had recommended the action because the list "was a sort of vestigial tail on the Federal Government's security programs." Mr. Saxbe said "it is now very apparent it no longer serves any useful purpose."

The list was widely criticized, and the Supreme Court in 1951 ruled that no group could be placed on the list without a hearing.

June 5, 1974

House Democrats Vote for Abolition Of Anti-Red Panel

By RICHARD D. LYONS
Special to The New York Times

WASHINGTON, Jan. 13 — Democratic Representatives voted today to abolish the House Internal Security Committee, which for 45 years, under various names, has been the spearhead of anti-Communist investigations on Capitol Hill.

With hardly a dissenting voice, members of the House Democratic Caucus voted to transfer to the House Judiciary Committee some of the functions and staff of the Internal Security Committee together with the files collected by its predecessor, the House Un-American Activities Committee, on the alleged subversive work of more than 750,000 Americans.

Congressional liberals had sought for several decades to kill the committee, which had its genesis in 1930 as the Select Committee to Investigate Communist Propaganda. Over the years the committee became the sounding board for such anti-Communist crusaders as Richard M. Nixon, Martin Dies and J. Parnell Thomas.

Committee interest hit its peak in the late nineteen-forties during the confrontation between Alger Hiss, a former State Department official, and the late Whittaker Chambers, who had confessed to having been a courier for a Communist spy ring.

Mr. Hiss was later convicted of perjury and served 44 months in prison.

The 1948-49 Hiss investigation, in which Mr. Nixon played a major role by using his position as a committee member to champion Mr. Chambers's cause, helped to give the then obscure Republican Representative from California national attention. He was elected to the Senate in 1950 and then went on to become Vice President and President.

Final action on abolition is to come Thursday and, while it must be ratified by the whole House, today's action made it seem certain that the work of the committee would end.

Moment in History

"This is a moment in history," said Representative Robert F. Drinan, the Massachusetts Democrat and Jesuit priest who has led the campaign to abolish the committee. A member of both the Judiciary and Internal Security Committees, Father Drinan originally sought a seat on the latter specifically to work for its abolition.

For years House liberals had been thwarted in their attempts either to kill or cut off financing for the committee. An attempt last year to transfer the functions to the Judiciary Committee was defeated by a vote of 246 to 164.

But today those members seeking abolition had the additional backing of most of the 75 new Democratic Representatives.

Representative James W. Symington, Democrat of Missouri, said, after the voice vote was taken by the Democratic Caucus, that the number of freshmen Congressmen "and their attitudes toward change" had an obvious impact.

A resolution to abolish the Internal Security Committee was introduced today by Father Drinan, then withdrawn when the chairman of the committee, Representative Richard H. Ichord, Democrat of Missouri, proposed one with similar wording. The differences were minor, mainly concerning the transfer of staff aides from the Internal Security Committee to the Judiciary Committee.

While Mr. Ichord was not immediately available for comment, members of the caucus said the chairman realized that he could not avoid the abolition of the committee.

Abolition of the committee had been proposed in a series of House reforms put forth last year by a special committee headed by a retiring Representative, Julia Butler Hansen, Democrat of Washington, which received the support of the House Democratic leadership.

Father Drinan predicted that had the issue come to a formal ballot, "We would have won by over 100 votes."

While the work of the Internal Security Committee, whose name was changed five years ago from Un-American Activities Committee, had dwindled in recent years along with the attention it drew, the group still had a 1974 budget of $725,000 and a saff of 39.

In addition to investigating Communist activities in this country, the committee over the years had also looked into the work of such right-wing groups as the German-American Bund and the Ku Klux Klan. Lately it had turned its attention to such radical organizations as teh so-called Symbionese Liberation Army.

But in recent years fewer and fewer Democrats have been willing to sit on the committee. Mr. Ichord currently is the party's member, leading Mr. Symington to comment that he is "the captain of a ship without a crew."

January 14, 1975

295

A Particular Vision of the Flag

By ELIOT FREMONT-SMITH

THE COMMITTEE: The Extraordinary Career of the House Committee on Un-American Activities. By Walter Goodman. Introduction by Richard H. Rovere. 564 pages. Farrar, Straus & Giroux. $10.

THE House Committee on Un-American Activities, better known initially as the Dies Committee (after its first chairman, Congressman Martin Dies of Texas) and lately by the scrabbled acronym, HUAC, has now been in business for 30 years. It has had fat years and lean years —the fattest dating roughly from the end of World War II to 1951 when the spotlight of publicity shifted onto the capers of Senator Joseph McCarthy; the leanest from the fall of McCarthy in 1954 to the present. Its tone was set from the beginning, when Martin Dies announced that the 1937 sit-down strikes in Detroit were "part of a Moscow - directed insurrection." The committee's first hearings, conducted in August, 1938,

Associated Press
Martin Dies in 1940

featured testimony against, among other things and people, the C.I.O., the American Civil Liberties Union, the Federal Theater, Harry Bridges, the Camp Fire Girls and the Indian Bureau of the Department of the Interior, which was accused of trying to spread "Communism and paganism."

From the first, the committee was out to expose not only agents of foreign powers— principally the Soviet Union, secondarily Nazi Germany—but more importantly, any and all domestic elements which it felt to be alien to its own nativist, white, Christian view of Americanism. Thus the prime targets included liberalism, labor, the New Deal, intellectuals, artists and the foreign-born. Committe member, and later chairman, John Rankin of Mississippi injected a strident racism into the committee's activities, and an anti-Negro bias and a more virulent anti-Semitism were to stain the committee throughout and beyond its heyday.

'Kids in a Swimming Hole'

Methodology was also set from the outset —or nearly from the outset. (Walter Goodman describes the Congressmen at the initial hearings as "splashing around like kids in a new swimming hole.") There were "friendly" witnesses and "hostile" witnesses, who were quickly disabused of the notion that they had courtroom rights. The best of the friendlies were the full-circle turncoats, recanted spies and subversives who could feed the committee both "expert" testimony and names. The first of these was one J. B. Matthews, a former Communist who in 1938 set the pattern of justifying further investigation.

As Mr. Goodman describes it, Matthews "demonstrated convincingly how the front organizations inflated their membership figures; then he used the inflated figures as evidence of national peril." This was a considerable improvement over the investigation of Communism conducted eight years previously by New York's arch-conservative Hamilton Fish. Mr. Fish was so proper and so ignorant that he could never credit the Communists' allegiance to Communism. "His strategy was to trip the witnesses up, make them admit that really, at bottom, they did too believe in God and capitalism"—just like all the Fishes did. Naturally, this didn't lead very far, and the Fish committee died within a year; Matthews's contribution has been good for 30.

Mr. Goodman, a social historian, has written what many will call the definitive account of the committee. It is, in fact, more of an outline for a definitive account, which would have to be many pages longer than this already lengthy book and include far more direct testimony. Mr. Goodman is especially enlightening on the little known and painfully ironic origins of the committee—fathered, as it was, by Samuel Dickstein, a zealous New York Congressman of Jewish descent who thought he was proposing an investigation primarily directed at Nazi activities in this country. (Richard Rovere, writing in an introduction, cites Mr. Dickstein's efforts as a classic example of "boomerang effects in politics.")

The hundreds of names in the book bring it all back—Dies, Rankin, Fritz Kuhn, Earl Browder, Robert Stripling, Louis Budenz, J. Parnell Thomas, Gerhart Eisler, "the Hollywood Ten," Richard Nixon, Karl Mundt, Elizabeth Bentley, Harry Dexter White, Alger Hiss and Whittaker Chambers, William Remington, Herbert Philbrick, Francis Walter, J. Edgar Hoover (who would come before the committee "like the Archbishop paying a call on a group of lay brothers: he patronized them, they fussed over him")— right on down to the students who went to Cuba and Mrs. Dagmar Wilson of Women Strike for Peace.

Vigilantes May Rise Again

Mr. Goodman classifies himself a "liberal" and believes that, for all its zaniness and squalor, the committee did serve the purpose of opening liberals' eyes to Communists in their midst. He writes fairly, or at least openly, and with suave good humor; but he fails to recapture either the drive of the investigators (the smell of blood) or the desperation of many of its victims. He makes it seem all quite hilarious, which it was, but only in part and not at the time.

He ends on a sterner note. The committee, he says, represented a genuine part or ethos or attitude of America, in which "common sense is mingled with common superstition." This part of America seems on the wane, as the committee is; but neither has disappeared. Mr. Goodman hints that some of the committee's functions—demanding loyalty to one particular vision of the flag, suggesting that an alien "Communist apparatus" influences dissident Americans— have currently been taken over by the President and the Secretary of State. And undoubtedly the revulsion against Joe McCarthy still exerts a weakening effect on the committee. The vigilantes, as Mr. Rovere suggests elsewhere, may rise once more; but it seems unlikely that they will ever again bemuse the country as they did during the committee's first two decades.

CHAPTER 4

In The Name of National Security

John Mitchell, one of President Richard M. Nixon's Attorneys General.

Courtesy The New York Times

Mississippi's Two Senators Say Communists Seek Negro Revolt

WASHINGTON, Feb. 3 (AP) —Senator James O. Eastland told the Senate today that Communist forces inside and outside the United States "are pressing for a Negro revolution in this country."

The Mississippi Democrat, who heads the Senate Internal Security subcommittee, said in a speech that the focal point for attack was Mississippi.

He said that the Communists long had hoped to "fan the fires of racial hatred, to use and pervert the racial and individual aspirations of Negroes and Negro groups, to manipulate Negro and racial organizations so as to bring them into the Communist sphere."

Both Say Agitators Rejected

Senator John C. Stennis, who is also a Democrat from Mississippi, joined Senator Eastland in the charge that the Communist party and its workers had infiltrated civil rights demonstrations in Mississippi.

Both Senators said that most Negroes in the state had rejected efforts of outside agitators to mix the races and stir up trouble.

"The better type of colored people did not like this conduct," Senator Stennis said, adding that they had refused to take the white agitators into their homes or to join in the disorders.

Both Senators quoted J. Edgar Hoover, Director of the Federal Bureau of Investigation, as saying that Communists had infiltrated racial relations in an attempt to foment disorder.

"It's an attempt to take over the state of Mississippi by the Communist party," Senator Eastland said. He added that efforts of the Freedom Demo-cratic party, a predominantly Negro group, to unseat the state's Democratic House members was "a Communist-planned attempt to influence the Congress of the United States."

Mr. Eastland said, however, that "aid and incitement for the Negro revolution is not coming entirely from Communist and pro-Communist sources."

He indicated that a group of lawyers who had announced that they would go to Mississippi to seek the ouster of the state's five House members was headed by Morton Stavis of Elizabeth, N. J.

The Senator said that Mr. Stavis had changed his name legally from Moses Isaac Stavisky in 1939, charged that he had been a member of the Communist party and had served as counsel for Communist party members in court and at hearings before the House Committee on Un-American Activities.

He said that Mr. Stavis and his wife had invoked the Fifth Amendment before the House committee in 1956 and had refused to answer all questions as to their past or present Communist party membership.

Denies Communist Links

Reached by telephone last night at his home in Elizabeth, N. J., Mr. Stavis said that "of course" he had never belonged to the Communist party.

He acknowledged that he had changed his name from Stavisky, and called Senator Eastland's mention of the change "ill-concealed anti-Semitism."

Mr. Stavis, who returned Tuesday night from Mississippi, said the Senator's attack was an "effort to get the American people back to the days of the late Senator McCarthy," and added:

"The country is not of a mind to tolerate again that type of paranoia."

The lawyer has been coordinator of the Lawyers' Legal Drive to unseat the five Mississippi Representatives.

February 4, 1965

Hoover Links Reds To Berkeley Strife

By The Associated Press

WASHINGTON, May 17 — J. Edgar Hoover and a spokesman for the International Association of Chiefs of Police have told Congress there was Communist involvement in the student demonstrations at the University of California last fall.

Testimony by Mr. Hoover before a House Appropriations subcommittee was made public today. The Director of the Federal Bureau of Investigation appeared March 4.

Charles E. Moore, public relations director of the police chiefs' group, appeared today before the Senate Internal Security subcommittee.

Mr. Moore testified that the student demonstrations and an accompanying "filthy speech" episode had been "dominated by a small hard-core group" of Communists and Communist sympathizers who generated new demands upon the university's administration as fast as "the university yielded or surrendered at every turn" to other demands.

He called this a typical Communist tactic.

The demonstrations were instigated by the campus Free Speech Movement, which has demanded virtually unlimited freedom on campus to espouse off-campus causes such as civil rights. The school has limited such activity.

Mr. Hoover testified that individuals with subversive backgrounds who participated in the demonstrations included five faculty members. Thirty-eight others, he said, were students or connected with the university in some capacity.

Charges Confusion

Mr. Hoover did not identify the individuals in his testimony.

The fall disorders on the Berkeley campus were cited by the F.B.I. chief as an example of "a demonstration which, while not Communist-originated or controlled, has been exploited by a few Communists for their own ends."

"In this instance," he said, "a few hundred students contain within their ranks a handful of Communists that mislead, confuse and bewilder a great many students to their own detriment.

"Communist party leaders feel that based on what happened on the campus of the University of California at Berkeley, they can exploit similar student demonstrations to their own benefit in the future."

Mr. Hoover said Mario Savio, spokesman for the Free Speech Movement and the demonstrators, had a previous arrest record for sit-in demonstrations.

He said Mr. Savio made a tour of Midwest and Eastern colleges last November accompanied by Bettina Aptheker, daughter of Herbert Aptheker, whom Mr. Hoover identified as a member of the National Committee of the Communist party.

A New Organization

Bettina Aptheker, Mr. Hoover said, is a member of the W.E.B. DuBois Club of Berkeley. The W.E.B., DuBois Club of America, Mr. Hoover said, is a Marxist-oriented youth organization founded in San Francisco last June and named in honor of Dr. William E. B. DuBois, a civil rights crusader who joined the Communist party at the age of 93.

Another witness before the Senate subcommittee was Dr. Stefan Possony, who testified that Communists had made student demonstrations such as those California a "spectator sport."

Dr. Possony, the Director of International Studies at the Hoover Institute at Stanford University, said "we must expect this is going to continue."

The subcommittee continues its hearings tomorrow.

Reds in Background

Mr. Moore, who was a special agent for the F.B.I. form 1951 to 1961, told the Senators that he had spent about a week in California investigating the Berkely campus disorders.

Mr. Moore testified that the real Communists had stayed in the background during the demonstrations, working mainly through others to whip student demonstrators to a type of frenzy." He said these others included many from "unusual backgrounds."

Mr. Moore termed the DuBois clubs "an obvious Communist apparatus" and said Mr. Aptheker very clearly "was behind Mario Savio."

Mr. Moore asserted that the whole demonstration provided the Reds with an exercise in "crowd manipulation" and how to contend with the police by trying to make them seem "the tactical enemy."

At one point, Mr. Moore protested that some magazines had published sympathetic articles portraying the student rebellion as a demonstration for their rights.

He said the American Broadcasting Company had paid the expenses of Mr. Savio to come East to participate in a program and that Mr. Savio used the trip to visit other campuses.

Mr. Hoover's wide-ranging testimony also said spies were included in virtually every Soviet group that visited the United States—diplomats, newsmen, scientists, businessmen, students and cultural exchange missions. He also said he opposed publicizing the testimony of Joseph Valachi, convicted murderer who broke a blood oath and divulged secrets of the Cosa Nostra.

"In regard to the Communist bloc espionage attack against this country, there has been no letup whatsoever," Mr.

Hoover told the House subcommittee.

Cites Consulates

"Our government is about to allow them to establish consulates in many parts of the country which, of course, will make our work more difficult."

Asked if he thought advantages in cultural exchange would offset this disadvantage, the man who has headed the F.B.I. for 41 years replied:

"We have found in practically every cultural exchange group or student group that has come to this country, there is always a member of the K.G.B., the intelligence service of the Russian Government. They are called students but some are 36, 37 or 38 years old."

Soviet press coverage, Mr. Hoover said, "is tailored for the intelligence work of the Soviets. [Newsmen] are in a business where they are expected to be where news is developing, to meet those persons having intimate knowledge, to ask questions and to seek information.

"As of Feb. 1, 1965, over half of the Soviet nationals posing as press representatives in the United States were known to be intelligence agents."

A favorite tactic of Soviet intelligence, Mr. Hoover added, is "disguising their intelligence personnel as legitimate trade representatives."

May 18, 1965

U.S. Asks to Have DuBois Clubs Registered as Communist Front

By FRED P. GRAHAM
Special to The New York Times

WASHINGTON, March 4—The Justice Department petitioned the Subversive Activities Control Board today to order the campus-oriented W. E. B. DuBois Clubs to register as a Communist-front organization.

The proceeding was the first under the Subversive Activities Control Act since 1963 and the 23d time that the Government has cited a group under the law. The previous 22 attempts failed to produce a registration, as the organizations either dissolved or bogged the proceedings down in the courts.

Organized to promote "Marxism, peace, civil rights and civil liberties," the clubs have been prominently involved in civil rights activities in the San Francisco area, demonstrations against the House Committee on Un-American Activities and demonstrations against the Government's Vietnam policy.

Attorney General Nicholas deB. Katzenbach said in a statement that the DuBois group had been formed in June, 1964 "under the plan, guidance and direction of the Communist party U. S. A." This was the result of a resolution passed by the 1959 party convention, which called for the establishment of a national Marxist youth organization, he said.

The Katzenbach statement said that a substantial number of the group's officers were members of the Communist party and "subject to its discipline."

Mr. Katzenbach said that the DuBois Clubs, with headquarters in San Francisco, claims a membership of about 2,500 and has about 36 chapters, most of them on college campuses. They are concentrated in California, New York, Wisconsin and Illinois.

The DuBois organization was named for Dr. William E. B. DuBois, a Negro historian and sociologist who was a co-founder of the National Association for the Advancement of Colored People. He broke with the N.A.A.C.P. in 1934, returned again in 1944 and quit again in 1948. He joined the Communist party in 1961 at the age of 93, two years before he died as an expatriate in Ghana.

Although Mr. DuBois pronounced his name DooBOYS, within the organization many of the individual clubs call themselves dooBWA clubs.

Historically, Mr. Katzenbach said, "Americans have the freedom to organize in dissent. At the same time, in accordance with the law, young people who might consider joining this organization are entitled to know its nature and sponsorship."

The action was taken after an extensive investigation by the Federal Bureau of Investigation.

A Communist front organization, as described in the 1950 law, is one substantially dominated, directed or controlled by a Communist organization, and operated principally to give aid and support to that Communist action group.

Under the law's procedures, the board now will hold hearings to determine whether the organization is a Communist front.

If so, it will be required to list its officers and the sources and distribution of its funds. Listing is required also for all printing equipment, including presses and duplicating machines.

Mr. Katzenbach made the point that the procedure "is a disclosure, not a criminal action."

Although the law has not resulted in any registrations, the Justice Department has found that when it proceeds against a group, membership falls off and the organization collapses.

The last group to be cited under the law was called the Advance and Burning Issues Youth Organization, described as a Marxist-Leninist youth group. It quickly dissolved, and the Justice Department asked the board to stay its proceedings.

In a test case, two groups—Veterans of the Abraham Lincoln Brigade and the American Committee for the Protection of the Foreign Born—appealed the board's finding that they were Communist front organizations to the Supreme Court.

In a decision handed down last spring, the Court ruled that the record was too stale for a ruling on the merits.

March 5, 1966

Nixon Terms Lawlessness Growing National Problem

CHICAGO, June 10 (UPI)—Richard M. Nixon said tonight that a nation that "accepts public lawlessness as a legitimate means of dissent has passed a significant milestone on the road to anarchy."

The former Vice President said that a growing threat to freedom in the United States was "a rising disregard for the rule of law which is the guarantee of all freedom." he called for "a national crusade" to restore respect for the law.

June 11, 1966

Inquiry on New Left Is Planned in Senate

By BEN A. FRANKLIN
Special to The New York Times

WASHINGTON, Oct. 25 — The Senate Internal Security Subcommittee disclosed plans today for a sweeping investigation of organizations of the New Left, including militant civil rights and antiwar groups.

The subcommittee's preparations for the inquiry were revealed when lawyers for two of the groups to be investigated charged that the subcommittee or its agents had stolen letters, files and documents on which part of the inquiry was to be based.

To counter this complaint, lawyers for the subcommittee introduced the formal, authorizing resolution for an inquiry in United States District Court here today.

The resolution, unanimously adopted in secret two weeks ago, was signed by the 10 Senators on the subcommittee. Lawyers for the panel asserted that the documents in question had been obtained as part of a legally authorized Congressional investigation.

At the same time, the House Un-American Activities Committee opened public hearings on the alleged role of Communists in last summer's urban rioting.

The first witness was Archie Moore, former light heavyweight champion prizefighter and a Negro. He said the rioters were black people crying out against the white man's injustices and that if the injustices were alleviated Communism could not thrive in the urban ghettoes.

He was supported by Clarence Mitchell, director of the Washington branch of the National Association for the Advancement of Colored People.

Another Senate Inquiry

Another investigation of the riots is being conducted—so far only at the staff level without public hearings — by the Permanent Investigations subcommittee headed by Senator John L. McClellan, Democrat of Arkansas.

Senator McClellan is also a member of the Internal Security subcommittee—the Senate's counterpart of the Un-American Activities Committee.

The Internal Security Subcommittee plans to focus its investigation on the so-called National Conference for New Politics, a meeting of New Left, black power, pacifist and militant student groups held in Chicago over the Labor Day weekend and coordinated by a two-year-old, New York-based group of the same name. It is this that will give the inquiry such broad scope.

Among the 200 organizations represented at the conference by delegations or observers were the National Mobilization Committee to End the War in Vietnam, Students for a Democratic Society, the Southern Christian Leadership Conference, the Student Nonviolent Coordinating Committee, the Congress of Racial Equality, Women Strike for Peace, the Summit County (Ohio) Adequate Welfare Committee, the Mississippi Freedom Democratic Party and the National Committee for a Sane Nuclear Policy.

The Communist Party, U.S.A., and various Trotskyite and Socialist groups were also involved.

The language of the Internal Security subcommittee's resolution authorizing the investigation directs the staff, headed by J. G. Sourwine, to "undertake immediately a full and complete investigation of the activities of the National Conference for New Politics and any organizations and individuals affiliated or associated therewith, with respect to all areas and spheres of activity where the basic authority of the subcommittee or any facet thereof is applicable."

Mr. Sourwine said in an interview today that the resolution was "pretty broad" but that preliminary checks of documents and interrogation of prospective witnesses would not include every organization that participated in the Chicago meeting. He said he could not specify which organizations would receive the subcommittee's closest attention.

However, in a Senate speech on Sept. 22, Senator James O. Eastland, Democrat of Mississippi and the subcommittee's chairman, indicated that the panel would bear down hardest on the conference itself and on the Mississippi Freedom Democrats, a nearly all-Negro organization seeking to run Negro candidates as independents for local offices in 20 Mississippi counties.

The Freedom Democrats, according to documents introduced by Senator Eastland, sought to raise $141,000 at the Chicago Conference to finance its independent political activities in Mississippi during the next year.

Senator Eastland declared in his speech that he "would not want to prejudice possible future hearings before the Internal Security subcommittee," but added: "Who can doubt the cooperation between the Communist party and the Conference for New Politics?"

The formal purpose of the subcommittee investigation is to determine whether there is a need for legislation to control allegedly subversive elements in the conference.

The resolution authorizes hearings later if Senator Eastland deems them appropriate. Such hearings would be closed to the press and the public under terms of the resolution, "except as the chairman may otherwise direct."

Besides Senators Eastland and McClellan, members of the Internal Security subcommittee are:

Senators Thomas J. Dodd of Connecticut, Sam J. Ervin Jr. of North Carolina, Birch Bayh of Indiana and George A. Smathers of Florida, all Democrats, and Everett McKinley Dirksen of Illinois, Roman L. Hruska of Nebraska, Hugh Scott of Pennsylvania and Strom Thurmond of South Carolina, Republicans.

The resolution was introduced today before Judge Matthew F. McGuire by lawyers for Senator Eastland and Mr. Sourwine.

They were responding to a petition seeking $500,000 in damages and an injunction against Mr. Eastland, Mr. Sourwine and Benjamin Mandel, research director of the subcommittee.

The petition filed by lawyers for the national conference and the Freedom Democrats, asks for damages for the alleged theft of letters, records and files from the Mississippians' temporary headquarters during the Chicago meeting.

The complaint contends that two persons it identifies only as "Joe Doe and Richard Roe . . . of state, local or Federal law enforcement and-or extra legal agencies" took the documents from a hotel room and gave them to Senator Eastland "wilfully and with intent, under color of Federal and state law, to deprive the plaintiffs" of their constitutional right to organize for political activity in Mississippi and elsewhere.

Judge McGuire did not rule today. The reason for introducing the subcommittee resolution was to show the court that the missing papers were duly authorized to be in the custody of a standing Senate subcommittee, and thus that Senator Eastland and the other officials were immune from suit.

Neither Senator Eastland nor the subcommittee would disclose how it came into possession of the missing documents.

October 26, 1967

Return to McCarthyism Feared By 7 Rights and Religious Aides

*Spock a Signer of the Letter
That Attacks 2 Committees
in Senate, One in House*

By EDITH EVANS ASBURY

A new wave of McCarthyism threatens the nation in the opinion of seven religious and civil liberties leaders.

Freedom of speech and political dissent is under attack by three Congressional committees at a time when the nation most needs discussion, the leaders declared in a letter released yesterday that recalled the anti-Communist charges of Senator Joseph R. McCarthy, Republican of Wisconsin, in the early nineteen-fifties.

The Rev. Dr. Martin Luther King Jr., the civil rights leader who was slain April 4, was a signer of the letter. The letter, which was prepared before Dr. King's death and made public at a news conference in the offices of the American Civil Liberties Union, 156 Fifth Avenue, was addressed to the public and each member of Congress.

Dr. Benjamin M. Spock, the pediatrician who is under indictment for antiwar activities, also signed the letter and attended the news conference.

The other signers were Roger Baldwin, founder of the A.C.L.U.; the Rev. John C. Bennett, president of the Union Theological Seminary; Robert F. Drinan, S. J., Dean of the Boston College Law School; Rabbi Maurice Eisendrath, president of the Union of American Hebrew Congregations, and Robert M. Hutchins, president of the Center for the Study of Democratic Institutions.

The Congressional panels criticized were the Senate Special Subcommittee on Internal Security, the House Committee on Un-American Activities and the Senate Permanent Subcommittee on Investigations.

The Internal Security Subcommittee is investigating the National Conference for New Politics held at Chicago in 1967, which included the Mississippi

302

Black Star
Dr. Benjamin M. Spock

Freedom Democratic party, the letter said. The party is challenging the political control of the committee's chairman, Senator James O. Eastland, the letter stated.

The House Committee on Un-American Activities is investigating "the New Left in general, and the Students for a Democratic Society in particular," the letter continued.

The Senate Investigations Subcommittee is looking into last summer's Negro riots.

McCarthy Recalled

The three committees, the letter said, "threaten to repeat the experience of the nineteen-fifties when the cry of Communism by Senator Mc-Carthy and his acolytes stifled all but the most orthodox politics" and may lead "as in the fifties, not only to silence but also to persecution, prosecution and loss of jobs."

The late Senator McCarthy, as the chairman of the Senate Committee on Government Operations, conducted numerous public hearings at which a large number of persons, including members of the State Department and the Army, were denounced as Communists on the basis of evidence that his critics called inadequate.

An increasing estrangement between blacks and whites, and fundamental disagreements over the war in Vietnam "threaten to rupture the nation," the letter asserted.

Various forms of protest have arisen, which, "whatever the Government believes about the merits of the opinions of the protesters," must not be disposed of "by fixing the label 'Communist,' 'agitation,' 'Hanoi' or 'Moscow' to them," the letter said.

However, it continued, the three Congressional committees have adopted the "discredited path" of "searching high and low for malevolent political influences — generally foreign — which are supposedly manipulating protests" instead of inquiring into basic causes.

April 25, 1968

Hoover Finds Peril In New Left Action

By The Associated Press

WASHINGTON, May 18— J. Edgar Hoover says that revolutionary stands taken by militant black nationalist groups and students of the New Left pose a threat to the nation's security.

He told Congress that the black nationalist groups he had in mind were the Student Nonviolent Coordinating Committee, the Black Muslims and the Revolutionary Action Movement. They are, he said, "a distinct threat to the internal security of the nation."

The Federal Bureau of Investigation director said that the New Left, typified by the Students for a Democratic Society, which has been active in campus disturbances, was "a new type of subversive, and their danger is great."

Mr. Hoover appeared before a House Appropriations subcommittee Feb. 23 and his testimony was released today. He was seeking approval of a $207.5-million budget for the fiscal year starting July 1.

The budget provides an $11-million increase for the F.B.I.

It will permit an increase in personnel from 15,638 to 16,-251. This would include 78 more agents for a total of 6,668 and 535 more clerks for a total of 9,583.

Mr. Hoover expressed concern over reports that black nationalist groups were stockpiling weapons "for use against the white man."

Cites Availability of Guns

He said these reports could well be true because guns were easily obtained and because of "the inflammatory urgings of such agitators as Stokely Carmichael, H. Rap Brown and James Forman of the Student Nonviolent Coordinating Committee."

Mr. Hoover also testified as follows:

¶Membership in racist groups like the Ku Klux Klan was dwindling in the heart of the South—Mississippi, Alabama and Louisiana. Klan membership was only about 14,000 but "there are thousands of sympathizers."

¶The F.B.I. investigated 29,-228 reported violations of the Selective Service Act last year. While many young people "noisily and brazenly advocated the burning and turning in of draft cards" to demonstrate opposition to the Vietnam war, "many just went through the motions with phony cards."

¶The Mexican Communist party has made plans to store weapons and ammunition in preparation for a revolution in Mexico and has already designated staging areas for the revolt. One unspecified area is 150 miles from Laredo, Tex.

¶The domestic Communist party has tried to link civil rights protests with its opposition to the Vietnam war as part of a program "to create one massive movement which they hope will ultimately change our government's policies, both foreign and domestic."

Finds Desire to Destroy

Mr. Hoover said that among young people, the New Left "can be expected to find wider fields of endeavor and to try to do all that it can to infect the rising generation with its anti-American prattle."

He said the mood of these organizations — as typified by Students for a Democratic Society, "is a mood of disillusionment, pessimism and alienation." He continued: At the center of the movement is an almost passionate desire to destroy, to annihilate, to tear down. If anything definite can be said about the Students for a Democratic Society, it is that it can be called anarchistic."

The student group, "infiltrated by Communist party members," has "seized upon every opportunity to foment discord among the youth of this country," Mr. Hoover said.

Of the militant black nationalist groups, Mr. Hoover said "some so-called civil rights groups preaching hatred of the white race, demanding immunity from laws and advocating violence constitute a serious threat to our country's internal security."

May 19, 1968

STUDENT LEADERS VOICE RADICALISM

New Left Advocates Back communism (With Small c)

By ANTHONY RIPLEY
Special to The New York Times

EAST LANSING, Mich., June 15—The national convention of Students for a Democratic Society has removed any lingering doubt about the purpose of its organization.

It is revolutionary communism with a small "c".

The convention, which ended today on the campus of Michigan State University, has elected three top national officers, two of whom call themselves communists.

Radicals in the group insist on the small "c" to differentiate themselves from Communist party affiliation. The group disavows Soviet Communism as bureaucratic and oppressive and, at its convention, roundly turned back the Progressive Labor party representatives who look to Communist China for revolutionary inspiration.

Instead, the group generally follows what its members call a "New Left radical political analysis" that looks for sources of discontent in the nation outside the traditional revolution of the proletariat of Marxism.

Questioned About Views

But beyond the complex talk of "Marxist analysis" and "New Left analysis," the words of two newly elected national officers stand forth with clarity.

While on the convention floor answering questions about basic beliefs, one of the candidates for national office was asked:

"Do you consider yourself a socialist?"

"I consider myself a revolutionary communist," the candidate, Bernadine Dohrn, replied.

Another new national officer was accused of being a Stalinist.

"Having only been a communist a few months, I have difficulty understanding that concept," the officer, Michael Klonsky, replied.

Elected as top officers of the group were Miss Dohrn, 26 years old, a graduate of the University of Chicago law school, interorganizational secretary; Mr. Klonsky, 25, of Los Angeles, a graduate of San Fernando State College, national secretary, and Fred Gordon, 24, of San Diego, Calif., a graduate of Harvard University, educational secretary.

Eight members elected to the

303

national committee, which helps direct the organization's chapters on 300 college campuses, were Mike James and Mike Spiegel, of Chicago; Carl Oglesby, of Yellow Springs, Ohio; Bartee Haile Jr., of the Texas region; Jeff Jones, of New York City; Chip Marshall, of the Niagara region; Morgan Spector, of the San Francisco Bay region, and Eric Mann, of the New England region.

Mark Rudd, the leader of the Columbia University demonstrations, was a candidate for the national committee but placed next to last in the final balloting.

"He's your man, not ours," a member of the organization told reporters.

Officers said at the convention that the group had "fraternal relations" with the Southern Student Organizing Committee, the University Christian Movement, the Student Nonviolent Coordinating Committee, the Liberation News Service, the National Community Union and a newspaper called The Movement.

In a statement issued at a news conference after the convention today, officers said that little structural change had been made in the organization. They said that much of the discussion had "centered on ways of extending the movement to new constituencies—to uncommitted students and high school students, and to workers, hippies, the American poor, college trained professionals and American G.I.'s."

The organization works from "a basic anticapitalist analysis," one speaker told the convention.

The essence of the group's differences with standard Communist belief is its view that the old working class revolution no longer applies to this wealthy nation, where many workers have become middle class.

One of the convention's last acts of business was to approve a resolution to "initiate and support activities directed toward creating a radical political consciousness among the members of the armed forces."

June 16, 1968

Hoover Charges Sabotage Workshop At New Left Parley

WASHINGTON, July 18 (UPI)—J. Edgar Hoover said today that workshops dealing with "sabotage and explosives" for possible use against Selective Service facilities were conducted last month at the national convention of Students for a Democratic Society.

The director of the Federal Bureau of Investigation said that participants in the meetings at Michigan State University in East Lansing had "explored the use of combustible materials and the various types of bombs which could be devised to destroy communications and plumbing systems of strategic buildings."

Mr. Hoover's comments were contained in a report on F.B.I. operations in the fiscal year 1968 that ended June 30.

Attorney General Ramsey Clark said in a foreword that the year was one of "outstanding advances" in the bureau's law enforcement activities.

Mr. Hoover characterized the Students for a Democratic Society as the core of a New Left subversive force comparable to the Communist party in its "concept of violence as an instrument to destroy the existing social order."

He said that the workshops "even discussed the finer points of firing Molotov cocktails from shotguns, as well as similar forms of so-called defense measures which could be used in defiance of police action."

Much of the "unrest and violence" on college campuses in recent months was "instigated and precipitated" by this New Left, Mr. Hoover said.

He gave no names and made no mention of the source of his report or the possibility of prosecuting participants.

July 19, 1968

Agnew Links Protesters With Reds

GOVERNOR POINTS TO MOSCOW TRIPS

By HOMER BIGART

Gov. Spiro T. Agnew of Maryland brought the issue of Communists-on-the-campus into the Presidential campaign yesterday.

The Republican Vice-Presidential candidate told a news conference here that he saw a "definite link" between the campus revolt and Communists.

He said the student uprisings were sponsored mainly by the Students for a Democratic Society, which contained "persons actively identified at least as Red sympathizers."

He said he was going to expose them during the campaign.

As evidence of the Communist link, Governor Agnew cited placards carried last spring by Columbia University students, placards that "indicated support for Ho Chi Minh and Castro." And he said that some of the instigators of the campus uprisings had traveled to Havana, Hanoi and Moscow.

Spoke at Nixon Office Here

He used the Nixon headquarters at Park Avenue and 57th Street as the rostrum for his remarks, perhaps the most conservative since he was nominated at Miami.

The first hint that he was about to take a tougher stand on youthful dissenters came Thursday night in York, Pa., where he told the state convention of Young Republicans that the protesters were caught up in what he called "unconscious anarchism."

Yesterday he saw them as "Communists or Communist sympathizers."

Besides seeing Reds on the campuses, Governor Agnew scolded doves for talking too much about Vietnam when they lacked facts to back up their judgments. He also criticized Chief Justice Earl Warren for a "rather precipitous resignation" that placed the Republican party in an "uncomfortable position."

The Republicans' discomfort, he said, sprang from their having to object to the confirmation of Associate Justice Abe Fortas, named by President Johnson to succeed Mr. Warren.

Some Republicans have said that the Warren resignation was timed to prevent a Republican President from naming a Chief Justice should the Republicans win in November.

As for Mr. Fortas, Governor Agnew said: "I've always felt he's a very fine gentleman."

Reminded that Richard M. Nixon once called Mr. Warren "a fine Republican Chief Justice," Governor Agnew said he was not criticizing Mr. Warren's "very competent" performance in the Supreme Court but only the timing of the resignation.

On the Communist issue, Governor Agnew said the alleged links between student demonstrators and Communists should be investigated but not in such a way as to revive "events in our recent past" — an apparent reference to the activities of the late Senator Joseph R. McCarthy, who charged widespread Communist infiltration of the Government in the early nineteen-fifties.

He said it was unfortunate that as a result of the Communist issue having been "played up too highly in former years" there was now "the tendency to play it down."

Commenting on the disorders that occurred during the Democratic National Convention in Chicago, Governor Agnew said that some of the leaders were, if not actually Communists, at least willing to travel to Communist capitals for what he termed "instruction."

He said that after watching the evolution of student disorders in the United States and abroad he had reached the conclusion that they revolved basically around the "sort of person willing to be identified with Communist causes."

In Paramus, N. J., last night, speaking before 3,000 cheering suburbanites at a spaghetti dinner, Mr. Agnew accused the Johnson Administration of fostering a "climate of permissiveness."

He denounced what he called "the appeasement of the militant minority in the ghettos," assailed a "minority of the clergy" who encouraged resistance to the draft, and cited in particular those who "encouraged the pouring of blood over draft records."

Mr. Agnew called J. Edgar Hoover, director of the Federal Bureau of Investigation, a great American. He said that when the Republicans took over the Government the streets would be safe again and a sense of patriotism would be restored to the land.

"Little old ladies now forced to wear tennis shoes so they can outleg criminals will once again be able to wear high heels," Mr. Agnew promised.

September 7, 1968

RISE IN TERRORISM FEARED BY HOOVER

WASHINGTON, Dec. 31 (UPI)—J. Edgar Hoover, director of the Federal Bureau of Investigation said today that the nation faced the prospect of increased terrorist tactics by the New Left aimed at the total destruction of the Government.

In a year-end report, he also said that the growth of Negro extremist organizations constituted "a potential threat to the internal security of the nation."

"There has been a marked increase in recent months in bombings and burnings of public buildings and other acts of terrorism," Mr. Hoover said.

"New Left leaders have constantly exhorted their followers to abandon their traditional role of 'passive dissent' and resort to these terroristic tactics as a means of disrupting the defense effort and opposing established authority."

Tomorrow Mr. Hoover becomes 74 years old and ready to embark on his 45th year in the job of F.B.I. director.

January 1, 1969

Wiretaps on Dr. King Made After Johnson Ban

By MARTIN WALDRON
Special to The New York Times

HOUSTON, June 6 — Testimony in Federal District Court has indicated that the Federal Bureau of Investigation continued to wiretap the telephones of the Rev. Dr. Martin Luther King Jr. and Elijah Muhammad after former President Johnson ordered an end to wiretaps except those authorized by the Attorney General for "national security" reasons.

The implication was that the F.B.I. either ignored the Presidential order or that Dr. King, the assassinated civil rights leader, and Mr. Muhammad, the Black Muslim leader, were being surveyed in connection with some security case.

The F.B.I. refused to comment. Aides of Mr. Johnson did not reply immediately to a request for clarification from him.

On June 30, 1965, President Johnson, in an "administratively confidential" memorandum to all Government departments, said that the "invasion of privacy of communications is a highly offensive practice which should be engaged in only where the national security is at stake."

No telephone tap, including those for national security reasons, could be maintained without prior approval of the Attorney General, the President said.

But Robert Nichols, special agent of the Atlanta F.B.I. office, testified this week at a hearing here that he had supervised a wiretap on the home telephone of Dr. King.

"I wasn't on it except until May, 1965," Mr. Nichols said.

Charles Morgan Jr., Southern director of the American Civil Liberties Union, then asked, "And the wiretap on Martin King's calls continued until his death on April 4, 1968?" Mr. Nichols replied:

"It was my understanding that it went on."

C. Barry Pickett, a special agent in the F.B.I. office at Jacksonville, Fla., testified that he had been a clerk in the Phoenix, Ariz., office of the F.B.I. from May, 1962, until May, 1966.

His assignment, he said, was to listen to the conversations of Black Muslim leaders.

The F.B.I. had a microphone in Mr. Muhammad's home as well as a wiretap on his telephone, Mr. Pickett said.

Neither Mr. Nichols, Mr. Pickett, nor Mr. Pickett's former superior, Frederick J. Brownell, a retired special agent, was required to testify as to the purpose of the wiretaps.

District Judge Joe Ingraham referred to the wiretaps as being illegal. But he said that if it were found that Cassius Clay had been convicted of draft dodging by the use of illegally gathered evidence it would not be necessary to decide the reasons for the wiretaps.

The wiretap testimony was presented as Judge Ingraham heard the appeal of Clay from his conviction in June, 1967. Clay alleges that the Government used "tainted" evidence.

Testimony in the appeal of the former heavyweight boxing champion from a five-year sentence was concluded yesterday. Judge Ingraham asked the two sides to submit briefs within two weeks. He said that he might ask for additional testimony after reading the briefs.

Mr. Pickett, who was one of a half dozen F.B.I. employes assigned to eavesdrop on Mr. Muhammad, said that he had been told to record all conversations at Mr. Muhammad's home, but that he had to make a synopsis only of what he considered to be "pertinent facts."

Attorneys for the Department of Justice fought for two days in Judge Ingraham's court to try to bar public disclosure of their wiretaps or anything connected with them.

The existence of the wiretaps was disclosed in the Supreme Court in March when the Solicitor General's office acknowledged that the F.B.I. had monitored five conversations involving Clay. Only one, the Government said, had been approved by the Attorney General and that one was involved in the gathering of "foreign intelligence information."

The Government lawyers argued that the four others should also be kept secret because "the unauthorized dissemination of the facts relating to these surveillances would prejudice the national interests and might prejudice the interest of third parties."

The Government attorneys, John S. Martin Jr. and Michael T. Epstein from the Justice Department, and United States Attorney Anthony J. P. Farris of Houston, said that their reasons for wanting the records kept secret could not even be advanced in open court.

After a closed session lasting 30 minutes, Judge Ingraham upheld the Government's position on the wiretap that involved "foreign intelligence," but he admitted the synopses of the four other wiretaps into evidence.

Attorney General John N. Mitchell has signed an affidavit stating that disclosure of the wiretap that involved foreign intelligence could prejudice the national interest. He did not mention the four other wiretaps.

None of the records of the four other wiretaps bore a date later than June 30, 1965, when President Johnson's order on wiretaps was issued.

The record of the conversation between Clay, who is also known as Muhammad Ali, and Dr. King was dated Sept. 4, 1964. The dates on the records of the conversation between the former boxer and Mr. Muhammad were in 1964 and early 1965.

Not until Mr. Morgan cross-examined the F.B.I. agents was it uncovered that the wiretaps had probably extended beyond the June 30, 1965, date.

Hoover Testimony Cited
Special to The New York Times

WASHINGTON, June 6—An F.B.I. spokesman, asked about wiretaps today, referred to the testimony of J. Edgar Hoover to the House Subcommittee on Appropriations on March 4, 1965, at which time Mr. Hoover testified as follows:

"In carrying out our investigative responsibilities, we have 44 telephone taps in operation. Each must be authorized in advance and in writing by the Attorney General. Their use is highly restrictive—that is, only in matters in which the internal security of the country is involved, and in kidnapping and extortion violations where human life is in jeopardy. All those now in operation fall in the internal security category."

A Department of Justice spokesman said Mr. Hoover's testimony was accurate in every respect.

June 7, 1969

U.S. CLAIMS RIGHT OF WIRETAPPING IN SECURITY CASES

Justice Agency Says Court Approval Is Not Needed If Subversion Is Feared

---

By FRED P. GRAHAM
Special to The New York Times

WASHINGTON, June 13—The Justice Department contended today that it had the legal power of eavesdrop without court approval on members of organizations that it believes to be seeking to "attack and subvert the Government by unlawful means."

In court papers filed in Federal District Court in Chicago and released here, the Government disclosed that it had used wiretapping or bugging to eavesdrop on some or all of the eight antiwar activists who have been indicted for inciting riots at the Democratic National Convention last summer in Chicago.

In disclosing the surveillance, the Justice Department said for the first time that it had the power under the Constitution to eavesdrop on domestic groups, free of court supervision and without regard for the Fourth Amendment.

"There can be no doubt that there are today in this country organizations which intend to use force and other illegal means to attack and subvert the existing forms of government," the Government brief argued.

"Moreover, in recent years there have been an increasing number of instances in which Federal troops have been called upon by the states to aid in the suppression of riots.

"Faced with such a state of affairs, any President who takes seriously his oath to 'preserve, protect and defend the Constitution' will no doubt determine that it is not 'unreasonable' to utilize electronic surveillance to gather intelligence information concerning those organizations which are committed to the use of illegal methods to bring about changes in our form of government and which may be seeking to foment violent disorders," the document stated.

32-Page Document

The latter reference, and others in the 32-page document, made it clear that the Government was saying it had the power to eavesdrop on black militant groups and other radical elements without going through the procedures established by the Crime Control Act that was passed by Congress last year, or those safeguards generally felt to be required by the Fourth Amendment.

These procedures require court approval before any eavesdropping is conducted. They also limit the time of eavesdropping and impose other restrictions on Government surveillance.

Today's assertion by the Government amounts to a statement that Federal agents may legally continue to carry out the kind of unregulated eavesdropping that was used for years against the Rev. Dr. Martin Luther King Jr. and Elijah Muhammad, the Black Muslim leader.

It came to light in court hearings in Houston last week that the two Negro leaders had been bugged and tapped for long periods by agents of the Federal Bureau of Investigation.

Arguing today that the Attorney General should not have to obtain court approval before conducting such surveillance, the Government argued.

"The question whether it is appropriate to utilize electronic surveillance to gather intelligence information concerning the activities and plans of such organizations in order to protect the nation against the possible danger which they present is one that properly comes within the competence of the executive and not the judicial branch."

In the papers filed today the Justice Department also said that some of the defendants had been overheard over listening devices being used in "foreign intelligence" investigations. This is a new term, which is used to designate Government counterespionage activity.

Many lawyers believe that the Supreme Court will eventually uphold the President's authority to wiretap without court approval in "foreign intelligence" situations, but the Government had not said until today that it could use the same methods to keep tabs on American citizens not affiliated with foreign powers.

One of the eight defendants, Jerry C. Rubin, 30 years old, a leader of the Youth International party from New York City, had previously been told by the Government that he was overheard over an electronic listening device.

Attorney General John N. Mitchell said in an affidavit attached to today's brief that four other defendants had also been overheard. He named David T. Dellinger, 53 years old, of Brooklyn, and Rennard C. Davis, 28, of Chicago, co-chairmen of the National Mobilization Committee to end the war in Vietnam; Thomas E. Hayden, 29, a founder of the Students for a Democratic Society organization, who is from New York City, and Bobby G. Seale, 32, a Black Panther leader from Oakland, Calif.

Mr. Mitchell said that these four and Mr. Rubin had been overheard over devices that were being used either in "foreign intelligence" investigations or revolutionary domestic organizations. The court was furnished with sealed copies of transcripts of the conversations.

The other defendants are Abbott H. Hoffman, 32, a Yippie leader from New York City; Lee Weiner, 29, of Chicago, and John R. Froines, 29, of Eugene, Ore.

June 14, 1969

POLICE IN JERSEY ORDERED TO QUASH FILES ON PROTESTS

Court Says Gathering Data on Civil Rights Militants Violates Constitution

---

By RONALD SULLIVAN
Special to The New York Times

TRENTON, Aug. 6—The State Attorney General and every other law enforcement official in New Jersey were ordered today to destroy the secret intelligence files they have been keeping on persons suspected of being involved in riots and and other "public demonstrations."

The order, which was signed by Superior Court Judge Robert A. Mathews and made public here by the State Department of Law and Public Safety, said that the keeping of the files violated the United States Constitution's First Amendment guarantees of freedom of speech and assembly.

"The secret files that would be maintained as a result of this intelligence-gathering system," Judge Mathews ruled, are inherently dangerous, and by their very existence tend to restrict those who would advocate, within the protected areas, social and political change."

State Attorney General Arthur J. Sills was not in his office here today. However, sources in the State House said Mr. Sills planned to appeal the court's decision, which was handed down in Superior Court in Hudson County.

There was immediate resistance to the judge's order. Steven Nestor, the chief of the Jersey City Police Department, said tonight that "we're still going to keep them." He said the only thing he would not do now would be to give out information from the files.

Chief Nestor is scheduled to appear in court Friday to respond to a complaint by the Black Panthers in Jersey City that the police there were conducting a systematic policy of harassment and intimidation against their organization.

Mr. Sills instigated the new intelligence system in April, 1968, when he sent a long memorandum to local law enforcement agencies. The memorandum, entitled, "Civil Disorders — The Role of Local, County and State Government" was drafted in the aftermath of the bloody rioting in Newark and Plainfield in 1967.

Mr. Sills said in a legal brief in support of the system last February that "on balance, the public need for information predominates over the individual's interest in not having the police compile information about him."

"In short," he added, "those who actively stand up for what they believe often do so in the face of certain negative factors which weigh against participation in organized political activity."

But in his decision, Judge Mathews held that the United States Supreme Court had repeatedly ruled that individual rights were paramount.

"When a state official, in exercising his power, comes in conflict with those individual liberties protected by the Bill of Rights, it is the delicate and difficult task of the courts to determine whether the resulting restriction on freedom can be tolerated." In this instance, he ruled, it could not.

Civil rights officials here said the decision probably would spur attacks on similar intelligence systems elsewhere in the country, particularly in those areas that had been hit by rioting.

The memorandum from Mr. Sills included two security dossiers — security summary reports and security incident reports—with which local officials were to maintian intelligence reports on suspected groups and activists and to turn them over to the state police.

The summary reports were to deal with any civil disturbance, as well as any rallies, demonstrations, marches and other forms of peaceful protest. The incident reports were to maintain exhaustive information on suspected activists, including the names and addresses of friends, employers, financial status, habits and traits, places frequented, and past activities.

In attacking the forms, the American Civil Liberties Union, acting in behalf of the Jersey City branch of the National Association for the Advancement of Colored People, called them the product of a "Gestapo-like network of police spies."

Judge Matthews asked, "what, for example, is to prevent a report being rendered on one who opposes an existing political regime in a city, county or state?"

Furthermore, he said, "it is not too difficult to imagine the reluctance of an individual to participate in any kind of protected conduct which seeks

publicly to express a particular or unpopular political or social view because of the fact that by doing so he might now have a record, or because his wife, his family, or his employer might also be included."

As for the organizational file, Judge Matthews said that it was "so broad and sweeping that any gathering or event could qualify for a write-up."

For the one on individuals, he said that Mr. Sills did not make clear how the personal information gathered in them would be helpful in preventing civil disorders.

August 7, 1969

City Has Its Own Special Police To Keep Dossiers on Dissidents

By DAVID BURNHAM

The Police Department unit responsible for collecting intelligence about dissident individuals and groups in New York is the Bureau of Special Services, known as Bossi to both its friends and enemies.

The work of Bossi, an acronym from the days when it was called the Bureau of Special Service and Investigations, became a matter of interest yesterday after a New Jersey judge, on Wednesday, ordered the destruction of all official intelligence files on persons suspected of being involved in riots and public demonstrations. The New Jersey Attorney General plans to appeal the Superior Court decision.

Although no other single police agency in New York City is as secretive as Bossi, it is known that the compilation of intelligence files on thousands of residents there is a major part of the bureau's work.

The bureau is commanded by Deputy Inspector William Knapp, a member of the Police

Department for 23 years. It is known that as of March, 1968, one captain, two lieutenants, five sergeants, 55 detectives and four patrolmen were regularly assigned to it. The salaries of these 68 men—a major part of any police agency budget—totaled $666,000.

Infiltration Unit Reported

But according to a 1967 report by the International Association of Chiefs of Police, the bureau had—and presumably still has—a temporary special assignment unit that in 1966 was composed of 55 men.

Though no salary figures are available for this second group, its existence suggests that the bureau's total budget may be more than $1-million a year.

The report by the chiefs' association suggested that the job of most men in the second Bossi group was to infiltrate various groups around the city.

An insight into Bossi's operations was provided last winter by Detective Adolph W. Hart when he testified before a largely unattended late afternoon hearing of the Joint Legis-

lative Committee on Crime.

Detective Hart's testimony—based on his experience as an undercover agent—was a key factor in the conviction of William Epton, the Harlem Progressive Labor party leader, for conspiring to riot and for advocating the overthrow of New York State. Epton was arrested on Aug. 5, 1964, shortly after making speeches and carrying posters during the two-day Harlem riot that year.

Recruiting Described

Detective Hart, who attended several colleges for short periods of time, said he had been recruited by Bossi when he was working in a steel mill in Pittsburgh in 1963.

He said that to conceal his identity, he had not received a badge, pistol or the usual Police Academy training before being sent to Harlem as an undercover agent.

The militant right-wing Minutemen, some Cuban refugee groups, the Columbia University unit of the Students for a Democratic Society, the American Nazi party and the Black Panthers also are said to have had — or have at present — Bossi undercover men as members.

One informed police source, however, indicated that militancy was not required to win a place in Bossi's files.

"They even have dossiers on

Mayor Lindsay and some of his guys," this source said. "I have never seen his name in the file, but someone like [Daniel Patrick] Moynihan is considered pretty far out by Bossi, and a lot of people like him are in the files."

Mr. Moynihan is urban-affairs adviser to President Nixon.

No reason could be learned why there might be a file on the Mayor. A spokesman for the Mayor said Mr. Lindsay would have no comment.

The same source said Bossi's files, while containing some information from undercover agents, consisted mostly of information typed directly from newspaper clips by detectives and then stamped "confidential."

The ultimate justification for Bossi's intelligence-gathering unit is to help the police cope with any group that might threaten physical harm to city officials or others in government. The guarding of visiting dignitaries is one of its chief functions.

In addition to the escort section, which helps the Secret Service guard the President when he is in New York, Bossi is divided into a permanent security section, labor section, confidential investigation section, general investigation section, administration section, and supply and equipment section.

August 8, 1969

Security Guidelines By Secret Service Could Affect Many

By RICHARD D. LYONS
Special to The New York Times

WASHINGTON, Nov. 7—The Secret Service has issued to the nation's Federal and local law enforcement agencies a set of guidelines, which, if lit-

erally interpreted, would have them collect negative information about vast numbers of Americans.

Labeled "For Official Use Only," the guidelines were apparently issued last summer to supplant another set that had stemmed from the Warren Commission's recommendations dealing with the protection of the President.

But the current guidelines apparently go far beyond those

envisioned by the Warren Commission, which investigated the assassination of President Kennedy.

Jack Warner, an assistant to the Secret Service director, said the guidelines were intended to facilitate the gathering of information to be used to protect the President and other high officials.

Yet the wording of the "U.S. Secret Service Liaison Guidelines" requests not only infor-

mation about obvious threats to the President and others protected by the service, but also this other information:

¶About attempts to "embarrass'" high officials.

¶"Regarding civil disturbances."

¶On people seeking "redress of imaginary grievances, etc."

¶On people making "irrational" or "abusive statements" about high Government officials.

¶"Regarding anti-American or anti-U.S. Government demonstrations."

A Secret Service official, who requested anonymity, commented: "The choice of language is certainly unfortunate and could mislead less sophisticated people into thinking that they should collect and send us information that certainly wasn't desired."

The guidelines direct the mailing of "routine reports" to Secret Service headquarters here and the telephoning of "emergency information, especially in reference to Presidential protection."

The guidelines have been sent to at least seven Federal law enforcement agencies, including the Federal Bureau of Investigation and the Central Intelligence Agency, as well as to many police departments.

Many Groups Protest

Many legal and scientific groups have protested the collection of such information and its use against persons seeking full or part-time Federal employment. They contend that the practice leads to blacklisting and that persons on such blacklists seldom, if ever, have the right to confront those who feed the information to Federal agencies.

The groups also contend that unsubstantiated reports of abnormal behavior and participation in political activities, usually left-wing, find their way into security "data banks" of many Federal agencies.

According to the contentions, the agencies then trade the information among themselves. Information that might be regarded as innocuous in one agency might be regarded as extremely damaging in another.

The groups concerned about blacklisting are seeking to determine who has access to the information, what criteria are used to judge its potential harmfulness to an individual and how it can be used against him.

The New York Times reported last month that blacklists of scientists nominated for part-time advisory positions had been drawn up within the Department of Health, Education and Welfare. The sources of the information that was used against the scientists have yet to be explained.

'Negative Information'

The legal and scientific groups also contend that in recent years participation in demonstrations protesting United States involvement in Vietnam has been regarded by the Department of Health, Educa-

tion and Welfare as "negative information." The practice, it is alleged, has the secondary effect of stifling legitimate protest.

In a suit filed in Federal court in Boston, Dr. Henry S. Kahn, a physician, is seeking to force the Department of Health, Education and Welfare to give him a commission in the Public Health Service.

Dr. Kahn charges that the commission was offered pending the outcome of a security check and that it was withdrawn when the results came in. He asserts that his opposition to the Vietnam war and his participation in protest demonstrations were the reasons for the withdrawal.

Among the pieces of information used against Dr. Kahn was a newspaper clipping stating that he was among the participants in an antiwar demonstration.

Mr. Warner, the Secret Service aide, said emphatically that the service would not allow information collected under the guidelines to be used in this manner.

Mr. Warner said the Warren Commission Report, Volume XVIII, Page 930, contained a "sample letter" that might be sent by the service to local police chiefs asking for infor-

mation needed for the protection of the President.

Aid to Protection Effort

The intent of the letter is to allow the Secret Service to amass and digest more easily information on persons who might threaten the President, members of his family or high officials. Congress has authorized the Secret Service to do this.

Yet the language of the guidelines contrasts sharply with that of the sample letter, which does not contain references to embarrassment, civil disturbances and other things mentioned in the guidelines.

Mr. Warner said the service routinely processed 6,000 to 7,000 pieces of information a month and had assessments of their potential value and importance.

He implied that if the guidelines were interpreted literally the Secret Service would be receiving much more information.

When two lawyers who served on the Warren Commission staff were asked for comment about the guidelines and the intent of the commission's recommendations, they replied that the guidelines appeared to have gone beyond the commission's intent.

November 8, 1969

Nixon Aide Opposes Camps of Detention

WASHINGTON, Dec. 3 (AP) --The Nixon Administration urged Congress today to repeal a law authorizing establishment of detention camps for use in internal security emergencies.

It said that repeal of a section of the McCarran Act was needed to put down rumors that the Government planned to use its provisions to detain war protesters and other citizens with minority views.

The position was made known by Deputy Attorney General Richard G. Kleindienst,

who was quoted earlier this year as saying that people who demonstrated in a manner to interfere with others "should be rounded up and put in a detention camp." Today he said that he had been misquoted.

He released a letter to The Atlantic in which he denied he had told the magazine's Washing editor that he favored detaining demonstrators.

The Emergency Detention Act was enacted as part of the Internal Security Law of 1950. It established procedures for apprehending and detaining persons who were considered likely to engage in espionage or sabotage in internal security emergencies.

December 4, 1969

The 'War' Between Panthers And Police

CHICAGO—The "war" between the Black Panther party and the police—a series of clashes that has resulted in the death, injury

or arrest of a number of Panthers—has all but decimated the party's leadership and has raised a host of disturbing questions.

Last Friday, Jerris Leonard, head of the Justice Department's Civil Rights Division, announced that he would head a special Justice Department task force to investigate whether the civil rights of two Black Panthers were violated when they were killed in a pre-dawn police raid here.

He also said that a Federal

grand jury would be called to look into that incident and a Nov. 13 clash in which a Black Panther and two policemen were shot to death on Chicago's South Side.

The announcement, which brought the number of official and unofficial investigations of the slaying to eight, was a recognition that very serious doubts had been raised about the police version of the raid, and that there was growing belief that the avowedly revolutionary Pan-

thers had been singled out for special attention by law enforcement agencies.

Black Skepticism

But the Justice Department's action was greeted with skepticism in some quarters because of a growing feeling, particularly in the black community, that the Federal Administration has had a hand in the recent wave of raids, arrests and shoot-outs involving the Panthers.

The Panthers recruit their

members from the jails, the streets, and the urban colleges. Formed originally for armed "self-defense" against the police, they have gone through a series of political evolutions and now regard themselves as the "vanguard of the revolution" and welcome white allies to the class struggle. The Panthers openly display weapons; adhere to a 10-point guerrilla-style program admonishing them to know their firearms and calling for bread, land, and justice; give free breakfasts and political indoctrination to school children; and speak in a rhetoric that is a heated ghetto Marxism tempered with slogans like "off the pig" (kill the police).

The Panthers charge that the Justice Department is leading a national conspiracy to wipe them out. In recent weeks, their contention has been echoed by more moderate civil rights leaders, including Roy Wilkins, executive director of the National Association for the Advancement of Colored People, who has said that the recent incidents "take on the aspect of a police vendetta."

And Jay A. Miller, executive director of the Illinois division of the American Civil Liberties Union, said Mr. Leonard told him last spring that "the Black Panthers are nothing but hoodlums and we've got to get them."

The Justice Department has issued a carefully worded statement saying that it has "never had any policy of concerted activity with local police in order to harass any member of the Black Panther party."

Clear Attitude

But the attitude of the Administration toward the organization is clear. Vice President Agnew, who frequently says bluntly what his colleagues may muffle in officialese, has called the Panthers

The symbol of the Black Panther party.

a "completely irresponsible, anarchistic group of criminals."

After Attorney General John N. Mitchell took over the Justice Department last January, he ruled that the Panthers were a threat to national security and thus subject to Federal Bureau of Investigation wiretapping under the controversial—and as yet untested—"Mitchell doctrine."

The Government actions appear to have at least contributed to a climate of opinion among local police, who hardly need encouragement to go after the flamboyant militants, that a virtual open season has been declared on the Panthers.

Throughout the summer and fall there had been raids, usually in the pre-dawn hours, on Panther offices and apartments in cities across the country. Usually the offices were torn apart in the process, and frequently charges, made after the raid, were later dropped for lack of evidence.

On Dec. 4, police assigned to the Cook County State's Attorney's office raided a West Side apartment at 4:40 A.M., and in the process Fred Hampton, the 21-year-old chairman of the Illinois Panthers and regarded as one of the most effective leaders still in circulation, and another black Panther were shot to death.

The police say that a woman opened fire on them with a shotgun and a fierce gun battle ensued, lasting at least 10 minutes. The Panthers say the police came in shooting, and that Hampton was "assassinated" while he slept.

There were no bullet holes visible in the places where the police said they were in the cramped five-room apartment, but there were many bullet holes in the places where the Panthers were. This made some persons suspicious. There were widespread demands for an investigation. A citizens group, which includes former Attorney General Ramsey Clark and former Su-

preme Court Justice Arthur Goldberg, has been formed to look into the Hampton slaying as well as other clashes between the police and Panthers.

The immediate effect of the incidents in Chicago and elsewhere has been a rallying of support for the Panthers by more moderate black organizations and by members of all segments of the Negro community who have previously felt little attraction for the Panthers' revolutionary doctrine.

A well-dressed Negro mother summed up the feeling of the black community here as she walked with her family to a packed rally in a church a few days after the shootings.

"They came in and killed Fred Hampton," she said in a soft, very even tone. "And if they can do it to him, they can do it to any of us."

—JOHN KIFNER

December 21, 1969

S.D.S. Militants Advocate A Rise in Violent Tactics

FLINT, Mich., Dec. 27 (Reuters)—Leaders of the militant Weathermen faction of Students for a Democratic Society called today for an escalation of violence and revolutionary tactics to overthrow the American power structure.

The keynote speaker, Barnardine Dohrn, national S.D.S. chairman, told the Weathermen at the opening of a five-day convention here that they must "unite with other white radical groups to overthrow the racist American power structure."

She said it was "obvious that peaceful demonstrations accomplish nothing, so it is time for more violence."

The faction's president, Mark Rudd, forecast "pitched battles between the militant groups and the pigs [police] on a scale that will make anything in the nineteen-sixties look like a Sunday School picnic."

December 28, 1969

Ex-Officer Says Army Spies on Civilian Activists

1,000 Plainclothesmen Said to Report on Virtually All Political Groups

Special to The New York Times

WASHINGTON, Jan. 15 — A former Army intelligence officer said in a magazine article today that nearly 1,000 plainclothes Army investigators keep track of civilian political activity across the country and submit regular reports to a collection headquarters at Fort Holabird in Baltimore.

Christopher H. Pyle, a former captain in Army Intelligence who is now studying for a doctorate in political science at Columbia University, said Army detectives attend political rallies, protest marches and other gatherings, but base most of their reports on the files of "municipal and state police departments and of the F.B.I."

"To assure prompt communication of these reports," Mr. Pyle said, "the Army distributes them over a nationwide wire service. Completed in the fall of 1967, this Teletype network gives every major troop command in the United States daily and weekly reports on virtually all political protests occurring anywhere in the nation."

Mr. Pyle said the investigators monitor "protest politics" ranging from Ku Klux Klan rallies in North Carolina to meetings of the Women's Strike for Peace in Philadelphia.

"Today, the Army maintains files on the membership, ideology, programs, and practices of virtually every activist political group in the country," he said.

The article was published today in The Washington Monthly, a magazine focusing on problems in American politics and government.

'Blacklist' Alledged

Mr. Pyle also said in the article that the Army "periodically publishes an eight-by-ten-inch glossy-cover booklet known within intelligence circles as the 'blacklist.'

Mr. Pyle said this is an encyclopedia of profiles of people and organizations who, in the opinion of the intelligence command officials who compile it, might 'cause trouble for the Army.'"

The surveillance program was started in 1965, Mr. Pyle said, but at that time was designed only to give military officials early warning of possible civil disorders. The program was gradually widened to include most forms of political protest activity, he said.

The investigators are all Army personnel, he said. About 75 per cent are enlisted men and 25 per cent are lieutenants or captains, Mr. Pyle added in a telephone interview, saying that the detectives have top-secret clearances.

The Army also plans, according to Mr. Pyle, to link its Teletype systems to a computerized data bank at Fort Holabird, to which Federal agencies such as the Secret Service, the Federal Bureau of Investigation and the Central Intelligence Agency will have access.

Spokesmen at the intelligence command at Fort Holabird and at the Pentagon declined comment on Mr. Pyle's article.

Mr. Pyle, 30 years old, received an Army commission upon graduation from Bowdoin College in Brunswick, Me., in 1961 after being in the Reserve Officer Training Corps. He obtained a delay on his active duty and received a law degree from Columbia as well as a master's degree in political science.

He entered the Army in 1966 as a first lieutenant and was assigned to the intelligence branch at Fort Holabird. Mr. Pyle was discharged in 1968.

January 16, 1970

ARMY GIVES REPLY ON ROLE OF 'AGENTS'

Special to The New York Times

WASHINGTON, Jan. 26—The Army acknowledged today that its Intelligence Command had about 1,000 "agents" across the country who conduct security checks of Army and Government personnel, but it denied that any widespread monitoring of civilian political activity took place.

The announcement came in response to an article, published in the current issue of The Washington Monthly, written by Christopher H. Pyle, a former captain in Army Intelligence. Mr. Pyle charges that nearly 1,000 plainclothes agents keep files on "virtually every activist political group in the country."

The Army said its agents' "primary duty and function is the conduct for security clearance purposes of background investigations on U.S. Army military members and Department of the Army civilian employes."

The announcement said that the Intelligence Command also had "the mission of providing the Army with planning and early-warning information relative to the possible development of a civil disturbance."

Such information is "limited" in scope, the Army added. "For some time," it said, "there has been a specific prohibition against military personnel undertaking such activities as undercover operations in the civilian community."

January 27, 1970

MAGAZINES' FILES UNDER SUBPOENA

Time, Life and Newsweek Data Involve S.D.S. Unit

By HENRY RAYMONT

The Federal courts have subpoenaed the unedited files and unused pictures of Time, Life and Newsweek magazines dealing with the Weatherman faction of Students for a Democratic Society. The small group of militant revolutionaries is being investigated by a Federal grand jury in connection with four days of disorders in Chicago last October.

The subpoenas, issued soon after the disorders, were disclosed for the first time by representatives of the three national magazines in separate interviews yesterday.

They said that Time and Life had complied with the subpoenas but that Newsweek hoped to work out an informal agreement to delete the names of any confidential informants before delivering its files.

The disclosure came amidst growing concern among newspaper editors and television network news executives across the country about what they believe to be an increasing effort by the authorities to collect intelligence about radical movements from the news media.

Denial in Washington

Some of this concern rose to the surface last week with the disclosure that the Government had subpoenaed the tapes and unused portions of a Columbia Broadcasting System television program about the Black Panther party, shown Jan. 6.

A Justice Department spokesman said in Washington yesterday that the recent actions in no way represented a change in policy. He said that for years the department had obtained information from the news media, particularly in civil rights cases in the South, sometimes voluntarily and sometimes through subpoenas.

But, in Chicago, spokesmen for the four major newspapers and television stations reported that there had been intensified Federal and local demands for photographs and notes of newspapermen, particularly in regard to recent incidents involving the Panthers and the Weathermen.

One television channel contended that the search for and reproduction of film strips requested by various courts had cost the station $155,000 in overtime and equipment.

J. G. Trezevant, general manager of the Daily News and The Sun-Times and president of Chicago's Newspaper Publishers Association, expressed concern over what he described as the practice of "dragnet subpoenas" under which the four newspapers were ordered last October to make available all their files in the hope that they would disclose some germane information.

He charged that this had led to "reckless fishing expeditions" through newspaper files and to "harrassment" of the editorial staff.

As a result, he said that the association was preparing steps to quash a subpoena in a test case designed to establish guidelines for a more orderly process of obtaining materials from the media.

"The big problem," Mr. Trezevant said in a telephone interview from Chicago, "is to find a way of fulfilling our civic duty to the judicial process without disrupting our normal operation or becoming an investigative agency for the prosecution or the defense."

Speaking as an executive of The Daily News and The Sun-Times, he said that the two newspapers were strongly opposed to any attempt to subpoena notes from reporters, a practice he described as "a dangerous restriction to freedom of the press."

Norman E. Isaacs, editor of The Louisville Courier Journal and president of the American

Society of Newspaper Editors, said yesterday he was "seriously disturbed" about the recent instances in which newspaper files had been subpoenaed by the courts.

'Sweeping' Actions Cited

"I am afraid this has all the marks of the domino theory," he said yesterday in Louisville. "If we start by accepting the jurisdiction of the Federal courts into our files, we can become vulnerable to all kinds of local or Congressional investigations. I am seriously dis-

turbed over the broad scope, the sweeping nature of the recent Federal court actions."

In response to inquiries, Time Inc. executives acknowledged yesterday that the company had been served supoenas for written and pictoral material concerning the Weathermen. They said that the files of both Time and Life dealt mainly with the street violence and contained no confidential information.

Hal Bruno, national editor of Newsweek, said here that a

similar order was handed to Newsweek in late October and that negotiations were in progress with the United States attorney's office in Chicago.

Indicating that Newsweek had assembled considerable material on the Weathermen from confidential sources, Mr. Bruno said the objective of the negotiations was to delete any identification of these sources from the file before it was presented to the court.

February 1, 1970

ARMY ENDS WATCH ON CIVIL PROTESTS

WASHINGTON, Feb. 26 (UPI) —The Army will no longer keep tabs on peaceful demonstrations or publish a list of individuals who "might be involved" in a riot, the chairman of the House Invasion of Privacy Subcommittee announced today.

Representative Cornelius E. Gallagher, Democrat of New Jersey, who said that the Pentagon had filed cards on 18.5

million people, released a letter from the Army general counsel, Robert E. Jordon 3d., saying that all copies of its civil disturbance list "have been ordered withdrawn and destroyed."

He said that the list was published from May 14, 1968, to Feb. 24, 1969.

The American Civil Liberties Union filed a suit against the Army last week asking a Federal court to stop the practice.

February 27, 1970

U.S. to Tighten Surveillance of Radicals

By JAMES M. NAUGHTON
Special to The New York Times

WASHINGTON, April 11—The Nixon Administration, alarmed by what it regards as a rising tide of radical extremism, is planning to step up surveillance of militant left-wing groups and individuals.

The objective, according to White House officials, is to find out who the potential bomb planters and snipers may be before they endanger others.

Preparations for expanding and improving the domestic intelligence apparatus — informers, undercover agents, wiretaps—were disclosed in a series of interviews with key officials, who requested anonymity.

According to these officials, President Nixon is disturbed by the rash of bombings and bomb scares, courtroom disruptions and reports of small but growing numbers of young people who feel alienated from the American system.

On March 12, the same day

that bombs exploded in three Manhattan office buildings, Mr. Nixon met over dinner in the White House with Irving Kristol, professor of urban values at New York University.

One aide who attended the dinner said the discussion included attempts to draw parallels between young, middle-class, white Americans who are resorting to violence and the Narodniki—children of the mid-19th century Russian aristocracy who murdered Czar Alexander II, and between militant black nationalists here and Algerian revolutionaries.

Mr. Kristol told the President it was not unrealistic to expect the Latin American resort to political kidnappings to spread soon to Washington. Mr. Kristol confirmed the dinner meeting and commented, "Some of these kids don't know what country this is. They think it's Bolivia."

Some, but not all, of Mr. Nixon's domestic advisers are

convinced that the situation is critical. One of the more conservative aides contended, "We are facing the most severe internal security threat this country has seen since the Depression."

The officials have concluded that attempts to bring militants back into society's mainstream are as futile, as one stated it, "as turning off the radio in the middle of a ball game to try to change the score."

The official view is that extreme radicals cannot be won over with welfare, electoral or draft reforms or by White House appeals. It wouldn't make a bit of difference if the war and racism ended overnight," said a highly placed Nixon assistant. "We're dealing with the criminal mind, with people who have snapped for some reason. Accordingly, the Administration sees its prime responsibility as protecting the innocent from "revolutionary terrorism." The President said last month, when he asked

Congress for broader Federal jurisdiction and stiffer penalties in bombing cases, that they were the work of "young criminals posturing as romantic revolutionaries."

Tougher Problem Today

To keep tabs on individuals referred to by the President as "potential murderers" will require updating an intelligence system geared to monitoring the Communists three decades ago, the aides said.

They said it was easy to keep track of the Communists because they had a highly organized system that undercover agents could penetrate easily. But today's alleged anarchists are disorganized, operating in groups of three or four, and difficult to detect.

'We know there are people training themselves in certain forms of guerrilla warfare and the use of explosives," said one official, "but it's extremely difficult to answer the who, when and how."

A Nixon aide who is aware of the Justice Department's intelligence operations said there was no advance warning of the arson that destroyed a Bank of America branch in Santa Barbara, Calif., last month. He said that "We knew of the New

311

York bomb factory" in a Greenwich Village townhouse, but only just before it exploded on March 6, killing three young people.

White House officials wonder aloud why one of the victims, Diana Oughton, 28 years old, once active in legitimate reform efforts, became a member of a militant faction of the Students for a Democratic Society.

"If we had a (phone) tap on Diana Oughton," a Presidential assistant said, "we might have arrested her before the bombs went off and nobody would have died."

Survivor Is Traced

The official said that Federal agents had traced a survivor of the Greenwich Village blast, Cathlyn Platt Wilkerson, to Canada, but he expressed distress that the intelligence system was not capable of pinpointing her activities before she became a fugitive.

Administration sources would not disclose details of the changes they are preparing in the intelligence mechanism, although they said a good deal of interdepartmental discussion about them was under way.

One suggestion was said to be the possibility of the Justice Department providing grants through the Law Enforcement Assistance Administration to local police departments for training in domestic intelligence gathering.

Only New York City and District of Columbia policemen have adequate intelligence systems, one official said, adding: "We need better trained people in metropolitan police departments so they can distinguish between a guy with a beard and a subversive."

The White House is aware of the political sensitivity of domestic intelligence gathering, which one aide described as "hangups in the question of snooping." He contended, however, that the Government was less interested in prosecuting individuals than in gathering information to "prevent the perpetration of an act of violence."

It would help to have "broader public awareness" of the need for improved surveillance techniques, he said. "One of the greatest disservices Senator [Joseph] McCarthy did to this country was to swing the pendulum so far that people no longer want to think about internal security," the official said.

He argued that it would, in fact, increase safeguards of the civil liberties of individuals to have a greater awareness of which members of society posed a threat.

"My concern is that sooner or later this is going to kill innocent people," the official said. "There will be tremendous public outrage and not enough time for restrained, measured response. People will demand that their police start cracking heads.

"The greatest safeguard for rights of individuals is to have good information on what the [radical fringes] are doing. Stop them before the bombings. Bomb legislation [with heavier penalties] is after the fact."

Mr. Nixon, who prefers to decide on Administration policy after receiving a set of clearly defined options, apparently has little choice but to adopt the recommendations of his more conservative staff members for increased surveillance. Liberal advisers have not provided him with alternatives.

Indeed, the liberals do not appear to have any answers to the problem of American radicalism. As one White House liberal put it: "What does Richard Nixon do for these people, short of resigning the Presidency?"

April 12, 1970

MOST IN POLL FAVOR LIMITING FREEDOMS

Special to The New York Times

WASHINGTON, April 15 —A majority of Americans appear ready to restrict basic freedoms guaranteed by the Bill of Rights, according to a poll by the Columbia Broadcasting System, the results of which were broadcast last night.

Even with no clear danger of violence, 76 per cent of those polled said they opposed the freedom of any group to organize protests against the Government.

Smaller majorities indicated they would favor restrictions on other criticism of the Government, freedom of the press, and double jeopardy, and would support preventive detention.

The poll was a random national telephone sample of 1,136 adults. The results were broadcast on the program "Sixty Minutes," together with excerpts from companion interviews conducted by C.B.S. in Bloomingdale, Ill.

Of 10 constitutional rights treated in the poll, C.B.S. said majorities favored limiting five and offered only mild support of two others.

Only three of the 10 protections won strong support. Trial by jury was endorsed by 82 per cent of those questioned. Secret trials were opposed by 75 per cent. Searches of homes without warrants were opposed by 66 per cent.

April 16, 1970

Mrs. Smith Warns of Repression

She Assails Militant Students and Their Critics in Capital

Special to The New York Times

WASHINGTON, June 1 — Senator Margaret Chase Smith spoke today of a "national sickness" pervading the land, and she denounced protesting student militants. She also attacked their critics in the Administration.

It was the 20th anniversary of a speech in which the Maine Republican, speaking from the same Senate desk, attacked the late Senator Joseph R. McCarthy of Wisconsin for irresponsible political tactics, and she recalled some of that speech today.

"I spoke as I did 20 years ago because of what I considered to be the great threat from the radical right—the threat of a government of repression," Senator Smith declared.

"I speak today," she said, "because of what I consider to be the great threat from the radical left that advocates and practices violence and defiance of the law—again, the threat of the ultimate result of a reaction of repression."

Recalling her floor speech of June 1, 1950, Senator Smith said: "We had a national sickness then from which we recovered. We have a national sickness now from which I pray we will recover."

While she was sharply critical of student demonstrators who commit crimes, the 72-year-old Senator indicated her belief that overreaction by Administration officials — she declined to name names—contributed substantially to the problem.

The Senator said she was "not proud of the way in which our national television networks and campuses have been made publicity platforms for irresponsible sensationalism— nor am I proud of the counter-criticism against the networks and the campuses that has gone beyond the bounds of reasonableness and propriety and fanned, instead of drenching, the fires of division."

Asked after the speech if this had been a reference to Vice President Agnew, Mrs. Smith replied that she was "not going into personalities" now although she might at a later date.

"Extremism bent upon polarization of our people is increasingly forcing upon the American people the narrow choice between anarchy and repression," the Senator warned. "And make no mistake about it, if that narrow choice has to be made, the American people, even if with reluctance and misgiving, will choose repression."

"Ironically, the excesses of dissent in the extreme left can result in repression of dissent," she added. "For repression is preferable to anarchy and nihilism to most Americans."

Mrs. Smith indicated that she regarded today's conflicts and criticism just as seriously as she did the excesses of McCarthyism 20 years earlier, whatever the official stance of the Administration may be.

"The President denies we are in a revolution," she said. "There are many who would not agree with his appraisal. Anarchy may seem nearer to many of us than it really is."

The Senator said that just as in the 1950's "the Senate was silenced and politically intimidated by one of its own members, so today many Americans are intimidated and made mute by the emotional violence of the extreme left."

"It is time that the greater

center of our people," she continued, "those who reject the violence and unreasonableness of both the extreme right and extreme left, searched their consciences, mustered their moral and physical courage, shed their

intimidated silence and declared their consciences."

Three weeks ago at Colby College in Waterville, Me., Mrs. Smith reported today, her efforts to answer questions were greeted in some instances with

hisses and obscenities.

Mrs. Smith's speech was well received by the small group of Senators on the floor to hear it. They ranged from liberals— Senators Edward M. Kennedy, Democrat of Massachusetts, and

Charles H. Percy, Republican of Illinois—to conservatives, Senators John C. Stennis, Democrat of Mississippi, and John J. Williams, Republican of Delaware.

June 2, 1970

Federal Computers Amass Files on Suspect Citizens

Many Among Hundreds of Thousands Listed Have No Criminal Records— Critics See Invasion of Privacy

By BEN A. FRANKLIN
Special to The New York Times

WASHINGTON, June 27 — The police, security and military intelligence agencies of the Federal Government are quietly compiling a mass of computerized and microfilmed files here on hundreds of thousands of law abiding yet suspect Americans.

With the justification that a revolutionary age of assassination, violent political dissent and civil disorder requires it, the Government is building an array of instantly retrievable information on "persons of interest."

The phrase is an agent's term for those citizens, many with no criminal records, whom the Government wants to keep track of in an effort to avert subversion, rioting and violence or harm to the nation's leaders.

Critics of this surveillance, so far few in number, believe that the collection and dissemination of such information on noncriminals — for whatever purpose — is unauthorized by law and raises the most serious constitutional questions.

The foremost among them, Senator Sam J. Ervin, Jr., Democrat of North Carolina, has said that computerized files already in existence here are leading the country toward a "police state."

Discussions with officials, an examination of some known data files and information supplied by the Senator show that the files often contain seemingly localized and mundane information reflecting events that today are virtually commonplace.

The leader of a Negro protest against welfare regulations

in St. Louis, for example, is the subject of a teletyped "spot report" to Washington shared by as many as half a dozen Government intelligence gathering groups.

The name of a college professor who finds himself unwittingly, even innocently, arrested for disorderly conduct in a police roundup at a peace rally in San Francisco goes into the data file.

A student fight in an Alabama high school is recorded— if it is interracial.

Government officials insist that the information is needed and is handled discretely to protect the innocent, the minor offender and the repentant.

The critics — including the Washington chapter of the American Civil Liberties Union and Representative Cornelius E. Gallagher, Democrat of New Jersey—charge that the system is an invasion of privacy and a potential infringement of First Amendment rights to free speech and assembly.

Mass Surveillance Systems

Senator Ervin, a conservative, a student of the Constitution, a former judge of the North Carolina Superior Court, and the chairman of the Senate Subcommittee on Constitutional Rights, says that the advent of computer technology in Government file keeping is pushing the country toward "a mass surveillance system unprecedented in American history."

In a recent series of Senate speeches, Mr. Ervin said that the danger was being masked by a failure of Americans to understand "the computer mystique" and by the undoubted sincerity and desire for "efficiency" of the data blank operators and planners.

The Government is gathering information on its citizens in

the following reservoirs of facts:

¶A Secret Service computer, one of the newest and most sophisticated in Government. In its memory the names and dossiers of activists, "malcontents," persistent seekers of redress, and those who would "embarrass" the President or other Government leaders are filed with those of potential assassins and persons convicted of "threats against the President."

¶A data bank compiled by the Justice Department's civil disturbance group. It produces a weekly printout of national tension points on racial, class and political issues and the individuals and groups involved in them. Intelligence on peace rallies, welfare protests and the like provide the "data base" against which the computer measures the mood of the nation and the militancy of its citizens. Judgments are made; subjects are listed as "radical" or "moderate."

¶A huge file of microfilmed intelligence reports, clippings and other materials on civilian activity maintained by the Army's Counterintelligence Analysis Division in Alexandria, Va. Its purpose is to help prepare deployment estimates for troop commands on alert to respond to civil disturbances in 25 American cities. Army intelligence was ordered earlier this year to destroy a larger data bank and to stop assigning agents to "penetrate" peace groups and civil rights organizations. But complaints persist that both are being continued. Civilian officials of the Army say they "assume" they are not.

¶Computer files intended to catch criminal suspects — the oldest and most advanced type with the longest success record—maintained by the Federal Bureau of Investigation's National Crime Information Center and recently installed by the Customs Bureau. The crime information center's computer provides 40,000 instant, automatic teletype printouts each day on wanted persons and stolen property to 49 states and Canada and it also "talks" to 24 other computers operated by state and local police departments for themselves and a total of 2,500 police jurisdictions. The center says its information is all "from the public record," based on local and Federal warrants and complaints, but the sum product is

available only to the police.

¶A growing number of data banks on other kinds of human behavior, including, for example, a cumulative computer file on 300,000 children of migrant farm workers kept by the Department of Health, Education and Welfare. The object is to speed the distribution of their scholastic records, including such teacher judgments as "negative attitude," to school districts with large itinerant student enrollments. There is no statutory control over distribution of the data by its local recipients—to prospective employers, for example.

Warning by Ervin

Senator Ervin has warned: "Regardless of the purpose, regardless of the confidentiality, regardless of the harm to any one individual [that might occur if there were no computer files], the very existence of Government files on how people exercise First Amendment rights, how they think, speak, assemble and act in lawful pursuits, is a form of official psychological coercion to keep silent and to refrain from acting."

But despite his sounding of such alarms, Senator Ervin has noted that there is "unusual public and Congressional complacency." When he speaks on the Senate floor of "techniques for monitoring our opinions" and of "grave threats to our freedoms," the chamber is more often than not nearly empty. He has gained little Congressional support and scant attention outside the Congress.

Meanwhile, various official and high-level pressures on Government agencies to acquire computers and to advance their surveillance are producing results.

The pressures include a stern recommendation for the broadest possible surveillance of "malcontents" and potential assassins by the Warren Commission, which investigated the assassination of President Kennedy. The commission's mandate is widely cited in the Government as the authority for citizen surveillance.

The commission, headed by former Chief Justice Earl Warren, disapproved as too narrow, the criteria for persons to be brought under "protective" surveillance proposed in 1964 by the Secret Service. The guidelines were "unduly restrictive," the commission declared, because they required

313

The Government and Dissent

evidence of "some manifestation of animus" by disgruntled and activist citizens before those persons could be brought under Secret Service surveillance as potential "threats to the President."

'Every Available Resource'

"It will require every available resource of the Government to devise a practical system which has any reasonable possibility of revealing such malcontents," the commission said.

The guideline was broadened. A computer was installed by the Secret Service last January. The commission's edict became a surveillance bench mark.

For surveillance of persons who may be involved in civil disturbances, the riots of 1967 and 1968 served the same purpose.

"The Warren Commission and the riots legitimatized procedures which, I grant you, would have been unthinkable and, frankly, unattainable from Congress in a different climate," one official said. "There are obvious questions and dangers in what we are doing but I think events have shown it is legitimate." The official declined to be quoted by name.

Senator Ervin contends that in the "total recall," the permanence, the speed and the interconnection of Government data files there "rests a potential for control and intimidation that is alien to our form of Government and foreign to a society of free men." The integration of data banks, mixing criminal with noncriminal files, is already under way, according to his subcommittee.

Integration of Files

The subcommittee has been advised by the Department of Housing and Urban Development, for example, that its data systems planners have proposed to integrate on computer tape files concerning the following: the identities of 325,000 Federal Housing Administration loan applicants; the agency's own "adverse information file;" the Justice Department's organized crime and rackets file, and F.B.I. computer data on "investigations of housing matters." The object, the Department said, is a unified data bank listing persons who may be ineligible to do business with H.U.D.

As another example of how computer data proliferates, the subcommittee cites a report it received from the Internal Revenue Service.

The I.R.S., with millions of tax returns to process, was one of the earliest agencies to computerize. It has also had a reputation as a bastion of discretion. The privacy of individual tax returns has been widely regarded as inviolate, to be overcome only by order of the President.

But the subcommittee has been told that the I.R.S. has

The New York Times

Senator Sam J. Ervin Jr., Democrat of North Carolina

"for many years" been selling to state tax departments—for $75 a reel—copies of magnetic tapes containing encoded personal income tax information. It is used to catch non-filers and evaders or state taxes.

The District of Columbia and 30 states bought copies of the I.R.S. computer reels covering returns from their jurisdictions in 1969, the service has told the subcommittee. Each local jurisdiction was merely "requested" to alert its employes that the unauthorized disclosure of Federal tax data was punishable by a $1,000 fine.

Firearms Data for Sale

The I.R.S. also sells at cost—apparently to anyone who asks—the copies of its data files of registrants under the various Federal firearms laws it enforces.

The Secret Service computer file is capable of instant, highly sophisticated sorting and retrieval of individuals by name, alias, locale, method of operation, affiliation, and even by physical appearance.

The agency's Honeywell 2200, with random access capability, makes it possible to detect, investigate and detain in advance "persons of interest" who might intend — or officials concede "they might not but we don't take chances"—to harass, harm or "embarrass" officials under its protection.

Unknown to most Americans, the names, movements, organizations and "characteristics" of

tens of thousands of them—criminals and noncriminals—are being encoded in the Secret Service data center here.

The names of other thousands have been inserted in less specialized computers operated by the Justice Department and the F.B.I. Although the agencies insist that they do not, the computers can—and Senator Ervin stresses that no law says they may not—"talk" to each other, trading and comparing in seconds data that may then spread further across the nation.

The Secret Service can now query its computer and quickly be forewarned that, say, three of the 100 invited guests at a Presidential gathering in the White House Rose Garden are "persons of protective interest."

Under current Secret Service criteria, they may have been regarded by someone as the authors of reportedly angry or threatening or "embarrassing" statements about the President or the Government. The action taken by the Secret Service may range from special observation during "proximity to the President" to withdrawal of the invitation.

What constitutes a computer-worthy "threat" thus becomes important. The Secret Service asserts that it applies relatively easy-going and "sophisticated" standards in deciding who is to be encoded. But the critics point out that the vast capacity of a computer for names and dossiers—unlike that of a paper fil-

ing system, which has a self-limiting ceiling based on the ability to retrieve—is an encouragement to growth.

The information or "data base" for a Secret Service computer name check flows into the protective intelligence division from many sources—abusive or threatening letters or telephone calls received at the White House, F.B.I. reports, military intelligence, the Central Intelligence Agency, local police departments, the Internal Revenue Service, Federal building guards, individual informants.

Much of it that may be "of interest" to the Federal monitors of civil disturbance data is screened out, Secret Service spokesmen say, or is merely name-indexed by the computer with a reference to data reproducable elsewhere.

According to guidelines distributed by the Secret Service last August, the types of information solicited for insertion in the computer—broadened at the insistence of the Warren Commission—included items about:

¶Those who would "physically harm or embarrass" the President or other high Government officials.

¶Anyone who "insists upon personally contacting high Government officials for the purpose of redress of imaginary grievances, etc."

¶Those who may qualify as "professional gate crashers."

¶Participants in "anti-American or anti-U. S. Government demonstrations in the United States or overseas."

In an interview, Thomas J. Kelley, assistant director of the Secret Service for protective intelligence, said the computer name insertions already totaled more than 50,000. The Secret Service is extremely careful, he said, both in evaluating the encoded subjects and in checking to determine that those who receive a printout are entitled to it.

But there apparently is no formal guideline or list of criteria for dissemination, as there is for insertion. And direct, automatic, teletype access to the computer from distant Secret Service bureaus — the system used by the airlines and the National Crime Information Center — may be the next step, Mr. Kelley said.

Nothing demonstrates how remote access multiplies the output of a computer better than the crime information center's system, started by the F.B.I. in 1966.

With direct-access teletype terminals in 21 state capitals and large cities, the information center computer here can be queried directly by local police departments on the names, aliases, Social Security numbers, license tag numbers and a broad array of stolen goods (including boats) that come hourly before the police

An officer in a patrol car tailing a suspicious car can

radio his dispatcher, ask for a check of a license number, and be told by teletype and radio in less than a minute that the automobile is stolen and that its occupants may be "armed and dangerous."

With one of the newest and most sophisticated random access computers in Federal service, the Secret Service data center can also perform some wizardry that no other equipment here can master. It can be ordered, for example, to print out a list of all potential trouble makers — "persons of protective interest"—at the site of a forthcoming Presidential visit. The random access scanning can be geographical.

Photographs and descriptions can be assembled for the traveling White House detail. Investigations, even detentions, can be arranged at the site.

"You take a waiter in a hotel dining room where the boss is going to speak," a Secret Service spokesman explained. "Let's say the computer turns up his name and we investigate and decide it would be better for him to be assigned to some

other duties. No one has a constitutional right to wait on the President, you know. That's how it works."

Cued by another more elegant electronic program, the same computer can also produce all the information it contains on the "characteristics" of subjects encoded on its tapes — all the short, fat, long-haired, young white campus activists in Knoxville, Tenn., for example. Only the Secret Service computer can do that.

The American Civil Liberties Union office here protested last October that the Constitution protects such acts as an effort merely to "embarrass" a Government official, the persistence of citizens in seeking redress even of "imaginary" grievances, and their participation in "anti-U.S. Government demonstrations." The Secret Service, however, has declined to withdraw or amend its intelligence reporting guidelines.

"They seem satisfactory to us," Mr. Kelley said. "If we weren't getting the information we want, we'd change them."

Under the heading, "Protective Information," the guide-

lines read as follows:

"A. Information pertaining to a threat, plan or attempt by an individual, a group, or an organization to physically harm or embarrass the persons protected by the U.S. Secret Service, or any other high U.S. Government official at home or abroad.

"B. Information pertaining to individuals, groups, or organizations who have plotted, attempted, or carried out assassinations of senior officials of domestic or foreign governments.

"C. Information concerning the use of bodily harm or assassination as a political weapon. This should include training and techniques used to carry out the act.

"D. Information on persons who insist upon personally contacting high Government officials for the purpose of redress of imaginary grievances, etc.

"E. Information on any person who makes oral or written statements about high Government officials in the following categories: (1) threatening statements; (2) irrational statements, and (3) abusive state-

ments.

"F. Information on professional gate crashers.

"G. Information pertaining to 'terrorist' bombings.

"H. Information pertaining to the ownership or concealment by individuals or groups of caches of firearms, explosives, or other implements of war.

"I. Information regarding anti-American or anti-U.S. Government demonstrations in the United States or overseas.

"J. Information regarding civil disturbances."

Senator Ervin, who is noted for a piquant sense of humor, said in a speech a few months ago: "Although I am not a 'professional gate crasher,' I am a 'malcontent' on many issues.

"I have written the President and other high officials complaining of grievances that some may consider 'imaginary.' And on occasion I may also have 'embarrassed' high Government officials."

Based on the guidelines, the Senator asserted, he himself is qualified for the computer.

June 28, 1970

F.B.I. Brands Black Panthers 'Most Dangerous' of Extremists

Report Also Hits Weathermen as Guiding Force Behind Violent Young People

Special to The New York Times

WASHINGTON, July 13—The Federal Bureau of Investigation today branded the Black Panther party as the country's "most dangerous and violence-prone of all extremist groups."

It also called the Weatherman faction of the Students for a Democratic Society "a principal force guiding the country's violence-prone young militants."

During the fiscal year 1970, the F.B.I. said in its annual report, "the Weatherman group was in the forefront of much of the activity deliberately calculated to provoke violent confrontations."

The 22-page report, issued by J. Edgar Hoover, director, covered the major activities of the agency during the last 12 months. It dealt separately with organized crime, aircraft hijackings and other areas of F.B.I. concern. A considerable section was devoted to protest demonstrations and militant activity.

"Mr. Hoover deplored the fact that, despite its record of hate, violence, and subversion, the Black Panther party continues to receive substantial

monetary contributions from prominent donors," the report said.

'Foreign Influences'

It also charged that "foreign influences" were making "inroads in certain black extremist groups in the United States, particularly the Black Panther party."

Although the nature of the "foreign influences" was not detailed, the report noted that Eldridge Cleaver, the party's Minister of Information, was presently living in Algiers to avoid criminal prosecution in this country. The report said Mr. Cleaver had traveled to North Korea last September and "has also developed close ties with Al Fatah, the Arab guerrilla organization."

Mr. Cleaver was the only Black Panther mentioned by name. Most of the other party leaders are in jail or in exile.

Although the report referred to pending criminal trials in New Haven, Baltimore and New York against Black Panthers, it made no mention of the Chicago police raid on a Panther apartment last December that aroused considerable resentment against police tactics.

A leader of the Panthers in Illinois, Fred Hampton, was killed in the raid. A special grand jury has been called to investigate the conduct of the police.

In discussing the Weatherman faction, the F.B.I. did not deal with numbers, but it said that leaders had apparently decided to build "a small paramilitary organization designed to carry out urban guerrilla warfare."

Weatherman members are believed to have gone "underground" following a general meeting in February, the report states.

The principal activities of Weatherman members were described as a number of demonstrations last October in Chicago, a demonstration the following month at the Department of Justice here and several publicized visits to Cuba.

"Mr. Hoover reported that there was a sharp increase in protest demonstrations on college campuses during the school year of 1969-1970," the report noted. It said 1,785 demonstrations took place.

According to the F.B.I.'s figures, sit-ins and building seizures numbered 313 and there were 281 attacks on Reserve Officers' Training Corps installations.

The report said that 462 injuries resulted from protest demonstrations on college campuses, "nearly two-thirds of which were sustained by police and college officials."

The report said "eight individuals" were killed in the disruptions, but it was not immediately clear whether they were students.

The injury figure was disputed by Dr. John Spiegel, director of the Lemberg Center for the Study of Violence at

Brandeis University.

"These figures can not possibly be accurate," Dr. Spiegel charged, since the police dutifully record every injury in their ranks, while students do not.

A preliminary count by the center reflects that injuries are about evenly divided between police and college officials on the one hand, and demonstrators on the other.

Other major areas listed by the F.B.I. were the following:

¶Communist party, U.S.A.—The report said the party had launched a new youth group, the Young Workers Liberation League, last February in an effort "to close the generation gap that exists today in the party."

¶The Yablonski murders — Mr. Hoover noted that five persons were arrested as a result of F.B.I. investigation into the deaths of Joseph A. Yablonski, his wife and daughter. Mr. Yablonski lost a heated race for the presidency of the United Mine Workers of America just before his death.

¶Organized crime — The report noted that two large gambling rings had been broken in December and May, one in Elizabeth, N. J., and the other in the Detroit area. Several Cosa Nostra "family" heads were prosecuted during the year, the report said.

Mr. Hoover also noted that "aircraft hijackings continued to represent a serious national threat," but no comparative figures were reported.

July 14, 1970

315

SECURITY OFFICIAL NAMED BY NIXON

President Also Meets With Top Political Advisers

By ROBERT B. SEMPLE Jr.
Special to The New York Times

KEY BISCAYNE, Fla., Nov. 7 —President Nixon today named Robert Mardian, former general counsel of the Department of Health, Education and Welfare, as the new Assistant Attorney General in charge of the Internal Security Division of the Justice Department.

Meanwhile, the President met with political and domestic advisers in what many regarded as in part a key political policy session.

The new security aide, Mr. Mardian, is regarded as a conservative, and is a close friend of Deputy Attorney General Richard G. Kleindienst. Both Mr. Kleindienst and Mr. Mardian worked in Senator Barry Goldwater's unsuccessful bid for the Presidency in 1964.

There were suggestions from some sources here that under Mr. Mardian's leadership the Internal Security Division, which has languished in recent years, would be given new and broader investigative responsibilties.

Terrorists Cited

These sources reported that the division would be given greater control over Justice Department activities dealing with domestic subversion involving terrorists and various militant groups. This is now the primary responsibility of the department's Criminal Division.

The Internal Security Division reached a high point of activity in 1956, when it employed 94 lawyers. It now employes 42. The decline was partly a reflection of various Supreme Court rulings involving subversive groups, including the Communist party.

Mr. Kleindienst will succeed J. Walter Yeagle, who has been nominated for a judgeship on the United States Court of Appeals for the District of Columbia. Mr. Yeagle, who has directed the Internal Security Division since 1959, is now 61 years old. Mr. Mardian is 47.

Mr. Mardian has also been serving as executive director of the Cabinet Committee on Education, informally known as the President's Cabinet committee on desegregation. The committee's main effort of the last few months has been to work with statewide committees of distinguished Southerners to insure a peaceful transition from the old dual school system to a desegregated school system. The fate of the Cabinet committee, headed by George P. Shultz, Director of the Office on Management and Budget, was not clear today.

Powerful Role Seen

There was also some speculation here that Mr. Mardian may in time become one of the most powerful members of the Justice Department, in view of his close relationship with Mr. Kleindienst.

Mr. Kleindienst is thought to be in line to succeed John N. Mitchell as Attorney General should Mr. Mitchell resign his post to direct planning for the 1972 Presidential campaign. There has been some speculation that he might do so.

The President, meanwhile, met with seven of his key political and domestic strategists for several hours at his bayside residence on Key Biscayne. The meeting was officially described here as a "long-range planning session" on Mr. Nixon's domestic legislative program for 1971, as well as the new budget that Mr. Nixon will submit to Congress early next year. It was also believed, however, given the participants in the meeting, that some portion of the discussion was devoted to the misfortunes of the Republican party at the polls last Tuesday.

Among those who participated in the meeting were Mr. Mitchell; Robert H. Finch, counselor to the President; John D. Ehrlichman, assistant to the President for domestic affairs; H. R. Haldeman, assistant to the President; Donald Rumsfeld, director of the Office of Economic Opportunity, and Charles Colson, special counsel to the President.

Mr. Mitchell was manager of Mr. Nixon's 1968 Presidential campaign, and Mr. Finch managed his 1960 race.

The White House press office refused to comment in any way on the meeting, but the participants were believed to have discussed, among other things, possible changes in the Administration's approach to the electorate in 1972 in view of the failure of its efforts to defeat the Democrats by charging them with permissiveness and weakness on the issue of law and order.

November 8, 1970

Big Man on the Campus: Police Undercover Agent

By ANTHONY RIPLEY
Special to The New York Times

ALBUQUERQUE, N. M., March 28—There is a new man on campus among the freaks and fraternity men, the athletes and the esthetes, the bookish types and the bomb throwers. He is the spy.

He has not come to study Russian or Chinese or to prepare himself to infiltrate some foreign nation. Instead, his mission is to watch the students, the faculty and the off-campus crowds.

Though such undercover activity was almost unheard of five years ago, it has now become almost a permanent institution on the American college scene.

It is the product of student turmoil—rioting, bombing, arson, strikes, demonstrations—and the widespread drug problem.

The police defend their undercover tactics as the only practical way to enforce drug laws and to keep watch on radical campus activities, which, they fear, might trigger disturbances in the surrounding community.

What is happening around the country shows up in sharp relief at the University of New Mexico. In fact, reports from college campuses coast to coast indicate there is nothing at all extraordinary about such incidents as these:

¶A semi-undercover state policeman, Jack F. Johnson, was seen on the campus from the fall of 1969 to the summer of 1970. He generally tried to blend in with the students and carried a Brownie Instamatic camera. His presence was publicly announced on several occasions. Once he was spotted and identified at a closed faculty meeting and was asked to leave. Mr. Johnson is now back on uniformed patrol duty near Albuquerque.

¶Two city narcotics agents were discovered by students living in Coronado Hall, a dormitory for men. The agents left quietly soon after they were identified and both city and university officials confirmed their presence.

¶A city policeman using false press credentials posed as an Associated Press photographer during demonstrations last spring protesting the invasion of Cambodia. Howard Graves, the AP bureau chief in Albuquerque, complained to the police, who promised it would not happen again.

¶Unspecified law enforcement agencies requested permission to place undercover agents on the campus but were refused by university officials.

Displeased but Helpless

Like most of the officials at the other colleges that reported similar incidents, school officials here were not pleased with the snooping but felt helpless in keeping undercover men from either enrolling as regular students or mixing with off-campus crowds.

"We do not condone or encourage such activity," said Harold W. Lavender, vice president for student affairs. "Neither can we prevent it. We've had opportunities to deliberately enroll undercover agents and we have, in high dudgeon, turned them down."

John S. Todd, an assistant to the Albuquerque city manager who is responsible for police matters, said undercover men were assigned to the university area whenever there were "specific instances of illegal activity" such as narcotics use. Agents are also assigned, he said, when "feeling is developing" over a campus political issue or national political issue.

Mr. Todd said it was only "prudent" to watch radical activities that might spill over from the campus to the surrounding city.

The bulk of the nation's undercover work is done by local police officers or outsiders hired by the state, county or city police, according to the campus reports. Probably the best known undercover man in the United States, M. L. Singkata Thomas Tongyai, known at Hobart College in Canandaigua, N.Y., as "Tommy the Traveler," was one of these.

He was hired by the local sheriff's office and, according to an Ontario County grand jury, "advocated violent forms of protest" among student radicals. He took part in a police drug raid on the Hobart campus last June 5.

Other Campus Watchers

But Federal agencies, particularly the Federal Bureau of Investigation and United States Army intelligence, have also been watching campuses.

A series of United States

316

Senate committee hearings have detailed the extensive surveillance activities of the Army at such widely separated places as New York University, Northwestern University and Colorado College. However, the Army, under public pressure, has announced it has cut back its civilian watching programs in the United States.

Recent public disclosure of the contents of F.B.I. files stolen March 8 from the bureau's office in Media, Pa., show that it has regularly used informants to watch radical activities at Haverford College.

The F.B.I. has been active elsewhere, too, according to the campus reports. "There's someone here I think you should meet," a University of Illinois student shouted last fall to a group of protesters in front of the Champaign, Ill., county courthouse. "That man there, in the blue jacket, with the camera, works for the F.B.I."

A young, clean-cut man in a blue windbreaker, whom the student identified by name, said nothing and continued to take pictures of the demonstrators, who were protesting acquittal of a former Champaign police officer charged with murder in the death of a black store clerk.

Charles Travelstead, special agent at the Urbana, Ill., office of the F.B.I., declined to comment on the incident but said the agency did use "confidential informants who share our concern in the vital areas of terrorism and bombings."

"If an individual cooperated with us and incurred expenses," he continued, "he would be reimbursed for out-of-the-pocket expenses."

Much of the undercover activity surrounds anti-drug efforts by the police, who insist that a man in uniform only scares away pushers and buyers.

A survey released in February by the National Institute of Mental Health reported one-third of the 10,000 students on 50 campuses who were interviewed admitted that they had smoked marijuana and one-seventh of the total reported that they were regular users.

At Yale University, an undercover agent named George Miller last November was involved in the arrest of 90 young people on assorted drug charges. Most were not students, but were drifters and dropouts among the so-called "street people" who gather near university campuses across the nation.

A leaflet called "View from Behind Bars" was circulated after the arrests and described the activities of Mr. Miller, who was hired by the New Haven police:

"Lots of people are still muttering how Good Ol' George couldn't possibly do that. The stark reality is that George Miller was an incredibly slick agent. He tripped with us, went to rallies with us, turned on with us. He dressed in purple and yellow and wore hip glasses. . . . He waved to us and smiled at us. He was accepted and trusted.

"Some people muttered a few things about not trusting him. But we're all paranoid, right?

"And in the end, George busted our friends. . . . So what does it all mean about our lives? About who we trust and how we really relate to one another? And how do we prevent another George Miller from coming around again?"

Other surveillance methods are also used.

In Miami, Seymor Gelber, chief assistant State's Attorney for Dade County, made a study of campus police at 210 colleges and universities for a doctoral degree from Florida State University. He said 14.1 per cent of those studied admitted using telephone recording devices. Among 28 colleges of over 20,000 students each, the use of wiretaps was 25 per cent.

Though some of the undercover men say infiltration is a difficult task, others find it easy in the open, accepting atmosphere of college life.

At the University of Kansas, a 19-year-old undercover narcotics agent told The Associated Press:

"I just went into the dorm and acted stupid. I got into conversations and got to know them. Then I asked where I could get the stuff and they told me."

His work led to a series of early morning raids by 150 agents on the campus at Lawrence, Kan.

At the University of Michigan, Ann Arbor Police Lieut. Eugene Staudenmaier makes no pretense of being undercover as he attends almost all political rallies.

Recently he attended a workshop during a campus peace conference. Someone recognized him and complained. He stood up, identified himself and the workshop members voted to allow him to stay. He left a short time later.

"I don't like this polarized situation where police and students are stereotyped as natural enemies," he said.

At Ohio State University last April, two young men up front in a crowd of rioting students were later identified as undercover state policemen. Their pictures were published in the student newspaper, The Lantern.

The university's 58-man campus police force, armed with .38 caliber revolvers, night sticks and chemical disabling agents, keeps an undercover squad of six men. They are supplemented by undercover Ohio State policemen and Columbus city policemen.

At the University of Texas at Austin there was "Duke," who arrived in a new car with mod clothes and who made fiery speeches during student union demonstrations a year ago. He was indicted, but never arrested, and the charges against him were later dropped.

At Northwestern University it was a girl, "Connie," who moved into the apartment of two off-campus radicals and, according to one Northwestern activist, "hung around the campus and was mildly friendly."

Last May, when the police were called during an argument between her and one of her roommates, she identified herself as a member of the "Red Squad" of the Chicago police department. She disappeared the next day.

At the University of California at Berkeley it was a city police officer, Roland Soliz, who had been on campus under the name of "Roland Guzman." He joined Students for a Democratic Society, the Young Socialist Alliance, the Radical Student Union and various Mexican-American groups before he was uncovered by the student newspaper, The Daily Californian.

Former undercover agents, though useless once identified, do have a future. Gerald Kirk, a University of Chicago student who said he worked for the F.B.I. from 1966 to 1969, has been touring the country in the last few months, speaking six nights a week. The topic of his speech is "Inside the Spider's Web."

March 29, 1971

MITCHELL SEEKS TO HALT SERIES ON VIETNAM BUT TIMES REFUSES

COURT STEP LIKELY

By MAX FRANKEL
Special to The New York Times

WASHINGTON, June 14— Attorney General John N. Mitchell asked The New York Times this evening to refrain from further publication of documents drawn from a Pentagon study of the Vietnam war on the ground that such disclosures would cause "irreparable injury to the defense interests of the United States."

If the paper refused, another Justice Department official said, the Government would try to forbid further publication by court action tomorrow.

The Times refused to halt publication voluntarily.

The Justice Department's request and intention to seek a court enjoinder were conveyed by Robert C. Mardian, Assistant Attorney General in charge of the internal security division, to Harding F. Bancroft, executive vice president of The Times.

They spoke by telephone at about 7:30 P.M., which was some two hours before tomorrow's first edition of the paper was scheduled to go to press with the third installment of the articles about the Pentagon study.

An hour later, a telegram from Mr. Mitchell asked that The Times halt further publication of the material and return the documents to the Pentagon.

The Times then issued the following statement:

"We have received the telegram from the Attorney General asking The Times to cease further publication of the Pentagon's Vietnam study.

"The Times must respectfully decline the request of the Attorney General, believing that it is in the interest of the people of this country to be informed of the material contained in this series of articles.

"We have also been informed of the Attorney General's intention to seek an injunction against further publication. We believe that it is properly a matter for the courts to decide. The Times will oppose any request for an injunction for the same reason that led us to publish the articles in the first place. We will of course abide by the final decision of the court."

Telegram From Mitchell

The telegram from Attorney General Mitchell, addressed to Arthur Ochs Sulzberger, president and publisher of The Times, said:

"I have been advised by the Secretary of Defense that the material published in The New York Times on June 13, 14, 1971, captioned 'Key Texts From Pentagon's Vietnam Study' contains information relating to the national defense of the United States and bears a top secret classification.

"As such, publication of this information is directly prohibited by the provisions of the Espionage Law, Title 18, United States Code, Section 793.

"Moreover, further publication of information of this character will cause irreparable injury to the defense interests of the United States.

"Accordingly, I respectfully request that you publish no further information of this character and advise me that you have made arrangements for the return of these documents to the Department of Defense.

Espionage Law Cited

The section cited by the Attorney General is labeled "gathering, transmitting or losing defense information."

The laws governing the disclosure of secret documents were described earlier in the day by a Pentagon spokesman as containing "certain ambiguities" about whether they apply to publications or only to their sources of information. Government lawyers were divided on the matter, the spokesman indicated, because there appeared to be no precedent for application of the law to a publication.

Both Mr. Mitchell and the Pentagon spokesman, Jerry W. Friedheim, cited sections of the Espionage and Censorship Chapter of the Federal criminal code. Mr. Friedheim mentioned Section 798, entitled "Disclosure of Classified Information." The Attorney General mentioned Section 793, headed "Gathering, Transmitting or Losing Defense Information."

Much of Section 793 refers to spying on defense installations and to obtaining code books, blueprints, maps or other defense-related documents.

Selections From Section

It goes on to state that "whoever having unauthorized pos-

session of, access to, or control over any document, writing, code book ... or information relating to the national defense which information the possessor has reason to believe could be used to the injury of the United States or to the advantage of any foreign nation, willfully communicates, delivers, transmits ... the same to any person not entitled to receive it, or willfully retains the same and fails to deliver it to the officer or employee of the United States entitled to receive it ... shall be fined not more than $10,000 or imprisoned not more than ten years, or both."

The Justice Department's request conveyed by Mr. Mardian was the first direct contact between the Government and The Times about the publication of the Pentagon papers.

The first group of materials, published in the Sunday issue of the paper, dealt with the clandestine warfare carried on against North Vietnam before the Tonkin Gulf incident in August, 1964. The second installment, in this morning's issue, covered the Johnson Administration's decision to begin open bombing of North Vietnam in February, 1965.

Before Mr. Mardian's call, the Administration had said only that the Justice Department was investigating the disclosures, at the request of the Defense Department.

Laird Sees 'Violation'

Secretary of Defense Melvin R. Laird said the disclosure "violated the security regulations of the United States."

The Secretary implied a difference between the violation of security regulations—by officials subject to these regulations—and violation of law. He said he had asked the Justice Department to determine the legal implications.

This morning, a formal Pentagon statement expressed concern about "this violation of security" but left determination of legal action to the Justice Department.

At the Justice Department this afternoon, a spokesman said the subject was still under consideration by Attorney General Mitchell. "We have yet to determine whether or not there is something to investigate," the spokesman added, explaining that Mr. Mitchell was dealing during the day with a statement on housing discrimination and had not yet considered the matter fully.

As of that time, there was said to have been no order for any Justice investigation, but other agencies of government reported intensive inquiries into the affair.

Authority Unchallenged

Mr. Mitchell, Secretary Laird and White House officials began to confer on Sunday on the disclosures in The Times. No official here challenged the authenticity of the account

of the Pentagon study and of the documents printed in The Times. Only a few members of Congress commented on their content.

The White House referred to the Pentagon all questions on the circumstances of the disclosure. Under vigorous questioning about the documents, it chose to emphasize that President Nixon had developed a "new Vietnam policy" and decided when he took office in 1969 "not to engage ourselves in a continuation or justification" of the policies of earlier administrations, which are the subject of the Pentagon papers.

Ronald L. Ziegler, the President's press secretary, said that a copy of the 1967-68 Pentagon study was brought to the White House this morning from the Defense Department.

Although Mr. Nixon and his aides were said to be unfamiliar with this "internal" archive, Mr. Ziegler stressed that the basic documents and information contained in them had been available to the new Administration and were fully considered in its own policy review in early 1969.

Asked whether The Times had informed the White House of its publishing plans, Mr. Ziegler said the newspaper "did not at any time check with us." Asked whether the President was concerned about the publication of secret documents, he replied:

"I'm not going to build up, by White House comment, the exposure of classified information."

The only formal public statement was that by the Pentagon referring the matter to the Justice Department. This came after Secretary Laird was drawn into a discussion of the affair by Senator Stuart Symington, Democrat of Missouri, at a hearing of the Senate Foreign Relations Committee on foreign aid.

Data Called Still 'Sensitive'

Senator Symington announced his intention to propose a "full examination of the origins of the war" for the benefit of future generations. Mr. Laird opposed the idea, arguing that a debate of the past "would not serve the interests of the country and would not help us disengage from Vietnam."

Stating a theme that he apparently hoped would dominate the reaction to The Times' disclosures, Mr. Laird said that "the divisions caused by debate of the past actions would not serve a useful purpose today." He has been trying to shift focus away from "Why Vietnam?" to the means of disengaging in an honorable way, he declared.

Mr. Laird said the disclosure of the Pentagon papers was "unauthorized" and "violates the security regulations of our Government." Although the study covers information only to 1968, he added, the information "remains sensitive" and its

publication does not serve "a useful purpose." The Secretary said the documents would remain classified and would not be made available to the Foreign Relations Committee.

Senator Symington observed that the committee had tried several times to obtain the material, on a confidential basis. He said it was "shocking" that Congress had been kept ignorant of the materials and that even now he had to read about them in the newspapers.

Asked whether he knew who might have passed the materials to The Times, Mr. Laird said, "No, I don't yet know." But since there were so few copies, he added, "it won't be hard to track down whoever was responsible.

"This is highly sensitive information and should not have been made public," he declared.

Legal Distinction Implied

Shortly afterward, Mr. Friedheim, the Pentagon briefing officer, read a statement that had been worked out after a full day of consultation among Mr. Mitchell, Mr. Laird, some White House officials and lawyers of the Defense and Justice Departments. Inferentially, the statement made a distinction between violation of Government security regulations and possible violations of law. It said:

"The Department of Defense must be and is concerned about the disclosure of publication of highly classified information affecting national security.

"The material remains classified and sensitive despite the fact that it covers a period that ended in 1968.

"It is our responsibility to call this violation of security to the attention of the Justice Department. We have done so.

"The Government has the responsibility to determine what individual or individuals, if any, violated the laws relating to national security information by unauthorized disclosure of classified material."

Mr. Friedheim said officials of the Justice and Defense Departments had had various discussions of the matter, face to face and also by telephone, since Sunday, when The Times began publication of its series of articles.

He said the relevant law was Title 18 of the United States Code, Section 798, noting that it contained "certain ambiguities" as to whether it applies to publications or only to their sources of secret information.

"Some lawyers are of the opinion that the publication is liable to prosecution as well as the official [source]," the spokesman said, "but there appears no precedent to establish that point. Justice is studying the whole matter to decide who, if anyone, to charge with law violation."

The section that he cited states: "Whoever knowingly and willfully communicates, furnishes, transmits, or otherwise makes available to an unauthorized person, or publishes, or uses in any manner prejudicial to the safety or interest of the United States or for the benefit of any foreign government to the detriment of the United States any classified information . . . shall be fined not more than $10,000 or imprisoned not more than 10 years, or both."

The section contains a list and definition of classified information as bearing on codes, weapons and materials, intelligence activities and material obtained from the communications of foreign governments.

Mr. Friedheim said the Pentagon had determined that there were "a dozen or so" copies of the papers and that half of these, at the Defense Department, "have remained under extremely tight control." He said he did not believe the Pentagon's copies had either been duplicated or shown to unauthorized persons. He refused to say where the other copies had been kept.

7,000 Pages of Material

There is a possibility, the spokesman remarked, that unauthorized duplicate copies were made at some point, "or even that a set of the study was stolen at some point." The materials run to about 7,000 pages of analysis and documentation.

As a practical matter, Mr. Friedheim said, the Pentagon regards individuals with authorized clearance to handle classified information as primarily responsible for the protection of such information.

He said Secretary Laird had been aware of the secret Pentagon study since he came into office in 1969 and had even once referred to its existence in public testimony before the Senate Foreign Relations Committee.

The spokesman then emphasized again Mr. Laird's "philosophical" conviction that it was more important to consider ways of disengaging from Viet-

United Press International

PRINTING OF PAPERS ASSESSED: Senator George S. McGovern, left, South Dakota Democrat, said Vietnam documents told story of "deception." Senate Minority Leader Hugh Scott called "release" of study a "crime."

nam than to "rake over the coals" of past policies.

At the State Department, a spokesman said he could not comment "on the accuracy of —or make any useful comment on the substance of — these papers until we have had an opportunity to check the original."

Checking was difficult, the spokesman, Charles W. Bray 3d, said this morning, because the department had not had time to locate its copy of the report, or even to determine whether it had one.

Several hours later, according to Mr. Bray, the papers were found in personal files that had been left behind by William P. Bundy, who served as Assistant Secretary of State for East Asian and Pacific Affairs during the Johnson Administration.

Secretary of State William P. Rogers had no comment on the matter today, but he is likely to be asked about the materials at a news conference scheduled for tomorrow.

In Congress, there were only a few other comments on the matter and no indication that

disclosure of the Vietnam materials would significantly influence the Senate vote Wednesday on legislation that would require withdrawal of American forces from the war zone by the end of this year.

Materials Called 'Instructive'

Senator George S. McGovern of South Dakota, a cosponsor of that measure and candidate for the Democratic Presidential nomination, said the documents told a story of "almost incredible deception" of Congress and the American people by the highest officials in Government, including the President.

He said that he did not see how any Senator could ever again believe it was safe to permit the executive branch to make foreign policy alone, and added:

"We would make a serious mistake to assume the kind of deception revealed in these documents began and ended with the Johnson Administration."

Senator Hugh Scott of Pennsylvania, the Republican leader, said that the "release" of the documents was "a bad thing,

it's a federal crime." But he described their content as "very instructive and somewhat shocking."

"I think the American people have never been told as much as they could digest about the war until President Nixon assumed office," he added. "He has been more than candid. This President has taken the people into his confidence more than anyone else."

Asked whether The Times should continue publication of its articles, Senator Scott said the paper would have to decide "on its good judgment."

Representative Paul N. McCloskey Jr. of California, who has talked of challenging Mr. Nixon for the Presidency in the Republican primaries next year discussed The Times article and underlying Pentagon paper on the floor of the House.

Deception Is Charged

He said "the issue of truthfulness in Government is a problem as serious as that of ending the war itself." He also complained of "deceptive," "incomplete" and "misleading" briefings given to him during a recent visit to Southeast Asia, often, he said, with officers who knew the statements to be incorrect standing mute in his presence.

"This deception is not a matter of protecting secret information from the enemy," Mr. McCloskey said. "The intention is to conceal information from the people of the United State as if we were the enemy."

Robert S. McNamara, the former Secretary of Defense, who commissioned the Pentagon study in 1967, was reported to have sent the copy later delivered to him to the National Archives.

Mr. McNamara turned down several invitations to make a public comment today on the ground that this was inappropriate to his present duties as President of the International Bank for Reconstruction and Development—the World Bank.

June 15, 1971

Ellsberg Yields, Is Indicted; Says He Gave Data to Press

By ROBERT REINHOLD
Special to The New York Times

BOSTON, June 28—Dr. Daniel Ellsberg declared today that he had given the Pentagon study of the Vietnam war to the press. Moments later he surrendered to the United States Attorney here for arraignment on charges of unauthorized possession of secret documents.

Later in the day a Federal grand jury in Los Angeles returned a two-count indict-

ment accusing Dr. Ellsberg of the theft of Government property and the unauthorized possession of "documents and writings related to the national defense."

The 40-year-old scholar and

former Defense Department official had been described as the source of the Pentagon documents that The New York Times drew upon for its Vietnam series, the publication of which began on June 13 and was stopped on June 15 by Federal Court order.

Times Silent on Source

The Times refused again today to discuss the source of its documents.

After a one-hour hearing before United States Magistrate Peter W. Princi, Dr. Ellsberg was released on $50,000 bail. The Government had asked that

bail be set at $100,000.

At almost exactly 10 o'clock this morning, as his lawyers promised Saturday, Dr. Ellsberg drove in a taxi to the Post Office Building, which houses the Federal courts.

Looking calm and confident and clutching his wife, Patricia, around the shoulders, he told the crushing throng of newsmen that in 1969 he gave the information contained in the documents to Senator J. W. Fulbright, chairman of the Senate Foreign Relations Committee.

"This spring, after two invasions and 9,000 more Americans deaths, I can only regret that at the same time I did not release them to the newspapers," he said. "I have now done so. I took this action solely at my own initiative.

"I did this clearly at my own jeopardy and I am prepared to answer to all the consequences of these decisions. That includes the personal consequences to me and my family, whatever these may be. Would not you go to prison to help end this war?"

In an interview later as he stood barefoot on the porch of his home in Cambridge, Dr. Ellsberg declined to discuss the details of how he gave the documents to the press. He would not confirm that The Times, the first newspaper to publish some of them, was the recipient of the 7,000-page study nor would he say whether he had a role in subsequent appearances of segments of it in other newspapers.

"I feel inhibited while there is litigation before the Supreme Court which turns in part on protection of sources," he said. "I don't want to say things that would make the case moot."

But, he added, "I was determined not to come forward without accepting responsibility."

First Appearance in 10 Days

It was Dr. Ellsberg's first public appearance in the 10 days since his name was mentioned publicly as The Times's source of the study, of which he was one of 30 or 40 authors. A warrant for his arrest was issued in Los Angeles late Friday, but his lawyers advised him to await a regular business day to surrender. Over the weekend he eluded an intensive search by Federal Bureau of Investigation agents.

The warrant charges Dr. Ellsberg, a former Marine Corps officer, who is now a research associate at the Massachusetts Institute of Technology, with possession and failure to return the secret papers, under Title 18, Section 793E, of the United States Code. He is not accused of transmitting documents to anyone else.

After pressing through an almost impenetrable crowd of newsmen and cheering well-wishers, Dr. Ellsberg and his lawyers, Leonard B. Boudin and Charles R. Nesson, both professors at the Harvard Law School, entered the 11th-floor offices of the United States Attorney Herbert F. Travers Jr.

There he was placed under arrest by F.B.I. agents and taken to the United States Marshal's office for photographs and fingerprinting. About 30 minutes later, with two Federal marshals holding his arms he was taken to a 12th-floor courtroom.

There Dr. Ellsberg sat alone behind a brass rail and listened

The New York Times/Donal F. Holway

SAYS HE RELEASED PENTAGON PAPERS: Dr. Daniel Ellsberg at news conference outside Federal building in Boston with his wife after he surrendered himself yesterday.

intently, his chin propped on his hand, as his lawyers and the Assistant United States Attorney, Lawrence P. Cohen, presented arguments over bail.

'Severity of the Crime'

Mr. Cohen argued for $100,000 bail because of the "severity of the crime as measured by the punishment"—up to 10 years in prison and a $10,000 fine, or both—and because Dr. Ellsberg did not turn himself in immediately upon issuance of the warrant, eluding the F.B.I. over the weekend. "This suggests the defendant has the resources to remain in hiding and frustrate this court," Mr. Cohen said.

In response Mr. Boudin asked that his client be released in his own recognizance. Magistrate Princi expressed some doubt, saying that if the defendant was proved guilty of being insensitive to laws protecting secret documents, then "might he not be also insensitive to his obligation to appear if he found things were not going as he anticipated."

Mr. Boudin sought to establish Dr. Ellsberg's reliability by reading a long list of his accomplishments and former positions—as special assistant to the Assistant Secretary of Defense and as a special assistant to the United States Ambassador to Vietnam. The lawyer added that the defendant waited until today to surrender to avoid the "Roman holiday" atmosphere that sometimes surrounds major F.B.I.

arrests.

The United States Attorney replied that it was a matter of public notice that Dr. Ellsberg "has been in concealment for two weeks."

"I'd like something concrete," the Magistrate said. "He is here this morning. Is there any reason to believe he would not be here next week?"

Eventually Dr. Ellsberg, a slim, intense-looking man, asked that he be allowed to "make myself responsible to appear." After several more minutes, he rose again and said, "I do ask that my responsibility for my appearance be accepted."

At this the Magistrate said: "I am going to take you at your word. I am going to put you on $50,000 bail without surety. You're going to walk out and be free." He then scheduled a hearing on July 15 for the removal of Dr. Ellsberg to Los Angeles, where the case will presumably be tried.

At the conclusion of the hearing Dr. Ellsberg and his wife, both smiling, descended to the street and held an impromptu news conference under the bright sun in the middle of Post Office Square, which was thronged with cheering supporters.

He urged everyone to read the documents and expressed the hope that the disclosures would help "free ourselves from this war."

Asked if he had any regrets,

Dr. Ellsberg replied, "Certainly not" and added that he was very pleased with the way the newspapers had defended the First Amendment.

"As a matter of fact, it's been a long time since I had as much hope for the institutions of this country," he continued. "When I see how the press and the courts have responded to their responsibilities to defend these rights, I am very happy about that as an American citizen."

Earlier he said that "as a responsible American I could no longer cooperate in concealing this information."

After having consented somewhat reluctantly to the interview, he discussed his motives for publicizing the documents.

"I have wanted for about two years to try to raise the issue of personal responsibility and accountability of officials," he said, "not to punish but to make current officials conscious of their responsibility."

He took pains to dispute press reports that he was racked by guilt over his role in Vietnam, where he was connected with the pacification program.

"The simple fact is that I never felt tortured by guilt by anything I did in Vietnam," he asserted. "The kind of things I do blame myself for is not informing myself earlier than I did about the origins of the conflict."

He went on to say that his knowledge of the contents of the study was what drove him because it gave him a responsibility.

He maintained that not a single page of the documents he had disclosed "would do grave damage" to the country. He said he had not released documents that recounted direct negotiations between the Johnson Administration and foreign governments.

Dr. Ellsberg said he would expand on his comments tomorrow afternoon at a news conference at Faneuil Hall here.

Coast Jury Acts

By STEVEN V. ROBERTS
Special to The New York Times

LOS ANGELES, June 28—Dr. Ellsberg was indicted by a Federal grand jury here today for the theft and possession of the secret Pentagon study.

The indictment of Dr. Ellsberg, who once worked for the Rand Corporation in nearby Santa Monica, supersedes a criminal complaint issued against him late Friday by the United States Attorney here.

Paul C. Vincent, the Justice Department attorney who has been handling the case here, told newsmen that Dr. Ellsberg could decide to be tried either in Los Angeles or Boston.

The first count of the indictment cited Section 793(E) of the United States Code and charged Dr. Ellsberg with "unauthorized possession of Defense information." It noted that in September and October of 1969 he "had access to and control over copies of certain documents and writings relating to the national defense."

Two Copies at Rand

This was during the time Dr. Ellsberg worked at Rand, the research organization that received two of the original 15 copies of the controversial Pentagon study. Last week Lynda R. Sinay, a friend of Dr. Ellsberg, told the grand jury that he had paid her $150 to make copies of certain documents on a Xerox machine, but that she did not know what the documents contained.

The indictment alleged that Dr. Ellsberg "did willfully, knowingly and unlawfully retain" the 47-volume study. All but one volume of the study was classified top secret, and the indictment said Dr. Ellsberg had failed "to deliver them to the officer or employe of the United States entitled to receive them."

The second count, citing Section 641 of the United States Code, charged that Dr. Ellsberg did "convert to his own use" the Pentagon study, which was entitled "United States-Vietnam Relations, 1945-1967." The study, the indictment said, had a value in excess of $100.

The grand jury will meet again on July 6, and other indictments are still possible.

June 29, 1971

SUPREME COURT, 6-3, UPHOLDS NEWSPAPERS ON PUBLICATION OF THE PENTAGON REPORT

BURGER DISSENTS

First Amendment Rule Held to Block Most Prior Restraints

By FRED P. GRAHAM
Special to The New York Times

WASHINGTON, June 30 — The Supreme Court freed The New York Times and The Washington Post today to resume immediate publication of articles based on the secret Pentagon papers on the origins of the Vietnam war.

By a vote of 6 to 3 the Court held that any attempt by the Government to block news articles prior to publication bears "a heavy burden of presumption against its constitutionality."

In a historic test of that principle — the first effort by the Government to enjoin publication on the ground of national security — the Court declared that "the Government has not met that burden."

The brief judgment was read to a hushed courtroom by Chief Justice Warren E. Burger at 2:30 P.M. at a special session called three hours before.

Old Tradition Observed

The Chief Justice was one of the dissenters, along with Associate Justices Harry A. Blackmun and John M. Harlan, but because the decision was rendered in an unsigned opinion, the Chief Justice read it in court in accordance with long-standing custom.

In New York Arthur Ochs Sulzberger, president and publisher of The Times, said at a news conference that he had "never really doubted that this day would come and that we'd win." His reaction, he said, was "complete joy and delight."

The case had been expected to produce a landmark ruling on the circumstances under which prior restraint could be imposed upon the press, but because no opinion by a single Justice commanded the support of a majority, only the unsigned decision will serve as precedent.

Uncertainty Over Outcome

Because it came on the 15th day after The Times had been restrained from publishing further articles in its series mined from the 7,000 pages of material—the first such restraint in the name of "national security" in the history of the United States—there was some uncertainty whether the press had scored a strong victory or whether a precedent for some degree of restraint had been set.

Alexander M. Bickel, the Yale law professor who had argued for The Times in the case, said in a telephone interview that the ruling placed the press in a "stronger position." He maintained that no Federal District Judge would henceforth temporarily restrain a newspaper on the Justice Department's complaint that "this is what they have printed and we don't like it" and that a direct threat of irreparable harm would have to be alleged.

However, the United States Solicitor General, Erwin N. Griswold, turned to another lawyer shortly after the Justices filed from the courtroom and remarked: "Maybe the newspapers will show a little restraint in the future." All nine Justices wrote opinions, in a judicial outpouring that was described by Supreme Court scholars as without precedent. They divided roughly into groups of three each.

The first group, composed of Hugo L. Black, William O. Douglas and Thurgood Marshall, took what is known as the absolutist view that the courts lack the power to suppress any press publication, no matter how grave a threat to security it might pose.

Justices Black and Douglas restated their long-held belief that the First Amendment's guarantee of a free press forbids any judicial restraint. Justice Marshall insisted that because Congress had twice considered and rejected such power for the courts, the Supreme Court would be "enacting" law if it imposed restraint.

The second group, which included William J. Brennan Jr., Potter Stewart and Byron R. White, said that the press could not be muzzled except to prevent direct, immediate and irreparable damage to the nation. They agreed that this material did not pose such a threat.

The Dissenters' Views

The third bloc, composed of the three dissenters, declared that the courts should not refuse to enforce the executive branch's conclusion that material should be kept confidential — so long as a Cabinet-level officer had decided that it should—on a matter affecting foreign relations.

They felt that the "frenzied train of events" in the cases before them had not given the courts enough time to determine those questions, so they concluded that the restaints upon publication should have been retained while both cases were sent back to the trial judges for more hearings.

The New York Times's series drawn from the secret Pentagon study was accompanied by supporting documents. Articles were published on June 13, 14 and 15 before they were halted by court order. A similar restraining order was imposed on June 19 against The Washington Post after it began to print articles based on the study.

Justice Black's opinion stated that just such publications as those were intended to be protected by the First Amendment's declaration that "Congress shall make no law . . . abridging the freedom of the press."

Paramount among the responsibilities of a free press, he said, "is the duty to prevent any part of the Government from deceiving the people and sending them off to distant lands to die of foreign fevers and foreign shot and shell.

"In my view, far from de-

321

serving condemnation for their courageous reporting, The New York Times, The Washington Post and other newspapers should be commended for serving the purpose that the Founding Fathers saw so clearly," he said. "In revealing the workings of government that led to the Vietnam war, the newspapers nobly did precisely that which the founders hoped and trusted they would do."

Justice Douglas joined the opinion by Justice Black and was joined by him in another opinion. The First Amendment's purpose, Justice Douglas argued, is to prohibit "governmental suppression of embarrassing information." He asserted that the temporary restraints in these cases "constitute a flouting of the principles of the First Amendment."

Justice Marshall's position was based primarily upon the separation-of-powers argument that Congress had never authorized prior restraints and that it refused to do so when bills were introduced in 1917 and 1957.

He concluded that the courts were without power to restrain publications. Justices Brennan, Stewart and White, who also based their conclusions on the separation-of-powers principle, assumed that under extreme circumstances the courts would act without such powers.

Justice Brennan focused on the temporary restraints, which had been issued to freeze the situation so that the material would not be made public before the courts could decide if it should be enjoined. He continued that no restraints should have been imposed because the

Government alleged only in general terms that security breaches might occur.

Justices Stewart and White, who also joined each other's opinions, said that though they had read the documents they felt that publication would not be in the national interest.

But Justice Stewart, a former chairman of The Yale Daily News, insisted that "it is the duty of the executive" to protect state secrets through its own security measures and not the duty of the courts to do it by banning news articles.

He implied that if publication of the material would cause "direct, immediate, and irreparable damage to our nation or its people," he would uphold prior restraint, but because that situation was not present here, he said that the papers must be free to publish.

Justice White added that Congress had enacted criminal laws, including the espionage laws, that might apply to these papers. "The newspapers are presumably now on full notice," he said, that the Justice Department may bring prosecutions if the publications violate those laws. He added that he "would have no difficulty in sustaining convictions" under the laws, even if the breaches of security were not sufficient to justify prior restraint.

The Chief Justice and Justices Stewart and Blackmun echoed this caveat in their opinions — meaning that one less than a majority had lent their weight to the warning.

Chief Justice Burger blamed The Times "in large part" for the "frenetic haste" with

which the case was handled. He said that The Times had studied the Pentagon archives for three or four months before beginning its series, yet it had breached "the duty of an honorable press" by not asking the Government if any security violations were involved before it began publication.

He said he found it "hardly believable" that The Times would do this, and he concluded that it would not be harmed if the case were sent back for more testimony.

Justice Blackmun, also focusing his criticism on The Times, said there had been inadequate time to determine if the publications could result in "the death of soldiers, the destruction of alliances, the greatly increased difficulty of negotiation with our enemies, the inability of our diplomats to negotiate." He concluded that if the war was prolonged and a delay in the return of United States prisoners result from publication, "then the nation's people will know where the responsibility for these sad consequences rests."

In his own dissenting opinion, Justice Harlan said: "The judiciary must review the initial executive determination to the point of satisfying itself that the subject matter of the dispute does lie within the proper compass of the President's foreign policy relations power.

"The judiciary," he went on, "may properly insist that the determination that disclosure of that subject matter would irreparably impair the national security be made by the head

of the executive department concerned—here the Secretary of State or the Secretary of Defense—after actual personal consideration.

"But in my judgment, the judiciary may not properly go beyond these two inquiries and redetermine for itself the probable impact of disclosure on the national security."

The Justice Department initially sought an injunction against The Times on June 15 from Federal District Judge Murray I. Gurfein in New York.

Judge Gurfein, who had issued the original temporary restraining order that was stayed until today, ruled that the material was basically historical matter that might be embarrassing to the Government but did not pose a threat to national security. Federal District Judge Gerhard A. Gesell of the District of Columbia came to the same conclusion in the Government's suit against The Washington Post.

The United States Court of Appeals for the Second Circuit, voting 5 to 3, ordered more secret hearings before Judge Gurfein and The Times appealed. The United States Court of Appeals for the District of Columbia upheld Judge Gesell, 7 to 2, holding that no injunction should be imposed. Today the Supreme Court affirmed the Appeals Court here and reversed the Second Circuit.

The Supreme Court also issued a brief order disposing of a few other cases and adjourned until Oct. 4, as it had been scheduled to do Monday.

July 1, 1971

EHRLICHMAN ORDERED '71 ELLSBERG INQUIRY

NIXON ROLE CITED

F.B.I. Quotes Aide as Saying Hunt, Liddy Were Given Job

By MARTIN ARNOLD
Special to The New York Times

LOS ANGELES, May 1—John D. Ehrlichman has told Federal investigators that the break-in at the office of Daniel Ellsberg's psychiatrist came as a result of a secret White House investigation he ordered at the request of President Nixon.

Mr. Ehrlichman, according to a Federal Bureau of Investigation report made public today

in the Pentagon papers trial, said that G. Gordon Liddy and E. Howard Hunt Jr., conspirators in the Watergate case, had

been "designated" to conduct the investigation.

The former Presidential assistant said that he did not

know that Liddy and Hunt had broken into the psychiatrist's office until after it had happened, did not agree with the

Associated Press
Dr. Daniel Ellsberg talking to newsmen outside the Federal courthouse in Los Angeles during a luncheon recess yesterday in the Pentagon papers trial.

"method of investigation," and told the two men "not to do this again," the F.B.I. report said.

An Independent Study

The bureau's report, based on an interview by agents with Mr. Ehrlichman in his White House office last Friday, said that in 1971 the President "had expressed interest" in the leak of classified information and "asked him to make inquiries independent of concurrent F.B.I. investigation which had been made relating to the leak of the Pentagon papers."

There was "information available that Ellsberg had emotional and moral problems and Liddy and Hunt sought to determine full facts" by preparing a "psychiatric profile" and conducting an "in-depth investigation of Ellsberg," the report said. It was apparently this effort that eventually resulted in the break-in.

The disclosure at the Pentagon papers trial led the defense to move immediately for a dismissal of the case "with prejudice." Judge William Matthew Byrne Jr. of the United States District Court said he would take the motion under submission.

"It may be renewed by the defendants" at a later time, he said, "or I may renew it myself." Then, in what was interpreted as a broad hint to the Government, he turned to the chief prosecutor, David R. Nissen, and said, "I assume that your superiors are evaluating the case."

Although the judge refused to dismiss the charges immediately, he said that he believed that the Ehrlichman material was exculpatory; that is, material in the hands of the prosecution that would tend to prove the innocence of the defendants.

This latest disclosure was the third major revelation to hit this trial during the last three trial days, and, like the others, it strengthened the link between this and the Watergate case.

According to the F.B.I. report, Mr. Ehrlichman said that a decision had been made "to conduct some investigation in the Pentagon papers leak matter 'directly out of the White House.'" The papers were first disclosed in The New York Times on June 13, 1971.

The report says that the investigation was "directed toward an 'in-depth investigation of Ellsberg to determine his habits, mental attitudes, motives, etc.'"

The quotes within the quotes are Mr. Ehrlichman's own words, according to the F.B.I. interview.

May 2, 1973

PENTAGON PAPERS CHARGES ARE DISMISSED

United Press International

Judge William Matthew Byrne Jr., above, threw out the Pentagon papers case and, left, defendants were freed. They are Anthony J. Russo Jr., left, and Dr. Daniel Ellsberg.

NEW TRIAL BARRED

But Decision Does Not Solve Constitutional Issues in Case

By MARTIN ARNOLD
Special to The New York Times

LOS ANGELES, May 11—Citing what he called "improper Government conduct shielded so long from public view," the judge in the Pentagon papers trial dismissed today all charges against Dr. Daniel Ellsberg and Anthony J. Russo Jr.

And he made it clear in his ruling that the two men would not be tried again on charges of stealing and copying the Pentagon papers.

"The conduct of the Government has placed the case in such a posture that it precludes the fair, dispassionate resolution of these issues by a jury," he said.

David R. Nissen, the chief prosecutor, said, "It appears that the posture is such that no appeal will be possible."

Defendants Not Vindicated

But the decision by United States District Court Judge William Matthew Byrne Jr. did not vindicate the defendants; it chastised the Government. Nor did it resolve the important constitutional issues that the case had raised.

The end of the trial, on its 89th day, was dramatic. The courtroom was jammed; the jury box was filled with news reporters; defense workers in the Ellsberg-Russo cause, mostly young people, sat in chairs lining the courtroom wall.

Dr. Ellsberg and Mr. Russo, surrounded by their lawyers, stared intently as Judge Byrne quickly read his ruling.

The Government's action in this case, he said, "offended a sense of justice," and so "I have decided to declare a mistrial and grant the motion for dismissal." The time was 2:07 P.M.

The courtroom erupted in loud cheering and clapping. The judge, barely hiding a smile, quickly strode out the door behind his bench.

Tension had been building for two days, since the sudden

disclosure by the Government yesterday that telephone conversations of Dr. Ellsberg were picked up by wiretapping in late 1969 and early 1970, and that all records and logs of those conversations had disappeared from the Federal Bureau of Investigation.

When this morning the Government was still unable to produce either the records or a legal authorization for the taps, it was evident that the case had ended.

The jury was not present when the judge read his decision. It had been sent home until Monday morning.

Before rendering his decision, the judge offered the defendants the opportunity to go to the jury for a verdict. He said that he would withhold his ruling on their motion to dismiss if they wanted. He indicated that if they did decide to go to the jury, he would probably dismiss some of the counts—six for espionage, six for theft and one for conspiracy.

He said that he believed enough of the case was left to litigate before the jury, if the defendants so desired. They did not, and then he read his ruling.

"A judgment of acquittal goes to all the facts," he said, but he added that if he ruled on that defense motion, "it would not dispose of all the issues." That, he said, "can only be done by going to the jury."

He did say, however, that his ruling was based not only on the wiretap disclosures, "or based solely on the break-in" of the office of Dr. Ellsberg's psychiatrist on Sept. 3, 1971, by agents in the employ of the White House.

Ellsberg May Sue Nixon

But Judge Byrne said that "on April 26 the Government made an extraordinary disclosure"— that of the break-in—and that was followed by disclosures that the break-in was done by a "special unit" reporting to the White House.

He said that the special unit "apparently operated with the approval of the F.B.I." and that the C.I.A. also became involved in the prosecution of this case at the "request of the White House."

Dr. Ellsberg and Mr. Russo were jubilant, and members of their families were in tears as the long ordeal, which started with Dr. Ellsberg's arrest on June 25, 1971, ended.

Dr. Ellsberg said that he would file a civil action against former and present high ranking officials of the Government, even perhaps against President Nixon.

Dr. Ellsberg and Mr. Russo contended that they had taken the papers and copied them to give them to Congress, which, they hoped, would bring pressure to end the war in Vietnam.

So in reality they were arguing in court not only constitutional issues, but their belief that the greater good required them to break some regulations to make the papers public.

This, too, was an issue that the jury would have decided.

"I am convinced by the record of the last couple of weeks, particularly the last couple of days," that the trial should not go on, the judge said.

"Governmental agencies have taken an unprecedented series of actions against these defendants," he said. He cited the special White House "plumbers" unit, which "apparently operated with the approval of the F.B.I."

"We may have been given only a glimpse of what this special unit did," the judge said. "The latest series of actions compound a record already pervaded by instances which threatened the defendants' rights to a fair trial.

"It was of greatest significance," he said, that the wiretap occurred during the period of conspiracy.

"Continued Government investigation is no solution," he added, "because delays tend to compromise the defendants' rights."

He precluded another trial against Dr. Ellsberg and Mr. Russo by including in his ruling this sentence:

"Under all the circumstances, I believe that the defendants should not have to run the risk, present under existing authorities, that they might be tried again before a different jury."

Dr. Ellsberg was asked if he

was disappointed that the case had not gone to the jury, and he replied, "I think that an American jury would have come to a judgment that is good for this country."

"Tony and I think we know we did something right," he added.

He was asked if he would disclose the Pentagon papers again, and he answered, "I would do it tomorrow, if I could do it."

Leonard B. Boudin, a defense attorney, said:

"I think that the court's ruling was appropriate, necessary, eloquent, justified and dispositive. The judgment was made not on the narrow issue of wiretapping, but on the totality of Government misconduct."

Dr. Ellsberg then added that "the trial isn't over until that bombing is over in Cambodia.

"Don't we have the right not to be tried under Nazi law," he asked. "This Administration has been very straight about where it is. It is up to us to tell them what it means to be an American.

"If facts prove to be what they appear to be, the President has led a conspiracy, not only against Tony and me, but against the American public."

Later today, the Judge's clerk notified the jurors by telephone that the case had ended and a quick poll this evening showed that at least half of them would have voted to acquit the defendants.

May 12, 1973

I.R.S. Team Collects Data On Extremists for Tax Use

By ROBERT M. SMITH
Special to The New York Times

WASHINGTON, Jan. 12—The Internal Revenue Service acknowledged tonight that it has a special seven-man unit whose sole job is to collect information on extremist political organizations of the left and right and their leaders to uncover situations where there may have been tax evasion.

Leon Levine, a public information officer for the revenue service, said that he was not clear what criteria were used to place people in the "extremist" category. But, he said, "because of the way some of these people behave in their everyday affairs, it's reasonable to believe some of them may be violating the tax laws."

The acknowledgement came from Johnnie Walters, Commissioner of Internal Revenue,

after a former agent of the Federal Bureau of Investigation said he had seen a soundproof room in which the special squad worked.

The former agent, Robert N. Wall, mentioned this while discussing some of the inner workings of the bureau.

He said bureau activities had included monitoring the telephone calls of the Israeli Embassy; investigating, and trying to place young informants in, a liberal research institute; soliciting information from banks and telephone companies without getting subpoenas, and attempting to foment strife within radical circles through such devices as anonymous letters.

Mr. Wall, a 33-year-old former naval officer who was an F.B.I. special agent for five

years, made the statements in an article, which will appear in The New York Review of Books, and in an interview at his home in Buffalo.

He described himself as so disenchanted with the American life style that he plans to move to a farm in Novia Scotia. He left the Federal Bureau of Investigation in April, 1970. He says he had become disillusioned with the bureau.

Almost all of Mr. Wall's allegations about the bureau have been independently verified by reliable sources inside and outside the Government.

An F.B.I. spokesman was asked today whether the bureau tries to create dissension in radical circles, whether it monitors the telephones of foreign embassies and whether it solicits information from banks and telephone companies without subpoenas.

The spokesman said the bureau would make "no comment whatsoever." A spokesman did confirm, however, that Mr. Wall had been a special agent.

A reliable source confirmed Mr. Wall's allegations about the bureau's attempts to sow dissension in extremist organizations. He said the tactic had been pursued effectively in

The New York Times
Robert N. Wall

the case of the Ku Klux Klan and that the technique had been borrowed from F.B.I. operations against organized crime. There, he said, an anonymous letter could result in gang warfare or the murder of a gangster.

Mr. Walters, the Internal Revenue chief, said that he did not know much about the special I.R.S. unit's operations because the existence of the unit came to his attention only about a week ago, in connection with a discussion of a possible reorganization of the agency. The Internal Revenue Service is an agency of the Treasury Department.

When the unit finds evidence that extremists have access to large sums of money, it passes on the information to the regular tax enforcement personnel at Internal Revenue. Among the items checked are whether the organization's leaders have filed tax returns and whether the organization itself is claiming a tax-exempt status that it does not actually have.

According to Mr. Wall, one purpose of the F.B.I.'s counterintelligence program "was to create dissent among the various groups involved in the New Left to prevent them from working together.

"In one case we addressed a letter to the leaders of the National Mobilization Committee which said that the blacks of Washington, D. C., would not support the upcoming rally of the N.M.C. [in 1969] unless a $20,000 'security bond' was paid to a black organization in Washington. At the same time we instructed some informants we had placed in the black organization to suggest the idea of a security bond informally to leaders of the organization.

"The letter we composed was approved by the bureau's counterintelligence desk and was signed with the forged signature of a leader of the black group.

"Later, through informants, we learned that the letter had caused a great deal of confusion and had a significant effect on the planning for the march."

Mr. Wall's article in the Jan. 27 issue of The New York Review of Books will also say that some of the agents in the Washington field office, where he worked, tried to confuse peace demonstrations by "handing out leaflets giving misleading information about the time and place when the marchers were supposed to meet."

'To Reduce Violence'

A source here acknowledged, "We do disrupt where possible. We do the same thing with the Ku Klux Klan. We do it only where there is a likelihood of violence, to reduce violence."

The source went on to say, however, that with the exception of a 1967 march led by the Rev. Dr. Martin Luther King Jr., "there never was a peace march on Washington that didn't have a potential for violence."

This source also reported that the Federal Bureau of Investigation tried to deepen factional conflicts within the radical Students for a Democratic Society by writing anonymous letters designed "to play one faction off against another."

In Buffalo Mr. Wall is a supporter of liberal causes ranging from the free-form Cause school—to which he sends his daughter—to sympathy for a radical college student arrested with the help of a police undercover agent.

For the last year and a half he has been a law student at the State University of Buffalo but is now leaving school for Nova Scotia because he feels "law cannot handle society's problems."

Mr. Wall, who is a tall, thin man, joined the F.B.I. in May, 1965, after graduating from St. Bonaventure University in Olean, N.Y., and serving as a lieutenant (jg.) in the Navy. After training, he worked in the bureau's Miami office. From March, 1966, to March, 1967, he says, he attended language school at the National Security Agency at Ft. Meade, Md., studying Hebrew.

Why Hebrew? "They told me the Israelis were trying to get American atomic secrets for their desalination project," he said. A reliable source here said that the American intelligence community did feel the Israelis wanted atomic information, but he said he did not know why.

Mr. Wall said he was trained to listen in on the telephone calls of the Israeli Embassy. That was also confirmed by this source, who said the Federal Bureau of Investigation also monitored and taped the conversations of Arab Embassies.

Mr. Wall said in the interview that during the six-day Israeli-Arab war of 1967, the bureau was short-handed and he was pressed into service at a switchboard set up by the F.B.I. to monitor all the calls being made to and from the Israeli Embassy. He said he did not overhear any interesting conversations.

'Think Tank' Investigation

Mr. Wall's article in The New York Review of Books also says that while he was a member of a security unit in the Washington field office he investigated the Institute for Policy Studies, a liberal "think tank" here headed by Marcus Raskin and Richard J. Barnet. Mr. Wall recalls that he himself opened that investigation:

"The Institute caught my attention shortly after I began investigating the New Left. Reports from F.B.I. informants showed that many of the leaders and spokesmen of the antiwar and civil rights organizations called at the Institute when they visited Washington.

"I reasoned that if there were a conspiracy that linked all these groups, the Institute was the logical place to look for it. I drafted a memo to that effect and requested that a case on the Institute be opened and assigned to me. My supervisor quickly agreed; he was then trying to increase the case load of the squad [called S-7] to justify a request for an increase in manpower."

Mr. Wall reports that he closed the investigation after becoming convinced the Institute "was not the secret mastermind of any conspiracy," but that another agent later reopened the file.

"He began monitoring the checking account of the Institute to determine where its money was going," Mr. Wall says. "He asked for telephone company records and compiled a list of the Institute's long-distance telephone calls. He attempted to place informants in the Institute as student interns and gathered every available paper published by it."

"Individual investigations," Mr. Wall reports, "were then opened on the people who worked for or received money from the Institute."

Mr. Wall concludes, "So far as I have been able to determine, the F.B.I. has found no evidence whatever of any illegal activity by the I.P.S., but it continues to be investigated."

Mr. Barnet, co-director of the Institute of Policy Studies, said yesterday he had not been aware the F.B.I. was investigating it until he met Mr. Wall recently. "It only suggests," he said, "that any organizations that do critical analysis are fair game for surveillance. We will continue to operate as we have, and we will take whatever measures we can to protect ourselves from this."

Tells of Affidavits

Mr. Barnet also said the Institute had affidavits from Mr. Wall saying that the bureau had seen bank records of the Institute. The Institute, said Mr. Barnet, is considering taking legal action against the Riggs Bank, the largest in Washington, for having made the records available without being served a subpoena.

John R. Cocker of the Riggs Bank said today, in response to a question, that "our practice has always been that we require a subpoena for any records from any Government agency whatsoever, including the Congress."

Mr. Wall also said the Chesapeake & Potomac Telephone Company in Washington gave the bureau telephone records without a subpoena ("It was a working relationship").

Frederick W. Langbein, general counsel for the telephone company, said today it was "absolutely untrue" that the telephone company gave the F.B.I. records of calls without a subpoena. He said that making known the existence of a message was a violation of Federal law.

Mr. Wall said, "We also had no problem in getting school records and hospital records—nothing is sacred. You could even get Social Security records, but you had to justify that quite heavily."

A reliable source confirmed that "the bureau does get financial information from banks on subjects."

"The relationship," he added, "is the same one you have to your confidential sources. Some won't go along with it and will request legal procedures. We also get stuff from the phone company. Years ago we got the stuff almost across the board."

"Recently," the source went on, "there was trouble in New York, a suit or something, and now many of them request legal procedures. It depends on the ingenuity and resourcefulness of the agent and the willingness of the man in charge. If an agent goes to the wrong individual in the company, well, he won't cooperate."

Mr. Wall said that he went to the Internal Revenue Service for information on one of the New Left people he was investigating sometime between April and June, 1969, and was taken to a soundproof room in the basement of the I.R.S. building.

"The room had no name on the door and it had several locks," Mr. Wall said. "Inside were two guys, who seemed surprised that I had shown up. On a long table in the middle of the room were piles and piles of manila folders. It turned out they were investigating the taxes of these people and my man's folder was on the table."

According to Mr. Wall, the I.R.S. investigators explained they had assembled files on "antiwar people and draft-card burners and black militants." They said they were preparing to open investigations on all of them, but were just getting started and were not sure where they were going, Mr. Wall said.

Mr. Wall said his squad, S-7, also handled "Racial Matters—an absurdly and frighteningly broad" category. "Investigations on almost anything done by or for black people could be opened simply by labeling it a racial matter," he said.

Mr. Wall said he resigned from the F.B.I. after investigating the Center for Black Education.

"My supervisor insisted it was a training ground for guerrillas. I was satisfied it was a school for black studies," he said. "After I sent in a memo recommending we close the case, a note came back saying either the agent was naive or the informants had duped him."

Having begun with the belief that the Federal Bureau of Investigation "was above all a protector of the innocent public," Mr. Wall came away convinced that "the bureau has become an ogre."

"It's repressive," he said, "but repression is such a trite word no one listens to it. The continuation of even the fiction of two-party democracy requires that the bureau stop repressing grass-roots, community-involved groups."

Recalling his own activities on the New Left squad, Mr. Wall maintains: "The biggest fiction is that the bureau is not political. It is a political force."

ERVIN QUESTIONS CHECK ON SCHORR

Criticizes White House for Ordering F.B.I. Inquiry

By RICHARD HALLORAN
Special to The New York Times

WASHINGTON, Feb. 1—Senator Sam J. Ervin Jr. asserted today that the Nixon Administration had acted with either "stupidity" or "duplicity" in ordering a personal investigation of Daniel Schorr, a television newsman.

Senator Ervin, chairman of the Subcommittee on Constitutional Rights, also charged at a Capitol Hill hearing that the White House was inconsistent in its explanations of a Federal Bureau of Investigation inquiry into the background of Mr. Schorr, who works for the Columbia Broadcasting System.

The North Carolina Democrat further criticized the Administration for refusing to allow three White House officials to testify as to whether the investigation was a prelude to the offer of a position in the Administration, as the White House has contended, or an attempt to intimidate Mr. Schorr.

The television newsman said in his testimony before the Senate subcommittee that the investigation had a "special dimension" since it came "in the context of other episodes of conflict between the Government and the press — the speeches of Vice President Agnew, the controversy over the publication of the Pentagon papers, the public discussion of Government credibility and news manipulation."

Mr. Schorr, who has been with C.B.S. for 19 years in Washington and abroad, said, "I should like to think that I have not been affected by the whole episode. The insidious thing about it is that I do not know what subtle effects it may have on me or on my colleagues."

The F.B.I. investigation of Mr. Schorr first came to light last November in a Washington Post article by Ken W. Clawson, who has since resigned from the newspaper to become a deputy to Herbert G. Klein, the executive branch's director of communications.

Hearings Resume

Subsequently, Senator Ervin asked the television correspondent to testify at his subcommittee's hearings on freedom of the press, which began last fall. The hearings resumed today and will continue into next week.

Mr. Schorr said that, on at least five occasions, President Nixon and senior officials of his Administration had criticized his reporting. On Aug. 19 of last year, he was asked to come to the White House to hear objections to a report that appeared the evening before.

The next day, Mr. Schorr testified, F.B.I. agents interviewed him as well as C.B.S. executives here and in New York, other newsmen, neighbors, previous employers and neighbors of a brother in New York. He said the agent had told him that he was being considered for a "high Government position" but did not know what it was.

The director of the F.B.I., J. Edgar Hoover, confirmed much of Mr. Schorr's recollections of the investigation in a letter to Senator Ervin made public today.

Mr. Hoover said that the F.B.I. was requested by a member of the White House staff on Aug. 19 to undertake a background investigation of Mr. Schorr. It began at 8:30 on the morning of Aug. 20 and ran until 3 P.M., when the F.B.I. learned that Mr. Schorr "desired the investigation be discontinued."

"Prior to the discontinuance of our investigation," Mr. Hoover wrote, "25 persons were interviewed concerning Mr. Schorr." He said that "the incomplete investigation of Mr. Schorr was entirely favorable to him and the results were furnished to the White House."

Mr. Schorr said today that he believed that the bureau "had acted quite properly, routinely, and on instructions." But he said he had never been offered any job in the Nixon Administration, either before or since the investigation. Given the Administration's complaints about his reporting, Mr. Schorr said, "it would have been an extraordinarily openminded thing for them to have done."

After The Washington Post article on the investigation, the White House press secretary, Ronald L. Ziegler, asserted that Mr. Schorr was being considered for a position in the Administration but declined to say which one.

There have been conflicting reports that Mr. Schorr was in line for a job with the Council on Environmental Quality, but Senator Ervin said today that the position in question had been filled, according to White House sources.

"Job or no job," Mr. Schorr said today, "the launching of such an investigation without consent demonstrates an insensitivity to personal rights."

"I think most Americans would feel more comfortable if there were legal safeguards against such arbitrary intrusion into their lives."

February 2, 1972

Wider Army Surveillance Of Top Officials Disclosed

By RICHARD HALLORAN
Special to The New York Times

WASHINGTON, Feb. 28—Senator Sam J. Ervin Jr. disclosed today that Army intelligence surveillance of civilian officials from late 1967 into 1970 was more extensive than had previously been revealed.

In a brief filed with the Supreme Court, the North Carolina Democrat said that the Army had watched the political activities of a Supreme Court Justice, "numerous Congressmen and United States Senators" and state officials.

The Senator did not name the subjects of the surveillance, the details of which were furnished by the Army to the Subcommittee on Constitutional Rights, which Mr. Ervin heads.

A spokesman for Mr. Ervin said, however, that the subjects included Mr. Ervin, Senators Edmund S. Muskie, George McGovern, Edward M. Kennedy, Harold E. Hughes and Fred R. Harris and former Senators Ralph W. Yarborough and Eugene J. McCarthy.

Members of the House listed as subjects included Representatives Philip M. Crane, Republican of Illinois; John R. Rarick, Democrat of Louisiana, and Don Edwards, California Democrat when he was a California State Senator, and former Representatives Adam Clayton Powell, Manhattan Democrat, and Allard K. Lowenstein, Nassau Democrat.

Governors said to have come under surveillance included Francis W. Sargent, Republican of Massachusetts, and Kenneth M. Curtis, Democrat of Maine. Former Gov. H. Philip Hoff of

The New York Times
Senator Sam J. Ervin Jr.

Vermont and Lieut. Gov. Thomas Hayes of Vermont, Democrats, were also on the list.

Senator Ervin's spokesman declined to name the Supreme Court Justice since his name was on a still-secret document furnished by the Army to the subcommittee. But other authoritative sources who have studied the documents indicated that it was Thurgood Marshall.

Whether the information was gathered before Mr. Marshall was named to the Court in 1967 or after he took his seat was not clear. He was the Solicitor General before going to the Supreme Court.

No details on what sort of information was collected about Justice Marshall or why he was investigated were available.

Earlier reports on the Army's civilian intelligence operation named Senator Adlai E. Stevenson 3d, Representative Abner J. Mikva, and former Gov. Otto Kerner, all Illinois Democrats, as subjects of surveillance.

The new names came from Army reports and computer printouts from intelligence data banks that Senator Ervin's subcommittee obtained from the Army and had declassified, or taken out of the secret category.

In most cases, the documents showed that Army agents in civilian clothes attended political rallies or listened to speeches given by the subjects and then filed "spot" reports on the event. The Army has consistently justified such surveillance as part of its responsibility for warning against the outbreak of civil disturbances.

The Army was ordered by

senior civilian officials of the Johnson Administration in 1967 to 1968 to use its internal counter-intelligence units to gather information that might indicate that civil disturbance was on the way. It was also ordered to collect information that might be useful to Army troops when they were sent into an area of strife.

Civilian officials and military officers involved in the operation conceded later that directives intended to control the surveillance had been drawn too loosely and that the operation had spilled over into watching legitimate political activity.

Among the main targets were persons and organizations that opposed the war in Vietnam, student radicals, blacks, civil rights militants and others considered to be anti-establishment. The Army also watched organizations considered to be conservative or right-wing, such as the Daughters of the American Revolution, the Ku Klux Klan and the American Nazis.

Senator Muskie of Maine and Senator McGovern of South Dakota are both candidates for the Democratic Presidential nomination and opponents of the war. Senators Kennedy of Massachusetts, Hughes of Iowa, Harris of Oklahoma, and former Senators Yarborough of Texas and McCarthy of Minnesota, all Democrats, have also spoken out against the American involvement in Vietnam.

However, Representative Crane is considered a militant conservative and Representative Rarick has been a hawkish supporter of American action in Vietnam. Representative Edwards has been a critic of the war, as has Mr. Lowenstein. Mr. Powell was generally considered anti-establishment.

Given the somewhat haphazard pattern of the surveillance, critics of the Army's operation have suggested that it often lacked direction and indiscriminately gathered information on public figures.

Senator Ervin's brief in the Supreme Court was filed as "friend of the court" brief in the case of Arlo Tatum v. Melvin R. Laird, the Secretary of Defense. Mr. Tatum, the executive secretary of the Central Committee for Conscientious Objectors, alleged that he had been put under surveillance by the Army.

He has filed suit against the Government asking for a court order enjoining such surveillance. His case was dismissed in the District Court here and then upheld by the Court of Appeals. It is scheduled to be heard by the Supreme Court this spring.

February 29, 1972

HIGH COURT CURBS U.S. WIRETAPPING AIMED AT RADICALS

Rules Warrant Is Necessary for Federal Surveillance in Domestic Matters

DECISION IS UNANIMOUS

Powell, Appointee of Nixon, Writes Opinion Upsetting Government Practice

By FRED P. GRAHAM
Special to The New York Times

WASHINGTON, June 19 — The Supreme Court declared unconstitutional today the Federal Government's practice of wiretapping, without first obtaining court approval, domestic radicals considered dangerous to the national security.

The Court, 8 to 0, rejected the Nixon Administration's assertion that the President's authority to protect the nation from internal subversion gives the Government the constitutional power to wiretap "dangerous" radical groups without obtaining court warrants.

"Fourth Amendment freedoms [against "unreasonable searches and seizures"] cannot properly be guaranteed if domestic surveillances may be conducted solely within the discretion of the executive branch," the Court declared.

Without ruling on the constitutionality of warrantless wiretapping against agents of foreign powers, the Court held that "national security" wiretapping of domestic radicals who have no foreign ties can be done only with the type of court warrants currently used in police wiretapping of organized crime.

The ruling was a stunning legal setback for the Justice Department, which failed to muster a single vote from a Court with four justices appointed by President Nixon.

Attorney General Richard G. Kleindienst announced after learning of the decision that he had "directed the termination of all electronic surveillance in cases involving security that conflict with the Court's opinion." He said that subsequent surveillance would be done "only under procedures that comply" with the decision.

Opinion Written by Powell

The opinion was written by Justice Lewis F. Powell Jr., who was appointed to the Court shortly after he wrote a newspaper article strongly supporting the President's "national security" wiretap power.

Justice Powell had termed the complaints against the Government's wiretapping "a tempest in a teapot" and had suggested that the distinctions between warrantless wiretapping of foreign agents and domestic subversives was "largely meaningless." But he assured the Senators at his confirmation hearing that his mind was still open.

His opinion today leaned heavily upon the threat to free speech that he saw in unbridled governmental wiretapping of dissenters.

"History abundantly documents the tendency of government—however benevolent and benign in its motives — to view with suspicion those who most fervently dispute its policies," he wrote.

"The price of lawful public dissent must not be a dread of subjection to an unchecked surveillance power," he continued. "Nor must the fear of unauthorized official eaversdropping deter vigorous citizen dissent and discussion of Government action in private conversation."

Justice William H. Rehnquist, another Nixon appointee who had made statements supporting the President's wiretap authority before joining the Court, did not participate in the decision. He had suggested that he would participate by remaining behind the bench when the case was argued. He gave no reason for stepping aside today.

By coincidence, the historic decision was announced only seconds after Attorney General Kleindienst, an aggressive proponent of warrantless wiretapping, formally presented the Supreme Court his credentials as the Government's chief legal officer.

Mr. Kleindienst, clad in the cutaway coat and striped trousers customarily worn by Government attorneys in the Supreme Court, was welcomed by Chief Justice Warren E. Burger in a brief statement as the Court session began.

Kleindienst Leaves

Then as the Justices settled back for the announcement of the first decision, Mr. Kleindienst strode from the courtroom, not waiting long enough to hear that the long-awaited wiretapping ruling was about to be handed down.

An important result of the decision is that any defendant in a Federal prosecution has a right to see complete transcripts of any conversations overheard on a warrantless "domestic security" listening device so that his lawyer can make certain that no illegally obtained information is being used by the prosecution.

Court records indicate that victims of such wiretapping could include defendants in the "Chicago Seven" riot-conspiracy case, the kidnapping conspiracy case involving the Rev. Philip F. Berrigan and other prosecutions of antiwar activists and black radicals.

Mr. Kleindienst said that his staff would screen all such cases to decide whether to disclose the wiretap transcripts or drop the prosecutions.

Today's ruling had its roots in a decision by President Roosevelt in 1940 that he had the power to wiretap suspected German spies. In 1946, President Truman broadened the practice to include American citizens suspected of espionage.

It was not until 1967, when the Supreme Court ruled that electronic surveillance was subject to the Fourth Amendment's warrant requirements, that the Government was confronted with the issue of what to do about this type of "national security" surveillance.

In 1968 Congress passed a law authorizing law enforcement officers to get court warrants to investigate a wide variety of crimes. The law stated that it would not affect any constitutional authority the President might have to wiretap in national security cases without warrants.

This confronted the Nixon Administration with the choice of trying to obtain court warrants for its national security surveillance or to take the chance that the Supreme Court would uphold warrantless eavesdropping.

Latter Course Taken

Attorney General John N. Mitchell took the latter course—one so controversial among career attorneys that when the case reached the Supreme Court no member of the Solicitor General's office argued the Government's case.

Robert C. Mardian, then Assistant Attorney General in charge of the Internal Security Division, made the argument. He was opposed by Arthur Kinoy of the Center for Constitutional Rights in New York, and William T. Gossett of Detroit.

327

Mr. Kinoy represented three members of the radical White Panther party who were accused of plotting to bomb a Central Intelligence Agency office in Detroit. Mr. Gossett argued for United States District Judge Damon Keith, who ordered the Justice Department to disclose the transcripts of the defendants' conversations obtained by wiretaps installed without court permission.

The United States Court of Appeals for the Seventh Circuit upheld Judge Keith.

Justice Powell's opinion held that the 1968 statute did not give the Government the power to wiretap without court authority, but merely left untouched any constitutional power it might have had anyway.

He stressed that the Court was leaving for another day a decision on whether warrants will be required to wiretap foreign spies and that the decision today covered only those with "no significant connection with a foreign power, its agents or agencies."

Justice Department officials are expected to argue that many of the radicals who have been wiretapped have had contacts with Communist countries, and the ruling could make left-wing groups more circumspect about their future dealings with foreign governments.

Legal experts disagree as to whether the Government can obtain warrants under the 1968 act for surveillance of radicals, because the Government must show probable cause that a specific law is about to be violated. National security surveillance is usually based upon more nebulous suspicions.

Justice Powell's opinion virtually invited Congress to pass a new law to allow for this special type of wiretapping, but any proposal so loaded with overtones of political surveillance would be expected to face difficulty on Capitol Hill.

Chief Justice Burger noted that he concurred only in the result. Justice Byron R. White, in a separate concurring opinion, said that the warrantless surveillance might have been legal under the "national security "exception of the 1968 law, but that the Justice Department's Court papers did not satisfy the statute.

Liberties Union Statement

In New York today, the American Civil Liberties Union hailed the wiretapping decision. A statement by the organization's executive director, Aryeh Neier, said:

"The Supreme Court has rejected the Government's boldest claim of powers to intrude upon individual liberties. The Government had claimed that in the undefined interests of 'national security' it could engage in a vast, lengthy, unsupervised and unchecked invasion of the privacy of people having only the remotest link with anything in any way criminal or even wrong.

"If this claim had been upheld, there would have been virtually no limits to the range of governmental intrusion on liberty that would have been implicitly authorized once the Government invoked the talisman of 'national security.'

"In rejecting the Government's claims, the Court has vindicated the constitutional liberties of all Americans."

June 20, 1972

Files Disclose More Army Snooping Under Johnson

By SEYMOUR M. HERSH
Special to The New York Times

WASHINGTON, Aug. 31 — Army files show that military electronic eavesdropping on civilians was far more extensive during the Johnson Administration than previously disclosed. They show it included monitoring of private radio transmissions during the 1968 Republican National Convention and during the trial that year of Huey Newton, the Black Panther leader.

A series of highly classified memorandums made available to The New York Times also show that high officials of the Nixon Administration withheld information on the electronic snooping during Senate hearings into Army surveillance last year.

Much information about the extent of Army spying on civilian antiwar groups has been made public since the first disclosure by a former agent in early 1970 and most recently in a Senate subcommittee report published earlier this week.

But, until today, only one incident of electronic surveillance has been cited. It involved the monitoring of private radio transmissions by personnel from the Army Security Agency during the Democratic National Convention in 1968.

Approved by General

The newly obtained documents show that the eavesdropping during the Republican convention and the Newton trial was authorized by Gen. William C. Westmoreland, Army Chief of Staff at that time.

The convention monitoring occurred from Aug 6 to Aug. 10, 1968, after Army counterintelligence personnel received "reports indicating that pro-Castro and other dissident elements might initiate disruptive tactics," a February, 1971, memo explained. The Newton trial, held in Oakland, Calif., was similarly monitored for "suspected dissident communications" during early September, 1968.

In both cases, the 1971 memo said, the operations were terminated "without obtaining any intelligence."

The documents show that General Westmoreland's predecessor as Chief of Staff, Gen. Harold K. Johnson, approved electronic eavesdropping on private radio communications for three earlier activities — the October, 1967, march on the Pentagon; the April, 1968, riots in Washington; and the May-June, 1968, Poor People's March. General Westmoreland replaced General Johnson on July 4, 1968.

Concern Expressed

The documents show that all of the electronic eavesdropping on events in the Washington area was conducted by Army Security Agency personnel working out of the Vint Hill Farms Stations, an installation in Warrenton, Va., that serves as a focal point for the Army's monitoring of foreign embassy radio communications.

Earlier memos dated in 1968 and 1969, show a repeated concern over the fact that the electronic monitoring was illegal, but the concern appeared to be mostly about the potential adverse publicity the Army could receive in case the activities were inadvertently made public.

For example, one 1969 memo notes straightforwardly that "Section 605 of the Federal Communications Act of 1934 prohibits monitoring of civilian radio transmissions not intended for public use." Elsewhere the three-page memo, apparently prepared in advance of a staff meeting, makes the following observation:

"Compromise of the fact that U.S.A.S.A. [United States Army Security Agency] units are engaged in monitoring civil communications either prior to or following Federal troop commitment, in violation of the law, would be politically embarrassing and would result in adverse publicity to both the U. S. Army and U.S.A.S.A."

Officials Were Informed

The memos also make clear that top officials of the Johnson Administration's Department of Justice, including Attorney General Ramsey Clark, were informed of both the eavesdropping program and its illegality.

One document, dated August, 1968, shortly before the Democratic National Convention, was entitled, "Possible Violations of Federal Communications Act in Connection With Civil Disturbances." It described a meeting in the Federal Communications Commission in which the Army decided to seek coordination with the Department of Justice because, as the memo stated, "exceptional sensitivity was attached to any monitoring activity."

An oral reply was received from Sol Lindenbaum, Mr. Clark's executive assistant, the memo stated, saying, "The matter had been discussed with the Attorney General." Because Federal law "unequivocally prohibits such action," the memo said, Army eavesdropping "would not be authorized—without specific approval or at least a specific indication that there was no objection by the Attorney General."

The classified memo went on to say: "Additional discussions indicated a desire not to record this denial in writing by the Attorney General's Office."

Sensitivity Stressed

Another memo, written three days later, concluded that the Justice Department was unwilling to flatly prohibit such activity, but would rule on eavesdropping on a case-by-case basis.

The matter was considered so delicate that one letter dealing with the apparent illegality of the monitoring activities was ordered withheld from the usual Department of the Army channels, "due to the extreme sensitivity of this proposed activity."

A later Army analysis of the eavesdropping activity concluded that the monitoring of radio calls, including the Republican convention and the Newton trial, was accomplished without any approval from higher officials, either in the Department of the Army or the Justice Department.

On March 2, 1971, during hearings into Army surveillance before the Senate Subcommittee on Constitutional Rights, Robert F. Froehlke, Assistant Secretary of Defense at the time, testified that Army intelligence had monitored citizens band broadcasts only once—at the 1968 Democratic National Convention in Chicago.

But one month before the testimony of Mr. Froehlke, who is now Secretary of the Army, an Army security official prepared a complete review of all electronic eavesdropping activities.

The memo, written specifically for future testimony at the Senate hearings, described all five other monitoring operations and concluded, "It is conceivable that more information about these matters could be made public. We cannot ignore the possibility that this may extend to our actions during the Republican convention and the Newton trial."

Lawrence M. Baskir, chief counsel of the Senate Subcommittee on Constitutional Rights, said that his staff had learned that the surveillance "went further than Secretary Froehlke had testified to at the hearings."

But he added, "Our attempts to get the Defense Department to give us full information about it were never answered."

September 1, 1972

C.I.A. Will Curb Training It Provides Police Forces

By DAVID BURNHAM

The new director of Central Intelligence has informed Congress that the agency has decided to curb the training it has been providing local police departments in the United States.

The director, James R. Schlesinger, announced the new policy in a letter to Representative Chet Holifield, Democrat of California, who is chairman of the House Government Operations Committee.

"In keeping with the sensitivity of this matter I have directed that such [training] activities be undertaken in the future only in the most compelling circumstances and with my personal approval," Mr. Schlesinger wrote.

The Central Intelligence Agency acknowledged last month that it had provided training to policemen from about a dozen city and county police forces about techniques to detect explosives and wiretaps, conduct surveillance of individuals and maintain intelligence files.

Legal Advice Sought

The acknowledgment of the domestic police training activities came after Representative Edward Koch, Democrat of New York, wrote the C.I.A. last Dec. 28 questioning whether such training did not violate the 1947 legislation creating the intelligence group. This law states, "The agency shall have no police, subpoena, law enforcement powers or internal-security functions."

In disclosing the C.I.A.'s statement that it had trained domestic police departments, Mr. Koch called upon Mr. Holifield's committee and the Senate Judiciary Subcommittee on Constitutional Rights to investigate whether these activities violated the law.

Mr. Schlesinger's brief letter did not attempt to define "the most compelling circumstances" that would lead him to authorize the agency to provide a local police agency with special training.

But Mr. Holifield, in a statement in yesterday's Congressional Record, said that they might involve "foreign criminals or international drug traffickers."

Mr. Holifield, though arguing that the C.I.A. should not be absolutely barred from conducting such training, said he did not agree with the C.I.A.'s contention that the training was authorized under the Omnibus Crime Control Act of 1968.

"The sensitive nature of the agency's work, and the mandate of its enabling legislation to refrain from engaging in domestic law enforcement activities, would seem to compel a reconsideration of the recently publicized activities in question," the California Democrat wrote Mr. Schlesinger.

Mr. Holifield also questioned the C.I.A.'s statement to Mr. Koch that the training was always given at the request of the local agencies. "There may be some arguments as to whether the initiative in every single case was local, since the agency may have offered some suggestions of its own or may have had some requests routed through the Law Enforcement Assistance Administration," he said.

Mr. Koch's initial request to the C.I.A. was prompted by an account in The New York Times about 14 New York policemen who had been given training in the handling and processing of intelligence information.

March 6, 1973

PRESIDENT LINKED TO TAPS ON AIDES

Nixon Said to Have Backed Action in '69 in Effort to Plug Security Leaks

---

By SEYMOUR M. HERSH
Special to The New York Times

WASHINGTON, May 15— President Nixon personally authorized the wiretapping of more than a dozen of his subordinates on the National Security Council and in the Pentagon beginning in 1969, reliable sources said today.

The sources said the wiretapping had been undertaken in response to a dispatch by William Beecher published in The New York Times on May 9, 1969, which reported for the first time that B-52 bombers were striking targets inside Cambodia.

A White House spokesman confirmed the report of Presidential authorization tonight. "It was a national security matter," the spokesman said. "The procedure was approved by the President and authorized in individual cases by the Attorney General in coordination with the director of the Federal Bureau of Investigation."

Well-informed Government officials defended the President's authorization as necessary, in view of what they termed a serious security breach. Mr. Beecher's dispatch told how the bombing was being conducted without any public protest from Prince Norodom Sihanouk, who was

Mr. Beecher's article was the first to indicate that the Nixon Administration was expanding the Vietnam war.

"The President's motives were honorable," one official said. "This had to be stopped and it [the wiretapping] turned out to be for the protection of the innocent." He was referring, he said, to the fact that most of those whose phones were wiretapped were found to not have violated security.

Another Government official aware of the wiretapping noted that it had been legal and added: "Hell, yes, I was aware that it was going on. To have done less would have been the highest order of irresponsibility."

Other Government sources contended that at least three White House and Pentagon officials whose phones were monitored turned out to be—as one put it—"blabbermouths" and were eventually eased out of their positions.

3 Aides Were Tapped

Specific approval for the operation, which involved the tapping of home and office telephones, was granted by the late J. Edgar Hoover, director of the Federal Bureau of Investigation, and John N. Mitchell, then the Attorney General.

Special F.B.I. reports of the overhead telephone conversation were provided to Dr. Henry A. Kissinger, Mr. Nixon's National Security Adviser, and then Col. Alexander M. Haig Jr., one Mr. Kissinger's key deputies who is now a four-star general and is serving as the temporary White House chief of staff.

Among those tapped, sources said, were three aides to Mr. Kissinger—Daniel I. Davidson, who left the Government later in 1969; Anthony Lake, who quit over the Cambodian invasion in May, 1970; and Winston Lord, who will be leaving this week.

Mr. Lake and Mr. Lord served as special assistants to Mr. Kissinger and participated in many secret peace talks with Le Duc Tho, the chief North Vietnamese negotiator, and other North Vietnamese officials prior to the peace agreement that was reached early this year.

William D. Ruckelshaus, the acting director of the F.B.I., told a news conference yesterday that records of 17 wiretaps placed on 13 Government officials and four newsmen had been found in a safe belonging to John D. Ehrlichman, the Persident's former chief assistant for domestic affairs. Mr. Ruckelshaus identified one of those overhead as Dr. Morton Halperin, who joined Mr. Kissinger's staff in 1969.

Meeting Described

Sources in the executive branch said that the wiretap logs had been sent routinely to

Mr. Kissinger's office until May, 1970. At that time, one official said, there was a meeting between President Nixon, Mr. Hoover and H. R. Haldeman, the former White House chief of staff, "to discuss these taps."

"They agreed to continue them," the official added, "but they also decided to have all of the mail [the logs and other products of the wiretaps] go to Haldeman." The wiretap program itself was ended in February, 1971, other officials said.

"We found out what we wanted to find out," one source said. "We found the people who were the weak links." He described the taps as being very productive. "They were a couple of guys who could have been prosecuted," he added, "but we just let them go out of the Government."

Mr. Lake, reached on vacation in Edgartown, Mass., said he was "disgusted" to hear that his phone had been tapped while working for the Government. "It's an invasion of privacy," he said. "I can't think of any grounds for them to have done that."

Mr. Lord, reached in the White House, said he had only learned from Mr. Kissinger a few minutes prior to the call that his phone had been tapped. He had no comment.

Mr. Davidson could not be immediately reached.

Mr. Halperin acknowledged in a telephone interview that he had been told by Mr. Kissinger that his security clearance had been protested by the Central Intelligence Agency and the F.B.I. The agencies complained that he had neglected to mention a trip to the Soviet Union while filling out a form. "As I told him [Mr. Kissinger] many times," Mr. Halperin said, "I had reported that trip three times previously and four times afterward."

Mr. Halperin quoted Mr. Kissinger as telling him at one point that he had been "advised not to hire any of the people" he hired.

Complaints Noted

After The Times dispatch on the Cambodia bombing was published, Mr. Halperin noted, he was told that three top Government officials — Secretary of State William P. Rogers, then Secretary of Defense Melvin R. Laird and Mr. Mitchell—complained to the President that he was the source for the article.

"Kissinger told me I was under suspicion for that," Mr. Halperin said. "I interpreted that at the time as meaning that they were mad at the leak because they were trying to keep from the American public that, while the Administration was claiming it was withdrawing, in fact it was escalating the war."

"Of course I told him I was not [the source]," Mr. Helperin said, "and of course he can find out if he wants to because Beecher is now a Pentagon official." Mr. Beecher left The Times last month to become a deputy assistant secretary of Defense for public affairs.

Mr. Halperin, who is associated with the Brookings Institution in Washington, said that despite the suspicion and the wiretapping, he remained on the National Security Council until September, 1969, when —despite urgings from Mr. Kissinger—he resigned.

Mr. Halperin said he continued to serve as a consultant to Mr. Kissinger until the spring of 1970, when he resigned in protest over the American and South Vietnamese invasion of Cambodia.

May 16, 1973

WHITE HOUSE UNIT REPORTEDLY SPIED ON RADICALS IN '70

Order to Set Up Intelligence Body on Continuing Basis Laid to Ehrlichman

DATA WERE SENT TO DEAN

Watergate Sources Indicate That Caulfield and Krogh Also Were Involved

By SEYMOUR M. HERSH
Special to The New York Times

WASHINGTON, May 20 — The White House established a secret intelligence unit in 1970 to collect and evaluate information about radical and antiwar groups, sources close to the Watergate investigation said today.

The unit, known as the Intelligence Evaluation Committee, is now clandestinely operated out of the Justice Department's Internal Security Division.

The sources said that the unit reported directly to John W. Dean 3d, the former White House counsel, and John J. Caulfield, a former New York City police detective who has been linked to an alleged Presidential offer of executive clemency to James W. McCord Jr.

Ehrlichman Role Cited

The sources said that the intelligence unit had been set up in response to an order from John D. Ehrlichman, who has resigned as chief adviser to President Nixon on domestic affairs because of the Watergate scandal. Egil Krogh Jr., an Ehrlichman aide, is believed to have been connected with the intelligence committee at varying times, the sources said.

Mr. Krogh resigned as Under Secretary of Transportation two weeks ago after his involvement in the burglary of Dr. Daniel Ellsberg's psychiatrist became publicly known.

The sources said that government investigators were now attempting to determine whether some of the intelligence committee's highly classified reports may have been used by other Justice Department agencies and the White House to justify undercover and double-agent activities against suspected opposition groups, including Democrats opposed to the Nixon Administration.

Previous Intelligence Units

Units to coordinate and analyze domestic intelligence were set up during the Johnson Administration and in the first years under Mr. Nixon, but the committee is believed to be the first to utilize all of the Government's intelligence resources in targeting future demonstrations.

Undercover intelligence activities against radical and antiwar groups are legal and have been routinely utilized by Federal and local police agencies. The Nixon Administration has been linked, however, to a number of illegal activities against Democratic candidates stemming from last year's primary elections. These included an allegation that an undercover agent employed by White House officials wrote bogus campaign literature accusing leading Democrats of sexual misconduct.

Reliance By Dean

Some investigators are known to suspect Mr. Dean may have relied on intelligence estimates produced by the committee to back up his belief that a White House intelligence operation was needed during the Democratic and Republican National Conventions at Miami Beach last year. The committee reports are based on wiretapping plus electronic eavesdropping by such agencies as the Pentagon's National Security Agency.

A number of highly classified documents known to contain electronically intercepted material have been turned over by Mr. Dean to a Federal District Court for safekeeping in connection with the ongoing Watergate investigation. The documents have not been publicly identified.

The intelligence group was publicly mentioned in an exchange at the Senate Watergate hearings Friday with McCord, a convicted member of the Watergate break-in team.

McCord testified that, in early 1972, officials of the Internal Security Division were supplying the Committee for the Re-election of the President with intelligence reports on antiwar and radical activities for possible political use. He also told of making a visit to the analysis and evaluation section of the Internal Security Division to receive the material.

At that point, Senator Lowell P. Weicker Jr., Republican of Connecticut, asked:

"And this, as you understood, you were with the Intelligence Evaluation Committee at that time, or with the officers of it?"

McCord replied, in effect, yes.

A high-ranking Justice Department official confirmed the existence of the intelligence committee and its political uses. He described it in an interview as "answerable only to the White House."

"This was set up by the Nixon Administration," the official said. "It's run out of the White House."

The group is operated in the Justice Department by Bernard Wells, said to be a former agent of the Federal Bureau of Investigation. Its members include officials of the F.B.I., the Central Intelligence Agency, the National Security Agency, and various other police and official units, the Justice Department official said.

The sources said that the intelligence committee had been set up in an attempt to meet what many Administration officials considered to be the extremely grave threat to democracy posed by various radical and antiwar groups who were demonstrating against the Vietnam war and calling for the overthrow of the Government.

To meet the reported threat, the sources said, an elaborate system of undercover activity, including infiltration and the use of double agents, was developed by the F.B.I. and the Internal Security division.

One Justice Department official close to the committee insisted, however, that the intelligence unit had been utilized solely for the collection and analysis of intelligence. "We weren't operational at all," he said in a interview today.

Government officials are now attempting to determine how much control and authority top-level White House officials, such as Mr. Ehrlichman and Mr. Krogh, had over such domestic intelligence operations.

Newsweek magazine reported in this week's edition that Anthony T. Ulasewicz, a former New York City policeman, began work in 1969 for Mr. Ehrlichman in the White House as a political undercover agent. The magazine report, confirmed by Government investigators, said that Mr. Ulasewicz had undertaken such sensitive assignments as an inquiry into a rumor that the brother of a possible Democratic Presiden-

tial candidate might have been involved in a homosexual incident.

Investigators said that Mr. Ulasewicz had been recommended to the White House staff by Mr. Caulfield, who was a bodyguard to former Attorney General John N. Mitchell before joining the White House staff himself in April, 1969. Last week, Mr. Caulfield was placed on administrative leave as assistant director of the Treasury Department Bureau of Alcohol, Tobacco and Firearms.

Sources also identified Mr. Ulasewicz, who was said by Newsweek to have been a streetcar conductor before joining the New York City police force, as the unnamed official who placed a telephone call to McCord in January to arrange for secret meetings with Mr. Caulfield. McCord told of the call in his televised Senate testimony.

Newsweek also reported that

Jeb Stuart Magruder, the former deputy director of the re-election committee, and Herbert L. Porter, another former campaign official, have told Senate investigators that they recruited demonstrators to disrupt Democratic primary campaigns.

Another source told The New York Times that on at least one occasion Republican funds were used by the Republican officials to fly demonstrators to Washington. Newsweek also said that Mr. Ulasewicz was paid in cash by Herbert W. Kalmbach, President Nixon's former personal attorney who has been linked to a number of clandestine Republican cash funds.

Government investigators are known to be closely scrutinizing the activities of Mr. Krogh, who was a key Ehrlichman aide for domestic security matters.

The sources said that Mr. Krogh, in secret Senate testi-

mony two weeks ago, denied knowing Mr. Caulfield, but officials later learned that his personal files at the Transportation Department included a separate dossier on Mr. Caulfield.

Mr. Krogh was also reported by his former White House associates to have been on good terms with J. Edgar Hoover, the late director of the F.B.I. He has repeatedly hinted of other White House operations similar in nature to the Ellsberg burglary, but told Federal investigators, according to reliable sources, that "some of these are things that a guy would just expire with."

Mr. Krogh has refused to discuss his White House activities with newsmen although he has acknowledged full responsibility for the operation against Dr. Ellsberg's psychiatrist.

May 21, 1973

Nixon '70 Domestic Security Plan Detailed

A BROAD PROGRAM

Panthers, Saboteurs Targets — Hoover Opposed the Plan

By SEYMOUR M. HERSH
Special to The New York Times

WASHINGTON, May 23— The White House urged the Federal Bureau of Investigation in 1970 to mount a massive counterinsurgency program, involving spying, wiretapping and burglaries, against the Black Panthers, potential Arab saboteurs, antiwar radicals and Soviet espionage agents, well-placed sources said today.

President Nixon briefly described the program in his statement yesterday and noted then that it had never been put into effect because of opposition by the late J. Edgar Hoover, then the director of the F.B.I. Extensive details about the project were provided to The New York Times today.

A Secret Report

The program was outlined in a secret report on domestic intelligence prepared in July, 1970, and approved by Mr. Nixon, his top White House

aides and the chief officers of the Central Intelligence Agency, the Defense Intelligence Agency and the National Security Agency.

The report was among a series of classified documents that were put in a safe deposit box by John W. Dean 3d, the former White House counsel, and released last week by a Federal judge to the Senate Select Committee on Presidential Campaign Activities and other Congressional committees now investigating the role of the C.I.A. in the burglary of the Democratic National Committee's headquarters at the Watergate office complex last June.

The White House has insisted that the documents are related to national security. They have not been made public.

Groups Infiltrated

The Nixon Administration repeatedly expressed its concern over the Black Panthers and the radical movement, and the Government is known to have infiltrated many such groups long before Mr. Nixon became President. But the details obtained by The Times today are the clearest indication to date of the depth of the Nixon Administration's concern over the problem of dissident groups and its plans to deal with them.

One high-level source who worked on the 1970 report said in a telephone interview that

"the facts we had available in this country then showed that we were faced with one of the most serious domestic crises that we've had."

"One of our greatest problems," the official added, "was that the informed public didn't understand it."

In his statement, Mr. Nixon suggested that the domestic program had been necessitated by deteriorating liaison between the F.B.I. and other intelligence agencies. He also said that the task of maintaining domestic security had been seriously hampered by the F.B.I.'s decision in 1966 to suspend "certain types of F.B.I. undercover operations." He did not elaborate.

The sources said, however, that Mr. Hoover opposed the project solely because Mr. Nixon would not grant him authority in writing for the use of F.B.I. agents in illegal wiretaps and illegal breaking-and-entering operations.

Those kinds of F.B.I. activities, the sources said, had been ruled out by Attorneys General Nicholas deB. Katzenbach and Ramsey Clark in 1965 and 1966.

The sources also revealed that F.B.I. agents had been engaging in burglaries and illegal forced entries since 1941 as part of a highly classified domestic intelligence operation.

"We'd been doing burglaries for years," a former high-ranking F.B.I. official said. "We did them regularly — as a matter of policy."

"Hoover never got approval

outside of the bureau for them," the official said of the burglaries. "After all, you really can't ask the Attorney General to approve an illegal operation." The official added that he and other F.B.I. officials assumed that higher officials did know of the procedure.

A high-level source who was involved in the preparation of the 1970 report confirmed that it called for breaking-and-entering operations on American citizens as well as burglaries of foreign embassies.

In addition, he said, the F.B.I. and National Security Agency, which handles most of the United States' electronic eavesdropping, were to monitor foreign embassies in the United States to ferret out information about potential disorders.

In his statement yesterday, Mr. Nixon said that Mr. Hoover had been directed to be chairman of the Inter-Agency Committee on Domestic Disorder. The President said this about the report:

"On June 25, the committee submitted a report which included specific options for expanded intelligence operations, and on July 23 the agencies were notified by memorandum of the options approved. The options initially approved had included resumption of certain intelligence operations which had been suspended in 1966. These in turn had included authorization for surreptitious entry — breaking and entering, in effect — on specified categories of targets in specified situations related to national security."

In a news briefing after the

President's statement was released yesterday, J. Fred Buzhardt Jr., a special counsel to Mr. Nixon, refused to say whether the report authorized breaking and entering in domestic security cases. "I would not address it further for the simple reason it is a classified document," he said.

Past Proposals Cited

Leonard Garment, the White House counsel, who also attended the press briefing, subsequently described the illegal entry recommendations as similar to those that had been "utilized on a clandestine basis, with the approval of Chief Executives, for many years."

One official who worked on the report described the most serious issue facing the Nixon Administration in mid-1970 as "the black problem."

He said intelligence indicated that Black Panther leaders were being covertly supported by some countries in the Caribbean and in North Africa. Some Government officials also believed, he said, that Algeria, which was vocal in its support of the Black Panthers in the United States, might become a main overseas base for the Panthers.

Another factor that concerned domestic White House advisers, the source said, was what he termed "the vigilante police action" by the Chicago police in the 1969 shooting of Fred Hampton, a Black Panther leader from Chicago. The apparently unjustified police shooting, he said, prompted many moderate black leaders to voice their support for the Panthers "and made it harder for blacks to understand that these guys [the Panthers] were thugs and murderers."

A Justice Department source who also was familiar with the 1970 report, which was prepared with the aid of Tom C. Huston, an aide to H. R. Haldeman, the former White House chief of staff, expressed concern about the activities of Eldridge Cleaver, the Panther leader who eventually fled to Algeria.

"He had a lot of money," the official said, "and we weren't able to find out who was financing him. We suspected the Arabs were involved."

This official complained that Mr. Hoover's decision to limit domestic intelligence operations as of 1966 had severely hampered the F.B.I.'s ability to penetrate radical black groups and other organizations. "Here is an agency [the F.B.I.]," the source said, "which has millions of dollars going into it — huge appropriations — and we did not know that there were going to be racial riots.

"The White House got very upset after learning about some of these riots from the newspapers," the official said. "The White House then felt, 'My God, we've got to do something about this.'"

Arab Problem

Both sources said that the second major area of concern, as expressed in the report, was the possibility of Arab sabotage before the Middle East talks at the United Nations in the late summer of 1970.

Those talks, initiated by Dr. Gunnar V. Jarring, who was then and still is a United Nations special representative for the Middle East, were scheduled to begin on Aug. 26, 1970. Palestinian radicals had been opposed to such negotiations.

Sources familiar with the 1970 report said the United States had received intelligence indicating that Arab money was flowing to students in the United States who were serving as intelligence agents.

"It was a serious problem," a Justice Department official said, "and we couldn't do anything about it. They were pushing the Arab position and trying to gather information that was to be used against Israel."

The spies "came in as students," the official added. "That was their cover," he said, noting that the State Department eventually cut down on the number of visas granted to such students.

"All these things going on and we were powerless," he continued, referring to Mr. Hoover's decision to curtail illegal operations in 1966.

Specifically, another source said, the White House believed that Arab commandos were attempting to penetrate the United States before the peace talks in order to conduct sabotage and assassinations.

Jewish Help Sought

White House officials were described as being so frustrated by the inabiilty of the F.B.I. to penetrate the Arab operations that Mr. Garment, then an adviser to President Nixon for civil rights, cultural and Jewish affairs, was urged to contact the Jewish intelligence community—and ask them about the threat.

The peace efforts, which were unproductive, took place without incident and there were no known attacks on Jewish leaders in the United States.

The sources said that the increase in radical activities and in the number of Soviet agents operating inside the United States was attributed by White House officials to the lack of effective F.B.I. domestic intelligence operations.

"Back in 1966," one source said, "we used to conduct entry operations into radicals' headquarters and—if you thought they had a bomb factory—you tried to find out what kind they were making."

Another source noted that the clandestine F.B.I. activities were conducted under a number of classified code names. He said that Mr. Hoover's 1966 decision to curtail illegal entry operations also cut off a number of other clandestine operations. These included, he said, the use of mail covers, a program by which F.B.I. agents would get from the Post Office a list of persons writing to suspects, and another project that involved the analysis of handwriting of immigrants to the United States in an effort to determine whether they had been educated in Soviet schools, and thus could be potential spies.

"He wiped out the whole domestic security system," the source said of Mr. Hoover.

Mr. Hoover's decision to curtail such activities apparently was well-known throughout the intelligence community. In grand jury testimony last month, E. Howard Hunt, a Watergate participant and former C.I.A. agent who also took part in the 1971 burglary of the office of Dr. Daniel Ellsberg's psychiatrist, noted that the F.B.I. had not been called upon to handle the burglary. The reason, he said, was that "in the last five or six years, under Mr. Hoover's aegis, the Federal Bureau of Investigation had ceased training its agents."

Agents Lost Skills

Hunt added: "The cadre that the bureau used to maintain for the type of operation was no longer in existence. It had dwindled away. The agents had been reassigned or lost their skills."

In a telephone interview today, Mr. Clark, who became acting Attorney General in late 1966, recalled that at that time he had refused the F.B.I. permission to conduct an entry operation into the offices of a foreign government in New York City.

"They wanted information that was in the office," Mr. Clark said, "but I said it would be a violation of the Constitution and Federal law and that it would utterly destroy their ability to prosecute."

During the mid-nineteen-sixties, the Supreme Court had been narrowing the scope of F.B.I. activity that could be justified on grounds of national security. The Court specifically ordered the Justice Department in 1965 to determine on whose authority an illegal wiretap had been placed by F.B.I. agents then investigating the Bobby Baker case.

One source recalled that an extensive search of Justice Department files produced a 1954 memorandum to Mr. Hoover by then Attorney General Herbert Brownell Jr., granting the F.B.I. director the right to determine when national security wiretaps could be implanted.

After a review led by Mr. Katzenbach, who was Attorney General in 1965, the F.B.I. was ordered to seek higher approval before any wiretaps were authorized.

May 24, 1973

PRECEDENTS CITED ON BREAK-IN PLANS

National Security Used as Justification in Past

Special to The New York Times

WASHINGTON, May 23 — While there is no explicit legal authority for Federal agents to engage in burglaries or wiretapping without a court order, successive Administrations have permitted such activities under the President's implied power to protect the country from internal and external threats.

Presidents have traditionally found their authority to protect the national security in executive and judicial interpretations of their constitutional mandates to conduct the country's foreign policy and, on the domestic front, to "take care that the laws be faithfully executed."

It was on this general authority that the so-called "1970 intelligence plan," which the President disclosed yesterday in a statement on the Watergate case, was based. The plan, if it had been put into effect, would have involved surveillance, wiretapping, and illegal burglaries against foreign and domestic radicals. It was created in response to domestic bombings and disorders on college campuses.

Among other things, the plan would have authorized "breaking and entering" by Federal agents "in specified situations related to national security." It was drawn up under the President's authority to protect the security of the nation, as implied in the Constitution and recognized by Federal statutes.

Citing such authority, Presidents from Franklin Roosevelt on have permitted covert electronic surveillance and have authorized illegal burglaries to protect the country against what they perceived as threats to its existence.

From 1941 until 1966, for example, the Federal Bureau of Investigation pursued a policy of making otherwise illegal entries in connection with domestic intelligence-gathering operations.

Until last year, the F.B.I. also engaged in placing, without the benefit of a court order, wiretaps on individuals who the Government believed were a threat to national security. Last June, however, the Supreme Court held that court orders were required for such wiretaps except where the individuals involved had connections with a foreign power.

Federal statutes generally circumvent the issue of the President's power to conduct otherwise illegal activities in the area of national security.

May 24, 1973

Mr. Nixon's Historic Alibi

By James Reston

WASHINGTON, May 24—President Nixon's latest explanation of his part in the Watergate scandal—which is quite different from his first two explanations—is that everything he did, or failed to do, was motivated by his concern for "national security."

In his mind it is probably true, and this is precisely the problem. In fact, it is the main theme of his political life. Whenever he has been charged with dubious political or executive decisions, he has always justified them on the ground that, right or wrong, they were done in the name of "national security."

Does he have constitutional authority to bomb Cambodia in order to keep the Lon Nol Government in power, or carry out the nation's commitments under the Southeast Asia Treaty, or try to compel North Vietnam to abide by the cease-fire agreement in Indochina? The Congress questions that he does, but he bombs anyway in the name of "national security."

Was he fair in his savage attacks on Harry Truman and Dean Acheson in questioning their motives in the Korean war? In his mind, he did it for "national security."

It is a very old Nixon story. He came into politics vilifying Helen Gahagan Douglas and Jerry Voorhis as "pinkos," and he wanted the United States to intervene in the French Indochina war at Dien Bien Phu, and he fought everybody who thought it might be possible to arrange an accommodation with Peking and Moscow—all for the same reason. He thought he was fighting for "national security."

More than that, he still feels he can use any blunt instruments at his command to serve his own notion of national security today. His latest statement on the Watergate was not a satisfactory explanation, or even a credible alibi, but a confession of wrongdoing, of losing control over the F.B.I., of executive negligence, and even of Presidential knowledge and approval of bugging and burglary—all in the name of "national security."

It is very easy and dangerous to guess at his motives, for he has invited all kinds of dubious speculations, but his judgments are the main thing. Assuming the best of motives, he thought, by his own testimony, that in the name of "national security" he could tap telephones, even of his own staff, authorize burglaries, ignore the disclosures of the press and the questions of the Congress, urge his staff to defend the "national interest" against its enemies, and then pretend to be surprised if they bugged the Watergate or raided Dr. Ellsberg's psychiatric files.

He asked for loyalty from his staff, and he got it. He had a chance to get campaign finance reform and he opposed it. After his spectacular victory last November, he had a chance for reconciliation with his old adversaries and he refused it. After the facts began to come out on the Watergate scandal and he announced that he wanted all the facts to come out and that he was going to get to the bottom of the whole thing, he ducked direct questioning and put out what can only be called a mystifying clarification, which raised more questions than it answered.

■

What the nation obviously wanted and needed was a plain and honest statement of the facts from the President. What it has had from the President is one statement last August and one in October that he didn't know anything about the Watergate and nobody on his staff was involved, and then on April 17 of this year that maybe he had been misled by his own loyal public servants, and now, in summary, that he really did know a lot about the cover-up but that it was done in the name of "national security," which must still limit the investigation in the Senate and the courts.

"In citing these national security matters," he said, "it is not my intention to place a national security 'cover' on Watergate, but rather to separate them out from Watergate. . . ."

But he is in fact putting on a cover. He is limiting the inquest. By his own testimony, he has created an atmosphere of fear, suspicion and hostility in the White House, which has infected not only the Haldemans and the Ehrlichmans and the Mitchells but all the other minor characters in the tragedy.

"To the extent," the President said, "that I may in any way have contributed to the climate in which they [the illegal activities] took place, I did not intend to; to the extent that I failed to prevent them, I should have been more vigilant."

This is probably the most candid confession he has made in this whole tragedy, but he did not rest his case on this confession. He rested it, as he has done throughout his long and remarkable political career, on the proposition that whatever he did was done for "national security."

And the tragedy is that more crimes and brutalities have been done in the name of "national security" in this country in the last quarter-century than in the name of anything else, and Mr. Nixon is still falling back on this excuse, as he has done throughout his long career.

May 25, 1973

ALIEN-RADICAL TIE DISPUTED BY C.I.A.

By SEYMOUR M. HERSH
Special to The New York Times

WASHINGTON, May 24—The Central Intelligence Agency reported in 1969 and 1970 that it could find no substantial evidence to support the Nixon Administration's view that foreign governments were supplying undercover agents and funds to radicals and Black Panther groups in the United States, White House and intelligence sources said today.

The C.I.A.'s findings were rejected, the sources said, by high-level White House aides who arranged in late 1970 for 35 agents from the Federal Bureau of Investigation to open overseas intelligence posts in 20 countries. The bureau's expansion is said to have angered Richard Helms, then the C.I.A. director, and other agency officials.

"We tried to show that the radical movements were homegrown, indigenous responses to perceived grievances and problems that had been growing for years," one official who worked on the agency's analyses recalled. "We said the radicals were clean and that we couldn't find anything. But all it turned out to be was another nail in Helms's coffin."

Mr. Helms was relieved as the agency's director late last year.

The C.I.A. said it would not comment on its 1969 and 1970 reports. One former White House official who worked on security matters in 1970 acknowledged that the agency's reports on student unrest had been available. But he added, "it was never our position that we had hard information" about the foreign link to domestic disturbances.

The intelligence sources said that the first C.I.A. study was submitted to the office of Henry A. Kissinger, the President's national security adviser, more than six months before Mr. Nixon decided to establish a special inter-agency committee to prepare recommendations for expanded domestic intelligence operations.

The New York Times reported today that the committee's report, approved by Mr. Nixon and his top intelligence advisers in July, 1970, called for the F.B.I. to mount a massive counter-insurgency program, involving spying, wiretapping and burglaries, against the Black Panthers, potential Arab saboteurs, radical students, and Soviet espionage agents.

The program was not put into effect because J. Edgar Hoover, then director of the bureau, refused to act without written authorization from Mr. Nixon.

'Foreign Support' Seen

Mr. Nixon, in discussing the proposal during his Watergate statement Tuesday, cited what he said was a wave of domestic bombings, campus disturbances and gun battles in early 1970 and added: "Some of the disruptive activities were receiving foreign support." He cited no evidence.

Elsewhere in his statement, Mr. Nixon characterized the 1970 report as one of "three important national security operations" that had become in-

volved in the Watergate scandal. The two other programs, he said, were the series of telephone wiretaps on newsmen and White House aides instituted in 1969 and the establishment of a special investigation unit in 1971 in connection with the Pentagon papers leak.

One intelligence official said that the White House had a "preoccupation" with the extent of foreign influence on domestic radicals and blacks. "Whenever kids went abroad," the source said, "there were those in the White House who were convinced that they were meeting with Communists and coming back with dope."

Student Patterns Scanned

The C.I.A. studied three distinct areas in both 1969 and 1970, the source said. It analyzed student patterns throughout Europe, North Africa and Latin America to determine whether there was any connection between activities there and the United States' disturbances. No significant connection was found, he said.

Another main area of study was in the Mideast, where nations — especially Egypt — were analyzed to determine whether the Arab student population in the United States was being drawn into radical activities under the leadership of the Arab bloc.

"For years there had been indications," the source said, "that there were Arab students in the United States who were probably financed by [Mideast] embassy money who were trying to draw support against Israel. To our knowledge there

were no serious efforts beyond that. By that I mean there were no illegal activities by those students—no recruiting American spies and no bomb-throwing."

The third main study area concerned possible Algerian support for the Black Panthers, the source said.

"That question was tracked back and forth 16 times over and over again," he noted. "Every intelligence agency said we know it's an interesting hypothesis but, by and large, the judgment of the intelligence community in 1970 was that there was no significant Algerian support for the domestic operations of blacks."

"History supports that judgment completely," the official declared. He noted that the Algerian Government apparently ousted Eldridge Cleaver, the Black Panther leader, and his followers late last year.

Both C.I.A. reports, which are still classified, the sources said, attempted to put the protest activities of blacks and students into a sociological context, the source said. "We thought that it was absolutely imperative that the causes of what was happening — the Vietnam war and racial injustice—had to be understood."

A White House official who worked on the 1970 domestic intelligence report characterized the agency studies as having "absolutely nothing to do with student activities."

The official said that none of the participants in the 1970 working group—including the C.I.A., which was represented

by Mr. Helms—"disagreed in any way with the threat assessment of that report."

One high-level agency source said in response that Mr. Helms's role during the White House discussions of domestic violence was to "calm them down, to keep things in perspective but yet at the same time to go through the motions of cooperation.

'He Made the Effort'

"So he made the effort," the source continued, "and two times those reports—each more than 200 pages long—went so far as to put in context the political activities of both the blacks and radical students."

"The response of the White House," he added, "was to move F.B.I. agents into C.I.A. activities."

Other sources said that the agents had been dispatched abroad after a White House meeting of Mr. Nixon, Mr. Kissinger and Mr. Hoover. "Apparently, it was a hush-hush deal," one former White House official said. "My impression was that the President and Mr. Kissinger had lost confidence in the C.I.A. and wanted to have a double-check on what was going on abroad."

The F.B.I. now spends about $3-million a year to maintain about 40 agents and more than 30 clerks in the overseas offices, one Justice Department source said. The offices are officially described as intelligence liaison units.

"It caused a tremendous furor in the agency," one intelligence official recalled. "Helms was furious."

May 25, 1973

DOCUMENTS SHOW NIXON APPROVED PARTLY 'ILLEGAL' '70 SECURITY PLAN

Laird Takes Ehrlichman White House Job

'RISKS' ARE NOTED

By JOHN M. CREWDSON

Special to The New York Times

WASHINGTON, June 6 — President Nixon approved a plan for expanded domestic intelligence gathering in July, 1970, after being cautioned that parts of it were "clearly illegal" and involved "serious

risks" to his Administration if the operations were ever discovered, according to White House documents.

The program, which Mr. Nixon described in part last month, was approved by him through H. R. Haldeman, then his chief of staff, after Tom Charles Huston, a staff assistant to the President, told Mr. Haldeman, "We don't want the President linked to this thing with

his signature on paper . . . [because] all hell would break loose if this thing leaks out."

In a statement issued May 22, Mr. Nixon said that he had rescinded his approval of the "1970 intelligence plan" five days after he ordered it put into operation. He attributed the switch to "reconsideration . . . prompted by the opposition of [F.B.I.] Director [J. Edgar] Hoover."

The President acknowledged in his statement that the "extremely sensitive" documents detailing the plan, some of which have been obtained by the New York Times, contained a provision for surreptitious entry" by Federal agents in the course of certain types of national security investigations.

But Mr. Nixon gave no hint that the Interagency Committee

The New York Times/Mike Lien

President Nixon in the White House Rose Garden yesterday, with Melvin R. Laird, left, new chief domestic adviser, and Gen. Alexander M. Haig Jr., Presidential chief of staff.

on Intelligence, which recommended in a 43-page report that the existing restrictions against breaking and entering by intelligence agents be removed, had warned that the "use of this technique is clearly illegal."

The New York Times obtained three memorandums written by Mr. Huston—one summarizing the committee's report to the President, another informing the heads of Federal intelligence agencies that the committee's recommendations had been approved, and a third providing Mr. Haldeman with background on the committee's deliberations and with a strategy for securing Mr. Hoover's cooperation.

The Times did not receive copies of the full report, or of the entire letter attached to the summarizing memorandum, also written by Mr. Huston, advising Mr. Haldeman that the President should not give the plan his written approval.

The committee's recommendations for the lifting of certain restrictions on intelligence gathering were summarized in a top-secret memorandum by Mr. Huston, who served as the committee's White House liaison.

The memorandum, sent to Mr. Haldeman for the President's approval in early July of 1970, notes that surreptitious entry, even by Federal agents, "amounts to burglary. It is also highly risky and could result in

great embarrassment if exposed."

Such burglaries, the memorandum continued, "would be particularly helpful if used against the Weathermen and Black Panthers," and against unspecified "diplomatic establishments."

But, it noted, "the deployment of the executive protector force has increased the risk of surreptitious entry" in diplomatic cases.

The Executive Protective Service, a uniformed branch of the Secret Service, was created by President Nixon in March, 1970, to guard foreign embassies in the Washington area.

The intelligence committee, of which Mr. Hoover was the chairman, also proposed, according to the Huston memorandum, that restrictions against both legal and illegal 'mail coverage' be removed.

A "legal" mail cover involves the examination, before delivery, of letters and packages addressed to suspect individuals, and the recording of the name of the sender, the date and place of posting, and other information that can be obtained without opening the seal.

"There is no valid argument against use of legal mail covers," Mr. Huston wrote, "except Mr. Hoover's concern that the civil liberties people may become upset."

But he added that the risk of such protests was "hardly serious enough to justify denying ourselves a valuable and legal intelligence tool."

The memorandum points out that "illegal" mail covers, or

the opening of sealed materials before delivery, presented "serious risks." But Mr. Huston said that the committee had recommended the implementation of such "covert coverage" on the ground that "the advantages to be derived from its use outweigh the risk."

In addition to asking the President to approve the use of covert mail covers, and illegal entry, the committee's report, as reflected in the Huston memorandum, requested the authorization of the following other measures:

¶Permission for the National Security Agency to monitor "the communications of U. S. citizens using international facilities," such as overseas telephone and telegraph circuits.

¶The intensification of such electronic surveillance against "individuals and groups in the United States who pose a major threat to the internal security."

¶An increase in the number of "campus sources" working for Federal intelligence agencies "in order to forestall widespread violence."

On July 15, 1970, Mr. Huston wrote a second memorandum to Mr. Hoover and the three other members of the committee — Richard Helms, then the Director of Central Intelligence; Gen. Donald V. Bennett, who headed the Defense Intelligence Agency, and Adm. Noel Gayler, at the time the N.S.A. director.

In that document, also marked "top-secret" by Mr. Huston, he told the four men that "the President has carefully studied the special report of the Interagency Committee

on Intelligence," and had approved all of its recommendations, including the use of illegal mail covers and the removal of restraints on surreptitious entry against foreign and "high priority internal security targets."

Opposition by Hoover

When Mr. Hoover received word of the President's decision, according to one participant in the report's preparation, "he went through the roof."

Mr. Hoover, the participant said, had objected to all of the committee's recommendations, but had not believed "that the President would read his footnoted objections," and then approve the plan.

The participant, who asked not to be identified, said that Mr. Hoover had "never made a principled objection to anything in the report."

Mr. Hoover's opposition to the intelligence plan, the participant said, and to the committee of representatives of Federal intelligence agencies that would oversee its operation, stemmed instead from the issue of "whether he was going to be able to run the F.B.I. any way he wanted to run it."

In his statement of May 22, President Nixon said only that the intelligence agencies, after having been told on July 23, 1970, that the plan had been approved, "were notified five days later, on July 28, that the approval had been rescinded" because of Mr. Hoover's "opposition."

Mr. Nixon said then that the genesis of the "unused" intelligence program had been the increase, in late 1969 and early 1970, of urban and campus unrest to a problem of "critical proportions."

The President noted that, in the months before he approved the plan, "a wave of bombings and explosions struck college campuses and cities," that "rioting and violence on American campuses had reached a new peak," and that "gun battles between guerrilla-style groups and police were taking place."

In some cases Mr. Nixon said, these activities "were receiving foreign support."

The participant noted, however, that to his knowledge the C.I.A. had been unable to find any significant connection between "revolutionary violence" in this country and foreign governments.

The recommendations approved by the President nevertheless included the monitoring of overseas communications by the N.S.A., and an increase in the "coverage of violence-prone campus and student-related groups" and in "C.I.A. coverage of American students [and others] traveling or living abroad."

The committee's report, as summarized by Mr. Huston for the President, noted that Mr.

Hoover had until then refused to permit individuals below 21 years of age to serve as "campus sources" for the F.B.I.

The reason, Mr. Huston said, was that "Mr. Hoover is afraid of a young student surfacing in the press as an F.B.I. source, although the reaction in the past to such events has been minimal. After all, everyone assumes the F.B.I. has such sources."

Publicity on Campus

When a campus source is exposed, Mr. Huston wrote, "the adverse publicity is moderate and short-lived. It is a price we must be willing to pay for effective coverage of the campus scene."

In his statement, Mr. Nixon noted that a copy of the intelligence plan and "related documents" were taken from the White House by John W. Dean 3d, shortly before he was dismissed on April 30 as the chief White House counsel.

On May 4, Mr. Dean put the plan and other documents, which were reliably reported to be a series of memorandums from Mr. Huston to Mr. Haldeman, in the safe deposit box of an area bank.

Ten days later, Chief Judge John J. Sirica of the Federal District Court here, to whom Mr. Dean's lawyers had given the keys to the box, turned copies of the papers over to the Justice Department and the Senate's Watergate investigating committee.

The papers have not been publicly released, but one official with access to the documents has said that the related memorandums, written by Mr. Huston after the President had withdrawn his approval for the plan, contain other intelligence-gathering proposals not included in the original program.

The official said that one memorandum, dated Sept. 21, 1970, contained a proposal by Mr. Huston that the Internal Revenue Service put together a small group of agents to use information gleaned from tax records "to harass or embarrass" certain individuals. He said there was no indication whether the proposal had been acted on, only that "some objection from the I.R.S. had been ironed out."

June 7, 1973

Protection for the President

To the Editor:

Ironically, President Nixon is being protected today by the doctrine established in a series of United States Supreme Court decisions reversing on First Amendment grounds the Smith Act convictions and public employment firings of members of the Communist party. The teaching of those cases is that American justice requires guilt to be personal and that merely because a person is a member of a political group that espouses, or some of whose members engage in, illegal activities he is not tainted unless he at least knowingly and actively supported such activities as evidenced by his own acts or statements.

The *strictissimi juris* rule established in these cases rejects guilt by association in political organizations. Without it, and under the proposition unsuccessfully argued by the Government in those cases, President Nixon would be guilty of all the criminal acts C.R.E.P. officials committed for the purpose of advancing his re-election campaign (and possibly also of conspiracy to advocate the overthrow of the Government by force or violence) even if the evidence never does come any closer to proving his personal involvement.

This consideration reaffirms the wisdom of those cases and the importance of the First Amendment vigorously enforced by a courageous Supreme Court. (Assoc. Prof.) BARRY NAKELL
University of North Carolina
Chapel Hill, N. C., June 12, 1973

June 23, 1973

BURGLARIES LAID TO AGENTS OF F.B.I. IN 30-YEAR PERIOD

National Security and Fight Against Crime Are Cited— Halt Reported in 1966

By JOHN M. CREWDSON
Special to The New York Times

WASHINGTON, Aug. 23 — Informed Justice Department sources disclosed today that what one of them called "illegal and unlawful" burglaries by agents of the Federal Bureau of Investigation had taken place in this country over a 30-year period that began under the Administration of President Franklin D. Roosevelt and ended in 1966.

One source, who like the others asked not to be named, said that the burglaries, "obviously" barred by the Fourth Amendment, had been conducted not only in connection with national security investigations, but also in criminal cases and against alleged crime figures.

The source said that the practice was "an old, established investigative technique," but that its use had never been known to any of the Attorneys General who served during the time it was employed, or to anyone else outside the F.B.I.

Disclosure Corroborated

The disclosure, which was corroborated by others familiar with the practice, followed a statement by President Nixon at a news conference in San Clemente, Calif., yesterday that such burglaries took place "on a very large scale" during the Administrations of Presidents Kennedy and Johnson.

Mr. Nixon made the remark, which brought rapid denials from two former Democratic Attorneys General, in response to a question about the constitutionality of the 1971 burglary of the office of a Los Angeles psychiatrist who had treated Dr. Daniel Ellsberg, the former Defense Department official who says he provided the Pentagon papers to the press.

Mr. Nixon said that such burglaries had been "authorized" in other Administrations, but did not say by whom. The sources said today, however, that approval of the technique had never come from any authority higher than J. Edgar Hoover, the late F.B.I. director, who ordered the practice ended in 1966.

Hunt for Codes Cited

The sources said that, in some instances, breaking and entering by specially trained F.B.I. men had been used against foreign embassies and missions in this country in hopes of finding "cryptographic materials," or code books.

Whenever code books were found, one source said, they were turned over to the National Security Agency, an arm of the executive branch that specializes in code-breaking, among other top-secret functions.

According to one former Justice Department official, Mr. Hoover halted the practice in 1966 because he disliked lending his agents to such a risky enterprise, and because "the benefits we got out of it were for the N.S.A., not the F.B.I."

He recalled that Mr Hoover had said several times after that, when the security agency appealed for further burglaries, "if they need it [the information], let them get it themselves" But, he said, the security agency was not "equipped to do that—it takes some pretty sophisticated equipment and years of training. "

Tom Charles Huston, a former adviser to Mr. Nixon on internal security matters, wrote in a memorandum to the President in July, 1970, that the technique of burglarizing foreign embassies should be resurrected.

"We spend millions of dollars attempting to break these codes by machine," Mr. Huston noted. "One successful surreptitious entry can do the job successfully at no dollar cost."

Another source said that the technique had not been "limited to national security matters." He said: "It's been done on criminal cases, too. You can catch a fugitive much quicker [that way] than by looking for him for a year and a half."

The source said that one rule employed by F.B.I. agents on such cases was that "you never take anything except information." In the case of a criminal fugitive, he said, agents breaking into a house or apartment might find "any number of" clues pointing toward his whereabouts, or "to look for a sign that an individual was there."

He said that organized crime figures had been the object of such burglaries as well. "They're not perfect — they leave documents behind them, too," he added.

All F.B.I. agents before 1966 "had the capability" to perform such burglaries, the source said, but those actually used were a more select group. "Just like a man has a special talent for playing the violin," he explained. "Well, it's the same with this business. For one thing, you need nerves of steel."

The source declined to name specific embassies or alleged criminals where the technique had been used, or to say how frequent it was, except that it was "done with prudence."

Asked whether the burglaries had in fact stopped in 1966, he said that "basically" they had, but that there had been a few "sporadic" approvals since then.

In a long statement on May 22 and again at his news conference yesterday, Mr. Nixon insisted that the practice had been halted in 1966.

The sources also said that periodic, illegal entries were made beginning in the early nineteen-sixties — at the time the Government began to intensify its fight against organized crime—to install concealed microphones, or bugs, in the homes or offices of suspected crime syndicate figures.

'Bugs on the Hoods'

"They had to do it to put the bugs on the hoods," the man, a former Justice Department official, said. "They had to break and enter to put them in," he said, adding that such events were not strictly burglaries, since nothing was taken, and that on some occasions entry was gained through false pretenses, "by bribing the janitor or someone to let them in."

One source said that the use of such bugs was also unknown outside the F.B.I. until it came to light during the Kennedy Administration, when one was discovered in a Las Vegas, Nev., casino, and that Attorney General Robert F. Kennedy had "never" approved their use. But another source said he was certain that the late Mr. Kennedy had au-

Associated Press

Ramsey Clark, an Attorney General under President Lyndon B. Johnson, said he had refused permission for unlawful entry of a foreign mission in New York.

thorized the use of "one or two" such devices, which, unlike telephone taps, cannot be installed without gaining physical entry to the room in question.

The planting of such bugs continues today, but since 1968, when the Omnibus Crime Control Act was passed, they cannot be installed without a court order.

Nicholas deB Katzenbach, who succeeded Robert Kennedy as Attorney General in 1964, declared today that if any "official" burglaries had taken place, he was unaware of them. Ramsey Clark, Mr. Katzenbach's successor, recalled in a telephone interview today that

he had been approached by Mr. Hoover on one occasion with a request to authorize the burglary of the New York City mission of what he believed was a "North African country," but that he had turned down the F.B.I. director.

Mr. Clark, who now practices law in Washington, said he believed that it was "most improbable" that Mr. Hoover might have continued the practice without his knowledge, something that apparently did take place.

Despite Mr. Nixon's assertion yesterday that the use of burglaries during previous Administrations was "quite well known," the practice appears to have been one of the best-kept secrets within the F.B.I.

Asked how the Nixon Administration might have learned of its prior existence, one source said he believed that the information had been included in a series of memorandums prepared over the last few months by William C. Sullivan, who recently retired from the Justice Department after having been a former assistant to the late Mr. Hoover. .

Although Mr. Nixon made a special point yesterday of the burglaries that had occurred during the two Administrations that preceded his, he was careful to point out that he believed that the September, 1971, break-in at the office of Dr. Ellsberg's psychiatrist had been "illegal, unauthorized," and "completely deplorable."

Gerald L. Warren, the deputy White House press secretary, fended off questions today from reporters with the President in San Clemente dealing with the prior burglaries.

"The President said it because it was a fact," Mr. Warren stated, and he would add no details.

Yesterday, Mr. Nixon also noted that "the height of the wiretaps was when Robert

Kennedy was Attorney General in 1963," and that the average number of taps installed each year in his own Administration and that of President Eisenhower, whom he served as Vice President, has been "about 110."

However, statistics released in June by Senator Hugh Scott of Pennsylvania, a Republican who is the minority leader, show that the greatest number of wiretaps, 519, were in place between 1945 and 1954, and that the average for each of the years of 1953 to 1960, when Mr. Eisenhower was President, was about 200.

Mr. Nixon also remarked yesterday that he had found a "rather complex situation set up" in the White House when he arrived there in 1969 that was designed to permit the tape recording of his conversations "in the President's office, the room outside of his office [and] also in the Cabinet Room and at Camp David."

He said that he had had "the entire system dismantled" then, but that it had been "put into place again in June of 1970" to provide a historical record of his Administration. It was this system that produced the tapes of conversations between Mr. Nixon and his former aides that have been subpoenaed by Archibald Cox, the special prosecutor in the Watergate case.

However, George Christian, a former press secretary to President Johnson, said in Austin, Tex., today that "what recording equipment there was at the White House was taken out before Mr. Nixon took office."

Mr. Christian added that he "never heard of any [equipment] at Camp David," the Presidential retreat in Maryland's Catoctin Mountains.

August 24, 1973

C.I.A. Will Seek to Excise Parts of Book by Ex-Aide

By JOHN M. CREWDSON
Special to The New York Times

WASHINGTON, Sept. 20 — The Central Intelligence Agency has told the American Civil Liberties Union that it will oppose the publication of about 100 pages of allegedly classified material contained in an account by a former C.I.A. official of the agency's internal workings.

Melvin L. Wulf, legal director for the A.C.L.U. in New York City, said today that he had been notified by the agency that officials there planned to excise "near to a hundred

pages" from a 530-page manuscript by his client, Victor L. Marchetti, a former assistant to the C.I.A.'s deputy director.

Mr. Wulf submitted the manuscript to the intelligence agency for review on Aug. 27, under the terms of a Federal court order handed down a year ago.

That occasion marked "the first time in the history of the United States," according to Mr. Wulf, that an author had been required by judicial order to submit a manuscript to the

Government for prior censorship.

Both Mr. Wulf and Mr. Marchetti, who are the only two individuals outside the C.I.A. to have seen the manuscript in its entirety, said that they believed it contained nothing that would jeopardize the national security.

But a knowledgeable Government official described some of the material in an outline for the Marchetti book, tentatively titled "The Cult of Intelligence," as dangerous, and said that, if the agency had allowed its publication, it "would have blown us out of the water in a lot of places—identities, operations, things like that."

Mr. Wulf said that he expected to receive from the C.I.A. next week a letter detailing the passages to which the agency objected. He said

that he and Mr. Marchetti would then meet with representatives of the Alfred A. Knopf Company, the prospective publisher, to decide on their response.

Mr. Marchetti said in a telephone interview that although he wanted to wait until he knew precisely which passages the agency was focusing on, "my feeling is to fight back as hard as we can to publish."

Mr. Wulf said that he anticipated the possibility of going "back to court [to] try again to raise the generic question of their power to do this." Mr. Marchetti added that if the courts upheld the C.I.A.'s opposition to the material it was possible that he "would go to jail before I would permit them to quash the book."

When the C.I.A. discovered last year that Mr. Marchetti intended to write both the book

337

and a magazine article on intelligence operations, it secured an injunction, based on a draft of the article and an outline for the book that prohibited him from presenting his writings to a publisher without allowing the agency to review the contents.

The Government maintained in its argument for the injunction that the agency was entitled to such prior review under an employment agreement signed by Mr. Marchetti in which he agreed not to disclose classified information obtained by reason of his employment with the agency.

The injunction, which stipulates that fiction, as well as nonfiction materials written by Mr. Marchetti must be submitted for review, was upheld by a Federal appeals court decision in August of last year.

The court also maintained that the issue was not one of Mr. Marchetti's First Amendment rights of free speech, as Mr. Wulf has argued, but rather one involving the terms of the contract that Mr. Marchetti entered into with the agency "by accepting employment with the C.I.A. and by signing a secrecy agreement."

The Supreme Court later declined to hear an appeal of the appellate decision, which stipulated that Mr. Marchetti could seek judicial review of any disapproval of a manu-script, or portions of one by the C.I.A.

Mr Marchetti, who spent 14 years with the C.I.A. before retiring in 1969, has previously published one novel. "The Rope Dancer," which concerns the activities of a fictional "national intelligence agency," and an article in the April 3, 1972, issue of The Nation magazine that was critical of some of the agency's activities.

He said today that he was currently working on a second novel that was based on a "purely fictional" insane asylum where wayward or "burned-out" operatives were sent to recover.

Although Mr. Marchetti submitted "The Rope Dancer" to the C.I.A. for review, another former agency employe, E. Howard Hunt Jr., wrote several dozen novels under different pseudonyms, during his service with the agency, many of which dealt with the exploits of fictional intelligence operatives.

A knowledgeable source said yesterday that Hunt, who pleaded guilty in January to charges of bugging the Democratic party's Watergate offices, was never required to submit his works for review because the agency was unaware that they were being published.

September 21, 1973

Misusing the CIA: A Final Report

Along with the confusion over the Presidential tapes last week came some clarification on another aspect of the Watergate imbroglio. The House Armed Services Committee Special Subcommittee on Intelligence — composed of four Democrats and three Republicans — probing into the CIA's role in Watergate and the Ellsberg case, concluded unanimously that, however reluctantly, the Agency had allowed itself to be used for "improper purposes" for which there was "no support in law or reason." Following are excerpts from its report:

•

Early on in his employment as a consultant, Mr. [E. Howard] Hunt [ex-CIA officer] requested through Mr. [Charles] Colson [former White House Counsel] that arrangements be made for certain alias and disguise gear in connection with an interview. . . . General [Robert] Cushman [former Deputy Director of the CIA] approved the request. . . . [Hunt then made] added demands on the Agency for technical assistance including disguise and alias material for Mr. George Gordon Liddy [former Counsel for the Committee for the Re-Election of the President]. On Aug. 27, 1971 . . . General Cushman . . . advised [Mr. John Ehrlichman, former White House staff member] that assistance to Mr. Hunt would have to end, since Hunt obviously was over-reaching the original agreement.

As future events graphically illustrated, the deed had then been done, and Mr. Helms [former CIA Director], General Cushman, and the CIA had become unwitting dupes for purely domestic White House staff endeavors that were beyond the realm of CIA authority.

•

Former CIA Director Richard Helms testified that often the Executive Office of the President made requests of the CIA for assistance and advice. . . . Witnesses associated with the CIA were unanimous in their views that *requests* from top level White House aides in the present Administration were, almost without exception, taken as *orders* from people who were speaking for the President. . . . In that setting, then, we have the *request* from the White House staff for the cooperation of the CIA with Howard Hunt. . . . General Cushman concluded that Hunt was hired to work on the security leaks problem, and "the CIA was being *ordered* to assist him" (emphasis added). . . .

In "hindsight," said Ambassador Helms, "maybe we should have asked (Hunt) a lot more questions."

. . . While E. Howard Hunt was making demands upon the CIA for additional technical material, he was doing it not for purposes of [an] interview, but rather for use in connection with the Room 16 Group's [Plumbers'] plan for the surreptitious entry into the office of . . . Dr. Henry Fielding [Dr. Daniel Ellsberg's psychiatrist]. . . .

Hunt asked CIA for a camera-concealing device for indoor photography. . . . Among other services, CIA provided Mr. Liddy with technical instructions for the use of camera and developing services when the job was completed. . . . In all fairness, it must be [said] that the CIA was not aware of the true purpose for which the camera and equipment was to be used.

•

[*The panel delved into the Watergate scandal and the complex "CIA-FBI-Mexican connection" and concluded that there was no direct CIA involvement:*]

• Efforts were made by Messrs. Haldeman, Ehrlichman and Dean of the White House staff to deflect the FBI investigation of the Watergate break-in by invoking nonexisting conflicts with CIA operations.

• Substantial efforts were made by Mr. John Dean, then White House Counsel, to involve CIA in the Watergate break-in without any foundation in fact. . . .

• Substantial evidence . . . leads to the inescapable conclusion that Mr. H. R. Haldeman, former White House Chief of Staff, and Mr. John Ehrlichman . . . were the sources of enormous executive authority and were considered by the Acting Director of the FBI and CIA officials to be speaking for the President.

•

The investigation has illustrated clearly that . . . there existed in the White House staff a propensity for using the CIA for purposes not intended by the Congress. . . . It is not only that the deeds were in fact done, but also the propensity of certain White House aides to dip directly into the CIA for improper purposes, leaving in doubt the serious questions of whether this was done with authorization. However, we are convinced that the CIA did not know of the improper purposes for which the technical materials provided were to be used and resisted later efforts to involve the agency.

It is clear, then, that the National Security Act must be strengthened to assure that the CIA not engage in any activity [not specified in its charter] except as is personally approved by the President.

November 4, 1973

U.S. ADMITS PLAN TO DISRUPT PARTY

Also Concedes Surveillance of Socialist Workers

By FARNSWORTH FOWLE

The Federal Government, replying to a suit against it, has acknowledged that it conducted "electronic surveillance" of Socialist Workers party members from 1945 to 1963 and that the Federal Bureau of Investigation had a program to disrupt the party from 1961 to 1969.

The Government's reply, filed Monday in Federal District Court as a result of the party's complaint last July 18, was made public yesterday at a news conference called by the Political Rights Defense Fund, which is raising money for the costs of the court action.

The Government said that the "basic purpose" of the disruption program had been "to alert the public to the fact that S.W.P. is not just another socialist group but follows the revolutionary principles of Marx, Lenin and Engels as interpreted by Leon Trotzky."

The reply followed the F.B.I.'s disclosure Dec. 6 of an order that its late director, J. Edgar Hoover, issued to all offices on May 10, 1968, to begin an attack against groups and individuals "who spout revolution and unlawfully challenge society to obtain their demands."

Unwarranted Taps Denied

This and other counterintelligence programs were terminated without explanation in a Hoover directive of April 28, 1971. The organizations and individuals were not identified by the bureau at the time.

In the document made public yesterday, submitted on behalf of United States Attorney Paul J. Curran, the Government issued a general denial that in 1972 and 1973 election campaigns it made unwarranted use of devices to intercept confidential conversations of party members, supporters and candidates.

It acknowledged knowing of only one such wiretap—in 1972, on the Los Angeles home of James P. Cannon, then national chairman. The tap was placed on the basis of a report to the bureau by the local police, the Government said.

The suit is a class action by the Socialist Workers party, its affiliated Young Socialist Alliance, Mrs. Linda Jenness, the party's 1972 Presidential nominee, and 14 other named individuals, as well as "all others similarly situated." They asked the Federal court for more than $27-million in damages because of alleged violations of party members' constitutional rights by the defendants—the Attorney General, other department and agency heads, President Nixon and several former Nixon associates.

Harassment Is Charged

The complaint charged a systematic campaign of excessive interrogation, employment discrimination and other harassment of party members and supporters and other illegal acts, which it said impaired the party's ability to participate effectively in Federal, state and local elections.

The complaint asked for a permanent injunction against wiretapping, mail monitoring and breaking into party offices. It also asked that the party be removed from the Attorney General's list of subversive organizations.

John Ratliff, of the legal staff of the Political Rights Defense Fund, called the Government's admissions "astonishing." He said that the fund had already asked for further documents about the disruption program and would take necessary legal steps "if the Government resists their motions."

"When the Government singles out and harasses a political group on the basis of its ideas and programs," he said, "it threatens everyone's First, Fourth and Fourteenth Amendment rights." Some Government assertions in the reply, he said, "go beyond what they were making before."

A memorandum with the Government reply argued the Federal District Courts lack jurisdiction over the President and that the complaint as to him should be dismissed. Mr. Ratliff called Mr. Nixon the "chief conspirator and ultimate authority for the illegal and unconstitutional acts" in the complaint, and said that the fund's lawyers would offer counterarguments on this motion.

Mrs. Jenness said there was "nothing secretive" about her party, calling it an "open, legal organization." Recalling past Government denials of interference, she said, "We always knew they carried out these activities." She declared that the Government was no longer "in a position to get away with the amount of lying."

Mrs. Jenness, asked about the size of the party, said that in the 1972 election it got about 100,000 votes in 23 states. She said the members, numbering about 2,000, were comparable to active party workers in the major parties. The weekly readership of the party's journal, The Militant, she estimated at 70,000. It is edited by her husband.

January 11, 1974

F.B.I. TELLS OF FILE ON JERSEY GIRL, 16

Admits It Saw Subversion in Letter to Socialists She Wrote in School Project

By JOSEPH F. SULLIVAN
Special to The New York Times

NEWARK, Jan. 27 — The Federal Bureau of Investigation has admitted it is keeping a "subversive" file on a 16-year-old high school girl who wrote a letter to the Socialist Workers party as part of a school project.

In papers filed in answer to a suit brought by Lori Paton of Chester, N.J., the F.B.I. also disclosed that it had ordered a criminal investigation into Miss Paton's activities. J. Wallace LaPrade, the agent in charge of the Newark office of the F.B.I., previously had denied that the girl was being investigated by the bureau.

The extent of the F.B.I. investigation and the existence of a "mail cover" on the Socialist Workers party headquarters in New York between Jan. 23 and May 16, 1973, were disclosed as a result of proceedings instituted by Frank Askin, a lawyer with the Constitutional Litigation Clinic at Rutgers University Law School.

Mr. Askin, a cooperating attorney with the New Jersey Chapter of the American Civil Liberties Union, is representing the girl in her action to force the F.B.I. to expunge her name from its records and to pay $65,000 in damages.

The suit also is termed a class action representing "all American citizens who wish to exercise their rights under the First Amendment to engage in lawful correspondence with minority political parties without being the objects of covert and overt surveillance and interception of their mail. . . ."

If the suit succeeds, it could lead to court-imposed limits on F.B.I. surveillance. Bureau officials in Newark and Washington have refused to comment on the case. Earl Kaplan, a lawyer with the internal security section in the Department of Justice, also has refused to let agents answer Mr. Askin's questions concerning routine bureau investigation procedures, asserting that they are privileged.

The Government's disclosure was the second it had made in the last month regarding surveillance of the Socialist Workers party. Last Jan. 7, also in replay to a suit, the Government acknowledged that it had conducted "electronic surveillance" of Socialist Workers party members from 1945 to 1963 and that the F.B.I. had a program to disrupt the party from 1967 to 1969.

Miss Patton became the target of inquiry as a result of a request on Jan. 11, 1973, by L. Patrick Gray 3d, then acting F.B.I. director, to the post office for a "confidential arrangement regarding a mail cover" on the national headquarters of the Socialist Workers party, 410 West Street, New York.

Mail Cover Explained

A mail cover is a type of surveillance in which all the data on the outside of first-class letters are copied and the contents of second- third- and fourth class mail examined before it is forwarded to the target of the surveillance.

About this time Miss Paton was enrolled in a social studies course at West Morris-Mendham High School. As part of a class project she wrote a letter to the Socialist Labor party but misaddressed it. The letter went to the Young Workers Alliance, an affiliate of the Socialist Workers party.

As a result of her letter, the organization sent her a copy of its newspaper and some printed material.

Special Agent John P. Devlin checked the Paton family's credit, the employment of the girl's father, Arthur Paton, and drew from Police Chief Edward Strait of Chester the information that no member of the family had a police record.

He then went to the high school to check the girl's background and interests. When the school principal, Richard Matthews, told him the girl was still a student and the contact with the political organization was part of a school exercise, the agent left before the girl or her teacher could reach the office.

January 28, 1974

Documents Hint Politics Played Role in Wiretaps

Evidence Released by House Judiciary Panel Appears to Challenge Nixon on National Security Justification

By SEYMOUR M. HERSH
Special to The New York Times

WASHINGTON, July 18 — The House Judiciary Committee published today a mass of evidence that appeared to challenge President Nixon's contention that national security was the sole basis for White House involvement in wiretaps and the so-called "plumbers" operations.

The documents, including internal Administration memorandums, depicted a pattern of clandestine White House activities that originated because of seemingly legitimate national security concerns but later became overtly political operations. These activities began with wiretaps in 1969.

The documents released in the impeachment inquiry also show that the President and his top aides were aware in March and April, 1973, of the illegality of the clandestine activities of the White House "plumbers." The investigative group's activities included a 1971 break-in at the office of the former psychiatrist of Dr. Daniel Ellsberg, the key figure in the Pentagon papers case.

"That's an illegal search and seizure that may be sufficient at least for a mistrial," John D. Ehrlichman, a top aide, told Mr. Nixon on March 21, 1973, one document showed.

Published with the documents was a White House rebuttal citing newspaper leaks of information, secret negotiations with foreign powers and Secretary of State Kissinger's concern about America's "credibility with its allies" in an effort to persuade the committee that the White House surveillance activities did not constitute an impeachable offense.

None of the wiretaps, according to the documents, produced any relevant material about leaks of national security information.

However, Mr. Nixon and his aides were shown to have expressed concern about the "lia-bility" to the Administration that could result from public disclosure of the extensive wiretapping.

The materials indicated that White House awareness of the illegality of the "plumbers" activities, coupled with blackmail threats from E. Howard Hunt Jr., a former member of the "plumbers," prompted the President to seek to withhold information from various Watergate investigators in the spring of 1973.

The Judiciary Committee released today the seventh volume in its evidence in the impeachment inquiry. This volume consisted of four separate books and was accompanied by the 225-page rebuttal by James D. St. Clair, Mr. Nixon's attorney for Watergate matters. So far, 12 books of evidence and two of rebuttal have been issued.

Besides documents dealing with the "plumbers" and the wiretaps on 13 Government officials and four newsmen, the documents also dealt with undercover political activities for the Republicans by Donald H. Segretti; activities by John J. Caulfield and Anthony T. Ulasewicz, who made clandestine inquires for the White House; and a plan for a major domestic intelligence and operations program against radicals.

Mr. St. Clair limited his defense of Mr. Nixon to a presentation of internal White House memorandums, including a previously unpublished affidavit from Mr. Kissinger, demonstrating grave concern in the White House over leaks of classified information from 1969 through 1971.

Tap on Political Aide

In addition, the White House rebuttal reprinted many of the newspaper articles that were alleged to have disclosed highly classified information and to have prompted the President to authorize both the wiretap program and the "plumbers," a White House special investigations unit set up to stop leaks of information.

The White House defense did not deal with what appeared to be the main thrust of the House Judiciary Committee's presentation — that the two major White House intelligence-gathering programs ultimately became highly politicized.

According to the evidence gathered in the inquiry into the possible impeachment of the President, Mr. Nixon, about 10 weeks after he ordered wiretaps on suspected Administration "leakers" of highly classified information, personally authorized a wiretap on a White House political aide whom he wanted "to set up."

The aide, John P. Sears, a deputy White House counsel and former Nixon law partner who had no day-to-day involvement in national security affairs, also was placed under 24-hour-a-day surveillance by agents of the Federal Bureau of Investigation

Similarly, the documents show, President Nixon personally ordered a wiretap and 24-hour surveillance placed on Marvin Kalb, a CBS News correspondent known to be held in displeasure at the White House.

The apparently political nature of the wiretapping was indicated by a December, 1969, letter to the President from J. Edgar Hoover, the late F.B.I. director, providing political information that had been over heard in a wiretap on Morton H. Halperin, a former aide to Mr. Kissinger.

The Hoover letter dealt with plans by Clark Clifford, who was Secretary of Defense under President Johnson, to publish an article highly critical of the Nixon Administration's Vietnam policy. Within weeks, the House documents showed, a number of key White House aides were involved in making elaborate "P.R." plans designed to combat the expected effect of the Clifford article.

Nearly six months earlier, the F.B.I. unsuccessfully urged the White House to turn off the wiretap on Mr. Halperin's telephone because Mr. Halperin "has said almost nothing on the telephone." By 1970, Mr. Halperin had become an adviser to Senator Edmund S. Muskie, then a potential Democratic Presidential challenger to Mr. Nixon.

The documents show that President Nixon was sent at least 34 top-secret summaries of wiretap conversations although an F.B.I. memorandum of May, 1973, also published today, concluded that "nothing [in the summaries] was found which would indicate that a violation of Federal law was determined from the electronic surveillance coverage, nor was there any specific instance of information being leaked in a surreptitious manner."

A similar pattern of politicization of a national security operation emerged in the documents dealing with the "plumbers" unit.

Included among those documents is the committee's transcript of a meeting July 24,

Raids in Cambodia By U.S. Unprotested

By WILLIAM BEECHER
Special to The New York Times

WASHINGTON, May 8— American B-52 bombers in recent weeks have raided several Vietcong and North Vietnamese supply dumps and base camps in Cambodia for the first time, according to Nixon Administration sources, but Cambodia has not made any protest.

In fact, Cambodian authorities have increasingly been cooperating with American and South Vietnamese military men at the border, often giving them information on Vietcong and North Vietnamese movements into South Vietnam.

Information from knowledge-

Start of New York Times article that helped prompt wiretaps on 17 U.S. officials and newsmen.

1971, involving the President, Mr. Ehrlichman, his key domestic aide, and Egil Krogh Jr., a co-director of the "plumbers," which was then beginning its operation.

"Polygraph him," the President said of a Pentagon aide suspected in a recent leak of information. "I don't care whether he's a hawk or a dove or a—if the son-of-a-bitch leaked, he's not for the Government."

At no point in the brief meeting, which took place on day after The New York Times published an account of the United States negotiating positions in disarmament talks, did the President specifically mention Dr. Ellsberg, who has said that he gave to The Times, and subsequently to others newspapers, the secret Pentagon study of United States involvement in Vietnam. Nor did Mr. Nixon authorize any clandestine operations.

But Mr. Nixon did state that the disarmament information "does affect the national security — this particular one." He added, "This isn't like the Pentagon papers. This one involves a current negotiation and its getting out jeopardizes the negotiating position."

"Now, God damn it," the President said, "we're not going to allow it. We just aren't going to allow it."

Decision to Investigate

No further transcripts were made available bearing on the President's statement de-emphasing the national security significance of the Pentagon papers, published by The New York Times beginning June 13 1971. It was that publication that led to the formation of the "plumbers" unit.

However, the documents showed that an article on disarmament in The Times in July, 1971, was apparently responsible for the President's decision to authorize the "plumbers" to begin active investigations in the field.

Despite the specific Presidential mandate, the documents showed, within two months Mr Krogh's "plumbers" operation was no longer concerned with finding the source of the disarmament report but instead was itself preparing a massive series of leaks of classified information to newspapers.

In a previously unpublished Sept. 20, 1971, "plumbers" memorandum to Mr. Ehrlichman, Mr. Krogh and his co-director, David R. Young Jr., discussed extensive plans to leak classified materials dealing with the 1963 assassination of President Ngo Dinh Diem of South Vietnam and the unsuccessful Bay of Pigs invasion of Cuba in 1961. Both incidents were to be presented in a way that would adversely reflect on the Democratic party and President Kennedy.

The documents included another Krogh-Young memorandum to Mr. Ehrlichman, dated Aug. 19, 1971, saying, "We were also told by Colson that the President was after him to get out something on the Pentagon papers."

Charles W. Colson, a former White House special counsel, received a one-to-three-year jail sentence last month for his admitted role in obstruction of justice against Dr. Ellsberg. Mr. Colson later declared that President Nixon urged him "on numerous occasions" to commit the acts for which he was imprisoned.

One memorandum from Mr. Hunt to Mr. Colson said that Mr. Hunt was involved in preparing a wide-ranging file of derogatory information on Dr. Ellsberg. "This basic tool," Mr. Hunt wrote, "is essential in determining how to destroy his public image and credibility."

In his "plumbers" work, Mr. Hunt also became involved in the collection of political information on Senator Edward M. Kennedy, Democrat of Massachusetts, considered another leading Presidential candidate.

The documents suggested that politically explosive and potentially incriminating knowledge possessed by Mr. Hunt prompted the White House concern in March, 1973, over his blackmail threats. The threats were made after Mr. Hunt pleaded guilty in connection with the Republican burglary of the Democratic headquarters in the Watergate complex.

Mr. Ehrlichman discussed Mr. Hunt's threats in separate meetings early that month with Mr. Krogh and Mr. Young, the documents revealed, at one point telling Mr. Krogh that, if Mr. Hunt's demand for money was not met, "he would tell all the seamy things that he had done for Ehrlichman." The President had assigned to Mr. Ehrlichman over-all supervision of the "plumbers."

A Watergate grand jury concluded that on March 21 Mr. Nixon approved a hush money payment to Mr. Hunt. That same day, a transcript showed, the President and Mr. Ehrlichman used the term "the burglary" in discussing the 1971 break-in at the psychiatrist's office to obtain information on Dr. Ellsberg.

"Let's suppose Hunt blows at some time," Mr. Ehrlichman told the President. "Our position on that is that, uh, 'Hunt was an investigator. He was sent out to do an investigation on Ellsberg. Uh, when we discovered what he was up to, we stopped him.'"

Mr. Ehrlichman added, "That was a national security situation."

The House committee included in its report a series of grand jury statements indicating that Mr. Ehrlichman, despite his definition of the operation as a "national security" matter, sought to destroy a series of potentially incriminating "plumbers" documents in late March. At the same time, the documents showed, he was urging Mr. Krogh to "hang tough" and "not do anything rash."

The documents released today focus on Mr. Nixon's five-week delay in reporting the Ellsberg break-in to the Justice Department for forwarding to California in connection with Dr. Ellsberg's conspiracy trial, which was then in progress. The President, in public state-

ments last year, acknowledged that he first learned of the burglary on March 17, 1973, but that, for "national security" reasons, he did not permit that information to be forwarded until April 25.

Federal District Judge William Matthew Byrne Jr. dismissed the charges against Dr. Ellsberg on grounds of Government misconduct after he eventually learned of the break-in and other activities.

Mr. Nixon's description of events is apparently contradicted a number of times by documents released today.

For example, in his news conference on Aug. 22, 1973, the President explained that for national security reasons he instructed Henry E. Petersen, an Assistant Attorney General, on April 18 to "stay out" of the Ellsberg break-in.

As the President recounted it, Mr. Petersen asked him whether any evidence had been developed from the break-in. The President added: "And I said, 'No, it was a dry hole.' He said, 'Good.'" The President went on to say that, in view of the fact that no information had been collected in the burglary, "there was no requirement that it be presented to the jury that was hearing the case."

In his grand jury testimony made available a few pages later in the documents, Mr. Petersen recalled no such exchange "There's nothing you have to do," he quoted Mr. Nixon as saying abruptly.

July 19, 1974

Saxbe Says Top Officials Had Some Knowledge of F.B.I.'s Drive to Disrupt Various Political Groups

By JOHN M. CREWDSON
Special to The New York Times

WASHINGTON, Nov. 13—Attorney General William B. Saxbe said today that some knowledge of F.B.I. efforts to disrupt domestic political groups had been made available to some Congressmen, senior Justice Department officials and possibly some Presidents.

Mr. Saxbe, in making public a report of the Federal Bureau of Investigation's secret counterintelligence operations known as "Cointelpro," said at a news conference that the Justice Department had believed until recently that the program's existence was unknown outside the bureau.

"We have since found memoranda to indicate that there was some fragmented information available to some Attorneys General and perhaps to the President about the bureau's undercover efforts," Mr. Saxbe said, adding that similar data had been provided to members of the Congressional Oversight Committees.

Mr. Saxbe was accompanied by Clarence M. Kelley, the F.B.I. director, who said in a statement that the late J. Edgar Hoover, his predecessor, had informed every Attorney General since 1958 of some of the techniques used by F.B.I. agents against groups selected as targets of its Cointelpro activities.

Mr. Kelley defended the program, which the Saxbe report said was made up of seven distinct efforts, as an appropriate response to "the anarchistic plans and activities of violence-prone groups whose publicly announced goal was to bring America to its knees."

Justice Department officials confirmed after the news conference that the targets of the disruptive activities, some of which Mr. Saxbe termed disturbing and "improper," included such civil rights organizations as the Student Nonviolent Coordinating Committee, the Congress of Racial Equality, and the Southern Christian Leadership Conference.

According to the 21-page report, the first Cointelpro efforts undertaken at Mr. Hoover's order were in 1956 against suspected members of the Communist party.

The program was later expanded to include the Socialist Workers party, so-called "white hate groups" such as the Ku Klux Klan, "black extremist" organizations such as the Black Panther party and "new left" groups such as Students for a Democratic society.

Mr. Kelley said that information about the Cointelpro activities had been furnished to Attorney General William P. Rogers in May of 1958, Attorney General-designate Robert F. Kennedy in January, 1961, and successive Attorneys General in 1965, 1967 and 1969.

Nicholas deB. Katzenbach, who served as Attorney General in 1965, said in a telephone interview that he had never heard the term Cointelpro, an abbreviation of counterintelligence program. Mr. Katzenbach said that he had known of "some of the activities that the bureau was doing with respect to the Klan," but that he was surprised to learn that such organizations as CORE, the S.N.C.C. and the S.C.L.C. had also been subjected to covert disruptions.

Ramsey Clark, who succeeded Mr. Katzenbach, said that "all I know about it is what I've read

341

in the papers."

"The idea that I would have tolerated any Government agent engaging in any disruptive activity is false and unthinkable," Mr. Clark said.

Mr. Saxbe gave assurances that Cointelpro was ordered discontinued by Mr. Hoover following a burglary in 1971 of the F.B.I.'s field office in Media, Pa., in which several sensitive bureau documents regarding the surveillance of political groups were taken and subsequently made public.

He said that as far as he knew, there had been no requests from the F.B.I. to resume such activities and that he could not foresee circumstances under which he would approve such requests.

Henry E. Petersen, head of the Justice Department's Criminal Division who directed the Cointelpro study, expressed concern over some of the techniques used by F.B.I. agents in the program.

Mr. Saxbe said the Justice Department might be subject to civil lawsuits by individuals whose civil rights may have been damaged.

The report noted that, between 1956 and 1971, F.B.I. officials had received 3,247 proposals for disruptive activity, of which 2,370 were approved and implemented.

"To the extent that there were, nevertheless, isolated excesses, we have taken steps to prevent them from ever happening again," he said.

November 19, 1974

C.I.A. - F.B.I.

HUGE C.I.A. OPERATION REPORTED IN U.S. AGAINST ANTIWAR FORCES, OTHER DISSIDENTS IN NIXON YEARS

FILES ON CITIZENS

Helms Reportedly Got Surveillance Data in Charter Violation

By SEYMOUR M. HERSH
Special to The New York Times

WASHINGTON, Dec. 21—The Central Intelligence Agency, directly violating its charter, conducted a massive, illegal domestic intelligence operation during the Nixon Administration against the antiwar movement and other dissident groups in the United States, according to well-placed Government sources.

An extensive investigation by The New York Times has established that intelligence files on at least 10,000 American citizens were maintained by a special unit of the C.I.A. that was reporting directly to Richard Helms, then the Director of Central Intelligence and now the Ambassador to Iran.

In addition, the sources said, a check of the C.I.A.'s domestic files ordered last year by Mr. Helms's successor, James R. Schlesinger, produced evidence of dozens of other illegal activities by members of the C.I.A. inside the United States, beginning in the nineteen-fifties, including break-ins, wiretapping and the surreptitious inspection of mail.

A Different Category

Mr. Schlesinger was succeeded at the C.I.A. by William E. Colby in September, 1973.

Those other alleged operations, in the fifties, while also prohibited by law, were not targeted at dissident American citizens, the sources said, but were a different category of domestic activities that were secretly carried out as part of operations aimed at suspected foreign intelligence agents operating in the United States.

Under the 1947 act setting up the C.I.A., the agency was forbidden to have "police, subpoena, law enforcement powers or internal security functions" inside the United States. Those responsibilities fall to the F.B.I., which maintains a special internal security unit to deal with foreign intelligence threats.

Helms Unavailable

Mr. Helms, who became head of the C.I.A. in 1966 and left the agency in February, 1973, for his new post in Teheran, could not be reached despite telephone calls there yesterday and today.

Charles Cline, a duty officer at the American Embassy in Teheran, said today that a note informing Mr. Helms of the request by The Times for comment had been delivered to Mr. Helms's quarters this morning. By late evening Mr. Helms had not returned the call.

The information about the C.I.A. came as the Senate Armed Services Committee issued a report today condemning the Pentagon for spying on the White House National Security Council. But the report said the Pentagon spying incidents in 1970 and 1971 were isolated and presented no threat to civilian control of the military.

The disclosure of alleged illegal C.I.A. activities is the first possible connection to rumors that have been circulating in Washington for some time. A number of mysterious burglaries and incidents have come to light since the break-ins at Democratic party headquarters in the Watergate complex on June 17, 1972.

Duping Charged

Throughout the public hearings and courtroom testimony on Watergate, Mr. Helms and other high-level officials said the C.I.A. had been "duped" into its Watergate involvement by the White House.

As part of its alleged effort against dissident Americans in the late nineteen-sixties and early nineteen-seventies, The Times' sources said, the C.I.A. authorized agents to follow and photograph participants in antiwar and other demonstrations. The C.I.A. also set up a network of informants who were ordered to penetrate antiwar groups, the sources said.

At least one avowedly antiwar member of Congress was among those placed under surveillance by the C.I.A., the sources said. Other members of Congress were said to be included in the C.I.A.'s dossier on dissident Americans.

The names of the various Congressmen could not be learned, nor could any specific information about domestic C.I.A. break-ins and wiretappings be obtained.

It also could not be determined whether Mr. Helms had had specific authority from the President or any of his top officials to initiate the alleged domestic surveillance, or whether Mr. Helms had informed the President of the fruits, if any, of the alleged operations.

Distress Reported

These alleged activities are known to have distressed both Mr. Schlesinger, now the Secretary of Defense, and Mr. Colby. Mr. Colby has reportedly told associates that he is considering the possibility of asking the Attorney General to institute legal action against some of those who had been involved in the alleged domestic activities.

One official, who was directly involved in the initial C.I.A. inquiry last year into the alleged domestic spying, said that Mr. Schlesinger and his associates were unable to learn what Mr. Nixon knew, if anything.

Mr. Colby refused to comment on the domestic spying issue. But one clue to the depth of his feelings emerged during an off-the-record talk he gave Monday night at the Council on Foreign Relations in New York.

The C.I.A. chief, who had been informed the previous week of the inquiry by The Times, said at the meeting that he had ordered a complete investigation of the agency's domestic activities and had found some improprieties.

But he is known to have added, "I think family skeletons are best left where they are—in the closet."

He then said that the "good thing about all of this was the red flag" was raised by a group of junior employees inside the agency.

It was because of the prodding from below, some sources have reported, that Mr. Colby decided last year to inform the chairmen of the House and Senate Intelligence Oversight Committees of the domestic activities.

Mr. Schlesinger, who became Secretary of Defense after serving less than six months at the C.I.A., similarly refused to discuss the domestic spying activities.

Anguish Reported

But he was described by an associate as extremely concerned and disturbed by what he discovered at the C.I.A. upon replacing Mr. Helms.

"He found himself in a cesspool," the associate said. "He was having a grenade blowing up in his face every time he turned around."

Mr. Schlesinger was at the C.I.A. when the first word of the agency's involvement in the September, 1971, burglary of the office of Dr. Daniel Ellsberg's former psychiatrist by the White House security force known as the "plumbers" became known.

It was Mr. Schlesinger who also discovered and turned over to the Justice Department a series of letters written to Mr. Helms by James W. McCord, Jr., one of the original Watergate defendants and a former C.I.A. security official. The letters, which told of White House involvement in the Watergate burglary, had been deposited in an agency office.

The associate said one result of Mr. Schlesinger's inquiries into Watergate and the domestic aspects of the C.I.A. operations was his executive edict ordering a halt to all questionable coun-

terintelligence operations inside the United States.

During his short stay at the C.I.A., Mr. Schlesinger also initiated a 10 per cent employe cutback. Because of his actions, the associate said, security officials at the agency decided to increase the number of his personal bodyguards. It could not be learned whether that action was taken after a threat.

Many past and present C.I.A. men acknowledged that Mr. Schlesinger's reforms were harder to bear because he was an outsider.

Mr. Colby, these men said, while continuing the same basic programs initiated by his predecessor, was viewed by some as "the saving force" at the agency because as a former high-ranking official himself in the C.I.A.'s clandestine services, he had the respect and power to ensure that the alleged illegal domestic programs would cease.

Some sources also reported that there was widespread paper shredding at the agency shortly after Mr. Schlesinger began to crack down on the C.I.A.'s operations.

Asked about that, however, Government officials said that they could "guarantee" that the domestic intelligence files were still intact.

"There's certainly been no order to destroy them," one official said.

When confronted with the Times's information about the C.I.A.'s domestic operations earlier this week, high-ranking American intelligence officials confirmed its basic accuracy, but cautioned against drawing "unwarranted conclusions."

Espionage Feared

Those officials, who insisted on not being quoted by name, contended that all of the C.I.A.'s domestic activities against American citizens were initiated in the belief that foreign governments and foreign espionage may have been involved.

"Anything that we did was in the context of foreign counterintelligence and it was focused at foreign intelligence and foreign intelligence problems," one official said.

The official also said that the requirement to maintain files on American citizens emanated, in part, from the so-called Huston plan. That plan, named for its author, Tom Charles Huston, a Presidential aide, was a White House project in 1970 calling for the use of such, illegal activities as burglaries and wiretapping to combat antiwar activities and student turmoil that the White House believed was being "fomented" —as the Huston plan stated— by black extremists.

Former President Richard M.

Nixon and his top aides have repeatedly said that the proposal, which had been adamantly opposed by J. Edgar Hoover, then the director of the Federal Bureau of Investigation, was never implemented.

Government intelligence officials did not dispute that assertion, but explained that, nonetheless, the C.I.A.'s decision to maintain domestic files on American citizens "obviously got a push at that time."

"Yes, you can say that the C.I.A. contribution to the Huston plan was in the foreign counterintelligence field," one official said.

'A Spooky Way'

"The problem is that it was handled in a very spooky way."

"If you're an agent sitting in Paris and you're asked to find out whether Jane Fonda is being manipulated by foreign intelligence services, you've got to ask yourself who is the real target," the official said. "Is it the foreign intelligence services or Jane Fonda?"

However, this official and others insisted that all alleged domestic C. I. A. operations against American citizens had now ceased and that instructions had been issued to insure that they could not occur again.

A number of well-informed official sources, in attempting to minimize the extent of alleged wrongdoing posed by the C.I.A.'s domestic actions, suggested that the laws were fuzzy in connection with the so-called "gray" area of C.I.A.-F.B.I. operations — that is, when an American citizen is approached inside the United States by a suspected foreign intelligence agent.

The legislation setting up the C.I.A. makes the director "responsible for protecting intelligence sources and methods from unauthorized disclosure."

One official with close access to Mr. Colby contended at length in an interview yesterday that the C.I.A.'s domestic actions were not illegal because of the agency's legal right to prevent the possible revelation of secrets.

'Gray Areas'

"Look, you do run into gray areas," the official said, "and, unquestionably, some of this fell into the gray area. But the director does have an obligation to guard his sources and methods. You get some foreigner snooping around and you have to keep track."

"Let's suppose as an academic exercise, hypothetically," the official said, "that a foreigner believed to be an intelligence agent goes to a Washington newspaper office to see a reporter. What do you [the C.I.A.] do? Because it's a Washington newspaper office and a reporter, do you scratch

that from the C.I.A.'s record?

"Sure, the C.I.A. was following the guy, but he wasn't an American."

A number of other intelligence experts, told of that example, described it as a violation of the 1947 statute and a clear example of an activity, even if involving a foreigner, from which the C.I.A. is barred.

Prof. Harry Howe Ransom of Vanderbilt University, considered a leading expert on the C.I.A. and its legal and Congressional authority, said in a telephone interview that in his opinion the 1947 statute included "a clear prohibition against any internal security functions under any circumstances."

Professor Ransom said that his research of the Congressional debate at the time the C.I.A. was set up makes clear that Congress expressed concern over any police state tactics and intended to avoid the possibility. Professor Ransom quoted one member as having said during floor debate, "We don't want a Gestapo."

Similar reservations about the C.I.A.'s role in domestic affairs were articulated by Mr. Colby during his confirmation hearings before the Senate Armed Services Committee in September, 1973.

Asked by Senator Stuart Symington, Democrat of Missouri, about the "gray" area in the 1947 legislation, Mr. Colby said:

"My interpretation of that particular provision is that it gives me a charge but does not give me authority. It gives me the job of identifying any problem of protecting sources and methods, but in the event I identify one it gives me the responsibility to go to the appropriate authorities with that information and it does not give me any authority to act on my own.

'No Authority'

"So I really see less of a gray area [than Mr. Helms] in that regard. I believe that there is really no authority under that act that can be used."

Beyond his briefings for Senator John C. Stennis, Democrat of Mississippi, and Representative Lucien N. Nedzi, Democrat of Michigan, the respective chairmen of the Senate and House Intelligence subcommittees of the Armed Services Committees, Mr. Colby apparently had not informed other Ford Administration officials as of yesterday of the C.I.A. problems.

"Counterintelligence!" one high-level Justice Department official exclaimed upon being given some details of the C.I.A.'s alleged domestic operations. "They're not supposed to have any counterintelligence in this country."

"Oh, my God," he said, "oh, my God."

A former high-level F.B.I. official who operated in domestic counterintelligence areas since World War I, expressed astonishment and then anger upon being told of the C.I.A.'s alleged domestic activities.

"We had an agreement with them that they weren't to do anything unless they checked with us," he said. "They double-crossed me all along."

He said he had never been told by his C.I.A. counterintelligence colleagues of any of the alleged domestic operations that took place.

Mr. Huston, now an Indianapolis attorney, said in a telephone conversation yesterday that he had not learned of any clandestine domestic C.I.A. activities while he worked in the White House.

Huston Disagrees

Mr. Huston took vigorous exception to a suggestion by intelligence officials that his proposed White House domestic intelligence plan resulted in increased pressure on the C.I.A. to collect domestic intelligence.

"There was nothing in that program that directed the C.I.A. to do anything in this country," Mr. Huston said. "There was nothing that they could rely on to justify anything like this. The only thing we ever asked them for related to activities outside the United States."

Two months ago, Rolling Stone magazine published a lengthy list of more than a dozen unsolved break-ins and burglaries and suggested that they might be linked to as yet undisclosed C.I.A. or F.B.I. activities.

Senator Howard H. Baker Jr., Republican of Tennessee, who was vice chairman of the Senate Watergate committee, has publicly spoken of mysterious C.I.A. links to Watergate. The White House transcripts of June 23, 1972, show President Nixon saying to H. R. Haldeman, his chief of staff, "Well, we protected Helms from one hell of a lot of things."

The remark, commented upon by many officials during recent interviews, could indicate Presidential knowledge about the C.I.A.'s alleged domestic activities.

The possible Watergate link is but one of many questions posed by the disclosures about the C.I.A. that the Times sources say they believe can be unraveled only by extensive Congressional hearings.

The C.I.A. domestic activities during the Nixon Administration were directed, the source said, by James Angleton, who is still in charge of the Counterintelligence Department, the agency's most powerful and mysterious unit.

As head of counterintelligence, Mr. Angleton is in charge of maintaining the C.I.A.'s "sources and methods of intelligence," which means that he and his men must ensure that foreign intelligence agents do not penetrate the C.I.A.

The Times's sources, who included men with access to first-hand knowledge of the C.I.A.'s alleged domestic activities, took sharp exception to the official suggestion that such activities were the result of legitimate counterintelligence needs.

"Look, that's how it started," one man said. "They were looking for evidence of foreign involvement in the antiwar movement. But that's not how it ended up. This just grew and mushroomed internally."

"Maybe they began with a check on Fonda," the source said, speaking hypothetically. "But then they began to check on her friends. They'd see her at an antiwar rally and take photographs. I think this was going on even before the Huston plan."

'Highly Coordinated'

"This wasn't a series of isolated events. It was highly coordinated. People were targeted, information was collected on them, and it was all put on [computer] tape, just like the agency does with information about K.G.B. [Soviet] agents.

"Every one of these acts was blatantly illegal."

Another official with access to details of C.I.A. operations said that the alleged illegal activities uncovered by Mr. Schlesinger last year included break-ins and electronic surveillances that had been undertaken during the fifties and sixties.

"During the fifties, this was routine stuff," the official said. "The agency did things that would amaze both of us, but some of this also went on in the late sixties, when the country and atmosphere had changed."

The official suggested that what he called the "Nixon antiwar hysteria" may have been a major factor in the C.I.A.'s decision to begin maintaining domestic files on American citizens.

One public clue about alleged White House pressure for C.I.A. involvement in the intelligence efforts against antiwar activists came during Mr. Helms's testimony before the Senate Watergate committee in August, 1973.

Mr. Helms told how the President's Foreign Intelligence Advisory Board had once suggested that the agency could "make a contribution" in domestic intelligence operations.

'No Way'

"I pointed out to them very quickly it could not, there was no way," Mr. Helms said. "But this was a matter that kept coming up in the context of feelers: Isn't there somebody else that can take on some of these things if the F.B.I. isn't doing them as well as they should, as there are no other facilities?"

The Times's sources, reflecting the thinking of some of the junior C.I.A. officials who began waving "the red flag" inside the agency, were harshly critical of the leadership of Mr. Helms.

These junior officials are known to believe that the alleged domestic spying on antiwar activists originated as an ostensibly legitimate counterintelligence operation to determine whether the antiwar movement had been penetrated by foreign agents.

In 1969 and 1970, the C.I.A. was asked by the White House to determine whether foreign governments were supplying undercover agents and funds to antiwar radicals and Black Panther groups in the United States. Those studies, conducted by C.I.A. officials who reportedly did not know of the alleged secret domestic intelligence activities, concluded that there was no evidence of foreign support.

"It started as a foreign intelligence operation and it bureaucratically grew," one source said. "That's really the answer."

The source added that Mr. Angleton's counterintelligence department "simply began using the same techniques for foreigners against new targets here."

Along with assembling the domestic intelligence dossiers, the source said, Mr. Angleton's department began recruiting informants to infiltrate some of the more militant dissident groups.

"They recruited plants, informers and doublers [double agents]," the source said. "They were collecting information and when counterintelligence collects information, you use all of those techniques.

"It was like a little F.B.I. operation."

This source and others knowledgeable about the C.I.A. believe that Mr. Angleton was permitted to continue his alleged domestic operations because of the great power he wields inside the agency as director of counterintelligence.

It is this group that is charged with investigating allegations against C.I.A. personnel made by foreign agents who defect; in other words, it must determine whether a C.I.A. man named by a defector is, in fact, a double agent.

Marchetti Book

Victor Marchetti, a former C.I.A. official, said in a book published this year that the "counterintelligence staff operates on the assumption that the agency — as well as other elements of the United States Government—is penetrated by the K.G.B.

"The chief of the C.I.A. staff [Mr. Marchetti did not identify Mr. Angleton] is said to keep a list of the 50 or so key positions in the C.I.A. which are most likely to have been infiltrated by the opposition, and he reportedly keeps the persons in those positions under constant surveillance," he wrote.

Dozens of other former C.I.A. men talked in recent interviews with similar expressions of fear and awe about Mr. Angleton, an accomplished botanist and Yale graduate who once edited a poetry magazine there.

He was repeatedly described by former C.I.A. officials as an unrelenting cold warrior who was convinced that the Soviet Union was playing a major role in the antiwar activities.

One former high-level C.I.A. official accused Mr. Angleton of a "spook mentality" who saw conspiracies everywhere. The official said that Mr. Angleton was convinced that many members of the press had ties to the Soviet Union and was suspicious of anyone who wrote anything friendly about the Soviet Union.

Another former official characterized counterintelligence as "an independent power in the C.I.A. Even people in the agency aren't allowed to deal directly with the C.I. [counterintelligence] people.

"Once in it," he said, "you're in it for life."

Most of the domestic surveillance and the collection of domestic intelligence was conducted, the sources said, by one of the most clandestine units in the United States intelligence community, the special operations branch of counterintelligence. It is these men who perform the foreign wiretaps and break-ins authorized by higher intelligence officials.

'Deep Snow Section'

"That's really the deep snow section," one high-level intelligence expert said of the unit, whose liaison with Mr. Helms was conducted by Richard Ober, a long-time counterintelligence official who has served in New Delhi for the C.I.A.

Despite intensive interviews, little could be learned about the procedures involved in the alleged domestic activities except for the fact that the operation was kept carefully shielded from other units inside the C.I.A.

One former high-level aide who worked closely with Mr. Helms in the executive offices of the agency recalled that Mr. Ober held frequent private meetings with Mr. Helms in the late sixties and early seventies.

"Ober had unique and very

confidential access to Helms," the former C.I.A. man said. "I always assumed he was mucking about with Americans who were abroad and then would come back, people like the Black Panthers."

'Nothing I Can Say'

The official said he had learned that Mr. Ober had quickly assembled "a large staff of people who acquired enormous amounts of data, more than I thought was justified."

After the unveiling of the domestic operations by Mr. Schlesinger last year, sources said, Mr. Ober was abruptly transferred from the C.I.A. to a staff position with the National Security Council.

"They didn't fire him," one well-informed source said, "but they didn't want him around. The C.I.A. had to get rid of him, he was too embarrassing, too hot."

The source added that Mr. Ober had vehemently defended his actions as justified by national security.

A Government intelligence official, subsequently asked about Mr. Ober, denied that his transfer to the National Security Council was a rebuke in any way.

Reached by telephone at his office this week, Mr. Ober refused to discuss the issue.

"There's nothing I can say about this," he said.

Mr. Angleton, also reached by telephone this week at his suburban Washington home, denied that his Counterintelligence Department operated domestically.

"We know our jurisdiction," he said.

Mr. Angleton told of a report from a United States agent in Moscow who was relaying information to the C.I.A. on the underground and radical bombings in the United States during the height of the antiwar activity.

A Source in Moscow

"The intelligence was not acquired in the United States," Mr. Angleton declared, "it came from Moscow. Our source there is still active and still productive; the opposition still doesn't know."

Mr. Angleton then described how the C.I.A. had obtained information from Communist sources about the alleged demolition training of black militants by the North Koreans. He also told of recent intelligence efforts involving the K.G.B. and Yasir Arafat, chairman of the Palestine Liberation Organization.

A number of former important F.B.I. domestic intelligence sources took issue with Mr. Angelton's apparent suggestion that the domestic antiwar activity was linked to the Soviet Union.

"There was a lot of stuff [on radicals in the United States] that came in from the C.I.A. overseas," one former official recalled, but he said a lot of it was worthless.

Amazement and Dismay

Other officials closely involved with United States intelligence expressed amazement and dismay that the head of counterintelligence would make such random suggestions during a telephone conversation with a newsman.

"You know," said one member of Congress who is involved with the monitoring of C.I.A. activities, "that's even a better story than the domestic spying."

One former C.I.A. official who participated in the 1969 and 1970 White House-directed studies of alleged foreign involvement in the antiwar movement said that Mr. Angleton "undoubtedly believes that foreign agents were behind the student movement, but he doesn't know what he's talking about."

The official also raised a question about the bureaucratic procedures of the C.I.A. under Mr. Helms and suggested that his penchant for secrecy apparently kept the most complete intelligence information from being forwarded to the White House.

"We dealt with Ober and we dealt with Angleton on these studies, went over them point by point," the official said, "and Angleton, while not exactly enthusiastic, signed off" —that is, he initialed the study indicating that it represented the views of the Counterintelligence Department.

The former C.I.A. official said that he could not reconcile Mr. Angleton's decision to permit the studies, which reported no evidence of foreign involvement, while being involved in an elaborate and secret domestic security operation to root out alleged foreign activities in the antiwar movement. The results of the studies were forwarded to Henry A. Kissinger, then President Nixon's national security adviser.

A number of former F.B.I. officials said in interviews that the C.I.A.'s alleged decision to mount domestic break-ins, wiretaps and similarly illegal counterintelligence operations undoubtedly reflected, in part, the long-standing mistrust between the two agencies.

In 1970, Mr. Hoover reportedly ordered his bureau to break off all but formal liaison contact with the C.I.A., forcing lower level C.I.A. and F.B.I. officials to make clandestine arrangements to exchange information.

By the late sixties, one former F.B.I. official said, all but token cooperation between the two agencies on counterintelligence and counterespionage had ended.

"The C.I.A. was never satisfied with the F.B.I. and I can't blame them," the former official said. "We did hit-or-miss jobs.

'Cutting Throats'

"We were constantly cutting the throats of the C.I.A. in our dealing with them. If the White House knew about it, they were too afraid of Hoover to do anything about it."

The former aide cited a case in the late sixties in which Mr. Angleton turned to F.B.I. for a domestic investigation because he "believed four or five guys were agents, including two guys still in the agency [C.I.A.] and three or four who had been high-level."

"They were suspected of having dealings with foreign intelligence agents," the former official said.

"We just went through the motions on our investigation. It was just a brushoff."

Before Mr. Hoover's decision to cut off the working relationship, the former official added, the F.B.I.—as the agency responsible for domestic counterintelligence—would, as a matter of policy, conduct a major clandestine inquiry into the past and present C.I.A. men.

Despite Mr. Hoover's provocative actions, the former F.B.I. man said, the C.I.A. still was not justified in taking domestic action.

"If they did any surreptitious bag jobs [break-ins]," he said, "they'd better not have told me about it."

December 22, 1974

Excerpts From '47 Law Creating C.I.A.

Special to The New York Times

WASHINGTON, Dec. 25— *Following is an excerpt from the 1947 law that created the Central Intelligence Agency, Title 50, Section 403 of the United States Code:*

§ 403. Central Intelligence Agency

There is established under the National Security Council a Central Intelligence Agency with a Director of Central Intelligence, who shall be the head thereof. The director shall be appointed by the President, by and with the advice and consent of the Senate, from among the commissioned officers of the armed services or from among individuals in civilian life. . . .

Powers and Duties

(d) For the purpose of coordinating the intelligence activities of the several Government departments and agencies in the interest of national security, it shall be the duty of the agency, under the direction of the National Security Council—

(1) To advise the National Security Council in matters concerning such intelligence activities of the Government departments and agencies as relate to national security;

(2) To make recommendations to the National Security Council for the coordination of such intelligence activities of the departments and agencies of the Government as relate to the national security;

(3) To correlate and evaluate intelligence relating to the national security, and provide for the appropriate dissemination of such intelligence within the Government using where appropriate existing agencies and facilities: *Provided,* That the Agency shall have no police, subpena, law-enforcement powers, or internal-security functions: *Provided further,* That the departments and other agencies of the Government shall continue to collect, evaluate, correlate, and disseminate departmental intelligence: *And provided further,* That the Director of Central Intelligence shall be responsible for protecting intelligence sources and methods from unauthorized disclosure;

(4) To perform, for the benefit of the existing intelligence agencies, such additional services of common concern as the National Security Council determines can be more efficiently accomplished centrally;

(5) To perform such other functions and duties related to intelligence affecting the national security as the National Security Council may from time to time direct.

December 26, 1974

Colby Said to Confirm C.I.A. Role in U.S.

By SEYMOUR M. HERSH
Special to The New York Times

WASHINGTON, Dec. 31—The Central Intelligence Agency has told President Ford that its agents maintained thousands of files on American citizens and participated in a wide program of electronic surveillances, break-ins and the surreptitious inspection of mail inside the United States, well-placed Government sources said today.

The sources said that William E. Colby, the Director of Central Intelligence, did not provide any specific instances of wrongdoing in his report on the spying allegations that was submitted to the President last week, but instead listed the domestic activities by category.

Mr. Colby's report, the sources said, reflected the fact that it had been ordered by the President in response to the spying allegations reported on Dec. 22 in The New York Times.

"The report says that The New York Times charges this or that, and then says here are the facts," one source noted, adding that the C.I.A. document seemed to be limitd to areas of wrongdoing outlined in the initial Times dispatch.

In its Dec. 22 report, The Times quoted well-placed sources as saying that the C.I.A. had violated its charter by mounting a massive intelligence operation in the late nineteen - sixties and early nineteen-seventies against the antiwar movement and other dissident groups in the United States. Intelligence files on at least 10,000 American citizens were compiled, the sources

were quoted as saying.

The Los Angeles Times said today that Mr. Colby's report acknowledged that the C.I.A. kept files on more than 9,000 Americans and stated that there were at least three illegal break-ins.

The New York Times's sources confirmed that account, but added that Mr. Colby had also told the President of electronic surveillances and the surreptitious opening of mail. The report did not say specifically whether the electronic surveillance involved bugging or wire-tapping or both.

In each case, however, the sources said, the Colby report did not say who was targeted inside the United States or for what reason. "It just said that there was X number of files and X number of break-ins," a source said.

In the case of the mail covers, which have not been used by the Federal Bureau of Investigation since the mid-nineteen-sixties, the source said, Mr. Colby stated that the operations were approved in advance by various Attorneys General or Postmasters General.

No such contention was made for the break-ins and buggings, the source said. Some of the illegal domestic activities are known to have taken place as long as 20 years ago.

Asked whether he considered the Colby report to be complete, one source who has had first-hand access to the document, said, "That depends on what you mean by complete."

"What it does," he added,

"is go into some detail on some of the charges in The Times."

"Basically Colby doesn't attempt to justify what was done," the source explained, "He just lays out the facts."

'Not the End-All'

Asked further whether the report appeared to be a satisfactory response, the source said, "It's satisfactory only insofar as it gives a factual description of the allegation in the first Times article."

"Clearly," the source said, "this [the Colby report] is not the end-all to the investigation. Obviously, there are questions left to be answered."

The Times's sources also described the C.I.A. report as being far less voluminous than was indicated by published reports last week. Those reports, which were not challenged by officials in the White House press office, depicted the Colby document as being more than 50 pages in length with various appendices.

In fact, the sources said, the document included a number of papers and materials not directly pertinent to the charges of domestic spying, and it was those pages that added to its bulk.

The sources further expressed bafflement over the concern expressed last week by the White House over the possible problems for some foreign countries that would result from publication of the Colby report. "This is only a problem for foreign governments in terms of 'Here's another example of how we can't keep our mouths shut,'" one official said.

Earlier today, The Associated Press quoted what it said was

a senior adviser to President Ford as saying that he understood that the Colby document substantially supported the allegations reported in The New York Times.

Those allegations have resulted in calls for at least four investigations by the next Congress, which convenes in two weeks. In addition, some Senators and officials have urged formation of a special prosecutor's office to investigate and possibly bring criminal charges.

President Ford, who received the Colby report Friday while on his ski-work visit to Vail, Colo., has made it known that he will not discuss the report or the C.I.A. until after his return to Washington Thursday. Mr. Ford will meet then with Secretary of State Kissinger and Mr. Colby to determine what steps to take.

At least four high-ranking former C.I.A. officials, all members of the counterintelligence division, which was alleged to have participated in the illegal activities, have resigned since the initial Times story.

Under the National Security Act of 1947, setting up the C.I.A., the intelligence agency was explicitly barred from internal security functions, even in the case of foreign espionage. That function was to be left to the Federal Bureau of Investigation.

In a related development, Vice President Rockefeller told newsmen today in San Juan, Puerto Rico, where he is vacationing, that the C.I.A. or any other institution that breaks the law should be punished.

But the newly confirmed Vice President added that the "C.I.A. is in Mr. Kissinger's area and I don't intend to interfere." Mr. Rockefeller and Mr. Kissinger have been vacationing with their wives since last week at the Dorado Beach Hotel in San Juan.

January 1, 1975

FORD SETS UP COMMISSION ON C.I.A.'S DOMESTIC ROLE; A JUSTICE DEPT. INQUIRY ON

By WALTER RUGABER
Special to The New York Times

WASHINGTON, Jan. 4—President Ford established today a commission to investigate allegations of illegal domestic spying by the Central Intelligence Agency.

Ron Nessen, the White House press secretary, said that Mr. Ford had interviewed several persons and hoped to make from five to seven appointments, all from outside the Government, sometime next week.

The President, in a statement describing the commission as a "blue ribbon panel," added that the Justice Department was also "looking into such aspects of the matter as are within its jurisdiction."

Mr. Ford took note, too, of

a number of prospective Congressional investigations. He said that "cooperative efforts" by the executive and legislative branches would produce "beneficial" results.

Balancing Requirements

"It is essential in this Republic that we meet our security requirements and at the same time avoid impairing our democratic institutions and fundamental freedoms," Mr. Ford said in his statement. "Intelligence activities must be conducted consistently with both objectives," he continued.

"To that end, in addition to asking the panel to determine whether the C.I.A. has exceeded its statutory authority, I have asked the panel to determine whether existing safeguards are adequate to preclude agency activities that might go beyond its authority and to make appropriate recommendations."

The President met for more than three hours today with Secretary of State Kissinger and for about 20 minutes with Richard Helms, the former Director of Central Intelligence, who is now Ambassador to Iran.

Earlier, the President had received a report on the C.I.A.'s domestic activity from the current director of the agency, William E. Colby, and had talked with the Secretary of Defense, James R. Schlesinger, a former C.I.A. director.

Based on these conversations and the Colby report, Mr. Nessen said, "It is fair to say . . . that enough questions have been raised to appoint a commission to look into this matter."

The New York Times, quoting well-placed sources, reported two weeks ago that the C.I.A. had conducted illegal domestic spying and had compiled dossiers on nearly 10,000 American citizens. The agency is barred by law from domestic activity.

Mr. Helms, who was chief of the intelligence agency during much of the time operations within the United States were alleged to have been under way, has "categorically denied" any illegal spying during his C.I.A. tenure.

Mr. Nessen avoided endorsing the former C.I.A. chief's denial.

"I don't have anything to say about Mr. Helms," the press secretary remarked.

The President's statement that the Justice Department was investigating also suggested that the White House was unwilling to dismiss the reports of law violations by the C.I.A.

Mr. Ford, whose Executive order establishing the commission was announced late this afternoon, said he was aware that a number of Congressional committees planned to hold hearings on C.I.A. issues.

"Whether hearings are undertaken by existing oversight committees, or should the Congress deem a joint House-Senate committee to be the best approach to avoid a proliferation of hearings, it is my strong hope that the committees consider the findings and recommendations of the commission."

The Executive order provides that the commission must make its final report to the President within three months and that it will go out of existence a month later.

"I am confident that through the cooperative efforts of the executive branch, particularly by the new commission, and of the Congress, the results will be beneficial both to our national security and to the traditions and institutions of this Republic," Mr. Ford said.

He announced that he would write to Government officials involved in intelligence activities and foreign policy "for the purpose of emphasizing that they are at all times to conduct their activities within the scope of their respective statutory authorities."

When he left the White House this afternoon, Secretary Kissinger said that "on the basis of what I now know there was no reason to discharge Mr. Helms as Ambassador. He predicted that Mr. Helms would return to Teheran "eventually."

Justice Agency's Inquiry

WASHINGTON, Jan. 4 (AP)— The Justice Department declined to comment on its inquiry into the C.I.A. A spokesman said that "we just don't comment on investigations."

However, it was learned that the Justice Department inquiry is aimed at possible violations of Federal civil rights statutes. The investigation was reported to be in its early stages.

A Justice Department official said that if solid evidence of criminal violations was developed, the matter would be submitted to a grand jury to determine whether indictments would be issued.

January 5, 1975

Views and Background of Ford Commission Investigating C.I.A.

By ANTHONY RIPLEY
Special to The New York Times

WASHINGTON, Jan. 13— The blue ribbon commission appointed by President Ford to sift the affairs of the Central Intelligence Agency is a heavily interconnected group with at least three members who have had an established relationship with the C.I.A.

Six persons on the eight-member panel, which held its first meeting today, occupied high Government posts in the turbulent nineteen-sixties when Government was confronted with widescale dissent and domestic unrest — unrest and dissent that the C.I.A. was apparently asked to monitor.

Four members are linked together in the vast Rockefeller business, political and charitable enterprises.

Following is a look at each of the eight men who are asked to report to President Ford on the C.I.A. by April 4. They are investigating allegations that the agency may have violated its charter by engaging in domestic spying.

Included are interrelationships among the eight. These ties do not necessarily suggest that because one man may have been close to C.I.A. affairs that the others may have been, too.

Also included are some of their public statements and actions that appear to bear on the task they have undertaken.

Nelson A. Rockefeller

Since 1969, Mr. Rockefeller has served as a member of the President's Foreign Intelligence Advisory Board. It is a high-level civilian review board for the C.I.A. and other intelligence programs.

Last Sept. 23, during his Vice-Presidential confirmation hearings, Mr. Rockefeller was questioned by Senator Mark O. Hatfield, Republican of Oregon.

"Do you believe that the Central Intelligence Agency should ever actively participate in the internal affairs of another sovereign country, such as in the case of Chile?" Senator Hatfield asked.

Mr. Rockefeller replied in part: "I assume they were done in the best national interest . . . I think the flexibility of the present potential actions by our Government are important in the event of some unforeseen circumstances. Therefore, I would question whether the potentiality of activity should be eliminated. . . . I think it would be a mistake.

"How they are conducting what is done is a matter for good judgment."

C. Douglas Dillon

Mr. Dillon is now chairman of the Rockefeller Foundation. As Under Secretary of State, he was part of a Cabinet-level group that reviewed C.I.A. activities. He also served as Secretary of the Treasury, which is involved in domestic intelligence matters through the Internal Revenue Service; the United States Customs Service, the Secret Service, the Consolidated Law Enforcement Training Center and the Bureau of Alcohol, Tobacco and Firearms.

Also, Mr. Dillon has been active with the Council on Foreign Relations. The council has been an object of scorn by both left and right-wing politicians. Some on the staff have old C.I.A. connections.

The council's membership includes some of the most influential men in government, business, education and the press. Though it has no formal role in American foreign policy, it is regarded as the most prestigious group of its kind. Mr. Rockefeller's brother, David, chairman of the Chase Manhattan Bank, is the council's chairman.

In 1960, Mr. Dillon told the world affairs conference of the American Federation of Labor and Congress of Industrial Organizations of the dangers of Communism, rejecting "peaceful co-existence."

"The primary issue today is nothing less than the survival of free men in a free civilization," he said. Later in the same speech he qualified this by saying that the United States must be strong but ready to negotiate.

Lyman L. Lemnitzer

As chairman of the Joint Chiefs of Staff from 1960 to 1963, General Lemnitzer was given daily briefings from the intelligence services, including the C.I.A. Between 1963 and 1969, he was Supreme Allied Commander in Europe, heading the military forces of the North Atlantic Treaty Organization.

As the nation's chief military officer, he presumably would have been aware of the many C.I.A. activities that are paid for through the Defense Department budget. The military services and military "cover" are used routinely for intelligence-gathering by means of military aid, military training missions,

347

electronic surveillance and overseas listening posts.

The general seldom spoke of matters beyond patriotism, duty and the concerns of the military. In 1971, he called the release of a top secret study on the war in Southeast Asia, known as the Pentagon papers, a "traitorous act."

John T. Connor

Mr. Connor is chairman of Allied Chemical Corporation, which has heavy overseas business interests. He is a director of the Chase Manhattan Bank, which is one of the Rockefeller family enterprises. He is also a member of the Council on Foreign Relations.

In 1964, he was one of the business leaders who supported President Johnson for re-election, and he was Mr. Johnson's first Cabinet appointee, as Secretary of Commerce.

In 1970, Mr. Connor spoke out against the invasion of Cambodia, telling presidents and board chairmen of some of the nation's largest corporations at a meeting in Hot Springs, Va., that he was "shocked and stunned" by the action.

He spoke then of the "tragic consequences" of President Johnson's escalation of the Vietnam war in 1964.

"Thousands and thousands of lives have been lost or ruined; our foreign relations have been jeopardized; serious social problems have been caused; our young people have become bitter, reckless and disillusioned, and disastrous inflation rages in the national economy, affecting us all," he said.

Ronald Reagan

The former Governor of California has often spoken on a wide range of national and international issues.

Mr. Reagan, stretching back to his days as an actor when he toured the country making speeches for the General Electric Corporation, has warned against the excesses of big government and against internal and foreign Communist threats.

In April, 1970, in a speech in Yosemite, Calif., he suggested that "if it takes a bloodbath" to silence militant campus demonstrators, "let's get it over with." Later, in Bakersfield, Calif., he said that the "bloodbath" remark "was just a figure of speech—I wasn't even aware I had used that expression."

"I certainly don't think there should be a bloodbath on campus or anywhere else," he said.

Just eight days ago, Mr. Reagan brought up the quotation again at a farewell news conference as Governor. He conceded that it had been "probably a poor choice of words" but insisted that he had never meant that the students would have to undergo a bloodbath.

"I said the administrators now are going to have to dig in their heels, stand firm and take their bloodbath, meaning they were going to have to undergo whatever repercussions from rioting students, and so forth there would be in putting their foot down and saying, 'No more of this.'"

In May, 1973, he attempted to draw a distinction between criminal and illegal behavior in discussing the Watergate affair.

"They did something that was stupid and foolish and was criminal — it was illegal," he said.

"Illegal is a better word than 'criminal' because I think criminal has a different connotation."

He said that those involved in planting electronic bugs at Democratic party headquarters in the Watergate complex were "well-meaning individuals" who were "not criminals at heart."

Erwin N. Griswold

As Solicitor General, Mr. Griswold argued cases for the Johnson and Nixon Administrations before the Supreme Court. He has supported the moral right of dissent against what are considered unjust laws but added that such dissenters should be prepared to go to jail.

He defended the Nixon Administration's use of wiretaps without court orders in cases of suspected subversion but lost the case before the Supreme Court.

He also defended the Government's attempts to prevent publication of the Pentagon papers and defended the Army's right to engage in domestic surveillance.

In an interview in August, 1969, in The Christian Science Monitor, he said, "I think it's terribly important that any repressive forces of society . . . **be thoroughly and carefully kept under public control, with ultimate responsibility back to top Government officials."**

Dr. Shannon, an expert on Tennyson, returned to full-time teaching and research last August after 15 years as presi-

dent of the University of Virginia. Like Mr. Connor, he opposed the Cambodian invasion in 1970. He signed a telegram of protest to Virginia's members of the United States Senate.

He and President Ford met at Williamsburg, Va., at Christmas time in 1973 and subsequently corresponded about the possibility of one of the Ford children attending the university.

He has told friends that he hopes to bring some "humanist concepts" to the work of the commission.

Lane Kirkland

Mr. Kirkland, secretary-treasurer of the A.F.L.-C.I.O. is second in command to George Meany, the president. He serves on the board of the Rockefeller Foundation and is on the National Commission on Critical Choices for Americans, a group organized by Vice President Rockefeller.

In an interview last week on the Public Broadcasting Service program "Washington Straight Talk," Mr. Kirkland stated: "I want no part of any domestic secret police operation in this country. I have those biases and those attitudes.

"As to what the facts of the matter are, as to what's actually been going on, what the truth is, I have no preconceived notions."

He was asked about reports that the C.I.A. had channeled money to A.F.L.-C.I.O. activities overseas. He replied that he knew nothing about it and would be opposed to it.

January 14, 1975

Ford Signs Bill to Avoid Misuse of Records on Citizens

VAIL, Colo., Jan. 1 (AP)—President Ford signed a privacy act today intended to safeguard individuals from the misuse of Federal records, and announced that James T. Lynn, Secretary of Housing and Urban Development, will replace Roy L. Ash as director of the Office of Management and Budget.

In other official action, Mr. Ford pocket-vetoed a bill to increase Government travel allowances and signed an energy research bill.

The President had greeted the

new year with friends and staff, holding a champagne toast at his rented vacation home here.

He went skiing this morning and watched the Rose Bowl game on television as he neared the end of his Vail vacation.

The privacy act was cited by Mr. Ford as "an initial advance in protecting a right precious to every American, the right of individual privacy."

The bill gives individuals the right of access to information on file about them and to have inaccurate data corrected. Ex-

ceptions are provided for law enforcement files and other sensitive records.

A commission will be set up to study how to protect privacy further, and is to submit recommendations within two years.

The bill provides for fines up to $5,000 for violations by Government employes and authorizes damage suits.

The measure restricts the use of Social Security numbers for identification and prohibits any government agency from selling a mailing list unless author-

ized by law.

"This bill, for the most part, strikes a reasonable balance between the right of the individual to be left alone and the interest of society in open government, national defense, foreign policy, law enforcement and a high quality and trustworthy Federal work force," Mr. Ford said.

However, the President said he felt it did not adequately protect the individual against unnecessary disclosures of personal information.

January 2, 1975

POLICE KEPT FILES ON HOUSTON CITIZENS

HOUSTON, Jan. 6 (AP) — Mayor Fred Hofheinz said today that the Houston Police Department had compiled dossiers on a substantial number of residents, including United States Representative Barbara C. Jordan, a Democratic member of the House Judiciary Committee.

Mayor Hofheinz declined to identify any others in the files but said that they included some of Houston's most distinguished citizens. He said that Police Chief Carrol M. Lynn had been asked to purge the files and deliver the dossiers to him.

Chief Lynn said, "I found numerous names of persons on file who were never suspects in any case under investigation and I was surprised to see them there."

"Those responsible for putting the files in the police department will be punished," Mayor Hofheinz said.

He added that the dossiers were compiled before he took office last January. He said that he understood a file on himself had been removed by the time he became mayor.

Mayor Hofheinz said that the files had been held in the police department's criminal intelligence division.

January 7, 1975

Police in Chicago Kept Dossiers On Civic Leaders and Newsmen

By SETH S. KING
Special to The New York Times

CHICAGO, March 22 — Undercover agents of the Chicago Police Department infiltrated several community action organizations during the last several years, and the department's intelligence unit has kept dossiers on scores of Chicago civic leaders, politicians and journalists.

The secret police surveillance of individuals was disclosed yesterday when The Chicago Daily News got the list of those on whom files were kept. The list had been obtained by lawyers through subpoena in an antidiscrimination court action brought by a black policemen's organization.

Earlier in the week The Daily News found that police undercover agents had become active members of such groups as the Metropolitan Area Housing Alliance, an umbrella for several community action organizations; the Rev. Jesse L. Jackson's People United To Save Humanity; the Citizen's Action Program; the Organization for a Better Austin, a community improvement group in that racially changing neighborhood; and the Alliance to End Repression, which concerned itself with cases of alleged police brutality.

The agent who infiltrated the Austin organization, Marcus W. Salone, worked so enthusiastically that he served as president from 1972 until 1974.

The surveillance list covered an incongruous range of persons active in the Chicago area. These included Gaylord Freeman, chairman of the First National Bank and Arthur Woods, chairman of Sears Roebuck and Company, who are reported to be contributors to the Black Strategy Center in 1969; the Rev. Theodore Hesburgh, president of the University of Notre Dame; Gayle Sayers, former star running back of the Chicago Bears; Alexander Polikoff and Marshall Patner, civil liberties lawyers; State Senator Richard Newhouse, a black lawyer who ran against Mayor Richard J. Daley in the recent primary; Len O'Connor, a television commentator, and Mike Royko, a Daily News columnist, both of whom have written books critical of the Mayor, and the Republican States Attorney, Bernard M. Carey.

Mr. Carey, who tried yesterday without success to obtain the dossier kept on him, announced he would present the police surveillance matter to a Cook County grand jury for investigation.

A Police Denial

CHICAGO, March 23 (AP)— James M. Rochford, the city Police Superintendant, flatly denied today that his department had kept intelligence files on Mr. Carey.

He said that he would not reply to charges that files were kept on various civic groups pending further study.

Mr. Rochford told newsmen that "There are no personal files," on Mr. Carey, State Senator Newhouse, or Father Hesburgh.

March 23, 1975

POLICE RED SQUAD TOLD TO DISBAND

Michigan Judge Also Orders Destruction of 50,000 Files

Special to The New York Times

LANSING, Mich., Jan. 18—A judge has ordered the Subversive Activities Unit of the Michigan State Police disbanded and its files on 50,000 persons destroyed after ruling that two state laws authorizing creation of the 29-member "Red Squad" violate the state and Federal constitutions.

Two attorneys of the American Civil Liberties Union said Friday that they would appeal the decision by Judge Thomas L. Brown of Ingham County Circuit Court because he did not require the state police to notify those on whom data were collected so that they could examine their files.

The Red Squad, which has an annual budget of more than $750,000, was created under a criminal syndicalism law of 1931 that makes it a crime to advocate terrorism as a means of achieving industrial or political reform. A subversive activity law of 1950 also authorized the unit.

Judge Brown described as "ridiculous" a section of the law of 1931 making display of a red flag a felony and prima facie evidence that one advocates anarchy.

He said both laws and the existence of the Red Squad had a "chilling effect" on rights of free speech, assembly and petitioning the government for redress of grievances.

The state police have acknowledged that no arrests have been made under either law. The Michigan Attorney General, Frank Kelly, agreed in court that the two statutes were unconstitutional.

Judge Brown ruled in a lawsuit to end the Red Squad, filed last April by Zolton Ferency, former Democratic candidate for governor, on behalf of the Human Rights Party of Michigan, which Mr. Ferency now heads.

Two years ago a separate lawsuit to disband the unit was filed in Detroit by 13 persons. They are represented by Richard Soble and George Corsetti, who said they wanted all people on whom files were kept to be given a chance to examine them before the files were destroyed.

Mr. Corsetti charged that the files had been used to ruin careers and reputations.

He said there was evidence that materials from the squad's files on workers who organized health and safety grievances at the Chrysler Corporation had been turned over to Chrysler security officials. A Chrysler spokesman said the company had no such material in its personnel files.

January 19, 1976

C.I.A.-F.B.I. INQUIRY VOTED BY SENATE

Church Is Expected to Be Named Chairman—Panel to Bar 'TV Spectacular'

By DAVID E. ROSENBAUM
Special to The New York Times

WASHINGTON, Jan. 27—The Senate voted, 82 to 4, today to create a special committee to investigate the operations of the Central Intelligence Agency, the Federal Bureau of Investigation and more than a dozen other intelligence and law enforcement agencies of the Government.

Senator Frank Church of Idaho, a severe critic of some practices of the C.I.A., is expected to be named chairman.

The other Democrats named today to the 11-member panel by Senator Mike Mansfield of Montana, the Democratic leader, were Philip A. Hart of Michigan, Walter F. Mondale of Minnesota, Walter D. Huddleston of Kentucky, Gary W. Hart of Colorado and Robert B. Morgan of North Carolina.

Senator Hugh Scott of Pennsylvania, the Republican leader, appointed the Republican committee members last week. They are John G. Tower of Texas, Howard H. Baker Jr. of Tennessee, Charles McC. Mathias of Maryland, Richard S. Schweiker of Pennsylvania and Barry Goldwater of Arizona.

The committee was created by a Senate resolution, the same procedure used two years ago to establish the committee that investigated the Watergate burglary and its aftermath.

Four Southern conservatives voted against creation of the panel. They were Jesse A. Helms of North Carolina, William L. Scott of Virginia and Strom Thurmond of South Carolina, all Republicans, and Herman E. Talmadge, Democrat of Georgia. None expressed his opposition in today's floor debate.

The inquiry results from disclosures of apparently illegal domestic operations of the C.I.A. involving American citizens and later disclosures of F.B.I. files on members of Congress.

Senators of both parties promised today not to allow the panel's hearings to develop into a "television spectacular" and they pledged to restrict the kind of unauthorized leaks of information that haunted the Watergate committee.

Nonetheless, it seemed likely that the committee's inquiry would permit the most extensive public inquiry ever into the activities of the C.I.A., the F.B.I., military intelligence agencies.

Meanwhile, today, President Ford's C.I.A. investigating commission, headed by Vice President Rockefeller, held a third day of closed hearings. It heard testimony from William E. Colby, Director of Central Intelligence, and a former official of the agency, Richard Ober.

Just as Sam J. Ervin Jr., the former Democratic Senator from North Carolina, set the tone of the Watergate committee's hearings in his role as chairman, so Senator Church is expected to impart his personal style and manner to the investigation of the intelligence erations.

Tops in Seniority

The six Democrats on the panel will select their chairman. Senator Church, who is 50 years old and has served in the Senate since 1957, has more seniority than the other Democrats on the committee, and there was little doubt that he would be chosen.

The six Democrats are scheduled to meet in Senator Church's office tomorrow to name the chairman formally and to plan for the investigation. Senator Philip Hart, who is second in seniority among the committee Democrats, said that he would nominate Mr. Church.

Two years ago, Mr. Church, who is chairman of the Foreign Relations Committee's Subcommittee on Mulinational Corporations, held highly publicized hearings into the International Telephone and Telegraph Corporation's attempts to promote United States intervention against the Chilean Government of Salvador Allende Gossens.

After it was disclosed that the C.I.A. had been secretly authorized to spend more than $8-million in an effort to make it impossible for Mr. Allende to govern, Mr. Church accused Government officials of having lied at his hearings about the extent of the covert operations in Chile.

Fair Inquiry Pledged

Mr. Church said today that he still could not reconcile the intelligence agency's activities in Chile "with the professed principles of the United States." But he said that his earlier criticism of the agency would not affect his ability to conduct a fair inquiry.

"We'll be dealing with very sensitive matters," Mr. Church said in an interview. "We must remain mindful of two responsibilities. One [is] the national security interest of the United States. The other is the right of the people to know what, if any, transgressions have taken place. I think the facts can be made public in such a way that they will not seriously impair the national security."

The other Democrats on the committee have had little experience with foreign affairs.

Senators Hart and Mondale are liberals who have been active for years in support of civil rights legislation and domestic social programs. Both operate quietly and have a reputation among their colleagues for sound judgment They opposed the Vietnam policies of the Johnson and Nixon administrations.

Senator Huddleston, who was elected to the Senate in 1972, is considered a moderate on most issues. In foreign affairs, he has tended to support the stands of liberal Democrats.

Senator Gary Hart and Senator Morgan were elected last November.

Gary Hart was the manager of Senator George McGovern's 1972 Presidential campaign and his views on foreign policy have been closely identified with Mr. McGovern's antiwar stand.

Senator Morgan is considered a conservative. He has considerable experience in law enforcement, having served for five years as Attorney General of North Carolina. He was elected to the seat vacated by Senator Ervin's retirement.

Among the Republicans, Senators Tower and Goldwater are conservatives who have said that they would have preferred that the inquiry into C.I.A. practices be left to the Armed Services Committee, on which they sit. Senator Tower will be the special committee's vice chairman.

Senator Baker is a moderate who was the ranking Republican on the Watergate committee. During that panel's investigation, he conducted a separate inquiry into the C.I.A.'s connection with the Watergate burglary and its cover-up.

Senators Mathias and Schweiker are among the most liberal Republicans in the Senate, and both have been critical of Government policy in Indochina.

Members Not Notified

Senator Mansfield said that he had not notified the Democratic members of the special committee before their names were announced on the Senate floor following today's vote.

"I wanted people who I thought would do a good, judicious job," Mr. Mansfield said. "I wanted youngsters in there, and I wanted people who would have a fresh, open outlook on intelligence activities over all."

Senator John O. Pastore, Democrat of Rhode Island, who sponsored the resolution creating the special committee, said in a floor speech that the various intelligence agencies were "absolutely necessary to the survival of the country."

But he said that there had been "serious abuses." The purpose of the investigating committee, he said, is "to find out how [the abuses] started, how far they went and to remedy these abuses and make sure it doesn't happen again."

The resolution was worded broadly enough to give the special committee considerable latitude in deciding what agencies to investigate.

The panel was authorized to investigate "the extent, if any, to which illegal, improper or unethical activities were engaged in by any agency or by any persons, acting either individually or in combination with others, in carrying out any intelligence or surveillance activities by or on behalf of any agency of the Federal Government."

Other Agencies Listed

In addition to the C.I.A. and the F.B.I., the agencies subject to scrutiny include the Defense Intelligence Agency, the National Security Agency, the Department of State's Bureau of Intelligence and Research, the intelligence branches of the Army, Navy and Air Force and the Treasury Department's Bureau of Alcohol, Tobacco and Firearms.

Senator Tower told his colleagues on the Senate floor that much of the committee's work would have to be done in closed session to provide "adequate safeguards" for intelligence operations.

But Senator Alan Cranston, Democrat of California, who worked actively for establishment of the special committee, argued that "the emphasis throughout should be on sharing the maximum amount of information with the public."

"There are some powerful incentives for a cover-up," he said. "Individuals and agencies involved in wrongdoing or questionable practices must be identified."

January 28, 1975

EX-F.B.I. OFFICIAL TESTIFIED AGNEW WAS INVESTIGATED

By NICHOLAS M. HORROCK

Special to The New York Times

WASHINGTON, Feb. 2—The former No. 3 man in the Federal Bureau of Investigation testified under oath in 1973 that the bureau investigated Spiro T. Agnew shortly before the 1968 election at the request of President Johnson.

In heretofore unpublished testimony, Cartha D. DeLoach, formerly assistant to the director of the F.B.I., asserted that shortly before Mr. Agnew was elected Vice President, President Johnson asked the bureau to investigate him on a matter of "the gravest national security" and that an investigation was conducted.

The testimony was taken by Senator Howard H. Baker Jr., Republican of Tennessee, and Senate Watergate committee staff investigators.

Of the F.B.I. investigation, Mr. DeLoach said "that the reason this was being done was because they felt the Republicans—and this was their [the White House] statement—the Republicans were attempting to slow down the South Vietnamese from going to the Paris peace talks and they wanted to know who either Mr. Nixon or Mr. Agnew had been in touch with from Albuquerque when they visited the city several days prior to that."

Mr. DeLoach said that the late J. Edgar Hoover had authorized an investigation and that the Domestic Intelligence Division of the F.B.I. had obtained the toll call receipts of persons on Mr. Agnew's staff in an effort to discover if anyone had called Mrs. Anna Chennault.

Mrs. Chennault, widow of the commander of the Flying Tigers in World War II, was alleged to have been an intermediary between the South Vietnamese and the Republicans.

Sources who worked on the White House staff in 1968 dispute the genesis of the investigation. They say it was the F.B.I. that first suggested Republican links to the South Vietnamese.

Mr. DeLoach also said in his testimony that Mrs. Chennault had been the subject of "physical surveillance" by the F.B.I. that involved following her with teams of agents.

According to sources within the bureau in 1968, it was President Johnson's concern over opponents of his Vietnam policy that resulted in a team of Washington field office agents being assigned to prepare reports for the White House on any political figures who entered the Soviet Embassy on 16th Street NW in Washington.

Published reports have long noted that the bureau maintained a constant physical surveillance of the embassy and filmed all persons who entered or left.

The bureau has declined comment on a number of allegations that it entered into widespread political activity in the last decade for its own purposes or at the behest of President Johnson and Nixon, pending the upcoming Congressional testimony of Clarence M. Kelley, the F.B.I. director.

As a matter of routine, the bureau made an index reference of each person who was seen at the Soviet Embassy and attempted to establish his identity and whether the visit involved a breach of national security.

When Mr. DeLoach ordered the special survey, Courtland J. Jones, a supervisor of the national security team in the Washington field offices, was put in charge of a survey of the index cards to detect the involvement of any prominent figures or politicians.

F.B.I. sources said they had been told that the special survey was on behalf of the White House.

The special survey went on for some time, according to one former F.B.I. official, "and it engendered numerous reports to the White House."

Mr. Jones declined comment. Mr. DeLoach was unavailable after repeated attempts to reach him.

Reports on Congressmen

One source said he believed that the operation might have resulted in reports on at least a dozen Senators and Representatives being sent to the White House. A White House aide during that period said he could not deny that such an operation had taken place, but he said that much of the data had been offered voluntarily by the F.B.I. and not because President Johnson had asked for it.

This source said that he could not recall seeing any stream of data on political figures involved with the Soviet Embassy coming into the White House.

One former bureau official said that such reports, particularly if the President passed them on to anyone, would compromise the F.B.I.'s then completely secret surveillance techniques at the Embassy.

This F.B.I. source said the operation had resulted in boxes of logs and records and that there were some indications that these may have been destroyed.

Domestic intelligence and political activities were laid to the bureau during the Senate Watergate hearings in 1973. The Chicago Tribune and the Scripps-Howard newspapers compiled major reports on F.B.I. activity and reported that bureau agents had been sent to the Democratic National Convention in Atlantic City in 1964 at the behest of President Johnson; that the bureau allegedly gathered material for Mr. Johnson on Senator Barry Goldwater, Republican of Arizona, his opponent in the 1964 Presidential race, and that the bureau routinely gave various Presidents information on political and public figures.

The first indication of the investigation of Mr. Agnew was given in these press reports.

Mr. DeLoach has denied that he was a protege of President Johnson's but he has acknowledged that the President requested him to assume liaison duties with the White House because Mr. Johnson had known him as a Senator.

Mr. DeLoach has also acknowledged that Mr. Johnson ordered a direct telephone line to the White House installed in the bedroom of Mr. DeLoach's home.

White House aides from the Johnson era said that an enormous amount of F.B.I. intelligence flowed in between 1964 and 1968 and was handled with the utmost secrecy.

It was reportedly delivered to Walter Jenkins, a Presidential aide, and when he left office it was delivered to a secretary, James Jones, now a Democratic Representative from Oklahoma, and W. Marvin Watson.

After Mr. Jenkins left government in October, 1964, following an arrest, Mr. DeLoach testified, the number of field investigations ordered on Johnson appointees was so great that Mr. Hoover complained of the burden.

During the Nixon era, the Watergate hearings brought out, the White House used a request for a background check on a CBS newsman, Daniel Schorr, as a method of harassing private citizens.

President Johnson was regularly supplied by the F.B.I. with confidential information, including details of a prominent Republican Senator's sexual activities, Time magazine reports in its current issue.

But Time said that Mr. Johnson sometimes denounced tapping telephones as "the worst thing in our society."

The magazine said the information had been given to the President by J. Edgar Hoover, then F.B.I. director.

The magazine also said that Mr. Johnson got the transcript and tapes of the late Rev. Martin Luther King, Jr.'s personal activities.

February 3, 1975

Levi Details Wide Scope Of Hoover's Secret Files

By NICHOLAS M. HORROCK

Special to The New York Times

WASHINGTON, Feb. 27—J. Edgar Hoover, as director of the Federal Bureau of Investigation, kept secret files of derogatory information on Presidents, members of Congress, Federal officials and those who simply tried to oppose him, Attorney General Edward H. Levi testified today.

Several of the occurrences confirmed in Mr. Levi's testimony have been hinted in published press accounts for years and others have been charged by former F.B.I. officials. But the description and detail on Mr. Hoover's private files was both startling and previously unrevealed.

In the first detailed, official account of the late Mr. Hoover's secret files, Mr. Levi said the Department of Justice had found evidence that in at least one case the F.B.I. director had disseminated derogatory information on a Congressman to members of the executive branch of Government.

The Attorney General told members of the House Subcommittee on Civil Rights and Constitutional Rights that he could also confirm a series of incidents in which the F.B.I. had been misused for political purposes or to serve the whim of past Presidents.

Deputy Attorney General

Laurence H. Silberman said after the hearing that it was President Kennedy, Johnson and Nixon who had made a misuse of the bureau's files and manpower.

The Justice Department cited specific incidents of misuse by President Johnson, but not by Mr. Kennedy and Mr. Nixon.

Midway through his testimony, Mr. Levi noted that "at this point I believe I must refer to a past practice of the bureau with respect to certain files, not with reference to their subject matter, but to their location."

He said the F.B.I. had found a group of files marked "official and confidential" or simply "OC" that were kept in Mr. Hoover's private office and were not part of the over-all bureau filing system.

These files, he said, consisted of some 164 file jackets or folders, dated back to 1920. When Mr. Hoover died on May 2, 1972, these files were moved to the office of W. Mark Felt, then associate director of the F.B.I.

It was not clear from Mr. Levi's testimony whether the two past acting F.B.I. directors, L. Patrick Gray 3d or William D. Ruckelshaus, were ever advised of the existence of the files, but bureau sources said privately that they were not.

The files apparently came into the hands of the current F.B.I. director, Clarence M. Kelley, fairly recently. They were never mentioned publicly during the term of Attorney General William B. Saxbe who stepped down last month to become Ambassador to India.

The secret Hoover files, Mr. Levi testified, contained, among other things, 48 folders on "public figures or prominent persons," which Mr. Levi said included "Presidents, executive branch employes and 17 individuals who were members of Congress." He said two of the men named in the files were still in Congress.

Mr. Levi said the files told of an instance in which an F.B.I. agent "forwarded derogatory information to Mr. Hoover concerning a Congressman who had attacked the director, "adding, "The file contains a document which indicates that Mr. Hoover disseminated the derogatory information to others in the executive branch."

There was also evidence in the files that Mr. Hoover used material from his files in meetings with Congressmen, Mr. Levi testified.

The files were also instructive about Mr. Hoover's personality, it was said. One file, for instance, covered "five decades" of activity and had been kept up year by year, Mr. Levi said.

He also said there were memorandums regarding efforts of various persons to have Mr. Hoover replaced, as well as information about an alleged smear campaign against him and derogatory remarks made about him. He also kept files on the poor attitude of an F.B.I. employe and letters from F.B.I. men on personal matters, Mr. Levi said.

According to Mr. Levi, Mr. Hoover had maintained such a personal file since 1920 but in 1941 pruced it up and reorganized it. At that time he described his secret file as "various and sundry items believed inadvisable to be included in the general files of the bureau."

Mr. Kelley testified that the bureau had no idea whether the material it found was complete. He said that Mr. Hoover had "purged" his personal files for "a year before his death" and that at the time of his death substantial material had been moved from the bureau to Mr. Hoover's home in the northwest area of Washington. •

Mr. Kelley said he believed the material moved to Mr. Hoover's home was in the nature of personal financial matters, correspondence and items of historical value, but he said he did not have a clear list.

Mr. Levi said that an internal review of F.B.I. files had revealed the instances of "misuse" of the F.B.I., including several involving Presidents. In one case, he said, the bureau was used to gather political intelligence.

Later Justice officials confirmed one such incident, in 1964, when a former White House aide, Bill Moyers, asked the bureau to gather data on campaign aides to Senator Barry Goldwater, the Republican Presidential candidate.

Mr. Moyers made the request on behalf of President Johnson a few weeks before Election Day, Mr. Silberman said, and no derogatory material was uncovered.

Mr. Levi said that in another instance "a President caused the F.B.I. to gather intelligence relating to a political convention under circumstances that, although cast in legitimate law enforcement terms, could—and some would say should—have been suspected of being politically motivated."

Later, department officials confirmed that Mr. Levi was referring to a 1964 case where President Johnson may have derived political information overheard from a wiretap of the late Rev. Dr. Martin Luther King Jr. at the Democratic National Convention.

Department officials also confirmed an incident in 1968 shortly before the election when President Johnson may have derived political advantage from an F.B.I. investigation.

Other Justice sources privately confirmed that this was the incident in which the F.B.I. obtained the telephone toll records of members of the staff of Spiro T. Agnew, then the Republican candidate for Vice President.

The toll records were obtained after a request came to the F.B.I. from a key aide to President Johnson, these sources said, adding that the request was made on the basis of national security at that time.

Mr. Levi cited instances in which incumbent Presidents had ordered the bureau to report on the activities of members of Congress. Justice Department officials later said that Presidents Kennedy, Johnson and Nixon had indulged in this practice.

In another instance, Mr. Levi testified, the F.B.I. was used to conduct an investigation of another Federal law enforcement agency. Justice Department officials later said the incident arose during the 1965 investigation of Bobby Baker, former Senate Democratic majority aide. At that time the Criminal Division of the Department of Justice requested the bureau to fit out an informer with a secret radio transmitter so that his conversations with principals in the case could be recorded.

The bureau refused to do so and, Justice officials said, the Criminal Division turned to the Treasury Department's Federal Narcotics Bureau.

In 1967 when President Johnson found out that the Narcotics Bureau had assumed this task in the case involving his long-time protégé, Bobby Baker, Justice officials said, he ordered the F.B.I. to conduct an investigation of the Treasury Department to determine if any of the officials involved were friends or supporters of then Attorney General Robert F. Kennedy.

Mr. Levi's nearly two-hour-long testimony was met with criticism and suspicion by several members of the committee, more on the ground of what it revealed about the general F.B.I. practice of accepting and filing unsupported allegations.

Mr. Kelley confirmed that the bureau receives and files allegations that have no connection with any criminal or national security investigation.

The rationale he and Mr. Levi offered was that the materia might be useful in the future. Neither man testified on just what proportion of the bureau's 6.5 million files (not counting criminal conviction and arrest records) are made up of such allegations.

Mr. Levi left the committee with a pledge that he and other Justice Department officials were working on "guidelines" to prevent the misuses of the F.B.I. in the future.

"I would be disturbed at the thought of an F.B.I. director maintaining files on specific individuals in his own personal offices with the unavoidable consequences that the files would be generally suspected of being "dossiers' with various connotations as to purpose or use . . . Director Kelley and I both agree that such files should not be so maintained."

February 28, 1975

F.B.I. HARASSED A LEFTIST PARTY

By NICHOLAS M. HORROCK
Special to The New York Times

WASHINGTON, March 18—The Federal Bureau of Investigation harassed the Socialist Workers party for a decade with efforts to have members dismissed from their jobs, with leaks to news media of unsavory items about their personal lives and attempts to encourage police agencies to press petty prosecutions, newly released bureau documents show.

As a result of a court order in a civil suit brought in Federal District Court in New York, the F.B.I. was compelled last week to release 3,138 pages of internal documents to the party and its youth arm, the Young Socialist Alliance.

It is one of the largest disclosures of internal F.B.I. workings in the history of the bureau and probably the most revealing set of documents since the theft of F.B.I. documents in Media, Pa., in 1971, laying bare bureau operations in Pennsylvania. The papers were made available to The New York Times today.

The documents have also been made available to the Senate Select Committee on Intelligence headed by Senator Frank Church, Democrat of Idaho, a Socialist Workers source confirmed.

The carton of papers sketched 31 years of bureau attention to the Socialist Workers party that included detailed investigations of virtually every officer or official the 2,500-member party ever had.

It also included 573 pages of documents on 41 operations of the bureau's Counter-intelligence Program against the party. The documents describe Cointelpro as trying to "disrupt" party activities and harass party members and their families.

A spokesman said the F.B.I. declined to comment on the questions raised by the documents because it involved a matter still in litigation. The rationale for the bureau's unusual attention to the Socialist Workers party could not be learned. The party was never publicly linked to the violence of the antiwar years or money and control from Communist nations abroad.

Despite three decades of intensive investigation and at least one period—from 1961 to 1971—of covert efforts to destroy the party and frighten its members, there is no indication that the bureau brought any charges. Two spokesmen for the Political Right Defense Fund, Catherine Perkus and Syd Stapleton, said that neither the party nor the youth group had been the subject of a Federal prosecution since several cases in 1945.

Sources within the Department of Justice confirmed that they had "no memory" of any Federal prosecutions of the party or its membership within the last two decades.

Most of the investigations of the party and its members appeared to have been conducted under the authority of Federal statutes covering rebellion and insurrection; seditious conspiracy advocating the overthrow of the Government; the Internal Security Act of 1950 and the Communist Control Act of 1954.

Portions of two of the main acts relied upon in the F.B.I. investigation as late as 1973, the McCarran and the Smith acts, had been declared unconstitutional. There appeared to be no legal justification for the Cointelpro techniques. In a report on Cointelpro issues last fall by then Attorney General William B. Saxbe, many of the techniques were called illegal.

Thus, it was the 573 pages on "disruption" of the Socialist Workers party that remained the most startling. The documents indicate that one of the earliest operations began in the fall of 1961. It was aimed at John Clearence Franklin, then the party's candidate for Borough President of Manhattan in New York City.

The papers indicate that the bureau discovered a record of criminal convictions in the files of the Albany, N. Y., Police Department that it believed to be Mr. Franklin's. The New York office of the bureau recommended that the record be given secretly to F.B.I. contacts in the press for publication.

In a cable from Washington, under the auspices of the Director of the F.B.I., the bureau gave this response:

"This suggestion is an excellent example of the type desired by the bureau under the disruption program. The bureau is pleased to note that the suggestion was well thought out and it is felt that if future suggestions are submitted with the same amount of preparation and planning, this program will be exceedingly successful."

In a bureau cable dated Nov. 8, 1961, the New York field office took credit for planting the Franklin police record in a column called "On The Town," written by Charles McHarry in The New York Daily News.

"The attention of (blank) was directed to this item on 11/7/61, without, of course, revealing the bureau as being the source," the F.B.I. cable said.

Jack Metcalfe, a spokesman for The Daily News, said the paper would have "no immediate comment" but the matter was being looked into.

The attempt to discredit Socialist Worker political candidates cropped up routinely in the documents. They show that the bureau mailed an anonymous letter on Clifton Deberry, a candidate for Mayor of New York in 1964, which said he had been convicted in Chicago for nonsupport of his first wife and raised questions about the legitimacy of his current marriage.

The letters were mailed to The New York Times, The Daily News, The Journal-American and the New York television outlets of C.B.S. and N.B.C., but there is no indication that any of these organizations used the material. Indeed, bureau documents show that agents were disturbed because the material had not been used.

On Oct. 29, 1965, the New York office reported to Washington: "Since the N.Y.C. elections will be held 11/2/65, it appears that no positive results have been obtained from this operation."

In Denver, the Bureau's field office obtained permission to mail an anonymous letter signed, "A Concerned Mother," to the president of the Denver school board hinting that Allen Taplen, a member of the party who in 1965 was a candidate for membership on the board, was a Communist. Mr. Taplen was not elected.

In 1968, the bureau circulated what it called an "uncomplimentary squib" about Fred Halstead, then the party's candidate for President, to military agencies to try to disrupt Mr. Halstead's attempt to campaign among American troops.

The documents revealed several operations where the bureau secretly tried to bring members of the party under local police and state pressure. In December, 1961, the bureau determined that a party vacation retreat called Mountain Spring Camp in Washington, N. J., did not have a liquor license, yet it apparently served beer and other alcoholic beverages.

In nine months of secret manipulations, the papers show, always trying to keep the bureau's role anonymous, the Newark field office encouraged a raid on the camp by the New Jersey Alcoholic Beverage Board and the state police.

The raid was conducted on Sept. 1, 1962, over the Labor Day weekend.

Sixteen bottles of liquor and 70 bottles of beer were "confiscated," and later two people pleaded guilty to liquor violations. "It is the opinion of the N.Y.O. [New York Office]," one F.B.I. document read, "that this had been a very successful disruptive tactic with both immediate and long-term results reflecting adversely upon the S.W.P."

In a similar operation in 1966, the papers indicate, the F.B.I. made an anonymous telephone report to the New York State Department of Labor alleging that a print shop operated by the party was attempting to defraud the state by creating bogus unemployment insurance claims for party members.

The bureau, the documents show, later developed a covert contact with an official of the department who reported that it had discovered one violation. Spokesmen for the Socialist Workers said party officials remembered that an audit of the records of the print shop was conducted in 1966 or 1967.

The F.B.I. also made several attempts to put pressure on party members who were not connected with political activity or a given party function, the documents indicate.

In one case outlined in the documents, the F.B.I. wrote an anonymous letter, with full approval from the director's office, to the management of The Paterson (N. J.) Morning Call, a now-defunct daily newspaper. The letter informed the Call that one of its reporters had allegedly been a member of the party.

A report from an informant, noted in the document, later said the reporter "is having difficulties at his job. . .because of his affiliation with the S.W.P." Another bureau document noted that the reporter "was told by his employer to discontinue his S.W.P. activities if he wants to hold his job as a newspaper man."

The Newark F.B.I. field office, the papers show, asked permission to mail a letter attacking the reporter's personal mores to the father of a woman friend of his but was not given permission by Washington. Washington said the idea might be resubmitted at a later date.

The reporter, Murray Zuckoff, is now a staff member of the Jewish Telegraphic News Agency in New York. He said today in a telephone interview that he had no knowledge that the bureau had sent a letter to his employers and he believed that reports of bureau documents indicating that his job had been threatened were exaggerated. He said he

thought that 1966 was a zenith year for his reporting and that he had remained with the Paterson paper until it was bought by another publication in 1969.

In another instance, according to the documents, the bureau had been in touch with the Boy Scouts of America and tried to have a scoutmaster in Orange, N. J., removed from his job because his wife was a member of the party.

The bureau authorized the Newark office, according to the papers, to "orally" inform the Boy Scouts of the man's alleged subversive background, yet none of the documents indicate what the background was except that the man's wife was associated with the party. One F.B.I. report noted, "Newark has advised that its files contain no public source information of a subversive nature concerning the man."

In July, 1968, the documents disclose the Newark office reported that the man had not been registered as a scoutmaster. The man's removal "from the scouting program, where he would have strong influence in the shaping of the minds of young boys, reflects the successful application of the disruption program for a worthy cause," the bureau report goes on.

The papers show that there was a constant attempt to disrupt internally the party's activities and to put it against other organizations in the left and civil rights movement.

In one instance, in 1964, the F.B.I., according to the documents, mailed an anonymous letter to several newspapers alleging that the party was capitalizing on a Southern civil rights legal case for its own profit. There was no indication that any of the publications wrote an article as a result of the letter.

In connection with the same operation, the bureau took an account of a robbery of one of the principals in a defense committee from the Charlotte Observer of Feb. 27, 1964, and added a limerick written by F.B.I. agents to make it appear the robbery was a cover for the socialist workers to abscond with the funds. The F.B.I.'s anonymous verse went as follows:

Georgie-Porgie, down in
    Monroe
Found himself alone with
    the dough,
Called the cops, and what
    did he say?
Bad guys came and took it
    away.

This piece of verse and the clipping also went to several newspapers and again there was no indication that it served as a base for a news article.

March 19, 1975

House Unit Is Told That C.I.A. Spied on Mail to Red Countries

WASHINGTON, March 21 (UPI)—The Central Intelligence Agency, with full cooperation from the Postal Service, illegally opened some mail that was sent between the United States and Communist countries between 1953 and 1973, Congressional testimony disclosed today.

The mail surveillance operation was outlined to the House Civil Liberties Subcommittee in closed session last Tuesday by the chief postal inspector, William J. Cotter, and elaborated on today by Dr. Melvin Crain, a former C.I.A. agent who was involved in the operation.

"The letters were opened, reproduced, resealed and sent on their way without interrupting mail flow or their opening in anyway being detected," Dr. Crain said.

According to law, any Government agency wishing to open first-class mail must obtain a search and seizure order from a Federal court.

The subcommittee chairman, Robert W. Kastenmeier, Democrat of Wisconsin, said the program "to intercept, open, and duplicate the mail of American citizens [was] in direct violation of the letter and spirit of the law."

Critical of Activity

"I find this program to be a reprehensible manifestation of the view that so-called 'national security' concerns outweigh the rights of citizens to privacy of their associations, papers and communications," Mr. Kastenmeier said.

In his Tuesday testimony, Mr. Cotter said the mail opening operation had taken place at Kennedy International Airport in New York and in San Francisco.

He expressed the belief that every President going back to Dwight D. Eisenhower was "aware of this activity conducted by the C.I.A." He also testified that during the Administration of Richard M. Nixon two top officials—Postmaster General Winton M. Blount and Attorney General John N. Mitchell—not only knew about the operation but also condoned it.

Dr. Crain said he was told at a C.I.A. briefing that the mail-opening activity was the result of a joint operation among the C.I.A., Federal Bureau of Investigation and the Post Office.

Dr. Crain, who said all covert intelligence activities by the United States should be stopped, detailed how he had "personally witnessed and handled" the letters that regularly came through his office.

"There were hundreds and hundreds of them," he said. "It must not continue. It must not recur. The 'mail must go through' all right—but unopened by spooks."

Mr. Cotter said he knew of the mail opening in his capacity as an assistant C.I.A. agent in the early nineteen-fifties. He said the C.I.A. activity was suspended in 1973 and to his knowledge, has not been continued since.

March 22, 1975

SUMMARY OF ROCKEFELLER PANEL'S C.I.A. REPORT

Special to The New York Times

WASHINGTON, June 10—Following is the text of the summary of the investigation conducted for President Ford by the Commission on C.I.A. Activities Within the United States. The report of the commission, headed by Vice President Rockefeller, was made public today.

The Fundamental Issues

In announcing the formation of this Commission, the President noted that an effective intelligence and counterintelligence capability is essential to provide "the safeguards that protect our national interest and help avert armed conflicts."

While it is vital that security requirements be met, the President continued, it is equally important that intelligence activities be conducted without "impairing our democratic institutions and fundamental freedoms."

The Commission's assessment of the CIA's activities within the United States reflects the members' deep concern for both individual rights and national security.

A. Individual Rights

The Bill of Rights in the Constitution protects individual liberties against encroachment by government. Many statutes and the common law also reflect this protection.

The First Amendment protects the freedoms of speech and of the press, the right of the people to assemble peaceably, and the right to petition the government for redress of grievances. It has been construed to protect freedom of peaceable political association.

In addition, the Fourth Amendment declares:

The right of the people to be secure in their persons, houses, papers, and effects, against unreasonable searches and seizures, shall not be violated. . . .

In accordance with the objectives enunciated in these and other Constitutional amendments, the Supreme Court has outlined the following basic Constitutional doctrines:

1. Any intrusive investigation of an American citizen by the government must have a sufficient basis to warrant the invasion caused by the particular investigative practices which are utilized;
2. Government monitoring of a citizen's political activities requires even greater justification;
3. The scope of any resulting intrusion on personal privacy must not exceed the degree reasonably believed necessary;
4. With certain exceptions, the scope of which are not sharply defined, these conditions must be met, at least for significant investigative intrusions, to the satisfaction of an uninvolved governmental body such as a court.

These Constitutional standards give content to an accepted principle of our society—the right of each person to a high degree of individual privacy.

In recognition of this right, President Truman and the Congress—in enacting the law creating the CIA in 1947—included a clause providing that the CIA should have no police, subpoena, law-enforcement powers or internal security functions.

Since then, Congress has further outlined citizen rights in statutes limiting electronic surveillance and granting individuals access to certain information in government files,[1] underscoring the general concern of Congress and the Executive Branch in this area.

---

1 Omnibus Crime Control and Safe Streets Act of 1968 (18 U.S.C. Secs. 2510-26) and Privacy Act of 1974 (5 U.S.C. Sec. 552a).

B. Government Must Obey the Law

The individual liberties of American citizens depend on government observance of the law.

Under our form of Constitutional government, authority can be exercised only if it has been properly delegated to a particular department or agency by the Constitution or Congress.

Most delegations come from Congress; some are implied from the allocation of responsibility to the President. Wherever the basic authority resides, however, it is fundamental in our scheme of Constitutional government that agencies—including the CIA—shall exercise only those powers properly assigned to them by Congress or the President.

Whenever the activities of a government agency exceed its authority, individual liberty may be impaired.

C. National Security

Individual liberties likewise depend on maintaining public order at home and in protecting the country against infiltration from abroad and armed attack. Ensuring domestic tranquility and providing for a common defense are not only Constitutional goals but necessary pre-conditions for a free, democratic system. The process of orderly and lawful change is the essence of democracy. Violent change, or forcing a change of government by the stealthy action of "enemies, foreign or domestic," is contrary to our Constitutional system.

The government has both the right and the obligation within Constitutional limits to use its available power to protect the people and their established form of government. Nevertheless, the mere invocation of the "national security" does not grant unlimited power to the government. The degree of the danger and the type of action contemplated to meet that danger require careful evaluation, to ensure that the danger is sufficient to justify the action and that fundamental rights are respected.

D. Resolving the Issues

Individual freedoms and privacy are fundamental in our society. Constitu-

tional government must be maintained. An effective and efficient intelligence system is necessary; and to be effective, many of its activities must be conducted in secrecy.

Satisfying these objectives presents considerable opportunity for conflict. The vigorous pursuit of intelligence by certain methods can lead to invasions of individual rights. The preservation of the United States requires an effective intelligence capability, but the preservation of individual liberties within the United States requires limitations or restrictions on gatherings of intelligence. The drawing of reasonable lines-where legitimate intelligence needs end and erosion of Constitutional government begins—is difficult.

In seeking to draw such lines, we have been guided in the first instance by the commands of the Constitution as they have been interpreted by the Supreme Court, the laws as written by Congress, the values we believe are reflected in the democratic process, and the faith we have in a free society. We have also sought to be fully cognizant of the needs of national security, the requirements of a strong national defense against external aggression and internal subversion, and the duty of the government to protect its citizens.

In the final analysis, public safety and individual liberty sustain each other.

and security rights of American citizens. But we cannot ignore the invasion of the privacy and security rights of Americans by foreign countries or their agents. This is the other side of the coin—and it merits attention here in the interest of perspective.

Witnesses with responsibilities for counterintelligence have told the Commission that the United States remains the principal intelligence target of the communist bloc.

The communists invest large sums of money, personnel and sophisticated technology in collecting information—within the United States—on our military capabilities, our weapons systems, our defense structure and our social divisions. The communists seek to penetrate our intelligence services, to compromise our law enforcement agencies and to recruit as their agents United States citizens holding sensitive government and industry jobs. In addition, it is a common practice in communist bloc countries to inspect and open mail coming from or going to the United States.

In an open society such as ours, the intelligence opportunities for our adversaries are immeasurably greater than they are for us in their closed societies. Our society must remain an open one, with our traditional freedoms unimpaired. But when the intelligence activities of other countries are flourishing in the free environment we afford them, it is all the more essential that the foreign intelligence activities of the CIA and our other intelligence agencies, as well at the domestic counterintelligence activities of the FBI, be given the support nesessary to protect our national security and to shield the privacy and rights of American citizens from foreign intrusion.

The Commission has received estimates that communist bloc intelligence forces currently number well over 500,000 worldwide.

The number of communist government officials in the United States has tripled since 1960, and is still increasing. Nearly 2,000 of them are now in this country—and a significant percentage of them have been identified as members of intelligence or security agencies. Conservative estimates for the number of unidentified intelligence officers among the remaining officials raise the level to over 40 percent.

In addition to sending increasing numbers of their citizens to this country openly, many of whom have been trained in espionage, communist bloc countries also place considerable emphasis on the training, provision of false identification and dispatching of "illegal" agents—that is, operatives for whom an alias identity has been systematically developed which enables them to live in the United States as American citizens or resident aliens without our knowledge of their true origins.

While making large-scale use of human intelligence sources, the communist collection of intelligence to an extraordinary degree of technology and sophistication for use in the United States and elsewhere throughout the world, and we believe that these countries can monitor and record thousands of private telephone conversations. Americans have a right to be uneasy if not seriously disturbed at the real possi-

The Need for Intelligence

During the period of the Commission's inquiry, there have been public allegations that a democracy does not need an intelligence apparatus. The Commission does not share this view. Intelligence is information gathered for policymakers in government which illuminates the range of choices available to them and enables them to exercise judgment. Good intelligence will not necessarily lead to wise policy choices. But without sound intelligence, national policy decisions and actions cannot effectively respond to actual conditions and reflect the best national interest or adequately protect our national security.

Intelligence gathering involves collecting information about other countries' military capabilities, subversive activities, economic conditions, political developments, scientific and technological progress, and social activities and conditions. The raw information must be evaluated to determine its reliability and relevance, and must then be analyzed. The final products—called "finished intelligence"—are distributed to the President and the political, military and other governmental leaders according to their needs.

Intelligence gathering has changed rapidly and radically since the advent of the CIA in 1947.[1] The increased complexity of international political, economic, and military arrangements, the increased destructiveness of the weapons of modern warfare, and the

advent of electronic methods of surveillance have altered and enlarged the needs for sophisticated intelligence. Intelligence agencies have had to rely more and more on scientific and technological developments to help meet these needs.

Despite the increasing complexity and significance of intelligence in national policymaking, it is also important to understand its limits. Not all information is reliable, even when the most highly refined intelligence methods are used to collect it. Nor can any intelligence system ensure that its current estimates of another country's intentions or future capacities are accurate or will not be outrun by unforeseen events. There are limits to accurate forecasting, and the use of deception by our adversaries or the penetration of our intelligence services increases the possibility that intelligence predictions may prove to be wrong. Nevertheless, informed decision-making is impossible without an intelligence system adequately protected from penetration.

Therefore, a vital part of any intelligence service is an effective counterintelligence program, directed toward protecting our own intelligence system and ascertaining the activities of foreign intelligence services, such as espionage, sabotage, and subversion, and toward minimizing or counteracting the effectiveness of these activities.

Foreign Invasions of United States Privacy

This Commission is devoted to analyzing the domestic activities of the CIA in the interest of protecting the privacy

[1] The CIA is only one of several foreign intelligence agencies in the federal government. Others include the National Security Agency, the Defense Intelligence Agency, the intelligence branches of the three military services and the State Department's Bureau of Intelligence and Research.

bility that their personal and business activities which they discuss freely over the telephone could be recorded and analyzed by agents of foreign powers. This raises the real specter that se-

lected American users of telephones are potentially subject to blackmail that can seriously affect their actions, or even lead in some cases to recruitment as espionage agents.

Summary of Findings, Conclusions, and Recommendations

As directed by the President, the Commission has investigated the role and authority of the CIA, the adequacy of the internal controls and external supervision of the Agency, and its significant domestic activities that raise questions of compliance with the limits on its statutory authority. This chapter summarizes the findings and conclusions of the Commission and sets forth its recommendations.

A. Summary of Charges and Findings

The initial public charges were that the CIA's domestic activities had involved:

1. Large-scale spying on American citizens in the United States by the CIA, whose responsibility is foreign intelligence.

2. Keeping dossiers on large numbers of American citizens.

3. Aiming these activities at Americans who have expressed their disagreement with various government policies.

These initial charges were subsequently supplemented by others including allegations that the CIA:

—Had intercepted and opened personal mail in the United States for 20 years;

—Had infiltrated domestic dissident groups and otherwise intervened in domestic politics;

—Had engaged in illegal wiretaps and break-ins; and,

—Had improperly assisted other government agencies.

In addition, assertions have been made ostensibly linking the CIA to the assassination of President John F. Kennedy.

It became clear from the public reaction to these charges that the secrecy in which the Agency necessarily operates, combined with the allegations of wrongdoing, had contributed to widespread public misunderstanding of the Agency's actual practices.

A detailed analysis of the facts has convinced the Commission that the great majority of the CIA's domestic activities comply with its statutory authority.

Nevertheless, over the 28 years of its history, the CIA has engaged in some activities that should be criticized and not permitted to happen again—both in light of the limits imposed on the Agency by law and as a matter of public policy.

Some of these activities were initiated or ordered by Presidents, either directly or indirectly.

Some of them fall within the doubtful

area between responsibilities delegated to the CIA by Congress and the National Security Council on the one hand and activities specifically prohibited to the Agency on the other.

Some of them are plainly unlawful and constituted improper invasions upon the rights of Americans.

The Agency's own recent actions, undertaken for the most part in 1973 and 1974, have gone far to terminate the activities upon which this investigation has focused. The recommendations of the Commission are designed to clarify areas of doubt concerning the Agency's authority, to strengthen the Agency's structure, and to guard against recurrences of these improprieties.

B. The CIA's Role and Authority (Chapters 4-6)

Findings

The Central Intelligence Agency was established by the National Security Act of 1947 as the nation's first comprehensive peacetime foreign intelligence service. The objective was to provide the President with coordinated intelligence, which the country lacked prior to the attack on Pearl Harbor.

The Director of Central Intelligence reports directly to the President. The CIA receives its policy direction and guidance from the National Security Council, composed of the President, the Vice President, and the Secretaries of State and Defense.

The statute directs the CIA to correlate, evaluate, and disseminate intelligence obtained from United States intelligence agencies, and to perform such other functions related to intelligence as the National Security Council directs. Recognizing that the CIA would be dealing with sensitive, secret materials, Congress made the Director of Central Intelligence responsible for protecting intelligence sources and methods from unauthorized disclosure.

At the same time, Congress sought to assure the American public that it was not establishing a secret police which would threaten the civil liberties of Americans. It specifically forbade the CIA from exercising "police, subpoena, or law-enforcement powers or internal security functions." The CIA was not to replace the Federal Bureau of Investigation in conducting domestic activities to investigate crime or internal subversion.

Although Congress contemplated that

the focus of the CIA would be on foreign intelligence, it understood that some of its activities would be conducted within the United States. The CIA necessarily maintains its headquarters here, procures logistical support, recruits and trains employees, tests equipment, and conducts other domestic activities in support of its foreign intelligence mission. It makes necessary investigations in the United States to maintain the security of its facilities and personnel.

Additionally, it has been understood from the beginning that the CIA is permitted to collect foreign intelligence — that is, information concerning foreign capabilites, intentions, and activities—from American citizens within this country by overt means.

Determining the legal propriety of domestic activities of the CIA requires the application of the law to the particular facts involved. This task involves consideration of more than the National Security Act and the directives of the National Security Council; Constitutional and other statutory provisions also circumscribe the domestic activities of the CIA. Among the applicable Constitutional provisions are the First Amendment, protecting freedom of speech, of the press, and of peaceable assembly; and the Fourth Amendment, prohibiting unreasonable searches and seizures. Among the statutory provisions are those which limit such activities as electronic eavesdropping and interception of the mails.

The precise scope of many of these statutory and Constitutional provisions is not easily stated. The National Security Act in particular was drafted in broad terms in order to provide flexibility for the CIA to adapt to changing intelligence needs. Such critical phrases as "internal security functions" are left undefined. The meaning of the Director's responsibility to protect intelligence sources and methods from unauthorized disclosure has also been a subject of uncertainty.

The word "foreign" appears nowhere in the statutory grant of authority, though it has always been understood that the CIA's mission is limited to matters related to foreign intelligence. This apparent statutory ambiguity, although not posing problems in practice, has troubled members of the public who read the statute without having the benefit of the legislative history and the instructions to the CIA from the National Security Council.

Conclusions

The evidence within the scope of this inquiry does not indicate that fundamental rewriting of the National Security Act is either necessary or appropriate.

The evidence does demonstrate the need for some statutory and administrative clarification of the role and function of the Agency.

Ambiguities have been partially responsible for some, though not all, of the Agency's deviations within the United States from its assigned mission. In some cases, reasonable persons will differ as to the lawfulness of the activity; in others, the absence of clear guidelines as to its authority deprived the Agency of a means of resisting pressures to engage in activities which now appear to us improper.

Greater public awareness of the limits of the CIA's domestic authority would do much to reassure the American people.

The requisite clarification can best be accomplished (a) through a specific amendment clarifying the National Security Act provision which delineates the permissible scope of CIA activities, as set forth in Recommendation 1, and (b) through issuance of an Executive Order further limiting domestic activities of the CIA, as set forth in Recommendation 2.

Recommendation (1)

Section 403 of the National Security Act of 1947 should be amended in the form set forth in Appendix VI to this Report. These amendments, in summary, would:

a. Make explicit that the CIA's activities must be related to *foreign* intelligence.

b. Clarify the responsibility of the CIA to protect intelligence sources and methods from unauthorized disclosure. (The Agency would be responsible for protecting against unauthorized disclosures within the CIA, and it would be responsible for providing guidance and technical assistance to other agency and department heads in protecting against unauthorized disclosures within their own agencies and departments.)

c. Confirm publicly the CIA's existing authority to collect foreign intelligence from willing sources within the United States, and, except as specified by the President in a published Executive Order,[1] prohibits the CIA from collection efforts within the United States directed at securing foreign intelligence from unknowing American citizens.

Recommendation (2)

The President should by Executive Order prohibit the CIA from the collection of information about the domestic activities of United States citizens (whether by overt or covert means), the evaluation, correlation, and dissemination of analyses or reports about such activities, and the storage of such information, with exceptions for the following categories of persons or activities:

a. Persons presently or formerly affiliated, or being considered for affiliation, with the CIA, directly or indirectly, or others who require clearance by the CIA to receive classified information;

b. Persons or activities that pose a clear threat to CIA facilities or personnel, provided that proper coordination with the FBI is accomplished;

c. Persons suspected of espionage or other illegal activities relating to foreign intelligence, provided that proper coordination with the FBI is accomplished.

d. Information which is received incidental to appropriate CIA activities may be transmitted to an agency with

appropriate jurisdiction, including law enforcement agencies.

Collection of information from normal library sources such as newspapers, books, magazines and other such documents is not to be affected by this order.

Information currently being maintained which is inconsistent with the order should be destroyed at the conclusion of the current congressional investigations or as soon thereafter as permitted by law.

The CIA should periodically screen its files and eliminate all material inconsistent with the order.

The order should be issued after consultation with the National Security Council, the Attorney General, and the Director of Central Intelligence. Any modification of the order would be permitted only through published amendments.

C. Supervision and Control of the CIA

1. External Controls (Chapter 7)

Findings

The CIA is subject to supervision and control by various executive agencies and by the Congress.

Congress has established special procedures for review of the CIA and its secret budget within four small subcommittees.[2] Historically, these subcommittees have been composed of members of Congress with many other demands on their time. The CIA has not as a general rule received detailed scrutiny by the Congress.

The principal bodies within the Executive Branch performing a supervisory or control function are the National Security Council, which gives the CIA its policy direction and control; the Office of Management and Budget, which reviews the CIA's budget in much the same fashion as it reviews budgets of other government agencies; and the President's Foreign Intelligence Advisory Board, which is composed of distinguished citizens, serving part time in a general advisory function for the President on the quality of the gathering and interpretation of intelligence.

None of these agencies has the specific responsibility of overseeing the CIA to determine whether its activities are proper.

The Department of Justice also exercises an oversight role, through its power to initiate prosecutions for criminal misconduct. For a period of over 20 years, however, an agreement existed between the Department of Justice and the CIA providing that the Agency was to investigate allegations of crimes by CIA employees or agents which involved Government money or property or might involve operational security. If following the investigation, the Agency determined that there was no reasonable basis to believe a crime had been committed, or that operational security aspects precluded prosecution, the case

was not referred to the Department of Justice.

The Commission has found nothing to indicate that the CIA abused the function given it by the agreement. The agreement, however, involved the Agency directly in forbidden law enforcement activities, and represented an abdication by the Department of Justice of its statutory responsibilities.

Conclusions

Some improvement in the congressional oversight system would be helpful. The problem of providing adequate oversight and control while maintaining essential security is not easily resolved. Several knowledgeable witnesses pointed to the Joint Committee on Atomic Energy as an appropriate model for congressional oversight of the Agency. That Committee has had an excellent record of providing effective oversight while avoiding breaches of security in a highly sensitive area.

One of the underlying causes of the problems confronting the CIA arises out of the pervading atmosphere of secrecy in which its activities have been conducted in the past. One aspect of this has been the secrecy of the budget.

A new body is needed to provide oversight of the Agency within the Executive Branch. Because of the need to preserve security, the CIA is not subject to the usual constraints of audit, judicial review, publicity or open congressional budget review and oversight. Consequently, its operations require additional external control. The authority assigned the job of supervising the CIA must be given sufficient power and significance to assure the public of effective supervision.

The situation whereby the Agency determined whether its own employees would be prosecuted must not be permitted to recur.

Recommendation (3)

The President should recommend to Congress the establishment of a Joint Committee on Intelligence to assume the oversight role currently played by the Armed Services Committees.[3]

Recommendation (4)

Congress should give careful consideration to the question whether the budget of the CIA should not, at least to some extent, be made public, particularly in view of the provisions of Article I, Section 9, Clause 7 of the Constitution.[4]

Recommendation (5)

a. The functions of the President's Foreign Intelligence Advisory Board should be expanded to include oversight of the CIA. This expanded oversight board should be composed of distinguished citizens with varying backgrounds and experience. It should be headed by a full-time chairman and should have a full-time staff appropriate to its role. Its functions related to the CIA should include:

1. Assessing compliance by the CIA with its statutory authority.

---

[1] The Executive Order authorized by this statute should recognize that when the collection of foreign intelligence from persons who are not United States citizens results in the incidental acquisition of information from unknowing citizens, the Agency should be permitted to make appropriate use or disposition of such information. Such collection activities must be directed at foreign intelligence sources, and the involvement of American citizens must be incidental.

[2] Subcommittees of the Appropriations Committees and the Armed Services Committees of the two houses.

[3] See statement by Commissioner Griswold, Chapter 7.

[4] "No Money shall be drawn from the Treasury, but in Consequence of Appropriations made by Law; and a regular Statement and Account of the Receipts and Expenditures of all public Money shall be published from time to time."

2. Assessing the quality of foreign intelligence collection.

3. Assessing the quality of foreign intelligence estimates.

4. Assessing the quality of the organization of the CIA.

5. Assessing the quality of the management of the CIA.

6. Making recommendations with respect to the above subjects to the President and the Director of Central Intelligence, and, where appropriate, the Attorney General.

b. The Board should have access to all information in the CIA. It should be authorized to audit and investigate CIA expenditures and activities on its own initiative.

c. The Inspector General of the CIA should be authorized to report directly to the Board, after having notified the Director of Central Intelligence, in cases he deems appropriate.

Recommendation (6)

The Department of Justice and the CIA should establish written guidelines for the handling of reports of criminal violations by employees of the Agency or relating to its affairs. These guidelines should require that the criminal investigation and the decision whether to prosecute be made by the Department of Justice, after consideration of Agency views regarding the impact of prosecution on the national security. The Agency should be permitted to conduct such investigations as it requires to determine whether its operations have been jeopardized. The Agency should scrupulously avoid exercise of the prosecutorial function.

2. Internal Controls (Chapter 8)

Findings

The Director's duties in administering the intelligence community, handling relations with other components of the government, and passing on broad questions of policy leave him little time for day-to-day supervision of the Agency. Past studies have noted the need for the Director to delegate greater responsibility for the administration of the Agency to the Deputy Director of Central Intelligence.

In recent years, the position of Deputy Director has been occupied by a high-ranking military officer, with responsibilities for maintaining liaison with the Department of Defense, fostering the Agency's relationship with the military services, and providing top CIA management with necessary experience and skill in understanding particular intelligence requirements of the military. Generally speaking, the Deputy Directors of Central Intelligence have not been heavily engaged in administration of the Agency.

Each of the four directorates within the CIA—Operations, Intelligence, Administration, and Science and Technology—is headed by a deputy director who reports to the Director and Deputy Director of Central Intelligence. These four deputies, together with certain other top Agency officials such as the Comptroller, form the Agency Management Committee, which makes many of the administrative and management decisions affecting more than one directorate.

Outside the chain of command, the primary internal mechanism for keeping the Agency within bounds is the Inspector General. The size of this office was recently sharply reduced, and its previous practice of making regular reviews of various Agency departments was terminated. At the present time, the activities of the office are almost entirely concerned with coordinating Agency responses to the various investigating bodies, and with various types of employee grievances.

The Office of General Counsel has on occasion played an important role in preventing or terminating Agency activities in violation of law, but many of the questionable or unlawful activities discussed in this report were not brought to the attention of this office. A certain parochialism may have resulted from the fact that attorneys in the office have little or no legal experience outside the Agency. It is important that the Agency receive the best possible legal advice on the often difficult and unusual situations which confront it.

Conclusions

In the final analysis, the proper functioning of the Agency must depend in large part on the character of the Director of Central Intelligence.

The best assurance against misuse of the Agency lies in the appointment to that position of persons with the judgment, courage, and independence to resist improper pressure and importuning, whether from the White House, within the Agency or elsewhere.

Compartmentation within the Agency, although certainly appropriate for security reasons, has sometimes been carried to extremes which prevent proper supervision and control.

The Agency must rely on the discipline and integrity of the men and women it employs. Many of the activities we have found to be improper or unlawful were in fact questioned by lower-level employees. Bringing such situations to the attention of upper levels of management is one of the purposes of a system of internal controls.

Recommendation (7)

A. Persons appointed to the position of Director of Central Intelligence should be individuals of stature, independence, and integrity. In making this appointment, consideration should be given to individuals from outside the career service of the CIA, although promotion from within should not be barred. Experience in intelligence service is not necessarily a prerequisite barred. Experience in intelligence service is not necessarily a prerequisite for the position; management and administrative skills are at least as important as the technical expertise which can always be found in an able deputy.

b. Although the Director serves at the pleasure of the President, no Director should serve in that position for more than 10 years.

Recommendation (8)

a. The Office of Deputy Director of Central Intelligence should be reconstituted to provide for two such deputies, in addition to the four heads of the Agency's directorates. One deputy would act as the administrative officer, freeing the Director from day-to-day management duties. The other deputy should be a military officer, serving the functions of fostering relations with the military and providing the Agency with technical expertise on military intelligence requirements.

b. The advice and consent of the Senate should be required for the appointment of each Deputy Director of Central Intelligence.

Recommendation (9)

a. The Inspector General should be upgraded to a status equivalent to that of the deputy directors in charge of the four directorates within the CIA.

b. The Office of Inspector General should be staffed by outstanding, experienced officers from both inside and outside the CIA, with ability to understand the various branches of the Agency.

c. The Inspector General's duties with respect to domestic CIA activities should include periodic reviews of all offices within the United States. He should examine each office for compliance with CIA authority and regulations as well as for the effectiveness of their programs in implementing policy objectives.

d. The Inspector General should investigate all reports from employees concerning possible violations of the CIA statute.

e. The Inspector General should be given complete access to all information in the CIA relevant to his reviews.

f. An effective Inspector General's office will require a larger staff, more frequent reviews, and highly qualified personnel.

g. Inspector General reports should be provided to the National Security Council and the recommended executive oversight body. The Inspector General should have the authority, when he deems it appropriate, after notifying the Director of Central Intelligence, to consult with the executive oversight body on any CIA activity (see Recommendation 5).

Recommendation (10)

a. The Director should review the composition and operation of the Office of General Counsel and the degree to which this office is consulted to determine whether the Agency is receiving adequate legal assistance and representation in view of current requirements.

b. Consideration should be given to measures which would strengthen the office's professional capabilities and resources including, among other things, (1) occasionally departing from the existing practice of hiring lawyers from within the Agency to bring in seasoned lawyers from private practice as well as to hire law school graduates without prior CIA experience; (2) occasionally assigning Agency lawyers to serve a tour of duty elsewhere in the government to expand their experience; (3) encouraging lawyers to participate in outside professional activities.

Recommendation (11)

To a degree consistent with the need for security, the CIA should be encouraged to provide for increased lateral movement of personnel among the directorates and to bring persons with outside experience into the Agency at all levels.

Recommendation (12)

a. The Agency should issue detailed guidelines for its employees further specifying those activities within the

IN THE NAME OF NATIONAL SECURITY

United States which are permitted and those which are prohibited by statute, Executive Orders, and NSC and DCI directives.

b. These guidelines should also set forth the standards which govern CIA activities and the general types of activities which are permitted and prohibited. They should, among other things, specify that:

—Clandestine collection of intelligence directed against United States citizens is prohibited except as specifically permitted by law or published Executive Order.

—Unlawful methods or activities are prohibited.

—Prior approval of the CIA shall be required for any activities which may raise questions of compliance with the law or with Agency regulations.

c. The guidelines should also provide that employees with information on possibly improper activities are to bring it promptly to the attention of the Director of Central Intelligence or the Inspector General.

D. Significant Areas of Investigation

Introduction

Domestic activities of the CIA raising substantial questions of compliance with the law have been closely examined by the Commission to determine the context in which they were performed, the pressures of the times, the relationship of the activity to the Agency's foreign intelligence assignment and to other CIA activities, the procedures used to authorize and conduct the activity, and the extent and effect of the activity.

In describing and assessing each activity, it has been necessary to consider both that activity's relationship to the legitimate national security needs of the nation and the threat such activities might pose to individual rights of Americans and to a society founded on the need for government, as well as private citizens, to obey the law.

1. The CIA's Mail Intercepts (Chapter 9)

Findings

At the time the CIA came into being, one of the highest national intelligence priorities was to gain an understanding of the Soviet Union and its worldwide activities affecting our national security.

In this context, the CIA began in 1952 a program of surveying mail between the United States and the Soviet Union as it passed through a New York postal facility. In 1953 it began opening some of this mail. This program was expanded over the following two decades and ultimately involved the opening of many letters and the analysis of envelopes, or "covers," of a great many more letters.

The New York mail intercept was designed to attempt to identify persons within the United States who were cooperating with the Soviet Union and its intelligence forces to harm the United States. It was also intended to

determine technical communications procedures and mail censorship techniques used by the Soviets.

The Director of the Central Intelligence Agency approved commencement of the New York mail intercept in 1952. During the ensuing years so far as the record shows, Postmasters General Summerfield, Day, and Blount were informed of the program in varying degrees, as was Attorney General Mitchell. Since 1958, the FBI was aware of this program and received 57,000 items from it.

A 1962 CIA memorandum indicates the Agency was aware that the mail openings would be viewed as violating federal criminal laws prohibiting obstruction or delay of the mails.

In the last year before the termination of this program, out of 4,350,000 items of mail sent to and from the Soviet Union, the New York intercept examined the outside of 2,300,000 of these items, photographed 33,000 envelopes, and opened 8,700.

The mail intercept was terminated in 1973 when the Chief Postal Inspector refused to allow its continuation without an up-to-date high-level approval.

The CIA also ran much smaller mail intercepts for brief periods in San Francisco between 1969 and 1971 and in the territory of Hawaii during 1954 and 1955. For a short period in 1957, mail in transit between foreign countries was intercepted in New Orleans.

Conclusions

While in operation, the CIA's domestic mail opening programs were unlawful. United States statutes specifically forbid opening the mail.

The mail openings also raise Constitutional questions under the Fourth Amendment guarantees against unreasonable search, and the scope of the New York project poses possible difficulties with the First Amendment rights of speech and press.

Mail cover operations (examining and copying of envelopes only) are legal when carried out in compliance with postal regulations on a limited and selective basis involving matters of national security. The New York mail intercept did not meet these criteria.

The nature and degree of assistance given by the CIA to the FBI in the New York mail project indicate that the CIA's primary purpose eventually became participation with the FBI in internal security functions. Accordingly, the CIA's participation was prohibited under the National Security Act.

Recommendation (13)

a. The President should instruct the Director of Central Intelligence that the CIA is not to engage again in domestic tutory authority in time of war. (See mail openings except with express statutory authority in time of war. (See also Recommendation 23.)

b. The President should instruct the Director of Central Intelligence that mail cover examinations are to be in compliance with postal regulations; they are to be undertaken only in furtherance of the CIA's legitimate activities and then only on a limited and selected basis clearly involving matters of national security.

2. Intelligence Community Coordination (Chapter 10)

Findings

As a result of growing domestic disorder, the Department of Justice, starting in 1967 at the direction of Attorney General Ramsey Clark, coordinated a series of secret units and interagency groups in an effort to collate and evaluate intelligence relating to these events. These efforts continued until 1973.

The interagency committees were designed for analytic and not operational purposes. They were created as a result of White House pressure which began in 1967, because the FBI performed only limited evaluation and analysis of the information it collected on these events. The stated purpose of CIA's participation was to supply relevant foreign intelligence and to furnish advice on evaluation techniques.

The CIA was reluctant to become unduly involved in these committees, which had problems of domestic unrest as their principal focus. It repeatedly refused to assign full-time personnel to any of them.

The most active of the committees was the Intelligence Evaluation Staff, which met from January 1971 to May 1973. A CIA liaison officer[4] attended over 100 weekly meetings of the Staff, some of which concerned drafts of reports which had no foreign aspects. With the exception of one instance, there is no evidence that he acted in any capacity other than as an adviser on foreign intelligence, and, to some degree, as an editor.

On one occasion the CIA liaison officer appears to have caused a CIA agent to gather domestic information which was reported to the Intelligence Evaluation Staff.

The Commission found no evidence of other activities by the CIA that were conducted on behalf of the Department of Justice groups except for the supplying of appropriate foreign intelligence and advice on evaluation techniques.

Conclusions

The statutory prohibition on internal security functions does not preclude the CIA from providing foreign intelligence or advice on evaluation techniques to nterdepartmental intelligence evaluation organizations having some domestic aspects. The statute was intended to promote coordination, not compartmentation of intelligence between governmental departments.

The attendance of the CIA liaison officer at over 100 meetings of the Intelligence Evaluation Staff, some of them concerned wholly with domestic matters, nevertheless created at least the appearance of impropriety. The Director of Central Intelligence was well advised to approach such participation reluctantly.

The liaison officer acted improperly in the one instance in which he directed an agent to gather domestic information within the United States which was

---

[4] The liaison officer was Chief of the CIA's Special Operations Group which ran Operation CHAOS, discussed in Chapter II of this Report.

reported to the Intelligence Evaluation Staff.

Much of the problem stemmed from the absence in government of any organization capable of adequately analyzing intelligence collected by the FBI on matters outside the purview of CIA.

Recommendation (14)

a. A capability should be developed within the FBI, or elsewhere in the Department of Justice, to evaluate, analyze, and coordinate intelligence and counterintelligence collected by the FBI concerning espionage, terrorism, and other related matters of internal security.

b. The CIA should restrict its participation in any joint intelligence committees to foreign intelligence matters.

c. The FBI should be encouraged to continue to look to the CIA for such foreign intelligence and counterintelligence as is relevant to FBI needs.

3. Special Operations Group—"Operation CHAOS" (Chapter 11)

Findings

The late 1960's and early 1970's were marked by widespread violence and civil disorders.[5] Demonstrations, marches and protest assemblies were frequent in a number of cities. Many universities and college campuses became places of disruption and unrest. Government facilities were picketed and sometimes invaded. Threats of bombing and bombing incidents occurred frequently. In Washington and other major cities, special security measures had to be instituted to control the access to public buildings.

Responding to Presidential requests made in the face of growing domestic disorder, the Director of Central Intelligence in August 1967 established a Special Operations Group within the CIA to collect, coordinate, evaluate and report on the extent of foreign influence on domestic dissidence.

The Group's activities, which later came to be known as Operation CHAOS, led the CIA to collect information on dissident Americans from CIA field stations overseas and from the FBI.

Although the stated purpose of the Operation was to determine whether there were any foreign contacts with American dissident groups, it resulted in the accumulation of considerable material on domestic dissidents and their activities.

During six years, the Operation compiled some 13,000 different files, including files on 7,200 American citizens. The documents in these files and related materials included the names of more than 300,000 persons and organizations, which were entered into a computerized index.

This information was kept closely guarded within the CIA. Using this information, personnel of the Group prepared 3,500 memoranda for internal use; 3,000 memoranda for dissemination to the FBI; and 37 memoranda for

distribution to White House and other top level officials in the government.

The staff assigned to the Operation was steadily enlarged in response to repeated Presidential requests for additional information, ultimately reaching a maximum of 52 in 1971. Because of excessive isolation, the Operation was substantially insulated from meaningful review within the Agency, including review by the Counterintelligence Staff—of which the Operation was technically a part.

Commencing in late 1969, Operation CHAOS used a number of agents to collect intelligence abroad on any foreign connections with American dissident groups. In order to have sufficient "cover" for these agents, the Operation recruited persons from domestic dissident groups or recruited others and instructed them to associate with such groups in this country.

Most of the Operation's recruits were not directed to collect information domestically on American dissidents. On a number of occasions, however, such information was reported by the recruits while they were developing dissident credentials in the United States, and the information was retained in the files of the Operation. On three occasions, an agent of the Operation was specifically directed to collect domestic intelligence.

No evidence was found that any Operation CHAOS agent used or was directed by the Agency to use electronic surveillance, wiretaps or break-ins in the United States against any dissident individual or group.

Activity of the Operation decreased substantially by mid-1972. The Operation was formally terminated in March 1974.

Conclusions

Some domestic activities of Operation CHAOS unlawfully exceeded the CIA's statutory authority, even though the declared mission of gathering intelligence abroad as to foreign influence on domestic dissident activities was proper.

Most significantly, the Operation became a repository for large quantities of information on the domestic activities of American citizens. This information was derived principally from FBI reports or from overt sources and not from clandestine collection by the CIA, and much of it was not directly related to the question of the existence of foreign connections.

It was probably necessary for the CIA to accumulate an information base on domestic dissident activities in order to assess fairly whether the activities had foreign connections. The FBI would collect information but would not evaluate it. But the accumulation of domestic data in the Operation exceeded what was reasonably required to make such an assessment and was thus improper.

The use of agents of the Operation on three occasions to gather information within the United States on strictly domestic matters was beyond the CIA's authority. In addition the intelligence disseminations and those portions of a major study prepared by the Agency which dealt with purely domestic matters were improper.

The isolation of Operation CHAOS within the CIA and its independence

from supervision by the regular chain of command within the clandestine service made it possible for the activities of the Operation to stray over the bounds of the Agency's authority without the knowledge of senior officials. The absence of any regular review of these activities prevented timely correction of such missteps as did occur.

Recommendation (15)

a. Presidents should refrain from directing the CIA to perform what are essentially internal security tasks.

b. The CIA should resist any efforts, whatever their origin, to involve it again in such improper activities.

c. The Agency should guard against allowing any component (like the Special Operations Group) to become so self-contained and isolated from top leadership that regular supervision and review are lost.

d. The files of the CHAOS project which have no foreign intelligence value should be destroyed by the Agency at the conclusion of the current congressional investigations, or as soon thereafter as permitted by law.

4. Protection of the Agency Against Threats of Violence—Office of Security (Chapter 12)

Findings

The CIA was not immune from the threats of violence and disruption during the period of domestic unrest between 1967 and 1972. The Office of Security was charged throughout this period with the responsibility of ensuring the continued functioning of the CIA.

The Office therefore, from 1967 to 1970, had its field officers collect information from published materials, law enforcement authorities, other agencies and college officials before recruiters were sent to some campuses. Monitoring and communications support was provided to recruiters when trouble was expected.

The Office was also responsible, with the approval of the Director of Central Intelligence, for a program from February 1967 to December 1968, which at first monitored, but later infiltrated, dissident organizations in the Washington, D.C., area to determine if the groups planned any activites against CIA or other government installations.

At no time were more than 12 persons performing these tasks, and they performed them on a part-time basis. The project was terminated when the Washington Metropolitan Police Department developed its own intelligence capability.

In December, 1967, the Office began a continuing study of dissident activity in the United States, using information from published and other voluntary knowledgeable sources. The Office produced weekly Situation Information Reports analyzing dissident activites and providing calendars of future events. Calendars were given to the Secret Service, but the CIA made no other disseminations outside the Agency. About 500 to 800 files were maintained on dissenting organizations and individuals. Thousands of names in the files were indexed. Report publication was ended in late 1972, and the entire project was ended in 1973.

Conclusions

The program under which the Office of Security rendered assistance to Agency recruiters on college campuses was justified as an exercise of the Agency's responsibility to protect its own personnel and operations. Such support activities were not undertaken for the purpose of protecting the facilities or operations of other governmental agencies, or to maintain public order or enforce laws.

The Agency should not infiltrate a dissident group for security purposes unless there is a clear danger to Agency installations, operations or personnel, and investigative coverage of the threat by the FBI and local law enforcement authorities is inadequate. The Agency's infiltration of dissident groups in the Washington area went far beyond steps necessary to protect the Agency's own facilities, personnel and operations, and therefore exceeded the CIA's statutory authority.

In addition, the Agency undertook to protect other government departments and agencies—a police function prohibited to it by statute.

Intelligence activity directed toward learning from what sources a domestic dissident group receives it financial support within the United States, and how much income it has, is no part of the authorized security operations of the Agency. Neither is it the function of the Agency to compile records on who attends peaceful meetings of such dissident groups, or what each speaker has to say (unless it relates to disruptive or violent activity which may be directed against the Agency).

The Agency's actions in contributing funds, photographing people, activities and cars, and following people home were unreasonable under the circumstances and therefore exceeded the CIA's authority.

With certain exceptions, the program under which the Office of Security (without infiltration) gathered, organized and analyzed information about dissident groups for purposes of security was within the CIA's authority.

The accumulation of reference files on dissident organizations and their leaders was appropriate both to evaluate the risks posed to the Agency and to develop an understanding of dissident groups and their differences for security clearance purposes. But the accumulation of information on domestic activities went beyond what was required by the Agency's legitimate security needs and therefore exceeded the CIA's authority.

Recommendation (16)

The CIA should not infiltrate dissident groups or other organizations of Americans in the absence of a written determination by the Director of Central Intelligence that such action is necessary to meet a clear danger to Agency facilities, operations, or personnel and that adequate coverage by law enforcement agencies is unavailable.

Recommendation (17)

All files on individuals by the Office of Security in the program relating to dissidents should be identified, and except where necessary for a legitimate foreign intelligence activity, be destroyed at the conclusion of the current congressional investigations, or as soon thereafter as permitted by law.

5. Other Investigations by the Office of Security (Chapter 13)

A. Security Clearance Investigations of Prospective Employees and Operatives

Findings and Conclusion

The Office of Security routinely conducts standard security investigations of persons seeking affiliation with the Agency. In doing so, the Office is performing the necessary function of screening persons to whom it will make available classified information. Such investigations are necessary, and no improprieties were found in connection with them.

B. Investigations of Possible Breaches of Security

1. Persons Investigated

Findings

The Office of Security has been called upon on a number of occasions to investigate specific allegations that intelligence sources and methods were threatened by unauthorized disclosures. The Commission's inquiry concentrated on those investigations which used investigative means intruding on the privacy of the subjects, including physical and electronic surveillance, unauthorized entry, mail covers and intercepts, and reviews of individual federal tax returns.

The large majority of these investigations were directed at persons affiliated with the Agency—such as employees, former employees, and defectors and other foreign nationals used by the Agency as intelligence sources.

A few investigations involving intrusions on personal privacy were directed at subjects with no relationship to the Agency. The Commission has found no evidence that any such investigations were directed against any congressman, judge, or other public official. Five were directed against newsmen, in an effort to determine their sources of leaked classified information, and nine were directed against other United States citizens.

The CIA's investigations of newsmen to determine their sources of classified information stemmed from pressures from the White House and were partly

a result of the FBI's unwillingness to undertake such investigations. The FBI refused to proceed without an advance opinion that the Justice Department would prosecute if a case were developed.

Conclusions

Investigations of allegations against Agency employees and operatives are a reasonable exercise of the Director's statutory duty to protect intelligence sources and methods from unauthorized disclosure if the investigations are lawfully conducted. Such investigations also assist the Director in the exercise of his unreviewable authority to terminate the employment of any Agency employee. They are proper unless their principal purpose becomes law-enforcement or the maintenance of internal security.

The Director's responsibility to protect intelligence sources and methods is not so broad as to permit investigations of persons having no relationship whatever with the Agency. The CIA has no authority to investigate newsmen simply because they have published leaked classified information. Investigations by the CIA should be limited to persons presently or formerly affiliated with the Agency, directly or indirectly.

Recommendation (18)

a. The Director of Central Intelligence should issue clear guidelines setting forth the situations in which the CIA is justified in conducting its own investigation of individuals presently or formerly affiliated with it.

The guidelines should permit the CIA to conduct investigations of such persons only when the Director of Central Intelligence first determines that the investigation is necessary to protect intelligence sources and methods the disclosure of which might endanger the national security.

c. Such investigations must be coordinated with the FBI whenever substantial evidence suggesting espionage or violation of a federal criminal statute is discovered.

Recommendation (19)

a. In cases involving serious or continuing security violations, as determined by the Security Committee of the United States Intelligence Board, the Committee should be authorized to recommend in writing to the Director of Central Intelligence (with a copy to the National Security Council) that the case be referred to the FBI for further investigation, under procedures to be developed by the Attorney General.

b. These procedures should include a requirement that the FBI accept such referrals without regard to whether a favorable prosecutive opinion is issued by the Justice Department. The CIA should not engage in such further investigations.

Recommendation (20)

The CIA and other components and agencies of the intelligence community should conduct periodic reviews of all classified material originating within those departments or agencies, with a view to declassifying as much of that material as possible. The purpose of such review would be to assure the public that it has access to all information that should properly be disclosed.

Recommendation (21)

The Commission endorses legislation, drafted with appropriate safeguards of the constitutional rights of all affected individuals, which would make it a criminal offense for employees or former employees of the CIA willfully to divulge to any unauthorized person classified information pertaining to foreign intelligence or the collection thereof obtained during the course of their employment.

2. Investigative Techniques
Findings

Even an investigation within the CIA's authority must be conducted by lawful means. Some of the past investigations by the Office of Security within the United States were conducted by means which were invalid at the time. Others might have been lawful when conducted, but would be impermissible today.

Some investigations involved physical surveillance of the individuals concerned, possibly in conjunction with other methods of investigations. The last instance of physical surveillance by the Agency within the United States occurred in 1973.

The investigation disclosed the domestic use of 32 wiretaps, the last in 1965; 32 instances of bugging, the last in 1968; and 12 break-ins, the last in 1971. None of these activities was conducted under a judicial warrant, and only one with the written approval of the Attorney General.

Information from the income tax records of 16 persons was obtained from the Internal Revenue Service by the CIA in order to help determine whether the taxpayer was a security risk with possible connections to foreign groups. The CIA did not employ the existing statutory and regulatory procedures for obtaining such records from the IRS.

In 91 instances, mail covers (the photographing of the front and back of an envelope) were employed, and in 12 instances letters were intercepted and opened.

The state of the CIA records on these activities is such that it is often difficult to determine why the investigation occurred in the first place, who authorized the special coverage, and what the results were. Although there was testimony that these activities were frequently known to the Director of Central Intelligence and sometimes to the Attorney General, the files often are insufficient to confirm such information.

Conclusions

The use of physical surveillance is not unlawful unless it reaches the point of harassment. The unauthorized entries described were illegal when conducted and would be illegal if conducted today. Likewise, the review of individuals' federal tax returns and the interception and opening of mail violated specific statutes and regulations prohibiting such conduct.

Since the constitutional and statutory constraints applicable to the use of electronic eavesdropping (bugs and wiretaps) have been evolving over the years, the Commission deems it impractical to apply those changing standards on a case-by-case basis. The Commission does believe that while some of the instances of electronic eavesdropping were proper when conducted, many were not. To be lawful today, such activities would require at least the written approval of the Attorney General on the basis of a finding that the national security is involved and that the case has significant foreign connections.

Recommendation (22)

The CIA should not undertake physical surveillance (defined as systematic observation) of Agency employees, contractors or related personnel within the United States without first obtaining written approval of the Director of Central Intelligence.

Recommendation (23)

In the United States and its possessions, the CIA should not intercept wire or oral communications[6] or otherwise engage in activities that would require a warrant if conducted by a law enforcement agency. Responsibility for such activities belongs with the FBI.

Recommendation (24)

The CIA should strictly adhere to established legal procedures governing access to federal income tax information.

Recommendation (25)

CIA investigation records should show that each investigation was duly authorized, and by whom, and should clearly set forth the factual basis for undertaking the investigation and the results of the investigation.

C. Handling of Defectors
Findings

The Office of Security is charged with providing security for persons who have defected to the United States. Generally a defector can be processed and placed into society in a few months, but one defector was involuntarily confined at a CIA installation for three years. He was held in solitary confinement under spartan living conditions. The CIA maintained the long confinement because of doubts about the bona fides of the defector. This confinement was approved by the Director of Central Intelligence; and the FBI, Attorney General, United States Intelligence Board and selected members of Congress were aware to some extent of the confinement. In one other case a defector was physically abused; the Director of Central Intelligence discharged the employee involved.

Conclusions

Such treatment of individuals by an agency of the United States is unlawful. The Director of Central Intelligence and the Inspector General must be alert to prevent repetitions.

---

[6] As defined in the Omnibus Crime Control and Safe Streets Act, 18 U.S.C. Secs. 2510-20.

6. Involvement of the CIA in Improper Activities for the White House (Chapter 14)

During 1971, at the request of various members of the White House staff, the CIA provided alias documents and disguise material, a tape recorder, camera, film and film processing to E. Howard Hunt. It also prepared a psychological profile of Dr. Daniel Ellsberg.

Some of this equipment was later used without the knowledge of the CIA in connection with various improper activities, including the entry into the office of Dr. Lewis Fielding, Ellsberg's psychiatrist.

Some members of the CIA's medical staff who participated in the preparation of the Ellsberg profile knew that one of its purposes was to support a public attack on Ellsberg. Except for this fact, the investigation has disclosed no evidence that the CIA knew or had reason to know that the assistance it gave would be used for improper purposes.

President Nixon and his staff also insisted in this period that the CIA turn over to the President highly classified files relating to the Lebanon landings, the Bay of Pigs, the Cuban missile crisis, and the Vietnam War. The request was made on the ground that these files were needed by the President in the performance of his duties, but the record shows the purpose, undisclosed to the CIA, was to serve the President's personal political ends.

The Commission has also investigated the response of the CIA to the investigations following the Watergate arrests. Beginning in June 1972, the CIA received various requests for information and assistance in connection with these investigations. In a number of instances, its responses were either incomplete or delayed and some materials that may or may not have contained relevant information were destroyed. The Commission feels that this conduct reflects poor judgment on the part of the CIA, but it has found no evidence that the CIA participated in the Watergate break-in or in the post-Watergate cover-up by the White House.

Conclusions

Providing the assistance requested by the White House, including the alias and disguise materials, the camera and the psychological profile on Ellsberg, was not related to the performance by the Agency of its authorized intelligence functions and was therefore improper.

No evidence has been disclosed, however, except as noted in connection with the Ellsberg profile, that the CIA knew or had reason to know that its assistance would be used in connection with improper activities. Nor has any evidence been disclosed indicating that the CIA participated in the planning or carrying out of either the Fielding or Watergate break-ins. The CIA apparently was unaware of the break-ins until they were reported in the media.

The record does show, however, that individuals in the Agency failed to comply with the normal control procedures in providing assistance to E.

Howard Hunt. It also shows that the Agency's failure to cooperate fully with ongoing investigations following Watergate was inconsistent with its obligations.

Finally, the Commission concludes that the requests for assistance by the White House reflect a pattern for actual and attempted misuse of the CIA by the Nixon administration.

Recommendation (26)

a. A single and exclusive high-level channel should be established for transmssion of all White House staff requests to the CIA. This channel should run between an officer of the National Security Council staff designated by the President and the office of the Director or his Deputy.

b. All Agency officers and employees should be instructed that any direction or request reaching them directly and out of regularly established channels should be immediately reported to the Director of Central Intelligence.

7. Domestic Activities of the Directorate of Operations (Chapter 15)

Findings and Conclusions

In support of its responsibility for the collection of foreign intelligence and conduct of covert operations overseas, the CIA's Directorate of Operations engages in a variety of activities within the United States.

A. Overt Collection of Foreign Intelligence within the United States

One division of the Directorate of Operations collects foreign intelligence within the United States from residents, business firms, and other organizations willing to assist the Agency. This activity is conducted openly by officers who identify themselves as CIA employees. Such sources of information are not compensated.

In connection with these collection activities, the CIA maintains approximately 50,000 active files which include details of the CIA's relationships with these voluntary sources and the results of a federal agency name check.

The division's collection efforts have been almost exclusively confined to foreign economic, political, military, and operational topics.

Commencing in 1969, however, some activities of the division resulted in the collection of limited information with respect to American dissidents and dissident groups. Although the focus was on foreign contacts of these groups, background information on domestic dissidents was also collected. Between 1969 and 1974, when this activity was formally terminated, 400 reports were made to Operation CHAOS.

In 1972 and 1973, the division obtained and transmitted, to other parts of the CIA, information about telephone calls between the Western Hemisphere (including the United States) and two other countries. The information was limited to names, telephone numbers, and locations of callers and recipients. It did not include the content of the conversations.

This division also occasionally receives reports concerning criminal activity within the United States. Pursuant to written regulations, the source or a report of the information received is referred to the appropriate law enforcement agency.

The CIA's efforts to collect foreign intelligence from residents of the United States willing to assist the CIA are a valid and necessary element of its responsibility. Not only do these persons provide a large reservoir of foreign intelligence; they are by far the most accessible source of such information.

The division's files on American citizens and firms representing actual or potential sources of information constitute a necessary part of its legitimate intelligence activities. They do not appear to be vehicles for the collection or communication of derogatory, embarrassing, or sensitive information about American citizens.

The division's efforts, with few exceptions, have been confined to legitimate topics.

The collection of information with respect to American dissident groups exceeded legitimate foreign intelligence collection and was beyond the proper scope of CIA activity. This impropriety was recognized in some of the division's own memoranda.

The Commission was unable to discover any specific purpose for the collection of telephone toll call information or any use of that information by the Agency. In the absence of a valid purpose, such collection is improper.

B. Provision and Control of Cover for CIA Personnel

CIA personnel engaged in clandestine foreign intelligence activities cannot travel, live or perform their duties openly as Agency employees. Accordingly, virtually all CIA personnel serving abroad and many in the United States assume a "cover" as employees of another government agency or of a commercial enterprise. CIA involvement in certain activities, such as research and development projects, are also sometimes conducted under cover.

CIA's cover arrangements are essential to the CIA's performance of its foreign intelligence mission. The investigation has disclosed no instances in which domestic aspects of the CIA's cover arrangements involved any violations of law.

By definition, however, cover necessitates an element of deception which must be practiced within the United States as well as within foreign countries. This creates a risk of conflict with various regulatory statutes and other legal requirements. The Agency recognizes this risk. It has installed controls under which cover arrangements are closely supervised to attempt to ensure compliance with applicable laws.

C. Operating Proprietary Companies

The CIA uses proprietary companies to provide cover and perform administrative tasks without attribution to the Agency. Most of the large operating proprietaries—primarily airlines—have been liquidated, and the remainder engage in activities offering little or no competition to private enterprise.

The only remaining large proprietary activity is a complex of financial companies, with assets of approximately $20 million, that enable the Agency to administer certain sensitive trusts, annuities, escrows, insurance arrangements, and other benefits and payments provided to officers or contract employees without attribution to CIA. The remaining small operating proprietaries, generally having fewer than ten employees each, make nonattributable purchases of equipment and supplies.

Except as discussed in connection with the Office of Security (see Chapters 12 and 13), the Commission has found no evidence that any proprietaries have been used for operations against American citizens or investigation of their activities. All of them appear to be subject to close supervision and multiple financial controls within the Agency.

D. Development of Contacts With Foreign Nationals

In connection with the CIA's foreign intelligence responsibilities, it seeks to develop contacts with foreign nationals within the United States. American citizens voluntarily assist in developing these contacts. As far as the Commission can find, these activities have not involved coercive methods.

These activities appear to be directed entirely to the production of foreign intelligence and to be within the authority of the CIA. We found no evidence that any of these activities have been directed against American citizens.

E. Assistance in Narcotics Control

The Directorate of Operations provides foreign intelligence support to the government's efforts to control the flow of narcotics and other dangerous drugs into this country. The CIA coordinates clandestine intelligence collection overseas and provides other government agencies with foreign intelligence on drug traffic.

From the beginning of such efforts in 1969, the CIA Director and other officials have instructed employees to make no attempt to gather information on Americans allegedly trafficking in drugs. If such information is obtained incidentally, it is transmitted to law enforcement agencies.

Concerns that the CIA's narcotics-related intelligence activities may involve the Agency in law enforcement or other actions directed against American citizens thus appear unwarranted.

Beginning in the fall of 1973, the Directorate monitored conversations between the United States and Latin America in an effort to identify narcotics traffickers. Three months after the program began, the General Counsel of the CIA was consulted. He issued an opinion that the program was illegal, and it was immediately terminated.

This monitoring, although a source of valuable information for enforcement officials, was a violation of a statute of the United States. Continuation of the operation for over three months without the knowledge of the Office of the General Counsel demonstrates the need for improved internal consultation. (See Recommendation 10.)

8. Domestic Activities of the Directorate of Science and Technology (Chapter 16)

Findings and Conclusions

The CIA's Directorate of Science and Technology performs a variety of research and development and operational support functions for the Agency's foreign intelligence mission.

Many of these activities are performed in the United States and involve cooperation with private companies. A few of these activities were improper or questionable.

As part of a program to test the influence of drugs on humans, research included the administration of LSD to persons who were unaware that they were being tested. This was clearly illegal. One person died in 1953, apparently as a result. In 1963, following the Inspector General's discovery of these events, new stringent criteria were issued prohibiting drug testing by the CIA on unknowing persons. All drug testing programs were ended in 1967.

In the process of testing monitoring equipment for use overseas, the CIA has overheard conversations between Americans. The names of the speakers were not identified; the contents of the conversations were not disseminated. All recordings were destroyed when testing was concluded. Such testing should not be directed against unsuspecting persons in the United States. Most of the testing undertaken by the Agency could easily have been performed using only Agency personnel and with the full knowledge of those whose conversations were being recorded. This is the present Agency practice.

Other activities of this Directorate include the manufacture of alias credentials for use by CIA employees and agents. Alias credentials are necessary to facilitate CIA clandestine operations, but the strictest controls and accountability must be maintained over the use of such documents. Recent guidelines established by the Deputy Director for Operations to control the use of alias documentation appear adequate to prevent abuse in the future.

As part of another program, photographs taken by CIA aerial photography equipment are provided to civilian agencies of the government. Such photographs are used to assess natural disasters, conduct route surveys and forest inventories, and detect crop blight. Per-

mitting civilian use of aerial photography systems is proper. The economy of operating but one aerial photography program dictates the use of these photographs for appropriate civilian purposes.

Recommendation (27)

In accordance with its present guidelines, the CIA should not again engage in the testing of drugs on unsuspecting persons.

Recommendation (28)

Testing of equipment for monitoring conversations should not involve unsuspecting persons living within the United States.

Recommendation (29)

A civilian agency committee should be reestablished to oversee the civilian uses of aerial intelligence photography in order to avoid any concerns over the improper domestic use of a CIA-developed system.

9. CIA Relationships With Other Federal, State, and Local Agencies (Chapter 17)

CIA operations touch the interest of many other agencies. The CIA, like other agencies of the government, frequently has occasion to give or receive assistance from other agencies. This investigation has concentrated on those relationships which raise substantial questions under the CIA's legislative mandate.

Findings and Conclusion

A. Federal Bureau of Investigation

The FBI counterintelligence operations often have positive intelligence ramifications. Likewise, legitimate domestic CIA activities occasionally cross the path of FBI investigations. Daily liaison is therefore necessary between the two agencies.

Much routine information is passed back and forth. Occasionally joint operations are conducted. The relationship between the agencies has, however, not been uniformly satisfactory over the years. Formal liaison was cut off from February 1970 to November 1972, but relationships have improved in recent years.

The relationship between the CIA and the FBI needs to be clarified and outlined in detail in order to ensure that the needs of national security are met without creating conflicts or gaps of jurisdiction.

Recommendation (30)

The Director of Central Intelligence and the Director of the FBI should prepare and submit for approval by the National Security Council a detailed agreement setting forth the jurisdiction of each agency and providing for effective liaison with respect to all matters of mutual concern. This agreement should be consistent with the provisions of law and with other applicable recommendations of this Report.

Findings and Conclusion

B. Narcotics Law Enforcement Agencies

Beginning in late 1970, the CIA assisted the Bureau of Narcotics and Dangerous Drugs (BNDD) to uncover possible corruption within that organization. The CIA used one of its proprietary companies to recruit agents for BNDD and gave them short instructional courses. Over two and one-half years, the CIA recruited 19 agents for the BNDD. The project was terminated in 1973.

The Director was correct in his written directive terminating the project. The CIA's participation in law enforcement activities in the course of these activities was forbidden by its statute. The Director and the Inspector General should be alert to prevent involvement of the Agency in similar enterprises in the future.

C. The Department of State

For more than 20 years, the CIA through a proprietary conducted a training school for foreign police and security officers in the United States under the auspices of the Agency for International Development of the Department of State. The proprietary also sold small amounts of licensed firearms and police equipment to the foreign officers and their departments.

The CIA's activities in providing educational programs for foreign police were not improper under the Agency's statute. Although the school was conducted within the United States through a CIA proprietary, it had no other significant domestic impact.

Engaging in the firearms business was a questionable activity for a government intelligence agency. It should not be repeated.

D. Funding Requests From Other Federal Agencies

In the spring of 1970, at the request of the White House, the CIA contributed $33,655.68 for payment of stationery and other costs for replies to persons who wrote the President after the invasion of Cambodia.

This use of CIA funds for a purpose unrelated to intelligence is improper. Steps should be taken to ensure against any repetition of such an incident.

E. State and Local Police

The CIA handles a variety of routine security matters through liaison with local police departments. In addition, it offered training courses from 1966 to 1973 to United States police officers on a variety of law enforcement techniques and has frequently supplied equipment to state and local police.

In general, the coordination and cooperation between state and local law enforcement agencies and the CIA has been exemplary, based upon a desire to facilitate their respective legitimate aims and goals.

Most of the assistance rendered to state and local law enforcement agencies by the CIA has been no more than an effort to share with law enforcement authorities the benefits of new methods, techniques, and equipment developed or used by the Agency.

On a few occasions, however, the Agency has improperly become involved in actual police operations. Thus, despite a general rule against providing manpower to local police forces, the CIA has lent men, along with radio-equipped vehicles, to the Washington Metropolitan Police Department to help monitor anti-war demonstrations. It helped the same Department surveil a police informer. It also provided an interpreter to the Fairfax County (Virginia) Police Department to aid in a criminal investigation.

In compliance with the spirit of a recent Act of Congress, the CIA terminated all but routine assistance to state and local law enforcement agencies in 1973. Such assistance is now being provided state and local agencies by the FBI. There is no impropriety in the CIA's furnishing the FBI with information on new technical developments which may be useful to local law enforcement.

For several years the CIA has given gratuities to local police officers who had been helpful to the Agency. Any such practice should be terminated.

The CIA has also received assistance from local police forces. Aside from routine matters, officers from such forces have occasionally assisted the Office of Security in the conduct of investigations. The CIA has occasionally obtained police badges and other identification for use as cover for its agents.

Except for one occasion when some local police assisted the CIA in an unauthorized entry, the assistance received by the CIA from state and local law enforcement authorities was proper. The use of police identification as a

means of providing cover, while not strictly speaking a violation of the Agency's statutory authority as long as no police function is performed, is a practice subject to misunderstanding and should be avoided.

10. Indices and Files on American Citizens (Chapter 18)

Findings

Biographical information is a major resource of an intelligence agency. The CIA maintains a number of files and indices that include biographical information on Americans.

As a part of its normal process of indexing names and information of foreign intelligence interest, the Directorate of Operations has indexed some 7,000,000 names of all nationalities. An estimated 115,000 of these are believed to be merican citizens.

Where a person is believed to be of possibly continuing intelligence interest, files to collect information as received are opened. An estimated 57,000 out of a total of 750,000 such files concern American citizens. For the most part, the names of Americans appear in indices and files as actual or potential sources of information or assistance to the CIA. In addition to these files, files on some 7,200 American citizens, relating primarily to their domestic activities, were, as already stated, compiled within the Directorate of Operations as part of Operation CHAOS.

The Directorate of Administration maintains a number of files on persons who have been associated with the CIA. These files are maintained for security, personnel, training, medical and payroll purposes. Very few are maintained on persons unaware that they have a relationship with the CIA. However, the Office of Security maintained files on American citizens associated with dissident groups who were never affiliated

with the Agency because they were considered a threat to the physical security of Agency facilities and employees. These files were also maintained, in part, for use in future security clearance determinations. Dissemination of security files is restricted to persons with an operational need for them.

The Office of Legislative Counsel maintains files concerning its relationships with congressmen.

Conclusions

Although maintenance of most of the indices, files, and records of the Agency has been necessary and proper, the standards applied by the Agency at some points during its history have permitted the accumulation and indexing of materials not needed for legitimate intelligence or security purposes. Included in this category are many of the files related to Operation CHAOS and the activities of the Office of Security concerning dissident groups.

Constant vigilance by the Agency is essential to prevent the collection of information on United States citizens which is not needed for proper intelligence activities. The Executive Order recommended by the Commission (Recommendation 2) will ensure purging of nonessential or improper materials from Agency files.

11. Allegations Concerning the Assassination of President Kennedy (Chapter 19)

Numerous allegations have been made that the CIA participated in the assassination of President John F. Kennedy. The Commission staff investigated these allegations. On the basis of the staff's investigation, the Commission concludes that there is no credible evidence of CIA involvement.

June 11, 1975

Report on C.I.A. Is Praised, but Recommendations Are Called Weak

By SEYMOUR M. HERSH
Special to The New York Times

WASHINGTON, June 11—The official who provided much of the basic information for the initial account in The New York Times of domestic spying last December praised the Rockefeller commission today for compiling what he termed an "exhaustive" report on the Central Intelligence Agency's illegal activities.

But the source, who spoke only under the continued guarantee of anonymity, criticized the commission's recommendations as being too weak and not providing for explicit statutory prohibition—with appro-

priate punishment—for future wrongdoing.

The official, who has had direct access to highly classified intelligence information, estimated that 90 per cent or more of the allegations he knew about had been described in the commission's report. "I was kind of shocked by the details," he said. "I didn't think the commission would turn out that much detail."

One conspicuous omission, he said, dealt with the C.I.A.'s domestic spying on members of Congress. The Rockefeller commission report made no mention of such files, although William E. Colby, Director of

Central Intelligence, told a House subcommittee last March 5 that files on at least four present and former members of Congress were maintained by the C.I.A.'s special domestic counterintelligence unit.

One such file showed that the agency had maintained a dossier on Representative Bella S. Abzug, Democrat of Manhattan, since 1953—17 years before she was elected to Congress—and had illegally opened some of her mail.

Mr. Colby further testified that "a number" of the domestic counterintelligence files had been destroyed, an assertion that also was omitted from

the Rockefeller commission's report.

Other sources with some independent knowledge of the domestic spying activities subsequently noted in telephone interviews that the commission's report did not mention the destruction in late 1974 of between 150 and 200 C.I.A. domestic files on black dissidents, nearly all of which included photographs of some kind.

No Cover-up Seen

Sources close to the Rockefeller commission conceded that such information had not been included in the final report, but emphasized—as one put it—that there was no evidence that this was an attempt to hide anything. "A lot of files on blacks were not destroyed," one source said.

"It would be a mistake," another source said, "to put a racist twist on this or to say that the ones [files] that were destroyed were the hot ones."

"We found everything that was humanly possible on that operation," he added.

In effect agreeing with that statement, The Times's basic intelligence source predicted that the Senate Select Committee on Intelligence, whose chairman is Senator Frank Church, Democrat of Idaho, would be unable to significantly advance the commission's findings—at least in the area of illegal domestic activities. "They're nice enough people," he said of the staff members of the Senate committee, "but not substantial enough to handle this."

Intensive Interviewing

Any further information about domestic spying, the source said, would have to result from intensive personal interviewing of C.I.A. domestic operatives who may not have officially reported all of their activities.

The Times's source attacked the 30 recommendations by the Rockefeller commission as being totally inadequate.

"There are too many recommendations that say that the C.I.A., the President and the director [of the C.I.A.] 'should not' do things without imposing criminal sanctions," he said.

"We need criminal sanctions to hold the bureaucracy in line," the source continued. "Times have a way of changing, and world views change. Without criminal sanctions, it's possible that conditions could arise which would involve activities like those now being criticized. Don't forget, justifications change with the times."

End to Further Inquiries

The source concluded the interview with what amounted to a plea for an end to further inquiries. "It's time to return to normal for the C.I.A.," he said. "This has been upsetting even more so for the analytical types than the covert types [in the agency]."

He added that many C.I.A. analysts, those who research data and prepare intelligence estimates, "were deeply disappointed to find out that their agency, which they have respect for, was involved in this kind of a thing."

The Rockefeller commission report also did not deal with the allegations, as published by The New York Times last Dec. 29, of a former C.I.A. domestic operative who said he had conducted break-ins, wiretap operations and other illegal activities while investigating antiwar groups in New York City in the late nineteen-sixties and early nineteen-seventies.

In Congressional testimony last February, Mr. Colby said the agency had been unable to identify the former C.I.A. man, who was not identified by name in The Times's account, and added: "I fear that the journalist has been the victim of what we in the intelligence trade call a fabricator."

Sources close to the Rockefeller commission said that, despite repeated checks, they had been unable to find any documentary evidence of such undercover C.I.A. activities in New York City. The former C.I.A. agent identified himself as having worked for the agency's domestic operations divisions there.

Skepticism Voiced

In a telephone interview this morning, the former C.I.A. operative—who depicted New York City as "a big training ground" for undercover agents —expressed skepticism that a full account of all the C.I.A.'s domestic activities would ever be compiled.

"It's so easy to cover up," he said. "You're never going to find out what really happened; all the details and all the people involved will never come out."

"They'll clean up their shop a little, but in 10 or 20 years it'll start again," he added. "It's all so cyclical."

The former C.I.A. man has refused thus far to agree to discuss his activities with members of the Rockefeller commission or the Senate committee headed by Mr. Church.

June 12, 1975

F.B.I. Reported to Have Listed Citizens to Detain During Crisis

By JOHN M. CREWDSON
Special to The New York Times

WASHINGTON, Aug. 2—The Federal Bureau of Investigation began in the early nineteen-fifties to compile a secret list, known as the "Security Index," of American citizens who were "targeted for detention" in a national emergency under the Subversive Activities Control Act, according to two sources who claim direct knowledge of the operation.

The sources said that the list, which at its peak contained about 15,000 names, included, in addition to suspected agents of hostile governments, virtually all known members of the American Communist party, some of whom were "quite elderly," several clergymen, and others who, according to the sources, posed no genuine internal security threat.

Although the detention provisions of the act under which the index was established were repealed by Congress in 1971, one of the sources said that the index — now reportedly much smaller—was still being maintained by the bureau's Domestic Intelligence Division, in anticipation of possible reinstatement of such authority.

The F.B.I. has never acknowledged that it has maintained an index of persons who might be detained, although the existence of such a list was widely rumored in radical and Communist party circles in the nineteen-fifties and in the late sixties by some black leaders who feared it might be employed to quell urban unrest.

But one of the sources, who termed the Security Index "a ridiculous thing," said it was known jocularly within the F.B.I. as the "pick-up list." The other source described its ostensible purpose as "to assist in rounding up people who might commit sabotage or espionage."

An F.B.I. spokesman, informed of the sources' accounts, said at first that the bureau maintained "no Security Index." Asked to check further, he later acknowledged that the F.B.I. does "maintain a list of individuals felt to be dangerous to the internal security of the United States."

He emphasized, however, that the list was "not for detention purposes, but is merely for administrative control within the F.B.I." He would not elaborate on the uses to which it was being put, if any.

Asked to characterize the individuals on the current list, one Justice Department official said that, in addition to suspected terrorists such as members of the Weather Underground, it was likely to include at any given time political dissidents and members of Marxist organizations ranging from the Communist party to the Pro - Chinese Revolutionary Union.

Never Heard of It

In a telephone interview, Melvin Wulf, the legal director of the American Civil Liberties Union's New York office, said that he had never heard of the F.B.I.'s Security Index.

But he called such a practice "clearly unconstitutional," especially in the absence of any legislative authority to detain individuals in the event of an emergency.

Under the First Amendment, he noted, "you're supposed to have a right to any political opinion you want to have."

According to one high Justice Department official, a group set up last March by Attorney General Edward H. Levi to study the F.B.I.'s intelligence-gathering operations has "considered" the legality of continuing the Security Index in the absence of any emergency detention authority.

It could not be learned, however, what recommendation the group had made to Mr. Levi on retention of the index.

The Federal statute under which the index was initially established provided that, in the event of an "internal security emergency" declared by the President, the Attorney General could detain individuals he considered likely to engage or conspire in "acts of espionage or sabotage."

One Justice official recalled that, after the repeal of that provision in September, 1971, the F.B.I. asked the department whether it could continue to maintain the index as a part of the bureau's record-keeping system, despite the repeal.

"We told them, 'Yeah, you can keep records,' " the official recalled, and another official said it was the Justice Department's understanding that the index, which now reportedly contains about one-tenth the number of names as at its peak, serves the bureau simply as a file of "potential troublemakers" that is "no longer in any way geared to a roundup."

The only official reference to the Security Index that has ever become public is contained in an F.B.I. report stolen with other documents from the bureau's office in Media, Pa., in early 1971.

The stolen report noted that a young woman, a student at

the University of California, would not be recommended for inclusion on the Security Index unless information could be found to corroborate the assertion of an anonymous informer that she was "an inveterate Marxist revolutionist."

The report, dated Feb. 26, 1971, contained no indication that the woman was suspected of any criminal activity or was being investigated for any other reason than her purported political beliefs.

One former Government official familiar with the index, which he said was known within the bureau as the "special list," conceded that the idea behind it "probably was sound years ago, when we would know a few weeks or a month in advance if a country was going to declare war on us."

But he said that, apart from the legal implications, the con-

cept of "rounding up people who might commit sabotage or espionage" in time of war made less sense in the nuclear age.

According to this source, until the late nineteen-sixties the Security index was compiled by the subversives control section of the F.B.I.'s Intelligence Division, which spent a good deal of time keeping track of the addresses and occupations of those on the list.

Because it was originally established as a "Communist index," he said, a member of the Communist party "would go on there almost automatically." But he and others said that the list was subsequently expanded to include members of other leftist organizations and of some on the right, such as the Ku Klux Klan, that had no obvious connection with any hostile foreign power.

The index was reportedly made up of three categories of individuals who were ranked

according to the potential seriousness of the threat they posed to internal security—leaders of allegedly militant or "subversive" organizations, members of such organizations believed prone to violence or espionage, and other members of such groups.

Not Warranted

One of the sources said that, because of what he characterized as the F.B.I.'s propensity for inclusiveness and its inherent reluctance to purge its files, the index "undoubtedly" listed some individuals whose views and activities did not warrant their inclusion under the now-defunct language of the Subversives Control Act.

The guiding principle under which the index was compiled, he said, "was who would be dangerous to the country."

"That's a very nebulous concept," he added, pointing out that, as late as 1971, the index

contained the names of "about a dozen" clergymen.

According to this source and others, in the late nineteen-sixties officials of the bureau's Intelligence Division became concerned that the index by then included a number of individuals who, if detained in the event of an emergency, could prove a subsequent embarrassment to the F.B.I.

As a result, they said, the index was pared back from around 12,000 names to 2,000, a figure from which it has since declined still further.

The 10,000 or so names that were weeded out, the sources said, were placed in a "reserve index," which for practical purposes served as an inactive file.

It could not be learned whether the reserve index was still in existence, or what its status was.

August 3, 1975

F.B.I. IS ACCUSED OF POLITICAL ACTS FOR 6 PRESIDENTS

Senate Intelligence Inquiry Names Leaders From Roosevelt to Nixon

ROBERT KENNEDY CITED

Secret Dossiers, Taps and Surveillance Reported— Newsmen Affected

By NICHOLAS M. HORROCK
Special to The New York Times

WASHINGTON, Dec. 3—The Federal Bureau of Investigation supplied secret dossiers, conducted wiretaps and carried out physical surveillance for "political" purposes at the behest of all six Presidents from Franklin D. Roosevelt to Richard M. Nixon, the staff of a Senate committee charged today.

In a 16-page report based on documents from F.B.I. files and testimony of former officials and other witnesses, the staff of the Senate Select Committee on Intelligence reported the following:

¶Attorney General Robert F. Kennedy authorized F.B.I. wire-

taps on correspondents of The New York Times and Newsweek magazine in the early 1960's in an effort to discover leaks of information.

¶Mr. Kennedy authorized F.B.I. wiretaps on six American citizens, including officials of a domestic Government agency, a Congressional staff member and two registered lobbyists for foreign interests, in an investigation of efforts by "foreign interests to influence United States economic policies."

¶The F.B.I. supplied to President Johnson materials from its files on seven newsmen. The report named three of them as David Brinkley of NBC, Peter Arnett of The Associated Press and the columnist, Joseph Kraft. Committee sources said that the agency also gave the White House information on Peter Lisagor of The Chicago Daily News and John Chancellor of NBC. The names of the two other newsmen were not disclosed.

The staff report also confirmed news reports of an effort by President Johnson to obtain background information on Senator Barry Goldwater's staff in 1964, when Mr. Goldwater was the Republican Presidential nominee.

It said that Presidents Roosevelt and Johnson had asked the bureau to check the backgrounds of persons who wrote to the White House opposing their foreign policy decisions.

The report came in the second phase of committee hear-

ings on the F.B.I. At today's session the committee made public a series of memorandums that made it appear that former Attorney General Nicholas deB. Katzenbach was aware of an electronic bug being planted in the room of the Rev. Dr. Martin Luther King Jr. in a New York hotel in 1965. In the three memorandums, singed by the F.B.I. Director, J. Edgar Hoover, and directed to Mr. Katzenbach, it was noted that the bureau had installed an electronic bug in hotel rooms occupied by Dr. King on three different occasions. Each memorandum noted that "this surveillance involved trespass."

The Hotels, all in New York City, were the Sheraton Atlantic, 34th Street and Broadway, on May 12, 1965; The Astor Hotel, at 44th Street and Broadway, on Oct. 14, 1965, and the Americana Hotel on the Avenue of the Americas, on Nov. 29, 1965.

Mr. Katzenbach said in testimony that he could not recall ever having received the memorandums although each carries what appear to be his initials in his handwriting.

Mr. Katzenbach, in a 63-page prepared statement, said that on March 30, 1965, he and Mr. Hoover agreed that the bureau should obtain prior authorization for the installation of electronic bugs.

According to F.B.I. records, the committee staff said, the F.B.I. installed five room bugs on Dr. King, after the March 30 order. It was unclear if the bureau sought or Mr. Katzenbach issued approval for these installations.

Former Attorney General Ramsey Clark, in testimony be-

fore the committee today, urged creation of a commission to investigate all Government activity relating to Dr. King.

In connection with "political abuse" of the F.B.I. and its political activities, the committee report said, the "F.B.I. intelligence system developed to a point where no one inside or outside the bureau was willing or able to tell the difference between legitimate national security or law enforcement information and purely political intelligence."

As early as 1940, the report said, the F.B.I. ran name checks (checks of its records), opened files and made reports on "hundreds of persons who sent telegrams to the President that were all more or less in opposition to national defense [according to a Hoover memo] or that expressed approval of Col. Charles Lindbergh's criticism of the President." Colonel Lindbergh was active in the isolationist movement that opposed any move to involve the United States in the war then going on in Europe.

There were similar incidents involving the mixing of political and national security matters in the Truman and Eisenhower Administrations according to the report. In 1949, for instance, the F.B.I. investigated the National Lawyers Guild, which was denouncing F.B.I. activities. The then Attorney General, J. Howard McGrath, passed this military affairs editor of The Truman, the report said.

The report said that President Eisnhower had asked Mr. Hoover to brief his Cabinet on racial tension early in 1956. But, according to the staff report, Mr. Hoover sent "a report not only of incidents of violence, but also on the activities of seven Governors and Congressmen in groups opposing integration, as well as the role of Communists in civil rights lobbying efforts and the N.A.A.C.P.'s [National Association for the Advancement of Colored People] plans to push legislation."

Purpose of Wiretaps

In the Kennedy Administration, the report said, the F.B.I. was sent to interview a steel company executive and several newsmen during a national steel strike. This too had been reported in the press.

The staff report said that in 1962 Attorney General Kennedy authorized that wiretaps be placed on Hanson W. Baldwin, military affairs editor of The New York Times, and his secretary. They lasted for about one month, the report said. Mr. Baldwin, now retired, was unavailable for comment.

The report said that the taps had been placed to discover his news sources in an attempt to plug Administration leaks of information.

A year earlier, the report said, Mr. Kennedy authorized a telephone tap on a Newsweek magazine reporter. The report did not name the reporter. A spokesman for Newsweek said the reporter might have been Lloyd Norman, its veteran Pentagon correspondent, who angered the Kennedy Administration by his disclosures in coverage of the crisis over the Berlin Wall in 1961. Mr. Norman was unavailable for comment.

The report said that President Nixon had used the bureau to get background information on Daniel Schorr, a CBS newsman, and charged that in the wiretaps of journalists and White House officials in the Nixon Administration at least one tap was conducted "solely for personal information about the target."

The report said that Mr. Kennedy had also ordered wiretaps on officials of the executive branch, lobbyists and a Congressional aide. The aide's telephone was tapped at his home and not in his Capitol Hill office, according to the report.

President Johnson appeared to have been an active user of the F.B.I., mainly through Cartha D. Deloach, then an assistant director. Mr. Deloach said in his testimony that he headed a "special squad" at the Democratic National convention at Atlantic City in 1964, but contended that the operation had been to detect and prevent violence.

A substantial part of the information passed on by the special squad dealt with the activities of Dr. King and the members of the Mississippi Freedom Democratic Party, which was attempting to gain seating.

"As Theodore White's account of the 1964 campaign makes clear, the most important single issue that might have disturbed President Johnson at the Atlantic City convention was the Mississippi challenge," the report noted. It left the question of whether the operation was entirely for political purposes up to the committee.

December 4, 1975

POWER TO PREVENT DOMESTIC THREATS SOUGHT FOR F.B.I.

A Justice Department Draft Asks Authority to Act in Advance of Crime

LEVI DESCRIBES PLAN

Tells of Control Procedures —Mondale Criticizes the Proposal as 'Vague'

By NICHOLAS M. HORROCK

Special to The New York Times

WASHINGTON, Dec. 11—The Department of Justice proposed today that the Federal Bureau of Investigation be permitted to "obstruct or prevent" groups that were plotting to use force or violence that might pose a threat to life or "interfere substantially" with the "essential functioning of government."

The proposal was among a series of draft "guidelines" prepared by a Justice Department study group designed to place controls over the bureau's domestic security activities.

It was the first time, several senior Congressional aides said, that a proposal had been made that the F.B.I. be permitted legally to act against a group or individual before a crime had been committed.

Proposal Criticized

Edward H. Levi, the Attorney General, testified today on the proposed guidelines before the Senate Select Committee on Intelligence. He said the F.B.I. would be able to open full domestic security investigations only where there was a "likelihood" that the activities of an individual or a group would involve illegal violence or that the subjects were supported by a foreign government or political group.

Senator Walter F. Mondale, Democrat of Wisconsin, strongly criticized the proposed guidelines as "vague" and said they would not help future directors of the F.B.I. withstand any direct orders by Presidents or Attorneys General to engage in improper conduct.

Without strong law, he said, the guidelines "would be swept away as quickly as a sand castle is overrun by a hurricane."

Other Senators, too, said the language of the proposals appeared broad.

A few moments later the Senator and the Attorney General entered into an angry exchange over whether the committee could obtain from Clarence M. Kelley, director of the bureau, further documents on the disruption program known as Cointelpro, which the F.B.I. operated from 1956 to 1971.

Mr. Mondale said the committee had received similar materials from the Central Intelligence Agency.

"I'm not in the C.I.A., have never been, and don't care to be," Mr. Levi snapped angrily.

"Do you consider that a good answer?" Mr. Mondale asked, his face flushed.

"I consider that as good an answer as the question," Mr. Levi said.

Senator Mondale, turning to Senator Frank Church, the committee chairman, said:

"Mr. Chairman, I think that kind of arrogance is why we have trouble with the executive branch [of Government]."

"I apologize to Senator Mondale if I appeared arrogant," Mr. Levi said in carefully controlled tones. "I thought somebody else was appearing arrogant."

An Example Cited

Mr. Levi said that another feature of the draft guidelines would place "strict controls" on any technique "by the F.B.I. which goes beyond the gathering of information."

"Nonetheless," Mr. Levi said, "there may be circumstances involving an immediate risk to human life or to extraordinarily important Government functions that could only be countered by some sort of preventive action."

Mr. Church asked the Attorney General what might be involved in "preventive action." Mr. Levi gave an example of two violence-prone columns of marchers heading toward one another with the potential for a confrontation. He said the bureau might block streets or change direction signs. "I take it that is a preventive action," Mr. Levi said.

Mr. Church offered a counter example of motor caravans and asked whether such a tactic as putting sand in the gasoline tanks would be acceptable.

"The answer is no, certainly not," Mr. Levi said.

The draft guidelines said that preventive actions "may not involve the commission of a crime, the origination of an idea for a crime or inducing others to carry out such ideas" and would be conducted so as not to limit the civil rights of individuals.

The F.B.I. now has no statutory authority to disrupt the activities of groups or individuals simply because they may contemplate violence. Nor is the F.B.I. legally permitted to hold radicals to prevent violence.

The United States does permit the prosecution of persons conspiring to violate Federal laws. By and large, law enforcement officials have argued, these laws can be invoked only after the fact, after a violation.

F.B.I. officials, including Mr. Kelley, have strongly urged that the bureau be given authority to deal with political violence such as airline hijackings and terrorist kidnappings.

The preventive action methods would have to be approved by the Attorney General or his designate and would have to be taken within specific time periods.

The draft guidelines are the first set of controls over F.B.I. domestic security operations ever proposed by the Department of Justice. They were prepared by a committee, headed by Mary Lawton, Deputy Assistant Attorney General in the legal counsel's office, that included F.B.I. officials.

The Senate panel asked for the guidelines as it began to prepare its proposals for controlling domestic security operations.

The committee ended today the investigative aspects of its public hearings and is expected to complete its report early in February.

In general the Justice Department draft would establish a role for the bureau to investigate threats to domestic security where the backing came from foreign intelligence services or groups or where violence was contemplated. The guidelines attempt to bar instances such as those uncovered by the committee where the bureau investigated peaceful dissidents.

The guidelines suggest two types of investigations. One, a preliminary inquiry could be instituted by bureau field offices to discover whether an individual or group contemplated violence or was backed by foreign powers.

In the preliminary investigation the bureau could not place a new informant in the group or conduct physical or electronic surveillance.

If a full investigation were authorized by the F.B.I. head-quarters, other techniques could come into play, but "mail covers"—copying down names from the face

of an envelope—and surveillance by an electronic listening device would have to be approved by the Attorney General under current statutes.

The guidelines also attempt to set ground rules for destroying information after its usefulness ended

and for controlling the dissemination of information.

Mr. Levi acknowledged that some portions of the guidelines might be better handled through the passage of new laws but said that others could be effected by department

regulations or executive orders.

Portions of the guidelines will presumably become part of a Ford Administration legislative package on domestic intelligence next year.

December 12, 1975

HOUSE COMMITTEE FINDS INTELLIGENCE AGENCIES GENERALLY GO UNCHECKED

SECRECY IS CITED

A Year's Investigation Uncovered Number Of Irregularities

By JOHN M. CREWDSON
Special to The New York Times

WASHINGTON, Jan. 25—The House Select Committee on Intelligence has concluded following a year-long investigation that the Federal intelligence agencies, as they are currently constituted, operate in such secret ways that they are "beyond the scrutiny" of Congress, according to the panel's final report.

The 338-page report, which has not been released but a copy of which was obtained by The New York Times, discloses a number of irregularities uncovered by committee investigators. These include an apparent violation by the Central Intelligence Agency of a 1967 Presidential directive prohibiting it from providing secret financial assistance to any of the nation's educational institutions.

Low Budget Figures

The House committee also concluded that secret budget figures given to Congress by

Federal intelligence agencies over the years were "three or four times" lower than the totals actually spent by the United States in gathering intelligence at home and abroad.

It put the total annual Federal intelligence budget at "more than $10 billion."

Many of those expenditures, it said, were obscured from Congress and were not adequately audited either by the Office of Management and Budget or by the agencies' own accountants, with the result that wastefulness and questionable expenditures had occurred.

The document is the third major government report in eight months detailing improper C.I.A. covert activities at home and abroad. On June 10 a Presidential commission headed by Vice President Rockefeller released its report on the agency's domestic spying activities and on Nov. 20 the Senate Select Committee on Intelligence issued its report that included assassination plots against foreign leaders.

9-to-4 Vote

The committee's investigation, the report on which was approved in final form by a 9-to-4 vote of the panel's members on Friday, but which will not be made public until the end of this month, also turned up the following revelations:

¶That the National Security Agency, which has the respon-

sibility for monitoring the communications of other nations and attempting to break their codes, illegally listened in on overseas telephone conversations of specific American citizens whose names or telephone numbers had been provided to it by "another government agency."

¶That the Federal Bureau of Investigation violated its own manual of regulations by preserving in its files "intimate sexual gossip" picked up by agents during a criminal investigation.

¶That Robert A. Maheu, a former top aide to Howard R. Hughes, the billionaire, arranged at the behest of the C.I.A. to supply King Hussein of Jordan and other foreign leaders wth female companions who were reimbursed for their efforts with Federal funds.

¶That "thousands, if not millions, of dollars of unwarranted mark-ups" were added to the cost of bugging equipment purchased by the F.B.I. through a private company whose president was a close friend of high bureau officials.

An F.B.I. spokesman said he would have no comment on the report's allegations until it was made public.

Colby Calls It Biased

But William E. Colby, the outgoing Director of Central Intelligence, said that a preliminary draft of the House report he had seen was "biased and irresponsible."

Mr. Colby said through a spokesman that the panel's disclosure of several of the agency's sensitive activities would

harm American foreign policy, and he criticized what he termed "a selective use of evidence" by the committee "to present a totally false picture of American intelligence as a whole."

A. Searle Field, the committee's staff director, responded that Mr. Colby had not yet seen the final version of the report approved by the panel on Friday, from which a number of names and other sensitive details were deleted.

The committee's three Republican members and one of its 10 Democrats voted on Friday against releasing the report in its present form. However, one source present at that meeting said that none of the four had objected to the report's tone or conclusions, only to the inclusion of sensitive information about three covert C.I.A. operations.

On Arms Shipments

The document contains long sections on the C.I.A.'s financing of political parties in Italy and its shipment of arms to anti-Communist forces in Angola and to Kurdish rebels in Iraq, although none of the countries is identified.

Mr. Colby pointed out today, however, that the unilateral release of that information, much of which has already appeared in news accounts, violated the committee's agreement with the White House to first seek President Ford's approval to make it public.

That agreement grew out of a dispute between the committee and the White House over access to classified information that was precipitated by the panel's disclosure of a phrase from a C.I.A. intelligence summary.

Mr. Ford halted the committee's access to documents and sensitive testimony by Administration officials and demanded the return of classified files already in the panel's possession. This move, the report noted, prompted Representative Otis G. Pike, the Long Island Democrat who heads the committee, to order the Capitol police "to prevent any takeover of files by the executive."

The committee discovered

later, the report said, that the situation described by the phrase — the employment of "greater communications security" by the Egyptians just before the 1973 Mideast war — had been fully described in a book about Secretary of State Henry A. Kissinger published a year earlier.

In a subsequent interview tonight with NBC, Mr. Colby, asked what he might do after leaving office later this week, replied that he was considering writing a book about "modern intelligence" methods.

The C.I.A. has also expressed private concern about the committee report's description of its failure to give foreign policy makers sufficient advance warning of the outbreak of the 1973 Middle East war, the 1974 political coups in Cyprus and Portugal, the Indian nuclear explosion that same year and the 1968 Soviet invasion of Czechoslovakia.

But a committee source said today that the intelligence agency had not responded to the panel's request for details on comparable intelligence successes, except to cite the "saving of Europe" from Communist control following World War II and the frustration of efforts by Prime Minister Fidel Castro of Cuba to "export revolution" to Latin America.

'In Compliance'

Told of the committee assertion regarding the violation by the C.I.A. of the 1967 Presidential directive, Mr. Colby replied through a spokesman that he believed the agency to have been in compliance with President Johnson's order to halt "any covert financial assistance or support, direct or indirect, to any of the nation's educational or private voluntary organizations."

The House report noted, however, that Carl Duckett, who heads the C.I.A.'s division of science and technology, testified to the panel last Nov. 4 that the agency "still has ongoing contracts" for research and development "with a small number of universities," and that some of them were covertly let—that is, that the institutions performing the work were unaware that they were working for the C.I.A.

The agency, the report declared, has "unilaterally reserved the right to, and does, depart from the [1967] Presidential order when it has the need to do so."

It quoted a June 21, 1967, memorandum to Richard Helms, then the Director of Central Intelligence, noting that the agency would try to conform to the Johnson guidelines "as rapidly as feasible and wherever possible," but that "the agency must retain some flexibility for contracting arrangements with academic institutions."

The panel also cited a study it requested from auditors for the General Accounting Office that concluded that significant portions of the Federal Intelligence budget had gone unreported to Congress in recent years.

The secret intelligence budgets given to Congress, the G.A.O. said, did not contain a number of important items, including 20 percent of the National Security Agency's annual budget, the budgets of the Pentagon's Advanced Projects Research Administration and the National Security Council, and the costs of domestic counter-intelligence functions performed by the F.B.I.

The expenditures of those funds, the report said, were largely unchecked by Congress

and even by the Office of Management and Budget, which assigned only six full-time auditors to the foreign intelligence agencies. It said this spending was also inadequately monitored by C.I.A. accountants, who told the committee that in many cases they had been forced to "rely solely on the integrity" of many agency officials.

One of the categories of inappropriate expenditures cited by the agency was Mr. Maheu's procurement of women, which a committee source said occurred around 1957. This was some years after he became a consultant to Mr. Hughes and about the same time that he produced for the agency a pornographic film, "Happy Days," which starred an actor who resembled Indonesian President Sukarno.

The report did not elaborate on the production of the film, or whether it was ever used to embarrass Mr. Sukarno, as the agency had intended.

Neither Mr. Maheu nor Mr. Sukarno were named in the report, from which all identities have been excised. But their names, like that of King Hussein, were provided by sources familiar with the House panel's investigation.

The committee's disclosure that the N.S.A. had monitored the overseas telephone conversations of American citizens at the request of another Federal agency is the first instance in which the N.S.A. has been found to have targeted individuals in this country.

Halted in 1973

There have been previous reports, including one by the Rockefeller commission, that agency incidentally overheard American citizens in monitoring foreign telephones before May

1973, when the practice was halted.

The N.S.A. listened to conversations that other Federal investigators believed to have some importance in connection with narcotics cases and radical anti-Vietnam war activity, but no evidence has been found that such interceptions were approved by the Justice Department or by a court order, as required by law.

The House committee's investigation focused mainly on the operations of the C.I.A. and touched on the F.B.I. only peripherally. But it turned up one instance, the bureau's investigation of a radical "think-tank" organization here, that the report said violated a number of F.B.I. regulations covering the conduct of criminal investigations by its agents.

Despite a bureau regulation that prohibits such inquiries from continuing beyond 90 days unless there is a likelihood of eventually uncovering criminal activities, the investigation of the organization, the Institute for Policy Studies, lasted from 1968 to 1973.

No criminal violations were found during that five-year period, the report said, and the bureau concluded in May 1974 that there had been "a paucity of information" to indicate that such violations had occurred.

Nonetheless, the report said, the bureau's agents at one point seized the institute's garbage and recorded in their reports "intimate sexual gossip" about the organization's members and others, despite a bureau regulation prohibiting the retention of such "social or personal" information "not relevant to subjects' subversive activities or affiliations."

January 26, 1976

HOUSE PREVENTS RELEASING REPORT ON INTELLIGENCE

By DAVID E. ROSENBAUM
Special to The New York Times

WASHINGTON, Jan. 29—The House of Representatives acceded tonight to the wishes of President Ford and the intelligence agencies and voted to withhold the final report of its Select Committee on Intelligence until it had been censored by the executive branch.

The action, which was opposed by the House Democratic leadership, came on a vote of 246 to 124.

Representative Otis G. Pike, the chairman of the select committee, said that the vote had made "a complete travesty of the whole doctrine of separation of powers."

He said that the House "probably will not ever have a strong oversight committee now" and that his committee's work had been "entirely an exercise in futility."

'I'm Not as Proud'

After the vote, the Suffolk County Democrat told reporters: "I'm not quite as proud of being a member of the House of Representatives today as I

was yesterday. I'm still proud, but not as proud."

A copy of the report was made available to The New York Times, which, earlier this week, published several articles based on it.

The President issued a statement tonight expressing pleasure over the vote.

"This action indicates that a large majority of House members shares my concern that our legitimate classified national security information be denied to our enemies and potential enemies," Mr. Ford said. "Today's vote shows the House members recognize that the American people want a strong and effective foreign intelligence capability."

Mr. Pike said that virtually all information that was of importance "interest-wise or titillation-wise" had already been published.

Major Implications

Nonetheless, in the view of representatives on both sides of the issue, the vote tonight had major implications.

Those who wanted the full document to be published officially said that the vote provided indications on whether the House seriously intended to oversee the activities of intelligence agencies in the future and of whether the House was willing to leave to the executive branch all decisions on what should properly be kept secret.

On the other hand, representatives who wanted to prevent immediate publication argued that there was a difference between an official document and one that had merely been reported on in newspapers. The House, they said, should not be party to the official publication of classified information and should not take steps that might endanger the national security.

Representatives Morgan F. Murphy of Illinois and Robert N. Giaimo of Connecticut, both Democratic members of the intelligence committee, gave impassioned speeches in favor of releasing the full document. Their speeches had all the more effect because both men are highly regarded by their colleagues and normally speak in an understated manner.

"If we are not a co-equal branch of this Government, if we are not equal to the President and the Supreme Court," Mr. Murphy asserted, "then let the President write this report, let the C.I.A. write this report, and we ought to fold our tents and go home."

Mr. Giaimo pointed his forefinger at Mr. Pike, who was sitting on the front row of the chamber, and declared, "If you think he is going to release anything that in his judgment would jeopardize the secrets of the United States, then you are wrong."

The White House and the intelligence agencies had "spread a smokescreen" about the secrets in the report, Mr. Giaimo said, and he asked his colleagues whether they placed their trust in Mr. Pike or the Central Intelligence Agency.

Pike Stand on Secrets

For his part, Mr. Pike conceded that the report contained classified information, but he said that there was "not the slightest question that we are giving away any dangerous secrets."

A secret, he said, was "some fact or opinion to which some bureaucrat has applied a stamp."

Mr. Pike's opponents were equally emotional in their speeches.

Representative James H. Quillen, a Tennessee Republican, declared, "My country comes first, and I will not take any action to release classified information to anyone domestically or abroad."

The ranking Republican on the intelligence panel, Representative Robert McClory of Illinois, said that the President and the intelligence agencies had provided the committee with information with the understanding of confidentiality.

"We don't have to spread out in the record all the secret information, including information that might jeopardize the lives of individuals and jeopardize our activities overseas," Mr. McClory argued. He continued:

"What agency will provide us with data and documents if we can't be trusted."

It would be "unworthy of Congress," Mr. McClory said, to "translate leaks into official documents."

One hundred twenty-two Democrats and two Republicans voted to publish the document immediately. One hundred twenty-seven Democrats and 119 Republicans voted against doing so until the President had cleared the document.

William E. Colby, the outgoing Director of Central Intelligence, urged the House earlier in the week not to publish the report on the ground that to do so would damage the nation's intelligence activities. Mr. Colby said that there was considerable potentially dangerous information in the report, although he never specified what it was.

Findings in Report

Among the findings in the report, according to accounts published in The Times, were the following:

¶The Navy conducted a program of intelligence gathering through submarines operating inside territorial waters of other nations and on at least nine occasions, these ships collided with other vessels.

¶The operations and funds of the intelligence agencies were virtually unchecked, and the agencies used deceptive accounting methods.

¶The extent of the United States involvement in the civil war in Angola had been understated by Mr. Colby.

¶Secretary of State Henry A. Kissinger and his wife had received personal gifts from the leader of Kurdish rebels, who had been supplied arms secretly by the C.I.A.

Normally, publication of a committee report, even a sensitive one, is a routine matter that is not voted on by the full House. The intelligence report came before the House because of an unusual set of circumstances.

Mr. Pike's committee is scheduled to go out of existence Saturday.

Because the House is not in session tomorrow, Mr. Pike asked Tuesday for unanimous consent to publish the report Friday and an extension until Feb. 11 for publication of the committee's recommendations.

After a junior House member objected to the extension, Mr. Pike was forced to take his request to the Rules Committee.

Yesterday, apparently without the knowledge of the Democratic leaders, who normally control the operations of the Rules Committee, that committee adopted a resolution prohibiting publication of the report until it had been cleared by the President.

The Rules Committee's action forced the House vote tonight.

One committee source said tonight that there was "a possibility" that some panel members would ask the House next week to reconstitute the select committee to rework the report.

The source said White House aides had indicated that they would excise "more than half" of the 338-page document before making it public.

In another development today, Senator Frank Church, chairman of the Senate Select Committee on Intelligence, introduced legislation that would create a permanent Senate committee to oversee the Government's intelligence activities.

The legislation would establish procedures to assure committee secrecy but specifies that the committee would be free to make public information if it found it was in the national interest to do so.

January 30, 1976

SCHORR RELIEVED OF DUTIES BY CBS

The Network Acts Pending Resolution of Inquiry Into Leak of House Report

By RICHARD D. LYONS
Special to The New York Times

WASHINGTON, Feb. 23—CBS News formally relieved Daniel Schorr today of all duties as a Washington correspondent pending resolution of a Congressional investigation of his leak of a House committee's intelligence report to The Village Voice.

Mr. Schorr will continue on the CBS payroll and maintain an office in the network's Washington bureau, but is forbidden to cover news events as an employee of the network.

Richard S. Salant, president of CBS News, said in a statement issued in New York that Mr. Schorr was being relieved of duties in "view of the adversary situation in which" he is placed in pending government investigations. He refused to elaborate on the statement, although Marcia Stein, a spokesman, said that the suspension would continue "until all litigation is out of the way."

Mr. Salant said in his statement that the network "will support Mr. Schorr by providing legal counsel insofar as investigations relating to his CBS News activities are concerned."

The statement added that CBS News would back Mr. Schorr "against attempts to require him to reveal the source through which he obtained the report."

"These aspects of the matter involve fundamental issues of press freedom," the statement said.

But Mr. Salant underscored the network's position that in making the report available to The Village Voice "Mr. Schorr acted as an individual."

Mr. Salant's statement, and one by Mr. Schorr, were agreed to today at a meeting in New York. Attending were Mr. Schorr, William J. Small, senior vice president for news of CBS News; Joseph A. Califano, Mr. Schorr's attorney, and lawyers for the network. Mr. Califano is a former counselor to President Johnson.

The scope of Mr. Schorr's legal problems may become known tomorrow morning when a committee of the House of Representatives meets in an effort to determine how to procede with its investigation of the newsman. The House called for the investigation last Thursday by a vote of 269 to 115.

In the resolution, which was introduced by Representative Samuel S. Stratton, Democrat of upstate New York, it was specifically stated that Mr. Schorr "may be in contempt of" the House, or to have abused his privileges as an accredited correspondent there.

Representative John J. Flynt, Democrat of Georgia, is chairman of the group that will consider the issue—the House Committee on Standards of Official Conduct, usually referred to as the House Ethics Committee.

One of the tangential issues involved in the complicated case is whether Mr. Schorr sought to have CBS News broadcast the report, and, if such an offer was rejected, how widely Mr. Schorr sought to distribute the report elsewhere.

Book Deal Failed

Mr. Schorr has said that he provided the report, that of the House Select Committee on Intelligence, to The Village Voice, a New York weekly, which published it in two installments earlier this month after the House voted on Jan. 29 not to make it public.

Sources at CBS News said that the network was satisfied that Mr. Schorr had broadcast as much of the report as it had wanted. Mr. Schorr is known to have then approached a book publisher in an effort to have

the report printed as a paperback. But the deal fell through, and he delivered the report to The Village Voice, rather than to other newspapers that had requested that he give it to them.

Mr. Schorr's first broadcast about the contents of the report, a detailed investigation and critique of the operations of the Central Intelligence Agency, coincided with the publication of the main details of it by The New York Times in its issue of Jan. 26. As early as Jan 20 The Times reported portions of the draft

of the report.

In a telephone interview here, Mr. Schorr said that he did not want to comment on the details of the case.

"I'm an inactive reporter fighting for the right to be an active reporter again," he said.

Mr. Schorr's statement, which was released earlier today in New York, said in part:

"Experience has quickly taught me that it is not possible to work as a reporter while personally involved in a controversy over reporters' rights, and I accept that reality.

"I do not seek the legal con-

tests which may lie ahead, but I am confident that, as they unfold, it will become clear that what is involved beyond specific details of my action is the public's continued right to know in the face of a secrecy backlash."

Mr. Schorr, who has a reputation here as a tenacious and productive newsman, last appeared on a CBS broadcast on Feb. 18. Last week, CBS News placed him on general reporting duties after the controversy broke out.

February 24, 1976

PRESIDENT LIMITS U.S. SURVEILLANCE OF CITIZENS' LIVES

Executive Order Restricts Intelligence Agencies in Collecting Information

INFILTRATION IS CURBED

But Congress Is Asked to Permit Some Methods to Assemble Foreign Data

By NICHOLAS M. HORROCK
Special to The New York Times

WASHINGTON, Feb. 18 — President Ford sharply restricted today the power of the intelligence agencies to intrude upon the lives and activities of American citizens.

In a 36-page executive order, which will go into effect on March 1, Mr. Ford limited the physical and electronic surveillance of Americans, issued tight new regulations on the collection and dissemination of information about them and barred such practices as burglaries, drug tests on unsuspecting humans, and the illegal use of tax return information.

He also limited the infiltration of any group—whether for intelligence purposes or to influence its activities— to those made up largely of foreign nationals or directly controlled by a foreign government.

Mr. Ford's order covered the Central Intelligence Agency, the National Security Agency

and the Defense Intelligence Agency and other agencies when they are engaged in collection of foreign intelligence. A separate set of guidelines is being prepared for the Federal Bureau of Investigation and is expected to be made public later this year by Edward H. Levi, the Attorney General.

No Legal Sanction

An executive order does not carry the sanctions of law. If it is violated, the employee is subject to dismissal, loss of pay and other administrative disciplinary actions.

The executive order was part of an informational package given to Congressional leaders late yesterday and outlined by Mr. Ford at a televised news conference last night. Today the White House sent to Congress a bill calling for a secrecy law to punish present and former employees who improperly disclose the "sources and methods" of gathering national security intelligence.

Mr. Ford's secrecy bill was accompanied to Capitol Hill by a 4-page statement to Congress in which he outlined his actions on intelligence matters and his hopes for legislation. In addition to secrecy, he called on Congress to pass legislation to specifically permit electronic surveillance in the United States for foreign intelligence purposes with a judge's approval.

The President said he would also ask Congress for authority to open the United States mails to gather foreign intelligence. However, until such a bill is passed, his executive order prohibits the intelligence agencies from continuing the practice.

He also said he would support legislation forbidding plots to assassinate foreign leaders.

Congressional reaction to Mr. Ford's message was wary. The Senate Democratic leader, Mike

Mansfield of Montana, called it a "good step in the right direction," and House Speaker Carl Albert, an Oklahoma Democrat, said he wated to study it before commenting.

In his executive order, the President decreed that Government agencies would require a "secrecy agreement" from employees anywhere in government who receive information that could be construed as containing "sources and methods" of intelligence.

The agreement would permit the Government to go to court to bar the disclosure of national security data. This would extend to large new areas of the executive branch the secrecy agreement system already in force at the Central Intelligence Agency and the Federal Bureau of Investigation. It would not cover employees of Congress or the courts.

The executive order did relatively little to change the planning and execution of covert operations such as the secret support for pro-Western Angolan forces. It renamed and formalized the activities of the "40 Committee," a branch of the National Security Council that passes on all covert operations.

Under the order, the members must meet and vote on proposed operations.

The President will then receive the recommendations of the new committee, to be called the Operations Advisory Group, and the positions of the members who may have opposed it. Mr. Ford, White House officials say, still firmly opposes the concept of informing Congress before a decision on a covert operation is made or permitting Congress to become part of the decision-making process.

The executive order does not bar any type of covert operation except plots to assassinate foreign leaders. But John O. Marsh, counselor to the President, said the White House believed the formalization of the decision-making process would prevent improper or unrealistic operations from gaining approval.

Presidential Pressure

Despite the massive disclosures of previous Presidential abuse of the intelligence agencies, there was little in Mr. Ford's executive order to protect the agencies from Presidential demands or prohibit improper pressures from a President.

At a White House briefing, Mr. Marsh said he believed that the three-member Oversight Board would be the place where agency officials could report improper Presidential requests.

Under the executive order, the board would receive periodic reports from the inspector generals of the intelligence agencies and would, in turn, make reports to the Attorney General. If the board received a report of what it regarded as abusive, illegal or improper activity, it could recommend that the Attorney General punish or prosecute the officials or employees involved.

The order calls for the Attorney General to report to the President on abuse and impropriety. But it left the power of sanctions within the executive branch and thus under the authority of the President.

The Oversight Board and the secrecy legislation were dovetailed as part of Mr. Ford's strategy to stop further leaks of information. By creating the board, his aides say, he has arranged a proper place for intelligence agency employees to report impropriety.

Thus, as one aide said at today's briefing, intelligence agency employees would no longer need to seek out the media to make abuses public. It was a series of disclosures in the press of improper C.I.A. activity that opened widespread investigations of the intelligence agencies last year.

The President used his executive order also to give George Bush, the recently appointed Director of Central Intelligence, more power than any of his predecessors. It is, nevertheless, not absolute power.

Mr. Bush will head a "committee on foreign intelligence,"

made up of himself, Robert F. Ellsworth, Deputy Secretary of Defense for intelligence, and William G. Hyland, of the National Security Council staff. This group will take over direction of the intelligence community, preparation of the budget and allocation of resources. In effect, the mechanism replaces the cumbersome United States Intelligence Board and centralizes command under the President.

The executive order instructed Mr. Bush's deputy director at the C.I.A. to take over the day-to-day management of the 15,000-employee agency. In effect, the President is trying to upgrade the office of Director of Central Intelligence to Cabinet level and give him responsibility and hegemony over the entire. intelligence community without having to change the governmental structure formally.

February 19, 1976

EXCERPTS FROM SENATE INTELLIGENCE REPORT

Special to The New York Times

WASHINGTON, April 28—Following are excerpts from "Intelligence Activities and the Rights of Americans," the final report of the Senate Select Committee on Intelligence Activities.

INTRODUCTION AND SUMMARY

The constitutional system of checks and balances has not adequately controlled intelligence activities. Until recently the executive branch has neither delineated the scope of permissible activities nor established procedures for supervising intelligence agencies. Congress has failed to exercise sufficient oversight, seldom questioning the use to which its appropriations were being put. Most domestic intelligence issues have not reached the courts, and in those cases when they have reached the courts, the judiciary has been reluctant to grapple with them.

Each of these points is briefly illustrated below.

1. The Number of People Affected by Domestic Intelligence Activity

United States intelligence agencies have investigated a vast number of American citizens and domestic organizations. F.B.I. headquarters alone has developed over 500,000 domestic intelligence files, and these have been augmented by additional files at F.B.I. field offices. The F.B.I. opened 65,000 of these domestic intelligence files in 1972 alone. In fact, substantially more individuals and groups are subject to intelligence scrutiny than the number of files would appear to indicate since, typically, each domestic intelligence file contains information on more than one individual or group, and this information is readily retrievable through the F.B.I. General Name Index.

The number of Americans and domestic groups caught in the domestic intelligence net is further illustrated by the following statistics:

Nearly a quarter of a million first class letters were opened and photographed in the United States by the C.I.A. between 1953-1973, producing a C.I.A. computerized index of nearly one and one-half million names.

At least 300,000 individuals were indexed in a C.I.A. computer system and separate files were created on approximately 7,200 Americans and over 100 domestic groups during the course of C.I.A.'s Operation CHAOS (1967-1973).

Millions of private telegrams sent from, to or through the United States were obtained by the National Security Agency from 1947 to 1975 under a secret arrangement with three United States telegraph companies.

An estimated 100,000 Americans were the subjects of United States Army intelligence files created between the mid-1960's and 1971.

Intelligence files on more than 11,000 individuals and groups were created by the Internal Revenue Service between 1969 and 1973 and tax investigations were started on the basis of political rather than tax criteria.

At least 26,000 individuals were at one point catalogued on an F.B.I. list of persons to be rounded up in the event of a "national emergency."

2. Too Much Information Is Collected for Too Long

Intelligence agencies have collected vast amounts of information about the intimate details of citizens' lives and about their participation in legal and peaceful political activities. The targets of intelligence activity have included political adherents of the right and the left, ranging from activist to casual supporters. Investigations have been directed against proponents of racial causes and women's rights, outspoken apostles of nonviolence and racial harmony; establishment politicians; religious groups, and advocates of new life styles. The widespread targeting of citizens and domestic groups and the excessive scope of the collection of information is illustrated by the following examples:

(a) The women's liberation movement was infiltrated by informants who collected material about the movement's policies, leaders and individual members. One report included the name of every woman who attended meetings, and another stated that each woman at a meeting had described "how she felt oppressed, sexually or otherwise." Another report concluded that the movement's purpose was to "free women from the humdrum existence of being only a wife and mother," but still recommended that the intelligence investigation should be continued.

(b) A prominent civil rights leader and adviser to Dr. Martin Luther King Jr. was investigated on the suspicion that he might be a Communist "sympathizer." The F.B.I. field office concluded he was not. Bureau headquarters directed that the investigation continue using a theory of "guilty until proven innocent":

"The bureau does not agree with the expressed belief of the field office that—— is not sympathetic to the party cause. While there may not be any evidence that——is a Communist, neither is there any substantial evidence that——is anti-Communist."

(c) F.B.I. sources reported on the formation of the Conservative American Christian Action Council in 1971. In the 1950's, the bureau collected information about the John Birch Society and passed it to the White House because of the society's "scurrilous attack" on President Eisenhower and other high Government officials.

(d) Some investigations of the lawful activities of peaceful groups have continued for decades. For example, the N.A.A.C.P. was investigated to determine whether it "had connections with" the Communist Party. The investigation lasted for over 25 years, although nothing was found to rebut a report during the first year of the investigation that the N.A.A.C.P. had a "strong tendency" to "steer clear of Communist activities." Similarly, the F.B.I. has admitted that the Socialist Workers Party has committed no criminal acts. Yet the bureau has investigated the Socialist Workers Party for more than three decades on the basis of its revolutionary rhetoric —which the F.B.I. concedes falls short of incitement to violence—and its claimed international links. The bureau is currently using its informants to collect information about S.W.P. members' political views, including those on "U.S. involvement in Angola," "food prices," "racial matters," the "Vietnam War" and about any of their efforts to support non-S.W.P. candidates for political office.

(e) National political leaders fell within the broad reach of intelligence investigations. For example, Army Intelligence maintained files on Senator Adlai Stevenson and Congressman Abner Mikva because of their participation in peaceful political meetings under surveillance by Army agents. A letter to Richard Nixon, while he was a candidate for President in 1968, was intercepted under C.I.A.'s mail opening program. In the 1960's President Johnson asked the F.B.I. to compare various senators' statements on Vietnam with the Communist Party line and to conduct name checks on leading antiwar senators.

(f) As part of their effort to collect information which "related even remotely" to people or groups "active" in communities which had "the potential" for civil disorder, Army intelligence agencies took such steps as: sending agents to a Halloween party for elementary school children in Washington, D.C., because they suspected a local "dissident" might be present; monitoring protests of welfare mothers' organizations in Milwaukee; infiltrating a coalition of church youth groups in Colorado, and sending agents to a priests' conference in Washington, D.C., held to discuss birth control measures.

(g) In the late 1960's and early 1970's, student groups were subjected to intense scrutiny. In 1970 the F.B.I. ordered investigations of every member of the Students for a Democratic Society and of "every black student union and similar group regardless of their past or present involvement in disorders." Files were opened on thousands of young men and women so that, as the former head of F.B.I. intelligence explained, the information could be used if they ever applied for a Government job.

In the 1960's bureau agents were instructed to increase their efforts to discredit "New Left" student demonstrators by tactics including publishing photographs ("naturally the most obnoxious picture should be used"), using "misinformation" to falsely notify members events had been canceled, and writing "tell-tale" letters to students' parents.

(h) The F.B.I. Intelligence Division commonly investigated any indication that "subversive" groups already under investigation were seeking to influence or control other groups. One example of the extreme breadth of this "infiltration" theory was an F.B.I. instruction in the mid-1960's to all field offices to investigate every "free university" because some of them had come under "subversive influence."

(i) Each administration from Franklin D. Roosevelt's to Richard Nixon's permitted and sometimes encouraged Government agencies to handle essentially political intelligence. For example:

¶President Roosevelt asked the F.B.I. to put in its files the names of citizens sending telegrams to the White House opposing his "national defense" policy and supporting Col. Charles Lindbergh.

¶President Truman received inside information on a former Roosevelt aide's efforts to influence his appointments, labor union negotiating plans and the publishing plans of journalists.

¶President Eisenhower received reports on purely political and social contacts with foreign officials by Bernard Baruch, Mrs. Eleanor Roosevelt and Supreme Court Justice William O. Douglas.

¶The Kennedy Administration had the F.B.I. wiretap a Congressional staff member, three executive officials, a lobbyist and a Washington law firm. Attorney General Robert F. Kennedy received the fruits of a F.B.I. "tap" on Martin Luther King Jr. and a "bug" on a Congressman, both of which yielded information of a political nature.

President Johnson asked the F.B.I. to conduct "name checks" of his critics and of members of the staff of his 1964 opponent, Senator Barry Goldwater. He also requested purely political intelligence on his critics in the Senate, and received extensive intelligence reports on political activity at the 1964 Democratic Convention from F.B.I. electronic surveillance.

President Nixon authorized a program of wiretaps which produced for the White House purely political or personal information unrelated to national security, including information about a Supreme Court justice.

3. Covert Action and the Use of Illegal or Improper Means
(a) Covert Action

Apart from uncovering excesses in the collection of intelligence, our investigation has disclosed covert actions directed against Americans, and the use of illegal and improper surveillance techniques to gather information. For example:

(i) The F.B.I.'s Cointelpro—counterintelligence program—was designed to "disrupt" groups and "neutralize" individuals deemed to be threats to domestic security. The F.B.I. resorted to counterintelligence tactics in part because its chief officials believed that the existing law could not control the activities of certain dissident groups and that court decisions had tied the hands of the intelligence community. Whatever opinion one holds about the policies of the targeted groups, many of the tactics employed by the F.B.I. were indisputably degrading to a free society. Cointelpro tactics included:

¶Anonymously attacking the political beliefs of targets in order to induce their employers to fire them;

¶Anonymously mailing letters to the spouses of intelligence targets for the purpose of destroying their marriages;

¶Obtaining from I.R.S. the tax returns of a target and then attempting to provoke an I.R.S. investigation for the express purpose of deterring a protest leader from attending the Democratic National Convention;

¶Falsely and anonymously labeling as Government informants members of groups known to be violent, thereby exposing the falsely labeled member to expulsion or physical attack;

¶Pursuant to instructions to use "mis-

information" to disrupt demonstrations, employing such means as broadcasting fake orders on the same citizens band radio frequency used by demonstration marshals to attempt to control demonstrations and duplicating and falsely filling out forms soliciting housing for persons coming to a demonstration, thereby causing "long and useless journeys to locate these addresses."

Sending an anonymous letter to the leader of a Chicago street gang (described as "violence-prone") stating that the Black Panthers were supposed to have "a hit for you." The letter was suggested because it "may intensify . . . animosity" and cause the street gang leader to "take retaliatory action."

From "late 1963" until his death in 1968, Martin Luther King Jr. was the target of an intensive campaign by the Federal Bureau of Investigation to "neutralize" him as an effective civil rights leader. In the words of the man in charge of the F.B.I.'s "war" against Dr. King, "No holds were barred."

The F.B.I. gathered information about Dr. King's plans and activities through an extensive surveillance program, employing nearly every intelligence-gathering technique at the bureau's disposal in order to obtain information about the "private activities of Dr. King and his advisers" to use to "completely discredit" them.

The program to destroy Dr. King as the leader of the civil rights movement included efforts to discredit him with executive branch officials, Congressional leaders, foreign heads of state, American ambassadors, churches, universities and the press.

The F.B.I. mailed Dr. King a tape recording made from microphones hidden in his hotel rooms which one agent testified was an attempt to destroy Dr. King's marriage. The tape recording was accompanied by a note which Dr. King and his advisors interpreted as threatening to release the tape recording unless Dr. King committed suicide.

The extraordinary nature of the campaign to discredit Dr. King is evident from two documents.

At the August 1963 march on Washington, Dr. King told the country of his "dream" that:

"All of God's children, black men and white men, Jews and Gentiles, Protestant and Catholics, will be able to join hands and sing in the words of the old Negro spiritual, 'Free at last, free at last, thank God Almighty, I'm free at last.' "

The bureau's Domestic Intelligence Division concluded that this "demagogic speech" established Dr. King as the "most dangerous and effective Negro leader in the country." Shortly afterwards, and within days after Dr. King was named "Man of the Year" by Time magazine, the F.B.I. decided to "take him off his pedestal, reduce him completely in influence," and select and promote its own candidate to "assume the role of the leadership of the Negro people."

In early 1968, bureau headquarters explained to the field that Dr. King must be destroyed because he was seen as a potential "messiah" who could "unify and electrify" the "black nationalist movement." Indeed to the F.B.I. he was a potential threat because he might "abandon his supposed 'obedience' to white liberal doctrines (nonviolence)." In short, a nonviolent man was to be secretly attacked and destroyed as insurance against his abandoning nonviolence.

(b) Illegal or Improper Means

The surveillance which we investigated was not only vastly excessive in breadth and a basis for degrading counterintelligence actions, but was also often conducted by illegal or improper means. For example:

(1) For approximately 20 years the C.I.A. carried out a program of indiscriminately opening citizens first class mail. The bureau also had a mail opening program, but canceled it in 1966. The bureau continued, however, to receive the illegal fruits of C.I.A.'s program. In 1970, the heads of both agencies signed a document for President Nixon, which correctly stated that mail opening was illegal, falsely stated that it had been discontinued and proposed that the illegal opening of mail should be resumed because it would provide useful results. The President approved the program, but withdrew his approval five days later. The illegal opening continued nonetheless. Throughout this period C.I.A. officials knew that mail opening was illegal but expressed concern about the "flap potential" of exposure, not about the illegality of their activity.

(2) From 1947 until May 1975, N.S.A. received from international cable companies millions of cables which had been sent by American citizens in the reasonable expectation that they would be kept private.

(3) Since the early 1930's, intelligence agencies have frequently wiretapped and bugged American citizens without the benefit of judicial warrant. Recent court decisions have curtailed the use of these techniques against domestic targets. But past subjects of these surveillances have included a United States Congressman, a Congressional staff member, journalists and newsmen, and numerous individuals and groups who engaged in no criminal activity and who posed no genuine threat to the national security, such as two White House domestic affairs advisers and an anti-Vietnam War protest group. While the prior written approval of the Attorney General has been required for all warrantless wiretaps since 1940, the record is replete with instances where this requirement was ignored and the Attorney General gave only after-the-fact authorization.

Until 1965, microphone surveillance by intelligence agencies was wholly unregulated in certain classes of cases. Within weeks after a 1954 Supreme Court decision denouncing the F.B.I.'s installation of a microphone in a defendant's bedroom, the Attorney General informed the bureau that he did not believe the decision applied to national security cases and permitted the F.B.I. to continue to install microphones subject only to its own "intelligent restraint."

(4) In several cases, purely political information (such as the reaction of Congress to an Administration's legislative proposal) and purely personal information (such as coverage of the extramarital social activities of a high-level executive official under surveillance) was obtained from electronic surveillance and disseminated to the highest levels of the Federal Government.

(5) Warrantless break-ins have been conducted by intelligence agencies since World War II. During the 1960's alone, the F.B.I. and C.I.A. conducted hundreds of break-ins, many against American citizens and domestic organizations. In some cases, these break-ins were to install microphones; in other cases, they were to steal such items as membership lists from organizations considered "subversive" by the bureau.

(6) The most pervasive surveillance technique has been the informant. In a random sample of domestic intelligence cases, 83 percent involved informants and 5 percent involved electronic surveillance. Informants have been used against peaceful, law-abiding groups; they have collected information about personal and political views and activities. To maintain their credentials in violence-prone groups, informants have involved themselves in violent activity. This phenomenon is well illustrated by an informant in the Klan. He was present at the murder of a civil rights worker in Mississippi and subsequently helped to solve the crime and convict the perpetrators. Earlier, however, while performing duties paid for by the Government, he had previously "beaten people severely, had boarded buses and kicked people, had [gone] into restaurants and beaten them [blacks] with blackjacks, chains, pistols." Although the F.B.I. requires agents to instruct informants that they cannot be involved in violence, it was understood that in the Klan, "he couldn't be an angel and be a good informant."

4. Ignoring the Law

Officials of the intelligence agencies occasionally recognized that certain activities were illegal, but expressed concern only for "flap potential." Even more disturbing was the frequent testimony that the law and the Constitution were simply ignored. For example, the author of the so-called Huston plan testified:

Question: Was there any person who stated that the activity recommended, which you have previously identified as being illegal opening of the mail and breaking and entry or burglary—was there any single person who stated that such activity should not be done because it was unconstitutional?

Answer: No.

Question: Was there any single person who said such activity should not be done because it was illegal?

Answer: No.

Similarly, the man who for 10 years headed F.B.I.'s Intelligence Division testified that:

". . . never once did I hear anybody, including myself, raise the question: is this course of action which we have agreed upon lawful, is it legal, is it ethical or moral. We never gave any thought to this line of reasoning, because we were just naturally pragmatic."

Although the statutory law and the Constitution were often not "[given] a thought," there was a general attitude that intelligence needs were responsive to a higher law. Thus, as one witness testified in justifying the F.B.I.'s mail opening program:

"It was my assumption that what we were doing was justified by what we had to do . . . the greater good, the national security.

5. Deficiencies in Accountability and Control

The overwhelming number of excesses continuing over a prolonged period of time were due in large measure to the fact that the system of checks and balances—created in our Constitution to limit abuse of governmental power—was seldom applied to the intelligence community. Guidance and regulation from outside the intelligence agencies—where it has been imposed at all—has been vague. Presidents and other senior executive officials, particularly the Attorneys General, have virtually abdicated their consitutional responsibility to oversee and set standards for intelligence activity. Senior Government officials generally gave the agencies broad, general mandates or pressed for immediate results on pressing problems. In neither case did they provide guidance to prevent excesses and their broad mandates and pressures themselves often resulted in excessive or improper intelligence activity.

Congress has often declined to exercise meaningful oversight, and on occasion has passed laws or made statements which were taken by intelligence agencies as supporting overly broad investigations.

On the other hand, the record reveals instances when intelligence agencies have concealed improper activities from their superiors in the executive branch and from the Congress, or have elected to disclose only the less questionable aspects of their activities.

There has been, in short, a clear and sustained failure by those responsible to control the intelligence community and to insure its accountability. There has been an equally clear and sustained failure by intelligence agencies to fully inform the proper authorities of their activities and to comply with directives from those authorities.

6. The Adverse Impact of Improper Intelligence Activity

Many of the illegal or improper disruptive efforts directed against American citizens and domestic organizations succeeded in injuring their targets. Although it is sometimes difficult to prove that a target's misfortunes were caused by a counterintelligence program directed against him, the possibility that an arm of the United States Government intended to cause the harm and might have been responsible is itself abhorrent.

The committee has observed numerous examples of the impact of intelligence operations. Sometimes the harm was readily apparent—destruction of marriages, loss of friends or jobs. Sometimes the attitudes of the public and of Government officials responsible for formulating policy and resolving vital issues were influenced by distorted intelligence. But the most basic harm was to the values of privacy and freedom which our Constitution seeks to protect and which intelligence activity infringed on a broad scale.

(a) General Efforts to Discredit

Several efforts against individuals and groups appear to have achieved their stated aims. For example:

A bureau field office reported that the anonymous letter it had sent to an activist's husband accusing his wife of infidelity "contributed very strongly" to the subsequent breakup of the marriage.

Another field office reported that a draft counselor, deliberately and falsely accused of being an F.B.I. informant, was "ostracized" by his friends and associates.

Two instructors were reportedly put on probation after the bureau sent an anonymous letter to a university administrator about their funding of an anti-Administration student newspaper.

The bureau evaluated its attempts to "put a stop" to a contribution to the Southern Christian Leadership Conference as "quite successful."

An F.B.I. document boasted that a "pretext" phone call to Stokely Carmichael's mother telling her that members of the Black Panther Party intended to kill her son left her "shocked." The memorandum intimated that the bureau believed it had been responsible for Carmichael's flight to Africa the following day.

(b) Media Manipulation

The F.B.I. has attempted covertly to influence the public's perception of persons and organizations by disseminating derogatory information to the press, either anonymously or through "friendly" news contacts. The impact of those articles is generally difficult to measure, although in some cases there are fairly direct connections to injury to the target. The bureau also attempted to influence media reporting which would have an impact on the public image of the F.B.I. Examples include:

Planning a series of derogatory articles about Martin Luther King, Jr., and the poor people's campaign.

For example, in anticipation of the 1968 "poor people's march on Washington, D. C.," bureau headquarters granted authority to furnish "cooperative news media sources" an article "designed to curtail success of Martin Luther King's fund raising." Another memorandum illustrated how "photographs of demonstrators" could be used in discrediting the civil rights movement. Six photographs of participants in the poor people's campaign in Cleveland accompanied the memorandum with the following note attached: "These [photographs] show the militant aggressive appearance of the participants and might be of interest to a cooperative news source."

Information on the "poor people's campaign" was provided by the F.B.I. to friendly reporters on the condition that "the Bureau must not be revealed as the source.

Soliciting information from field offices "on a continuing basis" for "prompt . . .dissemination to the news media. . .to discredit the New Left movement and its adherents." The headquarters directive requested, among other things, that:

"Specific data should be furnished depicting the scurrilous and depraved nature of many of the characters, activities, habits and living conditions representative of New Left adherents."

Field Offices were to be exhorted that "every avenue of possible embarrassment must be vigorously and enthusiastically explored."

Ordering field offices to gather information which would disprove allegations by the "liberal press, the bleeding hearts and the forces on the left" that the Chicago police used undue force in dealing with demonstrators at the 1968 Democratic convention.

Taking advantage of a close relationship with the chairman of the board—described in an F.B.I. memorandum as "our good friend"—of a magazine with national circulation to influence articles which related to the F.B.I. For example, through this relationship the bureau "squelched" an "unfavorable article against the bureau" written by a freelance writer about an F.B.I. investigation: "postponed publication" of an article on another F.B.I. case: "forestalled publication" of an article by Dr. Martin Luther King, Jr., and received information about proposed editing of King's articles.

(c) Distorting Data to Influence Government Policy and Public Perceptions

Accurate intelligence is a prerequisite to sound Government policy. However, as the past head of the F.B.I.'s Domestic Intelligence Division reminded the committee:

"The facts by themselves are not too meaningful. They are something like stones cast into a heap."

On certain crucial subjects the domestic intelligence agencies reported the "facts" in ways that gave rise to misleading impressions.

For example, the F.B.I.'s Domestic Intelligence Division initially discounted as an "obvious failure" the alleged attempts of Communists to influence the civil rights movement. Without any significant change in the factual situation, the bureau moved from the division's conclusion to Director Hoover's public Congressional testimony characterizing Communist influence on the civil rights movement as "vitally important."

F.B.I. reporting on protests against the Vietnam War provides another example of the manner in which the information provided to decision-makers can be skewed. In acquiescense with a judgment already expressed by President Johnson, the bureau's reports on demonstrations against the war in Vietnam emphasized Communist efforts to influence the anti-war movement and underplayed the fact that the vast ma-

jority of demonstrators were not Communist controlled.

(d) "Chilling" First Amendment Rights

The First Amendment protects the rights of American citizens to engage in free and open discussions and to associate with persons of their choosing. Intelligence agencies have, on occasion, expressly attempted to interfere with those rights. For example, one internal F.B.I. memorandum called for "more interviews" with New Left subjects "to enhance the paranoia endemic in these circles" and "get the point across there is an F.B.I. agent behind every mailbox."

More importantly, the Government's surveillance activities in the aggregate —whether or not expressly intended to do so—tend, as the committee concludes, to deter the exercise of First Amendment rights by American citizens who become aware of the Government's domestic intelligence program.

(e) Preventing the Free Exchange of Ideas

Speakers, teachers, writers and publications themselves were targets of the F.B.I.'s counterintelligence program. The F.B.I.'s efforts to interfere with the free exchange of ideas included:

¶Anonymously attempting to prevent an alleged "Communist-front" group from holding a forum on a Midwest campus and then investigating the judge who ordered that the meeting be allowed to proceed.

¶Using another "confidential source" in a foundation which contributed to a local college to apply pressure on the school to fire an activist professor.

¶Anonymously contacting a university official to urge him to "persuade" two professors to stop funding a student newspaper in order to "eliminate what voice the New Left has" in the area.

¶Targeting the New Mexico Free University for teaching "confrontation politics" and "draft counseling training."

7. Cost and Value

Domestic intelligence is expensive. We have already indicated the cost of illegal and improper intelligence activities in terms of the harm to victims, the injury to constitutional values and the damage to the democratic process itself. The cost in dollars is also significant. For example, the F.B.I. has budgeted for fiscal year 1976 over $7 million for its domestic security informant program, more than twice the amount it spends on informants against organized crime. The aggregate budget for F.B.I. domestic security intelligence and foreign counterintelligence is at least $80 million. In the late 1960's and early 1970's, when the bureau was joined by the C.I.A., the military and N.S.A. in collecting information about the antiwar movement and black activists, the cost was substantially greater.

Apart from the excesses described above, the usefulness of many domestic intelligence activities in serving the legitimate goal of protecting society has been questionable. Properly directed intelligence investigations concentrating upon hostile foreign agents and violent terrorists can produce valuable results. The committee has examined cases where the F.B.I. uncovered "illegal" agents of a foreign power engaged in clandestine intelligence activities in violation of Federal law. Information leading to the prevention of serious violence has been acquired by the F.B.I. through its informant penetration of terrorist groups and through the inclusion in bureau files of the names of persons actively involved with such groups. Nevertheless, the most sweeping domestic intelligence surveillance programs have produced surprisingly few useful returns in view of their extent. For example:

¶Between 1960 and 1974, the F.B.I. conducted over 500,000 separate investigations of persons and groups under the "subversive" category, predicated on the possibility that they might be likely to overthrow the Government of the United States. Yet not a single individual or group has been prosecuted since 1957 under the laws which prohibit planning or advocating action to overthrow the Government and which are the main alleged statutory basis for such F.B.I. investigations.

¶A recent study by the General Accounting Office has estimated that of some 17,528 F.B.I. domestic intelligence investigations of individuals in 1974, only 1.3 percent resulted in prosecution and conviction, and in only "about 2 percent" of the cases was advance knowledge of any activity—legal or illegal—obtained.

¶One of the main reasons advanced for expanded collection of intelligence about urban unrest and antiwar protest was to help responsible officials cope with possible violence. However, a former White House official with major duties in this area under the Johnson Administration has concluded, in retrospect, that "in none of these situations . . . would advance intelligence about dissident groups [have] been of much help," that what was needed was "physical intelligence" about the geography of major cities, and that the attempt to "predict violence" was not a "successful undertaking."

¶Domestic intelligence reports have sometimes even been counterproductive. A local police chief, for example, described F.B.I. reports which led to the positioning of Federal troops near his city as:

". . . Almost completely composed of unsorted and unevaluated stories, threats and rumors that had crossed my desk in New Haven. Many of these had long before been discounted by our intelligence division. But they had made their way from New Haven to Washington, had gained completely unwarranted credibility and had been submitted by the Director of the F.B.I. to the President of the United States. They seemed to present a convincing picture of impending holocaust."

In considering its recommendations, the committee undertook an evaluation of the F.B.I.'s claims that domestic intelligence was necessary to combat terrorism, civil disorders, "subversion" and hostile foreign intelligence activity. The committee reviewed voluminous materials bearing on this issue and questioned bureau officials and former Federal executive officials.

We have found that we are in fundamental agreement with the wisdom of Attorney General Stone's initial warning that intelligence agencies must not be "concerned with political or other opinions of individuals" and must be limited to investigating essentially only "such conduct as is forbidden by the laws of the United States." The committee's record demonstrates that domestic intelligence which departs from this standard raises grave risks of undermining the democratic process and harming the interests of individual citizens. This danger weighs heavily against the speculative or negligible benefits of the ill-defined and overbroad investigations authorized in the past. Thus, the basic purpose of the recommendations in this report is to limit the F.B.I. to investigating conduct rather than ideas or associations.

The excesses of the past do not, however, justify depriving the United States of a clearly defined and effectively controlled domestic intelligence capability. The intelligence services of this nation's international adversaries continue to attempt to conduct clandestine espionage operations within the United States. Our recommendations provide for intelligence investigations of hostile foreign intelligence activity.

Moreover, terrorists have engaged in serious acts of violence which have brought death and injury to Americans and threaten further such acts. These acts, not the politics or beliefs of those who would commit them, are the proper focus for investigations to anticipate terrorist violence. Accordingly, the committee would permit properly controlled intelligence investigations in those narrow circumstances.

Concentration on imminent violence can avoid the wasteful dispersion of resources which has characterized the sweeping (and fruitless) domestic intelligence investigations of the past. But the most important reason for the fundamental change in the domestic intelligence operations which our recommendations propose is the need to protect the constitutional rights of Americans.

In light of the record of abuse revealed by our inquiry, the committee is not satisfied with the position that mere exposure of what has occurred in the past will prevent its recurrence. Clear legal standards and effective oversight and controls are necessary to insure that domestic intelligence activity does not itself undermine the democratic system it is intended to protect.

RECOMMENDATIONS

Recommendation 1—There is no inherent constitutional authority for the President or any intelligence agency to violate the law.

Recommendation 2—It is the intent

of the committee that statutes implementing these recommendations provide the exclusive legal authority for Federal domestic security activities.

(a) No intelligence agency may engage in such activities unless authorized by statute, nor may it permit its employees, informants or other covert human sources to engage in such activities on its behalf.

(b) No executive directive or order may be issued which would conflict with such statutes.

Recommendation 3—In authorizing intelligence agencies to engage in certain activities, it is not intended that such authority empower agencies, their informants or covert human sources to violate any prohibition enacted pursuant to these recommendations or contained in the Constitution or in any other law.

Recommendation 4—To supplement the prohibitions in the 1947 National Security Act against the C.I.A. exercising "police, subpoena, law enforcement powers or internal security functions," the C.I.A. should be prohibited from conducting domestic security activities within the United States, except as specifically permitted by these recommendations.

Recommendation 5—The Director of Central Intelligence should be made responsible for "coordinating" the protection of sources and methods of the intelligence community. As head of the C.I.A., the Director should also be responsible in the first instance for the security of C.I.A. facilities, personnel, operations and information. Neither function, however, authorizes the Director of Central Intelligence to violate any Federal or state law or to take any action which is otherwise inconsistent with statutes implementing these recommendations.

Recommendation 6—The C.I.A. should not conduct electronic surveillance, unauthorized entry or mail openings within the United States for any purpose.

Recommendation 7—The C.I.A. should not employ physical surveillance, infiltration of groups or any other covert techniques against Americans within the United States except:

(a) Physical surveillance of persons on the grounds of C.I.A. installations;

(b) Physical surveillance during a preliminary investigation of allegations an employee is a security risk for a limited period outside of C.I.A. installations. Such surveillance should be conducted only upon written authorization of the Director of Central Intelligence and should be limited to the subject of the investigation and, only to the extent necessary to identify them, to persons with whom the subject has contact;

(c) Confidential inquiries, during a preliminary investigation of allegations an employee is a security risk, of outside sources concerning medical or financial information about the subject which is relevant to those allegations;

(d) The use of identification which does not reveal C.I.A. or Government affiliation, in background and other security investigations permitted the C.I.A. by these recommendations and the conduct of checks which do not reveal C.I.A. or Government affiliation for the purpose of judging the effectiveness of cover operations upon the written authorization of the Director of Central Intelligence;

(e) In exceptional cases, the placement or recruitment of agents within an unwitting domestic group solely for the purpose of preparing them for assignments abroad and only for as long as is necessary to accomplish that purpose. This should take place only if the Director of Central Intelligence makes a written finding that it is essential for foreign intelligence collection of vital importance to the United States, and the Attorney General makes a written finding that the operation will be conducted under procedures designed to prevent misuse of the undisclosed participation or of any information obtained therefrom. In the case of any such action, no information received by C.I.A. from the agent as a result of his position in the group should be disseminated outside the C.I.A. unless it indicates felonious criminal conduct or threat of death or serious bodily harm, in which case dissemination should be permitted to an appropriate official agency if approved by the Attorney General.

Recommendation 8 — The C.I.A. should not collect information within the United States concerning Americans except:

(a) Information concerning C.I.A. employees, C.I.A. contractors and their employees or applicants for such employment or contracting;

(b) Information concerning individuals or organizations providing or offering to provide assistance to the C.I.A.;

(c) Information concerning individuals or organizations being considered by the C.I.A. as potential sources of information or assistance;

(d) Visitors to C.I.A. facilities;

(e) Persons otherwise in the immediate vicinity of sensitive C.I.A. sites; or

(f) Persons who give their informed written consent to such collection.

In (a), (b) and (c) above, information should be collected only if necessary for the purpose of determining the person's fitness for employment or assistance. If, in the course of such collection, information is obtained which indicates criminal activity, it should be transmitted to the F.B.I. or other appropriate agency. When an American's relationship with the C.I.A. is prospective, information should only be collected if there is a bona fide expectation the person might be used by the C.I.A.

Recommendation 9—The C.I.A. should not collect information abroad concerning Americans except:

(a) Information concerning Americans which it is permitted to collect within the United States;

(b) At the request of the Justice Department as part of criminal investigations or an investigation of an American for suspected terrorist or hostile foreign intelligence activities or security leak or security risk investigations which the F.B.I. has opened.

Recommendation 10—The C.I.A. should be able to transmit to the F.B.I. or other appropriate agencies information concerning Americans acquired as the incidental byproduct of otherwise permissible foreign intelligence and counterintelligence operations whenever such information indicates any activity in violation of American law.

Recommendation 11—The C.I.A. may employ covert techniques abroad against Americans:

(a) Under circumstances in which the C.I.A. could use such covert techniques against Americans within the United States, or

(b) When collecting information as part of Justice Department investigation, in which case the C.I.A. may use a particular covert technique under the standards and procedures and approvals applicable to its use against Americans within the United States by the F.B.I.

(c) To the extent necessary to identify persons known or suspected to be Americans who come in contact with foreigners the C.I.A. is investigating.

C.I.A. Human Experiments and Drug Use

Recommendation 12—The C.I.A. should not use in experimentation on human subjects any drug, device or procedure which is designed or intended to harm, or is reasonably likely to harm, the physical or mental health of the human subject, except with the informed written consent, witnessed by a disinterested third party, of each human subject, and in accordance with the guidelines issued by the National Commission for the Protection of Human Subjects for Biomedical and Behavioral Research. The jurisdiction of the commission should be amended to include the Central Intelligence Agency and other intelligence agencies of the United States Government.

Recommendation 13—Any C.I.A. activity engaged in pursuant to Recommendations 7, 8, 9, 10 or 11 should be subject to periodic review and certification of compliance with the Constitution, applicable statutes, agency regulations and executive orders by:

(a) The Inspector General of the C.I.A.;

(b) The General Counsel of the C.I.A., in coordination with the Director of Central Intelligence;

(c) The Attorney General, and

(d) The oversight committee recommended [below].

All such certifications should be available for review by Congressional oversight committees.

Recommendation 14—N.S.A. should not engage in domestic security activities. Its functions should be limited in a precisely drawn legislative charter to the collection of foreign intelligence from foreign communications.

Recommendation 15—N.S.A. should take all practicable measures consistent with its foreign intelligence mission to eliminate or minimize the interception, selection and monitoring of communications of Americans from the foreign communications.

Recommendation 16—N.S.A. should not be permitted to select for monitoring any communication to, from or about an American without his consent, except for the purpose of obtaining information about hostile foreign intelligence or terrorist activities, and then only if a warrant approving such monitoring is obtained in accordance with procedures similar to those contained in Title III of the Omnibus Crime Control and Safe Streets Act of 1968.

Recommendation 17 — Any personally identifiable information about an American which N.S.A. incidentally acquires, other than pursuant to a warrant, should not be disseminated without the consent of the American, but should be destroyed as promptly as possible unless it indicates:

(a) Hostile foreign intelligence or terrorist activities, or

(b) Felonious criminal conduct for which a warrant might be obtained pursuant to Title III of the Omnibus Crime Control and Safe Streets Act of 1968, or

(c) A threat of death or serious bodily harm.

If dissemination is permitted, by (a), (b) and (c) above, it must only be made to an appropriate official and after approval by the Attorney General.

Recommendation 18 — N.S.A. should not request from any commercial carrier any communication which it could not otherwise obtain pursuant to these recommendations.

Recommendation 19—The Office of Security at N.S.A. should be permitted to collect background information on present or prospective employees or contractors for N.S.A. solely for the purpose of determining their fitness for employment. With respect to security risks or the security of its installations, N.S.A. should be permitted to conduct physical surveillances consistent with such surveillances as the C.I.A. is permitted to conduct, in similar circumstances, by these recommendations.

Recommendation 20—Except as specifically provided herein, the Department of Defense should not engage in domestic security activities. Its functions, as they relate to the activities of the foreign intelligence community, should be limited in a precisely drawn legislative charter to the conduct of foreign intelligence and foreign counterintelligence activities and tactical military intelligence activities abroad and production, analysis and dissemination of departmental intelligence.

Recommendation 21—In addition to its foreign intelligence responsibility, the Department of Defense has a responsibility to investigate its personnel in order to protect the security of its installations and property, to ensure order and discipline within its ranks and to conduct other limited investigations once dispatched by the President to suppress a civil disorder. A legislative charter should define precisely—in a manner which is not inconsistent with these recommendations—the authorized scope and purpose of any investigations undertaken by the Department of Defense to satisfy these responsibilities.

Recommendation 22—No agency of the Department of Defense should conduct investigations of violations of criminal law or otherwise perform any law enforcement or domestic security functions within the United States, except on military bases or concerning military personnel, to enforce the Uniform Code of Military Justice.

Control of Civil Disturbance Intelligence

Recommendation 23—The Department of Defense should not be permitted to conduct investigations of Americans on the theory that the information derived therefrom might be useful in potential civil disorders. The Army should be permitted to gather information about geography, logistical matters or the identity of local officials which is necessary to the positioning, support and use of troops in an area where troops are likely to be deployed by the President in connection with a civil disturbance. The Army should be permitted to investigate Americans involved in such disturbances after troops have been deployed to the site of a civil disorder to the extent necessary to fulfill the military mission and to the extent the information cannot be obtained from the F.B.I.

Recommendation 24 — Appropriate agencies of the Department of Defense should be permitted to collect background information on their present or prospective employees or contractors. With respect to security risks or the security of its installations, the Department of Defense should be permitted to conduct physical surveillance consistent with such surveillances as the C.I.A. is permitted to conduct, in similar circumstances, by these recommendations.

Recommendation 25—Except as provided in 27 below, the Department of Defense should not direct any covert technique (e.g., electronic surveillance, informants, etc.) at American civilians.

Recommendation 26—The Department of Defense should be permitted to conduct abroad preventive intelligence investigations of unaffiliated Americans, provided such investigations are first approved by the F.B.I. Such investigations by the Department of Defense, including the use of covert techniques, should ordinarily be conducted in a manner consistent with the recommendations pertaining to the F.B.I.; however in overseas locations where U.S. military forces constitute the governing power or where U.S. military forces are engaged in hostilities circumstances may require greater latitude to conduct such investigations.

Recommendation 27 — The I.R.S. should not, on behalf of any intelligence agency or for its own use, collect any information about the activities of Americans except for the purposes of enforcing the tax laws.

Recommendation 28—I.R.S. should not select any person or group for tax investigation on the basis of political activity or for any other reason not relavant to enforcement fo the tax laws.

Recommendation 29—Any program of intelligence investigation relating to domestic security in which targets are selected by both tax and nontax criteria should only be initiated:

(a) Upon the written request of the Attorney General or the Secretary of the Treasury, specifying the nature of the requested program and the need therefore, and

(b) After the written certification by the Commissioner of the I.R.S. that procedures have been developed which are sufficient to prevent the infringement of the constitutional rights of Americans, and

(c) With Congressional oversight committees being kept continually advised of the nature and extent of such programs.

Disclosure Procedures

Recommendation 30—No intelligence agency should request from the Internal Revenue Service tax returns or tax-related information except under the statutes and regulations controlling such disclosures. In addition, the existing procedures under which tax returns and tax-related information are released by the I.R.S. should be strengthened, as suggested in the following five recommendations.

Recommendation 31 — All requests from an intelligence agency to the I.R.S. for tax returns and tax-related information should be in writing and signed by the head of the intelligence agency making the requests or his designee. Copies of such requests should be filed with the Attorney General. Each request should include a clear statement of:

(a) The purpose for which disclosure is sought;

(b) Facts sufficient to establish that the requested information is needed by the requesting agency for the performance of an authorized and lawful function;

(c) The uses which the requesting agency intends to make of the information;

(d) The extent of the disclosures sought;

(e) Agreement by the requesting agency not to use the documents or information for any purpose other than that stated in the request, and

(f) Agreement by the requesting agency that the information will not be disclosed to any other agency or person except in accordance with the law.

Recmmendation 32—I.R.S. should not release tax returns or tax-related information to any intelligence agency unless it has received a request satisfying the requirements of Recommendation 31 and the Commissioner of Internal Revenue has approved the request inwriting.

Recommendation 33—I.R.S. should maintain a record of all such requests and responses thereto for a period of 20 years.

Recommendation 34—No intelligence agency should use the information supplied to it by the I.R.S. pursuant to a request of the agency except as stated in a proper request for disclosure.

Recommendation 35—All requests for information sought by the F.B.I. should be filed by the Department of Justice. Such requests should be signed by the Attorney General or his designee, following a determination by the department that the request is proper under the applicable statutes and regulations.

Post Office

Recommendation 36—The Post Office should not permit the F.B.I. or any intelligence agency to inspect markings or addresses on first class mail, nor should the Post Office itself inspect markings or addresses on behalf of the F.B.I. or any intelligence agency on first class mail, except upon the written approval of the Attorney Genral or his designee. Where one of the correspondents is an American, the Attorney General or his designee should only approve such inspection for domestic security purposes upon a written finding that it is necessary to a criminal investigation or a preventive intelligence investigation of terrorist activity or hostile foreign intelligence activity.

Upon such a request, the Post Office may temporarily remove from circulation such correspondnce for the purpose of such inspection of its exterior as is related to the investigation.

Recommendation 37—The Post Office should not transfer the custody of any first class mail to any agency except the Department of Justice. Such mail should not be transferred or opened except upon a judicial search warrant.

(a) In the case of mail where one of the correspondents is an American, the judge must find that there is probable cause to believe that the mail contains evidence of a crime.

(b) In the case of mail where both parties are foreigners:

(1) The judge must find that there is probable cause to believe that both parties to such correspondence are foreigners and or one of the correspondents is an official employee or conscious agent of a foreign power, and

(2) The Attorney General must certify that the mail opening is likely to reveal information necessary either to the protection of the nation against actual or potential attack or other hostile acts of force of a foreign power; to obtain foreign intelligence information deemed essential to the security of the United States, or to protect national security information against hostile foreign intelligence activity.

Recommendation 38—All domestic security investigative activity, including the use of covert techniques, should be centralized within the Federal Bureau of Investigation, except those investigations by the Secret Service designed to protect the life of the President or other Secret Service protectees. Such investigations and the use of covert techniques in those investigations should be centralized within the Secret Service.

Recommendation 39—All domestic security activities of the Federal Government and all other intelligence agency activities covered by the domestic intelligence recommendations should be subject to Justice Department oversight to assure compliance with the Constitution and laws of the United States.

Recommendation 40 — The F.B.I. should be prohibited from engaging on its own or through informants or others in any of the following activities directed at Americans:

(a) Disseminating any information to the White House, any other Federal official, the news media or any other person for a political or other improper purpose, such as discrediting an opponent of the Administration or a critic of an intelligence or investigative agency.

(b) Interfering with lawful speech, publication, assembly, organizational activity or association of Americans.

(c) Harassing individuals through unnecessary overt investigative techniques such as interviews of obvious physical surveillance for the purpose of intimidation.

Recommendation 41 — The bureau should be prohibited from maintaining information on the political beliefs, political associations or private lives of Americans except that which is clearly necessary for domestic security investigations as described [below].

Investigations of Committed or Imminent Offenses

Recommendation 42—The F.B.I. should be permitted to investigate a commited act which may violate a Federal criminal statute pertaining to the domestic security to determine the identity of the perpetrator or to determine whether the act violates such a statute.

Recommendation 43 — The F.B.I. should be permitted to investigate an American or foreigner to obtain evidence of criminal activity where there is "reasonable suspicion" that the American or foreigner has committed, is committing or is about to commit a specific act which violates a Federal statute pertaining to the domestic security.

Recommendation 44 — The F.B.I. should be permitted to conduct a preliminary preventive intelligence investigation of an American or foreigner where it has a specific allegation or specific or substantiated information that the American or foreigner will soon engage in terrorist activity or hostile foreign intelligence activity. Such a preliminary investigation should not continue longer than 30 days from receipt of the information unless the Attorney General or his designee finds that the information and any corroboration which has been obtained warrants investigation for an additional period which may not exceed 60 days. If, at the outset or at any time during the course of a preliminary investigation, the bureau establishes "reasonable suspicion" that an American or foreigner will soon engage in terrorist activity or hostile foreign intelligence activity, it may conduct a full preventive intelligence investigation. Such full investigation should not continue longer than one year except upon a finding of compelling circumstances by the Attorney General or his designee.

In no event should the F.B.I. open a preliminary or full preventive intelligence investigation based upon information that an American is advocating political ideas or engaging in lawful political activities or is associating with others for the purpose of petitioning the Government for redress of grievances or other such constitutionally protected purpose.

Recommendation 45 — The F.B.I. should be permitted to collect information to assist Federal, state and local officials in connection with a civil disorder either—

(i) After the Attorney General finds in writing that there is a clear and immediate threat of domestic violence or rioting which is likely to require implementation of 10 U.S.C. 332 or 333 (the use of Federal troops for the enforcement of Federal law or Federal court orders), or likely to result in a request by the governor or legislature of a state pursuant to 10 U.S.C. 331 for the use of Federal militia or other Federal armed forces as a countermeasure, or

(ii) After such troops have been introduced.

Recommendation 46—F.B.I. assistance to Federal, state and local officials in connection with a civil disorder should be limited to collecting information necessary for

(1) The President in making decisions concerning the introduction of Federal troops;

(2) Military officials in positioning and supporting such troops, and

(3) State and local officials in coordinating their activities with such military officials.

Background Investigations

Recommendation 47—The F.B.I. should be permitted to participate in the Federal Government's program of background investigations of Federal employees or employees of Federal contractors. The authority to conduct such investigations should not, however, be used as the basis for conducting investigations of other persons. In addition, Congress should examine the standards of Executive Order 10450, which serves as the current authority for F.B.I. background investigations, to determine whether additional legislation is necessary to:

(a) Modify criteria based on political beliefs and associations unrelated to suitability for employment; such modification should make those criteria consistent with judicial decisions regarding privacy of political association, and

(b) Restrict the dissemination of information from name checks of information related to suitability for employment.

Recommendation 48—Under regulations to be formulated by the Attorney General, the F.B.I. should be permitted to investigate a specific allegation that an individual within the executive branch with access to classified information is a security risk as described in Executive Order 10450. Such investigation should not continue longer than 30 days except upon written approval of the Attorney General or his designee.

Recommendation 49—Under regulations to be formulated by the Attorney General, the F.B.I. should be permitted to investigate a specific allegation of the improper disclosure of classified information by employees or contractors of the executive branch. Such investigation should not continue longer than 30 days except upon written approval of the Attorney General or his designee.

Recommendation 50—Overt techniques and name checks should be permitted in all of the authorized domestic security investigations described above, including preliminary and full preventive intelligence investigations.

Recommendation 51—All nonconsensual electronic surveillance, mail-opening and unauthorized entries should be conducted only upon authority of a judicial warrant.

Recommendation 52—All nonconsensual electronic surveillance should be conducted pursuant to judicial warrants issued under authority of Title III of the Omnibus Crime Control and Safe Streets Act of 1968.

The act should be amended to provide, with respect to electronic surveillance of foreigners in the United States, that a warrant may issue if:

(a) There is probable cause that the target is an officer, employee or conscious agent of a foreign power.

(b) The Attorney General has certified that the surveillance is likely to reveal information necessary to the protection of the nation against actual or potential attack or other hostile acts of force of a foreign power; to obtain foreign intelligence information deemed essential to the security of the United States, or to protect national security information against hostile foreign intelligence activity.

(c) With respect to any such electronic surveillance, the judge should adopt procedures to minimize the acquisition and retention of nonforeign intelligence information about Americans.

(d) Such electronic surveillance should be exempt from the disclosure requirements of Title III of the 1968 Act as to foreigners generally and as to Americans if they are involved in hostile foreign intelligence activity.

As noted earlier, the committee believes that the espionage laws should be amended to include industrial espionage and other modern forms of espionage not presently covered, and Title III should incorporate any such amendment.

Recommendation 53—Mail opening should be conducted only pursuant to a judicial warrant issued upon probable cause of criminal activity as described in Recommendation 37.

Recommendation 54 — Unauthorized entry should be conducted only upon judicial warrant issued on probable cause to believe that the place to be searched contains evidence of a crime, except unauthorized entry, including surreptitious entry, against foreigners who are officers, employees or conscious agents of a foreign power should be permitted upon judicial warrant under the standards which apply to electronic surveillance described in Recommendation 52.

Administrative Procedures

Recommendation 55—Covert human sources may not be directed at an American except:

(1) In the course of a criminal investigation if necessary to the investigation, provided that covert human sources should not be directed at an American as a part of an investigation of a committed act unless there is reasonable suspicion to believe that the American is responsible for the act, and then only for the purpose of identifying the perpetrators of the act.

(2) If the American is the target of a full preventive intelligence investigation and the Attorney General or his designee makes a written finding that he has considered and rejected less intrusive techniques and he believes that covert human sources are necessary to obtain information for the investigation.

Recommendation 56—Covert human sources which have been directed at an American in a full preventive intelligence investigation should not be used to collect information on the activities of the American for more than 90 days after the source is in place and capable of reporting unless the Attorney General or his designee finds in writing either that there are "compelling circumstances," in which case they may be used for an additional 60 days, or that there is probable cause that the American will soon engage in terrorist activities or hostile foreign intelligence activities.

Recommendation 57—All covert human sources used by the F.B.I. should be reviewed by the Attorney General or his designee as soon as practicable and should be terminated unless the covert human source could be directed against an American in a criminal investigation or a full preventive intelligence investigation under these recommendations.

Recommendation 58—Mail surveillance and the review of tax returns and tax-related information should be conducted consistently with the recommendations [above]. In addition to restrictions [above], the review of tax returns and tax-related information, as well as review of medical or social history records, confidential records of private institutions and confidential records of Federal, state and local government agencies other than intelligence or law enforcement agencies may not be used against an American except:

(1) In the course of a criminal investigation, if necessary to the investigation;

(2) If the American is the target of a full preventive intelligence investigation and the Attorney General or his designee makes a written finding that he has considered and rejected less intrusive techniques and he believes that the covert technique requested by the bureau is necessary to obtain information necessary to the investigation.

Recommendation 59—The use of physical surveillance and review of credit and telephone records and any records of governmental or private institutions other than those covered in Recommendation 58 should be permitted to be used against an American, if necessary, in the course of either a criminal investigation or a preliminary or full preventive intelligence investigation.

Recommendation 60—Covert techniques should be permitted at the scene of a potential civil disorder in the course of preventive criminal intelligence and criminal investigations as described above. Nonwarrant covert techniques may also be directed at an American during a civil disorder in which extensive acts of violence are occurring and Federal troops have been introduced. This additional authority to direct such covert techniques at Americans during a civil disorder should be limited to circumstances where Federal troops are actually in use and the technique is used only for the purpose of preventing further violence.

Recommendation 61—Covert techniques should not be directed at an American in the course of a background investigation without the informed written consent of the American.

Recommendation 62—If Congress enacts a statute attaching criminal sanctions to security leaks, covert techniques should be directed at Americans in the course of security leak investigations only if such techniques are consistent with Recommendation 55(1), 58(1) or 59. With respect to security risks, Congress might consider authorizing covert techniques, other than those requiring a judicial warrant, to be directed at Americans in the course of security risk investigations, but only upon a written finding of the Attorney General that there is reasonable suspicion to believe that the individual is a security

risk, he has considered and rejected less intrusive techniques and he believes the technique requested is necessary to the investigation.

Incidental Overhears

Recommendation 63—Except as limited elsewhere in these recommendations or in Title III of the Omnibus Crime Control and Safe Streets Act of 1968, information obtained incidentally through an authorized covert technique about an American or a foreigner who is not the target of the covert technique can be used as the basis for any authorized domestic security investigation.

Recommendation 64 — Information should not be maintained except where relevant to the purpose of an investigation.

Recommendation 65 — Personally identifiable information on Americans obtained in the following kinds of investigations should be sealed or purged as follows (unless it appears on its face to be necessary for another authorized investigation):

(a) Preventive intelligence investigations of terrorist or hostile foreign intelligence activities—as soon as the investigation is terminated by the Attorney General or his designee pursuant to Recommendation 45 or 69.

(b) Civil disorder assistance—as soon as the assistance is terminated by the Attorney General or his designee pursuant to Recommendation 69, provided that where troops have been introduced such information need be sealed or purged only within a reasonable period after their withdrawal.

Recommendation 66 — Information previously gained by the F.B.I. or any other intelligence agency through illegal techniques should be sealed or purged as soon as practicable.

Recommendation 67 — Personally identifiable information on Americans from domestic security investigations may be disseminated outside the Department of Justice as follows:

(a) Preventive intelligence investigations of terrorist activities—personally identifiable information on Americans from preventive criminal intelligence investigations of terrorist activities may be disseminated only to:

(1) A foreign or domestic law enforcement agency which has jurisdiction over the criminal activity to which the information relates, or

(2) To a foreign intelligence or military agency of the United States, if necessary for an activity permitted by these recommendations, or

(3) To an appropriate Federal official with authority to make personnel decisions about the subject of the information, or

(4) To a foreign intelligence or military agency of a cooperating foreign power if necessary for an activity permitted by these recommendations to similar agencies of the United States, or

(5) Where necessary to warn state or local officials of terrorist activity likely to occur within their jurisdiction, or

(6) Where necessary to warn any person of a threat to life or property from terrorist activity.

(b) Preventive intelligence investigations of hostile foreign intelligence activities—personally identifiable information on Americans from preventive criminal intelligence investigations of hostile intelligence activities may be disseminated only:

(1) To an appropriate Federal official with authority to make personnel decisions about the subject of the information, or

(2) To the National Security Council or the Department of State upon request or where appropriate to their administration of U.S. foreign policy, or

(3) To a foreign intelligence or military agency of the United States, if relevant to an activity permitted by these recommendations, or

(4) To a foreign intelligence or military agency of a cooperating foreign power if relevant to an activity permitted by these recommendations to similar

(c) Civil disorders assistance—personally identifiable information on Americans involved in an actual or potential disorder, collected in the course of civil disorders assistance, should not be disseminated outside the Department of Justice except to military officials and appropriate state and local officials at the scene of a civil disorder where Federal troops are present.

(d) Background investigations—to the maximum extent feasible, the results of background investigations should be segregated within the F.B.I. and only disseminated to officials outside the Department of Justice authorized to make personnel decisions with respect to the subject.

(e) All other authorized domestic security investigations—to governmental officials who are authorized to take action consistent with the purpose of an investigation or who have statutory duties which require the information.

Recommendation 68—Officers of the executive branch who are made responsible by these recommendations for overseeing intelligence activities and appropriate Congressional committees should have access to all information necessary for their functions. The committees should adopt procedures to protect the privacy of subjects of files maintained by the F.B.I. and other agencies affected by the domestic intelligence recommendations.

Attorney General Oversight of the F.B.I.

Recommendation 69—The Attorney General should:

(a) Establish a program of routine and periodic review of F.B.I. domestic security investigations to ensure that the F.B.I. is complying with all of the foregoing recommendations, and

(b) Assure, with respect to the following investigations of Americans, that:

(1) Preventive intelligence investigations of terrorist activity or hostile foreign intelligence activity are terminated within one year, except that the Attorney General or his designee may grant extensions upon a written finding of "compelling circumstances";

(2) Covert techniques are used in preventive intelligence investigations of terrorist activity or hostile foreign intelligence activity only so long as necessary and not beyond time limits estab-

lished by the Attorney General, except that the Attorney General or his designee may grant extensions upon a written finding of "compelling circumstances."

(3) Civil disorders assistance is terminated upon withdrawal of Federal troops or, if troops were not introduced, within a reasonable time after the finding by the Attorney General that troops are likely to be requested, except that the Attorney General or his designee may grant extensions upon a written finding of "compelling circumstances."

Recommendation 70—The Attorney General should review the internal regulations of the F.B.I. and other intelligence agencies engaging in domestic security activities to ensure that such internal regulations are proper and adequate to protect the constitutional rights of Americans.

Recommendation 71—The Attorney General or his designee (such as the Office of Legal Counsel of the Department of Justice) should advise the general counsels of intelligence agencies on interpretations of statutes and regulations adopted pursuant to these recommendations and on such other legal questions as are described below.

Recommendation 72—The Attorney General should have ultimate responsibility for the investigation of alleged violations of law relating to the domestic intelligence recommendations.

Recommendations 73—The Attorney General should be notified of possible alleged violations of law through the Office of Professional Responsibility by agency heads, general counsel or inspectors general of intelligence agencies.

Recommendation 74—The heads of all intelligence agencies affected by these recommendations are responsible for the prevention and detection of alleged violations of the law by or on behalf of their respective agencies and for the reporting to the Attorney General of all such alleged violations. Each such head should also assure his agency's cooperation with the Attorney General in investigation of alleged violations.

Recommendation 75—The F.B.I. and each other intelligence agency should have a general counsel, nominated by the President and confirmed by the Senate, and an inspector general appointed by the agency head.

Recommendation 76—Any individual having information on past, current or proposed activities which appear to be illegal, improper or in violation of agency policy should be required to report the matter immediately to the agency head, general counsel or inspector general. If the matter is not initially reported to the general counsel he should be notified by the agency head or inspector general. Each agency should regularly remind employees of their obligation to report such information.

Recommendation 77—As provided in Recommendation 74, the heads of the F.B.I. and of other intelligence agencies are responsible for reporting to the Attorney General alleged violations of law. When such reports are made the appropriate Congressional committees should be notified.

Recommendation 78 — The general counsel and inspector general of the F.B.I. and of each other intelligence

agency should have unrestricted access to all information in the possession of the agency and should have the authority to review all of the agency's activities. The Attorney General or the Office of Professional Responsibility, on his behalf, should have access to all information in the possession of an agency which, in the opinion of the Attorney General, is necessary for an investigation of illegal activity.

Recommendation 79 — The general counsel of the F.B.I. and of each other intelligence agency should review all significant proposed agency activities to determine their legality and constitutionality.

Recommendation 80—The director of the F.B.I. and the heads of each other intelligence agency should be required to report, at least annually, th the appropriate committee of the Congress on the activities of the general counsel and the Office of the Inspector General.

Recommendation 81—The director of the F.B.I. and the heads of each other intelligence agency should be required to report, at least annually, to the Attorney General on all reports of activities which appear illegal, improper, outside the legislative charter or in violation of agency regulations. Such reports should include the general counsel's findings concerning these activities, a summary of the inspector general's investigations of these activities and the practice and procedures developed to discover activities that raise questions of legality or propriety.

Office of Professional Responsibility

Recommendation 82—The Office of Professional Responsibility created by Attorney General Levi should be recognized in statute. The director of the office, appointed by the Attorney General, should report directly to the Attorney General or the Deputy Attorney General. The functions of the office should include:

(a) Serving as a central repository of reports and notifications provided the Attorney General, and

(b) Investigation, if requested by the Attorney General, of alleged violations by intelligence agencies of statutes enacted or regulations promulgated pursuant to these recommendations.

Recommendation 83—The Attorney General is responsible for all of the activities of the F.B.I., and the director of the F.B.I. is responsible to, and should be under the supervision and control of, the Attorney General.

Recommendation 84—The director of the F.B.I. should be nominated by the President and confirmed by the Senate to serve at the pleasure of the President for a single term of not more than eight years.

Recommendation 85—The Attorney General should consider exercising his power to appoint assistant directors of the F.B.I. should be nominated by the should be imposed on the tenure of the assistant director for the Intelligence Division.

Recommendation 86—The Attorney General should approve all administrative regulations required to implement

statutes created pursuant to these recommendations.

Recommendation 87—Such regulations, except for regulations concerning investigations of hostile foreign intelligence activity or other matters which are properly classified, should be issued pursuant to the Administrative Procedures Act and should be subject to the approval of the Attorney General.

Recommendation 88—The effective date of regulations pertaining to the following matters should be delayed 90 days, during which time Congress would have the opportunity to review such regulations:

(a) Any C.I.A. activities against Americans, as permitted above;

(b) Military activities at the time of a civil disorder;

.(c) The authorized scope of domestic security investigations, authorized investigative techniques, maintenance and dissemination of information by the FBI, and

(d) The termination of investigations and covert techniques as described [above].

Recommendation 89—Each year the F.B.I. and other intelligence agencies affected by these recommendations should be required to seek annual statutory authorization for their programs.

Recommendation 90—The Freedom of Information Act (5 U.S.C. 552 (b)) and the Federal Privacy Act (5 U.S.C. 552 (a)) provide important mechanisms by which individuals can gain access to information on intelligence activity directed against them. The domestic intelligence recommendations assume that these statutes will continue to be vigorously enforced. In addition, the Department of Justice should notify all readily identifiable targets of past illegal surveillance techniques and all Cointelpro victims and third parties who had received anonymous Cointelpro communications of the nature of the activities directed against them or the source of the anonymous communication to them.

Recommendation 91—Congress should enact a comprehensive civil remedies statute which would accomplish the following:

(a) Any American with a substantial and specific claim to an actual or threatened injury by a violation of the Constitution by Federal intelligence officers or agents acting under color of law should have a Federal cause of action against the Government and the individual Federal intelligence officer or agent responsible for the violation, without regard to the monetary amount in controversy. If actual injury is proven in court, the committee believes that the injured person should be entitled to equitable relief, actual, general and punitive damages and recovery of the costs of litigation. If threatened injury is proven in court, the committee believes that equitable relief and recovery of the costs of litigation should be available.

(b) Any American with a substantial and specific claim to actual or threatened injury by violation of the statutory charter for intelligence activity (as proposed by these domestic intelligence recommendations) should have a cause of action for relief as in (a) above.

(c) Because of the secrecy that surrounds intelligence programs, the committee believes that a plaintiff should have two years from the date upon which he discovers or reasonably should have discovered the facts which give rise to a cause of action for relief from a constitutional or statutory violation.

(d) Whatever statutory provision may be made to permit an individual defendant to raise an affirmative defense that he acted within the scope of his official duties, in good faith and with a reasonable belief that the action he took was lawful, the committee believes that to insure relief to persons injured by governmental intelligence activity this defense should be available solely to individual defendants and should not extend to the Government. Moreover, the defense should not be available to bar injunctions against individual defendants.

Criminal Penalties Should Be Enacted

Recommendation 92—The committee believes that criminal penalties should apply, where appropriate, to willful and knowing violations of statutes enacted pursuant to the domestic intelligence recommendations.

Recommendation 93—Congress should either repeal the Smith Act (18 U.S.C. 2385) and the Voorhis Act (18 U.S.C. 2386), which on their face appear to authorize investigation of "mere advocacy" of a political ideology, or amend those statutes so that domestic security investigations are only directed at conduct which might serve as the basis for a constitutional criminal prosecution under Supreme Court decisions interpreting these and related statutes.

Recommendation 94—The appropriate committees of the Congress should review the Espionage Act of 1917 to determine whether it should be amended to cover modern forms of foreign espionage, including industrial, technological or economic espionage.

Recommendation 95—The appropriate Congressional oversight committees of the Congress should, from time to time, request the Comptroller General of the United States to conduct audits and reviews of the intelligence activities of any department or agency of the United States affected by the domestic intelligence recommendations. For such purpose, the Comptroller General or any of his duly authorized representatives should have access to, and the right to examine, all necessary materials

of any such department or agency.

Recommendation 96—The committee re-endorses the concept of vigorous Senate oversight to review the conduct of domestic security activities through a new permanent intelligence oversight committee.

Definitions

For the purposes of these recommendations:

A. "Americans" means U.S. citizens, resident aliens and unincorporated associations, composed primarily of U.S. citizens or resident aliens; and corporations, incorporated or having their principal place of business in the United States or having majority ownership by U.S. citizens, or resident aliens, including foreign subsidiaries of such corporations, provided, however, "Americans" does not include corporations directed by foreign governments or organizations.

B. "Collect" means to gather or initiate the acquisition of information or to request it from another agency.

C. A "covert human source" means undercover agents or informants who are paid or otherwise controlled by an agency.

D. "Covert techniques" means the collection of information, including collection from record sources not readily available to a private person (except state or local law enforcement files), in such a manner as not to be detected by the subject.

E. "Domestic security activities" means governmental activities against Americans or conducted within the United States or its territories, including enforcement of the criminal laws, intended to:

1. Protect the United States from hostile foreign intelligence activity including espionage;

2. Protect the Federal, state and local governments from domestic violence or rioting, and

3. Protect Americans and their Government from terrorists.

F. "Foreign communications" refers to a communication between or among two or more parties in which at least one party is outside the United States or a communication transmitted between points within the United States if transmitted over a facility which is under the control of or exclusively used by a foreign government.

G. "Foreigners" means persons and organizations who are not Americans as defined above.

H. "Hostile foreign intelligence activities" means acts or conspiracies by Americans or foreigners who are officers, employees or conscious agents of a foreign power or who, pursuant to the direction of a foreign power, engage in clandestine intelligence activity or engage in espionage, sabotage or similar conduct in violation of Federal criminal statutes.

I. "Name checks" means the retrieval by an agency of information already in the possession of the Federal Government or in the possession of state or local law enforcement agencies.

J. "Overt investigative techniques" means the collection of information readily available from public sources or available to a private person, including interviews of the subject or his friends or associates.

K. "Purged" means to destroy or transfer to the National Archives all personally identifiable information (including references in any general name index).

L. "Sealed" means to retain personally identifiable information and to retain entries in a general name index but to restrict access to the information and entries to circumstances of "compelling necessity."

M. "Reasonable suspicion" is based upon the Supreme Court's decision in the case of *Terry v. Ohio,* 392 U.S. 1 (1968), and means specific and articulable facts which, taken together with rational inferences from those facts, give rise to a reasonable suspicion that specified activity has occurred, is occurring or is about to occur.

N. "Terrorist activities" means acts, or conspiracies which: (a) are violent or dangerous to human life; and (b) violate Federal or state criminal statutes concerning assassination, murder, arson, bombing, hijacking or kidnapping; and (c) appear intended to or are likely to have the effect of:

(1) Substantially disrupting Federal, state or local government, or

(2) Substantially disrupting interstate or foreign commerce between the United States and another country, or

(3) Directly interfering with the exercise by Americans of constitutional rights protected by the Civil Rights Act of 1968, or by foreigners of their rights under the laws or treaties of the United States.

O. "Unauthorized entry" means entry unauthorized by the target.

April 29, 1976

F.B.I. SOUGHT DOOM OF PANTHER PARTY

By JOHN KIFNER
Special to The New York Times

WASHINGTON, May 8—The Federal Bureau of Investigation carried out a secret, nationwide effort to "destroy" the Black Panthers, including attempts to

stir bloody "gang warfare" between the Panthers and other groups and to create factional splits within the party, according to the staff report of the Senate Select Committee on Intelligence Activities.

The bureau's efforts, part of the Cointelpro or counterintelligence program, contributed to a climate of violence in which four Black Panthers were shot to death, the report says.

[In Fulton, Mo., Saturday,

Clarence M. Kelley, the F.B.I. director, apologized to the American public for investigative abuses by the bureau in "the twilight" of J. Edgar Hoover's career, Page 20.]

Besides the four deaths of Black Panthers mentioned in the Senate Committee's report, independent police and Panther sources said there had been two other slayings of Panthers in intraparty rivalry in New York City.

The Cointelpro campaign was an effort to combat dissidents and radicals. The part involving the Panthers, the committee report said, included an attempt to drive a wedge between two Panther leaders, Eldridge Cleaver and Huey P. Newton, and to split the party by sending bogus divisive letters.

The bureau also used informers and bogus messages and cartoons to make trouble between the Panthers and a black nationalist group called US in southern California and be-

C.I.A. - F.B.I.

tween Chicago Panthers and the Blackstone Rangers, a heavily armed street gang, according to the report, released this week.

For example, a faked note was sent to the leader of the street gang Jeff Fort, telling him of the Panthers hostility toward his group, saying, "There's supposed to be a hit out for you."

In noting that this meant there was probably a contract to kill someone, the Chicago F.B.I. office said in a memorandum to headquarters that the letter "may intensify the degree of animosity between the two groups and occasion Fort to take retaliatory action which could disrupt the B.P.P. [Black Panther Party] or lead to reprisals against their leadership."

The report portrays a campaign in which the bureau used a legion of informers, sometimes as provocateurs, and close cooperation with local police antiradical squads to sow confusion, fear and dissension among the Panthers. Cartoons attacking them, purportedly from rival groups, were distributed to aggravate antagonisms. Stories were planted with newspaper and television outlets to put the Panthers and their supporters i na bad light. Bogus messages were sent to cause rifts between the party and its white leftist supporters.

After a series of clashes between the Panthers and Ron Karenga's US group — US stood for United Slaves—in southern California, which resulted in three deaths (one more would follow), the San Diego F.B.I. office sent to headquarters a message that the report says "pointed with pride" to the violence, saying:

"Shootings, beatings and a high degree of unrest continues to prevail in the ghetto area of southeast San Diego. Although no specific counterintelligence action can be credited with contributing to this overall situation, it is felt that a substantial amount of the unrest is directly attributable to this program."

The committee report said that the techniques used in Cointelpro "would be intolerable in a democratic society even if all the targets had been

involved in violent activity; but Cointelpro went far beyond that."

"The unexpressed major premise of the programs," the report went on, "was that a law enforcement agency has the duty to do whatever is necessary to combat perceived threats to the existing social and political order."

A separate committee report on the F.B.I. efforts against the Black Panthers said that, although the "claimed purpose" of the program was to prevent violence, some of the tactics "were clearly intended to foster violence, and many others could reasonably have been expected to cause violence."

The bureau, this report concluded, "itself engaged in lawless tactics and responded to deep-seated social problems by fomenting violence and unrest."

The report said that the Senate committee had not been able to determine "the extent to which Cointelpro may be continuing." The committee found three instances of similar operations, the report said, even though the program was supposed to have been abandoned "for security reasons" in April 1971, after the existence of Cointelpro had been made known when a radical band made off with documents from an F.B.I. office in Media, Pa. The report suggested that a search of the bureau's more than 500,000 case files might be "productive."

The report noted that in the current fiscal year the bureau had budgeted some $7.4 million for domestic intelligence informers, more than twice the amount budgeted for informers in organized crime.

The committee investigators had considerable difficulty, according to staff sources, in assembling their information.

For instance, these sources said, the F.B.I. declined to turn over documents in which its Chicago office said that their informer had been the sole source of information that led to the Chicago police raid in 1969 in which the state Panther leader, Fred Hampton, and an aide were killed.

Those documents were obtained only in the last week by the committee because they turned up in a civil damage suit filed in Chicago by the Panthers who survived the raid. They emerged there because testimony in the case indicated that documents were being withheld and a Federal district judge, Joseph Sam Perry, ordered a search that turned up more than 50 volumes of previously undisclosed files.

The Panthers became the primary focus of the "black nationalist hate groups" section of Cointelpro by July 1969, and were the target of 233 of the 295 actions authorized against black groups, the report says.

Mr. Hoover, then the F.B.I. director, sent a memorandum to 14 field offices in late 1968 noting that a "state of gang warfare" existed between the Karenga organization and the Panthers "with attendant threats of murder and reprisals." He ordered "imaginative and hard-hitting counterintelligence measures aimed at crippling the BPP" to be drawn up to "fully capitalize" on the rivalry and "exploit all avenues of creating further dissension" in the Panther ranks.

On Jan. 17, 1969, two Panthers, Alprentice Carter and John Huggins, were killed in a shootout with US members on the University of California, Los Angeles, campus. The F.B.I. helped stir the feud further, the report says, and on May 23 John Savage, a Panther, was killed and another, Sylvester Bell, was slain on Aug. 15, both by US members. There were other confrontations.

At one point, a bureau memorandum said, its informers in both camps would be used so the Karenga group would be "appropriately and discreetly advised of the time and location of B.P.P. activities in order that the two organizations might be brought together and thus grant nature the opportunity to take her due course."

Enmity Inflamed

Although it is not mentioned in the report, both the police and Panther sources say that in a split that developed in the

Panthers, Robert Webb, a member of the Cleaver faction in New York, was shot while selling the party newspaper on 125th Street on March 9, 1971, by Panthers loyal to Huey P. Newton. In retaliation, Samuel Lee Napier, circulation manager of the paper, controlled by the Newton faction, was slain in Queens on April 17, 1971.

The report heavily documents the efforts of the F.B.I. to exacerbate the split by sending false messages back and forth between Mr. Cleaver, who had fled to Algeria to avoid prosecution for parole violation, and the Newton group in Oakland, telling of alleged failings, deviations, high living and plots.

These F.B.I. efforts began, the report says, in March 1970 while Mr. Newton was in jail on a voluntary manslaughter conviction, later overturned, in connection with a gunfight in which an Oakland policeman was slain. The Panthers at that time were presenting a united front.

An anonymous letter was sent to Mr. Cleaver telling him that the California Panthers were seeking to undercut his influence. This prompted him to expel three party members, the report said.

What then followed, the report said, was a "barrage" of letters of various types to sow divisiveness, creating what an F.B.I. memorandum described as a "chaotic situation" that "must be exploited." Among them was a directive on false Panther stationery, attributed to the Newton group, declaring that Mr. Cleaver was "a murderer and a punk" and warning that anyone aiding "Cleaver and his jackanapes" would be "dealt with."

The Panthers' newspaper and their free "breakfast for children" program were particular targets of the F.B.I.'s efforts, the report said. In a memorandum disclosed in the civil damage suit in Chicago, Mr. Hoover said the breakfast program had generated publicity that showed the Panthers "in a favorable light and clouds the violent nature of the group and its ultimate aim of insurrection."

May 9, 1976

Spy Inquiries, Begun Amid Public Outrage, End in Indifference

BY LESLIE H. GELB.

Special to The New York Times

WASHINGTON, May 11—The Congressional and Presidential investigations into domestic spying and political assassination plots by the intelligence community began 16 months ago amid public outrage but are now ending

amid public indifference and Congressional uncertainty over whether there will eventually be adequate reforms.

"It all lasted too long, and the media, the Congress and the people lost interest," commented Representative Otis G. Pike, who headed the House Select Committee on Intelligence. The House voted against publishing

his committee's report and ignored its proposals for a basic structural overhaul of the intelligence community.

Administration officials take the position that President Ford has already done enough to reinforce and streamline policy control of intelligence activities and catch abuses, but mostly through changes that are being kept

secret, even from Congress.

Senator Frank Church, chairman of the Senate Select Committee on Intelligence, has argued that it is not enough for the President to put the Administration's own house in order. The Church committee has pushed for a new Congressional oversight committee on intelligence, to consolidate and strengthen the current system, which is fragmented among several committees.

What began with sensational publicity accompanying disclosures of the intelligence inquiries is ending now in compromises. Why this happened and how it

384

happened is a case study in the subtle ways in which the politics of this city work.

Perhaps most important, the political climate has changed since the start of the investigations. Congress, once on the offensive, was thrown back somewhat on the defensive by disputes over disclosures of classified information given to Congressional committees and over responsibility for the assassination in Greece of the chief of the Central Intelligence Agency operations there.

Then, as the details of covert operations, illegal wiretappings and mail openings became old news, public interest waned, and Congressional committees and executive agencies turned inward, settling their disputes along the usual lines of committee turf, bureaucratic tactics and access to information.

Equally fundamental, the personalities and strategies of the two Congressional investigating committees diverged sharply, and thus Congress was unable to face the Administration with a solid front.

Mr. Pike tried to operate in the open and to confront the White House, and he lost support in the House. Mr. Church and his Senate committee made compromises, doing some things in the open and other things in private, and generally tried to get along with the Administration.

Support Is Sought

Now, he must shepherd support among—and sometimes against—the Senate leaders whose committees have long handled intelligence matters and who are reluctant to surrender these prerogatives to the new oversight committee he proposes.

Throughout, the Congressional investigators have been hobbled by the difficulties of obtaining information on the inner workings of the intelligence community.

Some officials, noting the reluctance of the Administration to share information—and through it, power—with Congress, recalled that former Secretary of Defense James R. Schlesinger once told a White House meeting that sensitive information should not be given in the Pike committee because the committee contained unfriendly foreign operatives.

According to these sources, William E. Colby, then the Director of Central Intelligence, ironically commented that this was a good idea, and he was sure that Mr. Schlesinger had evidence to support his allegation and should turn it over to House Speaker Carl Albert. No more was said.

Even within the executive branch, rivalries and sensitivities affected the flow of information. Vice President Rockefeller reportedly lectured Mr. Colby once for having given too much information to the commission set up within the executive branch to investigate C.I.A. activities. Mr. Rockefeller headed that commission himself.

More common apparently, was the frustration of the executive branch investigators at the refusal of intelligence agencies to disclose enough about their past methods of operation. "There were times when we wished we had subpoena power here in the White House," one official said.

Another said that ultimately the executive branch investigation succeeded, because the White House was able to play off the intelligence agencies against one another. The White House, he said, "was able to pry information out of the agencies, because each agency didn't know what the White House was getting from the others, and they were afraid of getting caught in a lie."

Confirmation that this tactic was effective came from a C.I.A. official. "The biggest fear here," he said, "was the rest of the executive branch more than Congress." Officials from other agencies made the same points. Each was concerned about opening up its secret sources and methods to the others.

Providing sensitive information to Congressional committees was a separate problem. Early meetings of an inter-agency committee headed by John O. Marsh, Jr., the President's counselor, were punctuated by a lot of speechmaking on the need for being rough with the committees. Attorney General Edward H. Levy would often interrupt to say something like: "This is a fine speech for Broadway, but how will it sound when they throw you in a cell for violating the law?"

The general view among officials in the Administration and on Capitol Hill who have been involved with the various investigations is that the main obstacles to turning over information came from those concerned with policy at the State and Defense Departments, from the National Security Council staff and from the heads of operational staff.

Generally on the other side were the White House staff, which believed that President Ford had nothing to hide, and the leaders of the C.I.A., who believed that their agency could be saved only by being candid.

The President decided early to be more forthcoming with the Church committee than with the Pike committee. This was a reflection of the very different ways in which the committees sought to get information.

Mr. Pike was made chairman of the House committee largely because of the majority's conviction that representative Lucien Nedzi, the chairman of the House Armed Services Committee, had not been tough enough in his oversight. Mr. Pike hired a young staff with few Washington ties, and together they confronted the Administration at each step. Committee unity fell apart when Mr. Pike recommended citing Mr. Kissinger for contempt when he did not turn over certain policy papers.

Mr. Church, on the other hand, gave high priority to hold-

ing his committee together. He built a staff of experienced Congressional aides, and their approach was to cajole and co-operate with the Administration.

Diversion and Delay

For the Church committee, getting all the assassination material set an important precedent for obtaining additional documents. But the very volume of the assassination material forced diversion and delay. Months were spent preparing that report before the bulk of the committee got down to its assigned business.

But in the long run, the Pike committee's confrontation tactics may have hurt, leaving the Senate committee's campaign for stronger Congressional oversight of intelligence activities without a corresponding effort in the House. The tactics also changed the focus of debate in Washington from how much Congressional oversight is necessary to whether Congress can keep a secret.

Mr. Pike sees some advantage to his tough stance, however. "I think Church paid a price for cooperation," the Representative says. "Less information was made public."

In this respect, there was a dovetailing of strategies between the White House and the Church committee. "The President's attitude was that there was no reason to keep information respecting mistakes and abuses from Congress," one White House official explained, "but at the same time, the President felt he had the responsibility that it not be made public if it would damage the country."

Most Administration officials maintained that the President had no grand strategy for dealing with Congress, except to avoid any appearance of a cover-up and to conclude the investigations as quickly as possible. "The longer it went on, the more rocks would be turned over, the more worms would be found," one key participant said.

Delay was inherent in the practical steps taken by the Administration to insure its concepts of secrecy. One who took part in the process of negotiation said:

"If the committee asked for information, we'd brief them. If they demanded the documents, we'd give them a sanitized version. If this wasn't enough, we'd give them the rest on the condition that they would not publish without consent."

Others in the Administration sought delay, one official said, "much the same way a lawyer plays for time, hoping something will come up to save his client." Things did come up.

"Pike, Welch and Schorr, those were the three names that caused us to pull back, not because our constituents said you're going too far, but because those names came to have important symbolic importance in the currency of Washington," said a senator who did not want to be identified.

Richard S. Welch was the head of the C.I.A. office in Greece. He was murdered shortly after a magazine identified him. Daniel Schorr was a reporter for CBS who obtained and arranged for publication of the still-classified Pike committee report.

Senator Walter F. Mondale, Democrat of Minnesota, who was a member of the Church committee, said: "There was a sense of anarchy over in the House. Then came the Welch murder and what I believe to be the careful orchestration of the Welch funeral to tie the murder to the Congressional investigations."

Administration officials denied any orchestration, maintaining that all of the funeral arrangements were made by the Welch family.

"The Schorr matter," Mr. Mondale said, "further undermined confidence in Congress to deal with secret matters."

As the public became "numb with bad news," in Mr. Mondale's phrase, some members of the Pike committee apparently sought to revive public attention through unauthorized disclosures of information. Meanwhile, the Church committee continued to keep those secrets to show that Congress can do so and that Congressional oversight can work.

From the start, the Church committee's goals, according to committee members, was to generate support for standing Congressional oversight committees, with full legislative and budgetary authority and new laws governing intelligence activities.

To some members of the Pike committee, his goals, in some respects, went much deeper—to a basic restructuring of the intelligence community—and much beyond what the House and the Administration seemed prepared to support.

The Pike committee wanted to know how much intelligence costs the taxpayer and whether the results were worth the costs and the risks. The committee's report, which has been criticized by many people, came to the conclusion that the taxpayer was not getting his money's worth. The national intelligence budget is estimated at $4.5 billion.

The Senate is now about to consider the Church committee's plan for a standing oversight committee that would supersede the three existing committees—Armed Services, Appropriations and Foreign Relations — with authority over intelligence agencies.

The battle lines are drawn along these lines: On the one side are those who back the existing oversight committees and some who also feel that Congress ought not to get deeply involved in the President's business of running intelligence operations. On the other side are those who feel that the existing committees did not do the job.

A White House official who supports the President's proposal for a joint House-Senate oversight committee argued that the legislative and budgetary powers of the proposed new Senate committee go too far. "It makes the committee a participant in decisions, and how can it be both participant and judge?" he asked. "Who will then do the overseeing?"

The Church committee's report makes clear that it intended the proposed committee to be a participant and is less concerned about oversight as such. It is the power to decide that it wants to share with the President.

May 12, 1976

SENATE APPROVES WATCHDOG PANEL FOR SPY AGENCIES

Committee to Get Sole Power Over C.I.A. and Share In Control of Other Units

By RICHARD L. MADDEN
Special to The New York Times

WASHINGTON, May 19—The Senate, capping a 15-month investigation into abuses by the nation's intelligence agencies, today created a permanent committee with broad powers to monitor the activities of the agencies.

By a vote of 72 to 22, the Senate established a 15-member Select Committee on Intelligence with exclusive authority to oversee the activities of the Central Intelligence Agency and to authorize funds for that agency's operations.

In addition, the new committee would share with existing committees jurisdiction over other agencies, such as the Federal Bureau of Investigation and defense intelligence.

The outcome ended a long dispute among leading senators over what jurisdiction the new committee should have. Also, the one-sided vote today favoring the committee was regarded as a vindication of the work of a temporary committee, headed by Senator Frank Church, Democrat of Idaho, which investigated abuses by intelligence agencies and recommended creation of a permanent committee with broad powers.

A central finding of the Church committee in its reports last month was that Congress had exercised too little control over the intelligence agencies.

Restriction Is Defeated

Before approving the resolution establishing the committee, the Senate rejected, 63 to 31, an effort by Senators John C. Stennis, a Mississippi Democrat, who is chairman of the Senate Armed Services Committee, and John G. Tower, Republican of Texas, to remove the proposed committee's legislative jurisdiction over Defense Department intelligence operations. These included the Defense Intelligence Agency and the National Security Agency. Up to now the Armed Services Committee has had sole jurisdiction over those agencies.

Then, in a preliminary vote of 87 to 7, the Senate approved a compromise agreement worked out last week by Senate leaders establishing the permanent committee.

The eight Democrats and seven Republicans who will serve on the new committee will be named by the Senate majority and minority leaders. Speculation about a choice of chairman centered on Senators Walter F. Mondale of Minnesota, Walter Huddleston of Kentucky and Daniel K. Inouye of Hawaii, all Democrats.

"I'm not asking for that job," said Mr. Church, who is campaigning for the Democratic Presidential nomination. "I think I've done my work," he told reporters.

Senator Is Satisfied

Mr. Church expressed satisfaction that the new committee had the power it needed to monitor the intelligence activities properly, even though the House of Representatives has no such committee and it was unclear how the new Senate committee would work with the Congressional machinery. "One good committee can do the job," Mr. Church said.

Budgets for the intelligence agencies would be authorized annually by the new committee, but this budget authority would be shared with other committees in the case of the F.B.I., which would be shared with the Judiciary Committee, and the defense intelligence agencies, which would be shared with the Armed Services committee.

Senator Abraham A. Ribicoff, Democrat of Connecticut who was floor manager of the resolution, said that the Senate could debate these budget figures in secret and disguise them in other legislation, as is now the practice.

Two members each from the appropriations, Armed Services, Foreign Relations and Judiciary Committees would be among the 15 members of the new committee, and all the members of the committee would be limited to eight years of service.

The resolution sets up procedures to let the full Senate decide if the committee could make public classified information and it prohibits the unauthorized release of such information by a senator or staff member on the committee.

In unsuccessfully arguing against including defense intelligence agencies in the committee's jurisdiction, Mr. Stennis maintained that the resolution would result 'in a proliferation of involvement by Senate committees in intelligence matters and would inevitably lead to greater disclosures on the nature and scope of U.S. intelligence activities."

"I don't care if you have a committee of one, it's almost impossible to stop leaks," said Senator Barry Goldwater, Republican of Arizona.

Mr. Ribicoff argued that the resolution contained safeguards to protect sensitive information.

The 22 votes against the resolution were cast by 15 Republicans and 7 Southern Democrats.

May 20, 1976

F.B.I. Men Linked To 70's Kidnapping Of Domestic Radical

The following article was written by Nicholas M. Horrock and is based on reporting by him and by John M. Crewdson.

Special to The New York Times

WASHINGTON, June 24—Agents of the Federal Bureau of Investigation kidnapped a radical political figure within the last five years in an attempt to frighten the man and deter his political activity, a well-placed bureau source disclosed today.

That incident, about which few additional details could be learned, involved agents assigned to the F.B.I.'s New York City field office.

The F.B.I. source said the incident could become part of an intensive investigation by the Justice Department into the alleged use of other illegal techniques by the F.B.I., including burglary.

Another source, a former agent assigned to the F.B.I.'s New York office, said he could confirm that kidnappings were directed against domestic radicals as well as foreign espionage agents, raising the possibility that Justice Department lawyers may find evidence to support indictments on those charges as well.

The New York Times reported in March 1975 that the bureau had kidnapped and interrogated foreign agents it discovered operating covertly in this country.

These sources said in interviews that kidnapping was also used to get information from or to "disrupt" the activities of figures in domestic radical groups.

One source said he could cite at least one kidnapping that had occurred within the last five years, the period under scrutiny by the Justice Department. The source said that two agents had been involved in seizing a member of the radical New Left to "disrupt" activities planned by him. The victim, according to the source, would not know he had been kidnapped by F.B.I. agents and would probably think his abductors were members of radical right opponents of the anti-war movement.

The source said that the two agents had conducted the kidnapping without formal authorization from the bureau and may have done it "on their own." He said the victim was roughed up but was released "without permanent damage."

Grand Jury Cited

Both sources said that this was not an isolated incident over the past decade and that some of the men who had conducted illegal burglaries, and thus would come under the Department of Justice inquiry, knew about or had been involved in such kidnappings.

Meanwhile, a well placed Government source said that

evidence in the investigation of F.B.I. burglaries had already been presented to a grand jury, but he declined to disclose its location.

Another source, with extensive contacts among present and former F.B.I. agents, said that indictments were expected as early as September and might involve an initial group of 28 agents or officials.

"Street agents," however, had little specific knowledge of the pace of the investigation, according to one source. William L. Gardner, the lawyer in the Justice Department's Civil Rights Division, which is conducting this investigation, has told certain agents that they might have to go before a Federal grand jury.

He has also told agents, sources report, that the Government would grant them immunity from prosecution for their part in burglaries in exchange for their testimony. Mr.

Gardner, who heads the Civil Rights Division's criminal section, is investigating violations of laws that prohibit law enforcement officials from depriving a citizen of his civil rights or from making illegal searches and seizures.

Contempt Threat Warning

Mr. Gardner, according to F.B.I. sources, has told agents that they will not face administrative punishment by the bureau if they choose not to testify on the ground that they might incriminate themselves.

But he has warned them that the Government may get a court to grant them immunity and that if they then fail to testify, the government may move to have them held in contempt of court. One agent found this ironic since it was the method used in the early 1970's to try to get members of the anti-war movement to testify.

Within the F.B.I., sources said, there is vast difference between kidnapping used in foreign espionage cases and in investigations of domestic radicals. Kidnapping "illegals," the name for foreign agents here under false identity, is "part of the game" and is carried out by both foreign and American intelligence services, they said. But in domestic investigations, this was considered totally unacceptable.

"You can't have law enforcement officers doing that. The next step will be killing somebody," he said. This agent said he would have resigned from the bureau if he had been asked to kidnap someone.

The purposes for kidnapping varied from trying to frighten a member of the radical movement (used against Ku Klux Klan members in the 1960's) to trying to get information.

June 25, 1976

F.B.I. Was Not As Advertised And Won't Ever Be the Same

By JOHN M. CREWDSON

After five decades of virtual immunity from public criticism, the Federal Bureau of Investigation is in serious trouble from top to bottom. No one seems to think its survival is in jeopardy, but the F.B.I. that emerges from the current official scrutiny of its people and procedures will probably be a far cry from the venerated institution of crime-fighters and gang-busters that J. Edgar Hoover made a part of American folklore.

Not a week goes by now without new allegations of wrongdoing by agents and officials of the F.B.I., and last week was no exception. Testimony was made public in which an agent in New York told of scores of burglaries he had carried out, always under orders from his superiors. Two other agents, one retired, came under Justice Department scrutiny when it was learned that a paid informant they "handled" had also been a burglar for the F.B.I. (and for himself while on the Bureau's payroll). An investigation was under way of the possible misappropriation of medical insurance funds for purposes of high living. And the associate director of the Bureau acknowledged his technical responsibility for disruptive tactics against political militants while he headed the Minneapolis office in the late 1960s and early 70s. That operation was part of the now infamous Cointelpro, or counterintelligence program, characterized by Congressional investigators as "indisputably degrading to a free society."

The illegalities and improprieties may seem at first glance to be no more than random instances of overstepping by a few zealous or unscrupulous agents. But as the pieces continue to fit together, the picture they form threatens to

tarnish the badges of F.B.I. agents to a point where their sheen may never be restored.

As a veteran "street agent" reflected recently, "You cannot have law-enforcement officers become totally lawless. That's vigilantism. That just breaks down the whole system."

The Bureau could perhaps have lived with the disclosure of its shoddy investigation, under White House pressure, of the Watergate affair, and even with Congressional disclosures that were mainly historical: That the F.B.I. had been used for political purposes by successive Presidents since Franklin Roosevelt, had secretly tried for years to publicly discredit the Rev. Dr. Martin Luther King Jr., and had failed to investigate adequately the assassination of President Kennedy.

Such shortcomings might have been tolerable because they grew out of policy, dictated either from within the F.B.I. or from outside, and policies can be changed with the passing of those who make them. But what now promises to irreparably diminish the stature of the nation's foremost law-enforcement agency, in the gloomy view of several of its former officials, is the spectacle of individual agents acting without regard for the laws they were sworn to uphold, apparently with the knowledge and approval of their superiors, who in some cases seem themselves to have violated their fiduciary trust.

Morale is now described as dismal. The work of the Intelligence Division, the chief target of one of two separate Justice Department inquiries, is said to have suffered. And ordinary criminal investigations are reportedly encountering citizen resistance of a kind hitherto unthinkable.

That the Justice Department is now conducting not one but two investigations of the F.B.I. is in many ways remarkable. Such a thing probably would not have been possible while J. Edgar Hoover was in charge, and might not be possible even now without the combined effects of Watergate and the Congressional disclosures.

The investigations have been spurred mainly by a troubled Attorney General, Edward H. Levi, and three of his principal aides: Michael Shaheen, head of the department's new Office of Professional Responsibility; J. Stanley Pottinger, head of the Civil Rights Division, and Richard Thornburgh, the chief of the Criminal Division.

Kelley a Silent Partner

A fifth and somewhat more silent partner in the clean-up campaign is Clarence M. Kelley, the F.B.I. director since 1973, police chief of Kansas City before that, and before that an F.B.I. agent for 20 years.

Eugene Mihaesco

Mr. Kelley is by every account a decent and honorable man with a great deal of love for the institution. But he is said to have been badly stung by his recent discovery that some aides had allowed him to provide incorrect information to the public and the Congress about the F.B.I.'s use of burglaries.

Mr. Kelley had been saying for a year or so that the Bureau's practice of occasionally breaking into private homes and offices without a search warrant, to remove evidence and photograph documents in search of leads in domestic intelligence investigations, had been halted by Mr. Hoover in 1966.

But a month ago, Mr. Kelley acknowledged that some musty documents had been discovered last March 17 in the F.B.I.'s giant New York City office that proved him wrong. Illegal burglaries, the papers showed, had been carried out in 1972 and 1973 by agents there who were trying to trace the movements of members of the fugitive Weather Underground.

Mr. Kelley is understood to be trying now to find out which of his aides knew of the more recent burglaries and failed to advise him. And it remains unclear why that discovery was withheld from the Senate Intelligence Committee, which was investigating F.B.I. burglaries and did not publish its report on the Bureau until six weeks after the New York papers had been found.

After the recent burglaries became known — they apparently resumed almost from the moment of Mr. Hoover's death in May, 1972—F.B.I. sources suggested that the practice had continued well beyond 1973.

The illegal entries, the sources have said, were aimed at a wide variety of groups, including the Mafia and Puerto Rican nationalists, and the burglaries were described as just part of a broader range of illegal activity by F.B.I. intelligence agents that included at least one kidnapping of a new-left radical, unprovoked assaults, firebombings and illegal telephone taps.

Although L. Patrick Gray 3d, who headed the F.B.I. during the period now under investigation, is believed to have been too preoccupied with the Watergate investigation to be aware of the burglaries, there is a good chance that Mr. Pottinger and his Civil Rights Division lawyers will be able to trace knowledge of the break-ins almost to the top of Mr. Gray's command.

Some 30 F.B.I. agents have now been notified that they are targets of the Pottinger inquiry into the burglaries. Several officials at F.B.I. headquarters, including at least one assistant director, have retained lawyers and are negotiating for immunity from prosecution that would allow them to testify against their colleagues.

(Mr. Kelley's sudden dismissal last month of Nicholas P. Callahan, his top deputy and a veteran of four decades of service in the F.B.I., seems now to have been unrelated to the burglary investigation. Mr. Callahan, according to reliable Justice Department sources was discharged after other department lawyers discovered that he had somehow been involved in the misappropriation of a "recreational fund" financed by agents' dues.)

Apart from improprieties, the Bureau's vaunted efficacy is being challenged. David G. Trager, the United States Attorney for the Eastern District of New York, recently characterized the Bureau's criminal investigators as "geared up for gang-busters crime" and unable or unwilling to tackle more sophisticated cases of official corruption and white-collar crime. At least one House subcommittee is now planning to look into the F.B.I.'s general investigative operations and its use of 7,000 informants, like the admitted burglar identified this week, to keep track of radical groups.

All of this has combined to make it a difficult time for Mr. Kelley. Apart from his public concession that he had been wrong about the burglaries, his assertion last May that the F.B.I. was "truly sorry for some of its past activities," provoked a firestorm of criticism among the unrepentant inside the bureau and out.

In addition, he has personal problems. He has been confined to Bethesda Naval Hospital, suffering from a painful back ailment. His wife died recently after a lingering illness. And at 64 years of age, he is faced with the prospect that unless he manages to hold onto his job through the middle of 1978, his Government pension will be no more than a few thousand dollars.

Last month, the Justice Department was unable to quash a subpoena for Mr. Kelley's appearance—the first of its kind by an F.B.I. director that anyone could recall—at a criminal trial in Iowa where two Indians stood accused of killing two F.B.I. agents in South Dakota last year.

In the view of the defense lawyers, it was Mr. Kelley's admission from the witness stand that the F.B.I. had issued a nationwide alert of possible violence by Indians over the bicentennial weekend without any evidence that such violence would occur that tipped the scales in the defendants' favor. They were acquitted.

Mr. Kelley was nonetheless said to have been in excellent spirits after his dismissal of Mr. Callahan, and although his prospects of staying on at the F.B.I. after the November elections are not good, he apparently has resolved to work until then in concert with Mr. Levi in trying set the Bureau straight.

Late last month, Mr. Kelley appointed Richard G. Held, the head of the F.B.I.'s Chicago office, to replace Mr. Calla-han. Although Mr. Held is a 35-year F.B.I. veteran himself, he has not spent much time at F.B.I. headquarters and, unlike Mr. Callahan, has not been closely identified with the small clique of Hoover loyalists who now inhabit the Bureau's top echelons. Yet it was Mr. Held who acknowledged Friday that he had been responsible, as head of the Minneapolis office, for the program for disrupting political militants.

The choice of Mr. Held over James B. Adams, one of Mr. Callahan's younger and more impressive deputies and until recently the odds-on favorite to assume the director's mantle one day, may signal an end to Mr. Hoover's postmortem hold on the F.B.I.

If that is so, there may be nothing else seriously wrong with the Bureau that cannot, in time, be cured.

John M. Crewdson is a Washington correspondent for The New York Times.

August 1, 1976

Suggested Reading

Association of the Bar of the City of New York. *The Federal Loyalty-Security Program.* 1956.

Barth, Alan. *Government by Investigation.* Clifton, New Jersey: Augustus M. Kelley, 1955.

Barth, Alan. *The Loyalty of Free Men.* New York: The Viking Press, 1951.

Biddle, Francis. *The Fear of Freedom.* New York: Da Capo Press, 1951.

Blacklisting: Two Key Documents. (1952/1956). New York: Arno Press, 1972.

Blackstock, Nelson. *Cointelpro: The F.B.I.'s Secret War on Political Freedom.* New York: Vintage Books — Random House, 1976.

Bontecou, Eleanor. *The Federal Loyalty-Security Program.* Ithaca, New York: Cornell University Press, 1958.

Boorstin, Daniel J. *The Image: Or What Happened to the American Dream.* New York: Atheneum, 1962.

Brown, Ralph, S., Jr. *Loyalty and Security: Employment Tests in the United States.* New Haven, Conn.: Yale University Press, 1958.

Buckley, William F., Jr. and L. Brent Bozell. *McCarthy and His Enemies: The Record and Its Meaning.* Chicago, Ill.: Henry Regnery Company, 1954.

Budenz, Louis F. *The Techniques of Communism.* (1954). New York: Arno Press, 1977.

Chambers, Whittaker. *Witness.* New York: Alfred A. Knopf, 1951.

Clark, Jane Perry. *Deportation of Aliens From the United States to Europe.* (1931). New York: Arno Press, 1977.

Cogley, John. *Report on Blacklisting, Part 1: Movies.* (1956). New York: Arno Press, 1972.

Cooke, Alistair. *A Generation on Trial.* New York: Alfred A. Knopf, 1951.

Dies, Martin. *The Trojan Horse in America.* (1940). New York: Arno Press, 1977.

Dilling, Elizabeth. *The Red Network: A "Who's Who" and Handbook of Radicalism for Patriots.* (1935). New York: Arno Press, 1977.

Draper, Theodore. *The Roots of American Communism.* New York: The Viking Press, 1957.

Dubovsky, Melvyn. *We Shall Be All: A History of the Industrial Workers of the World.* New York: Quadrangle, 1969.

Eisenhower, Dwight D. *The White House Years: Mandate for Change.* Garden City, New York: Doubleday, 1963.

Freeland, Richard M. *The Truman Doctrine and the Origins of McCarthyism: Foreign Policy, Domestic Politics, and Internal Security, 1946-1948.* New York: Alfred A. Knopf, 1971.

The Fund for the Republic, Inc. *Digest of the Public Record of Communism in the United States.* (1955). New York: Arno Press, 1977.

Ghent, W.J. *The Reds Bring Reaction.* (1923). New York: Arno Press, 1977.

Goldman, Eric F. *The Crucial Decade—And After.* New York: Alfred A. Knopf, 1960.

Goodman, Walter. *The Committee. The Extraordinary Career of the House Committee on Un-American Activities.* New York: Farrar, Straus and Giroux, 1968.

Griffith, Robert. *The Politics of Fear: Joseph McCarthy and the Senate.* Lexington, Kentucky: University of Kentucky Press, 1970.

Harper, Alan D. *The Politics of Loyalty: The White House and the Communist Issue.* Westport, Conn.: Greenwood Press, 1969.

Hiss, Alger. *In the Court of Public Opinion.* New York: Harper & Row, 1957.

Hook, Sidney. *Heresy, Yes—Conspiracy, No!.* Westport, Conn.: Greenwood Press, 1953.

Hough, Emerson. *The Web.* (1919). New York: Arno Press, 1977.

Hughes, Emmet John. *The Ordeal of Power.* New York: Atheneum, 1963.

Kempton, Murray. *Part of Our Time. Some Ruins and Monuments of the Thirties.* New York: Simon and Schuster, 1955.

Latham, Earl. *The Communist Controversy in Washington from the New Deal to McCarthy.* Cambridge, Mass.: Harvard University Press, 1966.

McCarthy, Joseph. *McCarthyism: The Fight for America.* (1952). New York: Arno Press, 1977.

Murphy, Paul M. *The Constitution in Crisis Times.* New York: Harper & Row, 1972.

Murray, Robert K. Red Scare: *A Study in National Hysteria, 1919-1920.* Minneapolis, Minn.: University of Minnesota Press, 1955.

National Americanism Commission of the American Legion, Compiler. *Isms: A Review of Alien Isms, Revolutionary Communism and Their Active Sympathizers in the United States.* (1937). New York: Arno Press, 1977.

Nixon, Richard. *Six Crises*. New York: Doubleday, 1962.

Preston, William, Jr. *Aliens and Dissenters: Federal Suppression of Radicals, 1903-1933*. Cambridge, Mass.: Harvard University Press, 1963.

Rovere, Richard H. *Senator Joe McCarthy*. New York: Harcourt, Brace Jovanovich, 1959.

Schaack, Michael J. *Anarchy and Anarchists: A History of the Red Terror and the Social Revolution in America and Europe*. (1889). New York: Arno Press, 1977.

Stripling, Robert E. *The Red Plot Against America*. Edited by Bob Considine. (1949). New York: Arno Press, 1977.

Taylor, Telford. *Grand Inquest*. New York: Da Capo Press, 1955.

Tenney, Jack B. *Red Fascism: Boring from Within by the Subversive Forces of Communism*. (1947). New York: Arno Press, 1977.

Truman, Harry S. *Memoirs: Years of Trial and Hope*. Garden City, New York: Doubleday, 1956.

U.S. Committee on Education and Labor. *Documents Relating to Intelligence Bureau of Red Squad of Los Angeles Police Department*. (1940). New York: Arno Press, 1971.

Warren, Frank., III. *Liberals and Communism: The "Red Decade" Revisited*. Bloomington, Ind.: Indiana University Press, 1966.

Wechsler, James A. *The Age of Suspicion*. New York: Random House, 1953.

Index

Walker, Edwin A., 279-80
Wall, Robert N., 324-25
Wallace, Henry, 135, 156, 168